SHAKESPEARE SURVEY

67

Shakespeare's Collaborative Work

ADVISORY BOARD

SHAKESPEARE SURVEY

67

Shakespeare's Collaborative Work

EDITED BY

PETER HOLLAND

CO-EDITOR FOR THEMED ARTICLES:

TON HOENSELAARS

CAMBRIDGE
UNIVERSITY PRESS

CAMBRIDGE
UNIVERSITY PRESS

University Printing House, Cambridge CB2 8BS, United Kingdom

Cambridge University Press is part of the University of Cambridge.

It furthers the University's mission by disseminating knowledge in the pursuit of education, learning and research at the highest international levels of excellence.

www.cambridge.org
Information on this title: www.cambridge.org/9781107071544

© Cambridge University Press 2014

First published 2014

Printed in the United Kingdom by CPI Group Ltd, Croydon CR0 4YY

A catalogue record for this publication is available from the British Library

ISBN 978-1-107-07154-4 Hardback

EDITOR'S NOTE

Volume 68, on 'Shakespeare, Origins and Originality', will be at press by the time this volume appears. The theme of Volume 69 will be 'Shakespeare and Rome', of Volume 70 will be 'Creating and Re-creating Shakespeare', the theme of the World Shakespeare Congress in 2016, and of Volume 71 will be 'Shakespeare and London'.

Submissions should be addressed to the Editor to arrive at the latest by 1 September 2015 for Volume 69, by 1 September 2016 for Volume 70 and by 1 September 2017 for Volume 71. Pressures on space are heavy and priority is given to articles related to the theme of a particular volume. Submissions may be made either as hard copy sent to the Editor at The Shakespeare Institute, Church Street, Stratford-upon-Avon CV37 6HP, or as an e-attachment to pholland@nd.edu. All articles submitted are read by the Editor and at least one member of the Advisory Board, whose indispensable assistance the Editor gratefully acknowledges.

Unless otherwise indicated, Shakespeare quotations and references are keyed to *The Complete Works*, ed. Stanley Wells, Gary Taylor, John Jowett and William Montgomery, 2nd edition (Oxford, 2005).

Review copies should be addressed to the Editor as above. In attempting to survey the ever-increasing bulk of Shakespeare publications our reviewers inevitably have to exercise some selection. We are pleased to receive offprints of articles which help to draw our reviewers' attention to relevant material.

Three former members of the Advisory Board have died in the last year: Anne Barton joined the Board for Volume 26 (1973) and served until Volume 52 (1999); R. A. Foakes served from Volume 32 (1980) until Volume 60 (2007); and Terence Hawkes served from Volume 34 (1982) until Volume 60 (2007). All were of course outstanding scholars who contributed greatly to Shakespeare studies. Here I wish to mention only their generous and perceptive assistance to successive Editors of *Shakespeare Survey* over many years. Their wisdom was much missed when each decided to step down from the Board. Their friendship and kindness was deeply valued by so many of us right to the end.

I would also like to thank Ton Hoenselaars who co-edited the themed section in this volume with his customary energy and wisdom. Working with him was an enjoyable experience and I'm very grateful for his assistance.

P.D.H.

CONTRIBUTORS

JAMES P. BEDNARZ, *Long Island University*
WILLIAM C. CARROLL, *Boston University*
FRANCIS X. CONNOR, *Wichita State University*
TREVOR COOK, *York University, Canada*
GABRIEL EGAN, *De Montfort University*
JULIA GRIFFIN, *Georgia Southern University*
BREAN HAMMOND, *University of Nottingham*
RUI CARVALHO HOMEM, *University of Oporto*
SUJATA IYENGAR, *University of Georgia*
RUSSELL JACKSON, *University of Birmingham*
ISABEL KARREMANN, *University of Würzburg*
ARTHUR F. KINNEY, *University of Massachusetts Amherst*
TINA KRONTIRIS, *Aristotle University, Thessaloniki*
BARRY LANGSTON, *Independent Scholar*
STEPHAN LAQUÉ, *University of Munich*
DENNIS MCCARTHY, *Independent Scholar*
ELLEN MACKAY, *Indiana University*
RODERICK H. MCKEOWN, *University of Toronto*
SONIA MASSAI, *King's College London*
L. MONIQUE PITTMAN, *Andrews University*
JAMES PURKIS, *University of Western Ontario*
CAROL CHILLINGTON RUTTER, *University of Warwick*
JUNE SCHLUETER, *Lafayette College*
CHARLOTTE SCOTT, *Goldsmiths, University of London*
WILL SHARPE, *The Shakespeare Institute, University of Birmingham*
JAMES SHAW, *Bodleian Libraries, University of Oxford*
SIMON SMITH, *Birkbeck, University of London*
B. J. SOKOL, *Goldsmiths, University of London*
STEPHEN SPIESS, *University of Michigan*
GARY TAYLOR, *Florida State University*
LESLIE THOMSON, *University of Toronto*
SIR BRIAN VICKERS, *Institute of English Studies, University of London*
WILLIAM W. WEBER, *Yale University*

CONTENTS

CONTENTS

viii

ILLUSTRATIONS

LIST OF ILLUSTRATIONS

WHY DID SHAKESPEARE COLLABORATE?

GARY TAYLOR

Anyone interested in Shakespeare must care about collaboration. Modern attribution scholarship agrees that Shakespeare's writing can be found in at least forty plays: the thirty-six in the First Folio, plus *Pericles*, *The Two Noble Kinsmen*, *Edward III* and *Sir Thomas More*. Of those forty plays, the four not included in the Folio are undeniably collaborative.[1] Within the Folio itself, another four – *Timon of Athens*, *Henry VIII/All Is True*, *Titus Andronicus* and *1 Henry VI* – are now accepted as collaborative by all the leading attribution specialists.[2] Eight plays out of forty: that's twenty per cent of the canon. Hugh Craig and John Burrows have produced compelling new statistical evidence that the other two parts of *Henry VI* are also collaborative, as most attribution scholars in the eighteenth, nineteenth and early twentieth century contended.[3] Ten out of forty: that's twenty-five per cent of the canon. If we accept the growing consensus that Shakespeare wrote the additions to the *Spanish Tragedy* published in 1602, and parts of *Arden of Faversham* and *The History of Cardenio*, then he collaborated in 13 out of the extant 43 plays he worked on: that's 30 per cent.[4] Those who accept the claims of the 2013 RSC edition of *Collaborative Plays* would add five more.[5] Modern scholarship gives us a larger Shakespeare canon, but also a larger proportion of collaborative work. Moreover, two plays originally written by Shakespeare alone – *Macbeth* and *Measure for Measure* – were apparently adapted after Shakespeare's death.[6] That leaves just twenty-eight plays that survive in texts written entirely by Shakespeare.[7] Shakespeare's is the only

---

[1] For summaries and syntheses of earlier attribution scholarship, see Gary Taylor, 'The Canon and Chronology of Shakespeare's Plays', in Stanley Wells *et al.*, *William Shakespeare: A Textual Companion* (Oxford, 1987), pp. 69–144; and Brian Vickers, *Shakespeare, Co-Author: A Historical Study of Five Collaborative Plays* (Oxford, 2002).

[2] These eight plays were all identified as collaborative in Stanley Wells and Gary Taylor, gen. eds., *Complete Works*, rev. edn (Oxford, 2005). See Jonathan Hope, *The Authorship of Shakespeare's Plays* (Cambridge, 1994); Macdonald P. Jackson, 'Stage Directions and Speech Headings in Act I of *Titus Andronicus* Q (1594): Shakespeare or Peele?', *Studies in Bibliography*, 49 (1996), 134–48; 'Shakespeare's Brothers and Peele's Brethren: *Titus Andronicus* Again', *Notes and Queries*, 242 (1997), 494–5; 'Phrase Length in *Henry VIII*: Shakespeare and Fletcher', *Notes and Queries*, 242 (1997), 75–80; *Defining Shakespeare: Pericles as Test Case* (Oxford, 2003); W. E. Y. Elliott and R. J. Valenza, 'Oxford by the Numbers: What Are the Odds that the Earl of Oxford Could Have Written Shakespeare's Plays?', *Tennessee Law Review*, 72:1 (2004), 323–453; Hugh Craig and Arthur Kinney, eds., *Shakespeare, Computers, and the Mystery of Authorship* (Cambridge, 2009); Hugh Craig, 'Authorship', in *The Oxford Handbook of Shakespeare*, ed. Arthur F. Kinney (Oxford, 2012), pp. 23–30. These scholars do not agree on every scene or passage, but there is overwhelming evidence and a deep consensus among the established figures on the collaborative nature of these plays.

[3] Craig and Kinney, *Computers*, pp. 68–76; Elliott and Valenza, 'Oxford by the Numbers'; Paul Vincent, 'Inconsistencies in *2 Henry VI*', *Notes and Queries*, 246 (2001), 270–4; Hugh Craig and John Burrows, 'A Collaboration about a Collaboration: The Authorship of *King Henry VI, Part Three*', in *Collaborative Research in the Digital Humanities*, ed. Marilyn Deegan and Willard McCarty (London, 2012), pp. 27–65. The first scholarly case for their collaborative authorship was Edmond Malone's 'Dissertation on the Three Parts of *King Henry VI*' (1787), in *The Plays and Poems of William Shakspeare*, 10 vols. (1790), vol. 6, pp. 383–429.

hand in less than two-thirds of the plays that Shakespeare had a hand in.

We can be interested in collaboration without mastering Principle Component Analysis, Fisher's Exact Test, chi-square, degrees of freedom, historical sociolinguistics, plagiarism software, palaeography, chainlines or watermarks. Rowe did not believe that all of *Pericles* was written by Shakespeare, but 'some part of it certainly was, particularly the last Act';[8] Coleridge denied that Shakespeare could have written the first speech of *1 Henry VI* but conjectured that he did write the additions to *The Spanish Tragedy*; Tennyson identified John Fletcher as the author of some scenes of *Henry VIII*; Swinburne insisted on Shakespeare's presence in *Arden of Faversham*. On the basis of their own sensitivity to verse style, each poet floated an intuitive hypothesis, which has subsequently been tested and confirmed repeatedly, by a variety of independent empirical experiments, conducted by people who are not poets. Attribution scholarship is a determinedly dull technical discipline, like physical archaeology or the chemical analysis of pigments. Caravaggio signed only one of his paintings, but you can admire, teach and write about Caravaggio's art without becoming an expert in the scientific techniques that established his canon. Likewise, I will here take for granted the consensus of the leading living experts about *what* Shakespeare wrote, and begin with a different, critical question: *why* did he collaborate?

Both prevailing answers to that question are economic. The postmodernist answer celebrates collaboration because, it claims, proprietary individual authorship was a capitalist ideology not written into law until the Enlightenment, and therefore irrelevant to the cooperative *mentalité* of early modern playwrights. Shakespeare collaborated because he didn't know any better.[9] He belonged to the innocent race before the bourgeois flood. Undeniably, the evolution of copyright and the economics of the book trade affected the subsequent history of Shakespeare's reputation. But although theatre since the time of the Athenians has required actors, musicians, dancers, choreographers, painters, carpenters, costume-makers,

[4] On *Spanish Tragedy* see Craig and Kinney, *Computers*, pp. 162–80; Warren Stevenson, *Shakespeare's Additions to Thomas Kyd's 'The Spanish Tragedy': A Fresh Look at the Evidence Regarding the 1602 Additions* (Lewiston, 2008); Brian Vickers, 'Identifying Shakespeare's Additions to *The Spanish Tragedy*: A New(er) Approach', *Shakespeare*, 8:1 (2012), 13–43; Douglas Bruster, 'Shakespearean Spellings and Handwriting in the Additional Passages Printed in the 1602 *Spanish Tragedy*', *Notes and Queries*, n.s. 60:3 (September 2013), pp. 420–4. On *Arden* see Craig and Kinney, *Computers*, pp. 78–99, and Jackson, *Determining the Shakespeare Canon: Arden of Faversham and A Lover's Complaint* (Oxford, 2014). On *Cardenio* see Brean Hammond, ed., *Double Falsehood* (London, 2010); David Carnegie and Gary Taylor, eds., *The Quest for Cardenio: Shakespeare, Fletcher, Cervantes and the 'Lost' Play* (Oxford, 2012); Terri Bourus and Gary Taylor, eds., *The Creation and Re-creation of Cardenio: Performing Shakespeare, Transforming Cervantes* (New York, 2013).

[5] *William Shakespeare and Others: Collaborative Plays*, ed. Jonathan Bate, Eric Rasmussen *et al.*, The RSC Shakespeare (New York, 2013). However, Will Sharpe's essay on 'Authorship and Attribution', in that edition, pp. 641–745, acknowledges that it is 'highly unlikely to almost impossible' that *Locrine, Thomas Lord Cromwell, The London Prodigal* or *A Yorkshire Tragedy* 'contain Shakespeare's writing', and claims only that *Mucedorus* is 'worth considering' (642). By contrast, Sharpe endorses the consensus that Shakespeare 'almost certainly to very likely' wrote parts of *More, Arden, Edward III, Double Falsehood* and the *Spanish Tragedy* additions.

[6] For recent work on these long-suspected cases of adaptation, see Gary Taylor and John Lavagnino, gen. eds., *Thomas Middleton: The Collected Works* and *Thomas Middleton and Early Modern Textual Culture: A Companion to the Collected Works* (Oxford, 2007); Gary Taylor, '*Macbeth* and Middleton', in *Macbeth*, ed. Robert Miola (New York, 2014), pp. 294–303; Gary Taylor, 'Empirical Middleton: *Macbeth*, Adaptation, and Micro-Authorship' (forthcoming in *Shakespear Quarterly*); Terri Bourus and Gary Taylor, '*Measure for Measure*(s): Performance-testing the adaptation hypothesis', *Shakespeare*, 10:2 (2014).

[7] If Middleton had a hand in *All's Well That Ends Well*, as suggested by Laurie Maguire and Emma Smith in the *Times Literary Supplement*, 20 April 2012, then the figure would be 27 out of 43. But Brian Vickers and Marcus Dahl have strongly contested the conjecture and, as Maguire and Smith made clear from the outset, much further research is required to test the claim.

[8] Nicholas Rowe, ed., *The Works of Mr. William Shakespear*, 6 vols. (1709), vol. 1, p. vii.

[9] The most influential summation of this view is Jeffrey Masten's *Textual Intercourse: Collaboration, Authorship, and Sexualities in Renaissance Drama* (Cambridge, 1997): see especially the chapter 'Between gentlemen: homoeroticism, collaboration, and the discourse of friendship' (pp. 28–62).

financiers and all manner of back-stage crew, before Shakespeare's lifetime it had never routinely required more than one playwright per play. Even then, as Jeffrey Knapp has demonstrated, 'Collective play-writing was never the norm for Renaissance drama, practically or conceptually.'[10]

The collapse of the historically indefensible postmodernist hypothesis has led to a resurgence of the only available alternative: the neoclassical, formalist explanation, which denigrates collaboration as itself a capitalist intrusion upon the natural and desirable state of individual artistic autonomy. According to this theory, the economic dominance of actors and proprietors forced playwrights to collaborate. Shakespeare's plays include material by other writers because the men who paid the piper fiddled with the tunes. 'If we give into this opinion', Pope declared in 1725, 'how many low and vicious parts and passages might no longer reflect upon this great Genius, but appear unworthily charged upon him?'[11] Likewise, Bart van Es, in 2013, explains six of Shakespeare's collaborations in terms of 'Shakespeare's working conditions in the early 1590s', dominated by the 'financial pressure' and 'constant haste' of a system where writers 'were the employees of the acting companies'.[12]

But the neoclassical economic claim is as suspect as the postmodernist one. Since most commercial plays of the period were apparently written by a single author, the theatres were unsuccessful in imposing their alleged collaborative agenda. Anyway, *why* would theatres want multiple authors? When Knapp claims that 'collective playwriting helped speed up the process of satisfying' the commercial theatre's 'demand' for new material, he is simply echoing the assertion by Brian Vickers that 'the need to keep the theatrical companies supplied with material must have been one reason for co-authorship'.[13] Vickers himself supports this thesis by citing, more than once, a 1927 article by Charles Sisson.[14] Sisson discovered legal documents about a lost play called '*The late Murder in White Chappell, or Keepe the Widow Waking*', which 'was contrived and written by Wm Rowley, Jon ffoord, John Webster, and Tho: Decker'. This indisputably collaborative play was based upon two recent ('late')

and local ('White Chappell') events, which took place between April and August 1624; the play was licensed in September, and both Sisson and Vickers agree that it must therefore have been written 'at great speed' by all four authors. Vickers then notes, on the basis of Henslowe's account books, that the six weeks allowed for *Keep the Widow Waking* was 'a not-unusual period of time' for writing a play. Combining the evidence of Henslowe and Sisson, Vickers generalizes that collaborative dramatists 'must have worked in permanent haste'.

Can these grand claims be supported by a few self-serving depositions in a lawsuit about a lost late-Jacobean play? The timetable of composition is less certain than Sisson and Vickers assert.[15] But

---

[10] Jeffrey Knapp, *Shakespeare Only* (Chicago, 2009), p. 120. The book expands and develops the historicist argument of Knapp's 'What is a Co-author?', *Representations*, 89 (2003), 1–29. For a less temperate pummelling of postmodernist views of the author function, see Vickers, *Co-Author*, pp. 506–41.

[11] *The Works of Shakespear*, ed. Alexander Pope, 6 vols. (1725), vol. 1, p. xxi.

[12] van Es, *Shakespeare in Company* (Oxford, 2013), pp. 55, 44, 48, 54. He acknowledges 'The evidence of co-authorship' in the early '*Henry VI* plays, *Titus Andronicus*, and probably *Edward III*' (51, 284), and reverts to the early dating of *Sir Thomas More*, citing no source later than 1990 (313). He gives no reason for his rejection of more recent empirical scholarship that dates Shakespeare's collaborative work on *More* to the seventeenth century; that dating is simply inconvenient for his overall thesis (284). For confirmation of seventeenth-century composition, see most recently Hugh Craig, 'The Date of *Sir Thomas More*', in *Shakespeare Survey 66* (Cambridge, 2013), pp. 38–54.

[13] Knapp, *Shakespeare Only*, p. 120; Vickers, *Co-author*, p. 28.

[14] Sisson, '*Keep the Widow Waking*: A Lost Play by Thomas Dekker', *Library*, IV:8 (1927), 39–57. Sisson reprinted this as a chapter of *Lost Plays of Shakespeare's Age* (Cambridge, 1936), pp. 80–124. I cite the 1936 printing because Vickers does, both in *Co-Author*, pp. 32–4, and in 'Incomplete Shakespeare: Or, Denying Co-authorship in *Henry the Sixth, Part 1*', *Shakespeare Quarterly*, 58:3 (2007), 311–52, p. 315.

[15] Vickers claims that the co-authors 'had about six weeks to fulfil the commission', but we do not possess any documentary evidence that their commission specified a completion date. Sisson, followed by Vickers, assumes that the play was licensed before mid-September, but this specificity is not supported by N. W. Bawcutt's authoritative edition: see *The Control and Censorship of Caroline Drama: The Records of Sir*

even if we accept their conjectures, none of the very specific circumstances that encouraged rapid production of *Keep the Widow Waking* is relevant to any Shakespeare play that attribution specialists have identified as collaborative. Vickers is correct when he claims that, in Henslowe's accounts, 'plays were normally finished in four to six weeks' (*Co-author*, 43). But that sentence, tellingly, is about all plays, not just collaborative ones. Vickers cites Neil Carson for this statistic, but he omits Carson's preceding and following sentences: '*However organized*, the playwrights worked with considerable speed. Henslowe's accounts indicate that plays were normally finished in four to six weeks. Drayton promised to complete a book in a "fortnyght".'[16] Likewise, Vickers ignores the fact that Sisson's book also contains a chapter about another lost play produced in haste to exploit a topical scandal: *The Old Joiner of Aldgate*, written by George Chapman, alone. Nor were Drayton and Chapman the only playwrights capable of writing quickly. Ben Jonson 'fully penned' the very long text of *Volpone* in five weeks (85 lines per day), and the biggest hit of the entire period, Middleton's *A Game at Chess*, must have been written in five weeks or less (375 lines per week).[17] Shakespeare allegedly wrote *The Merry Wives of Windsor* in two weeks.[18] Noël Coward wrote his most admired play, *Private Lives*, in four days.[19] Alan Ayckbourn began writing his enormously popular *Bedroom Farce* on a Wednesday, completed it that Friday, typed it all up on Saturday, and began rehearsals on Monday.[20] Compositional velocity is not a function of the number of playwrights involved. Neither is commercial success.

Why should a theatrical demand for new material create a demand for collaboration? Carson pointed out that seven playwrights did all the writing for Henslowe's crowded fall and winter season of 1599–1600; an eighth actor-playwright (the older Robert Wilson) joined them to collaborate on one play. Seven playwrights working alone on separate plays should, theoretically, be able to produce as many plays as seven playwrights working together on collaborative plays. The only obvious gain in productivity here, created by

collaboration, is the single collaborative contribution of Robert Wilson. But Wilson worked on fifteen other Henslowe plays from spring 1598 to summer 1600, so he clearly belongs to the same ensemble of writers. From the perspective of theatre management, why not have eight playwrights writing separately, instead of eight playwrights writing collaboratively with each other?

With professional playwrights writing for commercial theatres, collaboration cannot be explained by simple economies of time or personnel. The motive cannot be quantitative. It's not about the numbers. It must be qualitative, and therefore phenomenological. Collaboration in some way improved the quality of the human experience. Analysing Henslowe's records, Carson could detect only one statistical difference between single-author plays and plural-author plays: the collaborative ones were more likely to get finished (57–8). If theatres had an economic motive for encouraging collaboration, it was not because co-authors worked faster, but because they were more often able to achieve closure. Why? Carson does not venture an answer. Finishing a play for which you were the sole author (and therefore the sole payee) would have provided a greater financial incentive to finish. Therefore, the economic motive cannot

---

Henry Herbert, Master of the Revels 1623–73 (Oxford, 1996), which gives only 'Sept. 1624' as the licence date, and does not place it between or after the entries of 3, 15, or 18 September (154–6). Moreover, Herbert licensed the play as 'A new Trag: call: a Late murther of the sonn upon the mother writt: by M<r> Forde Webster'. This title refers only to the earlier of the two scandals; Ford and Webster could have begun work on that tragedy before Dekker and Rowley joined them to incorporate the more recent comic material. Dekker's testimony was in response to charges of slander about the comic plot.

[16] Carson, *A Companion to Henslowe's Diary* (Cambridge, 1988), p. 59 (my italics).

[17] 'Canon and Chronology', in *Companion*, ed. Taylor and Lavagnino, pp. 440–1.

[18] T. W. Craik, ed., *The Merry Wives of Windsor* (Oxford, 2008), p. 4 (citing John Dennis in 1702).

[19] Philip Hoare, *Noël Coward: A Biography* (Chicago, 1995), p. 214.

[20] Prunella Scales, interviewed on *The National Theatre: 50 Years* (BBC, broadcast 2 November 2013).

have been paramount: playwrights apparently had greater or more effective incentives to finish plays for which they received smaller, divided payments. Why? Historically, some playwrights, some of the time, have found it stimulating, socially and imaginatively, to work with what Nashe called a 'fellow writer'.[21] Apparently, at least some of the time, the social relationship of one Elizabethan playwright to his fellows mattered more to him than his economic relationship to Henslowe. Some of the time, collaboration created a different, more satisfying working experience for the playwrights themselves.[22]

Collaboration might also, theoretically, have increased the quality of the product. Acting companies could have believed that collaboration produced scripts that improved the experience of acting in them, and therefore improved the experience of audiences watching and hearing them. Economic pressure might thus, theoretically, have created an incentive to produce a better product. This possibility may seem counter-intuitive, and many critics reject it out of hand. Sisson had nothing but contempt for *The Late Murder in Whitechapel, or Keep the Widow Waking*: 'Incongruous as was the linking together of these two stories into one play, in which no possible dramatic connection could give them any artistic unity, it was evidently sufficient for the dramatist exploiting topical interest that the two wretched criminals involved lay in the same gaol together and were led forth on the same day to stand at the bar of judgment' (82). Vickers, likewise, asserts that 'the speed with which the play was staged meant that the four dramatists had little time for consultation' with each other (315) – thus explaining what he sees as a lamentable lack of artistic unity in all collaborative plays.

It should be obvious that we can say nothing intelligent about the artistic unity of a lost play. Nor can we say anything useful about the lost conversations of one playwright with another. How does Vickers know that four professional playwrights, all living within the much smaller space of early modern London, in easy walking distance from each other, had 'little time' for interaction? In six

weeks *none* of them could find *any* time to talk to each other? Are we to imagine them, walled up in separate rooms for a month and a half, never venturing out to share a meal, an ale or a chat? Should we assume that playwrights, people who make a living writing dialogue, are by nature anti-social? Isn't it likely that some playwrights, then as now, were capable not only of 'empathic listening' but also of mutually productive and interactive 'dialogic listening'?[23] The fact that such conversations were not recorded does not mean that they never took place.

Vickers jumps immediately from *Keep the Widow Waking* to *Sir Thomas More* (*Co-author*, 34–43). Both plays provide documentary evidence of commercial theatre practice. Like the lost 1624 play, the manuscript adaptation of *More* contains the work of four playwrights, one of whom is Thomas Dekker; the others are Chettle, Heywood and Shakespeare.[24] However, the adaptation of *More* has not been linked to any topical scandal that needed to be exploited quickly. Even if speed had been necessary, adapting the play required much less work than writing a new one from scratch, and should have taken much less time to write. Moreover, for most of the period from spring 1603

---

[21] Nashe, *Strange Newes* (1592), sig. F1; *Have with you to Saffron-walden* (1596), sig. V2. See also John Foxe, *Actes and monuments* (1583), on the interestingly complicated writer Bishop Gardiner: 'standyng so much in a singularitie by hymselfe, neither agreeth wyth other hys fellow writers of his own faction, nor yet fully accordeth with hymselfe in certain cases' (p. 1792).

[22] My own experience is that a sense of ethical obligation to collaborators I know and respect encourages me to prioritize finishing a job that I might otherwise postpone or abandon.

[23] See John Stewart, Karen E. Zediker, and Saskia Witteborn, 'Empathic and Dialogic Listening', in *Bridges Not Walls: A Book about Interpersonal Communication*, ed. John Stewart, 11th edn (New York, 2012), pp. 192–207, and Cathy Turner, 'Hare in Collaboration: Writing Dialogues', in *The Cambridge Companion to David Hare*, ed. Richard Boon (Cambridge, 2007), pp. 109–22.

[24] John Jowett, ed., *Sir Thomas More* (London, 2011), pp. 415–60. Jowett summarizes, and expands, the compelling empirical evidence, accumulated by dozens of specialists over the course of more than a century, for the identification of those four hands in the manuscript.

to the end of 1604 (when Jowett and other recent scholars date the adaptation), plague closed the London theatres. No public performances means no urgent demand for new material. Time pressure, that catch-all economic explanation for collective writing, cannot explain the manuscript of *Sir Thomas More*. So, why four playwrights, instead of one? Why collaboration at all?

We could ask that question, and distinguish those four hands in the manuscript, even if we could not connect those hands to particular playwrights working simultaneously in the commercial theatres of early modern London. In the manuscript, authorship is not a theory about cultural authority. The manuscript does not contain Shakespeare's name, and the British Library originally acquired it without knowing that Shakespeare had anything to do with it. Of course, the value of the manuscript rocketed once scholars began to identify Hand D as Shakespeare, just as sales of a crime novel called *The Cuckoo's Calling* rocketed when its author, 'Robert Galbraith', was outed as a pseudonym for J. K. Rowling. Like Rowling, Shakespeare is a lucrative brand name. In the twenty-first century, many more people will buy an edition of *Sir Thomas More*, or buy tickets to a performance of *Sir Thomas More*, because the trademark 'Shakespeare' is attached to it. But that is a fact about the subsequent history of the text. It tells us nothing about Shakespeare, or collaboration, in the early modern London theatre.

Let's begin, therefore, with 'Hand C', which remains anonymous, but does appear in other extant playhouse documents. Hand C might be a theatrical scribe, or (less likely) an unidentified playwright, or some combination of the two. There needs no ghost, come from the grave, to tell us that theatre is a collaborative art-form, but Hand C usefully incarnates the commercial and intrinsically social institution of a joint-stock theatre company.[25] His handwriting illustrates one particular kind of collaborative interaction.

Shakespeare's three pages of the manuscript – the smallest of his known contributions to a collaborative play – contain 1266 words in his own handwriting, including stage directions and speech prefixes, but excluding the eighteen words that he himself deleted in the course of his writing. Hand C subsequently altered Shakespeare's 1266 words thirteen times. In nine places he changed Shakespeare's speech prefixes to bring them into line with the rest of the play, replacing Shakespeare's anonymous crowd with the specific individuals established by the other playwrights. Once, Hand C added the word 'Enter' before a speech prefix, to clarify the stage logistics. These ten changes clearly belong to the necessary business of performing a play: telling actors when to enter, identifying which lines are spoken by which actors. Another change corrects Shakespeare's tautology 'letts us' to 'letts'; this necessary correction might have been made by any scribe or editor. Together, these eleven interventions alter the text no more than Shakespeare himself did, deleting words when he changed his own mind. More significant, from an editorial or dramaturgical point of view, is Hand C's deletion of 26 consecutive words:

is safer wars than ever you can make, whose discipline is riot; in, in to your obedience; why, even your hurly cannot proceed but by obedience

In context, in the manuscript, with interlineations and deletions and an unpunctuated relationship to what goes before and after, this is a confusing and superfluous passage. Hand C replaced it with four unexciting but clear transition words of his own: 'tell me but this'. This is the kind of intrusion that, we can imagine, would make Ben Jonson furious. Nevertheless, these twenty-six deleted words constitute only 2 per cent of Shakespeare's original handwritten text, and Hand C's four added words are less than one third of one per cent. Hand C tinkers with what Shakespeare wrote – and with what the other playwrights wrote. Whether scribe or playwright, his function was to coordinate the work of all the other hands in the manuscript.

---

[25] Paul Werstine points out that the one element of universal consensus about *More* is that 'Hand C has as his goal the preparation' of the manuscript 'to use for performance': *Early Modern Playhouse Manuscripts and the Editing of Shakespeare* (Cambridge, 2013), p. 255.

Notoriously, Shakespeare's own contribution to *More* is not well connected to the work of the three other adapters; therefore, at the time he wrote his three surviving pages, he was not intensely interacting with Chettle, Dekker or Heywood, and his primary motive for writing those pages does not seem to have been social. Either he wanted to write that particular episode, or someone else thought that the play would be improved if he wrote that particular episode. We cannot know whether the initiative came from Shakespeare or someone else, but it hardly matters, because either way the motive was aesthetic, and either way Shakespeare was willing. He was not forced. Although for twenty years Shakespeare was what Gerald Bentley called the company's 'attached dramatist', he did not write the company's additions to their expropriation of Marston's *Malcontent*, which were provided instead by John Webster, a younger playwright with, at the time, no known previous connection to the company. If Shakespeare in 1603–4 chose not to write additions to *The Malcontent*, Shakespeare in 1603–4 could also have chosen not to write additions to *Sir Thomas More*. In fact, by 1603–4 Shakespeare had more economic and artistic freedom than any other professional playwright in London. Consequently, the best explanation for Shakespeare writing those three pages is that something about one episode in *Sir Thomas More* was particularly appealing or appropriate for him to write – by contrast with the material added to *Sir Thomas More* by Chettle, Dekker and Heywood, which seemed appealing or appropriate for each of them, but not for him.

So, what is it about that scene that seemed to him, or someone else, particularly Shakespearian? To begin with, it is not the beginning of the play. Shakespeare's three pages contribute to the sixth scene of the play; editors with a fetish for act divisions have placed it somewhere in the middle of Act 2. The play's original first scene of urban unrest had been so thoroughly eviscerated by the censor that it had to be replaced, or abandoned. Shakespeare did not write a replacement. Instead, Heywood added new material in scene 4, and a new scene 5 was supplied by Hand C (perhaps

copying and modifying something written by Chettle). Only then does Shakespeare appear.

Shakespeare's contribution to *More* fits a pattern found in all his known or suspected collaborations from the beginning of his career until the early Jacobean period.[26] According to the most recent attribution scholarship, Shakespeare did not begin *Arden of Faversham*, *Edward III*, *Titus Andronicus*, any of the three *Henry VI* plays or *Pericles*. For most of his career, Shakespeare was less interested, or less accomplished, in setting up a situation than in developing one. Playwright David Edgar, without any knowledge of this pattern, contends that 'Shakespeare wasn't skilled at exposition.'[27] No modern Shakespeare scholar would dare say so, but the Royal Shakespeare Company apparently agrees: their 2013 productions of *All's Well That Ends Well*, *Richard II* and *Othello* (the only ones I saw) all interpolated new material to jumpstart the play. So did the 2013 Chicago Shakespeare Theatre's *Henry VIII* and the Goodman Theatre's 2013 *Measure for Measure*. All productions at Shakespeare's Globe now begin with an interpolated, energetic musical performance; in their outstanding 2013 *Midsummer Night's Dream* director Dominic Dromgoole also added an introductory dumbshow of the war between Theseus and the Amazons. We might perhaps agree that 'Shakespeare wasn't *as* skilled at exposition' (much virtue in *as*). Certainly, he owes more of his global reputation to an extraordinary gift, demonstrated in *More*, for writing scenes of intense conflict.

In Shakespeare's three pages, *More* singlehandedly quells a rioting mob, one which shouts

---

[26] Shakespeare did write the opening scene of *Timon*, but scholars continue to disagree about that play's date: John Jowett's edition (Oxford, 2004) prefers 'spring 1606' (pp. 3–8), but Anthony Dawson and Gretchen Minton's edition (Arden Shakespeare, 2008) prefers '1607 or early 1608' (pp. 12–18). If *Pericles* preceded *Timon*, then Shakespeare's collaborations would neatly divide into two periods, distinguished by whether he began the play (as he did in *Timon* and in all three collaborations with Fletcher). But the transition need not have been so tidy, and in either case *More* belongs to the earlier pattern.

[27] Edgar, *How Plays Work* (London, 2009), p. 31.

down a sergeant, a mayor and two earls. Scholars have compared this episode to other mob scenes in Shakespeare's works, and in certain respects it does resemble two scenes in *Julius Caesar* and, especially, the opening scene of *Coriolanus*. Those parallels help establish Shakespeare's authorship of the episode, but they have also been used to explain Shakespeare's participation in the project: he had 'a specific expertise in staging popular uprisings' (Jowett, 379), in a way that excited spectators but did not disturb censors.

But the episode in *More* also differs from the mob scenes in *Caesar* and *Coriolanus* in one crucial respect, which connects it to Shakespeare's aesthetic much more broadly. Shakespeare's three pages are entirely dominated by the play's charismatic male protagonist, an 'abnormally interesting' person.[28] Thomas More speaks 788 of the 1213 words that Shakespeare wrote for actors to speak: 65 per cent of the dialogue, including one speech 44 lines long.[29] The consensus of attribution scholarship is that Shakespeare also wrote More's first meditative soliloquy, transcribed by Hand C in scene 8, a turning point for the play and for More's career. More recently, Jowett has argued that Shakespeare wrote parts of a second soliloquy for More, in scene 9, also transcribed by Hand C.[30] But even if we disregard those two soliloquies, the pattern is clear. What interested Shakespeare was Thomas More. From *Richard III* to *The Tempest*, Shakespeare wrote a succession of exceptionally long, exceptionally dominant roles for male protagonists. As Scott McMillin first pointed out, the part of More is comparably long, and must have been written for one of the few Elizabethan actors capable of memorizing and mastering so many lines. Edward Alleyn and Richard Burbage are the most plausible candidates.[31] But for *Othello* (1603–4) and *Volpone* (1605–6) the King's Men required two such actors, to play the paired protagonists Othello–Iago and Volpone–Mosca. This change in company practice might well be connected to the arrival of John Lowin, who at some point in the second half of 1603 left Worcester's Men (working for Henslowe at the Rose) to join the King's Men.[32]

Perhaps he brought the manuscript of *More* with him.[33]

More's dominance is nowhere more evident than in the three pages Shakespeare wrote. Like many of Shakespeare's most famous roles, More in this scene enacts, embodies, the political, imaginative and charismatic power of male eloquence. By contrast with Shakespeare's history plays, much of the rest of *Sir Thomas More* presents, as Jowett says, 'a strong sense of a London locality', of London as 'a city of the people', and of More himself as

---

[28] On 'hypermimesis' and 'charismatic art', see C. Stephen Jaeger, *Enchantment: On Charisma and the Sublime in the Arts of the West* (Philadelphia, 2012), pp. 3, 38. On 'abnormally interesting people', particularly in relation to seventeenth-century theatre, see Joseph Roach, *It* (Ann Arbor, 2007). Roach focuses on the Restoration, but admits that 'the most popular actors in Shakespeare's time enjoyed robust celebrity status' (30), and by the time the additions to *More* were written they also enjoyed royal patronage; Alleyn and Burbage (for either of whom the role of More might have been written) inaugurate the circulation of portraits of sexy leading actors; like other history plays, *More* required the recycling of aristocratic clothing on common stages.

[29] This is all the more remarkable because Shakespeare wrote 344 words before More speaks at all.

[30] Jowett, 'A Collaboration: Shakespeare and Hand C in *Sir Thomas More*', in *Shakespeare Survey 65* (Cambridge, 2012), pp. 255–68.

[31] Scott McMillin, *The Elizabethan Theatre and 'The Book of Sir Thomas More'* (Ithaca, 1987), pp. 61–3.

[32] Martin Butler, 'John Lowin', *Oxford Dictionary of National Biography* (Oxford, 2004), online, accessed 1 September 2013; Andrew Gurr, *The Shakespeare Company, 1594–1642* (Cambridge, 2010), pp. 233–4. McMillin suggested that Lowin could have been the actor paired with Burbage in *Othello* and *Volpone*.

[33] My conjecture about Lowin might resolve the continuing issue about the apparently conflicting relationship between Shakespeare (clearly tied to the Chamberlain/King's Men from 1594 to 1614) and Hand C (whose company affiliations, or movements between companies, remain disputed): see Jowett's discussion (*More*, 102–3). Worcester's Men became a London company in 1601, the year that Lowin would have completed his apprenticeship as a goldsmith; he first appears in Henslowe's account books during the winter of 1602–3, usually through business concerning the purchase of new plays. Jowett places composition of the original play 'in or around 1600' (424–32); both Munday and Chettle were working for someone other than the Admiral's Men from 19 June 1600 to 31 March 1601.

a Londoner among Londoners. Vittorio Gabrieli and Giorgio Melchiori go so far as to claim that London is the 'protagonist' of Act 2.[34] Twenty specific London localities are mentioned by name. But not in Shakespeare's three pages, which do not even contain the word 'London'. The original play, and the other additions, can be clearly linked to emergent genres of city comedy and of history plays with a strong local London interest, like Heywood's *Edward IV* and Dekker's *Shoemaker's Holiday*. The presence of Dekker and Heywood among the adapters makes perfect sense. They specialized in citizen pride and civic humanism. Shakespeare did not. His three pages echo, instead, with the names 'Surrey' and 'Shrewsbury', and evocations of 'the majesty of England'. Although editors describe the mob as citizens, in Shakespeare's pages they are addressed, instead, as 'countrymen', they first refer to their home not as London but as 'our country', and the imagery is not urban either, but imported instead from the natural world: herring, butter, beef, roots, parsnips, dung, pumpkins, a river's 'bank', shark, ravenous fishes, a hound, dogs, mountainish. Thomas More may be a Londoner speaking to Londoners, but Shakespeare still warbles his native woodnotes wild.

You can see the same pattern in *Timon of Athens*, another early Jacobean collaboration, written not long after the additions to *Sir Thomas More*. Shakespeare creates almost the entire long part of the eloquent tragic male protagonist Lord Timon, and Shakespeare completely dominates the play once Timon leaves the city for the countryside; Shakespeare's 'poesy is as a gum, which oozes / From whence 'tis nourished'. By contrast, his younger collaborator, the life-long Londoner Thomas Middleton, dramatizes the satiric, comic, urban ensemble world of servants, creditors and so-called 'senators' who are indistinguishable from the oligarchic commercial aldermen who ruled London. Shakespeare wrote most of the play, but MacDonald P. Jackson observes that Middleton 'created the scenes on which the plot pivots', and that 'Middleton's satirical cameos in Act 3 . . . mingling verse and prose, are the only scenes by a collaborator that Shakespeare could not have written better himself'.[35] Theatrically, Middleton's fast, energetic, urban scenes have always worked better than the magnificently metaphysical poetry of the long, slow, self-indulgent, emotionally static monologues of Timon in the woods. The National Theatre's award-winning 2012 production of *Timon*, directed by Nicholas Hytner, demonstrated how powerful and pertinent the play can be in performance. And if, for some critics, the play is a failure, that failure has to be attributed to the dominant playwright: Shakespeare's excessive focus on the protagonist and Shakespeare's lack of interest in the rest of the plot, including its conclusion.

The collaborative adaptation of *More* and the collaborative creation of *Timon* both recognize two things: first, that London audiences had a growing appetite for the city comedies and city histories being written by Shakespeare's younger contemporaries, and secondly, that Shakespeare himself was not the man to satisfy that appetite and needed a collaborator to do so. Did Shakespeare personally recognize his limitations? Or did the recognition come from Richard Burbage and the rest of the King's Men? Who knows? What matters is that we can see, here, the artistic logic of collaboration. An actor is cast in one role, and not another, because every actor does certain things especially well, and other things not quite so well; ideally, the producer or director or actor-manager or someone in the company aligns the skills of a particular actor with the requirements of a particular role. Casting is, according to a widespread theatrical and cinematic axiom, ninety per cent of directing. Casting is also, I would propose, ninety per cent of collaboration. In a collaborative work, each contributor is cast in a particular role; ideally, each is cast in a role that suits his or her particular talents. The achievement of *West Side Story* depends, for instance, on the music of Leonard Bernstein, the lyrics of Stephen Sondheim, the choreography of Jerome Robbins,

---

34 Gabrieli and Melchiori, eds., *Sir Thomas More*, Revels Plays (Manchester, 1990), p. 30.

35 MacDonald P. Jackson, 'Collaboration', in *The Oxford Handbook of Shakespeare*, p. 51.

the script by Arthur Laurents – and even, a little, on the precursory author, William Shakespeare.

Shakespeare was an actor, but he certainly knew – indeed, everyone knew – that Burbage was a better actor. Burbage was also a painter, which Shakespeare was not. Robert Johnson and Thomas Morley were accomplished composers, which Shakespeare was not. We are willing to admit that Shakespeare collaborated with other people, like Burbage and Johnson, because they were better at something than he was. Why then are we so resistant to accepting that another *writer* might have been better at some aspect of *writing* than Shakespeare was? We accept that Shakespeare incorporated traditional song lyrics, written by other people, into his plays. Why then has it taken Shakespeare's editors three centuries to recognize or accept the evidence of his collaborations?

Part of the explanation must be that human beings are hard-wired to seek the simplest possible cause of an effect, and therefore we typically focus on a single agent, even when we know there is more than one. Everybody talks about Verdi's operas, or Sondheim's musicals, even though neither Verdi nor Sondheim ever worked alone, or wrote what theatre credits call 'the book' of a musical play. Thus, modern productions and editions advertise 'William Shakespeare's' *Timon of Athens*, even when the inside of the book, or the programme, acknowledges that Middleton wrote parts of the play. Likewise, as David Nicol has pointed out, critics routinely praise the collaborative plays of Middleton and Rowley as though they had been written entirely by Middleton.[36] Jeffrey Knapp recognizes that *Pericles* and *The Two Noble Kinsmen* are collaborative plays, and indeed he interprets both as metatheatrical meditations on collaboration – but only in terms of *Shakespeare's* thoughts about collaborating.[37]

Another part of the explanation must be another, related illusion: what Thomas Carlyle called 'hero-worship', what Daniel Kahneman and other cognitive psychologists call 'the halo effect'.[38] This can be seen clearly in the first edition of Shakespeare's works to pay serious attention to the problems of attribution and collaboration. In 1725 Alexander

Pope correctly denied that Shakespeare had written '*Locrine, Sir John Oldcastle, Yorkshire Tragedy, Lord Cromwell, The Puritan*' or *The London Prodigal*. But in the very next sentence he conjectured that in some other plays '(particularly *Love's Labour Lost, The Winter's Tale* and *Titus Andronicus*)', Shakespeare wrote 'only some characters, single scenes, or perhaps a few particular passages' (xx). In the edition itself Pope marks as un-Shakespearian particular scenes in other comedies (*Two Gentlemen of Verona, The Comedy of Errors, Much Ado about Nothing, The Taming of the Shrew*) and the comic Porter's scene in *Macbeth*. Pope, a great satiric poet with a brutally sharp sense of humour, did not think this comic material was funny, and accordingly could not believe that Shakespeare wrote it.

As it happens, modern scholarship has found plentiful evidence of collaboration in Shakespeare's histories and tragedies, but no collaborator has been identified in any of his comedies – and although Middleton adapted *Macbeth*, Shakespeare created the Porter. In this respect, Samuel Johnson was a more accurate judge of Shakespeare's achievement than Pope. Shakespeare's 'natural disposition', Johnson famously intoned, 'led him to comedy. In tragedy he often writes with great appearance of toil and study, what is written at last with little felicity; but in his comick scenes, he seems to produce without labour, what no labour can improve. In tragedy he is always struggling after some occasion to be comick, but in comedy he seems to repose, or to luxuriate, in a mode of thinking congenial to his nature.'[39] On the basis of what we now know about Shakespeare's collaborations, we can modify Johnson's summary slightly by concluding that (like John Lyly) Shakespeare created his own mode of Elizabethan romantic comedy, which was

---

[36] Nicol, *Middleton and Rowley: Forms of Collaboration in the Jacobean Playhouse* (Toronto, 2012), esp. pp. 5–21.

[37] Knapp, *Shakespeare Only*, pp. 133–46.

[38] Kahneman, *Thinking, Fast and Slow* (New York, 2011), pp. 82–5.

[39] 'Preface 1765', in *Johnson on Shakespeare*, ed. Arthur Sherbo, 2 vols. (New Haven, 1968), vol. 7 in the *Yale Edition of the Works of Samuel Johnson*, p. 69.

particularly and happily self-sufficient. His histories, tragedies and tragicomedies, by contrast, contain more writing by other people, presumably because Shakespeare or someone else felt that he would profit from the partnership.

The halo-effect led Pope to deny Shakespeare's authorship of passages that Pope himself found aesthetically unsatisfying; in Pope's case, hero-worship preceded and directed attribution. That still happens; it's found, for instance, in the Folger Shakespeare's systematic denial of collaboration or adaptation; it's evident in the particular refusal to acknowledge a second author in the most recent Arden edition of *Titus Andronicus*, or the most recent Cambridge editions of *Pericles*, *Timon of Athens* and *Measure for Measure*; it's visible when Lukas Erne attributes to Shakespeare all of the 'first tetralogy' and calls it 'the most ambitious project the professional stage had yet seen'.[40] But hero-worship can also follow, and respond to, attribution. The growing empiricism of attribution scholarship as a technical discipline, beginning in the nineteenth century, inevitably impacted the preferences of Shakespeare fandom. Shakespearians now routinely deny the aesthetic achievement of passages in Shakespeare's works that Shakespeare turns out not to have written. Why would Shakespeare choose to collaborate with writers who were as incompetent as many of Shakespeare's editors and critics presume them to be?

Perhaps because Shakespeare did not consider his collaborators incompetent. At the beginning of his career, Shakespeare was learning from more experienced craftsmen, in the kind of apprenticeship relationship normal throughout medieval and early modern Europe. Coleridge recognized that the first lines of *1 Henry VI* do not sound like Shakespeare's verse – but Coleridge did not dismiss them as rhythmically or rhetorically monotonous, as Vickers does. Nashe's sequential short sentences and end-stopped lines in that scene can also be found elsewhere in his work, in passages that have been widely anthologized and admired:

> Beauty is but a flower
> Which wrinkles will devour;
> Brightness falls from the air;

> Queens have died young and fair;
> Dust hath closed Helen's eye.
> I am sick, I must die.
> Lord, have mercy on us!

The choric repetition of 'Lord, have mercy on us' in this famous lyric is echoed in *1 Henry VI*, when the dying Salisbury's 'O Lord, have mercy on us, wretched sinners!' is immediately followed by the dying Gargrave's 'O Lord, have mercy on me, woeful man!' (1.4.70–1). G. R. Hibbard, describing the blank verse in *Summer's Last Will and Testament*, the source of this lyric, acknowledges that 'The lines are largely end-stopped', but he also recognizes that much of it 'surprises by its lyrical grace and easy flow'. He praises the 'the argumentativeness' and 'sheer virtuosity' of Nashe's dialogue, 'the way in which the blank verse is handled to express and contain a veritable torrent of abuse and misrepresentation', 'the insistent use of hammering alliteration to convey scorn and contempt' and 'the way in which all the detail is integrated into a long verse paragraph, building up to the climax'. All these observations are just as relevant to Nashe's verse in Act 1 of *1 Henry VI*, as is Hibbard's recognition of 'two conflicting impulses' in Nashe's work, 'an affection for the past and an impulse to laugh at it. It is both naive and sophisticated.'[41]

In the 2013 production at Shakespeare's Globe, the first scene, by Nashe, was the most powerful in the play, much more memorable than the Temple Garden scene (2.4), or the scenes leading up to Talbot's death (4.2–4.5), which are all attributed to Shakespeare.[42] We may blame this disparity on the weakness of a particular production; earlier stagings, directed by Terry Hands

---

[40] Erne, *Shakespeare as Literary Dramatist* (Cambridge, 2003), p. 5.

[41] Hibbard, *Thomas Nashe: A Critical Introduction* (London, 1962), pp. 95–101.

[42] Gary Taylor, 'Shakespeare and Others: The Authorship of *Henry the Sixth, Part One*', *Medieval and Renaissance Drama in England*, 7 (1995), 145–205; Brian Vickers, 'Incomplete Shakespeare'; Paul Vincent, *When 'harey' Met Shakespeare: The Genesis of 'The First Part of Henry the Sixth'* (Saarbrücken, 2008).

(1977) and Michael Boyd (2008), better demonstrated the theatrical potential of those later Shakespeare scenes. But in those productions, too, the first scene was more brilliantly dramatic. And Pope, who preferred poetry to theatre, and who was not biased by our knowledge of who wrote what, degraded to the bottom of the page passages in both 2.4 and 4.2.

What Nashe brought to the history play, beyond a different music and a mind better equipped to start texts than to close them, was the vigorous xenophobia that we can also see in *The Unfortunate Traveller*.[43] We may not praise this, but English audiences still respond to the Francophobia (often with laughter), and it was an essential ingredient to the growth of history as an Elizabethan dramatic genre. We can easily distinguish Nashe's French-baiting from the humanist defence of (Catholic) 'strangers' in the speeches Shakespeare wrote for More. Shakespeare's scenes in *1 Henry VI* concentrate instead on flowers and hunting, on destructive factional divisions among the English themselves, on the tragedy of the charismatic male protagonist Talbot, on the relationship between fathers and sons, and on men generally. Indeed, no women appear in Shakespeare's scenes of *1 Henry VI*. This, too, is typical. Women play a much larger and more important role in the three (collaborative) *Henry VI* plays and the (collaborative) *All Is True* than in Shakespeare's single-authored 'second tetralogy'.[44] Nashe, the author of 'Choice of Valentines', introduces the play's first sexualized and ambiguous woman, Joan. Nashe is also more interested than Shakespeare in modern mechanized warfare: 1.4 is the only scene in Shakespeare where characters are killed, onstage, by artillery fire, which produces the grotesque mangling of bodies ('One of thy eyes and thy cheeks' side struck off!') that we can also find in Nashe's prose, fascinated as it is with the dissected human body. Nashe provides, too, the populist anti-Catholicism of the play's third scene, explicitly set in a London of rioting apprentices, which twice mocks Winchester's 'cardinal's hat' (1.3.36, 49), and rebels from 'Pope and dignities of Church' (50). Winchester, historically, should have been a bishop in that scene,

which notoriously contradicts 5.1.28–33, where Winchester's elevation to cardinal seems to have just occurred. But Nashe, who had written anti-Marprelate pamphlets in defence of English episcopacy, would have known that attacking Winchester as a 'bishop' would have come dangerously close to Marprelate's puritan position; attacking a cardinal, by contrast, was perfectly safe, indeed an endorsed public pleasure. Anti-Catholicism and Xenophobia go hand-in-hand and, together with their good friend Misogyny, they made *1 Henry VI* a huge popular success. The play is, if anything, *too* unified by these interrelated otherings; its failure, from our perspective, is primarily political, not aesthetic.

'It takes all sorts of playwrights', Harold Pinter acknowledged, 'to make a world.'[45] The Elizabethan history play also created a world, and often did so by combining different authorial voices in what Nina Levine calls 'a community constituted by difference' and by collaborative 'reciprocities of plurality'.[46] Michael Morpurgo, describing the National Theatre's acclaimed and beloved adaptation of his novel *War Horse*, was particularly struck by the company's ability to 'yoke people together with a common purpose', and thereby 'create a sense of community'. *War Horse* is, of course, an English history play, and its success depends less on puppets than on what Morpurgo called 'a togetherness about the whole thing'.[47] A history play answers the question 'Who *were* we?' and its causal corollary 'Why *are* we?', defining 'we' not as 'human beings in general', but as 'a particular community to which the spectators

---

43 Andrew Fleck, 'Anatomizing the Body Politic: The Nation and the Renaissance Body in Thomas Nashe's *The Unfortunate Traveller*', *Modern Philology*, 104 (2007), 295–328.

44 Jean E. Howard and Phyllis Rackin, *Engendering a Nation: A Feminist Account of Shakespeare's History Plays* (New York, 1997), pp. 217–18.

45 Pinter, 'Writing for the Theatre' (1962), in *Plays: One* (London, 1991), p. xi.

46 Nina Levine, 'Citizen's Games: Differentiating Collaboration and *Sir Thomas More*', *Shakespeare Quarterly*, 58 (2007), 31–64, esp. p. 45.

47 Interview with Morpurgo, *The Making of War Horse*, dir. Phil Grabsky and David Bickerstaff (National Theatre/Seventh Art Productions, 2009), DVD.

belong'.[48] The genre explores collective identity, not individuality. It should not surprise us that, of the twelve history plays in current definitions of the Shakespeare canon, half are collaborative – a larger proportion than for any other genre.

Shakespeare's last history, *All is True* (a.k.a. *Henry VIII*), decisively identified as a collaboration more than a century and a half ago, has suffered from the negative side of the halo effect longer than any other play. Pope never doubted Shakespeare's responsibility for the play, and he did not degrade a single passage to the sewer at the bottom of the page that he reserved for interpolations. Indeed, he singled out, typographically, four passages in the play as 'beauties' deserving of particular commendation and attention: three in speeches by Wolsey after his fall (3.2), and some lines in Queen Katherine's final scene (4.2). All four passages, it turns out, were written by Fletcher. The notoriously anti-theatrical Pope thought that the best poetry in the play was written by Fletcher. By contrast, modern critics consider Fletcher a poor poet, and compare these passages unfavourably with the complex versification, syntax and imagery of Shakespeare's scenes in the play.[49] But theatrical performances of the play, like the stunning 2013 production at the Chicago Shakespeare Theatre, directed by Barbara Gaines, always keep these speeches by Fletcher, and often heavily cut Shakespeare's incomprehensible poetry.[50] In *All is True*, as in *The Two Noble Kinsmen*, 'Shakespeare's poetry . . . invests the story with a sense of real gravitas', particularly in the portrayal of royal families and gods. But in performance Fletcher's scenes in both plays are more emotionally and theatrically powerful, and – as in *Timon of Athens* – Shakespeare's collaborator provides a stronger narrative drive.[51] In each case, the collaborator provides something valuable, and valuably different from Shakespeare.[52]

Fletcher is also accused of 'inconsistencies in characterization', and critics are particularly contemptuous of his 'trademark sudden reversals' when a character abruptly switches 'from one position, expressed in extravagant terms, to its opposite'.[53] But the sudden reversals of Fletcher's characters are compellingly true to my own

experience of other people. Perhaps I'm particularly dense, but haven't you ever had the experience of being completely stunned when someone you think you know does something or says something that contradicts, radically, who you think they are? Eventually I may, or may not, re-interpret their personality in a way that reconciles position A with position B, and therefore 'unifies' their character; but that retrospective intellectual hypothesis does not erase, or replace, the vivid, disturbing *experience* of inconsistency, which is also found often in the tragedies of Euripides.

The modern objection to Fletcher's characters belongs to a larger critique of his work which originates with Coleridge: 'the plays of Beaumont and Fletcher', declared the Romantic sage, 'are mere aggregations without unity'.[54] This Romantic celebration of the 'organic' unity of Shakespeare's plays, opposed to the merely 'mechanic' unity of Beaumont and Fletcher, has become a more

---

48 Gary Taylor, 'History. Plays. Genre. Games', in *The Oxford Handbook to Thomas Middleton*, ed. Gary Taylor and Trish Thomas Henley (Oxford, 2012), pp. 47–63, esp. p. 53.

49 For a collection of such negative judgements, see Vickers, *Co-author*, pp. 480–90. MacDonald P. Jackson, 'Collaboration', *Oxford Handbook of Shakespeare*, ed. Kinney, pp. 31–52, also laments the 'disparity in poetic power' between Shakespeare and Fletcher (pp. 36–43).

50 See the review of the Chicago production by Terri Bourus in *Shakespeare Bulletin*, 31:3 (2013), 485–9.

51 Jackson, 'Collaboration', p. 35. Jackson acknowledges that 'Fletcher's languid cadences, with their dying fall, are not unsuited to convey the changes in spiritual state'; he recognizes the 'pulpit eloquence' of Cranmer's oration in the last scene; he admits that 'Audiences have regularly been moved by' the 'plangent strains' of Wolsey's final soliloquy, 'as also by the elegiac cadences of Katherine's valedictory speeches in 4.2' (41). But these concessions culminate in the damningly faint praise of 'Fletcher's material is stageworthy' (41).

52 For more on Fletcher's contribution to collaborations with Shakespeare and others, see the essays by Christopher Hicklin, Huw Griffith and Terri Bourus in Bourus and Taylor, eds. *The Creation and Re-creation of Cardenio: Performing Shakespeare, Transforming Cervantes* (New York, 2013).

53 Jackson, 'Collaboration', in *Oxford Handbook of Shakespeare*, ed. Kinney, p. 39.

54 Quoted and discussed by Gordon McMullan, *The Politics of Unease in the Plays of John Fletcher* (Amherst, 1994), p. 137.

general critique of all collaborative plays, including Shakespeare's. The pioneering attribution scholar Cyrus Hoy declared: 'The crucial issue for the aesthetic appraisal of [a collaborative play] is how satisfactorily the multiple dramatic visions have fused into a single coherent one.' The postmodernist critic Jeffrey Masten, who disdains Hoy, insists that collaborators were dedicated to 'erasing the perception of difference' between them. The attribution scholar Brian Vickers, who disdains Masten, systematically catalogues and laments the inconsistencies of plotting and characterization in each of Shakespeare's collaborative plays.[55] Despite their other differences, these three influential experts on collaborative drama all agree that plays should be unified, all agree that collaboration is an apparent obstacle to unity, and all agree that collaborative plays can and should be judged, aesthetically, by the standard of unification.

In *Shakespeare, Co-Author* Vickers provided a valuable, monumental, polemical synthesis of the collaborative achievement of hundreds of nineteenth and twentieth century scholars, who established the presence of a collaborator in five of Shakespeare's plays. Unfortunately, that synthesis culminates in a chapter that denigrates the aesthetic achievement of those five plays, and indeed of all collaborative plays, because all such plays fail to deliver the 'unity' demanded by Horace, and by all the Elizabethan grammar schoolmasters who shoved Horace down their students' throats. Why would Shakespeare collaborate, when collaboration inevitably damaged the aesthetic unity of a play?

Perhaps because Shakespeare did not value certain kinds of unity. Horace was not a playwright. Ben Jonson translated Horace's *Ars Poetica*, compared himself to Horace, and was compared by his contemporaries to Horace, sincerely or satirically. But Shakespeare was compared to Ovid, not Horace. Shakespeare's favourite poet was Ovid, and his favourite work was Ovid's *Metamorphoses*.[56] No one ever read the *Metamorphoses* for unity. Ovid was not only far more popular than Horace in Western Europe throughout the middle ages and the Renaissance; he was also more characteristic

of classical culture generally, as anyone familiar with *The Odyssey*, Pindar or Herodotus should recognize. The classical scholar Malcolm Heath observes that '*poikilia*', diversity, is invoked more frequently in ancient Greek criticism than unity, 'and is an important principle of artistic construction in Greek tragedy'.[57] The Renaissance rediscovery of Aristotle's *Poetics* quickly led Italian critics to defend Ariosto's *Orlando Furioso* by challenging the Aristotelian insistence on unity. The foundational defence of Ariosto was written by a writer that Shakespeare certainly read, Giovambattista Giraldi Cinzio (who wrote the source of *Othello*). Whereas Homer in the *Iliad* and Vergil in the *Aeneid* had set out to describe 'a single action of one knight' ('*una sola attione de un cavaliero*'), Ariosto – like the authors of French, Provencal and Spanish romances – wished to treat 'many [actions] of many [men]' ('*molte de molti*').[58] Neither Aristotle nor Horace is of any use in understanding modern vernacular poets, who with their multiple plots 'relieve the satiety caused by always reading one same thing' ('*levare la satietà al lettore di sempre leggere una medesima cosa*').[59] Variety, not unity, was the fundamental criterion.[60]

Whether or not Shakespeare read *Orlando Furioso* and its Italian fans, Sidney and Spenser certainly did. Whether or not Shakespeare had ever seen a *commedia dell'arte* performance, he began his career in the century when licensed companies of professional players, first in Italy and then in England, subordinated the plots of humanist writers to the unpredictable onstage interactions of an ensemble of character-actors and clowns. After the work of Madeleine Doran on 'multiplicity and

---

[55] Hoy, 'Critical and Aesthetic Problems of Collaboration in Renaissance Drama', *Research Opportunities in Renaissance Drama*, 19 (1976), 6; Masten, *Textual Intercourse*, p. 17; Vickers, *Co-author*, pp. 433–50.

[56] See particularly Jonathan Bate, *Shakespeare and Ovid* (Oxford, 1994); Francis Meres, *Palladis Tamia* (1598), sig. Oo1v.

[57] Heath, *The Poetics of Greek Tragedy* (Stanford, 1987), p. 106.

[58] Cinzio, *Risposta a M. Giouambattista Pigna* (1554), p. 10.

[59] Cinzio, *Discorsi intorno al comporre dei romanzi* (1554), p. 42.

[60] Bernard Weinberg, *A History of Literary Criticism in the Italian Renaissance*, 2 vols. (Chicago, 1961), vol. 2, p. 969.

sequential action', after David Bevington's work on the sixteenth-century evolution of dramatic form to achieve 'panoramic inclusiveness' by means of doubling, after Richard Levin's work on the evolution of multiple plots from Terence to Middleton, after Scott McMillin and Sally-Beth MacLean on the Queen's Men, the dominant acting company of the 1580s, with a repertory defined not by recognizable classical genres but by what the actor-playwright Robert Wilson called a 'medley' – after six decades of collaborative scholarship, it should no longer be necessary to insist that the aesthetic of Shakespeare and his collaborators valued Ovidian variety more than Horatian unity.[61]

None of these critics was writing specifically about collaborative authorship. But the cultural logic that values romance narratives, stylistic variation, mixed genres, doubling actors and double plots also applies to the variety created by mixed authorial voices. The first Elizabethan collaborative plays were not written by hurried hacks, whipped into submission by the vile capitalist imperatives of Philip Henslowe. From 1562 to 1588, *Gorboduc*, *Jocasta*, *Gismond of Salerne*, *Estrild* and *The Misfortunes of Arthur* were all collaboratively written by humanist gentlemen, apparently for no financial reward.[62] Before he began collaborating in the London theatres, Thomas Nashe wrote one part of a student 'shew' at the University of Cambridge. Dr Johnson speaks of 'confederate authors' and, although that idiom disappeared after the American Civil War gave 'confederate' particularly negative connotations, Johnson's adjective does capture the sense that a collaborative work of art does not seek 'unity', but instead presupposes a 'federal' structure that allows for individual difference.[63] Early modern playwrights made temporary and shifting alliances, based on the needs of a particular narrative. The division of plays into acts, scenes, or sections of scenes, written by separate authors, gives each author imaginative autonomy within an agreed framework.

But how do we distinguish between a desirable multiplicity and an undesirable inconsistency? In highlighting the inconsistencies in Shakespeare's collaborative plays, Vickers violates one of the cardinal rules of attribution scholarship. Before we can attribute responsibility for a disputed work to a particular author, we must first examine the uncontested canon of candidate authors, in order to establish the constants that characterize all their work. In this case, we are trying to identify which characteristics, if any, distinguish collaborative plays from single-author plays. Vickers says, rightly, 'Scholars have long noticed many inconsistencies in Shakespeare's co-authored plays.'[64] But in fact scholars have noticed many inconsistencies in *all* Shakespeare's plays. Between 1982 and 1993 Kristian Smidt wrote four books on 'unconformities' in Shakespeare's histories, tragedies and comedies, collecting examples noticed by earlier critics.[65] In *Henry V* Pistol begins married to Nell, but ends married to Doll; Exeter is specifically ordered by the King to 'remain' behind in Harfleur (3.3.135), but then reappears on the battlefield at Agincourt (4.3, 4.6, 4.7, 4.8), without explanation. In *Two Gentlemen* Sylvia's father is both a Duke and an Emperor, living simultaneously in both Milan and Verona; *Othello* is only the most famous example of the incompatible time schemes found throughout

---

[61] Doran, *Endeavours of Art: A Study of Form in Elizabethan Drama* (Madison, 1954), p. 17; David M. Bevington, *From 'Mankind' to Marlowe: Growth of Structure in the Popular Drama of Tudor England* (Cambridge, 1962), p. 115; Levin, *The Multiple Plot in English Renaissance Drama* (Chicago, 1971); McMillin and MacLean, *The Queen's Men and their Plays* (Cambridge, 1998), p. 124.

[62] On *Estrild*, written by Charles Tilney with choruses by George Buc, see Sharpe, 'Authorship and Attribution', pp. 659–60.

[63] 'Life of Peter Sarpi' (1774), in *The Works of Samuel Johnson*, 12 vols. (1792), 12: 6 ('Cardinal Bellarmine with his confederate authors'). The idiom was also used by Richard Smalbroke in *The Reverence due to the house of God* (1722), xv, and by George Steevens (1780), cited in Henry Weber, 'Observations on the Participation of Shakespeare in *The Two Noble Kinsmen*', in *The Works of Beaumont and Fletcher*, ed. Weber, 14 vols. (Edinburgh, 1812), vol. 13, p. 164.

[64] Vickers, *Co-author*, p. 443.

[65] Smidt, *Unconformities in Shakespeare's History Plays* (London, 1982); *Unconformities in Shakespeare's Early Comedies* (London, 1986); *Unconformities in Shakespeare's Tragedies* (London, 1989); *Unconformities in Shakespeare's Later Comedies* (London, 1993).

Shakespeare's plays. A.C. Bradley took an interest in just this sort of contradiction in the notorious notes to *Shakespearean Tragedy*, and Tolstoy's condemnation of *Lear* shows what happens when a realist critic encounters Shakespeare's basic violations of narrative logic. Wherever we look in English Renaissance drama, we will find rampant inconsistency.

Attribution scholars are particularly likely to notice, and to be disturbed by, the kinds of inconsistency industriously collected and rhetorically displayed by Vickers. After all, the technical discipline of attribution scholarship consists of the systematic reading of recurring material signs; computers are often preferred because a computer reads material signs more consistently and systematically than humans do. The attribution scholar or the scholar's computer is particularly good at noticing small details that have hitherto been overlooked; in fact, details of which the author himself might have been unconscious provide particularly valuable evidence. Moreover, attribution scholarship depends on pattern recognition, the ability to connect details in different parts of a text. All these admirable skills and procedures enable attribution scholars to identify, empirically and objectively, who wrote a play or a significant part of one. But these same skills and procedures also make attribution scholars hypersensitive – indeed, obsessive compulsive – about inconsistencies of plot and characterization. Those inconsistencies are not likely to be noticed in the theatre; nor are they likely to be noticed by what we might call the common reader, that endangered species of creature who reads Shakespeare for the plot or the poetry, outside the professionalized 'domain dependence' of specialist attribution scholarship.

Spectators don't notice the inconsistencies that bother scholars. In the theatre, or in other unscripted environments, we 'only perceive a contradiction if we juxtapose a present moment with an incompatible antecedent moment; how many spectators perceive a contradiction therefore depends on the probability of this present moment being juxtaposed with that one particular incompatible antecedent moment, and no other'.[66] Our

ability to make such juxtapositions, in real time, is a function of immediate memory span. 'A great deal of experience does not survive the instant of its passing and is irretrievably forgotten the moment it is over', according to cognitive psychologists; 'in the next instant, the circumstances of which we need to take account are different.'[67] A book, by contrast, is an artificial memory device, which enables us to juxtapose any moment of a play with any other moment, and to notice the kinds of self-contradictions that have fuelled deconstructionist philosophy and criticism.

Long before laboratory experiments in the psychology of perception demonstrated our hard-wired liability to overlook such contradictions, professional theatre-makers knew how easy it was to trick an audience. A professional magician knows that we won't see the sleight of hand by which he exchanges one card for another. The protagonist of *Titus Andronicus* cuts off his own hand (in a scene written by Shakespeare, not Peele), an action that must be convincingly horrific, and that contributes to the pathos of the character's 'lamentable action of one arm' for the rest of the play.[68] But the actor playing Titus does not really cut off his hand at every performance, any more than the actor playing Lavinia has her hands and tongue amputated. The 2013 Royal Shakespeare Company production of *Titus* included, among its Creative Team, a professional 'illusionist', Richard Pinner, who was 'Stage and Close Up Magician of the Year' in 2003 and has worked in more than thirty countries. The success of magic tricks depends not only on the practised skills of the magician but on the human susceptibility to particular kinds of cognitive illusion.[69] We

---

66 Gary Taylor, *Moment by Moment by Shakespeare* (London, 1985), p. 146.

67 Ian M. L. Hunter, *Memory*, rev. edn (Harmondsworth, 1964), pp. 75, 79.

68 Thomas Middleton, *Father Hubburd's Tales*, ed. Adrian Weiss, in *Collected Works*, lines 946–7 ('for all my lamentable action of one arm, like old Titus Andronicus').

69 See for instance Stephen L. Macknik, Susana Martinez-Conde and Sandra Blakeslee, *Sleights of Mind: What the*

routinely tell our students and ourselves that a play is not 'real', that it is 'artificial', and we congratulate ourselves on our metatheatrical sophistication. We celebrate Shakespeare's 'magic of bounty' (*Timon*, 1.1.6) and recognize the playwright's self-description when Rosalind describes 'a magician, most perfect in his art and yet not damnable' (*As You Like It*, 5.2.58–9). But we are less happy about acknowledging that as a matter of routine actors and playwrights successfully con us, trick us, pick the pockets of our minds, dazzle and deceive us with what Middleton, in a speech he added to *Macbeth*, calls 'magic sleights' – tricks that 'raise such artificial sprites' as the supernatural figures in Shakespeare's plays, which wow us with 'the strength of their illusions' (3.5.26–8). Unfortunately, the magic tricks that create the illusion of narrative logic, psychological depth and aesthetic unity no longer work if we record them with a fixed camera, and then play them back, over and over again, at very slow speed – which is what happens when scholars read, over and over again, the printed text of a play.

The inconsistencies created by collaboration do not matter in the theatre; the variety created by the particular styles and talents of different collaborators do matter. That's perhaps why collaboration is not common in novels, but common enough in both theatre and film. The screenplay for *Birth of a Nation*, the first full-length motion picture, was co-written by D. W. Griffith and Frank E. Woods. *Casablanca*, consistently ranked among the top films of all time, had three credited screenwriters, and a fourth uncredited, and was based on a 'plot' co-written by two playwrights. *Some Like It Hot*, widely regarded as one of the greatest film comedies in English, was co-written by Billy Wilder and I. A. L. Diamond; Wilder, in fact, 'quite clearly *preferred* to collaborate', and all his great films were co-written.[70] The film of David Mamet's *Glengarry Glen Ross*, a 'constructive collaboration' based on a 'productive intersection' of talents, was a critical and commercial success; by contrast, the 'one-sided' film of *Oleanna*, completely dominated by the singular authorial intelligence of Mamet, was a critical and popular failure.[71] Screenplays that are collectively written, like screenplays with a single author, can 'produce the most engaging and the most turgid films'.[72] The same is true of early modern plays. Sometimes it works, sometimes it doesn't. But the fundamental motive is always the same: the recognition that, sometimes, 'collaboration has an explosive upside, what is mathematically called a superadditive function, i.e. one plus one equals more than two, and one plus one plus one equals much, much more than three'.[73]

Neuroscience of Magic Reveals About Our Everyday Deceptions (New York, 2011).

[70] McMullan, *Politics of Unease*, p. 133 (referring to Fletcher). For Wilder, see Terri Bourus, '"It's a Whole Different Sex!": Women Performing Middleton on the Modern Stage', in *Oxford Handbook to Thomas Middleton*, ed. Taylor and Henley, pp. 569–70.

[71] Christophe Collard, 'Adaptive Collaboration, Collaborative Adaptation: Filming the Mamet Canon', *Adaptation*, 3:2 (2010), 82–98.

[72] C. Paul Sellors, *Film Authorship: Auteurs and Other Myths* (London, 2010), p. 5.

[73] Nassim Nicholas Taleb, *Antifragile: Things that Gain from Disorder* (New York, 2012), p. 232.

WHAT IS NOT COLLABORATIVE ABOUT EARLY MODERN DRAMA IN PERFORMANCE AND PRINT?

GABRIEL EGAN

We often say that Shakespeare's plays are inherently collaborative because drama itself is a collective artform and that the processes of transmission by which the texts come down to us – scribal copying and printing – constitute additional layers of collaboration. On the assumption that Shakespeare welcomed or at least acquiesced to changes to his plays made by actors during rehearsal, the 1986 Oxford Complete Works edition attempted, where a choice existed, to reflect the plays as they were first performed rather than as first written. This article reconsiders the extent to which Shakespeare's plays may have been reshaped in the theatre, finding that it has recently been overstated and that his authority over his words is probably greater than is usually supposed. Howsoever they were altered in the theatre, the plays come down to us solely (with one small exception) in the form of early printed editions, and so to gauge how close we may come to Shakespeare's words we must consider what was changed in the process of printing. The idea that, like performance, textual transmission too was thoroughly collaborative rose to prominence in the 1980s and 1990s as the sociology-of-texts movement reached Shakespeare studies. This movement stressed that writers do not produce books as such on their own, but rather it takes a constellation of other individuals and institutions to constitute the necessary conditions and provide the additional contributions that result in print publication. This article argues that the collaborative nature of publication has also recently been overstated and calls for editors to return to the task of undoing the effects of scribes and compositors to recover the authorial labour.

ALTERATIONS IN THE THEATRE

The dominant editorial theory of all but the last decade of the twentieth century was the New Bibliography. Changes made to a Shakespeare play during rehearsal and in performance were, for the most part, characterized by New Bibliographers as unauthorized interference rather than collective reshaping. Despite occasional public acknowledgements that the collaborative nature of performance gives a post-rehearsal text a collective authority of its own,[1] the New Bibliographers generally privileged the author's intentions prior to rehearsal, which they treated as an activity that could only corrupt the text. New Bibliographical editors preferred as their copy text an early printed edition based on authorial papers rather than one based on a promptbook, although they derived complex rules for admitting into the modern edition readings from editions other than the copy text where these are more likely to reflect Shakespeare's original (pre-rehearsal) intentions.

---

[1] John Dover Wilson, '"The Genuine Text": A Letter to the Editor', *Times Literary Supplement*, no. 1737 (16 May 1935), 313; John Dover Wilson, '"The Genuine Text": A Letter to the Editor', *Times Literary Supplement*, no. 1739 (30 May 1935), 348; John Dover Wilson, '"The Genuine Text": A Letter to the Editor', *Times Literary Supplement*, no. 1741 (13 June 1935), 380; W. W. Greg, '"The Genuine Text": A Letter to the Editor', *Times Literary Supplement*, no. 1740 (6 June 1935), 364.

In his *Prolegomena for the Oxford Shakespeare*, however, R. B. McKerrow frankly acknowledged the editorial consequences of the changes to Shakespeare's scripts in the theatre:

Such alterations may have been made by the author himself or, if he was not available, they may have been made by others. He may, or may not, have regarded them as improvements: he probably merely accepted them as necessary changes, and it is quite likely that he never bothered about whether they introduced inconsistencies into what was originally conceived as a consistent whole. We must not expect to find a definitive text in the sense in which the published version of the plays of a modern dramatist is definitive.[2]

It remained editorially respectable, however, to treat the theatre as a wholly corrupting influence. A notorious late example is Philip Edwards's 'At this point what one can only call degeneration began, and . . . the nearer we get to the stage, the further we are getting from Shakespeare.'[3] At the same time as Edwards was making this assertion, McKerrow's successor as editor of the proposed Oxford Shakespeare, Stanley Wells, was finalizing his adaptation of New Bibliography to accommodate the increasing respect that theatrical practice was being afforded within Shakespeare studies.[4] Wells saw promptbook-derived early printed editions as having their own authority and, when choosing the moment for a 'snapshot' of a play to be represented in the modern edition,[5] his 'new' New Bibliography favoured – where there was a choice to be made – the script not as it left Shakespeare's hand but as it was first performed. Wells's adaptation of New Bibliography took the accommodation of editorial theory to theatrical concerns about as far as it reasonably ought to go.

The acknowledgement that a Shakespeare script was subject to authorized change has, in the years since the Oxford Shakespeare of 1986, been exaggerated into a claim that it was forever in motion. In Tiffany Stern's model of theatrical production, the place of the single authorized manuscript of the play has been taken by a play decomposed not only into actors' parts, but also songs (written out separately to be sent off to a composer for setting to music), prologues and epilogues (held on separate manuscripts and reused for different plays), and property documents such as letters to be read aloud during a performance.[6] All these documents were also 'the play', yet they circulated beyond the bounds of the authorized manuscript. The result is that we must consider a play not as a unified and coherent original creation but rather as a patch-work compilation forever being reworked into new patterns of combination:

The suggestion then is that a play is a collection of fragments taken from elsewhere and loosely held together . . . there was something 'patch-like' in the very way a play was written in the first place . . . the very method of creating the play seems to be, somehow, 'patchy' . . . There was a sense at the time that plays were not whole art-works in the way that poems were. Plays had the bit, the fragment, the patch in their very natures.[7]

Stern's method '"deconstructs" the text along certain lines and then, up to a certain point, "de-authors" it'.[8] The widespread appeal of Stern's approach lies in its apparent reconciliation of theatre-historical materials with a critical-theoretical disposition towards postmodernism. That is to say, a broad spectrum of Shakespearians feel a desire – perhaps not fully consciously – for what she says to be true because it appeals to current orthodoxies in English studies that arose in Anglo-American literary criticism with the dissemination and wide acceptance of high French theory from the late 1960s.

---

[2] R. B. McKerrow, *Prolegomena for the Oxford Shakespeare: A Study in Editorial Method* (Oxford, 1939), p. 6.

[3] William Shakespeare, *Hamlet*, ed. Philip Edwards, New Cambridge Shakespeare (Cambridge, 1985), p. 32.

[4] Gabriel Egan, *The Struggle for Shakespeare's Text: Twentieth-century Editorial Theory and Practice* (Cambridge, 2010), pp. 167–89.

[5] Stanley Wells, 'Editing Shakespeare', *Times Literary Supplement*, no. 4268 (18 January 1985), 63.

[6] Tiffany Stern, *Documents of Performance in Early Modern England* (Cambridge, 2009).

[7] Tiffany Stern, 'Re-patching the Play', in *From Script to Stage in Early Modern England*, ed. Peter Holland and Stephen Orgel, *Redefining British Theatre History* (Basingstoke, 2004), pp. 151–77, pp. 154–5.

[8] Stern, 'Re-patching the Play', p. 171.

In Stern's model, the dispersal of authorial authority was not merely conceptual but was physically embodied in dispersed pieces of paper. Unfortunately for this model, the hard evidence of early modern play licensing points in precisely the opposite direction. To be approved the play had to be presented to the state censor as a single, complete manuscript. Scripts were occasionally revised, but not routinely and seldom more than once, and revision required the script again to take a unified, singular form in order to be reassessed by the censor for a substantial fee, as we shall see. Before we explore the revision of scripts for revival, it is worth considering just how much freedom to revise was built into the parts-based system of lines-learning and preparation for first performance. We might suppose that the singularity and fixedness of the licensed script was merely a convenient fiction that the Master of the Revels and the playing companies shared in order to satisfy the official rules on theatrical regulation while proceeding with their prime objective of extracting wealth from the new industry. After all, would not actors be likely to depart from the official script whenever they saw need? Not all the evidence that has been adduced on this topic is strictly relevant, because then as now the word 'part' meant not only the document but also the human personality created by an actor, as when Shakespeare's Antonio metatheatrically calls the world a stage 'where every man must play a part' and his 'a sad one' (*The Merchant of Venice*, 1.1.78–9). With little direct evidence to go on, Stern treats every reference to a play's parts as gestures towards the physical documents and creates the impression that these were highly fluid documents that need not be closely tied to the licensed script.

Yet, sometimes 'parts' simply does mean just the portions of a whole. In April 1613 the dramatist Robert Daborne was contracted by Henslowe to write a play called *Machiavel and the Devil* (Dulwich College Manuscripts 1 Article 70)[9] and thereafter he began sending Henslowe bits of it as he completed them. On 25 June Daborne wrote to Henslowe 'for thear good & myn own J have took extraordynary payns wth the end & altered one other scean in the third act which they have now in parts' (Dulwich College Manuscripts 1 Article 81).[10] Assuming that the third act is the object of 'which they have', what does Daborne mean by the actors having it 'in parts'? Stern reads this as meaning that the actors had divided the portions of the play they received into cuescripts (another name for actors' parts) and begun learning them.[11] Even when read in isolation this letter makes that interpretation unlikely since, as Daborne indicates, he was still making alterations while composing fresh material and he had not completed the play. It would be tiresome indeed to learn a play while it was still being written and altered. The matter is established beyond doubt and against Stern's interpretation by looking at earlier letters in which Daborne makes clear that upon completion he wanted Henslowe and Alleyn to hear him read the whole play before giving a reading to the players who would decide whether to accept it (Dulwich College Manuscripts 1 Articles 74, 75).[12] No playing company that was efficiently run would have its members learn the parts for a play before it had been collectively agreed to purchase the script and mount a production.

Just when did the actors start to learn their parts? Learning them before the censor had given a performance licence would be risky, since the licence might be refused or made upon condition of extensive cuts or alterations. Yet in a letter to Edward Knight, scribe to the King's Men, Master of the Revels Herbert seems to imply that parts were made before licensing:

Mr. Knight, In many things you have saved mee labour; yet wher your judgment or penn fayld you, I have made boulde to use mine. Purge ther parts, as I have the booke. And I hope every hearer and player will thinke that I

---

9 W. W. Greg, ed., *Henslowe Papers: Being Documents Supplementary to Henslowe's Diary* (London, 1907), pp. 67–8.

10 Greg, ed., *Henslowe Papers: Being Documents Supplementary to Henslowe's Diary*, p. 73.

11 Simon Palfrey and Tiffany Stern, *Shakespeare in Parts* (Oxford, 2007), pp. 61–2.

12 Greg, ed., *Henslowe Papers: Being Documents Supplementary to Henslowe's Diary*, pp. 69, 70.

have done God good servise, and the quality no wronge; who hath no greater enemies than oaths, prophaness, and publique ribaldry, wh[ch] for the future I doe absolutely forbid to bee presented unto mee in any playbooke, as you will answer it at your perill. 21 Octob. 1633.[13]

Stern reads this as indicating that for a new play the actors might start learning the parts before the Master of the Revels has given his verdict on it.[14] That is not at all what is going on here. The preceding notes in Herbert's office book show that the play in question is John Fletcher's *The Woman's Prize, or the Tamer Tamed*, a sequel to Shakespeare's *The Taming of the Shrew*. It was first performed in 1611 and the King's Men revived it in 1633 without asking Herbert to look over the old book and give it a new licence. Hearing that it contained 'foule and offensive matters' Herbert suppressed the performance and demanded the promptbook, censored it and sent word that in future revivals must be licensed as well as new plays.[15] In such cases, 'The players ought not to study their parts till I have allowed of the booke', wrote Herbert.[16] Because the King's Men were reviving a play first performed 22 years earlier, the parts were already in existence. Herbert was warning the players not to learn their parts for a revival of an old play until he had read and relicensed the book, and this tells us nothing about what happened with new plays. Yet this piece of evidence is frequently misused to suggest that for new plays the actors might start to learn their parts before the script was licensed. We just do not know if they did, and there are obvious reasons why they should not have.

We usually assume that it was the playing company that took a newly purchased script to the Master of the Revels for licensing, but in the one firm case for which there is evidence the script was already licensed at the moment it was purchased. The details of this case strengthen our reasons for assuming that revision after licensing was firmly forbidden.[17] Early in 1603, a play by George Chapman called *The Old Joiner of Aldgate*, now lost, was performed by the boy actors at the St Paul's playhouse and it got its dramatist into trouble.[18] The story was a lightly disguised version of an

ongoing legal struggle between the father of the heiress Agnes Howe and various suitors hoping to marry her. Several of the parties represented in the play were offended by the satire and accused one another of having had a hand its production. The matter got to the Star Chamber court, where Chapman admitted writing the play but insisted it was all his own invention and that no-one had given him a particular plot to follow.[19] Thomas Woodford, who bought the play on behalf of the boys' company, deposed that 'he bought one playe booke of... George Chapman beinge Lycencede by the Mr of our Layte Soueringe Lady the quenes maiestyes Revels he not knowing that yt touchede any person lyvinge'.[20] This phrasing makes it plain that the script was already licensed at the point of purchase, so Chapman himself or his agent must have taken the play to Edmund Tilney to get it endorsed.

Chapman was asked under oath if he altered the play after it was licensed and he flatly denied doing so. Since the play was intended to mock several well-known Londoners, including Doctor John Milward the Preacher at Christ Church, Greyfriars, it would have been safest to submit an innocuous script to Tilney and then to introduce or amplify the satire by revision before performance. At least, that would have been the safest thing to do if, as Stern believes, alterations between licensing and performance were not uncommon and were tacitly permitted. Chapman's denial that this was done for *The Old Joiner of Aldgate* was echoed by the man

---

[13] N. W. Bawcutt, ed., *The Control and Censorship of Caroline Drama: The Records of Sir Henry Herbert, Master of the Revels 1623–73* (Oxford, 1996), p. 183.

[14] Tiffany Stern, *Rehearsal from Shakespeare to Sheridan* (Oxford, 2000), pp. 63–4; Tiffany Stern, *Making Shakespeare: From Stage to Page*, Accents on Shakespeare (London, 2004), p. 145; Palfrey and Stern, *Shakespeare in Parts*, p. 61.

[15] Bawcutt, ed., *Control and Censorship of Caroline Drama*, p. 182.

[16] Bawcutt, ed., *Control and Censorship of Caroline Drama*, p. 183.

[17] I am indebted to the anonymous reader of an earlier version of this article for pointing me towards this case.

[18] C. J. Sisson, *Lost Plays of Shakespeare's Age* (Cambridge, 1936), pp. 12–79.

[19] Sisson, *Lost Plays of Shakespeare's Age*, pp. 60–2.

[20] Sisson, *Lost Plays of Shakespeare's Age*, p. 62.

accused of commissioning it, John Flaskett, one of Agnes's thwarted suitors. Under oath, he likewise flatly denied the suggestion that after witnessing the first performance he made recommendations for the play's revision.[21] We might be tempted to treat Chapman's and Flaskett's denials with what has become known as the Rice-Davies Response: 'they would, wouldn't they?'[22] Yet if we suspect that they were lying and that the play was in fact revised after licensing, then the vehement denial of this by Chapman and Flaskett – who were prepared to perjure themselves on this point – itself constitutes strong evidence that such revision was not tacitly accepted as a routine part of the theatrical process. The licensed script really was supposed to govern what got performed.

In a study of the various kinds of revision that might be undertaken, Eric Rasmussen noted that: 'Along with adding new material to a finished script before the first production, playwrights might write additions for later revivals (see Knutson, 'Henslowe's').'[23] Where the reviser(s) was/were not the original dramatist(s), revision for revival would add a further layer of collaboration to the play. Rasmussen discussed some famous examples, but the essay by Roslyn L. Knutson that he here cited had itself concluded from the evidence in Henslowe's Diary covering the period 1592–1603 that what he described was rare: 'revision for the occasion of revival was neither commonplace nor economically necessary' and 'under normal circumstances companies did not pay for revisions of old playbooks'.[24] In a classic work on Shakespearian revision, John Kerrigan argued that we can tell authorial changes from non-authorial ones because the former tend to be 'small additions, small cuts and indifferent word substitutions' as well as larger changes, while authors revising another's work tend to insert or remove sizeable sections of text without touching the surrounding material.[25] Rasmussen denied this distinction in different revisers' interventions and he overstated the general prevalence of revision, ignoring an important reason to limit it. Revision was costly because it entailed a fee for relicensing.

With the zeal of a new appointee, Master of the Revels Henry Herbert established, upon taking up his post, that plays licensed by his predecessors would need relicensing for revival under his tenure and that he would do the work for free. On 19 August 1623 he recorded in his office book the relicensing of 'An ould play', now lost, called *The Peaceable King, or the Lord Mendall* (previously allowed by George Buc)' & because <itt was free from adition> or reformation I tooke no fee', and another 'olde play', Shakespeare's *The Winter's Tale* (also previously allowed by Buc), for which 'the allowed book was missinge' but 'on Mr. Hemmings his worde that there was nothing profane added or reformed' Herbert relicensed it and 'returned it without a fee'.[26] On 21 August 1623 Herbert took no fee for relicensing 'An Old Play', Thomas Dekker's *Match Me in London*, first performed *c.*1611–*c.*1613 and formerly allowed by Buc, presumably because it was unaltered.[27] On 7 July 1624 Herbert took ten shillings for relicensing Dekker and Massinger's *The Virgin Martyr*, performed in 1620, with an additional scene and he took the same amount on 13 May 1629 for relicensing an unnamed old play with 'a new act'.[28] Herbert appears to have charged ten shillings for relicensing revised plays until the 1630s when the fee jumped to £1.

[21] Sisson, *Lost Plays of Shakespeare's Age*, p. 68.

[22] Elizabeth Knowles, *Oxford Dictionary of Quotations*, 7th edn (Oxford, 2009), RICE 660:3.

[23] Eric Rasmussen, 'The Revision of Scripts', in *A New History of Early English Drama*, ed. John D. Cox and David Scott Kastan (New York, 1997), pp. 441–60, p. 448.

[24] Roslyn L. Knutson, 'Henslowe's Diary and the Economics of Play Revision for Revival, 1592–1603', *Theatre Research International*, 10 (1985), 1–18, p. 1.

[25] John Kerrigan, 'Revision, Adaptation, and the Fool in *King Lear*', in *The Division of the Kingdoms: Shakespeare's Two Versions of* King Lear, ed. Gary Taylor and Michael Warren, Oxford Shakespeare Studies (Oxford, 1983), pp. 195–243, p. 195.

[26] Bawcutt, ed., *The Control and Censorship of Caroline Drama*, p. 142.

[27] Bawcutt, ed., *The Control and Censorship of Caroline* Drama, p. 143.

[28] Bawcutt, ed., *The Control and Censorship of Caroline Drama*, pp. 153, 168.

In 1622–5 Herbert's standard fee for licensing a new play for performance was £1, for 1626–31 we have no evidence, and from 1632 it was £2.[29] Thus Herbert's fees for relicensing plays revised for revival, ten shillings and £1, are substantial and must have discouraged routine minor alteration ('re-patching') of plays when they were being revived. For plays licensed under Herbert's tenure, then, there was a powerful economic disincentive to revision, and if it was deemed desirable it might as well be substantial revision to justify the additional cost of relicensing. What about previous Masters of the Revels? We have no direct evidence, but we should not assume that they forewent the opportunity to earn extra fees that would follow from insisting that revivals-with-revision were relicensed. There is no evidence that plays would have been endlessly and haphazardly re-patched in the way that Stern supposes. Revision was costly and for that reason orderly and rare.

There are other reasons to temper the recent enthusiasm for treating Shakespeare's plays as essentially collaborations made in the theatre. Andrew Gurr's knowledge of just how theatre companies turned scripts into performances might be expected to make him scathing of the New Bibliographical preference for the authorial text over the promptbook that had supposedly been corrupted by rehearsal and performance. In fact Gurr could see merit in the New Bibliographical view, at least in the case of Shakespeare:

he, as a player in the company for which he was writing, knew exactly what he wanted to be put on stage, and that therefore his original version should prevail over the company's product after much rehearsal and modification. That suggests, though the case is not usually made that way, absolute primacy for the authorial text before the company got its hands on it and changed it ... aiming at the author's own version must be a target unique to Shakespeare's plays, since no other writer had the same inside role in his company or financial interest in its playhouses.[30]

That is to say, it is precisely because, as extensive theatre historiographical research has established,

Shakespeare was thoroughly a man of the theatre that his pre-rehearsal texts had rather more theatrical authority than those of other dramatists, and the promptbook – whose differences from the authorial papers reflected Shakespeare's wishes being overruled – rather less. Paradoxically, much the same conclusion arises from Lukas Erne's argument, which has nowhere been effectively refuted, that Shakespeare wrote with at least half an eye on his print readership and hence was not exclusively a man of the theatre.[31]

ALTERATIONS IN PRINTING

With the exception of several pages of the manuscript of *Sir Thomas More* in Shakespeare's handwriting (British Library Harley 7368), our sole access to his output is in the form of early printed editions. Since the 1970s there has emerged an argument that, like performance, publication is an inherently collaborative process. Just as the dramatist expected the actors to complete his play by adding their own labour in rehearsal and performance, so, the argument goes, he expected the printshop workers to complete his text by adding their labour in finalizing, editing and polishing it. When we inquire into the detail of just what the printers are supposed to have added, the claims are noticeably modest. In *Principles of Textual Criticism* James Thorpe wrote that 'In many cases, probably in most cases, he [the writer] expected the printer to perfect his accidentals; and thus the changes introduced by the printer can be properly thought of as fulfilling the writer's intentions.'[32] Philip Gaskell agreed: 'Most authors, in fact, expect

---

[29] Bawcutt, ed., *The Control and Censorship of Caroline Drama*, pp. 39–40.

[30] Andrew Gurr, 'A New Theatre Historicism', in *From Script to Stage in Early Modern England*, ed. Peter Holland and Stephen Orgel, *Redefining British Theatre History* (Basingstoke, 2004), pp. 71–88, p. 72.

[31] Lukas Erne, *Shakespeare as Literary Dramatist* (Cambridge, 2003).

[32] James Thorpe, *Principles of Textual Criticism* (San Marino CA, 1972), p. 165.

their spelling, capitalization, and punctuation to be corrected or supplied by the printer, relying on the process to dress the text suitably for publication, implicitly endorsing it (with or without further amendment) when correcting proofs.'[33] D. F. McKenzie and Jerome J. McGann extended this argument in order to claim that a printed book is entirely a collaborative (and hence in their terminology, a socialized) object.[34] Since they could not point to evidence of substantial rewriting by printers of the words of the books they produced, McKenzie and McGann had instead to argue that punctuation, spelling and (especially) layout themselves carry much more meaning than had hitherto been thought. Printers' input in those areas constitute collaboration, according to this sociology-of-text approach.

The socialized model of publication has considerable appeal for those who would valorize the artisanal labour embedded in artistic creation, but it does not in fact reflect how early modern printers thought of their work. It is often cited that in his handbook on printing Joseph Moxon characterized punctuation as the compositor's responsibility: 'As he *Sets* on, he considers how to *Point* his Work, viz. when to *Set* , where ; where : and where . where to make () and where [] ? ! and when a *Break*.'[35] The same idea about the final decisions regarding punctuation is witnessed seven decades earlier by James Binns in a study of the evidence for printshop practice surviving in books written in Latin. In 1617 an edition of Marco Antonio De Dominis's *De Republica Ecclesiastica* contained a note to other printers considering reprinting the book from this one, alerting them to its printing errors and remarking that 'They themselves can better punctuate with full stops and commas according to their own judgement.'[36] However, neither of these documents suggests that the authority for punctuation rested with the compositors. Rather the idea appears to have been that compositors should save writers from themselves when necessary.

The way Moxon put the matter is exactly how we think of it today, which is that printers do well to correct error but responsibility lies

with the author and is embodied in the supplied copy:

Nor (as afore was hinted) is a *Compositor* bound to all these Circumstances and Punctilio's, because in a strict sense, the Author is to discharge him of them in his *Copy*: Yet it is necessary the *Compositers* Judgment should know where the Author has been deficient, that so his care may not suffer such Work to go out of his Hands as may bring Scandal upon himself, and Scandal and prejudice upon the Master Printer.[37]

That is, the author discharges the compositor of responsibility by providing copy, yet a good compositor fixes what he can and not for the sake of the author's reputation but for the sake of the reputation of the printshop. Editors of journals will readily recognize the lines of responsibility being drawn here.

For our purpose, the key principle to take from this is that we should not conflate the labour of agents in the chain of transmission trying to eliminate mere error (their own and the author's) with the labour of true artistic collaboration that is meant to make the whole greater than the sum of its parts. Or, as Gary Taylor puts it in his article in this volume, $1+1=3$.[38] If the part of the *Sir Thomas More* manuscript in Shakespeare's

[33] Philip Gaskell, *A New Introduction to Bibliography* (Oxford, 1972), p. 339.

[34] D. F. McKenzie, 'Typography and Meaning: The Case of William Congreve', in *Buch und Buchhandel in Europa im Achtzehnten Jahrhundert: Fünftes Wolfenbütteler Symposium vom 1 bis 3 November 1977* [*The Book and the Book Trade in Eighteenth-century Europe: Proceedings of the Fifth Wolfenbütteler Symposium November 1–3 1977*], ed. Giles Barber and Bernhard Fabian (Hamburg, 1981), pp. 81–125; Jerome J. McGann, *A Critique of Modern Textual Criticism* (Chicago, 1983).

[35] Joseph Moxon, *Mechanick Exercises, Or, The Doctrine of Handy-works*, Wing M3014, 2 vols. (London, 1683), vol. 2: Applied to the Art of Printing, Hh2v.

[36] James Binns, 'STC Latin Books: Evidence for Printing-house Practice', *The Library* (=*Transactions of the Bibliographical Society*), 32 (1977), 1–27, p. 7.

[37] Moxon, *Mechanick Exercises, Or, The Doctrine of Handy-works*, vol. 2: Applied to the Art of Printing, Hh4v.

[38] Gary Taylor, 'Why Did Shakespeare Collaborate?' (above, p. 17).

handwriting is typical of what his printers received then they would indeed have had to provide the punctuation, since his autograph pages are almost entirely unpunctuated. But it is now well established that for most of the plays in the 1623 Folio the printers received non-authorial literary transcripts and in these the punctuation would have followed contemporary norms.[39] For the authoritative early quartos there is some evidence – primarily idiosyncratic spellings – that these were printed from Shakespeare's own papers, but we do not know if those were as devoid of punctuation as his autograph contribution to *Sir Thomas More*. If Erne is right that Shakespeare wrote specifically with print publication in mind, presumably it was usual for him to punctuate the documents he provided for that purpose. What is at stake here is not the punctuation itself, of course, but the idea that we should consider the printers to have been partners of the writers (albeit junior ones) in the production of books. Moxon's terminology does not warrant such a view.

Just how we judge the socialization claim depends in part on how much we think punctuation matters. Greg called the word choices of a text its substantives because they 'affect the author's meaning' and called the punctuation, spelling and styling its accidentals, 'affecting mainly its formal presentation'.[40] This distinction has been criticized on the grounds that punctuation affects meaning as much as word choice does.[41] Greg's distinction was not intended as a description of language – he was scarcely so naive about punctuation – but as a tool in the practical exploration of the authority, author's or printer's, lying behind certain choices. For Greg, punctuation belonged to a different layer of authority in the printed book precisely because printers were free to alter it to an extent that they would not do in the case of words chosen by the writer. Although New Bibliography in general and Greg in particular have a reputation for being antipathetical to theatre, it is worth noting that modern actors and directors share this idea that the authority in punctuation differs from the authority in word choices. Practitioners are aware that modern editions' punctuation reflects modern rules for sentence construction and they routinely ignore it. Shakespeare's autograph pages in *Sir Thomas More* suggest that he too thought that deciding where to pause and for how long, and how to use stress to articulate the relationships between clauses, are the actor's province, not the writer's. One obvious exception, of course, must be Quince's prologue to *Pyramus and Thisbe* (*A Midsummer Night's Dream*, 5.1.108–17), which Shakespeare presumably punctuated carefully to indicate the desired, 'incorrect', delivery. Complicating the issue, there are exceptions of the opposite kind too, where word choices are immaterial. As Taylor pointed out, the distinction between *pray thee* and *prithee* is 'entirely without semantic significance' and it is properly treated as accidental not substantive.[42]

If changes to texts made in the printshop were confined to punctuation, spelling and styling then the effects thereof would be relatively trivial. However, the limited studies so far undertaken indicate that compositors did change Shakespeare's choice of words too. For the most part, individual compositor's habits have not been established with the statistical rigour that is now rightly demanded when computational stylistics is used to establish collaborative authorship and determine the boundaries of the contributors' shares. The art has not developed sufficiently for us even to be able to say with confidence where one compositor's stint ended and another's began. Early confidence in the methods for making such distinctions derived largely from the physically impressive application of new opto-mechanical technology – especially space-age looking Hinman Collators – and from

---

[39] Gary Taylor, 'Post-script', in *Shakespeare Reshaped, 1606–1623*, ed. Gary Taylor and John Jowett, Oxford Shakespeare Studies (Oxford, 1993), pp. 237–43.

[40] W. W. Greg, 'The Rationale of Copy-text', *Studies in Bibliography*, 3 (1950–1), 19–36, p. 21.

[41] Tom Davis, 'The CEAA and Modern Textual Editing', *The Library* (=*Transactions of the Bibliographical Society*), 32 (1977), 61–74; Tom Davis, 'Substantives? Accidentals?', *The Library* (=*Transactions of the Bibliographical Society*), 3 (1981), 149–51.

[42] Gary Taylor, 'Copy-text and Collation (with Special Reference to *Richard III*)', *The Library* (=*Transactions of the Bibliographical Society*), 3 (1981), 33–42, p. 40.

the complexity of the evidence from which it appeared to be wringing new knowledge.[43] Confidence plummeted, however, once independent studies of the compositorial labour in one book produced wildly different divisions of stints, as happened with the 1598 edition of *Love's Labours Lost*.[44] McKenzie demonstrated that one of the so-called psycho-mechanical tests for discriminating compositors – based on choices for spacing around punctuation – is virtually worthless on its own because a compositor's practice in this regard may vary day by day.[45] Since McKenzie showed this weakness in much of the preceding scholarship, almost no-one has bothered making fresh studies in the field. MacDonald P. Jackson is a rare exception and is entirely alone in using a statistical understanding of chance to distinguish real habits from random variation in behaviour.[46]

Despite the limitations of the studies of compositorial labour, a couple of particular habits have been established beyond reasonable dispute. Paul Werstine showed that mislineation of Shakespeare's verse is far more prevalent in Folio compositor A's stints than in Folio compositor B's, so rather than attributing the resulting rough verse to the author's experiments in prosody we should assume that he lined his verse with metrical regularity that the printer occasionally wrecked.[47] The Oxford *Complete Works* editors showed that although the two expressions were equally acceptable in the period, Folio compositor B tended to modernize 'nor . . . nor' to 'neither . . . nor' even when metre required that the first word be monosyllabic.[48] The sociological model of publishing requires the modern editor to embrace these depredations as the inevitable effects of collaborative endeavour, but the correct editorial response is to undo them. Yet it is, of course, dangerous to undo them so long as the art of detecting compositorial interference remains in its infancy, and when we cannot be sure that we are not misreading interference at one stage in the process of transmission as interference at another. Ralph Crane is the only known scribe involved in the transmission of Shakespeare's texts who has left enough manuscript evidence for systematic study of his interventions to be

feasible.[49] Because Crane prepared copy for the Folio, knowledge of his habits has undermined what was previously thought to be a reliable distinction between the work of compositors D and F: evidence of the apparently distinct habits of two men might really be just one compositor changing his practice when setting from a Crane transcript.[50] This possibility draws our attention to an important difference between the constructive input of players turning a script into a performance and the essentially destructive input of scribes and compositors transmitting a manuscript. The latter's agencies are detectable only by the harm they do.

When they worked to the best practices of their professions, scribes and compositors left no trace on the words we are interested in. One way to detect scribal transmission is the provision of Latinate act and scene intervals that no one in the theatre would bother to add, but these do

[43] Egan, *Struggle for Shakespeare's Text*, pp. 38–99.

[44] George R. Price, 'The Printing of *Love's Labour's Lost* (1598)', *Papers of the Bibliographical Society of America*, 72 (1978), 405–34; Paul Werstine, 'The Editorial Usefulness of Printing House and Compositor Studies: Reprinted from *Analytical and Enumerative Bibliography* 2 (1978): 153–165 with a New Afterword', in *Play-texts in Old Spelling: Papers from the Glendon Conference*, ed. G. B. Shand and Raymond C. Shady (New York, 1984), pp. 35–64.

[45] D. F. McKenzie, 'Stretching a Point: Or, the Case of the Spaced-out Comps', *Studies in Bibliography*, 37 (1984), 106–21.

[46] MacDonald P. Jackson, 'Finding the Pattern: Peter Short's Shakespeare Quartos Revisited', *Bibliographical Society of Australia and New Zealand Bulletin*, 25 (2001), 67–86.

[47] Paul Werstine, 'Line Division in Shakespeare's Dramatic Verse: An Editorial Problem', *Analytical and Enumerative Bibliography*, 8 (1984), 73–125.

[48] Stanley Wells, Gary Taylor, John Jowett and William Montgomery, *William Shakespeare: A Textual Companion* (Oxford, 1987), *1 Henry VI*, 5.1.59n.

[49] T. H. Howard-Hill, 'Ralph Crane and Five Shakespeare First Folio Comedies', unpublished DPhil thesis, University of Oxford, 1971; Virginia J. Haas, 'Ralph Crane: A Status Report', *Analytical and Enumerative Bibliography*, 3 (1989), 3–10.

[50] Paul Werstine, 'Scribe or Compositor: Ralph Crane, Compositors D and F, and the First Four Plays in the Shakespeare First Folio', *Papers of the Bibliographical Society of America*, 95 (2001), 315–39.

no harm to the dialogue, stage directions and speech prefixes. Crane's interventions, however, extended to: massing a scene's entrance directions at the beginning of the scene no matter when the characters enter, destroying the evidence of where the dramatist placed his entrances; expanding the dramatist's contractions – *you'de* > *you would* and *they're* > *they are* – even when this damaged the metre; and rewriting stage directions to make them more literary. Likewise, by definition, when compositors were being careful, as they were in the first editions of *Venus and Adonis* and *Lucrece* printed by Shakespeare's fellow Stratfordian Richard Field, it becomes difficult to tell them apart.[51] Once co-authorship has been discounted, certain kinds of unevenness in a text are evidence of non-authorial agencies active in its transmission, so the very foundation of the socialized model of publication – the identification of labours other than the author's – should alert us to the risk of treating corruption as collaboration.

* * *

In place of the authority of the author, recent theatre historiography and textual criticism has tended to emphasize the collaborative, socialized labours of the players, the scribes and compositors, whose effects upon the surviving script are treated as though they are nearly as important as the author's labour. Because it is difficult to differentiate these various inputs when studying their collective output in an early printed play it is sometimes said to be virtually impossible to do so. A typical example is Jeffrey Masten's insistence that attempts to attribute parts of co-written plays to their respective co-writers are bound to fail because 'the collaborative project in the theatre was predicated on erasing the perception of any differences that might have existed, for whatever reason, between collaborated parts'.[52] Developing his argument, Masten decided that just as we cannot distinguish writers' individual inputs to a printed book, so we cannot distinguish the compositors' inputs from the writers':

compositor analysis . . . insists upon a precise individuation of agents at every stage of textual production, in ways that are often strikingly anachronistic. In this way,

compositor analysis closely parallels the work of scholars like Cyrus Hoy (and more recently Jonathan Hope) who have sought to discern and separate out of collaborative texts the individuated shares of particular playwrights . . . [53]

Since Masten wrote this, extraordinary successes in the field of computational stylistics have illustrated the importance of authorship in the teeth of postmodernism's denial of it. It turns out that authorship is indeed individualistic and discernible, and not at all a post-seventeenth-century construction. Hugh Craig makes this point pithily:

In the case of authorship, statistical studies might have revealed – were free to reveal – that authorship is insignificant in comparison to other factors like genre or period. In that case the theory that authors are only secondary to other forces in textual patterning would have been validated . . . As it happens, however, authorship emerges as a much stronger force in the affinities between texts than genre or period. Unexpectedly, perhaps uncomfortably, it is a persistent, probably mainly unconscious, factor. Writers, we might say, can't help inscribing an individual style in everything they produce. We need to take account of this in a new theory of authorship.[54]

Those who wish to insist that the processes of co-authorship so thoroughly mixed the styles of the writers that they cannot be disentangled must confront the mounting evidence that we can now distinguish quantitatively between the stints of different writers in one script. Independent studies working along different lines have shown the

---

[51] William Shakespeare, *Shakespeare's Poems*: Venus and Adonis, The Rape of Lucrece *and the Shorter Poems*, ed. Katherine Duncan-Jones and H. R. Woudhuysen, The Arden Shakespeare (London, 2007), pp. 471–89.

[52] Jeffrey Masten, *Textual Intercourse: Collaboration, Authorship, and Sexualities in Renaissance Drama*, Cambridge Studies in Renaissance Literature and Culture, 14 (Cambridge, 1997), p. 17.

[53] Jeffrey Masten, 'Pressing Subjects: Or, the Secret Lives of Shakespeare's Compositors', in *Language Machines: Technologies of Literary and Cultural Production*, ed. Jeffrey Masten, Peter Stallybrass and Nancy Vickers, Essays from the English Institute (New York, 1997), pp. 75–107, pp. 97–8.

[54] Hugh Craig, 'Style, Statistics, and New Models of Authorship', *Early Modern Literary Studies*, 15.1 (2009–10), 41, para. 3.

measurable unevenness, even if they cannot always precisely identify the joins, produced by Shakespeare's collaborative authorship of *1 Henry VI*, *The Contention of York and Lancaster / 2 Henry VI*, *Titus Andronicus*, *Timon of Athens*, *Pericles*, *All is True / Henry VIII*, *The Two Noble Kinsmen*, *Sir Thomas More*, *Edward III*, *Arden of Faversham* and *The Spanish Tragedy*.[55] In making these distinctions, non-authorial revision for revival presents essentially the same methodological problems as co-authorship at the point of original composition. The conclusion to be drawn from these studies' ability to discriminate between writers is not that upon entering the theatre the scripts went into a melting pot that blurred all boundaries. Quite the opposite: plays were relatively stable works that we can, centuries later, dismantle into their constituent parts. The challenge for those working on scribal and print transmission is to emulate the statistical rigour of these studies of authorship and so discover whether the unevenness arising from the combined labours of scribes and compositors can be turned into reliable distinctions of human agency in the resulting printed editions.

---

[55] Brian Vickers, *Shakespeare, Co-author: A Historical Study of Five Collaborative Plays* (Oxford, 2002); MacDonald P. Jackson, *Defining Shakespeare: 'Pericles' as Test Case* (Oxford, 2003); Hugh Craig and Arthur F. Kinney, *Shakespeare, Computers, and the Mystery of Authorship* (Cambridge, 2009); Brian Vickers, 'Identifying Shakespeare's Additions to *The Spanish Tragedy* (1602): A New(er) Approach', *Shakespeare*, 8 (2012), 13–43; MacDonald P. Jackson, *Determining the Shakespeare Canon: 'Arden of Faversham' and 'A Lover's Complaint'* (Oxford, forthcoming in 2014).

FRAMING SHAKESPEARE'S COLLABORATIVE AUTHORSHIP

WILL SHARPE

SHAKESPEARE–AUTHOR

Attempts to describe Shakespeare as an authorial figure are as variegated in the complexion of their particular nuance as they are apparently unending. Shakespeare's authorship, or Shakespeare as author, seems to dominate popular perceptions of his cultural standing and achievement far more than considered critical engagement with his works. His frequent appearances in the press, from Grub Street to Fleet Street, are almost invariably couched in questions of authorship as it relates to permanently out-of-reach notions of authenticity. Even in the month leading up to the release of *William Shakespeare and Others: Collaborative Plays*[1] (October, 2013), there was a story in *The Globe and Mail* about two Canadian Universities (York and Guelph) funding a conference in Toronto arguing for Edward De Vere's authorship of Shakespeare's plays[2] and a piece by John Sutherland in *The Guardian* in which he claimed:

Macbeth, for example, is a very easy play for unknowledgeable audiences to take on board (perhaps because it wasn't written by Shakespeare: OUP nowadays attribute it to Thomas Middleton).[3]

In addition there appeared a publicity piece in *The Times* on *Collaborative Plays*,[4] somewhat overstating our claims about which plays included we adjudge part-Shakespearian, and, again, urging the position that the Romantic anachronism of Shakespeare the genius is corrected and refined by recognition of the theatrical origins of his work. Rather than a mastermind in a lonely garret, he was a 'jobbing playwright' producing scripts by committee, both reorienting and tempering his cultural position and explaining why it is feasible to conceive of other plays of the period containing his words. Through this alone we get a convergence of discrete figurations of Shakespeare as authorial figure which are all too readily conflated. This article will expand upon work undertaken in *Collaborative Plays* in describing Shakespeare's activities as both single and co-author, and describe the necessity for a more nuanced understanding of the methodological boundaries between these ever-shifting, frequently imprecise attempts to frame Shakespeare's authorship.

John Sutherland's comment acknowledges the popular acceptance of attribution studies as a mechanism by which the Shakespeare canon is continuously reshaped and multi-authorship identified, though his understanding of the particular issue of *Macbeth* is badly garbled, presumably

---

[1] Jonathan Bate and Eric Rasmussen, with Jan Sewell, Will Sharpe, Peter Kirwan and Sarah Stewart, eds., *William Shakespeare and Others: Collaborative Plays* (Basingstoke, 2013).

[2] J. Kelly Nestruck, 'Amid Controversy, Two Canadian Universities Financially Back Debate Over Shakespeare's "True Identity"', *Toronto Globe and Mail* (16 October 2013), www.theglobeandmail.com/arts/theatre-and-performance/amid-controversy-the-debate-over-who-wrote-shakespeare-comes-to-toronto/article14889619/page=all.

[3] John Sutherland, 'All the World's a Stage for Shakespeare, but We No Longer Understand Him', *The Guardian* (11 October 2013), www.theguardian.com/commentisfree/2013/oct/11/shakespeare-understand-national-theatre-hytner-confusing.

[4] Jack Malvern, 'Computer Analysis Proves Shakespeare's Hand in Other Plays', *The Times* (19 October 2013).

referring to the play's appearance in the Oxford Middleton on the strength of the long-established identification of Middleton's hand as adapter within the text.[5] Other popular and recurrent positions are:

1) Shakespeare didn't write Shakespeare.
2) The play's the thing and authorship is of no consequence.
3) Shakespeare wrote for the theatre, and therefore all of his plays can be considered collaborative in some way.

The final point is based partly on understandings of theatre as a socially embedded art form and partly on an accretion of high profile stories in the press in recent years about Shakespeare attribution cases. Two prevalent offshoots of this are the ideas that collaboration was the default way for Shakespeare to work and, conversely, that scholars are going Shakespeare-attribution crazy with the licence this apparently affords. All three of these umbrella points and their many sub-arguments were seen amply represented on the comments board of another publicity piece for *Collaborative Plays* in *The Guardian*.[6] There was the inevitable weigh-in on the authorship controversy – 'This is just a power grab by the Stratford industry'[7] – suggesting that attempts to identify Shakespearian collaboration are in fact a kind of unethical annexing of the works of others by an insecure local tourism industry looking to reassert an already shaky position. And there was the inevitable sarcasm attending announcements of Shakespeare's hand discovered in 'new' places:

Perhaps all Elizabethan plays were written by Shakespeare, the better ones on his good days, the worse ones on his bad days... At best, this study advances the case for plays long since suspected of involving Shakespeare, and for the range of his professional activities thought to have begun – so why not continued? – of [sic] patching plays by others. Whatever its origins, the play's still the thing.[8]

This single post covers several positions, including over-attribution to Shakespeare. Despite some astute observations – we are indeed advancing old

arguments, and the account given of Shakespeare as patcher of scripts is not unreasonable – the conclusion that the play's the thing, something akin to Parolles's 'simply the thing I am / Shall make me live', still seems something of a non-sequitur. The existence or quality of a play renders the search for its author neither inconsequential nor obsolete, while equally knowing the play's author is not a precondition for enjoying it as an artwork. Still, establishing Shakespeare as an authorial presence within a play will invariably influence subsequent acts of literary criticism upon it, just as attempts to compare and contextualize an anonymous passage within his body of work are themselves literary critical acts intended to serve as attribution technologies.

Shakespeare as collaborator and theatre professional have arguably become the most influential framing devices in current non-academic thinking about Shakespeare's authorship, though other significant modes of understanding him as an authorial figure have proliferated in recent scholarly criticism. One distinct category of study seeks to view authorship as a consistent preoccupation of Shakespeare's craft, and Patrick Cheney has described 'how [Shakespeare] the literary poet-playwright recurrently puts his model of hybrid authorship centre stage'.[9] Lukas Erne's bibliographic analysis, *Shakespeare as Literary Dramatist*, reads authorship through its formulations in Renaissance print culture, challenging the notion that Shakespeare, as theatre professional, was concerned only with the publication of his plays in the form of live performance. He argues

---

5 The fact of Middleton's adaptation of *Macbeth* has been challenged by Brian Vickers in 'Disintegrated. Did Thomas Middleton really adapt *Macbeth*?' *Times Literary Supplement* (28 May 2010), 13–14.
6 Dalya Alberge, 'Shakespeare's Fingerprints Found on Three Elizabethan Plays', *The Guardian* (12 October 2013), www.theguardian.com/culture/2013/oct/12/shakespeare-new-plays.
7 Posted by alexcox (13 October 2013, 3.02pm).
8 Posted by Michael L. Hays (12 October 2013, 5.49pm).
9 Patrick Cheney, *Shakespeare's Literary Authorship* (Cambridge, 2008), p. 11.

for a reappraisal of Shakespeare the man in print, seeing him as deeply concerned with authorial self-fashioning and posterity, a position he has powerfully restated in *Shakespeare and the Book Trade*.[10] In addition to theatrical, bibliographic and page-to-stage/stage-to-page/stage-and-page formulations of Shakespearian authorship, we have Shakespeare as socially constituted creator, whose works are a kind of cultural palimpsest (what Russ McDonald describes as a 'reciprocity between the cultural field and literary artefact').[11] Through the tenets of New Historicism, Shakespeare was both locus of and conduit for myriad cultural and textual influences, though he is also acknowledged in turn as a reshaping force upon them; a figure who 'helped make the world that made him'.[12]

Yet in spite of the broadest sociology of text we might posit, Patrick Cheney identifies an emergent field of criticism that 'acknowledges the revisionist principle of social collaboration in the production of Shakespeare's plays, but simultaneously grants *individuated literary authorship* to "Shakespeare" himself'.[13] Much of this might be seen as a series of attempts to refocus and render more usable critical traditions stretching from the Romantics – Keats's 'negative capability', Coleridge's 'myriad-minded Shakespeare', through to Stephen Greenblatt's vision of a Shakespeare with the 'astonishing capacity to be everywhere and nowhere, to assume all positions and to slip free of all constraints' – seeking to describe the creative mystery of Shakespeare's ever-elusive authorial voice within his works; the indifference he shows to editorializing in print; and the extraordinary space for imaginative engagement and generation of meaning he renders his audience, as characteristic authorial traits.[14] Attribution study in fact shares many roots with Romantic tradition, averring features of Shakespeare's style and authorial presence as starting points for stylistic authorial analysis, seeking to work backwards from the most global of achievements to a local point of inception, carried out on a writing table, manually transcribed using the simplest pen and ink technology, and identifiably expressive of an individual creative consciousness. It might posit as characteristic a striking synthesis

of pragmatic theatrical design, complex narrative adaptation of source material, and a transformative revivification of the technical principles of composition learned through a Humanist education; an exceptional ability to observe, absorb and apply with vital resonance natural phenomena and behavioural characteristics derived both from literary precedent and from lived experience; an unusually rigorous and complex morality that seems to suspend judgement and dole out empathy to the highest and meanest characters in equal measure; an authorial voice that continually slips the net of constructed argument to be subsumed into the endless catacombs of the artwork itself, all filtered through an ever-shifting imaginative sense of the malleable expressiveness of English, of its unseen possibilities.

This is of course a loose, pseudo-Romantic, oft-described model of Shakespeare's poetic and dramatic achievements, just as we summon up images of a harsh, pugnacious intellectualism when we think of Jonson, a scathing comedy that is both aggressive and defensive. Yet it forms a series of stylistic impressions that stylometric analysis seeks to augment with more molecular observation of identifiably Shakespearian linguistic functions.

SHAKESPEARE'S THEATRICAL AUTHORSHIP

A recent revival of interest in the authorship 'controversy' and all it entails has seen, in *Shakespeare Beyond Doubt*, a cross pollination of many kinds of

[10] Lukas Erne, *Shakespeare as Literary Dramatist* (Cambridge, 2003); *Shakespeare and the Book Trade* (Cambridge, 2013).

[11] Russ McDonald, *The Bedford Companion to Shakespeare* (Boston, 2001), p. 27; see also Jerome J. McGann, *A Critique of Modern Textual Criticism* (Chicago, 1983); Stephen Greenblatt, *Shakespearean Negotiations: The Circulation of Social Energy in Renaissance England* (Berkeley, 1988), pp. 4–5, and the many writings of Louis Montrose. Julie Stone Peters, *Theatre of the Book: 1480–1880* (Oxford, 2000) is a forerunner of Erne's stage-to-page criticism.

[12] Richard Helgerson, *Forms of Nationhood: The Elizabethan Writing of England* (Chicago, 1992), p. 215.

[13] Cheney, *Shakespeare's Literary Authorship*, p. 6.

[14] Stephen Greenblatt, *Will in the World: How Shakespeare Became Shakespeare* (New York, 2004), p. 242.

authorship study reapplied to the job of asserting Shakespeare's identity as the author of his works. John Jowett, MacDonald Jackson, James Mardock and Eric Rasmussen contributed essays on Shakespeare as collaborator, as subject of stylistic and stylometric analysis, and as working theatre professional.[15] The fact of both Shakespeare's collaborative authorship and the many instances of the kinds of notation we might expect from theatrical manuscripts in surviving early textual witnesses of his work, in spite of their myriad putative transmission scenarios, position Shakespeare at work within the early professional theatres, and the practices of both textual criticism and stylometric analysis seek to recover and identify Shakespearian authorship as a material process within that context.

Textual criticism might posit authorial features based on the notational, orthographic and calligraphic signs within a manuscript, or through an attempt to reconstruct manuscripts underlying printed texts. How this relates to our knowledge of theatre history and Shakespeare's working practices is of course one of the central battlegrounds of modern editorial theory, though stylometrists are less concerned with describing theatrical practice than with locating individual minds and hands at work within a text.[16] The complex filters of transmission through which theatrical texts must pass – scribal copying, rehearsal, performance and revival – all leave multiple marks upon texts, but they are not assumed to account for the overall verbal and poetic textures of a play. A writer's favoured imagery, grammatical tropes and features of syntactical and rhetorical invention are taken to survive the processes of theatrical mediation, not to mention of printing, even if more localized authorial markers such as contractions, spellings, and substantive signifiers are commonly obscured, confused or written out. What survives, in other words, is style, and computational stylometry can be considered most simply as the 'numerical measurement of style'.[17] Yet stylometry must be recognized as but one way of practising textual criticism, one way of attending to a linguistic code with a particular outcome in mind, one way of framing an author. For example, Shakespeare as

literary author *pace* Erne is, as John Jowett points out, a construct, a figuration read through a bibliographic study of printed texts within a marketplace, without any clarity as to how this might be made compatible with the methodologies of textual editing, itself attached to a huge weight of contestation about the complex and varied origins of those texts and how they may or may not relate to their author.[18] We must consider how an author's identity, in all its complex and discrete manifestations, might be embedded and recovered, or indeed dispersed, in the labyrinthine linguistic codes of multiple imprints and the inferred texts their existence replaces, suggesting the search for Shakespeare as author is a potentially limitless struggle that cannot be neatly confined to any single methodology.

Framing Shakespeare as a professional at work within a necessarily collaborative medium is in part to emphasize how normal a facet of his working life acts of collaboration were. He was the company's principal writer, though his responsibilities also included acting, working with fellow sharers and actors on his and others' texts in what we might call rehearsals, not to mention the administrative responsibilities involved in the running of a business. So we might widen our sense of what Shakespearian collaboration involves beyond the joint composition of a play. It could mean the tailoring of his own writing in the light of group revelations about what did or did not work during rehearsals, or the reading of the play to the company, or its reading by others – not something we can ever prove or detect, but likely to have

---

[15] John Jowett, 'Shakespeare as Collaborator', MacDonald P. Jackson, 'Authorship and the Evidence of Stylometrics', and James Mardock and Eric Rasmussen, 'What Does Textual Evidence Reveal About the Author?', in *Shakespeare Beyond Doubt*, Stanley Wells and Paul Edmondson, eds. (Cambridge, 2013), pp. 88–99, 100–10, 111–20.

[16] See John Jowett, *Shakespeare and Text* (Oxford, 2007) for an overview of the complex history of attempts to categorize theatrical manuscripts from the New Bibliography to the present day; see also Paul Werstine, *Early Modern Playhouse Manuscripts and the Editing of Shakespeare* (Cambridge, 2012).

[17] Jackson, 'Authorship and the Evidence of Stylometrics', p. 100.

[18] Jowett, *Shakespeare and Text*, p. 114.

happened. It could mean the penning of the odd line, word or phrase here or there in other writers' works, if indeed Shakespeare, as many suspect, worked as an occasional script-doctor for his company, though additions of this minute nature, if they did exist, would again be almost impossible to detect. It could mean performing in a play: the 1616 Folio of Ben Jonson's *Works* claims that Shakespeare was an actor as well as a dramatist, naming him in the cast lists for performances of *Every Man in His Humour* and *Sejanus*. By these wide standards, then, we begin to see a highly reciprocal creative relationship between Shakespeare and his company, though the processes and material outcomes of co-authorship are not usefully conflated with overly permissive accounts of theatrical collaboration and what it might have entailed, as another *Guardian* comment illustrated well:

But [Shakespeare] was in a room full of other actors . . . who were also speaking, and coming up with lines. In such a scenario, Shakespeare's work would be down to a team effort, and of course those scribes, who might have had to ad-lib a garbled utterance more than once.[19]

This figuration is apt to suggest that plays were written extempore by the acting company as they rehearsed; that actors, with their minds steeped in poesy and pentameter, could contribute to and fill in the blanks of speeches and plays that Shakespeare initiated; that drama was somehow ushered into being by the very spirit of creativity of the age itself. This is to overstate radically the collaborative nature of theatrical rehearsal as it applies to authorship and to underestimate radically the labour and particular skill in the writing we recognize as Shakespeare's, or as Marlowe's, or Jonson's.[20] Perhaps cuts or words were inserted as a result of the dynamic group process of rehearsal, and the complexion of certain roles undoubtedly owed their inception to the particular talents and personalities of individual actors, but stylometric analysis posits that at some point the direct relationship between writers' minds and the blank sheets of paper they fill is the most fundamental locus of authorship. When confronted with words on a page, we might

reasonably search for specific individuals behind those words, and the syntactical, ideational makeup of the vast majority of plays have their only meaningful point of origin in their authors' unique creative faculties.[21] Within collaborative texts it is possible to tell writers apart; even if we can't identify them, we can nonetheless frequently posit shifts in authorial hands through local differentiation across a range of stylistic indicators, showing that at some level and at some point in any instance of textual creation, authorship is an individual process, and any writer's particular relationship to language as a conduit for expression is measurable in some way.

Locating Shakespeare within the early theatres is both to assert an incontrovertible biographical fact and to propose a set of contexts within which his authorship can be understood pragmatically. Yet a theatrical model of Shakespearian authorship is not adequate in all respects, as the conditions within which his work was produced cannot fully account for the quality of it. Jackson argues for the singularity of Shakespeare's writing even within the contexts of his working life: 'Shakespeare's dramatic verse is unmatched by that of his professional contemporaries. Its remoteness from the amateur compositions of noblemen proposed as "the real Shakespeare" is even greater.'[22] There are many contexts in which group human process serves precisely to offset and highlight the exceptional talents of individuals within it, and within the collaborative context of the professional theatres Shakespeare can be seen as both team player and solitary genius, in the sense that he frequently wrote without a co-author and that the material outcomes of his authorship manifested themselves in creative feats that his fellow writers were unable to match. While the latter stance is purely subjective it is nevertheless clear

---

[19] Posted by Gammerax (12 October 2013, 8.09pm).

[20] See Tiffany Stern, *Rehearsal from Shakespeare to Sheridan* (Oxford, 2000) for a detailed appraisal of the practices of rehearsal and the role of authors in relation to them.

[21] I do not intend to discuss the practices of stylometric analysis in any depth here, having done so in Bate *et al.*, eds., *William Shakespeare and Others: Collaborative Plays*, pp. 641–745.

[22] Jackson, 'Authorship and the Evidence of Stylometrics', p. 100.

that both writing alone and in collaboration were facts of Shakespeare's working life, and delineating between the two practices is a desirable outcome of studies of Shakespeare's material authorship.

The unwieldy understanding of collaboration and its relationship to early professional theatre, influenced by trends in Shakespeare scholarship over the past thirty years, has led to the commonly recycled statement that it was the norm for playwrights, Shakespeare included, although even the most cursory tallying of figures should disabuse us of this notion. Shakespeare collaborated, and Shakespeare was a man of the theatre, but his activities as a writer differ sharply from the picture we get of collaboration in Henslowe. Based on figures supplied by Alfred Harbage in *The Complete Pelican Shakespeare*, there are 84,528 lines in Shakespeare's solo-authored plays, not including plays in which co-authorship or adaptation is proven or suspected: *Titus Andronicus*, *1 Henry VI*, *Measure for Measure*, *Timon of Athens*, *Macbeth*, *Pericles*, *Henry VIII* and *The Two Noble Kinsmen*.[23] Of course this figure will vary between editions, but it is roughly correct, and to it can be added the 4,784 lines of *Measure* and *Macbeth*, minus the 250-odd lines of interpolated material (they are not collaborative plays in the same sense as the others), and the 5,205 lines of Shakespeare's accepted canonical poetry (*Venus*, *Lucrece* and the Sonnets), taking the figure to almost 95,000 lines. The total number of lines of Shakespeare's in his canonical collaborative plays, based on the lineation and authorial distribution models in the revised *Oxford Shakespeare* is 7,448: *1 Henry VI* (432), *Titus Andronicus* (2,009), *Timon of Athens* (1,442), *Pericles* (1,211), *Henry VIII* (1,169) and *The Two Noble Kinsmen* (1,185), less than a tenth of his solo-authored material. At its most permissive, the total number of lines we attribute to Shakespeare in *Collaborative Plays* is 1,622 across four plays: *Arden of Faversham* (164), *Edward III* (913), *The Spanish Tragedy* (354) and *Sir Thomas More* (191), fewer than the number of lines of Shakespeare's shortest play, *The Comedy of Errors* (1,756), and slightly more than the average contribution Shakespeare made to each of the four canonical collaborations from his King's Men

days. *Double Falsehood* cannot be measured in the same way, being largely made up of Theobald's writing and being so heavily cut: the whole play is 1,777 lines, and the scenes in which Jonathan Hope detects Shakespeare (up to and including 2.2) comprise 427 lines, though judging by *Henry VIII* and *Kinsmen* we might posit Shakespeare's contribution to *Cardenio* to have been in the region of 1,000–plus lines.

This is not to wrest Shakespeare the isolated genius back from the increasingly popular image of a working life analogous to that of a Hollywood screenwriter, but to work towards a realistic picture of his activities as a collaborator proportionate to his solo-authored work. It seems a fairly uncomplicated fact that the latter was Shakespeare's predominant mode of writing, and correcting this impression – in the same way as ideas about the size of Shakespeare's vocabulary are usefully reoriented – is aimed at supplying a platform for describing and understanding his artistic achievements more accurately.[24] The image of a Shakespeare with a smaller vocabulary forces us to consider his particular skill in manipulating and reframing ordinary language into extraordinary syntactical and semantic patterns, and similarly we might reappraise his particular skill as a collaborative author in relation to the works of his we know to be actually collaborative. Any authorial act is broadly collaborative and is the product of myriad influences – literary, lived, educational, interpersonal – but taking non-collaborative to mean solo-authored, the great majority of what we think of as the Shakespeare canon is the product of Shakespeare's individual effort. This acknowledgement is not hostile or pejorative towards collaboration but, if it is not accurate to identify a play as co-authored, then it is surely not desirable to do so.

---

[23] *All's Well* and *2* and *3 Henry VI* are included as the collaboration theories are still so nascent; without them the figure goes down to 75,804.

[24] David Crystal, *Think On My Words: Exploring Shakespeare's Language* (Cambridge, 2008); Hugh Craig, 'Shakespeare's Vocabulary: Myth and Reality', *Shakespeare Quarterly*, 62:1 (2011), 53–74.

SHAKESPEARE'S CANONICAL
CO-AUTHORSHIP

The usual standard for attributing a work to Shakespeare is of course inclusion in the 1623 First Folio, and yet the Folio's view of the canon has been increasingly exposed as incomplete in recent decades.[25] It reprinted all of the plays we now recognize as canonical that had appeared in quarto format – some attributed to him on their title-pages, others not – prior to its 1623 publication. It also included plays in which Shakespeare had shared the load with other writers, though, possibly through its desire to market the image of an isolated genius, obscured the collaborative origins of *Titus Andronicus*, *1 Henry VI*, *Timon of Athens* and *Henry VIII*. It also included texts of *Measure for Measure* and *Macbeth* that had been adapted by Thomas Middleton at some point between the time of Shakespeare's death in 1616 and 1623. Middleton was also almost certainly Shakespeare's collaborator on *Timon*, while *Titus* is now widely accepted as an early collaboration with George Peele, who might also have had a hand, along with Thomas Nashe and possibly another, in *1 Henry VI*, to which several scholars estimate Shakespeare's contribution to be as low as only twenty per cent of the entire play.[26] *Henry VIII* is chronologically the latest of the co-authored efforts preserved in the Folio, and the only Fletcher collaboration to make it in.

A number of plays that had appeared in quarto and had borne Shakespeare's name, however, were not included: *Locrine* (1595, ascribed to 'W.S.'); *Sir John Oldcastle* (1600, reprinted 1619); *Thomas Lord Cromwell* (1602, also 'W.S.'); *The London Prodigal* (1605); *The Puritan* (1607, also 'W.S.'); *A Yorkshire Tragedy* (1608) and *Pericles* (1609).[27] Whatever the book-buying public may have made of these imprints at the time, the Folio's editors seem to have been making a statement about them as spurious attributions by rejecting them from its canon. All seven of these plays were included in the second impression of the Third Folio (1664), presumably because of their title-page claims, ranging from the cryptically suggestive to the outright explicit, of Shakespearian origin. Of these, only *Pericles* has

been admitted by modern scholarship, a play now adjudged with some security to be a collaboration between Shakespeare, who was responsible for Acts 3–5, and the disreputable George Wilkins, a relatively unproductive dramatist who produced Acts 1 and 2 and wrote one other solo-authored play, *The Miseries of Enforced Marriage* (1606), for Shakespeare's company.[28] On the strength of *Pericles* alone we see the limitations of the Folio as a text which can tell us the whole truth about Shakespeare's authorship, both through what it chose to leave out, and, in some cases, through what it left in. In addition to *Pericles*, the Folio omits Shakespeare's Sonnets and the poem that accompanied them, *A Lover's Complaint*, which itself remains a controversial item in the Shakespeare catalogue; his narrative poems, *Venus and Adonis* and *The Rape of Lucrece*; *The Two Noble Kinsmen*, which appeared as a quarto bearing Shakespeare and Fletcher's names on its title-page in 1634; and two plays that are now lost, the mysterious *Love's Labour's Won*, which we know about through its mention in Francis Meres's *Palladis Tamia, or Wit's Treasury* (1598), and *Cardenio*, another Fletcher collaboration from the final

---

[25] See in particular Gary Taylor, 'The Canon and Chronology of Shakespeare's Plays', in *William Shakespeare: A Textual Companion*, ed. Stanley Wells and Gary Taylor, with John Jowett and William Montgomery (Oxford, 1987); Brian Vickers, *Shakespeare, Co-Author* (Oxford, 2002); Jowett, *Shakespeare and Text* (Oxford, 2007).

[26] MacD. P. Jackson, 'Stage Directions and Speech Headings in Act 1 of *Titus Andronicus* Q (1594); Shakespeare or Peele?', *Studies in Bibliography*, 49 (1996), 134–48; see also Vickers, *Shakespeare Co-Author* on *Titus*; Gary Taylor, 'Shakespeare and Others: The Authorship of *Henry the Sixth Part One*', *Medieval and Renaissance Drama in England* 7 (1995), 145–205.

[27] The 1600 edition of *Oldcastle* did not name Shakespeare, while the 1619 edition, which the publisher and printer falsely dated to 1600, did.

[28] He also collaborated on *The Travels of the Three English Brothers* with John Day and William Rowley, a play written for Queen Anne's – formerly Worcester's – Men at the Curtain theatre, performed and printed in 1607, and the prose novella *The Painful Adventures of Pericles, Prince of Tyre* (1608), apparently memorially reconstructed from the play on which he collaborated the previous year. See *Textual Companion*, p. 558, and MacD. P. Jackson, *Defining Shakespeare: Pericles as Test Case* (Oxford, 2003).

part of Shakespeare's career, which probably partially survives through *Double Falsehood*, as discussed at some length in *Collaborative Plays*.

So we can make three statements from this: that the Folio is not always right about Shakespeare's status as an author; that for the most part it is; and that Shakespeare wrote collaboratively during his career. It seems an awkward premise to accept that now-canonical works were excluded from the Folio because of their collaborative origins given that the Folio contains collaborative works, albeit that fact is swept under the carpet, though their inclusion might be explicable in the following, admittedly speculative, ways. *Titus* had been written before Shakespeare's company, the Chamberlain's/King's Men, was even formed, and Peele, a dramatist of no great notoriety, had died twenty years before Shakespeare, in 1596. Peele's involvement is mainly detected in the first act of the play, and whatever his posthumous reputation or the state of knowledge about his involvement in *Titus* in 1623, the play had followed Shakespeare into the repertory of the Chamberlain's Men in 1594, and ultimately found its way into the Folio. Charlton Hinman's epic study of the Folio showed that *Timon* occupies space meant for the solo-authored *Troilus and Cressida*, for which the publishers evidently had trouble acquiring the copyright (it had been printed in quarto in 1609), and Shakespeare and Middleton's collaborative effort was seemingly, reluctantly, brought in as a stopgap.[29] After *Timon*'s reinstatement authorization to print *Troilus* came through and it was inserted into the volume at the last minute, too late for it to be listed in the 'Catalogue'. In spite of their collaborative natures *1 Henry VI* and *Henry VIII* perhaps held a marketing appeal to strengthen the emphasis on Shakespeare as a writer, or *the* writer, of history plays. He was not the only playwright to deal with the reign of historical kings, but, the Folio seems keen to suggest, he was the best. All this can by no means be taken as definitive, but it at least begins to suggest plausibly the various reasons behind the inclusion of these collaborative plays.

For those excluded, we only have Meres's mention of the existence of *Love's Labour's Won* and its inclusion in a bookseller's catalogue of 1603 to go on.[30] We shall never know without a copy being discovered if it was a collaboration, hence its exclusion from the Folio, or, if not, why it was excluded. Despite the fact that *Cardenio* is likewise lost, we have records of the King's Men being paid on 20 May and 8 June 1613 for performances of it at court, and a Stationers' Register entry of 1653 ascribes the play's authorship to Shakespeare and Fletcher. If we apply the same logic to *Cardenio* as to *Pericles* and *The Two Noble Kinsmen*, as well as what we can infer about *Timon*'s laboursome petition for inclusion in the Folio, we can at least form the reasonable working hypothesis that collaboration was their downfall. The Folio does not purport to be a Complete Works in the sense that we now think of such volumes, including none of Shakespeare's extensive non-dramatic work either. It is concerned entirely with the image of Shakespeare as a stage poet; and, it seems, as a stage poet who worked alone.

As for the apocryphal plays naming Shakespeare on their title pages, they are: either correct attributions; or they are honest mistakes (Shakespeare was after all the company's chief dramatist); or Shakespeare's name was hot property, and printers and publishers, in the absence of genuine Shakespeare plays, tried to fulfil the demand in other ways. Lukas Erne argues for the latter, and points out that Shakespeare was a far more prominent figure in print prior to the Folio's publication than has traditionally been allowed. He has also shown that Shakespeare was in fact the first playwright in print to have works misattributed to him.[31] *The Passionate Pilgrim*, a collection of poems published in 1599 by William Jaggard – one of the eventual printers of the First Folio – almost certainly provides a useful analogue. According to the title-page it is a

---

[29] Charlton Hinman, *The Printing and Proof-Reading of the First Folio of Shakespeare*, 2 vols. (Oxford, 1963), vol. 1, pp. 177–8, vol. 2, pp. 261–4.

[30] Francis Meres, *Palladis Tamia, Wit's Treasury* (London, 1598), p. 282; T. W. Baldwin, *Shakspere's Love's Labor's Won* (Carbondale, 1957).

[31] Erne, *Shakespeare and the Book Trade*.

collection of poems by 'W. Shakespeare', a statement which stands up as partially true, containing as it does early versions of Sonnets 138 and 144 and three excerpts from *Love's Labour's Lost*. The more uncomfortable truth is that, alongside those that are still unattributed, appear works definitely by Richard Barnfield, Christopher Marlowe and Sir Walter Raleigh. In one of the very few records we have of Shakespeare the private person reacting to something, Thomas Heywood, in a fit of chagrin after the book's 1612 reprint had managed to subsume and give to his rival some of his writings, tells us that Shakespeare 'was much offended with M. Jaggard that (altogether unknown to him) presumed to make so bold with his name'.[32] Tellingly, a revised title-page was printed for the 1612 edition dropping Shakespeare's name altogether. The King's Men also seemingly took legal action against Thomas Pavier when he attempted to bring out a collection of Shakespeare's plays in 1619, including the falsely dated *Sir John Oldcastle*, attributed to Shakespeare.[33]

Protecting and preserving Shakespeare as an authorial brand on stage at least was an apparent long-term strategy of his company post-1599, though whether this was linked to any long-term plans to print his works is impossible to say. It is perhaps worth contextualizing title-page attributions to Shakespeare from the first decade of the seventeenth century within the company's overall printed output. For reasons which scholars continually debate, they seem to have cut off the supply of new Shakespeare plays to the presses at around the time they opened the doors of the Globe theatre to the public in 1599.[34] Of all the solo-authored and collaborative plays Shakespeare wrote following this move – beginning in all probability with *Julius Caesar* and followed by *As You Like It*, *Hamlet*, *Twelfth Night*, *Troilus and Cressida*, *Measure for Measure*, *Othello*, *All's Well That Ends Well*, *Timon of Athens*, *King Lear*, *Macbeth*, *Antony and Cleopatra*, *Pericles*, *Coriolanus*, *The Winter's Tale*, *Cymbeline*, *The Tempest*, *Cardenio*, *Henry VIII* and *The Two Noble Kinsmen* – only *Hamlet*, *Lear*, *Pericles* and *Troilus* found their way into print within his lifetime. All the others,

bar *Othello* – which appeared somewhat mysteriously in quarto in 1622, six years after Shakespeare's death – and *Kinsmen* made their debut in print in the 1623 First Folio, in which *Hamlet*, *Lear* and *Troilus* would also reappear, serving as confirmation of Shakespeare's authorship of those plays.[35] The omission of *Thomas Lord Cromwell*, *The London Prodigal*, *The Puritan*, *A Yorkshire Tragedy*, *Pericles* and *Kinsmen*, however, meant that the validity of these attributions would have to be settled, with extreme difficulty and controversy, through stylistic and stylometric arguments.

By way of contrasting this trend, of the nineteen solo-authored and collaborative plays written before the move to the Globe, only five – *The Two Gentlemen of Verona*, *The Taming of the Shrew*, *1 Henry VI*, *The Comedy of Errors* and *King John* – were not printed before 1623.[36] Normally a play would appear in quarto around two years after its first performance, a matter of some debate, which Roslyn Knutson plausibly argues signalled revival by the company.[37] Peter Blayney has also suggested that upward movements in the trend of play printing at c.1594 and c.1600 were intended to fulfil advertising functions and provide extra revenue, bolstering Erne's view that Shakespeare's company

---

32 Thomas Heywood, *An Apology for Actors* (London, 1612), G4v.

33 See Jowett, *Shakespeare and Text*, p. 71. The interpretation that the King's Men disapproved of Pavier's project is countered by Sonia Massai in *Shakespeare and the Rise of the Editor* (Cambridge, 2007), pp. 106–35.

34 See Erne, *Shakespeare as Literary Dramatist*, chapters 2 and 3; Jowett, *Shakespeare and Text*, pp. 10–12.

35 *Sir Thomas More* is omitted from this list because of the uncertain nature of its company auspices and of Shakespeare's relationship to it, just as *Arden of Faversham* and *Edward III* are not included in the count of the nineteen pre-Globe plays.

36 The others being *2* and *3 Henry VI*, *Titus Andronicus*, *Richard III*, *Love's Labour's Lost*, *A Midsummer Night's Dream*, *Romeo and Juliet*, *Richard II*, *The Merchant of Venice*, *1 Henry IV*, *The Merry Wives of Windsor*, *2 Henry IV*, *Much Ado About Nothing* and *Henry V*, all of which appeared during Shakespeare's lifetime.

37 Roslyn Lander Knutson, *The Repertory of Shakespeare's Company 1594–1613* (Little Rock, 1991), pp. 12–13, 81.

'actively supported' publication.[38] The two-year time gap is largely true of all the pre-1599 printed plays, though one anomaly is a slew of plays appearing in 1600 – *2 Henry IV*, *Much Ado About Nothing*, *Henry V*, *A Midsummer Night's Dream* and *The Merchant of Venice* – the latter two being then around five years old. Why they were put into print at this time is unclear, though Gary Taylor has conjectured that it may have been a company decision to help finance the move to the Globe.[39] The pattern thereafter is markedly different. *The Merry Wives of Windsor*, another pre-Globe play, appeared in a decidedly poor text in 1602 (the 1600 *Henry V* quarto was of similarly low quality) and *Hamlet*, the first play written after the company's move to the Globe to be printed, in an even poorer one the following year. The issue of a second 'good' quarto of *Hamlet* in 1604–5, advertised on the title-page as 'Newly imprinted and enlarged to almost as much againe as it was, according to the true and perfect Coppie', could have been an instance of the company reacting against what Hemings and Condell would come to term 'stolne, and surreptitious copies'.[40] Jowett suggests this and points out that it was the Chamberlain's company, and not Shakespeare, who had *As You Like It*, *Henry V*, *Much Ado* and Jonson's *Every Man In* 'stayed' in the Stationers' Register in 1600, a possible sign that they were protecting their interests in preventing the publication of those plays.[41]

The other three plays to appear in print in Shakespeare's lifetime, *Troilus*, *Lear* and *Pericles*, also apparently did so without the King's Men's approval. *Troilus* was entered in the Stationers' Register in 1603 by James Roberts who noted that he was waiting for 'sufficient authority' to print it.[42] This apparently never came. It was eventually printed in 1609 for Richard Bonion and Henry Walley with a title-page that claimed performance by Shakespeare's company. Strangely, the page was hastily reprinted to remove this information, with the suggestion also made in the epistle that the play was in fact never performed. Coupled with the complications surrounding its inclusion in the Folio, it seems again that *Troilus* is something of an unusual case. The version of *Lear* that appeared

in the Folio was considered different enough from its 1608 counterpart for the two plays to be edited as distinct entities in the 1986 Oxford edition of Shakespeare. Richard Preiss has elegantly argued that the first quarto texts of *Lear* and *Troilus* and perhaps *Pericles* were in fact published against the company's wishes.[43] Disaffection with *Lear*'s appearance in print may, indeed, account for the apparent revision of the play Shakespeare undertook around 1610, represented in the Folio text of the play. Edward Blount, who was also one of the Folio's publishers, entered *Antony and Cleopatra* and *Pericles* into the Stationers' Register in May 1608, though his failure to publish them has been a cause of some dispute, the entry interpreted variously as a 'blocking entry' on behalf of Shakespeare's company or as an attempt at publication which the company blocked in order to protect their own valuable

---

[38] Peter Blayney, 'The Publication of Playbooks', in *A New History of Early English Drama*, ed. John D. Cox and David Scott Kastan (New York, 1997), pp. 383–422; Erne, *Shakespeare as Literary Dramatist*, p. 128.

[39] Wells and Taylor, *Textual Companion*, p. 33.

[40] John Hemings and Henry Condell, 'To the Great Variety of Readers', *Mr. William Shakespeares Comedies, Histories, & Tragedies* (London, 1623). Gary Taylor in *Textual Companion*, p. 396, discusses the various theories regarding James Roberts's relationship to the 1602 entry of *Hamlet* in the Stationers' Register, none of which aver that he had a copy to print at the time; Erne suggests that Roberts already had the manuscript from which Q2 (1604/5) was set when Q1 (1603) appeared. See *Shakespeare as Literary Dramatist*, p. 81.

[41] Jowett, *Shakespeare and Text*, p. 10.

[42] From the entry in the Stationers' Register on 7 February 1603; see Wells and Taylor, *Textual Companion*, p. 424.

[43] Richard Preiss, 'Natural Authorship' in *Renaissance Drama*, n.s. 34 (2005), 69–104. Preiss argues that the texts of *Troilus* (which goes back on itself to deny the play's performance) and *Lear* (which emphasises on the title-page a very specific, private context for performance), both distance themselves from the public theatre, and therefore from company assets as performance texts, allowing a loophole for their printing without the company's approval. George Buc, the Master of the Revels from 1610, was granted the authority to license plays for publication in 1606, gaining control of the censorship of printed playbooks from the Church Court of High Commission, and apparently allowed both *Troilus* and *Lear* to be printed.

assets.[44] Indeed, *Pericles* was published in a very bad text the following year by Henry Gosson.

Of all other plays from the Chamberlain's/King's stable printed in that decade, two are by Jonson (*Sejanus* and *Volpone*); two are by other King's dramatists we know by name (Barnaby Barnes's *The Devil's Charter* and Wilkins's *The Miseries of Enforced Marriage*); two are Children of The Queen's Revels' plays, added to and performed by Shakespeare's company (Thomas Dekker's *Satiromastix* and John Marston's *The Malcontent*); five are reprints of Shakespeare's pre-Globe plays (Q4 and Q5 *1 Henry IV*, Q4 *Richard III*, Q4 *Richard II* and Q3 *Romeo and Juliet*); five are unattributed to any author, the latter two of which are also 'apocryphal' plays (*A Larum for London*, *The Fair Maid of Bristow*, *The Revenger's Tragedy*, *The Merry Devil of Edmonton* and Q3 *Mucedorus*); and the remaining three name Shakespeare as author (*Thomas Lord Cromwell* ['W.S.'], *The London Prodigal* and *A Yorkshire Tragedy*). Concerning collaboration then, the big question for the 'apocryphal' plays linked to Shakespeare's company, three of which were attributed to him on their title-pages, is whether they can be considered in the same ways as *Pericles* and *The Two Noble Kinsmen*. Can we explain their exclusion from the Folio yet guarantee the presence of Shakespeare's authorial hand nonetheless, by assuming they were plays on which he collaborated?

SHAKESPEARE AS WORKING AUTHOR

The position we adopted in *Collaborative Plays* is no. Alternatively, perhaps Shakespeare's professional responsibilities help explain his links to them; Jonathan Bate has argued that Shakespeare had to at least 'sign off' on plays in his capacity as company shareholder, as a way of stressing the likelihood of Shakespearian contact with plays not his own.[45] In these circumstances, Shakespearian collaboration in five of the 'apocryphal' Chamberlain's/King's plays — *Thomas Lord Cromwell*, *The London Prodigal*, *A Yorkshire Tragedy*, *The Merry Devil of Edmonton* and *Mucedorus* — is likely. And yet

whether or not the process Bate describes ever actually took place – there is no evidence of plays needing to be approved in-house in this way, though the Master of the Revels' approval of scripts was a kind of ancestral form of what in the modern world might be termed signing off on a document – it is nonetheless not possible to locate Shakespeare in any meaningful sense as an authorial presence within the first four plays in this list.[46] As for the Shakespearian contribution we all want to see in these plays – from the addition of small parts of a scene or speech, as with Hamlet's 'of some dozen or sixteen lines' to more substantial revisions – they are not the likeliest places to look, despite the various pieces of external evidence linking them to Shakespeare.

The additions to the Shakespeare canon we propose in our edition all come from works that bear no attribution to him in their earliest textual states. Much has been made in recent decades of Shakespeare's status as a collaborative author, though it has also been argued that he was not naturally given to it, with only six of the now-canonical thirty-eight plays being products of shared authorship.[47]

---

44 Roslyn Knutson, 'The Repertory', in Cox and Kastan, eds., *A New History of Early English Drama*, pp. 461–80, discounts the notion of blocking entries. Nonetheless, even Erne concedes: 'considering it cannot be taken for granted that the publication (or attempted publication) of any of these plays was authorized by the King's Men, it seems possible that their strategy in publishing Shakespeare's plays did significantly change some time after February 1603'. See *Shakespeare as Literary Dramatist*, p. 108. See Suzanne Gossett, ed., *Pericles* (Arden, 2004), pp. 16–18 for a compelling alternative discussion of the Blount evidence.

45 Quoted in 'Computer Analysis Proves Shakespeare's Hand in Other Plays', *The Times* (19 October 2013).

46 *Mucedorus* is a potential candidate for Shakespearian co-authorship; cases for all five plays are described at length in my 'Authorship and Attribution' section in Bate *et al.*, eds., *William Shakespeare and Others: Collaborative Plays*, pp. 641–745.

47 Charles Nicholl says as much in *The Lodger: Shakespeare on Silver Street* (London, 2008), p. 33; he also refers to Shakespeare having 'tacked and botched' in his early collaborations, and suggests that *Timon* displays 'irregularity' and that 'Shakespeare may have been edged into this collaboration by professional pressure', pp. 31, 33.

This number may well swell to nine as the theories of Hugh Craig, Laurie Maguire and Emma Smith about *2* and *3 Henry VI* and *All's Well That Ends Well* are tested and contested.[48] Still, the critical traditions behind *Titus Andronicus*, *1 Henry VI*, *Timon of Athens*, *Pericles*, *Henry VIII* and *The Two Noble Kinsmen* have tended subjectively towards their marginalization to the fringes of Shakespeare's canon, apparently strengthening the notion that collaboration was low on his list of artistic priorities, or that it was not a form of working likely to get the best out of him.

Shakespeare's motives for collaborating are often difficult to explain. He certainly only did so sporadically at best, *Timon* being perhaps his first joint effort since the formation of the Chamberlain's Men in 1594. His contributions to *1 Henry VI*, *The Spanish Tragedy* (if indeed he is, as we argue, the author of at least some of the Additions therein) and *Sir Thomas More* probably happened in 1594, *c*.1597 and 1604 respectively, though we might argue these were acts of revision rather than collaboration, which we could define as a decision to share the load of producing a play from scratch with another writer or writers. Henslowe's account books show that it was more normal than not for his dramatists to work together in this way, with teams of two or three often producing several plays in a matter of months or even weeks in exchange for one-off cash payments. Piecework necessitates hasty completion if it is to be economical, and in becoming a shareholder in his company Shakespeare was effectively freed from the creative sand trap of hand-to-mouth playwriting. Thereafter he did not want for money and for eleven years apparently did not collaborate, and, while the latter may be coincidence, financial security nonetheless accounts for one unusual feature of Shakespeare's writing: it took time.

The poetry of Shakespeare's plays is routinely praised, but we must also allow the extreme high quality of their structural crafting and plot management as likely functions of the patient and methodical manner in which he was able to write. Of course Shakespeare was not immune from mistakes, and many commentators have pointed out inconsistencies (Antonio's son in *Much Ado*, for

example) and errors (Bohemia's lack of a sea-coast) in his work, as well as more systematic plot-holing, Kristian Smidt's four-volume study being the most complete.[49] But these are relatively minor details that should not overshadow recognition of Shakespeare's supreme dramaturgical achievements; as Stephen Wittek contends, 'Shakespeare practised and perfected an impressionistic, non-realist style of drama that allowed for fluidity in spatio-temporal representation', arguing that what are perceived as 'mistakes' in a literal-minded fashion can in fact enhance the sensory effect of the play to the theatrical spectator.[50] All geography in Shakespeare really refers to the limits of the stage on which it was performed, and, in *Othello*, for example, the 'errors' in structural chronology actually work to build the famous double time scheme that renders the action both expansive and airless, the scheme of events both plausible and shockingly unreal and all consuming.

Michael Neill's edition explains how the moments of outright illogic in plot detail can both be absorbed and absolved, while the effect of the play's time-scheme is to tighten the screws upon a tragedy of unusual focus, an agonized rush of cause and consequence unfolding before the helpless spectator, longing to intervene.[51] There is a polymorphous quality to the treatment of time, with

---

[48] See Laurie Maguire and Emma Smith, 'Many Hands. A New Shakespeare Collaboration?', *Times Literary Supplement* (20 April 2012), 13–15; Hugh Craig and Arthur F. Kinney, eds., *Shakespeare, Computers, and the Mystery of Authorship* (Cambridge, 2009), pp. 40–77. In our edition we acknowledged these studies but declared it too soon to accept or reject their conclusions, unlike the plays for which we were advancing arguments which all have very long and varied Shakespeare-attribution histories. See also Brian Vickers and Marcus Dahl, '*All's Well That Ends Well*: An Attribution Refuted', *Times Literary Supplement* (11 May 2012), 14–16.

[49] *Unconformities in Shakespeare's History Plays* (New Jersey, 1982); *Unconformities in Shakespeare's Early Comedies* (New York, 1986); *Unconformities in Shakespeare's Tragedies* (New York, 1990); *Unconformities in Shakespeare's Later Comedies* (New York, 1993). See also John Sutherland and Cedric Watts, *Henry V, War Criminal? & Other Shakespeare Puzzles* (Oxford, 2000).

[50] Private communication (2 December 2013).

[51] Michael Neill ed., *Othello* (Oxford, 2006), pp. 33–6.

Shakespeare bending and shaping it to heighten the particular effects he sought to bestow on the play's narrative as it shifts through the gears. Iago's many interactions with the audience are considered analyses of events which may be happening over a period of some thirty-six hours, but which work to create the illusion of a more elastic timeframe. Such narrative and structural inconsistencies within Shakespeare's collaborative plays are frequently proffered as defects indicative of collaboration, though we must clearly rethink this approach. Shakespeare averaged roughly two well-laboured works a year over a twenty-year period. We have no idea how many other playwrights his company employed while he was writing, but we can see that they did not force him to rush out work or, for the most part, to change his habits. To assume they felt his plays were worth the wait is speculation; what is not is the fact that Shakespeare was unusually slow and, in the main, solitary compared with the busy hive of workers collaborating under Henslowe.

There is great sensitivity among Shakespearians to charges of Bardolatry, and emphasizing Shakespeare's works as products of a kind of hive-mind seems a secure way of sidestepping it. Acknowledging Shakespeare as a primarily slow, solitary author is neither helpless admiration nor is it to deny collaboration as a fact of his working life. *Collaborative Plays* in fact builds on many thousands of hours of careful work spanning multiple centuries seeking to expand the picture of Shakespeare as collaborator or at least reviser of works outside his traditional canon. And an accurate picture of Shakespeare's patterns of work can also help temper subjective reactions about tendencies towards over-attribution to him; that it is merely part of a wish-fulfilment to see him everywhere. Shakespeare was only slow by the standards of other contemporaries. Henry Chettle, for example, apparently wrote *Troy's Revenge* for Henslowe in nine days and, of the twenty new plays listed by Chambers as being completed for and acquired by the Admiral's company during 1599–1600, Chettle had a hand in seven of them.[52] Still, most years of Shakespeare's career saw him produce two to three plays of roughly 3,000 lines each, showing he was able to produce multiple works of extraordinary poetic and dramatic quality in a relatively short space of time. It is therefore not a great stretch of the imagination to see his output expanding by 1,600 or so lines over a fourteen-year period, as is the case with his apparent contributions to *Arden*, *Edward III*, *The Spanish Tragedy* and *Sir Thomas More*. A perceived lack of Shakespearian linguistic pyrotechnics within these contributions is frequently upheld as a precondition for excluding them from his canon, though this can work in the other direction too.

Our sense of the ease and speed with which Shakespeare could pen a few hundred lines increases if we – wrongly, I think – imagine him taking little care over their poetic quality, in turn increasing our sense of the likelihood they could be his, despite not 'feeling' unproblematically or recognizably Shakespearian. Certain non-stylistic features of the Hand D section of the *Sir Thomas More* manuscript – the extreme sloppiness of the orthography and calligraphy, the confusion over entrance directions leading from the previous section and resultant ambiguities created by the vagaries of speech prefix assignation, both of which Hand C attempts to correct – also apparently indicate hasty composition and a sense of authorial disconnect from the wider processes of collaborative revision on the play. That Shakespeare was less concerned with precision in such details when writing to order for others, though, is easily undermined by comparing the chaotic states of variance and vagary in speech prefixes in, for example, Q1 *Love's Labour's Lost* or Q2 *Romeo and Juliet*, texts apparently set from Shakespeare's authorial papers.[53] The case of *More* perhaps illustrates well a pre-theatrical and purely authorial moment of composition, assuming that the pragmatics of staging would be refined at a later date and subordinating them to the immediate necessities of the job of

---

[52] See Martin Wiggins, 'No Later than Munday, Chettle', *Around the Globe* 31 (Autumn, 2005), 26–7; E. K. Chambers, *The Elizabethan Stage* (Oxford, 1923), vol. 2, pp. 171–2.

[53] Wells and Taylor, *Textual Companion*, pp. 270–1, 288–90.

poetic composition.[54] And in it a unique figuration of Shakespeare as authorial entity becomes available. John Jowett notes that these leaves of paper 'disrupt . . . the image of Shakespeare as a dramatist available only in print and in isolation from the agency of theatre . . . [they] give . . . us Shakespeare as neither revered bard nor postmodern author function, but as dramatic author marking the paper with strokes of ink'.[55]

Through those strokes of ink we see a Shakespeare both recognizable and unfamiliar; one whose calligraphy can be linked to the patchy records we have in his six surviving signatures, albeit with the uncertainty intact that accompanies all biographical records of him. We have characteristic poetic and dramatic features – Jonathan Bate notes 'Shakespeare's unique poetic intensity' in the language, in the 'linguistic device of grammatical "conversion"' that abounds in the passage – as More conjures a series of stark mental images in his speeches, an extended and highly impressive deployment of the narrative trope of ekphrasis.[56] While the message differs radically from Mark Antony's incitement to riot in the other great crowd-control scene to which this is often compared, the understanding that emotional directives are the key to affective human response is powerfully shared. And yet there ultimately seems an exercise of linguistic restraint at work, a sense in which the passage is not radically distinct from the verbal texture of much of the rest of the play, a Shakespeare who is there and not quite there. We might more usefully consider Shakespeare's cooperativeness as co-author and how collaboration can help us understand this facet of his work. Erin Sullivan argues both that the image More offers of the 'wretched strangers' differs sharply from the thuggish characters of the first scene (penned by Munday), which, if Shakespeare knew, makes

the picture of More that he offers us especially interesting . . . a very learned, artful rhetorician – not entirely different from a Mark Antony, for instance – who is at once aware of the inequities and injustices in his social world and compelled to find ways to quiet objections to them . . . More than anything we are offered a character with a multi-faceted, even relativistic

way of understanding the worldliness of the world, who will eventually be compelled to articulate a much firmer, even intractable position on a particular matter that straddles worldly and godly existence over the course of the rest of the play.[57]

A qualitative, subjective taxonomy of Shakespeare's collaborative work, in which it is subordinated to his solo-authored canon, in which revision and smaller collaborative contributions are both treated with scepticism and perceived as slight, in which Shakespeare is seen 'phoning it in' or unconcerned with collaborative authorship as a process, is as unhelpful a model as one in which collaboration is overemphasized as a Shakespearian practice, or one in which fresh attribution is dismissed out of hand as a symptom of a wider obsession with Shakespearian authorship. Sir Brian Vickers stated in a *New York Times* article on Douglas Bruster's recent spelling evidence for Shakespeare's hand in *The Spanish Tragedy*, that 'Shakespeare wasn't a solitary genius, flying above everyone else. He was a working man of the theatre. If his company needed a new play, he'd get together with someone else and get it done.'[58] While a model of Shakespearian authorship based on the idea of 'genius' may of course yield little that is useful to the stylometrist or literary critic alike,

---

54 Grace Ioppolo has argued that the manuscript shows Shakespeare making adjustments to a copy he is making, though, as Jowett suggests, 'the more usual view is that it shows Shakespeare in the process of initial composition, see Ioppolo, *Dramatists and Their Manuscripts in the Age of Shakespeare* (Abingdon, 2004), pp. 102–9, and Jowett, *Shakespeare and Text*, p. 202, n.12.

55 John Jowett, ed., *Sir Thomas More* (Arden, 2011), p. 8.

56 Jonathan Bate in Bate *et al.*, eds., *William Shakespeare and Others: Collaborative Plays*, p. 23.

57 Erin Sullivan, 'Sir Thomas More', unpublished essay, 2011.

58 Jennifer Schuessler, 'Much Ado About Who: Is It Really Shakespeare? Further Proof of Shakespeare's Hand in *The Spanish Tragedy*', *The New York Times* (12 August 2013), www.nytimes.com/2013/08/13/arts/further-proof-of-shakespeares-hand-in-the-spanish-tragedy.html?pagewanted=all&_r=3&.&. See also Douglas Bruster, 'Shakespearean Spellings and Handwriting in the Additional Passages Printed in the 1602 *Spanish Tragedy*', *Notes and Queries* 60:3 (2013), 420–4.

the 'solitary' part of the formulation needs consideration, and should not be formulaically, even pejoratively bound to, and dismissed along with, notions of 'genius'. Assertions that Shakespeare's solo-authored work exhibits more of his genius than his collaborative are of course woolly and imprecise, though observations that it might function differently are not, and are starting points for more detailed formalist, stylistic analysis of Shakespeare's co-authored writing.

The postmodern fragmentation of Shakespeare across cultures and times asserts an impossibly irrecoverable presence, stripped of authorial agency, a figuration perhaps incompatible with attempts to locate him in the act of writing within specific works. Yet the wellspring of creative energy that we associate with Shakespeare's works was not an abstraction; it was a person, it was Shakespeare, and knowing what he did and did not write matters. His plays were not written by someone else just as they were not summoned into being by the whole acting company extempore, or by the culture of the age, and are not all explicable as acts of collaboration. Though some of them are. Our perception of Shakespeare's gifts as a writer will be deepened by appreciations of the range of particular stylistic, structural and ideational characteristics of his collaborative writing within a precisely defined body of his co-authored work, something we have attempted to provide with *Collaborative Plays*, though we accept that the body we have constructed may prove as friable as any other scholarly edifice against the erosion of subsequent inquiry. Our conceptions of Shakespeare the authorial craftsman and Shakespeare the collaborator and reviser, and the implications this has for Shakespearian biography, for our understanding of his activities as a writer, of his canon, as well as a broader philosophical ethic about intellectual property, must be as adaptable and nuanced in their particular complexions as were Shakespeare's own Protean experiments with authorial self-representation through poetic form.[59]

---

[59] This article was both aided and improved by the invaluable input of Peter Holland, Eric Rasmussen, Erin Sullivan and Stephen Wittek. My thanks also to a host of friends and colleagues for offering examples of structural problems in Shakespeare's plays, and helping me think through the issues they represent.

COLLABORATION AND PROPRIETARY AUTHORSHIP: SHAKESPEARE *ET AL.*

TREVOR COOK

Amicorum communia omnia[1]

It now remains to consider what the prince's methods and controls ought to be in handling his subjects and friends.[2]

Whenever Shakespeare is believed to have worked with another dramatist, he is generally presented as the lead author: Shakespeare and Thomas Middleton, Shakespeare and George Wilkins, Shakespeare and John Fletcher – to name just a few instances – or in the more inclusive title of a recent anthology: *William Shakespeare and Others*.[3] This practice makes sense in light of Shakespeare's elevated status. Shakespeare is the very image of the author function, the principle of thrift in a proliferation of hands.[4] For by him everything praiseworthy in these plays was contributed, on page and on stage, theatrical and literary, whether plots or scenarios or characters or lines – all these things were created through him and for him, if not his playing company. So if his name is the name above all names, it is because in him the many complexities of a largely invisible collaborative process hold together. Whether for good reasons or ill, Shakespeare has the pre-eminence. He is prince. Even the inclusion of *Timon of Athens*, *Measure for Measure* and *Macbeth* in the recent *Collected Works of Thomas Middleton* is premised on the belief that Middleton contributed to work that began with and still belongs substantially to Shakespeare; these are, after all, just some of '*Shakespeare's* Collaborative Works' (emphasis added). But who in Shakespeare's lifetime claimed credit for a play like *Pericles*? The title page of the

1609 quarto lists the King's Men as the actors and William Shakespeare as the author, but the play was not included in the First Folio and many scenes were evidently written by George Wilkins, who had only the year before published a prose version

---

1 Desiderius Erasmus, 'Adages', in *Collected Works of Erasmus*, vol. 31, trans. Margaret Mann Phillips, ed. R. A. B. Mynors (Toronto, 1982), p. 29. For the context of this adage, and the theories of property most relevant to the argument below, see Kathy Eden, *Friends Hold All Things in Common: Tradition, Intellectual Property, and the Adages of Erasmus* (New Haven, 2001).

2 Niccolò Machiavelli, *The Prince*, trans. and ed. James B. Atkinson (Indianapolis, 2008), p. 255. I also share Machiavelli's reservations: 'Because I know that many people have written about this topic, I fear that my writing about it too may be judged presumptuous – particularly since in discussing this matter, I depart from the precepts given by others. But the intention of my writing is to be of use to whoever understands it; thus it has seemed to be more profitable to go straight to the actual truth of matters rather than to a conception of it' (255). On the reception of Machiavelli in English prior to 1640 see Alessandra Petrina, *Machiavelli in the British Isles: Two Early Modern Translations of The Prince* (Farnam, 2009).

3 *William Shakespeare and Others: Collaborative Plays*, ed. Jonathan Bate and Eric Rasmussen (London, 2013). Also, Stanley Wells, *Shakespeare and Co.: Christopher Marlowe, Thomas Dekker, Ben Jonson, Thomas Middleton, John Fletcher and the Other Players in His Story* (London, 2006). The title-pages of single volume editions of Shakespeare's collaborative plays, notably in the *Oxford Shakespeare*, bear out my first point.

4 The most recent study to espouse (and epitomize) this view is James J. Marino, *Owning William Shakespeare: The King's Men and Their Intellectual Property* (Philadelphia, 2011), p. 128, *passim*.

(partly plagiarized) of the same story. Was it (or just parts of it) Shakespeare's work, Wilkins's, or a joint property? Or as any one of the interested parties might have put it: yours, mine, or ours?

Such questions are challenging because scholars have little evidence upon which to base an answer and still less of a shared understanding of what that evidence means; 'We don't even have adequate language to describe co-authorship' in Shakespeare's lifetime.[5] As a sharer in a professional playing company, Shakespeare was clearly not a solitary genius in the manner of the romantic myth that informs so much of our use of possessive forms today, as in the phrase 'Shakespeare's *Romeo and Juliet*'. Even in a play as original in plot as *A Midsummer Night's Dream*, Shakespeare avoids distinctions between mine and thine: the writer/director Peter Quince and others refer always to 'our play' (e.g. 1.2.11; 3.1.46–7), the star Bottom yields the spotlight to 'our company' (5.1.347–8) and the logic of penal appropriation does not apply: 'when the players are all dead', their patron Theseus concludes, 'there need none to be blamed' (5.1.350–1). The radically collaborative nature of staging a play requires each participant to relinquish his (or her) individual interests, just as presumably Shakespeare habitually did in the Lord Chamberlain's Men at the time. And with as many as half of the plays produced between 1590 and 1642 having been the work of two or more hands,[6] Shakespeare was probably accustomed to definitions of authorship, textual property and the individual very different from our own.[7] Yet, however much might be made of this disputed estimate,[8] it was at least equally common, if not more prevalent, for authors to work independently and to be acknowledged for that work.[9] Even co-authors sometimes claimed credit for their unique contributions. In a letter dated 5 June 1613, the struggling dramatist Robert Daborne explains to his creditor, the impresario Philip Henslowe, for instance, that he had 'given' part of 'my own play' to another writer in order to help him meet a deadline set by the playing company that had commissioned him.[10] To complicate matters further, some authors even adopted

different positions at different points in their career, keeping their literary property from others as rivals in one work, and then sharing it with them as collaborators in another. For example, Ben Jonson claimed to have physically 'beat' the dramatist John Marston, whom he accused of 'plagiary' in his play *Poetaster* (1602), 'and took his pistol from him', but the two also worked together on projects such as *Eastward Ho!* (1605), wrote prefatory poems for each other's plays, and were celebrated together by their peers.[11] Literary propriety was nevertheless constantly observed, both in terms of property and decorum. When Jonson revised the collaborative play *Sejanus His Fall* for publication as his own work in 1605 (listing Shakespeare among the performers), he acknowledged that he rewrote the

---

[5] James Shapiro, *Contested Will: Who Wrote Shakespeare?* (New York, 2010), p. 256. See also Heather Anne Hirschfeld, 'Early Modern Collaboration and Theories of Authorship', *PMLA* 116 (2001), p. 620.

[6] G. E. Bentley, *The Profession of Dramatist in Shakespeare's Time, 1590–1642* (Princeton, 1971), p. 199.

[7] Jeffrey Masten, *Textual Intercourse: Collaboration, Authorship, and Sexualities in Renaissance Drama* (Cambridge, 1997); Heather Anne Hirschfeld, *Joint Enterprises: Collaborative Authorship and the Institutionalization of the English Renaissance Theatre* (Amherst, 2004).

[8] Brian Vickers, *Shakespeare, Co-Author: A Historical Study of Five Collaborative Plays* (Oxford, 2004), p. 17; MacDonald P. Jackson, 'Collaboration', in *The Oxford Handbook of Shakespeare*, ed. Arthur Kinney (Oxford, 2012), pp. 32–3; John Jowett, *Shakespeare and Text* (Oxford, 2007), p. 23.

[9] Vickers, *Co-Author*, pp. 506–41; Jeffrey Knapp, *Shakespeare Only* (Chicago, 2009). Knapp argues that even in the case of *Dream* 'a collaborative ethos can do more than accommodate the desire to be distinguished from one's fellows, to be the writer, the leader, even to play all the parts; it can actually spur these ambitions, by encouraging each fellow to think of himself in collective terms, as exemplary of the group' (92).

[10] *Henslowe Papers: Being Documents Supplementary to Henslowe's Diary*, ed. Walter W. Greg (London, 1907), p. 72.

[11] Ben Jonson, 'Informations to William Drummond of Hawthornden', in *The Cambridge Edition of the Works of Ben Jonson*, vol. 5, ed. Ian Donaldson (Cambridge, 2012), p. 374 (see also p. 367); 'Poetaster', in *The Cambridge Edition of the Works of Ben Jonson*, vol. 2, ed. Gabriele Bernhard Jackson (Cambridge, 2012), p. 106.

'good share' of an anonymous 'second pen' (presumably George Chapman's), substituting lines of 'mine own', rather 'than to defraud so happy a genius of his right'.[12]

We hear no comparable statements from Shakespeare regarding the division of labour and distribution of credit in the plays associated with his name, though he was clearly no stranger to the give and take of dramatic authorship. On one occasion, in 1592, he was criticized for beautifying himself with others' 'feathers',[13] a possible reference to his collaboration with the university wit George Peele early in his career;[14] and on another, in 1599, he took offence at the association of his name with another's poetry, indicating that he was no less keenly aware than Jonson of what was and what was *not* his literary property.[15] We know also from Hamlet's request to add 'some dozen or sixteen lines' to 'the murder of Gonzago' that Shakespeare was familiar with revision as a form of collaboration (2.2.540, 543). This exchange is itself revised in 1605, when *Hamlet* was 'Newly imprinted and enlarged to almost as much againe as it was', most likely by Shakespeare himself.[16] But it was not uncommon for play texts to be revised by another dramatist and that dramatist to be credited, as in the King's Men's play *The Malcontent*, which, although ascribed to John Marston in one imprint of 1604, was in another the same year re-advertised as 'Augmented by Marston' and 'Written by John Webster'.

In the 'Dream of the Master Text', which introduces the Norton Shakespeare, Stephen Greenblatt cites the whole episode of the play-within-the-play in *Hamlet* as an example where the radically collaborative nature of drama precludes proprietary authorship for Shakespeare and his contemporaries. However, while Hamlet certainly takes very little control over the process, this is not because, as Greenblatt suggests, he had no interest in controlling the performance nor because like 'any other working English playwright' he had no 'public "standing", legal or otherwise, from which to do so'; rather, it is because the success of his plot in this instance depends upon his involvement being kept secret: he 'must be idle' (3.2.88).[17] In private,

Hamlet is otherwise keen to take possession of the play. In the first quarto, Hamlet requires that the players attend *to* him as much as they memorize a new speech *for* him ('for a neede study me / Some dozen or sixteene lines'); and in each of the early printed texts he not only assumes sole responsibility for altering the play to his purposes ('which I would set down and insert' (2.2.543–4), but also models for the players how to pronounce 'my lines' (3.2.1–4), as well as warns their 'clowns speak no more than is set down for them' (3.2.39). *Hamlet* is not the only work which enables conflicting definitions of authorship in the period. Shakespeare's first seventeen sonnets, in the order they were printed in 1609, suggest that he privileged sameness and so would have adhered to Jeffrey Masten's rightly influential definition of collaboration in the period as 'a dispersal of author/ity, rather than a simple doubling of it'.[18] In this, he would have been less like Jonson – possessive and only occasionally collaborating – and more like Francis Beaumont and John Fletcher, a frequent collaborator who worked closely enough with writers of like mind for his style to be easily conflated with theirs. But this does not account for the creative differences observed in the so-called rival poet sonnets (78–86), which are everywhere alert to *meum et tuum* – 'my Muse', 'my verse', 'my art' and 'every alien pen', 'others' works' – and as such remind us that Shakespeare did not conform to any one model of authorship throughout his career.

---

[12] Ben Jonson, 'Sejanus His Fall', in *The Cambridge Edition of the Works of Ben Jonson*, vol. 2, ed. Tom Cain (Cambridge, 2012), p. 215.

[13] Henry Chettle and Robert Greene, *Greene's Groatsworth of Wit: Bought with a Million of Repentance (1592)*, ed. D. Allen Carroll (Binghamton, 1994), p. 84.

[14] John Jowett, 'Shakespeare as Collaborator', in *Shakespeare Beyond Doubt: Evidence, Argument, Controversy*, ed. Paul Edmondson and Stanley Wells (Cambridge, 2013), pp. 89–92.

[15] Lukas Erne, *Shakespeare as Literary Dramatist*, 2nd edn (Cambridge, 2013), p. 27. The phrasing here is also Erne's.

[16] *Hamlet* Q2 (1605).

[17] 'Introduction', in *The Norton Shakespeare*, 2nd edn, ed. Stephen Greenblatt *et al.* (New York, 2008), p. 69.

[18] Masten, *Textual Intercourse*, p. 19.

Greenblatt clearly overstates the case when he remarks that 'there is no evidence that Shakespeare had an interest in asserting authorial rights over his scripts'.[19] He also confuses a dramatist's interests with his or her limitations when he adds that neither Shakespeare nor his contemporaries were capable of exerting authorial control over their texts. The fact that authors had no legal 'standing' in the early seventeenth century does not mean that some would not have wished it otherwise.[20] For new historicists in general, however, not even Shakespeare's signature indicates an interest in being identified as the author of the work in question.[21] Instead, Shakespeare's name functions as the guarantor of a particularly valued style in much the same way that a master painter's signature did in the Renaissance. Greenblatt's analogy with the visual arts is nonetheless instructive. A painter's signature does not necessary mean that he was the sole creator of the work that bears his name, and so in the case of a publication like *Pericles* it is possible to think of Shakespeare as the master dramatist and Wilkins as the uncredited apprentice.[22] Shakespeare's role in staging a play was, for Greenblatt, thus closer to that of Luca Signorelli's in painting the large-scale frescoes in Orvieto Cathedral than Piero della Francesca's in completing his more manageable panel painting *Madonna della Misericordia*. In 1499, Signorelli accepted a commission 'to paint all the figures to be done on the said vault, and especially *the faces and all the parts of the figures from the middle of each figure upwards*, and that no painting should be done on it without Luca himself being present', freeing him out of necessity to delegate every other task, excepting 'the mixing of colours', to anyone whose work was compatible with his own.[23] Della Francesca's contract stipulated instead that '*no painter may put his hand to the brush other than Piero himself*'.[24] Rather than taking full advantage of this analogy, however, Greenblatt both misrepresents drama as more collaborative than painting and privileges the author function over the functioning artists in his example. Greenblatt is right that there 'is no record of any comparable concern for exclusivity in the English theatre', and that Robert

Brome's rare surviving contract with the Salisbury Court Theatre in 1635 does not stipulate 'that the plays associated with his name be exclusively *his* but rather that he be exclusively *theirs*'.[25] But there are many instances in the visual arts where collaborators were individually credited for their contributions and just as much evidence in Henslowe's *Diary* and elsewhere that dramatists could reasonably expect the same, if not from the play-going public then at least from their peers. In the all-or-nothing rhetoric of recent authorship studies, we forget that everyone in the theatre deserved at least to be credited for something, as in the well-known imprint of *Gorboduc* (1561) which goes so far as to announce who wrote what: 'three Actes were wrytten by / Thomas Nortone, and the two laste by / Thomas Sackvyle'.

That Shakespeare was mostly silent about his working arrangements with his contemporaries does not mean that Jonson was the only one to question the implications of collaboration for crediting individual artists with specific contributions to a creative work, or that such concerns were unprecedented. In fact, such questions

---

[19] Greenblatt, 'Introduction', p. 69.

[20] As in the case of John Donne. See my '"The meate was mine": Donne's *Satyre II* and the Prehistory of Proprietary Authorship', *Studies in Philology*, 109:1 (2012), 103–31.

[21] This despite Michel Foucault's assertion that 'The author's name manifests the appearance of a certain discursive set and indicates the status of this discourse within a society and a culture. It has no legal status, nor is it located in the fiction of the work; rather, it is located in the break that founds a certain discursive construct and its very particular mode of being.' 'What Is an Author?' in *The Foucault Reader*, ed. Paul Rabinow (New York, 1984), p. 107. Or as Peggy Kamuf puts it: 'The undecidable trait of the signature must fall into the crack of the historicist/formalist opposition organizing most discourse about literature' (*Signature Pieces: On the Institution of Authorship* (Ithaca, 1988), p. 13).

[22] See Lisa Pon, *Raphael, Dürer, and Marcantonio Raimondi: Copying and the Italian Renaissance Print* (New Haven, 2004), pp. 1–14.

[23] Quoted in Michael Baxandall, *Painting and Experience in Fifteenth Century Italy: A Primer in the Social History of Pictorial Style*, 2nd edn (Oxford, 1988), p. 23 (original emphasis).

[24] Baxandall, p. 20 (original emphasis).

[25] Greenblatt, 'Introduction', p. 71.

commonly arose from partnership in the visual and plastic arts. Writing of sculpture, the elder Pliny had observed in the second century that in many exemplary works of Greco-Roman art the number of hands involved threatened to obscure the fame of each artist. He was especially troubled by the prized sculpture of Laocoön and his two sons, for, although this work deserved to be celebrated above all others, it was difficult for Pliny to know which of its three creators to praise for it: no one is able to take all the credit [quoniam nec unus occupat gloriam], nor can it be divided fairly among many [nec plures pariter nuncupari possunt].[26] A further problem for Pliny in the *Natural History*, as for critics of the so-called disintegrators in Shakespearian scholarship, was that collaboration prevented artists from pursuing a singular vision and so compromised the integrity of their work, a complaint that painters in the fifteenth century identified with the presence of multiple hands. In 1476, for example, a displeased patron petitioned the Duke of Milan to prevent an unfinished painting from being completed by 'so many hands', since the evidence of the three artists' collaboration had apparently deformed the work.[27] In contrast, the work of the brothers Lorenzo and Vittorio Ghiberti could be celebrated because their contributions to the Baptistery doors in Florence agreed so well together that they seemed 'to be by one and the same hand'.[28]

Beyond these examples, the most telling comment upon the implications of collaboration for individual credit in the dramatic arts occurs in the multi-authored English play, *The Spanish Gypsy*, which, dating to the first half of the seventeenth century, more closely resembles the kind of joint enterprise with which Shakespeare was at times involved. Scholars have carefully examined this play to determine who wrote which lines, and to test the soundness of their attribution methods, but have not yet considered the extent to which the play comments upon its own authorship. *The Spanish Gypsy* raises two important points relevant to the propriety of 'Shakespeare's' collaborative plays: first, that cooperation can occur between rivals with competing interests just as often as between

friends, or in the spirit of 'coopetition' what are known today as 'frenemies' (both neologisms of the past century); and second, that collaboration could accommodate the desires of either friend or foe to distinguish themselves or their particular contribution. There is then a third way for authorship studies with relevance to Shakespeare. As a co-author, he did not necessarily relinquish all (or fail to recognize any) desire to be identified as the author of a particular passage, nor did he necessarily assume complete control of the finished product. One argument that has been made in favour of Shakespeare's sole propriety is that much like Jonson he experimented with different models of authorship throughout his career, but it is just as important to recognize that these experiments took place with different authors and so did not always end in the same way. In the case of *Timon of Athens* (*c.*1605), Shakespeare met his match with Thomas Middleton who, as a rising star beginning to make a name for himself (since lauded as 'Our other Shakespeare'[29]), would not compromise his artistic vision in favour of his partner's, resulting in a conflicted text that can only be fairly identified as Shakespeare's and Middleton's. Shakespeare's co-author in *Pericles* (*c.*1607-8) was more compliant; George Wilkins was an inferior dramatist who during his brief time working for the King's Men must have been grateful to be acknowledged at all, though he seldom has been, leading to a general consensus that this play is Shakespeare's (and

---

[26] Pliny, *Natural History*, vol. 10, trans. D. E. Eichholz (London, 1938), p. 28; *Naturalis Historia*, 36.4.37.

[27] The nature of the complaint, as conveyed by the duke to the painters, was that their diverse hands had resulted in a work lacking unity: 'we say to you and desire that you take care of it according to your obligation, by arranging that the painting is not done by so many hands as it would seem to be done, so as to make the work unharmonious (*disforma*)' (Martin Kemp, 'Equal Excellences: Lornazzo and the Explanation of Individual Style in the Visual Arts', *Renaissance Studies*, 1:1 (1987), 1–26, p. 6).

[28] Kemp, 'Equal Excellences', p. 6.

[29] Gary Taylor, 'Thomas Middleton: Lives and Afterlives', in *Thomas Middleton: The Collected Works*, ed. Gary Taylor *et al.* (Oxford, 2007), p. 58, *passim*.

Wilkins's). It was only in Shakespeare and Fletcher's (alternatively Fletcher and Shakespeare's) *The Two Noble Kinsmen* (*c*.1613–14) that Shakespeare shared his work equally with another dramatist, in this case one with whom he enjoyed a friendly rivalry as the more senior partner. These attributions are supported by the plays themselves, if not on their title-pages. Like *The Spanish Gypsy*, 'Shakespeare's' collaborative plays comment on the conditions of their production, not because the authors involved necessarily took their working relationship as their subject but because these plays were subject always to those relationships.[30]

MEUM ET TUUM

One difference between Shakespeare's collaborative plays and *The Spanish Gypsy* is that, although scholars agree that the latter was collaboratively written, there is less agreement about the precise number and identity of the authors involved. It was licensed for performance on 9 July 1623 only months after Jonson's successful masque *The Gypsies Metamorphosed* (1621), suggesting an attempt to capitalize on his recent success, and was first published in 1653 by Richard Marriot as a quarto bearing the title 'THE SPANISH GIPSIE. / As it was Acted (with great Applause) / at the Privat House in Drury-Lane, / and SALISBURY COURT. / Written by THOMAS MIDLETON, / and WILLIAM ROWLEY. Gent.' A second quarto of 1661 similarity identified the writers as Middleton and Rowley, and in light of their previous work on *A Fair Quarrel* (1617) and *The Changeling* (written in 1622, published in 1653), there is little reason to doubt the external evidence for their co-authorship. The internal evidence for authorship, however, reveals similarities between the play's style and the works of John Ford and between its treatment of gypsies and the works of Thomas Dekker,[31] so that many scholars now favour Ford and Dekker as the most likely co-authors of the play, although, as Gary Taylor and the editors of the *Collected Middleton* maintain, there remains no reason to exclude Middleton and Rowley.[32]

With as many as four writers contributing to the play one might assume that each surrendered to the others the credit for his individual contribution (*unus pro omnibus, omnes pro uno*), but it is difficult to ignore the many themes related to interpersonal conflict and violations of property in the play. For one thing, the play begins with and revolves around a rape. When Roderigo forcibly removes Clara from her parents in the opening scene, his actions are construed as 'rape' before any sexual assault takes place, since rape in the period could mean the violent seizure of property in general or the sexual assault of a woman in particular (*OED* n.3.1).[33] In this respect, rape was synonymous with plagiary, which as the Latin legal word for kidnapping had only recently been introduced on the English stage as a metaphor for literary misappropriation in Jonson's *Poetaster* (1601). Nothing more might be made of this fact, since by Act 2 the play is primarily concerned with sexual violation, if it were not for the play's secondary concern with literary propriety throughout. The real threat in *The Spanish Gypsy* is domestic (among collaborators), not foreign: Spanish gypsies were notorious for theft but the English, in the play, are no better: 'they so pilfer' (2.1.39). These lines are thought to have been written by Thomas Dekker and, if so, have a particular resonance with some of his earlier compilations of cant, *The Bellman of London* (1608), *Lantern and Candlelight* (1608), and *O per se O* (1612). The literature of canting had been

---

[30] For similar approaches see Masten, *Textual Intercourse*, p. 58; Suzanne Gossett, 'Introduction: *The Spanish Gypsy*', in *The Collected Works of Thomas Middleton*, ed. Gary Taylor *et al.* (Oxford, 2007), 1725a and 'Editing Collaborative Drama', in *Shakespeare Survey 59* (Cambridge, 2006), pp. 214, 219. In other words, that they were 'historically embedded but personally inflected' (Hirschfeld, *Joint Enterprises*, p. 1).

[31] H. Dugdale Sykes, 'John Ford, the Author of *The Spanish Gipsy*', *Modern Language Review*, 19 (1924), pp. 11–24.

[32] Gary Taylor, 'Thomas Middleton, *The Spanish Gypsy*, and Collaborative Authorship', in *Words that Count: Early Modern Authorship: Essays in Honor of MacDonald P. Jackson* (Cranbury, 2004), pp. 241–73.

[33] *The Spanish Gypsy, The Collected Works of Thomas Middleton*, ed. Gary Taylor *et al.* (Oxford, 2007), p. 1729, 1.3.42. All subsequent references are to this edition and are cited in text.

for many years implicated in literary piracy,[34] and, in *Martin Mark-all* (1610), Dekker was publically accused of having plagiarized substantial portions of *Bellman*, in particular, from Thomas Harman's *A Caveat or Warning for Common Cursitors* (1566).[35] Whoever wrote these lines was thus right to suspect the presence of thieves in their midst.

The thematic links to proprietary authorship and textual property in the play thus far appear less circumstantial when one considers that the first verses to circulate in the play, as a stage property, immediately raise questions of attribution and ownership. When the Gypsy love-interest of the principal characters, Preciosa, opens a paper that contains love poetry by the clown Sancho and has been wrapped around a piece of gold, she is puzzled: 'Whose is this?' (2.1.158–9). She obviously means the gold, but Sancho is more concerned with the propriety of the verses, both in terms of their possession and quality: 'Whose but yours? If there be any fault in the verses, I can mend it extempore; for a stitch in a man's stocking, not taken up in time, ravels out all the rest' (2.1.160–2). Sancho's ability to answer for his verses, and if necessary revise them, depends upon his close proximity to them (*Phaedrus*, 275d4–e6), but his promise is frustrated by the presence of a collaborator with a different view of the situation. The tailor's metaphor is appropriate to texts (with their etymologic links to textiles), and a stitch in time may save the poet labour, but for his colleague Soto the hasty compilation of the extemporizing poet can only produce the kinds of patchworks identified as plagiarisms in the period and as signs of collaborative authorship today: 'Botcherly poetry, botcherly' (2.1.163). Sancho is subsequently given an opportunity to read his verses aloud, which, in keeping with a pun on distich, Soto matches line for line with critical commentary, prompting everyone in mock sympathy to object 'they're excellent' and the incredulous leader of the gypsies, in particular, to ask 'But are these *all* your own?' (2.1.195–6, my emphasis). In the context of the other player's mock enthusiasm for Sancho's verses, Preciosa's father seems scarcely able to believe that one person could compose so many excellent verses, while in the context

of Soto's criticisms it would seem that parts of what Sancho has read aloud do not sound as though they originated with him.

The theme of who owns what in a work with discernible seams becomes more pronounced as the play becomes increasingly Rowleyan in character, even if as some scholars believe Rowley never wrote a word of it.[36] It is difficult to dissociate Rowley completely from Sancho and Soto on account of their obvious similarities with Chough and Trimtram,[37] the two clowns he created for *A Fair Quarrel*, and at 4.2.87 Soto assumes the name 'Lollio' after the clown Rowley created and performed in *The Changeling*. So even if Rowley was not personally responsible for Sancho's and Soto's parts, whoever prepared them was clearly aware of his work. Either scenario is plausible. Rowley had not only worked closely with Middleton before, but also partnered with Dekker and Ford on *The Witch of Edmonton* in 1621 and *Keep the Widow Waking* in 1624 and, when *The Spanish Gypsy* was first performed in 1623 he had just joined Shakespeare's former company, the King's Men, in the same capacity as actor-dramatist that he had first occupied for the Queen Anne's Men and then for the Prince Charles's Men. Rowley was thus equally in a position to have written these parts as to have inspired them. In either case, the sense we get of Rowley's character both within *The Spanish Gypsy* and elsewhere is that he was protective of his work. As David Nicol has recently observed, the epistles that Rowley prepared for his collaborations with Middleton 'suggest a hint of possessiveness toward the text and of an awareness of his own stylistic individuality' (or what most modern commentators are too ready to dismiss as his inferiority),

---

[34] David Mayall, *Gypsy Identities 1500–2000: From Egipcyans and Moon-Men to the Ethnic Romany* (London, 2004), p. 69.

[35] S. R., 'Martin Markall', in *The Elizabethan Underworld*, ed. A. V. Judges (London, 1930), p. 398. See Elizabeth Hanson, *Discovering the Subject in Renaissance England* (Cambridge, 1998), pp. 111–14.

[36] E.g. David J. Lake, *The Canon of Thomas Middleton's Plays: Internal Evidence for the Major Problems of Authorship* (Cambridge, 1975), pp. 219–20.

[37] Norman Brittin, *Thomas Middleton* (New York, 1972), p. 97.

which in the case of a *Fair Quarrel*, in particular, arguably stems from his responsibilities managing literary affairs and finances as the chief spokesmen if not the leader of the Prince Charles's Men at the time.[38]

The point here is not to assert that Rowley did (or did not) contribute directly to *The Spanish Gypsy* but to remember the kinds of minor writers – like his quondam colleague Wilkins[39] – who sometimes collaborated with more established authors, and to imagine the kinds of challenges that they faced. These writers had as much reason, if not more, to receive credit for their contributions, however lowly those contributions might have been. There is more than a hint of possessiveness among the clowns in *The Spanish Gypsy*, for which someone like Rowley seems to have been responsible – while by most accounts Ford contributed the rape plot, Dekker supplied the gypsy scenes, and Middleton managed the main plot (and wrote a few minor passages) – and this possessiveness arguably stems from a perceived vulnerability to misappropriation. Nor is there reason to think that these writers thought of themselves the way we think of them today. Rowley, no less than Wilkins, is often regarded as a 'collaborating hack', but as Mark Hutchings and A. A. Bromham remark, 'his connection with plays such as *The Witch of Edmonton* (1621, with Dekker and Ford), and particularly *A Fair Quarrel* and *The Changeling* [both with Middleton], indicates that he deserves more serious consideration',[40] and the play's many allusions to *The Changeling*, in particular, suggest that someone involved with *The Spanish Gypsy* agreed. Whoever was responsible for writing the clowns' parts knew that playwrights were as eager, if not more so, to take credit for making the audience laugh as to make them cry or think, but that those who play to the crowd are never taken as seriously as those who write the more refined parts.

This perceived inequality between those who get the laughs and those who take credit for them is most evident when, in the lead-up to the play-within-the-play, the clowns Soto and Sancho assess the limitations of the aristocrat Roderigo in terms reminiscent of the more celebrated writers

associated with *The Spanish Gypsy*. Roderigo claims that he has played in the theatre before, but, when the clowns embrace him as 'A player! A brother of the tiring-house', he admits to not being their equal on stage: he 'can nor dance nor sing' no more than Ford, Dekker or Middleton is known to have (3.1.60, 62). All that Roderigo possesses of any use is his tool ('my pen') and found materials ('my invention'), which being of less value than the skills the clowns bring to the performance he surrenders in the spirit of collaboration: 'My head and brains are yours' (3.1.62–4). The clowns for their part are notably wary. They agree that his contributions are less valuable ('A calf's head and brains were better') and dismiss them as part food ('A rib of poetry'), part commodity ('A modicum of the Muses'), and part property ('A horseshoe of Helicon'), before identifying Roderigo himself not as a producer but as a consumer of such goods: 'A magpie of Parnassus!' (3.1.65–7). They then re-evaluate their partnership and invite him back to the project at hand: 'Welcome again!' Sancho exclaims, 'I am a fire-brand of Phoebus myself; we'll invoke together', though he is quick to clarify his reasons '– so you will not steal my plot' (3.1.67–70). Sancho, it would seem, knows to keep his friends close and his enemies closer but, in Cicero's *De Officiis*, a widely influential text throughout the Renaissance, he would also have learned the value of an extended partnership (*communitas*) for private property: 'For, although it was by Nature's guidance that men were drawn together into communities, it was in the hope of safeguarding their possessions that they sought the protection of cities' (2.21.73).[41] Unlike Cicero, who in referring to the protection of 'possessions' meant material objects (*custodia rerum suarum*), earlier maintaining that

---

[38] David Nicol, *Middleton and Rowley: Forms of Collaboration in the Jacobean Playhouse* (Toronto, 2012), p. 20.

[39] The two collaborated with John Day on *The Travels of the Three Brothers* (London, 1607).

[40] Mark Hutchings and A. A. Bromham, *Middleton and His Collaborators* (Horndon, 2008), p. 74.

[41] Cicero, *De officiis*, trans. Walter Miller, Loeb Classical Library (Cambridge, 1961), p. 249. See Eden, *All Things in Common*, pp. 100–1.

intellectual property was common to all, Sancho extends the definition of private property from *res publica* to *res literaria*, and its safeguarding from the city to the theatre, just as Erasmus had done before him and Milton would do after.[42] His response to Roderigo's objection that it is not his 'fashion' – 'But nowadays 'tis all the fashion' – further aligns the play's self-interested relationships with a developing notion of possessive individualism in the years leading up to Hobbes' and Locke's more influential formulations of the same. *The Spanish Gypsy*'s many allusions to *The Changeling* suggest that Sancho is himself Rowley's creation and by implication his property,[43] although any attention to particular persons and their interests here quickly gives way to the imminent arrival of 'our company' (3.1.71–7): the many still threaten to overwhelm the one.

In addition to the threat of theft, there is also an ensuing disagreement in the play as to whether contributions to a collaborative project are valuable for their usefulness or their returns, or whether they are to be regarded as gifts. When Roderigo is introduced to the company as a poet, for example, Precosia admits that she loves one that 'writes chastely', which is no less accurate of the rapist Roderigo than of Middleton (or for that matter Ford, Dekker or Rowley), and naively proceeds to solicit his services: if 'your pen' can 'sell me' anything of any use, she promises, he 'shall have bays and silver' (3.1.94–6). Roderigo rejects the exchange value placed upon his verses in such a transaction ('no selling'), assuring her instead that any contribution he might make will be 'free', but although this view is echoed by Sancho ('And me too') and embraced by her father, who values the poet's 'use' for their 'sports', it only has meaning within the proposed entertainment where it is possible (and indeed necessary) for authors to suspend their individual interests: 'one pleasure dulls' (3.1.97–100). Outside the play-within-the-play and beyond *The Spanish Gypsy* itself, credit and monetary gain were precisely the two things that professional writers like Ford, Dekker and Middleton (who lived by their pens) had most at stake and, in light of later attempts to discern the true authors of the play, the clown had reason to fear it would not be distributed equally.

Just as their first meeting with Roderigo provokes the clowns to recognize the likelihood of theft within the creative process, with both misappropriation and collaboration being understood as 'all the fashion', their second meeting prompts them to propose a solution in time for the-play-within-the-play. Nicol has suggested that Rowley did not perform in *The Spanish Gypsy*, and that allusions to his written work would have been a sad reminder of the absence of the actor, but if this was the case it is no less possible that Rowley's conspicuous absence on the stage would have reminded audiences of his role(s) as a writer.[44] There is an obvious contest between actors and authors in *The Spanish Gypsy*, whether it was instigated by Rowley or written by others with him in mind. Clowns were well known for their appeal to audiences and their ability to upstage the playwright by improvising dialogue, as Hamlet anticipated in his instructions to the players, and authors tended only to let actors take the credit when things went wrong.[45] When Soto fails to acknowledge Roderigo as the tenth and final member of the company he thus means to diminish the writer's role in comparison with his own. From Soto's perspective as a player, writers are seldom present on stage and so Roderigo counts only as the last digit in the number ten (zero): 'That's our poet; he stands for a cipher' (4.2.32–3), though from Fernando's perspective as the plotter (and Roderigo's father),

---

[42] Eden, *All Things in Common*, p. 162 *passim*.

[43] See Nicol, *Forms of Collaboration*, p. 125.

[44] Nicol, *Forms of Collaboration*, pp. 146–7.

[45] Robert Weimann, *Shakespeare and the Popular Tradition in the Theater: Studies in the Social Dimension of Dramatic Form and Function* (Baltimore, 1987), pp. 73–85 and pp. 208–52; Richard Helgerson, *Forms of Nationhood: The Elizabethan Writing of England* (Chicago, 1992), pp. 223–8. After Thomas Nashe had to answer for his involvement with the seditious *The Isle of Dogs*, a collaboration with Ben Jonson, he (somewhat disingenuously) noted 'I having begun but the induction and first act of it, the other foure acts without my consent, or the least guesse of my drift or scope, by the players were supplied.' *Nashes Lenten stuffe* (London, 1599), B1v.

Roderigo counts for more as he acts in a drama of his own making, in which case his presence as a zero increases the value of the whole performance, and a performance assumes the presence of a repertoire: 'Ciphers make numbers – What plays have you?' (4.2.34).

The opposition between performance and product here, as well as Sancho's earlier advocacy of practice ('invoke together') as the best means of safeguarding property ('my plot'), indicates a concern as much with the division of property as with the sharing of labour. Masten has remarked that 'there is no accounting of *intellectual property*' in the records of the period, like Henslowe's *Diary* which is concerned less with 'the precise attribution of intellectual property' than with 'the allocation of labour, and (co)laborers'.[46] But, as Tiffany Stern has recently documented, the many plot-scenarios listed in Henslowe's accounts were in fact treated like properties that could be bought and sold (or stolen) and were sometimes contracted out to dramatists who may have been at odds with, if not open rivals of the plot's originator.[47] In other words, Beaumont and Fletcher might have agreed upon 'our plot', as might have the majority of collaborating dramatists,[48] but some still insisted upon 'my plot'. Only in the case of *The Spanish Gypsy* it proves difficult if not impossible to privilege one role over another. However compelling his argument in favour of process might be, Sancho cannot remain on stage indefinitely – his last word in the play is notably 'leave' (5.3.110); and however 'neat and witty' his plan might be, Fernando has to rely more upon the players than he is willing to admit – he has only supplied 'some slight plot', nothing more than a 'subject' that the company has to 'extempore fashion out' (4.2.41–4). The least substantial contribution is Roderigo's as writer. Despite posing as the 'master poet' of Shakespearian stature,[49] he does not, in fact, produce anything – to 'save' him that 'labour', Roderigo's father supplies him with a paper containing his 'passage', 'drama', and 'scene' (4.2.45–7). In each case, as the clowns recognize, the collaborator is more likely to be credited with contributing than a contribution: for when he leaves the scene of

production, when he ceases to work, the credit goes to those who remain with(in) the work, or at the very least those who worked on it last.[50]

Distributing papers like Fernando's plot on stage, the author is also revealed to be as bound by place as the actor is by time, since he can only safeguard his property so long as he is present with it, although even then he can never be certain of others' intentions. In the spirit of collaboration, it is perfectly appropriate for the father to share this stage property with his son: if Roderigo were a member of a rival company, Fernando would have been careful to safeguard it from him. It is similarly reasonable to expect that co-workers will freely exchange the necessary materials. But there is no reason to assume that they are necessarily working towards the same end. Sancho was right to suspect Roderigo, as someone like Rowley would have been to suspect Middleton (*The Spanish Gypsy* is most often associated with Middleton in whose *Collected Works* it is, after all, included). In the context of this collaboration, Roderigo and his father are obviously working together on the same production, but they also have hidden motivations and different ideas about its purpose: Roderigo hopes it will improve his image, and Fernando knows it will expose him as a rapist. Their collaboration only has the appearance of being amicable, and each has arguably appropriated the other's work in much the same way that Sancho feared a co-author might.

It was not unknown for playwrights to acknowledge publicly that certain passages were not of their own devising, as when in 1604 Dekker, in a more charitable mood, credited Middleton with 'any glory to be won' from lines in *The Magnificent Entertainment* ('as his due' for having 'begotten'

---

46 Jeffrey Masten, 'Playwriting: Authorship and Collaboration', in *A New History of Early English Drama*, ed. John D. Cox and David Scott Kastan (New York, 1997), p. 367.

47 Tiffany Stern, *Documents of Performance in Early Modern England* (Cambridge, 2009), pp. 8–35.

48 Masten, *Textual Intercourse*, pp. 23–4.

49 Or, more precisely, Jonsonian. See Knapp, *Shakespeare Only*, p. 75.

50 See Marino, *Owning*, p. 30.

them), on the grounds that things done by people other than ourselves should never be credited to us: '*Quæ nos non fesimus ipsi, vix ea nostra voco.*'[51] But if the play within *The Spanish Gypsy* can be trusted to reflect the collaborative ethos, it seems also to have been fashionable, if not altogether inevitable, for credit to be misallocated among co-authors and for one author to be acknowledged for another's contributions, just as we see it is in attribution studies of the play nowadays, although like plagiarisms in the period these allegations had less to do with the alleged impropriety than the cultural status of the putative perpetrator.[52] When Dekker gave credit to Middleton he conceded the kind of authority that the clowns in *The Spanish Gypsy* anticipated would be abused by someone in Middleton's position, although twenty years earlier Middleton had found himself in a similar position when working with Shakespeare on *Timon of Athens.*

YOURS, MINE, AND OURS

If the play itself is any indication, Shakespeare and Middleton's sole collaboration in Shakespeare's lifetime was not a happy one: *Timon of Athens* is by most accounts uneven, corrupt and troubling beyond the tragic demise of its eponymous hero.[53] This may be because the text that survives is unfinished, the project was abandoned, and the play was never performed or printed in either of the authors' lifetimes, so its problems were never worked out by actors or editors. Or it may be because the play was meant to exhibit Timon's own tragic extremes. In either case, the play is subject to and takes as its subject the kinds of collaborative rivalry discussed above: first, it demonstrates that disagreements did exist between Shakespeare and his collaborators and that not everyone readily yielded to his preferences, whether for something as important as characterization or as inconsequential as spelling; and second, it dramatizes how creative differences arise when one contributor refuses to compromise his artistic vision because he believes himself to be the more generous partner and his collaborators the debtors who assist him. The play notably begins with a contest between artists. A merchant,

a mercer and three artists – a poet, a painter and a jeweller – walk onto the stage. The jeweller praises his art, the painter shows off his, the merchant seems enamoured of both and credit is presumably available for all (the mercer is silent); but none of them are in on the joke: the Poet created them all. The Poet is at this point the sole authority on stage; he alone sees past the commonplaces of exchanged pleasantries to the power of the 'Magic of bounty' (1.1.6), and he is prepared like Timon to let go of his property so as to gain control over others, property that might appear communal ('Our poesy') but nonetheless originates with him ('A thing slipped idly from me') (1.1.20–1). He has to explain what he means to those beneath him, even his fellow artists, but 'No levelled malice / Infects one comma in the course I hold' (1.1.47–8). His wit can be met only by the philosopher Apemantus. He is the big man in the gift economy of collaboration.[54]

Brian Vickers judges that the fault with *Timon of Athens* 'lay not with the co-authors, but with the "plot" from which they began',[55] but in a play so obviously concerned with gift giving, debts and the fault lines of friendship it is difficult to imagine that as Shakespeare thought about these things for his share in the work he was not also mindful of his working relationship with Middleton, a freelance writer sixteen years his junior whom Shakespeare, as a sharer in a professional playing company if not as the superior dramatist, had reason to think of as the lesser partner. (If scholars can discern unconscious habits of style that shape the form of each author's work and differentiate it from others',

---

[51] 'The Magnificent Entertainment', in *Thomas Middleton: The Collected Works*, ed. Gary Taylor *et al.* (Oxford, 2007), p. 264.

[52] Marilyn Randall, *Pragmatic Plagiarism: Authorship, Profit, and Power* (Toronto, 2001) and Laura J. Rosenthal, *Playwrights and Plagiarists in Early Modern England* (Ithaca, 1996).

[53] Wells, *Shakespeare*, p. 187.

[54] Perhaps not coincidently, his portrayal of Timon can be characterized as generous and Middleton's as prodigal. Peter Grav, *Shakespeare and the Economic Imperative: 'What's aught but as 'tis valued'* (New York, 2008), p. 137.

[55] Vickers, *Co-Author*, p. 480.

might we not also acknowledge unconscious attitudes towards others that inform the content of this same work, while still hopefully avoiding the *mise en abîme* of biographical readings?)[56] No one knows (or can know), of course, what Shakespeare was thinking when he wrote parts of *Timon of Athens*, but we do know with reasonable certainty what he wrote and can trust what the Poet says in the context of the play. For starters, the play resembles the Poet's description of the Painter's art: 'Artificial strife / Lives in these touches livelier than life' (1.1.37–8). Beginning with Charles Knight in the nineteenth century, scholars have noted a 'contrast of style' between scenes 1 and 2 that is especially indicative of another hand, but there has never been any doubt who wrote the dialogue between the Poet and Painter: 'It has all the equable graces of Shakspere's [sic] facility, with occasional examples of that condensation of poetical images which so distinguishes him from all other writers. For instance',[57]

> All those which were his fellows but of late,
> Some better than his value, on the moment
> Follow his strides, his lobbies fill with tendance,
> Rain sacrificial whisperings in his ear,
> Make sacred even his stirrup, and through him
> Drink the free air.   (1.1.79–84)

The easy movement from economic to ecological imagery here is identifiably Shakespearian, as is the Poet's subsequent foreshadowing of Timon's fate, which as Knight notes is consistent with 'the almost invariable system by which Shakespeare very early infuses into his audience a dim notion of the catastrophe, – most frequently indeed in the shape of some presentiment'.[58] Similar features of the text have enabled scholars since to validate these suspicions. However, the content of the Poet's speech from which these lines are taken is equally identifiable with Shakespeare.

In context, the Poet's speech on Fortune, though serving in many ways as 'the central fable of the play',[59] is not exclusively concerned with the affairs of Timon; it is partly an explanation of the Poet's own 'rough work' (1.1.43), which he compares for the Painter's benefit to the scene that is unfolding in front of them. Timon's situation is analogous to the Poet's creation, just as the poem metatheatrically represents the play itself. 'I have upon a high and pleasant hill / Feigned Fortune to be throned', the Poet explains (1.1.64–5). 'One do I personate of Lord Timon's frame, / Whom Fortune with her ivory hand wafts to her, / Whose present grace to present slaves and servants / Translates his rivals' (1.1.70–3). All of this can be understood as referring to the Poet, since this is at least partly how the Painter understands it: ''Tis conceived to scope' (1.1.73). Everything the Poet has just said 'would be well expressed / In our condition' (1.1.77–8). In other words, the Poet has commented upon his own bounty and present rival, provoking the Painter to assert that his art is every bit equal to the Poet's. Only now does the Poet, with the full force (and bounty) of Shakespeare's verse, demand to be heard correctly in the passage quoted above. Everyone who was previously equal, even those who deserve better, have to follow him, attend on him, flatter him, praise him, and by him achieve what they most desire.

When Knight singled out the passage above as a 'sufficiently striking' example of Shakespeare's voice, he would have done well to cite the line that precedes it: 'Nay, sir, but hear me on' (1.1.78).[60] If we can hear Shakespeare's voice here, it is because the Poet demands to be heard. Knight may have doubted that Apemantus in the first scene 'belongs

---

[56] Ton Hoenselaars similarly wonders what Shakespeare's response would have been to the apparent inferiority of his co-author's contribution in a play like *Titus Andronicus*. He proposes that one way for us to imagine an answer is to turn our attention to recent efforts to rewrite some of these same plays collaboratively today. 'Shakespeare: Colleagues, Collaborators, Co-authors', in *The Cambridge Companion to Shakespeare and Contemporary Dramatists*, ed. Ton Hoenselaars (Cambridge, 2012), pp. 112–14.

[57] Charles Knight, *Studies of Shakspere, Forming a Companion Volume to Every Edition of the Text* (London, 1849), p. 71.

[58] Knight, *Studies*, p. 71.

[59] Maurice Charney, Introduction, 'Timon of Athens', in *The Complete Signet Classic Shakespeare*, ed. Sylvan Barnet (New York, 1972), p. 1368.

[60] Knight, *Studies*, p. 71.

wholly to Shakespeare', but he was otherwise confident that the rest of scene 1 was written by Shakespeare – as he says of another example 'no one can doubt to whom these lines belong'.[61] The only person who could have been more certain to whom theses lines belong was Shakespeare. Most scholars agree that if *Timon of Athens* was co-authored, it was co-written concurrently, meaning that, unlike other examples of collaboration where dramatists revised the works of other dramatists or contributed scenes not knowing who else was involved, Shakespeare and his collaborator divided the play between themselves and worked on their respective parts at the same time. In this case, Shakespeare knew that another dramatist, almost certainly Middleton, would take over the next scene, and this knowledge is relevant to the Poet's speech on Fortune, if for no other reason than that as he foreshadowed the fate of Timon he had to be mindful of how this fate would later be depicted by his co-author. This speech should not be read biographically; there are no one-to-one correspondences between characters and their authors anywhere in the play. However, to the extent that he prepares audiences with a dim notion of the catastrophe to follow, there is a sense in which the Poet is himself aware that he too will be spurned by fortune as he describes his poem which is the play and profligates his talents. His dependants, who labour after him, await his fall, and in anticipation of the play's many irresolvable differences, have no intention of accompanying his declining foot (1.1.85–9). Other plausible explanations have been offered for why Shakespeare would begin this play with a contest between the arts.[62] I mean here only to suggest one effect that Shakespeare's choice to introduce the Poet as the superior artist has upon this collaborative play: it establishes Shakespeare's own bounty early on and distinguishes his contribution from those of a collaborator who in light of the play's lack of coherence proved as unwilling as he was to compromise on matters of form or content. The play does not wholly belong to Shakespeare, only parts of it do; the rest belong to Middleton, who was not Shakespeare's cipher but some one like him.

The only collaborative play involving Shakespeare that casts a particular co-author in a negative light is *Pericles*, wherein the chaste maid Marina, in a part penned by Shakespeare, converses with a bawdy house keeper that has many of the known defects of Wilkins's character. The first printed play text, as noted above, clearly identified Shakespeare as the author, but scholars have long noticed discrepancies of style in the play of the kind associated with collaboration and, as early as the nineteenth century, made a strong case for Wilkins's candidacy as co-author. There is a striking similarity in style between these first two acts and Wilkins's other known works, including the prose tale *The Painful Adventures of Pericles*, not to mention a striking dissimilarity between that style and Shakespeare's, though for anyone familiar with both writer's works the question remains why the celebrated author of *Hamlet* would willingly partner with the inferior author of *The Miseries of Enforced Marriage* (1607). For some, this is reasonable doubt enough to dismiss the claim for Wilkins's share in *Pericles*. As F. D. Hoeniger noted in 1963, while outlining the case for collaboration in his Arden edition of *Pericles*, 'Not a few scholars have rejected Wilkins primarily because the very idea that Shakespeare should have collaborated with such a minor dramatist near the end of this career was repugnant to them.'[63] In fact, this idea would prove so objectionable that, despite being originally inclined to accept the evidence,[64] Hoeniger himself later discredited entirely 'the notion that late in his career Shakespeare collaborated with such a hack writer as George Wilkins'.[65] For others, the idea that Shakespeare collaborated with

[61] Knight, *Studies*, p. 71.
[62] John Dixon Hunt, 'Shakespeare and the Paragone: A Reading of *Timon of Athens*', in *Images of Shakespeare: Proceedings of the Third Congress of the International Shakespeare Association, 1986*, ed. Werner Habicht, D. J. Palmer and Roger Pringle (Cranbury, 1988), pp. 47–63.
[63] F. D. Hoeniger, 'Introduction', *Pericles* (London, 2000), p. lix.
[64] Hoeniger, 'Introduction', p. lxii.
[65] F. D. Hoeniger, 'Gower and Shakespeare in *Pericles*', *Shakespeare Quarterly*, 33:4 (1982), 461–79, p. 462.

Wilkins is indefensible for reasons more distressing than the latter's inferior writing. Those who reject the co-authorship of *Pericles* are grateful for any opportunity to dismiss the 'preferred collaborator' and, as Doreen DelVecchio and Anthony Hammond observe in their Cambridge edition of the play, 'Happily, a good deal of light, much of it unflattering, has been shed on Wilkins.'[66] Court records show that Wilkins owned a tavern, which likely fronted a bawdy house; kept company with prostitutes; kicked a pregnant woman in the belly, stamped upon another; harboured or absconded with known criminals; abused constables; committed extreme outrages; and perpetrated several other felonies, including the theft of another's hat and cloak.[67] One can see why DelVecchio and Hammond entertain 'the *gravest* doubts that Wilkins had anything to do with *Pericles*' (emphasis added), but even they cannot deny that Wilkins was known to Shakespeare.[68]

Shakespeare crossed paths with Wilkins both within and without the theatre,[69] and so was presumably not unaware of his deficiencies both in writing and in character, but there is no reason to believe that by virtue of working with him Shakespeare necessarily tolerated such delinquencies. The belief that Wilkins does not deserve credit for any part of *Pericles* is not incompatible with evidence supporting his co-authorship. Instead, there is every indication in the bawdy house scenes that the likes of Wilkins, however necessary their roles might have been, were unwelcome partners and unsuitable proprietors, so long as they lacked the propriety of their superiors. In other words, Wilkins might have been uniquely qualified to craft such scenes, some of the 'lowest' in Shakespeare,[70] but only Shakespeare could have been responsible for the critical distance of Marina who, in the concluding scenes, begins to be identified as 'mine own' (21.201 and 22.70).[71] In scene 19, for instance, Marina notably refuses the sexual advances of her jailor, Bolt, because he is too 'bad' (his 'reputation' too foul) to be her companion and attempts to persuade him in a different direction (19.186, 189). She is simultaneously desperate and hopeful:

Do anything but this thou dost. Empty
Old receptacles or common sew'rs of filth,
Serve by indenture to the public hangman –
Any of these are yet better than this.
For what thou professest a baboon, could he speak,
Would own a name too dear. Here's gold for thee.
If that thy master would make gain by me,
Proclaim that I can sing, weave, sew, and dance,
With other virtues which I'll keep from boast,
And I will undertake all these to teach.
I doubt not but this populous city will
Yield many scholars.   (19.199–210)

Wilkins would have been a ready model for the likes of Bolt, and may have written parts of this scene,[72] but there is admittedly no proof that Shakespeare had his co-author in mind here. There is only a curious agreement, difficult to ignore in the unflattering light introduced above, between Marina's response to Bolt and the two main reasons for denying Wilkins co-authorship of *Pericles*. Like Bolt, Wilkins had to do something better with his life to gain the respect of others, despite his having perhaps limited options and, like Wilkins, Bolt lacks eloquence worthy of his proposed partner and so is barred ownership of a better name. The author of these lines may not have had Wilkins in mind, but certain readers and audiences are apt to, especially since Marina's counter offer further resembles the two most likely explanations for Shakespeare's decision to work with Wilkins. The offer

---

[66] 'Introduction', *Pericles*, ed. Doreen DelVecchio and Anthony Hammond (Cambridge, 2006), pp. 9–10.

[67] For the facts of Wilkins's life see Roger Prior's two articles 'The Life of George Wilkins', in *Shakespeare Survey 25* (Cambridge, 1972), pp. 137–52 and 'George Wilkins and the Young Heir', in *Shakespeare Survey 29* (Cambridge, 1976), pp. 33–9; as well as Mark Eccles, 'George Wilkins', *Notes and Queries*, 220 (1975), 250–2.

[68] DelVecchio and Hammond, 'Introduction', p. 9.

[69] Charles Nicholl, *The Lodger Shakespeare: His Life on Silver Street* (New York, 2007), pp. 197–248; Katherine Duncan-Jones, *Ungentle Shakespeare: Scenes from His Life* (London, 2001), pp. 205–13.

[70] Eric Partridge, *Shakespeare's Bawdy* (London, 1968), p. 58; Nicholl, *The Lodger*, p. 210.

[71] Knapp, *Shakespeare Only*, p. 138.

[72] MacDonald P. Jackson, *Defining Shakespeare: Pericles as Test Case* (Oxford, 2003), pp. 211–13.

of money suggests a purely financial arrangement, with both parties standing to gain (though perhaps not equally); and the offer of apprenticeship suggests a willingness to train others in the paths they should go. Even Katherine Duncan Jones, who goes so far as to imagine Shakespeare and Wilkins dining frequently together, questions what the latter 'had to offer' and assumes that they 'worked in collusion and friendly competition'.[73] In short, anyone who shares the prejudices of this passage, whether attributable to Shakespeare or not, is predisposed to judge Wilkins unworthy of proprietary authorship, and prepared instead to promote the more legitimate claims of his co-author.[74] Because of his moral and literary improprieties, Wilkins stands only as a cipher, the zero that adds greater value to the one.

The assertion that *Pericles* supports a negative view of someone like Wilkins in a part penned by Shakespeare is different from a biographical reading that assumes that Shakespeare wrote only about his own thoughts, feelings and first-hand experiences; such readings are founded on the Romantic myth of the solitary author and enable all kinds of fanciful theories of Shakespearian authorship (Bacon, Marlowe, Oxford *et al.*) that are at odds with the history of collaboration in his lifetime. Scholars should be sceptical like Masten of any attempt to 'secure an allegorical reading in which playwrights contend for the ownership/husbanding of the play'.[75] *Pericles* is not an allegory. For, as Masten remarks of *The Two Noble Kinsmen*, the last of Shakespeare's collaborative plays, there are no 'easy one-to-one' correspondences: 'Collaboration as practice (Shakespeare and Fletcher writing the *Two Noble Kinsmen*) does not necessarily result in collaboration as theme.'[76] There are, however, certain inevitable analogies, such as that between Wilkins and Bolt in *Pericles* or that between the eponymous characters and their co-creators in *The Two Noble Kinsmen*. In the same way then that it was 'viable' to interpret the latter as being about Shakespeare and Fletcher after an imprint of 1634 identified these two 'memorable Worthies' as co-authors, even if as Masten cautions it is not advisable,[77] it is possible to interpret the former as being about Wilkins in light of

the mounting evidence of his involvement and the known facts of his life. Correlation may not equal causation – the fact that Wilkins was a scoundrel did not necessarily incite Shakespeare to cast him as such – but there is nevertheless a correlation. Less certain is whether such correlations were apparent to early audiences and readers, not to mention the writers themselves. As Masten stresses repeatedly in his reading of *The Two Noble Kinsmen*, Palamon and Arcite are so similar that even characters within the play cannot tell them apart.

What I hope to have substantiated, with analogies from the visual arts, is that writers at the turn of the seventeenth century could and sometimes did observe proprietary authorship in the context of collaborative working arrangements. What we learn from Shakespeare and John Fletcher in *The Two Noble Kinsmen*, however, is that nobody wins when a collaborative plays stages itself as a contest between authors.[78] In this play, we return to the world of *A Midsummer Night's Dream*, governed by Theseus and Hippolyta, though one less disposed to share credit among play fellows. The fact that the two titular cousins, Palamon and Arcite, are alike in almost every manner does not predispose them to share. Instead, it provokes a crisis of sameness whereby each must distinguish himself. As Palamon remarks, there is no need 'to be fond upon /Another's way of speech, when by mine own / I may be reasonably conceived' (1.2.46–8). These lines, typically assigned to Shakespeare, are particularly relevant to Fletcher, whose distinctive style was, in the words of William Cartwright, 'So his owne/ That 'twas his marke, and he was by it knowne'.[79] Each cousin strives to make just such a mark, and although others in the play at times fail to observe it they are nevertheless driven by a belief in

---

[73] Duncan Jones, *Ungentle Shakespeare*, p. 208.

[74] Knapp, *Shakespeare Only*, pp. 133–8.

[75] Masten, *Textual Intercourse*, p. 58.

[76] Masten, *Textual Intercourse*, p. 58.

[77] Masten, *Textual Intercourse*, p. 58.

[78] Masten, *Textual Intercourse*, p. 55; Knapp, *Shakespeare Only*, pp. 143–6.

[79] 'Another', in *Comedies and Tragedies Written by Francis Beavmont and Iohn Fletcher Gentlemen* (London, 1647), d2r.

'the difference of men' (2.1.55), in the same way that scholars are motivated to identify who wrote what in a collaboration so effective that it is difficult, if not impossible, to tell. The problem with this play's co-authors is that, while 'They cannot both enjoy' the favour of audience and readers, 'They are both too excellent' to choose between (3.6.274, 285), and even if one of these 'Two emulous Philomels' were to disappear no one would think it winning (5.5.124).

There is no question that writing was fundamentally collaborative in Shakespeare's lifetime, as in a broader sense it still is today, but there is also no question that some authors strove to rise above mutual identification while at the same time recognizing its inevitability, through allegations of plagiarism. These tensions were not unique to drama. Visual artists at the time were also beginning to reject the similarities that arose from conventional modes of imitation, which they felt suppressed innovation in favour of tradition, and were favouring instead the differences that emerged from individual contributions. In Italy in the mid-1620s, for instance, the celebrated Roman painter, Giovanni Lanfranco, attempted to discredit his chief rival, Domenichino, by accusing him of plagiarizing his *Last Communion of Saint Jerome* (1614) from a little-known painting by their teacher Agostino Carracci from the 1590s. Domenichino, however, was simply following the example of his master. As one of three collaborating painters in the Carracci family, Agostino had carried out simultaneous commissions with his brother Annibale and their cousin Ludovico in the spirit of friendly rivalry.[80] Yet, while the Carracci brothers of Bologna were like Shakespeare and Fletcher celebrated for the harmony of their artistry, which reflected the consanguinity of kinship, their seventeenth-century biographer, Giovanni Pietro Bellori, felt that one still deserved more credit than the others:

for their style and their studies were so compatible that, there being no variance, each of them presented the very same image and the same traits of talent. Beyond this, it is believed that Annibale's character contributed more than a little, for he was without envy and without ambition, practicing with the other two in one and the same school, the school being the master. This one merit is to be credited to him alone, that he was the originator and the example to his brothers.[81]

Surely, Shakespeare's ability to surpass his peers and serve his own interests was no less compatible with his immersion in the workaday world and his commitment to the give and take of collaborative artistry.

---

[80] Elizabeth Cropper, *The Domenichino Affair: Novelty, Imitation, and Theft in Seventeenth-Century Rome* (New Haven, 2005), p. 56.

[81] Giovanni Pietro Bellori, *The Lives of the Modern Painters, Sculptors, and Architects*, trans. Alice Sedgwick Wohl, ed. Hellmut Wohl (Cambridge, 2005), p. 75.

TOPICAL SHAKESPEARE

BARRY LANGSTON

The First Part of Henry VI, as a title, is a lightly modernized version of 'The first Part of Henry the Sixt' in the 1623 First Folio. There is no warrant for the variations preferred by modern editors, though Philip Henslowe's short title 'harey the vj' is useful if a distinction is being made between the play as eventually published in 1623 and what was performed at the Rose in 1592–3. *The First Part of Henry VI* is now widely regarded as a collaborative effort, and the view that the three *Henry VI* plays were not conceived in historical-chronological order is also back in favour. While these developments might be seen as another swing of the pendulum, it must be said that the latest wave of disintegrators are undogmatic; little divides them from Michael Hattaway, who has defended solo-authorship and composition as a unified trilogy.[1] Michael Taylor, who effectively has a foot in both camps, argues that the so-called *First Part of Henry VI*, with its focus on the French Wars, was probably a collaborative 'prequel' to a successful two-parter about the Wars of Roses which was solo-authored. Why should Shakespeare, after demonstrating his ability to go it alone, have taken a retrograde step of this kind? Given our lack of hard evidence, in Taylor's view, 'it would not be hard to imagine a harassed author calling on friends and colleagues to help him construct an unexpectedly commissioned piece in a hurry'.[2] What follows is an attempt to place this hypothetical collaboration in a historical context and tease out implications for our understanding of the play and the early career of the man from Stratford who received a first favourable notice after 'harey the vj' was performed at Henslowe's Rose in the spring and early summer of 1592. Thomas Nashe, the collaborator who is identified with the greatest confidence, evoked audience reactions in *Pierce Penniless*, published later in the same year during a general 'restraint' of playing on account of the plague:

How would it have joyed brave Talbot (the terror of the French) to think that after he had lain two hundred years in his tomb, he should triumph again on the stage, and have his bones new embalmed with the tears of ten thousand spectators at least (at several times) who in the tragedian that represents his person, imagine they behold him fresh bleeding.

In an allusive fashion, he was probably conveying more information than is immediately apparent to readers who were not present at these performances. Also, though he was presumably puffing his own work, the more established writer with a university education seems to have had no regrets about working with the tyro Shakespeare. There is food for thought in both of these points.

* * *

The Rose on Bankside was closed for refurbishment during the winter of 1591–2. The capacity of the galleries from which the impresario Henslowe got most of his declared income was increased, and other improvements included a ceiling for 'my

---

[1] Michael Hattaway, ed., *The First Part of King Henry VI* (Cambridge, 1990), pp. 34–43.
[2] Michael Taylor, ed., *Henry VI, Part One* (Oxford, 2003), pp. 10–14.

lords Rome'.[3] Whether this is understood as 'my lord's room' or 'my lords' room', it sounds less impersonal than the lords' room, or rooms, whose location is an old bone of contention among theatre historians. When the playhouse reopened on 19 February 1592, the resident company was 'my Lord Strange's Men'. While it is often assumed that grandees who lent their name to troupes of players were not concerned with what they did, Ferdinando Lord Strange is a recognized exception to the supposed rule. Thomas Kyd claimed that he first met Marlowe because they both served 'my Lord although his Lordship never knew his service but in writing for his players'. Ferdinando is generally believed to have been the lord in question and, partly for that reason, is regarded as a proactive patron.[4] As the Rose's new galleries were rarely full if Henslowe's recorded receipts are anything to go by, Ferdinando – soon to become fifth Earl of Derby – may have promised to make up the shortfall. At all events, he was a big spender who died head over heels in debt in 1594.[5] As Sir Edmund Chambers observed in a different but related context, an Elizabethan patron 'was expected to put his hand in his pocket'.[6] Strikingly, nothing special seems to have been arranged for the reopening, which was also the company's debut at the Rose. For two whole weeks, they marked time with pieces like *The Jew of Malta* and *Friar Bacon and Friar Bungay*. The gala occasion – if there was one – took place on 3 March, when Henslowe's share of the take was £3 16s 8d, the best of the entire season. In his 'diary', or account book, the play performed was marked as 'ne'. By general if not universal assent this meant 'new' in the case of 'harey the vj'.[7] A compelling reason for the players marking time would have been if the offering which drew the crowds was not ready for performance until 3 March. Also, if it was specially commissioned, it was probably by Ferdinando with at least the intention of being present at the première. Though his actual presence cannot be proved, it is a reasonable inference if he was not demonstrably elsewhere. Since his father, Henry fourth Earl of Derby, was in Lancashire, the chances are that Ferdinando was in the metropolis running up more debts.[8] On this

analysis, unusual pressure on a writer has still to be explained. If a proactive and generous patron could wait for two weeks, why not longer?

The answer may well be that 'harey the vj' was an especially topical play with a specific thrust. Though there is often reluctance to accept that Shakespearian material was topical, *The First Part of Henry VI* is a partial exception to another rule. The point hardly needs to be laboured that audiences would have linked the fifteenth-century French enemy with a newer Spanish foe and, with varying degrees of enthusiasm, editors have accepted that the play's protagonist (insofar as it has one) was probably intended to suggest a living individual. According to John Dover Wilson, the play 'was connected with the fortunes of an expeditionary force dispatched from these shores under the leadership of the brilliant and popular Earl of Essex'. Essex's mission in 1591 was to aid Henry IV in his struggle against Catholic League forces who had thrown in their lot with the Spanish. In his view, brave Talbot, who died fighting against the odds rather than abandon a siege, stood for Essex, who had made valiant efforts to take Rouen.[9] While it is conceivable that the battle-scarred veteran who fell in the last battle of the Hundred Years War represented Elizabeth I's unscathed young favourite, this

---

[3] R. A. Foakes, ed., *Henslowe's Diary* (Cambridge, 2002), p. 13.

[4] Park Honan, *Christopher Marlowe: Poet & Spy* (Oxford, 2005), pp. 247–8. See also Peter Thomson, *Shakespeare's Professional Career* (Cambridge, 1992), pp. 33–4.

[5] Andrew Gurr, *The Shakespearean Stage* (Cambridge, 1992), p. 127. On the scale of Ferdinando's debts, see Barry Coward, *The Stanleys: Lords Stanley and Earls of Derby* (Manchester, 1983), p. 37.

[6] E. K. Chambers, *William Shakespeare: A Study of Facts and Problems*, 2 vols. (Oxford, 1930), vol. 1, p. 62.

[7] Foakes, *Henslowe's Diary*, p. xxxiv. See also Jonathan Bate, ed., *Titus Andronicus* (London, 1995), p. 70.

[8] On the problem of establishing where Ferdinando Strange was in 1591–2, see Charles Nicholl, *A Cup of News* (London, 1984), p. 90. For his father's whereabouts, see G. R. Batho, ed., *A Calendar of Shrewsbury and Talbot Papers in the Lambeth Palace Library and the College of Arms*, 2 vols. (London, 1971), vol. 1, pp. 205–6.

[9] John Dover Wilson, ed., *The First Part of King Henry VI* (Cambridge, 1952), pp. xv–xxi.

is effectively ruled out if Talbot had a more appropriate counterpart in the person of Essex's middle-aged rival, Sir John Norreys, known as 'Black John' (or 'Black Jack') for reasons to be discussed later. This seasoned campaigner, who had served in Ireland and the Netherlands, was sent to Brittany with an English force in April 1591 and had some success before Essex's arrival in Normandy led to the diversion of men and resources. Despite being given permission after Christmas to return to England, Norreys delayed during January and most of the following month. Though he eventually set out for Caen on 18 February, he probably did not reach London until 3 March.[10] His arrival on the same day as the première of 'harey the vj' would have made the new play an opening shot in a war of words against Essex. His presence at the Rose, presumably in 'my lordes Rome', would have emphasized the point for anyone who was exceptionally slow on the uptake. Plausibly, the way Nashe imagined Talbot's posthumous joy reflected actual pleasure exhibited by Norreys at the Rose. More certainly, the veteran commander established his headquarters across the river at Puddle Wharf and lobbied for fresh men and supplies with apparent success while Essex's demands fell upon increasingly deaf ears.[11]

Norreys, as a Calvinist fire-eater, might seem an unlikely associate for a big-spending patron whose background and sympathies were Catholic. The career of the young Earl of Southampton should remind us that hostility to Spanish imperialism and more outright Catholicism were not incompatible. Also, when war and peace were linked with the vexed issue of the succession, almost any unholy alliance was possible. Ferdinando Strange, by virtue of his descent from Henry VII, had a remote claim as Elizabeth's successor.[12] This might have entitled him to some input if informal decisions had to be made about who should succeed a childless Virgin Queen who refused to nominate a successor. If he saw himself as a viable claimant, however, he would have been badly mistaken and, though this is possible, it can probably be ruled out. Given his outlook and connections, he should have favoured the cause of James VI of Scotland's English-born

cousin, Lady Arbella Stuart, who was the preference of moderate Catholics and Catholic sympathizers. His own claims would have needed to be played down because they enabled those opposed to Arbella to encourage the suspicion that he was a traitor, secretly plotting to depose Elizabeth. The situation was made worse by the black sheep of his family, Sir William Stanley, who had defected to the Spanish in 1586, after his regiment in the Netherlands was treated badly. In 1591, it was even feared that Stanley was planning to kidnap Arbella on behalf of Spain.[13] Whether the rumours were true or false, or (more likely) somewhere in between, there was a good deal to be said for high-profile association with a Protestant paladin whose patriotic credentials were impeccable.

While Ferdinando's whereabouts in March 1592 are undocumented, we are a little better informed in the case of his friend Gilbert Talbot, seventh Earl of Shrewsbury, senior living descendant of the fifteenth-century hero. In 1591–2, following the death of his father, George, he was based in London, defending his interests against unscrupulous parties who included the sixth Earl's last mistress, Eleanor Breton. A further complication was that Shrewsbury House in Chelsea was occupied by the formidable Bess of Hardwick, Dowager Countess of Shrewsbury, who was Gilbert's mother-in-law as well as his stepmother. Though he had several options, he decided to accept the hospitality of another predatory, upwardly-mobile old woman, Lady Gresham, widow of the founder of the Royal Exchange, who lived in Bishopsgate, not far from where Shakespeare had lodgings for a time.[14] Without being a practising Catholic, Gilbert was a well-known sympathizer and his support for Arbella as Elizabeth's eventual successor was no secret. In the tussle with Bess of Hardwick

---

[10] John S. Nolan, *Sir John Norreys and the Elizabethan Military World* (Exeter, 1997), pp. 190–1.

[11] For a letter written by Norreys from Puddle Wharf in March 1592, see Rev. Joseph Stevenson, ed., *Correspondence of Sir Henry Unton* (London, 1847), p. 365.

[12] Charles Nicholl, *The Reckoning* (London, 2002), pp. 271–7.

[13] P. M. Handover, *Arbella Stuart* (London, 1957), pp. 91–5.

[14] Batho, *Shrewsbury and Talbot Papers*, vol. II, p. 167.

over who should be queen-maker, his wife Mary, whose loyalties might have been divided, took his side. In 1595, he would be warned off because his support for Arbella had become too obvious.[15]

In the present context, the most important fact revealed by a cache of Talbot papers at the College of Arms is that Gilbert Shrewsbury took a close interest in Norreys's Brittany campaign.[16] Norreys landed at St Malo on 5 May 1591 and joined forces with the Prince de Dombes. Guingcamp then surrendered after a short siege which ended on 24 May. Four days later, Gilbert's servant, Edmund Slater, who either accompanied the expedition or followed at an early opportunity, sent what was probably the first of a series of confidential reports from the front. Its importance is indicated by the fact that the bearer was Gilbert's chief of intelligence, Alexander Ratcliffe.[17] Though their employer did not become a Privy Councillor for almost a decade, it was useful for an aspirant to have his network of paid informants. My guess is that keen interest in Norreys was driven by concerns about the ongoing antics of the renegade, Sir William Stanley. On a visit to Spain, Stanley had urged the seizure of Alderney in the Channel Islands as a way of threatening Henry IV's flank. Philip II, as ever, was in two minds and Norreys's arrival in Brittany anyhow put paid to the scheme. Later, when Norreys returned to London, Stanley anticipated that his lobbying would be successful and proposed the invasion of England as a counter-measure.[18] Gilbert's public career might have taken off if his agents had struck gold. Emrys Jones shrewdly observed that 'the actors playing 1 Henry VI were inescapably paying a compliment to Talbot's Elizabethan successors'.[19] Though matters may be more complex than Jones realized, the point should remain valid when Talbot is seen as a Norreys rather than an Essex surrogate.

* * *

Recent editors who regard *The First Part of Henry VI* as a 'prequel' have taken it for granted that the play as published was what was originally performed. Older editors and commentators who favoured composition in historical-chronological

order suspected that this was not the case. On their view, 'harey the vj' at the Rose probably ended with York's 'solemn peace' with the Dauphin, not preliminaries to the young King's French marriage. One of the oddities of the play as it stands is the way Talbot is forgotten after an English herald, Sir William Lucy, has recovered the body from a stricken field. The most appropriate ending, when York has had the final word, would be the hero's funeral at Bordeaux, where he has supposedly fallen, though his actual death in 1453 took place at Castillon, some thirty miles away. *The First Part of Henry VI* begins with the funeral of Henry V. Shakespeare's version of the French wars that followed involves three sieges – invented or semi-invented – in which Talbot plays a leading role. When Orleans is retaken, the old Earl of Salisbury is buried in the cathedral, with Talbot taking charge of the funeral arrangements. When Regent Bedford expires during an apocryphal siege of Rouen, he is again responsible for the obsequies. Poetic justice, as well as symmetry, requires his own burial at Bordeaux, and the fact that this is completely unhistorical seems neither here nor there when so many other liberties have been taken with the chronicle accounts.

Evidence that a moving tableau of Talbot's funeral was the original ending of the play has been staring us in the face without being recognized for what it is. It is striking that the belief that there was a Talbot tomb in France only manifested itself after performances of 'harey the vj' at the Rose. In 1596, an English inscription which was supposedly 'ingrauen' on a tomb at Castillon appeared in the dedication to Gilbert Shrewsbury of *An Armor of Proofe*, a religiose poem by Roger Cotton. As a

15 Handover, *The Second Cecil* (London, 1959), p. 122.
16 Batho, *Shrewsbury and Talbot Papers*, vol. I, p. 205–6; vol. II, pp. 167, 170; E. G. W. Bill, ed., *A Calendar of Shrewsbury Papers in the Lambeth Palace Library* (Derby, 1966), pp. 105, 122.
17 Batho, *Shrewsbury and Talbot Papers*, vol. II, p. 166.
18 On Stanley, see Rory Rapple's article in the *ODNB*.
19 Emrys Jones, *The Origins of Shakespeare* (Oxford, 1977), p. 120.

native of Whitchurch in Shropshire, where Talbot's remains are actually interred, Cotton presumably knew the tomb which can still be seen and concluded that it was just a memorial.[20] A second version appeared in Richard Crompton's *Mansion of Magnanimitie* in 1599. Though Crompton was vague about the location, Bordeaux was probably implied. Unimpressed, the antiquary William Camden in 1605 observed that he had been unable to discover any Talbot funerary inscription.[21] By 1607, however, when an expanded edition of his *Britannia* was published, he had evidently made further inquiries and included a 'short' Latin inscription found at Whitchurch – on a brass plate subsequently lost – which seems to have been more authentic, even if Camden was not entirely accurate when it came to some of the details.[22] Unwilling to take tactful hints that Cotton and Crompton had been sold a pup, Camden's rival, Ralph Brooke, reproduced the English inscription in his *Catalogue and Succession of Kings, Princes, Dukes, Marquisses, Earles and Viscounts of the Realme of England since the Norman Conquest to the present yeare 1619*, adding that Talbot 'was buried in a Toombe at Roane'.[23] This was too much for Camden's follower, Augustine Vincent, who brought out *A Discoverie of Errours in the first edition of the Catalogue of Nobility published by Ralfe Brooke, Yorke Herald*, a comprehensive attack in which the entire work was reproduced verbatim and systematically taken apart. Regarding the supposed epitaph and tomb, he crushingly concluded that Talbot was unlikely to have been buried at Rouen three or four years after the city was surrendered to the French. The Latin inscription provided by 'Learned *Camden* (the Sunne-shine of whose iudicious knowledge hath enlightened these our latter days)' followed as Vincent's *coup de grace*.[24] The modern view is that Talbot was buried in France and repatriated later. There was no hint of this possibility when the rival heralds locked horns.[25]

For most practical purposes, the inscription dismissed by Vincent consisted of the titles and honours awarded to Talbot by Sir William Lucy in *The First Part of Henry VI* when he goes in search of the fallen hero's body:

> But where's the great Alcides of the field,
> Valiant Lord Talbot, Earl of Shrewsbury,
> Created for his rare success in arms
> Great Earl of Wexford, Waterford, and Valence,
> Lord Talbot of Goodrich and Urchinfield,
> Lord Strange of Blackmere, Lord Verdon of Alton,
> Lord Cromwell of Wingfield, Lord Furnivall of Sheffield,
> The thrice victorious Lord of Falconbridge,
> Knight of the noble order of Saint George,
> Worthy Saint Michael and the Golden Fleece,
> Great *Maréchal* to Henry the Sixth,
> Of all his wars within the realm of France? (4.7.60–71)

Previously in the play, even after Talbot is created Earl of Shrewsbury, titles, old and new, are ignored. In death, however, he has literally acquired more than his share. Strictly speaking, Talbot was merely lord of the honour of Wexford or Washford in Ireland, though he was called Earl of Shrewsbury and 'Weysford' in 1446 when he received letters patent creating him Earl of Waterford. The title Earl of Valence is adrift, though it may have been suggested by *Baron* Valence, listed as one of Gilbert's titles when he served as ambassador to France in 1596.

---

20 A visitor to Whitchurch in the reign of Charles II concluded that the 'tomb' was merely a 'Cenotaph or Honorary Monument'; see J. G. Nichols, ed., Thomas Dingley, *History from Marble*, 2 vols. (London, 1868), vol. II, pp. clxxvi–clxxviii.

21 William Camden, *Remaines of a Greater Worke* (London, 1605), p. 47.

22 Camden, *Britannia* (London, 1607), p. 453. Despite the impression given in this work, the lettering of the inscription was Gothic, not Roman, and, according to Dingley's account, the brass plate, now lost, had not been part of the 'tomb' as such.

23 Ralph Brooke, *A Catalogue and Succession* (London, 1619), p. 196.

24 Augustine Vincent, *A Discoverie of Errours* (London, 1622), p. 465.

25 A brief statement that Talbot's body was moved can be found in Joseph Edmondson, *Baronagium Genealogicum*, 6 vols. (London, 1764–84), vol. II, p. 83. Without references, the basic idea was fleshed out in Joseph Hunter, *Hallamshire* (London, 1819), p. 46. Historians are still evasive when it comes to identifying primary sources; for an example, see A. J. Pollard, *John Talbot and the War in France* (London, 1982), pp. 138–9.

Lord Talbot was certainly one of his ancestor's titles and, incidentally, the one by which Gilbert himself was known during his father's lifetime. Since John Talbot was brought up at Goodrich in Herefordshire, Lord Talbot of Goodrich is not wildly wrong; Archenfield was nearby. Lord Strange of Blackmere is uncontentious though it should not be confused with Ferdinando's title. During his father's lifetime, he was Lord Strange of Knockin, coincidentally also in Shropshire. Lord Verdun, without addition, was another authentic Talbot title. Lord Furnivall of Sheffield is uncontentious too, even if Furnivall (or Talbot) of Hallamshire might be preferred.[26] Lord Cromwell of Wingfield, however, is immediately ruled out. Though Wingfield in Derbyshire was acquired by John third Earl of Shrewsbury, properties did not come with a title and Ralph Lord Cromwell was still living at the time of Talbot's death. 'The thrice victorious Lord of Falconbridge' is another recognized anomaly. The real Lord Falconbridge – Falconberg in modern accounts – was one of Talbot's comrades in arms. More difficulties arise with non-hereditary honours. Talbot could not have belonged to the Order of St Michael, which was founded by Louis IX sixteen years after his death.[27] As a matter of fact, he was not a member of the Netherlandish Order of the Golden Fleece: he merely became a Knight of the Garter in 1424. Celebration of the Most Noble Order elsewhere in *The First Part of Henry VI* probably reflected the fact that Gilbert Shrewsbury and 'Black John' Norreys would both be nominated in 1592, though the latter was not elected, then or on a number of subsequent occasions.[28] Finally, there was no one who could properly have been called 'Great *Maréchal* to Henry the Sixth, / Of all his wars within the realm of France.' Historically, Marshal of France was a subordinate position which Talbot had held for a time under Richard Duke of York as Regent. Presumably, the real point was that Elizabeth I needed a veteran who had served in France and the Netherlands, to coordinate her war efforts.

Though we have repeatedly been told that a genuine inscription, somewhere in France, was the basis of Sir William Lucy's speech, this is effectively ruled out by errors which could not have

been made in the mid-fifteenth century. The most logical conclusion seems to be that a feature of the play as performed at the Rose was the source of the inscription. A Talbot 'funeral' would have sent a powerful message at a time when England's survival depended on the outcome of campaigns in France and so was likely to move audiences to tears, as described in *Pierce Penniless*.[29] In such a spectacle, an inscription on a board or tablet, like the one marking Sir Philip Sidney's grave in St Paul's, would probably have been one of the props.[30] Collections of epitaphs were popular reading in Shakespeare's day and, if a 'bad' one was copied by spectators after the show, it might well have taken more than Camden's or Vincent's expertise to get it out of the system.[31] It would also have been easy to assume that Talbot had been buried in France.

* * *

There is no hard evidence that 'harey the vj' was performed again, in any shape or form, after its final outing at the Rose on 31 January 1593.[32] If it was subsequently recast as the first part of a trilogy,

---

[26] Geoffrey H. White, ed., *The Complete Peerage by G. E. C.*, 13 vols. (London, 1949), vol. XI, pp. 698–701. Gilbert Shrewsbury's titles as ambassador to France in 1596 appear in William Dugdale, *The Baronage of England*, 2 vols. (London, 1675), vol. I, pp. 34–5.

[27] Vincent, *Discoverie of Errours*, p. 464.

[28] Garter elements are noted in Giorgio Melchiori, *Shakespeare's Garter Plays: 'Edward III' to 'The Merry Wives of Windsor'* (Newark, DE, 1994), pp. 96–9. Thanks to Miss Eleanor Cracknell for providing information from the Garter archive.

[29] The sort of emotionalism evoked by Nashe was shown on 21 June 1596 when Sir John Wingfield was buried in the cathedral at Cadiz, before the English torched the city and sailed away: see R. C. Bald, *John Donne: A Life* (Oxford, 1986), p. 84.

[30] Sidney's 1587 funeral was a likely inspiration for Henry V's in *The First Part of Henry VI*; see Ian Wilson, *Shakespeare: The Evidence* (London, 1993), pp. 97–8.

[31] On manuscript collections of epitaphs, see William Camden, *Remains*, ed. R. D. Dunn (London, 1984), p. 474.

[32] The only known performance of a version of *The First Part of Henry VI* until the nineteenth century took place at Covent Garden in March 1738; see Hattaway, *First Part of King Henry VI*, p. 43. The 1739 War of Jenkins' Ear between England and Spain followed.

it is possible that the published version was meant for the study rather than the stage, an example of Shakespeare as 'literary dramatist' in Lukas Erne's provocative phrase.[33] Since instant acclaim seems to have depended on its being more than usually topical, an inevitable price would have been paid when Norreys's moment had passed. Though he returned to Brittany towards the end of 1592, he was already yesterday's man before his final recall in 1594.[34] It does not follow, however, that the play which became *The First Part of Henry VI* was simply forgotten, since a popular pamphlet should have served as a reminder of it. After the play's initial success, while the playhouses stayed shut on account of the plague during the second half of 1592, Shakespeare was notoriously attacked as 'an upstart Crow' in *Greene's Groatsworth of Wit*. By 1623, this ephemeral work, which has little or no intrinsic merit from the point of view of modern readers, had been re-issued three times, and there were at least two more reprints before the coming of civil war in 1642 finally helped to kill off interest.[35] Soon after first publication, Henry Chettle denied that he was the real author, throwing in an apology of sorts to an offended party usually thought to have been Shakespeare himself. Nashe also denied being Greene's ghost in the preface to a new edition of *Pierce Penniless*. As Nashe was one of a trio who received barbed admonitions from the dying Robert Greene, the fact that he was still suspected of being the real author of the pamphlet is disturbing for the literally minded and, if it was at least conceivable that he had admonished himself, it also becomes possible that Greene's ghost and the 'upstart Crow' were one and the same. The attack, as Ronald Knowles has observed, probably served as an advertisement for a brilliant tyro whose natural superiority by implication was admitted.[36]

The verbal assault occurred in what was ostensibly a letter from Greene to three established playwrights whom he once knew. Though they were not named, the terms in which they were addressed suggest they were Marlowe, Nashe and George Peele; the first got a particularly rough ride. When Greene, or pseudo-Greene, turned on Shakespeare,

it sounds as if it was the players who were to blame for the threat posed to a dying man's old friends:

> trust them not; for there is an upstart Crow, beautified with our feathers, that with his *Tiger's heart wrapped in a Player's hide*, supposes he is as well able to bombast out a blank verse as the best of you: and being an absolute *Johannes fac totum* [Jack of all trades], is in his own conceit the only Shake-scene in a country.

The usual reading is that Shakespeare the player turned to writing plays which fellow performers and audiences preferred to offerings by the 'university wits'. An alternative which deserves consideration is that an ambitious newcomer struck a deal with the players enabling him to promote his wares as a performer in signature cameo roles. Though the 'upstart Crow' must have been a player as well as a poet, it is impossible to say for certain that performing came first.[37] On the contrary, the pamphlet itself arguably provides support for the priority of writing. It begins with the story of Roberto, who is later said to stand for Greene. Down on his luck, he is approached by an expensively dressed player who admits that he was just a 'country Author' before making his fortune by treading the boards. Peter Ackroyd wonders whether this might not have been another reference to Shakespeare.[38]

As a literary allusion 'upstart Crow' implies theft of some kind.[39] In a medieval Latin fable by Odo of

[33] Lukas Erne, *Shakespeare as Literary Dramatist* (Cambridge, 2003), pp. 1–25 and *passim*.

[34] For a short account of Norreys's decline, see Sidney Lee's article in the *DNB*, where his name is given as Norris – a possible spelling, but not the one he preferred.

[35] D. Allen Carroll, ed., *Greene's Groatsworth of wit, bought with a Million of Repentance* (New York, 1994), pp. 33–5.

[36] Ronald Knowles, ed., *King Henry VI Part 2* (London, 1999), pp. 109–10.

[37] Stanley Wells, *Shakespeare: A Dramatic Life* (London, 1994), p. 26. See also Thomson, *Shakespeare's Professional Career*, pp. 17–18.

[38] Peter Ackroyd, *Shakespeare: The Biography* (London, 2005), pp. 176–8.

[39] Dover Wilson, 'Malone and the Upstart Crow', in *Shakespeare Survey 4* (Cambridge, 1951), pp. 56–68.

Cheriton (one of a long line of pseudo-Aesops), the Crow steals the other birds' feathers. They complain to the Eagle, who orders restitution, leaving the Crow naked and humiliated.[40] In the context of an exchange of literary fire which presumably involved Ferdinando Strange, this is suggestive because the Eagle and Child was his family crest as well as the badge worn by his father's servants.[41] If Shakespeare was a 'thief', the question of what he literally did remains and must be settled before we can say whether the attack was made in earnest or not. If Taylor's collaborative scenario is combined with the suggestion that Shakespeare the poet played a signature role in 'harey the vj', a possible answer is that audiences jumped to the conclusion that the play was solo-authored when, in fact, it was not. A misunderstanding of this kind could have been cleared up without acrimony while becoming a talking point, because Shakespeare had been breaking the mould by identifying himself as the author of specific plays – something which other professionals generally avoided doing if early printed editions are anything to go by. When plays explicitly attributed to Greene or Marlowe were published, it was after their death.

The insult 'upstart Crow' has added meaning when Talbot has been recognized as a Norreys surrogate. The usual assumption is that 'Black John' was so called because of his complexion or notoriously bad temper. While there may be some truth in this, the obvious reference was to another family crest or badge. This was the Crow, a bird proverbially associated with blackness.[42] In September 1592, at the end of a progress, Elizabeth I visited Rycote, the home of Henry Lord Norreys, father of 'Black John'. This visit was the occasion of an entertainment later published as part of a pamphlet. At the beginning of the piece, old Henry Norreys greeted the Queen on behalf of himself and 'the Crowe my wife', who was one of her particular favourites. It was of course an affectionate usage, reflecting the fact that a new family crest had been borrowed from Lady Norreys's father, the late Lord Williams of Thame.[43] A mother's heart had been as 'blacke as her feathers' because of her fears for the safety of five valiant sons, all serving in Elizabeth's wars. Since the death of a sibling, 'Black John' was the eldest.[44] Appropriately, when Talbot describes his experiences as a prisoner in the market place at Orleans, he refers to himself as a 'Scar-crow'. This inevitably becomes 'scarecrow' in standard editions of the play – a rare occasion when a reference may have been missed because of modernized spelling.

The Norreys connection should now help us to identify the part played by Shakespeare in 'harey the vj' at the Rose. Michael Taylor observes: '*1 Henry VI* itself is full of upstart crows.' In his view, Talbot's antagonist, Joan, is the most engaging and interesting of them.[45] Joan herself applies the 'upstart' label to Sir William Lucy when he demands the body of the hero in very forthright terms. Before yielding, she says scornfully, 'I think this upstart is old Talbot's ghost, / He speaks with such a proud commanding spirit' (4.7.87–8). If Talbot is linked with 'Black John', the entire phrase 'upstart Crow' is implicit when Joan's put-down is followed by Lucy's description of the hero as 'the Frenchmen's only scourge, / Your kingdom's terror and *black* Nemesis' (4.7.77–8) – the italics are mine. Recent disintegrators maintain that this scene was written by Shakespeare himself because the herald's name was chosen as a tribute to Sir Thomas Lucy of Charlecote near Stratford. Though this is probably essentially correct, matters are complicated if the herald's name was borrowed from Sir William Lucy of Newington, whose namesake

---

40 Laura Gibbs, trans., *Aesop's Fables* (Oxford, 2002), pp. xxvii–xxix.

41 Leslie Hotson, *Shakespeare by Hilliard* (London, 1977), pp. 171–4.

42 According to Thomas Churchyard, evoking one of Norreys's campaigns in the Netherlands, his men 'bespredde the plaines, as thicke as the blacke crowes that flyes [*sic*] swarming out of the wilde wooddes'. *A Lamentable and Pitiful Description* (London, 1578), p. 68.

43 Hotson, *Shakespeare by Hilliard*, pp. 155–6.

44 Jean Wilson, ed., *Entertainments for Elizabeth* (Woodbridge, 1980), pp. 48–51.

45 Taylor, ed., *Henry VI, Part One*, pp. 39–50.

and contemporary William Lucy of Charlecote was not a knight according to Dugdale's *Antiquities of Warwickshire Illustrated*.[46] The real Sir William Lucy served in France but returned to England shortly before Talbot's death.[47] In Malone's editions of Shakespeare, a summary of casualties in the Wars of the Roses at the end of *The Third Part of Henry VI* reminds us that John second Earl of Shrewsbury and Sir William Lucy both fell at the battle of Northampton.[48] If a name was chosen for the herald which lends itself to confusion, it may have been a deliberate mistake or a genuine one. Either way, a hint of the Warwickshire family was probably intended, and we do not have to buy the old origins story according to which Shakespeare wrote his first verses after being persecuted by Sir Thomas Lucy, JP. Suggestively, the latter had a troupe of players who performed at Coventry in the mid-1580s, around the time Nicholas Rowe's poaching incident is supposed to have occurred.[49] If Sir Thomas was the young Stratford man's first patron, perhaps a tribute was paid when his protégé achieved wider fame. At all events, Talbot's herald was an appropriate part for Shakespeare to play. As he might have discovered from reading Chaucer's *House of Fame*, early heralds who served great men rather than the crown could be seen as *laudatores temporis acti* and, as such, had more in common with minstrels than with the squabbling officials of his own day. The College of Arms first got out of hand while George Shrewsbury was Earl Marshal. The running battles of Camden, Brooke and Vincent were a longer term consequence of this.[50]

Finally, it might be noted that a French chronicle is probably the ultimate literary-historical source for the discovery of Talbot's body by a herald.[51] Hall merely says his friends found the body and brought it back to Whitchurch, 'where it is intumulate'. Though Shakespeare in a hurry is unlikely to have made direct use of a foreign source still only available in manuscript, this is not an insuperable difficulty. Denys Hay observed that 'tales of the past were still told and traditions did not need the printed page to survive. One inference is obvious: a poet like Shakespeare need not have gone to history books for all the information he incorporated in his cycle of English historical plays.'[52] Much is explained if he drew on the family traditions of patrons, grander than Sir Thomas Lucy, with ancestors who had played a leading role in the foreign and domestic conflicts of the fifteenth century. At the same time, if Shakespeare the 'upstart Crow' as Talbot's herald conspicuously 'marshalled' the funeral, 'harey the vj' would have been very much his show.

---

[46] Dugdale, *The Antiquities of Warwickshire Illustrated* (London, 1656), p. 339.

[47] Hugh Talbot, *The English Achilles* (London, 1981), p. 159.

[48] Edmond Malone, ed., *The Plays and Poems of William Shakspeare* (London, 1821), vol. XVIII, p. 546.

[49] Mark Eccles, *Shakespeare in Warwickshire* (Madison, 1961), pp. 72–5.

[50] Sir Anthony Wagner, *Heralds of England* (London, 1967), pp. 3–20, 199–221.

[51] G. du Fresne de Beaucourt, ed., Mathieu d'Escouchy, *Chronicle* (Paris, 1865), vol. II, pp. 42–3.

[52] Denys Hay, *Polydore Vergil* (Oxford, 1952), p. 95.

SHAKESPEARE AFTER ALL?: THE AUTHORSHIP OF *TITUS ANDRONICUS* 4.1 RECONSIDERED

WILLIAM W. WEBER

The past decade has been host to a sudden shift in scholarly attitudes regarding the authorship of Shakespeare's first tragedy; a full century's worth of chaotically competing theories have collapsed into the relatively confident consensus that *Titus Andronicus* was co-authored by Shakespeare and George Peele. Agreement per se is nothing new, though. The original conviction that the play was Shakespeare's alone went unquestioned until Edward Ravenscroft justified his 1678 adaptation of the play by disparaging both the quality and authorial integrity of the original.[1] This doubt, coupled with the increasingly prudish tastes of the eighteenth and nineteenth centuries, led to a consensus that the honey-tongued bard could not possibly have been responsible for a play so bloody and barbarous.[2] The vogue for disintegration at the turn of the twentieth century brought new attention to the play, and for the first time scholars began to apply serious stylistic analysis in order to determine authorship, be it single or multiple.[3] Alongside this critical movement grew a new-found appreciation for the work's aesthetics, an appreciation that inevitably led certain more bardolatrous commentators to reassert Shakespeare's sole responsibility. The two-sided debate between disintegrationists and conservators raged for decades, with the latter group discounting the findings of the former by claiming that any non-Shakespearian features could be explained away as the result of a young actor/playwright imitating a mentor's method. The debate appeared to have reached an impasse.

Appearances are fickle, though, and the impasse is no more. For proof of this, we need look no further than Jonathan Bate. Arguably the most prominent of the conservators, Bate's 1995 Arden edition of *Titus Andronicus* considered a number of influential studies arguing in favour of multiple authorship, but still came down firmly on the side of Shakespeare *solus*.[4] When editing the same play for the RSC edition of 2007, though, Bate unequivocally concedes collaboration: 'modern scholarship has persuasively demonstrated . . . that *Titus Andronicus* was begun by another dramatist, George Peele'.[5] Bate is far from the only recent convert. Articles are being written about 'Peele and Shakespeare's *Titus Andronicus*', the latest Oxford edition of the *Complete Works* has also embraced Peele's

---

[1] Edward Ravenscroft, *Titus Andronicus, or, The Rape of Lavinia* (London, 1687), A2r.

[2] Exceptions to this trend were few, but included Edward Capell in the eighteenth century and Charles Knight in the nineteenth; German scholars throughout the years were commendably unmoved by the English habit of rejecting Shakespeare's hand in the play. For a fuller account of the critical tradition surrounding *Titus Andronicus*, see Brian Vickers, *Shakespeare, Co-Author* (Oxford, 2002), pp. 148–55.

[3] For the most thorough (and thoroughly misguided) example of this school of criticism's approach to *Titus*, see J. M. Robertson's full-length monograph *Did Shakespeare Write 'Titus Andronicus'?* (London, 1905).

[4] Cf. *Titus Andronicus*, ed. Jonathan Bate (London and New York, 1995), pp. 81–3.

[5] *The RSC Shakespeare*, ed. Jonathan Bate and Eric Rasmussen (New York, 2007), p. 1618. More recently, Bate and Rasmussen have collaborated on *William Shakespeare & Others: Collaborative Plays* (New York, 2013).

co-authorship for the first time.[6] We are all disintegrationists now.

The credit for this consensus regarding *Titus Andronicus* lies squarely with Brian Vickers and his monumental study of canonical collaboration, *Shakespeare, Co-Author*. Through copious assessment of prior scholarship, relentless argumentative assaults on conservators' scholarly shortcomings, and significant new rhetorical analyses of the play, Vickers makes an argument in Peele's favour that is both fierce and, in a word, overwhelming. Vickers's work, building on the historical and theoretical foundations laid by Bentley and Masten, has exerted a predominantly positive influence on contemporary criticism: for the first time the scholarly community is united in approaching dramatic collaboration as the normal endeavour that it was during Shakespeare's career; complete editions are including the entirety of works like *Edward III* and *Sir Thomas More* instead of decontextualized snippets; Shakespeare's genius is appearing all the more clearly in light of realistic professional practice as opposed to a romanticized ideal of creative isolation.[7] Shakespeare apparently felt no shame in sharing authorial responsibilities, and Shakespearian scholars should feel no shame in recognizing this: rather than seeing a collaborative play as somehow less pure, we should be embracing the co-authored text as an exciting new locus for historical, stylistic, and theoretical investigations alike.

The downside to a study as influential as Vickers's, though, is that overwhelmingly effective arguments threaten to usher in an uncritical orthodoxy of thought. This is an eventuality that should be shunned in any case, but especially so with a work as polemical as Vickers's — for in the furor of an argumentative battle nuance can become a casualty to rhetorical fire, no matter how noble the cause. In the laudable push to make a clear-cut division of labour between Peele and Shakespeare, Vickers severs *Titus Andronicus* into Part A and Part B, with the former comprised of the scenes supposed to have been written by Peele: 1.1, 2.1, 2.2, and 4.1. Despite the occasional touch of hedging on Vickers's part, these four scenes (arguably three, since 1.1 and 2.1 in the editorial tradition

are printed as one continuous scene in the original 1594 Quarto) become known as 'the Peele scenes', and are regularly combined for the purpose of statistical analysis. Vickers often credits critical tradition for the attribution of these particular scenes, and does not hesitate to chastise those critics who fail to employ a similar A/B dichotomy as being woefully ignorant of their forbears.

The questionable detail in Vickers's claim should be readily apparent: why do the Peele scenes appear in a continuous 600+ line section at the beginning of the play *as well as* a lonely scene in the penultimate act? What is it about 4.1 that sets it apart from its surroundings as being un-Shakespearian? One would hope that the counter-intuitive manoeuvre of assigning alternate authorship to a single isolated scene would be justified by especially strong internal evidence — or at least as much evidence as supports the attribution of the longer, consecutive passages that open the play. As I shall attempt to demonstrate in this essay, however, this is simply not the case. While virtually every authorship test applied to Act 1 has pointed squarely away from Shakespeare and at Peele, the battery of tests applied specifically to 4.1 has yielded no such clear answer: some tests suggest one author, some the other, and some are entirely non-committal. Given

---

[6] Cf. *William Shakespeare: The Complete Works, Second Edition*, ed. Stanley Wells and Gary Taylor (Oxford, 2005), pp. xx and 155, as well as Glenn Odom and Bryan Reynolds, 'Becomings Roman/Comings-to-Be Villain: Pressurized Belongings and the Coding of Ethnicity, Religion, and Nationality in Peele & Shakespeare's *Titus Andronicus*', in Bryan Reynolds, *Transversal Enterprises in the Drama of Shakespeare and His Contemporaries: Fugitive Explorations* (New York, 2006), pp. 183–226.

[7] Gerald Eades Bentley, *The Profession of Dramatist in Shakespeare's Time, 1590–1642* (Princeton, 1971); Jeffrey Masten, *Textual Intercourse: Collaboration, Authorship, and Sexualities in Renaissance Drama* (Cambridge, 1997). The critical tendency to embrace collaboration as emblematic of the breakdown of the traditional author function, as exemplified most clearly by Masten, has been helpfully resisted by Jeffrey Knapp, *Shakespeare Only* (Chicago and London, 2005). For a useful overview of the current critical status of collaboration and co-authorship, see Ton Hoenselaars, 'Shakespeare: Colleagues, Collaborators, Co-Authors', in *The Cambridge Companion to Shakespeare and Contemporary Dramatists*, ed. Hoenselaars (Cambridge, 2012), pp. 97–119.

this confusion in the objective measures applied to the scene, Vickers's attribution of it to Peele is premature and problematic. This particular scene deserves closer attention.

In order to get closer to establishing the authorship of 4.1, I aim to investigate the scene in several substantial new ways. First, I shall examine the scholarship that has led to a Peele attribution, paying detailed attention to the specific ways in which influential studies of the play as a whole reflect upon this individual scene; given this level of focus, the foundations of the Peele attribution appear increasingly unstable. Second, I propose applying a relatively new quantitative authorship test to the scene. This test, introduced by Mac-Donald P. Jackson and, importantly, endorsed by Vickers himself, analyses author-specific collocations and is uniquely designed to attribute relatively short disputed passages – just like 4.1.[8] Finally, I will engage with qualitative assessments of the scene's rhetoric in order to refine existing beliefs, challenge unverified assumptions, and build a more complete understanding of the scene's stylistic success; most centrally, I propose that a comparative analysis of the two playwrights' deployments of Ovidian allusions will shed new light on the nature of this contentious scene, a scene that I argue belongs to Shakespeare's share of the play.

* * *

The justification for doubting the Shakespearian nature of 4.1, while based on a range of assertions, derives ultimately from a single metrical criterion: a relative paucity of feminine endings. The scene's 128 blank verse lines include only three unstressed final syllables, a percentage that is significantly below Shakespeare's norm, but consistent with Peele's. The tactic of using feminine endings in order to assign authorship dates back to Victorian critic F. G. Fleay, but was not applied to *Titus Andronicus* on a scene-by-scene basis until T. M. Parrott did so in 1919; Parrott's findings were further refined in P. W. Timberlake's 1931 treatise examining the feminine ending in Elizabethan drama through 1595.[9] More contemporary scholars tend to consider Parrott and Timberlake together,

despite the fact that the two reached notably different conclusions regarding the proper application of metrical statistics. A closer look at each provides perspective on how valuable their findings continue to be.

Parrott's goal was to advance his own opinion of *Titus Andronicus*'s Shakespearian status, and the feminine ending was merely the tool he used to justify his theory of revision. Working from the assumption that Ravenscroft was correct in describing the play as having only been touched up by Shakespeare, Parrott's article attempts to determine where revision was heaviest via the recognition that Shakespeare used feminine endings more often than any other dramatist of the early 1590s. Using a straightforward scene-by-scene organization, Parrott combines this single metrical test with a battery of verbal parallels to argue that a scene's percentage of feminine endings correlates directly with its share of Shakespearian poetic genius. Parrott fails to find such genius in the first act, but (despite what Vickers would have us believe: 'Parrott ascribed to Peele two other scenes...2.1 and 4.1'[10]) he neither makes any specific claims as to the identity of the original author whose text he believes Shakespeare revised, nor limits

[8] MacDonald P. Jackson, 'Determining Authorship: A New Technique', *Research Opportunities in Renaissance Drama*, 41 (2002), 1–14. As shown below, I also draw on Jackson's fuller treatment of his technique in *Defining Shakespeare: Pericles as Test Case* (Oxford, 2003), pp. 190–215. For Vickers's endorsement as well as his fuller discussion of the method, see 'Identifying Shakespeare's Additions to *The Spanish Tragedy* (1602): A New(er) Approach', *Shakespeare*, 8 (2012), pp. 1–43, especially pp. 25–8. My own analysis was complete before Vickers's article was published, and therefore I have not employed his further refinements to the test, namely the application of plagiarism-detecting software. Advances in the search functionality of the *Literature Online* (*LION*) database, though, have ameliorated many of the same challenges that Vickers's turn to software was designed to avoid.

[9] F. G. Fleay, *Shakespeare Manual* (London, 1876), especially pp. 121–271; T. M. Parrott, 'Shakespeare's Revision of *Titus Andronicus*', *Modern Language Review*, 14 (1919), 16–37; P. W. Timberlake, *The Feminine Ending in English Blank Verse* (Menasha, 1931).

[10] Vickers, *Shakespeare, Co-Author*, p. 158.

his findings of non-Shakespearian verse to sharply defined scenes. Rather, Parrott argues for at least some Shakespearian revision in every scene except, tellingly, 1.1. Regarding 4.1, the low percentage of feminine endings causes Parrott to dismiss it swiftly as 'a recrudescence of the old rant', even while acknowledging moments of Shakespearian diction.[11]

Timberlake, unlike Parrot, does not attempt to push a particular attribution theory; rather, he simply presents the play's feminine ending statistics and then describes which authorship scenarios remain plausible in light of the evidence. Timberlake's approach to the feminine ending test is far more nuanced than anyone else's, based on the fact that his study accumulates scene-by-scene figures for every known English play written up to 1595. This wealth of specified knowledge keeps Timberlake from making such broad generalizations as Parrott's belief that a single scene's low rate of feminine endings was proof of non-Shakespearian authorship. Shakespeare's distinctiveness, according to Timberlake's figures, lies not in the fact that he always writes with a high frequency of feminine endings, but that he is the only dramatist of the period who ever achieves sustained high overall percentages over the course of multiple plays.[12] Even on the level of an entire play Shakespeare's range overlaps with that of Kyd and, notably, Peele (an inconvenient fact for Vickers, who gets around this difficulty by only considering plays in the tragic vein[13]). When it comes to individual scenes, Shakespeare was just as capable as any other playwright of writing even a long scene (i.e. 100 lines or more, following Timberlake's definition) with a very low percentage of feminine endings. According to Timberlake's figures, seven out of Shakespeare's thirteen early plays contain a long scene with a feminine ending percentage consistent with that found in a long scene in one of Peele's tragedies. If we count mid-length scenes of between 50 and 100 lines, that number expands to twelve out of thirteen; only *Richard III* displays a consistently high percentage. Every other early play has at least one scene that would comport with Peele's statistics. This shows that, when it comes

to scene-length passages, while a high percentage of feminine endings is indeed indicative of Shakespearian authorship, a low percentage is indicative of nothing at all. As Timberlake concludes of 4.1, the scene is '[l]ower than Shakespeare usually goes, but possible for any of the men suggested' – including Shakespeare.[14] Despite recognizing the scene's relative scarcity of feminine endings, Timberlake refuses to rule out the possibility of Shakespearian authorship.

Timberlake's findings, responsible as they were, drew the criticism of Hereward T. Price, who argued that variation of metrical statistics within a play was no reason to disperse authorship.[15] Unconvinced by scholars who, like Parrott, claimed the ability to distinguish a scene's authorship based solely on a high (Shakespearian) or low (non-Shakespearian) percentage of feminine endings, Price suggested that only a play's overall average should be taken into account, and that '*Titus* has just about the number of feminine endings that one would predict for a play by Shakespeare. They are unevenly distributed, as usual in Shakespeare.'[16] Vickers dismisses this as 'a confident-sounding but

---

[11] Parrott, 'Shakespeare's Revision', p. 32.

[12] The late plays by (or attributed to) Kyd are the only non-Shakespearian works that rival Shakespeare's high rate. Cf. Timberlake, *Feminine Ending*, pp. 46–53.

[13] To be entirely fair, discounting the figures from Peele's *Old Wives Tale* is forgivable, as that play is largely rhymed and only contains 128 lines of blank verse; as Timberlake points out, though, that play's 5.4% of feminine endings, while significantly higher than Peele's other dramas, is entirely in line with some of the blank-verse poetry ascribed to him from this period. In general, Peele's use of the feminine ending increased steadily over the course of his career. Why Vickers counts the *2* and *3 Henry VI* plays (10.4 and 10.7% feminine endings, respectively) while ignoring both *1 Henry VI* (6.3%) and *King John* (4.9%) is less understandable. While *1 Henry VI* could theoretically be written off due to its own collaborative authorship, no such claim can be made against *King John*, a play that, moreover, was written at about the same time as *Richard II*, which Vickers does include. For Timberlake's discussion of Peele, see *Feminine Ending*, pp. 15–24.

[14] Timberlake, *Feminine Ending*, p. 117.

[15] H. T. Price, 'The Authorship of *Titus Andronicus*', *The Journal of English and Germanic Philology*, 42 (1943), 55–81.

[16] Price, 'Authorship', p. 65.

vacuous and false judgment', claiming that Price has misrepresented the claims of earlier scholars in order to advance his own prejudiced conception of sole Shakespearian authorship.[17] Indeed, Price undercuts himself seriously by arguing, as evidence for his mistrust of metrical variation as an authorship test, that 'some scenes turn out to be better written than others'.[18] Subjective opinions as to quality have no place in a discussion of metrical tests, and Price's recourse to such unscientific language necessarily casts a pall over his assertions – but it does not entirely invalidate them. They deserve a closer look.

More important than Price's specific conclusion about *Titus Andronicus* is his broader claim that the authorship of a play should not be parcelled out according to a single metrical test, since even in cases of sole authorship metrics can vary significantly from scene to scene. Price writes:

The feminine ending is supposed to distinguish Shakespeare's work from that of his contemporaries. Scholars therefore assert that scenes with a low percentage (i.i, ii.i, iv.i) are not by Shakespeare, while they give to him the scenes with a high percentage (ii.iii, iii.ii, iii.iv, v.i, v.iii). The work of these scholars is vitiated by the underlying assumption that the percentage of feminine endings in a play ought to be fairly uniform.[19]

Vickers, citing only a portion of this passage, mistakenly substitutes 'Timberlake' for 'these scholars', and then responds to his own misrepresentation: 'But Timberlake never made such a claim.'[20] While it is true that Timberlake withheld judgement regarding *Titus Andronicus*, Price would have been entirely justified in accusing him of practising an identical methodology: Timberlake in fact claims that the sharp discrepancy between rates of feminine endings between the first two scenes of *A Comedy of Errors* is evidence that the text has been partially revised.[21] If this is not an example of the scholarly behaviour condemned by Price, then what is?

Having made clear his distrust for disintegration based solely on metrical discrepancies, Price cites Timberlake's figures to point out that plays of accepted Shakespearian authorship also contain significant scene-to-scene variation: 'In the *Two Gentlemen* the figures vary between 2.6 and 22.1 per cent and in *King John* between 3.8 per cent and 15.2 per cent.'[22] Vickers attacks this evidence: 'anyone able to check Price's account against Timberlake's will notice how distorted it is: the figure of 2.6 per cent comes from 1.1, a short scene (75 lines), and therefore likely to be untypical, and it is by far the lowest figure for the whole play'.[23] Vickers is right to point out how isolated this scene is (although calling a 75-line scene short is perhaps misleading, at least in the context of Timberlake, who classifies scenes between 50 and 100 lines as mid-length), but Price's point about scene-to-scene variation existing within a one-author play stands.

It is intriguing that Vickers chooses to attack the *Two Gentlemen* statistics for being 'distorted', since they are technically accurate while the *King John* ones are not. Scenes in that play vary not from 3.8 to 15.2%, as Price claimed, but from 0.0 to 15.2%. Moreover, in the case of that play (which is far closer generically to *Titus Andronicus* than is *Two Gentlemen*), it is the high figure that is more of an outlier. According to Timberlake's figures, the first scene achieves 15.2%, while the second highest tally is 6.9% in the 72-line 3.3. On the low end of the spectrum, three scenes are entirely devoid of strict feminine endings, with one of these (5.4) breaking the 50-line mark to qualify as mid-length. 4.3 measures over 150 lines and only contains 1.3% feminine endings. A set of three consecutive scenes contains only one feminine ending over the course of 96 lines. The play as a whole averages under 5%. Timberlake tries valiantly to deliver an explanation for how Shakespeare could have written a play with so few feminine endings at this point in his career; scholars attempting to attribute 4.1 to Peele based on this metric just ignore the inconvenient facts.

---

[17] Vickers, *Shakespeare, Co-Author*, pp. 165–6.
[18] Price, 'Authorship', p. 65.
[19] Price, 'Authorship', p. 65.
[20] Vickers, *Shakespeare, Co-Author*, p. 165.
[21] Timberlake, *Feminine Ending*, pp. 95–8.
[22] Price, 'Authorship', p. 65.
[23] Vickers, *Shakespeare, Co-Author*, p. 165.

Further investigation of Timberlake's statistics gives additional support to Price's position that a low percentage of feminine endings should not be used to deny Shakespeare's authorship of any single scene. As mentioned above, the majority of Shakespeare's early plays contain a long scene more consistent with Peele's overall metrics than Shakespeare's; if we were to pursue disintegration based on feminine endings to its logical conclusion, we would be searching for collaborators to such solidly Shakespearian plays as *1 Henry IV* and *A Midsummer Night's Dream*. Surely Price is right that this is not a responsible course to take. To say that Price is correct when it comes to the danger of attributing individual scenes is not to agree, however, with his conclusion that metrical figures are only useful at the level of an entire play. There exists a middle ground: the act.[24] When Timberlake's figures are applied not to scenes but to entire acts, a different picture of variability emerges.

As one would expect, looking at larger subsections of plays tends to minimize statistical extremes. Discounting *Love's Labour's Lost* and *A Midsummer Night's Dream*, the two rhyme-heavy comedies whose acts have only as much blank verse as a normal scene, the remainder of Shakespeare's early plays show remarkable regularity when their feminine endings are tallied by act. *Richard II* contains scenes that vary from 0.0 to 20.0% (with the 0.0 figure coming not from a very short scene, but rather the 80-line 5.1), but its acts group tightly around its average of 8.2%: 8.9, 9.5, 7.7, 7.3 and 7.2%, respectively. There are only two plays with striking variation across acts: *King John* and *Titus Andronicus*. The first of these should trouble us less, since its outlying act is both remarkably short (230 lines, less than half the length of any other act) and aberrant in a positive direction (15.2% feminine endings, compared to the play's overall average of 4.9%). As described above, a high percentage of feminine endings suggests only Shakespearian authorship; unless we want to doubt Shakespeare's hand in over 80% of the play, the discrepancy here should cause little worry. *Titus Andronicus* presents an entirely different situation: its first act is also atypical, but in a way that seriously suggests collaboration. The

figures by act show: 1.9, 7.1, 6.2, 8.1 and 11.2% with Folio act breaks; if we follow Q1 in reading F's 1.1 and 2.1 as a single uninterrupted scene, then the first two acts go up to 2.0 and 8%, respectively. In either case, the first act of *Titus* has a lower percentage of feminine endings than any other act-length section of blank verse in Shakespeare's early plays. This is strong evidence in favour of collaboration, made all the stronger in that it passes the negative test that the scene-by-scene analysis cannot: the majority of Shakespeare's early plays contain a low-percentage scene; only *Titus* has an entire act. If indeed Peele began the play and Shakespeare finished it, it should not surprise us that Shakespeare's far longer portion includes a single scene that resembles Peele's rate of feminine endings. In fact, it would be more statistically surprising if it did not.

Scholars who use the feminine ending test to yoke 4.1 together with the beginning of the play therefore act too hastily, and threaten to obscure the question by neglecting to give the scene the individual attention it deserves. The blame for popularizing the A/B division of the play lies with MacDonald P. Jackson, and with him also lies the credit for demonstrating its liabilities. Jackson first employed the A/B scheme (drawn, explicitly, from Parrott's figures for feminine endings, and including only 1.1, 2.1 and 4.1) in conjunction with his rare words test, and found a marked difference between the two sections of the play, with the A stratum showing much closer affiliation with

---

[24] It may reasonably be objected that *Titus* was not printed with act breaks until F, and that considering it in terms of that division is potentially anachronistic. However, as T. W. Baldwin says in *Shakespeare's Five-Act Structure* (Urbana, 1947), p. 347n: 'It will not do to assume – and I do not assume – that plays which are not now marked in five acts were not in fact constructed in acts.' That Peele and Shakespeare most likely had a five-act structure in mind while constructing the play is suggested by the acts marked in Peele's first printed play, *The Arraignment of Paris* of 1584, as well as the abundant evidence found in Baldwin's study that Shakespeare was well-aware of the five-act structure at this point in his career. That Henslowe records paying for plays by the act is further evidence that such a division of labor was not in the least unlikely; see *Henslowe's Diary, Second Edition*, ed. R. A. Foakes (Cambridge, 2002), pp. 100, 103.

Shakespeare's early vocabulary than Part B, which has more words anticipating later works.[25] As he does not give precise figures for each scene's contribution to the overall findings, it is impossible to see what effect 4.1 had on the outcome; regardless, Jackson found the overall results meaningful enough to justify continued use of the bipartite division strategy.

Doubts creep into the statistics with Jackson's next study of the play, 'Stage Directions and Speech Headings in Act I of *Titus Andronicus* Q (1594): Shakespeare or Peele'.[26] This article provides one of the most convincing arguments for Peele's authorship of the play's first act, basing its claim on an exhaustive comparative study of Peele and Shakespeare's respective uses of specific typographical and syntactical idiosyncrasies. These findings, powerful as they are, do not extend beyond the first act in Q1 (i.e. 1.1 and 2.1 in F); nothing in the stage directions or speech headings of 4.1 suggests Peele. The article, though, does not limit itself to bibliographic inquiry, but goes on to consider evidence drawn from Jackson's analysis of function words. The results of this radically different mode of inquiry align perfectly with the foregoing argument: Act I shows a statistically significant difference in the frequency of the words 'and' and 'with'.[27] As Jackson points out, the first of these words occurs more frequently in *Titus Andronicus* than in any other canonical play; its irregularity, however, is almost entirely due to the first act. In a footnote, Jackson suggests how the data would appear within his original A/B framework: 'For 2.1 the rate of *and* is also very high . . . for 4.1 it is normal, but there is certainly a highly significant disparity between parts A and B *in toto*, as originally defined.'[28] The same thing occurs for 'with', which also displays anomalously high frequency in this play compared to Shakespeare's others. Like 'and', 'with' appears more frequently in the first two scenes than elsewhere in the play, including 4.1. In fact, 4.1 is closer to Shakespeare's overall career average of 'with' usage (and further from Peele's) than is the average of the Shakespearian Part B. Nevertheless, Jackson points out: 'a notable disparity would remain if we were to revert to our

original lines of demarcation between Parts A and B'.[29] This realization provides precisely no justification for maintaining the Peelian attribution of 4.1, but does an excellent job demonstrating the troubling malleability of statistics: 1.1 is simply so atypical that combining it with *any* other scene would still result in a statistically significant difference from the rest of the play. Such statistical significance, therefore, is actually not significant at all.[30]

Further evidence as to the dubiousness of the A/B division exists in Brian Boyd's study of common words as a test of authorship in *Titus Andronicus*.[31] Boyd begins by following Jackson's breakdown of scenes, yet invariably winds up noting not how Part A differs from Part B but how the Shakespearian section contrasts with just Act I. For example, 'Rome' and its derivatives appear in 1.1 at a saturating rate of once in every 7 lines; comparatively, Part B uses these words only once in 36 lines, perfectly in line with Shakespeare's other

---

[25] MacDonald P. Jackson, *Studies in Attribution: Middleton and Shakespeare* (Salzburg, 1979).

[26] MacDonald P. Jackson, 'Stage Directions and Speech Headings in Act I of *Titus Andronicus* Q (1594): Shakespeare or Peele', *Studies in Bibliography*, 49 (1996), 134–48.

[27] Jackson, 'Stage Directions', pp. 144–5.

[28] Jackson, 'Stage Directions', p. 144n.

[29] Jackson, 'Stage Directions', p. 144n.

[30] One could reasonably object at this point that my line of argument here approaches hypocrisy – since I've made the claim above that 4.1's feminine endings shouldn't rule out Shakespearian authorship because the scene's eccentricity in this regard disappears upon considering it as part of its entire act; how is combining it with more Shakespearian scenes in order to erase its un-Shakespearianness any different from combining it with un-Shakespearian scenes in order to minimize its Shakespearianness? The distinction, I would suggest, lies in the relative argumentative weight that the admittedly similar observations claim: those who utilize the A/B distinction do so in order to prove Peele's authorship; my aim in rethinking the feminine ending test is only to cast doubt upon such hasty conclusions. I readily admit that 4.1's individual statistics cast doubt upon it, but those critics who go beyond mere doubt and arrive at positive assertion necessarily wind up ignoring or minimizing evidence that contradicts their viewpoints.

[31] Brian Boyd, 'Common Words in *Titus Andronicus*: The Presence of Peele', *Notes & Queries*, 42.3 (1995), 300–7.

Roman plays like *Julius Caesar* (one in 38) and *Coriolanus* (one in 34). The rate of 4.1, one in 32, is far closer to the characteristically Shakespearian Part B than to Act 1.[32] Boyd thankfully provides specific counts for each scene, for if he had chosen to follow the A/B division wholesale he would still have found a serious discrepancy: Part A as a whole registers just over 10.1 lines per usage, a fact that provides still more evidence that too broad a view can erase meaningful distinctions.[33]

It is unfortunate, given the unreliability of the A/B division, to see the enthusiasm with which Vickers embraces it. This enthusiasm is especially problematic during his assessment of J. C. Maxwell's mid-century article identifying a grammatical construction (possessive as antecedent to relative clause) that, Maxwell finds, is common in Peele but rare in Shakespeare.[34] Vickers approves of Maxwell's test and the collaborative conclusion it suggests, but feels the need to make it bolster his chosen attributive breakdown more explicitly (since Maxwell only concluded that the first act was clearly Peele's): 'Again we see the bad effect of limited knowledge: had Maxwell used the metrical studies by Parrott and Timberlake he would have realized that 2.1 and 4.1 are probably also by Peele.'[35] Vickers then proceeds to use Maxwell's data to produce a table showing how sharply differentiated parts A and B are, based on the frequency of the construction Maxwell identifies – one in 108.6 for A, one in 586.3 for B. These numbers are impressive (and made more so by the closeness with which they align with Peele's and Shakespeare's respective rates in other works), but they are also misleading: of the seven instances of the characteristic construction, precisely zero occur in 4.1. Rather than let Maxwell's findings speak for themselves, Vickers explicitly invokes the single criterion of feminine endings (in a way that misrepresents the claims actually made by Parrott and Timberlake, no less) in order to suggest that Maxwell's evidence says the opposite of what it actually does about 4.1.[36]

To be fair to Vickers, he does not only use the A/B division to misrepresent the specifics of other scholars' findings: he misrepresents his own

as well. At the end of his extensive review of previous scholars' attempts to ascertain the authorship of *Titus Andronicus*, Vickers introduces several new tests of his own devising: polysyllabic words, alliteration, vocatives, and rhetorical figures. The first three of these are purely quantitative, and thus allow the same kind of statistical analysis that forms the basis of almost all recent attribution tests. In each case Vickers provides scene-by-scene breakdowns of the stylistic features in question, but bases his attributive claims only upon the statistical distinction between A and B groupings. Unsurprisingly, this method provides further evidence for dual authorship; it also, however, fails to clarify the authorship of 4.1.

Vickers's analysis of polysyllabic words demonstrates that Peele employed three-, four-, and five-syllable words with greater frequency than Shakespeare, and that this fact is reflected in *Titus*

---

[32] Boyd, 'Common Words', p. 302.

[33] Like Jackson's contemporaneous findings concerning function words, Boyd's assessment of common words in the play shows that 1.1 is so strongly un-Shakespearian that it renders the particulars of the much shorter 4.1 irrelevant to a general claim about authorship. With this in mind, it becomes evident that studies based solely on the A/B division that fail to include data for individual scenes must not be taken to argue convincingly about 4.1 in either direction. Into this category fall Jackson's original findings from 1979 (see n.25 above), including both his rare word test and tests measuring the frequency of compound adjectives and the un- prefix, as well as the generally persuasive findings on metrics provided by Marina Tarlinskaja in *Shakespeare's Verse: Iambic Pentameter and the Poet's Idiosyncrasies* (New York, 1987), and the broader stylometric assessments made by the Shakespeare Authorship Clinic at Claremont McKenna College, as directed by Ward Elliott and Robert Valenza (see 'And Then There Were None: Winnowing the Shakespeare Claimants', *CHum* 30 (1996), pp. 191–245). Both of these important studies provide strong evidence that collaboration definitely occurred, but neither claims to be applicable to short enough passages to make a specific assertion about 4.1.

[34] J. C. Maxwell, 'Peele and Shakespeare: A Stylometric Test', *Journal of English and Germanic Philology*, 49 (1950), 557–61.

[35] Vickers, *Shakespeare, Co-Author*, p. 184.

[36] While of less pressing importance, it should also be pointed out that Vickers here chooses not to include 2.2 in his part A – presumably because it, like 4.1, is devoid of Maxwell's construction – despite the fact that he includes it in part A elsewhere in his chapter.

Andronicus: the 'Peele scenes' of part A feature polysyllabic words at a rate of one per 2.8 lines, compared to a 3.3 frequency for the rest of the play.[37] This difference, while significant, is hardly striking. One reason for this is 4.1, which happens to make the least frequent use of polysyllabic words of any scene in the play: only once per 5.4 lines. Were we to assign Peele only the first uninterrupted scene from Q1, the distinction between authors would become much more pronounced: once per 2.5 lines for Peele (even more frequent than in Vickers's control, *The Battle of Alcazar*), one in 3.4 for Shakespeare. Yet again, the first act is so very irregular that it appears statistically distinct even when combined with 4.1, the scene that is the most Shakespearian of all according to this particular test. This realization, combined with the similar findings of Jackson and Boyd, should prompt us to reassess the wisdom of continuing to rely on the feminine ending test as the all-powerful measure of authorship. Surely either the feminine ending test is wrong, the polysyllabic word test is wrong, or a scene as relatively short as 4.1 cannot be responsibly attributed based on these statistical measures alone. Since both measures agree with all other stylistic tests in recognizing the first act as Peele's, it is unlikely that they are entirely invalid; therefore, the problem must lie not with the tests, but with the application of them to this particular passage.

The danger of drawing conclusions about individual scenes based on the results of tests better suited to large swaths of text gains further nuance when we look at another of Vickers's quantitative rhetorical tests: vocatives. In this case the scene-by-scene numbers do indeed suggest that 4.1 is more typically Peelian than Shakespearian, as Peele tends to use vocatives at a higher rate – and 4.1 certainly has abundant vocatives:

> Help, *grandsire*, help! My aunt Lavinia
> Follows me everywhere, I know not why.
> *Good uncle Marcus*, see how swift she comes.
> Alas, *sweet aunt*, I know not what you mean.
> (4.1.1–4, emphasis added)

This opening speech by a frantic Young Lucius, with three vocatives in its four lines, proves representative of just how saturated the scene is with rhetorical figures of address. There are 41 vocatives in the scene's 128 lines, a rate of 1 per 3.2 lines. This, Vickers shows, is even more frequent than the Part A average of 1 per 4.2, and far indeed from Shakespeare's Part B rate of 1 per 8.7.[38] This appears to be strong evidence for Peele's hand in the scene.

Like feminine endings, though, the rate at which a playwright employs vocatives is not necessarily uniform throughout a play, and Shakespeare in particular tends to vary his use of the feature. As Vickers's data show, the 1 in 8.7 frequency of Part B results from averaging together individual scene rates that go as low as 1 in 19 lines for the 57-line 2.4 and 1 in 18.6 for the 205-line 5.2, and as high as 1 in 3.8 for the 121-line 4.3. This last scene, interestingly, uses vocatives even more frequently than Peele's 1.1, where the rate is 1 in 4.[39] This realization alone should be sufficient to cast significant doubt upon the usefulness of this particular test when it comes to attributing individual scenes, but I believe a closer look at Shakespeare's high-frequency scenes will help shed further light on the matter.

Unlike feminine endings, which are relatively neutral in terms of their connection to the content of a passage and therefore a good indicator of a playwright's unconscious metrical style, vocatives often correlate with the subject of a given scene – the example of courtiers addressing their sovereign as 'my lord' or 'your highness' with their every speech comes easily to mind. As Vickers points out, following Marco Mincoff, 4.1 is not this kind of formal scene at all; quite the opposite: 'Even in the intimate family scene . . . Peele makes his characters constantly address each other by their name or kinship term.'[40] It does seem strange that a scene like 4.1, occupied only by intimate family members, should employ so many

---

37 Vickers, *Shakespeare, Co-Author*, pp. 220–1.
38 Vickers, *Shakespeare, Co-Author*, p. 227.
39 Vickers, *Shakespeare, Co-Author*, p. 227.
40 Vickers, *Shakespeare, Co-Author*, p. 229. See also Marco Mincoff, *Shakespeare: The First Steps* (Sofia, 1976), p. 131.

vocatives that '[i]t is as if the actors don't know to whom they should address their lines'.[41] I would suggest, though, that there may well be a logical explanation for this counter-intuitive feature of the scene: the presence of a child.

While exploring the full historical and dramaturgical complexity of the roles that child actors played on the Elizabethan stage is beyond the scope of this discussion, it is not difficult to imagine that the participation of an adult company's inexperienced child actor in a scene would increase the likelihood that at least one character would be less likely to 'know to whom they should address their lines', and that the inclusion of extra vocatives in the script would function like embedded stage directions in order to keep the novice's attention directed properly. Looking back at the opening lines of 4.1, it is apparent how the vocatives direct Young Lucius to address first Titus, then Marcus – both of whom are presumably in front of him as he runs onto the stage – and then to whirl about to face the pursuing Lavinia behind him. This dynamic blocking is inherent in the language, so that anyone able to memorize the lines would already have memorized the manner in which they were to be delivered. What sounds needlessly repetitive to us may have been simply pragmatic for a theatre company in the process of training young, inexperienced actors. Rather than Peele using vocatives simply because he knew no easier way to fill out pentameter lines, 4.1 may instead be an example of Shakespeare writing with a mind to the abilities – and inabilities – of his cast.

To test this hypothesis, I have conducted a limited survey of vocative use in Shakespearian scenes containing child actors. Following Mark Lawthorn's catalogue of children in Shakespeare's plays, and specifically his two categories of children that most closely resemble Young Lucius (viz., 'Innocent and Noble Victims' and 'Children Who Are Silent or Say Very Little'), I have made a comparison of the frequency of vocatives during passages in which children speak or are spoken to with those passages in the same scenes in which the children are silent and away from the action.[42]

The results, from across the entirety of Shakespeare's career, are remarkably consistent and strikingly divergent: in scenes with children on stage, Shakespeare uses vocatives more than twice as often when a child is involved in the scene than when only adults are speaking.

The one scene in *3 Henry VI* involving the young Rutland (and involving him throughout) contains 12 vocatives in its 52 lines, for a rate of 1 in 4.3. *Richard III* provides significantly more material, with children appearing in three separate scenes but dominating none of them as Rutland did his. Between Clarence's children in 2.2, young York in 2.4, and both York and his elder brother Prince Edward in 3.1, the play has a total of 215 lines involving children, with 60 vocatives – a rate of 1 in 3.6. The remaining 214 lines of these same three scenes contain only 32 vocatives – a rate of 1 in 6.7. The boy Arthur has a substantial role in *King John*, appearing in 2.1, 3.1, 3.3 and 4.1. These scenes have 47 vocatives in the 218 lines involving Arthur, but only 112 in the 946 without him; 1 in 4.6 versus 1 in 8.4. This pattern continues with the young Latin student William in *The Merry Wives of Windsor* (1 in 3.7 for his one scene, 4.1, with no adult-only lines), Macduff's son in *Macbeth* (1 in 3.6 versus 1 in 14 in his one scene, 4.2), and Mamillius in the *Winter's Tale* (1 in 4.0 versus 1 in 8.6 over two scenes, 2.1 and 3.1). This sample of scenes from six different plays adds up to 2,436 lines – roughly the length of an entire play. The 695 lines involving children include 185 vocatives, for an overall frequency of 1 in 3.8. The 1,741 lines without children have only 210 vocatives, a rate of 1 in 8.3.

These findings receive further confirmation in the rest of *Titus Andronicus*. Aside from the disputed 4.1, Young Lucius only appears in Shakespearian scenes, being involved in the dialogue as either speaker or addressee in 3.2, 4.2, 4.3 and 5.3. Each

---

[41] Vickers, *Shakespeare, Co-Author*, p. 229.

[42] Mark Lawthorn, 'Children in Shakespeare's Plays: An Annotated Checklist', in *Shakespeare and Childhood*, ed. Kate Chedgzoy, Susanne Greenhalgh and Robert Shaughnessy (Cambridge, 2007), pp. 233–49.

of these scenes contains multiple (often familial) vocatives that closely resemble those of 4.1: compare 'Lavinia, go with me' (3.2.80) with 'Lavinia, come' (4.1.119); 'your honourable youth, / The hope of Rome' (4.2.12–13) with 'sweet boy, the Roman Hector's hope' (4.1.87); 'To it, boy! Marcus, loose when I bid' (4.3.59) with 'How now, Lavinia? Marcus, what means this?' (4.1.30); and 'Come hither boy, come, come' (5.3.159) with 'my boy . . . / Come, come' (4.1.113,116). Young Lucius almost never has a speech in which he fails to address one (or more) of his elders with a vocative, and he is almost never addressed without being called by his name or, most often, simply 'boy'. Out of 121 combined lines featuring him, there are 33 vocatives, a rate of 1 in 3.7 – far more frequent than the overall Part B average of 1 in 8.7; if we subtract these lines and vocatives from the totals, the figure for child-free Shakespeare passages becomes 1 in 9.7. Thus, we see that when it comes to vocatives in *Titus Andronicus*, there's actually a greater discrepancy between Shakespeare writing about a child and Shakespeare not writing about a child than there is between overall Shakespeare and Peele.

Moreover, the particularly familial nature of so many of Shakespeare's vocatives elsewhere in the play aligns 4.1 more closely with Part B than with the rest of Part A; beyond the examples given above, it is difficult to find more similarly constructed lines than 'Look Marcus, ah, son Lucius, look on her' (3.1.110) and 'Sit down, sweet niece. Brother, sit down by me' (4.1.64). Both contain a repeated imperative surrounding two familial vocatives and ahead of a terminal pronoun, creating a tight chiasmus that focuses the respective scenes' tragic energy within the Andronici clan; the line from 4.1, by including the previously external Lavinia within the formal unit and shifting the final pronoun from the third-person 'her' to the first-person 'me', acts as a further compression of the image, an intensification of the theme that marks the play's transition from internalized grief to externalized vengeance. The vocatives in 4.1, therefore, may actually be best described not as a return to Peele's formulaic rhetoric, but as a

dynamic development of Shakespeare's emotionally charged – and yet still pragmatically novice-friendly – language.

Making an attribution based on a qualitative reading of a single rhetorical feature is premature in the extreme, of course, and I do not expect anyone to be convinced by it alone. However, I do believe that the foregoing analyses of the feminine ending test, the A/B division, and the purely quantitative vocatives test have shown that, to date, no convincing attribution of 4.1 has been proven. A low percentage of feminine endings is suggestive but by no means conclusive, and demands further study of the scene in isolation. Sadly, the tendency to use the inconclusive feminine endings test as the justification for applying the A/B division has done precisely the opposite, and therefore there is no valid scholarly consensus as to the attribution of 4.1. It is time to end as much of the uncertainty as possible.

* * *

While the failure of a century's worth of scholarly ingenuity is daunting indeed, it should not stop us from seeking out new ways of solving this conundrum. It should hardly be surprising that methods intended to identify collaboration within the play as a whole have been less successful at attributing an individual scene; it should be less surprising still, given the far greater relative importance of establishing the fact of collaboration versus the local details regarding its manifestation, that no one has yet applied a test specifically designed to deal with shorter passages. In order to remedy this oversight and, hopefully, shed new light on the authorship of this pivotal scene, I would like to end the present study by applying two new tests to *Titus Andronicus* 4.1. One computerized and quantitative, the other philological and qualitative, both suggest that William Shakespeare is the most likely author of this scene after all.

An exciting potential solution to the problem of applying quantitative measures to relatively short pieces of text can be found in MacDonald Jackson's twenty-first century resurrection of the decidedly old-fashioned method of identifying verbal parallels.[43] Rather than rely on traditional methods of reading and remembering in order to compile lists of subjectively determined similarities between an uncertain text and an author's known corpus, Jackson's method utilizes the tremendous resource that is the Chadwyck-Healey *Literature Online* (*LION*) database, an advance that has the potential 'to revolutionize old practices'.[44] The process is simple but painstaking: in the case of testing a passage with two potential authors, one advances through the text line by line, entering every word, phrase and collocation of nearby words into the database's search field, with results limited by author to 'Shakespeare OR Peele'. When a given phrase or collocation appears in one author's works but not the other's, it counts as a single 'hit', regardless of how many times it may appear in that one author's works.[45] While results were recorded based on the entire Shakespeare canon (excepting only *The Passionate Pilgrim*, *A Funeral Elegy*, *Edward III* and *Sir Thomas More*), in order to make a fair comparison with Peele's smaller canon the test was also applied only to a restricted portion of Shakespeare's works, chosen (following Jackson) so as to match Peele's output as much as possible in terms of size, period, and genre: *The Comedy of Errors*, *Love's Labour's Lost*, *Richard II*, *Richard III*, *Romeo and Juliet*, *The Taming of the Shrew*, *The Two Gentlemen of Verona* and *Venus and Adonis*.[46]

Jackson demonstrates the efficacy of this method in identifying the author of a very short passage by applying it to two relatively uncontroversial parts of *Titus Andronicus*: the very beginning of the play (1.1.1–17), almost certainly by Peele, as well as an excerpt from a scene widely accepted to be Shakespeare's (2.3.10–29). Things seem muddled at first, as the opening speeches contain 5 hits for Peele, but 6 for Shakespeare. When the 'restricted' Shakespeare canon is employed, however, the numbers become 10 to 2 (83.3%) in favour of Peele – as we would expect. Similarly, a raw count of Tamora's speech to Aaron in 2.3 yields 20 Shakespeare hits and only 2 for Peele, and the restricted tally still winds up 7 to 2 (77.9%) for Shakespeare. Jackson goes on to apply this method to the entirety of

Pericles, and finds that it supports the supposition that Wilkins wrote the first two acts (75% of hits) and Shakespeare the final three (60.8%).[47] These percentages for long portions of the play are remarkably similar to those in individual scenes similar in length to 4.1 of *Titus Andronicus*; in general, one can expect the true author to receive about 75% of hits.

When applied to *Titus Andronicus* 4.1, this method delivers striking results. A raw count, including the full Shakespeare and Peele canons, shows 139 hits for Shakespeare (more than one per line) and only 9 for Peele: 93.9% Shakespeare.

---

43 Jackson, *Defining Shakespeare*, pp. 190–215. As Jackson's chapter points out, this method has been successfully applied to a number of complicated attribution problems, including the collaborative plays *The Spanish Gypsy* (by Ford, Dekker, Rowley and Middleton), *A Cure for a Cuckold* (by Webster, Rowley and Heywood), and *Anything for a Quiet Life* (by Webster and Middleton), among others. More recently, teams employing this collocation-seeking method performed admirably in an attribution competition and, as mentioned above, Brian Vickers has used a revised variant of it to argue persuasively for Shakespeare's hand in the 1602 additions to *The Spanish Tragedy*: see Vickers, 'Identifying Shakespeare's Additions', and Patrick Juola, 'Authorship Attribution', *Foundation and Trends in Information Retrieval*, 1.3 (2006), 233–334. Consistently, the method manages to identify the author of even short passages. Any reader desiring a fuller explanation of the method as I have applied it should consult Jackson, whose instructions are clear and comprehensive. The only significant departure I have made from Jackson's experiment is that I used the new 'search variant spellings' feature of *LION* instead of manually entering each and every possible typographical and orthological variant. This new technological feature streamlines the search process greatly but should be used with caution: as comprehensive as the database's list of variant spellings seems to be, I nevertheless found more than one example of missing variants. As the database is a digitization of original editions, one should always consult original texts and facsimiles as much as possible while conducting searches.

44 Jackson, *Defining Shakespeare*, p. 190.

45 In order to be included in the results, a matching phrase must be either a compound word or a collocation of two or more separate words, with pronoun/verb units discounted.

46 See Jackson, 'Determining Authorship', p. 9 for a fuller explanation of his reasoning in choosing these particular works.

47 Jackson, *Defining Shakespeare*, pp. 195–203.

Implementing the restricted Shakespeare canon makes the results less overwhelmingly one-sided, but they are still compelling: 65 Shakespeare hits, 22 hits for Peele, or 74.7% Shakespeare.[48] If Vickers's claim that the scene was probably written by Peele were correct, we would expect precisely the inverse of this outcome. There can be no doubt that the author of 4.1 employed a vocabulary and idiolect much more closely aligned with Shakespeare's than with Peele's and the only conclusion that can follow is that Shakespeare most likely wrote the scene.

Closer analysis of the test's data only strengthens the argument. One intriguing revelation is how many of the Shakespeare hits are instances of *epizeuxis*, or immediate repetition of a word. It has long been a critical commonplace that Peele was the more repetitive of the two authors, and that a high frequency of rhetorical repetition was therefore a sign of his hand. 4.1 is remarkably full of *epizeuxis*: 'see, see' (54); 'never, never' (55); 'what, what' (78); and 'come, come' (116). Shakespeare employs all four of these elsewhere in his writing, while Peele only utilizes the last. Specifically, 'see, see' shows up in no fewer than eleven other plays by Shakespeare, as well as an undoubtedly Shakespearian (and yet epizeuxis-heavy) speech in a later scene of *Titus Andronicus*: 'Ha, ha! Publius, Publius, what hast thou done? / See, see, thou has shot off one of Taurus' horns' (4.3.68–9). The next repetition, 'never, never', can be found in four other plays. The third, 'what, what', in eleven yet again. The fourth, 'come, come', does show up in Peele – but only once, in *Edward I*. And Shakespeare? He uses 'come, come' over one hundred times in over thirty plays. This particular brand of repetition appears to be nothing if not wholly Shakespearian.

Also of interest in the *LION* findings, while not included in the statistics, is the number of individual words from this scene that appear elsewhere in one author's canon but not the others. Proponents of a Peele attribution have long pointed to the fact that 4.1 includes the word 'fere', which Peele used in his 'War of Troy', but which does not appear in any Shakespearian work besides the late collaborative plays *Pericles* and *The Two Noble Kinsman*. This fact is interesting indeed and seemed especially so in the days before electronic databases made it possible to search the entire Peele canon with ease. Shakespeare concordances have long made it simple to identify words he used infrequently, and when one of those rare Shakespearian words happens to appear in the earlier works of a known or suspected co-author the fact certainly merits attention. As a *LION* search shows, though, 'fere' is far from the only word in the scene that is rare or unique to one or the other author's known vocabulary. The only word form used by Peele but never Shakespeare is 'playeth' – Shakespeare used the verb, of course, but never this particular conjugation. A few other rather innocuous examples arise if we limit ourselves to the restricted Shakespeare canon: 'Hecuba', 'Philomel', 'gloomy', 'slunk', 'camp', 'traitorous' and 'whelps'. Shakespeare used all of these words multiple times, often in early plays and poems, just not in the specific subset used by Jackson to create parity with Peele's works; additionally, Shakespeare used the words 'glooming' and 'encamp' in *Romeo and Juliet*, as well as 'Philomel' and 'traitorous' in his known section of *Titus Andronicus*. The list of words unique to Shakespeare is significantly more substantial: 'aunt', 'frenzy', 'causeless', 'sequence', 'confederate', 'Ovid', 'Metamorphosis', 'culled', 'Tereus', 'quote', 'Tarquin', 'Lucrece', 'performers', 'dominator', 'mutiny', 'sware' (past tense), 'prosecute', 'Sybil' and 'armoury'. Not only is this list over twice as long as that of Peele's, it requires fewer qualifications – namely that 'Lucrece' appears in the potentially Peelian *Titus Andronicus* 2.2 and that 'Tereus', 'Tarquin', 'performers', 'sware' and 'Sybil' do not appear in the restricted Shakespeare canon. So, to summarize: there is only one word in 4.1 truly unique to Peele, and it is the specific, pedestrian verb form 'playeth.' Conversely, there are over a dozen significant words

---

48 Space constraints will not permit a full record of the results of this test to appear here. Anyone interested in consulting the specifics can find them on the author's personal homepage, www.williamweatherfordweber.wordpress.com.

that are unique to Shakespeare. The evidence mounts.

* * *

As convincing as the quantitative results of the *LION* test appear, there will surely be those who object based on qualitative grounds: 4.1 simply seems to lack the poetic imagery and elegance that strikes many as Shakespearian, and some of its rhetorical components seem particularly Peelian. To assess the rhetorical signature of the scene – above and beyond its prosody and vocabulary – we must turn one last time to the example of Brian Vickers. Vickers ends his discussion of *Titus Andronicus* with a qualitative analysis in the context of Henry Peacham's 1593 rhetorical manual, *The Garden of Eloquence*. Peacham provides a seemingly exhaustive list of rhetorical schemes and figures, with each one receiving both a 'use' describing its proper function and a 'caution' warning against potential abuses. Vickers's general hypothesis is that Shakespeare was more likely to live up to the uses and avoid the cautions than was Peele, so that even if the two playwrights utilized a given figure with similar frequency, authorship can be determined by assessing the relative rhetorical success of a given passage. While this method is necessarily subjective, and perilously close to the bardolatrous assumption that anything deemed good must be Shakespeare's (and vice versa), I believe that a carefully comparative study of rhetorical quality – as understood in the particular historical context of Peacham's guidebook – can indeed provide worthwhile results auxiliary to those provided by more objective quantitative methods.

I propose applying a similar method to a rhetorical device central to the scene but not listed by Peacham and therefore largely ignored by Vickers: literary allusion. As the writers of rhetorical guidebooks were more interested in ecumenical and oratorical speech than they were in the imaginative endeavour of poetic playwrighting, it should come as little surprise that they overlooked the common literary tactic of alluding to a source text. The various ways in which allusion can function cause it to be splintered, with different instances of recognizable intertextual connection being listed by Peacham among figures such as *metaphora*, *paradigma*, *noema*, *mimesis*, *epicrisis*, *hyperbole* and several others. If Peacham had considered a unified figure of *allusio*, we can safely assume, based on the plethora of highly formulaic examples, that its 'use' would have been something like: allusion praises or dispraises a figure by comparison, gives gravity to a situation and delights the audience by reminding them of a well-known work; the 'caution' would be: a poet should avoid allusions that lack apt comparisons, are merely ornamental or that an audience cannot apprehend. If we look at the allusive tendencies of Shakespeare and Peele, it quickly becomes clear that the former is illustrative of the use, the latter the caution.

That Shakespeare was a master of deploying allusion for meaningful dramatic purposes is obvious enough that a brief summary should suffice – from Talbot's grimly foreshadowing reference to Icarus in *1 Henry VI* all the way through to Prospero's complicated quotation of Ovid's Medea in *The Tempest*, Shakespeare's classical allusions always serve a deeper purpose than mere rhetorical ornamentation. Falstaff's transformation at the end of *The Merry Wives of Windsor* loses much of its moral complication if a reader fails to grasp the allusion to Actaeon, and knowledge of the same myth is necessary for understanding the full, and troublesome, depths of Orsino's passion in *Twelfth Night*. For Shakespeare, allusion does not serve as self-congratulatory proof of erudition, but as a serious way in which his plays take on deeper meanings via purposeful intersections with well-known source texts, particularly Ovid's *Metamorphoses*.[49]

---

[49] For two of the best accounts of Shakespeare's rich allusive engagement with Ovid, see Leonard Barkan, *The Gods Made Flesh* (New Haven, 1990), and Jonathan Bate, *Shakespeare and Ovid* (Oxford, 1993); for *Titus* in particular, see Eugene M. Waith, 'The Metamorphosis of Violence in *Titus Andronicus*', in *Shakespeare Survey 10* (Cambridge, 1957), pp. 26–35; Grace Starry West, 'Going by the Book: Classical Allusions in Shakespeare's *Titus Andronicus*', *Studies in Philology*, 79 (1982), 62–77; and Niall Rudd, '*Titus Andronicus*: The Classical Presence', in *Shakespeare Survey 55* (Cambridge, 2002), pp. 199–208.

For Peele, the opposite is usually the case: most of his plays are indeed full of mythological imagery, but very, very rarely does it serve any meaningfully allusive purpose. The clear majority of his classical references are atmospheric, drawing on the vocabulary of Hades to drive home the point that his tragedies are tragic. *The Battle of Alcazar*, for example, contains almost 40 explicit verbal allusions to classical myth, and fully 25 of them are to the scenery or inhabitants of classical hell – Pluto and Proserpina, Sisiphus and Tantalus, Phlegethon and Styx, etc. The lone classical allusion in this play that clearly refers to a specific narrative source (and thus at least has the potential to import a complex literary meaning into the text, rather than serve as mere atmospheric ornamentation), comes at the end of the first act, where the villainous Moor, in soliloquy, compares himself to 'Envy at Cecropes gate', a clear allusion to a story from the second book of Ovid's *Metamorphoses*.[50] The problem is that Ovid's story is in no way relatable to the character who invokes it – not through similarity, not through irony; it simply does not work. All that the Moor means is that he is envious, and he decides to beautify his pronouncement of that fact with a gratuitous flourish of his erudition.

While the Moor is entirely serious in this unsuccessful attempt at allusion, Peele elsewhere appears self-aware regarding the vacuity of his classicism, revelling in the meaninglessness of his references. In his clever travesty of courtly romances, *The Old Wives' Tale*, Peele gives us the grotesquely blustering knight Huanebango and his self-effacingly overblown allusivity: 'Now by Mars and Mercury, Jupiter and Janus, Sol and Saturnus, Venus and Vesta, Pallas and Proserpina' – and so forth.[51] The alliterative logic of this litany of divinity is clearly rhetorical, not meaningful. It matters not what a given god represents, but only that the name suits the aural effect the knight desires. While the parodic nature of this speech does show that Peele was cognizant of how terribly allusion could be misused, he nevertheless remained guilty of artless allusion throughout his career.

Unless, that is, he wrote *Titus Andronicus* 4.1. This scene is one where allusion surpasses ornamentation, surpasses even the meaningful contextuality that is the usual aim of a well-deployed allusion, and becomes the very vehicle of the play's action. The scene begins with Lavinia, Titus's daughter who has been raped and had her hands and tongue cut off, chasing her schoolboy nephew in a desperate attempt to communicate the full extent of her suffering. Words of her own devising have been denied her by her attackers, so she must make recourse to the words of another – Ovid. In a striking display of overt intertextuality, Lavinia plays the alluding author by drawing her audience's attention to a relevant passage in an outside text – specifically, the well-known story of Philomela from Book VI of the *Metamorphoses*. This conscious, deliberate evocation of the tale does what her ravaged appearance could not, and alerts her relatives to the full extent of her suffering. Her uncle Marcus had already guessed that she had been raped (and did so by creating his own elaborate poetic allusion to Philomela), but as his supposition was based on apparent similarity rather than any perceivable authorial connection, he saw no need to worry his brother with such a horrific, but unprovable, suspicion. It is allusion, not echo, that creates action.

The power of Ovid's text becomes even clearer later in the scene, as the presence of the book inspires Marcus to help Lavinia engage in direct, rather than allusive, communication. Marcus's thought that Lavinia use a stick to scratch her rapists' names in the sand seems obvious enough; why didn't anyone think of it before? Because, I would argue, no one had been reminded of the *Metamorphoses*, and the story of another rape victim, Io. The evocation of one story – Philomela's – makes it possible to apply lessons drawn from the larger, tacit context – the whole of Ovid's poem. One allusion leads to another, creating layer upon layer of metatextual interplay, all of it serving to

---

[50] George Peele, *The Battle of Alcazar* (London, 1594), B2v, line 8. I have modernized Peele's spellings here and in following quotations.

[51] George Peele, *The Old Wives' Tale* (London, 1595), B4v, lines 12–14.

advance and inform the play's overall structure of imitative revenge.

This complexity of allusive practice is far beyond anything Peele ever attempted in his own work, but it fits in perfectly with what we know of Shakespeare's intertextual tendencies. When Shakespeare brought Ovid's text – and indeed the Philomela myth itself – onto the stage in *Cymbeline*, was he remembering Peele's one idiosyncratic moment of allusive depth, or was he adding yet another layer of genius to his own dramatic engagement with his favourite poetic predecessor? The latter seems far more likely. This realization, considered alongside the unambiguous results of the *LION* collocation test – the only test to date designed specifically to provide accurate results for a specific scene – as well as the problematic nature of the evidence that led to a Peele attribution in the first place, lead to only one possible conclusion. *Titus Andronicus* 4.1 is Shakespeare's.

A SHAKESPEARE/NORTH COLLABORATION: *TITUS ANDRONICUS* AND *TITUS AND VESPASIAN*

DENNIS McCARTHY AND JUNE SCHLUETER

I

In what may have been the most significant literary event to occur at the dawn of English theatre, Jasper Heywood published translations of three tragedies by the Roman dramatist Lucius Annaeus Seneca: *Troades* (1559), *Thyestes* (1560) and *Hercules Furens* (1561). In his preface to *Thyestes*, Heywood exhorted the best young writers at the Inns of Court to try their hand at Senecan tragedy. His prefatory poem packages the challenge in a dream meeting with Seneca, in which he recommends several law students by name to the ancient tragedian. At the top of his list is Thomas North:

In Lincoln's Inn and Temples twain, Gray's Inn, and other m°, . . .
There shalt thou see the self-same *North*, whose work his wit displays,
And *Dial* doth *of Princes* paint, and preach abroad his praise.
There *Sackville's* sonnets sweetly sauced and featly finèd be;
There *Norton's* ditties do delight, there *Yelverton's* do flee . . .   (emphasis added)[1]

The effect was powerful and immediate. Surviving plays indicate that three of those students – Thomas Norton, Thomas Sackville and Christopher Yelverton[2] – responded by producing tragedies in the Senecan style. And, though his play has not survived, we believe North did as well. It was North's play, we will argue, that, thirty years later, Shakespeare adapted, either on his own or, as Sir Brian Vickers has proposed, in collaboration with George Peele.[3] North's play was *Titus*

and Vespasian, revived by the Lord Strange's Men in 1592; Shakespeare's (or Shakespeare and Peele's) was *Titus Andronicus*, performed by the Pembroke's Men and printed in 1594.

At the time of Jasper's challenge, North was already well-acquainted with Seneca as a philosopher of stoicism: his translation of *The Dial of Princes* (1557) references Seneca's teachings a number of times. But now Heywood's translations of Seneca's plays were a reminder that the ancient Roman was also a dramatist whose work served to instruct the Roman upper class. It did not take much for the ambitious young *literati* at London's law courts to realize that playwriting could provide a means to offer advice and advertise their wisdom to the wealthy and powerful. As Jessica Winston observes, in the 1560s there was 'intense interest' in Seneca at the Inns of Court, where ambitious young men preparing for political careers translated his work and wrote Senecan-style plays to reflect and influence political events. Many

---

[1] Jasper Heywood, Preface to *The Seconde Tragedie of Seneca entituled Thyestes faithfully Englished by Jasper Heywood fellowe of Alsolne College in Oxforde* (London, 1560). Citation, given parenthetically in modern spelling, follows *Elizabethan Seneca: Three Tragedies*. MHRA Tudor and Stuart Translations, vol. 8, ed. James Ker and Jessica Winston (London, 2012), pp. 142–3.

[2] In 1566, Christopher Yelverton helped pen the Senecan tragedy *Jocasta* for Gray's Inn. See *The Cambridge History of English and American Literature in 18 Volumes*, ed. W. W. Ward, et al., 5: *The Drama to 1642, Part One* (New York, 1910), 4: *Early English Tragedy*, 10: *Jocasta*.

[3] Brian Vickers, *Shakespeare, Co-Author: A Historical Study of Five Collaborative Plays* (Oxford, 2002), pp. 148–243.

of the students 'saw Senecan tragedy as a classical version of advice-to-princes poetry', Winston
wrote, adding that '[o]ther works of counsel literature by men associated with the law schools in
this period include Thomas North's *The Dial of
Princes*'.[4]

Norton and Sackville were apparently the first
to respond to Heywood's challenge, penning, in
1561, the first known five-act blank verse English
tragedy, a politically-oriented Senecan play entitled *Gorboduc* (or, as it was originally known, *Ferrex and Porrex*).[5] Students of the Inner Temple performed the work in December 1561 for Elizabeth's
advisors, including Robert Dudley, then twenty-
nine (one year older than the new queen). The
handsome and charming Dudley, the future Earl of
Leicester, had quickly become the trusted confi-
dante and presumed lover of Elizabeth, and, since
1559, aristocrats on both sides of the Channel had
quietly speculated he would soon be king. These
whispers must have intensified when Dudley's wife
died under mysterious circumstances in September 1560. Amy Dudley (*née* Robsart) was found
in their home at the bottom of a flight of stairs
with a broken neck and two small wounds in her
head. Dudley had been at court at the time of her
death, and the coroner ruled the incident 'death
by misadventure'.[6] But a contemporaneous letter
from the Spanish Ambassador, Alvaro de la Quadra,
claimed that Elizabeth's chief counsellor, William
Cecil, had informed him that Elizabeth and Dudley had plotted her murder.[7] Regardless of how
Amy died, speculation among those in the know
was that Dudley had the greatest chance of anyone to become the next King of England and so
was the most important person to impress with
a play. The young student authors of the Inns of
Court, including North, certainly understood this.
They also knew that Dudley was not the only
serious and persistent suitor of Elizabeth at that
time.

Repeatedly, from 1559 to 1562, Eric XIV, King
of Sweden, Gothland and the Vandals, had sent
ambassadors to woo the queen; at one point, in
the autumn of 1561, he had even planned to come
to England himself. Although weather interrupted

his journey, some of Eric's ships arrived, bringing
twenty pied horses and thousands of pounds worth
of gold bullion.[8] We know from records of the
time that Dudley was concerned about these pro-
posals and considered the Goth king a worrisome
rival.[9]

It is thus not surprising that both *Gorboduc* and a
masque that accompanied the play on that December night in 1561 dealt with the marriage question.
The masque specifically warned the young queen
about the dangers of not producing an heir, suggested Dudley as a suitable choice for king, and
urged her not to marry a foreign ruler, especially
not Eric XIV.[10] The play itself was as forthright
as the masque in addressing the dangers of taking
a foreign ruler as a spouse, especially the King of
Sweden and the Goths, and in suggesting instead
someone from the home soil, someone like Dudley.
A speech in act five of *Gorboduc* encourages 'your
chosen kynge' to be 'borne within your Natyve
Lande', to avoid the 'heavie yoke of foreine gov-
ernaunce', to 'withstande the proude invadynge
foe', shun the 'Unnatural thraldome of straungers
reigne', and refuse to let 'Your Mother Lande to

---

[4] Jessica Winston, 'Seneca in Early Elizabethan England',
Renaissance Quarterly, 59:1 (2006), 29–58, pp. 30, 41.

[5] Thomas Norton, *The Tragedie of Gorbodvc, whereof three Actes
were wrytten by Thomas Nortone, and the two laste by Thomas
Sackvyle. Sett forthe as the same was shewed before the Qvenes most
excellent Maiestie, in her highnes Court of Whitehall, the .xviii.
day of January, Anno Domini. 1561. By the Gentlemen of Thynner
Temple in London*. Imprynted at London in Fletestrete, at the
Signe of the Faucon by William Griffith: And are to be sold
at his Shop in Saincte Dunstones Churchyarde in the West
of London. Anno. 1565. Septemb. 22.

[6] Simon Adams, 'Dudley, Robert, Earl of Leicester (1532/3–
1588)', *Oxford Dictionary of National Biography* (Oxford,
2004); online edn, May 2008, www.oxforddnb.com.gate.lib.
buffalo.edu/view/article/8160, accessed 23 December 2010.

[7] Adams, 'Dudley, Robert'.

[8] Norman Jones and Paul Whitfield White, '*Gorboduc* and
Royal Marriage Politics: An Elizabethan Playgoer's Report
of the Premiere Performance', *English Literary Renaissance*,
261 (1996), 3–17, p. 9.

[9] Jones and White, '*Gorboduc* and Royal Marriage Politics',
pp. 7–10.

[10] James Emmanuel Berg, '*Gorboduc* as a Tragic Discovery
of "Feudalism"', *Studies in English Literature, 1500–1900*, 40
(2000), 199–226, p. 200.

serve a foreine Prince'. An eyewitness account (one of the few from this era) testifies to the play's agenda: 'Many things were handled of mariage'; 'yt was better for the Quene to marye the L. R. knowen than wyth the K. of Sweden'.[11] By 'L. R.', the writer meant the 'Lord Robert' (Dudley).

This clever counsel obviously pleased the would-be king, who immediately encouraged Elizabeth to have the play performed at court. Three weeks later, the Inner Temple students brought *Gorboduc* to Whitehall Palace. Evidently, the success of Norton and Sackville's play, combined with Heywood's naming of him in his preface to *Thyestes*, was too much for North to resist, and, following the lead of Heywood and Norton and Sackville, he soon started work on his own Senecan tragedy. The result, we contend, was *Titus and Vespasian*, a lurid, bloody, overwrought drama that recalled elements of both *Gorboduc* and *Thyestes* and imported legends and language from North's own translation of *The Dial of Princes*. We have no eyewitness account of *Titus and Vespasian*. Nor do we have North's play. But we do have *Titus Andronicus*, which, we contend, contains substantial traces of it.

That *Titus Andronicus* is reminiscent of 1560s Senecan-style plays is indisputable. J. Dover Wilson famously describes the play as a 'broken-down cart, laden with bleeding corpses from an Elizabethan scaffold'; G. B. Harrison writes that it 'is little more than an experiment in horror'; and Jack E. Reese dismisses the work as 'an immature exercise in sensationalism'. Tellingly, T. M. Parrott notes how antiquated the play seems for the 1590s: 'On the face of it *Titus* is a melodrama of the pre-Shakespearean school', and Geoffrey Bullough agrees: 'Certainly *Titus* was old-fashioned in themes and style for 1594.'[12]

Could such a play be explained by the young dramatist's inexperience? In his New Cambridge Shakespeare edition of the play, Alan Hughes identifies passages that 'feel like the work of a young poet'; and Peter Alexander tries to excuse the play's excesses by calling Shakespeare 'a beginner at the beginning of English tragedy'.[13] But Alexander's comment, though an accurate depiction of North

at the Inns of Court, hardly fits Shakespeare, who began writing around 1589–90, when such dramas had nearly a thirty-year tradition. Indeed, according to some conventional chronologies, Shakespeare wrote *Titus Andronicus* after the *Henry VI* plays, even after *Richard III*. Of course, if our argument holds, it was North, not Shakespeare, who, at the age of twenty-six or twenty-seven, was the 'beginner at the beginning of English tragedy', and it was North's Senecan-style tragedy that *Titus Andronicus* reprises.

II

Scholars have long recognized the similarities between Seneca's *Thyestes* and *Titus Andronicus*. The horrific ending of the Shakespeare play, in which Titus exacts his revenge by feeding Queen Tamora her wicked sons baked in a meat pie, at a supposed banquet of reconciliation, recalls the climax of *Thyestes*, in which Atreus cooks up a similar stew, feeding Thyestes his sons at a banquet. Both works even focus on the elaborate preparations for the feast. In his source study of *Titus Andronicus*, Bullough shows that Titus's appeal to Pluto for revenge (4.3) and the disturbing and creepy woods that are the setting for the foulest deeds also come from *Thyestes*,[14] the very work that Heywood used

---

[11] See Jones and White, '*Gorboduc* and Royal Marriage Politics', p. 4. According to this spectator, the actions in the second dumb show, which is not specifically described in the surviving texts of *Gorboduc*, were particularly clear about its message, urging the queen to marry Dudley and not the King of Sweden.

[12] J. Dover Wilson, ed., *Titus Andronicus* (Cambridge, 1948), p. xii; G. B. Harrison, *Shakespeare's Tragedies* ([1952], New York, 1969), p. 45; Jack E. Reese, 'The Formalization of Horror in *Titus Andronicus*', *Shakespeare Quarterly*, 21 (1970), 77–84, p. 78; T. M. Parrott, 'Shakespeare's Revision of *Titus Andronicus*', *Modern Language Review*, 14 (1919), 16–37, p. 23; Geoffrey Bullough, ed., *Narrative and Dramatic Sources of Shakespeare*, vol. 6 (New York, 1966), p. 4.

[13] Alan Hughes, ed., *Titus Andronicus*, New Cambridge Shakespeare (Cambridge, 1994), p. 6; Peter Alexander, *Shakespeare's Life and Art* (London, 1939), p. 77.

[14] Bullough, ed., *Sources*, vol. 6, p. 26.

to challenge the Inns of Court students to write Senecan plays.

Titus Andronicus also shares features with *Gorboduc*: both are pseudo-historical, five-act revenge dramas featuring political intrigue, soliloquies, classical allusions, allegorical characters, dumb shows and gruesome finales. The eponymous character of *Titus Andronicus*, like Gorboduc, is an elder patriarch who feels too old to rule his nation. The queen in each play is a passionate woman who turns vengeful, cruel and murderous after her sons are threatened. Each tragedy focuses on the fall of a once proud noble family, showing the near total destruction of an ancient family line, and each includes the repeated themes of rebellion and civil war and the fatalistic concept of an inescapable curse. In one searching analysis, James D. Carroll found so many similarities between *Gorboduc* and *Titus Andronicus* that he suggested Shakespeare likely had the 'text by his side' as he wrote the play.[15]

More likely, Shakespeare had *Titus and Vespasian* by his side and the features *Titus Andronicus* shares with *Thyestes* (1560) and *Gorboduc* (1561) were all part of the play penned at the Inns of Court in response to Heywood's translation and Norton and Sackville's tragedy. This would explain why *Titus Andronicus* feels like an old-fashioned throwback to the bloody, rhetorically-inflated Senecan tragedies of the 1560s and why it appears to involve 1560s court politics. *Gorboduc* had emphasized the point that foreigners were naturally hostile to England and that marrying one would be like yielding to an invasion, allowing the foe to destroy the country from within. As noted by Norman Jones and Paul Whitfield White, *Gorboduc* preaches that a 'marriage to Eric XIV would result in the "Unnatural thraldome of straungers reigne"'.[16] And to this end, it would seem that North's play exceeded *Gorboduc*. Indeed, judging from treatments of the Titus story in other early modern works and, especially, in *Titus Andronicus*, it may not be an exaggeration to state that no work in the English language has ever detailed more horrific consequences resulting from a marriage to a foreign ruler. Once the Emperor of Rome took Tamora as his wife, she set

in motion a course of action that occasioned catastrophic events, including the rape and mutilation of Titus's daughter, the murder of the Emperor's brother, the butchery of Titus's sons, the rise of a rebel army, and the eventual horrific ending in which Titus, Lavinia, Tamora and the Emperor all end up dead.

Gorboduc's court audience would not have overlooked the fact that the evil queen was a Goth and that her wicked sons were Goth princes. While in modern historical texts Eric XIV is often referred to as King of Sweden, Eric was also king of the southern end of the peninsula, known then as Gothland, so named because it was supposed to be the ancestral home of the Goths. In official documentation, Eric XIV was known as *Sveriges, Götes och Vendes Konung*, or 'King of the Swedes, Goths and Wends', as were all Swedish Kings until 1973.[17] Even more significantly, while the appeals of Eric XIV to England may have been charming, he was a particularly aggressive and militaristic king bent on growing his empire. German scholar Johannes Burkhardt noted that such Nordic expansionism of the era fit neatly into the 'Swedish cult of the Goths' and that warlike Swedish kings enjoyed emphasizing their 'descendence from the Gothic heirs of the Roman Empire'.[18] In other words, we believe *Titus and Vespasian* was both a warning about marrying a foreign ruler and a calculated fictional treatment that amplified the savagery of Goths in general and the Swedish king's ancestors in particular.

Denunciations still resonate in Shakespeare's adaptation of the play. The Goths are 'barbarous' (1.1.28) in the first act, 'warlike' (2.1.61) and 'Lascivious' (2.3.110) in the second, and 'traitorous'

---

[15] James D. Carroll, '*Gorboduc* and *Titus Andronicus*', *Notes and Queries*, 51.3 (2004), 267–9, p. 267.

[16] Jones and White, '*Gorboduc* and Royal Marriage Politics', p. 10.

[17] Axel Johan Guinchard and Sydney Charleston, *Sweden: Historical and Statistical Handbook*, 2nd edn (Stockholm, 1914), p. 188.

[18] Johannes Burkhardt, 'The Thirty Years' War', in *A Companion to the Reformation World*, ed. R. Po-chia Hsia (Oxford, 2004), p. 279.

(4.1.93) in the fourth.[19] The cunning, barbaric, and flattering Tamora was a substitute for the war-like Eric XIV who had sent such showy displays of affection to England. And when Marcus Andronicus asks warily, 'How comes it that the subtile Queen of Goths / Is of a sudden thus advanc'd in Rome?' (1.1.392–3), the play's original audience would have recognized the not-so-subtle allusion to Eric's ambitions.

The tragedy would have played into Dudley's growing resentment of the Swedes in 1562. In January, a few weeks after the *Gorboduc* performance, Dudley and his faction snubbed the Swedish Ambassador by not attending his dinner party. A few months later, Dudley threatened an *attaché* to the Swedish embassy with imprisonment unless he revealed the purpose of his recent negotiations with the queen.[20] Thus, as the possible royal marriage of Elizabeth to a Goth king continued to alarm certain members of the English court, especially Robert Dudley, North, having studied the examples of *Thyestes* and *Gorboduc*, proceeded to write his viciously anti-Goth play. And we believe 1562 is the precise year not just because of the proximity and topicality of Norton and Sackville's play but also because the possibility of marriage to Erik XIV had become more remote by the end of that year.

III

Thomas North's *The Dial of Princes*,[21] the earliest of his three surviving translations, provides compelling support for our proposal that North was the author of the lost *Titus and Vespasian*. We know, of course, that Shakespeare's other Roman plays include storylines, characters and passages from North's translations, especially *Plutarch's Lives* (1579).[22] As George Wyndham observes in his introduction to that text:

Shakespeare . . . borrowed three plays almost wholly from North. . . . in *Antony and Cleopatra*, as in *Coriolanus* and in *Julius Caesar*, Shakespeare's obligation is apparent in almost all he has written. To measure it you must quote the bulk of the three plays. . . . Shakespeare, that

is, not only copies North's picture, he also uses North's palette.[23]

Moreover, we know that Shakespeare often used old sources, as, for example, with *King John, King Lear, Hamlet, 1 Henry IV, 2 Henry IV, Henry V, The Merchant of Venice, Julius Caesar, The Two Gentlemen of Verona* and *The Two Noble Kinsmen*. As Giorgio Melchiori wrote in his New Cambridge edition of *2 Henry IV*, 'Shakespeare was an expert at remakes of old plays for the Chamberlain's/King's

---

[19] Citations from *Titus Andronicus*, given parenthetically, follow *The Riverside Shakespeare*, 2nd edn, ed. G. Blakemore Evans with the assistance of J. J. M. Tobin (Boston and New York, 1997), pp. 1069–96.

[20] Jones and White, '*Gorboduc* and Royal Marriage Politics', p. 10.

[21] Antonio de Guevara, *The Diall of Princes. Compiled by the reverende father in God, Don Anthony of Gueuara, Bysshop of Guadix. Preacher and Chronicler, to Charles the fyft Emperoar of Rome. Englysshed oute of the Frenche, by Thomas North, seconde sonne of the Lorde North. Ryght necessary and pleasaunt, to all gentylmen and others whiche are louers of virtue. Anno. 1557.* Imprinted at London by John Waylande. Citations, given parenthetically in modern spelling, follow the 1619 edition, which is fully searchable in EEBO; Antonio de Guevara, *Archontorologion, or The Diall of Princes: Containing The Golden and Famovs Booke of Marcvs Avrelivs, Sometime Emperour of Rome. Declaring What Excellency consisteth in a Prince that is a good Christian: And what euils attend on him that is a cruell Tirant.* Written By the Reuerend Father in God, Don Antonio of Gueuera, Lord Bishop of Guadix; Preacher and Chronicler to the late mighty Emperour Charles the fift. First translated out of French by Thomas North, Sonne to Sir Edward North, Lord North of Kirthling: And lately reperused, and corrected from many gross imperfections. With addition of a Fourth Booke, stiled by the Name of The fauoured Courtier. London, Imprinted by Bernard Alsop, dwelling by Saint Annes Church neere Aldersgate, 1619.

[22] Plutarch, *The Lives of the Noble Grecians and Romanes, Compared together by that graue learned Philosopher and Historiographer, Plutarke of Chæronea:* Translated out of Greeke into French by Iames Amyot, Abbot of Bellozane, Bishop of Auxerre, one of the Kings priuy counsel, and great Amner of Fraunce, and out of French into Englishe, by Thomas North. Imprinted at London by Thomas Vautroullier dwelling in the Blacke Friers by Ludgate, 1579.

[23] George Wyndham, introduction to *Plutarch's Lives of the Noble Grecians and Romans*, Englished by Sir Thomas North (London, 1895), pp. lxxxviii, xc.

Men.'[24] In the case of some of these, *King John* and *King Lear*, for example, the presumed source play is extant, enabling us to see that Shakespeare's borrowings were hardly incidental. Regarding *King John*, Scott McMillin and Sally-Beth MacLean, in *The Queen's Men and Their Plays*, wrote that Shakespeare's play 'resembles *The Troublesome Reigne* virtually scene for scene'.[25]

Despite such knowledge, and despite Shakespeare's debt to North's translation of *Plutarch's Lives*, scholars have not explored *The Dial of Princes* in relation to any of Shakespeare's plays. Interested in determining the extent of any possible relationship between *The Dial* and *Titus Andronicus*, we followed the lead of recent authorship studies and searched the two texts with WCopyfind,[26] then combined that search with a cross-referencing of the online database Early English Books Online (EEBO). The result was an astonishing inventory of shared legends, plot elements, descriptions and phrases, many rare or exclusive to these two texts.

The tale of Lavinia provides an example. Scholars have long recognized that the story of Titus's daughter, whose husband is murdered and who herself is raped and mutilated, derives from the story of Philomel in Book VI of Ovid's *Metamorphoses*. But it is now clear that North's *Dial*, which provided Lavinia's name, also played a role. In that text, the beautiful and virtuous Lavinia is the symbol of agonizing widowhood, a woman who is emotionally destroyed by the battlefield death of her husband, Claudinus (486–9). The emperor, Marcus Aurelius, wrote letters intended to soothe her, warning of the self-destructive depression that was typical of Roman widows: 'Ladie *Lavinia*, most earnestly I desire thee, so vehemently not to pierce the heavens with thy so heavie sighes, nor yet to wette the earth with thy so bitter teares' (488). The passage resonates in the lament in *Titus Andronicus* concerning Lavinia's plight:

When heaven doth weep, doth not the earth o'erflow? . . .
I am the sea; hark how her sighs doth [blow]!
She is the weeping welkin, I the earth:
Then must my sea be moved with her sighs,

Then must my earth with her continual tears
Become a deluge, overflow'd and drown'd . . .

(3.1.221, 225–9)

Shakespeare's tragedy also relates an episode in which Titus, in the depth of misery, shoots his arrows at heaven (4.3). He puts messages on the arrows, imploring the gods to exact vengeance against the Emperor and the Goths. When he and his fellow Andronici shoot the messages heavenward, the arrows fall upon the Goths instead. North's *Dial* recounts a similar episode in which Brennus, a Goth Captain, justifies his desire to rob from the temples by arguing 'that Gods should give unto men, & not men unto Gods, . . . But as they began to rob the Temple, there fell a multitude of arrows from heaven, that the Captain *Brennus* died there, and all his men with him, not one left alive' (63). In *Titus Andronicus*, the arrows falling from heaven signal the upcoming demise of the wicked Goths just as they do in the story of the Goth Captain.

Resemblances, though, proved most explicit and dramatic in the accumulation of rare or exclusive phrases common to *The Dial* and *Titus Andronicus*. Take, for example, the scene in which Lavinia accuses Tamora's sons of being raised from the teats and milk of a tiger. This startling image was often repeated by writers who followed Shakespeare, but much of the wording in *Titus Andronicus* clearly derives from *The Dial*. Indeed, the exchange between Tamora and Lavinia in *Titus Andronicus* (2.3.138–52, 173–5) shares not only the nursing-tiger image with *The Dial* but also four different sets of word-groupings and verbal echoes that are either rare or exclusive: (1) *Dam, milk, teat* and *mother* (unique to *The Dial* and *Titus Andronicus*); (2) *tiger's, milk* and *sucked* (occurs in only one other

---

24 Giorgio Melchiori, ed., *The Second Part of King Henry IV*, updated edn, New Cambridge Shakespeare (Cambridge, 2007), p. 10.
25 Scott McMillin and Sally-Beth MacLean, *The Queen's Men and Their Plays* (Cambridge, 1999), p. 161.
26 WCopyfind is distributed by Lou Bloomfield of the University of Virginia. See http://plagiarism.bloomfieldmedia.com/z-wordpress/software/wcopyfind/.

sixteenth-century work); (3) *moved with pity* and *endure* (occurs in only one other work, from the late seventeenth century); and (4) *my tongue to tell* in the context of a speaker trying to keep *from lust* (unique to *The Dial* and *Titus Andronicus*).

The *dam-milk-teat-mother* passage in *The Dial* also includes the term *youngling*: 'it knoweth the dam which brought it forth which is apparent for so much as if the mother have milk, the *youngling* forthwith doth seek her teats' (470). The word also appears twice in *Titus Andronicus* but in only one other place in the Shakespeare canon. The nursing-tiger passage in *The Dial* also includes the phrase *nourished . . . and brought up*: 'Pyrrhus was born in Greece, *nourished* in Arcadia, *and brought up* with Tiger's milk . . . for to have sucked Tiger's milk, he was very proud and cruel' (258). The same phrase also appears in another section of *The Dial*, in which we find advice on how noblemen ought '*to nourish and bring . . . up*' their children (174); in *Titus Andronicus*, Aaron asks that the Roman soldiers 'save my boy, *to nourish and bring* him up' (5.1.84).

Among other links are:

(1) *God forbid* (that) *I should be so bold to*. A search of EEBO for all works that place *God forbid* NEAR *I should be so bold to* yields no results other than North and Shakespeare. *The Dial* – '*God forbid* that *I should be so bold to* say, they have been so long time in Spain without days of learning, as they were in Rome . . .' (543); *Titus Andronicus* – '*God forbid I should be so bold to* press to heaven in my young days' (4.3.91).

(2) *youth can better* (handle suffering) *than* an elder person. In EEBO, only one other work uses the phrase *youth can better*, and it is a late seventeenth-century work in which the context is not the same. Only *The Dial* and *Titus Andronicus* refer to the fact that someone's *youth can better* recover from or deal with an uncomfortable situation *than* an older person. *The Dial* – '[The] new come Courtier, whose *youth can better* away with an ill night's lodging *than* the gray hairs of the old Courtier' (596); *Titus*

Andronicus – 'My *youth can better* spare my blood *than* you' (3.1.165).

(3) *eyes are* (fed/cloyed) *with view of*. An EEBO search for *eyes are* NEAR *with view of* gives no other results. In fact, it results only in *The Dial* because Shakespeare's line mistakenly has the word *are* dropped from the printing. *The Dial* – 'his *eyes are* fed *with view of* faire dames of Court' (592); *Titus Andronicus* – 'Mine *eyes* [*are*] cloy'd *with view of* tyranny' (3.2.55).

(4) *teares shed on the Earth*. As EEBO confirms, the phrase *shed on the Earth* was uncommon, appearing only ten other times in the entire database. But nine of those works refer to *blood* being *shed on the Earth*, and the tenth to *water*. It is only *The Dial* and *Titus Andronicus* that refer to *tears* being *shed on the Earth*. *The Dial* – 'and the obedience of their people: but with many *Tears shed on the earth*' (549); *Titus Andronicus* – 'And at thy feet I kneel, with *tears* of joy / *Shed on this* [*the*] *earth* for thy return to Rome' (1.1.161–2).

(5) *I have been troubled in my* (sleep/mind). A search of EEBO for all works that include the phrase *I have been troubled in my* yields only two results: *The Dial* – 'For in these three days that *I have been troubled in my* mind' (543); *Titus Andronicus* – '*I have been troubled in my* sleep this night, / But dawning day new comfort hath inspir'd' (2.2.9).

(6) the juxtaposition of *tremble/trembling* with *my joints* and *my heart* (originally spelled *hart*). A search of EEBO for *joint* NEAR *my hart* NEAR *tremble* (and all variant forms) gives only one result other than North and Shakespeare. The same search using *heart* gives six results, one of which is Shakespeare's First Folio, in which editors evidently changed the spelling from that in the quarto. *The Dial* – '*my joints* shiver, *my heart trembles*, and my flesh consumeth' (371); *Titus Andronicus* – 'A chilling sweat o'erruns *my trembling joints*, / *My heart* suspects more than mine eye can see' (2.3.212–13).

(7) the juxtaposition of *a goodly gift* with *husband* and used in the same context. EEBO confirms that *a goodly gift* appears 18 times in 15 records,

but North and Shakespeare account for five of these. And it is only with North and Shakespeare that the context is the same: in reference to a married woman caught outside the home, alone, and so suspected of cheating and injuring the reputation of her husband. A search for *a goodly gift* within 99 words of *husband* yields only *The Dial* and *Titus Andronicus*. *The Dial* – 'Whether the *husband* be present or absent, it is a most necessary and honest thing that the wife be for the most part in the house: for by this means the household shall be well governed, and from the heart of the *husband* shall be withdrawn all kind of suspicions . . . Oh, God giveth *a goodly gift* and grace to that man which hath such & so good a wife that of her own nature loveth to keep herself within the house' (198); *Titus Andronicus* – 'Lavinia: Under your patience, gentle Emperess, / 'Tis thought you have *a goodly gift* in horning, / And to be doubted that your Moor and you / Are singled forth to try thy experiments. / Jove shield your *husband* from his hounds to-day! 'Tis pity they should take him for a stag' (2.3.66–71).

(8) the juxtaposition of *between two friends* and *enemy/enmity*. A search of EEBO for *between two friends* NEAR either *enemy* or *enmity* yields only two results other than North and Shakespeare. *The Dial* – 'to judge *between two Friends*, the one is made an enemy' (61); *Titus Andronicus* – 'Set deadly *enmity between two friends*' (5.1.131).

Nearly all the links between *The Dial* and *Titus Andronicus* that WCopyfind uncovered are exclusive or nearly exclusive, appearing in no other work. In a database of 128,000 texts, this cannot be coincidence.

We also tested our 1562 date for the composition of *Titus and Vespasian*, comparing *Titus Andronicus* to North's other two translations, *The Moral Philosophy of Doni* (1570)[27] and *Plutarch's Lives* (1579). We expected that these two later works would not contain the unique, context-related verbal fingerprints we had found in *The Dial*, written during North's years at the Inns of Court. The analysis proved

us right, but with one exception. And though that exception added more evidence that North was involved in writing the source play for *Titus Andronicus*, it challenged our 1562 date. The passage is from the last act of *Titus Andronicus*, where a Goth notes that Aaron can recite his evils 'and never blush'. Aaron responds, 'Ay, like a black dog' (5.1.121–2). This same expression, *blushing like a black dog*, also appears in North's *The Moral Philosophy of Doni*, where the temerity of another evil black character, the Raven, is described (204). An EEBO search of all works printed at any time that include *blush* within 20 words of *like a black* dog yields only six other results, four of which are from seventeenth-century post-Folio books on proverbs or rhetoric. So North, Shakespeare and one other sixteenth-century work use the expression.

The finding sent us back to our claim that *Titus and Vespasian* was penned eight years before the publication of *Doni*. But when we examined the issue more closely, we found that the expression does not appear in Anton Francesco Doni's Italian original but is an embellishment by North. Here is the corresponding line:

DONI'S LINE: 'Il ser Corbo, con una fronte altiera rispose galantemente . . .'

---

[27] Anton Francesco Doni, *The Morall philosophie of Doni: drawne out of the auncient writers. A worke first compiled in the Indian tongue, and afterwardes reduced into divers other languages: and now lastly englished out of Italian by Thomas North, Brother to the right Honorable Sir Roger North Knight, Lorde North of Kyrtheling* (London, 1570). Citations, given parenthetically in modern English, follow *The Moral Philosophy of Doni popularly known as the Fables of Bidpai*, ed. Donald Beecher, John Butler and Carmine Di Biase (Ottawa, 2003). North dedicated *Doni* to Leicester. See Tom Lockwood, 'North, Sir Thomas (1535–1603?)', *Oxford Dictionary of National Biography* (Oxford, 2004); online edn, January 2008 www.oxforddnb.com.gate. lib.buffalo.edu/view/article/20315, accessed 7 December 2012. Also, Beecher *et al.* identify North as part of Leicester's writing circle in the 1560s and 1570s (199–202). At one point, Leicester wrote to Lord Burghley on behalf of a penniless Sir Thomas (whose father's estate went to his elder son), describing him as 'a very honest gentleman & hath many good things in him wch are around only by pov^er tie' (see Lockwood).

ENGLISH TRANSLATION: 'Sir Raven, with a haughty
face, gallantly replies . . .'
NORTH'S EMBELLISHED TRANSLATION: 'Master
Raven, blushing like a black dog, set a good face on
the matter and boldly answered him.' (68v)

Evidently, it was North, not Doni, who used this
rare expression for shameless, dark-complexioned
characters. Since it was not Doni's *Filosofia Morale*
that motivated the phrase, then, our 1562 date
could stand.

Events at the Inns of Court in the early 1560s,
then, and WCopyfind's discovery of the dozens of
rare or exclusive word-groupings and phrases *Titus
Andronicus* shares with *The Dial of Princes* are at the
heart of our argument that *Titus and Vespasian* dates
from 1562, that North wrote *Titus and Vespasian*
and that this Senecan-style play served as the source
play for *Titus Andronicus*.

IV

But Shakespeare's *Titus Andronicus* is not the only
surviving telling of the Titus story. For more than a
century, scholars have argued over the relationship
between and among Shakespeare's play and two
other Titus-related works from the era:

(1) a ballad, *Titus Andronicus' Complaint*, a 30-
stanza poem in rhymed-couplet quatrains,
entered in the Stationers' Register in 1594,
extant in a manuscript dated *c*.1602, and published in Richard Johnson's *The Golden Garland
of Princely pleasures and delicate Delights* in 1620,
and

(2) a prose history, *The History of Titus Andronicus, The Renowned Roman General*, believed
to be a late Elizabethan work, published
(with the ballad) in an eighteenth-century
chapbook.[28]

As Richard Levin pointed out in 2000, the
chronology of these works had been the subject
of 'a spirited debate' lasting 'many years'.[29] Participants in the dispute included Eugene Waith and
G. Harold Metz, who argued that the prose his-

tory was the source for Shakespeare's work,[30] and
Marco Mincoff, G. K. Hunter, MacDonald P. Jackson and Brian Boyd, who contended that the prose
history came after the ballad, which followed the
play.[31] We expanded this analysis by adding *Eine
sehr klägliche Tragaedia von Tito Andronico und der
hoffertigen Kayserin* (*A Very Lamentable Tragedy of
Titus Andronicus and the Haughty Empress*), a drama
brought to the Continent by English actors, translated into German prose, and printed in a collection in Leipzig in 1620.[32] Using WCopyfind, we
learned that, in a number of instances where one
of these texts differs from another, it agrees with
yet another.

For example, neither the ballad nor *Titus
Andronicus* mentions the Roman General's

---

28 Citations from the ballad and the prose history, given parenthetically, follow Bullough, ed., *Sources*, vol. 6, pp. 35–48.
29 Richard Levin, '*Titus Andronicus* and "The Ballad Thereof"',
   Notes and Queries, n.s. 47:1 (2000), 63–8, p. 63.
30 Eugene M. Waith, ed., *Titus Andronicus*, Oxford Shakespeare
   (Oxford, 1984), pp. 28–31; G. Harold Metz, 'The History of
   Titus Andronicus and Shakespeare's Play', *Notes and Queries*,
   n.s. 22:4 (1975), 163–6, and 'Titus Andronicus: Three Ver-
   sions of the Story', *Notes and Queries*, n.s. 35:4 (1988), 451–5.
31 M. Mincoff, 'The Source of *Titus Andronicus*', *Notes and
   Queries*, n s 18·4 (1971), 131–4; G. K. Hunter, 'The
   "Sources" of *Titus Andronicus* – Once Again', *Notes and
   Queries*, n.s. 30:2 (1983), 114–16; MacD. P. Jackson, '*Titus
   Andronicus*: Play, Ballad, and Prose History', *Notes and
   Queries*, n.s. 36:3 (1989), 315–17; Brian Boyd, 'The Black-
   amoor Babe: *Titus Andronicus*, Play, Ballad, and History',
   Notes and Queries, n.s. 44:4 (1997), 492–4.
32 Albert Cohn, *Shakespeare in Germany in the Sixteenth and
   Seventeenth Centuries: An Account of English Actors in Germany and the Netherlands and of the Plays Performed by Them
   during the Same Period* ([1865] New York, 1971), pp. 156–
   235. Citations from the German play, given parenthetically, follow this edition. For a modern reprint of the collection, see *Spieltexte der Wanderbühne*, ed. Manfred Brau-
   neck, 4 vols. (Berlin, 1970), vol. 1, *Engelische Comedien und
   Tragedien*, pp. 461–522. The German play has attracted less
   attention, though in 1999 June Schlueter noted the similarity between the Peacham drawing, thought to be of a
   scene or scenes from *Titus Andronicus*, and the German play,
   reviving the idea that Shakespeare's play might derive from
   the lost *Titus and Vespasian*. See June Schlueter, 'Rereading the Peacham Drawing', *Shakespeare Quarterly*, 50 (1999),
   171–84.

battlefield heroics. Yet both the prose history and the German play not only detail his wartime exploits, they also recount the same events, in the same order. In the prose history, the action occurs in two different but consecutively described battles in which Titus fights Totillius, King of the Goths. The German play conflates the events of the prose history's battles, and the fight is between Titus and Morian (Shakespeare's Aaron), who describes the combat in a monologue, but the action is the same. Both works describe Titus as (1) causing confusion or disorder in the rebel army, (2) charging the leader of the army, (3) throwing him off his horse, (4) wounding him greatly, (5) killing many other men in the process, (6) confiscating the wealth of the camp, (7) then taking all of it and the queen to Rome – in that sequence.

The fact that the prose history and the German play share elements not found in *Titus Andronicus* refutes the view that the Titus story in the German play and the prose history comes exclusively from the Shakespeare play. Hence if we were to neglect the possibility that these works were derived from the same source play, we would have to suppose either (1) that the author of the German play was not only familiar with *Titus Andronicus* but also had access to the prose history and then borrowed elements from both or (2) that the prose history author was the borrower and had access not only to *Titus Andronicus* but also to the German play.

But such explanations remain incomplete because the ballad and the German play share still other elements that are absent from both *Titus Andronicus* and the prose history. In scene 4.1 of *Titus Andronicus*, for example, Marcus Andronicus gives a staff to Lavinia so she can write the names of her attackers on the ground. The prose history also describes Lavinia's 'taking a Wand between her Stumps' (43) and writing the lines on the ground. But the description in the German play is noticeably different. In it, Titus's son, Vespasian, enters with a staff and a basket of sand and suggests the idea to his father and Lavinia. Titus, after referring to the pain of his 'old heart', tells Vespasian to 'spread the sand on the floor [ground]' (197–8),

and his son obliges. One would assume that Titus's reference to his old heart and the spreading of the sand was an invention of the author of the German play, yet the ballad also speaks of Titus's aged heart and the spreading of sand: 'We spread a heap of Sand upon the ground' (46–7). The shared juxtaposition of *spread . . . sand on the ground* with *old* or *aged heart* in both the German play and the ballad is certainly no coincidence.

Also, in *Titus Andronicus*, the Goth queen has three sons brought to Rome, one of whom is executed in the first scene. But in the other three renditions, the Goth queen has only two sons brought to Rome, and there is no execution of a Goth son at the beginning.

One cannot argue that one of the other extant Titus tales served as the source for the other three because each one shares elements with *Titus Andronicus* that are absent in one or more of their counterparts. To illustrate, in both the German play and *Titus Andronicus*, the Moor gives a list-of-evils speech. In the German play, he concludes, 'Thousands and thousands of villainies and robberies have I committed, and yet it appears to me that I have not had enough of them' (168). This is clearly the counterpart to Aaron's 'But I have done a thousand dreadful things, / As willingly as one would kill a fly, / And nothing grieves me heartily indeed, / But that I cannot do ten thousand more' (5.1.141–4). But nothing like this occurs in the ballad or prose history. Conversely, in the German play, Titus's daughter is named Andronica, but, in the three other versions, it is Lavinia.

This shifting pattern of agreements and disparities persuasively argues that none of the four tellings of the Titus story was the source for any of its counterparts. Rather, such results can only be explained if all four works were based on a common source. In that source, the Goth queen would have had only two sons (it was Shakespeare who added another son and had him executed in the first act, while the other three writers kept to the source). Likewise, the source would have named Titus's daughter Lavinia, recounted Titus's battlefield exploits, and spoken of sand spread on the ground for Lavinia's canvas – features that were kept in some of the derivative tales but not in others.

Titus Andronicus, then, was not based on the prose history, the ballad or the German play but on another source. But was that source *Titus and Vespasian*? The play, of course, is lost, but we did submit North's *The Dial of Princes* to our software analysis, comparing it with the prose history, which, because it details essentially the entire plot of the fall of the Andronicus family, has been thought by many to be based on Shakespeare's play. But WCopyfind revealed that the prose history not only has points in common with *Titus Andronicus*, it also shares elements with *The Dial* that are absent from the Shakespeare play.

In *The Dial*, for instance, Lavinia is counselled against displaying the gestures of mourning – tearing her hair, scratching her face, shedding floods of tears, refusing all company – the very gestures that the suffering Lavinia in the prose history is described as exhibiting. We found other elements as well that are common to the prose history and *The Dial* but not to *Titus Andronicus*, including the Emperor Theodosius; the Goth Rulers, Totilla and Alaricus; the descriptions of the barbaric Goth revolts; and the manner of defeat of King Totilla in battle.

The prose history, for example, begins with a detailed history of the Goth–Roman conflict that is absent from other Andronican works:

When the Roman Empire was grown to its Height, and the greatest Part of the World was subjected to its imperial Throne, *in the Time of Theodosius*, a barbarous Northern People out of Swedeland, Denmark, and Gothland, came into Italy, in such Numbers, under the leading of *Tottilius, their King*, that *they overrun it with Fire and Sword, plundering Churches, ripping up Women with Child, and deflowring Virgins in so horrid and barbarous a manner*, that the People fled before them like Flocks of Sheep.

(35) (emphasis added)

Those who argue that *Titus Andronicus* (or the ballad) was the basis for the prose history must contend that its author originated this background story. Yet this is not pure invention. Moreover, with software assistance, it is not difficult to track down its

source. An EEBO search for all works that refer to the peculiar Goth names of the prose history – Theodosius, Totillius (Totilla) and Alaricus – yields twenty-four results, only a handful of which date from the sixteenth century. A closer look reveals that many of the elements found in the prose history are similar to the chapters on the Goths in *The Dial of Princes*: North's translation records the history of Totilla, King of the Goths, who was routed in battle in a manner similar to that involving Totillius, King of the Goths, in the prose history. And though the German play does not refer to Totilla, the description of the Goth–Roman battle in that text is also comparable.

Also, the prose history locates the Goth–Roman conflict 'in the Time of Theodosius', and it is the corresponding Theodosius-related chapters in *The Dial* that provide much of its Goth history. Interestingly, those chapters recount the story of Emperor Valent and Captain-General Theodosius, father to Emperor Theodosius, which parallels the relationship between the Emperor Saturninus and Titus Andronicus. The noble Theodosius, like the noble Titus, was a leader of the Roman army, succeeding in vanquishing an enemy of Rome and becoming much loved by the people and respected by the Senate. Similarly, Valent, like the Emperor, lived 'ever in jealousy and suspicion' (81). He ended up accusing Theodosius of treason and eventually had him beheaded. According to *The Dial*, this and other vile acts led to Valent's overthrow and execution by the Goths.

The chapters on Valent and Theodosius contain still other elements that are uniquely relevant to *Titus Andronicus*. *The Dial* refers thrice to Valent as *this wicked emperor*, a rare phrase that appears nowhere else in North's translations; it is the same phrase that Titus uses to refer to the Emperor in Shakespeare's play (4.3.23), and it, too, appears nowhere else in the canon. In fact, an EEBO search for *this wicked emperor* yields only 18 occurrences in 13 records: three of these are from the description of the Emperor Valent in *The Dial*; another three are in the quarto and Folio texts of *Titus Andronicus* and Edward Ravenscroft's 1687 adaptation. In other words, six of the

18 uses of *this wicked emperor* comprise the North and Shakespeare references. One of the passages from *The Dial* that describes the Emperor Valent as *this wicked emperor* also includes a reference to *the Princes of the Goths*, another rare phrase that occurs in only two works other than *The Dial* and *Titus Andronicus*. North and Shakespeare also juxtapose this phrase with *Emperor* and *bring/brought with him* (74/5.2.124–7).

We should add that the prose history, like the German play, also has different names for some of the characters, such as the Goth prince: Alaricus in the prose history, but Alarbus in Shakespeare. While the difference between *Alaricus* and *Alarbus* is slight, it is significant that the prose history is the one with the historically accurate name. This necessarily gives *Alaricus* priority and confirms that the author could not have been relying exclusively on Shakespeare's play. It also returns our attention to North's *Dial*, in which a Goth king is named Alaricus.

The results clearly suggest that the author of the prose history was not only familiar with numerous elements now found in *Titus Andronicus*; he also, directly or indirectly, borrowed from North's *Dial*. If that borrowing was direct, though, we would have to accept a remarkable coincidence: that in writing their respective Titus tragedies, the author of the prose history and Shakespeare independently mined a text that had no *prima facie* connection to the Titus tale. It is more reasonable to believe that, in both cases, exposure to the phrases, images, characters and plot elements in *The Dial of Princes* was indirect, through the source play that clearly announces its connection to the Titus story.

Finally, we would point out that the prose history provides additional support for our proposal that *Titus and Vespasian* was designed to dissuade the queen from marrying the King of the Swedes. The work stresses the Swedish origin of the Goths, introducing them as 'a barbarous Northern People out of Swedeland, Denmark, and Gothland' (35), and it emphasizes the controversy over the decision of the Emperor to marry the Goth queen, focusing on the fact that Titus Andronicus opposed such a marriage and reproducing *Gorboduc*'s warning against monarchs wedding foreigners:

> but those barbarous People still encreasing in their Numbers, the Emperor, desiring Peace, it was agreed to, in consideration he should marry Attava, Queen of the Goths, and in case he should die without Issue, her Sons might succeed in the Empire. Andronicus opposed this very much, as did many other; knowing, through the Emperor's weakness, that she being an imperious Woman, and of a haughty Spirit, would govern him as she pleased, and enslave the noble Empire to Strangers. (38)

V

One hundred and fifty years ago, the prevailing scholarly view was that *Titus and Vespasian* was the source of Shakespeare's play. Having just translated the German play, Albert Cohn, in 1865, declared: 'we should have to acknowledge *Titus and Vespasian* as the original on which Shakespeare's play was founded'.[33] Henry Morley, who edited *Titus Andronicus* prior to the 1904 discovery of the quarto, agreed: 'Thanks to Mr. Albert Cohn, we have restored to us, in mangled form, the old [lost] play of *Titus and Vespasian*, with absolute certainty that it was the original of *Titus Andronicus*.'[34] Cohn and Morley's view prevailed until 1926, when both Eleanor Grace Clark and A. M. Witherspoon decided that the lost play must have been about the siege of Jerusalem. As Clark put it: 'It will be clear that the story of *Titus and Vespasian* has nothing whatsoever in common with *Titus Andronicus* except the name *Titus* occurring in both titles.'[35] But this is not true. Titus Vespasian was the patriarch of the doomed Flavian dynasty that ruled Rome between 69 and 96 AD, and there

---

[33] Cohn, *Shakespeare in Germany*, p. cxiii.

[34] H[enry]. M[orley]., ed., *Titus Andronicus with The True Tragedie of Richard the Third* (Philadelphia, n.d. [1901?]), p. 8.

[35] Eleanor Grace Clark, '*Titus and Vespasian*', *Modern Language Notes*, 41:8 (1926), 523–7, p. 526.

are at least two important commonalities between the Vespasians and the Andronici that are difficult to dismiss as coincidence. The first is that, as in *Titus Andronicus*, the tragic downfall of Titus and his sons began when the noble wife of the leader of a Germanic (i.e. Goth) rebellion, her captured children at Titus's feet, tearfully begged him to pardon them from execution, and he rejected her pleas. This, according to Plutarch's *Moralia* (1603), would become the seminal event that led to the tragedies that would soon engulf the family. The following is Cassius Dio's account of this notorious episode:

[Pepoila] threw her children at Vespasian's feet and delivered a most pitiful plea in their behalf: 'These little ones, Caesar [Vespasian], I bore and reared in the monument, that we might be a greater number to supplicate you.' Yet, though she caused both him and the rest to weep, no mercy was shown to the family.[36]

Plutarch marked this callous judgement as the start of the Vespasian downfall, eventually leading to the tragedies that beset Titus and his sons. The passage that follows is Plutarch's analysis of the event in *Moralia*, as translated by Philemon Holland:

Howbeit, for all this, Vespasian caused this lady to be put to death; but for this murder of his he dearly paid, and was punished accordingly: for within a while after, his whole posterity was utterly destroyed and rooted out from the face of the earth, so as there remained not one of his race.[37]

Surely there is something familiar in Plutarch's association of the tragedies that overwhelmed the family Vespasian, leaving 'his whole posterity ... utterly destroyed and rooted out from the face of the earth', with a kneeling, noble, Germanic (Goth) woman begging in vain. In *Titus Andronicus*, Queen Tamora also vows that Titus and family will suffer utter destruction and for the same reason:

> I'll find a day to massacre them all,
> And rase their faction and their family,
> The cruel father and his traitorous sons,
> To whom I sued for my dear son's life;

> And make them know what 'tis to let a queen
> Kneel in the streets and beg for grace in vain.
>
> (1.1.450–5)

Second, the choice of the name *Saturninus* for an emperor who challenged the selection of Titus for the imperial diadem also finds its origin in the history of the Vespasian dynasty. The Governor of Germania Superior, Saturninus, confronted Titus's son for rule of the empire, and his troops and German supporters did, at one point, declare him emperor, making him the only non-Vespasian ruler during the Vespasian reign.

Finally, one of the most spectacular processions in the history of the Roman Empire celebrated the victory of Titus Vespasian and his son of the same name over a rebellion in Judea. The famous Roman landmark, the marble Arch of Titus, was one of two triumphal arches that the Romans built as a memorial of Titus's victory. And today, one can still observe on the Arch of Titus the reliefs that depict images of the spectacle: the wreathed Titus standing upon a four-horse chariot and the procession of soldiers carrying the treasures of the defeated rebels. This is reminiscent of the opening of *Titus Andronicus* in which the General Titus returns to a similar celebratory procession after a similar victory over a rebellion. Given the famous Arch of Titus, it is difficult to see how the first scene of Shakespeare's play could avoid comparisons to the father-and-son Vespasian rulers.

This is not to suggest that *Titus and Vespasian* was historical in the sense that, say, *Richard III* is. Instead, it was a kind of pseudo-history in the style of Norton and Sackville's *Gorboduc*. Evidently, the original dramatist took Titus and Vespasian, their triumphal procession, and the fateful

---

[36] Cassius Dio, *Roman History*, trans. Earnest Cary (Cambridge, MA, 1925), vol. 8, p. 293. Cassius Dio refers to her as 'Pepoila', but Plutarch and most other references use her Gallic name, 'Empona'.

[37] *The philosophie, commonlie called, the morals vvritten by the learned philosopher Plutarch of Chaeronea*, trans. Philemon Holland (London, 1603), p. 1158.

interaction with a Gothic rebellion for the purposes of a framework narrative, then added elements as he saw fit, including a hodge-podge of lurid Roman storylines. *Gorboduc*, though taking place in England, also received a similar Senecan-makeover in a tragic, Roman-styled fictionalization.

If we deny any connection between *Titus and Vespasian* and *Titus Andronicus*, we must explain why the two main characters of the German play are the father and son, Titus and Vespasian. To date, the two explanations scholars cite are by Witherspoon and Clark. Witherspoon merely stated that the 'mental association' of Lucius with Vespasian was 'explicable',[38] and Clark suggested that the English actors who performed the play on the Continent were simply confusing the name with that of the character in the Henslowe play.[39] The problem with both views is that this is not the only work that connects Vespasian to *Titus Andronicus*. There are what appear to be allusions to *Titus Andronicus* in three late Elizabethan works: *Christ's Tears Over Jerusalem*, *The Jew of Malta* and *A Knack to Know a Knave*. In the next section, we will revisit each.

VI

In 1984, J. J. M. Tobin noted some obvious connections between Thomas Nashe's *Christ's Tears Over Jerusalem* and *Titus Andronicus*, writing that Nashe's 1593 tract also contains 'both a "Titus" and a "Saturninus", together with a Thyestean-like banquet in which a mother eats her son'.[40] In 2000, Adrian Streete referenced these similarities and added his view that Titus's agonizing speech from Act 3 (3.1.219–33) 'seems especially indebted, both linguistically and thematically, to *Christs Teares*'.[41] Importantly, however, in these familiar passages in *Christ's Tears*, Nashe was relating a story about Titus and Vespasian.

A number of scholars have argued that Shakespeare based Aaron on the character of Ithamore, the Turk in Christopher Marlowe's *The Jew of Malta*, noting especially the connection between the two servants' list-of-evils speeches. In his Arden

edition of *Titus Andronicus*, Jonathan Bate argues that 'Aaron's catalogue of misdeeds (5.1.124–44) is modeled on the exchange between Barabas and Ithamore in which they outdo each other in outrageous ill-doing.'[42] It is undeniable that the speeches are related, but in the same scene in Marlowe's play, prior to the speeches by Barabas and Ithamore, Barabas refers to 'Titus and Vespasian'. It would be difficult to argue that this is a coincidence, for a search of the massive database Literature Online for all dramas that use the phrase 'Titus and Vespasian' yields only two results, only one of which – Marlowe's – is from the sixteenth century.

Finally, E. K. Chambers observed that an allusion in the anonymous *A Knack to Know a Knave* 'points to knowledge of Titus and the Goths . . . in 1592, and no such combination is known outside *Titus Andronicus*':[43]

> As Titus was unto the Roman Senators,
> When he had made a conquest on the Goths:
> That in requitall of his service done,
> Did offer him the imperiall Diademe;
> As they in Titus, we in your Grace still fynd,
> The perfect figure of a Princelie mind.[44] (F3)

The passage appears to be a reference to the opening scene of *Titus Andronicus*. But this is not what occurs in Shakespeare's play, where it is only the people and Titus's brother, Marcus, who express

---

[38] A. M. Witherspoon, ed., *The Tragedy of Titus Andronicus*, Yale Shakespeare (New Haven, 1926), p. 113.

[39] Clark, '*Titus and Vespasian*', p. 526.

[40] J. J. M. Tobin, 'Nomenclature and the Dating of *Titus Andronicus*', *Notes and Queries*, n.s. 31.2 (1984), 186–7, p. 186.

[41] Adrian Streete, 'Nashe, Shakespeare and the Bishops' Bible', *Notes and Queries*, n.s. 47:1 (2000), 56–9, p. 56.

[42] Jonathan Bate, ed., *Titus Andronicus*, Arden Shakespeare Third Series (London, 1995), p. 87.

[43] E. K. Chambers, *William Shakespeare: A Study of Facts and Problems*, vol. 1 (Oxford, 1930), p. 319.

[44] *A most pleasant and merie new Comedie, Intituled, A Knack to know a Knave. Newlie set foorth, as it hath sundrie tymes bene played by Ed. Allen and his Companie, With Kemps applauded Merrimentes of the men of Goteham, in receiving the King into Goteham* (London, 1595).

a desire to have Titus made ruler. More importantly, as Paul E. Bennett points out, *A Knack* includes three mentions of Vespasian, suggesting that the work was referring to *Titus and Vespasian*.[45] The Lord Strange's Men first performed *A Knack* in June 1592, right after their two-month run of *Titus and Vespasian*; these two plays were also the Lord Strange's Men's most frequently performed works of January 1593.[46] It seems unlikely that the Lord Strange's Men's playwright would advertise a competing Titus play owned by another company rather than the company's own popular *Titus and Vespasian*, which would run concurrently with *A Knack*. Bennett's position seems particularly sound given that we know that *A Knack* also alludes twice to *A Looking Glass for London*, another Lord Strange's Men's play that, like *Titus and Vespasian*, played in the two months prior to the opening of *A Knack*.[47]

We close our discussion of these three plays with Bate's comment on the reference in *A Knack* to a Titus who was offered the 'imperial Diadem' after he 'made a conquest on the Goths':

If this incident was dramatized in the lost play, the possibility for confusion is immediately apparent: replace 'Goths' with 'Jews' and you have an allusion to *Titus and Vespasian* as precise as that in the received text appears to be to *Titus Andronicus* – perhaps more precise, since in Shakespeare's play the offer comes not from the senate but from the people via their tribunes.[48]

This is exactly our view. The only difference is that Bate attributes the Goth substitution to actors who confused the two plays – 'If the same actors were simultaneously learning their lines for the new *Titus* and remembering the lines of the old *Knack*, contamination from one to the other is eminently plausible'[49] – while we have shown it was no mistake. The Goths were also the subject of the original play.

Such mutually reinforcing evidence should end the scholarly debate about the relationship of *Titus Andronicus* to other Titus-related works from the era. Evidently, just as he did with *Henry V*, *Hamlet*, *The Two Gentlemen of Verona*, *Julius Caesar* and numerous other dramas, Shakespeare also used a source play for *Titus Andronicus*, and it appears *Titus and Vespasian* was that play.

VII

Before concluding, we need to tie up two loose ends. First, is it reasonable to claim that a play written in 1562 would have been revived in 1592, as an entry in Henslowe's Diary indicates it was? A look at other revivals confirms that Henslowe was, indeed, interested in plays that were thirty or even forty years old. In 1594, Richard Edwards's *Palamon and Arcite* (1566), which Shakespeare and Fletcher likely used as a source for *The Two Noble Kinsmen*, was revived, as was *Gorboduc* (*Ferrex and Porrex*) in 1600.[50] In the early 1590s, the Rose theatrical manager also produced *A Taming of a Shrew* and *Henry VI* as well as renditions of *King Lear* and *Henry V*, all four of which are Shakespeare-related plays that currently exist in two versions. We believe *Titus and Vespasian* and *Titus Andronicus* provide another example of closely related sister-plays produced by Henslowe and Shakespeare. In fact, Henslowe's Diary indicates that the Lord Strange's Men performed *Henry VI* and *Titus and Vespasian* concurrently throughout the spring of 1592 and winter of early 1593, often on consecutive days.[51]

Second, how do we explain the notation 'ne' alongside Henslowe's *tittus & vespacia* entry when 'ne' has traditionally been taken to mean 'new'? But 'new', as many have noted, does not necessarily mean 'recently written'; it could mean that the

[45] Paul E. Bennett, 'An Apparent Allusion to *Titus Andronicus*', *Notes and Queries*, 200 (October 1955), 422–4, p. 423.

[46] See Neil Carson, *A Companion to Henslowe's Diary* (Cambridge, 1988), p. 86.

[47] Arthur Freeman, 'Two Notes on *A Knack to Know a Knave*', *Notes and Queries*, n.s. (1962), 326–7, p. 327.

[48] Bate, ed., *Titus Andronicus*, p. 73.

[49] Bate, ed., *Titus Andronicus*, p. 73.

[50] Carson, *A Companion to Henslowe's Diary*, pp. 82, 83, 89–90, 110, 111.

[51] See *Henslowe's Diary*, 2nd edn, ed. R. A. Foakes (Cambridge, 2002), and Carson, *Companion*.

play was new to the repertory or that it had been substantially revised before being revived. *2 Tamar Cam*, after all, is marked 'ne' twice, and 'ne' was also assigned for dated plays: Henslowe marked the 1594 revival of *Palamon and Arcyte* 'ne'. Moreover, individual scholars have proposed that 'ne' stood for the venue in which the play was performed, i.e. Newington Butts, or that it was associated with high box office returns, as in the case of *Alexander and Lodowick*, which, in two entries marked 'ne', took in 55s and 65s, more than double the average takings. Whatever the meaning, the fact that a 1566 play was marked 'ne' by Henslowe shows that the same designation for *Titus and Vespasian* is not inconsistent with an early date for the tragedy.

VIII

Shakespearians who have followed the scholarship on *Titus Andronicus* know that the three early modern retellings of the Titus tale, the prose history, the ballad and the German play, and the three late Elizabethan works that seem to allude to *Titus Andronicus*, *Christ's Tears Over Jerusalem*, *The Jew of Malta* and *A Knack to Know a Knave*, have been a necessary but divisive part of the conversation. Any effort to clarify the genealogy of *Titus Andronicus*, therefore, needs to explain particular details of these works and reconcile the relationships among them. We believe that our analysis has done just that. We also believe that our WCopyfind search has made it untenable to maintain that *Titus Andronicus* was the source of the prose history, the ballad or the German play: the evidence strongly suggests that all four texts had an earlier, common source.

In presenting our case for *Titus and Vespasian* as the source play for *Titus Andronicus* and for North as its author, we considered carefully the results of our WCopyfind search, which uncovered a substantial inventory of Goth legends, plot elements, descriptions and rare or exclusive phrases that *Titus Andronicus* shares with *The Dial of Princes*, a work not previously studied in connection with Shakespeare's play. We also discovered that the prose history contained other Goth-related elements borrowed from North's translation, e.g. the Emperor

Theodosius, King Totilla, Alaricus and the description of the distraught Lavinia, a fact suggesting that it was the author of the source play who was intimately familiar with *The Dial* and echoed it frequently. Intrigued, we had a closer look at the Inns of Court in and around 1560, where we discovered Heywood's challenge to the law students in his translation of *Thyestes* and saw, for the first time, Norton and Sackville's *Gorboduc* in relation to that challenge. It did not take long for us to realize that Thomas North, the translator of *The Dial*, whom Heywood particularly named, must also have responded, with a play imitating the Senecan style and, like *Gorboduc*, attending to its young author's political desires.

Titus and Vespasian, of course, is a lost play, and even Cohn's contemporaries, who thought beyond a doubt that it served as Shakespeare's source, could not verify its contents. Nonetheless, our argument rests on a well-established support structure: the notions that Henslowe would revive a 1560s play, that Shakespeare would adapt an old work for his own company and that Shakespeare would borrow liberally from North are all consistent with what we already know. Moreover, Jones and White's analysis of the political purpose of *Gorboduc*, the eyewitness account of its performance and Winston's work on the Senecan revival at the Inns of Court in the 1560s credibly establish the political and literary environment that shaped North's early years. Certainly, it seems a great coincidence that a work so intricately connected to a pair of early 1560s tragedies also appears to be focused on an issue that was a topical concern in the early 1560s – the possible marriage of Elizabeth to a Goth monarch. One could counter that another ambitious Inns of Court student could have written *Titus and Vespasian*, but Heywood's callout to North in the preface to *Thyestes* and the numerous rare or exclusive verbal fingerprints that *The Dial of Princes* and *Titus Andronicus* share are compelling.

Our concluding proposal, then, is that Thomas North be recognized as the author of the lost *Titus and Vespasian*, penned in 1562, and that *Titus Andronicus* be added to Shakespeare's list of 'borrowed' Roman plays. Ironically, although scholars place little weight on the rumour repeated by Edward Ravenscroft in the preface to his 1687 adaptation of *Titus Andronicus* – 'I have been told by some anciently conversant with the Stage, that it was not Originally [Shakespeare's] but brought [wrought?] by a private Author to be Acted, and he [Shakespeare] only gave some Master-touches to one or two of the Principal Parts or Characters'[52] – Ravenscroft may have gotten it right.

---

[52] Edward Ravenscroft, prefatory note to Reader, *Titus Andronicus, or the Rape of Lavinia* (London, 1687), reprinted in *William Shakespeare: The Critical Heritage*, ed. Brian Vickers, vol. 1 (London and Boston, 1974), pp. 238–9.

THE TWO AUTHORS OF *EDWARD III*

BRIAN VICKERS

I

On 1 December 1595 Cuthbert Burby entered in the Stationers' Register 'A book Intitled *EDWARD the THIRD and the Blacke Prince their warres with kinge JOHN of Fraunce* vjᵈ' (Arber, iii.55). When published the following year, however, the references in the title to 'the Blacke Prince' (Prince Edward, who is never described as such in the play, though called 'blacke Edward' at 4.5.111[1]) and the French King had been dropped,[2] and the Quarto was offered for sale as '*The Raigne of King Edward the third: As it hath bin sundrie times plaied about the Citie of London.*' The 1596 Quarto was reprinted in 1599, with heavy and largely helpful corrections, but thereafter the play sank out of sight until 1760, when Edward Capell, the greatest of the eighteenth-century Shakespeare editors, included it in his *Prolusions* (or 'precursors') as an example of correct textual editing.[3]

The main or outer plot concerns the most notable events in the first half of the reign of Edward III, as related in the chronicles of Holinshed and Froissart, from the declaration of war against France in 1337 to the triumph of Poitiers in 1356. The historical matter fills the opening scene, where King Edward asserts his right to rule in France, a resolve strengthened by the insolent demands of the French King John that he should give up his claims and swear allegiance to France. King Edward orders an army to be levied 'for our wars in France' (1.1.140), and in Acts 3 to 5 we follow a series of English victories, from the naval battle of Sluys to the ultimate triumph at the battle of Poitiers. But before he can set off the King must first deal with the Scottish violation of a peace treaty, their army having taken Berwick and Newcastle, and laid siege to the castle of Roxborough. There, the Countess of Salisbury, daughter to the Earl of Warwick (a loyal supporter of Edward), is beleaguered and the King sets off to rescue her. The episode that follows, three scenes in which the King falls in love with the Countess, is taken from Froissart's *Croniques de Frances* (1513), as translated by Berners in 1523–5, and amplified in William Painter's *The Palace of Pleasure* (1567), who had drawn the story from Bandello.[4] These scenes may appear to be a diversion, but they are thematically linked with the main story.

In the late nineteenth century some pioneer scholars had discovered that the verse style of the episode differed in several measurable ways from

---

[1] I quote from *Edward III*, ed. C. F. Tucker Brooke, in Brooke, *The Shakespeare Apocrypha* (Oxford, 1908), with lineation keyed to the *Riverside Shakespeare*, ed. G. B. Evans and J. J. M. Tobin (Boston and New York, 1997).

[2] I thank Richard Proudfoot for drawing my attention to this point, and for many helpful comments on an earlier version of this article.

[3] Capell, *Prolusions; or select pieces of antient Poetry, compil'd with great Care from their several Originals, and offerd to the Publick as Specimens of the Integrity that should be found in the Editions of worthy Authors . . . with a Preface*, pp. ix–x.

[4] The source material is conveniently summarized in Giorgio Melchiori, ed., *King Edward III* (Cambridge, 1998), 'Appendix: The Use of Sources', pp. 171–215. See also G. Harold Metz, *Sources of Four Plays Ascribed to Shakespeare* (Columbia, MO, 1989).

the main plot. In 1874 F. G. Fleay argued that two discrete parts could be distinguished:

one, which forms the main bulk of the play, relates to the foreign wars of King Edward; the other, which consists of two scenes and part of a third, contains a narrative of an attempted seduction of the Countess of Salisbury by the same monarch. These parts are distinctly different in general style and poetic power; so much so, that none but the dullest of prosaic readers could fail to note the differences; they are also clearly separated by metrical characteristics of the most pronounced kind. They are equally distinguished by the use or disuse of special words . . . . In my opinion, the episode is by Shakespeare; the main part of the play not.[5]

Fleay pointed out that the verse in these scenes contained many more 'double' or 'feminine' endings (lines having 11 syllables, not 10) than in the main plot. In 1901 Gustav Liebau, comparing several versions of the 'King and the Countess' story, recalculated Fleay's ratios as percentages and divided the scenes into two groups, showing distinctly differing rates: 10% in the episode and 4.3% in the main plot.[6] In 1931 P. W. Timberlake published the first detailed quantitative study of the feminine ending, giving the more accurate figures of 9.5% for the episode and only 2.1% for the main plot, written in 'the stiff blank verse of the older school'.[7]

Having analysed all the plays produced up to 1595, Timberlake could affirm that Shakespeare was the only dramatist who used such freedom in his blank verse. Since 'an impressive list of critics' had already suspected Shakespeare's hand in these scenes, Timberlake's analysis endorsed that attribution. Indeed, the difference in verse style between the two portions of the play is so great that they cannot possibly have been written by the same dramatist. For a dramatist working with the three verbal media of blank verse, lyric verse and prose, his patterns of usage within the conventions of prosody reveal more of his individuality than do computations of the frequency with which he uses such 'function words' as *of*, *the*, *while* or *whatsoever*. Data of this kind can play a useful supporting role, but it is not of primary evidential value. By contrast, the indication of two separate hands in this

play, provided by empirical analyses of its verse, is so decisive that we can simply dismiss any reading of *Edward III* which ignores this fact and claims that only one author was involved. The roll-call of commentators who could only find evidence of one hand, and who can therefore be ruled out of court, extends from J. P. Collier in 1874 and includes Tucker Brooke (1908), Karl Wentersdorf (1960), Eliot Slater (1988), Fred Lapides (1980) and Eric Sams (1996).[8] I am aware that in taking a firm line on this issue I am not following 'the tune of the time' in this relativistic age. But in authorship studies clear demarcations must be made when the evidence supports them, as it does

---

[5] 'On "Edward the Third"', *Academy*, 25 April 1874; reprinted in F. G. Fleay, *Shakespeare Manual* (London, 1876), pp. 303–6, p. 303.

[6] See Liebau, *King Edward III von England und die Gräfin von Salisbury Dargestellt in ihren Beziehungen nach Geschichte, Sage und Dichtung, unter eingehender Berücksichtigung des pseudo-Shakespeareschen Schauspiels 'The Raigne of King Edward the Third'* (Berlin, 1900), pp. 191–3. All translations from foreign language texts are my own, unless otherwise stated.

[7] See Timberlake, *The Feminine Ending in English Blank Verse: A Study of its Use by Early Writers in the Measure and its Development in the Drama up to the Year 1595* (Menasha, WI, 1931), pp. 78–9. Unfortunately, Timberlake lumped 4.4 (Shakespeare's dramatic presentation of Prince Edward on the eve of battle, receiving a *consolatio* from Audley on how to face death) with Kyd's scenes 5 to 8 on the grounds that 'they are to all intents one scene dealing with the battle of Poitiers'. He correctly cites the opening of scene 5 ('A sodaine darknes hath defast the sky | The windes are crept into their caves for fear') as an example of 'the earlier style'. However, he claims that the same style is found in 4.4.101–9, not noticing that this is a speech by the French Herald (bringing the ironic 'gift' of a prayer book for the prince's last hours), delivered in an appropriately formal style.

[8] Karl P. Wentersdorf, 'The Authorship of *Edward III*', Ph.D. dissertation, University of Cincinnati (1960); Eliot Slater, *The Problem of the Reign of King Edward III: A Statistical Approach* (Cambridge, 1988), with summary conclusions at pp. 124–5, 134–5; Tucker Brooke, ed., *The Shakespeare Apocrypha* (Oxford, 1908), pp. xx–xxiii; Fred Lapides, ed., *The Raigne of King Edward the Third: A Critical, Old-Spelling Edition* (New York, 1980), pp. 7, 15, 24, 55; Eric Sams, *Shakespeare's Edward III* (New Haven and London, 1996). Reviewing Sams's book, MacDonald Jackson revealed his own uncertainty whether or not '*Edward III* is Shakespeare's unaided work, though it may be', *Shakespeare Quarterly*, 49 (1998), 91–3, p. 92.

so overwhelmingly in differentiating Shakespeare's scenes from the rest of the play. There is nothing to be gained from blurring the issue. Two opposing interpretations cannot both be right.

Several scholars attributed the love story to Shakespeare. G. C. Moore Smith did so,[9] as did E. K. Chambers, at first tentatively, then with more confidence,[10] ascribing to Shakespeare not only the three scenes of the love plot (1.2, 2.1, 2.2), but also the scene in which the young Prince Edward prepares for battle (4.4). The first detailed stylistic study of Shakespeare's authorship of these scenes was made by the Danish scholar V. Østerberg in a German journal,[11] and failed to receive the attention it deserved. Chambers did not cite it, and it was unknown to Kenneth Muir, whose two-part study of the play remains essential reading.[12] Subsequent studies have strengthened the case for Shakespeare's authorship of these four scenes, and it can now be taken as established.[13] It has been confirmed by the play's appearance in the second editions of both the Riverside Shakespeare (1997) and the Oxford Shakespeare (2005), and in the one volume series of the New Cambridge Shakespeare, ed. Giorgio Melchiori (1998), the third Arden Shakespeare, ed. Richard Proudfoot and Nicola Bennett (forthcoming), and no doubt others.

2

As to the identity of Shakespeare's co-author, no such consensus exists. On the quality of his contribution, both in characterization and verse style, several disparaging accounts have been given, by F. J. Furnivall, G. C. Moore Smith and Kenneth Muir.[14] After the Countess episode, Muir judged, 'the remaining three acts of the play are something of an anti-climax, not merely because they are generally inferior in style, but because the qualities they possess are epic rather than dramatic' (p. 39). In characterizing the unidentified co-author Muir detected a discrepancy between his vivid sense of spectacle and his inferior control of dramatic poetry. The Crécy scenes (3.3.3–4), he judged, 'are certainly exciting. The arming of the Prince, the King's refusal to send aid, the despair of his friends

who think him doomed, and his triumphant entrance form an obviously effective sequence of incidents; but the actual poetry is disappointing.' Similarly, the two scenes relating to Audley 'contain some superb passages' but also severe lapses. Audley, mortally wounded, is asked how he fares, and replies: 'Even as a man may do / That dines at such a bloudie feast as this' (4.8.1–2). Muir found these two lines 'magnificent' but the rest of the scene 'a sad anti-climax'. Muir guessed that 'the author of these scenes was a young poet, "able to bombast out a blank verse as the best" of the University Wits, as Greene said of Shakespeare, but liable to strange lapses; one whose sense of situation was superior to his power of characterization' (53).

The identity of this 'poet', whether young or not, has often been discussed, and the usual suspects – Marlowe, Peele, Greene – have been proposed, but without any convincing evidence. The possibility of Kyd's co-authorship was first broached by Gregor Sarrazin, a leading scholar of his day in Shakespeare studies, and author of the first serious monograph on Kyd.[15] Sarrazin agreed with Liebau that some scenes in Edward III bore unmistakable signs of Shakespeare's hand, and was sure that he could identify a co-author in one scene, at least: 'The author of the battle description (3.1) must have been either Thomas Kyd or an imitator

[9] See Moore Smith's edition of Edward III (London, 1897), for the Temple Dramatists series, pp. x–xxiii.

[10] See Chambers, The Elizabethan Stage, 4 vols. (Oxford, 1923), vol IV, pp. 9–10, and William Shakespeare, 2 vols. (Oxford, 1930), vol I, p. 516.

[11] See Østerberg, 'The "Countess Scenes" of Edward III', Shakespeare Jahrbuch 65 (1929), 49–91.

[12] See Muir, Shakespeare as Collaborator (London, 1960), which includes 'Shakespeare's Hand in Edward III' (pp. 10–30), originally in Shakespeare Survey 6 (Cambridge, 1953), pp. 39–48, and 'Edward III' (pp. 31–55).

[13] See, e.g., Richard Proudfoot, 'The Reign of King Edward III (1596) and Shakespeare', PBA, 71 (1985), 169–85.

[14] See Furnivall, Introduction to The Leopold Shakespeare. The Poet's Works, in Chronological Order, from the text of Professor Delius, with 'The Two Noble Kinsmen' and 'Edward III' (London, 1877), p. c; Moore Smith's edn of Edward III, pp. xiii–xiv; Muir, Shakespeare as Collborator, pp. 32–3, 52–3.

[15] Sarrazin, Thomas Kyd und sein Kreis: eine litterarhistorische Untersuchung (Berlin, 1892).

of his, since it has striking resemblances in style and mode of presentation to the battle described in *The Spanish Tragedy*, Act 1' (124). As far as I can see, no scholar followed up Sarrazin's observation until 1951, when Felix Carrère discussed it briefly, conceding that the two scenes showed resemblances, but ascribing the *Edward III* passage to an unknown imitator of Kyd.[16] Sarrazin's observation was not taken seriously until 1963, when Guy Lambrechts published an essay in which – regrettably – he ascribed the whole of *Edward III* to Kyd.[17] Lambrechts knew the work of Liebau, Østerberg and Muir which attributed four scenes to Shakespeare, but disregarded it. Unsurprisingly, the consensus of scholars who accept Shakespeare's presence in the play has disregarded Lambrechts in turn. But Lambrechts did establish some genuine links with Kyd's canonical plays, starting with that battle scene.

In order to present my argument that Kyd was the main author of *Edward III* I shall need to remind readers of Kyd's debt to 'Senecan' influences in *The Spanish Tragedy* (1587) and *Cornelia* (1593), both of which, I shall argue, share so many elements of dramatic structure and language with *Edward III* (1593) as to identify Kyd as Shakespeare's co-author. I place the term Senecan within quotation marks to make the point that some aspects of Elizabethan tragedy owe just as much to his predecessors Virgil and Ovid.[18] In *The Tragedie of Dido, Queen of Carthage* (1588),[19] Aeneas's account of the fall of Troy derives from *Aeneid* Book 2,[20] while in the opening scene of *The Spanish Tragedy* the Ghost of Andrea's account of his descent to Hades, partly modelled on Seneca's *Thyestes*, owes much to *Aeneid* Book 6.[21] But the dramatic convention that I wish to discuss here is specific to Senecan tragedy: the narration of an off-stage event, usually a catastrophe, conveyed by a Nuntius. In his *Agamemnon*, for example, Eurybatus (Agamemnon's herald) delivers an enormously detailed description of the Greek fleet's shipwreck returning from Troy, extending over 158 lines (421–578) or about 16 per cent of the play.[22] The Senecan messenger's speech included a feature often overlooked in modern discussions, although influential in the Renaissance, which might be called 'the invitation

to narrate'. When the messenger arrives on the scene, the chief character formally invites him to deliver his news. This can be a brief request or imperative order, such as: '*Quis cladis modus?*' (*Med.* 884; 'What is the extent of the disaster?'), '*Ede quid portes novi*' (*Oed.* 914; 'Tell us the news you bring'), '*Altrix, profare quid feras*' (*Phaed.* 358; 'Nurse, tell us your news'), or '*quid sit quod horres ede et auctorem indica*' (*Thy.* 639; 'Tell us the source of your horror and name the culprit'). But the invitation can also be more extended, setting up the speaker at centre stage, and sometimes anticipating the tenor of his speech. The messenger is given permission to deliver bad news, as it were, without fear of interruption or punishment (and in Renaissance plays sometimes with a promise of reward). In *Phaedra* the Nuntius arrives weeping, bewailing his duty to 'announce an unspeakable

---

[16] Carrère, *Le théâtre de Thomas Kyd: contribution à l'étude du drame élizabéthain* (Toulouse, 1951), pp. 291–2.

[17] '*Edward III*, Oeuvre de Thomas Kyd', *Etudes anglaises*, 16 (1963), 160–74.

[18] Howard Baker's pioneering *Induction to Tragedy. A Study in a Development of Form in 'Gorboduc', 'The Spanish Tragedy' and 'Titus Andronicus'* (Baton Rouge, LA, 1939; New York, 1965) made an effective challenge to conventional literary history, emphasizing the importance of Virgil, Ovid and *The Mirror for Magistrates*. For an extension of Baker's thesis see G. K. Hunter, 'Seneca and the Elizabethans: A Case-study in "Influence"', in *Shakespeare Survey 20* (Cambridge, 1967), pp. 17–26, also 'Seneca and English Tragedy', in C. D. N. Costa, ed., *Greek and Latin Studies: Clssical Literature and Its Influence* (London and Boston, 1974), pp. 166–204, both repr. in Hunter, *Dramatic Identities and Cultural Tradition: Studies in Shakespeare and his Contemporaries* (Liverpool, 1978), pp. 159–73 and 174–213.

[19] All dating of plays in this article derives from Martin Wiggins, ed., *British Drama 1533–1642: A Catalogue*, 10 vols. (Oxford, 2012–).

[20] See *Dido*, 2.1.400–596, in C. F. Tucker Brooke, ed., *The Works of Christopher Marlowe* (Oxford, 1910). Dido's invitation, 'May I entreate thee to discourse at large, / And truely to, how Troy was ouercome' (401–2), translates *Aeneid*, Book 1, 753–6.

[21] See F. S. Boas, ed., *The Works of Thomas Kyd* (Oxford, 1901), pp. xxix, 394–5.

[22] *Thyestes*, 24. I quote from the Loeb *Seneca VIII–IX, Tragedies I–II*, ed. and trans. John G. Fitch (Cambridge, MA, and London, 2002, 2004). This excellent edition includes many notes indicating Senecan imitations in Elizabethan tragedy.

fate', but Theseus encourages him: 'Do not fear to tell boldly of harsh calamities. I have a heart not unprepared for distress' (991–4). In *The Trojan Women* the Messenger bewails having to 'tell with tears' the 'cruel deaths' of Astyanax, Andromache's son, and Hermione, Helen's daughter, but Andromache expresses her readiness to hear: 'Detail the sequence of killing, detail the double crime; great pain enjoys dwelling on its sorrows in full. Speak out, recount everything' (1056–8, 1065–7).

Although Seneca was not often studied in the classroom, a general Elizabethan interest in his plays by non-academic readers was met in *Seneca his Tenne Tragedies* (1581), Thomas Newton's collection of translations by various authors.[23] In the Inns of Court drama, which drew on both Senecan and Italian Renaissance models, the Nuntius played a significant role. Two are needed for *Gorboduc*, three for *Gismond of Salerne*, while in Thomas Hughes's *The Misfortunes of Arthur* (1588), a treatment of Arthurian legend consisting in 'the imitation of Seneca's form and the wholesale adoption of his material',[24] the Nuntius twice narrates the outcome of a battle, the first victorious for Arthur (2.1.1–76), the second fatal, a lengthy 'report of the whole battaile, with the death of Mordred and Arthurs and Cadors deadly wound' (4.2.1–236).[25] While Senecan elements influenced the plays written for the public theatres,[26] few dramatists took over this genre of 'circumstantial' or 'heroic narrative', as J. M. Nosworthy termed it.[27] Shakespeare undoubtedly knew Seneca's plays, and made much use of messenger speeches, but he seldom adopted the full convention of the addressee inviting the narrator to deliver his news. He preferred the brief question, in the mould of '*Quis cladis modus?*' or '*Ede quid portes novi*'. Even in *Richard III*, where Seneca was an influence, Shakespeare had begun to adapt the messenger's role to other functions, and he did so inventively throughout his career.[28]

Thomas Kyd, however, in his far briefer working life, remained loyal to the older conventions. *The Spanish Tragedy* contains three separate 'circumstantial' or heroic narratives describing the battle between the Spanish and the Portuguese on which the whole plot turns. Here Kyd's model was the French closet tragedy of Robert Garnier (1544–90), which adopted many elements from Seneca.[29] Garnier enjoyed a brief popularity in Elizabethan England: his *Marc Antoine* was translated by Mary, Countess of Pembroke in 1592, and Kyd's version of Garnier's *Cornélie* was probably made the following year, and published in 1594.[30] I use the term 'version' since Kyd translated freely, to the puzzlement of earlier scholars, who accused him of producing a paraphrase due to an inadequate

[23] See Charles Whibley, ed., *Seneca his Tenne Tragedies translated into English edited by Thomas Newton Anno 1581 With an Introduction by T. S. Eliot*, 2 vols. (London and New York. 1927). With the exception of *Thebais*, added by Newton in 1581, these translations were made between 1557 and 1562.

[24] J. W. Cunliffe, ed., *Early English Classical Tragedies* (Oxford, 1912), p. xc.

[25] See Cunliffe, *Early English Classical Tragedies*, pp. 241–3, 272–9.

[26] See Frederick Kiefer, 'Seneca's Influence on Elizabethan Tragedy: An Annotated Bibliography', *Research Opportunities in Renaissance Drama*, 21 (1978), 17–34, with a 'Supplement', *Research Opportunities in Renaissance Drama*, 28 (1985), 129–42.

[27] See Nosworthy, 'The Bleeding Captain Scene in *Macbeth*', *Review of English Studies*, 22 (1946), 126–30. As Nosworthy observed, this scene 'perpetuates the Senecan tradition of the fifteen-nineties, and its genre is that of circumstantial narrative, or, more precisely, heroic narrative', as used in *The Spanish Tragedy* or in 'the long narrative of the fall of Troy' in Marlowe's *Dido*, which was the inspiration both for this scene and for the Player's speech in *Hamlet* (p. 127).

[28] See, e.g., Gary J. Scrimgeour, 'The Messenger as a Dramatic Device in Shakespeare', *Shakespeare Quarterly*, 19 (1968), 41–54, who counted 'some seventy-five messengers' in the Shakespeare canon. This essay dealt with the early plays, promising an additional study for 'the later plays', which has not been forthcoming. See also Wolfgang Clemen, 'Shakespeare's Use of the Messenger's Report', in Clemen, *Shakespeare's Dramatic Art: Collected Essays* (London, 1972), pp. 96–123 (German original version 1952), and Robert S. Miola, in *Shakespeare and Classical Tragedy: The Influence of Seneca* (Oxford, 1992), pp. 73–4, 96–7, 147–9.

[29] See Cunliffe, *Early English Classical Tragedies*, pp. lvi–lix, and A. Witherspoon, *The Influence of Robert Garnier on Elizabethan Drama* (New Haven and London, 1924; New York, 1968).

[30] On the place of *Cornelia* in Kyd's canon see Arthur Freeman, *Thomas Kyd, Facts and Problems* (Oxford, 1967), pp. 167–70, and Lukas Erne, *Beyond 'The Spanish Tragedy'. A Study of the Works of Thomas Kyd* (Manchester, 2001), pp. 203–17.

knowledge of French. Fortunately, the recent re-evaluation by Josephine A. Roberts and James F. Gaines showed that Kyd regularly translated correctly but often enlarged the emotional scope of the original, making 'nearly 400 amendments'.[31] Kyd's invention showed itself in the many piecemeal additions to Garnier which display some of his own preoccupations, adding five lines at a key point in the fifth act to magnify the role of Cornelia's filial devotion to her dead father.[32] He inserted a long passage (largely in blank verse) at the start of Act 3, a description of nature contrasted with his own miserable condition, which Lukas Erne judged to be 'among the finest [lines] in the play';[33] he amended Garnier's neo-classical Rome by transforming pagan into Christian concepts; and eliminated obscure foreign references in favour of those more familiar to the English reader. Kyd regularly amplified the force of lamentations by adding gestures to tears, as in these three 'amendments' to *Cornélie*:

And thrice detain'd, with dolefull shreeks and cryes,
(With armes to heaven uprear'd) I gan exclaime . . .
                                                    (2.1.197–8)

With folded armes I sadly sitte and weepe   (2.1.207)

With blubbred eyes and hands to heaven uprear'd
                                                    (5.1.130)

Roberts and Gaines noted that in these passages Kyd echoed a similar line he had written for *The Spanish Tragedy*:

With mournefull eyes and hands to heaven upreard
                                                    (3.12.68)

Readers will notice the identical syntactical and metrical template underlying those four descriptions of grief, producing formulaic utterances, a typical feature of Kyd's style. While Englishing Garnier Kyd drew on his own mental repertoire of collocations and word associations, revealing the homogeneity of his linguistic resources; how could he do otherwise? *Cornelia* is simultaneously a translation and an original work. A recent dismissal

of it as 'second-hand', and therefore of no relevance in establishing the Kyd canon, is singularly ill-informed.[34]

Although Garnier had refashioned some elements in Seneca's plays, he preserved the messenger speech, together with the preliminary invitation to deliver news, whether good or bad. In *Hippolyte* (1573), the Messenger who brings news to Thésée of his son's death makes three attempts to utter his bad news, and Thésée has to twice reassure him before he can deliver a lengthy narration of the disaster.[35] In the final act of *Cornélie* (1574) an enormously long messenger's speech (513 lines in the original) brings news that Cornelia's father, Metellus Scipio, has been killed in the battle of Thapsus.[36] Here Garnier varies the sequence by making the heroine break into a lament as soon as she first hears that her father is dead. The Messenger apologizes that (in Kyd's translation)

These misfortunes yet
Must I report to sad Cornelia,
Whose ceaseless griefe (which I am sorry for)
Will agrauate my former misery.[37]

---

[31] Josephine A. Roberts and James F. Gaines, 'Kyd and Garnier: The Art of Amendment', *Comparative Literature*, 31 (1979), 124–33, p. 125. They conclude that *Cornelia* has its own originality: Kyd's 'amendments constitute a second text, which can be considered independently of Garnier's version, and where the work of the writer can be examined on many planes' (p. 133).

[32] The second issue of the play (1595) had the expressive title, *Pompey the Great, his faire Cornelia's Tragedie: Effected by her Father and Husbandes downe-cast, death, and fortune.*

[33] Erne, *Beyond 'The Spanish Tragedy'*, p. 214.

[34] See Will Sharpe, 'Authorship and Attribution', in Jonathan Bate and Eric Rasmussen, eds., *William Shakespeare and Others: Collaborative Plays* (London, 2013), pp. 641–745, p. 651. Sharpe also believes that 'fairly brittle evidence is all that links' Kyd with the anonymously published *Soliman and Perseda*, a conservative view at least a century out of date.

[35] Cf. *Hippolyte*, Acte V, 1965–2160, in C. M. Hill and M. G. Morrison, eds., *Robert Garnier, Two Tragedies 'Hippolyte' and 'Marc Antoine'* (London, 1975), pp. 92–8.

[36] Cf. Raymond Lebègue, ed., *Robert Garnier: Porcie, Cornelie* (Paris, 1973), pp. 221–32.

[37] *Cornelia*, Act 5, 16–19, in F. S. Boas, ed., *The Works of Thomas Kyd* (Oxford, 1901), p. 148.

Cornelia continues to lament, and the Chorus has to urge her to hear his news:

> *Chorus.* The manner of his end
>   Will haply comfort this your discontent.
> *Cornelia.* Discourse the manner of his hard mishap,
>   And what disastrous accident did breake
>   So many people bent so much to fight.   (42–6)

The Messenger then delivers a remarkably vivid 'circumstantial narrative' of the combat at sea and on land (47–329).

The Spanish Tragedy and *Edward III* both contain vivid battle narratives retaining the Senecan tradition of the Messenger first expressing an apologetic diffidence and then being invited to deliver his news. The two plays share another, more striking feature in that they represent action on both sides of a conflict, each with its own messenger report. In *The Spanish Tragedy* we first see the Spanish King greeting a General bringing news from the war against the Portugese, with a 'cheerefull countenance' already portending that 'fortune hath given us victorie' (1.2.5-6).[38] The Messenger briefly confirms the good news, and is then formally invited to go into detail:

> *King.* But Generall, vnfolde in breefe discourse,
>   Your forme of battell and your warres successe.
>   (16–17)

The messenger does so, relatively briefly by the standards of Senecan tragedy (1.2.22–84), also reporting that the Portuguese Prince has been captured. But to our surprise, Kyd then shows us the matching scene in the enemy court, as the distraught Viceroy awaits news of his son Balthazar. No messenger arrives from the battle front, but a Portuguese nobleman, Villuppo – whose name displays his nature[39] – claims to know what happened there. In accordance with Senecan convention, he apologises for the news he brings and requests permission to speak:

> *Villup.* My soueraign pardon the Author of ill newes,
>   And Ile bewray the Fortune of thy Sonne.
> *Vice.* Speake on, Ile guerdon thee what ere it be,
>   Mine eare is ready to receiue ill newes,

My hart is growne hard gainst mischiefes battery,
Stand vp I say and tell thy tale at large   (1.3.53–9)

Here Kyd extends the convention, for Villuppo delivers a false report, accusing Alexandro, another Portugese noble, of having shot Balthazar in the back. Villuppo reveals his villainy to the audience in an aside at the end of the scene (1.3.93–5), and when we see Alexandro next he is about to be executed (3.1.31–57). Fortunately, the Portuguese Ambassador returns with news that 'Balthazar doth liue', and the malicious Messenger is taken away to his punishment.

In this carefully plotted play, recreating the slow and devious process by which news travels, both true and false, Kyd now moves from the male, public world of the Spanish and Portuguese courts to a private house, where Bel-Imperia can finally receive a true account of her fiancé's death from Horatio, who had also fought in that battle. In accordance with Senecan convention, she formally invites the messenger to deliver his narrative:

> Signior Horatio, this is the place and houre,
> Wherein I must intreat thee to relate,
> The circumstance of Don Andreas death:
>   (1.4.1–3)

Like many Senecan messengers, Horatio laments 'this heavy dolefull charge', but gives a third account of the battle, adding a crucial detail. Andrea had been fighting Balthazar 'hand to hand' on horseback when a troop of Portuguese halberdiers arrived who 'pauncht [Andrea's] horse and dingd him to the ground'. Seizing his advantage, 'with ruthless rage' Balthazar killed Andrea, an unchivalric act that caused Horatio to enter

---

[38] Quotations are from W. W. Greg and D. Nichol Smith, eds., *The Spanish Tragedy (1592)*, Malone Society Reprints (Oxford, 1949), with lineation from Philip Edwards, ed., *The Spanish Tragedy* (London, 1959).

[39] As Joseph Schick noted, '*Viluppo* is an Italian word, meaning *confusion, entanglement*' (*The Spanish Tragedy: Kritischer Text und Apparat*, ed. Josef Schick (Berlin, 1901), p. 140).

the battle, rescue Andrea's corpse and take Balthazar prisoner.[40] This third version links the human action to the spirit world of the Prologue, where Andrea's Ghost has been promised revenge for this foul deed.

Edward III includes the same deployment of messengers on the opposite sides of the conflict, also with a false message that confuses those awaiting news. First, in the French camp, before the naval battle of Sluys, we see their king complacently waiting 'till our Nauie of a thousand saile / Haue made a breakfast to our foe by sea' (3.1.1–2). Unannounced, a Mariner enters and describes 'the glorious bright aspect' of the English fleet, against which the French have sailed, 'puft with rage' (62–86). The French King rewards him for his news, but invites him to return and narrate later events:

> And if thou scape the bloody strooke of war
> And do suruiue the conflict, come againe,
> And let vs heare the manner of the fight.   (91–3)

The French King and his teenage son sit to their meal, '*The battell hard a farre off*', and appeal to 'sweet fortune' to bring victory. But at this point, as requested, the Mariner returns, to the King's alarm:

> My hart misgiues: – say, mirror of pale death,
> To whome belongs the honor of this day?
> Relate, I pray thee, if thy breath will serue,
> The sad discourse of this discomfiture.   (137–40)

Having been formally invited, in the proper Senecan mode, the Messenger delivers a vivid description of the English victory and French defeat (141–84). Later in the play, however, the situation is reversed. In a scene invented by the dramatist,[41] Salisbury brings to King Edward both good news – the English army has defeated the French in Brittany – and bad:

> *Sal.* But now, my Lord, as this is ioyful newes,
>   So must my voice be tragicall againe,
>   And I must sing of dolefull accidents.
>
>   (5.1.104–6)

Salisbury metamorphoses into the Senecan messenger, deeply conscious of the effect his news will have, as he describes at length how, from a hill overlooking Poitiers, he had seen Prince Edward surrounded and outnumbered by the French, an apparently hopeless situation. When battle joined, the smoke from the cannon fire was so thick that they could no longer 'Discerne the difference twixt the friend and fo, / So intricate the dark confusion was' (151–2). In response to his narrative Queen Philippa collapses in grief, while the King starts to plan his son's funeral. At this point the grieving parents experience a peripeteia, for a Herald enters with news that the Prince was victorious, and he appears in person. This is the same dramatic reversal, brought about by an erroneous messenger speech, that we saw in *The Spanish Tragedy*, with this difference: Salisbury's was a genuine error, while Villuppo (whose name is echoed in the 'intricate . . . dark confusion' here) made a false report.

3

The importance of the Senecan messenger speech, bringing news of good and evil fortune, whether true or false, links *Edward III* with both of Kyd's Senecan dramas, *Cornelia* and *The Spanish Tragedy*. On its own, of course, that would be insufficient ground for attributing the English history play to Kyd, but major evidence for his co-authorship of *Edward III* exists in the form of an extraordinary number of collocations, sequences of three or more words that it shares with *The Spanish Tragedy* and *Cornelia*.[42] My evidence for these matches derives partly from close reading of the three texts, and partly from using software programs designed to detect student

---

[40] These events are dramatized in *1 Hieronimo* (3.2.105–14, ed. Boas). This fragmentary play (only 1200 lines), published in 1605, is a hybrid of a tragedy and a burlesque. The best discussion is in Erne, *Beyond 'The Spanish Tragedy'*, pp. 14–46.

[41] See Melchiori, ed., *King Edward III*, p. 164 n.

[42] I limit myself to these plays due to lack of space. A considerable number of unique collocations can be found linking *Edward III* with Kyd's *Soliman and Perseda* (1588; published c.1593–4).

plagiarism.[43] When electronic versions of two texts are loaded, these programs 'read' them in parallel and automatically highlight every instance where they share the same three consecutive words, or 'trigrams', as they are known in Corpus Linguistics. Typically, two Elizabethan plays might share several hundred identical collocations, most of which are common expressions, such as 'Yes my Lord' or 'by your leave'. The researcher must then check the list of matching collocations against a database, in this case the texts of all plays performed in the London theatres up to and including 1596,[44] rejecting the common phrases and saving the unique matches. By comparing an anonymous or co-authored play against one of known authorship using this method, if a sufficient number of unique matches is identified that will constitute a very strong case for the known author being responsible for all or part of the target text. This is essentially a verbal, not a numerical or statistical method, with the great advantage of staying within the linguistic world of the play texts, recreating in miniature their verbal fabric, without having to transpose verbal details into a non-verbal medium of mathematical quantities. It is not possible to specify in advance what would constitute 'a sufficient number of unique matches', but of course the more such matches are found the smaller the possibility becomes of the matches being due to coincidence, imitation or plagiarism. One could probably formulate this principle in statistical terms, but the result might be too complex for non-specialists. In any case, mathematics is not the only arbiter of probability.

When I investigated the authorship of *The Troublesome Raigne of King John* (1589) I was struck by its frequent use of alliteration on single consonants (up to five or six times within a line) and, more unusually, on double consonants, such as *'gr'*, *'tr'* or *'pr'*, which reminded me of Peele. When I used anti-plagiarism software to check this text against the canon of Peele's plays and poems (including his share of *Titus Andronicus*) I found that they had in common 219 instances of unique three-word matches.[45] This fact, together with other linguistic and prosodic details, allowed me to attribute the play to Peele. Coincidentally, Charles Forker was

editing the play for the Revels series and not only accepted my attribution (the 'massive totality' of the evidence 'virtually clinches the case for Peele') but printed all of the matching collocations.[46] The great advantage of collocation matching as an authorship attribution tool is that it works on quite short text samples, where other methods need at least a thousand lines of text. The passages added to *The Spanish Tragedy* in 1602 consist of only 320 lines, but with the help of the anti-plagiarism software I was able to identify 116 unique collocations shared with Shakespeare's plays and poems, allowing an attribution to him with some confidence.[47] I cite the success of these previous studies to assure readers that, despite hostile criticism,[48] the

---

[43] I have used the free software programs *Pl@giarism*, designed for the Law Faculty at the University of Maastricht (no longer available) and *WCopyfind* (University of Virginia), happily still extant. For a fuller account of the methodology see Brian Vickers, 'Identifying Shakespeare's Additions to *The Spanish Tragedy* (1602): a new(er) approach', *Shakespeare*, 8 (2012), 13–43.

[44] With the help of Dr Marcus Dahl I have constructed an electronic database of 55 plays performed in the public theatres before 1596. To search this resource I used the free software program *InfoRapid Search & Replace*.

[45] See Brian Vickers, '*The Troublesome Raigne*, George Peele, and the date of *King John*', in Brian Boyd, ed., *Words That Count. Essays in Honor of MacDonald P. Jackson* (Cranbury, NJ, 2004), pp. 78–116.

[46] See Charles R. Forker, ed., George Peele, *The Troublesome Reign of John, King of England* (Manchester, 2011), pp. 9–28 and Appendix 1: 'Unique matches of three consecutive words in *The Troublesome Reign* with comparable word strings in other plays by Peele' (pp. 335–56).

[47] See Vickers, 'Identifying Shakespeare's Additions to *The Spanish Tragedy*'. This essay was the catalyst for Douglas Bruster's decision to include the Additions in the next edition of the *Riverside Shakespeare*: see Bruster, 'Shakespearean Spellings and Handwriting in the Additional Passages Printed in the 1602 *Spanish Tragedy*', *Notes and Queries*, 60 (2013), 420–4.

[48] See MacDonald P. Jackson, 'New Research on the Dramatic Canon of Thomas Kyd', *Research Opportunities in Medieval and Renaissance Drama*, 47 (2008), 107–27, and 'Reviewing Authorship Studies of Shakespeare and his Contemporaries, and the Case of *Arden of Faversham*', *Memoria di Shakespeare*, 8, Special issue on Authorship, ed. Rosy Colombo and Daniela Guardamagna (Rome, 2012), pp. 149–67. A reply is forthcoming.

evidence provided by unique matching three-word collocations is a great advance on all previous methods used in authorship attribution. It also has a firm theoretical foundation in the relatively new discipline of Corpus Linguistics, for when linguists began to use vast electronic concordances of actual language use they discovered a hitherto unexpected role played by recurrent phrases. Where earlier linguistic theories held that users of natural language selected single words to be placed within a syntactical and semantic structure, it now became clear that we also use groups of words, partly as a labour-saving device, partly as a function of memory.[49] Such verbal economy is particularly prevalent in the drama written for the public theatres, where constraints of time demand speedy composition, characters fall into a set of roles with attendant speech patterns, and the verse line easily admits ready-made phrases. It is hardly surprising that many dramatists frequently repeat themselves.[50]

A considerable number of passages in *Edward III* match the two Kyd plays selected here and no other plays written for the public theatres before 1596. To return to the Senecan messengers' speeches, and the Spanish General's account of the carnage in the battle with the Portugese:

> Heere falles a body scindred from his head,
> There legs and armes lye bleeding on the grasse,
> Mingled with weapons and vnboweld steeds:
> That scattering ouer spread the purple plaine.
>
> (1.2.59-62)

As I briefly noted, Kyd had echoed Garnier's *Cornélie* several times in *The Spanish Tragedy*, showing that he must have given it special attention.[51] When he came to translate *Cornélie* with its graphic account of the battle of Thapsus, Kyd followed the text carefully for the first part, describing how all over the battle field

> Lay Armed men, ore-trodden with their horses,
> Dismembered bodies drowning in their blood . . .
>
> (5.249-50)

But when he reached a more restrained verse by Garnier, describing a thigh and a shoulder

'abbattue',[52] Kyd recalled his earlier and more violent formulation:

> Here lay an arme, and there a leg lay shiuer'd'   (258)

In *Edward III* the messenger's speech describing the French naval defeat at the battle of Sluys has uncanny echoes of both passages:

> Heere flew a head, disseuered from the tronke,
> There mangled armes and legs were tost aloft . . .
>
> (3.1.165-6)

Plagiarism might seem an easy explanation for these echoes, but the parallel verbs, 'scindred', 'shiuer'd' and 'disseuered' are inventive and individual variants on an unusual word choice to describe a body part violently torn away; a plagiarist is more likely to have repeated one or the other. Kyd used the same violent word for Hieronimo's prayer that Proserpine might grant:

> Reuenge on them that murdered my sonne
> Then will I rent them thus and thus
> Shiuering their limmes in peeces with my teeth.
>
> (3.13.20-3)

But all that he can vent his anger on are the petitioners' bonds, as the stage direction records: '*Teare the paper*' – '*with his teeth*', editors should add.

Other significant parallels point to Kyd's authorship of all three plays, beginning with the terms used to elicit the report. Cornelia invited the messenger to 'Discourse the manner of his hard mishap'. The Spanish King invited his general to 'vnfolde in breefe discourse' his news. In *Edward III* the French King invited the mariner to return and 'let vs heare the manner of the fight'; when he returned, however, he was asked to 'Relate . . . /

---

49 For a brief discussion, with further references, see Brian Vickers, 'Shakespeare and Authorship Studies in the Twenty-First Century', *Shakespeare Quarterly*, 62 (2011), 106–42, pp. 134–41.
50 See, e.g., Cyrus Hoy, 'Verbal Formulae in the Plays of Philip Massinger', *Studies in Philology*, 56 (1959), 600–18.
51 See Boas, *The Works of Thomas Kyd*, pp. xxxii, 395, and Erne, *Beyond 'The Spanish Tragedy'*, p. 55.
52 'Aux uns la cuisse estoit, ou l'espaule abbattue' (*Cornélie*, ed. Lebegue, L. 1765).

The sad discourse of this discomfiture'. These formulaic invitations to 'discourse' (three times) 'the manner of' (twice) are typical of Kyd, but not Shakespeare. Further, Shakespeare never used the word 'discomfiture'. Its only occurrence in the accepted canon comes in Act 1 of *1 Henry VI*, probably written by Nashe:[53] 'Sad tidings bring I to you out of France, / Of loss, of slaughter, and discomfiture' (1.1.58–9). Kyd, however, used the noun in the Argument to *Cornelia*, referring to 'the discomfiture of the Romans against the Parthians' (4). He also used the verb form four times in the play itself: in Cornelia's concern lest her father's 'braue regiments' should 'Be so discomfited' (3.1.111–15), in a description of how Sylla 'had discomfited and chas'd' his enemies (4.1.84), a similar outcome befalling Caesar's enemies, who are now 'discomfited' (4.2.98), and in the Messenger's speech describing how Scipio 'beheld / His people so discomfited and scorn'd' (5.274–5). Its appearance in *Edward III*, then, is another pointer to Kyd's hand.

In both plays the battles take place partly on land, partly by sea, where the combatants are at the mercy of the elements. In *Cornelia* the messenger recounts how Scipio found himself 'Besieg'd, betraide by winde, by land, by sea' (5.1.299). In *Edward III* the French messenger describes how 'both Sunne, the Winde and tyde / Reuolted all vnto our foe mens side' (3.1.180–1). In the naval battle between the English and the French blood flowed copiously:

> Purple the Sea, whose channel fild as fast
> With streaming gore that from the maimed fell.
> (3.1.161–2)

In *Cornelia*, Caesar recalls a battle

> When the Thessalian fields were purpled ore
> With either armies murdred souldiers gore
> (4.2.63–4)

In *The Spanish Tragedy* the carnage on the battlefield is so great that the bodies lie,

> Mingled with weapons and vnboweld steeds,
> That scattering ouer spread the purple plaine.
> (1.2.62)

These are formulaic descriptions, of course, but they point to the same author at work; indeed, one could interchange some components of these messenger speeches without damaging them. A more individual feature emerges when the amount of blood spilled on the battlefield inspires Kyd to create a complex metaphor of level open countryside, 'champaign' (in variant spellings), being turned into a quagmire of blood:

> Thys day, we see, the father and the sonne
> Haue fought like foes Pharsalias miserie;
> And with their blood made marsh the parched plaines
> (*Corn.* 1.1.38–40)

> They hewe their Armour, and they cleaue their casks,
> Till streames of blood like Riuers fill the downes;
> That being infected with the stench thereof
> Surcloyes the ground, and of a Champant[54] Land
> Makes it a Quagmire, where (knee deepe) they stand.
> (*Corn.* 5.1.173–7)

> This Champion fielde shall be a poole of bloode,
> And all our prospect as a slaughter house.
> (*Edw. III* 3.3.116–7)

This unique collocation of pools of blood and open country can only come from the same creative consciousness.

Other elements in *Edward III* share unique similarities of phrasing with Kyd's canonical plays. In *The Spanish Tragedy* the Messenger describes the opposing armies as 'Both furnisht well, both full of hope and feare' (1.2.25); the Messenger in *Edward III* reports that the French and English navies are 'Both full of angry spleene of hope and feare'(3.1.146), identical formulations. In *The*

---

53 See Brian Vickers, 'Incomplete Shakespeare: Or, Denying Coauthorship in *1 Henry VI*', *Shakespeare Quarterly*, 58 (2007), 311–52. I argued there that the original version, Henslowe's 'harey the vi', performed at the Rose theatre in 1592, was co-authored by Nashe (Act 1) and Kyd (Acts 2–5), and that subsequently (after 1594, when the Chamberlain's Men acquired the play) Shakespeare added three scenes (2.4, 4.2, 4.5) that turn it from a Talbot play to one dealing at least in part with the Wars of the Roses.

54 This spelling, 'in a Champant Countrey', recurs in Kyd's translation of Tasso, *The Housholders Philosophie*: cf. *Works of Thomas Kyd*, ed. Boas, p. 270.

Spanish Tragedy the Messenger describes how 'shi-uered Launces darke the troubled aire' (1.2.54), while his fellow narrator in *Cornelia* tells how

> The shyuered Launces (ratling in the ayre)
> Fly forth as thicke as moates about the Sunne
>
> (5.1.170–1)

In *Edward III*, after the English victory in the battle of Crécy, we find the stage direction '*Enter* Prince Edward *in tryumph, bearing in his hand his shiuered Launce*' (3.5.60). The co-occurrence of *shiuer* and *Launce* in three plays written within six years of each other, and in no other dramatic texts dating before 1596, exceeds the bounds of coincidence. In Kyd's lexicon a distinctive metaphor for a decisive act is the moment when the labourer's sickle initiates the harvest. As Revenge rebukes the impatient Ghost of Andrea:

> Thou talkest of haruest when the corne is greene,
> The end is crowne of euery worke well done:
> The Sickle comes not till the corne be ripe.
>
> (2.6.7–9)

So King Edward offers the French envoy one last chance to avoid battle:

> wilt thou yet resigne,
> Before the sickles thrust into the Corne,
> Or that inkindled fury turne to flame?
>
> (3.3.111–13)

The words 'sickle' and 'corn' are collocated in these plays and nowhere else in the pre-1596 drama corpus.

The matching collocations between *The Spanish Tragedy* and *Edward III* often take the form of single-line utterances in which at least three consecutive words are identical in both instances, with others matching in either a semantic or a syntactical function.[55] The neatness of patterning shows Kyd's tendency to formulaic utterance. Other unique matches extend over several lines, using a more complex structure. Thus both Hieronimo and King Edward formulate a vow of violent action while considering, and rejecting, an alternative course:

> *Hier.* And to conclude, I will revenge his death,
> But how? not as the vulgare wits of men,
> With open, but inevitable ils:
> As by a secret, yet a certain meane
>
> (*Sp. T.* 3.13.20–3)

> *King.* I meane to visit him as he requests.
> But how? not servilely disposed to bend,
> But like a conquerer to make him bowe
>
> (*Edw. III* 1.1.73–5)

This is neither imitation nor plagiarism but one of many instances of self-repetition. Another, truly unusual example of mental association in Kyd's lexicon found in both plays concerns a formation used in battle. The Spanish general describes their army's deployment as a squadron, that is, 'A body of soldiers drawn up in square formation':

> Our battels both were pitcht in squadron form
> Each corner strongly fenst with wings of shot
>
> (1.2.32–3)

In *Edward III* the French army, awaiting battle, is shocked to hear an ominous '*clamor of rauens*', as the stage direction puts it (4.5.18.0), in fulfilment of an earlier prophecy. The French prince Philip enters bearing bad news, as his father perceives: 'What fearefull words are those thy looks presage?' The young prince is so panic stricken that he cannot even utter the normal Senecan messenger's apology:

> *King.* Awake thy crauen powers, and tell on
> The substance of that verie feare in deed,
> Which is so gastly printed in thy face:
> What is the matter?
> *Phil.*   A flight of vgly rauens
> Do croke and houer ore our soldiers heads,
> And keep in triangles and cornerd squares
> Right as our forces are imbatteled.
>
> (*Edw. III* 4.5.25–31)

The significance of this scene in *Edward III* lies partly in its use of conventions representing changing fortunes on the battlefield, as used by Kyd elsewhere, but also in the fact that it shares with the

---

55 See Appendix 1.

quoted passage from *The Spanish Tragedy* a collocation unique in Elizabethan drama pre-1596, the co-occurence of the words *cornerd / corner*, *squares / squadron, imbatteled / battels*, together with the personal pronouns *our / Our*. The chance of two different dramatists producing such matching collocations is infinitesimal.

Cornelia will be an unfamiliar work to many readers, but it shares with *Edward III* a surprising range of expressions. Both plays seem to have been written, or at least completed, in the same year, and Kyd may have worked on them simultaneously.[56] Some of the significant matches consist of a single word, such as 'imbost'. In *Edward III* the French barricade 'Was thicke imbost with brasen ordynaunce' (5.1.135); in *Cornelia* the word is used to describe both the 'fearefull' defences of Carthage, with its 'Temples, Pallaces, and walls embost' (2.1.270), and 'our Emperor (at all points armed)' holding 'his Targe of steele embost' (5.1.105). In the corpus of pre-1596 plays 'e/imbost' is used three times to refer to animals and humans, while in *1 Tamburlaine* we find 'Embost with silke'. These are the only instances where the word is used in connection with defences or warfare. Other single word matches include unusual compound adjectives: 'my scarse-appearing strength' (*Edw.III* 3.3.202) matches 'a scarce-seen skyn' (*Corn.* 3.1.86), while 'fire-containing flint' (*Edw.III* 4.6.13–14) matches 'fier-darting eyes' (*Corn.* 5.1.179–80) and 'fire-sparkling eyes' (*Corn.* 5.1.214). There are many matches consisting of a single line of verse, for which space is lacking,[57] so I shall pick out some longer sequences, such as this description of the effects of war:

> I might perceave five Cities all on fire,
> Corne fieldes and vineyards burning like an oven
> *(Edw.III* 3.2.56–7)

> All sad and desolate our Citty lyes
> And for faire Corne-ground are our fields surcloid
> *(Corn.* 1.1.215–16)

Those are the only instances in the pre-1596 play corpus where 'city' and 'cornfield' are collocated. Another unique analogy shared by these two plays compares a troop of soldiers to a swarm of troublesome ants:

> and as a household Campe
> Of creeping Emmets in a Countrey Farme,
> That come to forrage when the cold begins,
> Cover the earth so thicke . . .
> Even so our battails.   *(Corn.* 5.1.72–9)

Here Kyd was translating Garnier, who had in turn borrowed the analogy from Virgil.[58] The fact that he used the same analogy in *Edward III* suggests that the history play was composed later:

> The snares of French, like Emmets on a banke,
> Muster about him; whilest he, Lion like
> Intangled in the net of their assaults
>   *(Edw.III* 3.5.28–30)

That analogy is so distinctive, the swarms of ants as hindrances (despite a difference in scale, and a mixed metaphor) that only one explanation is possible – common authorship.

Other extended collocations, associations of words and ideas that spread over several lines, suggest that Kyd turned to *Edward III* after translating *Cornélie*. In the opening scene of Garnier's play Cicero addresses Rome in an apostrophe, using the second person form:

---

[56] Freeman dates the composition of *Cornelia* to 1593, between May and December (*Thomas Kyd, Facts and Problems*, pp. 168–9); Erne judges that it was 'probably written in the second half of 1593' (*Beyond 'The Spanish Tragedy'*, p. 211). It was entered in the Stationers' Register on 26 January 1594. Martin Wiggins suggests that the references to the Earl of Derby in *Edward III* indicate that it was written for Lord Strange's / Derby's Men, in which case it is 'unlikely to date from before Ferdinando Stanley becoming Earl of Derby on Tuesday 25 September 1593'. He concludes that Shakespeare 'contributed to the play at the end of 1593, not long after finishing *Richard III*, during a short-lived period working for Derby's Men' after Pembroke's Men collapsed in that autumn: see *British Drama Vol. 3: 1590–1597* (Oxford, 2013), p. 228. Wiggins cites *Titus Andronicus* and *Richard III* as evidence for Shakespeare's move to Derby's Men (pp. 180, 220).

[57] See Appendix.

[58] Cf. *Cornélie*, 1600ff., 'Tout s'espand par les champs, comme un camp mesnager / De caverneux Fourmis, venus pour fourrager / Lors que l'hiver prochain ses froideus appreste' and *Aeneid*, Book 4, 402–7.

Romme, helas! Que te sert d'assugettir le monde?
Que te sert d'ordonner de la terre et l'onde?
Que te sert d'ordonner sous le pouvoir Latin . . .

(65–7)

Kyd translates this faithfully:

But Rome (alas) what helps it that thou ty'dst
The former World to thee in vassalage?
What helps thee now t'haue tam'd both land and sea?
What helps it thee that vnder thy controll . . .

(*Corn.* 1.1.68–70)

In *Edward III* the English King addresses France in
an apostrophe, also in the second person:

Ah Fraunce, why shouldest thou be this obstinate,
Agaynst the kind imbracement of thy friends,
How gently had we thought to touch thy brest
And set our foot vpon thy tender mould . . .

(3.3.27–30)

Another unique collocation, however, may suggest
the reverse sequence of composition. In *Cornélie*
the Messenger describes Caesar's decisive assault
on her father's troops: 'Les ennemis sur eux fon-
dre comme un tonnerre' (1785). As often, Kyd's
English is wordier than the French original, and to
describe the noise of battle he changes the analogy from thunder to a man-made cause, a hail of
flintstones used as weapons:

And when he saw the enemies pursuite,
To beate them downe as fierce as thundring flints . . .

(*Corn.* 5.1.280–1)

The word 'flints' is rare in the pre-1596 play
canon,[59] the only other match coming from *Edward
III* in the episode where the English archers, having no more arrows to fire, find another weapon.
Prince Edward, realizing that 'the ground it selfe
is armd | With Fire-containing flint', urges his
troops: 'to it with stones' (4.6.13–16), and they
win a victory against all odds. The French prince
is ashamed to report that

Some twentie naked staruelings with small flints,
Hath driuen back a puissant host of men (4.7.20–1)

The source of this episode was Holinshed's account
of the Cardinal of Périgord's fervent desire to
bring peace between the combatants, or else 'shall
the verie flintstones crie out of it'. This seeming
'prophesie' was fulfilled when the English archers
'toke vp pebbles from the place where they stood,
being full of those kind of stones, and approaching their enimies, they threw the same with such
violence on them, that lighting against their hel-
mets, armor and targets, they made a great ringing
noise'.[60] Perhaps Kyd dramatized this episode in
Edward III before completing his translation.

Whatever the sequence of composition, it seems
to me undeniable that *Edward III* and *Cornelia* came
from the same pen. One final unique matching collocation will, I hope, clinch the issue. In Garnier's
play Cornélie recounts a dream, in which she had
seen her dead husband, 'Le funebre Pompé d'un
visage piteux / Palle et tout decharné' (678–9):
that is, with a 'dismal', 'piteous', 'pale and hag-
gard' appearance. Garnier doesn't actually call him
a ghost; Kyd does, and adds a verb of his own to
describe the spectre's movement:

And loe (me thought) came glyding by my bed
The ghost of Pompey, with a ghastly looke . . .

(*Corn.* 3.1.73–4)

The same unique association of 'ghost' and 'glid-
ing' recurs in *Edward III* to describe the 'six poore
Frenchmen', emaciated by the English siege of
Calais:

You wretched patterns of dispayre and woe,
What are you, living men or gliding ghosts
Crept from your graves to walke upon the earth?

(*Edw. III* 4.2.12–14)

That this association is indeed a valid authorship
marker for Kyd can be seen from his Turkish
tragedy, written five years earlier, and the dying
words of his tyrant, having just killed his beloved:

---

59 The only other instance comes from *The Spanish Tragedy*,
Hieronimo's vow to pursue his son's murderers for whatever
time it takes, 'Wearing the flints with these my withered
feet' (3.7.71), but that refers to the road surface.
60 See Melchiori, ed., *King Edward III*, p. 211.

And sweete Perseda flie not Soliman,
When as my gliding ghost shall follow thee
With eager moode, thorow eternall night:[61]

Taken together with the other evidence presented here – and more could be cited – we may conclude, with a high degree of probability, that Shakespeare wrote the four scenes in *Edward III* traditionally attributed to him, but that the remainder of the play should be ascribed to Thomas Kyd.

APPENDIX I
UNIQUE MATCHES BETWEEN
THE SPANISH TRAGEDY
AND *EDWARD III*

It is not surprising to find many unique collocations shared by *The Spanish Tragedy* and *Edward III*, since war is central to both plays. Between them they contain a lexicon of collocations covering the whole sequence of battle, from exhortations to bravery, preparation for engagement, all the way to victory or defeat.

The opposed fighters threaten violence and bloodshed:

Stand from about me**, ile make a** pickaxe **of my** poniard
(*Sp. T.* 3.12.75)

Ile make a Conduit **of my** dearest blood
(*Edw. III* 3.1.112)

Face to face with their enemies, they are unmoved:

And therefore, **in despight of all thy** threats
(*Sp. T.* 4.4.189)

Then, Edward, here, **in spight of all thy** Lords,
I doe pronounce defyaunce to thy face
(*Edw. III* 1.1.87–8)

They celebrate the qualities that will be needed by a successful army:

Friendship and hardie valour **joynd in one**
(*Sp. T.* 1.2.75)

That, courage and experience **joynd in one**[62]
(*Edw. III* 3.3.223)

Those who survive can relate the onset of fighting:

Both **battailes joyne and** fall to handie blowes
(*Sp. T.* 1.2.47)

The **battailes joyne: and**, when we could no more
(*Edw. III* 5.1.150)

But the fortunes of war favour none, not even princes:

But straight **the Prince was** beaten from his horse
(*Sp. T* 1.2.79)

And saie, **the prince was** smoothered and not slaine
(*Edw. III* 4.5.122)

The capture of a prisoner brings renown to the victor, but also further conflict:

Thats none of mine, but his that **tooke him prisoner**
(*Sp. T.* 2.3.34)

What was he **tooke him prisoner** in the field?[63]
(*Edw. III* 4.2.48)

A successful army must maintain its numbers:

Brought rescue and encouragd **them to stay**
(*Sp. T.* 1.2.69)

If we can counsell some of **them to stay**
(*Edw. III* 3.4.13)

Once an enemy has been recognized, Kyd's combatants express impatience with delay and hasten to get on with the matter at hand, in an inter-related set of collocations:[64]

And not to **spend the time in** trifling **words**
(*Sp. T.* 2.1.44)

And not to **spend the time in** circumstaunce
(*Edw. III* 3.1.8)

---

[61] *The Tragedye of Solyman and Perseda*, ed. John J. Murray (New York and London, 1991), 5.4.147–9.

[62] Cf. also 'To ioyne our seuerall forces al in one' (*Edw. III* 3.1.186).

[63] Cf. also 'meeting with the Lyon in the feeld' (*Edw. III* 1.1.99), 'till thou hast won it in the fielde' (*Edw. III* 3.3.205).

[64] Cf. also 'so the Grashopper doth spend the time / In mirthfull iollitie, till Winter come' (*Edw. III* 3.2.16–17).

These English faine would **spend the time in words**
(*Edw.III* 3.3.138)

Some of the combatants risk their youth on the battle field, in the hope to win fame:

To gratious fortunes **of my tender youth**
(*Sp.T.* 1.1.7)

The painfull traffike **of my tender youth**
(*Edw.III* 5.1.230)

Some become victors on the battlefield, and are duly recognized:

For **well thou hast deserved** to be honored
(*Sp.T* 1.4.131)

I, **well thou hast deserved** a knighthood, Ned!
(*Edw.III* 3.5.88)

They consider ways of improving their position:

And make your late discomfort **seeme the lesse**
(*Sp.T.* 1.4.149)

By this revenge that losse will **seeme the lesse**
(*Edw.III* 4.3.82)

They offer each other consolation for loss:

Heere, take my hand-Kercher and **wipe thine eies**
(*Sp.T* 3.13.83)

Away with mourning, Phillip, **wipe thine eies**
(*Edw.III* 5.1.185)

Given that the majority of his sole and co-authored plays include scenes of battle, it is not surprising that the martial element bulks so large in Kyd's repertoire of collocations. But he could also draw on a store of more polite formulae, courteous phrases expressing deference and respect. Here, too, the phraseognomy of *The Spanish Tragedy* and *Edward III* is interchangeable:

Yes, to **your gratious selfe** must I complaine
(*Sp.T.* 1.4.93)

Your gratious selfe, the flower of Europes hope
(*Edw.III* 1.1.15)

Had but **your gratious selfe** bin there in place,
(*Edw.III* 5.1.82)

My gratious father, beleeve me so he doth
(*Sp.T.* 3.14.86)

My gratious father, and these other Lordes
(*Edw.III* 1.1.92)

My gratious father and yee forwarde peeres
(*Edw.III* 3.3.206)

That which may comfort both **your King and you**
(*Sp.T.* 1.4.148)

For this kind furtherance of **your king and you**
(*Edw.III* 4.1.5)

APPENDIX 2
UNIQUE MATCHES IN THE PRE-1596 CORPUS BETWEEN *CORNELIA* AND *EDWARD III*

(a) Single words

Wherewith they study to **exclude** your grace
(*Edw.III* 1.1.27)

Can bondage true nobility **exclude**?
(*Corn.* 2.1.295)

No sepulcher shall ere **exclude**
(*Corn.* 4.1.214)

Hot courage is **engendred** in my *brest*
(*Edw.III* 1.1.45)

Till jealous rage (**engendered** with *rest*)
Returnes them sharper set then at the first.
(*Corn.* 5.1.211–12)

[Note. These are the only instances in the pre-1596 corpus that combine the past participle 'engendred' with an emotion (also echoing 'brest' and 'rest'); in both plays it forms the prelude to war.]

England was wont to harbour malcontents,
Blood thirsty and seditious Catelynes
(*Edw.III* 3.1.13–14)

Blood-thirstie Discord, with her snakie hayre
(*Corn.* 5.1.178)

[Note: the association of 'blood thirsty' with civil unrest is unique in the pre-1596 corpus.]

May, peradventure, for *his* **negligence**

(*Edw.III* 3.2.22)

But still increaseth by *his* **negligence**

(*Corn.* 4.1.180)

But we may shorten time with **negligence**

(*Corn.* 4.2.148)

As ancient custome is of **Martialists**

(*Edw.III* 3.3.174)

As those brave Germans, true borne **Martialists**

(*Corn.* 4.2.46)

In sign whereof receive this **Coronet**

(*Edw.III* 4.1.7)

Presents your highnes with *this* **Coronet**

(*Edw.III* 5.1.100)

With many a fresh-flowrd **Coronet**

(*Corn.* 4.2.191)

(b) Collocations

Perhaps it will be thought a heynous **thing,**
That I a French man should discouer this,

(*Edw.III* 1.1.30–1)

No, t'is a secrete crosse, and vnknowne **thing,**
That I receiu'd, from heauen at my birth,

(*Corn.* 2.1.61–2)

'Tis **not a petty** Dukedome that I claime,

(*Edw.III* 1.1.82)

Perceiue we **not a petty** vaine, | Cut from a spring

(*Corn.* 2.1.370)

March, **and once more** repulse the trayterous Scot

(*Edw.III* 1.1.155)

And once more unjust Tarquins frowne

(*Corn.* 2.1.390)

Neere to the coast I have discride, my Lord

(*Edw.III* 3.1.62)

Ile pitch my tent **neere to the sandy** shore.

(*Edw.III* 4.2.61)

And casts him up **neare to the Coasts** of Hyppon

(*Corn.* 5.1.295)

Father, **range** your **battailes**, prate no more

(*Edw.III* 3.3.137)

Then this our steelde **Battailes** shall be **rainged**

(*Edw.III* 3.3.219)

So many enemies in **battle ranged**

(*Corn.* 2.1.92)

Why, **is it lawfull for a man** to kill,

(*Edw.III* 4.3.35)

Now, as **it is** not **lawfull for a man,**

(*Corn.* 2.1.223)

By this revenge that losse will **seeme the lesse**

(*Edw.III* 4.3.82)

My sorrow yet would never **seeme the lesse**

(*Corn.* 2.1.322)

For **when we see** a horse laid down, to die

(*Edw.III* 4.5.46)

And (sooth to say) why feare we **when we see**

(*Corn.* 2.1.331)

What need **we fight, and** sweate, and keepe a coile,

(*Edw.III* 4.6.11)

For Rome **we fight, and** those that fled for feare.

(*Corn.* 5.1.124)

That in the crimson braverie **of my** bloud,

(*Edw.III* 4.8.7)

That in the midst **of** this **my** mournfull state,

(*Corn.* 4.2.121)

To contradict our royall Queenes desire?

(*Edw.III* 5.1.70)

Who dares **to contradict our** Emporie?

(*Corn.* 3.1.16)

That now **are turnd to** ragged heaps of stones

(*Edw.III* 5.1.204)

Whose sweeter sleepes, **are turnd to** fearefull dreames.

(*Corn.* 5.1.359)

SHAKESPEARE, POETIC COLLABORATION AND *THE PASSIONATE PILGRIM*

FRANCIS X. CONNOR

Any literary endeavour requires collaboration, but not all collaborators deserve topline or title-page credit. To read a literary text *may* mean we engage intellectually with a publisher, typesetter, actor or any other agent responsible for such collaborations; that is, such non-authorial agents may inform our reading of the text in a way that seems important to understanding the text, or we may know through external evidence that the author intended for these elements to be necessary for the interpretation of his text. However, reading a text *must* mean that we engage with the author. Because of this, co-authorship – which I define as two or more authors sharing responsibility for writing a single work – is almost certainly the mode of collaboration of most interest to Shakespearians. In identifying Shakespeare's contributions to plays in which he is supposed to have contributed as an author, co-authorship (perhaps somewhat paradoxically) places William Shakespeare, the flesh-and-blood author, unambiguously at the centre of literary studies of his work.

Recent studies of co-authorship may be understood, to some degree, as a rejoinder to what Jeffery Knapp characterizes as a critical over-reaction to the 'uncertainty' of the authorial role in a theatrical culture, in which 'playwriting involved collaboration by definition'.[1] The Foucauldian arguments put forth by Jeffrey Masten and others claiming collaboration as the primary mode of authorship, one that mutes the singular authorial voice by rendering it historically contingent, have been challenged on theoretical and historical grounds by Knapp, Brian Vickers, John Jowett and others in the course of thinking about co-authorship, attribution study or other such concepts that insist upon the centrality of the historical author.[2] Most aggressively, Gabriel Egan's *Struggle for Shakespeare's Text* 'aims to help push the pendulum back from a currently fashionable dispersal of agency and insist upon authors as the main determinants of what we read', ultimately doing so by advocating the contemporary dominance of 'the single-author paradigm' and Lukas Erne's account of Shakespeare's 'literary consciousness' as encompassing, rather than distinguishing, literary and theatrical modes.[3]

Having re-affirmed that Shakespeare – the man who was born and died in Stratford, and made a

---

[1] Jeffery Knapp, 'What Is a Co-Author?', *Representations*, 89 (2005), 6–7.

[2] Jeffrey Masten, 'Playwrighting: Authorship and Collaboration', in *A New History of Early English Drama*, ed. John D. Cox and David Scott Kastan (New York, 1997), pp. 357–82; Brian Vickers, *Shakespeare, Co-Author* (Oxford, 2002), esp. pp. 506–41; John Jowett, *Shakespeare and Text* (Oxford, 2007), esp. pp. 6–26. More immediately relevant to *Passionate Pilgrim* is James P. Bednarz, 'Canonizing Shakespeare: *The Passionate Pilgrim, England's Helicon* and the Question of Authenticity', in *Shakespeare Survey 60* (Cambridge, 2007), pp. 252–67. Bednarz rejects Joseph Loewenstein's and Margreta De Grazia's arguments defending William Jaggard's attribution of *PP* to Shakespeare by rejecting their 'Foucauldian paradigm' which is 'severed from any notion of even the most historically contingent authorial agency' (254).

[3] Gabriel Egan, *The Struggle for Shakespeare's Text* (Cambridge, 2010), p. 3, pp. 228–9.

living writing plays and poems – remains the central figure in studies of the plays and poems we can identify as his, it is worth moving beyond co-authorship and thinking about how other modes of collaboration may (or may not) be relevant in particular cases. D. F. McKenzie's proposal for 'a new and comprehensive sociology of the text', encompassing 'the history of the book, its architecture, and the visual language of typography' remains an attractive approach, potentially offering fresh approaches to collaboration.[4] However, Egan has described this 'socialized approach' as one that 'treats the material objects created by writers, actual books, as more authoritative than the intentions that preceded them',[5] revealing an anxiety that approaches to collaborative authorship that extend beyond co-authorship constitute an act of Foucauldian dispersal, in this case sublimating the author to the process and products of publication. Heather Hirschfeld, specifically discussing collaboration, acknowledges the 'importance of composition or production processes that accrue around or alongside a text's written creation', while suggesting that this 'deliberately broad definition of collaboration as any kind of cooperative endeavor behind a literary or performative text . . . inadvertently [risks] neglecting the particular activity of shared composition as an object of study'.[6] This focus on co-authorship, however, may actually encourage attention to other modes of collaboration; since co-authorship was demonstrably an important theatrical practice, the focus on this mode offers a verifiable perspective on collaborative practices in the theatre. As MacDonald P. Jackson writes, 'understanding of "the social production" of dramatic texts and Renaissance England is surely increased by any information we can glean about the ways in which collaborating playwrights divided their labours'.[7]

Co-authorship, understandably, has little to tell us about Shakespeare's poetry; his major poetic works, *Venus and Adonis*, *Lucrece* and the Sonnets are all single-author works. Egan, Hirschfeld, Jackson and most of the other critics mentioned so far generally discuss Shakespeare's authorship in the context of the drama, the genre where such collaborations were most common. Yet poetry may also be a collaborative art, specifically lyric poetry circulated in manuscript. Arthur Marotti observed that 'in the manuscript environment the roles of author, scribe, and reader overlapped' within a system 'far less author-centered than print culture'.[8] At least some of Shakespeare's poetry circulated in manuscript, as evinced by Francis Meres's mention of Shakespeare's 'sugared Sonnets among his private friends', and by the manuscript record of some of Shakespeare's sonnets.[9]

Although discussions of Shakespeare as collaborator will necessarily focus on the plays, one printed book in his poetic canon may be understood as aligned with the practices of manuscript publication as described by Marotti and, as such, may be usefully considered with a broad definition of 'collaboration' in mind: *The Passionate Pilgrim* (hereafter *PP*), published in 1599 by William Jaggard and attributed on its title-page to 'W. Shakespeare'. *PP* includes at least five poems elsewhere attributed

---

4 D. F. McKenzie, 'Typography and Meaning: The Case of William Congreve', *Making Meaning*, ed. Peter McDonald and Michael J. Suarez (Amherst, 2002), p. 236. McKenzie's work is often paired with Jerome McGann's, particularly McGann's idea that 'bibliographic codes', such as paper, typography, illustrations, etc., can contribute to the meaning of a literary text, see *Textual Condition* (Princeton, 1991), pp. 59–72. For the most cogently argued critique of this approach, see G. Thomas Tanselle, 'Textual Criticism and Literary Sociology', *Studies in Bibliography*, 44 (1991), 83–143, esp. pp. 87–101.

5 Egan, *Struggle*, p. 152.

6 Heather Hirschfeld. *Joint Enterprises* (Amherst, 2004), p. 2.

7 MacDonald P. Jackson, 'Early Modern Authorship: Canons and Chronologies', *Thomas Middleton and Early Modern Textual Culture*, ed. Gary While and John Lavagnino (Oxford, 2007), pp. 86–7.

8 Arthur Marotti, *Manuscript, Print, and the English Renaissance Lyric* (Ithaca, 1995), p. 135.

9 For the manuscript circulation of Shakespeare's sonnets in the 1590s and beyond, see also Gary Taylor, 'Some Manuscripts of Shakespeare's Sonnets', *Bulletin of the John Rylands Library*, 68 (1985–6), 210–46; Arthur Marotti, 'Shakespeare's Sonnets and the Manuscript Circulation of Texts in Early Modern England', *A Companion to Shakespeare's Sonnets*, ed. Michael Schoenfeldt (Malden, 2007), pp. 185–203.

to Shakespeare: versions of its first two sonnets are later reprinted in *Shakespeares Sonnets* (1609), and versions of three poems had appeared in the 1598 quarto *Love's Labour's Lost* (hereafter *LLL*) printed by William White for Cuthbert Burby. Several poems in the collection had been published in books by other authors, B[artholomew] Griffin and Richard Barnfield, and others had been widely circulated before the book's publication and were not likely to originate with Shakespeare, notably the lyric 'Live with me and be my love'.[10] *PP* is unlikely to have been a co-authored work, in the sense that Shakespeare and Barnfield or any other poet planned the work and wrote poems to complete it. However, as a book that includes some work indisputably by Shakespeare and that is attributed to him, in what sense can we consider *PP* a collaborative work?

PP has hardly registered in recent, influential accounts of Shakespeare as a literary author: Lukas Erne, as I will discuss below, cordons it off as primarily Jaggard's commercial endeavour; Patrick Cheney, in proposing Shakespeare as a 'literary poet-playwright', a 'hybrid form of authorship articulated through the medium of both printed poetry and staged theatre, legibly registered in the Shakespearean poet-playwright author-figure', does not consider it.[11] The book is thus seen as playing only a marginal role in the development of Shakespeare's career; a by-product of his emerging popularity. However, by understanding it as a Shakespearian text resulting from the co-creative system of manuscript publication, *PP* can be recovered as a work that contributed to Shakespeare's development as a 'literary poet-playwright'. Having done so, I turn from *PP* to a dramatic text, *LLL*, to argue that the presentation of certain poems in the playbook, particularly one lyric, uniquely marked with a pilcrow and subsequently reprinted in *PP*, similarly demonstrates the potential for the social textuality of the lyric to intrude upon his plays, suggesting another form of collaboration in the plays. To call such practices 'collaborative' is not to diminish Shakespeare's creative or intellectual agency, but to identify one relatively minor

aspect of Shakespeare's career in which a socialized approach to textual analysis may be warranted.

PP has, because of the unknown circumstances of its production, rarely been considered collaborative. Lois Potter presents some grounds upon which we may consider Shakespeare a collaborator in the volume, concluding that, if Shakespeare offered William Jaggard, publisher of *PP*, his poems for inclusion in *PP*, 'in that case, Shakespeare himself would have been a collaborator on what – however it happened – can surely be called a collaborative volume'.[12] Potter distinguishes between the collaborative work (the indisputable fact that several authors' poems appear therein) and an author's active collaboration (the practice of authors agreeing to and participating in joining other authors with the shared goal of producing a coherent literary work). This maps onto Potter's distinction between sequential collaboration (authors working simultaneously on a playtext) and concurrent collaboration, when 'one writer took over a job that another writer had left unfinished, or revised it at a later stage'.[13] Because we have little empirical evidence of the history of *PP*'s production, we cannot know whether Shakespeare actively contributed to it voluntarily. This is fair; however, the caveat in Potter's conclusion again affirms co-authorship as the dominant mode of collaboration: 'in that case',

---

[10] Poem four, 'Sweet Cytherea', appeared in B. Griffin's *Fidessa* (1596); Poemeight, 'If Musicke and sweet Poetrie agree', appeared in Barnfield's *The Complaint of Poetrie, for the Death of Liberalitie*, published in 1598 by John Jaggard (brother of William). Poem twenty, 'As it Fell vpon a day', is also Barnfield's, from his 1598 *The Encomion of Lady Pecunia*. 'Live with me' had been circulating since the mid-1590s; its textual history is most conveniently outlined in Fredson Bowers' edition of Marlowe, although his narrative of the text's textual history has not been widely accepted.

[11] Patrick   Cheney,   *Shakespeare's   Literary   Authorship* (Cambridge, 2008), p. 11.

[12] Lois Potter, 'Involuntary and Voluntary Poetic Collaboration: *The Passionate Pilgrim* and *Love's Martyr*', in *Shakespeare and His Collaborators over the Centuries*, ed. Pavel Drabek, Klara Kolinska and Matthew Nichols (Newcastle Upon Tyne, 2008), pp. 12–13.

[13] Potter, 'Involuntary and Voluntary', p. 5.

if Shakespeare gave his work to Jaggard, only *then* is he a collaborator. In this sense, poetic collaboration is assumed to function in a manner similar to dramatic co-authorship.

Part of the reason *PP* has not been accepted as a collaborative work is its reputation as a book made against Shakespeare's wishes and thus a book that cannot be said to include an authorial role for Shakespeare. The book has long been identified as Jaggard's attempt to 'deceive unwary buyers' and 'a shady publishing venture by William Jaggard'.[14] James P. Bednarz blames Jaggard for including 'inferior' versions of the two Shakespeare sonnets alongside other unattributed or less popular poems that he 'fraudulently attributed' to Shakespeare (257). Jaggard did so not to create a new Shakespearian work but to cobble together a commercially viable anthology, one that, according to Bednarz, 'owes more to market forces than to the mentality of the scriptorium'.[15]

Despite this perception of the book as resulting from Jaggard's deception, we do not know whether Shakespeare approved or participated in the volume, as Bednarz himself acknowledges.[16] H. R. Woudhuysen recently suggested that it 'is worth considering' whether 'Shakespeare may have had a part in the publication' of *PP*.[17] Whether or not we agree with this assessment, the evidence for Shakespeare's reticence about the volume is as equivocal as the evidence that he may have actively contributed to the volume. The key external evidence for Jaggard's questionable practices is Thomas Heywood's complaint about the inclusion of excerpts from *Troia Britanica* in the 1612 edition of *PP*, which indicate that Shakespeare may have been similarly displeased about this act of appropriation. Heywood writes of a 'manifest injury' done to him by Jaggard's taking excerpts from his folio poem and reprinting them 'in a lesse volume, under the name of another, which may put the world in opinion I might steale from him'. Shakespeare, Heywood claims, was 'much offended with M. *Jaggard* (that altogether unknown to him) presumed to make bold with his name'.[18] This passage reveals that early modern writers were cognizant of plagiarism and wary about having their works misattributed,

and as such it demonstrates, *contra* Foucault, that 'modern' notions of authorship were recognized in the early modern period.[19] However, it is not clear whether Shakespeare is 'offended' specifically with the inclusion of Heywood's verses in the 1612 edition, or with *PP* as a whole; and, even if the latter is the case, we cannot be certain that Shakespeare felt similarly about Jaggard and *PP* in 1599, when he had only recently established his name as something someone would want to make bold with.[20]

Even accepting this reading of Heywood's comment, we still cannot completely recover Shakespeare's degree of involvement in *PP*. Nevertheless, there is room to treat the work as collaborative if we consider the manuscript origins of Shakespeare's poetry in the context of the period. Arthur Marotti laid the groundwork for such a view, noting that at least some of Shakespeare's sonnets were circulating in the late 1590s, and thus this 'manuscript-circulated verse was ready to be appropriated by enterprising publishers' with no obligation to seek Shakespeare's permission.[21] Since Shakespeare's sonnets were not exclusively his own literary property, publishers could and did publish them in a variety of contexts, none of them necessarily representing Shakespeare's final intentions.[22] Shakespeare tacitly agreed to have his sonnets circulate in such a manner; aside from the narrative

---

[14] J. Q. Adams, ed., *The Passionate Pilgrim* (New York, 1939), p. xiv; James M. Osborne, Louis L. Martz and Eugene M. Waith, 'Introduction', in *Shakespeare's Poems* (New Haven, 1964), p. 8.

[15] Bednarz, 'Canonizing Shakespeare', pp. 257, 255.

[16] Bednarz, 'Canonizing Shakespeare', p. 264.

[17] H. R. Woudhuysen, 'The Foundations of Shakespeare's Text', *Proceedings of the British Academy*, 125 (2004), 80.

[18] Thomas Heywood, *An Apologie For Actors* (London, 1612), G4r. Original spelling has been maintained, save for modernizing 'I' to 'j' and 'u' to 'v' when appropriate.

[19] See Vickers, *Shakespeare Co-Author*, pp. 522–3.

[20] Colin Burrow gives Jaggard a fair hearing in his edition of Shakespeare's *Complete Sonnets and Poems* (New York: Oxford, 2002), pp. 77–9.

[21] Arthur Marotti, 'Shakespeare's Sonnets as Literary Property', *Soliciting Interpretation*, ed. Elizabeth D. Harvey and Katharine Eisaman Maus (Chicago, 1990), p. 154.

[22] Marotti, 'Literary Property', pp. 165–6.

poems, for which he contributed prefatory epistles, Shakespeare did not seem inclined to collect and print his sonnets and shorter poems, and he was probably less so towards the end of the 1590s when his creative energies had turned primarily to the theatre. Nevertheless, it would not have hurt his career to cultivate attention for his lyric poems; just as he may have been involved with creating literary and dramatic versions of plays like *Hamlet* to appeal to reading and theatre audiences, he may have allowed some short lyrics to fly freely, allowing him to maintain a foothold in courts, coteries or whatever other circuits of manuscript publication, while continuing to cultivate his public, theatrical fame.[23]

Although *PP* may have been a by-product of manuscript circulation, the book does not read as a hastily assembled anthology or commonplace book. Instead, recent critics have recognized *PP* as an interesting book, and its poetry understood as maintaining a coherent thematic focus. Reassessments of the book itself by Potter (who believes that the 'publishing gimmick' of printing poems on rectos only was well-received)[24] and H. R. Woudhuysen (who observes that the small octavo 'has a feeling of something "special" and distinctive about it', and raises the possibility of it being a private publication)[25] have recuperated its reputation, encouraging us to think of it as a rather posh item rather than Jaggard's cash-grab. The critical reassessments of the poetry by Patrick Cheney, who argues that the work 'coheres with the general project of Shakespeare's poetry',[26] and Sasha Roberts, who interprets it as a sequence concerned with 'literary skill and artifice',[27] both emphasize ways in which Shakespeare remains paramount in the work; even the poems he certainly did not write are consistent with his literary work. If Shakespeare did not actively, willingly contribute to its production, the final product is a thoroughly Shakespearian text, one that could plausibly be read (and indeed was plausibly read) as Shakespeare's.

Although the book comes from a textually unstable and inherently collaborative system of manuscript publication, the organization of *PP*

actually complements Shakespeare's emerging reputation, identifying him with genres and styles with which he had already established himself. It is in this sense that recognizing *PP* as a collaborative work of Shakespeare does not diminish his authorial agency; instead it enhances such agency. This is particularly apparent in the first fifteen poems in *PP*, in which the only thing that betrays non-Shakespearian authorship is the appearance of several poems in other printed texts. *PP* begins like a sonnet sequence: the first six poems are conventional fourteen-line sonnets, as are poems 8 ('If sweet music and poetry agree'), 9 ('Fair was the morn') and 11 ('Venus with Adonis sitting by her'). Poems 7 ('Fair is my love'), 10 ('Sweet rose, fair flower'), 13 ('Beauty is but a vain . . .') and 14 ('Good night, good rest') all employ the stanza form Shakespeare used in *Venus and Adonis*. 'Crabbed Age and Youth' is the only outlier among the first fifteen poems, being a twelve-line song that seems to have been a version of a popular song; it would fit in the 'Sonnets to only twelve lines of music' section, and perhaps it was intended to go there.[28] All together, fourteen of the first fifteen poems that appear before the 'Sonnets' section of the book are plausibly 'Shakespearian'. This is not to claim that Shakespeare wrote the poems by Griffin and Barnfield that appear here but that there is clearly an attempt to edit the volume as a Shakespearian poetic work. The authentic Shakespeare poems are not simply appropriated and

---

23 On Shakespeare's possible literary and dramatic versions of *Hamlet*, see Lukas Erne, *Shakespeare as Literary Dramatist* (Cambridge, 2003), pp. 177–81, 220–44.

24 Potter, 'Involuntary and Voluntary', p. 10.

25 Woudhuysen, 'Foundations', p. 80.

26 Patrick Cheney, *Shakespeare, National Poet-Playwright* (Oxford, 2004), p. 159.

27 Sasha Roberts, *Reading Shakespeare's Poems in Early Modern England* (New York, 2003), p. 156.

28 'Crabbed Age' may have appeared in print as early as 1591, and possibly under Thomas Deloney's name in a lost edition of his *Garland of Good Will*. Burrow suggests that it may have been included because a later version of the song addresses Adonis (*Complete Sonnets and Poems*, p. 353); Woudhuysen offers a parallel with the Nurse and Juliet's dialogue in *Romeo and Juliet* 2.5 (*Shakespeare's Poems* (London, 2007), p. 400).

bulked out to make a book; they are shaped into a singular literary work, one consistent with the themes and prosody in Shakespeare's then-in-print poems.[29]

The work also appears structured in a way to distinguish the Shakespearian and quasi-Shakespearian material from the final five poems, which include poems less likely to be identified with Shakespeare. At least the second edition of the book includes a second title-page, 'SONNETS To sundry notes of Musicke', which may have explicitly served as such a partition.[30] This section includes several poems that appear to have been popular: most obviously, 19 ('Live with me and be my love'), was circulating in manuscript and appearing in plays before 1599. Poem 17 ('My lambs feed not') first appeared in Thomas Weelkes's 1597 Madrigals and also may have been circulating in manuscript. Sonnet 18 ('When as thine eye') may also have had circulated in manuscript before publication of PP. While this section still gestures towards Shakespeare – it includes 'On a day (alack the day)' from LLL, and Sonnet 18 uses the Venus and Adonis verse structure – there seems to be less of an attempt to imitate Shakespeare.[31] It seems significant that two of these lyrics had appeared, in some form, in a recent Shakespeare play: 'On a day' and 'Live with me and be my love', a snippet of which is sung by Sir Hugh Evans in The Merry Wives of Windsor 3.1.16–20, a play staged c.1597. The final poems in PP may not be as obviously Shakespearian as the first fifteen, but their inclusion in PP may gesture to his dramatic authorship; perhaps other songs in this section appeared in Lord Chamberlain's Men's productions.

Because of this emerging acknowledgement of PP's coherence, William Jaggard's work may be reassessed. These more charitable accounts of PP may inform Lukas Erne's account of the book in his recent Shakespeare and the Book Trade, which summarizes its production thus:

The Passionate Pilgrim . . . furnishes a fictionalized version of Shakespeare, fictionalized by a smart publisher, that is, who rightly anticipated that Shakespeare, the passionate pilgrim, would sell. (88)

While rightfully admiring his business acumen, Erne stops short of attributing any creative agency to that 'smart publisher'. For Erne, Jaggard smartly creates a book that can be plausibly attributed to Shakespeare to cash in on his contemporary popularity; if he is gifted, it is as a businessman rather than an artist. Indeed, although Erne has presented the most credible case that Shakespeare and his dramatic partners were involved in the publication of his work, Erne still keeps Shakespeare from any involvement in PP; instead, it is Jaggard who 'barely disguised that this miscellany was designed to cash in on the success of Venus and Adonis' (149), who was 'shrewd in fabricating a "Shakespeare" volume' (86) by 'connect[ing] his volume to Shakespeare by means of intertextuality', that is, by including poems linked to authentic Shakespeare works, including Venus and Adonis and Romeo and Juliet (88). For many scholars, Jaggard's motivation for publication remains primarily commercial.

However, if PP can be understood as a coherent work, albeit a work with which Shakespeare perhaps had nothing to do, we should attribute not simply a capitalist genius, but perhaps a creative genius, to William Jaggard. Bednarz

---

[29] Colin Burrow, offering four hypotheses for how Jaggard obtained copy for PP, speculates that Jaggard was encouraged to publish PP when he obtained two previously unpublished Shakespeare sonnets and 'decided to bulk them out with a mixture of poems that had previously appeared in print and others derived from manuscript sources' (Complete Sonnets and Poems, pp. 76–7); in his edition of Shakespeare's poems, Woudhuysen calls this theory the 'most cogent' of those Burrow outlines; Burrow himself notes that 'most editors incline' to this theory.

[30] J. Q. Adams proposed that the second title-page did not appear in the first edition. Since the first octavo exists only as a fragment, this is speculative; however, even if the first edition did not include a half-title page, the shift from recognizably Shakespearian verse to songs is notable.

[31] An earlier book published under similarly sketchy circumstances may provide some precedent for PP's structure: Thomas Newman's 1591 edition of Philip Sidney's Astrophel and Stella – soon recalled at the behest of the Sidney estate – follows the titular sonnet sequence with a page headed 'Other Sonnets of variable verse' (F4v), after which unattributed work by other poets, most notably by Samuel Daniel, begins.

calls this approach an 'anachronistically postmodern' defence, because, compared to Nicholas Ling, Jaggard's 'standards of attribution' were less reliable.[32] But Bednarz's account presumes that the mercenary capitalist cannot be a skilful editor and that the sorts of lyrical collaboration associated with manuscript publication could not have translated to print. Jaggard could easily have published the authentic Shakespeare poems as a commonplace book or an anthology akin to some of Ling's collections, surrounding his work with that attributed to other authors; instead, he chose Shakespeare-like texts to create a Shakespeare-like work. The thematic coherence outlined by Woudhuysen and Roberts imply the influence of some agent – an editor, author, publisher, perhaps Jaggard in this case – who selected, perhaps edited, and organized the poems to have a coherent thematic and authorial unity. As Colin Burrow suggests, 'Jaggard did not just invent a volume of poems by Shakespeare: he gave his readers just enough of Shakespeare to make them collaborate with his invention.'[33]

Indeed, the organization and design of Jaggard's book do seem to further encourage readers' collaboration. *PP* was printed with poems on rectos only (barring a few poems begun on rectos but continued on versos, presumably to save space).[34] This copious blank space is virtually unprecedented; Woudhuysen finds only two books similarly printed.[35] While Jaggard may be accused of printing the book so in order to pad its bulk, the blank pages could easily encourage readers to add their own work in the book, a kind of pre-fab interleaving.[36] Additionally, the small size of the book made it easily amenable to being bound with other books, especially the recent octavo editions of *Lucrece* (1598) and *Venus and Adonis* (1599), both published by Peter Short, who was associated with several books sold by *PP*'s bookseller, William Leake.[37] The example of Folger STC 22341.8, a *Sammelband* including *Passionate Pilgrim*, Shakespeare's *Lucrece* and *Venus and Adonis*, Thomas Middleton's *The Ghost of Lucrece*, and E. C.'s *Emaricdulfe*, and Huntington 59000–59002, where it is bound with *Venus and Adonis* and

Epigrammes and Elegies by I. D. and C. M., may indicate how it proved amenable to further collaboration. Discussing this book, Jeffrey Todd Knight says *PP* proved 'amenable to compilation' and summarizes its thematic links to the texts with which it was bound.[38]

In several ways, then, *PP* can be considered collaborative: the work itself combines Shakespeare's legitimate work with other authors, creating a text that can be read, at least in part, as a unified work; this work requires the agency of William Jaggard, who chose to print Shakespeare's poems in a book that emphasizes genres and styles associated with Shakespeare; the form of the book itself invites readers to collaborate. Such collaborations are not explicitly 'literary' in that they would change our interpretation of Shakespeare's texts, or that it would somehow override or supersede Shakespeare's intention for his literary work. But it may be a necessary consideration in the emerging paradigm of Shakespeare as 'literary' author, because publishers do act as intermediaries between authors and their readers. *Passionate*

---

[32] Bednarz, 'Canonizing Shakespeare', p. 260.

[33] Burrow, *Complete Sonnets and Poems*, p. 82.

[34] Adams, *Passionate Pilgrim*, pp. xxxiii–xxxv, offers a convenient chart of the book's outlay. In the extant second edition, only poems 19 and 20 appear on rectos and versos, although Adams suspects that more poems appeared thus in the first edition, which is extant only in a fragmentary state.

[35] Those books are William Drummond's *Poems* (c.1614) and John Day's 1570 *Pandectae locorum communium*. Woudhuysen considers the former, which is possibly a private publication, 'perhaps the closest comparison' to *PP* (*Shakespeare's Poems*, p. 80).

[36] For interleaving, the practice of binding blank leaves into a printed book, see Heidi Brayman Hackel, *Reading Material in Early Modern England* (Cambridge, 2005), pp. 142–3. Adams, discussing Folger STC 22341.8, records that an early owner of *PP*, George Fallowes, wrote a few notes in his copy: 'blank versos wherever they appeared would have been tempting to our idle scribbler' (*Passionate Pilgrim*, p. xxi).

[37] Leake is listed as the bookseller of the 1599 *Venus and Adonis*; ESTC lists ten other books printed or published by Short and sold by Leake.

[38] Jeffrey Todd Knight, *Bound to Read: Compilations, Collections and the Making of Renaissance Literature* (Philadelphia, 2013), p. 72; for discussion of these *Sammelbände* see pp. 70–5.

Pilgrim may be understood as the result of this kind of collaboration: a book that Shakespeare may not have actively participated in making, but one that contributed to his aspiration of literary authorship. Such collaboration would not diminish, but would rather enhance Shakespeare's literary reputation because, as Marotti writes, Jaggard, despite any commercial motivations, by identifying Shakespeare 'acknowledged the importance of a living author'.[39] There is therefore no need to turn to Foucault in defending *PP* as a Shakespearian collaborative work or in defending Jaggard's motives, nor should the historical author be abstracted into an author-function. Established Elizabethan models of collaboration justify its publication.

So *PP* plausibly offers a Shakespearian work; Shakespeare only authored a few of its poems, but the book ultimately affirms his authorial persona, consisting primarily of poems indicative of Shakespeare's authentic work. It seems unsurprising that it appeared during a boom period for Shakespeare publication in 1597–9, in which three editions of poetry and thirteen editions of plays, including first editions of *Romeo and Juliet*, *1 Henry IV* and *Richard II*, appeared. Among the newly published Shakespeare plays was *Love's Labour's Lost*, first printed in 1597, although the earliest extant copy of the play is the 1598 second edition. Cuthbert Burby published the second and likely, although not certainly, the first edition. *PP* and *LLL* also appeared at the beginning of a brief vogue for commonplace books and poetic anthologies at the end of the 1590s. Shakespeare's work would be well represented in these books; *Venus and Adonis* and *Lucrece* particularly, but *LLL* would be excerpted as well. Burby's prominence as a stationer may have contributed to the play's immediate popularity as a reading text. Neil Rhodes notes that *LLL*'s 'combination of romance and satire aligns it perfectly with the rest of Burby's list', and proved a natural fit with then-fashionable collections of wit such as Meres's *Palladis Tamia*, a Burby publication that mentions Shakespeare's play (216). *LLL* includes many sententious statements and, even though the 1598 quarto includes no commonplace markers like those in *Lucrece* or Q1 *Hamlet*,

sententiae from *LLL* appear in the printed commonplace books *England's Parnassus* (1600) and Bodenham's *Belvedere* (1600) and Robert Tofte's 1598 poem *Alba: The Month's Mind of a Melancholy Lover*. The latter employs the stanza form of Shakespeare's *Venus and Adonis* and includes four stanzas in which he recalls a performance of the play. Other allusions appear in John Weever's *Faunus and Melliflora* (1600) and I. M.'s *A Health to the Gentlemanly Profession of Servingmen* (1598).[40] These references to the play indicate the many ways the *LLL* quartos intersected with an audience also interested in printed poetry.

There may be some evidence of a more explicit engagement with the practices of printed poetry in Burby's *LLL*. In a play filled with lyric poetry, Act 4 particularly showcases Shakespeare's talent; scenes 2 and 3 include five lyric poems read by the scheming men who pine for their unattainable loves. These poems include all three lyrics reprinted in *PP*. Illustration 1 is Longueville's sonnet to Maria, as it appears in the 1598 *LLL* on E3r. This text differs substantively from the *PP* text in several places, and it is difficult to determine whether the versions are both set from a common copy, or *PP* from the earlier *LLL* copy. Notable here is the curved-stem pilcrow mark that introduces the poem. There is only one other similar mark in White's *LLL*; the other is an Aldine leaf set before another poem in 4.2, 'The prayfull Princesse' on E1r (see illustration 2).

These are not the inverted commas or manicules usually associated with commonplacing, nor do they mark *sententiae*; instead they introduce entire poems.[41] If the commonplace markers in *Lucrece*

---

39 Marotti, 'Literary Property', 154.

40 The relevant passage from Tofte, and information about other allusions to the play may most conveniently be found in H. R. Woudhuysen's Arden edition of *LLL* (1998), pp. 74–8.

41 *LLL* appears just before the boom in commonplacing printed plays, which, as Zachary Lesser and Peter Stallybrass have demonstrated, began in 1600 with Ben Jonson's *Every Man Out of His Humour*. Lesser and Stallybrass do not include *LLL* as a play with commonplace markers when they identify *Lucrece* as the only pre-1600 Shakespeare text with such

Long. This same shall go. *He reades the Sonnet.*

¶ Did not the heauenly Rethorique of thine eye,
 Gainst whom the world cannot holde argument,
 Perswade my hart to this false periurie?
 Vowes for thee broke deserue not punishment.
 A Woman I forswore, but I will proue,
 Thou being a Goddesse, I forswore not thee.
 My Vow was earthly, thou a heauenly Loue.
 Thy grace being gainde, cures all disgrace in mee.
 Vowes are but breath, and breath a vapoure is.
 Then thou faire Sunne, which on my earth doost shine,
 Exhalst this vapour-vow in thee it is:
 If broken then, it is no fault of mine:
 If by mee broke, What foole is not so wise,
 To loose an oth, to winn a Parradise?

1. Longueville's sonnet to Maria, *Love's Labour's Lost*, Q1 (1598).

or Q1 *Hamlet* identify these works as texts of particular importance, as Zachary Lesser and Peter Stallybrass have argued, then, although these odd marks in *LLL* do not mark *sententiae*, they may perform some of the functions of more conventional commonplace markers, and, in doing so, reveal the collaborative activities Shakespeare engaged in while writing both the play and his contributions to *PP*.

It is not immediately apparent why a compositor would add a pilcrow or aldine leaf at the beginning of these poems and nowhere else in the book, unless they are simply copying a mark in the manuscript.[42] Most editors believe the quarto *LLL* was set from an authorial manuscript, possibly in Shakespeare's hand.[43] At this point in the play, Longueville needs to read his 'stubborn lines' (4.3.52), and he entered carrying his poem on

markers. Zachary Lesser and Peter Stallybrass, 'The First Literary *Hamlet* and the Commonplacing of Professional Plays', *Shakespeare Quarterly*, 59 (2008), 394.

[42] The lost *LLL* Q0 complicates this argument, because the compositor likely set from printed copy, and it is unclear whether these marks appeared in the first edition. The pilcrow may be a sign of a corrected text; it has been suggested that the *PP* version of its associated sonnet was set from Q0. A compositor may thus have simply included a mark by an editor of Q0. That said, it is also possible that more marks appeared in the lost Q0 – in the case of *Lucrece*, each subsequent edition contained fewer commonplace marks; *LLL* could similarly have suffered such attrition. Alternately, they could have been added to the second edition of *LLL*, perhaps to call attention to poems that were circulating elsewhere.

[43] The lost first quarto makes assessing copy for the first edition difficult, but the quarto's extraordinary lapses of speech-prefix confusion make authorial copy highly plausible. For the most recent assessment of the play's text, see William Carroll, ed., *Love's Labour's Lost* (New York, 2009), pp. 181–90.

Holo. I wil fomthing affect the letter, for it argues facilitie.

The prayfull Princeffe pearſt and prickt
a prettie pleaſing Pricket,
Some ſay a Sore, but not a ſore,
till now made ſore with ſhooting.
The Dogges did yell, put ell to Sore,
then Sorell iumps from thickett
Or Pricket-ſore, or els Sorell,
the people fall a hooting.
If Sore be ſore, then el to Sore,
makes fiftie ſores o ſorell:
Of one ſore I an hundred make
by adding but one more l.

2. Holofernes's poem, *Love's Labour's Lost*, Q1 (1598).

a sheet of paper – 'wearing papers', as Berowne mockingly describes him (45).[44] Tiffany Stern has argued that plays may have been 'transcribed, kept, learned, revised, and even written, not as wholes, but as a collection of separate units to be patched together in performance', with songs particularly likely to be included on papers separate from the main playbook.[45] The lyric poems in Act 4 of *LLL* potentially offer such patchwork: the King, Longueville and Dumaine all read the love-sonnets onstage, offering an opportunity for Shakespeare to include just about any 'sugared sonnet' in the act. It is possible that, when composing the play, Shakespeare did not write poems specifically for the scene but he would contribute them later when it needed to be staged.

'The prayfull Princess' does not appear to have been printed elsewhere or to have circulated in manuscript. Unlike 'heauenly Rethorique', 'prayfull Princess' refers specifically to the action of the play; it is the epitaph on the death of the 'pricket' requested by Holofernes. It may still have been separate from the main text, but may not have been intended to be circulated elsewhere. On the other hand, since 'Did not the heuenly Rethorique' appeared in *PP* and since it is a sonnet, the sort of Shakespearian lyric we know circulated in manuscript, its pilcrow may take on additional significance. The curved-stem pilcrow is not there by accident; White does not use the mark at all in any of his contemporaneous dramatic texts;

---

44 Citations from Woudhuysen's Arden edition.
45 Tiffany Stern, 'Re-Patching the Play', *From Script to Stage in Early Modern England*, ed. Peter Holland and Stephen Orgel (New York, 2004), p. 156.

I have yet to find it in his non-dramatic texts. Pilcrows generally mark the beginning of a section or paragraph and sometimes they are used for references: Thomas Tusser's 1580 *Fiue hundred points of good husbandrie*, for instance, begins with 'A lesson' for readers 'how to finde out huswiferie verse by the *Pilcrowe*',[46] but White seems more inclined to use asterisks rather than a pilcrow (or an Aldine leaf) for references within his own books. The pilcrow (or a pilcrow-looking mark), in this circumstance, may have been designed to mark the sonnet intended to appear in the play and a printer, faithfully following copy, included it. The 1600 anthology *England's Helicon*, which includes four lyrics from *PP* (all of them, perhaps not coincidentally, from the 'Sundry Notes of Music' section), places a pilcrow at the beginning of many of its poems, connecting the mark with anthologizing.

In contrast to the commonplace markers in Q1 *Hamlet* that, according to Lesser and Stallybrass, distinguish it as 'a play for reading and even for study'[47] – a distinction that actually distances the printed play from its collaborative, theatrical versions – the pilcrow in *LLL* tethers the play to the collaborative activities of the theatre and manuscript publication. The sonnet, appearing in both *LLL* and *PP*, both possibly deriving from some iteration of Shakespeare's 'sugared sonnets', serves as a nexus between collaborative worlds of manuscript poetry and the theatre. Its appearance in the 1598 quarto suggests a possible modularity about it, perhaps a 'patch' in *LLL*'s copy, and a contribution to *PP*. Perhaps the pilcrow demonstrates that Shakespeare left some space in his playtext where he – or even other poets/playwrights – would add a relevant poem, whether written specifically for the play or not. If the pilcrow, or some similar mark, originated in Shakespeare's holograph *LLL*, it could reveal that Shakespeare did not initially write 'Did not the heauenly Rethorique' as part of *LLL*. It is part of the version captured in the 1598 quarto but that is not the only poem that could appear there. Where *LLL* is a coherent text aside from these possible patches, *PP* is a work comprised of such modular moments, a collection pieced together from work by Shakespeare and others.

I do not intend to argue or prove that Shakespeare actively participated, or even acquiesced, in contribution to *PP* and I am certainly not attempting to re-diffuse Shakespeare. Instead, I want to point to *Passionate Pilgrim* as a text, perhaps the only one in Shakespeare's career, that we can understand as a work of social collaboration, put into being by an author entering a field (lyric manuscript circulation) associated with non-authorial collaboration, and having a publisher take advantage of this system by creating a work that, deceptively or not, maintains the prosody and themes of that author's work, and, in the process, actually augmenting Shakespeare's reputation by affirming his skills as an Ovidian lyricist and sonneteer. I do want to suggest that, if we are newly inclined to understand Shakespeare as someone interested in printing his work, as someone who understood print publication as key to identifying himself as a literary author, it may have very well helped his career to participate in a small, elegant volume of poetry, one that demonstrates his influence as a poet and perhaps includes songs from his plays, at a time when he may have decided to turn from producing poetry to concentrate on theatre.

Brian Vickers concludes his argument about the need to heed the evidence of historical scholarship in this way: 'simply to open these sources is to notice not just the presence of the author but his centrality, in creating the play texts without which no theatrical production could take place'.[48] Similarly, authors remain central to the circulation of manuscript poetry, in part because the name of the poet would be necessary for admission to the rarified coteries and courts where such poetry would circulate. It is in this spirit that I want to read *PP* as a text where Shakespeare is central, and thus a text where we may see others – certainly

---

46 Thomas Tusser, *Fiue hundred pointes of good husbandrie* (London: Henrie Denham), A2v.
47 Lesser and Stallybrass, 'The First Literary *Hamlet*', p. 378.
48 Vickers, *Shakespeare, Co-Author*, p. 539.

Jaggard – collaborating with Shakespeare as revisers or perhaps editors, shaping some of his raw material into a coherent literary work while keeping it essentially Shakespearian. This does not mean Shakespeare co-authored the work, although he certainly authored some of its poems, and, considering the lack of clear evidence about the book's production, we cannot entirely dismiss the possibility that he may have agreed to contribute to the quasi-anthology. The critical reassessment of *PP* has begun, and hopefully a new understanding of *PP* as a Shakespearian collaborative work will help us continue to see the work as more than a minor Shakespeare curio.

CONTEXTUALIZING 'THE PHOENIX AND TURTLE': SHAKESPEARE, EDWARD BLOUNT AND THE *POETICAL ESSAYS* GROUP OF *LOVE'S MARTYR*

JAMES P. BEDNARZ

Although the authority of E. K. Chambers had been formidable enough to render suspect the 'disintegrators' who identified other hands in the canon for most of the twentieth century, by Mac-Donald P. Jackson's recent count 18 per cent of Shakespeare's extant plays, seven of thirty-nine (if one includes *Edward III*), 'are now widely thought to have been co-authored'.[1] And although it is now generally acknowledged that Shakespeare, with the possible exception of *Sir Thomas More*, collaborated with other dramatists only early and late in his career (before 1594 and between 1605 and 1613), we lack a viable account of his extraordinary collaborative experiment in print at its midpoint, when he joined what might be called 'the *Poetical Essays* group' of *Love's Martyr*. The evidence for Shakespeare's participation in this band of poets who wrote interconnected verses on a shared literary conceit is overwhelming. In or soon after June of 1601, his 67-line untitled elegy, which begins with the line 'Let the bird of lowdest lay' (now traditionally called 'The Phoenix and Turtle'), was published in a 17-page anthology of thematically related poems appended to Robert Chester's 167-page Elizabethan epic, LOVES MARTYR: / OR, / ROSALINS COMPLAINT. / *Allegorically shadowing the truth of Love,* / in the constant Fate of the Phoenix / *and Turtle.*[2] There, in a collection introduced on its internal title-page as, 'HERE-AFTER / FOLLOW DIVERSE / Poeticall Essaies on the former Sub- / iect; viz: the *Turtle* and *Phoenix*', Shakespeare's poem appears with verses by the still unknown 'Ignoto', John Marston, George Chapman and Ben Jonson. The title-page of *Love's Martyr* alerts readers to expect, in addition to Chester's poem, '*some new compositions, of severall moderne Writers* / *whose names are subscribed to their severall workes, upon the* / *first Subject*: viz. *the* Phoenix *and* / Turtle'. The poems in this short collection respond to Chester's central archetype, the mystical union-in-death of its allegorical lovers. Yet only the internal title-page of the *Diverse Poeticall Essaies* indicates what truly sets this book apart: the twelve poems that its publisher Edward Blount describes as having been composed by '*the best and chiefest of our* moderne writers'. Blount's *Poeticall Essaies* of 1601, the most elaborately self-referential of all Elizabethan verse miscellanies, both demonstrates Shakespeare's direct involvement with his fellow poet-playwrights in the book trade and documents his status as one of the period's most famous authors. Why then had Shakespeare and the others agreed to contribute? Four reasons, aside from financial gain, are plausible: they knew Sir John

---

[1] MacDonald P. Jackson, 'Collaboration', *The Oxford Handbook of Shakespeare*, ed. Arthur F. Kinney (Oxford, 2012), p. 33.

[2] Quoted from Robert Chester, *Loves Martyr* (London, 1601). The book was re-issued without its front matter by Matthew Lownes in 1611 as *The Anuals* [sic] *of Great Brittaine*. Its only modern editor is Alexander B. Grosart, *Robert Chester's Loves Martyr* (London, 1878). One of the two known exemplars of the first edition (STC 5119) is at the Folger Shakespeare Library. I quote from this edition in the library's Digital Image Collection at www.folger.edu.

Salusbury, to whom the volume was dedicated; they believed that it would be politically efficacious to be seen as his allies; they seized the opportunity to create lyric poetry imbued with a new philosophical density; and they were intrigued by the possibility of engaging each other as writers. The subject of this essay is the nature of their unique competitive collaboration and its implications for an understanding of early modern literary history.

I

When Shakespeare wrote 'The Phoenix and Turtle' for the *Diverse Poeticall Essaies*, he adapted his lyric to the requirements of a collaborative print publication that shaped its meaning. But at present the dominant interpretation of its production is predicated on a false analogy with dramatic 'plotting' that inhibits a full appreciation of its formal and philosophical subtleties. Tiffany Stern observes that early modern English dramatists, acutely aware of how 'careful advanced plotting was the secret to any successful play', designated it a separate phase of preliminary composition.[3] In dramatic collaboration, this preconceived plot-scenario was divided into 'parts' individually executed by writers whose scripts might then be subjected to overwriting and revision. Jonson, Marston and Chapman used this kind of plotting four years later when they composed *Eastward Ho!* for the Children of the Queen's Revels.[4] One can consequently understand why William Empson as well as Katherine Duncan-Jones and H. R. Woudhuysen, applying this dramatic collaborative template to the composition of the *Poeticall Essaies*, describe it as having a single master plot subdivided between Shakespeare and the rest, with Shakespeare commissioned to 'enact the funeral rites of both Phoenix and Turtle' and Marston, Chapman and Jonson designated to celebrate the 'wondrous creature, arising out of the Phoenix and Turtle Doves ashes'.[5] Yet a different collaborative paradigm is necessary to account for its dialogical structure, because Marston alone finds life in the cinders of Shakespeare's verse. Chapman and Jonson, whose poems complete the collection, *never* mention the birth of a new phoenix;

they manipulate the symbolism of the Phoenix and Turtle solely to define the moral obligation true love imposes in exchange for the benefit it bestows. Instead of signalling a unified narrative, the title of the *Diverse Poeticall Essaies* advertises its philosophical and stylistic multiplicity. Although orchestrated through editing, the artistic process that produced it was less restrictive than dramatic collaboration, since it was the result of a mode of 'Invention' that the dedication describes as being '*freer then the* Times' (line 15).[6] The celebrity poets were allowed so much independence that they were not even required to praise Salusbury or Chester in their individual contributions. Further, because each of the miscellany's major contributions is designated by an authorial 'subscription', the collaboration's formula was essentially competitive, with critical fault-lines dividing the reinterpretations of Chester's myth that Blount combined to produce the following sequence:

---

[3] Tiffany Stern, *Documents of Performance in Early Modern England* (Cambridge, 2009), p. 10.

[4] Suzanne Gossett and W. David Kay, editors of *Eastward Ho!* in *The Cambridge Edition of the Works of Ben Jonson*, ed. David Bevington *et al.*, 7 vols. (Cambridge, 2013), vol. 2, p. 537, acknowledge the 'lively critical debates' about the play's division of authorship, but conclude that: 'Most investigators . . . have agreed upon a largely sequential composition, with Marston primarily responsible for 1.1–2.1, Chapman for 2.2–3.3, and Jonson essentially for 4.2 to the end.' They qualify this conclusion by admitting that certain scenes, such as 2.1, remain in dispute and that 4.1 might show touches of all the collaborators, and they also note that occasionally there are 'parallels to the work of one author in scenes assigned to another'.

[5] William Empson, *Essays on Shakespeare* (Cambridge, 1986), p. 25; Katherine Duncan-Jones and H. R. Woudhuysen, eds., *Shakespeare's Poems* (London, 2007), p. 114. In *Ungentle Shakespeare: Scenes from the Life* (London, 2001), p. 142, Duncan-Jones had previously written that Shakespeare as 'the senior poet was specifically given the delicate assignment of writing an elegy, while the other, younger writers had the task of celebrating the re-born Phoenix'. Chapman, however, who was born around 1559, was the oldest of the group.

[6] Charles Cathcart, *Marston, Rivalry, Rapprochement, and Jonson* (Aldershot, 2008), p. 26, notes that in Marston's *What You Will*, Quadratus refers to Lampatho (whom I take to be a parody of Jonson) as 'an essayist' and that, in Jonson's answer, *Poetaster*, Crispinus (Marston's surrogate) speaks of 'an essay of my poetry'.

INVOCATIO, *Ad Apollinem & Pierides. Vatum Chorus.*
To the worthily honor'd Knight
Sir John Salisburie.   Vatum Chorus.
The first.
The burning.   *Ignoto.*
Untitled poem beginning 'Let the bird of lowdest lay',
followed by *Threnos.*   *William Shake-speare.*
A narration and description of a most exact wondrous
creature, arising out of the Phoenix and Turtle Doves ashes.
The Description of this Perfection.
To Perfection. A Sonnet.
Perfectioni Hymnus.   *John Marston.*
Peristeros: or the male Turtle.   *George Chapman.*
Praeludium.
Epos.   *Ben: Iohnson.*
The Phoenix Analysde.
Ode ἐνθουσιαστική.   *Ben: Iohnson.*

Twenty-first century readers might find the phrase 'diverse poetical essays' bland or trite. But at the turn of the seventeenth century it was as startlingly 'moderne' as the book's celebrity poets. It alerted readers to expect a set of exploratory poems based on multiple interpretations of a shared myth. Literary historians commonly assume that either Jonson or Marston served as Salusbury's agent in gathering and 'editing' the collection. Colin Burrow, for instance, speculates that Jonson 'orchestrated the efforts of the other poets', while Duncan-Jones suggests that Marston 'recruited' them.[7] But a shift in critical focus from poet to publisher, from text to book, and from 'part' to 'essay' provides keener insight into the social processes that produced these interactive poems. R. A. Small in 1899 suggested an alternative to this excessively author-based analysis when he assumed that 'the compiler of the book' had 'asked these four poets for verses'.[8] Its publisher served as what we now call its 'editor'. Publishers were, as Zachary Lesser observes, 'the primary readers and interpreters of the early modern book trade'.[9]

Blount alone possessed the literary judgement and artistic distance to craft a balanced presentation of Marston's and Jonson's works at a time when their views of each other's writing were so mutually antagonistic. He alone would have seemed capable of incorporating the competing poetics of Shakespeare and Jonson, whose literary programmes and styles register such different reconceptualizations of Chester's myth. Of the major Elizabethan miscellanies, Elizabeth W. Pomeroy notes, only *A Poetical Rhapsody* was 'published under the direction of a gentleman rather than a printer'.[10] As an outside arbiter, Blount would have been better able to define, frame and coordinate these polyvocal revisions of Chester's allegory. 'Rarely', writes Sidney Lee, 'have publishers exercised larger powers of control over the fruits of the author's pen.'[11] If we conceive of 'The Phoenix and Turtle' as a product of the book trade, Blount is the person most likely to have supervised its integration into *Love's Martyr*. At the end of the nineteenth century, Edward Arber remarked that the time had come for 'the English Printer and the English Publisher' to 'take their due place in the national estimation'. But the typical Elizabethan stationer is still frequently considered to have been merely venal or obtuse, stereotypes of A. W. Pollard's 'impecunious copy-snatcher' and Leo Kirschbaum's professional tradesman, almost entirely devoid of intellectual aspirations.[12] The stationers, according to Peter Ackroyd, were 'tradesmen principally concerned to earn a profit', who can 'in no sense be seen as "patrons" to the dramatists'.[13] With the turn towards cultural

---

7   Colin Burrow, ed., *William Shakespeare: Complete Sonnets and Poems* (Oxford, 2002), p. 88, and Duncan-Jones, *Ungentle Shakespeare*, p. 143.

8   R. A. Small, *The Stage-Quarrel between Ben Jonson and the So-Called Poetasters* (Breslau, 1899), p. 127.

9   Zachary Lesser, *Renaissance Drama and the Politics of Publication: Readings in the English Book Trade* (Cambridge, 2004), p. 23.

10 Elizabeth W. Pomeroy, *The Elizabethan Miscellanies: Their Development and Conventions* (Berkeley, 1973), p. 71.

11 Sidney Lee, 'An Elizabethan Bookseller', in *Bibliographica*, 12 vols., ed. A. W. Pollard (London, 1895), vol. 1, p. 474.

12 Edward Arber, *A Transcript of the Register of the Company of Stationers, 1554–1640*, 5 vols. (Birmingham, 1894), vol. 1, p. xiii. A. W. Pollard, *Shakespeare's Fight with the Pirates and the Problems of the Transmission of His Text* (London, 1917), p. 40, and Leo Kirschbaum, *Shakespeare and the Stationers* (Columbus, 1955).

13 Peter Ackroyd, *Shakespeare: The Biography* (New York, 2006), p. 422.

bibliography, however, the decisive role played by early modern stationers in constructing the English literary canon is taken more seriously.

Blount, under the direction of Salusbury, need not be considered the sole agent responsible for assembling the *Poeticall Essaies*. The influence of others, especially Jonson, who wrote about half of the collection's lines of verse, is also essential. The 'role of the publishers, and, in particular, the extent to which they were responsible for decisions concerning typography and format is not self-evident', Mark Bland wisely observes.[14] After all, the only unquestionable mark Blount left on *Love's Martyr* is his curt identification of himself on its title page: 'Imprinted for E.B.' Inference is made uncertain by the variable nature of the undocumented financial and editorial transactions among patrons, poets and stationers who brought books to the press. But inflection points are visible. In 1598, Francis Meres, honouring the best contemporary writers in *Palladis Tamia*, noted that in antiquity a person who handled 'grave and necessary matters' was entitled to be called a 'Vates' (a 'prophetic poet' or 'bard')'.[15] Expressing an equivalent enthusiasm for Shakespeare, Marston, Chapman and Jonson, Blount imagined them as a chorus of prophetic poets – a '*Vatum Chorus*' – and staged their philosophical colloquy as a kind of poetic symposium in the pages of *Love's Martyr*.

II

Recently Gary Taylor has revived interest in Blount as a stationer who exhibited outstanding literary taste as well as an active involvement with the books he published. Blount is, of course, particularly distinguished as a principal member of the syndicate that produced the Shakespeare First Folio in 1623. This followed his publication of the first English translation of Montaigne's *Essays* in 1603 and, with William Barrett, Cervantes's *Don Quixote* in 1612. Educated alongside Edmund Spenser at the Merchant Taylors' School and apprenticed to Henry Ponsonby, one of the most important stationers of the English Renaissance, Blount brought

superb training to his profession. Never purchasing his own press, he opened his business in 1594, acting primarily, in Sonia Massai's words, 'as a procurer and presenter of copy'.[16] A member of the Stationers' Company, he specialized in acquiring manuscripts that he either sold to other stationers or else, if he meant to publish them himself, brought to a printer, such as Richard Field in the case of *Love's Martyr*. Field's device of an anchor encircled by the motto '*Anchora Spei*' ('Anchor of Hope') adorns the book's internal title page. His former Stratford neighbour, Field had been the first person to publish Shakespeare when he issued *Venus and Adonis* in 1593, and it is possible that Blount sought him out for the occasion in part because of this nostalgic association.[17] After his apprenticeship to Ponsonby ended in 1588, Blount was still employed by his shop in 1590 when it produced prestigious editions of two contemporary masterpieces: Sir Philip Sidney's *Arcadia* and Edmund Spenser's *Faerie Queene*. (Field

---

14 Mark Bland, *A Guide to Early Printed Books and Manuscripts* (Chichester, 2013), p. 208.

15 Francis Meres, *Palladis Tamia, or, Wit's Treasury*, in G. Gregory Smith, ed., *Elizabethan Critical Essays*, 2 vols. (Oxford, 1904), vol. 2, p. 313.

16 Sonia Massai, *Shakespeare and the Rise of the Editor* (Cambridge, 2007), p. 160. Gary Taylor's article on Blount in the *ODNB*, ed. H. C. G Matthew and Brian Harrison, 60 vols. (Oxford, 2009), vol. 6, pp. 297–8, is the best overview of his career.

17 Having worked on George Silver's *Paradoxes of Defence* (1599) for Blount, Field later printed only William Alexander of Menstrie's *Aurora* (1604) and *A Paraenesis to the Prince* (1604) for him. Coincidentally, the first Latin edition of the *Amores* published in England, in 1583 (the one probably used by Marlowe), was issued by Thomas Vautrollier in a collection of Ovid's erotica, while Richard Field was an apprentice in his shop. Field (who married Vautrollier's widow and took over his press) then printed for John Harrison a Latin edition of Ovid's *Metamorphoses* in 1589 and a second book consisting of the *Heroides* and sections of the *Amores*, the *Ars Amatoria* and *Remedia Amoris* in 1594. Harrison stocked these with *Venus and Adonis* and *Lucrece*. Lukas Erne, *Shakespeare and the Book Trade* (Cambridge, 2013), p. 148, notes that Harrison therefore sold in his bookshop 'the chief poems of Ovid and the English Ovid'. See also Adam G. Hooks, 'Shakespeare at the White Greyhound', in *Shakespeare Survey 64* (Cambridge, 2011), pp. 260–75, pp. 267–72.

would print the second instalment of Spenser's epic in 1596.) Ponsonby even assigned Blount to be the employee responsible for collecting the first payment of Spenser's pension, on Lady Day, 25 March 1591, sequent to the poet's departure for Ireland.[18] A self-described friend of Christopher Marlowe, Blount styled himself the dead poet's literary 'executor' when he spearheaded a Marlowe revival in 1598 by publishing *Hero and Leander* with a touching dedication to Sir Thomas Walsingham. A huge success, *Hero and Leander* became a 'publishing event' when it was supplemented in the same year by two other stationers with an adaptation by George Chapman and a sequel by Henry Petowe.[19] Two years later, Thomas Thorpe dedicated his publication of Marlowe's translation of the first book of Lucan's *Pharsalia* to Blount, from whom he had obtained the manuscript. Like his friend Blount, Thorpe had a taste for Marlowe and Shakespeare, whose *Sonnets* he published in 1609. Indeed, Blount guided his taste so absolutely 'that of the eighteen titles Thorpe entered or published between 1604 and 1610', Lukas Erne notes, 'eleven were plays or masques by Jonson, Marston, and Chapman'.[20] Thorpe specialized in the celebrity authors of the *Poetical Essays* group.

One sign of Blount's involvement with the *Poeticall Essaies* is its signal generic nomenclature. Around the time that *Love's Martyr* was printed, the 'essay' was a revolutionary new genre with which Blount's career as a publisher was centrally involved. It is to this literary innovation, rather than to the theatrical practice of collaborative scriptwriting, that we must turn to account for the collection's mode of production. By the end of the sixteenth century, the word 'essay' had become a fashionable generic marker for both modern prose and poetry. The trend was sparked by the appearance of Francis Bacon's *Essayes* in 1597 and 1598, followed by the *Essayes* of Sir William Cornwallis in 1600 and 1601, along with the *Essaies* of Robert Johnson in the latter year. In the middle of this onrush, on 4 June 1600, Blount entered for publication John Florio's translation of Michel de Montaigne's *Essayes* (published 3 years later), providing English readers with a version of the book that had

invented the genre in the 1580s. By the time Blount chose this rubric for the collection in 1601 he certainly knew that Samuel Daniel (Florio's brother-in-law, who wrote a commendatory poem for his influential translation) had previously applied it to verse in the title of his own *Poeticall Essayes* of 1599, which includes: *The Civil Wars, Musophilus, The Epistle of Octavia to Antonius, The Tragedy of Cleopatra* and *The Complaint of Rosamond*.[21] Daniel's rubric conjoins history, literary defence, epistle, tragedy and complaint. The same designation, promising variety, was used in 1605 by John Davies of Hereford's WITTES PILGRIMAGE, / *(by Poeticall Essaies)* / Through a World of amorous Sonnets, *Soule-passions, and other Passages,* / Divine, Philosophicall, Morall, / *Poeticall, and Politicall.* Jean Starobinski traces one etymological root of the word 'essay' to the Latin '*exagium*' (scale), which suggests a 'weighed consideration'.[22] And this sense powerfully resonates with Shakespeare's provocative use of the word 'Session' (line 9) to describe the gathering of the Eagle, Swan and Crow, in what is otherwise depicted as an 'obsequie' (line 12). Elsewhere in Shakespeare's work this word denotes either 'the sitting of a court of law in trial' or

---

18   See Herbert Berry and E. K. Timings, 'Spenser's Pension', *Review of English Studies*, 11 (1960), 254–9, p. 255.
19   For a study of the poem's complex transfers of ownership, see W. W. Greg, 'The Copyright of *Hero and Leander*', *Library*, 3–4 (1944), 165–74.
20   Erne, *Shakespeare and the Book Trade*, p. 156.
21   John Pitcher, 'Essays, Works and Small Poems: Divulging, Publishing and Augmenting the Elizabethan Poet, Samuel Daniel', in *The Renaissance Text: Theory, Editing, Textuality*, ed. Andrew Murphy (Manchester, 2000), p. 11, states that Daniel used the 'essay' genre to characterize his collection as a series of 'trials, experiments, assays into different ways of thinking' in 'rhymed verse and stanzas rather than prose'. In 1620, Blount also found this generic rubric useful when he introduced *Horae Subsecivae* (London, 1620) as 'of mixt matter, by the way of observations, or Essayes, and Discourses' (A2ᵛ–A3ʳ), the virtues of which were 'matter and variety' (A3ʳ). And he returned to this formula again in 1628 when he published John Earle's *Micro-cosmographie, Or A Peece of the World Discovered; in Essays and Characters*.
22   Jean Starobinski, 'Can One Define the Essay?' *Essayists on the Essay: Montaigne to Our Time*, ed. Carl H. Klaus and Ned Stuckley-French (Iowa City, 2012), pp. 110–11.

'a political conference to determine matters of state'.[23] Such an occasion requires a trumpeter, not a church bell. In using the word 'Session' to describe his memorial rite, Shakespeare risks disrupting the narrative surface of his fiction to underscore a key epistemological paradox concerning 'the truth of love' represented by the Phoenix and Turtle: that Reason, the faculty of judgement we ordinarily employ to determine such matters, can never comprehend it.

> Reason in it selfe confounded,
> Saw Division grow together,
> To themselves yet either neither,
> Simple were so well compounded.
>
> That it cried, how true a twaine,
> Seemeth this concordant one,
> Love hath Reason, Reason none,
> If what parts, can so remaine.   (lines 41–8)

Proposing the impossible, the session's pressure to judge confronts the incapacity of Reason to understand what is only accessible to the non-rational Reason of Love. Under these conditions, the meaning of Shakespeare's essay is its mystery.

Bibliographers have shown a keen interest in Blount's role in publishing Shakespeare's drama in the First Folio of 1623 but they have neglected his interest in Shakespeare's poetry in 1601. Worse yet, when Sidney Lee first drew attention to Blount in 1895, he mistakenly assumed that the stationer had pirated 'The Phoenix and Turtle' through which he had 'first associated, although not by mutual consent, with the most commanding figure of his generation'.[24] Because Blount published the works of Robert Dallington in 1605, William Cavendish in 1620 and John Earle in 1628 without their initial permission, Lee assumed that he had acted as a 'snapper-up of unconsidered trifles' in filching 'The Phoenix and Turtle' as well.[25] His guess was based on his mistaken belief that 'Shakespeare, except in the case of his two narrative poems, showed utter indifference to all questions touching the publication of his works'. This misconception, however, has been recently countered by Lukas Erne's demonstration of the extent to which Shakespeare and the Lord Chamberlain's Men assisted stationers in bringing about his overwhelming bibliographic presence in late Elizabethan culture.[26] 'The Phoenix and Turtle' could only have been written for this volume.

The driving force behind *Love's Martyr* was unquestionably Sir John Salusbury, a patron of poets at Lleweni, his estate in Denbighshire, and in London.[27] And the most plausible reason for

---

23 Shakespeare uses 'session' eight times and 'sessions' three times in his works. The sense here is close to Angelo's request in *Measure for Measure* that the Duke, 'No longer session hold upon my shame' (5.1.363). Leontes in *The Winter's Tale* convenes his 'sessions' (3.2.1) to judge Hermione's virtue, and Edgar tells Albany in *King Lear* that he will appear 'where you shall hold your session' (5.3.55). In Sonnet 30, the poet internalizes it as a juridical metaphor for memory in evoking the 'sessions of sweet silent thought' (line 1), as does Iago in *Othello* when he asks: 'Who has a breast so pure / But some uncleanly apprehensions / Keep leets and law-days and in sessions sit / With meditations lawful?' (3.3.143–6). Burrow, *Complete Sonnets and Poems*, p. 373, in his note on line 9 of 'The Phoenix and Turtle' mentions that 'Session' refers to an 'ecclesiastical gathering' in Scotland, but this meaning appears nowhere else in the canon.

24 Sidney Lee, 'An Elizabethan Bookseller', *Bibliographica*, vol. 1, p. 482.

25 Lee, 'Elizabethan Bookseller', vol. 1, p. 474, condemned Blount for being 'destitute of all modern conceptions of the rights either of his authors or of his rivals in the trade'. In a remarkable re-attribution, Quentin Skinner, 'Hobbes and the Humanist *Studia Humanitatis*', *Writing and Political Engagement in Seventeenth-Century England*, ed. Derek Hirst and Richard Strier (Cambridge, 1999), p. 74, maintains that of the four 'Discourses' of Cavendish's *Horae Subsecivae* (1620), Thomas Hobbes 'almost unquestionably' wrote the third.

26 Sidney Lee, *A Life of Shakespeare* (London, 1908), p. 412; Lukas Erne, *Shakespeare as Literary Dramatist* (Cambridge, 2003) and *Shakespeare and the Book Trade* (2013).

27 For Salusbury as a patron, see Carleton Brown, *Poems by Sir John Salusbury and Robert Chester* (London, 1914), pp. xi–xxvii; E. A. J. Honigmann, *Shakespeare, The Lost Years* (Manchester, 1985), pp. 90–113; Katherine Duncan-Jones and Henry Woudhuysen, eds., *Shakespeare's Poems* (London, 2007), pp. 102–7, and James P. Bednarz, *Shakespeare and the Truth of Love: The Mystery of 'The Phoenix and Turtle'* (Basingstoke, 2012), pp. 73–6. Salusbury also composed verse, although G. Blakemore Evans, *The Poems of Robert Parry* (Tempe, 2005), pp. 10–34, disproves Brown's attribution of some of *Sinetes Passions* (1597) to him.

its publication is that Salusbury wanted to use the book to commemorate the knighthood that Queen Elizabeth granted him in June of 1601.[28] To this end, he apparently contacted Blount with the objective of having him publish a long, diffuse, allegorical epic, loosely based on *The Faerie Queene*, cobbled together with ancillary poems, by his protégé Robert Chester. Probably a member of Salusbury's household, Chester was an unknown and largely untalented poet. Blount, recognizing the immense disparity in quality between *The Faerie Queene* and *Love's Martyr*, would not have published Chester's poem without some kind of subvention.[29] As part of their agreement, he and Salusbury probably decided that *Love's Martyr* could be made more prestigious and vendible by appending a short collection of poems by famous authors the knight knew. That Salusbury sought to dignify Chester's poem through the addition of the *Poeticall Essaies* is a forceful reminder of the increased sociocultural status of professional writers such as Shakespeare, whose celebrity is construed as symbolic capital, an honour conferred on his patron. Chester's dedication to Salusbury seeks protection and legitimation, but the volume's great poets add their assumed dignity to his. The format Blount contrived, in two parts, freed its celebrity poets from the perversity of having to write hyperbolic commendatory poems extolling the merits of Chester's verse. First, in the invocation and dedication, the members of the '*Vatum Chorus*' invoke Apollo and the Muses for assistance in honouring the newly knighted Salusbury and 'consecrate' their work to him by offering their 'mutuall palmes' of victory to 'gratulate' an '*honorable friend*' (lines 15–16) on his triumph. And, second, in the main body of the collection, after 'Ignoto' establishes the traditional myth, the named members of the chorus display their speculative and stylistic genius in reconfiguring Chester's signature allegory. Their 'subscribed' essays can best be understood as 'answer poems', unique reinterpretations of Chester's myth conceived in a spirit of literary, philosophical and stylistic experimentation. What makes Blount's collection particularly compelling, however, is the extent to which

its interactive poetics was energized by emulation and position-taking. Elizabethan print miscellanies are usually secondary recontextualizations of material initially produced for other purposes. But the *Poetical Essays* group was directly commissioned to participate in a work-in-progress. Salusbury might have been in a particularly generous mood in June of 1601 when celebrating his new status as a '*true-noble Knight*' (Z1ʳ), and the collaboration between patron, publisher, printer and poets his commission entailed culminated in the period's most meticulously designed miscellany, a collection that first unites and then disperses its poets' responsive voices.

III

Jonson based '*Praeludium*' on '*Proludium*', a poem he had previously written to introduce '*Epos*', his 116-line major contribution to the volume, when he first presented these two poems to Salusbury in manuscript in 1600. Two extant manuscript versions of this prior coupling are preserved in National Library of Wales MS 5390D and Folger Shakespeare Library MS x.d.246. Jonson's main goal in transforming '*Proludium*' into '*Praeludium*' was to make it contextualize '*Epos*' more effectively in the *Poeticall Essaies*, and his revision provides a privileged glance at how the collection was assembled. On the title-page of the *Diverse Poeticall Essaies* Blount claims that its contents were '*never before extant*', but when Salusbury approached him about publishing *Love's Martyr*, probably between

---

[28] Duncan-Jones and Woudhuysen, *Shakespeare's Poems*, pp. 107–9, equate Chester's 'Parliament of the Gods' in *Love's Martyr* and Shakespeare's 'Session' (line 9) of 'The Phoenix and Turtle' with the actual parliament to which Salusbury was admitted on 16 December 1601, a few days before it ended. But the idea that Chester's 'Parliament' and Shakespeare's 'Session' can be interpreted in so literal a manner strikes me as an unconvincing imposed allegory. Salusbury is however twice identified as a worthily honoured knight (A3r and Z2v).

[29] Subsidies seem to have been common. Thomas Coryate, for example, is said to have paid Blount and his partner William Barrett to publish *Coryats Crudities* for him in 1611.

late February and June of 1601, he already possessed the 16-line discarded 'Proludium' and 'Epos', the latter of which was only altered slightly for publication. We know this because by 2 October 1600, when Robert Allott registered *England's Parnassus* (his miscellany of poetic excerpts), he had already read and quoted the longer poem's closing line: '*Man may securely* [i.e. overconfidently] *sinne, but safely never.*'[30] The existence of 'Epos' by October of 1600 indicates that even before the Earl of Essex's execution the following February, an event which inexorably led to Salusbury's knighthood and the publication of *Love's Martyr*, Jonson had independently incorporated Chester's iconography into his 'epode' (as he calls the poem) in order to describe its idealized male lover as 'a person like my dove / gract wth a phoenix love' (lines 91–2). '(Though thy wild thoughts wth sparrowes wings do flie)', Jonson had originally written to Salusbury in 1600, 'turtles will chastly die' (lines 73–4).[31] The National Library of Wales and Folger Library copies provide evidence of the earliest link between any of the celebrity poets and *Love's Martyr*; they stem from versions of Jonson's poems in existence before the *Poeticall Essaies* was planned. Since Jonson was soliciting patrons with verse epistles at the time, it is possible that the idea for a collection was sparked by the acclaim his poems enjoyed in manuscript. In 'Epos', based on the epodes of Pindar and Horace, with their alternating long and short lines of verse, Jonson embeds Chester's peculiar iconography in a cutting-edge neoclassical experiment. Delighted by the result, Salusbury might have invited the other three poets to compose their versions. Jonson's connection to the new knight is firmly established, but Salusbury's to Shakespeare and Marston is apparent as well. Salusbury was the brother-in-law of the late Ferdinando Stanley, Lord Strange, who was probably one of Shakespeare's earliest patrons. William Stanley, the Earl of Derby, Ferdinando's younger brother, was at the time financing the Children of Paul's, for which Marston wrote. Only Salusbury's connection with Chapman, who expressed admiration for the late Ferdinando Stanley, is less clear.[32]

'Epos', as previously mentioned, was little changed in the process of its transposition into print. But Jonson drastically revised 'Proludium', which he had originally styled as a stern rejection of amorous 'elegy', a genre which he described as being 'too loose and capering' for his 'stricter vein' (lines 1–2). Since all of the *Poeticall Essaies* glorify 'chaste' love, however, he replaced the 16-line 'Proludium' with the 30-line 'Praeludium' to make a far more provocative claim: the assertion that he possessed a more profound source of inspiration than that of his collaborators.[33] Unlike them, he suggests in 'Praeludium', he did not need the assistance of the Olympian gods or the Muses that the '*Vatum Chorus*' had collectively evoked, since, he writes, '*we bring owne true Fire*' (line 29). Acknowledging his poem's place at the end of the volume, Jonson begins his new 'Praeludium' with feigned surprise, pretending to be caught off-guard by a request to chant his verses now that the rest have finished theirs:

> We must sing too? what Subject shal we chuse?
> Or whose great Name in Poets Heaven use,
> For the more Countenance to our Active Muse?
>
> (lines 1–3)

Jonson's first-person plural self-reference, here and throughout the poem, is not a sign of fellowship with the other poets, but a witty testament to his independence. His 'royal we' (the Latin '*pluralis maiestatis*') sets him apart from the rest of the '*Vatum Chorus*' as the expression of an imperial

---

[30] See *England's Parnassus, or the Choysest Flowers of our Moderne Poets*, ed. Charles Crawford (Oxford, 1913), p. 198, number 1497, attributed to 'B. Ihonson'.

[31] National Library of Wales, Aberystwyth MS 5390D, pp. 502–3. Jonson's poems can be viewed in digital format online at the library's website: www.llgc.org.uk. Jonson's revision is analysed by William H. Matchett in *The Phoenix and the Turtle: Shakespeare's Poem and Chester's 'Loves Martyr'* (The Hague, 1965), pp. 95–7.

[32] See Bednarz, *Shakespeare and the Truth of Love*, pp. 71–89.

[33] Jonson's improvisation on Horace's Ode 1.12 in 'Praeludium' is analysed by Victoria Moul, *Jonson, Horace and the Classical Tradition* (Cambridge, 2010), pp. 25–7. My subsequent quotations are from *Horace, Odes and Epodes*, trans. C. E. Bennett (Cambridge, MA, 1978).

literary self.[34] Blount apparently afforded Jonson an opportunity to complete 'Praeludium' after Shakespeare and Marston had produced their verses and the 'Vatum Chorus' poems were being set in place. It was then, in revising 'Proludium', that Jonson probably added 'The Phoenix Analysde' and 'Ode ἐνθουσιαστική'. 'The Phoenix Analysde' provides a kind of epilogue for the collection by provocatively questioning whether it is a symbolic 'type' or a person, and 'Ode ἐνθουσιαστική', tempering wonder with judgement, unsuccessfully seeks to domesticate the rhapsodic power of Shakespeare's tetrameter poetry. Since Jonson's two sets of lyrics constitute separate units, his name is printed twice, after each two-part submission, with each subscription including the 'h' he used to spell his surname before 1604. Either disappointed by the result or assuming they were too contextually bound to the collection, he never re-published the last pair.

IV

How closely then was Shakespeare connected with the *Poeticall Essaies*? At the beginning of the twentieth century Joseph Quincy Adams rejected Lee's supposition that 'The Phoenix and Turtle' was accidentally associated with *Love's Martyr* only to replace it with the equally implausible assumption, subsequently popularized by E. K. Chambers, that Shakespeare had probably not read Chester's work carefully enough to know its ending.[35] This is proven, Adams maintains, by the fact that Shakespeare's poem states that the Phoenix and Turtle left 'no posteritie' (line 59), while Chester describes the birth of a new phoenix whose presence reincarnates the virtues of her self-sacrificing progenitors:

> From the sweet fire of perfumed wood,
> Another princely *Phoenix* upright stood;
> Whose feathers purified did yeeld more light,
> Then her late burned mother out of sight,
> And in her heart restes a perpetuall love,
> Sprong from the bosome of the *Turtle-Dove*. (S3ᵛ)

What Adams fails to realize is that of the four celebrity poets Shakespeare is actually the *most* attentive to Chester's mythology, which he skilfully adapts to answer *Love's Martyr* in an enigmatic style that compels readers to judge for themselves if 'Truth and Beauty' are permanently 'buried' (line 64). Shakespeare's answer to Chester's poem invites and resists interpretation. Is his 'bird of lowdest lay' (line 1) a new phoenix presiding over the ritual of its own transformation, as some critics assume and others deny? Should Reason's conclusion that 'Death is now the phoenix nest' (line 56) be accepted as authoritative, or should Reason be wholly discredited for being incapable of comprehending 'the truth of love'? *Love's Martyr* had such a decisive impact on 'The Phoenix and Turtle' that it should have been awarded a prominent place in Geoffrey Bullough's *Narrative and Dramatic Sources of Shakespeare*. *Love's Martyr* is yet another unexceptional text that Shakespeare's revision transformed. As Robert Miola, commenting on Shakespeare's assimilative writing practice, has recently observed, 'He freely borrowed characters, plots, and ideas from other writers and just as freely ignored or contradicted them when it suited.'[36] 'The Phoenix and Turtle' is, however, a unique instance of his work being published together with its primary source.

Shakespeare probably composed 'The Phoenix and Turtle' between Essex's execution on 25 February and Salusbury's knighthood in June. If he had not previously read 'Proludium' and 'Epos' in manuscript, which is unlikely, Blount might have supplied him with a draft, because Shakespeare's answer to Jonson – mediated through Chester's iconography – is decisive. Whereas Jonson's Horatian epode proclaims Reason, 'our *Affections* King'

---

[34] Margaret Healy, *Shakespeare, Alchemy and the Creative Imagination: The Sonnets and 'A Lover's Complaint'* (Cambridge, 2011), p. 205, is wrong to suggest that 'the poets intermittently claim to be speaking together as a "vatum chorus", as one', *after* the invocation and dedication. When Jonson states that, 'we bring / Our owne true Fire; Now our Thought takes wing' ('Praeludium', lines 28–9), he speaks for himself alone.

[35] Joseph Quincy Adams, *A Life of William Shakespeare* (New York, 1923), p. 341, and E. K. Chambers, *William Shakespeare, A Study of Facts and Problems*, 2 vols. (Oxford, 1930), vol. 1, p. 550.

[36] Robert S. Miola, *Shakespeare's Reading* (Oxford, 2000), p. 2.

(line 13), Shakespeare's Ovidian elegy derides judgement in favour of the mysterious 'Reason' of Love. Once he completed his 'essay', it was handed to Marston, who opens his quartet of verses with a direct rejoinder to 'Threnos' (sig. Z4ᵛ) that praises Reason's eloquence, but rejects its bleak conclusion that the Phoenix and Turtle have died childless (sig. 2Aʳ). 'O twas a moving *Epicedium*!' Marston exults, using a synonym for 'threnody' or 'dirge', before insisting that, whatever Reason might assume, a 'new creature' never explicitly identified as a phoenix (allowing for its mystery) has arisen from the ashes of Shakespeare's 'Co-supremes' (line 51). In order to reinforce this philosophical dialogue typographically Field instructed his compositor to insert ornamental borders ('vinets') at the head and foot of the 15-line 'Threnos' with its conspicuously large ascription to '*William Shake-speare*'.[37] This filled out the left page, balancing it against Marston's 26-line retort to its right. One of the unanticipated consequences of this layout is that it has fostered the false impression that '*Threnos*' is independent from the rest of Shakespeare's verse. The primary purpose for putting '*Threnos*' on its own page, however, was to create a reading protocol linking Shakespeare's and Marston's adjacent poems. Marston's '*A narration and description of a* most exact wondrous creature, arising *out of the Phoenix and Turtle Doves* ashes' might be said to complete Shakespeare's account by contradicting Reason's conclusion that 'Death is now the *Phoenix* nest' (line 56). Yet those who examine this *mise-en-page* (digitally reproduced on the Folger Shakespeare Library website) will notice how the oversize attribution to '*William Shake-speare*' firmly marks the end of his contribution from the beginning of Marston's. This makes Marston's work assume the form of an adaptation or sequel, much like Chapman's and Petowe's additions to *Hero and Leander*. The large font size used to print Shakespeare's name might even be interpreted as a full stop, attesting to his disavowal of responsibility for what Marston had written in their 'collaboration' within a collaboration.

We cannot be certain if Shakespeare anticipated Marston's supplement or if Marston devised it on his own. Did he surprise Shakespeare by linking his first poem with 'Threnos'? In 'finishing' Shakespeare's verse, was he acting as a collaborator or rival? To what extent did Marston's reaction to 'The Phoenix and Turtle' involve his own unique interpretation of Chester's, Jonson's and Shakespeare's variations? Katherine Duncan-Jones imagines that Shakespeare and Marston's 'friendly emulation' was secured by a unity of purpose.[38] But if we leave conjecture about their personal relationship aside, a full range of dialogical reactions to Shakespeare can be detected in Marston's partially derivative poetry and drama. It is difficult to gauge the degree of collusion, if any, their print collaboration entailed, although Marston's poetics can best be understood by staying attuned to the degree of their difference from Shakespeare's. In a theatrical market dominated by Shakespeare and Jonson between 1598 and 1601, it is to Marston's credit that he managed to make a name for himself by providing something new, beyond mere *bricolage*, for London theatregoers and readers. With Shakespeare's and Marston's poems in place, Jonson would then have written '*Praeludium*', with its explicit acknowledgement of their submissions in its opening line, as well as '*The Phoenix Analysde*' and '*Ode ἐνθουσιαστικη*', with their tetrameter response to Shakespeare.

In *Shakespeare as Literary Dramatist*, Lukas Erne explains that because of 'the suddenness and the frequency with which Shakespeare's name appears on the title pages of printed playbooks from 1598 to 1600' it might be said that 'in one sense, "Shakespeare", author of dramatic texts, was born in the space of two or three years at the end of

---

[37] John Kerrigan, 'Reading "The Phoenix and Turtle"', in *The Oxford Handbook of Shakespeare's Poetry*, ed. Jonathan Post (Oxford, 2013), p. 552, observes that these vignettes in a pattern of lace or flowers were known in the period as '*arabesques*' and derive, like the Phoenix on 'the sole *Arabian* tree' (line 2) of Shakespeare's poem, 'from the orient'. He consequently suggests that they are 'semiotically charged', supplying 'a continuation of the patterning of the verse by other means'.

[38] Duncan-Jones, *Ungentle Shakespeare*, p. 144. She describes Marston as a member of Shakespeare's 'fan club' (p. 143).

the sixteenth century'.[39] Discretion, however, prevented Blount from printing Shakespeare's name on either of the two title-pages of *Love's Martyr*. Following the precedent set by Richard Field and John Harrison in publishing *Venus and Adonis* and *Lucrece* without Shakespeare's name on their title-pages, Blount observed a stringent decorum of non-dramatic patronage poetry (never universally adopted) according to which the author's name appears conjoined with the book's patron only within its pages. So that even though Blount played a crucial role in inventing Elizabethan bardolatry by imagining Shakespeare as a *vates*, the title-page he designed for *Love's Martyr* only hints at its celebrity authors' identities through an epigraph from Martial: '*Mutare dominum non potest liber notus*' ('A famous book cannot change its master [i.e. author]', line 9 of *Epigrams* 1.66). If the book succeeds, its authorship, the motto suggests, will be so apparent that no one will be able to plagiarize it.[40] Title-page advertising is, however, only one measure of Shakespeare's growing reputation. Theatregoers who attended the contemporaneous Poets' War plays were engaged in the same process of authorial recognition, since in order to comprehend its ongoing literary debate they were required to distinguish the relative merits of Jonson's *Cynthia's Revels*, Shakespeare's *Twelfth Night* and Marston's *What You Will*, which were performed as an interlocked self-referential sequence between late 1600 and early 1601. Late in 1601, Thomas Dekker indicates how readily identifiable commercial dramatists had become when in *Satiromastix* he makes his caricature of Jonson swear not to 'venter on the stage, when [his] Play is ended, and to exchange curtezies, and complements with Gallants in the Lordes rooms, to make all the house rise up in Armes, to cry . . . that's he, that's he, that's he'.[41] It has been falsely claimed that theatre frustrates literary aspirations because it disperses authority among diverse agents, and that publication concentrates it in the hands of an autonomous author. But the spirited dialogue on the nature of poetic authority and the purpose of mimetic representation conducted by Jonson, Shakespeare and Marston on the stages of

Blackfriars, the Globe and Paul's during the Poets' War flows in and out of their 'essays' in *Love's Martyr*. One of Marston's strategies to further his reputation at Paul's between 1600 and 1601 was to play Shakespeare's and Jonson's dramatic paradigms off each other, triangulating recent productions at the Globe and Blackfriars. In *What You Will*, Shakespearian festive comedy accordingly critiques Jonsonian comical satire, even as Jonsonian comical satire undermines festive comedy. He had to be agile, in such company, to survive.

Marston and Jonson's engagement with each other's work was more confrontational, but Marston could not have survived merely by serving as Shakespeare's devoted acolyte. From the beginning of his career he embodied a kind of outrageousness and sensationalism, different from Shakespeare, which continues to be an element of his unique attraction. *Troilus and Cressida*, written later in the year, records the first sure sign of Shakespeare's interest in his drama. But until he composed *The Malcontent*, Marston had written nothing interesting enough to impress Shakespeare, nothing to equal the impact this innovative tragicomedy (itself influenced by *Hamlet*) left on *Measure for Measure*. Marston's play, which he dedicated to Jonson in 1604, was so successful that it was adapted by the King's Men, with additions by John Webster, for presentation at the Globe. Before *Measure for Measure*, Marston systematically reconfigured Shakespeare's work. He is never subservient, however, because he understood that his success depended on his providing something new. Marston used Shakespearian antecedent forms for ends that are variably alienated from their prior literary, theatrical and philosophical valences. Between 1600 and 1601, *Hamlet* and *Twelfth Night* at the Globe were followed by

---

[39] Erne, *Shakespeare as Literary Dramatist*, p. 63.

[40] Jonson cites the same line in his notes to *Hymenaei* (1606) in order to define his specific role in the masque's joint production (*The Cambridge Works of Ben Jonson*, vol. 2, p. 690).

[41] *Satiromastix, or the Untrussing of the Humorous Poet* (5.2.303–7) in *The Dramatic Works of Thomas Dekker*, ed. Fredson Bowers, 4 vols. (Cambridge, 1953), vol. 1, p. 389.

Antonio's Revenge and *What You Will* at Paul's, as Shakespeare's generic choices were recapitulated, adapted and even undermined in Marston's corresponding dramas. Their interrelated plays were not collaborative but they are essentially relational, and Blount's collection re-mediates their interplay in print by allowing Marston to comment on Shakespeare's poetry, just as he had done as a dramatist at Paul's. It is true that Marston was far more vocal about his differences with Jonson. But he was careful to distance himself sufficiently from Shakespeare, with whom he has such strong affinities.

It is difficult, for this reason, to find a language to express Marston's curious ambivalence. I consider *Antonio's Revenge* and *What You Will* 'variations' on *Hamlet* and *Twelfth Night*, even though Bart van Es wonders if this word registers the extent of Marston's originality.[42] Misunderstandings are bound to arise on this issue, since we lack a clear vocabulary to chart Marston's revisionary *ratios*. One also tends to feel a sense of uncertainty about the point at which emulation becomes satire in his work. Shakespeare's and Marston's verses in *Love's Martyr* can be read as either: a collaboration composed of a single poem divided into two parts, with Shakespeare detailing the phoenix and turtle's union-in-death and Marston announcing a mysterious resurrection; or two separate but interconnected meditations on the same subject, divided by the imprint of Shakespeare's name in a firm declaration of artistic ownership. In a collection so centrally involved with philosophical speculation about the relation of self and other, it would be surprising if this thematic core did not also reverberate with its mode of production. And yet its collaborative format coincides with authorial divisions that make the elision of Shakespeare's and Marston's verses problematic. Together they pose the mystery of incorporation that Shakespeare ponders in which 'Single Natures double name, / Neither two nor one was called' (lines 39–40). His signed poem, like his Phoenix and Turtle, never dissolves into an undifferentiated One.

Marston's scene of writing paralleled Shakespeare's: each improvised on Chester's poem in the wake of a strong predecessor. Shakespeare would have noticed how Jonson had woven allusions to *Love's Martyr* into the texture of his epode. And like him, Shakespeare responded to Chester's allegory with a two-part lyric, but in a radically new oracular mode that posed a bold conceptual and stylistic alternative to Jonson's neoclassicism. 'Epos' and 'The Phoenix and Turtle' are of major significance for literary historians because they illustrate the emergence of two versions of lyric – the neoclassical and metaphysical – that would dominate the genre's most powerful modes of expression for most of the seventeenth century.[43] Shakespeare and Jonson were in this instance collaborators whose literary relationship was mediated by competition. Their shared assignment was not to praise Chester's allegory in commendatory verse but to make it and its subject – 'the truth of love' – their own, a feat they achieved in remarkably different ways. Shakespeare made a more concerted effort to rework Chester's narrative material. He was adept at transforming second-rate antecedents into works of genius and updating slightly archaic genres. Jonson only alludes to Chester's phoenix and turtle in passing, but Shakespeare composed his poem as if it were an alternative ending to Chester's. At the conclusion of *Love's Martyr*, after the Phoenix and Turtle immolate themselves, the Pelican, a symbol of self-sacrificial love, offers both a choric lament for their passing and a joyful account of the new female Phoenix's birth from their ashes. Shakespeare rewrote Chester's ending to balance the paradoxical interplay of tragic and comic interpretations central to its mystery: the hope that a new Phoenix has risen or will arise and the suspicion of its extinction in a world impoverished by its absence. Their dialogue was made possible by Blount's collaborative 'essay' format.

V

As 'editor' of the *Poeticall Essaies*, Blount would have had to devise a strategy for integrating

---

42 Bart van Es, *Shakespeare in Company* (Oxford, 2013), p. 240.
43 See Bednarz, *Shakespeare and the Truth of Love*, pp. 163–91.

Shakespeare and Jonson's work in a single format during a period in which their poetics were so self-consciously opposed. The next time he would combine their writing would be in the First Folio. In 1601, his goal would have been to design a collection that was as generously accommodating as possible to their deliberately differentiated poetics.[44] Gary Taylor portrays Blount as a talented editor positioned at the crossroads of commerce and culture: a crucial reader, transmitter and interpreter of what he produced. Blount published some of the most innovative literature of his age and his involvement with the celebrity writers of the *Poetical Essays* group is an early indication of the scope of his ambition. What Taylor finds remarkable is his commitment to dialogue, the fact that he saw himself as 'a spectator judging verbal performances', an 'impartial observer', who enjoyed 'watching the play of ideology, and reporting it from a position which seemed outside ideologies'.[45] He dedicates a treatise on Portuguese history to the Earl of Southampton in 1600 with the proviso: 'For the subject it selfe I dare say nothing; since it is out of my element to judge.'[46] Blount's artistic detachment encouraged collaborative polyphony, and under his direction the *Poeticall Essaies* translated the social bonds that forged its occasional verse into a dialectical series of philosophical and stylistic textual substitutions and displacements. The meaning of 'The Phoenix and Turtle' will always remain, for this reason, inextricably embedded in the material text of *Love's Martyr*.

One strategy that Blount used to coordinate the collection's inclusion of verse by Shakespeare and Jonson, its most important contributors, was to counterpoise references to the classical Roman poets Ovid and Horace in its paratexts. Jonson would have been pleased to see Horace's authority prominently evoked in the motto of the *Poeticall Essaies*, a line from his ode to Censorinus, lauding his military success: '*Dignum laude virum Musa vetat mori*', ('A man worthy of praise the muse forbids to die') (*Odes* 4.8.28). Nothing can declare more gloriously a victor's fame, Horace writes, than 'the Muses of Calabria' (line 20).

The hero's 'due reward' would be unrealized, if 'worthy deeds' were left 'unheralded' (lines 21–2). 'The powers of gifted bards, their favour, and their voice ['*virtus et favor et lingua potentium / vatum*']', Horace explains (using that key word applied to the celebrity poets), 'rescue Aeacus from the Stygian waves' (lines 26–27). 'It is a fitting motto', Charles Cathcart observes, 'implicitly equating Salusbury with Censorinus – and the activities of the *Love's Martyr* poets with Horace.'[47] Jonson strongly identified with this poetic credo. He had previously quoted the same line in Latin to commend Thomas Palmer's *The Spirite of Trees and Herbes* (1598–99) and paraphrased it in his 'Epistle, to Elizabeth, Countess of Rutland' (sent to her on New Year's Day of 1600). 'It is the muse alone can raise to heaven', Jonson had written to Sir Philip Sidney's daughter, 'and, at her strong arm's end, hold up and even / The souls she loves' (lines 42–4).[48]

But whatever pride of place the collection gives Horace, it is Ovid who inspires the '*Vatum Chorus*'. The collection's invocation to Apollo and its dedication to Salusbury are based on Ovid's *Amores* (1.15.35–6), the very lines that Shakespeare had instructed Field to print on the title page of *Venus and Adonis*: '*Vilia miretur vulgus: mihi flavus Apollo / Pocula Castalia plena ministret aqua*' ('Let the vulgar admire worthless things: may golden Apollo serve me cups full of Castalian water'). Instead of a Pindaric choral ode to Salusbury's victory, we find a prayer, couched in familiar Ovidian terms, asking Fate, the Muses and Apollo to

---

[44] For a treatment of Shakespeare, Jonson and Marston's participation in the *Poetomachia* from 1599 to 1601, see James P. Bednarz, *Shakespeare and the Poets' War* (New York, 2001).

[45] Lee, 'An Elizabethan Bookseller', p. 474. Gary Taylor, 'The Cultural Politics of Maybe', in *Theatre and Religion: Lancastrian Shakespeare*, ed. Richard Dutton, Alison Findlay and Richard Wilson (Manchester, 2003), pp. 253–4.

[46] Blount's introduction to a translation of Girolamo Franchi di Conestaggio's *The Historie of the Uniting of the Kingdom of Portugall to the Crowne of Castill* (London, 1600), A2r.

[47] Cathcart, *Marston*, p. 27.

[48] *The Cambridge Edition of the Works of Ben Jonson*, ed. Bevington, vol. 5, p. 236.

propagate,
With your illustrate faculties
   Our mentall powers; Instruct us how to rise
In weighty Numbers, well pursu'd,
And varied from the Multitude:
   Be lavish once, and plenteously profuse
   Your holy waters, to our thirstie *Muse*,
That we may give a Round to him
   In a *Castalian* boule, crown'd to the brim.

(lines 16–24)

The '*Vatum Chorus*' follows Ovid in evoking the 'holy waters' of the Castalian spring at Delphi on Mount Parnassus as a source of symbolic nourishment. In Ovid's time, drinking from the spring was said to bring inspiration from Apollo, the god of poetry, and the Muses, the goddesses of inspiration he led. Unlike Ovid, however, the '*Vatum Chorus*' prays to be allowed to share their '*Castalian*' bowl in the fashion of a 'loving cup'. Ritual toasts were as common a form of social bonding in early modern England as they were in antiquity, and the chorus concludes their 'Round' by handing the bowl in the next poem 'To the worthily honor'd Knight'. However, now its 'juice' (in a commonly mistaken conflation of locales) is said to have come from the Muses' sacred spring at Pieris, near Mount Olympus, in Macedonia:

Noblest of minds, here do the Muses *bring*
   Unto your safer judgements tast,
Pure juice that flow'd from the Pierian *springs,*
   Not filch'd, nor borrow'd, but exhaust
     By the flame-hair'd Apollos *hand:*

(lines 1–5)[49]

Both Horace's *Ode* 4.8, quoted in the opening epigraph of the *Poeticall Essaies*, and Ovid's *Amores* 1.15 are eloquent defences of poetry. Indeed, *Amores* 1.15 parallels Horace's claim in *Odes* 3.30 to have built a monument more lasting than bronze. Evocations of Horace and Ovid add gravitas to the collection's 'consecration' of its verses to Salusbury. But while each commemorates the power of poetry to eternize, Ovid's elegy does not glorify a patron. Its sole concern is the poet's immortality. Rejecting military honours or law, Ovid has only one goal, which Christopher Marlowe translates

as: 'eternal fame, / That all the world may ever chant my name'.[50] To those who would ask him to compromise, Ovid/Marlowe replies:

Let base-conceited wits admire vile things,
Fair Phoebus lead me to the Muses' springs.
About my head be quivering myrtle wound,
And in sad lovers' heads let me be found.

(lines 35–8)

The '*Vatum Chorus*' transforms Ovid's self-regard into an act of homage to Salusbury that conforms to the title-page's Horatian epigraph. What is particularly intriguing about the use of *Amores* 1.15.35–6 in these poems allegedly written by the four celebrity poets is that Ovid's verses are thought to have served as a prior site of contention between Shakespeare and Chapman, when the latter used it to distinguish the Platonic uplift of *The Shadow of Night* (1594) from the fleshy sensuality of *Venus and Adonis* (1593). There, in 'Hymnus in Cynthiam', Chapman appears to mock his competitor (under an initial evasive plural) for identifying himself with the source of poetic inspiration, the sacred water of the Castalian spring, and instructs him to gaze into Chapman's own 'deepe fount' to see his error:

Presume not then ye flesh confounded soules,
That cannot beare the full Castalian bowles,
Which sever mounting spirits from the sences,
To look in this deepe fount for thy pretenses:
The juice more cleare then day, yet shadows night,[51]

---

[49] The Muses are called the '*Pierides*' in the invocation's title. Cathcart, *Marston*, pp. 21–2, emphasizes the similarity between the phrase '*Pure juice*' in line 3 and 'The pur'st elixèd juice of rich conceit' in *Antonio and Mellida* and '*the purer juice of love*' in *What You Will*. Jonson implicates Marston in the trivialization of such language in *Poetaster*, when Crispinus/Marston swears 'By Phoebus' that 'your city ladies . . . sit in every shop like the muses', offering 'Castalian dews and the Thespian liquors', before he asks Horace/Jonson, 'Did you never hear any of my verses?' (3.1.23; 28–31).

[50] This translation of Ovid's *Elegies* is quoted from *Christopher Marlowe: The Complete Poems and Translations*, ed. Stephen Orgel (Harmondsworth, 1971), lines 7–8.

[51] 'Hymnus in Cynthiam', lines 162–6, in *The Poems of George Chapman*, ed. Phyllis Brooks Bartlett (New York, 1962), p. 34.

Since Shakespeare and Chapman were among the celebrity poets to whom the 'Vatum Chorus' poems were attributed, we can only guess the extent to which they represent a momentary synchronicity of interest as they both engaged in a philosophical inquiry into the nature of ideal love. Chapman, however, would play only a supporting role in the Poeticall Essaies, with a short poem that parallels Jonson's contention that love should be ruled by judgement.

The Ovidian subtext of the 'Vatum Chorus' might be seen as biasing the collection towards Shakespeare, since it not only recalls the Latin epigraph for Venus and Adonis but also serves as the perfect introduction to 'The Phoenix and Turtle', the primary classical model for which is Amores 2.6.[52] Elaborating on Chester's theme of the mystical love-death of the phoenix and turtle, Shakespeare remembered Ovid's mock funeral elegy on the death of Corinna's parrot, a poem that opens and closes with a call for avian mourning at the dead bird's monument. Here, all 'unclean fowls' (line 52) are banned, as a parrot, instead of a phoenix, is paired with a loyal turtle-dove. 'Full concord all your lives was you betwixt', Ovid laments, 'And to the end your constant faith stood fixed' (lines 13–14). The dead bird now abides with the swans of Apollo and the solitary phoenix in Elysium. By relating the 'exequies' (line 2) of Amores 2.6 to the phoenix of the Metamorphoses (15.391–407), Shakespeare brought a new seriousness to the motif. Viewed from this grander perspective, the union of his Phoenix and Turtle is a meditation on the ecstasy or terror of selves that defy conventional categories of being and thought. But how much Shakespeare participated in the planning and composition of the 'Vatum Chorus' poems, which were probably written as a framing device after his work had been submitted, is unknown.

VI

The Poeticall Essaies provides the strongest evidence we possess of Shakespeare's direct engagement with the book trade after 1594. It also enhances our understanding of two subsequent events in English literary history, one immediate and the other remote, that are directly connected to Blount's creative management of Shakespeare and Jonson's competitive collaboration. First, Blount's synthesis elicited an immediate rejection by Jonson, who reacted to it by devising his own uncompromising contrast between Ovidian and Horatian poetics in Poetaster, staged later that year by the Children of the Chapel at Blackfriars at the culmination of the Poets' War. The Poeticall Essaies is particularly valuable in supplying a viable explanation as to why Jonson's 'Ovid' in Poetaster is strongly highlighted with allusions to Marlowe and Shakespeare's poetry and drama. And, second, Blount's editorial work on the Poeticall Essaies suggests, in miniature, why John Heminges and Henry Condell of the King's Men selected him, along with William Jaggard and his son Isaac, to be one of the principal publishers of the First Folio. In the final two sections of this essay, I examine in turn each of these influences.

Once the Poeticall Essaies had been assembled, Jonson must have felt dissatisfied with the extent to which its Ovidian 'quotations' overwhelmed their Horatian counterparts. We do not know who wrote the two 'Vatum Chorus' poems. If they had not been ghostwritten, some or all of the collection's authors might have had a hand in their composition or revision. Yet Jonson apparently felt that they did not adequately reflect his poetics, leading him, as we have seen, to draw a firm distinction in 'Praeludium' between his personal source of inspiration and that of his compeers. He would have wanted to be included as one of the 'Vatum Chorus' in the opening tribute to Salusbury but he had originally described his epode in 'Proludium' of 1600 as an explicit rejection of Ovidian elegy:

> An elegy? No, muse; it asks a strain
> Too loose and cap'ring for thy stricter vein.
> Thy thoughts did never melt in amorous fire,

---

[52] Hyder E. Rollins, ed., The Poems. A New Variorum Edition of Shakespeare (Philadelphia, 1938), p. 571, notes that Ovid's Amores 2.6 was first cited as a primary source for 'The Phoenix and Turtle' in Alfred von Mauntz's edition of Shakespeare's Lyrische Gedichte in 1893.

Like glass blown up and fashioned by desire.
The skilful mischief of a roving eye
Could ne'er make prize of thy white chastity.
Then leave these lighter numbers to light brains,
In whom the flame of every beauty reigns;
Such as in lust's wild forest love to range,
Only pursuing constancy in change.
Let these in wanton feet dance out their souls.

(lines 1–11)

For Jonson, in this context, 'elegy' and 'epode' are irreconcilable expressions of false and true love, and he must have felt compromised in being represented by the illicit *Amores*. The 'elegy' as a literary kind is based on the Greek '*elegeia*' or 'lament'. But Jonson was particularly concerned about what it had become in the work of Augustan poets from Propertius and Tibullus to Ovid, who had transformed it into a series of meditations on two main themes: the vagaries of uncontrollable sexual desire and the pursuit of literary fame. In English, for the sake of modesty, the generic title *Elegies* was often used in place of *Amores* (*Love Poems*), even though Ovid employed elegiac verse in other works as well. *Poetaster* accordingly stages the difference between 'Ovid', a brilliant but morally flawed poet whose ethical failure leads to his banishment, and 'Horace', Jonson's idealized self-projection, who is rewarded with patronage. The primary difference between Ovid and Horace, Jonson maintained, is that Ovid misunderstands the moral responsibility his vatic role involves. Sensing a fundamental contradiction in the conflation of Ovidian and Horatian paradigms in the *Poeticall Essaies*, Jonson dramatized their difference in meticulously self-referential literary criticism contrasting his new Horatian persona with the transgressive Ovidianism of Marlowe and Shakespeare.

The relevance of Jonson's Ovid for Marlowe and Shakespeare's poetics is underscored by his first appearance in *Poetaster*, as he puts the finishing touches on *Amores* 1.15, all 42 lines of which he recites (1.1.37–78). What makes his appearance so fascinating is that he recites an emended version of Marlowe's translation of the lines Shakespeare had used to identify his Ovidian poetics on the title page of *Venus and Adonis* and that the '*Vatum Chorus*' had echoed a few months earlier in responding to 'The Phoenix and Turtle', his brilliant improvisation on *Amores* 2.6:

Kneel hinds to trash; me light bright Phoebus swell
With cups full flowing from the muses' well.

(1.1.71–2)

'Ovid. Lib 1 Amo. El. 15', Jonson helpfully notes in the margin of the first edition of *Poetaster* in 1602 for readers eager to explore the play's classical intertexts. He would have expected his most judicious readers to understand the implications of the passage's triple authorship. When *Amores* was published as part of the Marlowe revival it became involved in a literary scandal. A surreptitiously published combined edition of John Davies's *Epigrams* and Marlowe's *Elegies* is listed on the Stationers' Register in June 1599 among the books called in by ecclesiastical order and then burned. Thus, Jonson's embedding of his 'improved' version of this censored high-profile translation in his printed play was provocative.[53] His strategy, in part, was to overlay his representation of Ovid's literary biography with a brief commentary on the Roman poet's influence on Elizabethan culture. Its scope in *Poetaster*'s plot, accordingly, begins with Ovid's recitation of Marlowe's translation of *Amores* 1.15 and ends with him standing beneath Julia's window, the evening before his exile, voicing an eloquent but spurious rhetoric of high romantic passion which combines the despair of Ovid's *Tristia* with the pathos of *Romeo and Juliet*:[54] 'Banished the court? Let me be banished life' (4.8.1), Ovid laments, thinking of Julia, 'the abstract of the court', before they console each

---

53 See David Riggs, *The World of Christopher Marlowe* (New York, 2004), pp. 102–15. Jeffrey Todd Knight, *Bound to Read: Compilations, Collections and the Making of Renaissance Literature* (Cambridge, 2013), p. 73, examines a contemporary bound volume combining 1599 editions of *Venus and Adonis* and *The Passionate Pilgrim* with the *Epigrammes and elegies. By I.D. and C.M.*, probably from the same year (Huntington Library shelf marks 59000–59002).

54 See Anne Barton, *Ben Jonson, Dramatist* (Cambridge, 1984), p. 84.

other for the last time. In his commentary on the play, Tom Cain writes that of Ovid's Elizabethan followers 'Marlowe loomed largest in 1601',[55] yet one could make an equally valid case for Shakespeare. Shakespeare had identified himself with Ovid by quoting *Amores* as his epigraph to *Venus and Adonis*, a narrative poem based on a tale from the *Metamorphoses*. In 1598, Francis Meres revived this association by stating that Shakespeare possessed Ovid's 'soul'.[56] William Jaggard even thought of Marlowe and Shakespeare as interchangeable when he published a garbled version of Marlowe's famous lyric 'Come live with me and be my love' as Shakespeare's in *The Passionate Pilgrim* of 1599. By 1600, in *As You Like It*, Shakespeare himself set the stage for Jonson's literary triad – Ovid, Marlowe, Shakespeare – by naming Ovid, exiled 'among the Goths' (3.3.6), and eulogizing Marlowe as the 'Dead shepherd', before quoting line 176 of *Hero and Leander* (3.5.82–3).[57]

'Ovid' in *Poetaster* is not a parody of either Marlowe or Shakespeare. In a drama populated by caricatures, Jonson never makes Ovid topically identifiable, even though he emphatically aligns him with the Elizabethan alpha and omega of 'Ovidianism'. 'Ovid' is a literary marker for a set of quotations, linguistic imitations and thematic analogies linking him with Marlowe and Shakespeare in a manner more subtle than the blatant technique of 'personation' (or 'personal mimicry') that Jonson deploys elsewhere in the play. That is why, as Janet Clare cogently explains, studies that focus solely on 'personation' cannot satisfactorily account for the theoretical strategies and literary objectives that make the Poets' War more than celebrity gossip.[58] Shakespeare's collaboration on the *Poeticall Essaies* did nevertheless have a decisive impact on Jonson's representation of himself as 'Horace', Ovid's literary equal and moral better, at the stage-quarrel's climax.[59] In 1599 John Weever's epigram '*Ad Io: Marston, & Ben: Iohnson*' claimed that Marston's 'Muse' (not Jonson's) 'enharbours *Horace*['s] vaine'.[60] After *Poetaster*, however, no matter how varied his borrowings from the classics remained, Jonson permanently crystallized his public persona around the *vates* that Dekker in *Satiromastix* (registered on 11 November 1601) mocked as 'Horace, the second'.[61] His reaction to Shakespeare, however, would be very different twenty-two years later, when Blount and Isaac Jaggard commissioned him prominently to commend the collected drama of a great poet he lamented in death as a 'beloved' friend.

VII

John Heminges and Henry Condell, on behalf of the King's Men, had reason to welcome Blount's professional involvement with 'MR. WILLIAM SHAKESPEARES COMEDIES, HISTORIES, & TRAGEDIES. Published according to the True Originall Copies'. The sole publishers mentioned on its title-page, Blount and Isaac Jaggard were the investors primarily responsible for managing its production.[62] Since Isaac Jaggard, in his twenties, supervised the book's printing at his father William's shop, it seems likely that his

---

55 Introduction to Ben Jonson's *Poetaster*, ed. Tom Cain (Manchester, 1995), p. 19.

56 Francis Meres, *Palladis Tamia*, in Smith, *Elizabethan Critical Essays*, vol. 2, p. 317.

57 Quoted from *The Oxford Shakespeare: The Complete Works*, ed. Stanley Wells, Gary Taylor *et al.*, 2nd edn (Oxford, 2005).

58 Janet Clare, 'The "Complexion" of *Twelfth Night*', in *Shakespeare Survey 58* (Cambridge, 2005), pp. 199–207, p. 200.

59 Jonson must have been surprised to find his version of *Amores* 1.15 lifted from *Poetaster* (1602) and printed after Marlowe's translation in *All Ovids Elegies* (STC 18933).

60 John Weever, Epigram 6:11 in *Epigrammes in the Oldest Cut and Newest Fashion* (London, 1599), F8ᵛ.

61 Thomas Dekker, 'To the World', *The Dramatic Works of Thomas Dekker*, vol. 1, p. 309.

62 The Folio's colophon states that it was 'Printed at the Charges of W. Jaggard, Ed. Blount, I. Smithweeke, and W. Aspley'. Smethwick and Aspley only controlled rights to six plays, and William Jaggard died before the Folio was published. On 8 November 1623 Blount and Isaac Jaggard sought to register sixteen previously unpublished Shakespeare plays only to discover that Blount already owned the rights to *Antony and Cleopatra*, having previously entered it on 20 May 1608, and that Jaggard had inherited the rights to *As You Like It*. See Peter W. M. Blayney, *The First Folio of Shakespeare* (Washington, DC, 1991), pp. 18–21. Blount registered *Pericles*, the only other Shakespeare play he had acquired earlier (and then apparently sold) on that same day in 1608.

well-connected partner Blount, an expert broker of texts in his fifties, would have negotiated issues of copyright with those stationers who owned the rights to plays by Shakespeare already in quarto. But acknowledging Blount's entrepreneurial risk-taking and business acumen does nothing to illuminate the standard of connoisseurship he brought to the Folio's construction. He was a crucial player in the King's Men's attempt to create credible versions of the plays from a combination of print and manuscript sources. The problem that the King's Men faced was that, although they had agreed to use William Jaggard's printing establishment to produce the First Folio, they were apparently aware that its proprietor had over the course of two decades repeatedly published either apocryphal or inferior versions of Shakespeare's plays and poems that he ostentatiously attributed to him on their title-pages. Between 1598 and 1599, Jaggard published two editions of mostly fake Shakespeare poems in a collection entitled *The Passionate Pilgrime*, and in 1612 he again misappropriated Shakespeare's name by releasing a third, expanded edition with poems by Thomas Heywood, who objected to the publisher's many 'dishonesties' and recorded Shakespeare's dissatisfaction as well.[63] Under pressure, Jaggard agreed to take Shakespeare's name off unsold copies. Then, in 1619, he worked on the so-called 'Pavier quartos', the first attempt to issue a volume of Shakespeare's collected plays, which featured the misattributed *Sir John Oldcastle* and *A Yorkshire Tragedy* along with maimed versions of the second and third parts of *Henry VI* and *The Merry Wives of Windsor*. Jaggard's *Passionate Pilgrime* and Blount's *Poeticall Essaies* represent irreconcilable approaches to authenticity, and the difference between them indicates why Blount was so crucial in securing greater accuracy for the First Folio.

Although the details are unclear, Isaac Jaggard's involvement with the First Folio began with his father William's publishing alliance with Thomas Pavier. William, who might have become blind as early as 1611, found in Pavier a business partner and estate executor upon his death in November of 1623, shortly before the Folio's completion.

The substitution of Blount for Pavier – whatever its terms and conditions – made a significant difference in the quality and accuracy of the texts the Jaggards printed. From Heminges and Condell's perspective, the problem of authenticity was mitigated by enlisting Blount's expertise in ensuring that a credible effort was made to consolidate and conflate the best available printed plays with playhouse manuscripts, a goal offset by the project's cost, magnitude, editorial complexity and compositor error. As in the case of 'The Phoenix and Turtle', he was called upon to exercise his almost invisible editorial touch in presenting Shakespeare's work. The publisher who had once summoned Shakespeare and Jonson to the 'exequies' of the 'Phoenix and Turtle' now commissioned Jonson to officiate at Shakespeare's apotheosis. The publisher who had characterized himself as Marlowe's literary executor now silently assumed the same role for Shakespeare.[64] Jonson obliged by extravagantly praising Shakespeare, a writer whom he described as having equalled or exceeded the ancients and outstripped even his best contemporaries. This was only the second time that Jonson had been asked to come to terms with Shakespeare's imposing bibliographical presence. But whereas in 1601 the two poets had engaged in a brilliant dialogue, alone in 1623, Jonson, confronting this change, did something remarkable. Seizing the occasion to assume his old vatic persona, exercising a

---

[63] See James P. Bednarz, 'Canonizing Shakespeare: *The Passionate Pilgrim*, *England's Helicon* and the Question of Authenticity', in *Shakespeare Survey 60* (Cambridge, 2007), pp. 252–67.

[64] Leah Scragg, 'Edward Blount and the Prefatory Material to the First Folio of Shakespeare', *Bulletin of the John Rylands Library*, 79 (1997), 117–26, p. 120, proves that Blount was responsible for commissioning at least some of the Folio's paratexts. 'To the memorie of M. *W. Shake-speare*' by I. M. (James Mabbe), for example, was added because Blount knew him, having published his translation of Mateo Alemán's *Guzmán de Alfarache* as *The Rogue* in the same year as the Shakespeare Folio. Like the Folio, it featured commendatory poetry by Jonson and Leonard Digges. More controversially, Scragg maintains that the Folio's dedication and address to the reader were ghostwritten, respectively, by Blount and Jonson.

Prospero-like power, he called his dead friend back to life – immortalized in the pages of his book – with his haunting command: '*My* Shakespeare, *rise*' (line 19). Despite being frequently omitted from accounts of Shakespeare's participation in the book trade, Blount's publication of 'The Phoenix and Turtle' among the collaborative essays of *Love's Martyr* in 1601 represents an important event in English literary history, the implications of which we are just beginning to understand.

SHAKESPEARE'S SINGULARITY AND
SIR THOMAS MORE

JAMES PURKIS

SHAKESPEARE'S SINGULARITY

For around one hundred years, the three pages of the manuscript of *Sir Thomas More* (BL MS Harley 7368) supposed to be in Shakespeare's hand have testified to his singularity. Shakespeare's perceived singularity, to take Gary Taylor's formulation of a term derived from Kenneth Muir, resides in part in his 'pre-eminence, his superlative uniqueness'.[1] Such singularity also, the reception of the *More* manuscript would suggest, manifests itself in something of an anti- or non-collaborative spirit. These senses of singularity are at work in W. W. Greg's influential description of the revision in Hand D, as his 1911 Malone Society Reprint designates the passages on folios 8a, 8b and 9a commonly attributed to Shakespeare's pen.[2] After describing the collaborative work on the preceding folios of the agents that he labels B and C, Greg continues his description of the revisions thus:

and then comes the astonishing addition by D. Round this much controversy has centred. The writer has no respect for, perhaps no knowledge of, the play on which he is working. His characters are unrecognizable. He is indifferent to the personae. He writes 'other' and leaves it to C to assign the speech to whom he pleases ... Yet these hasty pages of D's have individual qualities which mark them off sharply from the rest of the play. There is wit in the humours of the crowd, there is something like passion in More's oratory. So striking indeed are these qualities that more than one critic has persuaded himself that the lines in question can have come from no pen but Shakespeare's. The possibility acquires additional interest from the fact that the passage is undoubtedly autograph.

Here possibly are three pages, one of them still legible, in the hand that so many have desired to see. (xiii)

Greg does not join in the 'controversy' over the Hand-D addition's authorship beyond commenting that it seems to him 'an eminently reasonable view that would assign this passage to the writer who ... foisted certain of the Jack Cade scenes into the second part of *Henry VI*' (xii–xiii). Nevertheless, his image of 'D' as an author both aloof from and superior to his collaborators (apparently in more senses than one) remains foundational to the reception of Shakespeare's supposed part in the play's revision. The following pages question some of the aesthetic assumptions that lie behind Greg's description of D's work and take another look at the manuscript for evidence of how the passage was written. I argue that it is certainly possible, and perhaps even necessary, to conceive of the Hand-D addition in another manner to that instantiated by Greg's scholarship. This alternative account of Shakespeare's writing sees him as an engaged collaborator whose work is entangled within the complex textual interminglings of the manuscript. Such an image of Shakespeare's collaborative writing may occasion a reconsideration of how the play is attributed to Shakespeare, how

---

[1] Kenneth Muir, *The Singularity of Shakespeare* (Liverpool, 1977), p. 124. Gary Taylor, *Reinventing Shakespeare: A Cultural History from the Restoration to the Present* (London, 1991), p. 374.

[2] W. W. Greg, ed., *The Book of Sir Thomas More* (Oxford, 1911: repr. 1991). All references to the manuscript are cited from Greg's edition.

it should be incorporated among the established works, and even force a rethinking of the integrity of the Shakespeare canon itself.

If the Hand-D addition is indeed written in the manner that Greg describes, it is truly singular in another sense. The rest of the manuscript is deeply collaborative and the other contributions are so complexly interrelated that attributing individual agency becomes impossible at times. The original text of the play is in Anthony Munday's hand, but most critics assume that Munday is not the sole author of the original play.[3] Munday's text has been subject to the most extensive revision discernible in any extant theatrical manuscript of the period. At least one leaf of the original text has been removed and now lost after folio 5 and one or more has been similarly cast away after folio 11. The retained sheets also bear a number of cancellations.[4] In the place of the cancelled text, the revisers produced material on seven new leaves and two slips. Munday's text has also been supplemented in further ways by the making of small cuts, the addition of short passages of dialogue and the inscription of other marks, made by at least three, and possibly several more, agents.

Of the other hands that appear in the manuscript, three may be identified with confidence: those of Edmund Tilney, the Master of the Revels, Henry Chettle and Thomas Dekker. Another, which subsequent scholarship has come to know as 'Hand C' from its designation in Greg's Malone Society Reprint, is almost certainly that which wrote the plots for the second parts of *The Seven Deadly Sins* and *Fortune's Tennis*, as well as the cover of, and perhaps some or all of the annotations in, the manuscript of *John a Cumber and John a Kent* (Huntington MS 500), which is also in Munday's hand. Another hand, labelled as B in Greg's edition, may be that of Thomas Heywood.[5] Hand D may, of course, be Shakespeare's.

D aside, the work of each theatrical reviser incorporates material from another agent in some way and demonstrates a knowledge of and concern for the play in stark contrast to the image of D's participation presented by Greg. B writes a short scene that may be entirely original and also, as detailed below, rewrites another that is mainly comprised of material reproduced from Munday's text. B also inscribes some other lines in the margins of Munday's pages. Dekker pens a short passage added to the end of the revised version of a scene in which More plays host to Erasmus and disciplines a long-haired ruffian called Falkner. It is also a widely held assumption that Dekker rewrote the rest of the material that features Falkner, although its transcription in Hand C makes this uncertain. Dekker may further have been responsible for much of the transposition, rewriting and shuffling of old and new material that makes up the revised passages in which More receives Erasmus, first of all by instructing his man, Randall, to play a joke on his guest by pretending to be his master. Here, the possibility of determining and even defining agency frequently breaks down, as the rewriting becomes a compound of original and new material. To cite just one example, when Randall reassures his master that he will impersonate him effectively, in Munday's text he insists, 'if I doo it not in kew, let your Lordship bannishe me from the wearing of a golde chaine for euer' (lines 762–3). The equivalent line in the revised text is inflated to: 'If I doe not deserve a share for playing of yor Lo. well. lett me be yoeman

---

3 For a discussion of the authorship of the original text, see John Jowett, ed., *Sir Thomas More*, Arden Shakespeare, Third Series (London, 2011), pp. 415–23. Richard Proudfoot argues that 'we may have to consider the possibility that Munday, who did write plays, may also have had a job that entailed copying them out, whether or not he was their author': *Shakespeare: Text, Stage, Canon* (London, 2001), p. 86.

4 In addition to text lost to some short local revisions, nearly the whole of folio 3a, over a third of folio 3b, most of folio 5b, most of folio 11b, all of folio 14a, at least twenty-nine lines from folio 17b, and a little over half of folio 19a have been cancelled by various agents, although the cancelled text remains legible beneath the deletion marks. It may be that at one point in the revision process cancelled material from folios 3, 17 and 5b, was intended to be reinstated.

5 The case for identifying B as Heywood is made by Jowett, *Sir Thomas More*, pp. 433–7. However, the objections to the identifications raised by J. M. Nosworthy are still worthy of serious consideration: 'Hand B in *Sir Thomas More*', *The Library*, 5th ser., 2 (1956), 47–50.

vsher to yor Sumpter and be banisht from wearing of a gold chaine for ever' (Add. IV, lines 21–2).

Four-and-a-half folio sides, and both addition slips, are written in Hand C. While in 1928 Greg entertained the possibility that C may have been 'part-author' of the play, C is not considered to be the author of any of the work in his hand by subsequent critics (and the earlier Greg) on the less than self-evident assumption that some of his work elsewhere in the document involves transcription and because he has been identified as a 'bookkeeper' or 'theatrical scribe'.[6] In fact, on the one occasion where C's exemplar survives, it is apparent that C is not a simple 'copyist', as Greg labels him in his Malone Society Reprint (xvii). Reproducing a five-line speech drafted by B, C adds a word, 'hether', in order to perfect the meter (Add. VI, lines 68–73; Add. V, lines 2–7); he also determines the speaker of the lines. C also twice edits D's dialogue, at one point replacing three of D's lines with his own short phrase 'tell me but this' (Add. II, lines 235–7). To what extent C contributed non-derivative material elsewhere into the manuscript may only be conjectured. What is clear is C's importance to the incorporation of the additions. He writes entrance directions for the additions in Hands B and D, adds further stage directions and a number of speech headings to D's addition.

Chettle's contribution to the manuscript is the most puzzling. He may be one of the authors of the original text. One folio sheet, that offers an alternative version of a conversation between More and his wife, is in his hand. The material is almost entirely new, but it does incorporate the rewriting of the original text's 'Now shall you heare me speake, / like Moore in melanchollie' as 'Now will I speake like Moore in melancholy' (lines 1480–1; Add. I, line 1). The sheet is incorrectly placed and, although there is evidence that it was once in its correct place, Greg and Vittorio Gabrieli and Giorgio Melchiori query whether it was ever properly incorporated into the manuscript as part of the revision process.[7] Peter W. Blayney argues that Chettle was also responsible for the cutting of six passages and a marginal inscription that calls for the rewriting of the Erasmus scene.[8] As detailed below, Jowett also claims that Chettle is the author of another of the revision's scenes. Chettle may thus have contributed only a single passage that was never incorporated into the manuscript, or he may have been a co-author of the original text and a reviser responsible for making cuts, identifying a scene that required rewriting and providing two significant passages to the revision. The difficulty in determining Chettle's contribution captures something of the impossibility of defining the bounds of each contributor's participation in the manuscript's writing and rewriting.

GREG'S LEGACY

Greg's isolation of D from the densely collaborative revisions and rewritings that make up the other additions to Munday's original text of the play has determined how the passage has been attributed to Shakespeare. Critics have advanced a range of palaeographic, orthographic and stylistic arguments for the authorship of the Hand-D addition on the logic that, as the passage is a singular autograph work, the arguments converge to establish that Shakespeare wrote the material on folios 8 and 9. This form of argumentation was established by the essays collected in A. W. Pollard's *Shakespeare's Hand in the Play of Sir Thomas More* (1923), to which Greg contributed an agnostic essay that focused on the other contributors to the *More* manuscript.[9] But even the most recent advocates of the attribution, advancing computer-assisted stylistic arguments, have sought recourse to the accumulation of arguments from different perspectives. Timothy Irish Watt, for instance, states that his

---

[6] W. W. Greg, 'Reviews and Notices', *The Library*, 5th ser., 9 (1928), 202–11, p. 202.

[7] Peter W. M. Blayney, 'The Booke of Sir Thomas Moore Re-examined', *Studies in Philology*, 69 (1972), 167–91, pp. 180–1; Greg, ed., *Sir Thomas More*, p. xi; Vittorio Gabrieli and Giorgio Melchiori, eds., *Sir Thomas More* (Manchester, 1990), p. 22.

[8] Blayney, 'Re-examined', pp. 171–2.

[9] W. W. Greg, 'The Handwritings of the Manuscript', in A. W. Pollard, ed., *Shakespeare's Hand in the Play of Sir Thomas More* (Cambridge, 1923), pp. 41–56.

computational analyses 'can be added to the many indications [of Shakespeare's authorship of folios 8 and 9] already in existence, from parallel passages, image clusters, rare words, idiosyncratic spellings, and indeed from handwriting'.[10] MacDonald P. Jackson, too, draws on the arguments established in Pollard's collection to defend the Shakespearian attribution of the Hand-D passages against the negative verdict for Shakespeare's authorship offered by Ward E. Y. Elliott and Robert J. Valenza.[11] Reiterating the arguments put forward in Pollard's volume, supplemented by Giles E. Dawson's work that operates on an identical logic, Jackson insists that '[d]iverse objects of investigation – handwriting, spelling and bibliographical links, the development of ideas and imagery, collocations – all lead to the same conclusion': Shakespeare's authorship of the Hand-D addition.[12]

Such dependence on a convergence or combination of evidence may betray a continuing uncertainty about how convincing is each line of evidence in itself. Reviewing the palaeographic evidence for Shakespeare's authorship of the Hand-D addition in 1927, Greg observes that it is doubtful 'whether the available data are extensive enough to make complete proof possible'.[13] Indeed, implicitly expressing doubt about the strength of each line of argumentation, Greg concludes that attribution of the addition to Shakespeare 'must . . . be on the ground of the convergence of a number of independent lines of argument – palaeographic, orthographic, linguistic, stylistic, psychological – and not on any one alone' (908). This approach was attacked most succinctly by Alois Brandl just two years after the publication of Pollard's volume when he offered that 'a hundred unreliable arguments . . . do not together make a reliable one', and has been addressed most effectively in more recent years by Paul Werstine.[14] The following pages explore what may be a more troubling problem with the argument through cumulative lines of evidence. While advances in computer-assisted attribution methods have made arguments for Shakespeare's participation in the Hand-D addition's writing on the ground of word choices and collocations more persuasive than ever, the 'letter

or other undoubted autograph of Shakespeare' that could put beyond doubt the identification of his hand still stubbornly has not come to light.[15] And as Michael Hays puts it, with flawless if seldom-recognized logic, 'non palaeographic arguments may reach the same conclusion as palaeographic ones, but they cannot strengthen palaeographic arguments themselves'.[16] In a manuscript as complexly collaborative as is Harley 7368, the coincidence of hand and mind may not be assumed with comfort. As I argue below, another look at the manuscript indicates that the conclusion that the Hand-D passage is an autograph passage has been drawn too quickly by scholars, with the result that other possible ways in which the passage may have come into being have not been sufficiently explored.

Greg's insistence on D's indifference towards, or ignorance of, the rest of the play has held similarly powerful sway over accounts of the play's revision, even as Shakespeare's assumed involvement in the revisional process has grown in scope

---

[10] Timothy Irish Watt, 'The Authorship of the Hand-D Addition to *The Book Of Sir Thomas More*', in Hugh Craig and Arthur F. Kinney, eds., *Shakespeare, Computers, and the Mystery of Authorship* (Cambridge, 2009), pp. 134–61; p. 156.

[11] Ward E. Y. Elliott and Robert J. Valenza, 'Two Tough Nuts to Crack: Did Shakespeare Write the "Shakespeare" Portions of *Sir Thomas More* and *Edward III*? Part I', *Literary and Linguistic Computing*, 25 (2010), 67–84; 'Part II: Conclusion', pp. 65–78.

[12] MacDonald P. Jackson 'Is "Hand D" of *Sir Thomas More* Shakespeare's? Thomas Bayes and the Elliott–Valenza Authorship Tests', *Early Modern Literary Studies*, 12 (2007) pp. 1–36; http://purl.oclc.org/emls/12%13;3/jackbaye.htm., para. 25.

[13] W. W. Greg, 'Shakespeare's Hand Once More', *Times Literary Supplement*, 24 November and 1 December 1927, pp. 871, 908.

[14] Cited in R. W. Chambers, *Man's Unconquerable Mind: Studies of English Writers, from Bede to A. E. Housman and W. R. Ker* (London, 1939), p. 208; Paul Werstine, 'Shakespeare, *More* or Less: A. W. Pollard and Twentieth-Century Shakespeare Editing', *Florilegium*, 16 (1999), 25–45.

[15] The phrase is taken from S. J. Warner's letter to A. W. Pollard, dated 3 April 1919, now stored with the *More* manuscript.

[16] Michael Hays, 'Shakespeare's Hand in *Sir Thomas More*', *Shakespeare Studies*, 8 (1975), 241–53, p. 242.

from that implied by Greg's edition.[17] In 1931, R. C. Bald effectively reintroduced into criticism of the play the notion that Shakespeare was responsible for a soliloquy of twenty-one lines spoken by More on folio 11*b that appears in the document, apparently transcribed, in Hand C. In this short soliloquy, More, recently elevated to the Chancellorship, reflects on the corruptive dangers of 'honor office wealth and calling' and what appears to be a breach of the very order that he defends in his address to the rebels just two scenes earlier (Add. III, line 16). Bald preserves the disconnected singularity of Shakespeare's contribution to the play by insisting that the soliloquy on folio 11*b 'is written with even less reference to its surroundings than Addition II (the ill-May-Day scene attributed to Shakespeare)'.[18] While Bald's perception is repeated by such an important student of the manuscript as Peter W. Blayney, who remarks that the speech 'is virtually useless dramatically, for it neither fits the context in which it is placed, nor any other point in the play',[19] several critics have found More's soliloquy an effective 'prologue' to his swapping places with Randall to test if Erasmus 'can distinguishe / meritt and outward Cerimony' in the action that follows (Add. IV, lines 19–20).[20] If Shakespeare wrote More's soliloquy, it is difficult to insist on his ignorance of the rest of the play.

One hundred years after the publication of Greg's Malone Society Reprint, John Jowett's Arden 3 edition of the play added to the emerging image of a Shakespeare more engaged with the work of his fellow collaborators. Jowett proposes that *More* includes further Shakespearian matter in the shape of a speech written on the manuscript's other added slip, folio 13*, again penned by C. The short exchange between More and a messenger, Jowett argues, presents a revision of a speech that Shakespeare had originally written as another soliloquy for More.[21] Jowett interprets Shakespeare's contributions on the addition slips as fully participant within the manuscript's revision. The two short Shakespearian revisions, according to Jowett,

show the revisers' desire to give a stronger coherence to the play's fragmented middle scenes. They both use More

as the adhesive, placing him in a semi-choric role. They both also develop the audience's awareness that he is the play's central figure, and they both elaborate on his state of mind. They are, indeed, More's only soliloquies in the entire play. In all these respects the design is palpable.[22]

The design may be palpable but according to Jowett's conjecture it was not permanent as the revision of the second soliloquy reduces the 'semi-choric' effect of the addition. Despite interpreting Shakespeare's part in the revision of the middle scenes as demonstrating such deep intellectual and practical engagement with the play, Jowett continues to see the Hand-D addition much in line with Greg's view. When Shakespeare came to write the Hand-D addition, 'the purely circumstantial and local difficulty arising from the distribution of sheets of paper was not overcome' and his engagement lessened as his information about the rest of the play was circumscribed.[23] Indeed, in his Arden edition Jowett remarks that 'Shakespeare's writing practices in the passage show a dramatist perhaps uncertain as to how the scene would fit into the play' (20). The rest of this essay argues that the Hand-D section may be more like these other supposedly Shakespearian additions, as well as the contributions of the other revisers.

ERRING REBELS

Greg's perception of D's textual isolation is described for the most part through literary or aesthetic observations, in the form of his descriptions of D's possible ignorance of, and indifference to,

[17] Greg offers in the introduction to his Malone Society Reprint that 'the individuality of his style makes it quite evident' that D was responsible only for the three pages in his hand (xvii).
[18] R. C. Bald, 'Addition III of *Sir Thomas More*', *Review of English Studies*, 7 (1931), 67–9, p. 67.
[19] Blayney, 'Re-examined', p. 179.
[20] John Jowett, 'A Collaboration: Shakespeare and Hand C in *Sir Thomas More*', in *Shakespeare Survey 65* (Cambridge, 2012), pp. 255–68, p. 260.
[21] Jowett, ed., *Sir Thomas More*, p. 457.
[22] Jowett, 'A Collaboration', p. 260.
[23] Jowett, 'A Collaboration', p. 268.

the rest of the play, and his characters being 'unrecognizable'. Giorgio Melchiori, the most prolific critic of the play in the last decades of the twentieth century, similarly draws on character criticism in arguing for what he sees as D's isolation from the rest of the revision process. Melchiori contends that in writing his addition, D 'read the original scene rather hastily'.[24] Having done so, he almost entirely ignored or forgot the drawing of characters in the earlier iteration of the action that folios 8 and 9 replace and chose 'to present all the rebels, and especially their leaders, as clownish figures', reducing John Lincoln, in particular, 'from the indignant, dignified and purposeful character presented by Munday in the rest of the play' to 'an exact copy of the malicious and foolish Jack Cade'.[25] The appropriateness of character for interpreting early modern dramatic writing has lost much currency since the publication of Greg's edition. Critics are now more likely to recognize that the 'impression of continuous consciousness' that Alan Sinfield suggests represents a dramatic character may break down when contrary to the needs of the drama as a whole.[26] But it is worth examining such an argument for D's ignorance or indifference seriously, not least because the Hand-D passages perhaps show that in the hands of competent dramatists characters may err a little when circumstances require. Rereading folios 8 and 9 without an exclusive interest in its Shakespearian singularity reveals that D's work coincides with that of the other revisers of the ill-May-Day scenes in a manner quite contrary to the accounts of Greg and his followers. Specifically, the pages in Hand D participate in a shift in the representation of Lincoln and his followers that paints them with an increasing simplicity as their actions become more rebellious. This change was probably motivated in part by an attempt to 'discredit the seriousness of the rebellion' for the sake of getting the approval of the censor for the revised play, but fulfilled other practical dramatic purposes too.[27]

If the first scene of Munday's text survived the play's revision, the opening action of the revised drama follows quite closely Holinshed's account of the events of 1517.[28] (If the scene was in fact abandoned due to the evident displeasure that it caused Edmund Tilney, then arguments for D's ignorance of the Londoners' early representation are of course profoundly compromised.) Scene 1 begins by bringing together two instances of the foreigners' abuses reported separately in the source. The Frenchman Caveler enters having taken possession of two doves from Williamson while the Lombard de Barde attempts to abduct Williamson's wife, Doll. As Nina Levine remarks, in their dealings with the Londoners the strangers are presented 'not as refugee artisans but as imperious courtiers helping themselves to the citizens' property and wives'.[29] As the scene progresses, the audience is informed of past injuries done to the native Londoners by the foreigners and their lack of recourse to justice as the power of the foreign 'Lord Ambassadour' silences effective complaint (line 32). The initial representation of the native English characters thus shows them justifiably aggrieved at the foreigners' behaviour and their own circumstances. Melchiori's description of Lincoln as 'indignant, dignified and purposeful' is undoubtedly apt at this point. Lincoln's questioning 'must these wrongs be thus endured?', as he looks on at the foreigners' mistreatment of his fellow Londoners, and his description of himself as a man who has for a 'long time winckt at [the] vilde ennormitees' committed by the strangers, mark him as a sympathetic character moved by unendurable provocation and

---

[24] Giorgio Melchiori, 'Hand D in "Sir Thomas More": An Essay in Misinterpretation', in *Shakespeare Survey 38* (Cambridge, 1985), pp. 101–14, p. 112.

[25] Giorgio Melchiori, '*The Book of Sir Thomas More*: Dramatic Unity', in T. H. Howard-Hill, ed., *Shakespeare and 'Sir Thomas More': Essays on the Play and its Shakespearian Interest* (Cambridge, 1989), pp. 77–100; p. 84.

[26] Alan Sinfield, *Faultlines: Cultural Materialism and the Politics of Dissident Reading* (Oxford, 1992), p. 66.

[27] Melchiori, 'Dramatic Unity', p. 83.

[28] As Jowett states, it 'may well be that the revisers assumed that, unlike the other insurrection scenes, this one [Scene 1] was beyond recovery, for in the MS as it survives there is no revision or transcript of it': *Sir Thomas More*, p. 361.

[29] Nina Levine, 'Citizens' Games: Differentiating Collaboration and *Sir Thomas More*', *Shakespeare Quarterly*, 58 (2007), 31–64, p. 48.

injustice (lines 30, 62). The play's third scene reinforces the sympathies likely to have been occasioned by the opening action. Shrewsbury, Surrey, Palmer and Cholmeley express indignation at the strangers' 'highe-creasted insolence' and recount and condemn some of the foreigners' abuses in terms echoing those used by the Londoners (line 327). The nobles further take on a jingoistic tone, with Surrey speaking of the danger facing the strangers 'if the Englishe blood be once but vp' (line 372). And Cholmeley virtually absolves Lincoln and his followers of blame, remarking that the foreigners' 'base abuse' is the fault of the nobles who do not inform the monarch of the 'dayly wrongs [that] are offered to his subiects' (lines 382, 383). The scene is sufficiently sympathetic to Lincoln's rebels that Tilney cancels Surrey's and Cholmeley's lines.

Hereafter, though, the drama requires something else. The play must depart from its main source for the opening scene because, as Melchiori acknowledges, it is central to the drama's structure that More succeeds in 'what Holinshed said he failed to do, persuading the people'.[30] This change of history requires an attendant change in the representation of the rebels. If their presentation in the 'insurrection scene', as well as in the scene set in St Martin's that follows the meeting of the nobles, continues to show the same sympathy towards their grievances as do the opening scenes it is hard to see how More's intervention can be successful or how he can remain perceptible as the friend of the common people (and perhaps of the audience). The revised text must also be agreeable to the censor and, as Tilney's intercession in scene 3 indicates, this too requires the representation of the uprising to depart from its initial appearance by making Lincoln's followers come across as less threatening and their actions less sympathetic than they earlier appear. The revisions in Hands B, C and D work together to effect these necessary changes.

B's first contribution to the revision is the rewriting on folio 7a of a scene from the original text that depicts the put-upon London craftspeople congregating in St Martin's and determining to set fire to the strangers' houses. As Munday's iteration of the scene remains legible under the crossings out on folio 5b, it is possible to determine the nature of B's rewriting. B reproduces almost verbatim thirty-nine of the original text's forty-one lines. Only small changes – a 'then' for a 'come', an interpolated 'no', a dropped 'all' and, at the higher end of possible significance, 'lets stand vppon oᵗ swords' for Munday's 'Lets stand vppon our Guarde' – make their way into B's reproduction of original material. But B also adds eleven new speeches in order to introduce a clown into the play, which he neatly manages by employing a previously mute character, Ralph Betts, for the role. The new speeches are shuffled among the passages of material repeated from Munday's text. Three new speeches between the clown and his brother, George, begin the scene before B's sheet begins the interrupted repetition of Munday's original text. First by replacing the two speeches given to 'All' in Munday's text with speeches for the clown (the second of which takes the phrase 'fier the howses' from the replaced line (line 426; Add. II, line 25)), and then by interspersing six further speeches for the clown, as well as one new, single-word speech for Doll as the Clown's interlocutor, over the course of the short scene, B's task is completed.

Through B's supplementations, Lincoln's rebels are already on the way to becoming, to use Melchiori's word for their supposedly anomalous appearance in the Hand-D addition, 'clownish'. Even without B's added lines, the rebels in Munday's original text of the scene differ markedly from their previous appearance in the play. As Munday's Lincoln urges the rebels to 'Add rage to resolution', as Scott McMillin notes, 'a change begins to occur [in their representation] in the direction of mob hysteria' (line 417).[31] The Londoners' resolve to 'fire the houses' of the strangers is, for Jowett, 'excessive in relation to the wrongs the citizens themselves have suffered [and] arbitrary in its targeting' (l. 426).[32] But the danger and indignation of

---

[30] Melchiori, 'Hand D', p. 111.

[31] Scott McMillin, *The Elizabethan Theatre and The Book of Sir Thomas More* (Ithaca, 1987), p. 141.

[32] Jowett, ed., *Sir Thomas More*, p. 46.

Lincoln's angry mob is offset by the rebels simultaneously becoming a little buffoonish and, as Walter Cohen describes them in the Hand-D addition, belittled.[33] Doll's second speech includes the scatological command to 'bumbast' the strangers 'till they stinck againe' (lines 432–3). In other words, they are to be beaten until they defecate. And once George Betts proposes 'Let some of vs enter the straungers houses, / and if we finde them there, then bringe them foorth', Doll further defuses the insurrection's threat with insipid comedy, replying: 'If ye bringe them foorth before ye finde them, Ile neuer allowe of that' (lines 434–5, 436).[34] B's other contributions to the revision of the ill-May-Day scenes are the addition of a further three quips for the clown, this time written in the margins of three folios retained from the original text that follow the inserted sheets in Hands B, C and D, and a brief exchange between the clown and a sheriff, where the former pleads with the sheriff to hang Lincoln and Doll before him and, indeed, to not hang him at all. These contributions appear identical in purpose to the revision of the St Martin's scene in 'defus[ing] the effect of the rioters' aspirations' through clownage.[35] B's marginal contributions lie as uneasily alongside Lincoln's 'dignified' death in Munday's original text as anything charged to D.

C's contribution is closely interrelated to that of B and D. C adds a possibly incomplete or placeholder entrance direction for B's rewriting of the St Martin's scene in the margin of folio 5b, adds a notation '*Manett Clowne*' in the margin of folio 7b and alters one of B's speech headings where his (near) transcription of the original text diverges from its (near) exemplar (Add. II, line 42). C also writes an entrance direction for the Hand-D addition at the foot of folio 7b, adds another later in the scene, amends some of D's speech headings and twice alters D's dialogue. C's greatest material contribution to the revision, though, is the penning of a scene that fits between the rewritten St Martin's scene and the material in Hand D. The scene in Hand C, often referred to as the 'Guildhall scene', shows the Mayor, More and the nobles, who in scene 3 recount the abuses perpetrated by

the foreigners, determining to address Lincoln and his followers to 'appease / wth a calm breath this flux of discontent' (Add. II, lines 107–8).

The scene in Hand C further effects the transformation in the presentation of the rebels and their relationship to the strangers. Shrewsbury, Palmer, Surrey and Cholmeley, who in scene 3 condemn the 'pride' of the 'saucie Aliens', make no reference to the provocation under which the London citizens act (line 375). The objects of the Londoners' ire are presented in a sympathetic light as 'the amazed Lombards' (Add. II, line 82). At the same time, Lincoln's protestors are described not as abused subjects, as they were before, but 'rebells' and participants in a 'mutinie', as the focus of the nobles' concern shifts from the injuries heaped upon the native Londoners to the threat of 'this most dangerous Insurecion' (Add. II, lines 87, 101, 97). Both changes of emphasis allow More's later intervention in the Hand-D addition, where he quells the rebellion, to appear more sympathetic. Indeed, the scene in Hand C neatly accommodates the two particular strains of argumentation used by D's More: that the rebels empathize with the foreigners' plights as fugitives and that they, the rebels, are 'in armes gainst g<o>d' (Add. II, line 218). As Melchiori notes, the scene on 7b also sees the action of the play depart from Holinshed in having the assembled figures of authority report that the prisoners released by the rebels and 'cleav[ing]' to Lincoln's 'Lawles traine' are 'fellons and notorious murderers', rather than solely 'the citizens guilty only of "hurting the strangers"' as

---

[33] Stephen Greenblatt, Walter Cohen, Jean E. Howard and Katharine Eisaman Maus, eds., *The Norton Shakespeare: Based on the Oxford Edition*, 2nd edn (New York, 2008), p. 2031.

[34] A further, Cade-like menace (at least to a modern sensibility) also enters the scene through B's revision. As Cade calls that 'He that will lustily stand to it shall go with me and take up these commodities following – item, a gowne, a kirtle, a petticoat, and a smock' (4.7.143–6) so B's Clown quips 'now marsse for thie honner dutch or frenshe so yt be a wenshe ile vppon hir' (Add. II, lines 40–1).

[35] Janet Clare, '*Art made tongue-tied by authority': Elizabethan and Jacobean Dramatic Censorship*, 2nd edn (Manchester, 1999), p. 57.

Holinshed had it (Add. II, lines 89, 90).[36] Good reason is provided for further change in 'Lincolne Sherwine and ther dangerous traine' by the time that the drama reaches D's material (Add. II, line 75).

Most significantly, the scene in Hand C further signals that the rebels are to be reinterpreted by the audience not primarily in terms of danger, but, as in the St Martin's scene, in terms of a disparaging or belittling of the rebels. This shift in representation is achieved through explicit reference to the simplicity that has already begun to characterize their actions and dialogue in B's scene. Reflecting on the rebels' intention to 'fier the Lumbards howses', Surrey ponders 'oh power what art thou in a madmans eies / thou makst the plodding Iddiott Bloudy wise' (Add. II, lines 104, 105–6). If Surrey's words remain general rather than specifically addressed to the rebellion, even if the association is unavoidable, More's description of the rebels leaves no room for doubt as to how they are to be perceived. As he resolves to address 'oᵗ privat foes', More remarks (Add. II, line 119):

> letts to thes simple men for many sweat
> vnder this act that knowes not the lawes debtt
> wᶜʰ hangs vppon ther lives. for sillie men.
> plodd on they know not ~~ow~~ how. ~~like a fooles penn~~
> that ending showes not any sentence writt
> linckt but to common reason or sleightest witt
> thes follow for no harme but yett Incurr
> self penaltie wᵗʰ those that raisd this stirr
>
> (Add. II, lines 111–18)

The sense of the speech as it stands in the final text is complicated by a cancellation line that runs from line 113 to line 116, although, as Greg notes, 'a subsequent mark after 113 may be intended to make the omission begin at 114 only' (1911, p. 73). The reference to the rebels as 'sillie men' may have been cut, or refer to those that follow rather than 'raisd' the 'stirr'. The 'simple men' of More's initial couplet, however, remains untouched by the revision, and evidently refers to all of Lincoln's train, shaping the audience's perception of the rebels that are about to enter at the start of the pages in Hand D.

Identifying the author or authors of the Guildhall scene, and whether it is comprised of material from the original text, derives solely from the revision process or involves the intermingling of original and revisional matter, appears beyond present means. There are, as I have suggested above, grounds to believe that C may have played more than a purely scribal part in the preparation of folio 7b. Jowett attributes the 'Guildhall scene' to Chettle as part of the main revision process, although he admits that his assumption is 'weakly evidenced'.[37] However, as Melchiori states, the scene's close adherence to events as related by Holinshed, even to the extent of following 'the order in which they are recorded there', is typical of Munday's text and points to the possibility that the scene is 'modelled to a large extent' on material from the original text of the play.[38] The transformation of the strangers into 'Lombards' hints that C, and any other revisers involved in the scene's production, may have worked from an iteration that had passed before Tilney's eyes, which would mean that the scene at least in part derives from the original text.[39]

D's initial treatment of Lincoln and his followers connects suggestively with the Guildhall scene's emphasis on their simplicity, whatever the latter's genesis. When Lincoln declares that the rebels will 'accept of the king[es] mercy' but will 'showe no mercy vppon the st<raungers>', D's sergeant calls the rebels 'the <simplest> thing[es] that eu' stood in such a question' (Add. II, lines 141–2). His insult elicits the enraged responses from Lincoln and 'all' respectively, 'how say yoᵘ now prenti prentisses symple downe wᵗʰ him' and 'prentisses symple prentisses symple' (Add. II, lines 143, 144, 145). It

---

[36] Melchiori, 'Dramatic Unity', p. 81.

[37] Jowett, ed., *Sir Thomas More*, p. 453.

[38] Melchiori, 'Dramatic Unity', p. 81. It is of course possible that Chettle wrote or had a hand in an initial iteration of the scene that was later revised by another agent. Alternatively, Chettle may have rewritten the scene as part of the main revision process rather as B rewrote the St Martin's scene, by incorporating some or much material from the original scene.

[39] The altered sympathies in the scene may equally account for this change.

may be more than coincidence or D's awareness of the Guildhall scene that lies behind these lines. The only three lines that remain from the material that D's addition replaces, the three lines cancelled at the head of folio 10a to accommodate the new sheets, indicate that the emphasis on the rebels' simplicity found in the contributions in Hands C and D may have been a feature of the first iteration of the scene that D in part rewrites. The end of a speech by an unknown character (the speech evidently began on the preceding sheet so its prefix is now lost) informs the rebels: 'no doubt, what <punish> ment you (*in simplicitie* haue incurred, his high-nesse in mercie will moste <graciously> pardon' (lines 473–5, emphasis added). It is not much to go on, but it is highly suggestive. D's engagement with, if not dependence on, an earlier iteration of the scene emerges as a distinct possibility.

The rebels at the beginning of the Hand-D section may differ from their counterparts in the opening scene, then, but their erring may credibly, perhaps even best, be interpreted as evidence of D's informed and responsive participation in the joint collaborative process that effects a dramatically necessary shift in the presentation of the rebellion. It is important to note here, moreover, that the rebels' 'clownish' appearance in the Hand-D revision does not last for the duration of the addition. As D's More reminds them of their duties as subjects – of which they are acutely aware in the opening scene – and calls on them to recognize the strangers' plights as those of houseless refugees, they offer assent and practically summarize More's call for hospitality towards the foreigners by calling out 'fayth a saies trewe letts vs [*sic.*] do as we may be doon by' (Add. II, line 264). Through D's work, the play may revert easily to the original end of the scene written in Munday's hand on folio 10, where the rebels yield and appeal for the King's mercy and, according to Cohen and McMillin, find again the 'decency' that characterizes their initial behaviour in the play.[40]

D's contribution does not fit seamlessly with the work of his fellow revisers. In particular, as McMillin and Melchiori both point out, D appears ignorant of the introduction of the clown into the revised text.[41] It may simply be that D knew of B's role in the revisions and assumed that he would add material for the clown later. Alternatively, B and D may have written their revisions simultaneously, which would leave B, in introducing the clown, just as out of step with the revision process as D, who did not incorporate the clown character. The contributions of B and D thus may be construed as diverging from the same starting-point but demonstrating a similar intention: the toning down of the rebellion through comedy. It may be revealing of some sort of coordinated co-labouring in this regard that D's Lincoln's supposedly incongruous expression of concern with the ill brought by 'straing rootes' and the dangers brought by 'the eating of p[er]snyps' is intriguingly close to B's added dialogue for the Clown on 7b (Add. II, lines 130, 137). The clown's first words are 'come come wele tickle ther [that is, the strangers'] turnips' (Add. II, line 1). It is also of note that D's possible ignorance of the clown's development may have been shared by C. C's entrance direction for B's revised text of the St Martin's scene on folio 5b does not explicitly mention the clown, as he does in the entrance on folio 7b. It may be, as McMillin offers, that C's 'Betts' 'is meant to be plural'.[42] The original entrance in Munday's hand denotes both characters with a single 'Betses' (line 410). In this case, at the point of inscribing the entrance direction – which would have to have been written as a placeholder or guide prior to receiving B's new sheet – C may still have considered Ralph Betts as the same silent character as in the original iteration, indicating that D's supposed ignorance of the clown's development was not unique. C's stage directions are far from exhaustive, however. He also omits Sherwin from the direction even though he has a fairly prominent role in the scene, and anything inferred from C's entrance direction must be considered as suggestive at best.

---

[40] McMillin, *Elizabethan Theatre*, p. 141; Greenblatt *et al.*, eds., *The Norton Shakespeare*, p. 2031.

[41] Melchiori, 'Dramatic Unity', p. 85. McMillin, *Elizabethan Theatre*, p. 142.

[42] McMillin, *Elizabethan Theatre*, p. 24.

WRITING THE HAND-D ADDITION

If, as I have argued may be the case, D is a more engaged reviser than Greg's description determines him to be, it may be worth considering whether his work is closer to that of B and C in another way, as I have already begun to suggest. In his Malone Society Reprint, Greg writes that the Hand-D addition is 'unquestionably autograph' (xvii). The vast majority of critics have followed this supposition. Yet the common purposes of the work of the three ill-May-Day revisers – including the suggestive emphasis on 'simplicitie' that runs across from the C-penned 'Guildhall scene', through the material in Hand D, to the cancelled lines at the head of folio 10a – invite speculation over whether the pages in Hand D may have been written in a similar manner to the contributions of B and C, and thus whether folios 8 and 9 may not be purely autograph, or at least, as Greg described the passage in 1923, 'an entirely new version' of the dramatic action (47). In addition to the three lines at the head of folio 10a, the manuscript may offer further evidence pointing away from D's singularity.

The Hand-D passage undoubtedly exhibits features consistent with an author having second thoughts in the midst of composition. The end of Lincoln's third speech, for example, reads: 'for what[es] a watrie or sorry p[er]snyp to a good hart' (Add. II, line 131). Similarly, a speech attributed to 'Bett' reads that the rebels seek 'the removing of the straingers wch cannot choose but much helpe advauntage the poor handycraftes of the Cytty' (Add. II, line 193–4). The *currente calamo* status of these alterations constitute persuasive evidence of spontaneous literary revision on D's part. E. A. J. Honigmann, perhaps less convincingly, further proposes that the three lines of More's speech eventually replaced by C's 'tell me but this' include 'several false starts' (which he states are characteristically undeleted by Shakespeare) of the kind assumed typical of original composition.[43]

However, other alterations in the passage suggest something else is going on too. Several of the blots, crossings out and alterations in Hand D look like anticipations and eyeskip errors, and hence evidence of possible transcription. The inscription of the phrase 'twere in no error yf I told yo^u all you wer in armes against g<od>', for instance, sees D mistakenly writing 'in' after 'twere', seemingly anticipating the 'in' after the similar, later 'wer' (Add II, line 218). Likewise, when D has More call on the rebels to imagine themselves in the position of the strangers, he writes:

> what Country by the nature of yor error
> shoold gyve you harber go yo^u to ffraunc or flanders
> to any Iarman p[ro]vince, to spane or portigall
> nay any where why yo^u that not adheres to Ingland
> why yo^u must need[es] be straingers; . . .
>
> (Add II, ll. 249–53)

The first alteration is readily attributable to a transcribing writer faltering over the repetition of the word 'to'. Disruption in the metre further hints that D may have departed from an exemplar in his confusion. The second change, the crossing out of 'why yo^u', plainly invites anticipation as an explanation.

On another occasion, the sense of a passage is lost where it appears that a transcribing D is more aware of the repeated 'ands' of the passage than of its sense.

> ymagyn that yo^u see the wretched straingers
>   w^t
> their babyes at their back[es], and their poor lugage
> plodding tooth port[es] and cost[es] for tranportacion
> and that yo^u sytt as king[es] in your desyres
> aucthoryty quyte sylenct by yor braule
> and yo^u in ruff of yor yo opynions clothd
> what had yo^u gott, Ile tell yo^u, yo^u had taught
> how insolenc and strong hand shoold prevayle
>
> (Add II, lines 197–204)

As Gerald Downs puts it, '[l]uggage loses itself, but it doesn't plod. A scribe loses his way by picking up a word from the next line or by mistakenly anticipating a conjunction' and this appears to be D's

---

[43] E. A. J. Honigmann, 'Shakespeare's Deletions and False Starts', *Review of English Studies*, new ser., 56 (2005), pp. 37–48, p. 42.

error here.[44] The cancellation of 'yo' four lines later in the speech is also readily explicable as a transcription error, caused by the copyist being influenced by, or momentarily skipping to, the repeated 'yo^u s' of the following line which, with its earlier 'yo^u' and the similarity of the superscript *us* and *rs*, looks a lot like the preceding line.[45]

Distinguishing between changes introduced in original composition and during transcription is fraught with difficulty. The possible scribal errors in the Hand-D addition could be explained through alternative micro-narratives.[46] Is the cancelled 'why yo^u' cited above an instance of anticipation in copying, or is the clause that follows it – 'that not adheres to Ingland' – an embellishing phrase that occurred to the composing author immediately after he wrote 'why yo^u' for the first time? Does the further instance 'he ... hath not le only lent' represent a scribe momentarily missing a word crucial to the sense of the passage or a composing author's pen running on too quickly (Add. II, line 225)? Critics may make of such instances what they will, but as Levin L. Schücking remarked of the Hand-D addition almost ninety years ago, '[t]here are some points in the script which, to say the least, allow as well of the explanation of it being a copy, none that *force* us to take it for the original'.[47]

If the presence of transcription errors in the Hand-D addition is accepted, it may still be a Shakespearian autograph, even if regarding it as a fair copy means the loss of the attractive image of Shakespeare, as Greg describes D's work, composing 'probably with great fluency'.[48] Grace Ioppolo has argued precisely this point, while Henry Woudhuysen also writes of the impossibility of determining whether the Hand-D addition is a draft or a transcription.[49] Thomas Heywood's *Captives* manuscript (BL MS Egerton 1994, fols. 52 to 73), which appears to be 'a transcript "fouled" by frequent bursts of free composition', offers a potentially illuminating analogous example of what appears to be an author intermingling original material with transcription of his own earlier iteration (as well as more complex forms of rewriting).[50] However, once the possible coexistence of transcription and new writing in the Hand-D passage is recognized, it again starts to look a lot more like the work of the *More* manuscript's other agents. Without the comforting support of the aesthetic argument for D's detachment from the revision process, folios 8 and 9 appear as a possible site for the comingling of different agents' writings, like folio 7a and, probably, 7b.

Exactly what forms of collaborative writings may make up the Hand-D addition – as well as the role played in the passage's composition by D, the person in whose hand the addition is written – must remain open to conjecture. Shakespeare may have penned the passage in a manner similar to one of the several forms of rewriting that can be found in the rest of the manuscript. Alternatively, B. A. P. Van Dam considers D's interlined, and metrically disruptive, 'alas alas' an 'obvious actors' interpolation', and concludes that 'the three pages must have been written by a scribe' making occasional additions (and mistakes).[51] A similarly disruptive 'Alas, alas!' that may be found in *Measure for*

---

44 Gerald Downs, 'A Question (not) to be Askt: Is Hand D a Copy', *Shakespeare Yearbook*, 16 (2007), 241–66, p. 247.

45 In *Dramatists and their Manuscripts in the Age of Shakespeare, Jonson, Middleton and Heywood: Authorship, Authority and the Playhouse* (London, 2006), Grace Ioppolo reads the source of error differently, but reaches the same conclusion: '[t]he deletion of the seventh word is almost certainly due to correcting the inadvertent repetition of either the second or sixth word in the line while the author was looking at the original copy. That is, he wrote out 'yor', glanced at his original text (but at the wrong place) saw either 'yo^u' or 'yor' and accidentally began to copy this incorrect word' (107).

46 In his Arden edition, Jowett states that 'the few items of evidence for eyeskip from one point to another in the supposed copy are interpretable in ways that do not require a pre-existing draft', but he does not trouble the reader with any such interpretations (439).

47 Levin L. Schücking, 'Shakespeare and Sir Thomas More', *Review of English Studies*, 1 (1925), 40–59, p. 59.

48 Greg, 'Handwritings', p. 45.

49 Ioppolo, *Dramatists*, p. 104; H. R Woudhuysen, ed., *Love's Labour's Lost*, Arden Shakespeare, Third Series (Walton-on-Thames, 1998), p. 320.

50 E. A. J. Honigmann, *The Stability of Shakespeare's Text* (London, 1965), p. 206.

51 B. A. P. Van Dam, *The Text of Shakespeare's 'Hamlet'* (London, 1924), p. 371.

Measure presumably renders Van Dam's interpretation less probable (3.1.133), but D's work is not incompatible with the minor revisions made by C.[52] As palaeographic arguments cannot establish whether the passage is in Shakespeare's hand or not, one further possibility that emerges is that the passage is rewritten, 'transcribed' with some alteration, by an agent other than Shakespeare. It is of note, though, that one of D's revisions does point gently towards Shakespeare as the agent in whose hand the passage is written. Jowett observes that when D replaces the word 'warrs', he introduces 'the Shakespearean word "hurly" . . . in a context that is itself Shakespearean'.[53] 'Hurly', as Jowett argues, 'is found in no other play from the English public theatre, except for three occurrences in Shakespeare' (443). It is an arresting coincidence, if meagre grounds on which to take on the apparently insoluble task of identifying Hand D. If the passage is in Shakespeare's hand, of course, this still does not resolve how he wrote it and whether he reproduced or leaned heavily on material from another writer.

ATTRIBUTING THE SHAKESPEARIAN

The questions that I have raised about the Hand-D addition's writing may usefully be brought into contact with what is probably the most important attempt to establish Shakespeare's authorship of the revision. Jackson entered the text of the Hand-D addition into the searchboxes of the Chadwyck-Healey 'Literature Online' database 'phrase by phrase, collocation by collocation, and even content word by content word', and recorded all of the instances where the search term was shared by five or fewer plays other than *More* performed between 1590 and 1610.[54] Fifteen plays, according to the search, have four or more links with the Hand-D addition, and Shakespeare plays dominate the list. Significantly, Jackson's search finds Shakespearian links throughout the addition. If the Shakespearian mingles with the non-Shakespearian in the Hand-D addition, Jackson's findings suggest a more sustained and substantial contribution to the addition on Shakespeare's part than, for instance, B's part in revising the St Martin's scene.

However, while Jackson's findings indicate that caution may be appropriate in speculation over how much non-Shakespearian material may be included in the passage (even as what may be called Shakespearian and non-Shakespearian becomes a harder question to address), the *More* manuscript also challenges aspects of Jackson's methodology and, as a consequence, his findings. He concludes his study by claiming that the links that he uncovers mean that '[t]extual scholars can continue to study Hand D's pages in the confidence that they are his [i.e. Shakespeare's] autograph draft of *Sir Thomas More*'s best scene [*sic*] as he was composing it and committing it to paper' (78). The preceding pages indicate that such 'confidence' may be misplaced and the problem of attempting to identify the author of the passage through what is, in effect, a first-past-the-post method is plain, as the complexly interrelated writings of parts of the manuscript challenge the assumption of authorial purity on which Jackson's method depends. One is thus left wondering what, if anything, is to be made of links between the Hand-D addition and other plays that are not by Shakespeare? Is it significant that the Mayor first addresses the rebels with a line identical to one appearing in *Sir John Oldcastle*, a play that Munday co-wrote? Or is it indicative of some form of collaborative writing that the Mayor's second speech to the rebels includes (when

---

[52] This instance, and its connection to *More*, is discussed by John Jowett, *Shakespeare and Text* (Oxford, 2007), p. 15.

[53] Jowett, ed., *Sir Thomas More*, p. 440.

[54] MacDonald P. Jackson, 'The Date and Authorship of Hand D's Contribution to *Sir Thomas More*: Evidence from "Literature Online"', in *Shakespeare Survey 59* (Cambridge, 2006), pp. 69–78, p. 70. Jackson makes an exception of 'three cases where a phrase occur[s] in more than five plays' because they show a concentration in the work of a single playwright: '"Peace ho" . . . occurs eleven times in six Shakespeare plays, and only once outside Shakespeare . . . "Peace I say" . . . occurs six times in five Shakespeare plays and once in each of two plays by other dramatists. "shall we hear" . . . is found in five Shakespeare plays and in only one other' (77).

modernized) the apparently Shakespearian 'Peace ho', but also 'I charge you keep the peace' (Add II, line 50), which appears in *1 Honest Whore*, co-written by Dekker? Many of the revisional writings of the manuscript are too intricate to be detected by Jackson's, and possibly any other, method. Indeed, the coincidences of different agents' writings are sufficiently complex that what begins as the epistemological question of who wrote what ends as a conceptual one. In what senses the line 'If I doe not deserve a share for playing of yoʳ Lo. well. lett me be yeoman vsher to yoʳ Sumpter and be banisht from wearing of a gold chaine for ever' – or even B's 'then gallant bloods', which departs from Munday's text in its first word – may be attributed to an individual agent, be it Munday, Chettle, Heywood, C, or Dekker, is not self-evident.[55]

The preceding pages do not prove that Shakespeare cannot have written the Hand-D passages in the isolated, singular manner in which almost the entirety of a century's scholarship on the play supposes. But they do indicate that the grounds on which such an image of Shakespeare's anti-collaborative writing rests are less secure than almost a century of scholarship has supposed, and it may as a consequence be time to suspend the assumption of D's Shakespearian singularity. With such a deferral come new questions for defining Shakespeare's writing and for the integrity of his canon. Since C. F. Tucker Brooke attempted to explain its inclusion in his edition of the *Shakespeare Apocrypha* three years before the publication of Greg's Malone Society Reprint of the play, *More* has proven difficult to place in relation to the Shakespeare canon.[56] Included in some editions and one series, excluded from others, and almost invariably marked in some way as different from the other plays, *More*'s treatment by editors challenges the terms under which collaborative work may be given canonical status. But even this troubling reception may not recognize the real problem of the manuscript. The commonplace practice of reproducing 'Passages Attributed to Shakespeare', or 'The Additions Ascribed to Shakespeare', or 'A Scene from *Sir Thomas More*' has sustained

the assumption that the passages represent Shakespeare's individual work, identifiable and separable – or indeed already marked off through his singularity – from the rest of the manuscript.[57] Even as the second edition of the Oxford *Complete Works* and now the third series of the Arden Shakespeare take the almost unprecedented step of including the complete text of *More* in a Shakespeare edition or series, Shakespeare's supposed contributions remain divisible from the rest of the manuscript through the identification of the agent or agents considered responsible for each section of the manuscript.[58] But if the

---

55 Further problems weaken Jackson's method. C, of course, has no (known) texts on the LION database and must remain undetectable. It is a cause of discomfort that his interpolated 'tell me but this' registers as a match for *Othello* according to Jackson's search criteria (Add. II, line 237). As Jackson's method counts links per play, those authors who wrote mostly in collaborations – and the *only* thing that we really know of D is that he participates in the revision of a collaboratively-produced play – are unlikely to make an impression on the search. Chettle has only one single-authored play on the database compared to Shakespeare's thirty-six. As Chettle is considered by several critics to be a co-author of the original play, and hence may have written the first iteration of the scene that D rewrites, his effective invisibility to such searches is a particular worry, not least because both Peter Blayney ('Re-examined', pp. 182–8) and Gary Taylor have detected similarities between Chettle's work and the Hand-D addition that, in Taylor's words, 'seem too numerous and striking to arise from coincidence' (Gary Taylor, 'The Date and Auspices of the Additions to *Sir Thomas More*', in *Shakespeare and 'Sir Thomas More': Essays on the Play and its Shakespearian Interest*, T. H. Howard-Hill, ed. (Cambridge, 1999), pp. 101–29, p. 119). It is of note here too that Jackson's method cannot establish Chettle's authorship of the addition in his hand.

56 C. F. Tucker Brooke, ed., *The Shakespeare Apocrypha: Being a Collection of Fourteen Plays which have been Ascribed to Shakespeare* (Oxford, 1908).

57 Greenblatt *et al.*, eds., *The Norton Shakespeare*, p. 2031; G. Blakemore Evans, ed., *The Riverside Shakespeare*, 2nd edn (Boston, 1997), p. 1775; Jonathan Bate and Eric Rasmussen, eds., *William Shakespeare: Complete Works* (New York, 2007), p. 2464.

58 The exception and precedent is Charles Jasper Sisson's *William Shakespeare: The Complete Works* (New York, 1953), which does include the play.

matter in the play to which he may have contributed is not the singular work of Shakespeare, in the various forms in which this term functions, the document poses a new question. The critical challenge presented by *More* is not just one of what to do with a piece of dramatic writing by an indifferent and ignorant Shakespeare that features as a small part of a play written in the main by other dramatists. It enforces a rethinking of what, on epistemological and conceptual grounds, we choose to recognize as 'Shakespearian'.

DOUBLE FALSEHOOD: THE FORGERY HYPOTHESIS, THE 'CHARLES DICKSON' ENIGMA AND A 'STERN' REJOINDER

BREAN HAMMOND

Since the publication, in 2010, of my Arden edition of *Double Falsehood*, one skein of controversy has threaded around the closely argued case made by Professor Tiffany Stern to the effect that *Double Falsehood* could be, with the strong probability that it is, a forgery entirely concocted by Lewis Theobald, whose recorded statements about the play would therefore be a tissue of lies. Since this view has apparently convinced Shakespeare's most recent biographer, it should be as trenchantly opposed.[1] To date, chapter ten of Gary Taylor and Terri Bourus's *The Creation and Re-Creation of Cardenio*, by Taylor and entitled 'Sleight of Mind: Cognitive Illusions and Shakespearian Desire', is the most systematic refutation of Stern.[2] Taylor catalogues various kinds of attribution error as well as more general errors in her theatrical history, convicting her of 'confirmation bias', 'affective bias' and other forms of mistaken thinking. I do not think that Stern's misprision needs to be understood in complex logical and psychological terms. I think her arguments need to be carefully and closely investigated. I believe the time is right for me also to engage in the debate. My particular concern is the respect in which Stern's method of argument resembles that of an attorney leading a witness, putting points in a tendentious manner that appears to rig a particular case and at times to lack the objectivity and detachment required for a clear-headed investigation of the question whether *Double Faleshood* as presented by Lewis Theobald could conceivably be a forgery. I will cast doubt upon − I hope refute − individual strands of argument pursued in her articles and I will re-articulate the strength of the case against her. There is one strand of disputed evidence that I have pursued in greater depth, because, eerily, it produces an adaptation study that has some suggestive parallels with the *Double Falsehood* case, albeit of a play by Massinger and Field rather than by Shakespeare.

THE FORGERY HYPOTHESIS

Stern's way of proceeding has structural similarities to that of the anti-Stratfordians. Beginning from an iconoclastic position ('Shakespeare wasn't Shakespeare'; 'Lewis Theobald forged *Double Falsehood*'), they find evidence to support the contention without confronting the accumulated case against their initial presumption. Stern's form of argument is a relentlessly positivist one: she kicks stones everywhere, as she attempts to refute the evidence and conclusions of other scholars convinced that something more venerable lies behind the eighteenth-century text of Theobald's

---

[1] See Michael P. Jensen, 'Talking Books with Tiffany Stern', *Shakespeare Newsletter*, 62:1 (Spring/Summer, 2012), 9: 'Published as we prepared our interview is, "The Forgery of Some Modern Author?" . . . which powerfully queries the notion that Lewis Theobald had a manuscript copy of a play by Shakespeare and John Fletcher when he wrote *Double Falsehood*. It convinced me that he did not.' See also Lois Potter, *The Life of William Shakespeare: A Critical Biography* (Malden, MA, 2012), p. 392 ('convincing').

[2] Gary Taylor and Terri Bourus, *The Creation and Re-Creation of Cardenio: Performing Shakespeare, Transforming Cervantes* (New York, 2013), especially ch. 10, pp. 125–70. I am grateful to Gary Taylor for permitting me to see a pre-publication copy.

adaptation.[3] She is not the only serious scholar who believes that the play may be forged, though her contention that there is an established critical tendency in favour of that view seems to me to be exaggerated.[4] Much more economically than does Stern, Robert Folkenflik rehearses those aspects of *Double Falsehood* that might lead us to think it a hoax, in a review of my edition published in the *Huntington Library Quarterly* – though ultimately he himself does not believe the play to be a forgery.[5] Folkenflik has one particular point that is more potent than most of those made by Stern, to wit that the rare word 'absonant', cited by myself and others as an unlikely lexical item for Theobald to have forged, is to be found in two seventeenth-century dictionaries where there is independent evidence for Theobald knowing them.[6] Stern is apparently unaware of the work of one of the forgery school's subtlest proponents, Neil Pattison, so I would wish to focus attention on his view:

'forgery' is not a term sufficiently precise to account for the cathected interrelations of proprietorial, filial and authorial rights densely cross-hatching Theobald's text. Or rather, it is too precise. *Double Falshood* is exactly what it says it is: in truth, an edition and adaptation. But its original lies not in a lost and fragmented play of Shakespeare, or someone else, which may or may not have existed, and which Theobald may or may not have read, or not only there. It lies in Theobald's sense for the meaning of *Shakespeare*, and the negotiation of that meaning through the complex demands, ambitions and anxieties entailed by that meaning's conception in him.[7]

Put simply, *Double Falsehood*, according to Pattison, is a play about the search for a father produced by a writer who was himself in search of a father, both natural and literary. If Shakespeare was his father, think Stern and Pattison, then Theobald was a bastard son. So it would be timely to remind ourselves of just what a high hill the forgery hypothesis has to climb.

Stern's position is set out in two key articles: 'Fletcher and Theobald as Collaborators' published in a volume of essays edited by David Carnegie and Gary Taylor on *The Quest for Cardenio* and a piece published simultaneously in 2012 but written later, '"The Forgery of Some Modern Author'"?: Theobald's Shakespeare and Cardenio's Double Falsehood' in *Shakespeare Quarterly*. It is necessary to scrutinize those in detail.

The first half of the piece in *The Quest for Cardenio* deals with early modern material, asking the question 'whether we can ever be sure that *Cardenio* contained textual material written by both Fletcher and Shakespeare' (115). Stern's argument is that an understood distinction between 'plotters' – those who were notable for composing plots – and writers, who represented the plots in written dialogue, was emerging in the early modern period. Her 2009 book *Documents of Performance in Early Modern England* had mounted a case for considering that the 'plot' and the 'language' of early modern plays were 'created as separate documents'.[8] On this premise, she argues that Shakespeare could have been the 'plotter' of a putative *Cardenio* play without having written a line of the actual dialogue, which may have been Fletcher's contribution. She concedes that Shakespeare was considered to be much the weaker plotter of the duo, reducing the likelihood that this is the way the job was

---

[3] Tiffany Stern, '"Whether one did Contrive, the Other Write, / Or one Fram'd the Plot, the Other did Indite": Fletcher and Theobald as Collaborators', in *The Quest for Cardenio: Shakespeare, Fletcher, Cervantes, & the Lost Play*, ed. David Carnegie and Gary Taylor (Oxford, 2012), pp. 115–32; and '"The Forgery of some modern Author"?: Theobald's Shakespeare and Cardenio's Double Falsehood', *Shakespeare Quarterly*, 62 (2011), 555–93.

[4] See Rudolph Schevill, 'Theobald's *Double Falsehood* ?', *Modern Philology*, 9 (1911), 269–85; Leonard Schwartzstein, 'The Text of *The Double Falsehood*', *Notes and Queries*, 169 (1954), 471–2; Harriet Frazier, *A Babble of Ancestral Voices: Shakespeare, Cervantes, and Theobald* (The Hague, 1974); Jeffrey Kahan, *Shakespeare Imitations, Parodies and Forgeries, 1710–1820*, 3 vols. (London, 2004).

[5] Robert Folkenflik, '"Shakespearesque": The Arden *Double Falsehood*', *Huntington Library Quarterly*, 75 (2012), 131–43.

[6] Folkenflik, 'Shakespearesque', p. 140. The dictionaries are Thomas Blount's *Glossographia* (1661) and Edward Phillips's *A New World of English Words* (1658).

[7] Neil Pattison, '"O Brother! We shall sound the Depths of Falshood"', p. 8 (unpublished, on file with author).

[8] Tiffany Stern, *Documents of Performance in Early Modern England* (Cambridge, 2009), p. 9.

carved up: but her main objective is to exclude Shakespeare's presence in the *Cardenio* palimpsest, so she does not worry about this inconsistency overmuch. Moreover, the examples she gives of existing 'plots' – detailed accounts of a play's story existing independently of any written-out acts and scenes – all postdate Shakespeare's period. In the earlier period, documents termed 'plots' seem to be for playhouse use – they mark entrances and exits for actors: 'the title of "plot" is a misnomer in modern terms, for although broken into acts and scenes, these plots do not provide a summary or outline of the play's scene-by-scene action for the sake of potential audience members'.[9] Even if Stern may now be setting the standard for our understanding of this aspect of collaboration, there is no hard evidence offered for questioning what editors have established as the situation in the other collaborative plays, that Shakespeare wrote specific scenes and also 'mended' or touched up others.[10] Since Shakespeare and Fletcher worked together on two other plays, we have evidence for their working methods. We know, for example, that collaborating playwrights portioned plays off into acts and scenes and that some playwrights gained reputations for being able to write scenes in particular genres.[11] In the case of *Henry VIII*, our best guess is that the dramatists' influence was reciprocal. In that of *Two Noble Kinsmen*, Lois Potter's hypothesis is that 'the two dramatists began writing concurrently, but that Fletcher constructed the final draft. In 1.4, 2.2, possibly 2.5, and 5.1, he seems to have been working on, or in the light of, Shakespearian material; nothing suggests that Shakespeare was ever working on Fletcher's'. This, Potter thinks, is because Shakespeare was not in London when the play was being finished.[12]

Stern's second line of argument, further developed in her *Shakespeare Quarterly* article, is a forensic attempt, in the manner of an aggressive trial prosecutor, to discredit Theobald as a credible witness to his own testimony regarding *Double Falsehood* – a compilation of reasons for mistrusting him. This commences (122) in a way not likely to inspire confidence, with the claim that Theobald's *The Censor* was his 'regular contribution to *Mist's Weekly Journal*'. In fact, *The Censor* began in April 1715. It was independent of the *Weekly Journal* and commenced a decade before *Mist's*.[13] She quotes from *The Censor* a passage in which Theobald is said to be 'dictating' on the supreme importance of plots, but actually Theobald is quoting from Aristotle at this point, not writing in his own voice. Overall, *The Censor* is, as Peter Seary argues, 'important for its emphasis on language and character at the expense of neo-Aristotelian concerns with plot and poetic justice', precisely the opposite of what Stern asserts.[14] Similarly, when she later wants to illustrate Theobald's unusual degree of assimilation to his role models, Stern writes that Theobald 'regularly subsumed those early modern writers he most looked up to: he had it in *The Censor* that his satirical style revealed him as "lineally descended from *Benjamin Johnson*"' (124). But she omits to clarify that Theobald says this in the *Spectator*-like persona of the 'British Censor' and specifically *not in propria persona*. Her endeavour is to establish Theobald's 'plot-neediness' and

---

9 See Grace Ioppolo, *Dramatists and their Manuscripts in the Age of Shakespeare, Jonson, Middleton and Heywood: Authorship, Authority and the Playhouse* (London, 2006), pp. 53–5.

10 Gordon McMullan's account of attribution and composition for *Henry VIII* shows a consensus that Shakespeare was responsible for 1.1, 1.2, 2.3, 2.4, 3.2 (first part) and 5.1: *King Henry VIII*, ed. Gordon McMullan, Arden Shakespeare, Third Series (London, 2000), pp. 448–9.

11 Ioppolo, *Dramatists and their Manuscripts*, pp. 32–3. These conclusions would seem to be borne out by both the recent Oxford and the recent Arden editions of *Timon of Athens*, even if the Arden editors are more cautious about assigning portions than is the Oxford editor. See John Jowett, ed., *Timon of Athens* (Oxford, 2004); and Anthony B. Dawson and Gretchen E. Minton, eds., *Timon of Athens*, Arden Shakespeare, Third Series (London, 2008), pp. 1–10 and Appendix 2, pp. 401–7. The cautious Arden editors consider that most of Act 3 is Middleton's and all of Act 5 is Shakespeare's.

12 Lois Potter, ed., *The Two Noble Kinsmen*, The Arden Shakespeare, Third Series (London, 1997), p. 32.

13 Stern may mean *The Weekly Journal or Saturday's Post* founded by Nathaniel Mist on 15 December 1716. The periodical known as *Mist's Weekly Journal* did not commence until May 1725. In either event, Theobald's *Censor* did not originate with Mist.

14 Peter Seary, *ODNB* entry, 'Lewis Theobald'.

hence his unscrupulous attitude to other people's plots. One aspect of that is said to be his failure to acknowledge Warburton's help in annotating the Shakespeare edition: 'Warburton joined the crowd who saw Theobald as a textual predator' (123). To subpoena Warburton as a witness for the prosecution against Theobald is like calling Bonnie Parker as a witness against Clyde Barrow. To list the number of controversies in which Warburton was embroiled, several of them resulting from his sense of being slighted or overlooked, would require the remainder of my space. Edward Gibbon wrote in his *Memoirs* that 'the real merit of Warburton was degraded by the pride and presumption with which he pronounced his infallible decrees; in his polemic writings, he lashed his antagonists without mercy or moderation; and his servile flatterers . . . exalting the master-critic far above Aristotle or Longinus, assaulted every modern dissenter who refused to consult the oracle, and to adore the idol'.[15]

Stern's character assassination of Theobald, designed to represent him as a man capable of forging Shakespeare, continues in her *Shakespeare Quarterly* article, where Theobald is introduced thus: 'attorney, translator, and hack playwright, best known for his pantomimes, [he] was on the fringes of society in the 1720s'. That would be like saying that Andrew Lloyd Webber was on the fringes of society after writing his most famous musicals. The phrase 'best known for his pantomimes' *could* give the impression, to those unfamiliar with the form that Rich and Theobald pioneered, that it resembles modern pantomime in the more trivial and juvenile aspects of that evolved genre. From its inception at the turn of the century, the form characteristically combined scenes of classically inspired pantomime dancing developed by John Weaver and others, with *commedia dell'arte* characters drawn from the Théâtre Italien in Paris, operating within scenarios drawing on continental and English theatre texts and traditions. In Theobald's hands, however, as Neil Pattison has argued, pantomime aspired to the condition of total art, a multimedia 'whole show' – it combined popular spectacle with exceptional literacy and erudition, as elements of classical mythology, chorus dances, ballad singing

or Italianate airs, accompanied recitative dialogue and extravagant stage effects were added.[16] Aware of his schizophrenic position as a creator of commercial theatre that was impeding performance of serious drama on the one hand, and as an editor of Shakespeare on the other, Theobald's compromise was to try to 'achieve a harmonious integration of the serious and grotesque, the literate and illiterate, the native and foreign elements of the drama' – in *Harlequin Doctor Faustus*, for example, to graft in direct elements of the Marlowe play.[17]

Later in her article, Stern describes Theobald's working methods in such a way as to suggest that he could have been a forger. She retails the story of the Mesteyer plagiarism accusation against his play *The Perfidious Brother* (1715). It is difficult to find a major author in this period who *was not* so accused, and that is owing to the changing regard in which notions of literary property were held and the changing legal framework governing copyright. I have argued elsewhere that multiplying plagiarism accusations in the period post-1670 were testimony to a 'thickening' concept of literary property that would over time replace tradition and allusion with originality as a supreme aesthetic good.[18] Although her chronology of Theobald's

---

[15] Cited in James E. Tierney ed. *The Correspondence of Robert Dodsley 1733–1764* (Cambridge, 1988, repr. 2004), p. 214. Tierney is at this point footnoting Warburton's unpleasantness of manner in corresponding with Robert Dodsley over the publication of Pope's *Works*. B. W. Young's *ODNB* entry on William Warburton cites David Hume: 'It is petulance, and Insolence and abuse, that distinguish the Warburtonian School, even above all other Parsons and Theologians . . . I remember Lord Mansfield said to me that Warburton was a very opposite man in company to what he was in his Books; then, replyd I, he must be the most agreeable Companion in Europe, for surely he is the most odious Writer.'

[16] Neil Pattison, '"King Tibbald": The Writing of Lewis Theobald in Alexander Pope's The Dunciad Variorum', Ph.D. dissertation, University of Cambridge (2007), ch. 5. Although Pattison has serious doubts about *Double Falsehood*, he has none about Theobald's brilliance as a writer of upmarket entertainments embodying some of the ambition of earlier forms such as court masque.

[17] Pattison, '"King Tibbald"', p. 7.

[18] Brean S. Hammond, *Professional Imaginative Writing in England 1670–1740: Hackney for Bread* (Oxford, 1997), ch. 3. See

writing (577) that has him writing *Orestes* (1731) before he wrote *Double Falsehood* (1727) does not lead us to trust the investigator implicitly, the problem is not so much one of scholarly accuracy as of *ad hominem* argument. For example, where, to illustrate Theobald's Autolycus-like propensity to snap up the trifles of other authors, she condemns the breadth of his reading – 'to start with the dead: Theobald used various of the "above 800 old *English* Plays" that he had read by 1733 to provide plots for his dramas' (575) – one might rather commend him, along with other pioneers in early drama, such as William Oldys and Robert Dodsley, for creating an interest in pre-Shakespearian drama and for developing a newly systematic approach to editorship. It would be difficult to imagine, from Stern's account, that Theobald is still regarded as one of the greatest editors of Shakespeare who ever lived.[19]

There follows a lengthy section in which Theobald is made to claim that he possessed a 'single Shakespearean manuscript' whereas in his scholarly work (his edition of Shakespeare), he 'repeatedly, and contradictorily, maintained . . . that no such manuscript existed' (562). This is said to demonstrate his self-contradictory malfeasance. This argument seems disingenuous. I am unaware of any claim that Theobald made, in respect of *Double Falsehood*, to possess a Shakespeare *holograph*. That, in the course of his editorial work, Theobald never encountered a Shakespearian manuscript does not invalidate his claim to have had *some materials* that pre-exist his own working papers for *Double Falsehood*.[20] There are certainly some difficult questions to be asked about Theobald's account of his manuscript holdings, but how does it advance a putative forger's credibility to claim to have multiple copies rather than a single copy of a source? What Stern commits herself to, in levelling the charge of forgery, is that an attorney-at-law such as Theobald was, would procure a Royal licence, having the status of a Royal affidavit, for the genuineness of a set of forged documents. Notoriously in 1777 the clergyman William Dodd was hanged for forging a bill supposedly drawn up by the Earl of Chesterfield, despite Samuel Johnson's interces-

sion. Procuring a Royal licence is not a capital forgery detrimental to the financial stability of the realm, but making the King a liar is not something a man well versed in the law would undertake lightly.

A similar sleight of hand mars Stern's account of the evidence for the textual transmission of a *Cardenio* play down into the eighteenth century. This is a major point. Until recently, the only documentary evidences attesting to the transmission of the text of a lost *Cardenio* play were the near-contemporaneous annual accounts prepared for the Treasurer of the King's Chamber, John Stanhope (the payments, though not the play titles, being mirrored in a Pipe Office document) and the Humphrey Moseley entry in the Stationers' Register of 1653. My edition brought forward more evidence, so Stern must minimize its importance. When she treats my supposition that Jacob Tonson knew of a *Cardenio* play in 1718, she weakens my case by making no reference to the documentary evidence that I bring forward in support of it. When she treats my evidence based on newspaper reports in 1770, that an 'original manuscript' was 'treasured up' in the Covent Garden Theatre

---

also Hammond, 'Plagiarism: Hammond vs. Ricks', in *Plagiarism in Early Modern England*, ed. Paulina Kewes (London, 2003), pp. 41–55.

[19] A typical estimate of Theobald's importance as an editor might be Michael Taylor's: 'It is with [Theobald] that the writing of scholarly and critical notes became a significant feature of the editor's duty, and one has only to turn to any current scholarly edition of any of Shakespeare's plays . . . to see how important Theobald's innovation has become' ('The Critical Tradition', in *Shakespeare*, ed. Stanley Wells and Lena Cowen Orlin (Oxford, 2003), pp. 323–32, pp. 326–7). In *Shakespeare, Milton and Eighteenth-Century Literary Editing* (Cambridge, 1997), Marcus Walsh shows that Theobald 'worked on the basis of informed and by no means untheorized choices amongst a range of possible editorial orientations' (p. 112).

[20] As John Jowett observes, 'it should be remembered that Shakespeare is not unique [in having no surviving manuscripts.] Of the hundreds or even thousands of plays written during the period, only a small handful survive in manuscript. We have no theatrical manuscripts of plays by Christopher Marlowe, Thomas Kyd, George Chapman, Ben Jonson, John Webster': *Shakespeare and Text* (Oxford, 2007), pp. 11–12.

Museum, by a typical slippery elision she emends to 'original text', permitting her the more easily and breezily to assert that 'the library probably had Theobald's original text, acquired in 1740 when *Double Falshood* had its first Covent Garden production, or in 1741 when it was put on again for the author's benefit (570)'. Why then 'treasured up'?

THE 'CHARLES DICKSON' ENIGMA

In Charles Gildon's *The Post-Man Robb'd of his Mail* (1719), there is what Stern calls a 'vague account that may perhaps ratify the existence of one manuscript' (565). Gildon's throwaway title is perhaps one reason why the reference to an unknown play by Shakespeare tends not to be taken seriously. Pursuing this 'vague account' yields interesting results, particularly if we contextualise it from Gildon's writing and the detailed theatre history of its moment of inscription. So, in Gildon's eccentrically titled book, a passage occurs that refers to

a valuable Jewel, lately brought to [the Drury Lane theatre managers] by a Friend of mine, [that] might have had a Chance of obliging the Town with a noble Diversion. I mean, a Play written by *Beaumont* and *Fletcher*, and the immortal *Shakespear*, in the Maturity of his Judgment, a few Years before he dy'd. A Piece so excellent, that a Gentleman, who is allow'd a Master of the Stage, tells me, that after reading it seven times, it pleas'd and transported him, and that it is far beyond any of the Colleague Poets, and inferior to few of the other Poets which are in Print. There is infallible Proof that the Copy is genuine; yet this Rarity, this noble Piece of Antiquity, cannot make its way to the Stage, because a Person that is concern'd in it, is a Person, who of all Persons Mr. C[ibber] does not approve.[21]

Dismissing this intriguing reference as 'vague', as noted above, Stern goes on to wonder why, if Charles Gildon had an undiscovered play by Shakespeare in 1718, he did not publish extracts from it in his *Complete Art of Poetry*. Gildon's *Postman Robb'd* title becomes less whimsical when we recognize that the 'postman robbed' was a Gildon 'brand'. He published his first 'postman' collection, *The Post-Boy rob'd of his Mail*, in 1692.[22] Composed at the moment and in the manner of John Dunton's

Athenian Society and *Athenian Mercury* (the work sometimes credited with having invented the gossip column), Gildon's *Post-Boy* significantly anticipates *The Spectator*. His narrator claims to belong to a Club that, unlike the physical scientists or 'virtuosos', is interested in examining 'the Secrets of the *Rational World*', that is to say, human affairs. The members routinely find that 'no man almost is what he appears to be; we are all *Ianus*'s and have two or more Faces in all our Actions, as well as Designs' (p. 4). Spurred on by the discoveries of a club member who, having been impolitely jostled by a postman, has purloined his sack of letters and on perusal has found them to be a catalogue of venery and hypocrisy, some of them betraying the crapulous secrets of their own circle, the others decide to turn footpad and rob posts up and down the land. The resulting collection of letters comprises the main body of the work. The Duntonian nature of the collection is indicated by such titles as 'From a Whore to a young Spark that was forsaking her, on pretence of living soberly, with one inclos'd to the same, written to him by a grave Philosopher which he lost in a Bawdy House'; and indeed John Dunton was the publisher. The format proving successful, Gildon published another set of such letters in 1706 and another in 1719, the collection in which we have an interest.

Predominantly fictional, the 1719 collection nevertheless contains material that bears much more directly on contemporary culture than had its prequels. Stern's account of the textual situation in Gildon's *Post-Man* is not as careful as it needs to be. Although she claims that Gildon is 'writing under the pseudonym Charles Dickson', he is in fact writing under the pseudonym Sir Roger de Whimsey, a character clearly modelled on Sir Roger de Coverly in *The Spectator*. Cashing in on the recent success of

---

[21] Charles Gildon, *The post-Man robb'd of his mail: or, the packet broke open. Being a collection of miscellaneous letters, serious and comical, amorous and gallant* (London, 1719), pp. 267–8.

[22] *The Post-Boy rob'd of his Mail, or, The pacquet broke open consisting of five hundred letters to persons of several qualities and conditions, with observations upon each letter publish'd by a gentleman concern'd in the frolick* (London, 1692).

the literary periodicals, this latest *Post-Man* incarnation solidifies the 'club' narrative vehicle. Since, in a more moralistic era, the idea of robbing the mail would not go down well, the club members now find the letters abandoned, presumably by thieves, in a ditch. Book III letter V offers advice to a young author, the burden of which is that talent doesn't get you anywhere in an age when '*a Tale of a Tub* spreads immediately into every Corner of the Nation, and the Wicked and the Godly join to propagate its Sale' (147–8). After teaching the neophyte the tricks of the young dramatist's trade, the epistolarist ('Hugh Jean') delivers his own opinions of the drama of the Caroline era:

Massinger is far a better poet than *Beaumont* and *Fletcher*, yet we find the Plays of the latter are printed and reprinted, while it is a difficult thing to meet with those of the former. 'Tis true, the Dramatick Poets of the foregoing Times were not worthy of that Name, as being at most Dialogists; except the immortal *Ben Johnson*, in some of his Comedies: Yet on that Bottom *Beaumont* and *Fletcher* deserve the very least Praise, since they never design'd a just Character in their serious Plays; their Kings are all Footmen, or of the Mob, and have nothing Royal; and their Women seldom Modesty enough for a Whore in a Comedy. (149–50)

And 'Jean' then claims the personal authority of Dryden, who apparently told him that Beaumont and Fletcher were supported on the shoulders of partisan politics and later propped up by good actors. Their plays are now simply received by 'Prescription' and would have to be altered to succeed. We note here the predisposition in Massinger's favour, the omission of mention of Shakespeare and, specifically connected with *Double Falsehood*, the degree of discount that a play by Shakespeare might have to take if Fletcher's hand were discovered in it.[23]

Book IV has a sequence of letters directly concerned with cultural matters. Letter IX, signed 'Robert Grangoust', is devoted to tragedy, commencing with a letter he has received from London praising a new play in that genre. His correspondent's taste is, however, '*Gothick*', foregrounding as it does the language of tragedy to the detriment of plot and character. A tragic plot must prove 'some one important *Moral*' (243), asserts Grangoust. About tragic character, he speaks with great assurance. If a tragic protagonist is to solicit the audience's pity, he must have defects arising from passion, but must not be a '*Jago*' – an irredeemable villain. Grangoust deplores the fact that there is even a tragedy *called* 'The Villain'.[24] Neither should a tragic victim be entirely innocent because the innocent ought never to suffer on stage. Cowardice in men and unchastity in women are both unrepresentable. Grangoust appears to be anticipating *l'homme moyen sensuel* as his ideal tragic protagonist.

Grangoust is clearly a Gildon alias. His views are identical to those expressed in the essay that Gildon annexed to the so-called 'Volume the seventh' of Shakespeare's poems that Curll published in 1710, trying to pass it off as a continuation of Rowe's six-volume edition of the previous year. What he says about Milton's diction in *Paradise Lost* being unsuitable for the stage, in contrast to the more suitable diction of *Samson Agonistes*, directly echoes the earlier essay.[25] Although he does not say which dramatist he has in his sights, his views are, again, entirely compatible with those expressed by Charles Gildon in his *A New Rehearsal, or Bays the Younger* (1714). A satirical analysis of Nicholas Rowe's plays prompted by the success of *The Tragedy of Jane Shore* (1714), it draws lightly on the hugely successful format of Buckingham's *The Rehearsal* (1671), recasting Mr Bays as Rowe. It takes the form of a

---

23 One important line of argument embraced in my Arden introduction was that Theobald lost confidence in his Shakespeare 'find' when he became ever more convinced that it was a collaborative work, showing Fletcher's hand. Since Theobald did not work with any reliable chronology of Shakespeare's plays, he could not have known that Shakespeare and Fletcher were regularly collaborating around the time of a putative *Cardenio* play.

24 He probably has in mind Thomas Porter's frequently reprinted tragedy *The Villain* (London, 1663), though Lewis Theobald's *The Persian Princess* (London, 1715) has 'the Royal Villain' as its subtitle.

25 'Essay on the Art, Rise and Progress of the Stage in Greece, Rome and England' prefaced to *The works of Mr. William Shakespear. Volume the seventh* (London, 1710). See p. lvii for Gildon's remarks on Milton.

conversation between five disputants at the Rose Tavern in Covent Garden, two of whom are men of wit (Freeman, Truewit), one an indolent aristocrat (Sir Indolent Easie), one ('Sawny Dapper') a conceited versifier and another ('Bays') a pedantic and narcissistic 'Reciting' poet.[26] The last two characters are easily identified as Pope and Rowe.

In the discussion both of *Jane Shore* and *The Fair Penitent* (1703), the true critics express their outrage at the success of Rowe's 'she-tragedies' that have moved their audiences' compassion for protagonists who are no better than whores and cowards. In respect of the latter play, Freeman in Gildon's dialogue immediately recognizes what Rowe nowhere acknowledges, that it is 'built on a much better Play of *Massinger's*, call'd the *Fatal Dowry*'.[27] This is exceptionally discerning because the resemblance, given Rowe's wholesale makeover, is not easy to spot, there being no character names in common and only one or two fundamental plot similarities.[28] Freeman is outraged that Rowe's protagonist, Altamont, is a contented cuckold (despite being *Italian*), whose wife, Calista, is a whore from the play's outset. Rowe has therefore managed to represent both male cowardice and female unchastity, the two no-go areas, in the same play. Despite Sawny Dapper's case for the defence, Freeman and Truewit remain implacable that penitence, in Rowe's treatment of it, cannot be genuine and cannot legitimately move pity. Readers are treated to a parodic Prologue ridiculing the play and its coward-whore leading couple.

A consistent cultural identity is therefore emerging through those letters in the *Post-Man* devoted to the contemporary stage, an identity that carries the hallmarks of the real-life Charles Gildon. Contemporary conditions of authorship are being deplored, Massinger is being sponsored, Pope ridiculed and recent tragedies owing their success to the impressiveness of their diction and sentiments and the prosaic regularity of their verses, rather than to convincing plots and characters, are being critiqued. The abomination that was *The Fair Penitent* (in Gildon's opinion) presumably spurred him on to create his own version of Massinger's play, as emerges in Letter XII of Book IV. It is signed by one Charles Dickson and is a response to criticism that this author has received from Mr C – C – (Colley Cibber, one presumes) of a play that he has submitted for performance. That play can be identified as an altered version of Massinger and Field's *The Fatal Dowry* (1632, written *c.*1619) distinct from Rowe's. We can discern Dickson's main alteration: he has gone for a middle way between Massinger in whose play Beaumelle commits adultery with Young Nouall more or less for fun and as an assertion of her independence from her husband Charalois, who himself kills her – and Rowe, in whose play Calista has lost her honour to Lothario even before the play commences, and marries Altamont knowing she is already a whore. Altamont is willing to suffer all for love, however, and Calista has to go to the trouble of killing herself. What Gildon has clearly done, in a play now retitled *The Guiltless Adultress*, is to insert a plot device involving a maidservant that ensures the heroine's innocence – compromised, but not lost, by trickery. Justifying this device from Otway's *The Orphan* (1680), Dickson defends his diction from a charge of vulgarity by comparison with other plays: Dryden's *All for Love* and Cibber's own *Perolla and Izadora* (1706). The diction of *Ibrahim the Thirteenth*, he asserts plaintively, 'wou'd make a Cat spew, (as the saying is)' (262).[29] Dickson has retained resonances of Massinger's character names (Chalons, Beaumele) but has altered others (Renault, Castalio – a resonance of Rowe – and Amelia, the new name of the female lead).

---

[26] It was substantially reprinted in the following year as *Remarks on Mr. Rowe's Tragedy of the Lady Jane Gray, and All his other Plays* (London, 1715).

[27] Gildon, *The post-Man robb'd*, p. 57.

[28] Although Gildon does not make the accusation of plagiarism against Rowe in this place, it *was* made later in the century, for example by Richard Cumberland in his comparison between Rowe and Massinger undertaken in *The Observer*, 77–9 (1785). As Roger Lonsdale notes in his edition of Samuel Johnson's *Life of Rowe*, Hester Thrale thought that Johnson had overpraised Rowe's play, because it was not original. See Samuel Johnson, *The Lives of the Poets*, ed. Roger Lonsdale, 4 vols. (Oxford, 2006), vol. 2, p. 418.

[29] Presumably Mary Pix's apparently emetic tragedy *Ibrahim, the Thirteenth Emperour of the Turks: A Tragedy* (London, 1696).

There is little doubt that the letter is based on real events and that 'Charles Dickson' is the pseudonym for a living would-be playwright who really did have rough treatment at the hands of the Drury Lane management – almost certainly an *alter ego* for Gildon himself. The unusual term 'Fautors', meaning 'adherents' or 'partisans', deployed in Dickson's essay (245), connects it to Gildon's preface to *A New Rehearsal*, which opens with the phrase 'the common Cry of the Poetasters of the Town and their Fautors'.[30] It so happens that we can follow the fate of this unstaged adaptation to its eventual première in March 1758. In the preface to the published version of Aaron Hill's posthumously performed play *The Insolvent*, the story of the text's transmission is told:

Above thirty years ago, Mr. WILKS (then one of the Patentees of the Theatre Royal) gave an old manuscript play, call'd, *The Guiltless Adultress; or, Judge in his own Cause*, to Mr. THEOPHILUS CIBBER, who was then manager of what us'd to be call'd *the summer company* . . . By the hand, and the long time it had been in possession of the Managers, it was suppos'd to have been one of Sir WILLIAM D'AVENANT's (formerly a Patentee) and, by the opening of the piece, palpably was founded on a play of MASSENGER's, call'd, *The Fatal Dowry* —(this last piece has often been enquired after in vain).[31]

We learn that the play 'lay by some time', but was intended to be staged in 1733, when it was prevented by events that led to the shutting out of the actors from the Drury Lane theatre by their managers and baulked again in 1734, when the main house manager (Fleetwood) was jealous of the summer company's success and prevented all further acting. More than ten years later, Theophilus Cibber planned to perform the play and sent it to Aaron Hill for retouching. Since the letters between Cibber and Hill of 1746 survive, as does the play itself, albeit with linguistic changes throughout and a final act entirely composed by Hill, we can reconstruct the Gildon adaptation to an extent. Hill, we discover, wanted to call the play *Amelia, or the Fatal Bribery* because, in his version, the protagonist is actually not an adulteress at all.

He worked from manuscripts, referring as he does to the original play's lines being legible through 'a sad pale *ink*'; and the editor of Hill's letters asserts that 'both the Manuscripts remain in the possession of Mr. C . . . . r'.[32] Hill also claims to be aware of very many more unprinted old plays that could be revived without fear of piracy from the other house. Surprisingly, however, he does not appear to have been aware of the play's original author and inquires about that more than once.

For whatever reason, the play did not appear in the 1740s, having instead to await the deaths of Hill and Colley Cibber before appearing in March 1758, equipped with a prologue in which Theophilus Cibber laments his august father's recent demise, itself an example of filial piety as is the play to follow. Some character names are again altered (Old Aumele, Young Aumele, Valdore), though Chalons and Amelia are retained from Gildon. Much closer to Massinger than Rowe, the play is nevertheless radically sentimentalized, awash with fashionable tears. It seems likely that the plot device for protecting the heroine's chastity briefly referred to in IV.xii of Gildon's *Post-Man* is the action in Hill's play that has Amelia's bribed maid Florella leading Aumele to Amelia's bedchamber, only to be intercepted and murdered by Chalons before Amelia's chastity can be assaulted. The suspicious circumstances are clarified by Florella's confession, but not before Amelia tries to take her own life, unable to survive her husband's likely construction of events. It remains unclear whether Gildon or Hill was responsible for the tragicomic ending in which Amelia's life is saved by the medical savvy of Belgard, but the money would be on Hill because he claims to have entirely reworked the fifth act.

What is particularly striking about this transmission story is the similarity it bears to that of

---

[30] Charles Gildon, *A New Rehearsal, or Bays the Younger* (London, 1714), p. A2.

[31] *The Dramatic Works of Aaron Hill*, 2 vols. (London, 1760), vol. 2, p. 331. The statement also appears in the earlier separately published play quarto: Aaron Hill, *The insolvent: or, filial piety. A tragedy* (London, 1758), A2.

[32] *The Works of the Late Aaron Hill, Esq.*, 4 vols. (London, 1753), vol. 2, pp. 317, 313.

Double Falsehood. Here also is an old play, adapted, it appears, during the Restoration and surviving in a manuscript form that possibly dates back to the period of Davenant – although *The Fatal Dowry* appears to have been assigned as the exclusive property not of Davenant but of Killigrew after January 1669.[33] Further adapted by Gildon some-time around 1719, it was refused by the Drury Lane management but continued to be considered a possibility for performance well into the cen-tury until Aaron Hill, working presumably from the Gildon manuscript (though the mention of 'both the Manuscripts' might suggest an earlier ver-sion also), produced an adaptation acceptable to the mid-century theatre. The differences are that the Massinger and Field original had been printed – had not, like *Cardenio*, entirely disappeared, though it was not well known – and that Shakespeare's name was not involved. If we take seriously Aaron Hill's suggestion made in a letter to Theophilus Cibber of 22 April 1746 that he could 'find means to get ready *two* [old, unprinted plays] for before, and *two* for after *Christmas*, against every season', we would not think such survivals as that of *Carde-nio* in *Double Falsehood* as miraculously unlikely as Tiffany Stern's argument makes them out to be.[34]

Returning to Gildon's *The Post-Man*, we find the attack on Cibber and what we might call 'play-ers' theatre' continuing in the next letter, num-ber XIII again signed by Dickson. The narrative instance here is curiously contorted. Addressed to one 'Reverend Goodly', the salutation is never-theless to Isaac Bickerstaff of *The Tatler*. Since Sir Roger's group comment on the circumstance, we must assume that it is not accidental, but it is enigmatic, in view of the fact that Steele's *Tatler* ceased publication on 2 January 1711. Sympathiz-ing with Bickerstaff, who himself admits to hav-ing been snubbed by the theatre managers in *The Tatler*, Dickson proceeds to cite Cervantes on the corruption of the stage being the result of the man-agement of players.[35] This descends to individual detail: 'honest Will Pierre' not rising higher than a property man, Mr Bright having to go strolling, the long-serving prompter Downes being pensioned off. The detail here suggests that this passage was composed earlier, around 1708, because Downes had retired in October 1706, George Bright was released from the Marshalsea in 1707 and not re-employed at Drury Lane, and it appears to have been around 1708 that Will Peer (Pierre), having grown fat, dwindled into being a property man.[36] The lost Shakespeare play reference cited earlier follows, in the context of Dickson's ironic sugges-tion that Cibber might as well choose his plays by throwing dice, a method that would have given at least a chance to 'a valuable Jewel' etc.

The salient point here is that, *pace* Stern, there is nothing at all 'vague' about this, even if its splicing in of older material unrevised makes for some unclarity. Gildon/Dickson takes great care to present the hitherto unknown Shakespeare play in the context of a firmly established, detailed account both of the general theatre and of a particular case of a rejected script, easily identifiable by contempo-raries in the know and attributable to a writer then living. One is struck by the fact that Cervantes, of all authors, is invoked as guarantor for Dickson's opinion of theatre managers; and when the next letter goes on to praise Gildon's recent *Art of Poetry* and letter XV to attack 'Little Sawny the Poet', to wit, Alexander Pope, we seem to be inhabiting the same structure of feeling as would recur in 1727/8 around *Double Falsehood*. Stern appears to think

---

33 Philip Edwards and Colin Gibson, eds., *The Plays and Poems of Philip Massinger*, 5 vols (Oxford, 1976), vol. 1, p. 10, citing Allardyce Nicoll's *History of English Drama*. They wrongly attribute the correspondence between Cibber and Hill to Colley Cibber.

34 Aaron Hill, *Works*, vol. 2, p. 315.

35 Gildon was an enthusiastic admirer of Cervantes. In the 'Essay on the Art, Rise and Progress of the Stage in Greece, Rome and England' that he included in the so-called seventh volume of Rowe's Shakespeare edition, he quotes extensively from the discussion between the cathedral priest and the curate about the Spanish theatre in *Don Quixote* (vol. 1, ch. 48 in modern editions). Overall, Gildon's essay is a sponsorship of the need for rules and shares a purpose with Dennis's *Essay on the Genius and Writings of Shakespear*.

36 Information taken from the entries in *A Biographical Dictio-nary of Actors, Actresses, Musicians, Dancers, Managers and other Stage Personnel in London, 1660–1800*, ed. Philip H. High-fill, Kalman A. Burnim and Edward A. Langhans, 16 vols. (Carbondale, 1973–93).

that *Gildon* possessed this manuscript and raises questions about why he did not publish it. As I clarify, however, Gildon does not say that *he* has it. He says that Charles Dickson's *friend* has it. Even if we concur that Gildon is Dickson, an identification that my discussion above proposes, we need not deduce that Gildon himself ever possessed this play. In fact, the passage that so tantalizingly refers to 'a Play written by *Beaumont* and *Fletcher*, and the immortal *Shakespear*, in the Maturity of his Judgment, a few Years before he dy'd' indicates that there are *two* other interested parties, Dickson's friend who has the manuscript and is Cibber's *bête noire*, and 'a Gentleman, who is allow'd a Master of the Stage', who has read it seven times with transport.

Who might have been the 'Person, who of all Persons Mr. C[*ibber*] does not approve', the person who presented him with the lost play, and who might have been the 'Master of the Stage'? Since the publication of a series of letters in *The Spectator* in 1711 on 'the Genius and Writings of Shakespear' by John Dennis, written just after Rowe's 1709 edition was published, Dennis had been regarded as one of the emerging Shakespearians of the early century. Already his adaptation of *Coriolanus* as *The Invader of his Country* had been composed; his *Spectator* essays are mainly a justification of his adaptation principles. As previously noted, Gildon had, through the doubtful auspices of Edmund Curll, produced a volume titled *The Works of Mr. William Shakespear. Volume the seventh* (1710) that published Shakespeare's poems and sonnets (the latter all given individual titles) alongside several poems not actually by Shakespeare.[37] But by late 1719, John Dennis was the individual quarrelling with Cibber most acerbically. The premature withdrawal, after only three nights, of *The Invader of his Country*, had resulted in a pamphlet war. The two 'Sir John Edgar' pamphlets published by Dennis in 1720, primarily targeting Steele, took the attack on Cibber's supposed atheism and profligacy to new depths of vitriol: ''Tis credibly reported, that he spit on the Face of our Saviour's Picture at the *Bath*, with Words too execrable and too horrible to be repeated.'[38] Plagiarism is, in Dennis's value-system,

next to atheism and a consequence of it: 'nothing ought to be so sacred as a Man's Thoughts and Inventions: And . . . the impudent Plagiary . . . has dar'd to violate all that is Sacred among Men' (2.192). As does Gildon in the *Post-Man*, Dennis attacks Cibber's tragedies, *Perolla and Izadora* (1706) and *Ximena: or, The Heroick Daughter* (1719, though performed in 1712) for plagiarism and generic miscegenation: 'He has writ two Tragedies, the Language of which is peculiarly adapted to excite Laughter' (2.199). Dennis, Gildon and Theobald were all on good terms at this crucial juncture and were commonly identified in their attack on the theatre Patentees and in Dennis's campaign to have the Lord Chamberlain regulate the theatre more robustly. All three had an interest in the editing, adapting and performing of Shakespeare. Theobald may have been the 'third man'.

Stern's 'most troubling' rabbit produced out of her hat (566) is that by 1719 Gildon was blind, 'so unless he had possessed the manuscript for some time, his testimony is not based on seeing the text'. One really wonders whether this is a tasteless joke. One might ask, on the same grounds, how he managed to write his account of it! The answer, in part, is that he worked via an amanuensis named Lloyd, and in part that he trusts the evidence of his friend Dickson and Dickson's adviser.

A STERN REJOINDER

It is not unfair to say that Stern manipulates the evidence to support her position – which is that what we may have in *Double Falsehood* is 'Theobald stripping a story from *Don Quixote* and then consciously writing it up in the style

---

[37] Titling this 'Volume the seventh' makes it purport to be a continuation of Rowe's six-volume edition published by Tonson, and it is too often taken at its own estimate. Tiffany Stern asks 'why did Gildon also not mention the text when he published the unauthorized seventh volume to Rowe's edition in 1725?' (pp. 565–6), the answer to which is that he actually published the volume in 1710.

[38] John Dennis, *The Characters and Conduct of Sir John Edgar* (1720) in *The Critical Works of John Dennis*, ed. E. N. Hooker, 2 vols. (Baltimore, 1943), vol. 2, p. 189.

of Shakespeare whilst also unconsciously writing it in the style of Beaumont/Fletcher' (130). To understand how desperate this position is, we need to confront the full force of the accumulated scholarship that tells against it – and it is the most effective critique of Stern's case that she does not do this. The strongest aspect of the forgery argument espoused by Stern (and Kahan, Frazier and others before her) is the demonstrable gap in the record of textual survival and transmission: in particular, the absence of a performance record during the Restoration, the non-discovery of any of the three manuscripts that Theobald claimed to possess, and the failure of anything to materialize when Edmond Malone and others began serious digging in the 1770s. The record of textual survival of a *Cardenio* play has, however, been improved recently by the work of Gary Taylor and of Gerald Baker. Taylor's contribution to the *Quest for Cardenio* volume first provides additional evidence for thinking that the Robert Johnson song 'Woods, rocks, and mountains' was written by John Fletcher for a *Cardenio* play, and then goes on to argue that Edmund Gayton, who published the first extended critique of *Don Quixote* in English as *Pleasant Notes upon Don Quixote* (1654), must have witnessed a Caroline performance in which that song was presented because certain of his musical comments cannot be referring to either the Spanish original or Shelton's translation.[39] Baker has argued that there is a reference to a dramatized version of *Don Quixote*, to be found in a letter dated 29 October 1630, that the diplomat and parliamentarian Sir Thomas Roe wrote to Elizabeth Stuart, the Winter Queen, and that this could be a reference to *Cardenio*, suggesting that the play persisted in the repertory of the King's Men around 1629/30.[40] There certainly seems to have been a Caroline 'moment' for *Cardenio*.

And the question of the lacunae in the records has been tackled on a wide variety of fronts. In my *Quest for Cardenio* essay,[41] I speculated on the reasons why a Cardenio play might not have made it into the First Folio, and on why Betterton, if he had such a play, might not have performed it. Robert Hume estimates that we possess only

around 7% of the performance records for plays between 1660–1700.[42] Sometimes the reasons were adventitious. Thomas Heywood commented on the fact that none of his plays had been collected:

> many of them by shifting and change of Companies, have been negligently lost, Others of them are still retained in the hands of some Actors, who thinke it against their peculiar profit to have them come in Print, and ... it never was any great ambition in me, to bee in this kind Voluminously read.[43]

A play with a Spanish source (and with at least some possibility of sustaining a pro-Howard family and crypto-Catholic interpretation) could have run into censorship problems, or more generally problems of reception and changing public taste post-1619, after Frederick had lost the Palatinate to the Spaniards and the King was trying to effect reconciliation by brokering a marriage between the Spanish *Infanta* and his son Charles.[44] Anti-Spanish, anti-Catholic feeling ran very high in the run-up period to the compiling of the first Folio and even more so afterwards.[45] And after all, material objects

---

[39] Carnegie and Taylor, *Quest for Cardenio*, pp. 33–7.

[40] Gerald Baker, 'Quixote on the English Stage: A New Glimpse of *The History of Cardenio*?', in Bourus and Taylor, *Creation and Re-creation*, ch. 4, pp. 47–60.

[41] 'After Arden', in *Quest for Cardenio*, pp. 62–80.

[42] Robert D. Hume, 'Before the Bard: "Shakespeare" in Early Eighteenth-Century London', *English Literary History*, 64 (1997), 41–75: 'We can reconstruct only about 7 per cent of the performance calendar 1660–1700, and more than half the known dates fall in the 1660s' (p. 74).

[43] Ioppolo, *Dramatists and their Manuscripts*, p. 31.

[44] Richard Wilson's contention that the lost *Cardenio* play must have had a pro-Spanish, pro-Catholic tendency deriving from its source, Shelton's translation of *Don Quixote* (dedicated to Lord Howard de Walden, son of the Earl of Suffolk and the leader of England's strongest pro-Catholic family), has not commanded wholesale assent. See his 'Unseasonable Laughter: the Context of *Cardenio*', in Jennifer Richards and James Knowles, eds., *Shakespeare's Late Plays: New Readings* (Edinburgh, 1999), pp.193–209, reprinted in *Secret Shakespeare: Studies in Theatre, Religion and Resistance* (Manchester, 2004), pp. 230–45.

[45] On the other hand, Fletcher continued to use Spanish sources throughout this period, and Blount continued to publish translations of Spanish books. The King was pro-Spanish, and so was much of the court. Other plays printed

do disappear. Theobald's own blank verse translation of the first book of Homer's *Odyssey*, undertaken to rival Pope's in 1715, itself survives in only two known copies though it appears that 500 were printed. Even printed books disappear.[46] A footnote cited in Gerald Baker's essay in Taylor and Bourus's collection makes a nice point about disappearing manuscripts:

For those still sceptical that it is likely [Theobald] might possess multiple copies, it may be salutary to mention an item in the Abraham Hill list of manuscript plays (B.M. Add. MS. 2893), discussed by Bentley, *The Jacobean and Caroline* Stage, IV. 864–6. At some point between 1677 and 1703, Hill possessed *two* copies of *The Cloudy Queen and Singing Moor*, a script of which no other record survives. In the light of this, it is entirely reasonable to suppose Theobald could have had several copies of a manuscript of a play with the comparatively high profile a *Quixote* adaptation would have.[47]

Additional to advances made by those in search of the 'smoking gun' are those made by stylometrists that I can only rapidly recapitulate here. Stern's *Shakespeare Quarterly* article makes a cursory and unsystematic attempt to address them, but it is only when we see the aggregate, especially of work done since the Arden edition, that we perceive how unconvincing her claim is that all the arguments used to suggest Theobald really did have some *Cardenio* texts can equally be used to suggest that he had none. In the *Quest for Cardenio* volume, there are two landmark stylometric studies. MacDonald P. Jackson, basing his analysis on the ascription of hands by Oliphant, examines a range of stylistic indicators embracing: regulated and non-regulated uses of the auxiliary 'do' (already surveyed by Jonathan Hope); monosyllabic double-endings; position of pauses in the iambic pentameter line resulting from change in speaker turn; hath/doth evidence; words, phrases and collocations studied across the canons of the three suspected hands. All of this yields evidence of Fletcher's hand that Jackson considers to be beyond forgery and beyond reasonable doubt. When he looks, in the scenes that Oliphant considered non-Fletcherian, for material that seems both Shakespearian and

clearly beyond Theobald's power to imitate, he is perceptibly on less objective and more aesthetic ground. Somewhat surprisingly, because the outlook does not seem bright for most of the article, Jackson detects Shakespeare's presence, based on the concentration of diverse Shakespearian features in several parts of the text. 1.3.53–6 reveals several such features. His analysis demonstrates that the *prose* of the opening of 1.2 between Camillo and Julio reveals exclusive links to Shakespeare and none to Theobald. *Pace* Stern's statement in *Shakespeare Quarterly* (586), Jackson does consider evidence for the possibility of writers other than those of the 'big three', and discounts it.

In two respects, Jackson's work has been extended by other analysts. John Nance, in the Taylor/Bourus volume, has picked up on Jackson's hint that it may be in the *prose* of *Double Falsehood* and not in its verse, that Shakespeare's hand is most readily detectable. The prose survival in *Double Falsehood*, he shows, is greater than in other Theobald adaptations: Fletcher wrote very little prose and Theobald confined its presence to comedy. In 1.2.179–224, Nance suggests, the oscillation between verse and prose has many of the characteristics of Shakespeare as determined by Brian Vickers.[48] Richard Proudfoot's contribution to *The Quest for Cardenio* is particularly rich and suggestive. His conclusion is resounding: 'No forger, unequipped with modern evidence for the authorship not only of *The Two Noble Kinsmen*, but also and more significantly of *Henry VIII*, could possibly have confected the extant text of *Double Falsehood*' (165). This conclusion is based on comparison of the polysyllabic line-endings found in line-end positions in *Double Falsehood* with the same words in the same metrical position in the

---

in the Folio, it may be argued, are pro-Catholic. *The Tempest*, which begins the volume, resolves political conflict through a dynastic marriage, just as the Spanish Match was supposed to do.

46 Shef Rogers, 'Uncovering Wycherley's *Miscellaneous Remains*', *Printers and Readers: BSANZ Bulletin*, 25:1, 2 (2001), pp. 150–1.

47 Baker, 'Quixote on the English Stage', note 36.

48 Taylor and Bourus, *Creation and Re-creation*, ch. 9.

post-1602 plays of Shakespeare and Fletcher and in a body of Theobald's other writing. The matching rate of nearly 80 per cent in the years around and leading up to 1613 suggests that the vocabulary of *Double Falsehood* is deeply ingrained in the metrical and stylistic habits of Fletcher and Shakespeare in the period. It has always been an important observation that Theobald was writing long before Malone's pioneering *Attempt to Ascertain the Order in which the Plays attributed to Shakespeare were Written* (1778) gave us our first quasi-reliable ideas of Shakespearian chronology, and therefore those generic, lexical and other markers aligning *Double Falsehood* with the Shakespeare/Fletcher collaborations assume particular significance.

An aspect of Proudfoot's methodology deserves foregrounding: as he writes, 'the decision to end a line with a polysyllable would have been taken on a level somewhere between reflex based on habit and conscious metrical and stylistic decision-making' (164). For stylometrists, the holy grail is to isolate stylistic markers that could not be within the conscious control of a forger – that would be below the radar. This leads me to draw attention to an essay by Giuliano Pascucci that is not easily accessible. I have sometimes referred to the presence of Shakespeare's 'DNA' in *Double Falsehood* but have always been speaking analogically. Pascucci, though, has found an approach to attribution that uses machine-generated methods based on an algorithm that compresses recurrent patterns of symbols into a zip file, working with units of coding somewhat similar to the protein strings in the human genome.[49] Putting a text sample of two different authors together and measuring the extent of 'redundancy', that is, the material that makes the compression optimal, can test, he believes, for different hands in a writing sample when analysed against a control set. There is insufficient space to outline his method in detail; suffice it to say that his results by and large agree with those produced by Jackson and Proudfoot.

And finally, re-enter Gary Taylor. Taylor is not exactly a neutral observer in all of this. He has a very large stake in it, because over many years

he has been refining his stage reconstruction of the lost play, working back from *Double Falsehood* and imagining what time and adaptation might have done to an early modern treatment of the Cardenio story, which principally involves reintroducing a subplot involving Don Quixote and Sancho Panza. Vitally important to Taylor are the suppositions that there *was* a lost play, that *Double Falsehood* mediates what remains of it, and that the Don Quixote/Sancho Panza subplot was a victim of the rewriting. Interested party or not, the essays he has contributed to his and Bourus's *The Creation and Re-Creation of Cardenio* do some outstanding work. In Chapter 10, Taylor makes the important point that attribution in this case involves a chain of dependencies, and picking away at bits of each of them is not a satisfactory response:

Stern's forgery hypothesis requires the simultaneous conjunction of four different claims: one about *Don Quixote*, and another about Shakespeare, and another about Fletcher, and another about Shelton. *If any one of those claims is false, Stern's forgery hypothesis cannot be true.*
(138)

The final pages of the chapter do a great deal to establish that Shakespeare wrote the passage 1.2.109–16, as earlier pages have established that 5.2.251–7 was apparently written by Theobald and 5.2.94–101 was apparently written by Fletcher. Taylor's 'disintegrationism' is supported in a way that meets one of Stern's principal objections to stylometric efforts thus far: that they do not utilize samples from Theobald's writing sufficiently large to be statistically significant. Listen to Taylor's statistics with respect to 1.2.109–16:

Statistically, setting Shakespeare parallels against Theobald parallels, there is only about one chance in 350,000 that this passage belongs to the same population as the two Theobald imitations, and only one in six million that *Double Falsehood* 1.2.109–16 and 5.2.251–7

---

[49] Giuliano Pascucci, '*Double Falsehood/Cardenio*: A Case of Authorship Attribution with Computer-Based Tools', in *Memoria di Shakespeare*, 8, ed. Rosy Colombo and Daniella Guardamagna (Roma, 2012), pp. 351–72.

('The righteous Pow'rs') have the same origin. By contrast, the probability that 1.2.109–16 has the same origin as 1.1.1–7 is 100%. Finally, since 5.2.251–7 apparently belongs to the same population as Theobald's two Shakespeare imitations, and since the two passages we have examined in 1.1 and 1.2 of *Double Falsehood* also apparently belong to a homogenous set, we can statistically compare those two composite populations. The chances that *Cave of Poverty* 1–7, *Orestes* 1.1.1–7 and *Double Falsehood* 5.2.251–7 (three examples of Theobald imitating Shakespeare) have the same origin as *Double Falsehood* 1.1.1–7 and 1.2.109–16 (as Stern's forgery hypothesis would force us to believe) is less than one in twenty-four *billion*.

I must leave to others the task of validating the use of a statistical tool, Fisher's Exact Test, by means of which Taylor comes up with those daunting numbers, and return to Tiffany Stern. Although from time to time she says that she is not asserting forgery, there is really no other plausible authorial hypothesis that she can embrace – and of all possible authorial theories this is the least persuasive. Her version of it is no man of straw, and that is to her credit. She has done an excellent job in keeping the pot boiling. From a commercial point of view, if she did not exist, I would have needed to invent her. But she is wrong.

NOSTALGIC SPECTACLE AND THE POLITICS OF MEMORY IN *HENRY VIII*

ISABEL KARREMANN

In what is probably the best-known contemporary defence of the early modern stage, a passage from Thomas Nashe's *Pierce Pennilesse* (1592), we are also presented with an anatomy of nostalgia and its politics of memory and affect:

Nay, what if I prooue Playes to be no extreame, but a rare exercise of vertue? First, for the subject of them (for the most part) it is borrowed out of our English Chronicles, wherein our fore-fathers valiant actes (that haue lyne long buried in rustie brasse and worme-eaten bookes) are reuiued, and they them selues raysed from the Graue of Obliuion, and brought to pleade their aged Honours in open presence: than which, what can bee a sharper reproofe, to those degenerate, effeminate dayes of ours? How would it haue joyd braue Talbot (the Terror of the French) to thinke that after he had lyne two hundred yeare in his Tomb, he should triumph againe on the Stage, and haue his bones new embalmed with the teares of ten thousand spectators at least, (at seuerall times) who in the Tragedian that represents his person, imagine they behold him fresh bleeding.[1]

Nashe's defence of the stage, and of history plays in particular, is habitually quoted in critical discussions that seek to assess the role of the early modern theatre. Usually, the emphasis falls where Nashe placed it: on the straightforwardly mnemonic and didactic function of historical drama. In this reading, the theatre is a medium of national memory as well as of national identity. In resurrecting the medieval hero Talbot 'from the Graue of Obliuion', as did, for example, Shakespeare's *Henry VI, Part 1*, it salvages his memory from death and forgetfulness, and gives the English audience a sense of the nation's past as well as an example for virtuous,

manly conduct in the present. This goes hand in hand with an unabashedly nationalist impetus, harnessing remembrance of the past to the project of building a community in the present. Admiring and mourning for Talbot, the audience is united in a nostalgic remembrance of past glories that forges them into an 'imagined community'[2] in the here and now of theatrical performance.

I would like to challenge this somewhat superficial reading and complicate it in two respects. First, Nashe and his latter-day readers too easily conceive of the theatre exclusively as a medium of memory in the service of a collective identity of 'Englishness'. Yet the constitution of a national identity is just as much brought about through acts of *forgetting* as through acts of remembrance, as critics like Ernest Renan and Benedict Anderson have forcefully pointed out. Renan, for example, observed in his famous 1882 lecture 'What is a nation?' that the decisive factor in fusing a heterogeneous population into a united nation is precisely the obliteration of mutual acts of violence from collective memory:

Forgetting, I would even go so far as to say historical error, is a crucial factor in the creation of a nation . . . The essence of a nation is that all individuals have many things in common, and also that they have forgotten many things. No French citizen knows whether he is a Burgundian, an Alan, a Taifale, or a Visigoth, yet every

---

[1] Thomas Nashe, *Pierce Pennilesse, his Supplication to the Divell*, ed. G. B. Harrison (Edinburgh, 1966), pp. 86–7.

[2] Benedict Anderson, *Imagined Communities: Reflections on the Origin and Spread of Nationalism* (London, New York, 1991).

French citizen has to have already forgotten the massacre of Saint Bartholomew or the massacres of the Midi in the thirteenth century . . .[3]

The erasure of the past, and in particular of past tragedies that would impede a peaceful coexistence as one people, is thus a precondition for nation formation. When Nashe's account chooses to remember *only* the 'valiant actes', it effectively erases the more disgraceful and potentially disruptive episodes of the nation's past. This is certainly due to Nashe's immediate aim of defending the stage as the medium of resurrecting a glorious past that may serve as a glowing example for the present. But such a nostalgic view clearly does not adequately represent the full range of historical events nor the content of the history plays with their villainous, amoral protagonists and bloodthirsty battle scenes. Nashe's strategic blindness towards this raises the interesting question of what must be obliterated from the past so that it can serve as a rallying point for present concerns of nationhood.

Yet nostalgic oblivion is not only a question of content in the formation and deformation of the nation's past, it seems to me, but also a structural moment in the performative production of a passion for that past in the theatre. Thus when Nashe speaks of 'our forefathers', he presupposes an imagined community, a 'we' which actually has come about as a stage-induced effect of obliterating the social, gender, religious and regional differences among a rather heterogeneous audience. That Nashe offers 'braue Talbot, the terror of the French' as a figure of identification is a case in point: celebrating this kind of English masculine virtue excludes other subject positions and with it other, perhaps dissenting, perspectives from the range of possible reactions to the spectacle on stage.

What lends authenticity and authority to this nostalgically selective version of national history, Nashe seems to claim, are its physical manifestations on and off the stage: the living, breathing body of the actor, the audience's tears embalming his 'fresh bleeding' wounds. Nostalgic representation, in the words of Linda Hutcheon, turns the absent past 'into the site of immediacy, presence, and authenticity'.[4] When Nashe obliquely acknowledges the difference between presence and representation in his reference to the figure of Talbot as 'the Tragedian that represents his person' on stage, he hints at a point I wish to foreground here: that the affective investment in the nation's past is an effect of dramatic representation.

This raises the issue of the role of the theatre in recreating the nation's past and a national identity. I do not mean to imply that the early modern stage was a straightforward instrument of nation building nor that being swept away by a passion for the past was the only response available to watching historical drama. But if nostalgic spectacle is what induces a passion for the past in the audience, if it is indeed a device for producing mimetic emotions, shared among the spectators, then the theatre surely is a privileged site of nation building through nostalgia. At the same time, I would contend, the open display of such passion, both on and off the stage, may threaten that very effect precisely when this passion becomes obvious *as* spectacle. This is what happens during metatheatrical moments which, by drawing attention to the nostalgic spectacle the audience is emotionally caught up in, create an ironic distance. Opening up a space between nostalgic spectacle and affective identification, these scenes reveal, if only for a moment, the memory politics of nostalgia as well as its policy of affect.

In what follows, I would like to discuss how Shakespeare and Fletcher's *Henry VIII; or, All is True* (1613), while it undoubtedly participated in a nationalist agenda and rhetoric, offers critical insights into the political and affective workings of nostalgic spectacle. In so doing, I will pay special attention to the interplay of remembering and forgetting that actively constructs what is remembered of the past, and to the interplay of

---

[3] Ernest Renan, 'What is a Nation? [1882]', in *Nation and Narration*, ed. Homi Bhabha (London, New York, 1990), pp. 8–22, p. 11.

[4] Linda Hutcheon, 'Irony, Nostalgia, and the Postmodern', 1998, no pagination, online at www.library.utoronto.ca/utel/criticism/hutchinp.html#N26, accessed 11 November 2013.

mimetic representation and affective identification. This double approach, I hope, challenges all-too simplistic notions of the authenticity and authority of nostalgic memories. But first a few observations on nostalgia in general are in order.

The word 'nostalgia' would not have been known to an Elizabethan audience. The term was probably coined in 1688 by the Swiss physician Johannes Hofer as a medical expression for a lethal kind of severe homesickness. Its Greek etymology defines it in spatial and affective terms: *nostos* means 'return home'; *algos* denotes 'pain, sadness'.[5] While the word itself did not exist around 1600, the feeling of nostalgia was voiced in many texts that looked back, rather wistfully, to a period of the past. One example that springs to mind is the passage about 'The Four Ages' of the world in Arthur Golding's translation of Ovid's *Metamorphoses*, which longingly evokes the glories of the lost Golden Age from a perspective of despair about the all too brazen present. Nostalgia for the past was not only a topic for poetry but indeed its very form and function, at least according to Philip Sidney's *Apology for Poetry*, which maintained that while the natural world around us is 'brazen, the poets only deliver a golden'.[6] This longing for a Golden Age was a topos of early modern thought, in particular in England where the break with the customary past, entailed by the Reformation and the dissolution of the monasteries, proved particularly traumatic.[7] Indeed, for Erwin Panofsky, a 'nostalgic vision born of a sense of estrangement as well as a sense of affinity . . . is the very essence of the Renaissance'.[8] As appealing and, I believe, convincing as this account of nostalgia as the spirit of the early modern age may be, we do well to investigate the specific implications of nostalgia first so that we can see how it might work as a political practice of building a nation along with that nation's past.

Nostalgia, Christoper Shaw and Malcom Chase point out in their introduction to *The Imagined Past: History and Nostalgia*, is 'a protean and pervasive' concept, a cultural 'site occupied by ideas and structures of feeling which have a family resemblance'.[9] Despite its inchoate nature, two characteristic aspects can be isolated: its time-structure and its affect-structure. Nostalgia is a specific mode of connecting the past to the present. It is premised on a sense of teleological time in which past and present are clearly distinguished: there can be no longing for the past if it is not perceived as crucially different from the present. Typically, the present is seen as deficient or degraded while the past is idealized and aestheticized. This structural doubling-up of two different times, an inadequate present and an idealized past, is 'so characteristic . . . of nostalgic experience that it can perhaps be regarded as its distinctive rhetorical signature'.[10] It is indeed apt to speak of a *rhetorical* signature here, since this opposition of beautiful past and grim present is above all a rhetorical effect, existing in language and in the imagination. In Linda Hutcheon's analysis, nostalgia invariably refers us to 'the past as imagined, as idealized through memory and desire. In this sense, however, nostalgia is less about the past than about the present . . . the ideal that is not being lived now is projected into the past. It is "memorialized" as past, crystallized into precious moments selected by memory, but also by forgetting, and by desire's distortions and reorganizations.'[11] Trading on comfortable and conveniently reassuring images of the past, nostalgia at the same time suppresses both its variety and its negative aspects. In other words, nostalgia remembers and simultaneously forgets the past.

---

5 On the etymological roots and the cultural history of nostalgia, see Jean Starobinski, 'The Idea of Nostalgia', *Diogenes* 54 (1966), 84–103, pp. 84–86; Diego Muro, 'Nationalism and Nostalgia', *Nations and Nationalism*, 11:4 (2005), 571–89, pp. 571–3.

6 Philip Sidney, 'The Defence of Poesy', *The Major Works*, ed. Katherine Duncan-Jones (Oxford, 2002), p. 216.

7 Philipp Schwyzer, *Literature, Nationalism, and Memory in Early Modern England and Wales* (Cambridge, 2004), p. 73.

8 Erwin Panofsky, *Renaissance and Renascences in Western Art* (New York, 1972), p. 210.

9 Christopher Shaw and Malcolm Chase, *The Imagined Past: History and Nostalgia* (Manchester, 1989), p. 2.

10 Fred Davis, *Yearning for Yesterday: A Sociology of Nostalgia* (New York, 1979), p. 16.

11 Hutcheon, 'Irony'.

While this is true for the constitution of memory in general, nostalgia is special in that it connects memory with affect. As a 'historical emotion',[12] it provides us with a sense of time passing just as it allows us to register that very fact emotionally. Nostalgia is predominantly an affective or, as Shaw and Chase put it, an 'affectionate' mode of connecting past and present.[13] This emotional attitude can take different forms: a dissatisfaction with the present situation which motivates nostalgia in the first place; a longing for past glories which distances one from the present; an elation triggered by remembering former feats which authenticates the imagined past as 'true'. Indeed, it is above all 'its visceral physicality and emotional impact' that lends nostalgia its power.[14] Nostalgia seems to touch one immediately, on a very personal, even bodily level, as is testified by its original, medical meaning of home-sickness. While it is primarily an effect of language and the imagination, as noted above, its emotional and physical impact make it feel authentic. Yet we should be aware, Hutcheon cautions us, that nostalgia does not describe the quality of the past itself, but rather ascribes a certain quality to one's response to the past. It is what one feels when two temporal moments, past and present, come together: 'It is the element of response – of active participation, both intellectual and affective – that makes for the power' of nostalgia.[15]

Taken together, nostalgia's signature time- and affect-structure can help us understand its psychic as well as social functions. While nostalgia may be a very personal experience, it is a deeply social emotion as well. As such, it 'derives from and has implications for our lives as social actors'.[16] A distinctive way of negotiating the difference between past and present, it performs 'the never ending work of constructing, maintaining, and reconstructing our identities'.[17] Yet the functions of nostalgia can be differentiated further. In one sense it offers consolation: the reason for nostalgia is invariably found in dissatisfaction with the present situation, and this dissatisfaction is typically counter-balanced by an image of the past that offers 'a consolation for the [perceived] loss of status and power'.[18] Related to

this is the function of a critique of the present, which draws legitimacy and authority from the idealised past as a counter-image. The imagined past also provides a rallying-point for the dissatisfied, enabling them to form an imagined community. The element of emotional and intellectual response, which Hutcheon considers so crucial for nostalgia, becomes indeed a formative element of personal and group identity. Nostalgia thus fuses not only memory and affect but also 'affect and agency, or emotion and politics'.[19] It articulates a selective memory of the past, charges it emotionally and, through this, enables agency and authorizes political stances.

By the same token, nostalgia is not innocent. We therefore need to recognize and examine the 'politics of nostalgia', that is, the vested interests which are both served and disguised by its seemingly natural, authentic 'visceral physicality'.[20] As so often, the question 'who speaks?' is a reliable hermeneutic method for sifting the political uses of nostalgic rhetorics. In keeping with the longing for past glories, it is likely that individuals or groups who have lost their place in a territory (exiles or migrants) or in history (empires or classes on the decline) will develop nostalgia. Yet nostalgia can also emerge in sovereign nations that cultivate admiration for group traits of their ancestors and feel the need to live up to a glorious past.[21] This suggests that the political valence of nostalgia is per se undetermined, that it is 'transideological' – if never unideological – in the sense that it can be made 'to happen by (and to) anyone of any political persuasion'.[22] In other words, nostalgia is a tool that can be seized

---

[12] Svetlana Boym, *The Future of Nostalgia* (New York, 2001), p. 10.
[13] Shaw and Chase, *The Imagined Past*, p. 2.
[14] Hutcheon, 'Irony'.
[15] Hutcheon, 'Irony'.
[16] Davis, *Yearning*, p. vii.
[17] Davis, *Yearning*, p. 31.
[18] Shaw and Chase, *The Imagined Past*, p. 3.
[19] Hutcheon, 'Irony'.
[20] Hutcheon, 'Irony'.
[21] Muro, 'Nationalism', p. 575.
[22] Hutcheon, 'Irony'.

for very different political purposes. On the one hand, nostalgia is 'fundamentally conservative in its praxis, for it wants to keep things as they were – or, more accurately, as they are imagined to have been.'[23] By providing consolation for the frustration suffered over the loss of prized values, nostalgic feeling, much like a safety valve, thus also manages to stabilize a disappointing present situation.[24] On the other hand, nostalgia can trigger revolutionary political programmes advocating the restoration of political kingdoms, traditional lifestyles, religious beliefs and so on.[25] The one constant factor in both cases, I think, is its ability to forge imagined communities through an imagined past.

Nostalgia is a powerful tool of nationalism in that it offers a selective, idealized vision of the distant past and charges it with a deeply nationalist, patriotic sentiment.[26] In so doing, nostalgia does not simply manipulate the nation's past but actually produces both the nation and its past in the same act of remembering and forgetting. The idealizing and sentimentalizing rhetoric of nationalist nostalgia provides the nation, above all, with an image of past unity. David Lowenthal argues that nostalgia conjures up 'a past that was unified and comprehensible, unlike the incoherent, divided present' and that 'what we are nostalgic for is the condition of having been'.[27] This vision of national unity can only be achieved through an act of forgetting, as Renan insists, for while the past usually has been just as 'incoherent [and] divided' as the present, this fact must be forgotten if one wants to forge unity in the present and for the future. As a selective form of remembering and hence also a form of forgetting, nostalgia is a specific way of connecting the past with the present, which usually serves as an instrument or technique for creating and expressing a 'désir d'intégration',[28] resulting in what we might term, in response to Benedict Anderson's work, an 'affective community'.

But nostalgia is not only a tool of national unification. It can also run counter to the dominant propaganda of unity, for as a desire to return to an idealized past it also casts an unfavourable light on the present as somehow deficient. This was especially the case with a body of Jacobean history plays that looked back longingly to the Elizabethan reign as a golden era. Staging desire for Elizabeth, they also upstaged the 'deliberate attempts of the Stuart kings to define their rule of reunited Britannia as the fulfilment of all past history'.[29] In the changed context of the Stuart reign, Elizabeth, far from being a locus of national unity for England, was in fact a potentially destabilizing memory, at least for her successor.[30] From the very beginning of his reign James I was troubled by the memory of his Tudor predecessors. In particular, Queen Elizabeth's posthumous status as the heroine of a militant Protestantism was at odds with James's own ecumenical, conciliatory policy, and hence needed to be regulated. The broad range of his attempts at controlling the memory of the Tudors through historiography, ritual and political as well as popular discourse testifies to the scope and depth of his anxiety.[31] Fearing that recent political history might be written in his disfavour, James dissolved the Society of Antiquaries in 1607 and prevented its revival in 1614. When Fulke Greville wanted to write a history of Elizabeth's reign in 1610, he was denied access to state papers necessary to his research. But James sought to control the memory of his predecessor not only by suppressing its articulations. He also actively shaped it through

---

23 Hutcheon, 'Irony'.
24 Davis, *Yearning*, p. 99.
25 Muro, 'Nationalism', p. 576.
26 Davis, *Yearning*, p. 98; Muro, 'Nationalism', p. 574.
27 David Lowenthal, *The Past is a Foreign Country* (Cambridge, 1985), p. 29.
28 Paul Zumthor quoted in Jonathan Gil Harris, *Untimely Matter in the Time of Shakespeare* (Philadelphia, 2009), p. 69.
29 Teresa Grant, 'Drama Queen: Staging Elizabeth in *If You Know Not Me You Know Nobody*', in *The Myth of Elizabeth*, ed. Susan Doran and Susan Freeman (Basingstoke, 2003), pp. 120–42, p. 125.
30 Jonathan Baldo, 'Forgetting Elizabeth in *Henry VIII*', in *Resurrecting Elizabeth I in Seventeenth-Century England*, ed. Elizabeth H. Hageman and Katherine Conway (Madison, 2007), pp. 132–48, p. 145.
31 The traumatic memory of his mother's death and the fact that he succeeded the woman who was responsible for her execution seem to have haunted King James beyond a measure accountable for by reasons of state policy and legitimation only; see Baldo, 'Forgetting', pp. 134–6.

commissioning William Camden to continue writing his history of Elizabeth's reign, with the stipulation that it include a sympathetic account of the life and death of his own mother, Mary Stuart, and buttress James's own authority by presenting his reign as a continuation of Elizabethan policy.[32] In 1606, he ordered that Elizabeth's corpse be removed from the altar under the chapel built by Henry VII in Westminster Abbey and reburied in the same vault as her half-sister Mary Tudor. This reorganization of the Abbey effectively marked the Tudor monarchs since Henry VII as a mere digression and carved out both a material and a discursive space in which James could represent himself as the true heir of the Tudors' founding father instead.[33]

One might think that the concerted attempts of the royal mnemonic policy to lay the memory of Elizabeth to rest would have been successful. 'Elizabeth, though, however carefully reburied, just wouldn't lie down.'[34] In fact, the first decade after James's accession to the throne saw an increasing nostalgia for Elizabeth. It was articulated across a wide range of popular cultural media including stained-glass windows, prints, pictures, verse and monuments.[35] Most relevant to my topic is a number of history plays that staged the reign of the Tudor monarchs: Samuel Rowley's *When You See Me You Know Me* (1604), Thomas Heywood's two-part *If You Know Not Me, You Know Nobody* (1604/05), Thomas Dekker's *The Whore of Babylon* (1607) and *All is True (Henry VIII)*, written by Fletcher and Shakespeare in 1613.[36] These plays present the Tudors, and especially Elizabeth as the model Protestant princess, in a nostalgic light that cast a dubious shadow on the monarchical abilities and Protestant loyalties of James and his Catholic queen. They all call for a topical reading that highlights the analogies as well as the differences between the history staged and contemporary politics. Titles like *If You Know Not Me, You Know Nobody* and *When You See Me You Know Me* alert the audience to use their knowledge of current political figures and discover who is behind the mask of the persona. This highlighted topicality corresponds with nostalgia's time and affect-structure:

an imagined past, 'idealized through memory and desire',[37] invariably casts a bleak light on the present that is perceived as inadequate. Desire for Elizabeth, in other words, articulated dissatisfaction with James. In this case, then, stage-nostalgia did not work as a technique of domination as it did for Shakespeare's *Henry V* and, by extension, for the then reigning queen. The glorification of the Elizabethan past ran counter to the mnemonic policy of the current monarch, James I.[38] Given this tension between royal mnemonic policy and popular nostalgic commemoration, the question of the politics of nostalgia for Elizabeth is a vexed one, as many critics have noted. Curtis Perry, for example, cautions that far from being univocally critical of James, depictions of Elizabeth stand in a variety of relationships to Jacobean orthodoxies. He suggests that particular texts from the beginning of his reign rather tended to stress the continuity between the 'queen of famous memory'

---

32 While Camden's measured Tacitean account in Latin (1615) presents Elizabeth as an eminently politic ruler – prudent, wise but also devious and cold – who could hardly give rise to nostalgic feelings, the translators of his work into English (1625, 1629, 1630 and 1635) transmuted his cool appraisal of Elizabeth into a glittering panegyric; see Patrick Collinson, 'William Camden and the Anti-Myth of Elizabeth: Setting the Mould?', in *The Myth of Elizabeth*, pp. 79–98.

33 Michael Dobson and Nicola Watson, *England's Elizabeth: An Afterlife in Fame and Fantasy* (Oxford, 2002), p. 46.

34 Dobson and Watson, *England's Elizabeth*, p. 47.

35 Doran and Freeman, *The Myth of Elizabeth*, p. 8.

36 The Dekker–Webster play *Sir Thomas Wyatt* (pr. 1607) is often included in this canon but will not receive any attention here because its early form, the two-part play *Lady Jane*, was already written in 1602, before Queen Elizabeth's death, and no substantial changes were made to the printed version afterwards.

37 Hutcheon, 'Irony'.

38 Curtis Perry also discusses 'an oppositional critical strain of Elizabethan nostalgia' that indeed had serious political repercussions, as the later example of Oliver Cromwell shows. Cromwell based his concept of parliamentary freedom on an inaccurate, idealized notion of Elizabeth's governmental practice, a nostalgic notion that was an element in the climate of opinion that made the Civil War possible; see Curtis Perry, 'The Citizen Politics of Nostalgia: Queen Elizabeth in Early Jacobean London', *Journal of Medieval and Renaissance Studies*, 23 (1993), 89–111, pp. 110–11.

and her successor, using the appeal of the queen's memory to ratify his policies. Moreover, the uses of Elizabethan nostalgia in Jacobean England varied according to the milieus in and for which they were produced, and to the interests that they served. And finally, Perry notes, the social implications of this nostalgia changed and developed over time. In the beginning, comparison with Elizabeth helped to articulate contemporary notions about the role of the monarch and to set expectations against which James's style and policies were judged. Only later did it become a conventionalized vehicle for expressing dissatisfaction with the government of James and, still later, of his son Charles.[39]

While Perry's revisions of the nostalgia for Elizabeth are apt, they bear some revision themselves. For one, I do not quite agree with his assessment of nostalgia as a celebration of continuity, because the idea of continuity is itself at odds with the basic impetus of glorifying the past, namely discontent with the present.[40] This is precisely why James was so wary of the nostalgia for Elizabeth and sought to by-pass or redeploy memory of the Tudors rather than encourage it. Praise for James in these texts should accordingly be read rather as a cautious bowing to authority, since criticizing a king is a risky business at best. Because of this, praise for the present ruler may indeed function as a fully integral part and tactical aspect of the nostalgic mode, at least in the case of such a pronounced tension between royal policy and popular memory. It is this discrepancy in interests served by nostalgia that motivates my second revision of Perry's reading: where he holds only the divergent interests of King James and Prince Henry responsible for different images of Elizabeth, I would include the common citizens (which constituted the majority of spectators in the public playhouses after all) in the picture. While the audience surely got caught up in the patriotic enthusiasm that is so typical of nostalgia and that so effectively covers up its vested interests, their perspective may also have provided a critical angle on the royal politics of remembering and forgetting at work in the representation of history.[41] As Gordon McMullan

has noted, nostalgic history plays like *Henry VIII* invite 'the members of its audience to interpret their own history, giving them the choice of seeing the play either as a celebration of Stuart power or a questioning of the state of the Reformation ten years into James's reign'.[42] I would add that nostalgic plays even of a later date did not necessarily deteriorate into a mere 'conventional tool' for criticizing James,[43] but self-critically examined the mnemonic and affective politics of nostalgic spectacle.

In particular, Shakespeare and Fletcher's play about Henry VIII evinces such scepticism towards the truth of nostalgic spectacle.[44] Covering similar chronicle ground to Rowley's earlier play, it presents the downfall of Cardinal Wolsey, the divorce trial of Queen Catherine, the coronation of Queen Anne and the birth of Princess Elizabeth. Yet despite its subject matter, *Henry VIII* does not so much cater to nostalgic spectacle as critically interrogate the politics of remembering and forgetting it entails.[45] This preoccupation is already signalled by the play's original title, *All Is True*. Recalling titles such as *When You See Me, You Know Me* and *If You Know Not Me You Know Nobody*, which draw attention to the fact

---

[39] Perry, 'Citizen Politics', pp. 90–2, 109–11.
[40] This does not mean that popular nostalgia is necessarily subversive either; in its desire to return to the way things were, or were imagined to have been, it is essentially conservative; see Ivo Kamps, *Historiography and Ideology in Stuart Drama* (Cambridge, 1996), p. 67.
[41] Janette Dillon, *Shakespeare and the Staging of English History* (Oxford, 2012), p. 67.
[42] Gordon McMullan, ed. 'Introduction', *King Henry VIII*, Arden Shakespeare Third Series (London, 2000), pp. 1–199; p. 93.
[43] Perry, 'Citizen Politics', p. 109.
[44] This scepticism is one reason why Rudnytsky identifies *Henry VIII*, despite its use of 'the romantic elements of masque and spectacle', as 'Shakespeare's final history play' (Peter L. Rudnytsky, '*Henry VIII* and the Desconstruction of History', in *Shakespeare Survey 43* (Cambridge, 1991), pp. 43–58; p. 45). I follow his assessment, yet would hold that it is precisely through – and not in spite of – the conspicuous use of masque and spectacle that the play articulates its sceptical stance.
[45] Baldo, 'Forgetting Elizabeth', p. 141.

that looking is not seeing,[46] *All Is True* invites the spectators to question their own perception of nostalgic spectacle: Are we meant to take what is shown on stage as the truth? Does the play fulfil the promise of delivering historical truth, or does it critically comment on such expectations? In other words, if *all* is true then this would suggest that '*any* interpretation of the past may be true if one thinks it so'.[47] Critical readings of the play so far have tended, quite rightly, to focus on the tension between truth and representation.[48] I would like to add a concern with the passions that are evoked in performance to make this truth feel authentic and authoritative. What can this play, that so insistently reflects on history as a stage-managed spectacle, tell us about how emotions are stage-managed to make that spectacle authoritative?

The relation between theatrical spectacle, truth and nostalgic feeling is already addressed in the Prologue. At the very outset of the play, it sets the frame of mind as well as the emotional attitude with which the audience should receive the show:

> *Prologue*. I come no more to make you laugh. Things now
> That bear a weighty and a serious brow,
> Sad, high, and working, full of state and woe –
> Such noble scenes as draw the eye to flow,
> We now present.   (0.1–5)

The Prologue then proceeds to outline expected motivations for the audience that have come to see this play: some come to indulge their emotions, some seek for historical truth, others merely an entertaining spectacle:

> *Prologue*.   Those that can pity here,
> May, if they think it well, let fall a tear.
> The subject will deserve it. Such as give
> Their money out of hope they may believe,
> May here find truth, too. Those that come to see
> Only a show or two, and so agree
> The play may pass, if they be still, and willing,
> I'll undertake may see away their shilling
> Richly in two short hours.   (0.5–13)

In ending on a description, or perhaps rather a prescription, of acceptable responses, the Prologue emphasizes that nostalgic spectacle takes a tearful,

gullible audience to unfold the authority of its 'chosen truth' (0.18), or at least one prepared to accept it 'still, and willing[ly]' (0.11). Echoing Nashe's rhetoric in his defence of the historical stage, the Prologue links the affective and mnemonic workings of nostalgia with the issue of producing national memory. To make the audience sad is here rhetorically and, I would add, structurally linked with making it accept a selective version of history as truth. In order 'To make that only true we now intend' (0.21), the audience needs to 'Be sad as we would make ye' (0.25). The means to achieve this is verisimilitude and emotional identification:

> *Prologue*.   Think ye see
> The very persons of our noble story
> As they were living; think you see them great,
>   . . . then, in a moment, see
> How soon this mightiness meets misery.
>   (0.25–30)

What would ruin the nostalgic affect as well as its ideologically unifying effect is a noisy, disrespectful audience, 'That come[s] to hear a merry bawdy play' (0.14) such as Rowley's *When You See Me*, revived earlier that year, would have been.[49] In making these distinctions, the Prologue also articulates a subtle politics of class that is interesting for

---

[46] Teresa Grant, 'History in the Making: The case of Samuel Rowley's *When You See Me You Know Me* (1605/06)', *English Historical Drama, 1500–1660: Forms Outside the Canon*, ed. Teresa Grant and Barbara Ravelhofer (Basingstoke, 2008), pp. 125–57, p. 130.

[47] Rudnytsky, '*Henry VIII*', p. 46.

[48] For an overview see McMullan, 'Introduction', pp. 57–106.

[49] Rowley's play presented Henry VIII in the 'bluff King Hal' tradition as a swaggering, jovial ruler, with scenes of 'fool and fight' (*Henry VIII*, 0.19) that show Henry moving in disguise among his subject or getting into brawls and even being arrested, inviting the kind of rumbustious audience reaction rejected here. Since the play is set in the time of Prince Edward's birth and education, the topical comparisons invited tend to be between Henry VIII and James I, Queen Catherine Parr and James's Queen Anne, as well as the princes Edward Tudor and Henry Stuart, with the nostalgic emphasis falling on the Protestant fervour of Prince Edward and the Lutheran Catherine, as Teresa Grant (2008) has shown.

our topic. For it is not the uneducated groundlings that constitute the ideally gullible, emotional audience for nostalgia, but those that can afford the more expensive, genteel seating bought at the price of a shilling (0.12). The lower-class spectators, by contrast, who mix up 'our chosen truth with such a show / As fool and fight is' (0.18–19), 'Will leave us never an understanding friend' (0.21), the word 'understanding' referring to both the intellectual capacity and the physical location of the lower-class groundlings who stand under the raised stage. This comment hints at the possibility of a part of the audience being resistant to, or at least unaffected by, the nostalgic spectacle.

At the climax of the play, the christening of Princess Elizabeth and Cranmer's prophecy of England's glorious future under her reign and that of James I, we are presented with such a noisy audience. Fittingly, we do not see but hear the '*Noise and tumult within*' as the Porter is trying to keep an excited, festive crowd from storming the palace out of sheer joy at the arrival of an heir. The unruly multitude outside, composed of 'brazier[s]' (5.3.39), 'haberdasher's [wives]' (46), and 'youths that thunder at a playhouse' (58) is associated with popular festivities and spectacles such as the bear- and bull-baiting going on at Paris Garden (in the immediate vicinity of the Globe), May Day celebrations or the militia training at Moorfields. These clearly provide rival spectacles to the royally sponsored ritual of the christening, nostalgically staged by the play. In fact, the Porter scene interrupts the series of ceremonial shows that constitute the end of *Henry VIII*, the trial of Cranmer and the christening of Elizabeth. The nostalgic mood is bracketed in order to present a very different attitude to what will become a glorious event in the nation's past. While the unseen rabble in the Porter scene might serve only as a negative foil to a more appropriate response, it nevertheless could also remind the audience at the Globe that other reactions than nostalgic tearfulness and obedient acceptance of what is presented as truth are possible.

Another reaction that would also spoil the nostalgic mood is not mentioned at all in the Prologue, but enacted several times throughout the play: a sceptical, ironic distance towards the spectacle of history. As in *Henry V*, where the martial rhetoric of the Chorus is counter-acted by the scenes depicting war as a messy, bloody and thoroughly un-heroic business, so does the Prologue's aligning of nostalgic spectacle, truth and affective identification get punctured by scenes that separate truth from spectacle and thus carve out a space for ironic distance. This deconstruction of historical truth already begins with the opening scene. It presents us with Norfolk's report of the historical events on the Field of the Cloth of Gold, where the kings of England and France met to sign a peace treaty. Norfolk's description focuses on the splendour this encounter entailed, which he watched and now retails with admiration:

> Norfolk.   Today the French,
>   All clinquant all in gold, like heathen gods,
>   Shone down the English; and tomorrow they
>   Made Britain India. Every man that stood
>   Showed like a mine.   (1.1.18–22)

Only a few lines on, the sartorial competition of 'two kings / Equal in lustre' (28), is revealed as a mere show: the pact is quickly broken, and the peace did 'not value . . . / The cost that did conclude it' (88–9). What could be seen on the field that day was not all true. Yet even if one saw through the spectacle, one could not say so openly: 'no discerner / Durst wag his tongue in censure' (33). As Lee Bliss – one of the first critics to recognize the discrepancy between truth and spectacle as a structural feature of the play – remarks, 'In the beginning all had seemed true to Norfolk and, in his report, to us; only in retrospect can we see how false, how truly unstable . . . that appearance was.'[50] While Norfolk initially confessed himself a 'fresh admirer' of the spectacle (1.1.3), we are quickly made to see that his admiration 'did not signify wonder in the sense of approbation, but rather an ironic sense of amazement at the disparity'

---

[50] Lee Bliss, 'The Wheel of Fortune and the Maiden Phoenix in Shakespeare's *King Henry the Eighth*', *English Literary History*, 42 (1975), 1–25, p. 3.

between spectacle and truth.[51] This disillusionment with spectacle is arrived at only by hindsight, a cautionary tale that seems out of place with a nostalgic play that operates by idealizing the past in retrospect. It is in keeping, however, with a reading of this play as a critical inquiry into nostalgic spectacle and the truth it serves to obfuscate.

Such a reading is offered by Jonathan Baldo, who argues that, despite its insistence on the visual aspect typical of costume drama, the play above all 'draws attention to that which is not given view. Some of *Henry VIII*'s most noticeable features are its omissions.'[52] Even the persons and events it does include are primarily used to highlight their eventual 'omission or deletion from the pageant of history': in presenting the downfall of the Duke of Buckingham, Queen Katherine and Cardinal Wolsey, and their eventual deletion from the dramatic narrative that goes on to celebrate the memory of the king, the play dramatizes the process of history-making 'under monarchical control as a process of obliteration'.[53] With the representatives of alternative accounts of history silenced, what remains in the end is the 'univocal and undivided'[54] version of official royal historiography. Yet I would add that this process of obliteration and adjustment of popular to official memory is not only staged but also upstaged by the play as the spectacle of nostalgic truth is punctured again and again by alternative, contradictory perspectives.

The scene immediately following Wolsey's demise furnishes an illustrative example. Two nameless gentlemen, standing in the crowd that is watching Queen Anne's coronation procession, comment on what they – and the audience in the playhouse – see represented as an elaborate pageant on the stage. The First Gentleman identifies the members of the procession and their position at court to the Second Gentleman. Obviously unfamiliar with the inner circle of the royal household, as the common audience at the playhouse would also have been, the Second Gentleman is nevertheless not dazzled by the spectacle but proves a rather cynical, savvy observer. He reacts to the sight of Queen Anne with what might easily be mistaken as a paean to her beauty, were it not for the recurrence of a catchword that recalls the opening scene with its critical dissection of royal shows. 'Our King', the Second Gentleman states, 'has all the Indies in his arms, / And more, and richer, when he strains that lady.' (4.1.45–6) Again, the riches of India are evoked in order to describe a victory that might have come at too great a price. Just as the costly peace with France was quickly broken, so Anne's status as queen already seems precarious: Anne's star and that of her ladies have risen quickly, yet those may be 'sometimes falling ones' (56), as the First Gentleman insinuates. The sexual pun on 'falling' ties into a pattern of innuendos about Anne's chastity throughout the play, suggesting that her display of modesty, godliness and saintliness at the coronation (71–86) is again nothing more than a stage-managed spectacle. The dangerous truth of this insinuation may be measured by the Second Gentleman's warning reply: 'No more of that' (56).

The pageant is followed by a report of the coronation ceremony itself, structurally recalling the opening scene in that the subject is again a ceremonious occasion whose splendour comes to us as a second-hand historical narrative. It even contains a direct textual reference to the ability of spectacle to render the participants indistinguishable in the eyes of the spectators, just as was the case with the kings on the Field of the Cloth of Gold. Now a Third Gentleman describes how Queen Anne deliberately put herself on display 'some half an hour or so – / In a rich chair of state', and how 'the beauty of her person' excited such passion in the people that 'No man living / Could say "This is my wife" there, all were woven / So strangely in one piece [of cloth]' (4.1.68–9, 81–3). In Jonathan Baldo's view, what is most remarkable about this scene is that '[n]o one challenges the veracity of the Third Gentleman's report or the accuracy of his memory', and he takes this as evidence that memory is now entirely under the king's

---

[51] Bliss, 'Wheel', p. 3.
[52] Baldo, 'Forgetting Elizabeth', p. 141.
[53] Baldo, 'Forgetting Elizabeth', p. 132.
[54] Baldo, 'Forgetting Elizabeth', p. 142.

control.[55] Yet I think that in recalling the rhetoric and the structure of the opening scene, the audience may as well recall that some scepticism about the truthfulness of spectacle is in order. No figure on stage voices that scepticism, for this role has been shifted to the audience. Moreover, the scene draws our attention to the dynamic of forgetting and remembering that underpins this royal spectacle. The Third Gentleman's report closes with the information that, after the ceremony, the new queen withdrew to 'York Place, where the feast is held', when the First Gentleman cuts in:

First Gentleman.   Sir,
    You must no more call it York Place – that's past,
    For since the Cardinal fell, that title's lost.
    'Tis now the King's, and called 'Whitehall'.
                                            (4.1.96–7)

'I know it,' the Third Gentlemen concedes, 'But 'tis so lately altered that the old name / Is fresh about me' (99–101). This brief moment of forgetfulness, which is in actual fact motivated by an inability to forget the established name and remember a new one, highlights how popular memory has to adjust to new political and material circumstances. Where this is not so or not yet accomplished, it creates a tension with official royal memory and may offer a critical perspective on it. A moment of conspicuous forgetfulness on stage alerts the audience that the spectacle they are watching is not a straightforward representation of historical truth, however authentic it may appear.

Henry VIII is one of the few plays of which actual spectator reports exist. Sir Henry Wotton's description of the play and the fire that destroyed the Globe during a production in the summer of 1613 is famous for giving us a view of the early modern stage through the eyes of a contemporary. It also suggests that at least some of the audience took their cue from the critical onstage spectators discussed above. Instead of being reduced to pity and tears by the 'Pomp and Majesty' of the nostalgic spectacle, or dazzled into an easy acceptance of it as historical truth, Wotton notes that the play presents quite another truth about royalty 'sufficient . . . to make greatness very familiar, if not ridiculous'.[56] In keeping with this sentiment, his report of the fire – an event of potentially tragic stature – closes on a farcical note when the burning breeches of one spectator are doused with a bottle of ale, collapsing the 'sad, high' matters of 'state and woe' (0.3) into a 'merry, bawdy' (0.14) show indeed. What this eye-witness report of one of the first performances of All is True lacks utterly, however, is the kind of awed submission to the spectacle of nostalgia the Prologue claimed so confidently and comprehensively. This contemporary report affirms that while its subject matter makes Henry VIII qualify as a nostalgic play, this is self-reflexively and effectively qualified by the play itself as it repeatedly makes the issue of theatrical spectacle – and its fraught relation to historical truth and nostalgic feeling – its subject. In so doing, it provides those who care to look and see with a disillusioning insight into the mnemonic and affective politics of nostalgia that, as Wotton's report suggests, endows them with the authority to discern 'sufficient truth' not to succumb to its appeal.

---

55 Baldo, 'Forgetting Elizabeth', p. 142.
56 Quoted in McMullan, 'Introduction', p. 59.

ROYAL ENTRIES AND THE FORM OF PAGEANTRY IN *ALL IS TRUE*

RODERICK H. McKEOWN

All Is True suffers from its reputation as the play that brought the house down – quite literally – and for much of the twentieth century was often more remembered for an historic accident or the question of its authorship than its own merits, until Lee Bliss turned critical attention to the role of pageantry in the play.[1] Recent discussions of *All Is True*, however, have turned to its explorations of the legitimacy of Henry's reign and the strategies used by the Henrician state within the play to establish and affirm that legitimacy. Ivo Kamps's persuasive reading of the play's use of historiography attempts to consider the issue of royal legitimacy separately from the issue of Henry's character and conduct, complaining that 'critics cannot quite abandon their search for the "great men" of the Elizabethan plays'.[2] More recently, Gordon McMullan has considered the play's closing impression of Henry as 'an intemperate, and therefore finally unmanly, monarch'[3] participating in an 'improvised public mythologising'[4] to assert the legitimacy of Elizabeth's line of succession. I wish to consider the intersection between these two approaches by examining more closely that 'public mythologising' – in other words, royal pageantry. Royal pageantry is, self-evidently, a tactic for the legitimation and reification of royal power. One genre of royal pageantry of special relevance to both Kamps's and McMullan's readings of the play is the royal coronation entry, the first grand pageant of a reigning monarch or – particularly important for *All Is True* – his consort. As Germaine Warkentin has argued, such entries were designed to assert the king's legitimacy as a ruler, in particular by

affirming his *virtù*, and a queen consort's legitimacy by affirming her chastity,[5] questions that tie directly in with the action of the play. In such entries and in *All Is True*, royal conduct and character are inseparable from claims to royal legitimacy, and the play is crucially concerned with how such claims are made.

Before considering how royal entries specifically inform the structure of *All Is True*, I want to examine the role of pageantry in general in the play, by returning to the very first – and very astute – critical response to *All Is True*. Far from being simply spectacular, the play is about spectacle; specifically, the play holds up for scrutiny the mechanics of royal pageantry in forms as varied

---

[1] Lee Bliss, 'The Wheel of Fortune and the Maiden Phoenix of Shakespeare's *King Henry the Eighth*', *English Literary History*, 42 (1975), 1–25.

[2] Ivo Kamps, *Historiography and Ideology in Stuart Drama* (Cambridge, 1996), p. 112.

[3] Gordon McMullan, '"Thou hast made me now a man": Reforming Man(ner)liness in *Henry VIII*', in *Shakespeare's Late Plays: New Readings*, ed. Jennifer Richards and James Knowles (Edinburgh, 1999), pp. 40–56, p. 56.

[4] McMullan, 'Thou hast made me now a man', p. 55.

[5] See Germaine Warkentin, ed., *The Queen's Majesty's Passage and Related Documents* (Toronto, 2004), esp. p. 31, where Warkentin argues that the entries of queens regnant provided challenges to their organizers, 'for the customary ritual was designed to display a male monarch who was a fighting leader, resplendent in his military *virtù*'. Whether it is accurate to assign *virtù* so consistently central a place in the virtues showcased by royal entries is debatable; the civic sponsors of the entries would have wished to emphasize different traits of kingship depending on differing political climates, and the virtues of *virtù* would have been context-dependent.

as the masque, execution processions, coronations and royal christenings.

Sir Henry Wotton records that it was the play performed when the first Globe theatre burned to the ground on 29 June 1613:

Now, King Henry making a masque at the Cardinal Wolsey's house, and certain chambers being shot off at his entry, some of the paper, or other stuff, wherewith one of them was stopped, did light the thatch, where being thought at first but an idle smoke, and their eyes more attentive to the show, it kindled inwardly, and ran around like a train, consuming within less than an hour the whole house to the very grounds.[6]

Wotton is the first, but by no means the last, person to comment on the prominence of pageantry in the play; indeed, his account seems to take note of little else. The dramatic business of the fire comes after an equally involved description of the costumes and setting, an extensive catalogue of the various visual splendours that distracted the audience from the growing blaze. The fact that the audience's eyes were 'more attentive to the show' allowed the fire to spread unchecked, testifying to the spectacular nature of that early performance. The passage may dwell on the visual elements, but it is also a clear-eyed critique of the show:

The King's players had a new play, called *All is True*, representing some of the principal pieces of the reign of Henry VIII, which was set forth with many extraordinary circumstances of Pomp and Majesty, even to the matting of the stage; the Knights of the Order, with their Georges and garters, the Guards with their embroidered coats and the like: sufficient in truth within a while to make greatness very familiar, if not ridiculous.[7]

Wotton's choice of words is significant. He describes the play as 'representing some of the principal *pieces*' (emphasis added) – suggesting that at least one member of the original audience saw it not so much as a staging of the principal events from Henry's reign as a staging of its principal theatrical events. There is no battle of Agincourt here. Rather, the events depicted in the play are chosen because of their theatrical aspects. In invoking the kinds of public spectacle with which the original audience would have been familiar, Shakespeare

and Fletcher were doing more than staging spectacle for its own sake. *All Is True* relentlessly exposes the mechanism of pageantry, foregrounding both its presentation and its interpretation. The effect, as Wotton comments, is to make 'greatness very familiar, if not ridiculous'. Kamps has noted that the play's engagement with historiographical methods 'teases out some of the politically significant ambiguities inherent in projects of royal legitimation';[8] I wish to make the same claim for the play's engagement with pageantry. The play gives as much attention to pageantry's failures as it does to its successes, and it does so by both invoking and subverting the conventions of various genres of pageant. It opens with the description and analysis of a pageant that is quickly revealed as nothing but show, the Field of the Cloth of Gold, and closes with a rousing pageant, the baptism of Elizabeth. In each case, the play seems to offer opportunities for totalizing readings, only to undermine them.

This frustration of expectations has led to critical dissatisfaction with the play's structure, leading John Margeson to find that

the most difficult aspect of the structure to justify is the final act where Wolsey and Katherine are no longer part of the action, and where Cranmer takes Wolsey's place, somewhat inadequately, at centre stage with Henry.[9]

But I argue that pageantry offers the play more than its theme – it gives the play its structure, and this dramaturgical choice is determined by the particular form of pageantry that influences the play: as I have suggested above, while individual scenes draw on many different forms of pageantry *All Is True* shares many similarities of theme and overall structure with royal entries (particularly coronation entries), the highly theatrical celebrations enacted to welcome monarchs to towns and cities (particularly London). Structurally, there are suggestive

---

[6] Sir Henry Wotton, *The Life and Letters of Sir Henry Wotton*, ed. Logan Pearsall Smith (Oxford, 1907), vol. 2, p. 33.

[7] Wotton, *Life and Letters*, vol. 2, pp. 32–3.

[8] Kamps, *Historiography*, p. 12.

[9] John Margeson, 'Introduction', *Henry VIII* (Cambridge, 1990), p. 11.

similarities between *All Is* True and a royal entry: a royal entry consists not of one monolithic pageant, but a series of displays for the monarch. The play, too, presents a series of loosely connected pageants. Even more suggestively, the play's dramatic arc is similar to that of a king's progress into a city: Henry is at first faintly glimpsed, the focus of speculation, and the largely passive audience for a series of spectacles, initially interpreted for him by Katherine and Wolsey. Throughout the course of the play, Henry moves in from the margins of the action to become the central actor – and, crucially, the interpreter of others' actions. Finally, the fifth act then proceeds to overturn that movement, as the King remains a key figure on the stage but is replaced by the infant Elizabeth as the focus of attention, and by Cranmer as the privileged interpreter of action.

To a modern audience, the play's relation to royal entries is not, perhaps, immediately apparent. Although the end of Anne's coronation entry is staged, it omits the series of pageants that welcomed a king or queen into the city. To an audience in 1613, however, the oldest members of which might remember several such events, the emphasis on spectacle and the structural echoes of royal entries in *All Is True* may well have been evocative. If Shakespeare and Fletcher make greatness 'familiar', that is in part because they were writing for an audience regularly exposed to civic and royal displays. As Marissa Greenberg memorably phrases it,

Familiarity, of course, creates *expectation*: principles, patterns, and conventions may become so well known that a form's contents, trajectory, and outcome can be anticipated. But whereas familiarity gestures backward to collective memories, expectation points forward to shared notions of formal possibilities.[10]

But if the play's structure is reminiscent of a royal entry, what 'shared notions of formal possibilities' would that have provoked in a Jacobean audience? A king's first entry into London has as its climax the coronation, intended to ritually identify the king as 'the society's center and affirm its connection with transcendent things'.[11] But once

again, the play shows how such display can fail to convince. *All Is True* does not lend itself to any easy conclusions about Henry; McMullan, for example, recognizes and teases out the contrast between the King's apparent triumph over his adversaries, and his compromised masculinity. My argument about the structure of the play gives added weight to McMullan's reading. For the focal point of the final scene is not the King, but rather the infant Elizabeth, and Henry's importance in this scene is as the source of a line of succession, the progenitor of future kings. His position in the closing tableau is therefore not that of a king at all. *All Is True* may take its structure from a royal entry, but its structure is crucially off-centre, and it more closely resembles the royal entry of a consort, with Henry in that secondary role.

ROYAL ENTRIES

While no genre of pageantry is monologic, what sets royal entries apart from other politically charged pageants is the sheer plurality of voices they include. Although the form evolved over centuries, they were consistently mounted as joint ventures between city and court – but collaboration does not always imply cooperation. The city would hope to influence the monarch in its favour; the monarch would hope to win the loyalty of the city. The monarch, entering London for the first time, would be welcomed by a series of allegorical tableaux sponsored by the guilds of the city, and their allegorical function was naturally supportive of the city's interests. While they introduced the monarch to his or her people – establishing the tone of the reign – they also introduced the people to

---

[10] Marissa Greenberg, 'Crossing from Scaffold to Stage: Execution Processions and Generic Conventions in *The Comedy of Errors* and *Measure for Measure*', in *Shakespeare and Historical Formalism*, ed. Stephen Cohen (Ashgate, 2007), pp. 127–46, p. 129.

[11] Clifford Geertz, 'Centers, Kings, and Charisma: Reflections on the Symbolics of Power', in *Culture and Its Creators: Essays in Honor of Edward Shils*, ed. Joseph Ben David and Terry Nichols Clark (Chicago, 1977) pp. 150–71, p. 153.

the monarch, and frequently instructed or even admonished their royal star.

Elizabeth's coronation entry into London in 1559 is one of the best-documented – and most extensively studied – instances of Tudor civic drama. I wish to note the points of Elizabeth's entry that made it so successful. David Bergeron casts light on royal influence on the planning, noting that Elizabeth provided materials for her 1559 entry: 'Elizabeth is thus not only a recipient of the pageant, spectator and "actor" in it, but also a provider... She is accordingly part patron of this drama.'[12]

Just as important as all this preparation was Elizabeth's performance on the day. The moment when the presenters of each individual pageant at a royal entry turn to the monarch for a response is a moment of both opportunity and danger: the monarch will decide upon an agreed meaning for the pageant that is amenable to both court and city, or reject the implied ideological agenda, or refuse to engage, denying the pageant real resolution. Drawing on Maidstone's account of a 1392 royal entry, Anne Lancashire argues that in such events, 'interpretation was a major source of interest for the audience',[13] and this conclusion makes dramatic sense; on a day when so much is so heavily scripted, the reaction of king (as royal audience) and the crowd's reception of that reaction would be nervously anticipated as the only elements not susceptible to stage-management. For the first audience of All Is True, the most recent example of a coronation entry would have highlighted that risk; in contrast to Elizabeth, James famously tolerated, rather than enjoyed, his own entry. C. E. McGee argues that Shakespeare uses a moment of failed pageantic reciprocity as the climax to the relationship between Falstaff and Hal. Henry's rejection of his old companion is patterned on a royal entry in which the King refuses to accept the role offered him.[14] The dramatic tension of this reciprocity, central to the climax of 2 Henry IV, informs the structure of every scene in All Is True.

The tension in this dual role for the monarch – at all theatrical events, not just entries – is captured by Stephen Orgel. The performance is pitched to the king, but the king must then perform as a spectator:

In a theater employing perspective, there is only one perfect focal point, one perfect place in the hall from which the illusion achieves its fullest effect. At court performances this is where the king sat, and the audience around him at once became a living emblem of the structure of the court...

The central experience of drama at court, then, involved not simply the action of a play, but the interaction between the play and the monarch, and the structured organization of the other spectators around him... The king must not merely see the play, he must be seen to see it.[15]

This dynamic is true of any public appearance by a monarch but particularly so in the case of royal entries. What is important about a royal entry, as Germaine Warkentin notes, is that it presents 'a moral vision, not of the monarch's rule as it was, but as its presenters would like it to be',[16] and the monarch's response to that suggestion. The entry is thus not an event so much as a process, the beginning of a relationship. When the monarch draws closer to the end of the progress, he or she emerges with greater clarity in the people's eyes, both by being nearer, and by being subject to closer scrutiny in the political sense, as the crowd hears the royal response to each of the various displays along the route. Clifford Geertz describes the dynamic suggestively: the end of the entry, the next day's coronation, is the final, decisive shift, where the monarch assumes the central physical and political point in the pageant – never to relinquish it.

---

12 David M. Bergeron, 'Elizabeth's Coronation Entry (1559): New Manuscript Evidence', *English Literary Renaissance*, 8 (1978), 3–8, pp. 5–6.

13 Anne Lancashire, *London Civic Theatre: City Drama and Pageantry from Roman Times to 1558* (Cambridge, 2002), p. 46.

14 See C. E. McGee, '*2 Henry IV*: The Last Tudor Royal Entry', in *Mirror up to Shakespeare: Essays in Honour of G. R. Hibbard*, ed. J. C. Gray (Toronto, 1984), pp. 149–58.

15 Stephen Orgel, *The Illusion of Power: Political Theater in the English Renaissance* (Berkeley, 1975), pp. 10–16.

16 Warkentin, *The Queen's Majesty's Passage*, p. 21.

READING PAGEANTRY

This dynamic is reproduced in *All Is True*, as Henry participates in, and is the intended audience of, a series of highly theatrical set-pieces. Hardly a scene goes by without some instance of pageantry, whether staged, described or echoed by the structure of the scene. The first instance of pageantry in the play is described, rather than staged, evidence of the play's focus on interpretation. The opening conversation between Buckingham and Norfolk, reflecting on the Field of the Cloth of Gold, subtly anatomizes what is needed for pageantry to be a successful tool of political propaganda: impressive display, and an active collaboration between the presenters and the audience to determine an agreed upon meaning for the show.

The first fifty lines of the exchange are the reaction of two of the most sophisticated courtiers in the country to a spectacle. Despite this, and despite the fact that few members of the English delegation would not have seen aspects of the event in preparation, Norfolk relates the details of the event with breathless enthusiasm, seemingly caught up in the display in spite of his reservations. Alexander Leggatt suggests that the 'spectators' disinclination to analyze them [the various pageants] implies familiarity and acceptance'.[17] Wotton might demur at this point, arguing as he does that familiarity can make pageantry 'ridiculous'. Familiar the Dukes may be, but that does not explain Norfolk's attitude, who claims to have had on the Field

> The view of earthly glory . . .
>   Now this masque
> Was cried incomparable; and th'ensuing night
> Made it a fool and beggar. The two kings
> Equal in lustre, were now best, now worst,
> As presence did present them. Him in eye,
> Still him in praise, and being present both,
> 'Twas said they saw but one, and no discerner
> Durst wag his tongue in censure.   (1.1.14–33)

This is not quite a 'disinclination to analyze'. Rather, Norfolk – clearly casting himself as a 'discerner', not fully convinced by the spectacle – is refraining from overt or immediate analysis: that will come later, when he comments on the failure of the pact. Latent in his speech is a clear sketch of the functions and limitations of pure spectacle – again, paraphrasing Wotton, it is sufficient to make greatness familiar, if not ridiculous. The spectacle in France has been successful on one front; it has clearly been impressive enough to earn good reviews from a jaded courtier. The endless succession of shows, each one greater than the last, induces a sort of sensory overload – but it also undercuts itself. If any given display is grander than the one before it, another, still grander one may yet come along. Competitive magnificence is a self-consuming artifact; the very terms by which it succeeds are those that threaten to undo it.

Can such pageantry then be an effective tool of the state, if it is inherently self-deflating? Two aspects of this speech make apparent the mechanisms that are necessary for the opulence of the Field of the Cloth of Gold to have any pragmatic effect. The first element is the description of the kings, each better than the other 'as presence did present them'. In other words, such display is effective only when considered in isolation. Each king is supreme only when alone, and when no longer 'in eye' is no longer 'in praise'. Prolonged reflection or the chance to see a still more impressive display – either of these can wipe out the calculated effect of the pageant.

The final element of a successful pageant is revealed by a single word: 'durst'. The choice of modal is significant. Implicitly, there are 'discerners' in the crowd – Norfolk among them – who are quite capable of maintaining perspective on the splendour in front of them. But Norfolk, like those around him, censors his response; he can and may wag his tongue in censure, but he dares not. Buckingham too withholds his opinion until it is revealed that Wolsey is the author of the event. Just as the nobles have been coerced into bankrolling the venture, so too have they been coerced into paying it lip service; the Field of the Cloth of Gold loses its effectiveness as soon as its

---

[17] Alexander Leggatt, *Shakespeare's Political Drama: The History Plays and the Roman Plays* (London, 1988), p. 223.

intended audience have the time – and the sense of security – to reflect on it.

Norfolk elaborates obliquely on the precarious nature of pageantry's effectiveness, presenting a startlingly astute observation about the function of spectacle and symbolism.

> As I belong to worship, and affect
> In honour honesty, the tract of ev'rything
> Would by a good discourser lose some life
> Which action's self was tongue to. All was royal.
> To the disposing of it naught rebelled.
> Order gave each thing view. The office did
> Distinctly fill his function.   (1.1.39–45)

To say that 'Order gave each thing view' can be a comment on the physical arrangement of the audience and the pageant: in modern terms, the blocking was well done and everyone had a clear line of sight. More significantly, it means that the spectacle as a whole was arranged with regard for a more abstract order, that everything was received in relation to its status. As a display of kingly power, then, pageantry is another form of truth; it is a carefully selected and arranged event. Clearly all pageantry requires a certain complicity on the part of its audience, whether coerced or not, to make sure that they take the correct 'truth' from the spectacle.

And yet, by any standard other than the purely aesthetic, the Field of the Cloth of Gold, both historically and in the play, must be adjudged a failure. The peace it was supposed to cement between England and France was short-lived, both historically and in the play. Norfolk reports that already 'France hath flawed the league, and hath attached / Our merchants' goods at Bordeaux' (1.1.95–6). Moreover, as Gordon McMullan argues, the spectacle of the Field carries with it other risks, that 'the grand, masculine display that dominated the celebrations has placed English manhood . . . under severe threat from an incursion of foreign manners and customs'.[18] The competitive displays of wealth and military prowess, intended to establish Henry's *virtù* and add to his legitimacy as king, paradoxically expose him to elements that threaten to undermine 'English manhood' and, consequently, that very legitimacy.

DEBATE AT COURT

Royal pageantry is self-evidently both a display of, and an attempt to reify, kingly power and legitimacy. New historicist criticism has productively explored how the exercise of royal authority took on highly theatrical forms. The historical King Henry was effectively the constant object of the gaze of courtiers, ambassadors and the general public; the actual events where pageantry was a formal element of presentation were simply the most literal instances of a trend. James I would caution his son less than a century after Henry's reign in the *Basilikon Doron*: 'a king is as one set on a stage, whose smallest actions and gestures all the people do gazingly behold'.[19] The most telling word in this advice is 'gazingly'. The king is reduced to the object of a gaze, while his subjects (in the political sense of the word) become subjects (in the grammatical sense of the word) – whether as more or less passive observers, or as Norfolk's discerners. Part way through the play, Suffolk and Norfolk enter to find the King reading:

King Henry draws the curtain and sits reading pensively

Suffolk. How sad he looks! Sure he is much afflicted.
King. Who's there? Ha?
Norfolk.   Pray God he be not angry.
King. Who's there, I say? How dare you thrust yourselves
  Into my private meditations?
  Who am I? Ha?   (2.2.63–7)

The King's rhetorical question is highly ironic. 'Who am I?' The simple answer is that he is the King. But that very fact means that the question of who he is and what he is thinking will always be foremost at court. Because he is King, he has no 'private meditations'. His every move is scrutinized and interpreted, as Suffolk and Norfolk anxiously

---

[18] McMullan, 'Thou hast made me now a man', p. 43.

[19] King James, *The True Law of Free Monarchies and Basilikon Doron*, ed. Daniel Fischlin and Mark Fortier (Toronto, 1996), p. 155.

seek any insight into his mood or thoughts. At one and the same time, everyone knows who he is – and no one knows.

In this context, the propaganda value of pageantry seems less a sinister political exercise than it does a form of self-preservation. If Henry's (or James's) every action is subject to interpretation, then it is natural that he should wish to circumscribe the available interpretations. The 1996 RSC production of the play made this uncomfortably literal, as 'the bulk of the cast' opened the play 'gliding onstage in stiff formal poses' for a staged Field of the Cloth of Gold.[20] The stiffness of the poses underlines the necessity for rigid self-control in self-presentation at a court where the actions of most of the characters are calculated for public rather than private perceptions.

Katherine's appeal to Henry in 1.2 is accordingly not only an exercise in logical persuasion; it is a public, rhetorically sophisticated and highly theatrical presentation to the King, and its success depends on his acceptance of her chosen 'truth'. The business of court is enacted in a theatrical, highly symbolic manner, an instance of royal and judicial pageantry. If 'order gave all things view' at the Field of the Cloth of Gold, the Folio stage directions in this scene give a clear idea of just how important that order is:

Cornets. Enter King Henry, leaning on the Cardinal's shoulder, the Nobles, and Sir Thomas Louell: the Cardenall places himselfe under the King's feete on his right side. (317–20)[21]

A noyse within crying roome for the Queene, usher'd by the Duke of Norfolk. Enter the Queene, Norfolke and Suffolk: she kneels. King riseth from his State, takes her up, kisses and placeth her by him. (329–33)

These directions – unusually elaborate for Shakespeare – give insight both into Henry's role and into the thematic concerns of the scene. Henry, early in the play, is dependent on Wolsey and Katherine to mediate between him and the country. Each presents advice and counsel, for the King to accept or reject – but Henry significantly enters '*leaning on the Cardinal's shoulder*' hinting at Wolsey's influence,

and foreshadowing the cardinal's victory over both Buckingham and Katherine.

Wolsey and Katherine both make astute use of the space available to them.[22] The Cardinal positions himself, visually, as Henry's right-hand man. Katherine adopts a different strategy. Rather than displaying confidence in her political stature, '*she kneels. King riseth from his State, takes her up, kisses and placeth her by him*'. Katherine's gesture of submission has forced the King into action and prompts him to step away from the chair of State where he has occupied the visual focus of the scene. Secure in her influence over her husband, she exacts from him an acknowledgement of that influence by performing an uncertainty that she may or may not feel. His gesture of raising her up displays for all the court that she is to be seen as his equal, and his extravagant protestation that she has 'half our power' in response to her gesture of submission shows the power of theatrical displays of humility. But as the scene progresses from the issue of taxation – where Katherine scores an easy victory over Wolsey – to the trial of Buckingham, there are clear indications that Katherine's influence at court is not as extensive as her initial success might suggest. Her opening display may not merely be a *sign* of her influence over Henry, that display may rather, through its efficacy as a coercive theatrical gesture, have been a *source* of short-lived influence. Her second confrontation with Wolsey shows the ultimate weakness of her position, and careful presentation of her self and her case – again echoing pageantic conventions – will not be sufficient to prevent her divorce.

---

[20] Gordon McMullan, 'Introduction', in *Henry VIII* (London, 2000), p. 56.

[21] Where stage directions are cited alone, I revert to the Folio text. Modern editions revise stage directions for clarity in terms of staging, and in *All Is True* this can actually efface traces of early stage practices.

[22] My sense of the centrality of space in the play as a principal index of meaning draws on Janette Dillon's 'The Trials of Queen Katherine in *Henry VIII*', in *Shakespeare Survey 63* (Cambridge, 2010), pp. 149–61, particularly Dillon's use of the historical example of Lord Burghley's careful *mise en scène* for the trial of Mary Queen of Scots (pp. 149–50).

THE TRIAL OF KATHERINE

While Katherine becomes in many productions the stand-out role, one of the few voices of passion and sincerity in a court where calculation and artifice rule, it is important not to overlook just how stylized and ritualized her passion actually is. I draw on Anny Crunelle-Vanrigh's argument in seeing certain elements of Shakespearian staging as reminiscent of royal entries. Crunelle-Vanrigh reads Henry V's tour of the camp on the night before Agincourt as analogous to the King's tour of pageant sites in a royal entry.[23] At a bare minimum, Katherine's circuit of the court is a royal progress in miniature; more specifically, I read her tour of the stage in her trial scene as echoing the royal entrance of a queen consort, who processes past her subjects, on her way to be greeted and accepted by the King.

This is not to say that Katherine's use of ritual makes her insincere. She must speak as a queen, for otherwise she will be seen to have conceded her case. And in this scene, the most important spectator is the King himself; all the players in the court are performing for his benefit. Although Katherine's speech may be the verbal centre of the scene, the layout of the stage indicates that its visual focus is – or at least is intended to be – on the King, listening to her testimony: 'The King takes his place under the Cloth of State. The two Cardinalls sit under him as Iudges. The Queene takes place some distance from the King' (1343–6). The King is simultaneously the focus of the visual attention, surrounded by the trappings of state power, and the interpreter of the drama that is to unfold in front of him, both actor and audience. The cardinals may sit 'as judges', but they are very much subordinated to the King. It is not to them that Katherine addresses her pleas, but to Henry himself: 'The Queene makes no answer, rises out of her chair, goes about the court, comes to the King and kneeles at his Feete. Then speakes' (1362–5).

One of the dominant structural principles, both of a consort's entry and of this brief miniature drama, is delay, in keeping with Lancashire's argument that 'interpretation was a major source of interest for the audience' – theatre must first be performed, and then interpreted; action is followed by exegesis. Likewise, the spectators closest to the centre of the action, to the culmination of the entry, have the longest to wait. An entry is a journey from margin to centre, both literally and symbolically.

The circuit of the court, with its evocation of the traditions of a queen consort's entry makes sense as a tactical choice on Katherine's part, since those entries fulfilled a particular propagandistic function. As Germaine Warkentin has observed, king's entries were intended to assert the new monarch's virtù. For a queen, the relevant attribute was her chastity, 'generously defined as her capacity to produce offspring to inherit the kingdom'.[24] The two qualities, considered separately, are the reason for the divorce proceedings. Historically, Henry's obsession with securing a male heir drove his obsession with annulling his marriage; in the play, Suffolk centres his praises of Anne Bullen on hope that 'from her / Will fall some blessing to this land' (3.2.50–1). In history, as in the play, the reasons given for divorce centre around the putative incest of the King's first marriage: 'It seems the marriage with his brother's wife / Has crept too near his conscience' (2.2.16–17). In asserting her rightful status as the King's wife, Katherine is asserting her chastity in both its ideal and its pragmatic sense.

The ironies of this scene are particularly cruel. Katherine is forced to defend the legitimacy of her marriage in a court that has been convened as a result of Henry's immoderate desire for Anne. Cardinal Wolsey's comment to the King in 1.4 – 'Your grace / I fear with dancing is a little heated'

---

[23] Anny Crunelle-Vanrigh, 'Henry V as a Royal Entry', *SEL: Studies in English Literature, 1500–1900*, 47 (2007), 355–77.

[24] Warkentin, *The Queen's Majesty's Passage*, p. 32. See also Gordon Kipling's consideration of Anne Boleyn's entry, and 'the ambivalent and conditional nature of the citizens' acclamation. Pageant after pageant thus addresses the claim which justifies Anne's accession as queen. She can provide for the nation what Katharine could not: "a new son of the king's blood"' ('"He That Saw It Would Not Believe It": Anne Boleyn's Royal Entry into London', in *Civic Ritual & Drama*, ed. Alexandra F. Johnston and Wim Hüsken (Atlanta, 1997), pp. 39–79, p. 69).

(102–3) – leaves little doubt that Henry's attraction is palpable. The conversation between Anne and the Old Lady in the preceding scene makes it quite apparent that the outcome of Henry's campaign to be divorced is a foregone conclusion, and that Katherine is already 'a stranger now again' (2.3.17). Finally, there is the fact that one of the most successful pageants in the play will be Anne's coronation entry. Although the historical record is ambiguous, there is evidence that Anne's reception was less than fully enthusiastic.[25] In the play, though, the audience is treated to a spectacular procession, followed by uniformly approving evaluations: 'Sir, as I have a soul, she is an angel' (4.1.44) affirms the Second Gentleman, after Anne processes across the stage *'in her hair'* – with her hair hanging down – the traditional symbol of virginity. Historically, at least, Anne was six months pregnant at the time; the choice must be made in production whether to gloss over this fact, or to allow Anne's pregnant body to underscore the power of a well-crafted pageant to obscure inconvenient truths. The crowd at Westminster, at least, is convinced, and their reception of Anne is so enthusiastic that

> such a noise arose
> As the shrouds make at sea in a stiff tempest,
> As loud and to as many tunes. Hats, cloaks, –
> Doublets, I think – flew up . . .   (4.1.73–6)

Anne's entry is one of the few pageants of the play where organizers and onstage audience are in agreement about the 'chosen truth' of the spectacle. Katherine's performance is more complex, less supported by pageantic display, and less successful.

Katherine is at once a queen, displaying herself to her subjects as she processes to meet her husband, and a subject, presenting a show to her King. Her procession around the court serves as a visible sign of her contempt for its proceedings, symbolically reducing the judges and nobility to her subjects. Her kneeling before Henry is the gesture of a submissive subject and a submissive wife. Considering that Henry is arguing that she is not legitimately his wife, and therefore, 'a stranger now again', to kneel before Henry as she does is

at once an assertion of her continued status and an acknowledgement of where the real power in the room is. It hardly matters that Katherine has 'reverend fathers, men / Of singular integrity and learning, / Yea, the elect o' th' land' (2.4.56–8) to plead her case. The Cardinals may sit as judges, but it is to the King that Katherine addresses her arguments. Her judgement is borne out, too, as Henry dissolves the court when it does not rule as he wishes.

After the debate between Katherine and Wolsey – in which Henry says nothing – Katherine's departure from the court allows the audience's aural and visual attention to be reunited – and oriented towards Henry. He is at once a participant in his wife's mock-entry, and a king at court, observing an elaborate appeal for judgement by two parties. The King's refusal to speak removes him from his first role. In 1.2, Katherine's gesture of submission earns her an instant promise that her suit will be granted. In her trial, although the King may react physically, the text offers no verbal cue. He is not the King welcoming a consort. His final judgement confirms this; his valedictory speech, however flattering, is an act of divorce. Katherine may have her consolatory masque-like vision of angels but it is entirely private. It is Anne whose entry is effective, establishing in the eyes of 'the crowd i'th'Abbey' that she has 'all the royal makings of the queen' (4.1.89).

WOLSEY AND CRANMER

From the trial scene on, Henry assumes a steadily growing role in driving the action. We are informed by Suffolk of his discovery of Wolsey's treachery. Rather than simply confronting the Cardinal with his evidence, the King lays a theatrical trap. Just as Elizabeth was part sponsor and patron of her own entry, Henry puts in place the props – the packet of letters – and lays the scene for not only exposing Wolsey but moreover for exposing him publicly. As with the earlier case against

---

[25] See Kipling, 'He That Saw It', pp. 67–8.

Buckingham, evidence is presented, and then two sides compete to offer their interpretation. For all the confidence of the nobles, and in the teeth of Henry's obvious anger, Wolsey still can claim that 'spotless shall mine innocence arise / When the King knows my truth' (3.2.301–2). As with Katherine's trial, though, persuasion yields to the King's determination of the case.

In his rescue of Cranmer in Act 5, Henry exhibits a similar affinity for the theatrical. Arming Cranmer with his ring, the King secretly watches as the council lay their false charges against the archbishop. Cranmer then produces the ring, and the councillors rightly understand that they are outmatched – in the detailed stage directions typical of the play, '*Enter King frowning on them, takes his Seate*' (3181). As always, the King's demeanour is the object of the court's anxious gaze. On this occasion, there is little difficulty in determining the import of his looks. Henry himself offers the moral of his little drama:

> Well, well, my lords – respect him,
> Take him and use him well, he's worthy of it.
> I will say thus much for him – if a prince
> May be beholden to a subject, I
> Am for his love and service so to him.
> Make me no more ado, but all embrace him.
> Be friends, for shame, my lords.   (5.2.187–93)

Henry's comments, as well as resolving the Cranmer thread of the plot, offer a suggestive inversion. Just as subjects are 'beholden' (the Folio spelling is 'beholding') to their king, so too they 'gazingly do behold' him. Henry's tenure as the principal actor in the Cranmer episode is short-lived; the closing scene sees him once again in place as the royal audience for an extravagant spectacle – but his role will be different from earlier in the play.

At the christening of Elizabeth, the King's delayed entry establishes him as the audience for the spectacular display. But where a monarch on royal progress would then offer response, the bulk of the interpretation is left to Cranmer. The visual centre of the scene is the infant Elizabeth, under a canopy. The aural centre of the scene is the archbishop's prophecy of England's future under Elizabeth and James. His speech makes Elizabeth an icon of masculine virtue – or even *virtù*.

> All princely graces
> That mould up such a mighty piece as this is,
> With all the virtues that attend the good,
> Shall still be doubled on her.   (5.4.25–8)

At the end of *All Is True*, the masculine virtue of a monarch is celebrated – but in prolepsis, and that monarch is not Henry, but rather Elizabeth.

Although Henry is given the last word, his speech is curiously self-effacing, allowing Cranmer's prediction of Elizabeth's greatness to stand as the public 'truth' of the occasion. As Gordon McMullan has pointed out, the play offers us 'a king whose intemperance can only be seen as a failure of true manliness' participating in 'improvised public mythologising of a baby girl as a vision of England's future'.[26] Henry confines his comments to a definition of his own role and his speech casts him in a particularly feminine role:

> O lord Archbishop,
> Thou hast made me now a man. Never before
> This happy child did I get anything.   (5.4.63–5)

Henry's point of pride, his interpretation of this show, is that he has begotten an heir. In one respect, his deference to Elizabeth is entirely in keeping with her unexpected role as monarch whose legitimacy is affirmed in the final moments of the play, and with his own odd, hybrid position. On the other hand, Anne is specifically absent, and in this scene the King stands as sole begetter of the child. His assumption of both paternal and maternal roles only serves to highlight the problematic question of his own masculinity. If this is the end of his progress, then the quality that he celebrates in himself is that quality usually celebrated in a queen consort: the establishment of a line of succession.

What has happened to Henry? For the duration of *All Is True*, he has been the focus of audience attention and speculation – both from the onstage audience, and the audience of the play.

---

26 Gordon McMullan, '"Thou hast made me now a man"', p. 55.

Once again, this sudden shift in attention correlates strongly with the tone of a consort's entry. As Gordon Kipling has observed, 'queens' triumphs, it is true, carefully limit their acclamation: the consort must never seem more glorious than the king'.[27] A king's entry provides a steady intensification of attention paid to the king, as he assumes his place at the physical and political centre of the event. The same intensity of attention is granted to the king's consort in her entry, but always tempered by the fact that her status derives from him. She is the centre of attention, until the end of the spectacle, but she may never displace the king's political centrality.

The Prologue invites the audience to watch the King's Men's 'chosen truth' (line 18) – but what is that truth? In making pageantry the subject of *All Is True*, Shakespeare and Fletcher so thoroughly expose the propagandistic side of the genre, and its susceptibility to interpretation, that they make the play itself highly resistant to any totalizing reading. Even the figure of Henry, the supposed centre of interpretive authority in the play, remains to the end a highly ambivalent figure. To an early modern audience, attuned – whether consciously or not – to the conventions and expectations of a royal entry, Henry's marginalization in the final scene would be impossible to ignore. The very generic conventions that ensure that he is the locus of interpretation throughout the play finish by undermining his stature.

---

[27] Kipling, 'He That Saw It', p. 69.

ACTING HISTORICAL WITH SHAKESPEARE, OR, WILLIAM-HENRY IRELAND'S OAKEN CHEST

ELLEN MacKAY

My raptures are not conjured up
To serve occasions of poetic pomp,
*   But genuine.*

William Cowper, *The Task*

This article begins with a claim and a disclaimer: first, that a forger of Shakespeare might be classified as his collaborator and, second, by way of a hasty rejoinder, that this revision is no mitigation of his academic high crime, but a way of excavating the tacit cues and patterns that inform our broader practice of Shakespearian inquiry. Working backward from William-Henry Ireland's fraudulent creations, I mean to show that the drive to recover Shakespeare's lost evidence authorizes strange acts of hypostasy that centre on the figure of the chest or box. Given this ambition, the spirit of collaboration this inquiry explores is well removed from the early modern dramatic poets' compositional practice. Its domain is instead the receiving end of Shakespeare's literary legacy and, more particularly, the complex interplay of deprivation, inspiration and invention that constitutes the making of an authorial corpus out of meagre biographical and bibliographical remains.[1] Ireland's productions illustrate the degree to which knowing Shakespeare remains a performance of collecting an unpreserved past, underwritten by a dramaturgy of impossible recovery.

To be sure, the acts of recovery perpetrated by Ireland make him an unlikely figure with whom to generalize about a Shakespearian *mentalité*. As a pre-eminent case of who we scholars aren't and what we don't do, his transgression occupies a certain disciplinary centrality: Chapter Four

in Samuel Schoenbaum's supplement to his documentary biography, Chapter One in James Shapiro's history of the authorship debate, it even presides over the assistant to the director's office at the Folger Shakespeare Library in George James de Wilde's painting of *The Seven Ages of Man*, where Ireland's work epitomizes the foolishness of callow youth.[2] The continued recollection, not to say moralizing, of this fiasco says much about the desire to keep scholarship untainted by the ersatz or bogus; now as then, the experts taken in by this fraud are made 'fixed figures of the time of scorn, to point his slow unmoving finger at' to preserve the profession from the catastrophic implication that it cannot distinguish its own object.[3] And yet, as George Chalmers protested in his *Apology for the Believers*, given that the 'whole *Archeology*' of

---

[1] This formulation is loosely indebted to the title of Michael Dobson's definitive study, *The Making of a National Poet, Shakespeare, Adaptation, and Authorship, 1660–1769* (Oxford, 1992).

[2] James S. Shapiro, *Contested Will: Who Wrote Shakespeare?* (New York, 2010), pp. 17–51; Samuel Schoenbaum, *William Shakespeare: Records and Images* (New York, 1981), pp. 117–54. My thanks to Karen Lyon, who occupies this office, for providing me access to the painting.

[3] George Chalmers, *An Apology for the Believers in the Shakspeare-papers Which Were Exhibited in Norfolk-Street* (London, 1797), p. iii. The uncited quotation is from *Othello* (4.3.52–3), William Shakespeare, *Othello*, ed. Richard Proudfoot (London, 2002). On the moralizing of the hoax, see for example, William Cobbett's *Advice to Young Men and (incidentally) to Young Women* (London, 1796), II, p. 1, who preaches from the hoax's example, 'pay little attention to the decision of those who call themselves critics'.

the discipline was built on the premise that 'much was still to be found with regard to Shakespeare', and even that 'every moment was *expectancy* of more *arrivance*', the victims of Ireland's fraud were not simply dupes by their own poor diligence, but martyrs to an adventist outlook intrinsic to Shakespearian inquiry, seemingly fuelled by the prognostications of the Bard himself.[4]

The Ireland episode and its attendant embarrassments can therefore be seen to preside over a shift in the history of Shakespeare studies when the anticipation of discovery gave way to the recognition of its futility. As Edward Capell describes it in 1793, the lot of the modern scholar is to dream of a biography that can never be written:

How much is it to be wish'd, that something equally certain, indeed worthy to be intitl'd – a Life of Shakespeare, could accompany this relation . . . The truth is, the occurrences of this most interesting life (we mean the private ones) are irrecoverably lost to us.[5]

The question this essay explores is the shadowy underside of Capell's pragmatism: the persistent difficulty of letting loss be loss. Though Chalmers's claim that 'some fragments of Shakspeare may even yet be found, if curiosity would prompt diligence to search the repositories of concealment' now seems quaint, the undiscovered fragments and repositories of Shakespeare continue to orient the discipline.[6] By inventorying in its fullest array Shakespeare's unrecorded past, Ireland brings to light the scriptive force of the archive's lack.

Those seeking a full account of Ireland's story will find that it has been often and deftly told elsewhere.[7] For the purposes of this essay, suffice it to say that William-Henry Ireland was an undistinguished nineteen-year-old law clerk who spent most of 1795 retrieving a succession of Shakespeare's legal documents, correspondence, manuscripts, drawings and sundries from the oaken chest of an anonymous 'gentleman of *considerable property*'.[8] His tragedy of *Vortigern and Rowena* was both the zenith and the nadir of this recovered hoard, the most anticipated of his discoveries and the tipping point of the young man's overreach.

Performed at Drury Lane under Sheridan's management and featuring Philip Kemble in the leading role, the play was put before its audience as a 'wonder' of recuperation and revivification:

---

4 Chalmers, *Apology*, pp. 5–6, p. 8. The uncited quotation is again from *Othello* (2.1.42).

5 Edward Capell, 'Mr Capell's Introduction', in *The Plays of William Shakespeare*, ed. Samuel Johnson and George Steevens, 4th edn, 15 vols. (London, 1793), vol. 1, p. 320. James Shapiro cites this text from Capell in his account of the shift to biographical readings of the plays (a practice begun by Malone) in *Contested Will*, p. 51.

6 Chalmers, *Apology*, p. 7. Though perhaps not indicative of the state of the discipline, Ian McEwan's comments in an interview in the *New York Times Book Review* ('By the Book', 6 December 2012) is indicative of the shaping force of Shakespeare's absence.

'Every time I watch the curtain come down on even a halfway decent production of a Shakespeare play I feel a little sorrowful that I'll never know the man, or any man of such warm intelligence. What would I want to know? His gossip, his lovers, his religion (if any), the Silver Street days, his thoughts on England and power in the 17th century – as young then as the 21st is for us. And why he's retiring to Stratford. The biographies keep coming, and there's a great deal we know about Shakespeare's interactions with institutions of various kinds. England was already a proto-modern state that kept diligent records. But the private man eludes us and always will until some rotting trunk in an ancient attic yields a Pepys-like journal. But that's historically impossible. He's gone.'

7 See Derek Bodde, *Shakespeare and the Ireland Forgeries* (Cambridge, MA, 1930); Zoltan Harazsti, *The Shakespeare Forgeries of William Henry Ireland* (Boston, 1934); John Dunbar Mair, *The Fourth Forger: William Ireland and the Shakespeare Papers* (Freeport, NY, 1938, repr. 1971); Bernard Grebanier, *The Great Shakespeare Forgery: A New Look at the Career of William Henry Ireland* (New York, 1965); Samuel Schoenbaum, *Shakespeare's Lives*, 2nd edn (Oxford, 1991), pp. 30–68; Jeffrey Kahan, *Reforging Shakespeare: The Story of a Theatrical Scandal* (Bethlehem, PA, 1998); Joseph Rosenblum, *Practice to Deceive* (New Castle, 2000); Nick Groom, *The Forger's Shadow* (London, 2002); Patricia Pierce, *The Great Shakespeare Fraud: The Strange, True Story of William-Henry Ireland* (Stroud, 2004); Jack Lynch, *Becoming Shakespeare* (New York, 2007) and *Deception and Detection in Eighteenth-Century Britain* (Aldershot, 2008); Doug Stewart, *The Boy Who Would Be Shakespeare: a Tale of Forgery and Folly* (Cambridge, MA, 2010). Two novels also treat this history: Peter Ackroyd, *The Lambs of London* (London, 2004) and Arthur Phillips, *The Tragedy of Arthur: A Novel* (New York, 2011).

8 Walley Chamberlain Oulton, *Vortigern Under Consideration* (London, 1796), p. 36.

From deep oblivion snatched, this play appears:
It claims respect, since Shakespeare's name it bears;
That name, the source of wonder and delight,
To a fair hearing has at least a right.
We ask no more. With you the judgment lies
No forgeries escape your piercing eyes![9]

Accounts vary of the 'dread' verdict that ensued.[10] Contemporary reviews say that despite a 'liberal hearing',[11] the 'audience sought in vain . . . for the just impersonification and glowing description of our immortal bard'.[12] Ireland and his father blamed Kemble for letting his disbelief colour his performance and Edmond Malone for agitating against it – the latter's ferocious rebuttal of the Ireland papers was published a mere two days before the production. Whether the play failed on its own merits or whether it was brought down by the malevolence of its opponents is open to question, though it is worth noting that experts on the subject including Jeffrey Kahan and Doug Stewart incline to the latter view. What is certain is that with the curtain's fall, the audience's disapprobation grew so loud that the management was prevented from announcing a second presentation, and the family and its miscellanea descended into ignominy.

The forty-year remainder of William-Henry's life was spent excusing, repenting and monetizing this fraud.[13] His best effort on all three counts is his *Confessions* of 1805, in which Ireland describes himself driven to forgery by his father, Samuel, an engraver by trade, a passionate Bardolater by inclination and a withholding, severe parent to his Walter Mitty-ish son. The elder Ireland visited Stratford in 1794 to make drawings and notes for his *Picturesque Views on the Upper, or Warwickshire Avon* – his illustrations of the Hathaway cottage, the poet's birthplace, the exequial bust, etc. are foundational of this genre of Shakespeariana[14] – and he took William-Henry with him. The trip was formative in two respects: first, for an embarrassing scene that occurred at Clopton House, in which the elder Ireland, driven thither by the promise of Shakespearian bounty, inquired of its inhabitants whether they might have any undiscovered literary

treasures on their premises. Their deadpan response was that come to think of it, they had been in possession of 'several baskets full of letters and papers' with 'Shakespeare's name wrote upon them', but needing the space to raise some partridges, they had put them to the fire within the last fortnight.[15] The gullible Samuel was brought to his knees by this exchange – 'By God,' he is said to have said, doubtless with high tragic intonation, 'you are not aware of the loss the world has sustained.'[16] But he went on to find some consolation at Anne Hathaway's cottage, the site of the second scene that his son takes some pains to convey. Under the assurance that it was the very seat upon which 'our bard was wont to sit in courtship with Hathaway on his knee', Samuel bought an old oak chair there that he then set in a place of honour in the library of his London home (see illustration 3).[17] Like the mulberry-wood '*bagatelles*' that his father selected from Thomas Sharpe's shop,[18] William-Henry

---

[9] William-Henry Ireland, *The Confessions . . . Containing the Particulars of His Fabrication of the Shakspeare Manuscripts, Together with Anecdotes and Opinions of Many Distinguished Persons* (New York, repr. 1805), p. 145.

[10] Ireland, *Confessions*, p. 146.

[11] *The Bombay Courier*, 5: 212, 108; see also 'They heard with candour, and expected with ungratified attention. Their decision was in the end as absolute as it must be irrevocable.' *The Lady's Magazine; or, Entertaining Companion for the Fair Sex, Appropriated Solely to their Use and Amusement*, April 1796, vol. 27, p. 147.

[12] *The Lady's Magazine*, p. 147.

[13] Ireland died 17 April 1835 at the age of fifty-nine.

[14] On the importance of Samuel Ireland's pictures of the chief Shakespeare sites, see Samuel Schoenbaum, *William Shakespeare: Records and Images* (Oxford, 1981), p. 117.

[15] Ireland, *Confessions*, p. 31.

[16] Ireland, *Confessions*, p. 31.

[17] Ireland, *Confessions*, p. 33.

[18] Though William-Henry forgets the name of the 'old shop-keeper, who resided nearly opposite to our inn' and who claimed 'the remains of the mulberry tree, together with tobacco stoppers, busts, wafer seals, &c., all carved from the wood', the description is plainly of Thomas Sharpe, who had purchased the remains of the tree back in 1756. The younger Ireland's scepticism as to the authenticity of these objects is conventional: 'I much fear a dozen full-grown mulberry trees would scarcely suffice to produce the innumerable mementoes already extant.' Still, he believes the

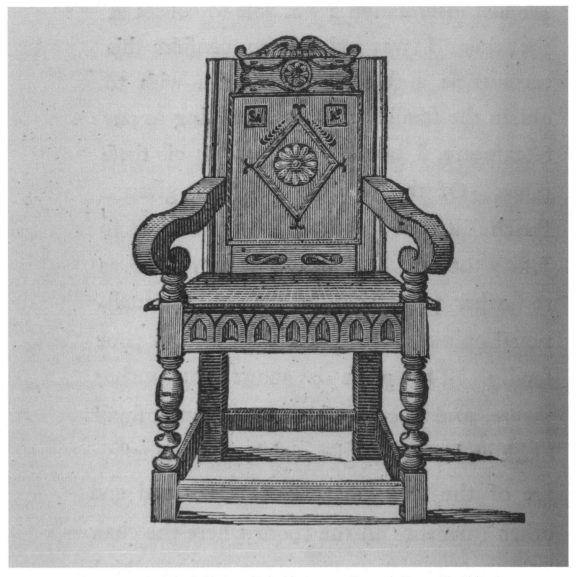

3. 'The Courting Chair', sketched by Samuel Ireland for *Picturesque Views on the Upper, or Warwickshire Avon*.

regarded the chair as a patent humbug; with uncharacteristic irreverence, he reports restraining his laughter at the sight of London's worthies 'settl[ing]' their 'physiognomies' upon it.

As a rationale or rationalization, all this is clear enough. Samuel's futile quest for Shakespeare's written remains and his subsequent willingness to purchase for veneration whatever Shakespeare might have seen, touched or sat on, set the scene for William-Henry's fabrications. But there is more to the tale. Equally prominent among the 'various pursuits' that the forger says 'occupied [his] boyish mind' during the lead-up to his crime was

goblet of sufficient age to have derived 'in all probability from the original tree' (*Confessions*, p. 20).

Thomas Chatterton, the martyr-saint of all forgers, dead by his own hand in 1770.[19] Immediately preceding his account of the Stratford visit, William-Henry describes a trip he subsequently took to Bristol to inspect the ancient chests in the turret chamber of the church of St Mary Redcliffe, where young Chatterton claimed he discovered his forged medieval verses.[20] Unsurprisingly, the search proved unavailing. The chests were 'empty', Ireland reports, and the chamber turned out to be 'a cheerless stone room'.[21] In effect, then, the Stratford trip was not Ireland's only pilgrimage to a literary interior voided of its contents; cast in the *Confessions* as foretelling precedent, Chatterton's barren casket is like Clopton House's emptied basket or ashy hearth: a site of history's loss, and the provocation for its imaginative refurbishing.

A book of poems Ireland went on to write on the subject of 'Neglected Genius' makes the turn to conjuration the inevitable result of this sort of disappointment. In retreat from the 'dismal vacuum' of Chatterton's chamber, the speaker seeks the 'spirit' vanished from it:

With measured pace and melancholy air
I'gan descend the turret's winding stair,
And oftimes listened to the echoing sound,
That seem'd to speak some following foot's rebound;
I paused, methought his spirit wander'd near;
I listen'd – but no sound broke stillness drear.[22]

This impulse is not Ireland's invention, however. Its fullest realization is in the nineteenth-century pictorial tradition of the prodigy-counterfeiter at work, amid tables, desks, cabinets, baskets and chests that spill forth the papers that Ireland quixotically sought.[23] If, as Susan Stewart argues, forgery is the fullest recognition of 'the limiting contingency of all representation as "standing for" and "standing in"' the place of a lost or uncapturable original, Chatterton, in his painted recollection, is the icon of this precept: a counterfeiter of British antiquity whose garret rooms and empty chests act as prompts and place holders for a fantasy of manuscriptural abundance.[24] As a touchpoint in Ireland's *Confessions*, he thus stands in for the 'doomed search for originals by

continuously auditioning stand-ins' that defines William-Henry's self-described 'performances'.[25]

Caught in Chatterton's thrall, or so Ireland confesses ('I used frequently to envy his fate, and desire nothing so ardently as the termination of my existence in a similar cause'[26]), he goes about his business with gusto. By Kahan's count, William-Henry produced 'well over ten thousand lines' of ersatz Shakespeare, the first and most famous instances of which Samuel Ireland illustrated and published as *The Miscellaneous Papers and Legal Instruments Under the Hand and Seal of Shakespeare*.[27] The miscellany began modestly enough, in the form of an 'Autograph Subscribed to a Mortgage-Deed'.[28] Having heard his father 'frequently assert, that such was his veneration for the bard that he would willingly give half his library to become possessed even of his signature alone', William-Henry cut some parchment from 'an old rent-roll' and copied nearly verbatim

---

[19] Ireland, *Confessions*, p. 18.

[20] I am grateful to Jeffrey Kahan for clarifying this chronology, which Ireland purposefully disarranges in his *Confessions*.

[21] Ireland, *Confessions*, p. 13.

[22] William-Henry Ireland, *Neglected Genius. A Poem. Illustrating the Untimely and Unfortunate Fate of Many British Poets; from the Period of Henry the Eighth to the Æra of the Unfortunate Chatterton* (London, 1812), pp. 80, 81.

[23] These include Henrietta Mary Ada Ward's *Chatterton, 1765* (c.1873); Richard Jeffreys Lewis's *Chatterton Composing the Rowleian Manuscripts* (c.1845); John Joseph Barker's *Thomas Chatterton in his Garret* (c.1845); W. B. Morris's *A Holiday Afternoon* (c.1875); and Henry Wallis's *The Death of Chatterton* (1856), which is by far the most famous of the works mentioned, and in which the poet, though no longer at work, is nonetheless surrounded by his furnishings and output. All but the Morris can be seen at the BBC's web catalogue, 'Your Paintings'.

[24] Susan Stewart, *Crimes of Writing: Problems in the Containment of Representation* (Durham, NC, 1994), p. viii.

[25] Joseph Roach, *Cities of the Dead: Circum-Atlantic Performance* (New York, 1996), p. 3. Ireland calls his forgeries both 'creations' and 'performances' in the *Confessions*.

[26] Ireland, *Confessions*, p. 11.

[27] Jeffrey Kahan, *Reforging Shakespeare: The Story of a Theatrical Scandal*, p. 36.

[28] William Henry Ireland, *Miscellaneous Papers and Legal Instruments Under the Hand and Seal of William Shakespeare: Including the Tragedy of King Lear, and a Small Fragment of Hamlet, from the Original Mss. in the Possession of Samuel Ireland, of Norfolk Street* (London, 1796), unpaginated.

the Blackfriars house deed and signature from the facsimile in Johnson and Steevens's 1793 edition of Shakespeare.[29] By pure happenstance, the seal he scavenged from his employer's legal muniments and attached to this document featured the impression of a quintain – a 'machine' once 'used by the young men, to instruct them in the art of tilting on horseback with the lance'.[30] This device was seen by an excited readership to 'bear so great an analogy to the name *Shake-spear*' that the document was immediately deemed authentic, and William-Henry's course was set.[31] As he writes,

it was hinted, that in all probability many papers of Shakspeare's might be found by referring to the same source from whence the deed had been drawn. This suggestion was frequently uttered in my presence: and being thus urged forward to produce what really was not in existence, I then determined on essaying some composition in imitation of the language of Shakspeare.[32]

Highlights from the ensuing pseudo-biographica include 'Queen Elizabeth's Letter' to Shakespeare complementing 'goode Masterre William' on his 'prettye Verses', and inviting him to 'Hamptowne' Court; 'The Profession of Faith', written to prove the poet 'a sincere votary of the protestant religion' (this is the document that James Boswell is said to have knelt and kissed, notwithstanding its closing line: 'O cherisshe usse like the sweete Chickenne thatte under the coverte offe herre spreadynge Wings Recyves herre lyttle broode'); 'A Letter' and 'Verses to Anna Hatharrewaye', featuring the immortal couplet, 'Is there on earthe a Manne more trewe / Thanne Willy Shakspear is toe you?', and supplemented with a lock of hair of unillustrious provenance.[33] There is also the 'Sketch of Shakespeare by his own hand', which is more or less a doodle of the Folio's Droeshout portrait, and a 'complete manuscript of Lear', revised to prove that any scurrility in that work was the interpolation of naughty players, but which had the inadvertent effect of making Shakespeare a less metrically assured poet than was heretofore the case.[34] Finally, the most brazen of Ireland's inventions was a 'deed of gift to one William-Henry Ireland', the ancestor and namesake of the clerk who, as luck

would have it, chanced to rescue Shakespeare from drowning in the Thames. For this service, Shakespeare bequeaths his good Samaritan and any like-named descendents the rights to *Henry IV* (one presumes both of them), *Henry V, King John*, and *King Lear* in perpetuity, along with a lost play the forger had on the boil, the history of *King Edward III*. As Ireland confesses, this outrageous fable was the means he dreamed up to 'claim [his] own productions' and cut the anonymous gentleman, in whose oaken chest they supposedly lay, out of the picture.[35] It was also the means to take centre stage in the history of his own invention, not only as Shakespeare's heir, but as his effusively thanked preserver: 'O Modelle of Virtue, Charity's Sweet Child, Thy Shakespeare thanks thee.'[36]

It is in this role, as the prop or stay against Shakespeare's obliteration, that Ireland would have his sins remembered, and the gambit is at once his most shameless and his most apt. As a forger, history has judged William-Henry a mediocre talent. By recovering evidences to furnish every gap that biographers, historians and enthusiasts of Shakespeare had cause to lament – indeed, by

---

[29] Ireland, *Confessions*, pp. 45, 47. See *The Plays of William Shakespeare*, ed. Samuel Johnson and George Steevens, vol. 1, pp. 88–93.

[30] Ireland, *Confessions*, p. 52.

[31] Ireland, *Confessions*, p. 53.

[32] William-Henry Ireland, *Confessions*, p. 55.

[33] The titles of these objects are taken from Samuel Ireland's *Miscellaneous Papers*. Authorial commentary is from William-Henry Ireland, *Confessions*, 59, 82, who says the hair was recycled from a 'gage d'amour' from his 'boyish days', but it may well have been his own (83).

[34] James Boaden's condemnation of the *Lear* emendations is irresistible: 'It at once converted the PLAYERS into the most elaborate and polished masters of versification, and SHAKSPEARE into a writer who . . . lost the supreme ascendancy in his art, from the not being able to number ten syllables upon his fingers' (*A Letter to George Steevens, Esq Containing a Critical Examination of the Papers of Shakspeare; Published by Mr. Samuel Ireland. To Which Are Added, Extracts from Vortigern. By James Boaden, Esq* (London, 1796), p. 7).

[35] William-Henry Ireland, *Confessions*, 229.

[36] William Henry Ireland, *Miscellaneous Papers and Legal Instruments Under the Hand and Seal of William Shakespeare* (London, 1796), sig. B5.

corroborating all the qualities that Englishmen of the late eighteenth century were likely to admire in their national poet, from financial prudence to nuptial affection to upright Anglican belief – William-Henry manufactured an archive that is plainly the wish-fulfillment of his bardolatrous age. But as a seeker of Shakespeare, and thus as a person 'urged forward to produce what really was not in existence', he is considerably more interesting. Though critics have mocked the 'power of *prophetic illumination*' that called Ireland to 'save the life of his friend SHAKESPEARE' some 'TWO CENTURIES *before his birth*', the rescue mission that William-Henry twice mounted (if we recall that it is via the same figure that *Vortigern* is 'from deep Oblivion snatched') is a faithful recapitulation of the Shakespearian leitmotif of foiled loss.[37] Ireland thus figures forth a resolution to the antinomy at the root of the Shakespearian condition: the near-utter perdition of an author-object unrivalled in his dramatization of 'the demand that the lost thing, in all its nature-born warmth, be preserved'.[38]

Undrowning Shakespeare, I am arguing, is therefore not just the twee and jejune result of a young forger's fancy but an act of imaginary recuperation that derives from the oeuvre of the author it saves. The literal evidence for such a claim might start with *The Tempest*, in which the play's villains anticipate the miracle they disbelieve in the precise idiom of Ireland's fable:

> Antonio. 'Tis as impossible that he's undrown'd
> As he that sleeps here swims.
> Sebastian. I have no hope
> That he's undrowned. (2.1.231–4)[39]

But the influence of such a passage on Ireland's 'deed of gift' is less a matter of literary debt than anachronic collaboration. Such a partnership has been called intrinsic to the reader-author relation; in *Dreaming by the Book*, Elaine Scarry describes 'the way in which a poem or a novel is a set of instructions for mental composition' that succeeds to the degree that 'the image seem[s] to come into being by an agency not one's own'.[40] In Shakespeare's drama, this co-imaginative process is something of a hallmark, made famous by

Henry V's Prologue ('let us . . . / On your imaginary forces work' (Prologue 17–18)) and by Theseus's lines before the mechanicals' play within *A Midsummer Night's Dream* ('The best in this kind are but shadows / And the worst no worse if your imagination amend them').[41] What William-Henry's tale adds to this operation is his demonstration of the shaping force it exerts upon the search for Shakespeare, inasmuch as the ambient promise of miraculous preservation that attaches to the author of *The Comedy of Errors*, *The Merchant of Venice*, *Twelfth Night*, *Cymbeline*, *Pericles* and *The Tempest* (to name only the most obvious of the plays in which apparently irrecuperable losses are restored) is given its means of fulfilment in this command to jointly conjure forth what cannot otherwise be shown. The mental composition that Shakespeare orchestrates – or rather, the manner of collaborative composing that he explicitly spells out – is thus a historiographic fantasy that can be taken as posthumous instructions for his own fashioning: an instigation to produce what is not really in existence by reaching into the void and reclaiming him from disappearance.

The protocols of this collaboration are most memorably set out in *Richard III*, a play that might be said to take the past's miraculous indissolubility as its motoring philosophy. Its first fearful explicator is the Duke of Clarence, who recounts as a nightmare from which he cannot awaken his descent to the 'slimy bottom of the deep', where he sees spread before him things that were seemingly lost for good:

> Methought I saw a thousand fearful wrecks;
> Ten thousand men that fishes gnaw'd upon;
> Wedges of gold, great anchors, heaps of pearl,

---

37 Boaden, *A Letter to George Steevens*, fn 4–5.

38 G. Wilson Knight, *The Crown of Life* (Oxford, 1947), p. 121.

39 William Shakespeare, *The Tempest*, ed. Alden T. Vaughan and Virginia Mason Vaughan (London, 2011).

40 Elaine Scarry, *Dreaming by the Book* (Princeton, 1999), p. 224.

41 William Shakespeare, *King Henry V*, ed. T. W. Craik, Arden Shakespeare (London; New York, 1995); William Shakespeare, *A Midsummer Night's Dream*, ed. Harold Fletcher Brooks, Arden Shakespeare (London, 1979).

Inestimable stones, unvalued jewels,
All scatter'd in the bottom of the sea . . . (1.4.24–8)

The guilty Clarence shrinks from this undissolved bounty, recognizing it as a sign of the reckoning to come ('Ah keeper, keeper, I have done these things, / That now give evidence against my soul' (1.4.66–7)). Prince Edward, on the other hand, advocates for the same vision of a past that endures independent of human efforts to save or lose it:

Methinks the truth should live from age to age,
As 'twere retail'd to all posterity,
· Even to the general all-ending day. (3.1.76–8)

It is apt, of course, that Edward should speak for a history that is 'not register'd' (3.1.75), and passes from age to age untouched by the warp or slant of a written 'record' (3.1.72). As the prince whose terrible fate is undocumented yet everywhere known, he is a powerful representative of a past that will not stay 'buried' in either 'the deep bosom of the ocean' or an unmarked grave (1.1.4). But especially salient to a discussion of Ireland's collaborative practice is the widespread remediation of this characterization, for once scripted by Shakespeare as a critic of authorized history, Edward becomes a personage whose fate is undocumented yet relentlessly *shown*. A remarkable array of paintings, Romantic to pre-Raphaelite, as well as an *animé* series, a *Doctor Who* spin-off, an episode of *The White Queen*, a scene in Madame Tussaud's waxworks and a Universal horror film starring Boris Karloff, Basil Rathbone and Vincent Price, depict the captivity or murder of the prince and his younger brother.[42] From this rich and unstinting visualization, it seems fair to conclude that the effect of Shakespeare's dramatizing facts unknown ('The chaplain of the Tower hath buried them; / But how or in what place I do not know' (4.3.29–30)), after questioning the value of the historical record in the first place, is to invite the audience or readership to fill in history's blanks, and what is more, to view such fillings-in as faithful renderings of a past that descends from age to age uncontaminated by authorized practices of record-keeping. The Princes in the Tower – a

Shakespearian scene that Shakespeare never dramatizes – is thus a particularly vivid demonstration of the *fort-da* of his historiographic process, in which the mind leaps from the impossibility of recovering hard facts (e.g.: 'may we cram / Within this Wooden O the very casques / That did affright the air at Agincourt?' (Prologue, 14)) to the necessity of imagining then (e.g.: 'Piece out our imperfections with your thoughts' (23)).

By this light, Ireland's *Miscellaneous Papers* are twice indexical of the creative anachronism authorized by a dramatist who in dramatic content and dramaturgical practice insists upon the transience of loss. First, by showing again and again that from evanescence must follow recrudescence, Shakespeare conditions the lack of his own remains to be read as the cue to 'piece out' a past that official repositories could not or would not contain – hence the profusion of 'title deeds, . . . letters of royal and noble personages, signatures and writings', etc., that Ireland 'recovers' from his imaginary oaken chest.[43] And second, by couching this philosophy in the conceit of undrowning, Shakespeare makes the hypostasizing of this absent matter an act of preservation. Ireland's fable is therefore also legible as the consummation of a distinctly Shakespearian wish: that the dark backward and abysm of time should yield up its gains as readily as the sea returns Antonio's argosies, or Viola's brother, or Pericles's wife, or the 'inestimable stones' and 'unvalued jewels' of Clarence's dream.

The aptness of Ireland's forgeries to evidence such a claim does not end with the *Miscellaneous Papers*, however. It is the story of their inspiration in Stratford and its environs that shows the force of Shakespeare's historiographic fantasy more generally applied, for it is not just William-Henry who

---

[42] The major paintings are by James Northcoate (1786); Paul Delaroche (1830); Charles Robert Leslie (1837); Henrietta Mary Ward (1861); John Everett Millais (1878); 'The Princes in the Tower' is episode 9 of season 1 of *The White Queen*, April 2006; *Tower of London*, dir. Rowland V. Lee (Universal Pictures, 1939).

[43] This list comes from Chalmers's *Apology*, p. 10.

exhibits signs of diminished agency in his quest 'to produce what really was not in existence'. Samuel Ireland's fruitless search of the places Shakespeare once occupied is no less illustrative of the fact that the archive *qua* repository is not a neutral concept in the field of Shakespeare studies, but instead a 'scriptive thing', a term Robin Bernstein reserves for objects that 'assert themselves in the field of matter' by activating some telling, because not wholly voluntary, action or response.[44] Bernstein makes a distinction between the routine or citational behaviours provoked by objects – for example, the opening of a book, the turning of its pages – and the conditions under which the scriptive thing triggers the 'kinesthetic imagination', Joseph Roach's phrase for 'thinking through movements . . . the otherwise unthinkable, just as a dance is often said to be a way of expressing the unspeakable'.[45] By way of example, Bernstein takes as her insurgent thing a knife that cuts the finger of its user, catching her or him in 'a dance of pain that is stylized through its citation of gender, class, age, race, and other categories of analysis'.[46]

The force of this notion in Shakespearian precincts is illustrated by the fact that Samuel Ireland's response to Clopton House's empty basket is just such a dance: a histrionic stylization of the pain of Shakespeare's inexorable loss, and a citation that verges on parody of the apposite response to this recognition from an English gentleman of taste and learning. Yet its value in this case is not 'as a heuristic tool for dealing with incomplete evidence', but rather as a tool for excavating the encounter with the impossibility of recovering anything like an evidential or complete record when it comes to Shakespeare.[47] That is, whereas Bernstein employs the scriptive thing to find 'historically located meanings' in the minefield of America's racial history, where information is often 'unstable and inconsistent, unspoken or unspeakable', the empty archive in Shakespeare studies is an implacable constant, to the extent that the revelation of this lack constitutes what could be described as the discipline's primal scene.[48] Particularly across the tortured history of Shakespearian biography, 'dealing with incomplete evidence', or finding a

way of not dealing with it, is a command performance: every searched repository foists upon the searcher the unwelcome *anagnorisis* that 'historically located meanings' will not be found.

For all its histrionics, then, the scene Ireland's father makes during his Warwickshire peregrinations is a dance that is broadly shared by all those who search out 'Some Account of the Life, etc. of William Shakespeare', as Nicholas Rowe first put it. This 'path of movement' from high-blown anguish to the compensatory purchase of Sharp's carved goblet and the Clopton House chair describes what I want to call the *mise-en-boîte* of Shakespeare's memorialization, a sort of pilgrim's progress from the recognition that the archive is bare to the investment in receptacular objects, from thimbles to trunks, that circumscribe, in sundry more or less hallowed woods, mulberry to Herne's oak, the lack of Shakespeare's remains.[49] As a 'thinking through' of the outrage of Shakespeare's irretrievability, this practice has the advantage of producing an interiority of sorts, for even as it recapitulates the lack of Shakespearian matter, it holds open a space in which to imagine furnishing that absence.

Thus exampled, as the impulse both whetted and slaked by the wily watchmaker-*cum*-heritage industry entrepreneur Thomas Sharp, the *mise-en-boîte* is bound to seem a late eighteenth-century phenomenon – a lingering effect of the Jubilee's

---

44 Robin Bernstein, 'Dances with Things: Material Culture and the Performance of Race', *Social Text*, 101 (2009), 67–94.

45 Roach, *Cities of the Dead*, p. 27, cited in Bernstein, 'Dances with Things', p. 70.

46 Bernstein, pp. 69–70.

47 Bernstein, p. 76.

48 Bernstein, p. 68.

49 The household stuffs produced from Shakespeare's trees are itemized in the seller's cry in David Garrick's play *The Jubilee*: 'Toothpick cases, needle cases, punch ladles, tobacco stoppers, inkstands, nutmeg graters, and all sorts of boxes made out of the famous Mulberry Tree', *The Plays of David Garrick*, ed. Harry William Pedicord and Fredrick Louis Bergmann, 7 vols. (Carbondale, 1980–82), vol. 2, p. 111, quoted in Jack Lynch, 'All Shall Yield to the Mulberry Tree', *Lumen*, 29 (2010), p. 28.

Cassolette made from Shakspeare's Mulberry Tree.

4. Robert Bremmel Schnebbelie, 'Cassolette made from Shakespeare's Mulberry Tree'.

distinctive practice of relic-seeking bardolatry. It is worth pointing out that this periodization is not strictly true; the *realia* classified under the Folger call number 'Wood' (some thirty-two items) range in date from 1700 to 1898, even if the mulberry phenomenon remains, as Jack Lynch writes, a 'current' that animates 'eighteenth century British intellectual life'[50] (see illustration 4). But what is more, the dance of pain that evinces from Sharp's genre of artifact is merely the most explicit expression of the drive to encase the poet's missing form. Later moments yield up variations on its theme.

For instance, in the nineteenth century, when the residence was reconceived, as Walter Benjamin writes, into 'a receptacle for the person' who dwelt within it, Shakespeare's (alleged) birthplace becomes the first among England's literary houses to be held in trust for the edification of a nation desperately seeking its most famous literary resident (see illustration 5).[51] Though picked clean of

---

50 Lynch, 'All Shall Yield', p. 22.
51 Walter Benjamin, *The Arcades Project*, trans. Howard Eiland and Kevin McLaughlin (Cambridge, MA, 1990), p. 220,

5. Henry Wallis, *The Room in Which Shakespeare Was Born*, 1853.

any Shakespearian traces decades earlier, this build-ing and its appurtenances were then furnished by curators who tapped into the period's *Sense of an Interior* to carve from its empty boxes of house-hold space 'theatres of composition', Diana Fuss's term for places that take and make the imprint of the 'intellectual labor' that happened there.[52] As it happens, among the props lately acquired to enhance this impression is the oak chair Samuel Ireland purchased at Clopton House, subsequently ornamented with the initials 'W. & A. S'.[53] The fake Shakespearian monogram (for 'William & Anne Shakespeare'), no less than the Shakespear-ian chair or the Shakespearian house, demonstrates the degree to which the preservation of the poet remains a process of carving him out of negative space.

In the twentieth century, the stage becomes the proper site for the management of this

impulse. The rebuilt Globe, and the many other Shakespeare theatres built in the image of its lost original, supply the material conditions with which to deduce the playwright's dramaturgical *habitus*. And yet, as the tourist industries in these sites prove, new Globes are containers for a broad spectrum of imagined Shakespearianism; stamped indelibly by the invitation to mental composition that *Henry V* orchestrates, subsequent wooden O's stand in for the authorization of supposition and surrogation within the girdle of their walls. When

quoted in Diana Fuss, *The Sense of an Interior* (New York and London, 2004), p. 9. On this genealogy see Lynch, 'All Shall Yield', pp. 29–30.

[52] Diana Fuss, *Sense of an Interior*, p. 1.

[53] An engrossing history of the migration of Ireland's chair to Ireland's study and back to Anne Hathaway's cottage can be found at http://findingshakespeare.co.uk/224, the blog hosted by the curators of the Shakespeare Birthplace Trust.

6. Photograph of the Malek-Lansing model of Shakespeare's Globe Theatre in the Brander Matthews Dramatic Museum, Columbia University.

shrunk, this characteristic is more pronounced; the models of the Globe that crop up in advance of its Bankside reconstruction invite the daydream that Susan Stewart finds to be the miniature's chief characteristic: that it will 'open itself to reveal a secret life'.[54] The effect is partly a matter of perspective: by affording the user a 'transcendent viewpoint' of a lost world, the model stage promises to unfold a scene not unlike the dream of recovered loss revealed to Clarence, in which 'narrativity and history' can unfold 'outside the given field of perception'.[55] Perhaps as a result, its appeal is wide-ranging, from theatre historians like Brander Matthews, who has a sumptuous specimen built in 1911 for Columbia University's Dramatic Museum (see illustration 6), to the amateur 'fellow-student of Shakespeare' to whom one Edward Alleyn Loomis markets the first 'generally available' blueprints for a do–it–yourself

Globe in 1948, devised to illuminate 'points missed by the "Absent Minded Professor"'.[56]

---

[54] Susan Stewart, *On Longing: Narratives of the Miniature, the Gigantic, the Souvenir, the Collection* (Durham, NC, 1993), p. 54.

[55] Stewart, *On Longing*, p. 54.

[56] Matthews's model, built under a London architect's direction, was profiled at the time of its completion in the *New York Times*, 30 July 1911, p. 9. Neither it nor its second iteration (depicted above) survive. The quotations from Loomis come from promotional writings and a typewritten letter enclosure for Loomis Laboratory, 'Blueprints for making a model of Shakespeare's Globe Theatre', Cambridge, MA, 1952, collection of the Folger Shakespeare Library, Sh. Misc. 1811. Models of the Globe continue to be published; Roger Puttenden's card-stock version, produced to coincide with the opening of the New Globe in 1997, is said by its creator to have sold 65,000 copies in its first year of issuance; see www.papermodelkiosk.com/php/forum/entry.php/99-From-Shakespeare-s-Globe-to-Sir-Christopher-Wren-s-St-Paul-%97-Heritage-Models-Roger-Pattenden.

Necessarily, there are iterations of the *mise-en-boîte* that undermine my loose chronology. One beguiling example is 'Miss Clara Fisher's Shakespearean Cabinet', a woodworked wonder in which twenty sites from the life and afterlife of the poet, including the birthplace, the Grammar School (enclosing 'Shakespeare's writing desk'), the 'Remains of the Church Where Shakespeare and Anne Hathaway Were Married' ('now a blacksmith's shop'), 'Shakespeare's Crab Tree', the Fortune, the Globe and the Jubilee Rotunda, are carved in miniature.[57] Completed by 1830 for the child actress from whom it takes its name, Fisher's cabinet is a perfect composite of the receptacular object, the domestic interior, and the wooden O, and is thus a useful reminder of the persistence and polymorphism of *emboîtement* across the long history of the search for Shakespeare. A partial inventory of its recurring objects would include rooms and buildings which the poet once inhabited, trees he may have planted or perched in, furnishings that he might have sat on, rambles that he could have taken, gardens that he must have loved, and the grave that contains his imperturbable remains, each of which encloses a site from which the poet has poignantly and irretrievably vanished.[58] In the place of an archive there thus emerges a collection of spaces, represented and real, in which to project Shakespeare's missing impression.

It will seem that William-Henry Ireland's forgeries supply an alternative to this phantasmatic practice, not least because Ireland as much as says so: dismissive of chairs and goblets, he shows an unrivalled zeal for producing impressional remains, beginning with the quintain seal and encompassing an astonishing array of manuscriptural and artifactual 'evidence'. Generously construed, these are repudiations in young Prince Edward's spirit to the problem of paucity, negligence and disappearance that dogs the Shakespearian archive. The gesture was short-lived, however, since as 'miscellaneous papers and legal instruments under the hand and seal of William Shakespeare', Ireland's fabrications did not persuade for long. A mere eighteen months after William-Henry presented his father with the first mortgage-deed,

his discoveries were categorically debunked. It is therefore a surprising feature of the Ireland forgeries that they were not subsequently discarded. Quite the reverse, in fact. William-Henry Ireland's papers have gone on to become some of the more fetching manuscript holdings of some of the most venerable literary repositories in the English-speaking world, among them, the British Library, the Bodleian Library, the Folger Shakespeare Library, the Huntington Library, The Boston Public Library, Harvard University's Houghton Library, The University of Birmingham Library, The University of Iowa Library, the New York Public Library, The Lilly Library of Indiana University, the University of Edinburgh Library, the Princeton University Library and the Library of University College, London.

The reason for this ubiquity owes to the fact that the discovery of their fraudulence did not mark the end of Ireland's Shakespearian performances. As early as 1797, and with the aid of his sisters, Anna Maria and Jane Ireland, William-Henry refabricated his manuscripts and assembled them in annotated scrapbooks, usually interleaved with selections from the *Miscellaneous Papers* and/or the published *Confessions*. So persuasively do these albums convey the impression of singularity and collectability that until a year ago, when Arthur Freeman traced Samuel Ireland's papers to the

---

[57] These titles and descriptions are taken from a publication titled 'Clara Fisher's Remembrances of Shakspere' (London, but *c.*1830), including a detailed list, with engravings, of each item in her 'Shakespearean Cabinet'. I encountered this work interleaved in a dismembered, manuscript copy of Ireland's *Miscellaneous Papers* held by the Folger, W.b.497.

[58] For an account of the Shakespearian ramble, see Nicola Watson's 'Shakespeare on the Tourist Trail', in *Shakespeare and Popular Culture*, ed. Robert Shaughnessy (Cambridge, 2007), pp. 199–226. On the Shakespeare Garden (in general and as exemplified by the one planted at the Birthplace in 1920), see Esther Singleton, *The Shakespeare Garden* (New York, 1922). On the tantalizing prospect of recovering the true physiognomy of Shakespeare from his gravesite, see Clement Ingleby, *Shakespeare's Bones: A Proposal to Disinter Them* (London, 1883).

Hyde collection, now at the Houghton Library at Harvard, there was no way of knowing which was a forgery of a forgery of a recovered past, and which was the forgery itself.[59]

Such a circumstance must in itself put to question the orienting values of priority, originality and authenticity within the Shakespearian archive. The effect is much enhanced, though, by the painstaking, hand-crafted construction of the albums of Miscellaneous Papers that Ireland prepared for the collector's market.[60] On the one hand, this fastidious presentation of nugatory contents – these are, after all, belated copies of defrocked 'originals' – is disarmingly charming: like a really earnest middle school student, Ireland dresses up his ersatz evidences in all the finery he can muster, as if he believed that the importance of his 'finds' rested on the fanciness of their presentation. On the other, the surprising cuteness of these albums reflects the financial exigencies that Ireland faced: the careful staging of each artifact, like each custom-carved niche in Fisher's Shakespearian Cabinet, conveys the necessity of collecting whatever it circumscribes. But regardless of the spirit in which it was fostered, the resulting attachment to Ireland's proliferating Papers, made explicit in the grip they maintain on special collections around the world, foments a crisis of factuality within the Shakespeare archive.[61]

In the classic sense, the effect is surreal. Like one of Marcel Duchamp's 'Boîtes-en-Valise', a William-Henry Ireland compendium of 'Original Forgeries' amounts to a provocation to consider the curatorial fantasy it performs, for Ireland's albums, like Duchamp's miniaturized and self-curated exhibits, turn inside-out the relation of a collection's contents to the custodial actions of collecting and putting on display.[62] Illustrative of this inversion is Ireland's practice of announcing each category of specious evidence on its own page, the title hand-written within an ornate, *découpage* device, so that the aesthetic highlight of each scrapbook is its performance of the institutional protocols of heritage culture, in the form of the framing and naming of its tendered relics (see illustrations 7(a) and (b)). The result is that the

signs of meticulous curation are rendered startlingly prominent, while the curatorial object – Shakespeare's manuscriptural archive – is, by the compiler's frank admission, nowhere to be found.

One way to describe the afterlife of the Ireland hoax is therefore as a museology of Shakespearian absence. The status of the forgeries as non-evidence and, more specifically, as exemplifications of what the poet did not leave behind has the effect of rendering the scrapbooks collections of the fantasy of a Shakespearian collection: they provide the means to enact Shakespearian historiography, irrespective of the lack of actual facts. The invitation to performance can be surprisingly overt; for instance, in several of Ireland's albums, the reader is not only shown examples of the Elizbethan-era paper that Ireland used, he or she is directly instructed to verify their marks: 'By holding this leaf up to the light the Jug Water Mark prevalent in the reign of Elizabeth will be perceptible'.[63] And yet, as the Ireland hoax famously demonstrated, a watermark

---

59 Arthur Freeman, 'The Actual Originals: William Henry Ireland's "Authentic Forgeries" Rediscovered', *Times Literary Supplement*, no. 5716 (2012), 14.

60 The date is ventured by Freeman, 'Actual Originals', p. 15.

61 Ruth Rosengarten, 'Between Memory and Document', Sem Titulo 6 (Museo Coleçâu Bernardo), unpaginated. For an account of the relation of Duchamp's series to the domestic interior, see T. J. Demos, 'Duchamp's Boîte-en-Valise: Between Institutional Acculturation and Geopolitical Displacement', *Grey Room*, 8 (Summer 2002), 14.

62 The confusion caused to owners and cataloguers is considerable. The Folger Library's extensive collection of Ireland forgeries includes a bound 1805 manuscript with the title 'S. Ireland's Original Forgeries' impressed on its spine (call number S.b.118). In pencil in a nineteenth-century hand is the following note: '*A companion volume to this is in the collection of R. M. Milnes, esq & M. P. It contains several exact duplicates of these forgeries.*' Another bound scrapbook in the Folger collection is titled 'Original Manuscripts of W. H. Ireland' (call number W.b.497).

63 This instruction is found in the Lilly Library *Collection of the Ireland Fabrications* at Indiana University (call number NLC 1542, 1805). Another in a similar vein can be found in the Folger ms. S.b.118, an especially lush album assembled and gifted to Mrs Ireland in 1805: 'By holding this leaf against the light, three several jug watermarks will become apparent to the observer.'

7(a). Title Page for the 'Signature of Michael Fraser & Quintin Seal' in *A Collection of the Ireland Fabrications*, 1805.

7(b). Title-page for the 'Deed Between Shakespeare & Fraser with the Quintin Seal'.

proves nothing; the observer who holds the leaf against the light can only rehearse the recognition of Chalmers and his cohort that the application of historical expertise – at least, as it relates to the manufacture of sixteenth-century paper – has nothing to say about the authenticity of the object scrutinized. The peculiar naiveté of Ireland's reforged forgeries owes partly to the expectation that readers will go through the motions anyway, performing their verificationism in the absence of any matter to fact-check. And the peculiar canniness that also evinces from them owes to the fact that Ireland was right, for it so happens that in the fifth volume of the Hyde Collection of Irelandiana there is a list in a nineteenth-century hand describing every watermark in the enclosed copy of the manuscript 'Kynge Lear'.[64] As evidence of the use of Ireland's collections of non-evidence, this is admittedly anecdotal, though I can add to it my own surrender to the charismatic interactivity of Ireland's scrapbooks. Still, I put it forward as an uncommonly legible trace of the scriptive force of Shakespeare's missing archive. From its inventory of facts untethered to any informational purpose, this kinesthetic response to Ireland's papers demonstrates the incitement to *act historical* that emanates from the lack of the poet's remains.

It is an open secret that Shakespearian scholarship is littered with examples of this sort of performance. An early case in point is Lewis Theobald, whose zealous prosecution of a *Shakespeare Restored* from (Pope's) unresearched editorial speculation culminates in his 'discovery' of the manuscript – in the end, three or four manuscripts – of the lost play *Cardenio*. Revised by its finder to suit contemporary tastes, the play was performed in December of 1727 and published the following year, yet it is mysteriously absent from Theobald's 1733 edition of Shakespeare's *Works*, and its original specimens, though hailed as treasures 'dug from the Rubbish by an excellent *Connoisseur*', are in turn mysteriously absent from Theobald's estate; as Tiffany Stern drily observes, 'the manuscripts do not have a post-Theobald history', but instead disappear into the same trash-heap from which they were once supposedly rescued.[65]

A figure equally problematic but differently entailed by the performance of history is James Orchard Halliwell-Phillipps, another gentleman scholar and indefatigable Shakespearian best known for his *Outlines of the Life of Shakespeare* (1881). Like Theobald, Halliwell-Phillipps is guided by the philosophy that any 'attempt' to recover Shakespeare should emerge 'strictly out of evidences and deductions from those evidences', 'scanty' as they are.[66] Yet this rigorous historicism, applied to a figure so poorly preserved, seems to have incited in him an urge to curate the whole of the literary atmosphere in which Shakespeare lived.[67] Halliwell-Phillipps's collections, now held at the Folger, comprise 56 scrapbooks and 43 'scrapboxes' of evidences clipped from a vast array of printed sources, including more than 800 books published before 1701.[68] This profligate scissoring

---

[64] This sheet is found at the front of Houghton MS. 2003JM-150, before the first page. For another account of the perplexed acts of authentication solicited by the Ireland forgeries, see Adam G. Hooks, 'Faking Shakespeare (Part 3): Authentic Shakespeare, Authentic Ireland' at www.adamghooks.net/2011/11/faking-shakespeare-part-3-authentic.html. Hooks describes the punctilious annotations in the Iowa volume of forged forgeries to argue that 'there may be no better demonstration of the depth and significance of our investment in Shakespeare – and indeed in the concepts of authorship and authenticity – than this authentic fake'.

[65] The description is taken from an advertisement for the play by an anonymous 'lover of Shakespeare' ('Philo-Shakespear') whom Tiffany Stern identifies as probably 'Theobald himself'. Philo-Shakespear, *Mist's Weekly Journal* (London), 2 December 1727, quoted in Tiffany Stern, '"The Forgery of Some Modern Author?": Theobald's Shakespeare and Cardenio's *Double Falsehood*', *Shakespeare Quarterly*, 62:4 (2011), pp. 560, 561.

[66] James Orchard Halliwell-Phillipps, *Outlines of the Life of Shakespeare* (Brighton, 1880), pp. xiii, vii.

[67] As Halliwell-Phillipps concedes, 'in the absence of some very important discovery, the general and intense desire to penetrate the mystery which surrounds the personal history of Shakespeare cannot be wholly gratified', *Outlines*, p. vi.

[68] These statistics are taken from an unpublished paper by Peter Blayney delivered at the Shakespeare Association of America Conference in 1995, cited in Alan Somerset, 'James Orchard Halliwell-Phillipps: The Life and Works of the Shakespearean Scholar and Bookman (review)', *Shakespeare Quarterly*, 54:2 (2003), p. 225.

of rare and unique old works suggests a kind of mania; indexing them in the service of the REED project, Alan Somerset describes the scrapbooks as the products of a curatorial frenzy: 'one's impression is that everything in Halliwell-Phillipps's possession on the subject is here, no matter how ephemeral, how lunatic, how repetitious'.[69]

Finally, there is the notorious example John Payne Collier, whose penchant for 'literary cookery' reached its peak with the Perkins Folio, a 'corrected' version in a seventeenth-century hand of the 1632 issue of Shakespeare's complete plays, and the authority for two editions of the *Works* he brought out in 1853 and 1858.[70] The marginalia Collier discovered were eventually proved to be his own creation, and subsequently the innumerable manuscript and print archives that he handled as a leading antiquarian and Shakespearian of his day were discovered to be larded with false emendations, additions, attributions and provenances. All who follow in Collier's wake therefore labour under G. F. Warner's admonition, from his 1887 *DNB* entry: 'None of his statements or quotations can be trusted without verifying, and no volume or document that has passed through his hands . . . can be too carefully scrutinised.'[71] Among the works cast in doubt by Collier's distortive and inventive tendencies is Simon Forman's 'Bocke of Plaies' (1611), the only surviving account of Shakespeare in performance during his lifetime, uncovered during the cataloguing of Ashmolean manuscripts in 1832 and published by Collier from a transcript in 1836. Although the consensus of scholars is now for the Bocke's authenticity, Forman's testimony cannot escape the taint of its discoverer, perhaps not least because the rescue of this lost manuscript, written by an 'astrologer-cum-wizard' said to have died by drowning in the Thames, recapitulates too neatly the Shakespearian fantasy of mystical, ahistorical preservation.[72]

In rounding up these twilight figures, each of whom gives over his career and (to varying degrees, at varying moments) his reputation to the search for Shakespearian evidence, I have sought to show the contours of a compositional practice that doubles as an impossible recuperation of historical loss.

It may seem like blaming the victim to assert that Shakespeare is the enabling partner in such a practice. But if his dramaturgy of undrowning does not extenuate forgery and bibliocide, it can offer a script with which to think about the scriptivity of his absent remains – specifically, the oscillation between adumbrating the author's lack and auditioning stand-ins to fill it that happens in Shakespeare's name, under circumstances that suggest diminished or compromised volition. The participation in this movement, moreover, is surprisingly pervasive. Though Ireland's, Halliwell-Phillips's, Collier's and (less certainly) Theobald's historiographic practices are deemed so far from correct as to be pathological – as Schoenbaum remonstrates, 'What obscure object of desire tempted Collier down the devious path that led to his undoing?' – it turns out to be quite difficult to see where deviation ends and disciplinary normalcy begins.[73]

Among the evidence one could take for this claim is the Courting Chair – the object of William-Henry's derision, now restored to Anne Hathaway's cottage by the Shakespeare Birthplace Trust – or *The Double Falsehood*, scorned by Pope in the *Dunciad*, now published under the aegis of

---

[69] J. A. B. Somerset, 'James Orchard Halliwell-Phillipps and his Scrapbooks', *Records of Early English Drama Newsletter*, 2 (1979), 12.

[70] 'Literary Cookery' is the title of A. E. Brae's anonymously published pamphlet attacking Collier for his forgeries in 1855.

[71] G. F. Warner, 'Collier, John Payne', *Oxford Dictionary of National Biography* (Oxford, 2004), www.oxforddnb.com/view/article/5920, accessed 3 Nov 2013, cited in R. A. Foakes, *Coleridge on Shakespeare: The Text of the Lectures of 1811–12* (2013), p. 4; Jeffrey Kahan, 'The Enigma of J.P. Collier', *Literary Imagination*, 7:2 (2005), p. 263.

[72] Barbara A. Mowat, 'Prospero's Book', *Shakespeare Quarterly*, 52:1 (2001), p. 25. On Forman's rumoured drowning, in fulfilment of his own prophecy no less, see James Walter, *Shakespeare's True Life* (Longmans, Green, 1890), p. 365: 'according to some, he expired suddenly in a boat whilst crossing the river; others averred that he was drowned; but so great was the dread of increasing necromancy, that the drowning was denied'.

[73] Schoenbaum, *Records and Images*, p. 153.

the Arden Shakespeare series. Like Ireland's forgeries, these recovered Shakespearian objects have circulated promiscuously across the categorical division of artifice from artifact and, like Ireland's forgeries, they therefore burden us with a certain embarrassment, not least because, some two hundred and twenty years after Capell pronounced him 'irrecoverably lost', they show us still enthralled to the idea of attempting Shakespeare's rescue. Like Ireland's forgeries, they therefore bring out of the shadows the persistence of a hope largely extinguished from confessable scholarly practice but deeply imprinted in the kinesthetic register of Shakespeare studies, that from some overlooked repository the missing poet might appear, or be traced in silhouette by the careful curation of sites he could have (or should have) occupied. They show us, in other words, the continued impulse to act historical despite, or perhaps because of, the irrevocable condition of Shakespeare's archival paucity, forgery and loss.

To many, this impulse will sound like a contamination of the very grounds of history; in her seminal article on performance and reenactment, Vanessa Agnew describes historians who throw up their hands in despair at the 'eclipsing of the past' by the 'theatricality' of its emulators.[74] But what of a past that can only gain grounds by theatrical means? It is Shakespeare's ingenuity to show us that what we constellate around the longing for an absent presence can be as definitive of history as it is of performance. Perhaps, then, forgeries of Shakespeare, like the myriad boxes retrofitted for his spectral occupation, are best regarded not as specious evidence but as examples of the Shakespearian art of making the past. Brazen as they are, they shine light on posterity's collaboration with a poet who seldom granted time's dark abysm the final word.[75]

---

[74] Vanessa Agnew, 'Introduction: What is Reenactment?' *Criticism*, 46:3 (2004) p. 335, quoted in Rebecca Schneider, *Performing Remains: Art and War in Times of Theatrical Reenactment* (London and New York, 2011), p. 36.

[75] I allude to Stephen Greenblatt's list of abjurations that succeeds from his famous opening sentence in *Shakespearean Negotiations*, 'I began with a desire to speak with the dead' (Berkeley, 1988), pp. 12, 1.

RE-COGNIZING SHAKESPEARIAN TRAGEDY

ARTHUR F. KINNEY

Over half a century ago, Paul MacLean proposed a diagram of the brain's organization that was both evolutionary and topographical. It remains one of the simplest and clearest introductions to the brain largely unchanged by subsequent findings. At the base of the brain, formed earliest, is the brain stem that controls the body's basic metabolic functions such as heart-rate and breathing. It functions through primitive instinct and repetition. The layer above the brain stem is the limbic system, or ring-like peripheral region comprised of the amygdala, the hippocampus and the hypothalamus. This is the home of emotions and memory. The four primary emotions – love, fear, sadness and joy – are awakened here by incoming stimuli that are associated with past events stored in the hippocampus or amygdala. Atop both the brain stem and the limbic system is the neocortex, spread like a coating over the two halves of the brain's architecture. This is where long-term interests and long-term memory react with incoming neural impulses allowing us to 'think' – that is, to *combine* immediate actions with long-term interests, to develop abstract thoughts, and to think and speak in complex sentences. It is the neocortex that distinguishes the human species from other forms of life.

In the early 1960s, Stanley Schachter and Jerome Singer of Columbia University proposed that the cognitive part of the brain also gives definition and direction to the emotions in direct line with classical Galenic thought that was also predominant in the Renaissance. Today's continuing research in cognitive science and developmental psychology has taught us considerably more about emotions (or what the Renaissance called passions). Since emotions are activated automatically and often unconsciously along subcortical pathways by charged neurons connected by dendrites and axons, we know more physiologically than Galen or Vesalius in the sixteenth century, yet still can experience emotions without consciously reasoning why. Scientists have shown that such precognitive information can be continually processed, leading to emotional states that influence perception, cognition, annexation – the bases of seeing, hearing, thinking, judging, remembering, coping and even imagining. Such emotions are registered in two ways. They may arise as private data, such as feeling cold air or hearing loud noise. Or such conditions may arrive instead as higher-order cognitive awareness by the neocortex which assesses, evaluates and integrates the new information by determining an appropriate response – shutting the window, stopping the noise. Once emotion is activated, emotion and cognition influence each other. How people feel affects what they perceive, think, do and vice versa. 'We're not used to thinking of feelings as the source of our conscious decisions, but research leaves no doubt', according to Daniel Gardner in *The Science of Fear*.[1] The parietal cortex accumulates evidence and integrates it to

---

This article is a companion piece to my 'Re-cognizing Leontes', in *Shakespeare Survey* 63 (Cambridge, 2010), pp. 326–37.

[1] Daniel Gardner, *The Science of Fear* (London, 2009).

determine whether or not an emotion is desirable. Such neural signs can travel about 100 metres per second. Decisions often remain below the threshold of consciousness, however. Such observations were not voiced in the Renaissance but a similar study of bodily and mental health had its correspondent way of recording them following Galen's theory of humours. As Nancy Sirasi has confirmed, 'Humoral theory is probably the single most striking example of the habitual preference in ancient, medieval, and Renaissance medicine for materialist explanations of mental and emotional states.' It was of great use to Shakespeare.

Humoral theory can be traced back to Alcmaeon of Croton (a follower of Pythagoras), to Plato's *Laches* and to Cicero's *Tusculan Disputations* among others. In the Renaissance, Juan Luis Vives connected passions to the imagination or fantasy in his *De Anima et vita beata* of 1538, writing:

a mere commotion of our fantasy bearing some resemblance to an opinion or judgement that a given object is good or bad, is enough to disturb our soul with all emotions: we fear, rejoice, cry, feel sad. This is also why our emotions converge toward that part of the body where the fantasy prevails, and also why we will actually attribute bodily qualities to emotions and call them warm, cold, dry or a mixture of those. Internal and external causes can exacerbate and repress the influence of our bodily temperament. Among the internal causes we find emotions themselves: sadness makes us cold and dry, joy makes us warm and wet. Emotions both reflect and contribute to the temperament of the body.[2]

In England, the logician Thomas Wilson, in *The Rule of Reason* (1553; sig. D3v), and Ralph Lever, in *The Arte of Reason, Rightly Termed, Witcraft* (1573) enumerate the passions while Thomas Blundeville argues in *The Arte of Logick* (1617) that the chief passions or affections of the mind are joy, lust, sorrow, fear. Timothy Bright in his *Treatise on Melancholy* (1586) considers melancholy in detail, from the medieval perspective drawn from Vives to external conditions where emotions are seen as a way of apprehending the world. For Bright, the corruption and transformation of blood or yellow bile into black bile could overstimulate the passions, overturn reason, disturb cognitive functions and initiate

extreme states of fear and despair. Other works on humours that have come down to us include la Primaudaye's *The French Academy*, translated into English in 1586 by Thomas Bowes, and *Batman Vppon Bartholome* (1582), Sir John Davies's *Nosce Teipsum* (1599), John Davies of Hereford's *Microcosmos* (1603), Thomas Coffeteau's *Optick Glasse of Humours* and, most especially, Nicholas de Coffeteau's *A Table of Humane Passions*, translated by Edward Grimestone into English in 1624. Pictured on Walkington's title-page is a human heart above four standing women representing the four primary humours: Pleasure holding birds, Pain holding her aching tummy and head, Hope leaning on an emblematic anchor and Fear hugging herself in terror. According to Coffeteau, 'when the spirits which we call vital' are interrupted by these passions, 'the whole body feels itself moued, not only inwardly, but also outwardly', always displaying 'some visible trace'. Aroused passions cause sudden altercation, 'contrary to the laws of nature', that 'transports the heat beyond the bounds, which nature hath prescribed it, and doth agitate it extraordinarily'.

Early in the seventeenth century, in 1604, just as Shakespeare was writing his major tragedies, Thomas Wright proposed the necessary relationship between cognition – what we know – and emotion – what we feel – in the dedicatory epistle to the Earl of Southampton prefacing his popular book on *The Passions of the Minde in Generall*. 'Some Seauen yeares ago right Honorable', he tells Southampton,

I was requested by divers worthy gentlemen, to write briefly some pithie discourse about the passions of the minde; because (as they sayd) they were things ever in vse, and seldome without abuse: they were daily, yea and almost hourly felt no less craftie, then dangerous, much talkt of, and as yet never well taught. Their demaund seemed to me so reasonable, honest, profitable, and

---

[2] Quoted Debora Shuger, 'The "I" of the Beholder: Renaissance Mirrors and the Reflexive Mind', in *Renaissance Culture and the Everyday*, ed. Patricia Fumerton and Simon Hunt (Philadelphia, 1999), p. 33.

delightfull, as I deemed it discourtesie, and incivilitie, not to condescend to satisfie their sute.[3]

Early on and throughout his study, however, Wright is quick to employ the lexicon of the four humours derived from Galen:

Me thinkes the passions of our minde – (pleasure, pain, hope, and fear – are not vnlike the foure humours of our bodies, whereto Cicero well compares them [in the *Tusculan Disputations*] for if blood, flegme, black bile or yellow bile exceed the due proportion required to the constitution and health of our bodies, presently we fall into some disease even so, if the passions of the Minde be not moderated according to reason (and that temperature virtue requireth) immediately the soule is molested with some maladies. But if the humours be kept in a due proportion, they are preservatives of health, & perhaps, health it selfs. (17)

For Wright, passions arise in the mind as the humours that answer to the soul so that mental, physical and spiritual health are all irremediably related, an indivisible conjunction that lies at the centre of human nature and of Shakespearian tragedy in its own time. In another basic passage, Wright associates passions with perturbations or temporary troubles of the mind. In *Microcosmographia* (1618) Helkiah Crooke adds that these troubles are distributed from the brain, heart and liver by 'veines, arteries, and sinews [nerves]' (825).

Wright's work was enlarged and widely circulated and makes observations similar to those found in Robert Burton's *Anatomy of Melancholy* (1628). Burton's massive and continually expanding work also grows from his continual analysis of humours – 'liquid and fluent part[s] of the body, comprehended in it, for the preservation of it'[4] – hot, sweet temperate blood from the heart; cold and moist phlegm from the liver; hot and dry choler [or yellow bile] from the gall; and cold and dry, thick and sour black bile from the spleen. Physiologically, there were also spirits or 'most subtle vapour[s]' initiating in the liver, dispersed through the veins and responsible for natural actions; vital spirits brought up to the brain and then diffused through the nerves.

Wright's clear association of the emotions with the mind combines sensitive appetites with common sense, imagination and memory. He then joins the will to the sensitive appetite and joins the imagination and understanding. Moreover, the imagination acts as a mediator between the body and the mind. To sum up, cognitive science of the seventeenth century sees passion as elemental and universal and directly linked to the will and to the imagination, to activities of the mind. We have in Thomas Wright, then, a recipe for Renaissance drama which, we shall also discover, is very much like our current state of cognitive science.

II

There are numerous examples throughout Shakespeare's works in which his characters express their states of being through references to their humours as their expression of passion. The most prominent, Corporal Nim, thinks all his passions are humours.

I have an humour to knock you indifferently well. If you grow foul with me, Pistol, I will scour you with my rapier, as I may, in fair terms. If you would walk off, I would prick your guts a little, in good terms, as I may, and that's the humour of it . . . I will cut thy throat one time or other, in fair terms, that is the humour of it.

(*Henry V*, 2.1.48–63)[5]

His appearance in *The Merry Wives of Windsor* turns that Middletonian city comedy into a Jonsonian comedy of humours. 'I have operations which be humours of revenge', he tells Pistol (1.3.79); 'I will discuss of [Falstaff's] love to Ford' (1.3.82); 'My humour shall not cool' (1.3.89). Consistently choleric, Nim later tells Mistresses Ford and Page, 'I love not the humour. Of bread and

---

[3] Thomas Wright, *The Passions of the Minde in Generall* (1604), ed. Thomas O. Sloan (Urbana, 1971).

[4] Robert Burton, *The Anatomy of Melancholy*, ed. Floyd Dell and Paul Jordan-Smith (New York, 1938).

[5] My text for *Henry V* and all Shakespeare texts in this essay is *The Norton Shakespeare*, edited by Stephen Greenblatt, Walter Cohen, Jean E. Howard and Katharine Eisaman Maus, 2nd edn (New York, 2008).

cheese' (2.1.121); 'I like not the humour of lying' (2.1.114).

Bottom can be equally fierce. At the casting of the mechanicals' play in *A Midsummer Night's Dream*, he tells Quince, 'my chief humour is for a tyrant, I could play "erc'les rarely, a part to tear a cat in, to make all split' (1.2.21–23). Pistol is choleric. Bottom would follow suit. But the choleric humour is employed with more thought, more venom, and more purpose when Shylock defends his right to take Antonio's flesh:

> You'll ask me why I rather choose to have
> A weight of carrion flesh than to receive
> Three thousand ducats. I'll not answer that,
> But to say it is my humour. Is it answered?
> 　　　　　　(*The Merchant of Venice* 4.1.41–3)

Petruccio would cure a choleric Katherine with deprivation: 'I'll curb her rude and headstrong humour', he says to himself and then, to the audience, 'He that knows better how to tame a shrew, / Now let him speak. 'Tis charity to show' (*The Taming of the Shrew*, 4.1.190–1), while Antipholus of Syracuse would cure melancholy with the sanguinity of his Dromio (*The Comedy of Errors*, 1.2.20–1).

But fear is most often the common factor. Tamora makes much of this as Revenge.

> No vast obscurity or misty vale
> Where bloody murder or detested rape
> Can couch for fear, but I will find them out
> And in their ears tell them my dreadful name
> 　　　　　　(*Titus Andronicus*, 5.2.36–9)

There is the Bastard's premonition:

> I find the people strangely fantasied,
> Possessed with rumours, full of idle dreams,
> Not knowing what they fear, but full of fear.
> 　　　　　　(*King John*, 4.2.144–6)

In prison, Claudio finds a stalwart Isabella:

> Death is a fearful thing...
> Ay, but to die, and go we know not where;
> To lie in cold obstruction, and to rot.
> 　　　　　　(*Measure for Measure*, 3.1.116–19)

Fear becomes the significant force in Shakespeare's tragedies, too. Where Aristotle informed the Renaissance that tragic dramatic art resulted in catharsis – pain and fear in the audience beholding the play – Galen taught Shakespeare that the primal passion of fear alone lay at the heart of tragedy for the characters in the play.

III

The tragedy of Macbeth, for instance, erupts suddenly at 1.3.45 when, on their journey home, after Macbeth and Banquo have been unexpectedly confronted by three weird sisters, Macbeth addresses them: 'Speak if you can. What are you?' Two more surprises follow. The three sisters greet Macbeth with three titles, only one of which is rightfully his. Banquo is surprised even more. 'Good sir, why do you start and seem to fear / Things that do sound so fair?' (1.3 49–50). It takes the Thane of Glamis, normally at ease with words, time to find a response and when he does, he inquires for the source of 'this strange intelligence'. He asks, 'why / Upon this blasted heath you stop our way. / With such prophetic greeting?' (1.3.74–6). The key word here, which Banquo has already supplied for us, is fear.[6] According to Wright, 'Fear is a flight of probable euill imminent: wherefore two things must be proved & amplified to enforce fear: first, that the euill is great, secondly, that it is very likely to happen' (274). The display of fear that Banquo sees in Macbeth's face is also interior; the sisters pronounce circumstances which threaten him, not because of what he has publicly said or done, but because of what he has privately thought:

> This supernatural soliciting
> Cannot be ill, cannot be good. If ill,
> Why hath it given me earnest of success

---

6 'The effect of tragedy is fear or terror', in J. V. Cunningham, *Woe or Wonder: The Emotional Effect of Shakespearean Tragedy* (Denver, 1951, 1964), p. 56; cf. 'Fear, sorrow, and wonder are the emotions explicitly associated with tragedy not only in *Hamlet*, but generally in the tradition of literary criticism of Shakespeare's day' (p. 36).

Commencing in a truth? I am Thane of Cawdor.
If good, why do I yield to that suggestion
Whose horrid image doth unfix my hair
And make my seated heart knock at my ribs
Against the use of nature. Present fears
Are less than horrible imaginings.
My thought, whose murder yet is but fantastical,
Shakes so my single state of man that function
Is smothered in surmise, and nothing is
But what is not.   (1.3.129–41)

'Present fears' is an admission of what so deeply disturbs Macbeth. Wright goes on to remark that 'The vicinity also of the euill moueth much, for a far off danger we little esteeme, as subiect to sundry casualties and encounters: but when they are neere. And at the doore, then it is time to be stirring' (274). Already Macbeth is illustrating Wright's observation that fear will 'bring more Paine to the minde' because it is 'more danger-ous to the body' (61). Fear continues to distract Macbeth. When Duncan offers him a new title, his present fears deepen. 'Stars, hide your fires, / Let not light see my black and deep desires; / The eye wink at the hand; yet let that be / Which the eye fears, when it is done, to see' (1.4.50–3). On hearing the news of Macbeth's elevation, his wife has doubts grounded in Macbeth's fears. '"Thus thou must do" if thou have it, / And that which rather thou dost fear to do / Than wishest should be undone' (1.5.21–3). She addresses his fears by addressing their opportunity with the King as guest in their castle: 'To alter favour ever is to fear' (1.5.70). Still fear reigns in Macbeth's mind. He defends himself against her attacks: 'Prithee, peace. / I dare do all that may become a man; / who dares do more is none' (1.7.45–7). He questions possible consequences: 'If we should fail?' (1.7.59). He hallucinates sights: 'Is this a dagger which I see before me?' (2.1.33). He hears sounds: 'Hear not my steps which way they walk, for fear / The very stones prate of my whereabout' (2.1.57–8).

Such fear is contagious. Lady Macbeth cannot kill the King because he reminds her of her father; she did not kill the 'surfeited grooms' (2.2.5) but drugged their possets of mulled milk and wine. Macbeth fares little better. Fear prevents his saying

'Amen' when the grooms cry 'God bless us' (2.2.26–7); 'I am afraid to think what I have done' (2.2.49). Such fear is a major passion for Robert Burton, too. In *The Anatomy of Melancholy*, Burton notes that 'Many lamentable effects . . . Fear causeth in men, as to be ready, pale, tremble, sweat, it makes sudden cold and heat to come all over the body, palpitation of the heart, syncope, &c.', adding,

It amazeth many men that are to speak, or shew them-selves in publick assemblies, or before some great person-ages, as Tully confessed of himself, that he trembled still at the beginning of his speech . . . Many men are so amazed and astonished with fear, they know not where they are, what they do, and which is worst, it tortures them many days before continual frights and suspicions . . . They that live in fear are never free, resolute, never merry, but in emotional pain: that, as Vives truly said, no greater mis-ery, no rack, no torture like unto it ever suspicious, anxious, solicitous, they are childishly drooping without reason, without judgment.   (227)

Macbeth tells his wife:

We have scorched the snake, not killed it . . .
But let the frame of things disjoint, both the worlds
    suffer,
Ere we will eat our meal in fear, and sleep
In the affliction of these terrible dreams
That shake us nightly. Better be with the dead,
Whom we to gain our peace have sent to peace,
Than on the torture of the mind to lie
In restless ecstasy . . .
O, full of scorpions is my mind, dear wife!
                                           (3.2.15–37)

'Fear is certainly the most effective way of gluing memory in place', Daniel Gardner writes in his recent book:

Any emotional content makes a memory stick . . . Human fears are particularly apt to stick in our minds, at least if they're expressing emotions, because scientists have found such images stir the amygdala just as fright-ening images do. And these effects are cumulative. Thus, a visually striking, emotion-drenched image – particu-larly one involving a distraught person's face – is almost certain to cut through the whirl of sensations we expe-rience every moment, grab our attention, and burrow deep into our memories.   (49–50)

Fear is endemic in the play of *Macbeth*: the word and its cognates appear an unprecedented 42 times in this one play. Banquo confesses to Macduff that 'Fears and scruple shake us' (2.3.125) while Banquo remains, for Macbeth, the only living witness to the prophecy of the three sisters that may have started the whole chain of fatal events. This haunts Macbeth with his now 'fruitless crown' and 'barren scepter' (3.1.63). For Macbeth, to be unsafe is to fear nihilism.

> Our fears in Banquo
> Stick deep, and in his royalty of nature
> Reigns that which would be feared. 'Tis much he dares,
> And to that dauntless temper of his mind
> He hath a wisdom that doth guide his valour
> To act in safety. There is none but he
> Whose being I do fear, and under him
> My genius is rebuked . . .   (3.1.50–7)

Again, Burton is apposite. In his chapter on 'Fear, a Cause', he says that fear 'causeth oftentimes sudden madness' (227). Macbeth's hired men sent to slaughter Banquo and Fleance prepare for another ghastly vision borne of fear, as the chiding Lady Macbeth points out to her husband when the coronation banquet is suddenly arrested:

> O proper stuff!
> This is the very painting of your fear;
> This is the air-drawn dagger which you said
> Led you to Duncan. O, these flaws and starts,
> Impostors to true fear, would well become
> A woman's story at a winter's fire
> Authorized by her grandam. Shame itself,
> Why do you make such faces? When all's done
> You look but on a stool.   (3.4.59–67)

We can measure such terrible fear when Macbeth describes what the passions of his mind have brought forth:

> Blood hath been shed ere now, i'th' olden time,
> Ere human statute purged the gentle weal;
> Ay, and since, too, murders have been performed
> Too terrible for the ear. The time has been
> That, when the brains were out, the man would die,
> And there an end. But now they rise again
> With twenty mortal murders on their crowns,

> And push us from our stools. This is more strange
> Than such a murder is.   (3.4 74–82)

And he adds, 'when now I think you can behold such sights / And keep the natural ruby of your cheeks / When mine is blanched with fear' (3.4.113–15). Burton sees such cognitive moments as 'the most wonderful effects and power' of the imagination, of peculiar force, 'most especially . . . in melancholy persons, in keeping the species of objects so long, mistaking, amplifying them by continual & strong meditation, until at length it produceth in some parties real effects [that] causeth this and many other maladies. And although this fantasy of ours be a subordinate faculty to reason, and should be ruled by it, yet in many men, through inward or outward distemperatures, defect of organs, which are unapt or hindered, and hurt' (220). The most incendiary part of this scene of cognitive breakdown (but which has often gone unremarked by critics) is that, in their distracted fantasy, Macbeth and his wife ('This is the air-drawn dagger which you said / Led you to Duncan'; 'when the brains were out, then the man would die') publicly confess to their conspiracies with murder. The scene concludes with their startling ignorance.

Lady Macbeth. You lack the season of all natures, sleep.
Macbeth. Come, we'll to sleep. My strange and self-abuse
> Is the initiate fear that wants hard use
> We are yet but young in deed.   (3.4.140–4)

'Fear makes our imagination conceive what it list', Burton writes. 'Many men are troubled with future events, fore-knowledge of their fortunes, destinies' (228). The next time we see Macbeth he is alone, swiftly making his way to the weird sisters, now in a cave before a burning cauldron. With them he will 'conjure' (4.1.66), that is, conspire. He wants information; he wants control; he wants the total annihilation of the enemy beginning with the supposed next in line to elected succession, Macduff, Thane of Fife, and his family (4.1.166–9). Macbeth's steadfast fear counters Macduff's more southerly flight into England; 'do not fear. Scotland hath foisons to fill up our will / Of your mere own' (4.3.88–90).

The satisfying (and victorious) response to fear is fearlessness.

Steven Johnson's recent work on the mind and cognitive science helps point to the substance of Acts 4 and 5 of Shakespeare's play. He writes:

Perhaps the most important insight to come out of the growing understanding of our brain's chemistry is what researchers call 'mood incongruity', because the brain is an associative network [of neurons] and because our memories record not just specific details of events but also our feelings about them; when the brain is under the influence of emotion, it habitually makes connections to past events that triggered the same emotional response. When you're experiencing distress, your brain is more likely to recall stressful memories from your past than it is upbeat ones. When something frightens you, your mind is more likely to become filled with thoughts of other, apparently unrelated threats than it is of examples of feeling safe. This is the essence of mood congruity: your memory system tends to serve up recollections of past events that are themselves congruous with your current mood. (146–7)

Macbeth's second confrontation with the weird sisters is matched by their responses when his initial motive that produced fear, Duncan's assassination, is extended well into the present and future with the show of eight kings (ending, emblematically, with James I). Their serial predictions – 'beware Macduff'; 'none of woman born / Shall harm Macbeth'; 'Macbeth shall never vanquished be until / Great Birnam Wood to high Dunsinane Hill / Shall come against him' (4.1.87; 96–7; 108–10) – grow increasingly longer but only seemingly more remote. As Johnson writes more generally, 'Emotions affect the way we feel, but they also affect the way we remember' (201).

Departing the cave, Macbeth realizes there is no escape. Wherever he turns, he finds new fearful embodiments or their fearful absence. His castle is besieged. Macduff has disappeared. Malcolm is alive. His wife's mind is beyond treatment. His 'lily-livered boy' does not share his face 'over-red [with] fear' (5.3.15). Yet he will 'Hang those that talk of fear' (5.3.38); he will himself 'not be afraid of death and bane', at least until Birnam Wood actually moves (5.3.61–3). The greatest terror, perhaps,

is 'the cry of women' which Seyton identifies as the death of Lady Macbeth: 'I have almost forgot the taste of fears', Macbeth says (5.5.9), a statement of utter candour that is also a necessary lie. Macbeth's final words – 'Lay on, Macduff, / And damned be him that first cries 'Hold, enough!' (5.10.33–34) – form a last-ditch cry of despair. All the past deaths – of Duncan, the grooms, Banquo, Lady Macduff and her children, Lady Macbeth – give awful urgency to his final duel and predict its outcome. A great relief washes through the play with Macduff's victory, producing for the moment a world suddenly without fear. 'The time is free' (5.11.21), Malcolm tells us.

IV

This conceptual patterning in *Macbeth* – to interrupt events with a startling incident that will lead to uncertainty and fear before it is resolved in death – is both elemental in its construction and bare bones in its presentation. Fleshed out, it is a pattern which informs other Shakespearian tragedies. His first real experiment with this formulation came earlier with *Hamlet*, another play which illustrates Wright's fundamental contention that 'feare and heaviness, no doubt are passions of the minde' (15). For *Hamlet*, it is introduced with the appearance of the ghost of King Hamlet on the battlements of Elsinore Castle where guards are protecting Denmark against the anticipated invasion of Fortinbras. Although the Prince willingly follows the Ghost to understand the cause of his appearance, Hamlet's fear is nonetheless manifest.

> What may this mean,
> That thou, dead corpse, again in complete steel,
> Revisitst thus the glimpses of the moon,
> Making night hideous, and we fools of nature
> So horridly to shake our disposition
> With thoughts beyond the reaches of our souls?
>   (1.4.32–7)

'He waxes desperate with imagination', Horatio observes (1.4.64). But he is wrong. It is not his imagination; we now know that the vibrant emotions of the neocortex may ally themselves with suspicions of the amygdala, and his thoughts are at once fearful but also resolute:

> from the table of my memory
> I'll wipe away all trivial fond records,
> All saws of books, all forms, all pressures past,
> That youth and observation copied there,
> And thy commandment all alone shall live
> Within the book and volume of my brain
>
> (1.5.98–103)

Robert Burton, in The *Anatomy of Melancholy*, tells us how Shakespeare's first audiences might have interpreted Hamlet's reaction: 'Thus in brief, to our imagination cometh, by the outward sense of memory, some object to be known [residing in the foremost part of the brain]' (219). Hamlet's fear and bewilderment over his father's death are transformed and empowered by a new purpose, by renewed energy. 'Now to my word', he says, 'It is "Adieu, adieu [Good-bye; to God], remember me"./ I have sworn 't' (1.5.111–13). Such quickened resolution temporarily tackles a number of fears – the fear of his uncle's involvement with his father's death; the fear at the Ghost's appearance; the fear of the command to kill; the fear of failing his father; the fears of being less than a man, less than a son.

Hamlet's vow at first is instant and absolute, but the philosophy student from Wittenberg, his mind always formulating, has second thoughts. The Ghost may be a trick, an agent of the devil, which misinforms his mind and heart. The greater tumult of his anxiety, apprehension and fear are partly put aside by reflection, by the entertainment of plural possibilities. Still the Ghost's apparent suffering remains a heavy burden and Hamlet is overcome with suspicion and obsessed with death, not unlike Macbeth meeting with the weird sisters. Hamlet's thoughts move away from revenge against Claudius to centre in himself, on his own life and death.

> To be or not to be; that is the question:
> Whether 'tis nobler in the mind to suffer
> The slings and arrows of outrageous fortune,
> And, by opposing, end them. (3.1.58–62)

The source of all grievances – the Ghost's reported death by his brother's hand while sleeping – grows into pervasive perturbations concluding in thoughts of suicide.

> To die, to sleep,
> To sleep, perchance to dream. Ay, there's the rub,
> For in that sleep of death what dreams may come
> When we have shuffled off this mortal coil
> Must give us pause. (3.1.66–70)

The heart, mind and imagination of Wright and Burton – the neocortex, thalamus and amygdala of Johnson and Gardner – join forces to disclose something more fearful than death: the thought that it might not mean eternal sleep:

> the dread of something after death
> The undiscovered country from whose bourn
> No traveler returns, puzzles the will,
> And makes us rather bear those ills we have
> Than fly to others that we know not of...
>
> (3.1.80–4)

The will intervenes between heart and mind although the cost of consequent thought is great for one who believes in conscience:

> thus the native hue of resolution
> Is sicklied o'er with the pale cast of thought,
> And enterprises of great pith and moment
> With this regard their currents turn awry,
> And lose the name of action. (3.1.86–90)

The brain falters. Inaction is disobedience to the Ghost of his father, an irresponsibility to himself. This does not mitigate Hamlet's fear; it strengthens and prolongs it.

'Some life is left to be imployed to vnderstanding, albeit not so great', Wright teaches us, 'because the soule is distracted with a Passion, the which inforceth the wit only to consider, what may conduce to the continuation and preseruation thereof', that is, preventing the undiscovered country, adding, 'the imagination representeth to the vnderstanding, not onley reasons that may fauor the passion, but also it sheweth them very intensiuely, with more shew and appearance than they are indeed' (51). The passion of fear blocks decision. Obsessed on the one hand with the memory of his father's Ghost and, on the other, with the underlying fear of the undiscovered country, Hamlet's will is momentarily frozen, suspended when his imagination goes to work on the occasion of another interruption: the arrival of a company of travelling players. Hamlet knows these players and their plays, among them *The Murder of Gonzago*, and he offers to add a speech of a dozen or sixteen lines that will 'amaze indeed / The very faculty of eyes and ears' (2.2.542–3). We do not know what lines Hamlet supplied the visiting actors, but the revealing, if muddled, speech of the Player Queen is a good possibility.

> So many journeys may the sun and moon
> Make us again count o'er ere love be done.
> But woe is me, you are so sick of late,
> So far from cheer and from your former state,
> That I distrust you. Yet, though I distrust,
> Discomfort you my lord it nothing must.
> For women's fear and love holds quantity,
> In neither aught, nor in extremity,
> Now what my love is, proof hath made you know,
> And as my love is sized, my fear is so.
> *When love is great, the littlest doubts are fear:*
> *Where little fears grow great, great love grows there.*
> (3.2.145–54.2)

This strange and awkward concoction of sorrow, illness, distrust, discomfort, fear, extremity and love folds uneasily on the Player Queen's character but it projects tellingly and incisively the various forms Hamlet's basic passion of fear is taking in its turbulent confusion. 'When we are moued with a vehement passion', Wright tells us, 'Our soules are then, as it were infected with a pestilent ague, which both hindereth the sight of our eyes, and the tast of our tongues, that is, corrupteth the judgment, and preserueth the will . . . passions make the passionate to iudge all those things which tend to favour of his passion, reasonable, great, and worthy, and all that stands against it, base, vile and naughty' (89). Such is the coinage of Hamlet's brain.

It is fitting, then, given the state of Hamlet's mind – still obsessed by death, still somewhat anxious and fearful if now more determined – that

upon returning to Denmark he goes at once to the castle graveyard. Meeting Horatio there, he is distracted by the gravediggers and, more precisely, by the skulls – the memento mori – they throw up from the grave. Burton's *Anatomy* tells of a child 'beyond the Rhine, [who] saw a grave opened, & upon the sight of the carcass was so troubled in mind, that she could not be comforted, but a little after departed, and was buried by it' (287–8). Hamlet also becomes distraught by the sight of the third skull, his jester and childhood playmate Yorick. This skull he picks up and examines: 'Where be your gibes now, your gambols, your songs, your flashes of merriment that were wont to set the table on a roar? . . . Quite chop-fallen?' (5.1.175–8). It might be a little difficult to identify such decaying bones; in the aggregate, they now belong to those in the undiscovered country with Polonius and Rosencrantz and Guildenstern. And Ophelia, about to receive maimed rites. What is new and different here is Hamlet's lack of fear and anxiety. What replaces them is fascination. What replaces them is a new mental disposition at rest with the fragility and transience of life. 'If it be now, 'tis not to come. If it be not to come, it will be now. If it be not now, yet it will come. The readiness is all' (5.2.158–69). Beyond fear and free of it, he like Macbeth is resigned to his human condition but, unlike Macbeth, he is not simply resigned; he is enabled to keep his vow to the Ghost, to kill a king who has killed his mother, and to assure the peaceful rule of a strong successor in Denmark who, like himself, came to the support of his father. Hamlet lives long enough to become the country's prince and in his remaining time select a successor in another mirror of princes and, with Horatio, finds his place in history and in legend. In Denmark as in Norway and Scotland, the time is free.

V

At first *Othello* would seem to depart from such a pattern. Initially warned by Iago of Brabanzio's enmity, Othello is not the portrayal of fear but of calmness and confidence:

Let him to his spite.
My services which I have done the signory
Shall out-tongue his complaints . . .
My parts, my title, and my perfect soul
Shall manifest me rightly.   (1.2.17–19, 32–3)

When Brabanzio and his companions are at the point of attacking Othello in the streets of Venice, he is unperturbed.

Keep up your bright swords, for the dew will rust
'em . . .
                    Hold your hands,
Both you of my inclining and the rest.
Were it my cue to fight, I should have known it
Without a prompter.   (1.2.60, 82–5)

Brabanzio will learn in 1.3 that they are joined through Othello's marriage.

It is otherwise in Cyprus. Here Iago is attuned, even as he has been throughout the play from its outset, to what is said by others as he plots desecration. What he sees and hears when Othello arrives ashore and is reunited with his bride is this:

It gives me wonder great as my content
To see you here before me. O my soul's joy,
If after every tempest come such calms,
May the winds blow till they have wakened death, . . .
'Twere now to be most happy, for I fear
My soul hath her content so absolute
That not another comfort like to this
Succeeds in unknown fate.   (2.1.180–9)

Othello's soul is hostage to his content with Desdemona, and she may well prove an easier victim for Iago, a way to get revenge on Othello for appointing Cassio as his lieutenant. But Iago need not wait. That very night Othello's herald reads a proclamation that invites all his men to the celebration of his nuptials, the consummation of his marriage: 'every man put himself into triumph: some to dance, some to make bonfires, each man to what sport and revels his addiction leads him' (2.2.3–5). The unexpected and ill-timed interruption of such a celebration, during which Cassio gets drunk and is unable to gain authority, surprises Othello. Now his own men grow unruly, noisy and disobedient. Othello's repeated inquiries to learn the cause of

the fray grow ever more heated but provide him no answers (2.3.146, 152, 171, 200). Such an altercation threatens the town itself, according to Othello:

What, in a town of war
Yet wild, the people's hearts brimful of fear,
To manage private and domestic quarrel
In night, and on the court and guard of safety!
'Tis monstrous.   (2.3.196–200)

Seizing on Othello's interpretation, Iago manages to renew it in his accusations of Cassio: 'The town might fall in fright' (2.3.215). Othello does what he presumably always does as a commander: he acts swiftly and decisively, dismissing Cassio, 'never more be officer of mine' (2.3.232). The fear Iago has suddenly aroused in Othello is the fear of betrayal which questions his very authority as a general. Such an act has dreadful consequences. Othello, until now always the confident general, has made the wrong choice in his lieutenant. These public errors in judgement, and this public admission of it, will eat away at Othello's recitation and self-confidence. His anxiety will grow under Iago's fostering to a fear of his whole world – the world of Venetian custom and the world of marriage, as well as the world of trusting others, the world of military order and tradition, the world of hierarchy and obedience.

Sensing the fact that Othello, if not an unquestioned leader, now becomes a questioned outsider, Iago builds on Othello's growing sense of insecurity, an alien in background and culture. For Othello, the overriding universal sense of a world betraying him is repeatedly emphasized in the particulars.

Othello. Was not that Cassio parted from my wife?
Iago. Cassio, my lord? No, sure, I cannot think it,
    That he would steal away so guilty-like
    Seeing your coming.   (3.3.36–9)

But Othello's doubts have been aroused:

Therefore these stops of thine frighten me the more;
For such things in a false disloyal knave
Are tricks of custom, but in a man that's just,
They're close dilations, working from the heart
That passion cannot rule.   (3.3.125–9)

Iago's destabilization of Othello's thoughts is relentless. Othello's suspicions and fears are not allowed to subside.

> Poor and content is rich, and rich enough,
> But riches fineless is as poor as winter
> To him that ever fears he shall be poor.
>
> (3.3.176–8)

> I do not in position
> Distinctly speak of her, though I may fear
> Her will, recoiling to her better judgement,
> May fall to match you with her country forms
> And happily repent.   (3.3.239–42)

> Note if your lady strain his entertainment
> With any strong or vehement importunity
> Much will be seen in that. In the mean time,
> Let me be thought too busy in my fears –
> As worthy cause I have to fear I am –
> And hold her free . . .   (3.3.255–60)

Cassio, encountering Othello, teaches him to fear disloyalty. Eavesdropping on Cassio with Bianca, Othello is prepared for yet another betrayal. The absence of the handkerchief he claims to have given Desdemona at their wedding only furthers his suspicions. Such moments are subjected to his growing imagination of Desdemona's unfaithfulness and fear of her betrayal. Disturbing Othello's witness, Iago gives Othello's fear new force. Robert Burton glosses such changes in his *Anatomy of Melancholy*: 'some ascribe all vice to a false and corrupt imagination, anger, revenge, lust, ambition, covetousness, which prefers falsehood before that which is right and good . . . Some will laugh, weep, sigh, groan, blush, tremble, sweat, at such things as are suggested unto them by their imagination' (221). Such escalating fear – 'she did deceive her father, marrying you' (3.3.210), Iago reminds Othello – leads Othello to reposition Desdemona as a faithless whore, her bedchamber as the site of her iniquity:

Come, swear it, damn thyself,
Lest, being like one of Heaven, the devils themselves
Should fear to seize thee. Therefore be double-damned:
Swear thou art honest.   (4.2.37–40)

Such a skewed and misinformed appropriation of events to regain control in a world full of betrayal accords with the findings of modern cognitive science. The 'intriguing property of fear-leaning', Steven Johnson writes, is what scientists call 'flashbulb memory':

During traumatic events, your brain stores not only a trace of the specific threat . . . but also contextual details surrounding that threat. This is a classic expression of the brain's associative architecture, captured by the famous slogan 'cells that fire together wire together' [that is, the brain's neural pathways grow stronger through repeated use]. Different incoming stimuli trigger in specific constellations of neurons; when these neurons fire in sync with one another, they are more likely to form new connections. As the connections grow stronger, a given neuron has an easier time triggering another connected neuron.   (58)

Seeing in his mind's eye how Othello's stories woo Desdemona, Iago stresses what Othello can see in his mind's eye as he tells of Cassio's sexual mumbling in his sleep as testimony (3.3.422–30) or Desdemona's reported acts of infidelity in strongly visible terms ('to be naked with her friend in bed / An hour or more', 4.1.3–4). Such clearly drawn images burn their way into Othello's brain. As Johnson writes,

The trouble with such emotional memories is that they can be fiendishly difficult to eradicate. The brain seems wired to prevent the deliberate overriding of fearful responses. Although extensive neural pathways link the amygdala to the neocortex, paths running in the reverse direction are sparse. That is, passion races to conquer reason, but reason does not race back. Our brain seems to have been designed to allow the fear systems to take control in threatening situations while preventing the reign of our conscious, deliberate selves.   (64–5)

Finally, in the mounting tension of the closing scene, it is when Desdemona identifies her fear as the sum total of Othello's own –

And yet I fear you, for you're fatal then
When your eyes roll so. Why I should fear I know not,
Since guiltiness I know not, but yet I feel I fear
          (5.2.39–41)

– that we too feel totally helpless. What follows is uncontrollable, senseless, homicide. Here there

ARTHUR F. KINNEY

can be no sense of freedom or release at a moment of such overwhelming fear.

VI

This overt mention of fear is largely absent from *King Lear*, the last of the great tragedies, yet it is nevertheless a powerful part of the drama. The play also opens with a scene that erupts in colour and ceremony from the hushed inconclusive suppositions of Kent and Gloucester. Before the play finally ends with his death, Lear will wander homeless through the Kentish countryside, presumably without purpose, undergoing fits of madness. But such a journey is sharply defined by his scene of abdication when he is, if elderly and weakened, also astute and strategic.

> Meantime we shall express our darker purpose.
> Give me the map there. Know that we have divided
> In three our kingdom; and 'tis our fast intent
> To shake all cares and business from our age,
> Conferring them on younger strengths, while we
> Unburthened crawl toward death.   (1.1.34–9)

Formally presented, nearly lost in the folds of ritual, Lear's public act of transferring rule upon his daughters reveals his unspoken design. Always conscious and deeply apprehensive of his own mortality, of his own death, Lear is nevertheless preparing to die. He wants to assure a planned succession, however, in his final months and days, that will not subject his country to battle. He wants to forestall rebellion among his heirs 'that future strife may be prevented now' (1.1.42–3). Confronted with the tradition of primogeniture, he will avoid conflict by passing equal authority to Goneril and Regan, but placing the more trusted and peaceful Cordelia between them. He will give to his youngest daughter an 'ample third of our fair kingdom, / No less in space, validity, and pleasure, / Than that conferred on Goneril' (1.1.79–81).

Much rides on the ceremony of abdication as a precaution, and when Cordelia hesitates he makes a fatal mistake, adding 'A third more opulent than your sisters' (1.1.85). Perhaps unaware of this, perhaps to salvage the error by returning to his plan,

Lear resumes the love test with Cordelia he has performed with her sisters. He wants their public confessions of love – not as private confessions of daughters to father, but rather as public declarations to the king as a commitment of love for his position and for their country which his ceremonial presence embodies. That is his second error: all three of them misconstrue the point Lear wishes to make. Loving the state is an imperative condition of ruling it – he shows his own love in his description of the land – and five times he asks Cordelia to fulfil the ritual that will qualify her as ruler. Misunderstood, he tries one last attempt to prevent future strife now. He will replace Cordelia as insurance against battle by constantly visiting the two daughters in turn. Lear has offered each of them a portion of everything – 'interest of territory, cares of state' (1.1.48) – and he has received, from Cordelia, nothing.

His rapidly revised plan of a shuffling diplomacy in the company of some of his loyal troops is the first thing Goneril challenges.

> Not only, sir, this your all-licensed fool,
> But other of your insolent retinue
> Do hourly carp and quarrel, breaking forth
> In rank and not-to-be-endured riots. Sir,
> I had thought, by making this well known unto you,
> To have found a safe redress; but now grow fearful,
> By what yourself too late have spoke and done.
>   (1.4.175–81)

Moreover, she shares such a 'particular fear' with Regan (1.4.315), removing the king's support and increasing his sense of doom. His sense of preserving the kingdom after his abdication by preserving the state with younger and abler leaders is denied at each early turn. The subsequent demonstrations of loyalty by Kent, Gloucester, the Fool and Poor Tom suggest a possible counterforce, but they prove inadequate to compensate for his loss and to assuage his fears.

Lear's wits stray but he is not witless. He recognizes the sardonic wit of the Fool. He recognizes the impoverishment of Poor Tom through the veil of his own suffering: 'Hast thou given all to thy two daughters? And art thou / Come to

232

this?' (3.4.49–50), and he struggles to accept enormously depleted circumstances: 'Thou art the thing itself; unaccommodated man is no more but such a poor, bare, forked animal as thou art' (3.4.98–100), a man who is nothing personified. He struggles to impose order and substance on a disordered and largely empty world as he once had at his failed abdication by holding a trial in the hovel of Poor Tom. He struggles before a damaged mirror in the blinded Gloucester.

Ha! Goneril, with a white beard! They flattered me like a dog; and told me I had white hairs in my beard ere the black ones were there. To say 'aye' and 'no' to everything that I said. 'Aye' and 'no' too was no good divinity. When the rain came to wet me once, and the wind to make me chatter; when the thunder would not peace at my bidding; there I found 'em, there I smelt 'em out. Go to, they are not men o' their words. They told me I was everything. 'Tis a lie, I am not ague-proof. (4.6.95–103)

They told me I was everything; then they told me I was nothing. Lear's deepened sense of a lack of self-worth is denied in the testimony of Cordelia (4.4.16–21). Their reunion is a powerful scene of Lear's attempt to regain sufficient stature to confront his exiled daughter, to bring her back to life; more aware than ever of the reality of that mortality he initially feared – his undiscovered country that puzzles the will – he can nevertheless attempt to rescue them both.

> Pray, do not mock me.
> I am a very foolish fond old man,
> Fourscore and upward, not an hour more nor less;
> And, to deal plainly,
> I fear I am not in my perfect mind.
> Methinks I should know you, and know this man;
> Yet I am doubtful; for I am mainly ignorant
> What place this is; and all the skill I have
> Remembers not these garments; nor I know not
> Where I did lodge last night. Do not laugh at me;
> For, as I am a man, I think this lady
> To be my child Cordelia.   (4.7.60–71)

The fear of his own death has taught Lear the force of life's crucible. The fear that is a part of Shakespearian tragedy is never far from the surface of this play; it resonates throughout.

For Robert Burton, Lear suffers from phrenitis:

Which the Greeks derive from the word phren . . . a disease of the mind, with a continual madness or dotage, which hath an acute fever annexed, or else an inflammation of the brain, or the membranes or kells of it, with an acute fever, which causeth madness and dotage.

(121)

For Steven Johnson, however, Lear's state of mind may result from 'the memory . . . stored in some secure, undisclosed location of the mind inaccessible to conscious awareness . . . The cortex can forget, but the amygdala can keep the fear alive, albeit somewhere below the radar of awareness' (61–2). In the end, Lear cannot escape the memory of an abdication gone horribly wrong. Cordelia attempts to take Lear off to prison to reunite the royal family: 'Shall we not see these daughters and these sisters?' (5.3.7). His reply is not what she expected, nor the best of what he has learned.

> No, no, no, no! Come, let's away to prison.
> We two alone will sing like birds i' the cage,
> When thou dost ask me blessing, I'll kneel down,
> And ask of thee forgiveness. So we'll live,
> And pray, and sing, and tell old tales, and laugh
> At gilded butterflies, and hear poor rogues
> Talk of court news; and we'll talk with them too,
> Who loses and who wins; who's in, and who's out;
> And take upon 's the mystery of things,
> As if we were Gods' spies; and we'll wear out,
> In a walled prison, packs and sects of great ones,
> That ebb and flow by the moon.   (5.3.8–19)

The trauma of his recent past defeats him, and his mind drifts back to a court life of factions which he is helpless to correct. Lear and Cordelia forgive each other, but there is little change from the anxieties that separated them.

VII

Hamlet has long seemed the epitome of melancholy. His inky cloak, his bewilderment over his mother's untimely remarriage despite canon law, his anxiety concerning the role of Claudius, his uncertainty of the true nature of King Hamlet's ghost, his madness (real or feigned) in which his father resembles Hyperion and his mother Niobe, his persistent moodiness and ability to play different parts all join in the anxiety over the undiscovered country from which no one returns. In part, his mind and heart suffer from the fundamental humoral passion of fear, the fear of a son's insufficiency, of the anxiety of his ability to take on the princely qualities of a Fortinbras. Othello, too, feels the fear of private betrayal by Desdemona alongside public defeat at the inabilities of Cassio for a job Othello thought most fit. Both Hamlet and Othello would prove the fool, as Macbeth and Lear would.

Michael Neill writes that 'As early as *Richard II*, Shakespeare has created a king who brooded Hamlet-like on the vulnerable humanity that underlies the theatre of royal self-presentation.' He continues,

Looking at the soliloquy that immediately precedes Richard's murder – 'Nor I, nor any man that but man

is, / With nothing shall he be pleased till he be eased / With being nothing' (5.5.39–41) – we can begin to see the extent to which the development of interior monologue grew out of Shakespeare's preoccupation with the fearful enigma of being and with death's undoing the differences by which humans make sense of their world.[7]

For Shakespeare, fear could be the essential ingredient of witnessing the world, producing thoughts that could not be erased from the mind. As an emotion of the mind, as cognitive passion, it is one way by which Shakespeare continues his remarkable relevance. The cortex allows man to forget what he wishes to avoid in thought and feeling, but the amygdala can make it irrefutable.

---

[7] Michael Neill, 'Shakespeare's Tragedies', in *The New Cambridge Companion to Shakespeare*, ed. Margreta de Grazia and Stanley Wells (Cambridge, 2010), p. 133.

SHAKESPEARE'S LITERATURE
OF EXHAUSTION

STEPHAN LAQUÉ

Shakespeare's plays are revered for their richness – whether believed to be inherent in the texts themselves or only obliquely present as so much semantic potential to be realized on stage, by the audience or in the minds of readers. There appears to be an almost cornucopian quality to these plays which invariably seem to offer a new reading, a new opportunity for theatrical realization, a new reason to leave scholarly verities behind and to reinvent Shakespeare's age, our own age and any conceivable concept from the history of human thought. This wealth may be our own making at least as much as that of Shakespeare, but its source still tends to be implicitly or explicitly construed as springing from the fullness of an artistic mind or from the receptiveness of a mind steeped in a culture that was particularly rich in fruitful tension, doubt and conflict. At something like the opposite extreme, I would like to suggest here that the cornucopia we find in the plays just might spring not from any pregnant potential or overabundance but, on the contrary, from a kind of tiring surfeit and from a powerful sense of exhaustion.

As I want to argue, Shakespeare's work registers exhaustion in the sense which John Barth described in his much-discussed and much-maligned essay 'The Literature of Exhaustion' of 1967.[1] The essay has been misread and vilified as an uncalled-for death notice of literature, as a dismissal of its potential and relevance. But when Barth speaks of 'the used-upness of certain forms or exhaustion of certain possibilities – it is by no means necessarily a cause for despair' (Barth, 1), he is not being nihilist or even pessimistic. He may be detecting a dead end, but he is intent on demonstrating not its depressing finitude but its rich potential. In Barth, exhaustion is the direct source of replenishment. Unfortunately, by publishing 'The Literature of Replenishment', the companion essay to 'The Literature of Exhaustion', Barth did everything he could to make sure this central idea of his is missed. This later essay provides very much a bathos and culminates in the disarming banality of stating that he was talking all along about the 'exhaustion' 'not of language nor of literature but of the aesthetic of high modernism' (39). Of course, writers of introductions to postmodern literature were going to lap up this kind of bite-sized definition and were in the process content to miss the entire thrust of the previous essay. Exhaustion was neatly remedied by a return to literature, by the author's embeddedness in previous epochs and by a new openness and freedom of recombination. But the replenishment which Barth's exhaustion-essay envisages is more specific, more incisive and much more fruitfully applicable to the work (if not to the postmodern mind) of William Shakespeare. This is how I would like to put Barth's drift in a nutshell: The exhaustion and tiredness of a genre, of an aesthetic tradition or of a medium can be tackled by affirming and embracing their very finitude. Narrating or staging exhaustion is a way of overcoming exhaustion. This is, surely, not the only option available to the fatigued producer of texts, but it is one which

---

[1] John Barth, *The Literature of Exhaustion and The Literature of Replenishment* (Northridge, CA, 1982).

has kept the literature of late modernity and, as I am claiming, the literature of early modernity in business.

When Shakespeare's writing career began in the 1590s, the genres he was going to contribute to had already run their course. This is nowhere more evident than in the sonnets. The sonnet had by Shakespeare's time been invented, established and transformed and all that was left to do was exaggerate, inflate or parody its conventions. Sonnets 129 and, of course, 130 may serve as cases in point. Sonnet 129 starts on a note of exhaustion:

Th'expense of spirit in a waste of shame
Is lust in action; and till action, lust
Is perjured, murd'rous, bloody, full of blame,
Savage, extreme, rude, cruel, not to trust...

(lines 1–4)

The subject to line 1 is delayed until the beginning of line 2 which serves to place the initial stress on 'expense' – according to the *OED* on 'the state of being expended or used up'.[2] The poem deplores the fact that 'lust in action' is tantamount to a squandering or 'expending' of energy and of the forces of life. At the same time as it rehearses this insight, however, it runs through twelve breathless lines without turn, *volta* or argument, collecting in condensed form the stock phrases of the poetic cliché of the transports of love. Hence the first line of the couplet states with a subtle note of disdain: 'All this the world well knows, yet none knows well / To shun the heaven that leads men to this hell' (lines 13–14). Rather than add new images to this tradition, Shakespeare's sonnet tears through a catalogue of well-known descriptions of these ravages and in the process offers not only a striking sense of driven intoxication but, as I would argue and as the poem's initial position of 'expense' would suggest, primarily a sense of exhaustion, of the used-upness of the genre.[3] The exhaustion of what love and love poetry have to offer is in the poem fittingly described and performed as a breathless orgiastic rush – very much reminiscent of the dizzying over-abundance of baroque art. This is the 'heaven' of joyous exhausting and using-up which according to the couplet

ineluctably leads men to 'this hell', to a state where the surfeit becomes 'despised' (line 5) and 'hated' (line 7). This, then, is a poem about exhaustion – both sexual and poetic – and its powerful lines testify to the lyrical productivity which can result both from the 'heavenly' succumbing to the exquisite rush of exhaustion and from the 'hellish' regrets which this rush leaves behind. Though 'this hell' is semantically quite unmistakeably there in the description – 'perjured, murd'rous, bloody' (l.3), 'a very woe' (l.11) – it is the ravages of the 'heaven' which the poem has presented and it is the fruit of the 'heaven' which we as readers have been given to taste: the poetic fruit which results from a rapturous engagement with exhaustion.

Sonnet 130 follows a different path in order to harvest poetic force from the exhaustion of the sonnet genre by famously parodying the Petrarchan blazon. Again, the relentless rehearsal and exposure of a convention spent through overuse yields poetic gain. After twelve lines of debunking the clichés of the Petrarchan sonnet, lines which are no less 'exhausting' than the quatrains of Sonnet 129, the speaker of Sonnet 130 can triumphantly declare that he can think his love 'as rare / As any she belied with false compare' (lines 13–14) – indicating that there just might be a more truthful form of comparison out there. But it is not his strategy to fill the space which his sustained exposing of the exhaustion of the sonnet has afforded him with an alternate poetic vision. All he does is enumerate at disarming length the pile of clichés which he has chosen to dismiss without attempting to offer an alternative and less 'belying' set of comparisons. And, indeed, there is no need for innovation. The speaker of Sonnet 130 can with full justification claim his sometimes clever and sometimes cruel dismissal as a poetic achievement in itself – and

---

[2] *OED*, 'Expense' 1.b.

[3] As H. E. Rollins noted in his *New Variorum* edition in the 1940s, the subject of the 'ravages of lust' had for a long time been 'a favourite topic with sonneteers'. William Shakespeare, *The Sonnets. A New Variorum Edition of Shakespeare*, ed. H. E. Rollins (Philadelphia and London, 1944), p. 330.

it is an achievement which not only satisfies aesthetically, but also accomplishes the rather conventional sonneteering ambition of proclaiming that his love is 'rare'.

At the tail-end of the sonnet tradition, Shakespeare was in a sense writing sonnets after the sonnet – and that is what he had to do, since writing poems in the Petrarchan mode would have been nothing short of embarrassing. As John Barth remarks in his essay: 'Beethoven's Sixth Symphony or the Chartres Cathedral if executed today would be merely embarrassing' (3). Romeo's amorous and poetic contortions in Shakespeare's tragedy are a caustic lampooning of this embarrassingly outdated form of writing and Romeo appears to consider his achievements in sonnet-writing to be of the scale of symphonies and cathedrals:

> Why then, O brawling love, O loving hate,
> O anything of nothing first create;
> O heavy lightness, serious vanity,
> Misshapen chaos of well-seeming forms,
> Feather of lead, bright smoke, cold fire, sick health,
> Still-waking sleep, that is not what it is!
> This love feel I, that feel no love in this.
> Dost thou not laugh?   (*Romeo and Juliet*, 1.1.173–9)

The sonneteer's clichéd antitheses and *contradictiones in adjectio* ('loving hate', 'heavy lightness', etc.) form the irrelevant ferment ('nothing') out of which the lover's pathetic self and his poetry are first created – 'Oh anything of nothing first create'. Romeo is patently unaware of the fatuous outdatedness of his gestures and his proclamation that he feels 'no love in this' is not only a sign of unrequited love but also of his incapacity to derive joy from 'this', his wallowing in bygone ways of thinking and writing. The exasperated Benvolio's laughter at the jadedness of Romeo brings tears to his eyes – tears, maybe, also of genuine compassion for someone who has been left behind while literature, thought and the culture of love have moved on. The solution lies in the context which the play imposes on the love-theme: *Romeo and Juliet* is not a conventional love-comedy nor does the play present the equally conventional blissful suffering of unrequited love.

What it is is a fully-fledged tragedy complete with malicious forces, misfortune and death. The play, then, does not come up with a new form of love or even a new genre of poetry about love, but uses a well-established genre (tragedy) in order to drive home the notion of the exhaustion and used-upness of one form of love and love poetry.

Tragedy is the genre of finitude, of resolutions which put a halt to vital progress and negate anything as simple as a happy replenishment 'ever after'. This is not the traditional realm of love and there is both a pleasing simplicity and an admirable boldness in this recontextualization which transplants the subject of love into the genre of tragedy; it is an experiment which waits to see what the outcome of the new constellation will be rather than offering a new and alternative concept of love. The play, then, is only in part about the prospects of the young and socially unacceptable love between Romeo and Juliet, but centrally about the untenability of an outdated form of love and of outdated forms of writing about love. Its emphasis is on exhaustion and in the last scene it almost cynically offers an entirely inappropriate and aesthetically outdated set of golden statues as the only form of representation in which a new form of love can live and exist. In the case of the parents of Romeo and Juliet, their reflection on exhaustion and finitude is nostalgic and arrives at the appropriately nostalgic text which is the golden statues. In the case of the play, however, this reflection happens in the process of its movement, of its diversions and contradictions, of its accelerations and its retardations – and produces a contemplation on exhaustion which resists interpretative exhaustion to this day.

At the start of *Romeo and Juliet*, love is felt by its champion Romeo Montague as so much exhaustion and fatigue. As Romeo replies to the eager partygoer Mercutio:

> You have dancing shoes
> With nimble soles; I have a soul of lead
> So stakes me to the ground I cannot move.
>   (1.4.14–16)

The experience is less one of being overwhelmed by pain than of being weighed and pinned down by a cumbersome burden – like a dead butterfly in a cabinet:

> I am too sore empiercèd with his shaft
> To soar with his light feathers, and so bound
> I cannot bound a pitch above dull woe;
> Under love's heavy burden do I sink.   (1.4.19–22)

Love, its poetry and its conventions, is a 'heavy burden' which threatens to tie down the vital spirit. This, then, is a play about overuse, about exhaustion, about the finitude of a genre, of a way of feeling and relating to one's feelings. Despite the fact that the young couple defies not only the stars but all manner of social convention, the play ends with the erection of the golden statues, with a return to outdated forms of commemoration. At the same time, however, the play has managed to produce a new and important piece of drama. As John Barth says of Jorge Luis Borges, his foremost exhibit of the literature of exhaustion:

> [Borges] writes a remarkable and original work of literature, the implicit theme of which is the difficulty, perhaps the unnecessity, of writing original works of literature. His artistic victory, if you like, is that he confronts an intellectual dead end and employs it against itself to accomplish new human work.   (8)

The overcoming – or 'replenishment' in Barth's terminology, if not in his second essay – of literary and cultural exhaustion or fatigue is not something to be narrated or staged in a straightforward manner. It is a performative act which produces newness even as it exposes and celebrates exhaustion. Thus Romeo's last and dying words:

> O, here
> Will I set up my everlasting rest,
> And shake the yoke of inauspicious stars
> From this world-wearied flesh.   (5.3.109–12)

Replenishment is a process which can and must never be completed. It is a product of rather than a reaction against exhaustion and Shakespeare's play derives much of its force from this careful and almost caring consideration of fatigue, from the 'world-wearied flesh' of spent conventions.

I am not claiming that all of Shakespeare's plays share this fascination with finitude, but it is a conspicuous element throughout his work and above all else in the tragedies. One particularly striking case of exhaustion is the figure of the revenger in *Hamlet*. Even before the prince has met the ghost of his father, he proclaims his fatigue:

> O God, O God,
> How weary, stale, flat, and unprofitable
> Seem to me all the uses of this world!
> (*Hamlet*, 1.2.132–4)

All the customary roles at Hamlet's disposal, such as that of surrogate husband to his mother or of chief mourner at court, have either been denied him or have been exhausted. His role as royal son has been depleted of meaning by the loss of his father and the infidelity of his mother whom he now cannot help but despise. Gertrude's sex life would force him back into the 'stale and unprofitable' role of being a son when he senses that he is already 'too much i'th' sun' (1.2.67), already weary of being the next in line.

However, the play will offer Hamlet new roles from the rich and much-used tradition of drama, most notably the two highly conventional ones of the revenger and of the fool. These roles are indeed far from being 'new'. They had been rehearsed, recast, established and re-established before Hamlet is offered the parts and he is therefore given the choice of two pretty much exhausted dramatic formats. Yorick's empty skull in Act 5 is probably the most tangible illustration of this sense of depletion.

> Here hung those lips that I have kissed I know not how oft. Where be your gibes now, your gambols, your songs, your flashes of merriment that were wont to set the table on a roar? Not one now to mock your own grinning? Quite chop-fallen?   (5.1.183–8)

The role of the jester had been an empty shell well before Hamlet decided to 'put an antic disposition on' (1.5.173). The post of the jester at the Danish court was vacant and his jests were no more than a fond and commonplace memory of precisely the kind which Hamlet dismisses in his tables-speech: 'I'll wipe away all trivial fond records, / All saws of books, all forms, all pressures past, / That youth and observation copied there' (1.5.99–101). Tired with the roles he has been given to play so far, Hamlet duly makes a mess both of being a proper revenger and of being a proper fool. Again, the play does not innovate, it does not point towards a new form of revenger or towards a new species of fool, but is content to explore the exhaustion of these moulds. The two dramatic roles fail to work for Hamlet and they signally do not come to fruition during the performance of *The Murder of Gonzago*. Hamlet's fooling comments on the play meet with Ophelia's and Claudius's stubborn incomprehension. Thus, Hamlet's wry comment that the players 'do but jest, poison in jest. No offence i'th' world' (3.2.223–4), is answered by Claudius with an exceedingly banal question: 'What do you call the play?' (3.2.225) and Ophelia misses the subversive thrust of Hamlet's caustic ruminations altogether: 'You are as good as a chorus, my lord' (3.2.233). After this ineffectual fooling, Hamlet decides to be a revenger at last – 'Now might I do it pat' (3.3.73) – but goes on to miss his best shot at filling that role when he fails to kill Claudius in the chapel. There seems to be no place for the conventional fool at the performance and even the most unmissable opportunity in the entire play cannot bring Hamlet's revenge to fruition. For five acts the play dwells upon the fact that the two roles which Hamlet is trying on are exhausted to the point where they cannot have a place within the play.

Hamlet eloquently and dramatically fails to fill the roles which convention offers him and he is very impatient with the bumbling attempts of those who confidently try to meet the requirements of their chosen genre. Laertes, Hamlet's rival revenger, is very much at ease with convention. When upon his return to the Danish court in Act 4 he proclaims 'Let come what comes. Only I'll be revenged / Most thoroughly for my father' (4.5.133–4), Claudius knows that he means business, but he also knows that he means business according to the long-established and long-exhausted etiquette of revenge. In order to predict and control Laertes's actions, it therefore suffices for him to know which set of conventions Laertes intends to follow:

> Good Laertes,
> If you desire to know the certainty
> Of your dear father's death, is't writ in your revenge
> That, sweepstake, you will draw both friend and foe,
> Winner and loser? (4.5.138–42)

Laertes is not an innovator, but is following a course of revenge that has long been 'writ' and laid down.[4] Even were he to strike and kill indiscriminately, he would still be following an established path of action – in that case the 'kind of wild justice' of which Francis Bacon famously warns.[5] Laertes does not shrink back from exhaustion but happily adopts convenient clichés, whether they are patterns of behaviour or images and rhetorical flourishes. In this he is strikingly unlike his friend Hamlet who keenly feels the exhaustion which the world and the Danish court would foist upon him and whose refusal to pick up and reuse in a straightforward manner the many empty shells of deed and speech fuels the captivating (in)action of the play.

In the graveyard-scene, Laertes's comfortable recycling of exhausted tropes clashes with Hamlet's contempt for stock responses and images. Laertes uses mountain imagery to illustrate the magnitude of his grief:

> O, treble woe
> Fall ten times treble on that cursèd head
> Whose wicked deed thy most ingenious sense
> Deprived thee of! – Hold off the earth a while,
> Till I have caught her once more in mine arms.
> *He leaps into the grave*
> Now pile your dust upon the quick and dead
> Till of this flat a mountain you have made
> To o'ertop old Pelion, or the skyish head
> Of blue Olympus. (5.1.240–9)

---

[4] A variety of forms of revenge had been 'writ' both in drama and in the books of law, where private revenge was illegal in England but in certain cases permissible in Italy (see R. A. Foakes, *Shakespeare and Violence* (Cambridge, 2003), pp. 108–9).

[5] Francis Bacon, *Essays*, ed. Michael J. Hawkins (London, 1972), p. 13.

The invocation of Mount Pelion and the notion of being buried underneath it has a very long tradition indeed and is a conventional mixing of ancient mythemes. After the Gigantomachia, Zeus trapped the giants under mountains, Typhoeus most famously being stuck under Etna whose eruptions were taken to testify to the giant's presence. Also, Zeus was challenged by other giants who piled mountains (Olympus, Pelion and Ossa, the mountain which Hamlet is going to introduce in his retort) one upon the other in an attempt to conquer heaven. The idea of stacking mountains would hardly have surprised Elizabethan audiences[6] and watching Laertes's grand gesture as he asks the grave-filling to be stopped while he jumps in and histrionically declaims a mishmash of classical mythology while holding Ophelia's body in his arms, is simply too much for Hamlet to bear. The prince jumps out from his hiding place:

> 'Swounds, show me what thou'lt do.
> Woot weep, woot fight, woot fast, woot tear
>   thyself,
> Woot drink up eisel, eat a crocodile?
> I'll do't. Dost thou come here to whine,
> To outface me with leaping in her grave?
> Be buried quick with her, and so will I.
> And if thou prate of mountains, let them throw
> Millions of acres on us, till our ground,
> Singeing his pate against the burning zone,
> Make Ossa like a wart. Nay, an thou'lt mouth,
> I'll rant as well as thou.   (5.1.271–81)

The time-honoured image of being buried alive under heaps of mountains simply will not do and Hamlet pointedly exposes its vacuity by offering the plainly bizarre challenges to 'drink up eisel' and 'eat a crocodile' as worthy matches. But, rather than step outside the well-used motif of piled-up mountains, he simply increases the quantity: 'let them throw / Millions of acres on us'. Again, an exhausted trope is not developed into or superseded by a fresher image, but explored and celebrated in its very exhaustion in order to produce a fresh piece of art.

The image of mountains being hurled about and piled upon the opponent was going to be employed to great baroque effect by John Milton when in Book VI of *Paradise Lost*, the heavenly host and Satan's army engage in a bootless and tiresome battle between equally invulnerable and invincible forces. When God's angelic army realize that their arms are not fit to decide the battle, they run to the hills and pick up mountains:

> Light as the lightning glimpse they ran, they flew,
> From their foundations loosening to and fro
> They plucked the seated hills with all their load,
> Rocks, waters, woods, and by the shaggy tops
> Up lifting bore them in their hands: (VI, 642–6)[7]

When the rebel army sees 'all their confidence / Under the weight of mountains buried deep' (VI, 651–2), they also begin to tear mountains from the ground and to hurl them about as giant projectiles:

> The rest in imitation to like arms
> Betook them, and the neighbouring hills uptore;
> So hills amid the air encountered hills
> Hurled to and fro with jaculation dire . . .   (VI, 662–5)

The result is a noisy exchange of mountains and Milton has to try very hard to confer some sense of martial dignity on this patently ridiculous scene: 'war seemed a civil game / To this uproar' (VI, 667–8). Mountain-throwing angels are extremely funny because extremely uncivil, but they can also be rather tedious and predictable if one is aware of the tradition of the trope or if one happens to be all-knowing. It is the absolute authority of God himself which in *Paradise Lost* registers the exhaustedness of this form of battle:

---

[6] Milagro Ducassé-Turner has pointed out that 'the myth of Zeus's imprisoning of the giants (in which the Elizabethans often confused the giants with the Titans) had already become a commonplace and proverbial', in 'Far-Off Mountains Turned Into Clouds' (*A Midsummer Night's Dream*, 4.1.187): Mountains of the Mind in Shakespeare's Drama', in *Mountains Figured and Disfigured in the English-Speaking World*, ed. Françoise Besson (Newcastle, 2010), pp. 261–81, p. 268.

[7] John Milton, *Paradise Lost*, ed. Alastair Fowler (Harlow, 2007).

War wearied hath performed what war can do,
And to disordered rage let loose the reins,
With mountains as with weapons armed, which
   makes
Wild work in Heav'n, and dangerous to the main.
                                        (VI, 695–8)

After the two armies and, of course, Book VI of John Milton's poem have employed and explained a wide variety of conceivable strategies and weapons (including chariots, gunpowder and some devilish engine), war has been exhausted and is now itself proclaimed 'wearied'. In epic detail, everything that 'war can do' has been used up and so, finally, God, the author of all and everything, steps in to save his creation by sending his son in to battle. The throwing about of mountains, which in its clichéd excess disgusts Hamlet when Laertes rambles on about it in his graveside histrionics, is in *Hamlet* as in Milton's *Paradise Lost* the culmination of an exhausting tour of exhausted tropes. The result of the respective tours may at times be bizarre and funny but it is above everything else a dramatic and poetic success.

Book VI of *Paradise Lost*, then, is like the tragedies of *Hamlet* and *Romeo and Juliet* a text about finitude and exhaustion. Out of this contemplation of fatigue, all three texts produce utterly new and remarkable pieces of literature. John Barth has pointed towards this productive concern with finitude as the salient feature of both Borges and Beckett:

One of the modern things about these two [i.e. Beckett and Borges] is that in an age of ultimacies and 'final solutions' – at least felt ultimacies, in everything from weaponry to theology, the celebrated dehumanization of society, and the history of the novel – their work in separate ways reflects and deals with ultimacy.   (5)

The early modern period is very much an age of ultimacies: not only of almost apocalyptic doubt and radical uncertainty, but also of a keenly felt overuse of certain genres and conventions – including the use of mountains as weaponry. While Shakespeare's plays were undoubtedly showing ways ahead in drama, in philosophy and, more broadly, in human thought, a lot of the energy which fuels these forays into new territory derives from precisely this kind of reflection on ultimacy, from this fascination with fatigue.

Beyond the tragedies, the last example I want to raise is the last play which Shakespeare authored on his own: *The Tempest*. It is the last play and it is in striking and often noted ways about ultimacies: the end of a career (Prospero's political career and Shakespeare's career in the theatre), the end of thraldom (to colonial rulers, to theatre directors and to the demands of audiences), the end of magic and the end of acting. Prospero pulls every conceivable stop at his disposal to expose the exhaustion of these occupations. He starts out by narrating his past to Miranda in some 160 drawn-out lines and he really needs no Ariel or magic spell to put his daughter (or, for that matter, his audiences) to sleep:

> Here cease more questions.
Thou art inclined to sleep; 'tis a good dullness,
And give it way. I know thou canst not choose.
> *Miranda sleeps*   (1.2.185–7)

Prospero's story of humanist ambition, of a usurping brother and his plotting, of a good Samaritan and of a hapless sea journey is a jumble of clichés. Even Miranda who has never been to the theatre and who should be unaware of the used-upness of these plot elements is put to sleep – a dramatic necessity for Ariel's entrance but at the same time a strong acknowledgement of Prospero's entanglement in old-fashioned plotlines. In the course of the play he proceeds to stage pastoral scenes, masques and allegories, many of which are tinged with a similar sense of depletion.

With the help of Ariel Prospero plays pranks which are very much reminiscent of Faustus's vain and empty practical jokes which he performs with the help of Mephistophilis in Marlowe's play. Prospero seems to be at least in part aware of a certain lack of originality in his dealings when he instructs Ariel:

> Thou and thy meaner fellows your last service
Did worthily perform, and I must use you
In such another trick.   . . . for I must

Bestow upon the eyes of this young couple
Some vanity of mine art. It is my promise,
And they expect it from me.   (4.1.35–42)

Prospero goes on to treat his daughter and her new-found boyfriend to some 70 lines of edifying but tiresome speeches by Ceres, Iris and Juno. It is highly unlikely that Miranda and Ferdinand indeed 'expect' or wish for anything of this sort and Prospero himself lets his mind wander rather than focus on his own display. In her final lines, Iris assumes a new height of clichéd pastoral irrelevance:

You sunburned sicklemen, of August weary,
Come hither from the furrow and be merry;
Make holiday, your rye-straw hats put on,
And these fresh nymphs encounter every one
In country footing.   (4.1.134–8)

Weary like the 'sunburned sicklemen' of his own pageant, Prospero suddenly remembers that Caliban and his new allies are plotting against him and breaks off the display. To dispel the bewilderment of Miranda and Ferdinand, he produces one of the most celebrated metatheatrical speeches in the Shakespeare canon:

Our revels now are ended. These our actors,
As I foretold you, were all spirits, and
Are melted into air, into thin air;
And like the baseless fabric of this vision,
The cloud-capped towers, the gorgeous palaces,
The solemn temples, the great globe itself,
Yea, all which it inherit, shall dissolve;
And, like this insubstantial pageant faded,
Leave not a rack behind. We are such stuff
As dreams are made on, and our little life
Is rounded with a sleep.   (4.1.148–58)

Beyond the obvious statement about the playfulness and the transitory nature of theatre, this is also an admission of finitude and exhaustion. The revels are at an end; they have produced nothing and they leave nothing behind apart from an inevitable tiredness which makes sleep necessary to produce a 'rounded' experience. But even as he contemplates the exhaustion or emptiness of his revels, Prospero produces one of the most memorable passages in the play, a passage which celebrates the force which can spring from fatigue.

Famously, the ending of the play is also about the end of the theatre. Prospero looks back upon his life as stage-director and decides to renounce his powers. His claim that he has performed necromancy, though, is surprising:

             the strong-based promontory
Have I made shake, and by the spurs plucked up
The pine and cedar; graves at my command
Have waked their sleepers, oped, and let 'em forth
By my so potent art. But this rough magic
I here abjure.... I'll break my staff,
Bury it certain fathoms in the earth,
And deeper than did plummet sound
I'll drown my book.   (5.1.46–57)

We have nowhere seen Prospero bringing the dead back to life – throughout the play, he has been putting people to sleep rather than waking any sleepers. It seems, therefore, that Prospero left the impetus and power for black magic and for rousing sleepers in some distant past before the start of the play – he had been done with the obvious forms of magic even before his first entrance. Claiming to have performed every known form of magic in his past thus serves to heighten the sense of exhaustion upon which a great deal of the force of the play we have witnessed rests. According to a definition by Borges which Barth quotes in part, Prospero's handling of exhaustion is here prototypically baroque: Borges defines the Baroque as 'that style that deliberately exhausts (or tries to exhaust) its own possibilities, and that borders on self-caricature . . . I would venture to say that the baroque is the final stage in all art, when art flaunts and squanders its resources.'[8] I feel that in his project 'to please' (Epilogue, line 13) Prospero is here indeed not shrinking back from his own caricature, and herein lies the remedy for exhaustion. Like the speakers in Sonnets 129 and 130, like Hamlet and like Romeo,

---

[8] Jorge Luis Borges, *A Universal History of Iniquity*, trans. Andrew Hurley (London, 2001), p. 4.

Prospero has flaunted and squandered his resources, he has celebrated exhaustion and in the process produced poetic and dramatic newness. Exhaustion and finitude, the used-upness of images, conventions and genres, then, are important sources of Shakespeare's works. Much of his greatness resides not in an innovative vision, but in his awareness of and engagement with exhaustion.

BIG-SHOULDERED SHAKESPEARE:
THREE *SHREWS* AT CHICAGO
SHAKESPEARE THEATER

L. MONIQUE PITTMAN

'Stormy, husky, brawling,
City of the Big Shoulders'
                  – Carl Sandburg, 'Chicago'[1]

'Stories about places are makeshift things.'
      – Michel de Certeau, *The Practice of Everyday Life*

Michel de Certeau's assertion that 'Stories about places are makeshift things' derives from his conceptualization of cities as locations where the logic and stability of institutional strategy meets the flux and fragment of everyday human tactic.[2] For Certeau, 'a tactic is determined by the *absence of power* just as a strategy is organized by the postulation of power' (38). In other words, by demarcating and naming places as sites of power, strategies establish and control difference and the governing gaze, whilst tactics reside in the mercurial of time and movement (36). Cities map an 'accepted framework, the imposed order' (107), but human lived movement within that frame exceeds and resists in its multifarious individual trajectories, blind alleys and intersecting networks that 'constructed order' (93, 107). Certeau elaborates: 'The long poem of walking manipulates spatial organizations, no matter how panoptic they may be: it is neither foreign to them (it can take place only within them) nor in conformity with them (it does not receive its identity from them). It creates shadows and ambiguities within them' (101). Thus, in cities, the stolid and finite structure meets the fluid and infinite individual walker, an embodiment of absence and lack in a grid of concrete presence that has been designed to materialize and maintain power (103).

Stories about theatrical performance within cities are also makeshift narratives that echo Certeau's dynamics of urban presence and absence. Theatrical ontology embodies paradox. As an art form that evanesces in its moment of fullest being, theatre survives primarily as a memory individual to each spectator. Often housed in substantial, enduring and costly spaces, any given theatrical production transpires for a few hours' duration only. For most of its elusive afterlife, theatre performance exists as a memory but not a uniform memory. Rather theatre remains as a recollection

---

Profound thanks go to the friends and colleagues whose conversation fuelled the thinking in this article: Karl Bailey, Vanessa Corredera, Kristin Denslow and Ante Jeroncic. Organizer D. J. Hopkins and members of the Shakespeare and Hollyworld seminar at Shakespeare Association of America (Boston, 2012) asked probing questions that focused theoretical development. Marilyn Halperin and her staff at the Chicago Shakespeare Theater were patient beyond imagining with each of my requests for more information from the theatre archives. Associate Dean Gary Burdick and the Office of Research and Creative Scholarship at Andrews University provided a generous travel grant. Lastly, I owe a particular debt of gratitude to the team of field researchers who accompanied me to Chicago Shakespeare in the Parks productions and gathered data: Theron Calkins, Vanessa Corredera, Arianna Lashley, Paul D. Smith, Jr., Samantha Snively and Lydia Weiso.

[1] Carl Sandburg, 'Chicago', in *Chicago Poems* (New York, 1916), p. 3.

[2] Michel de Certeau, *The Practice of Everyday Life*, trans. Steven Rendull (Berkeley, 1984), pp. xix, 107.

distinct in its scope and precision to each individual who witnessed the production. Acknowledging both the fragility and persistence of memory, Peter Holland characterizes the theatre as a series of forgettings: 'Theatre is a space of memory haunted by its own forgetfulness, by what we cannot remember when we leave the theatre, by the actor's memory that is visible only when it fails to work, by the texts that haunt the stage as unperformed and those that haunt through their performance.'[3] Holland's formulation articulates the way in which the ontology of theatre and its infinite generation of memory as well as its insistence on what cannot be recalled produce epistemological uncertainty. This heterogeneous afterlife of the theatre defies monolithic absolutes while the institutional materiality of performance spaces themselves typically represents an elite network of authority that underprops the homogenizing ideology of the dominant class.[4]

The 'Shakespearian' theatre introduces yet another layer of complexity to the makeshift narrative of performance in the city. In 'Shakespearean Performativity', W. B. Worthen articulates an informing relationship between the source text and theatrical production: 'What distinguishes Shakespearean performativity from some other modes of theater today is the premium placed – by performers and audiences, in conventional and experimental productions – on the identity of the verbal text, and the belief that its meanings inform, guide, or are animated by stage performance.'[5] Worthen's formulation cannily acknowledges shifting agential possibilities in the theatrical transaction (denoted by the active and passive verb structures he employs) – either the text *guides* the interpretive enactment on stage or *is given life by* embodied representation. On the one hand, the text-as-agent determines and, on the other hand, a theatrical subjectivity acts upon the text-as-object to create meaning. The stakes of this mutually constitutive subject/object relationship between Shakespearian text and theatre escalate when performance takes place in a space named for and devoted to the playwright's canon. In the case of a 'Shakespearian Theatre', each production asserts directly or indirectly an understanding of the poet and oeuvre that gives identity to that space; in other words, the theatre derived from Shakespeare also generates with each staging 'Shakespeare' as an originary source. Peggy Phelan astutely points out that the compulsion to the origin endemic to theatre founders repeatedly on the conditions of theatre performance itself, explaining that realistic theatre, reliant upon 'properties which reproduce the effects of the real', demonstrates a powerful 'desire to experience a first cause, an origin, an authentic beginning which can only fail because the desire is experienced and understood from and through repetition'.[6] The cultural capital of William Shakespeare intensifies this aspiration for beginnings, but the observable institutional efforts to craft the 'Shakespearian' highlight the self-generative fictionalizing of that endeavour. Because the idea of 'Shakespeare' becomes the mechanism of self-perpetuation, the forms of theatrical representation possible may all too often be limited to performances that justify in their construction of

---

[3] Peter Holland, 'On the Gravy Train: Shakespeare, Memory and Forgetting', in *Shakespeare, Memory and Performance* (Cambridge, 2006), pp. 207–34, p. 234.

[4] Pierre Bourdieu identifies the artist as the dominated figure within the dominant class, a figure who possesses cultural capital but little economic capital. See his *The Field of Cultural Production: Essays on Art and Literature*, ed. Randal Johnson (New York, 1993). The struggle for the right to be classified as an artist or a writer centres on the question of legitimacy, and Bourdieu notes that in the scramble for artistic dominance, members of the dominated classes can be the losers (41). Bourdieu summarizes: 'In short, the fundamental stake in literary struggles is the monopoly of literary legitimacy' (42). He argues that, as dominated members of the dominant class, artists bear a natural affinity with the dominated in society at large but that acts of 'bad faith' may still be possible in the contest over legitimacy (44). In other words, while the artist and the socially marginal experience a similar state of domination by the powerful, the quest for legitimacy on the part of the artist can efface analogies between the two forms of dominated classes.

[5] W. B. Worthen, 'Shakespearean Performativity', in *Shakespeare and Modern Theatre: The Performance of Modernity*, ed. Michael Bristol, Kathleen McLuskie and Christopher Holmes (New York, 2001), pp. 117–41, p. 119.

[6] Peggy Phelan, *Unmarked: The Politics of Performance* (New York, 1993), 126.

'Shakespeare' the amount of capital expenditure invested in temples to his service.

The Chicago Shakespeare Theater (CST) presents one notable American example of this identity transaction, wedding in its title the great Midwestern city to the great English playwright. Through the herculean efforts of founder and Artistic Director Barbara Gaines, the Chicago Shakespeare Theater has forged an identity and a place within the arts and entertainment scene of the Windy City when few thought such a venture viable. After thirteen seasons that began in 1986 with one play performed on a pub terrace, Gaines transformed the status and significance of her theatre with a massive building project during the late 1990s.[7] Rather than choose a site in close proximity to the established theatre district of the city, the Chicago Shakespeare Theater opted for an amusement park site on the city's waterfront.[8] At the 1998 groundbreaking for her new facility, Gaines justified her theatre's prominence on the Chicago skyline by a familiar claim about Shakespeare's worth: 'We are here to celebrate the building of a permanent home for the world's greatest humanist.'[9] As Gaines formulated a new identity for her theatre company, which until the relocation to Navy Pier had gone under the designation 'Shakespeare Repertory Theatre', she crafted a 'Shakespeare' to warrant the city's investment of $12 million into the project.[10] Calling upon the familiar construction of Shakespeare as benevolent humanist, Gaines elevated her adopted city to a titular position and dropped the British spelling of 'theatre' for the distinctly American 'theater' as part of planting on the Navy Pier amidst its carnival attractions.[11] Repeatedly in interviews and in theatre promotional materials, Gaines has lauded Shakespeare's works as manifestations of a humane consciousness, one drawn to the essential human values of equity, social justice and ethical relationships with others.[12]

Gaines's Navy Pier theatre instantiates the tension between institutional strategy and individual tactic characteristic of Certeau's city. A bricks-and-mortar structure built in large part by the city purse, the theatre belongs to totalizing 'socioeconomic and political strategies' (95), but located on Navy Pier amidst carnival topsy-turvy, it exists within the pedestrian's field of individual variance and resistance.[13] While the amusement

7 See Richard Christiansen, 'Shakespeare is Alive in Chicago', *Chicago Tribune*, 8 October 1987, http://articles.chicagotribune.com and Chris Jones, 'The Location is the Thing', *Chicago Tribune*, 1 February 1998, http://articles.chicagotribune.com.
8 At least one reporter, Rebecca Paller, noted the unspoken similarity between Gaines's location choice and that of another theatre attraction: 'Just as London has its newly constructed Globe theatre overlooking the Thames, Chicago will soon have a sparkling new Shakespeare theatre at the Navy Pier overlooking Lake Michigan.' See her 'Foundation to be Laid in Jan. 1998 for Chicago's Shakespeare Theatre', *Playbill News*, 26 November 1997, www.playbill.com.
9 Jonathan Abarbanel, 'Chicago's Shakespeare Bard's Repertory Theatre Breaks Ground', *AllBusiness.com*, 9 October 1998, www.allbusiness.com.
10 See Jones, 'The Location'.
11 In contrast to Gaines's rhetoric, more material concerns motivated the development company responsible for the renewal of Navy Pier, the Metropolitan Pier and Exposition Authority. Navy Pier general manager at the time, John Clay, explained the appeal of a Shakespeare theatre: 'We think that the Shakespeare productions will attract people to the other forms of entertainment on the Pier, especially during our slower times in the winter. We fit together very well' (quoted in Jones, 'The Location'). To the financiers behind the Navy Pier development, Shakespeare meant tapping into a moneyed Gold Coast audience that might not otherwise frequent the pier and enhancing income during the months when the frigid winds off Lake Michigan make fair-going wholly untenable.
12 Gaines's approach corresponds with the same tendency to associate the poet and his works with 'general or universal human interests . . . with social and cultural goodness' that Michael Bristol has located in much Shakespeare scholarship: *Shakespeare's America, America's Shakespeare* (New York, 1990), p. 16. David G. Brailow's study of the Ghost in Gaines's 1996 *Hamlet* notes the ahistorical interpretive impact of the director's 'universalist view of Shakespeare', in '"Tis here. 'Tis gone", The Ghost in the Text', in *Stage Directions in 'Hamlet': New Essays and New Directions*, ed. Hardin L. Aasand (Madison, 2003), pp. 101–14, p. 109. In *Authorizing Shakespeare on Film and Television: Gender, Class, and Ethnicity in Adaptation* (New York, 2011), I trace a similar construction of the liberal-humanist Shakespeare in Michael Radford's film adaptation of *The Merchant of Venice* (2004).
13 Here I posit for the amusement park a familiar carnival ancestry thoroughly articulated by Mikhail Bakhtin. See Mikhail Bakhtin, *Rabelais and His World*, trans. Helene Iswolsky

park Ferris wheel turns slowly outside the theatre and visitors wander in and out of Pier fun houses, Gaines leads the theatre's efforts to fulfil its stated mission 'to bring to life the plays of William Shakespeare, and to present other great performances for audiences from all walks of life and from around the world'.[14] In its final prepositional phrases, the theatre's mission glances at the educational, economic and ethnic differences that the demographics of Navy Pier visitors manifest. However, even as Gaines cites a populist, 'for-the-people' ethos in her understanding of Shakespeare the Humanist, she mystifies the very forces of authority that perpetuate social disequilibrium and injustice. Such a formulation tacitly ignores a well-known history in which Shakespeare has long been appropriated as a means to enforce conformity to hegemonic power structures – colonial, economic, religious and social. So, what happens inside the doors of the theatre? Do the tactical variations of the city walker on the Pier infiltrate the theatre's productions? What happens when a given play text threatens to expose the vulnerability of Gaines's self-justificatory rhetoric? How might the Chicago Shakespeare Theater treat a play that spotlights conflicts over power and hierarchy, a play such as *The Taming of the Shrew* (1593/94) that in so many ways defies ready alignment with Shakespeare the Humanist? *The Taming of the Shrew* certainly resists reconciliation with the marketable image of the liberal-humanist playwright essential to the Shakespeare impresario as Graham Holderness points out in his discussion of the play's performance history: 'Given the specific historical context, it seems to me impossible, despite the sustained efforts of a huge critical and theatrical project of naturalising and domestication, to elicit from the given text of the *Shrew* a body of meanings and values compatible with modern progressive thought or with contemporary feminism.'[15] A play deeply imbricated in systems of hierarchy and oppression, *Shrew* exerts tremendous pressure on the Chicago Shakespeare Theater's assertion of Shakespearian value and authority. When Gaines herself directed *Shrew* in 1993, she insisted, 'But I don't think Shakespeare was capable of writing a sexist play. He was, of course, a humanist, which transcends feminism, racism or any ism.'[16] Three productions of *Shrew* dating from CST's rise to prominence on the Navy Pier skyline manifest the means by which the theatre aligns production content with its construction of Shakespearian authority even when that 'Great Humanist' label experiences tactical resistance from below.[17]

Since its arrival on Navy Pier, CST has staged two full-scale productions of *Shrew*, one led by American David H. Bell (an experienced musical theatre director) that opened the 2003 season[18] and one directed by Josie Rourke (Artistic Director of London's Bush Theatre) that featured purpose-written induction matter by playwright Neil LaBute (2010).[19] As with most productions of *Shrew*, the central interpretive dilemma evident in both Bell's and Rourke's approaches was how to handle a plotting whose origins can be

---

(Bloomington, 1984). As a choreographed capitalist enterprise, Navy Pier can only dimly echo the practices of 'temporary liberation from the prevailing truth and from the established order...the suspension of all hierarchical rank, privileges, norms, and prohibitions' of folk carnival (10). Nonetheless, an analysis of Navy Pier must acknowledge that the amusement park's modes of entertainment trace back to the range of festive disruptions from the lower ranks examined by Bakhtin.

[14] *Shakespeare Lives in Chicago* (Chicago Shakespeare Theater Annual Report, 2007).

[15] Graham Holderness, *The Taming of the Shrew* (New York, 1991), pp. 22–3. CST's production history demonstrates the perennial popularity of a play that nonetheless troubles the humanist label; at Gaines's theatre, only *Romeo and Juliet* and *A Midsummer Night's Dream* rival *Shrew* for total number of full-length or Short Shakespeare! productions. In the twenty-six years of the company, *Shrew* has been mounted six times – three full-scale productions and three Short Shakespeare! offerings.

[16] Quoted in Clifford Terry, 'Shaking up Shakespeare: Barbara Gaines Takes on the Bard', *Chicago Tribune*, 28 November 1993, http://articles.chicagotribune.com.

[17] Here I reference obliquely Certeau's assertion that 'The ordinary practitioners of the city live "down below" (93) – below, between, and within the proper sites of power, the buildings and skyscrapers and structures that form the city.

[18] The Bell production ran from 5 September to 23 November 2003.

[19] The Rourke production ran from 7 April to 6 June 2010.

found in the troubling shrew-taming *fabliaux*.[20] The lavish Bell staging channelled a wistful nostalgia and softened the gender troubles of the play by driving towards images of loving mutuality. Bell's production accepted the stereotypes underlying the Shakespearian text with a wink and a nod to the audience, suggesting in the jokey familiarity of back-slapping misogyny that, political correctness aside, women and men will always battle for supremacy *and* discover desire in that conflict. In contrast, Rourke's *Shrew*, characterized by an austere cynicism, projected an interrogatory attitude towards Shakespeare's sacral authority, an intervention much more threatening to the theatre's self-image as guardian of Shakespeare the Humanist. During the Summer of 2012, as part of Chicago's fledgling Cultural Plan initiative, the theatre launched a Chicago Shakespeare in the Parks outreach that transferred a Short Shakespeare! production of *Shrew* (directed by Rachel Rockwell, Spring 2012) from the theatre's main stage to parks in neighbourhoods underserved by the city's major arts institutions. In the itinerant parks *Shrew*, elements of institutional strategy met the pedestrian's tactics of resistance, demonstrating just how difficult it can be to extricate high art from its institutional moorings and how vexed the authorizing imprimatur of Shakespeare the Humanist can be in the face of a city's socioeconomic realities.

SINGING OUR TROUBLES AWAY

In 2003, the Bell production deployed modes from a variety of popular culture representational forms to produce an interpretation in keeping with the genial humanity of CST's 'Shakespeare'. Taking inspiration from Federico Fellini's *La Dolce Vita* (1960), the chic, Italian staging reminiscent of the Via Veneto gave a mod accessibility to the dangerously outdated story.[21] In addition, song and dance numbers so dominated the Bell production that reviewers identified it as akin to a Shakespearian Broadway musical.[22] The stereotypical categories of gender endemic to musical theatre went hand-in-glove with the visual coding

of the production. Featuring ironwork balconies, striped awnings, flowers in bloom and climbing the walls, and recessed spaces under soft-pastel lighting gels, the deeply romantic stage design implied the inevitability of an amorous plot outcome. Indeed, how could love not flourish in such an insistent and over-signified environment? In this space, men and women conformed readily to familiar stereotypes – an Italian machismo in the men; a feminine Mob Princess in Bianca; and the put-upon 'Mama' in Katharina. In the 1960s setting, the play's drive towards images of loving mutuality and equality seemed an accommodation designed to preserve the status and popularity of Shakespeare while transforming a fractious text into an anticipation of reassuring heterosexual values. When interviewed, the actors playing Katharina and Petruchio respectively, Kate Fry and Ryan Shively, affirmed this reading of the text. Interviewer Metz summarized: 'both actors agree that the play is, at its core, a true-blue love story'. Shively asserted, 'When they [Katharina and Petruchio] leave at the end of the play, I think they're definitely in love. They're beginning this really exciting relationship, and I think that's the appeal of the play.'[23] Through carefully choreographed representational intertexts, Bell balanced his production between stereotypes generative of laughter and a celebration of compatibility through difference in keeping with CST's construction of Shakespeare.

---

[20] John C. Bean, 'Comic Structure and the Humanizing of Kate in *The Taming of the Shrew*', in *The Woman's Part: Feminist Criticism of Shakespeare*, ed. Carolyn Ruth Swift Lenz, Gayle Greene and Carol Thomas Neely (Urbana, 1983), pp. 65–78, p. 66.

[21] The promptbook's wardrobe chart stresses the Fellini connection by describing Petruchio's first look as 'Marcello Mastroianni'.

[22] *Chicago Tribune* reviewer Michael Phillips observed that the production 'boasts enough onstage music and vocalizing to qualify as a semi-musical, with original score by Henry Marsh as arranged by Alaric Jans': 'Shakespeare's *Shrew* Obscured by Brim Reality', *Chicago Tribune*, 15 September 2003, http://articles.chicagotribune.com.

[23] Quoted in Nina Metz, 'A Modern, Possibly PC, Look at *Shrew*', *Chicago Tribune*, 5 September 2003, http://articles.chicagotribune.com.

8. *The Taming of the Shrew*, 3.2. Chicago Shakespeare Theater, Courtyard Theater, 2003, directed by David H. Bell. Petruchio (Ryan Shively) and Katharina (Kate Fry).

The dramaturgical techniques utilized in the Act Four country house sequence illustrate the accommodations made by Bell to soften *Shrew* in ways suited to the theatre. Overlapping performance modes from film, musical theatre and movie-musical tradition gave a romantic gloss to these scenes depicting the emotional and physical abuse of Katharina that constitute her taming and renaming as Kate, 'conformable as other household Kates' (2.1.278).[24] Bell translated to stage the split-screen film technique and song montage to wring sentimental romance from the bitterness on the page. Intercutting the abuse strategies of 4.1 with the blooming romance of Lucentio and Bianca in 4.2, Bell implied a basic similitude between the couples despite the observably different power dynamics. Dividing the stage space in half, Bell interpolated extra-textual glimpses of Katharina and Petruchio in bed stage right and then placed

Lucentio and Bianca stage left as they planned their elopement. Brightening and fading spotlights created a visual rhythm carrying the audience back and forth between the two depictions of love's flowering. In 4.1 after throwing away the prepared food, Petruchio stood opposite Katharina across an enormous bed placed prominently on the thrust. Miming a defiant striptease, they each undressed – the shirtless Petruchio shimmied out of jeans while Katharina unzipped her soiled wedding dress and kicked it away, revealing a pink underslip. Spotlights rose on Lucentio and Bianca in 4.2, who kissed and flirted at a café table overlooked by Hortensio and Tranio. Meanwhile, a gently crooning Grumio warbled, 'Mystery is to know what to tell a woman'. At one moment in the song,

---

[24] Quotations from *Shrew* are taken from *The Riverside Shakespeare*, ed. G. Blakemore Evans (Boston, 1974).

a wakeful Katharina rested on an elbow to look longingly at the sleeping Petruchio. Another spotlight shift to Bianca served to parallel the growing desire of each sister for her respective partner. Yet another lighting return to Petruchio emphasized mutuality since he looked at the supine Katharina, touched her hair, kissed it, and inhaled her fragrance. Within this heightened romantic context, Petruchio at last delivered his 'Thus have I politicly begun my reign' (4.1.188–211) but did so in a soft bedroom voice, almost absurd given the claims of the speech itself.

This staging of what amounted to a crosscut song montage employed several techniques to smooth out the rougher edges that might well belie Shakespeare's status as cultivated by Gaines. The alternating striptease and wakefulness of Katharina and Petruchio implied a mutual attraction and desire that would soon trump the posturing for power by both individuals. In addition, Grumio's song suggested that the difficulties between Petruchio and Katharina were not born of a masculine prerogative to dominance but rather from the eternal mystery of womankind; the song included the nonsensical claim typical of such pabulum, 'Even when she's wrong, she's right'. In fact, the song's thematic through-line centred on the difficulty of communicating with a being as impenetrable and changeable as woman and hinted that Petruchio's problem was not a cruel imperiousness but rather genuine befuddlement over how best to speak his feelings to Katharina.

Such a reading of this crucial scene prepared for the couple's exit from the play as equals both in power and in love, allowing viewers to conclude that Shakespeare was not a misogynist nor an advocate of spousal abuse.[25] At the conclusion of the 5.2 wager, an emotionally vulnerable Katharina signalled to Petruchio her disappointment in his laddish callousness by briefly clutching the wager money piled on the nearby table and looking pointedly at her husband. During Katharina's submission speech, Petruchio walked to her, touched her gently and seated himself to listen attentively. Punctuating the logical shape of the speech with movement, Katharina appeared almost

to weep by the final lines, prompted by Petruchio's betrayal of her newly offered love. The force of Katharina's words and affective display compelled the sincerely loving Petruchio to kneel down and prevent Katharina from placing her hands beneath her husband's foot. After a long embrace and a scolding look from Katharina, Petruchio threw his ill-gotten gains in the air before the happy couple exited to the tuneful accompaniment of violins and accordion. The harmonious and mutual transformations of each character – Petruchio who abandoned his machismo posturing and Katharina who expressed a desiring and desirous nature at last – thus fulfilled the predestined promise of the romantic visual and aural landscape. A significant discrepancy between the promptbook and the performance further demonstrated the production's subtle commitment to patriarchal authority albeit of the benevolent variety. The promptbook directed Katharina to take up the winnings and toss them in the air. However, in performance, this final task was left to Petruchio, focusing on him as the agent of change one last time.

Bell's accommodation of the play's difficulties managed to preserve the cultural authority of the humanist Shakespeare and to render a fairly conservative construction of gender seemingly progressive. Opting for an escapist reading of the play that avoided the stark inequities of the source text, the theatre company exerted mighty agential rights to conceal the worrisome truth that the venerable poet-playwright might have been complicit with the gender inequities of his time and, sadly, of our own, rather than a trailblazer questioning those practices. In doing so, the theatre manifested Pierre Bourdieu's schema in which the artist's choices underscore the authority of the dominant power; while preserving CST's image of

---

[25] In his various accommodations, Bell followed a well-worn revisionist staging orthodoxy identified by Lynda E. Boose, 'reimagining an ending that will at once liberate Kate from meaning what she says and simultaneously reconstruct the social space into a vision of so-called "mutuality"' (see her 'Scolding Brides and Bridling Scolds: Taming the Woman's Unruly Member', *Shakespeare Quarterly*, 42 (1991), 179–213, p. 180.

a humane Shakespeare, the production neutered female resistance to constraint and naturalized the gender hierarchies essential to patriarchal culture. The contrivances of the staging presented Shakespeare as advocate of mutuality and equality as they simultaneously resorted to essentialist assumptions about gender identity. That so much window dressing was required reveals, in part, the stakes of the debate over Shakespearian identity. For, in its accommodations, the Bell production validated established gender hierarchies – benevolent though they might seem in a chastened and loving Petruchio – even as it appeared to embrace a resistant 'from below' call for equality. Bell's staging deployed song and dance in ways that echoed the carnivalesque context of Navy Pier but in the service of long-institutionalized hierarchies endemic to the unseen network of power authorizing the theatre itself.

WALKING OUT THE DOOR

The protesting too much of Bell's representation certainly finds parallels in the long performance history of this play but, in 2010, CST employed two artists, Josie Rourke and Neil LaBute, to launch a direct attack on the Great Humanist status of Shakespeare so strenuously and problematically defended by Bell's staging. In doing so, the Rourke and LaBute *Shrew* provided theatrical space for the pedestrian's tactics of resistance to institutionalized strategies, even privileging the act of 'walking out' in its dénouement. In contrast to Bell's cheerful accommodations, the LaBute framing material of the Rourke production functioned as an invitation to interrogate the status of Shakespeare's play and its steady confinement of the titular shrew.[26] According to CST Director of Education, Marilyn Halperin, the fresh framing material, which replaced the Christopher Sly Induction, underwent a series of revisions and negotiations by Rourke, LaBute and the cast in the run-up to the production.[27] Both author and director aimed for a more radical frame than ultimately was performed or could be supported by the demographic of the theatre's typical audience

and, more importantly, its donors.[28] Perhaps not since its early years had the financial viability of the theatre been in such great jeopardy as in 2010 in the full force of the Great Recession. Ticket

---

[26] Known for a tendency to misanthropy and accused of misogyny by some critics, LaBute may seem a surprising choice to revisit critically the brutality of Shakespeare's text: see Pat Jordan, 'Neil LaBute has a Thing About Beauty', *The New York Times Magazine*, 29 March 2009, http://www.nytimes.com. *Chicago Tribune* theatre critic Chris Jones concurs in his review: 'And thus, in one of the more unusual theatrical choices of the moment, Chicago Shakespeare decided that the way to alleviate (or explore) the play's discomforting sexual politics was to hire the politically incendiary playwright Neil LaBute to write an original outer frame. Yet more bizarrely, LaBute, a writer known for his brilliant depictions of mercurial men, came up with a new backstage love plot involving two broadly drawn lesbians' (Chris Jones, '*Taming of the Shrew* at Chicago Shakespeare: LaBute's Frame Doesn't Fit Battle of the Sexes', *Chicago Tribune*, 14 April 2010, http://leisureblogs.chicagotribune.com).

[27] Marilyn Halperin, Personal Interview, 29 September 2011. By re-voicing the Sly Induction's theatricalized context, the Rourke and LaBute production thus capitalized on a resistance inherent in the text and followed a more recent *Shrew* performance trend identified by Barbara Hodgdon: '*Shrew*'s frame has come into focus as the key to re-viewing as well as re-staging the scene of taming and as a site for its critique': 'Katharina Bound, or Play(K)ating the Strictures of Everyday Life' in *The Taming of the Shrew: Critical Essays*, ed. Dana E. Aspinall (New York, 2002), pp. 351–87, p. 372. Leah S. Marcus similarly notes that a recent performance tendency to import from the quarto *A Shrew* text (1594) the concluding Sly material 'is gaining increasing popularity' because 'it softens some of the brutality of the taming scenes . . . [and] distances late twentieth-century audiences from some of the most unacceptable implications of Kate's pronouncements on male sovereignty' (*Unediting the Renaissance: Shakespeare, Marlowe, Milton* (New York, 1996), p. 104).

[28] Just a few months after the play's run, the *Financial Times* published an op-ed piece by Alan Davey, chief executive of Arts Council England, regarding the forms of arts funding. Davey cites the Chicago *Shrew* as an example of the pressures that private funding can exert over artistic integrity and freedom. Davey writes: 'A reliance on the goodwill of wealthy donors can provoke self-censorship, too. In Chicago this year, a production of *The Taming of the Shrew*, by exceptional British director Josie Rourke, ran into difficulties due to apprehension over a benefactor's response to a scene portraying gay characters. This fear was misplaced and ultimately no donor withdrew – but the willingness to self-censor was real' ('Arts Cannot be Funded by Big Donors Alone', *Financial Times*, 5 August 2010, www.ft.com).

sales fell precipitously between 2007 and 2008 from $7.5 million to $6.3 million and bottomed out in 2010 at $5.6 million, a decline of 25.1 per cent over a four-year period.[29] The promptbooks for the 2003 and 2010 productions tell a similar story of declining resources: the Bell promptbook enumerates a total cast and crew of 74 personnel while the 2010 production lists 61. The difference in cast numbers is particularly striking, 30 in 2003 and 22 in 2010, numbers that may reflect the opposing aesthetics of the two directors as well as the shrinking production budget in 2010. With investments trending down with the market and public support and private donations remaining flat or decreasing slightly, *Shrew*'s director, writer and cast worked in this fragile financial context to arrive at a frame script true to the resistant stance of the production and acceptable to theatre subscribers and walk-in ticket purchasers.[30] As it was, the content of the frame, which included idiomatic slang and contemporary expletives as well as dramatizations of non-heteronormative relationships, prompted a warning letter from the theatre to schools bringing students to the production. The theatre marked its concern about the content of the frame by offering a no-questions-asked refund to any school group rendered uncomfortable by the adult nature of the production.[31]

In contrast to Bell, Rourke's set designed by Lucy Osborne exposed the theatrical means by which shrew-taming becomes entertaining and acceptable to an audience. Rourke's staging featured a fixed Italianate backdrop that changed little over the course of the performance. While Bell's stage included wings extending on the sides and utilized the deep recesses of backstage to create a generous expanse for action, Rourke's flat concealed the backstage and left much of the playing on a shallow main stage and the thrust. The shrunken world of Rourke's production constricted its human subjects to a narrower space than the fantasy experienced by the characters of Bell's run. The familiar backstage trope of LaBute's framing shone a light on the constructed nature of the world under scrutiny. A centrally positioned door on the backstage flat had not been fully installed

and leaned against the back wall flanked by bright yellow 'Caution' tape. The unfinished state of the stage was heightened by actors who would stamp their feet to mime knocking whenever 'entering' through the absent door. A similar exposure of theatrical mechanics occurred when stagehands rushed to secure in place a missing *Venus de Milo* statue with cordless DeWalt drills. While typical of the harried backstage genre, such obvious disruption to the theatrical spectacle also stressed the constructedness of the performative world outside the frame, CST's own season of productions on Navy Pier. Furthermore, the brokenness of the stage suited the riven and imperfect play text being performed.

In fact, much of the LaBute frame material articulated the impossibility of salvaging the gender dynamics of this 1590s comedy. Set during a technical rehearsal and preview performance of *The Taming of the Shrew*, the frame centred on a director and actor duo with a long history of domestic and artistic partnership, a relationship that had survived despite the actor's tendency to dalliance. LaBute's frame created a parallel between the taming endeavoured by Petruchio (Ian Bedford) and the strident efforts of the Director (Mary Beth Fisher) to control her lover and star whom she called by her stage name throughout, 'Kate' (Bianca Amato). Battles between the two women punctuated the technical and dress rehearsals of *Shrew* in which the two argued over the actor's habits of

---

[29] For accessing the *GuideStar* database and providing detailed financial analysis of CST's IRS Form 990 Return of Organization Exempt from Income Tax, I am indebted to my beloved partner, Paul D. Smith, Jr., CPA, MSA. *GuideStar*, 2012.

[30] Long-term investments declined from $10.5 million in 2007 to $8.5 million in 2010.

[31] The production homepage on the CST website included a parental advisory icon and short explanation of the frame content, closing with this directive: '*If you attend the theater with a young person*, please consider their sensitivity to coarse language and sexual themes. While our twenty-first century ears may not pick up on the many bawdy references in Shakespeare's *Shrew*, contemporary language and situations are more vivid' ('*The Taming of the Shrew*: A Note to Our Audience').

infidelity, the social roles of women, and the merits of long-term relationships.

DIRECTOR. I want you. Maybe kids. I want stability and a woman I can trust and that's not asking too much. Is it?

KATE. Why? Why do you want the same junk that your mother had? Look at her – she's so unhappy! So was mine before she died – died without ever doing one thing she wanted to for herself.

DIRECTOR. That's completely different . . .

KATE. No, it's not! (BEAT) Look at this goddam play we're doing – the way that women are treated. Right? And now look just how far we've come . . .

DIRECTOR. Not very.

KATE. People always bitch about it not being far enough and maybe that's so, but I'll take it. You know? I'm glad I'm here right now and can kiss and hug and love anybody I want . . . . (LaBute)

In the frame material, Kate's emphatic reference to 'this goddam play' as contrastive evidence of the twenty-first century's radical improvements in women's social and political status strongly diverged from the Bell production in which such a reading of the early modern text as deeply flawed was not even countenanced. LaBute chose to spotlight the play's strategies of shrew-taming by echoing them in the actions of the Director who continually humiliated her star as punishment for a failure to meet her ideals of loving fidelity. Most notably, the Director repeatedly tested lighting and blocking choices that objectified and disempowered her lover so unfeelingly that the viewer might well have suspected that, instead of one shrew, this production had delivered two.[32]

Much of the 'talking back' at Shakespeare took place in scenes where the Director and 'Kate' debated the merits of staging what 'Kate' described as this 'stupid excuse for a play'. In many ways, the fictional Director mouthed a familiar line of defence when questioned about the play's relevance and ethical worth; however, so much of the frame revealed her own dubious motivations to circumscribe her errant partner through the act of performance that she became an unredeemably compromised instrument defending the choice to stage *Shrew* yet again. LaBute's Director explained

the goals of the approach to her lover and star: 'I think we're going to have a show that's really special, one that is unafraid to tackle the problems of a text that's outdated by looking them squarely in the eye . . . You're not just this really fun and engaging "Kate" but you're giving us a new reading of a difficult role.' In an interview, Rourke echoed LaBute's Director as she articulated her own perspective on *Shrew*:

I think this play has many fascinating things to say about relationships, about control, about marriage, about gender. However, because of when it was written, it is a play in which a series of unacceptably repressive acts are committed against a woman. In putting a contemporary frame around Shakespeare's play, one of the things I am trying to do is to acknowledge the difficulties that *Shrew* presents to us in the twenty-first century in a way that is funny, raw and engaging.[33]

While the publicity interviews and tone of the 2003 *Taming* allowed very little room for such a candid acknowledgement, here Rourke pinpointed the failings of the text. However, she did so in ways that preserved the status of Shakespeare for the theatre. Although steering much closer to the 'sexist' label, Rourke stopped short of attributing the play's problematics to the poet. By placing the drama's title rather than 'Shakespeare' in the subject

---

32 The portrayal of a lesbian relationship raised critical comment: 'Judging the play as a whole using Rourke's own wish that it be "raw, funny and engaging", I say here that it failed utterly, unless "*lesbians* can be misogynist, just like men" counts as an urgent new insight. This was Shakespeare by way of Joe Eszterhas, and I found the play's depiction of homosexuality cartoonish and crude' (Andrea Stevens, review of *The Taming of the Shrew*, *Shakespeare Bulletin*, 28 (2010), 491–5, p. 492). The critical response to the new induction material was not surprising, given LaBute's reputation for misanthropy; in an earlier profile of the playwright at the time of a New York production of his *Reasons to be Pretty*, Pat Jordan wrote: 'LaBute's plays are, in fact, so provocative that some past audience members have walked out midplay or screamed out "kill the playwright" or slapped an actor's face after a performance.'

33 Josie Rourke, 'A 21st Century Lens', interview by Marilyn Halperin, in Playbill for *The Taming of the Shrew* (April 2010), p. 9.

position of a sentence naming the text's irresolvable gender trouble, Rourke maintained a useful gap between the revered playwright and the vexed artwork, one essential if her production was not set to undermine entirely the grounding principles of the theatre's self-construction. Nonetheless, that Rourke's assessment matched in many ways the argument attributed to the frame's compromised Director left open, perhaps unintentionally, the question of whether or not this perspective on *Shrew* was authoritative.

Such ambiguous cross-currents ebbed during the production's final scene. LaBute's and Rourke's most direct confrontation of the playwright occurred at the end of Katharina's submission speech in Act 5. Just as Petruchio extended a hand towards her and repeated twice, 'Now there's a wench', the actress stood, declared, 'No, no, no', and began to remove the skirting of her costume. With a grandness of movement, her hands reached upwards to punctuate a definitive, 'Fuck this. We are done here.' Clapping her hands, she marched in leggings and top down the centre aisle of the theatre to laughter and audience applause and thrust upward a valedictory hand gesture.[34] In her review, Caitlin Montanye Parrish wrote, 'By all means, see this glorious ensemble's work. But don't look for meaning in the contemporary scaffolding. "Fuck this!" is neither a thesis nor a revelation. It's a weak response to the joke played on women for ages: Their tragedy is men's comedy.'[35]

Whether or not 'Fuck this' constitutes a thoughtful or satisfying thesis, the defiance of LaBute's dénouement emphatically shaped a very different rhetorical position vis-à-vis Shakespeare's authority and the meaning of *Shrew* than the earlier Bell staging. Less than ten years later, the theatre that had once encouraged its audience to laugh away any discomfort with the play's content now schooled its patrons in a more combative stance towards Shakespeare's cultural capital. That CST would risk committing what Paul Yachnin has labelled 'bardicide' within the costly and secular-sacred of a 'Shakespeare Theatre' in Middle America, that it would 'kill' the thing that gives it being and identity might well surprise during the year

2010 when financial capital proved in such dangerously short supply.[36] Taking a significant financial risk, the production endeavoured to face up to the troubling dynamics of a play inconsistent with the theatre's Great Humanist image of Shakespeare. While some viewers might object to the mouthpieces chosen for this interrogative approach – cartoonish stereotypes of feminist lesbians – the production's final moment did manifest the individual tactic of resistance possible in Certeau's city. Quite literally, LaBute and Rourke's Katharina enacted the prerogative of Certeau's pedestrian to choose an alternate route through the city's

---

[34] LaBute-Rourke's 'Kate' ruptured what James C. Scott has called the 'public transcript', 'the open interaction between subordinates and those who dominate' (2), by voicing the 'hidden transcript', the 'offstage' discourse of resistance carefully guarded by the oppressed: *Domination and the Arts of Resistance: Hidden Transcripts* (New Haven, 1990, pp. 4–5). Scott describes explosions such as Kate's as 'a declaration that breaches the etiquette of power relations, that breaks an apparently calm surface of silence and consent, [and] carries the force of a symbolic declaration of war' (8). I am grateful to Ante Jeroncic for pointing out the relevance of Scott's work to this discussion.

[35] Caitlin Montanye Parrish, review of *The Taming of the Shrew*, *Time Out Chicago*, 18 April 2010, http://timeoutchicago.com. Similarly, the reviewers for *Early Modern Literary Studies* observe that previous interpolations designed to reimagine the partnership of Petruchio and Katharina have traditionally been one dramatic method of solving the misogyny of the play's end. Suggesting that such interpolations might be an equivalent of the LaBute–Rourke aborted ending, the reviewers refine the comparison: 'However, the undeniable difference between the two is that interpolations do not avoid the final scene, but rather they interpret it. There is little interpretation in omission' (M. G. Aune, Desiree Helterbran and Brandon Zebrowski, review of *The Taming of the Shrew*, *Early Modern Literary Studies*, 15:2 (2010–11), http://extra.shu.ac.uk/emls/15-2/revcts.htm).

[36] Yachnin explains that 'the revisionist artist prosecutes a brief against Shakespeare, who emerges as an author of and for the social elite or, more often, as an apologist for patriarchal or imperialist violence. In each case, the revisionist's implicit claim to value is founded on an artistic revolution against the politico-moral authority of Shakespeare – the poet-kingpin of the Western tradition' (Paul Yachnin, '"To kill a king": The Modern Politics of Bardicide', in *Shakespeare and Modern Theatre: The Performance of Modernity*, ed. Michael Bristol, Kathleen McLuskie, and Christopher Holmes (New York, 2001), pp. 6–54, p. 33).

9. *The Taming of the Shrew*, 2.1. Chicago Shakespeare Theatre, Courtyard Theater, 2010, directed by Josie Rourke. Katharina (Bianca Amato) and Petruchio (Ian Bedford).

institutionally delineated concrete, glass and steel, walking off the set and out the doors of the theatre.

Furthermore, unsatisfying and reductionistic as some elements of the frame may have been, LaBute did trouble a familiar trope of Shakespeare performance, the 'Shakespop sub-genre' that narrates 'the backstage struggles of a company to mount a Shakespeare show'.[37] Douglas Lanier explains that this trope often celebrates a communal regeneration prompted by the great author's work and manifested by the interactions of a theatre company (159). However, LaBute thwarted this self-justifying metatheatrical narrative in his truncated ending; even when in desperation the Director called out to halt 'Kate' and addressed her at last by her right name, 'Angela', this concession to the actor's identity came too late. By daring to rename Shakespeare as something less than the Great Humanist, the LaBute–Rourke production questioned, albeit briefly, the founding and self-constituting assumptions of the Chicago Shakespeare Theater.[38] Such inversion may well constitute carnival topsy-turvy as surely as the Ferris wheel and rides just outside the theatre's Navy Pier doors and approximate something like the individual tactic of resistance from below articulated by Certeau.

TAKING SHAKESPEARE TO THE PARKS

The LaBute–Rourke *Shrew* closed with its Katharina walking out the door and refusing to participate in the act of institutionalized oppression embodied by Shakespeare's play and its life on the stage. Two years later, the rest of the company walked out as well but with a difference – opting to bring Shakespeare along with them. The summer Chicago Shakespeare in the Parks initiative packed its bags and stowed its set, sound system and costumes on a tractor-trailer truck to move through the city and its neighbourhoods, abandoning the concrete and glass Navy Pier house for the open air. These parks productions in which audience members came and went with a casual ease not afforded by theatre architecture allowed CST

to acknowledge some of the sociocultural barriers that prevent proselytizing a broader demographic into the church of the fine arts. Essentially, the movement to the parks constituted a tacit admission that even planting in the context of Navy Pier does not eliminate the classist associations that limit access to and interest in the fine arts. In an endeavour to operationalize more fully its stated mission – 'to bring to life the plays of William Shakespeare, and to present other great performances for audiences from all walks of life and from around the world' – CST joined forces with the Chicago Park District to launch 'Chicago Shakespeare in the Parks' in the summer of 2012. Made possible by a Boeing Company grant and other corporate sponsorships, this mobile, 75-minute production aimed to bring Shakespeare to a wider Chicago demographic than typically served by the Navy Pier location despite its populist aspirations. Gaines and Criss Henderson (CST Executive Director) summarized the goals of the project in an emailed letter to patrons: 'As Chicago's home for Shakespeare, we now look forward to bringing our work into the diverse neighborhoods of our great city and uniting the community through the timeless and universal themes expressed by one of the world's greatest playwrights.'[39] Once again, the theatre's promotional materials, which burnished Shakespeare's credentials as a trans-historically relevant tool for civic union, were anchored in the Great Humanist construct. The universalizing instinct of the promotion downplayed the cultural and material particularities of Shakespeare and his oeuvre

[37] Douglas Lanier, *Shakespeare and Modern Popular Culture* (New York, 2002), p. 157.

[38] Kim Solga's recent study of director Peter Hinton's work at the Stratford Shakespeare Festival examines dynamics quite similar to those at Chicago Shakespeare. She notes a marked risk-aversion at the festival where administrators must balance profitability and concern for return patrons against artistic license and a more robust creative exploration ('Realism and the Ethics of Risk at the Stratford Shakespeare Festival', *Shakespeare Bulletin*, 28 (2010), 417–42, p. 422).

[39] Barbara Gaines and Criss Henderson, 'Introducing Chicago Shakespeare in the Parks', email to CST patrons, 15 June 2012.

in the service of a vaguely idealized civic unity. Such well-meaning cultural evangelism neatly side-stepped the reality that unity of the many often comes at the expense of the few and, in this case, given the play selected, indeed would come at the expense of a portion of the target demographic – women. The creative team behind the parks project selected an abridgement of *The Taming of the Shrew* as its cultural ambassador to the city of Chicago.

The Chicago Shakespeare in the Parks initiative grew out of a city-wide drive to extend the reach of fine arts institutions to its highly diverse and highly segregated population.[40] According to Halperin, the impetus came from a 2006 University of Chicago cultural mapping that indicated significant urban population swaths were not participating in the city's largest cultural institutions.[41] With funding supplied in part by the Joyce Foundation, the Cultural Policy Center and the Irving B. Harris Graduate School of Public Policy Studies joined forces to produce *Mapping Cultural Participation in Chicago*, a study that charted participation data from Chicago-area arts outlets onto maps of the city's neighbourhoods and overlaid ethnic identity, socioeconomic status and household structure data from the US 2000 Census.[42] The study's executive summary articulates the ethnic divide present: 'We find that participation in Chicago's largest arts and cultural organizations is highest in predominantly white, high-income areas of the metropolitan area' (9). However, while the gap in arts participation between Caucasian neighbourhoods and African-American and Latino neighbourhoods appears wide, the study also notes significant under-utilization in white neighbourhoods and concludes that rather than ethnicity, 'The socioeconomic attributes of a neighborhood are the most important predictors of the density of arts participation' (9). Because the extent and quality of data from the city's largest cultural institutions exceeded that from smaller, underfunded entities, the study's 'core data are those from the twelve largest not-for-profit cultural institutions in Chicago, supplemented by a sample of forty-nine smaller institutions' (9).[43] The study's conclusion diagnoses a failing of larger cultural institutions in

the city that appears a direct mandate for initiatives such as Chicago Shakespeare in the Parks:

Currently, however, Chicago's large arts organizations are not successfully engaging households in areas with poor socioeconomic backgrounds. Both predominantly minority and predominantly white areas with relatively low household incomes, low levels of educational attainment, and large households participate in the city's large arts organizations at relatively low rates. This finding suggests that to engage such households, these organizations may have to reconsider how they deliver their services, their pricing structure, and the times they make their services available to this audience.   (51)

In addition to the University of Chicago study, Mayor Rahm Emanuel's draft cultural plan fuelled the summer 2012 CST walk in the parks.[44] For the first time since 1986, the Windy City would have a working cultural plan, and during the summer months of 2012, the draft plan was under debate at town hall meetings throughout the city.[45] In the foreword to the draft version of the *City of Chicago Cultural Plan 2012*, Mayor Emanuel weds the interests of culture and economics: 'This plan matters. Financially, Chicago has the third largest

---

[40] Recent census studies have shown that 'Chicago remains the most segregated big city in America' despite having made significant strides in reducing segregation. In fact, 'Of the 10 largest cities, Chicago has seen the second-largest declines in segregation between 2000 and 2010' (Stefano Esposito, 'Chicago Tops Nation for Segregation, but Sees 2nd-largest Decline in U.S.', *Chicago Sun Times*, 31 January 2012, www.suntimes.com).

[41] Marilyn Halperin, Personal interview, 2 July 2012.

[42] Robert LaLonde *et al.*, *Mapping Cultural Participation in Chicago* (Chicago, 2006), p. 11.

[43] Those twelve largest institutions central to the study are The Art Institute of Chicago, Auditorium Theatre Council, Chicago Historical Society, Chicago Shakespeare Theater, Chicago Symphony Orchestra, Chicago Theater Group, Inc. (The Goodman Theatre), The Field Museum, Joffrey Ballet of Chicago, Lyric Opera of Chicago, Museum of Contemporary Art, Museum of Science and Industry and Steppenwolf Theatre Company (all defined as 'large' by virtue of 'annual revenue in excess of $8 million') (LaLonde, *Mapping Cultural Participation*, pp. 11, 53).

[44] Halperin, Interview, 2 July 2012.

[45] *City of Chicago Cultural Plan 2012*, draft (Lord Cultural Resources, 2012) www.chicagoculturalplan2012.com, p. 18.

10. *The Taming of the Shrew*, 3.2. Chicago Shakespeare Theatre, Chicago Park District, 2012, directed by Rachel Rockwell. Petruchio (Matt Mueller) and Katharina (Ericka Ratcliff).

creative economy in the U.S., with 24,000 arts enterprises, including nearly 650 non-profit arts organizations, generating more than $2 billion annually and employing 150,000 people. Chicago's creative vibrancy creates jobs, attracts new businesses and tourists, and improves neighborhood vitality and quality of life.' He adds in a final rhetorical flourish: 'The Chicago Cultural Plan 2012 will chart a roadmap for Chicago's cultural and economic growth and become the centerpiece for building Chicago's reputation as a global destination for creativity, innovation and excellence in the arts.' Imagined with a life span of 10–15 years, the document articulates the need for and purpose of a cultural plan: 'A cultural plan translates the cultural needs and identity of a community into a tool for implementing recommendations. These recommendations seek to: address gaps in cultural service delivery; expand participation; broaden the impact of culture on the wider community; identify new opportunities for a city's future audience; and stake out a city's identity through cultural expression' (16). The Fact Sheet summarizes plan initiatives including a specific focus on arts rooted in the distinct neighbourhoods of the city (10). Heartily welcomed by arts advocates such as Halperin at CST, the cultural plan (finalized in October 2012) argues for the civic and financial value of the arts as well as establishing an agenda for supporting and sustaining institutional arts enterprises.

Chicago Shakespeare in the Parks was a good-faith if vexed effort to jump-start this renewed commitment to the city's arts outlets.[46] Halperin explained that when a Boeing grant came through to fund a summer Shakespeare programme the theatre had to act quickly to prepare a run. A Short Shakespeare! *Shrew* had just been staged successfully (25 February to 7 April 2012) and, it was assumed, could transition most readily to the planned outdoor venues.[47] Performing during July and August at eleven area parks from the south to the north side of the city, the CST production, adapted and directed by Rachel Rockwell, starred Ericka Ratcliff as Katharina and Matt Mueller as Petruchio. The press release announcing the

performances articulated the assumptions underlying the open-air productions: 'The wildly spirited Kate and the machismo-driven Petruchio will scream, fight and woo their way into one another's heart in Shakespeare's verse and Elizabethan dress, underscored with original rock-inspired music to connect contemporary audiences with the characters' journeys.'[48] Perhaps in an attempt to suit its casting to the multicultural landscape of the Chicago Park District, the summer *Shrew* featured an inter-ethnic pairing, a Katharina of African descent and a Caucasian Petruchio, and included a Latino Grumio who also served as 'host' of the productions I attended.[49]

---

46 Both Ric Knowles and Michael McKinnie have recently examined urban cultural policies and plans in relationship to performance practices in Toronto and London respectively; they raise crucial questions about how underlying ethnic biases and global capital colour funding patterns and promotional rhetoric; see Ric Knowles, 'Multicultural Text, Intercultural Performance: The Performance Ecology of Contemporary Toronto', in *Performance and the City*, ed. D. J. Hopkins, Shelley Orr and Kim Solga (New York, 2011), pp. 73–91; Michael McKinnie, 'Performing the Civic Transnational: Cultural Production, Governance, and Citizenship in Contemporary London', in *Performance and the City*, pp. 110–27. Similarly, Kate Rumbold charts the influence of British governmental cultural policy on audience development and outreach by major Shakespeare institutions in the United Kingdom (Kate Rumbold, 'From "Access" to "Creativity": Shakespeare Institutions, New Media, and the Language of Cultural Value', *Shakespeare Quarterly*, 61 (2010), 313–36). These critical approaches drive the current project's investigation into Chicago's incipient cultural planning and experiment with the Chicago Shakespeare in the Parks initiative.

47 Halperin, Interview, 2 July 2012. The Short Shakespeare! production of *Shrew* ran on Saturday mornings throughout the spring of 2012. Halperin described it as one of the most successful 'abridgements' staged by CST, one that played well in the Courtyard Theater to a widely varying audience.

48 Chicago Shakespeare Theater, 'Cultural, Civic and Corporate Partnership Launches Bold Initiative: Chicago Shakespeare Theater, Chicago Park District and the Boeing Company present Chicago Shakespeare in the Parks' (12 June 2012, Press Release).

49 The Chicago Shakespeare in the Parks *Shrew* visited eleven neighbourhoods but produced a total of seventeen performances with repeats at four parks (Gateway Park at Navy Pier, Welles Park, Humboldt Park and Frank J. Wilson Park). The rest of the parks (South Shore Cultural Center, Tuley

Much about the Parks initiative was well-intended. Residents of the Tuley and Dvorak park districts genuinely appreciated the effort made by the city of Chicago and the theatre to bring Shakespeare to the neighbourhoods. In fact, even at a location that is more tourist attraction than 'neighbourhood' park, Gateway Park at Navy Pier, Halperin's pre-show welcome, which referenced the 2012 Cultural Plan's focus on arts in the neighbourhoods, drew rousing applause. After the Tuley Park performance, a number of attendees approached CST employees and thanked them for the production, only gently scolding CST for a failure to better publicize the event. While the series of email announcements sent to subscribers and previous ticket-purchasers made theatre regulars aware of the productions, such a strategy would, of course, not work with the underserved populations targeted by the initiative and highlighted in the University of Chicago cultural mapping.

The CST production relied on several methods throughout the run to mitigate the inevitably patronizing dynamic of a well-endowed and powerful arts company condescending to set up shop for one day only in the city's neighbourhoods. In an example of mutually beneficial collaboration, the neighbourhood productions began with a green show that typically featured children and adolescents involved in the parks' summer activity programmes.[50] Ward aldermen or their representatives introduced the performances and welcomed the theatre cast and crew to the neighbourhood. The Dvorak Park Advisory Council capitalized on the presence of additional park visitors to run a fund-raising concession stand and to promote their upcoming march on City Hall to request additional fiscal support. With tents providing only a very limited backstage space, cast members typically entered the playing area at the start of productions by walking through the crowd from temporary dressing rooms within the parks' main structures. Their exposed entrance thus disrupted the show's mimetic illusion before it had even begun and placed the performative act in close proximity to spectatorship, even blurring the difference as cast members stood or lounged on the

grass, watching and applauding during the green shows. Such prolegomenon management briefly levelled the distinction between 'us' and 'them' freighted on a high arts production that has travelled to an underserved community. Cast members similarly and very deliberately appeared to mingle with the audience after *Shrew*, soliciting feedback and thanking patrons for joining the occasion. At Tuley Park, a significant number of attendees crowded round the cast members post-performance with the largest cluster circling Ratcliff and seeking her autograph on the Shakespeare fans (cut-outs of Droeshout's Shakespeare) distributed to keep patrons cool in the heat wave temperatures and unmerciful sun.

In its approach to introducing the productions, CST attempted to wed its Great Humanist Shakespeare to the multicultural landscape of the city. Jose Antonio Garcia who played Grumio introduced the production and made the familiar appeal to turn off cell phones and focus attention on the performances. He also offered a bit of audience coaching by urging listeners to allow time for the ear to adjust to the music of Shakespeare's language. At each performance, his introduction concluded with a reminder that Shakespeare 'was writing about us', an appeal that echoed the Great Humanist construct of the theatre's self-image. This commitment to the Great Humanist Shakespeare, however, once again meant that the production blithely insisted on a cheerful and universal relevance by means of humorous stage business,

---

Park, Dvorak Park, Austin Town Hall Park, Douglas Park, Garfield Park Conservatory and Ridge Park) hosted single performances. I observed stagings at three locations: the largely African-American Tuley Park (30 July), the multicultural but predominantly Hispanic Dvorak Park (31 July), and Gateway Park located at the west end of Navy Pier and attracting a mixed audience of Gold Coast inhabitants and tourists (8 August).

50 Perhaps because the production start time at Gateway Park was 6:30 pm rather than the 3:30 pm and 4:00 pm respectively of Tuley and Dvorak, no green show featuring children took place at the 8 August performance. More of a tourist destination than a local service, Gateway Park may not offer the full range of summer programming that could populate a green show.

11. *The Taming of the Shrew*, Chicago Shakespeare Theatre, Garfield Park Conservatory, 2012, directed by Rachel Rockwell.
Mayor Rahm Emanuel and the cast of *The Taming of the Shrew*.

preventing direct confrontation of material that should be troubling to a modern and diverse audience.

In the extra-performance components, the Chicago Shakespeare cast, crew and staff members appeared to achieve considerable good will. However, the actual production remained disappointingly riddled with abuses of Katharina rendered decidedly uncomfortable by the colour difference between Katharina and Petruchio. Cuts necessitated by the 75-minute running time further stripped nuance and complexity from a text already characterized by a paucity of such and, thanks to the 'colour-blind' casting, made the now ethnically coded sexual and power dynamics between the leads more starkly problematic. While an integrated cast affirms the many voices with which Shakespeare can and should speak, in the context of Chicago's segregated neighbourhoods,

this piece of casting did not appear 'blind' unless 'blind' is taken to mean casting without an eye to unintended interpretive consequences, namely the visual implications of a Caucasian man imposing his will on an African-American woman. Ayanna Thompson has thoroughly troubled the concept of colour-blind casting by pointing out that because audiences still perceive colour, directors may inadvertently underscore ethnic stereotypes or set in motion unintended interpretive trajectories in their efforts to integrate a cast.[51] As Thompson notes, thoughtful colour-blind casting can provoke an important if painful dialogue about race (17),

---

[51] Ayanna Thompson, 'Practicing a Theory/Theorizing a Practice: An Introduction to Shakespearean Colorblind Casting', in *Colorblind Shakespeare: New Perspectives on Race and Performance*, ed. Ayanna Thompson (New York, 2006), pp. 1–24, p. 11.

but the CST parks production fell short of this ambition. First, it did little to code the performative nature of identity that even a play as restrictive as *Shrew* allows. By eliminating the theatrical framing of Christopher Sly's gulling, the production succeeded in creating a performance the requisite length for the exigencies of a parks staging. However, that decision dismissed a component of the text that could have signalled a more distanced and interrogatory spectatorship to the unfolding taming. In some ways, the choice to situate actors in the audience during the green show functioned as a replacement of the metatheatrical Sly frame; unfortunately, positioning actors as observers for a ten-minute pre-show proved too weak a gesture to combat and undermine the still-potent fantasy of the fictive taming.

Furthermore, the light-rock-infused underscoring composed by Kevin O'Donnell that played between scenes implied a unified complacency with the plot's action and provoked an upbeat geniality that urged laughing acceptance of the dynamics between Katharina and Petruchio rather than an interrogation of gender and, now, ethnic inequities. In a short online video, director Rockwell explained the juxtaposition of rock score against Elizabethan costuming as central to the production's aesthetic and a crucial means of rendering relevant the emotional content of the play: 'This whole thing for me is about contrast . . . We're putting it in an Elizabethan setting where the music that we're going to use for the show is a lot of really hardcore rock music.'[52] For Rockwell, while the audience members might not follow the language of Shakespeare, they would find emotional resonance in the 'crazy rock score underneath' the performance. The parks playbill quoted composer O'Donnell stressing the purpose of his scoring: 'Music offers an opportunity to help lift the story into the same time and space as the audience. Any good story must have some aspect of timelessness in it, in my opinion. So even if we see characters in period costumes speaking Shakespearean English, we should be able to see how the relationships are the same as our own. Right?'[53] However, the scoring did not quite match the edginess promised

and much more consistently captured the cheerful tunefulness and frequent insipidity of romantic comedy film idiom. Such an essentially harmonious aural landscape actually normalized dramatic content rather than highlighted dissonance in what could have been provoking ways.

In addition to music, the production deployed a range of anachronistic details to enliven the play content and heighten relevancy to the contemporary audience: Bianca's pink feather fan and fur handcuffs, the Kanye West shades worn by Lucentio and Tranio, the fraternity house and hot pepper boxers and zebra suspenders revealed when Lucentio and Tranio exchanged clothing, and the fast food hamburger used to torture Katharina during the country house scenes. The multicultural casting (Garcia as Grumio, Ratcliff as Katharina, and Tiffany Yvonne Cox as Bianca) likewise deliberately attempted to cross the high arts ethnic divide made evident in the University of Chicago cultural mapping project. While Garcia's Grumio enjoyed elevated status as the 'host' of the production and Ratcliff's Katharina as the titular lead, the three actors of colour still played figures significantly lower on the social scale than many members of the *dramatis personae* – a servant and daughters circumscribed by their father and husbands.

While Ratcliff delivered a spirited performance designed to preserve Katharina's personal agency, the spectre of American slavery and the sexual exploitation of slave women by their Caucasian masters still shadowed this production. Perhaps the worst example of this was when during his rough wooing (2.1) Petruchio disabled Katharina by sitting on her while she was face-down on the stage; in that position, Petruchio appeared to 'ride' the entirely dominated Katharina. A close second for tone-deaf awkwardness was the blocking of their wedding, when Petruchio finally hoisted a

---

52 Rachel Rockwell, 'Director Rachel Rockwell on *The Taming of the Shrew* for Chicago Shakespeare in the Parks', *YouTube*, 12 June 2012.

53 'Meet the Composer', Programme Notes for *The Taming of the Shrew*, Chicago Shakespeare in the Parks, Chicago, Summer 2012.

recalcitrant Katharina like a piece of meat over his shoulder and marched her unwillingly out of Padua.[54] In the performances I witnessed, these scenes received the most disapproving audience reactions at Tuley Park.[55] A small gathering of approximately 150 attendees composed primarily of African-American women in their 50s exchanged knowing glances and raised eyebrows throughout these scenes, and they further evidenced their ire in a series of verbalized 'humphs' during Katharina's submission speech highlighting 'love, honour, and *obey*', the final word in the trinity prompting vocal, good-natured, yet resistant responses. However, at the other two parks, Dvorak and Gateway, the blocking appeared to achieve its desired aim of laughter at the expense of the uppity shrew. Such blocking choices presented as amusing entertainment the violent logic of patriarchal power – that assumed physical superiority grants rights of dominance to the male sex.

At the same time, the costume design that placed Katharina in a gown referencing Elizabeth I's iconography strove against such disempowering staging choices. At her wedding, Ratcliff's Katharina emerged in a Ditchley Portrait-inspired white gown featuring high pleated ruff, cascading pearls and a substantial farthingale. Thus, the production staged a woman of colour wearing her hair in a natural, short-cut afro in a costume associated with an icon of Caucasian female power, Shakespeare's own monarch. Since the newspaper-style playbill featured a cartoon drawing of Elizabeth that merged elements of the Ditchley and the Rainbow portraits, the alignment of Ratcliff's Katharina with imagery of Elizabeth I could not be missed. Thus, even though the production made vexing choices that either blindly mimed social disequilibriums or merrily glossed those problems with contemporary trimmings, it did pause to imagine an African-American woman as an embodiment of historical power and precedence, and that should not be ignored, even when, only moments later, that embodiment of Elizabeth I was hoisted aloft by Petruchio and carted off to domestic servitude.

With such multivalent iconography as subject matter, assessing the parks Shakespeare in

relationship to Certeau's dynamic of institutional strategy and individual tactic necessarily means negotiating contradiction. As part of a citywide cultural initiative prompted by Mayor Emanuel's office and funded by the substantial resources of Chicago commerce, how could the parks productions be anything but another institutional strategy, one quite cynically designed to extend the soft power of the arts into potentially resistant neighbourhoods? I would contend, however, that the individual freedom to select another route and to move within and around the stolidity of the powerful is inherent in the very nature of dramatic performance, where theatrical practitioners *and* the audience together create the artwork. Baz Kershaw insists that 'Theatrical performance is the most public of all the arts because it cannot be constituted without the direct participation of a public.'[56] He has persuasively argued that the public's capacity to deliver a critique of drama has been steadily diminished by the transformation of theatre audiences into 'customers' who must applaud performance as a validation of their own capital investment in the ticket purchase (141). To restore the radical sociopolitical potential of theatre, Kershaw calls for a return of the 'unruly' audience, and in a very modest way that audience could be found at the Chicago Shakespeare in

---

54 Interestingly, the LaBute–Rourke *Shrew* choreographed this exact blocking move with the same lines in the same scene, Petruchio's defiant, 'She is my goods, my chattels, she is my house, / My household stuff, my field, my barn, / My horse, my ox, my ass, my any thing' (3.2.230–2). Whereas the 2010 production spotlighted this combination of words and demeaning blocking (inherited from the long performance history of the play) by breaking the dramatic action as Katharina scrambled down from Petruchio's shoulders in protest, the parks Shakespeare resorted to this familiar assertion of masculine rule predicated upon physical supremacy without irony or question.

55 At Tuley Park, my four undergraduate research assistants (Theron Calkins, Arianna Lashley, Samantha Snively and Lydia Weiso) were invaluable in scanning the audience during the performance and ensuring the accuracy of recorded observations.

56 Baz Kershaw, 'Oh for Unruly Audiences! Or, Patterns of Participation in Twentieth-Century Theatre', *Modern Drama*, 42 (2001), 133–54, p. 151.

the Parks productions. Characteristic of all the parks performances was a freedom of audience movement atypical of indoor theatrical venues. Such movement quietly assessed the value of the performance and elevated other personal priorities over the demands of a singular focus on the enacted narrative. With great frequency, audience members opted to slip away to concession stands and return laden with nachos and beverages, while others stayed for a time, then folded up their chairs and departed. Some audience members arrived late and appeared, on occasion, to be coming from work, joining a friend or partner, and settling down to enjoy only a fragment of the performance. Not only in the audience reaction can the disruptions of the individual tactic be seen but also in the very makeshift quality of the parks productions themselves. Plagued by occasional long pauses between last lines and scene exits, too few microphones and speakers for listening ease and a noticeable lack of ensemble chemistry early in the run, Chicago Shakespeare in the Parks made manifest the means of production itself. Thus, although the Short Shakespeare! production deleted *Shrew*'s Sly frame, it nonetheless displayed the mechanics of fiction-making, a tactic that threatens the hermetic inviolability of institutional narrative as surely as does an audience member's choice to walk away.

JOURNEY'S END

This story about *Shrew* in Chicago is a makeshift thing. Like Certeau's pedestrian, I have taken some routes and not others, wandered across terrain others might have ignored, and missed landmarks of significance to another's peregrinations. Performance, like the infinite possibilities of movement through the urban landscape, will always necessitate caveat and qualification. The story that emerges from these distinct movements illustrates that institutional Shakespeare must more seriously scrutinize the self-justifying constructs that perpetuate and market the playwright's authority at the expense of those on the social margins. Writing about performance means residing in the space of memory, the place of uncertainty, the location of ambiguity, the very liminal space so wonderfully disruptive of institutional strategy. By examining performance, even as we acknowledge its complicity with power, we pursue a form whose infinite and shifting echoes whisper the impossibility of monoliths. As the LaBute–Rourke and Rockwell *Shrew*s demonstrate, we can always walk away. And in that walking can be found the defiant resistance of Carl Sandburg's big-shouldered and labouring Chicagoan who knows that while institutions may strategize, the individual persists, and 'under his wrist is the pulse, / and under his ribs the heart of the people'. In contrast to the earlier Bell staging, the most recent Chicago *Shrew*s embodied in their fissures, gaps, failings and stereotyped misdirections, an effort to de-situate Shakespeare from the hegemonic centre and unmoor the Bard from his high culture marina along Lakeshore Drive. That very imperfection showed a kind of bravery – to appear as the less-than-perfect manifestation of the mighty Navy Pier edifice. Back on the pier where ticket prices and capital investment must be justified by perceived 'quality', the Chicago Shakespeare Theater may always resort to a defensive position behind the palisade of Shakespeare the Great Humanist, a position which blinds the theatre to the ethical problematics inherent in the poet's work. But its more recent productions and its walk through the parks brave places of discomfort on the frontlines and admit even tacitly the limits of the 'Shakespeare' that defines and authorizes the Chicago Shakespeare Theater.

WHY GANYMEDE FAINTS AND THE DUKE OF YORK WEEPS: PASSION PLAYS IN SHAKESPEARE

SUJATA IYENGAR

This article revisits contemporary critical debates surrounding the presence of cross-dressed boys as women on the early modern stage – in particular the question of whether or to what extent boy-actors could or should be said to represent 'women' or 'femininity' – through the Shakespearian emblem of the bloody rag or handkercher. In all but one instance, these soiled napkins appear alongside what the plays call 'passion' of various kinds. I will examine bloody rags on Shakespeare's stage in the light of early modern anti-theatrical polemics, medical disputes about sex-difference and the conflicted cultural status of printed paper in order to argue that these besmirched tokens bring together early modern 'passions' in multiple senses: strong or overpowering, embodied feeling; the fluid dynamics of early modern bodies; the Passion of Christ; erotic suffering; and, crucially, the performance on stage of all of the above.[1]

With the aid of Fran Teague's useful tables in *Shakespeare's Speaking Properties*, I count the following blood-stained or red-marked rags on Shakespeare's stage: in *The True Tragedy of Richard Duke of York and the Good King Henry the Sixth* (*3 Henry VI*), the monstrous, magnificent Queen Margaret forces tears from the captured Duke of York by asking him to wipe his face with a handkerchief imprinted with the dying blood of his youngest son.[2] In *A Midsummer Night's Dream*, or rather, in the parodic play of 'Pyramus and Thisbe' performed by the rude mechanicals in Act 5, Pyramus broaches his boiling bloody breast after catching up Thisbe's bloodstained mantle. In *As You Like It*, Rosalind, disguised as the boy Ganymede, faints

when faced with a cloth sodden with Orlando's blood. We could include the napkin 'spotted' with strawberries in *The Tragedy of Othello, the Moor of Venice* that the eponymous hero takes as a token of his wife's infidelity, although the napkin is not presented theatrically as specifically stained with blood. In *Cymbeline King of Britain*, Posthumus Leonatus keeps safe about his body a cloth coloured with, as he believes, the blood of the wife whose murder he has sanctioned.

These bloodied, reddened, marked or spotted handkerchiefs, napkins and cloths have received some critical attention, mostly surrounding their semiotic significance as religious relics and proxies for female uncontrollability. Stained cloths and rags on Shakespeare's stage, and particularly in *Othello* and *Cymbeline*, critics suggest, control women both by standing in for their chastity or sexual temperance and by drawing attention to what Gail Kern Paster has called women's humoral 'leakiness'.[3] Will Fisher identifies handkerchiefs (new to England in the sixteenth century) as portable, transferable bearers of gender, important in 'materializing early modern notions of femininity' through

---

[1] I would like to thank Peter Holland, Katharine Craik and the members of the seminar 'Passionate Shakespeare' at the International Shakespeare Conference in 2012 for their responses to this article.
[2] Frances N. Teague, *Shakespeare's Speaking Properties* (Lewisburg, Toronto, and London, 1991), pp. 191–6.
[3] Gail Kern Paster, *The Body Embarrassed: Drama and the Disciplines of Shame in Early Modern England* (Ithaca, 1993), esp. ch. 3, 'Laudable Blood', pp. 64–112.

their ability simultaneously to absorb unmentionable or unwelcome female or feminizing fluids and to display wealth and social status.[4] Teague reads the spotted handkerchief on *Othello* in multiple ways, as a 'symbol of self or of jealousy, emblem of treachery, and literal magic token'.[5] Marion Lomax comments upon the 'conflicting, yet here, strangely compatible notions of human sexual passion and Christ's Passion' through the bloody cloth that Posthumus takes as evidence of Innogen's death in *Cymbeline* and through the five 'crimson' spots under Innogen's left breast: stigmata, Lomax suggests, that connect the saintly wife to icons of female virtue. For Lomax, the bloody rag as relic beatifies the wounded wife, and Posthumus's remorse at the sight of this token redeems him.[6] Valerie Wayne argues more explicitly for Posthumus's recuperation through the stained cloth, describing the stage-tradition that Posthumus wears the cloth on his body and associating the cloth with both 'the bloodstained sheets of a marriage bed – like the handkerchief spotted with strawberries in *Othello* . . . as well as with menstruation'.[7] Richard Wilson analyses bloody or spotted handkerchiefs on Shakespeare's stage, and particularly in *Othello*, as emblems of Catholic relics, rags steeped in the blood of martyrs, and as 'the despised supplement of menstruation', markers of an uncontrollable or 'leaky' femininity and of, Wilson continues, a polylingual or 'leaky' paronomasia (first identified by Patricia Parker) that connects the *Moor* of Venice, *moresca* embroidery, the Catholic martyr Sir Thomas *More* and the latter's joking emblem, the mulberry tree or *morus* that changes colour from white to red to black as it ripens.[8] Ariane Balizet (in a series of essays and in her recent monograph) outlines the associations of menstruation with blood that connotes contamination, contagion and inferiority, that is, that which is culturally, medically and religiously subordinated and feminine, although she considers stained napkins as hymeneal signifiers of domesticity in a Reformed church: 'Just as the strawberry-spotted handkerchief in Shakespeare's *Othello*, for example, could signify the bloodied wedding sheets that seal the marriage pact, the bloody handkerchief in *The*

Duchess of Malfi stands in for the bloodied birthing-bed linens. In both cases, the bloody handkerchief becomes a miniaturized version of a private act that cannot be shown onstage (sex and birth) and signifies the initiation of a domestic realm unique to its inhabitants.'[9]

Wilson helpfully adduces Garry Wills's observation that 'Handkerchiefs were associated with the public execution of Jesuits [in England], since the emptying of all a man's blood in the savage disemboweling, castrating, and quartering of the hanged bodies of traitors prompted pious Catholics to dip handkerchiefs and other bits of cloth in the martyrs' saving blood.'[10] Wilson, however, unnecessarily opposes the two categories of holy relic and menstrual rag when he contrasts the work of 'feminists who see only hymeneal connotations' to accounts that emphasize Shakespeare's engagement with debates about Catholicism.[11] In fact – as Wilson's own fine work implies and as I will go on to discuss – a long-standing tradition within Protestant writing pejoratively compares Catholic

---

[4] Will Fisher, 'Handkerchiefs and Early Modern Ideologies of Gender', *Shakespeare Studies*, 28 (2000), 199–207, p. 201.

[5] Teague, *Shakespeare's Speaking Properties*, p. 27.

[6] Marion Lomax, *Stage Images and Traditions: Shakespeare to Ford* (Cambridge, 1987), pp. 107–9, esp. p. 107.

[7] Valerie Wayne, 'The Woman's Parts of *Cymbeline*', in *Staged Properties in Shakespeare's Drama*, ed. Jonathan Gil Harris and Natasha Korda (Cambridge, 2002), pp. 288–315, p. 298.

[8] Richard Wilson, '"Dyed in Mummy": Othello and the Mulberries', in *Performances of the Sacred in Late Medieval and Early Modern England*, ed. Susanne Rupp and Tobias Döring (Amsterdam, 2005), pp. 135–54, p. 146; Patricia Parker, *Shakespeare from the Margins* (Chicago, 1996), p. 275 n.11; Patricia Parker, 'What's in a Name: and More', *Sederi* XI (Huelva, 2002), 101–49.

[9] Ariane Balizet, '"Drowned in Blood": Honor, Bloodline, and Domestic Ideology in *The Duchess of Malfi* and *El médico de su honra*', *Comparative Literature Studies*, 49.1 (2012), 23–49, p. 44. See also Balizet's forthcoming book, *Blood and Home in Early Modern Drama* (2014), which independently comments upon blood-stained napkins in *The Tragedy of Othello, the Moor of Venice*, *As You Like It* and *Cymbeline King of Britain* as indicators of the 'liminality' of binary gender.

[10] Garry Wills, *Witches and Jesuits: Shakespeare's Macbeth* (Oxford and New York, 1996), p. 99.

[11] Wilson, 'Dyed in Mummy', p. 150.

practices of image-worship and even the performance of good works not just to blood-soaked rags or relics of martyrdom in general but to women's menstrual cloths in particular: the Passion of Christ to what Stephen Batman, translating the medieval medical authority Bartolomeus Anglicus and synthesizing other early Christian medical texts, calls 'the passion menstruall'.[12] Moreover, at moments of gender and sexual crisis, the bodies of Shakespearian characters express the 'wrong' gender for their circumstances when faced with bloody rags, although they do so with different degrees of 'passion'.

'NO MAN HATH THE PASSION MENSTRUALL'

Thomas Laqueur's influential *Making Sex* argued that a so-called 'one-sex' model predominated in England and Western Europe during the sixteenth and early seventeenth centuries in which orthodox early modern Galenic medicine (which, he suggests, was itself a modification of the Aristotelian theory that women were 'imperfect' men who had not fully developed in utero because they lacked sufficient heat) considered both men and women part of a single-sex continuum, with women as merely 'inverted' men who could, under the appropriate stimuli, develop organs thought to belong to the opposite sex. Moreover, suggests Laqueur, humoral theory meant that both genders were able to perform functions that we now consider specific to a single sex. For example, women could ejaculate seed during orgasm, stimulated by heat-generating friction or other methods of arousal (some authorities, indeed, maintained that sexual climax was necessary for conception to occur because women's seed would not be available for fertilization without it), and men, given sufficient chill and moisture, could lactate.[13] Gail Kern Paster, Katharine Park, Winfried Schleiner and Helen King have, however, challenged Laqueur's larger argument by identifying early modern medical beliefs that considered certain aspects of embodiment to be inescapably female: women's bodily integrity, bodily fluids and the social policing of these bodies and fluids (Paster); newly 'discovered' female organs such as the clitoris (Park); Galenic proto-feminism that saw women not as 'imperfect men' but as 'perfect in their own sex' (Schleiner); and an Aristotelian discipline of 'gynecology', a specific science pertaining to a definitively female sex with its own distinct maladies (King).[14] In addition, Paster and Schleiner argue that menstruation contributed to an ongoing belief in sexual dimorphism, both medical and popular. Paster observes the stigma associated with women's (implicitly menstrual or child-bearing) blood, in contrast to men's 'laudable' bloodshed through the wounds of war. Schleiner argues for an early modern, proto-feminist Galenism: women menstruated not as a sign of their innate pathology – not because they were imperfect men who bled away the precious sanguine humour since they had a plethora of too much blood or a cachochymia, an overdose of moist phlegm, as Laqueur maintains – but because healthy, fertile femininity required women to make more blood in preparation for a potential fetus and to purge this blood when it became too old or corrupted. Bethan Hindson, a social historian, surveys early modern diaries, histories and printed texts to investigate popular attitudes towards menstruation and, although she disagrees with Paster about the stigma of women's blood, finding female menstruation less 'embarrassing'

---

[12] Bartolomeus Anglicus, *De Proprietatibus Rerum, newly corrected, enlarged and amended: with . . . additions*, trans. and ed. Stephen Batman (London, 1582), D2v, col. 2.

[13] Thomas Laqueur, *Making Sex: Body and Gender from the Greeks to Freud* (Cambridge, MA, 1990), esp. ch. 2, 'Destiny is Anatomy', pp. 26–62.

[14] Gail Kern Paster, *The Body Embarrassed: Drama and the Disciplines of Shame in Early Modern England* (Ithaca, 1993), *passim*; Katharine Park, 'The Rediscovery of the Clitoris', in *The Body in Parts*, ed. David Hillman and Carla Mazzio (London and New York, 1997), pp. 175–9; Winfried Schleiner, 'Early Modern Controversies About the One-Sex Model', *Renaissance Quarterly*, 53:1 (2000), 180–91; Helen King, *Midwifery, Obstetrics, and the Rise of Gynaecology: The Use of a Sixteenth-Century Compendium* (Farnham, 2007), esp. 'Introduction: Towards Gynaecology' and ch. 1, 'Prefacing Women: Owners and Users', pp. 1–64.

than routine in early modern life, she concurs that menstruation marks a distinctly female sex.[15] Although Laqueur parallels male episodic bleeding from the anus to female monthly bleeding from the vagina, Hindson and others find that accounts of so-called male menstruation refer to sporadic anal bleeding from haemorrhoids or bloody flux (dysentery), rather than to the periodic evacuation of fetal sustenance from the body. Physicians and lay-people alike recognized that only women menstruated and sustained pregnancies.

Women's relationship to blood necessarily affected their experience of passion. Passions and perturbations disrupted the balance of humours in all bodies, male and female. Under the strain of great emotion, blood rushed to the heart from the liver (where it was manufactured) in order to sustain and support it. Joy, delight and pleasant emotions expanded or opened the heart, while fear, misery and hatred contracted or tightened it. Although pleasurable feelings might temporarily affect one's reason, they were, on the whole, beneficial to the health because they helped the formation of pure blood and of natural, vital and animal spirit in the liver, heart and brain respectively. Spirit both nourished these organs and was further refined by them; more importantly, spirituous blood provided the link between body and soul. A surfeit of joy, however, would enlarge the heart to dangerous levels and create a plethora, or overload, of blood within it; the resultant heat could turn the blood into choler (the thin, sharp, hot, dry humour, which weakened the heart and could cause deaths after fits of laughter) or into choler adust (burned choler) or melancholy (the thick, sour, cold, dry humour, which caused the depression that some experienced after excessively radiant pleasure). But far more perilous were the passions of fear and sorrow, in which heavy, dull melancholy overwhelmed the sanguine humour of blood and slowed the movement of spirit through the body. When the heart retained blood in this manner, the blood congealed into melancholy proper, which cooled and dried the whole body. An excess of *any* emotion, however – any passion or perturbation – would o'ercharge the heart. Shakespeare's

Angelo describes the process as he almost swoons with desire for Isabel:

> Why does my blood thus muster to my heart,
> Making both it unable for itself,
> And dispossessing all my other parts
> Of necessary fitness?
> So play the foolish throngs with one that swoons –
> Come all to help him, and so stop the air
> By which he should revive . . .
>
> (*Measure for Measure*, 2.4.20–6)

Angelo's heart is overwhelmed by too much blood, too quickly: it can neither mix the blood with air to produce the vital spirit necessary for the heart's nourishment and also as the precursor to the animal or rational spirit in the brain ('dispossessing all my other parts / Of necessary fitness'), nor can it continue beating regularly and consume the blood that would normally sustain it ('making . . . it unable for itself'). The blood musters to his heart as concerned bystanders crowd around a fainting man who then, like his blood itself, cannot obtain the air he needs in order to recover.

Helkiah Crooke observes in his discussion of 'passions of the mind' that women are more liable than are men to swooning and fainting. He argues that women's hearts resemble their wombs in that they, too, are vulnerable to environmental stimuli and emotional upset (as in the specifically female and uterine disorder of *hysterica passio*).[16] I have argued elsewhere that 'it is mostly Shakespeare's women who swoon' (although men feel apt to swoon when overwhelmed with erotic desire) but that 'both Shakespeare's men and women might faint'.[17] Shakespearian swoons stem from passion

[15] Bethan Hindson, 'Attitudes towards Menstruation and Menstrual Blood in Elizabethan England', *Journal of Social History*, 43:1 (2009), 89–114.

[16] Helkiah Crooke, *Microcosmographia* (London, 1615), Book 7, Vv6r; Book 4, Zr. On *hysterica passio*, see Kaara Peterson, *Popular Medicine, Hysterical Disease, and Social Controversy in Shakespeare's England* (Farnham and Burlington, VT, 2010), ch. 1, 'Early Modern Medicine and the Case History of *King Lear*', pp. 37–69, esp. pp. 62–9.

[17] Sujata Iyengar, *Shakespeare's Medical Language* (London, 2011), p. 133.

and perturbation – the result of the body's consuming vital and rational spirit more quickly than the heart and brain can produce them, whether because the heart contracts under negative emotions, or because blood or spirit rushes too quickly to the heart, preventing rational spirit from reaching the brain – but Shakespearian faints might come from passionate stimuli (especially when cowardice, grief or fear have used up vital spirit in the heart) as well as from external physical events such as blood loss in battle, weakness from travel or starvation (and women might faint in pregnancy, given the growing hunger of the uterus for vital blood). Stephen Batman connects men's greater fortitude and strength to their larger hearts and their greater blood- and spirit-volume:

Also Constantine sayth, that in males the heartes be large and great, therefore they be able to receiue much plentie of spirites and of bloud: And therefore through the great abundaunce of spirits and hot bloud, a man is more hardy then a woman, for in her the cause is contrarie: And through strength of heate and vertue of drie complection, no man hath the passion menstruall as women haue. All superfluities that bee bread in mens bodyes, are eyther consumed by greate heate, or els turned into haire, or are voided by businesse and trauaile.[18]

In keeping with then-standard belief, Batman concludes that men can tolerate extreme emotions and hardship more effectively than can women because of a combination of their humoral composition (their greater heat, which allows an excess of blood to be burnt off without ill effects as sweat or vapour, or turned into what were called the 'excrements' such as hair or nails) and their social status: hard-working men required, and diffused, more blood and heat as they conducted physical labour. Philip Barrough (1583) adds that '[W]omen of a hote temperature, that be wilde, and who vse strong exercises' (for example, 'barraine women and dauncers') were known to have similar needs, to such an extent that such women often failed to menstruate at all, because they had burned off all their excess blood through their vigorous activity.[19] Oddly enough, women's greater supposed ability to weep tears of joy and sorrow –

another 'excrement' – at times of great emotion apparently did not prevent them from swooning. So we might think of gendered passions in bloody terms: if one faints or swoons, it is because one lacks blood in the appropriate organs, as blood abandons the brain in order to try to protect the heart. But if a woman menstruates, she does so from plethora or too much blood – either pathological or (in proto-feminist Galenism) necessary for perfection or completion in her own sex.

'BAWDY PLAYERS' AS 'MENSTRUOUS RAGGES'

Given that menstruation is one of the few bodily functions specifically gendered female in early modern England, it is worth pausing to explore the range of figurative allusions to this process. As Sara Read has observed, references to menstrual cloths and rags in early modern religious treatises, sermons and so on repeat (through citation, commentary and creative transformation) two verses from the Biblical book of Isaiah.[20] In the Geneva Bible, Isaiah 30:22 urges the Israelites to 'pollute the couering of the images of siluer, and the riche ornament of thine images of golde, *and* cast them away as a menstruous cloth, and . . . say vnto it, Get thee hence'; and Isaiah 64:6 claims, 'we haue all bene as an vncleane thing, and all our righteousnes *is* as filthie cloutes, and we all doe fade like a leafe, and our iniquities like the winde haue taken vs away'. Note *h* explains, 'our righteousnes, and best vertues are before thee as vile clouts, or, (as some reade) like the menstruous clothes of a woman'.[21]

A quick look through Chadwyck-Healey's *Bible in English* database suggests that earlier English

---

[18] Stephen Batman, *Batman Upon Bartholome* (London, 1582), D2v, column 2.

[19] Philip Barrough, *The Methode of Phisicke* (London, 1583), Book III, Chapter 53, Nr.

[20] Sara Read, '"Thy Righteousness is but a menstrual clout": Sanitary Practices and Prejudice in Early Modern England', *Early Modern Women*, 3 (2008), 1–26.

[21] *The Bible* (Geneva, 1560), 'To waite for the lord', p. 293 col. 1, Ccciiir; 'Mans righteousness', p. 303v col. 2, Fff2v.

Protestant English translations of Isaiah specifically identify the contaminant in Isaiah 64:6 as menstrual blood: our righteousness is as 'the cloth of the womman roten blod flowende' (Wycliff, Early), 'the cloth of a womman in vncleene blood' (Wycliff, Late), 'the clothes stayned with the floures of a woman' (Coverdale), a 'cloth fyled wyth the floures of a woman' (Great), or 'the clothes defyled with the floures of a woman' (Thomas Mathew), while Isaiah 64:6 in the three major Protestant translations of Shakespeare's lifetime appears as 'filthie cloutes' (Geneva) and 'filthy ragges' (Bishops', KJV).[22] The late sixteenth- and early seventeenth-century Protestant consensus for 'filthy' over 'blood' or 'flowers' might seem to support Paster's assertion that menstruation in the late sixteenth-century becomes overwhelmingly identified with female bodies (thus, perhaps, the translators attempt to make universal an image that had become too specific to a limited range of persons) and that leaking female fluids became increasingly invisible or shameful, thus the term 'filthiness' rather than 'menstruous rag'. Read observes that seventeenth-century commentators, especially Protestants, prefer the less specific word 'filthy', to describe menstrual rags and suggests that the shift to filth, as it were, reflects an increasing disgust for the open display of women's bodies and discharges through the seventeenth century, that women themselves use the figure of filthiness less frequently than men do, and that the association with filth contributes to women's own relative silence about their own bodily wastes and their disposal.

But there is precedent for using 'filthy' to mean 'soiled with menstrual blood' as early as Coverdale's 1535 Bible, for the earlier reference, in Isaiah 30:22: 'Morouer yf ye destroye the syluer workes of youre Idols, and cast awaye the golden coapes that ye deckt them withall (as fylthynes) and saie, get you hence'.[23] In addition, Isaiah 30:22 remains 'menstruous' in Geneva and KJV, even though Bishops' is (as is its wont) a little more elliptical, replacing the explicit 'menstruous' with the more general 'filthyness': 'euen as filthynesse shalt thou put them away: And thou shalt say vnto it, Get thee hence'. In contrast, the Catholic Rheims-Douai in 30:20 conflates the filthy cloth and the polluted woman whose bodily discharges have contaminated it: 'And thou shalt contaminate the plates of the sculptils of thy siluer, and the garment of the molten of thy gold, and shalt scatter them as the vncleannes of a menstruous woman'; and in Isaiah 64:6 it retains the specifically female, and fertile, 'cloth of a menstrued woman'.[24]

Does 'filthy' in Geneva, Bishops' and KJV serve as intensifier or as euphemism? Or does the very use of euphemism imply obscenity and disgust? On the one hand, perhaps Bishops' and KJV wished to make clear that the verses referred to all Christians, not just to Catholics who venerated relics. On the other, Geneva provides one of its notorious 'bitter notis' to observe that '(some read)' that the filthy cloth was a menstrual rag, a parenthetical aside that Protestant divines transform into a figure to express disgust at Catholic robes and idolatry.[25] Astutely, Read notes the transformation of 'menstruous' to 'monstrous' in these texts, and connects it to the putting off of showy, contaminating Catholic idolatry but, surprisingly, she does not link this habit in the Protestant texts to the debates surrounding representation, decoration or even to the emerging split between public and private that she otherwise identifies as characteristic of menstruation (a private process that threatens to make female fertility public).

---

[22] *The Holy Bible . . . in the earliest English versions made from the Latin Vulgate by John Wycliffe and his Followers* [Wycliff, Early], ed. the Rev. Josiah Forshall (Oxford, 1850); *The Holy Bible . . . in the earliest English versions made from the Latin Vulgate by John Wycliffe and his Followers* [Wycliffe, Late], ed. the Rev. Josiah Forshall (Oxford, 1850); Myles Coverdale, *Biblia* ([n.p.], 1535); *The Byble in Englysh* [Great Bible] (London, 1540); *The Bible* [Thomas Matthew Bible] (London, 1549); *The Holie Bible* [Bishops' Bible] (London, 1568), all reprinted in Chadwyck-Healey, *The Bible in English* (Cambridge, 1996), last accessed through GALILEO, University of Georgia, 1 December 2012.

[23] Miles Coverdale, *Biblia* ([n.p.], 1535), Chapter XXX, Fo. xi, Bbb5r, col. 2.

[24] *The Holie Bible* ([n.p.], 1610), Ooo2v, Vuu3v.

[25] *Records of the English Bible*, ed. Alfred W. Pollard (London and New York, 1911), pp. 297–8.

In the pens of Protestant commentators, how-ever, these Biblical verses about idol-worship and righteousness become evidence of God's disgust towards the trappings of the Catholic mass, the sacralization of relics and the performance of good works. In opposition, Protestants offer humble, even abased, prayer, the importance of words rather than things and the experience of personal faith. Most of the Protestant examples I have found (from slightly earlier than Read's) connect the verses from Isaiah to clothing, display and *performance* (the per-formance of good works, and the performance of, as we shall see, stage-plays). Anthony Gilby, urging his fellow-Protestants to put away priestly apparel along with 'images' and 'ornaments', cites Isaiah 30:22 in his justification:

You shall, sayth he, put out the couerynge of the Imagis of syluer, & the precious vestyme[n]ts of the golde[n] Imagis, and thou shalt caste them awaye lyke a menstrous clowte, and saye vnto yt: Auawnte, or get the hence. Fynallye when all godly men abhorre the monstrous apparell of Fryers, Monkes, Chanons, I can not se, by what order they shulde exteme the ornaments of Popishe Preastes, whose order is as wyckyd as Freyers, Monkes, or any other.[26]

Richard Cavendish cites Isaiah to argue, once more, against works or doings, which are '*as men-struous clothes*'.[27] Laurence Tomson exhorts, 'what is he vpon the earth, that doth employ these wholy, [tha]t hath not alwayes [th]e flesh pricking against the spirit? then the work [tha]t is done of such, is it not as a menstruous cloth?'[28] And 'Our workes are al as the cloth [tha]t is defiled with menstruous bloud', writes the anonymous I.B. (possibly John Bale or John Bradford) in 1547.[29] John Foxe's *Acts and Monuments* quotes Sir John Borthwick's argu-ments in the second article of his charges, against indulgences, as the latter attributes to the devil any good works done by saints:

I pray you, who taught those saints to worke or deserue for other, but only Sathan, who would vtterly haue [th]e merits of Christ extinguished and blotted out, which he knoweth to be the onely remedy of saluation? For if the Scripture do teache vs that no man of himselfe can deserue or worke their saluation, how did the saints then

worke or merit for others . . . Besides this, all that which may be deserued or merited in the righteousnes of man, in the 64. chapter of Esay, they are compared vnto the garment menstruous & defiled, to be cast out.[30]

There are many more examples – such as those in the 1574 English translation of Niels Hem-mingsen's *The Preacher*; the 1581 edition of John Foxe's response to the Portuguese bishop Joseph Osorio (translated into English by James Bell and compiled by Walter Haddon), which refers to men-struous cloths in the context of humble Protestant piety and histrionic Catholic pomp no fewer than seven times; Michael Drayton's 1610 *Heavenly Har-mony*; or Bartimaeus Andrewes's commentary on the Song of Songs. The Protestant church, writes Andrewes, is black with afflictions and neglect, but luckily the 'painted harlottes' of Catholicism toil in vain: Jesus, the divine Bridegroom, 'wil not be taken in their beauty for it is but a menstruous cloth unto him'.[31] Some writers develop the figure further by contrasting rags stained with menstrual blood to pieces of whole-cloth dipped into and dyed in the blood of Christ. If the performance of works comprises stinking clouts sodden with menstrual flux, then faith, in the words of John Prime, is the fragrant 'peece of purple died in the bloud of Christ' and, according to the sermons of Nicholas Byfield, 'our practise should be died in the blood of Christ, and [s]auour of the vertue

---

[26] Anthony Gilby, *To my louynge brethren that is troublyd about the popishe aparrell* (Emden, 1566), B1r–v.

[27] Richard Cavendish, *The image of nature and grace* (London, 1571), P2v.

[28] Laurence Tomson, *An ansvvere to certein assertions* (London, 1570), J1v.

[29] I.B., *A bryefe and plaine declaracion* (London, 1547), A3v.

[30] John Foxe, *Actes and monuments* (London, 1583), KKK4v, p. 1261.

[31] Niels Hemmingsen, *The preacher, or Methode of preachinge* (London, 1574), H1r; Michael Drayton, *A Heauenly Har-monie* (London, 1610), F1v; Walter Haddon, John Foxe and James Bell, *Against Ierome Osorius Byshopp of Siluane in Portin-gall* (London, 1581), *passim*; Bartimaeus Andrewes, *Certaine very vvorthy, Godly and profitable sermons vpon the fifth chapter of the Songs of Solomon* (London, 1595), H2v.

of his death'.[32] (And if the new sandalwood dyes were used to colour the wool 'brick red', the vat might indeed 'sauour' or be perfumed with faith.[33])

The most interesting translation of this figure for Shakespearians appears in the anti-theatrical literature, as low-church ministers transformed the Protestant prohibition on images, relics and Catholic vestments used in worship into a Puritan ban on representation, props and costumes used in stage-plays (compare the attacks and defences surrounding ornament in poetry that are also current at this time).[34] Philip Stubbes compares the sin of pride to menstrual rags, not directly in his diatribe against 'filthie plays and enterluds' but in his sections on pride of heart and pride of apparel.[35] Philoponus defines 'pride of the heart' as the state of mind

whe[n] as a man lifting him selfe on highe, thinketh of himself, aboue that which he is of himselfe: dreamyng a perfection of himselfe, when he is nothyng lesse: And in respect of himselfe, contempneth, vilefieth and reproacheth all men, thinking none comparable to him selfe, whose righteousnes, notwithstanding, is lyke to the polluted cloth of a menstruous woman.[36]

Later, when his interlocutor Spudeus asks about whether people in other times cared so much for fashion as do, Spudeus claims, sixteenth-century townsfolk, without respect to age, sex or calling, Philoponus responds pithily, 'King *Pirrus* sente riche attyre to the Matrones of Rome, who abhorred them, as menstruous clowtes.'[37]

The anonymous 'I.H.' in 1615 deploys the comparison as part of a conceit that compares the city of London to a woman and its theatres to her sexual organs, both breasts and genitals. *The World's Folly* complains that London is full of the seven deadly sins, especially swearing, as citizens emulate the 'obscaene and light ligges, stuft with loathsome and vnheard-of Ribauldry, suckt from the poysonous dugs of Sinne-sweld Theaters'.[38] In a section that specifically discusses play-houses, the author complains that more persons attend 'playing houses, than praying houses', where they hear 'Roaring Meg (not Mol)', Scythian barbarisms and oaths on stage.[39] He singles out the Curtain theatre in a pun that characterizes audience-members as sexually voracious clients and popular playwrights as their paramours, eager to satisfy them, and concludes with an admonition to the city authorities:

Those also stand within the stroke of my penne, who were wont to *Curtaine* ouer their defects with knauish conueyances, and scum off the froth of all wanton vanity, to qualifie the eager appetite of their slapping Fauorites. Then surely neither can Gods wrath be qualified, nor his pestilential arrows, which fly amongst vs by day, & lethally wound vs by night, be quiuer'd vp, till these *Menstruous Ragges* be torne off (by the hand of *Authority*) from the Cities skirts, which so besoyle and coinquinate her whole vesture.[40]

In case we fail to understand the analogy, he glosses 'menstruous ragges' with a marginal note: 'Bawdy players'. So London is what we might call (with acknowledgement to Patricia Parker) a 'Literary Fat Lady':[41] the suburbs are her outskirts or outer garments; the theatres are her breasts engorged not with sustaining maternal milk but with 'loathsome . . . poyson'; the stage or playing space is her pudendum; the plays they perform are a sexualized or obscene discharge such as menstrual blood or (in the description of the Curtain) 'froth' or semen provoked from male observers by her actions, or from her own body as she pleasures herself; and the actors upon that stage are the rags sewn to the skirt

---

[32] John Prime, *A Fruitefull and briefe discourse in two bookes* (London, 1583), G3r; Nicholas Byfield, *Sermons vpon the first chapter of the first epistle generall of Peter* (London, 1617).

[33] Eric Kerridge, *Textile Manufactures in Early Modern England* (Manchester, 1985), p. 167.

[34] Barbara Lewalski's *Protestant Poetics and the Seventeenth-Century Religious Lyric* (Princeton, 1984) provides the definitive overview of this debate.

[35] Philip Stubbes, *Anatomie of Abuses* (London, 1583), L5v.

[36] *Anatomie of Abuses*, B6r–v.

[37] *Anatomie of Abuses*, D3v.

[38] I.H., *The World's Folly* (London, 1615), B1v–B2r.

[39] *The World's Folly*, B2r.

[40] *The World's Folly*, B3r.

[41] Patricia Parker, *Literary Fat Ladies: Rhetoric, Gender, Property* (London, 1987).

or to the shift to absorb the contaminating fluid (the rare and obsolete word 'coinquinate', meaning to defile or pollute, nicely evokes 'iniquity' although the latter is not part of its etymology). The account has a certain interest for social historians, too, since it suggests that, despite the debate surrounding whether or not women wore underwear on their lower bodies in this era, they did *not* (as a few twentieth-century popular accounts have it) leave an uninhibited trail of blood wherever they went, or bleed into their outer clothing.[42] Read (who does not discuss this example) remains carefully neutral on this topic, suggesting that menstrual protection might vary from one woman to another depending on class, health, profession and so on, so that prostitutes might insert sponges as absorbent pessaries while they menstruated so that they could continue serving clients; nobly-born women might use folded linen clouts or rags that were attached to a girdle; poorer women with no linen to spare might bleed into their shifts, which might or might not be knotted between the legs. She writes that there is no evidence that women sewed cloths for menstrual protection. But this anti-theatrical tract, and Rainolds's, below, clearly imagine the rag as something separate from the skirt, that can be removed from it – perhaps a bit like a bum-roll (a cushion tied around the hips to pad them, in lieu of a farthingale).[43]

Finally, the well-known anti-theatrical tract, *The Overthrow of Stage Plays* (1599) by John Rainolds, President of Corpus Christi, Oxford, combines three concerns of early modern life – anti-theatricalism, sexual dimorphism and the rag-paper cycle – when he compares putting actors on stage to perform plays to giving Phaedra a 'menstruous cloth' to hold during her 'amorous speech' in Seneca.[44] The analogy appears within a passage that contrasts Quintilian's restricted curriculum for students with the licentious programme of present-day teachers and scholars. On the one hand, argues Rainolds, Quintilian prohibits both literature, such as 'amatorie poemes', and certain methods of delivery, such as 'imitat[ing] the voices of Women, or old men' because 'such as those

are whom we imitate much, such our selves become'.[45] On the other, continues Rainolds,

you, as if Phaedras amorous speech expressed by Seneca were nothing without a peece of menstruous cloth sowed to it, doe occasion yours to make them selves familiar and well acquainted with Plautus, one farre beneath the best. He would haue his youth to practise their style in good things, as in weapons, which they may vse when neede shall be: you practise yours in speeches entising men to Uenerie, to ribauderie, to scurrilitie, to hoordom, to incest, to other abominations. He would haue his youth to commit most excellent thinges and wordes to memorie; you pester yours with filth, such filth in Rivales (I am ashamed to reherse it) as can not be matched, I thinke, sure very hardly, throughout all Plautus. Hee would not haue his youth to counterfeit a womans voice: you procure Minerva, Penelope, Euryclea, Antonoë, Eurynome, Hippodamia, Melantho, Phaedra, the Nurse, the Nymph, besides I know not whom in the vnprinted Comedie, to bee played by yours.[46]

Rainolds's 'menstruous cloth' evokes disgust and contamination, the viscerally physical, through the incongruity of high classical culture and low material object, manly verbal swordplay and feminine logorrhoea, tragic, extraordinary love and banal, monthly bleeding. Rainolds chooses this image because what menstruous rags and stage-plays share is their ability to foreground – obscenely – gender and binary sexual difference in the observer's mind.

The analogy breaks down somewhat when we take it apart. For one thing, the passage begins by comparing both stage-acting and the works of Plautus to menstrual rags, but then attempts to recuperate Plautus somewhat by implying that where written (printed?) tragedy and the works

---

42 See, for example, Harry Finlay's online *MUM: Museum of Menstruation*, which misrepresents or misunderstands Read's argument to suggest that 'When [women] menstruated, they left a trail of blood behind them', www.mum.org/pastgerm. htm, accessed 22 November 2013.

43 *OED*, bum, sb.1, C2.

44 John Rainolds, *The Overthrow of Stage-Plays* (London, 1599), Q3v.

45 *The Overthrow of Stage-Plays*, Q3r.

46 *The Overthrow of Stage-Plays*, Q3v.

of Seneca might immortalize 'the best', or 'good things', or even 'excellent thinges and wordes', in contrast, 'unprinted Comedie[s]' or extempore performance that includes female impersonation is even *worse* than Plautus's comedies. The common stage-property of the bloody handkerchief becomes a functional and overwhelmingly female object, the product of material processes rather than the work of imagination.

Rainolds's metaphor additionally suggests that the acting of 'unprinted comedies' threatens to turn printed paper – Seneca's tragedies – back into the rags from which paper was made. The obscene parody extends to bibliography: bookbinders folded and sewed printed sheets into books just as women folded and sewed 'menstruous cloth[s]' into absorbent pads. These rags' limited ability to absorb blood flow leads to our only direct Shakespearian reference to menstruation, the 'good old Lord' Gonzago's description of a sinking ship as 'leaky as an unstanched wench' (*The Tempest* 1.1.45–6). Rainolds seems to say by his analogy that stage-plays make visible something that should be excluded or hidden, that is, they evoke sex in both its (modern) senses, erotic contact and sexual difference.

The menstrual stain in anti-theatrical literature corresponds to what Jonas Barish calls the 'fearful aversion to anything . . . that might suggest active or interested sexuality, this being equated with femininity, with weakness, with the yielding to feeling, and consequently with the destruction of all assured props and boundaries' that he finds in the work of William Prynne and other anti-theatrical writers.[47] Stage-plays can't represent women's bodies but they make viewers think about them all the more, all the same, as Stephen Orgel has argued.[48] One could respond that women's bodies are more vividly objectified and estranged through their representation, as does Dympna Callaghan in *Shakespeare Without Women*.[49] But these gendered bodies on stage are also estranged from supposedly inherent or corporeal moral, social, intellectual qualities. Shakespeare's bloody rags foreground the art and act of representation in order to critique gender that is socially enforced.

'BLOODY PASSION'

We know that cross-dressed boys who played women's parts stimulated a high level of cultural anxiety around questions of gender, sexuality and representation in early modern England; Shakespeare's plays artificially sustain and develop this anxiety as they combine references to cross-dressing with the stage-property of the bloody or stained rag and the experience of what is (with one exception, with which I'll conclude) called 'passion'. Let's take Shakespeare's stained and spotted napkins in order once more. In *3 Henry VI*, 1.4, Queen Margaret taunts the imprisoned Duke of York by mocking him on a mole-hill, crowning him with paper, and – cruellest of all – bidding him weep and wipe his tears with a handkercher steeped in the blood of his murdered child the young Duke of Rutland. Many have noted the evident parallels with Christ's Passion and Crucifixion – the crown of thorns becomes a crown of paper, the mole-hill stands for Calvary, and the bloody rag parodies St Veronica's vernicle or handerchief mystically imprinted with the image of Christ's face after she mops his brow. Northumberland responds to York's tears as to a Passion Play: 'Beshrew me, but his passion moves me so / That hardly can I check my eyes from tears' (*3 Henry VI*, 1.4.151–2).[50] York's response to Margaret, however, focuses upon her sex and gender, upon her unnatural relationship to blood and to the bloody rag she waves in his face, in particular. Margaret is a 'she-wolf of France', 'ill-beseeming . . . in [her] sex', an 'Amazonian trull', and thus, in the

---

47 Jonas Barish, *The Anti-Theatrical Prejudice* (Berkeley, 1981), p. 85.

48 Stephen Orgel, *Impersonations* (Cambridge, 1996).

49 Dympna Callaghan, *Shakespeare Without Women* (London and New York, 2000).

50 Northumberland's phrase presents a crux: the octavo *The True Tragedie of Richard Duke of York* (London, 1595) gives 'passions moue' (B2v), but F gives 'passions moues' (TLN 552). I follow the New Cambridge emendation 'passion moves' here because the scene so clearly establishes York as a Christ-figure and his suffering as a passion. See *The Third Part of King Henry VI*, ed. Michael Hattaway (Cambridge, 1993).

false and common early modern etymology for *Amazon*, lacking a breast, the source of that most benign of early modern female fluids, mother's milk (1.4.112–15). Where true women are 'soft, mild, pitiful and flexible', Margaret is 'stern, obdurate, flinty, rough, remorseless' (1.4.142–3).

In the comic register, the parodic play of Pyramus and Thisbe in *A Midsummer Night's Dream* 5.1 prominently features Thisbe's bloodstained mantle, as the Prologue informs us:

> as she fled, her mantle she did fall,
> Which Lion vile with bloody mouth did stain.
> Anon comes Pyramus, sweet youth and tall,
> And finds his trusty Thisbe's mantle slain;
> Whereat, with blade – with bloody blameful blade –
> He bravely broached his boiling bloody breast.
>
> (5.1.141–6)

The alliterative repetition of 'bloody' with 'bravely', 'blameful' and 'boiling' comically emphasizes the stage-property, as does Pyramus/Bottom's rant when he discovers it, in clumsy dimeter: 'Thy mantle good /What, stain'd with blood', an ejaculation that almost immediately prompts Theseus's mock-sympathetic riposte, 'This passion – and the death of a dear friend – would go near to make a man look sad' (5.1.277–8, 283–4). More mysterious is Demetrius's comment, 'A mote will turn the balance which Pyramus, which Thisbe, is the better – he for a man, God warrant us; she for a woman, God bless us' (5.1.313–5). The Folio stops at 'better', omitting both the profanity (the name of God) and the obscure reference to sexual difference. Ronda Arab suggests that Demetrius accuses the asinine Bottom/Pyramus of being only as close to a man (that is, a human being) as Flute/Thisbe is to being a woman (that is, a female).[51] Certainly the play has made much of the technologies of female impersonation that the mechanicals use, and of the secondary sexual characteristics that, Flute claims, will impede his performance: 'let me not play a woman. I have a beard coming'; and Thisbe's lament, which Theseus characterizes as 'her passion [which] ends the play' describes Pyramus in terms more traditionally associated with the female mistress of Petrarchan poetry, as Harold Brooks notes in his Arden 2 edition (1.2.43–4, 5.1.310).[52] There may also be (as in *As You Like It* and in Sonnet 20) a pun on 'for a man' and 'for a woman': both Pyramus and Thisbe are equally unappealing sexually, to men and to women.[53] The mantle works to gender neither Flute as fainting female nor Pyramus as valiant swain, managing to evoke a monstrous parody of the Passion and an impersonation of sexual difference played 'most obscenely and courageously' (1.2.100–1).[54]

As You Like It calls attention to Rosalind/Ganymede's swoon at the sight of the 'napkin' stained with Orlando's blood as a mark of her femininity and of her heteroerotic love for Orlando (4.3.94). Both Oliver and Celia draw attention to the relationship between blood, gender and passion (I quote at length and intersperse commentary because the play, and Rosalind, just won't let it go):

> *Oliver.* He sent me hither, stranger as I am,
> . . . to give this napkin,
> Dyed in his blood, unto the shepherd youth
> That he in sport doth call his Rosalind.
>
> (4.3.153–7)

Note that Oliver couples the name of Rosalind with blood both times he utters it, first as he seeks out Ganymede and introduces himself, 'to that youth he calls his Rosalind / He sends this bloody napkin', and second as he intensifies the echoes of the sacrificial Biblical passion through the phrase 'dyed in his blood' and the evocation of the 'shepherd' and the 'rose' in Rosalind (4.3.93–4).

CELIA. Why, how now, Ganymede, sweet Ganymede!
OLIVER. Many will swoon when they do look on blood.

---

51 Ronda Arab, *Manly Mechanicals on the Early Modern English Stage* (Cranbury, NJ, 2011), p. 110.

52 *A Midsummer Night's Dream*, ed. Harold Brooks, Arden Shakespeare, Second Series (London, 1979), pp. 121–2.

53 *As You Like It*, Epilogue; Sonnet 20, line 9.

54 Patricia Parker argues that the scene additionally parodies Christ as Divine Bridegroom: 'What's in a Name: and More', pp. 101–49.

CELIA. There is more in it. Cousin Ganymede!
OLIVER. Look, he recovers.   (4.3.158–61)

Celia instinctively rallies Rosalind with her boy-name, Ganymede, although she cannot resist correcting Oliver's misapprehension when he assumes that Ganymede swoons from cowardice (which makes his heart quail or shrink, preventing it from producing enough vital spirit for its own sustenance) when faced with the sight of blood. Instead, she implies (and the audience knows), 'the more in it' is female perturbation, fear and sorrow, and the inability of Rosalind to voice her grief to vent the excess blood that has rushed to sustain her fainting heart, that makes Ganymede swoon. Oliver offers a diagnosis that is more apt than he realizes: 'Be of good cheer, youth. You a man? You lack a man's heart' (4.3.165–6). She does indeed 'lack a man's heart', and Rosalind's smaller heart is overwhelmed or o'ercharged by emotion. Rosalind responds, 'I do so, I confess it. Ah, sirrah, a body would think this was well counterfeited. I pray you, tell your brother how well I counterfeited. Heigh-ho!' (4.3.167–9). Ganymede overcompensates for the pair of feminine signifiers: a bloody rag and, as Oliver goes on to say, 'passion of earnest' (4.3.171–2). Even as Ganymede insists he was 'counterfeiting', Rosalind responds to Oliver's injunction, 'Well then, take a good heart, and counterfeit to be a man', with the joke, 'So I do; but, i'faith, I should have been a woman by right' (4.3.174–7). Perhaps Celia's observation, 'you look paler and paler' is both medically accurate (as the blood retreats to Rosalind's heart during her passion) and tactful (4.3.178). Oliver's exit lines hail Ganymede straightforwardly as Rosalind, as if the masquerade is over definitively in his mind: 'I must bear answer back / How you excuse my brother, Rosalind' (4.3.180–1). Ganymede still claims to be 'counterfeit[ing]', but Oliver probably realizes that the former's faint was more than a feint.

Although Desdemona's handkerchief is strawberry-spotted, rather than explicitly blood-stained, the play uses it to associate women and blood with performance. This handkerchief's blood-stains are figurative, not literal, because its characters remain trapped within a web of representation.[55] If the play seems less overtly concerned with gender exchange than As You Like It or 3 Henry VI, then both the images of Desdemona's body 'tasted' by the whole camp and Othello himself 'eaten... with passion', and the famous textual crux, 'Her (My) name, that was as fresh / As Dian's visage, is now begrimed and black / As mine own face' mix up the lovers' identities in the 'chaos' that Othello himself dreads (3.3.391–3). Throughout the play Othello's excessive jealousy, his public and private anger and (by Iago) his 'grief' are called 'passions'. The development, or rather, the degradation of these 'passions' tracks Iago's theatrical plot, as does the figurative staining or contamination of the handkerchief, from a token of love to a token of jealous and bloody murder. '[P]assion... Essays to lead the way' as Othello, angered, strives to discover 'How this foul rout [Cassio's drunken aggression, instigated by Iago] began' (2.3.199–200, 203). In the so-called temptation scene, 3.3, Othello praises Iago as one whose 'heart / ... passion cannot rule' (128–9); Iago's insinuations trigger the headache that Desdemona tries vainly to heal by binding her husband's brows with her 'too little' napkin (291). (If Othello suffers from epilepsy, the strawberry-spotted handkerchief resembles to some degree the blood-soaked linen plasters bandaged around the temples of epilepsy sufferers in the new Paracelsian therapies, or recalls the menstrual blood to be drunk, warm, by epileptics in the new pharmacopoeia.[56]) After we learn that Iago has long planned to steal the handkerchief, and watched Emilia take it up, Othello returns to the stage, where, Iago observes, he is 'eaten up with passion' (3.3.396). Othello's 'trance' in 4.1 follows a well-known speech that

[55] On representation, rhetoric and identity in Othello, see Joel Altman's magisterial The Improbability of Othello: Rhetorical Anthropology and Shakespearean Selfhood (Chicago and London, 2010).

[56] Louise Noble, 'The Fille Vièrge as Pharmakon: The Therapeutic Value of Desdemona's Corpse', in Disease, Diagnosis, and Cure on the Early Modern Stage, ed. Stephanie Moss and Kaara L. Peterson (Aldershot, 2004), p. 149 n.43.

associates the handkerchief with Passion (with 'God's wounds', abbreviated into the common profanity) and passion:

Lie with her? Lie on her? We say 'lie on her' when they belie her. Lie with her? 'Swounds, that's fulsome! Handkerchief – confessions – handkerchief. To confess and be hanged for his labour. First to be hanged and then to confess! I tremble at it. Nature would not invest herself in such shadowing passion without some instruction. It is not words that shakes me thus.   (4.1.34–40)

The 'shadowing passion' is both the looseness of Cassio, in his alleged erotic dream, where night shadows or reflects the events and thoughts of the day, and the convulsive 'grief' ('A passion most unsuiting such a man', reproves Iago) that cripples Othello himself, where Iago's words cloud Othello's reason (put him in shadow) and call up, as instructions to an actor, the emotions demanded by the script (4.1.76). To Othello, Desdemona now merely shadows or plays 'well-painted passion', like an actor, when she weeps (4.1.258), and to Lodovico, Othello's fall from 'the nature / Whom passion could not shake' denotes that he must have lost his 'wits' (4.1.267–8, 271). Lodovico almost suspects a script – that 'letters [did] work upon his blood / And new-create his fault' – but cannot conceive of the true author (277–8). Finally, Desdemona calls Othello's jealous rage in 5.2 his 'bloody passion', and Othello just a few lines later returns to harping on 'That handkerchief' (5.2.47, 50), whose 'work' could not be 'ta'en out' (3.3.300) as easily as Emilia had imagined.

When we move to *Cymbeline*, Shakespeare includes the characteristic pattern of gender reversal, metatheatrical reference and spotted rags that I have described in *3 Henry VI* and *As You Like It*, but crucially omits a term that hitherto has accompanied it. I end this survey of bloody Shakespearian passions with a development or maturity in Shakespeare's career or at least an imaginative response to the exigencies of the emerging genre of tragicomedy. The bloodstained napkin in *Cymbeline* provides the (faked) evidence of Innogen's death that Pisanio somehow gets to Posthumus in the Roman camp. Posthumus finds the supposed

'testimonies [of Innogen's infidelity] lie bleeding in [him]' (3.4.22–3); Innogen 'forget[s] to be a woman' (3.4.155) and dresses as the youth Fidele, and Posthumus (at least according to the stage-tradition discussed by Valerie Wayne) wears on his body Innogen's bloody rag. But this play lacks passion, despite its 'bloody cloth' (5.1.1). I mean that literally: the word 'passion' does not appear in this play. Innogen is chaste to a fault, some argue, denying her husband even the 'lawful pleasure' of marital intercourse, even as she displays (in a phrase that is at best salacious and at worst pornographic) 'a pudency so rosy the sweet view on't' would have charmed Saturn himself (*Cymbeline* 2.5.9, 11). Innogen perhaps remains amenorrhoeic, free from the 'passion menstruall' as from the passion sexual.

More appealing, however, is the surmise that this play lacks not mutual erotic passion but *suffering* passion (from the Latin *patior, passus sum*, I suffer, I suffered, but also I allowed, and I am patient). Faced with Pisanio's evidence, Posthumus (to our surprise and relief, if we are familiar with the plot of the slandered lady from *Ado* and *Othello*) repents his jealousy almost instantly, even if he imagines his wife to have been possibly 'wrying but a little' (5.1.5): he experiences no 'bloody passion' such as tortures Othello. Similarly, Innogen suffers patiently rather than passionately: unlike Desdemona, she does not cry 'Am I that name?' but resists her misogynistic hailing by performing a different sex (*Othello*, 4.2.121); unlike Juliet (Thisbe's tragic counterpart), neither when she finds herself accused of adultery nor a seeming widow does she think to kill herself. Perhaps the play lacks Passion, too – Innogen does not need to become a redemptive sacrifice as does Desdemona and nor does Posthumus need to kill himself as does Othello. The play also lacks the imagery of eating and consumption that, as Stephanie Moss and others have noted, characterizes *Othello*, and Desdemona's sacrificed or mummified corpse in particular.[57] Instead, perhaps *Cymbeline*'s hero is

---

[57] Stephanie Moss, 'Transformation and Degeneration: The Paracelsian/Galenic Body in *Othello*', in *Disease, Diagnosis and Cure on the Early Modern Stage*, pp. 151–170.

'Posthumus' in its adjectival sense, in the sense that he, like Innogen, is reborn from the dead (since Innogen believes he is dead, having mistaken Cloten's headless corpse for Posthumus's body earlier in the play). This is Redemption *without* Passion but with and through the Play – Passionately Secular, Passionately Theatrical and Passionately Pagan, Shakespeare.

THE MERCHANT OF VENICE AT THE NATIONAL THEATRE OF GREECE (1945) AND THE SILENCING OF THE HOLOCAUST

TINA KRONTIRIS

Can Shylock write/erase history? His role in *The Merchant of Venice* is a relatively short one; he appears only in five scenes and speaks a total of about 355 lines. Yet he has almost always been regarded as the central figure of the play, a fact acknowledged by most critics who have traced his history. John Drakakis observes in his recent edition of *The Merchant*: 'The sense that this is Shylock's play – indeed his tragedy – is given added emphasis from the beginning of the eighteenth century onwards in criticism and performance . . . and has remained remarkably resilient.'[1] The resilience of this tendency is due to the fact that Shakespeare involves the Jewish moneylender in a potentially tragic confrontation which far exceeds his fiscal role in the plot: Shylock appears to represent his 'nation' in an age-old conflict between Jews and Gentiles. The comic resolution of this conflict and the harsh treatment of the Jew have always presented a problem to interpreters of the play. The severity of the punishment imposed on Shylock in the fourth act, and especially his compulsory religious conversion (which is not found in Shakespeare's main source), carries political/ideological implications and raises important questions about the play's attitude towards Jews as an ethnic-religious group. Hence from the time of its inception, and throughout its long afterlife, the play has been bound up with the history of the Jews and the issue of anti-Semitism.

This has never been more evident than in the post-Holocaust era. As Dennis Kennedy observes, the crimes committed against the Jews under Hitler and 'our almost continual subsequent awareness' of these crimes have transformed the play and our way of reading it: 'The external events of the Second World War have affected *Merchant* so thoroughly that it is fair to say that since 1945 we have been in possession of a new text of the play, one which bears relationships to the earlier text but is also significantly different from it.'[2] Indeed, the way the play has been staged in postwar times is often used as a gauge of sensitivity both to the important issues it poses about racial/religious tolerance and to the question of responsibility towards the fate of the Jews historically. Attempts to displace, subdue or contain Shylock are likely to be interpreted as a politically conservative stance. As Drakakis says, 'So long as we keep the plight of Shylock at a distance, as the Elizabethan audiences may have done, then the laughter that the play generates will be of a conservative kind.'[3] This statement applies as much to artists and critics today as to those who lived closer in time to the end of the war and became secondary witnesses of the horrific genocide. Indeed, it applies especially to them, I would argue, since by their choices they determined what was passed on as memory and registered as history. There is ample evidence to suggest that performances of *The Merchant of Venice* within the first decade from the end of the war followed an escapist path.

---

[1] John Drakakis, 'Introduction', *The Merchant of Venice*, Arden 3 edn (London, 2010), p. 1.

[2] Dennis Kennedy, *Looking at Shakespeare*, 2nd edition (Cambridge, 1993), p. 200.

[3] Drakakis, 'Introduction', p. 110.

In this essay I purpose to examine a 1945 production of this play at the Greek National Theatre in order to show that it strategically avoided an allusion to the mass murder of the Jews by the Nazis, even though Greece had recently lost most of its long-established Jewish communities. In 1940, just before Greece's entry in the Second World War, Shylock appeared as a hero on the national stage; but in 1945 he came back as a comic, semi-grotesque figure, who was not allowed to claim the audience's primary attention. Through its choice of an apolitical, escapist interpretation of *Merchant*, the National Theatre's first postwar production participated in the silencing of the Holocaust and the subsequent suppression of the history of Jews in Greece. As we shall see, the tendency to treat the play from a noncommittal perspective in the early postwar period was not a uniquely Greek phenomenon, though the significance of this perspective was different in the Greek context.

THE ESCAPE FROM ACCOUNTABILITY AFTER THE SECOND WORLD WAR

In the decade immediately following the Second World War most European theatre directors avoided a direct allusion to war crimes or to postwar reality. There was a general tendency towards extravagant performances, largely of the classics. Shakespeare in particular held the lead in many countries. Yet his plays were approached in ways that manifested a need to get away from the present and to look back to the traditional values of the remote and largely imaginary past. According to Dennis Kennedy, in the first twenty years after the war, 'Shakespeare was used in Western and Central Europe as a site for the recovery and reconstruction of values that were perceived to be under threat, or already lost.'[4] Jean Vilar, the French actor and director who opened the Avignon Festival in 1947 with Shakespeare's *Richard II*, invested all his talent and economic means, Kennedy tells us, in a 'utopian scheme' to celebrate timeless themes and to reaffirm human values.[5] Vilar's choice of a

Shakespeare history play as well as his interpretation of the main character as representative of all humanity expressed a much-needed belief in the future.[6] The expression of faith in this case was accompanied not by any revolutionary impetus, as after World War I, but by a flight into past traditions, symbolized by the medieval setting of the play and the performance. As Kennedy correctly observes, such escapist approaches to the classics may be read as evidence of a 'retirement from accountability'.[7]

One would expect that the *Merchant of Venice* would have formed an exception to the escapist tendency, since it is a play where a major character, the dramatically powerful Shylock, claims to speak on behalf of a wronged Jewish people. The loss of his daughter, the contemptuous attitude of the Christians towards him as well as his forced conversion and humiliation at the end of the play are painful experiences which would carry a strong resonance among audiences in postwar times. Occasionally, the resonance was felt and voiced. Alluding to Shylock's experience, *New York Times* theatre critic Brooks Atkinson had said in 1947: 'In the twentieth century we know better than Shakespeare did how painful a tragedy it is.'[8] Yet theatre artists did not apparently feel compelled to interpret Shakespeare's Jew in this light. It took them a long time to confront the play with the kind of sensitivity it deserved and to view it in *relation* to the Holocaust. In England and North America the play continued to be staged with Shylock as a conventional villain of the kind that Michael Redgrave had portrayed in 1953 at the Stratford Memorial Theatre.[9] In fact, it was not until Guthrie's modern interpretation, produced for Canada's

---

[4] Dennis Kennedy, 'Shakespeare and the Cold-War', in *Four Hundred Years of Shakespeare in Europe*, ed. A. L. Pujante and Ton Hoenselaars (Nebraska, 2003), p. 163.

[5] Kennedy, 'Shakespeare and the Cold War', p. 164.

[6] Kennedy, 'Shakespeare and the Cold War', p. 165.

[7] Kennedy, 'Shakespeare and the Cold War', p. 170.

[8] Quoted in Charles Edelman, 'Introduction', *The Merchant of Venice*, Shakespeare in Production (Cambridge, 2002), p. 55.

[9] Vicki K. Janick, '*The Merchant of Venice*': A Guide to the Play (Westport, CT, 2003), p. 230.

Stratford Festival in 1955, that the tendency towards the comic villain began to change.[10]

Even in Germany, Holocaust-sensitive stagings of *Merchant* did not appear in the early postwar period, despite the fact that by 1954 the play had (re)gained, at least in West Germany, a notable position in the Shakespeare repertoire of the theatres.[11] Sabine Schülding, who studies at length the confrontational function of *Merchant* in postwar Germany (the use of the play as a site for the country's coming to terms with its recent past), locates the beginning of this function in the late 1950s or early 1960s.[12] Zeno Ackermann, who focuses on the earlier years, convincingly argues that in the aftermath of the war German 'productions of *Merchant* were not necessarily informed by an unequivocal urge to remember'.[13] 'Rather, their *primary* [sic] concern consisted in imaginatively reconstructing a shattered nation by utilizing the restorative plot of the comedy',[14] whose final resolution contains the conflict by avoiding the wound on Antonio's body and offering a retreat to mythical Belmont. Ackermann also reminds us that the cancellation of the plans to stage *Merchant* at Frankfurt's City Theatre in 1946 – usually cited as an example of German sensitivity towards the play close in time to the end of the war – was actually due to the intervention of the American occupation authorities present in Germany at the time.[15]

THE MERCHANT OF VENICE
ON THE GREEK STAGE BEFORE
THE WAR

The same evasive attitude towards the Holocaust prevailed in a historically significant production of *Merchant* staged by the National Theatre of Greece, Athens, in 1945. Contrary to a 1940 production that had emphasized the tragic aspect of the play through the portrayal of a revengeful but heroic Shylock, the production of 1945 downplayed the potentiality of the play's dramatic conflict and presented an invigorating harmonious world in which the Jew was little more than an unpleasant intruder. The comparison of these two diametrically opposed stage interpretations of the play offered below sheds light on the interconnection of historical events, national priorities and theatrical performances. In order to facilitate the discussion of these two key productions, I shall review briefly the interpretation of *Merchant* and of Shylock in particular during the 1930s, for the decade preceding the war became a reference point for Greek theatre when the war was over.

---

[10] Edelman, 'Introduction', pp. 57–8.

[11] Zeno Ackermann and Sabine Schülting, 'Einführung', *Shylock nach dem Holocaust: Zur Geschichte einer Erinnerungsfigur* (Berlin and New York, 2011), p. 5.

[12] Sabine Schülting, '"Remember Me": Shylock on the Postwar German Stage', in *Shakespeare Survey 63* (Cambridge, 2010), p. 293. Schülding sees the year 2005, which marks the sixtieth anniversary of the end of the Second World War, as a chronological break in the general pattern of postwar German *Merchant*s: 'the association with the Shoah, which has shaped the German reception of Shakespeare's "comedy" for six decades is slowly giving way to a wider range of interpretations' (298). In an earlier article, Schülting considers George Tabori's production/adaptation of *Merchant* (Munich, 1978) as paradigmatic of the relationship between the treatment of Shakespeare's 'comedy' in Germany since the Second World War and the country's attempt to piece together its postwar identity ('"I am not bound to please thee with my answers": *The Merchant of Venice* on the Post-war German Stage', in *World-Wide Shakespeares: Local Appropriations in Film and Performance*, ed. Sonia Massai (London, 2005), pp. 69–71).

[13] Zeno Ackermann, 'Performing Oblivion/Enacting Remembrance: *The Merchant of Venice* in West Germany, 1945 to 1961', *Shakespeare Quarterly*, 62 (2011), p. 369. Through nuanced analyses of contemporary reviews, production programmes and other forms of writing, Ackermann interrogates the heretofore widely accepted assumption that German productions of *The Merchant of Venice* in the first years that followed the end of the Second World War were characterized by attitudes or feelings which manifested a desire to make reparation for the damage caused to the Jews by the Germans during the war. Working on the premise that a culture's turn at any point is subject to the 'complex dialectical process of continuity and change' (368), the author adduces evidence to show that at least until the end of the 1950s, and possibly later, 'the subtext of the play's reception was constituted by the conflicting needs of both confronting and warding off guilt' (p. 383).

[14] Ackermann, 'Performing Oblivion', p. 369.

[15] Ackermann, 'Performing Oblivion', p. 374.

In Europe, Henry Irving's 'tragic' view of Shylock had prevailed in various forms up until 1930.[16] Max Reinhardt's 1921 production – where a buffoon-like Shylock, who talked loudly and laughed boisterously, moved in an enchanting Venice set in blue and white cubist construction[17] – constituted the exception rather than the rule of its time. In the early 1930s, however, there appeared a number of rival interpretations, which aimed to dispense with the inherited stage sentimentality, to undercut the tragic potential of the character of Shylock, particularly in the trial scene, and to reinforce the comic aspect of the play. After Reinhardt, two artists were especially influential in this new emphasis on comedy: Harley Granville-Barker and Theodore Komisarjevsky. The first showed – through an intricately close, theatrically realistic analysis of the text – that sentimentality is foreign to the dramatic design of Shakespeare, who displays awareness of the fairy-tale nature of his material and carefully monitors the tragic potential of Shylock. The second used carnivalesque sets and *commedia dell'arte* acting techniques to remove the play entirely from the Irving stage tradition. In the *Merchant* that Komisarjevsky directed for the Stratford Memorial Theatre in July 1932, Shylock was portrayed by Randal Ayrton as a dehumanized comic devil and the whole play was given a burlesque turn.[18] This performance marked a turning point in the stage history of *Merchant* because it showed that the play could be staged effectively as theatrical entertainment, without regard to its serious social/ideological issues.

In Greece *Merchant* had an episodic history before the 1930s. Although the play was repeatedly performed in the late nineteenth century, its popularity receded during the first three decades of the twentieth century.[19] The relatively few performances that took place between 1900 and 1927 adopted the 'tragic view' of Shylock, which had its source in European theatre. The serious portrayal of the character of Shylock, usually played with a Hebraic accent, was set on a lavish naturalistic stage, which was customarily used in Greek productions of Shakespeare at that time. According to theatre historian Yiannis Sideris, there may

have been some individual actor here or there (e.g. Nikolaos Lekatsas) who played the role in a comic tone, 'yet no one in those years [before 1927] found it reasonable not to consider the play a tragedy, or at least a work with scenes of "terror and horror"'.[20]

The interpretation of *Merchant*, as of other Shakespearian plays, turned a page in the late 1920s with the work of a highly influential figure in the history of Greek theatre. This was Fotos Politis (1890–1934), author, critic, translator, drama teacher and, in 1932, Director of the newly established National Theatre of Greece. Educated in Germany before the First World War, Politis became an admirer of Max Reinhardt's theatre and acquired the German love for the classics. In his brief but productive theatrical career, Politis staged a great number of plays from ancient to modern times. Of the three Shakespeare plays he tackled on stage – *The Merchant of Venice*, *Julius Caesar*, *Othello* – the first apparently held a long-lasting fascination for him; within a five-year span he staged *Merchant* twice, in 1927 for the Professional School

---

[16] Irving constructed a sentimental Jew by introducing significant changes in the text, the most striking of which was the return of Shylock to his home after his daughter Jessica had run away; see James Bulman, *The Merchant of Venice*, Shakespeare in Performance (Manchester, 1991), ch. 2, esp. pp. 37–8.

[17] John Russell Brown, 'Introduction', *The Merchant of Venice*, Arden Shakespeare (London, 1994), p. xxxvi; see also Andrew Bonnell, *Shylock in Germany: Antisemitism and the German Theatre from the Enlightenment to the Nazis* (London, 2008), pp. 72–3.

[18] Edelman, 'Introduction', p. 49; Janick, *The Merchant of Venice*, p. 227.

[19] The first Greek performance of *Merchant* took place in Athens on 10 January 1882. The play was presented by actor-director Nikolaos Lekatsas, who took on the role of Shylock. From then on to the end of the nineteenth century, Lekatsas performed the play repeatedly in Athens as well as in the urban centres of the Greek Diaspora of those times (Constantinople, Smyrna, Cyprus, etc.). In the twentieth century, the play's popularity waned. Apart from the odd, one-night performance here or there, there are just four or five regular productions recorded for the period 1900–1927: see Yiannis Sideris, 'O Saixpir stin Ellada II', *Theatro*, 14 (March–April 1964), p. 60.

[20] Yiannis Sideris, 'O Saixpir stin Ellada VI', *Theatro*, 18 (November–December, 1964), p. 24.

of Theatre and in 1932 for the National Theatre, thus lifting the play out of its relative obscurity in Greece up to that time. A prolific writer as well as director, Politis wrote numerous articles in the daily and weekly press, offering his analyses as guides to the performances he directed or as critique to the work of others. In an article for his 1927 production of *Merchant*, Politis argued that Shylock is a grotesque, dark and sorrowful figure peripheral to the play's dramatic design (as necessary as the Prince of Morocco) and that the lyrical and joyful fifth act represents the quintessential spirit of the play. Those who view the Jew as the protagonist of the play, Politis supported, are often led to the ridiculous choice of cutting the last act, and so they distort the Shakespearian text.[21] Overall, he saw a balance of roles among the major dramatic persons in the comedy, whom he considered to be Antonio, Bassanio and Portia. As theatre historian Yiannis Sideris informs us, the Greek artist did not quite manage to apply his ideas effectively, that is, to prevent the actor who played Shylock from dominating the stage.[22] Yet Politis's analysis reveals that, at least on the conceptual level, his Jew had something of the comic/satiric outlook that Reinhardt had introduced earlier.[23]

Five years later, when Politis restaged *Merchant* for the institution he headed, he changed his view of the character of Shylock – possibly as a result of Granville-Barker's influence on the Greek artist.[24] In his second article on *Merchant*, published on the same day as the opening of the performance on 5 October 1932, Politis still maintained that this play is 'the song of beautiful and carefree youth' and as such has little to do with serious conflict.[25] But he now considered Antonio as the central character or 'nucleus' of the play. Most importantly, he now viewed Shylock as a complex figure, 'a unique mixture of Prophet and Devil, ideologue and materialist, hero and little man',[26] deserving the audience's understanding, if not sympathy, and occasional admiration. Accordingly, in his new stage production the Greek director illuminated various aspects of Shylock's character – including the Jew's feelings about the loss of his wife's ring. Altogether, Politis presented a complex

Jewish moneylender – vindictive but dignified and at times even heroic. This heroic element was new in Politis's consideration,[27] as well as in Greek theatre at the time. Yet the director did not concede the play to Shylock. While he granted the Jew his due complexity and depth, he denied him a central position in the drama. To this effect, Politis toned down the tragic potential of Shylock's response to the loss of his daughter, emphasizing instead the lyricism and harmony of the play. It was evidently a harmony that incorporated or spoke through wealth and grace. A memorable feature for at least one critic was Portia's elegant living-room, which

---

21 Fotos Politis, 'O Emporos tis Venetias', *Politeia*, 14 April 1927, repr. in *Theatro*, 16, 1 (July–August 1964), p. 97. Here and throughout, the translation of quoted material from Greek sources is mine.

22 Sideris, 'O Saixpir stin Ellada VI', p. 25.

23 The influence of Max Reinhardt on Politis's theatrical work has not been fully documented though always acknowledged. The earliest example of such influence was seen in Politis's 1919 production of Sophocles's *Oedipus*, a landmark performance in the history of ancient tragedy in Greece. Later on, Reinhardt's influence on the Greek director became less obvious as it became heavily modified by the latter's own idea about the pedagogical function of the theatre. In a 1926 article entitled 'Reinhardt', Politis praises the Austrian director for his stage innovations and his creation of 'ensemble theatre'; in the same article, however, Politis criticizes his famous colleague for allowing the spectacular aspect of the stage to 'swallow' the poetry of the text as well as the art of acting: Fotos Politis, 'Max Reinhardt', in *Epilogi Kritikon Arthron: Ta Theatrika*, ed. Nikos Politis (Athens, 1983), pp. 247–51. In 1931, after his trip to Vienna and Munich, where he attended several performances (including Reinhardt's *Everyman*), Politis became even harsher in his critique. He still admired Reinhardt, and even sent promising Greek actors to attend his seminars, but he now considered the Austrian artist 'a symbol of theatrical decadence' (Politis, 'Taxidevontas', *Proia*, 6 September 1931).

24 Politis seems to echo Granville-Barker's 'satanic heroism' and 'prophetic dignity', as well as the idea of a wronged Jew (*Prefaces to Shakespeare*, vol. 5 (London, 1930), pp. 117, 120–1). Since the Greek artist kept abreast of developments in theatre and criticism, it is likely that in 1932 he had read the recently published *Prefaces* of the English critic and theatre director.

25 Politis, 'O Emporos tis Venetias', p. 181.

26 Politis, 'O Emporos tis Venetias', p. 182.

27 Sideris, 'O Saixpir stin Ellada VI', p. 32.

was filled with people in the final scene – 'beautiful people, richly and elegantly dressed', says the critic, 'an image seen for the first time in a Greek theatre'.[28]

In Autumn 1940, *The Merchant of Venice* was staged again at the National Theatre, this time by a different director, Dimitris Rondiris,[29] and in a different historical context. Although Greece had not yet entered the war when rehearsals of the play were in progress, there was a great deal of anxiety about the possibility of the Nazi military operations spreading to the south. The play opened on 21 October on the main stage of the National Theatre that carried on with its business as usual, but soon, as German and Italian warplanes began to cross the Greek sky, performances moved to the nearby Palace Theatre, which offered a bomb shelter. When a week later Mussolini officially declared war on Greece and fighting began at the Greek–Albanian border, *Merchant* came off the stage to give place hurriedly to more patriotic productions, like Aeschylus's *Persians* and, a few months later, Shakespeare's *Henry V*.[30] Due to the war, the 1940 production of *Merchant* did not number many performances and did not receive much attention from the critics. Yet the limited evidence clearly suggests that it focused on Shylock. Angelos Terzakis, author, critic, and in 1940 director of repertory at the National Theatre of Greece, writes in the single essay included in the performance programme:

If *The Merchant of Venice* occupies a distinct, unique place among Shakespeare's comedies, this is certainly due to the figure of Shylock alone . . . The quantitative size of the role is almost insignificant, and its place within the central plot, which is clearly about love as in the other comedies, nearly episodic. But the few words that come out of Shylock's mouth in the comic atmosphere of romance sound heavy, tragic, like the bells of a night alarm.[31]

Terzakis centralizes Shylock by arguing that this character's relatively small but 'heavy, tragic' part is strong enough to threaten the comic atmosphere of the love plot and to leave its mark on the whole play. Although the critic sees the play as presenting an antithesis between two divergent worlds with Antonio (the 'truly mature man') as the link and the arbitrator between them, he does not discuss this contrast. His focus remains steadily on Shylock, who among the play's characters attracts the critic's almost exclusive attention. Terzakis views Shylock as an inconsistent, even contradictory character, but considers the contradiction a desirable aspect of Shakespeare's psychological realism and very central to the play's effect on the spectator. In the closing paragraph of his essay the critic keeps a grip on the audience, by suggestively superimposing the image of Shylock on the idyllic atmosphere of the fifth act and making an impassioned plea for the admiration of the Jew:

Lorenzo and Jessica, in spite of him [Shylock] sing of their love beneath the moon, and Bassanio, liberated from the Jew's crooked shadow, leans carefree on Portia's tender lap. But we, as we leave [the theatre], always hear the echo of the lingering anguish of Shylock as he beats his breast in the ghetto; and we don't feel like laughing at him. For he is a bitter and poisonous being, because we have poisoned him, one who possesses the power to elicit something much more difficult [to give] than our piteous sympathy or philanthropic love: our awe and our admiration.[32]

Awe and admiration were indeed the prominent features of Shylock in the National Theatre's production of *Merchant* on the eve of Greece's entrance

---

28 Gregoris Xenopoulos, 'To Theatron: Ethnikon Theatron' (performance review of *Merchant*), *Nea Estia*, vols. 11–12 (1932), p. 114.

29 Rondiris had succeeded Politis as Director of the National Theatre in 1934. Although he lacked his predecessor's experimental spirit and intellectual acumen, Rondiris was extremely fond of Shakespeare and usually included at least one Shakespearian play in the theatre's yearly repertory.

30 For a discussion of how this English history play was used in support of the war cause before the German invasion of Greece in the spring of 1941, see Tina Krontiris, 'Henry V and the Anglo-Greek Alliance in World War II', *Shakespearean International Yearbook*, 8 (2008), 32–50.

31 Angelos Terzakis, 'O Emporos tis Venetias', performance programme for *The Merchant of Venice*, National Theatre of Greece (October 1940), p. 14 (see digital archive, www.nt-archive.gr/playMaterial.aspx?playID=310#programs).

32 Terzakis, 'O Emporos tis Venetias', p. 18.

in the war. Alexis Minotis, the star actor who played the role, presented a defiant, dignified and heroic Jew.[33] This interpretation owed much to Fotos Politis's revised analysis;[34] but whereas in 1932 a justifiably wrathful Jew had been prevented from rising over the play's comic world, in 1940 he was given all the opportunity to dominate the stage. Minotis, who possessed a flaming temperament by nature, released all his energy on stage and thus brought out the role's full power. His Jew appeared fierce and revengeful, potentially tragic but not in the least sentimental. Full of passion and unquenched hatred, Minotis's Shylock was not the man to accept intimidation; he fought tooth and nail to avenge the wrongs against his race. Clearly, it was not sympathy that Minotis aimed to elicit in portraying this Shylock but admiration for the defiance and justification for the hatred. This portrayal suited Minotis's dramatic style while it also responded to the spirit of the times by satisfying the audience's taste for heroic drama as well as their sense of justice formed in relation to current events. Without altering the text, the production had succeeded in associating Shylock with the war conditions and the Nazi violence against the Jews, evident in pogroms like that of Kristallnacht. 'The persecution of the Jews in recent years imparted a paradoxical topicality to the role of Shylock', said one critic, and Minotis 'without at all seeking to present him as sympathetic projected vividly his justification.'[35] The production allowed Shylock to show all his hatred for Christian Venice, stressing especially his ethnic consciousness. It gave him unrestrained expression, confronting conflict head on rather than evading it. This was on the eve of Greece's involvement in the Second World War, when collision seemed inevitable and shrinking from it amounted to national humiliation.

THE RETURN TO HARMONY IN A DISCORDANT ATHENS: *THE MERCHANT OF VENICE*, 1945

Some nine months after the withdrawal of the Nazi forces from Greek soil and only a month after the Liberation of Europe, the National Theatre of Greece returned to Shakespeare and to his *Merchant of Venice*. As a result of the war, the conditions of performance this time were radically different. The sense of relief that people felt right after the war and their optimism for the future (evident in the high release of energy in all kinds of activity) could not hide the dire reality.

In 1945 Greece was economically run down, socially unsettled, politically unstable and ideologically divided.[36] During the Occupation, Hitler's commanders had used up all of the Greek resources and had even forced the collaborationist government in Athens to grant a 'loan' to Germany for its military operations.[37] The Resistance, in which the communists played a leading role, had inspired hopes for the democratization of Greek society. Upon Liberation, there was an unleashing of social pressures that had been accumulating for years, even before the war. But hopes for social justice were soon crushed by the failure of the reinstated bourgeois politicians to punish the Nazi collaborators. A civil conflict, signs of which were evident even before the withdrawal of the Germans,

---

[33] One of the pre-eminent Shakespearian actors in Greece at the time, Minotis had been employed by the National Theatre ever since its establishment in 1932. Although he had not been given a role in the 1932 *Merchant* specifically, he was very much influenced, like most actors, by the ideas of the enlightened Fotos Politis. Before 1941, Rondiris relied on Minotis for the interpretation of the great Shakespearian roles, including the role of the young prince in the very popular *Hamlet* of 1937. According to Yiannis Sideris, Rondiris owes much of his success as director of Shakespearian drama to the talented Minotis, who followed his own inspiration 'as if there were no stage director at all': Yiannis Sideris, 'O Saixpir stin Ellada VII', *Theatro*, 19 (January–February 1965), pp. 31, 38.

[34] Sideris, 'O Saixpir stin Ellada VII', p. 36.

[35] Alkis Thrilos, *To Elliniko Theatro*, vol. 2: 1934–1940 (Athens, 1977), p. 530.

[36] The historical events summarized in this paragraph can be found in many Greek sources. For an authoritative account in English, see Mark Mazower's book *Inside Hitler's Greece* (Yale University Press, 1993), especially ch. 23 and the Epilogue.

[37] This compulsory loan was never repaid and remains a political issue between Germany and Greece even today.

12. *The Merchant of Venice*, National Theatre of Greece, directed by Dimitris Rondiris, October 1940. Scene 4.1. Shylock (Alexis Minotis) presents himself to the court of justice, presided by Portia (Eleni Papadaki), who speaks from the podium with the Duke (Elias Destounis) behind her. Notice Minotis's upright, dignified posture and the scale hanging from his sleeve.

came to a head on 4 December 1944, when British and Greek government forces opened fire in central Athens against the communist-led National Liberation Front (EAM) and its military affiliate (ELAS).[38] For longer than a month, the Greek capital was shaken by a fierce battle, which ended with the retreat of the communists and many casualties. The peace agreement, signed by the representatives of the two sides on 12 February 1945, ended temporarily the military confrontation but did not much ease the polarized political climate. Six different governments were formed between Greece's Liberation in October 1944 and the first national elections held in early March 1946. All

proved unable to handle the conflict, which in 1946 erupted into a full-scale civil war.

These conditions had a direct impact on theatre in general and the state-funded National Theatre in particular. The latter had lost most of its artistic personnel in the hard years of the occupation and during the battle of Athens it had been

---

[38] According to Mazower, the Battle of Athens constitutes a unique instance in the Second World War, where Allied (British) forces fought literally against the Resistance, represented in this instance by the Greek communists. The December 1944 battle is also one of the key events in the early history of the Cold War (*Inside Hitler's Greece*, p. 369).

13. *The Merchant of Venice*, National Theatre of Greece, directed by Dimitris Rondiris, October 1940. Scene 4.1: Shylock (Alexis Minotis), hand raised, is ready to stick the knife into the breast of a submissive Antonio (Manos Katrakis), dressed in black.

used by the communists as a fortress or point of attack. Indeed the situation was so bad that in mid-November 1944 the Ministry of Education decided to close down the theatre for a three-month period.[39] As shall be explained later, the theatre had also changed its general policy, initiating a process of democratization. Hence, though the chronological distance between the two major productions of the *Merchant of Venice* that frame the Second World War is small, the 1945 production actually belongs to a different era – the postwar, post-Holocaust era.

Contrary to what one might expect, the affinity of the postwar performance was not to the heroic Shylock version staged in 1940, nor was it yet an entirely new approach. It was, interestingly enough, a return to Politis's 1927 interpretation of the play as a joyful and harmonious comedy whose grotesque Jewish figure must not be allowed to spoil its comic vision. Pelos Katselis,[40] director of the 1945 performance and in his younger years a student of Politis, had staged *Merchant* for the National Theatre's touring company in late 1939 or early 1940.[41] He had then adopted his teacher's first view of the play, focusing on the playfulness of youth, positioning Antonio as the protagonist and presenting Shylock as the odd figure of the comedy, something between a victim and a villain.[42] Katselis maintained the same interpretation in 1945, almost uninfluenced by the intervening historical events. In an extensive note, printed in the performance programme and published in the press on the day, he explained his view of the play and what he aimed to do with it on stage. Like Politis, Katselis saw *Merchant* as a musical symphony, whose oppositions must be harmonized and whose confrontational elements must be reconciled on stage. According to Katselis, the play presents the harmonious unity of two opposites – the dream of a joyous life based on love and friendship and the reality of money dealings and unpaid debts. 'We can't say in words where the one stops and the other begins', he admitted, 'but from the study of the play we do know that the reality with its rawness exists in order to enhance the dream.'[43] In this 'harmonious view of life', he contended,

'ideological and social prejudices have no place'.[44] Shylock has no place. 'He is like a cloud that passes over a joyful sky; his presence was caused by some playful events and he must go away.'[45] Then, towards the end of the note, in a kind of apologetic postscript, the director stated:

Shylock with his tiger-like instincts is justified too... The performance in this aspect will attempt, without risky textual interventions... to keep the balance equally between the Jews and the Christians... And it will do so in the secret hope that along with aesthetic pleasure a great social lesson will come out of this charming play, *a lesson that our times have paid dearly with much human blood.*[46]

---

[39] Tina Krontiris, *O Saixpir se Kairo Polemou, 1940–1950* (Athens, 2007), pp. 90–1.

[40] Katselis (1907–1981) attended the Professional School of Theatre in the late 1920s – when Politis taught there – and played the role of Iago in his teacher's production of *Othello* (1929). That Politis exercised a formative influence on Katselis is evident especially in the latter's writings on selected Shakespeare plays. Katselis was well-read in Stanislavski and closely familiar with the staging practices of Max Reinhardt, whose work he had seen during his theatrical studies in Germany and Austria in 1937–1939 (Yiannis Sideris, 'O Saixpir stin Ellada VIII', part A, *Theatro*, 20 (March–April 1965), p. 25; Walter Puchner, 'O Pelos Katselis analytis tou Saixpir', in *Klimakes kai Diavathmiseis* (Athens, 2003), pp. 143–4 and *passim*).

[41] The touring company, or 'Arma Thespidos', as it was called, moved in lorries round the country and staged performances in provincial towns and the capital's suburbs from September 1939 to December 1941. Among the nine plays performed by the Arma in its first theatrical season, there were two of Shakespeare's, *Othello* and *The Merchant of Venice*, the first premiering in Corinth on 15 September 1939 and the second probably in Patras on 5 January 1940. In the Arma's *Merchant*, the role of Shylock was played alternately by Tzavalas Karousos and Nikos Paraskevas.

[42] Sideris, 'O Saixpir stin Ellada VIII', part A, p. 27.

[43] Pelos Katselis, 'Me nea skinothesia *O Emporos tis Venetias*', *Theatro*, 12 (June 1945), p. 4. (See also the performance programme, pp. 12–13, in the digital archive www.nt-archive.gr/viewfiles1.aspx?playID=743&programID=.)

[44] Katselis, 'Me nea skinothesia', p. 4.

[45] Katselis used this characteristic phrase in an interview he gave to Yiannis Sideris, 'Synomilies me tous skinothetes tou theatrou mas': Pelos Katselis, *O Eonas mas*, 1 (March 1947), p. 27.

[46] Katselis, 'Me nea skinothesia', p. 4 (italics added).

Here the director makes it clear that he doesn't read *The Merchant* as an anti-Semitic play: Shakespeare, he implies, is on Shylock's side. But at the same time the Greek artist de-politicizes Shylock's powerful reaction by referring to his animal instincts. Aware of the fact that in some way he has to deal with the play's conflict, Katselis declares his intention to keep a balance between the opposing sides, without 'textual interventions', which would place him in the 'risky' position of having to take a political stance on the racial conflict dramatized in the play and by extension on its recent historical analogue. While in the above statement the director acknowledges the killing of the Jews in the Holocaust, the social lesson he expects his spectators to derive from the performance (a lesson presumably on the destructive effects of racial hatred) is suggestively expressed in the form of a 'secret hope', not an intention or purpose.

Angelos Terzakis, who had been reappointed director of repertory in the postwar reconstitution of the National Theatre, subscribed to Katselis's escapist perspective. In a revised essay on the *Merchant of Venice*, printed in the performance programme along with the director's note, he emphasized the play's fairy-tale atmosphere and dream-like quality. This quality, he argued, is not associated with the real, geographically defined Venice, but 'the Venice of a dream, the emotional extension of an excellent fantasy'.[47] In comparison with his 1940 view, Terzakis still maintained that *The Merchant* is a play of contrasts and divergent elements superficially connected in the plot but he now discovered an 'inner unity' in the play's 'lyrical disposition, atmosphere, and general tone'.[48] Terzakis's shift of emphasis towards the comic (escapist) view was reflected in the structure of his essay: the long, politically committed discussion of Shylock in the 1940 piece was replaced by a single paragraph where only a concise analysis of the character was dryly given. Although Terzakis had not changed his view of Shakespeare's Jew, it was now evident that he was trying to maintain a distance from him. In 1940 he had encouraged the spectators to identify with Shylock, whereas in 1945 he seemed to try to prevent them from doing

so. Indicatively, Terzakis ended his 1945 essay with a summary of the play's themes – 'joy, youth, humanity, poetry, fantasy'[49] – from which Shylock is noticeably absent. The displacement of Shylock from centre to periphery was also signalled by changes in the list of roles. Whereas the 1940 performance programme had placed Shylock first on the list, the 1945 programme relegated him to the tenth position, following Q3, which lists the *dramatis personae* according to their rank in the social hierarchy.

The performance opened on 12 June in the gardens of Klathmonos Square, central Athens, where the National Theatre had set up its summer stage. The relocation of the stage was a matter of necessity rather than choice, since the theatre's main premises, the neoclassical building on Saint Constantine Street, had suffered damage during the December 1944 events and was still under repair several months later. Thus, coincidentally, the green surrounding of the stage enhanced the escapist interpretation of the play.

Visually, the performance aimed to create a joyful atmosphere in a dream-like world. Instead of the two-tier stage that had been customarily used, the French-trained stage designer, George Vakalo, had created a slightly raised small platform with steps in the back of the stage and an ample room in the front, where the actors moved in all directions, communicating a sense of freedom. Neither the sets nor the costumes alluded to a specific historical period; the sets even gestured towards the exotic as the semi-permanent background set with the spiral columns were reminiscent of a Mauritanian rather than a Venetian court.[50] Colour and light were profusely used in various combinations, creating a

---

47 Angelos Terzakis, 'O *Emporos tis Venetias*', performance programme for *The Merchant of Venice*, National Theatre of Greece (June 1945), p. 5. (See digital archive www.nt-archive.gr/playMaterial.aspx?playID=743#programs).

48 Terzakis, 'O *Emporos tis Venetias*' (1945), p. 4.

49 Terzakis, 'O *Emporos tis Venerias*' (1945), p. 5.

50 Ioannis Stoyiannis, 'To Ethniko Theatro: O *Emporos tis Venetias*' (performance review), *Vradini*, 30 June 1945; Alexis Solomos, 'Athinaika Theatra' (performance review), *Angloelliniki Epitheorisi*, 1 (July 1945), pp. 28–9.

14. *The Merchant of Venice*, National Theatre of Greece, directed by Pelos Katselis, June 1945. Scene 3.2: Bassanio (Nikos Dendramis) presents himself as a suitor to Portia (Aleka Mazeraki). The Mauritanian-style columns and the fairy-tale outlook of the scene are visible.

kind of phantasmagoria that enhanced the sense of harmony and became the spectacular expression of the love game.[51] The elaborate costumes, which contributed to the spectacular aspect of the performance, alluded generally to fairy-tales and only vaguely to sixteenth-century dress fashion. Both stage sets and costumes 'appeared like a colourful page from a fairy-tale book', remarked Alexis Solomos, in a production that 'tended towards escape'.[52] In this respect, the gondolas, the only explicit symbol of Venice that was used, constituted an incongruous element in the total stage conception.

On such a stage, Shylock must indeed have looked like an intruder. The role of the Jewish moneylender was played alternately by two well-known actors, Nikolaos Paraskevas and Tzavalas Karousos, a split that was made in order to keep both actors happy. The National Theatre had announced that it would give two première performances, a week apart from one another. The

[51] Michalis Rodas, 'E ermenia dyo Shylock' (performance review), *To Vima*, 22 June 1945. Some critics considered this display of colours overdone; one of them said that the stage resembled a 'dancing' hall, while another called it 'a barbarous chromatic orgasm' (Kostas Oiconomidis, 'Ethnikon Theatron: *O Emporos tis Venetias* tou Saixpir' (performance review), *Ethnos*, 13 June 1945; Alkis Thrilos, 'Afou ekleise e avlaia: *O Emporos tis Venetias* sto therino Vasiliko Theatro' (performance review), *Elliniko Aima*, 14 June 1945).

[52] Solomos, 'Athinaika Theatra' (performance review), *Anglo-elliniki Epitheorisi*, 1 (July 1945), p. 28.

first première featured Paraskevas and not solely because he was the senior in the couple. Karousos, an avowed socialist and political activist, had taken part in the December events, fighting on the side of the communists, and the theatre feared reprisals, justifiably as it turned out. On the first day of Karousos's appearance as Shylock, and as he was counting his 3000 ducats on stage, a group of right-wing hooligans stormed into the theatre shouting, 'down with the traitors, out with the murderers' and similar slogans.[53] Although this incident did not have any further repercussions on the performances of the play, it does show the flammable political climate in which the play was produced. It also explains, perhaps, why the vast majority of theatre critics, if they attended the second première, did not write about it.

Paraskevas played Shylock in a mixed style, without offering a coherent interpretation of this character. For example, he rendered the character's famous tirade in 3.1 ('Hath not a Jew eyes . . . ') with a dramatic tone reminiscent of the old tragic style. Elsewhere, he used stereotypical images, like whetting his knife on the sole of his shoe, to give his character a comic bent. In the trial scene of the fourth act (treated as parody in this production), Paraskevas transformed the Jew into a quasi-grotesque figure, 'who made continuous, punctuating gestures in front of the Duke's court'.[54] As he traversed between these two extremes, the actor, following the demands of his director, tried to crush or keep down the parts of his role that could potentially dominate the play's comic world. This is apparent in the review of at least one critic, who complained that in 3.1 Paraskevas failed to maintain the Jew's 'cry of anguish' all the way to the end.[55] The scanty evidence on Karousos's rendering of the role does not permit a valid comparison. Perhaps he was more responsive to the Jews tragic moments, as one reviewer observed.[56] But in the production's overall projection of Shylock it probably made small difference. Splitting the role and assigning it to two actors had the effect of further shattering the figure of a Jew who was ill at ease on a phantasmagoric stage dominated by the spirit of comedy.

On the whole, this was a performance that aimed at offering pleasure through escape, the kind of pleasure one gets from reading fairy-tale books. It appealed to the imagination and the senses, engaging especially the spectator's sight and hearing.

Music was an integral part of this spectacle. The production's orchestra, directed by George Lykoudis, contributed to the fairy-tale atmosphere and the harmonization of the scenes. Engelbert Humperdinck's musical scores,[57] which had been used also in the 1940 performance, were now enriched by the addition of various pieces by Henry Purcell, including two entitled 'moonlight', which were used in the final act.[58] Reconciliation, mercy, harmony, love – these were the themes stressed in the 1945 performance. The conflict between Jews and Gentiles, so central to the play and to the Second World War, had been evaded. There was no allusion made on stage to the 'social lesson' that was 'paid dearly with much human blood'. Nor were the discordant echoes of the current political turmoil allowed to reach the stage. Indeed The Merchant of Venice must have appeared an outlandish show to those who attended the evening performances in the summer of 1945.

Theatre critics who saw The Merchant of Venice performed at both ends of the war, in 1940 and 1945, stated that the two stood in complete contrast to one another.[59] For one reviewer, prewar productions of Merchant (collectively) were 'more

---

53 Vassilis Kanakis, Ethniko Theatro (Athens, 1999), pp. 59–60.
54 Rodas, 'E ermenia dyo Shylock'.
55 Petros Haris, 'O Emporos tis Venetias', Eleftheria, 14 June 1945.
56 Rodas, 'E ermenia dyo Shylock'.
57 Humperdinck originally composed the music for Reinhardt's 1905 production of Merchant, where music, and sounds more generally, played an important role in the total sensational effect of the performance upon the spectator; see Erika Fischer-Lichte, 'Theatre as Festive Play: Max Reinhardt's Productions of The Merchant of Venice', in Jews and the Making of Modern German Theatre, ed. Jeanette Malkin and Freddie Rokem (Iowa City, 2010), p. 223.
58 See the online archive of the National Theatre of Greece and specifically the paragraph 'Comments' on the musical scores for the 1945 Merchant of Venice, http://www.nt-rchive.gr/playMaterial.aspx?playID=743#music.
59 Solomos, 'Athinaika Theatra', 28.

15. *The Merchant of Venice*, National Theatre of Greece, directed by Pelos Katselis, June 1945. Scene 4.1: Shylock (Nikos Paraskevas) is about to cut one pound of flesh from the breast of Antonio (Thanos Kotsopoulos). Notice the grotesqueness of Shylock's searching for the cutting spot.

muscular in tone', having made of him 'the kind of impression that is left by a masculine figure', whereas the postwar production of the play was excessively refined and effeminate: 'Yesterday, this dense style was replaced by feminine elements, a playful elegance and an air of "spectacle".'[60]

From such comments we understand that *Merchant* had been associated with a heavier, 'masculine' style of staging, used for the performance of

---

[60] Stoyiannis, 'To Ethniko Theatro'.

Shakespearian tragedy, which had its heyday at the Greek National Theatre in the late 1930s. According to the reviewer just cited, the postwar emphasis on comedy did not bring the play into line with the less problematic Shakespearian comedies; rather, it placed it into a feminized, hence weaker position. In the Greek postwar context, this sense of feminization could suggest a refusal to come to grips with the important problems left behind by the war. Indeed, Katselis's emphasis on the play's dream world, almost at the exclusion of its reality, appears to have emptied out *Merchant*, rendering it rather shallow. Alkis Thrilos, a conservative but discerning critic who compared the 1940 and 1945 productions, stated that the interpretation of Shylock in the later production was narrow because it failed to establish and project to the audience the implied motives of the Jew's hatred for the Christians:

Minotis had presented a richer interpretation, more complex and powerful. He had shown that the meanness, the hatred of the Jews stems from the persecution of their race. He had then justified Shylock . . . Of course, the interpretation of Mr Paraskevas was not equally uplifting; it was much more narrow. It underlined almost exclusively the repulsion that Shylock provokes without disclosing the factors that formed his character and demand [our] lenience.

This is perhaps the most valid critique of the 1945 production: in presenting Shylock as a semi-grotesque figure, peripheral to the play's main theme, it failed to explain the reality and the history of his existence, including the recent history. Indicatively, the 1945 Shylock appeared without a characteristically Jewish gabardine, while his skullcap resembled the hat worn by the Venetians.

THE MERCHANT OF VENICE AND THE SILENCING OF THE HOLOCAUST

The diverse Jewish communities that spread around Greece before the Second World War were some of the oldest in the Mediterranean region.[61] The largest of these was the predominantly Sephardic community of Thessaloniki (aka Salonica), which had emigrated to the Macedonian city from Spain in the late fifteenth century, and in 1941 numbered 45,000 members. A largely autonomous community, Salonican Jews had seen the collapse of the Ottoman Empire, under which they enjoyed relative safety, and the annexation of Thessaloniki to Greece in 1912, after the victorious campaign of the Greek army in the Balkan Wars. Because of its large size, and also because Thessaloniki was allotted to the Germans in the tripartite division of occupied Greece,[62] this historic community became the first to suffer in a series of Nazi persecutions in Greece. Hitler's intelligence/security service (SD) started its atrocious work in early February 1943, when all Salonican Jews, marked with a yellow star, were forced to remain in fenced and guarded ghettos. With the help of a special police which they formed by recruiting low-life Jewish elements, SD officials began the process of deportation. From mid-March to mid-May 1943 thousands of Jews were stacked like cargo in convoy trains bound for Auschwitz. The community's spiritual leader, Grand Rabbi Zvi Koretz,[63] cooperated with the Nazi authorities, possibly thinking that he would thus gain their leniency, appeased his flock and advised them not to disobey German orders. The noncommittal, passive attitude

---

[61] For a detailed history of the origin and socio-political context of Greek Jews, see Steven Bowman, *The Agony of Greek Jews, 1940–1945* (Stanford, CA, 2009), chs. 1–2.

[62] When Hitler occupied Greece in March 1941, he divided the country into three zones – the Italian, the German and the Bulgarian – so as to gratify his allies. The chances of survival for Greek Jews during the occupation depended to a large extent on whether the occupier of the specific geographical area was German or Italian (the latter blocked Hitler's attempts at 'Judenrein'), as well as on the degree of Jewish assimilation into the Greek culture and accessibility to the resistance networks: Barbara Axiopoulou, 'Allilegyi kai voithia pros tous Evreous tis Elladas kata ti diarkeia tis Katohis, 1941–1944', in *Oi Evreoi tis Elladas stin Katohi*, ed. Rika Benveniste (Thessaloniki, 1998), pp. 13–28, p. 27.

[63] A controversial figure, Koretz has been severely criticized for his passive attitude. He has even been accused of consciously collaborating with the Nazis, whose plans he would have been able to understand since he was a native speaker of German.

of the Christian Salonicans, some of whom were refugees from Asia Minor and held grudges against the economically dominant Jews, also facilitated the Nazi's almost complete destruction of the age-old Sephardic community.[64] The same fate awaited the Jewish communities of Jannina and Corfu, which suffered 90 per cent losses. The Jews of these areas, like those of Thessaloniki, were socially autonomous (not integrated into Greek culture) and they too adopted an obedient stance towards the Nazi authorities.[65]

In contrast to Thessaloniki, Athens moved quickly in support of its Jews, who were assimilated into the mainstream social fabric and lived dispersed throughout the city. Headed by Archbishop Damaskinos, the Christian Orthodox Church organized an official protest (gathering signatures for petitions and letters addressed to the occupation authorities), while clandestinely it saved the lives of many Jews by providing (mostly false) baptismal evidence. When in March 1944 the SD carried out its last round of persecutions, many Athenian Jews hid in Greek homes and as many others followed their chief Rabbi, who fled to the guerilla-controlled mountains. Yet, as has often been acknowledged by historians, the greatest practical assistance to the Jews of Athens and southern Greece more generally, was provided by underground resistance groups, especially EAM, which was run by the communists but had wider popular support.[66]

The theatre played a small but significant role in EAM's mobilization to save the Greek Jews. Olympia Papadouka, an actress who took part in the resistance, wrote many years later:

Along with the other slogans for Freedom, 'Save the Jews' entered the list. The command came from the leadership of the resistance and we its members turned it into action with our personal initiatives. In my own neighbourhood, Metaxourgio, our squad went around and wrote on walls: 'Save the Jews – EAM'.[67]

She then describes how she reproduced the slogan on small pieces of paper, using the mimeograph of Rex Theatre where she worked, how she would drop batches of them on the streets at the right moment, and how she would reload her inner pockets with the help of the theatre's night watchman.[68] Nevertheless, by the end of the war, Greece had paid a heavy toll to the Nazi Moloch. Before the country's entry into the Second World War there were approximately 72,000 Jews living in Greece. At the conclusion of the war the number was down to 12,500. Obviously, only a small percentage of the Greek Jewry had survived.[69]

The participation of theatre people in the resistance movement and their awareness of what had happened to the Jews in Greece and the rest of Europe would seem, in retrospect, to have raised expectations about the stage's taking up the plight of the Jews at the end of the war. Yet it is an important fact that it did not, even when the opportunity arose. As we have seen, the National Theatre's first postwar production of *The Merchant of Venice* expatiated on the play's harmony theme, downplayed the Jewish–Christian conflict and so it silenced the racial issue. Why did it do so?

The answer to this question has partly to do with the way the extermination of Jews was represented in Greece and abroad from the spring of 1945 onwards. In a substantial essay entitled 'On the Social Construction of Moral Universals: The "Holocaust" from War Crime to Trauma Drama', Jeffrey Alexander shows how the most dire event of the twentieth century came to be the 'Holocaust' as we know it today. He identifies the beginning of the event as the moment of discovery of

---

[64] Rena Molho believes that an active concern on the part of the Greek Salonicans would have reduced the number of Jewish casualties: *O Politis*, 133 (May 2005), 31–39, p. 6 and *passim*.

[65] Hagen Fleischer, 'Greek Jewry and Nazi Germany: The Holocaust and its Antecedents', in *Oi Evreoi ston elliniko horo*, ed. Effie Abdela et al. (Athens, 1995), pp. 185–206, pp. 197–8.

[66] Fleischer, 'Greek Jewry and Nazi Germany', p. 198.

[67] Olympia Papadouka, *To Theatro tis Athinas: Katohi, Antistasi, Diogmoi* (Athens, 1999), pp. 61–3.

[68] Papadouka, *To Theatro tis Athinas*, pp. 61–2.

[69] Historians disagree on the numbers, but they all agree on a low survival rate. In this study I use the estimate of Hagen Fleischer, who considers all factors, not just the 1940 census: 'Greek Jewry and Nazi Germany', pp. 194–5.

the death camps by the American GIs on 3 April 1945 (perhaps arbitrarily, since some death camps had been already discovered by the Soviet Army in the summer of the previous year) and observes that even though the reports of the mass murder of the Jews were received with a shock and recognized as an unprecedented gross injustice, the terrible fate of the Jewish people 'did not itself become a traumatic experience for the audience to which the mass media's collective representations were transmitted'.[70] He correctly posits that symbolic extension and psychological identification are required in order for members of an audience to be traumatized (i.e. to be rendered secondary witnesses) by an event which they did not experience directly. Such identification did not occur and so trauma did not become a universal experience. Possibilities for universalizing the trauma were blocked, he argues, because the mass murders were related to other war horrors and the survivors were depersonalized, presented as a mass, rather than as individuals with personal lives.[71] Alexander links the American reluctance to identify with the victims as Jews to a latent anti-Semitism (which was not eradicated by the anti-anti-Semitism of the 1930s) and to the Anglo–American conceptualization of the war as a fight against evil, which was Nazism. The struggle for prevalence, the victory and the forward-looking project of recovery formed what Alexander calls 'the progressive narrative of the war against Nazism',[72] which engulfed all other considerations. In other words, there was a displacement of focus from the genocide as such to the victory and the construction of the future.

The press in Britain and the US had presented the anti-Jewish genocide in a way that amounted to a silencing of the issue. As Laurel Leff shows in her recent book *Buried by The Times*, America's leading newspaper downplayed news about the mass murders with the result that 'the horrible story was not told'.[73] The press's detachment broke down in spring 1945, with the 'liberation' of the concentration camps. 'The American press, which for so long had barely whispered of mass murder and extermination, exploded with news of the German camps.'[74] Detailed descriptions of the camps, accompanied by gruesome photographs, featured for several weeks in the American papers, and it appeared as if the topic was given its proper significance – except for the fact that the ethnic identity of the crime was concealed. Victims were referred to as 'citizens' of various nations or targeted groups (communists, POWs); the words 'Jews' or 'Jewish' were rarely, if at all, used and by 8 May (Armistice Day) there was a return to silence.[75]

In Greece the Jewish genocide was all but absent from the press.[76] In the entire month of April 1945, which marked the height of interest in British and American media, most Greek newspapers featured only two or three brief reports on the subject (usually near the bottom of the first page), with the right-wing papers making the least mention.[77] Rarely were photographs used to accompany these brief reports and none that portrayed the tragic conditions of the victims. As in the American papers, the victims of the atrocities were devoid of a clear ethnic identity. They were referred to as 'workers' in slave-labour camps, and they were

---

[70] Jeffrey Alexander, 'On the Social Construction of Moral Universals: the "Holocaust" from War Crime to Trauma Drama', *European Journal of Social Theory*, 5:1 (2002), 5–85, p. 8.

[71] Alexander, 'On the Social Construction of Moral Universals', p. 8.

[72] Alexander, 'On the Social Construction of Moral Universals', p. 16.

[73] Laurel Leff, *Buried by The Times: The Holocaust and America's Most Important Newspaper* (Cambridge, 2006), pp. 330–58.

[74] David Wyman, *The Abandonment of the Jews: America and the Holocaust, 1941–1945* (New York, 1984), p. 325.

[75] James Carroll, 'Shoah in the News: Patterns and Meanings of New Coverage of the Holocaust', Discussion Paper (The John F. Kennedy School of Government, 1997), pp. 5–6 (http://shorensteincenter.org/wp-content/uploads/2012/03/d27_carroll.pdf).

[76] The information I give here about the coverage of the Holocaust in the Greek press is based on my own browsing of representative daily papers from the months of April and May 1945.

[77] The political right included in its ranks many anti-Semites, who propagandized against Jews by linking them with the communists (Bowman, *The Agony of Greek Jews*, pp. 218–19).

completely depersonalized, presented as statistics or aspects of a repulsive, macabre spectacle.[78] There was no attempt to link the discovery of the camps with the deportation of the Greek Jews or inquiry about their fate. There was no worry expressed about them and no reference made to their return home. The only exception to the rule of detachment and misrepresentation was the communist daily *Rizospastis*, which refered to Greek Jews directly and demanded answers from the government. But like the other Greek papers, it treated the subject sporadically and devoted a minimum of space to it. All in all, the daily papers of the specific period in Greece provided no consistent narrative about the mass murder of the Jews and treated the subject with conspicuous detachment.

On this important issue the Greek press apparently supported the government position, as expressed by a top official in the summer of 1945. In response to the question why Greece was not offering assistance to the 2,000 Greek Jews who had been 'liberated' from the Polish concentration camps and sought means to return home, the vice-prime minister Kyriakos Varvaressos had stated: 'In this country the problems of Jews and Christians are alike and therefore we are not planning a special treatment of the Jews.'[79] This expedient homogenization was tantamount to a silencing of the Greek Holocaust (making it sound as if Christians and Jews were in the same boat) and was practically intended to put a lid on a developing social problem after the dissolution of the camps. When the surviving Greek Jews returned 'home' from Dachau and Auschwitz, they found no place to stay: their community had been dissolved, their family and friends were missing and, with few exceptions, their houses were occupied by squatters, refugees or even German collaborators.[80] Meanwhile, those Jews who were in hiding within Greece had come out and they too were trying to find their bearings. By summer of 1945 some 12,000 Jewish men and women had gathered in Athens, where employment opportunities were expected to be greater after the war.[81] The sight of many Jews wandering in the streets in search of jobs, food and shelter was not uncommon.[82] Apart from passing a law

concerning the return of Jewish property to its original owners (a law that turned out to be ineffective and difficult to apply), the Greek state did very little for the relief of the Greek Jews and rather encouraged their emigration to avoid the responsibility of providing for them.

The wider Greek public appears to have acquiesced in the state's abandonment of the Jews. One might discern a collusion among the public who knew about the appropriation of the Jewish property, the state which was unable and/or unwilling to deal with the situation, and the press which kept silent on the issue. At the same time, there was a problem of communication between the non-Jewish Greeks and the camp survivors, who did not find the understanding they expected and so resorted to silence.[83] Without the aid of the press that could supply the outline of a larger, coherent narrative, individual victims could not easily tell their horror stories or find sympathetic listeners. Nor could much sympathy be elicited from a people that had been largely desensitized by the effects of the war. Poverty and famine, the characteristics of the occupation period, had forced Greeks to become familiar with the spectacle of undernourished individuals and human corpses.[84]

The answer to the question why the National Theatre's 1945 *Merchant* silenced the racial issue has

---

78 For example, in a report entitled 'The liberation of foreign workers' the daily *Eleftheria* writes: 'The problem is not only the 20 million homeless people in the Third Reich, but also the drama of the 4.5 million foreign workers who were liberated from German territories [and] who now must be sheltered, fed, and transported back to their countries . . . Many of the workers were found to suffer from tuberculosis due to bad nutrition and terrible living conditions in rundown buildings. There are also instances of typhoid fever, but a special committee is taking measures to prevent it from spreading' (*Eleftheria*, 18 April 1945, p. 1).

79 Quoted in Karina Lampsa and Joseph Simpi, *E zoe ap' tin archi* (Athens, 2010), p. 135.

80 Lampsa and Simpi, *E zoe ap' tin archi*, pp. 122–4.

81 Bowman, *The Agony of Greek Jews*, p. 228.

82 Lampsa and Simpi, *E zoe ap' tin archi*, p. 127.

83 Hagen Fleischer, 'E Saloniki sti skia tis swastikas', *Macedonia*, 20 March 2011, p. 32.

84 Mark Mazower, *Inside Hitler's Greece: The Experience of the Occupation* (New Haven, CT, 1993), ch. 3.

also to do with the current political and theatrical situation. With some exceptions, Greek theatre was generally immersed in the ideo-political broils of the time, as already discussed, and so stage directors were unable to air postwar issues with the requisite degree of clarity and objectivity. Despite the polarized political climate in the spring of 1945, there was a certain theatrical euphoria, accompanied by a burst of creative energy that was invested in putting into practice ideas about a radical revitalization of the stage that had been inspired by the resistance movement and partly tested during the occupation. Like some of the privately owned theatre companies, the National Theatre of Greece, under the direction of the politically liberal, European-minded George Theotokas, attempted to participate in the postwar project of renewal.[85] Specifically, it set out to democratize the national stage and this meant, among other things, the inclusion of a greater number of contemporary Greek plays in the repertory and a new approach to the European classics, one that would render them more accessible to the masses. Shakespeare would still be given pride of place in the repertory. His head position in the first postwar season signified continuity with the past as well as commitment to the ideals of western culture. Also, the bard would continue to be produced with deference to the text, 'without risky textual interventions', while the style of staging his plays would signal a clear break with the immediate, prewar past. The lighter and more colourful sets, the idealistic interpretations and the comic bent would recall not the ostentatious, tragic Shakespeare of Rondiris, who catered to the elite, but the comic Shakespeare of Fotos Politis, who represented a happier, more creative period for Greek theatre generally and the National Theatre particularly.

This approach to the Elizabethan dramatist at the Greek National Theatre did not in any way include an attempt to make his works more relevant to the public by suggesting parallels with contemporary reality. Shakespeare's plays would be used to show a visually renewed postwar stage and to cool down political passions, but they would not be presented in a way that would encourage the audience to connect them with the recent historical events. Of course, the creation of a stage that would contemporize the classics effectively was a very difficult task, requiring, among other things, talent and experimentation. Greek theatre lacked the requisite human and material resources for such a project at that point in time. Moreover, the engagement with a radical reconsideration of the classics was altogether outside the National Theatre's range of goals. Other theatre companies, like the United Artists (*Julius Ceasar*, 1945) and the Avlaia (*The Tempest*, 1945), did state in their artistic manifestos their intention to politicize or contemporize Shakespeare,[86] but not the leaders of the national stage. An interpretation of *The Merchant of Venice* in the light of the as yet unshaped Holocaust (representationally speaking) would have been a daring act in 1945, possibly incomprehensible to an unprepared audience, certainly subversive of the government's policy on the Jewish issue and hardly relevant to the National Theatre as a state institution. On the other hand, a harmonious and joyful production of *Merchant* that stressed the principles of mercy and forgiveness (voiced especially by Portia in 4.1) could broadcast the politically advantageous message of reconciliation, so urgently needed after the December 1944 civil bloodshed that had caused an extreme animosity between ideologically opposed factions.

---

[85] For a complete account of the National Theatre's aims in this project, see George Theotokas, 'E proti metapolemiki periodos tou Ethnikou Theatrou', *Nea Estia*, 39 (1946), 460–73.

[86] The socialist-oriented United Artists staged *Julius Caesar* in June 1945 with the intention to present the play as a champion of the people's struggle for freedom and justice, without, however, introducing any great changes in stage design or acting. The politically moderate Avlaia, which produced *The Tempest* in October 1945 using cubes and squares in the sets and semi-modern dresses for the actors, attempted to put into practice ideas about the modernization of the classics voiced much earlier in the twentieth century by the proponents of poetic symbolism and Russian constructivism. Neither of the two groups succeeded in their respective projects but it is interesting that they attempted them so soon after the war. See Krontiris, *O Saixpir se Kairo Polemou*, pp. 103–27.

A harmonious *Merchant* could also offer the audience an opportunity to enjoy an escapist and optimistic spectacle that signalled, at least visually, a fresh beginning and looked back reassuringly to a remote and bright Renaissance.

The first postwar production of *The Merchant of Venice* in Greece stands symbolically at the beginning of a long series of silences about the Holocaust in Greek history. Until the 1990s Greece had failed to recognize officially the destruction of its Jewry during the Second World War. War commemorations usually emphasized the Nazi atrocities committed against the Greek citizens but hardly accounted for the absence of the Jewish communities that had enriched the cultural and commercial life of the country before the war. Even when a commemorative monument was finally erected in Thessaloniki in 1997, it was first placed in a peripheral, obscure part of the city, and only after protests by Greek Jews was it moved in 2006 to the central Freedom Square, where it stands today. The Greek Holocaust has also been absent from the officially approved schoolbooks, which selectively register and maintain collective historical memory. These silences suggest that in Greece the concepts of national identity and justice excluded the Jewish constituent.[87] Hence Jeffrey Alexander's point that there is a link between latent anti-Semitism and the reluctance to identify the victims of Hitler's mass murders as Jews is applicable here. The 1945 Greek *Merchant* discussed in this essay makes clear

that the Jewish genocide could not be addressed at the end of the war from a national stage because it was not considered then (or later) to be a national issue. It was viewed as a *war* crime committed specifically and only by the Germans; the Greeks were supposedly beyond racial prejudice that could lead to inhuman acts. This is the kind of distance that Alexander notes in his study of the American response to the Jewish tragedy.

Indeed, what is particularly interesting about the first postwar production of *Merchant* in Greece is its ability to symbolize, reflect and register certain obscure and/or suppressed aspects of history. As a piece of stage art, which recirculated selected tendencies of the prewar theatrical past (with all its European connections), it reflects the desire for continuity; as a production of Shakespeare it symbolizes the universal values then attached to the Elizabethan bard; and as a performance of a play about a defeated Jew in a state-controlled institution, right after the Holocaust, it registers national narratives and national strategies for negotiating humanitarian values, political expediency and ideologies of exclusion.

---

[87] Gabriela Etmektsoglou, 'To Olokaftoma ton ellinon Evreon', in *Istoria tis Elladas ston eikosto eona: B pagosmios polemos, 1940–1945*, ed. by Christos Hatziiosif (Athens, 2007), vol. 3, part 1, p. 176. For the relationship of the Holocaust to the Greek historical memory, see also Odette Varon-Vassar, *E anadysi mias dyskolis mnemis: keimena gia ti genoktonia ton Evraion* (Athens, 2012).

CINNAS OF MEMORY

JULIA GRIFFIN

The two poets of *Julius Caesar*, joint starting-points for this article, are something of a paradox in the history of Shakespearian reception. Cinna, carried off to be dismembered in Act 3, and the unnamed character thrown out by Brutus in Act 4, have in the last 50 years attracted multiple and extended critical discussions, including four articles devoted entirely to them.[1] And yet, in the play, both exist to be silenced: most of their time on stage is spent in getting off it; they are easily cut from performance, and usually have been. Acting texts of the play from the late seventeenth century to the early eighteenth tend to pick them for exclusion; they are also absent from some early translations.[2] The Duke of Buckingham, rewriting and dividing Shakespeare's tragedy some time before 1720, omits both of them, one from each of his two plays.[3] Both characters were reintroduced on stage by the Meinigen Court Company, which performed in London in the 1880s, but this did not catch on;[4] even when Orson Welles changed Cinna's fortunes, making his death a climax of the famous 1937 production, the second poet remained out. Neither appears in either of the two big-budget films of the play.[5]

They seem to exist in a rarefied state: more on the page than on the stage. This state is reflected in the way that critics choose to write about them. They are seen to provide pleasing allegories for the poet in society, for the modern critic and sometimes for Shakespeare himself. Thomas Pughe, in an essay devoted to them, 'indulges in the speculation' that both poets might originally have been played by Shakespeare: 'The point would probably

[1] For the full-length treatments, see: Norman N. Holland, 'The "Cinna" and "Cynicke" Episodes in *Julius Caesar*', *Shakespeare Quarterly*, 11:4 (1960), 439–44; Thomas Pughe, '"What Should the Wars Do with these Jigging Fools?": the Poets in Shakespeare's *Julius Caesar*', *English Studies*, 69 (1988), 313–22; Gary Taylor, 'Bardicide', first publ. in Tetsuo Kishi *et al.*, eds., *Shakespeare and Cultural Traditions* (Newark, 1994), pp. 333–49; Margaret Maurer, 'Again, Poets and *Julius Caesar*', *The Upstart Crow*, 28 (2009), 5–16. Significant discussions occur also in Alan Sinfield, 'Theatres of War', in *Faultlines* (Oxford, 1992), pp. 10–28; Dennis Kezar, '*Julius Caesar* and the Properties of Shakespeare's Globe', *ELR*, 28 (1998), 18–46; and Kenneth Burke, at the end of his flamboyant essay, 'Antony in Behalf of the Play', in *The Philosophy of Literary Form*, 2nd edn (Baton Rouge, 1967), where Antony asserts that the audience 'somehow know[s] that the poetic Cinna will suffer no fundamental harm' (p. 343). (Testimony suggests that most of us somehow know the opposite.)

[2] They are both omitted from the 'Smock Alley' text (before 1676) and the 'Dryden–Davenant' version of 1719; they are also both absent from the first Italian translation, by Domenico Valentini (1756) and the second German translation (admittedly very free) by Wolfgang Heribert von Dalberg (1785). For the English texts, see John Ripley, *Julius Caesar on Stage in England and America, 1559–1973* (Cambridge, 1980).

[3] He divided the action of Shakespeare's play into two: *The Tragedy of Julius Caesar* and *The Death of Marcus Brutus* (both before 1720).

[4] For a full account of their performance, see Ripley, *Julius Caesar on Stage*, pp. 147–50, and John Osborne, *The Meiningen Court Theatre 1866–1890* (Cambridge, 1988), pp. 87–110.

[5] The Mankiewicz film of 1953 and the 1970 film by Stuart Burge omit both. See Ripley for the stage history to 1970. In the last twenty years, Cinna has become a regular; the other Poet is still, I suspect, unusual. For descriptions of Cinna's death in the Welles productions (he also recorded a version for radio), see Michael Anderegg, 'Orson Welles and After: *Julius Caesar* and Twentieth-Century Totalitarianism', in Horst Zander, ed., *Julius Caesar: New Critical Essays* (New York and London, 2005), pp. 295–306.

not have been lost on the audience.'[6] To Pughe, the poets 'represent the element of imagination and intuition' suppressed, to everyone's detriment, by the main characters. Alan Sinfield takes a more sardonic line; in a well-known essay, he proposes taking the whole play as 'Cinna's dream' – 'the anxious fantasy of the Shakespearian intellectual, despised by the military-industrial complex and scapegoated by the people'. Bringing this figure still closer to home, he adds: 'he would look like Shakespeare'.[7] A hundred years earlier, Bernard Shaw had done something similar with the other poet:

In one of the scenes of *Julius Caesar*, a conceited poet bursts into the tent of Brutus and Cassius, and exhorts them not to quarrel with one another. If Shakespear had been able to present his play to the ghost of the great Julius, he could probably have had much the same reception. He certainly would have deserved it.[8]

Shakespeare as his own failed poet: Shaw's barbed vignette makes a pair with Sinfield's 'anxious fantasy'. To both, the poets are essentially irrelevant to their context; it seems appropriate that Shaw's remark occurs in his review of Beerbohm Tree's production of 1898, a production in which neither poet appeared.[9]

Although Sinfield and Shaw are very different in their political sympathies, and both, in their impatience with the poets, very different from Pughe, all three critics are alike in responding to the characters as 'poets' in the purest sense – poets only, with no connexion to their contemporary world, and thus transferable across history. Margaret Maurer seems to be the only critic to take an interest in who the two figures originally were: their historical prototypes. One reason for this general indifference is surely Shakespeare's own occlusion of their identities, which has encouraged a perception of them as ahistorical symbols. This article will consider first how Shakespeare detached them from history, and then how other playwrights annexed and repoliticized them to tell some different stories. I conclude with a brief look at some of the real-life poets whose careers intersect in some way with these protean, poeticized Romans.

1. ENTER CINNA THE POET

Shakespeare takes the basis of his account from Plutarch's *Brutus* 20.7–11. On his way to Caesar's funeral, a poet named Cinna, friend to Caesar, is killed by a furious mob who mistake him for his namesake, another Cinna who has spoken bitterly against the dead Dictator. The incident is described in six ancient sources, including two of Plutarch's *Lives*; only in *Brutus* is the murdered Cinna called a poet. All the sources except Plutarch (in either of his accounts) give him, instead, a full name: Gaius Helvius Cinna. This odd discrepancy has led some scholars to question whether Plutarch, like the crowd, had confused two different Cinnas; but the matter seems to be clinched by Ovid, some forty years later, in a poetic curse:

like the author of tardy Myrrha, whose surname wrought him harm, mayst thou be found in countless parts of the city.   (*Ibis*, 539–40)[10]

We know from Catullus that his friend, the poet Gaius Helvius Cinna, had spent nine years writing a poem about Myrrha, also called Zmyrna – the mythical princess who fell in love with her father;[11] here Ovid says that the author of a long-gestated poem on Myrrha was harmed by his *cognomen*, 'surname', and found all over Rome – that is, he suffered just as Helvius Cinna does in the historian Appian's account, and as the Poet will do, apparently, in Shakespeare's play:

---

[6] Pughe, 'Poets in Shakespeare's *Julius Caesar*', p. 322.

[7] Sinfield, 'Theatres of War', pp. 25, 27.

[8] Bernard Shaw (1898), in Peter Ure, ed., *Shakespeare: Julius Caesar. A Casebook* (London, 1969), pp. 40–1.

[9] See Ripley, *Julius Caesar on Stage*, ch. 7 for a full account of Tree's spectacular production.

[10] '*Conditor ut tardae, laesus cognomine, Myrrhae, / Urbis in innumeris inveniare locis*' (text and translation from J. H. Mozley, ed., *Ovid: The Art of Love and Other Poems* (Loeb Classical Library, repr. 1985), pp. 280–1. The context is a terrific curse directed by the speaker at his enemy, Ibis.

[11] I follow the standard numbering of Catullus's poems; text quoted from the edition by Kenneth Quinn, 2nd edn (London, 1973), Poem 95.

Tear him to pieces . . . his name's Cinna   (3.3.28, 32)[12]

Did Shakespeare realize that Plutarch's Cinna was this poet – the elegist of Myrrha; the friend of Catullus?[13] Only three lines of Cinna's poetry survive, but Catullus gives us an idea what it was like. To him, Cinna's style – allusive, esoteric, compressed – made him the antithesis of popular taste: 'let turgid epic be the people's pleasure', he declares, distinguishing his friend's productions as something very different.[14] If Shakespeare was aware of that, he may have been struck, like T. P. Wiseman, by the special irony of his fate.[15]

But Helvius Cinna was not only a poet. The non-Plutarchan accounts of his death all identify him, instead, as a tribune, one of the ten holders of the office. This might also provide an ironic angle to his death. The role of tribune was traditionally populist – defender of the popular interest: Flavius and Marullus, who stripped Caesar's statues of their triumphant regalia, were tribunes. The gesture cost them their positions.[16] According to the historian Dio Cassius, it was their colleague Cinna who proposed the punishment; for Cinna, as most of the ancient reporters on his death point out, was Caesar's friend.[17] The apparent paradox of Caesar's career – a politician who had always espoused popular causes, finally entrenched as Dictator for Life – is expressed, in Plutarch's *Caesar*, through his interactions with the tribunes: he is given an excuse for crossing the Rubicon when his tribune supporters (including Antony) are driven out of the Senate; he obtains money from the treasury by threatening another tribune, Metellus; his triumph over the last of the Pompeians is opposed by Flavius and Marullus.[18] Cinna then opposes them. The fact that Shakespeare, alone among all the playwrights who have written on the assassination, chose to begin his play with the tribune resistance suggests that he had a sense of the significance of their role; like Catullus and Ovid, however, he disregarded Cinna's political position – if he knew about it. Since it could have provided him with some piquant contrasts, it would be nice to know whether he did – whether his omission, in other words, was a conscious choice. Plutarch did not supply the information but Appian did and Shakespeare may well have known his account.[19]

Even if he knew nothing beyond Plutarch, he was selective. Plutarch, in both of his accounts, says Cinna was one of Caesar's 'companions', a 'friend'.[20] In the play, he is simply 'the poet' – a generic successor, as Alexander Leggatt and others have observed, to the musical, murdered Orpheus.[21] His poetry becomes a cause, or excuse, for his death: 'Tear him for his bad verses!' (3.3.31).

---

[12] For sources on Cinna's death, and the question of his identity, see the title essay in T. P. Wiseman, *Cinna the Poet* (Leicester, 1974), pp. 44–6; J. D. Morgan, 'The Death of Cinna the Poet', *Classical Quarterly*, 40:2 (1990), 558–9. For Appian's account of the dismemberment, see *Bellum Civile* II.147. Appian had been translated into English in 1578; he is the only source to give Antony a Funeral Oration, a fact which has made some scholars believe that Shakespeare read him; see Ernest Schanzer, 'A Neglected Source of *Julius Caesar*', *Notes and Queries*, 199 (1954), 196–7 (see more on this below).

[13] Margaret Maurer assumes so: 'Again, Poets and *Julius Caesar*', p. 12.

[14] Catullus 95b.2.

[15] 'It is a particularly brutal irony that in Cinna's case the people accidentally had the last word': Wiseman, *Cinna the Poet*, p. 58.

[16] Shakespeare, of course, has them 'put to silence' (1.2.286), suggesting something worse than their historical fate.

[17] Dio Cassius, 44.10.3.

[18] See *Caesar*, 31.2–3, 35.6–8, 61.8 (here and below I follow the numbering of the Loeb edition of Plutarch).

[19] See above, note 12. For another glimpse of Caesar Dictator versus the tribunes, see Suetonius, *Div. Jul.* 78.1–2, where Pontius Aquila refuses to stand up for him. Caesar speaks to him with angry sarcasm: '*Repete ergo a me Aquila rem publicam tribunus!*' – 'Take the republic back from me then, Aquila, tribune!' (Latin text quoted from the Loeb edition by J. C. Rolfe, 1914).

[20] Companion: '*hetairos*' – *Caesar* 68.3; friend: '*philos*' – *Brutus* 20.8.

[21] Leggatt, *Shakespeare's Political Drama: The History Plays and the Roman Plays* (London and New York, 1988), p. 157; see also Taylor, 'Bardicide', p. 334. Maurer, 'Again, Poets and *Julius Caesar*', p. 13, elegantly connects the Orpheus story with Cinna's subject, Myrrha, via Ovid's *Metamorphoses*. Valerius Maximus and Suetonius add the gruesome and rather Orphean detail that his head was afterwards carried around the city on a spike: Val. Max. IX.9; Suet. *Div. Jul.* 85; something Shakespeare's character seems to be spared.

Even his personal relationship with Caesar almost disappears: he remarks that he has dreamed of Caesar, as Plutarch says he did, but anyone might dream of a just-killed Dictator; when challenged, he says he is going to the funeral as 'friend', but since the alternative offered is 'enemy', that does not claim very much. And, as critics have noted, Shakespeare excises the immediate significance of his death. Plutarch presents his death as a turning-point for Brutus and his faction, who are now frightened enough to withdraw from Rome.[22] In the play, by contrast, it has no impact on any of the great politicians: Brutus and Cassius have already fled Rome; Antony is already in control (3.2.261–73). Cinna appears from nowhere and vanishes into it, becoming thus an easy symbol of the doomed poet: self-absorbed, out of touch (has he forgotten about the other Cinna when he tells the threatening strangers his name?), misunderstood by a jeering mob – and evoking various degrees of sympathy from the critics who are his usual audience.[23]

As a coda to this, we might note that editors face a choice with Cinna, and their decision will influence the reaction of the reader – and also, perhaps, of the audience reading the programme. There is no cast list in the Folio; the first text to supply a full one seems to have been published in 1684, the version supposedly acted at the Theatre Royal.[24] In it, Cinna is identified: 'Cinna. The Poet'. This is the phrasing adopted by Nicholas Rowe, in the first scholarly edition of the play (1709), and has remained the usual practice in English editions.[25] Abroad, however, the situation is more varied. Pierre LeTourneur, the second French translator of the play (1776), lists him as 'Helvius Cinna, poet and friend of Caesar'. Listing him by two names like this encourages the reader to think of 'The Poet' rather differently – less as an archetype; more as an historical person. The play itself offers little encouragement to do so.

2. ENTER A POET:
MAD FAVONIUS

Cinna's death ends the first half of the play – the half that takes place in Rome. Encamped at

Philippi, in the second half, Brutus and Cassius are confronted by another unfortunate, this time without a name, who bursts in to end their quarrel, is laughed at by Cassius for his 'vile' rhyming, and thrown out by Brutus. Who is this character? In the play itself, Cassius describes him as a 'cynic', and Brutus as a 'jigging fool' – that is, a bad rhymer; the stage directions for F1, maybe and maybe not authorial, identify him simply as 'a Poet'. The earliest cast lists do not include him at all. When he first appears, in the mid-eighteenth century, he is called 'Another Poet' – a sort of supplement to 'The Poet', Cinna.[26] And so the situation remains. (Critics sometimes refer to him as 'the cynic poet',

---

22 *Caesar* 68.7; *Brutus* 21.1.

23 The older response was strongly sympathetic. The Variorum edition quotes the French critic Paul Stapfer: 'The blackest action committed by the people, in all Shakespeare's Roman plays, is the murder of the poet Cinna in the midst of the tumult . . . [Shakespeare] shows us the amazing unreasonableness, and lets us hear the loud bursts of stupid and ferocious laughter of a populace in revolt': H. H. Furness, ed., Variorum (Philadelphia, 1913), p. 188, first publ. 1880. Recent critics of the left have been cooler towards Cinna's plight, feeling that Shakespeare ought to have made the elite directly responsible, rather than the people: 'the plebeians are not the enemies of poetry' (Taylor, 'Bardicide', p. 343). To Dennis Kezar, Cinna represents 'an obsolescent mode of poetic subjectivity': *Julius Caesar* and the Properties of Shakespeare's Globe', p. 42. Maurer finds in his dialogue with the plebeians 'the kind of poet particularly given to incidentally witty display' ('Again, Poets and *Julius Caesar*', p. 11), which rates those panicky little quips rather high.

24 A copy of the 1691 edition in the British Library contains a manuscript cast list probably from some time in the 1670s, including 'Cinna the Poet' but not the other poet: see Edward A. Langhans, 'New Restoration Manuscript Casts', *Theatre Notebook*, 27 (1973), 149–57, pp. 151–2.

25 The most recent Arden edition by David Daniell (1994) lists him as 'Cinna. A Poet', and explains him in a note on the next page as 'Gaius Helvius Cinna, poet and friend of . . . Catullus' (p. 153). The Cambridge edition by Martin Spevack (rev. 2004) lists him as 'Cinna, a poet (Caius Helvius Cinna, probably the poet and the tribune are one and the same)' (p. 74). He makes nothing more of this point.

26 According to the Variorum, he is first included in the cast-list of Capell's edition (1761). Late eighteenth-century editions commonly had him share a line with Cinna: 'Cinna, a Poet. Another Poet' (see, for example, Malone's edition of 1794). The latest Arden by David Daniell has 'A Poet'; Spevack has 'Another Poet'.

or, rather endearingly, 'the camp poet'.) Plutarch's account of him is different. He calls him an old friend of Cato – a *soi-disant* philosopher, who adopted a bold, unrestricted style of behaviour. This man, says Plutarch (via North),

would needes come into the chamber, though the men offered to keepe him out. But it was no boote to let Faonius, when a mad mood or toye tooke him in the head: for he was a hot hasty man, and sodaine in all his doings, and cared for never a Senator of them all. Now, though he used this bold manner of speeche after the profession of the Cynick Philosophers, (as who would say, doggs) yet this boldnes did no hurt many times, bicause they did but laugh at him to see him so mad.[27]

'Faonius' or 'Phaonius' in Plutarch's Greek, in Latin Marcus Favonius, he appears a few times in Plutarch's *Lives*. His most memorable contributions before the assassination of Caesar occur in the *Life of Pompey* – first, another piece of plain-speaking to authority:

There was one Phaonius in the companie, who otherwise was no ill man, saving that he was somewhat too bolde, thinking to counterfeate Catoes plaine maner of speech: he bad Pompey then stampe his foote apon the ground, and make those souldiers come which he had promised them.[28]

Despite this brusqueness, however, Favonius was deeply loyal to Pompey:

Faonius seeing Pompey for lacke of men to waite on him, washing of him selfe: ran unto him, washed him, and annointed him, and afterwards continued still to waite upon him, and to doe such service about him, as servaunts do to their masters, even to washing of his feete, and making ready of his supper.[29]

Like Cinna, Favonius was a victim of the civil conflict: Brutus and Cassius left him out of the conspiracy against Caesar, because he considered civil war worse than illegal monarchy,[30] but he sided with the Liberators after Caesar's assassination; he was taken prisoner at Philippi and put to death. According to Suetonius, he honoured his principles to the last, abusing Octavius for his wartime brutalities as he was led out in chains.[31]

In the case of Cinna, it is not certain exactly how much Shakespeare knew about him; here things are clearer. Unlike Cinna, Favonius was not a poet, and Shakespeare must have known this perfectly well.[32] He did indeed, according to Plutarch's *Brutus*, break into the Liberators' camp spouting verse; but the verse, Plutarch tells us, was by Homer – not, as the play implies, by the intruder himself. Plutarch has him mocked not for his poetry but for his style of delivery. Shakespeare, by contrast, gives the pseudo-poet his own pseudo-poetry to speak.[33] Favonius, like Cinna, loses his political character (Shakespeare is silent on his relationship with Cato) to become, instead, an isolated *littérateur*, to whom no one has the time to listen.[34] Cinna's fate is often seen as a comment by Shakespeare on the common people; it is not usually noted that Favonius is pushed out from above, rather than below. Both find themselves overwhelmed and 'put to silence', but differently:

---

[27] Plutarch, *Brut.* 34.4–5 = Bullough, *Narrative and Dramatic Sources of Shakespeare*, vol. 5 (New York, 1966), p. 114.

[28] Plutarch, *Pomp.* 60.4 = North, ed. G. Wyndham (1896), IV, pp. 271–2. Pompey had boasted that he could fill Italy with soldiers just by stamping his foot. Favonius is mentioned also in the Life of Cato the Younger. His death is reported by Dio Cassius, 47.49.4.

[29] *Pomp.* 73.6–7 = North, IV, p. 285.

[30] Plutarch, *Brut.* 12.3.

[31] Suetonius, *Div. Aug.* 13. He underlined the point by saluting Antony and calling him 'Imperator'.

[32] See Taylor, 'Bardicide', p. 338. Taylor says that the character is a 'philosopher' in Plutarch; in fact his story supports Taylor's general argument more strongly, as Plutarch says he is not only a would-be philosopher, but a veteran supporter of the anti-Caesarean side – no wispy apolitical.

[33] His two lines are clumsy fourteeners, very close to North's version of the Homeric verse; the laughter they evoke from Cassius is perhaps a (rather ungrateful) comment by Shakespeare on North's own poetic style.

[34] In Plutarch's account of the Philippi scene, Favonius's intervention makes a difference: 'His comming in brake their strife at that time, and so they left eche other' (Plutarch, *Brut.*, 34.7 = Bullough, V, p. 114. Not so in the play, where the quarrel had already died down before his entry. Compare Cinna, whose death, in the play, loses its political effect. (This is remarked by Holland, 'The "Cinna" and "Cynicke" Episodes', p. 441, Taylor, 'Bardicide', p. 338, and Maurer, 'Again, Poets and *Julius Caesar*', p. 9.)

the one by an irrational mob, the other by high-handed authority.

Shakespeare effaces the two poets' historical identity; most critics have followed suit; few audiences (relatively) have had a chance to see them. But, thus stripped down, they underwent some surprising metamorphoses. The second half of this essay will follow them as they resurface in the theatre, and acquire new political identities.

3. AFTER CINNA

Cinna, as we have seen, appears in the narratives of his death either as poet (Plutarch's *Brutus*, Ovid) or as political office-holder (the rest): never both. There is no evidence, amid the sparse testimony surviving from others or the exiguous fragments of his own work, to suggest that he combined the two roles and wrote poems about Caesar, but the possibility must have occurred to him. Senior politicians of the late Republic were notoriously keen to have their public achievements celebrated by poets: at least four poets wrote epics on Caesar's conquests in Gaul, including Cicero;[35] Cinna's friend Catullus wrote some scurrilous verses against Caesar, and an epigram announcing that he did not wish to please him,[36] but even he worked in a flattering reference to his Gallic conquests, in a short poem about love.[37] Shakespeare chose to isolate Cinna, but two less famous plays, Aaron Hill's *The Roman Revenge* (1738) and J. J. Bodmer's *Marcus Brutus* (1768), both influenced by Shakespeare, bring on poets much more engaged with their political surroundings.

i) The Roman Revenge: *Torbilius, the Caesarean Satirist*

Aaron Hill, an acquaintance and part-time friend of Alexander Pope, meditated for some years on how a play about Caesar should be written. The result, *The Roman Revenge*, is a descendant of Shakespeare's by a rather complex genealogy: it is a free adaptation of *La Mort de César* (1731), Voltaire's tragedy on the subject, inspired (at least in part) by half-friendly rivalry with Shakespeare.[38] Hill was not satisfied with Voltaire's treatment of the

titular hero, nor Shakespeare's either; in a series of essays published in *The Prompter*, the periodical he edited, he complained that neither playwright had fitly expressed Caesar's greatness.[39] *The Roman Revenge* sets out to remedy this. Caesar here is noble-minded and patriotic, determined to restore the Republic and committed to a deistic notion of religion close to that of Lord Bolingbroke, the intended addressee of the work. This represents quite a change from his personality in Voltaire's play, where he is testy and autocratic, determined to hold onto power at all costs. An internal allegory of the transformation is provided by a character in *The Roman Revenge* who begins by distrusting and attacking Caesar and ends up believing and supporting him: the character, invented by Hill, of Torbilius the Poet.

Torbilius makes his entry with Cassius, in the first scene. We are led to understand that he is a retainer in the house of Brutus and has also written satires against Caesar; Cassius urges him to work on Brutus, not yet involved in the conspiracy, but in

---

35 'Epics on the Gallic Wars', in Wiseman, *Cinna the Poet*, p. 37 n.79. Cicero succumbed to pressure from his brother Quintus, who was on Caesar's staff: see W.W. Ewbank, *The Poems of Cicero* (London, 1933), pp. 19–22.

36 Catullus 93.

37 Catullus 11, lines 10–11.

38 Voltaire asserted in his Preface (1736) that the play was written in the English taste, by which he meant that it was fierce, austere and lacking in love interest; he still contrived to maintain the unities essential to the French taste by ending the play with Antony's Funeral Oration, before Brutus and Cassius have left Rome. His rivalry with Shakespeare would later become much less friendly. See further my chapter 'Shakespeare's *Julius Caesar* and the Dramatic Tradition', in M. T. Griffin, ed., *A Companion to Julius Caesar* (Oxford, 2009), pp. 371–98.

39 For a discussion of Hill's engagement with Voltaire's play, expressed in his articles in *The Prompter* and letters to Pope and Bolingbroke, see Dennis J. Fletcher, 'Aaron Hill, translator of *La Mort de César*', *Studies in Voltaire and the Eighteenth Century*, 137 (1975), 73–9. There is a bracingly unsympathetic account of his adaptation in Thomas R. Lounsbury, *Shakespeare and Voltaire* (New York and London, 1902), pp. 116–17: 'It has about every fault which can be found in Voltaire's play without any of its merits' (p. 117). (The work was neither published nor performed in Hill's lifetime.)

the course of the scene Torbilius is so disgusted by Cassius's obvious malice that he decides to go over to Caesar's side: 'He, who forgave my guilt', he says, 'demands my virtue.'[40] In Act 2 scene 2, he is ushered into Caesar's presence: Hill has some gentle humour at his expense, as he discovers that the Dictator has not, after all, been upset by his satires (I only remember my friends, Caesar reassures him, crushingly);[41] but Torbilius takes it in his stride, informs on Cassius, and is given the task of spying on him. He finally impresses Caesar by his refusal to take any money for the information. As he proudly says:

> The *grateful* make no *claims*. – A mindful debtor
> *Pays* – not *obliges*: – never met, in one,
> The *Poet*, and the *Miser*. – The same fire,
> That sparkles, in his fancy's native blaze,
> Glows, at his honest *heart*; and burns out baseness;
> True genius will not – cannot, stoop to bribes:
> And he, who sells his *passions*, ne'er had wit –
> Or had it, for a curse, unmix'd with judgment.
> Caesar. 'Tis nobly said . . .   (II, pp. 281–2)

He enters into his new allegiance with vigour. As Brutus is soliloquizing on his duties to the Republic (3.3) – a soliloquy taken straight from Voltaire – Torbilius bursts in on him, urging him to break with Cassius. Brutus charges him with venality, a charge he rejects; at last, seeing him 'strangely mov'd', Brutus agrees to do nothing before consulting him. Torbilius's last appearance, in 5.5, shows him involved in the elaborate, unsuccessful attempt to warn Caesar – a sequence lacking from Voltaire's play: he hands the Dictator a scroll with the names of the conspirators but Caesar refuses to read it, on the grounds that 'Life is not *worth preserving*' without trust.[42] The poet thus fails to divert the course of history; but not without a struggle.

In creating this character, Hill adds a familiar-looking element to Voltaire's play but does something new with it. Torbilius is conceived as a satirist, perhaps a Catullus-like figure (*Nil nimium studeo, Caesar, tibi belle placere* – 'I don't much care, Caesar, about pleasing you');[43] he is a sort of dependant but not a servant (the cast list defines him as 'a Roman, favour'd by Brutus'), and he exercises

the right to choose his patrons. He goes to Caesar before he knows Caesar will employ him, and then he actually refuses to take payment. Hill ends the play with Antony's Oration; readers of Shakespeare (though not, perhaps, eighteenth-century theatre-goers) would know that the next scene is the murder of the Caesar-favouring poet. The future of Torbilius must raise some doubts: having replaced the poet Cinna, he must endure the shadow of his fate.

ii) Marcus Brutus: Cinna Switches Sides
Hill himself admired Caesar, and he created a poet who embraced his point of view. Late in his life, the Swiss poet J. J. Bodmer wrote three plays on the end of the Roman Republic, all of which manifest the opposite response:[44] he is consistently Republican, anti-Caesarean. The main source for all three plays was Plutarch, but Bodmer availed himself also of a range of poetry, both in Latin and in English; his political agenda leads him to some creative variations on his sources. This is especially clear in the scene that concludes *Marcus Brutus*, the scene that stars the poet Cinna.

Bodmer's Cinna is an extraordinary reversal of Shakespeare's, and Plutarch's. He is not a supporter of Caesar; and he is not killed. Instead he gets to declaim, after the assassination, in praise of Brutus – thanks in part to an ode by Abraham Cowley. Cowley had described Caesar as the 'ravisher' of Rome, and Bodmer's Cinna repeats this in a verbatim translation.[45] (We will return to Cowley

---

[40] *The Roman Revenge* in *The Dramatic Works of Aaron Hill Esq.* (London, 1760), vol. II, p. 263.

[41] Hill was perhaps thinking here of Catullus, whose scurrilous epigrams Caesar recognized by inviting him to dinner: Suetonius, *Div. Jul.* 73.

[42] II, p. 324.

[43] Catullus 93.

[44] Bodmer's three plays: *Marcus Brutus* (1761), *Julius Cäsar* (1763) and *Brutus und Kassius Tod* (1782). He also wrote a play on the death of Cicero, *M. T. Cicero* (1763). For a discussion of them, see Anthony Scenna, *The Treatment of Ancient Legend and History in Bodmer* (New York, 1937).

[45] See J. J. Bodmer, *Marcus Brutus* published in *Politische Schauspiele* (Zürich, 1768), p. 102: 'Wer ist der fuhllose, der zugegen stehet, und siehet, wie seine Mutter beraubet, gebunden,

later.) Brutus responds with a radical variation on Virgil's first *Georgic*: he turns flattering lines about Augustus Caesar's godlike future – 'the constellation Scorpio has left you more than your share of the sky!' – into a reprimand for Cinna's flattery: '*Don't talk about Scorpio . . . !*'[46] Bodmer chooses to end his play in Republican triumph: he includes Brutus's speech to the populace, and stops before Antony's. He almost makes one believe the Liberators might get away with it, that Virgil's praise of Caesar's heir might never be seriously written. In its place, we get Cinna's praise of Brutus, praise that goes on at such gushing length that Brutus asks him to stop. This Cinna, however, cannot be silenced by anyone, and he gets the last word – a Shakespearian one:

In centuries to come these great scenes will be performed on stage in states not yet existent and in languages not yet known.[47]

The sophisticated irony here – the repeat, in a foreign language, of the speech that prophesies exactly that – gives Bodmer a claim to being the first postmodernist reader of Shakespeare. His Cinna spoke still more truly than he knew: when Shakespeare's Cinna finally returned to the stage after nearly two hundred years of excision, it was under the auspices of the Meiningen Theatre Company, who performed in German. It would be forty more years before an audience would hear Cinna speak in English.

4. *BRUTUS UND KASSIUS TOD*: HORACE AT PHILIPPI

Of the playwrights, it was Bodmer, again, who made the most inventive use of Shakespeare's second poet. Favonius as poet in the camp was not available to any later playwright who wanted to follow Classical sources; Bodmer, however, found a very ingenious way to combine Shakespeare's scenario with historical truth. *Brutus und Kassius Tod* (1782), the last of his Brutus plays, picks up shortly after *Marcus Brutus* left off: with Brutus and Cassius encamped at Philippi. In the camp of Brutus, anxious to cheer him up, is an old friend of

his, Horaz – Quintus Horatius Flaccus, the poet Horace.

This is historically possible. Horace did indeed fight for the Liberators at Philippi, although Plutarch does not mention him. Horace himself speaks of it openly in his poetry: a refined sort of compliment to the victorious Augustus, who clearly did not object.[48] In Bodmer's play, he is never called a poet and he speaks no verse. He is a fellow-soldier, only, and he enters with two prisoners of war, identified as Saculio and Volumnius, a 'Wirkling' and a 'Pantalon' – buffoonish characters.[49] Both of these appear in Plutarch's *Brutus*: in North's translation, they are called a 'jeaster' and a 'common player'.[50] They enrage everyone in Brutus's camp with their ill-timed scurrility – everyone, that is, except the patient Brutus himself. But he does not protect them when Casca protests against their frivolity, coming soon after the death of Cassius. His testy response – do what you like with them! – is taken as their death warrant: they are hastily killed, and no one mourns for them. Bodmer, however, follows none of this; he gives the two nothing to do. He has brought them in here, and invented their relationship with Horace,

---

gefangen ist, und von der Schönheit des Raubers geblendet, stehet er an zu ihrer Rettung zu eilen?'; this is a close translation of Cowley's 'Brutus Ode' (published 1656), 'Can we stand by and see/Our *Mother* robb'ed, and bound, and ravisht be,/Yet not to her assistance stir,/Pleas'd with the *Strength* and *Beauty* of the *Ravisher*?' See the end of this article.

[46] Bodmer, *Marcus Brutus*, p. 103: 'du befiehlest in deinem Enthusiasme dem Scorpion im Thierkreise nicht, dass er seine Arme ein wenig an sich ziehte, damit er deinem Helden in dem poetischen Himmel Platz mache'. Cf. *Georgic* I. 34–5 '*ipse tibi iam bracchia contrahit ardens / Scorpius et caeli iusta plus parte reliquit*': R. A. B. Mynors, ed., *P. Vergili Maronis Opera* (Oxford, 1969), p. 30.

[47] p. 103: 'Späte Jahrhunderte sollen diese grosse Scene in Staaten, die noch nicht sind, und in Sprachen, die noch nicht geredet werden, auf die Schaubühne bringen.'

[48] See *Odes* II. 7, XXI. 4; *Satire* I. 7; *Epistles* II. 2.

[49] 'Pantalon', 'pantaloon', is the stock figure of a foolish old man from *commedia dell'arte*; the word 'Wirkling' is more obscure, but is perhaps related to '*wirr*' – confused, crazy.

[50] Plutarch, *Brutus* 45.6–9 = Bullough, V, p. 125. 'Common player' represents '*mimos*' in the Greek.

in memory, not of Plutarch, but of Horace's Satire I. 7, a poem which describes two litigants involved in a contest of wits before Brutus, sometime *before* Philippi. Horace discreetly keeps himself out of the scene, limiting his role to narrator; Bodmer, in his syncretic way, has him physically introduce the two characters onto the stage.

'Of your philosophy you make no use', remarks Shakespeare's Cassius to his Brutus, 'if you give place to accidental evils' (4.3.143–4). Exactly what Shakespeare took Brutus's philosophy to be has been a subject of some disagreement: some critics refer to him as a 'Stoic', but Plutarch says that 'he loved Platoes sect best' – the Academic sect.[51] By Brutus's time, this had diversified: the branch that he followed had modified its original mild scepticism to a position hardly distinguishable from Stoicism.[52] Horace, in the play, is welcomed as an old friend of Brutus, a former fellow-student at the Platonic Academy in Athens. But he disagrees with his old friend regarding the existence of Caesar's Ghost, when others in the camp say that Brutus has seen it:

It was nothing but the insubstantial birth of an image, its ghost, working upon exceptional strain . . . The voice, too, did not come to his ear from without, but resounded in his inmost heart.[53]

Why this elaborate declaration? We might call it biographical verisimilitude: despite his Academic training, the historical Horace belonged, as he said, to the 'stye of Epicurus' (Epistle I. 4, 16), and here Bodmer gives him the same sort of argument that Plutarch gives to the committed Epicurean Cassius:

In our secte, Brutus, we have an opinion, that we doe not always feele, or see, that which we suppose we doe both see and feele: but that our senses beeing credulous . . . are induced to imagine they see and conjecture that, which they in truth doe not.[54]

But something beyond biography is discernible here. 'There are more things . . . / Than are dreamt of in your philosophy': the historical Horace has fused not only with the historical Cassius but with another, fictional character. Bodmer replaces the nameless 'Poet' of *Julius Caesar* with a famous

poet of the same historical period, remembering at the same time that poet's Shakespearian near-namesake – Hamlet's Horatio, another sceptical old college-friend. The antique Roman once more becomes a Dane; the sheeted, cited dead arise; textual spectres walk again.[55]

EPILOGUE: CIVIL WAR POETS

Better-known poets have crowded into this article than the semi-anonymous characters who began it. Let us end with something more on two of these, from each chronological side of the play: one who succeeded with the challenges of political reality, and one who fared less well.

First, Horace: poet, survivor, and inspiration for a later age. In Satire I. 7, as we have seen, he remembers two litigants who appealed to Brutus in Asia, shortly before the Battle of Philippi. One, in the poem, is a sycophant; the other a slanderer. Neither emerges with much credit – the sycophant wins, in a sense, because Horace gives him the last word, but Brutus's own response, essential to his success, is not supplied. Horace himself is the narrator, above this verbal jockeying. So he appears in Ben Jonson's *Poetaster* (1602), where he serves both as a persona for the playwright, and a champion against his rivals and detractors, corralled into the play under Classical names. *Poetaster* directs most of its fire against them, but the character Horace himself declares that he is quite unbothered by their abuse: 'I take no knowledge that they do malign

---

[51] Plutarch, *Brutus* 2.2–3 = Bullough, V, p. 90.

[52] See M. L. Clarke, *The Noblest Roman: Marcus Brutus and his Reputation* (Ithaca, 1981), pp. 12–14.

[53] 'Es war nichts anders als eine leiblose Geburt der Einbildung, sein Geist, der in der äussersten Anstrengung arbeitete, schuf dieses Gebilde vor seiner entzündeten Stirn und gab ihm eine Gestalt, die nicht würklich und nicht berührbar war. Die Stimme kam auch nicht von aussen in sein Ohr, sondern klang in seine innern Sinnen' (Bodmer, *Brutus und Kassius Tod*, p. 20).

[54] Plutarch, *Brutus* 37.2 = Bullough, V, p. 116.

[55] '[T]he cited dead' is a Miltonic phrase: *Paradise Lost*, Book III, 327. The passage describes resurrection; the words echo Shakespeare.

me' (5.3. 172).[56] Nevertheless, he triumphs over them, thanks to the express protection of Caesar, who has two of them whipped, and backs Horace in his suggestion that the third should be given emetics to bring up his bad language. The two condemned to whipping are guilty of trying to inform on Horace: he has made an emblem, they say, that shows an eagle, and thus is directed at Caesar; Horace responds that the bird is a vulture, directed at the common people – 'the base and ravenous multitude' (5.3.76). We might remember the beginning of his famous Ode, III. 1, '*Odi profanum vulgus et arceo*' – I hate the uninitiated crowd and shun it; we might also remember Cinna, who could not escape it. Jonson's character avoids trouble from above by scorning those below; he is protected from the crowd by the favour of Caesar. Cherished though he is by power, however, he also stakes out a claim to some independence even from his great benefactor: 'And for my soul, it is as free as Caesar's' (5.1.90). Caesar applauds him:

Thanks, Horace, for thy free and wholesome sharpness,
Which pleaseth Caesar more than servile fawns.

(5.1.94–5)

Caesar supportive, the poet still independent: the scene seems ideal, almost to the point of wistfulness. Horace, the poet who once opposed Augustus but then flourished under his reign, here enables Jonson's scene, becoming a model or a fantasy for the public poet with Classical credentials.[57]

Even though the scene seems ideal, however, it still conveys a faint sense of constraint, of over-protestation. The play is filled with echoes of Horace; one line never audibly echoed is that apparent throw-away in Satire I. 3: '*Caesar, qui cogere posset*': Caesar, who might have forced an intransigent poet to perform (but chose not to do so, on this occasion). The cost, and the easiness, of annoying authority appears from the career of another poet, less fortunate in his civil war experience: Abraham Cowley, who has left a ghostly trace in the legend of Julius Caesar.

We have seen how, in Bodmer's *Marcus Brutus*, Cowley's hostile account of Caesar's career is given to the poet Cinna to speak. This account occurred in a eulogy for Brutus – Cowley's so-called 'Brutus Ode', a poem, first published in 1656, that achieved a curious dramatic afterlife. It made its way not only into Bodmer's play, but back into Shakespeare's too. In the so-called 'Dryden-Davenant' version of 1719, the Ghost's promise to return at Philippi (4.3.283) is fulfilled on stage: on this second appearance, lacking any Shakespearean words to speak, it quotes Cowley's Ode, 'Next, ungrateful *Brutus*, do I call'. Brutus counter-quotes from the same ode: 'Ungrateful, *Caesar*, that wou'd Rome enthral'; providing, thus, a neat substitution: a poetical addition, made at just the time that Shakespeare's two poets were being extracted from the play.[58]

But Cowley's involvement with Caesar had implications beyond the textual. The ode is a eulogy for Brutus, the republican; and the poet, despite his Royalist activism, seems to have suffered directly for it in 1660, when the monarchy resumed. After Cowley's death, his friend Thomas Sprat offered an elliptical account for his loss of royal favour: 'A paragraph and a metaphor'.[59] The phrase sounds like a memory of an earlier poet's troubles: Ovid, banished from Rome, on his own account, for '*carmen et error*': a poem and a mistake.[60] In Cowley's case, the 'paragraph' is

---

[56] Quotations taken from Tom Cain, ed., *Poetaster* in the *Revels Plays* series (Manchester, 1995).

[57] For a fine discussion of the figure of Horace in the play, see Victoria Moul, *Jonson, Horace and the Classical Tradition* (Cambridge, 2010), ch. 4.

[58] See, for a discussion of this version, John Ripley, *Julius Caesar on Stage*, pp. 124–6 (Ripley does not remark on the debt to Cowley, which was probably recognized by much of the contemporary audience). The Duke of Buckingham's Shakespearian *Caesar* plays also co-opt Cowley; *Julius Caesar*, the first of them, was published with a preface in which Caesar is described as a 'lovely Ravisher' whom a 'Nymph' could 'scarce refuse', a deliberate inversion of Cowley's censure of Caesar the Rapist (see above, under Bodmer's *Marcus Brutus*). Buckingham also wrote his own Ode on Brutus (first published in *Poems on Affairs of State*, vol. III (1704)); this reverses Cowley's argument, making Caesar the hero.

[59] Thomas Sprat, 'An Account of the Life and Writings of Mr. Abraham Cowley', prefixed to his edition of *The Works of Abraham Cowley* (London, 1668), sig. a4.

[60] *Tristia*, II. 207.

presumably a reference to part of the volume's preface, cut in the second edition, where Royalists are described as 'the Conquered'; the 'metaphor' is not clear, but perhaps it gestures towards the 'Ode', for which, according to a long-lived rumour, he was sharply reproved by Lord Clarendon.[61] Critics in the last forty years have emphasized the ambiguity of praising Brutus in the Interregnum: can we be sure that he represents the usurper Cromwell, rather than the Royalists, defenders of the *status quo* (monarchist in England but republican in Rome)?[62] T. R. Langley and others have stressed the corresponding anomaly of Caesar's own position, as ruler and revolutionary, an anomaly brought out so powerfully in Shakespeare's play. But politics has less room than literary criticism for such complexities. Whatever Cowley meant by his Ode, it cannot have pleased the returning *triumphator*, Charles II; subsequently the poet represented himself as 'melancholy', disappointed and a victim of the Muse. Like Shakespeare's second Poet, he had been cast away.[63]

'A paragraph and a metaphor'. The summary applies itself more generally to the situation of writers in a time of upheaval and uncertainty. Shakespeare's treatment of the two Roman poets anticipates Cowley's summary. By etymology, a 'metaphor' is a transferral; Cinna, the luckless homonym, and Favonius, the play-made poet, might be considered cases of transferred identity: metaphors embodied. They might also be seen as dramatic paragraphs: two short, discrete episodes. Taken as a whole, the phrase supplies an appropriately reticent epitaph for the Poet Out of Place – for the blunderer, thrown out of Brutus's camp in contempt; for the innocent, who set out for Caesar's funeral, and found it was his own.

---

[61] Matthew Tindal, *The Judgement of Dr. Prideaux in Condemning the Murder of Julius Caesar* (London, 1721), p. 41. The book is a reply to two articles by 'Cato' in the *London Journal* (2 and 9 December, 1721). The first defends Brutus against the charge of ingratitude to Caesar; it ends by quoting Cowley.

[62] See in particular T. R. Langley, 'Abraham Cowley's "Brutus": Royalist or Republican?' *YBES*, 6 (1976), 41–52 and J. G. Keough, 'Cowley's Brutus Ode: Historical Precepts and the Politics of Defeat', *TSLL*, 19:3 (1977), 382–91.

[63] See his Ode 'The Complaint' (publ. 1663), and several of the essays, e.g. 'Of Myself', where he describes himself as being 'made' a poet in childhood 'as irremediably as a child is made an eunuch'. (In the Errata to the volume, Cowley corrects 'irremediably' to 'immediately'; the original text seems greatly superior.)

THE MEASURE OF SEXUAL MEMORY

STEPHEN SPIESS

Duke. You were not bid to speak.
Lucio.   No, my good lord,
    Nor wished to hold my peace.
                                    (*Measure for Measure*, 5.1.77–9)

In the dizzying, chaotic finale of *Measure for Measure* – moments before Lucio unwittingly discovers the Duke, catalysing a famously unsettling resolution – the play's dramatic energy intensifies during a sharp repartee between Vienna's most prominent male figures. Fuelled by the disguised Duke's presence-in-absence, the dialogue draws energy from the tensions inherent within competing memory narratives: those of Lucio and the Duke, but also of Escalus, Angelo, their fellow citizens and even playgoing audiences. Dramatic irony reaches its apogee, however, neither in Escalus's torturous threats nor the Duke-as-Friar's critique of Viennese corruption, but rather in a basic memorial inquiry:

Lucio. . . . Come hither, goodman Baldpate. Do you know me?
Duke. I remember you, sir, by the sound of your voice. I met you at the prison, in the absence of the duke.
Lucio. O, did you so? And do you remember what you said of the Duke?
Duke. Most notedly, sir.
Lucio. Do you so, sir? And was the Duke a fleshmonger, a fool, and a coward, as you then reported him to be?
Duke. You must, sir, change persons with me ere you make that my report. You indeed so spoke of him, and much more, much worse.   (5.1.324–35)

Punning upon absence and substitution, dominant motifs throughout the play, the dialogue pulls *Measure for Measure*'s dramatic past into its immediate present: as the two characters debate previous roles, they replay the humorous inequality of their situational understanding – Lucio knows not to whom he speaks. Yet irony derives not only from Lucio's ignorance, nor solely his memorial reconstructions, but also from the memory work of playgoing audiences, who presumably recall that Lucio 'so spoke' of the Duke's alleged sexual histories and desires. Although playgoers likely perceive the friar's true identity, the characters within the play remain, at this moment, oblivious to the immense power imbalance between the two interlocutors. Before the Duke reveals himself, Viennese citizens hear competing recollections, either of which could prove valid. Escalus and Angelo, the Duke's avatars, take neither side on this particular aspect of the debate, responding instead to the 'Friar's' preceding comments: his 'Slander to th' state!' (5.1.320). The central contention of the Lucio–Duke exchange – the latter's status as a fleshmonger, fool and coward – falls into silence.

Lucio's charges of sexual immorality, intellectual impotence and masculine incapacity disappear, at least rhetorically, as the play concludes. Imbued with social and political authority, the Duke goes on to identify subjects, order social and sexual relations, and organize the play's dramatic narrative in relation to his personal recollections: he remembers Lucio's slanders, Marina's virtuous confessions, Escalus's 'goodness' and the Provost's 'care and secrecy' (5.1.527–9). His memory, quite literally, matters: these recollections provide the bases for Vienna's official narrative and – conjoined as well to questions of torture, imprisonment, execution and enforced marriage – are inscribed upon Viennese bodies. Having encouraged Friar Thomas to 'throw away [the] thought' of an alleged sexual past (1.3.1), the Duke moreover aligns memory production with processes of forgetting, whether natural or enforced.[1] Throughout, he works to dissociate his bodies natural and politic from the very 'thought' of sexual practice or desire. The only character who explicitly challenges this official narrative – Lucio, who remembers the Duke as 'One of all luxury, an ass, a madman' – is subjected to public discipline and forcibly married to a 'whore' (5.1.500–14).

Such practices may enable the play's ordered resolution, yet the call to memory bespeaks the traces of that which has been sacrificed (or violently suppressed) to achieve social, sexual, familial and dramatic coherence. Indeed, where the dénouement stages the labour of memorial production, it construes memory not simply as an individual and cognitive phenomenon, but also as an ongoing, collaborative and contestatory process. By associating the Duke's authority with his control – or lack thereof – of sexual memory, the play encourages consideration of how cultures remember and forget their sexual histories, including practices, such as prostitution, once licensed by state authority.

As Foucault reminds us, battles over cultural memory disclose relations of power but also questions of signification and knowledge production. 'Do you know me?' Lucio asks, to which the Duke-as-Friar replies, 'I remember you, sir, by the sound of your voice.' What are the relations of memory and knowledge in *Measure for Measure* and how are they informed by alleged sexual statuses or practices? As noted, the Duke recalls the sound of Lucio's voice but also the content of his slanders – his allegations that the former had 'some feeling of the sport' and 'his use was to put a ducat in her clack-dish', that he would 'eat mutton on Fridays' and 'mouth with a beggar' (3.1.383–442). What is

recollected in such claims? How do they signify, to whom, and to what effects? To pose such questions seeks neither to 'know' nor concretize the Duke's – or any other character's – sexual practices or desires; rather, I argue that *Measure for Measure* renders them significant precisely in their epistemological opacity. Indeed, by pursuing questions of memory, signification and knowledge rather than those of 'sexuality',[2] I demonstrate how historical epistemology – the study of knowledge production and dissemination in specific cultural contexts, with particular attention given to the modes and media through which meanings are forged and contested[3] – can refract hegemonic understandings of early modern sexual practices and meanings, especially those related to London prostitution. To do so, I examine acts of sexual remembrance and forgetting as they span four distinct, if interrelated, registers: in scholarly studies of the *ars memoria*, in *Measure for Measure*, in modern editorial practices, and in other early modern textual practices such as English chorography, chronicle history and state proclamation.

FORGOTTEN MEMORIES

In her analyses of the classical, medieval and early modern arts of memory, Frances Yates describes a remarkable, if strikingly grotesque, mnemonic promoted by the Franciscan priest John Ridevall. To recall the sin of idolatry, preachers should, Ridevall argues, construct a deformed prostitute

---

[1] On the politics of forgetting, see esp. Lina Perkins Wilder, *Shakespeare's Memory Theatre* (Cambridge, 2010); Peter Holland, ed., *Shakespeare, Memory and Performance* (Cambridge, 2006); Garrett Sullivan, *Memory and Forgetting in English Renaissance Drama: Shakespeare, Marlowe, Webster* (Cambridge, 2005); Jonathan Baldo, 'Wars of Memory in Henry V', *Shakespeare Quarterly*, 47 (1996), 132–59.

[2] Cf. Carolyn E. Brown, 'The Homoeroticism of Duke Vincentio: "Some Feeling of the Sport"', *Studies in Philology*, 94 (1997), 187–220.

[3] Cf. Lorraine Daston, 'Historical Epistemology', in James Chandler, Arnold I. Davidson and Harry Harootunian, eds., *Questions of Evidence: Proof, Practice, and Persuasion across the Disciplines* (Chicago, 1991), pp. 282–9.

in their minds – her face painted and disfigured, her ears mutilated and her body conspicuously diseased.[4] As with exceptionally beautiful recollections, such ghastly images, it was believed, would impress themselves upon a practitioner's brain, ensuring their preservation and effortless recollection. This affective intensity might inspire socially sanctioned behaviour, stirring the memory artist to virtuous conduct or, at the very least, away from lascivious comportment. Even the horrific 'similitude' served a pedagogic function: the recollection of vices and virtues, it was hoped, would induce a 'moral habit... used to remember past things with a view to prudent conduct in the present, and prudent looking forward in the future' (62). Ridevall's imagined harlot was thus a moral mnemonic, derived from the social and characterized by the sexual, that sustained and reproduced contemporary gendered and sexual ideologies: this 'strikingly hideous' harlot is conspicuously female, a 'common woman' who embodies specific sins.

Although there is little evidence to suggest that Ridevall's treatise was well known in late Elizabethan and early Jacobean England, the text proves interesting for its emphases on personification as mnemonic practice. Indeed, the use of personae – especially those marked by sexual practices or reputations – as mnemonics has been overlooked in modern scholarly accounts regarding the classical arts of memory, which have tended to foreground spaces, material objects, rituals and iconography.[5] While scholars have rightly noted the centrality of memory to medieval and early modern European cultures, relations of memory and sexual practice – especially at the cultural level – remain underexplored. Yet traces of Ridevall's practice, wherein individual types serve as embodied mnemonics with social, sexual and religious meaning, persist well into the sixteenth century, ranging across a variety of cultural forms. These include, of course, medieval morality and mystery plays, where audiences were encouraged to remember cardinal virtues and deadly sins by ritualistically observing eponymous characters who personified specific traits, but also an array of sixteenth-century

print texts,[6] such as Peter of Ravenna's *The Art of Memory, that Otherwyse is called the Phenix* (London, 1548), that likewise incorporated sexually personified mnemonics. In this extraordinarily popular text, Ravenna proffered 'maydens and vyrgyns' as especially effective moral and sexual mnemonics,[7] and even encouraged practitioners to model these constructions after individuals known personally to the memory artist. If not a dominant trope in the medieval and early modern arts of memory, the Ridevall harlot – and its virginal/chaste correlatives in Ravenna – nonetheless suggests how the *ars memoria* participated in, and drew energy from, contemporary sexual ideologies and cultures.

Among the Ridevall harlot's most striking aspects are its combined social and individual characteristics. Lacking a proper name and body, she functions as an abstraction, the personification of a general vice. Whereas – in accordance with the scholastic memory tradition – the text lacks a visual image, the memory artist must therefore draw from a rhetorical description to produce this harlot in his mind, around whom he then clusters various attributes and meanings associated with the sin of idolatry. While it is unclear whether Ridevall's preachers directly transmitted this mnemonic to parishioners – that is, encouraged them to use it in their everyday lives – the image clearly draws

---

[4] Frances Yates, *The Art of Memory* (Chicago, 1966), pp. 96–7. For a fuller account of Ridevall's career and works, see Beryl Smalley, *English Friars and Antiquity in the Early Fourteenth Century* (Oxford, 1960), esp. pp. 109–32.

[5] See esp. Stephen Greenblatt, *Hamlet in Purgatory* (Princeton, 2001); Ann Rosalind Jones and Peter Stallybrass, eds., *Renaissance Clothing and the Materials of Memory* (Cambridge, 2000); Eamon Duffy, *The Stripping of the Altars: Traditional Religion in England, c.1400–c.1580* (New Haven, 1992); David Cressy, *Bonfires and Bells: National Memory and the Protestant Calendar in Elizabethan and Stuart England* (Berkeley, 1989).

[6] In addition to works reviewed in Yates and Smalley, see also those discussed in Mary Carruthers, *The Book of Memory: A Study of Memory in Medieval Culture* (Cambridge, 1990).

[7] Wilder, *Shakespeare's Memory Theatre*, pp. 35–41. On the erotics of chastity and virginity, see especially Karma Lochrie, *Heterosyncrasies: Female Sexuality When Normal Wasn't* (Minneapolis, 2005).

upon a collective social typology in the pursuit of an explicitly communal objective.[8] Of course, page and pulpit were not the only discursive arenas through which early moderns could access, recall and imagine the bodies of English prostitution. By the turn of the seventeenth-century, 'prostitutes', 'harlots', 'whores' and an array of related figures saturated the scripts and stages of London dramaturgy. Such figures encouraged playgoers to contemplate their own desires and anxieties,[9] as well as the gender, politics and prices of early modern sexual commerce,[10] but also, in the case of Shakespeare's *Measure for Measure*, to consider how the histories of English prostitution itself have been – and might be – shaped, remembered and forgotten.

THE AUTHORITY OF MEMORY IN *MEASURE FOR MEASURE*

Traces of illicit sex permeate the social and corporeal landscapes of Shakespeare's Vienna. Written across its citizens' bodies, inscribed in the laws of the land, enshrined within buildings razed or repurposed, present and absent in the bawdy languages of its subjects, sexual memory saturates the contours of Viennese life. Although criminality, transgression and authority in *Measure for Measure* have received ample scholarly attention,[11] their relations to cultural memory have gone unnoticed. The play, however, both begins and concludes at sites of remembrance, constructing the Duke's memory practices as the manifestation of his social authority. He opens by praising the deputy Escalus, noting that 'The nature of our people, / Our city's institutions and the terms / For common justice, you're as pregnant in / As art and practice hath enriched any / *That we remember*' (1.1.9–13, emphasis added). Locating in his counterpart those 'qualities essential to the office of ruling',[12] the Duke qualifies this praise by stressing that Escalus's authority depends upon, and indeed emerges from, the parameters of official memory, the boundaries of the Duke's recollection.

This caveat sheds light upon the passage's otherwise enigmatic concluding sentiment: 'there is our commission', the Duke goes on to note, 'from which we would not have you warp' (1.1.13–14). What, exactly, is this commission, and how does it relate to the 'no more . . . but that' which Escalus has been entrusted to perform? The question turns upon an obscure editorial crux, yet one that centres precisely upon the acknowledgement – or elision – of memory as a central category in *Measure for Measure*. Here is the passage in full, with the 1623 Folio alongside a present-day Oxford edition (emphasis added):

Folio (1623)	Oxford (1986)
Of Gouernment, the properties to vnfold,	Of government the properties to unfold
Would feeme in me t'afect speech & difcourfe	Would seem in me t'affect speech and discourse;
Since I am put to know, **that** your Science Exceeded (in **that**) the lists of all aduice	Since I am put to know that your owne science Exceeds in that the lists of all advice

---

8 Cf. Mario DiGangi, *Sexual Types: Embodiment, Agency, and Dramatic Character from Shakespeare to Shirley* (Philadelphia, 2011).

9 Valerie Traub, *Desire and Anxiety: Circulations of Sexuality in Shakespearean Drama* (London, 1992), esp. pp. 71–87. Joseph Lenz, 'Base Trade: Theater as Prostitution', *ELH*, 60 (1993), 833–55.

10 Jyotsna Singh, 'The Interventions of History: Narratives of Sexuality', in Dympna Callaghan, Lorraine Helms and Jyotsna Singh, eds., *The Weyward Sisters: Shakespeare and Feminist Politics* (Oxford, 1994), pp. 7–58. Jean E. Howard, *Theater of a City: The Places of London Comedy, 1598–1642* (Philadelphia, 2007), esp. pp. 114–61.

11 On criminality, transgression, and authority in the play, see Singh, 'Interventions'; Jonathan Dollimore, 'Transgression and Surveillance in *Measure for Measure*', in Jonathan Dollimore and Alan Sinfield, eds., *Political Shakespeare: Essays in Cultural Materialism*, 2nd edn (Ithaca, 1994), pp. 129–53; Steven Mullaney, *The Place of the Stage: License, Play, and Power in Renaissance England* (Chicago, 1988); Jonathan Goldberg, *James I and the Politics of Literature: Jonson, Shakespeare, Donne and Their Contemporaries* (Baltimore, 1983).

12 The gloss comes from J. W. Lever's Arden 2nd series edition of the play. See William Shakespeare, *Measure for Measure* (London, 1965), p. 3.

My strength can giue you:
  Then no more remains,
But **that**, to your
  sufficiency, as your
  worth is able
And let them worke: The
  nature of our People,
Our Cities Institutions,
  and the Termes
For Common Iustice,
  y'are as pregnant in
As Art, and practise, that
  inriched any
That we remember:
  There is our
  Commiſſion
From which, we would
  not haue you warpe
        (TLN 6–17)

My strength can give you.
  Then no more remains,
But **this**: to your
  sufficiency, as your
  worth is able,
And let them work. The
  nature of our people,
Our city's institutions and
  the terms
For common justice,
  you're as pregnant in
As art and practice hath
  enriched any
That we remember.
  There is our
  commission,
From which we would
  not have you warp
        (1.1.3–14)

In both versions, the stated 'commission' delineates Escalus's cognitive authority: his advanced understanding of the nature, institutions and terms of Viennese life. It also hearkens back to the Duke's earlier, seemingly inscrutable assertion that 'no more remains but **this**: to your sufficiency, as your worth is able, and let them work' (1.1.7–9). This lineation emends the Folio's 'then no more remains but **that**, to your sufficiency, as your worth is able, and let them work'. The deictic shift proves critical. In the Oxford construction, the clause looks forward, functioning as instruction: Escalus must 'go to' or 'rely on' his sufficiency, letting 'them work'. His commission, as it were, is to use this knowledge to the best of his abilities – an obtuse charge at best. The emendation generates further problems: object (sufficiency) and pronoun (them) fail to agree, and the command disrupts the balance of the speech: the Duke's subsequent lines prove unnecessary (quite literally, no more 'remains' – only a retrospective inventory of Escalus's 'science') and the passage loses a critical verbal echo.

Editions drawn from the Folio retain this overlooked rhetorical device and produce – by way of the pronoun 'that' – a commission directly connected to Escalus's memory practices. In the Folio,

the pronoun refers not forwards but backwards – to the Lord's 'owne Science', a knowledge base which 'exceeds (in *that*), the lists of all aduice / My strength can giue you'. The term's second citation, positioned parenthetically in the Folio, moves even further back, remembering the 'properties' identified in the speech's first line. A restored Folio construction, therefore, has the Duke offer an entirely different commission, summarized thus: 'it would appear vain of me to expound upon the properties of Viennese governance, as I am aware that your knowledge (in this particular realm) exceeds mine own; nothing more do you possess, so use these faculties to the best of your ability. *This* knowledge – regarding the nature of our people, our institutions, and the codes of our legal system – is as deep and thorough as that possessed by any person in my memory. *That* is your commission – to understand how the state functions – from which you must not deviate.' Escalus thus possesses no official powers beyond a unique capacity to know, acknowledge and remember how power operates in the Duke's Vienna. 'Pregnant' in this capacity, he is a repository of state memory, embodying its critical interrelations with authority and power in Vienna. Such an understanding proves invaluable in its own right, as other citizens will learn to their benefit or detriment: one's status and livelihood, the savvy Escalus knows, depends upon 'that' which 'we' – the state – 'remember'. In forgetting the Folio, the Oxford edition elides memory itself.

Angelo's election only reiterates the potent and capricious nature of official memory in Vienna. Turning to this alternative deputy, the Duke declares 'there is a kind of character in thy life / That to th'observer doth thy history / fully unfold' (1.1.27–9). The statement may appear benign, coming only moments after Escalus affirms Angelo's honourable reputation, but the Duke's assertion rings a discordant note. Based upon conspicuously vague evidence – a 'kind of character' observed – he declares his counterpart a capable and qualified ruler. Angelo himself immediately challenges this memorial construction; noting his own lack of experience, he responds, 'Let there be more test made of my metal / Before so noble and so great a figure / Be stamped upon it.' The Duke pithily discards this self-history: 'No more evasion. / We have with a leavened and prepared choice / Proceeded to you' (1.1.47–52). While the stately proclamation, with its emphases upon prudence and circumspection, appears to settle the case, the Duke's haste unsettles his declared discretion. Two scenes later, the conceptual framework for Angelo's election – that he possesses the proper character to oversee Vienna – crumbles when the Duke acknowledges, to Friar Thomas, that he does not know whether Angelo will govern responsibly: 'Hence we shall see / If power change purpose, what our seemers be' (1.3.53–4). Angelo's 'history fully unfold' thus unfolds not the deputy's histories – his past, present or future – but those of the Duke and Vienna, one wherein the state produces and enforces certain memory narratives, to pointedly material consequences: Claudio, Juliet, Pompey and Froth are all detained or imprisoned under Angelo's reign, while Mistress Overdone stresses its potential effects upon her trade and livelihood.

Measuring the material effects of official memory, *Measure for Measure* exposes the labour necessary to reproduce dominant social narratives. But it also encourages audiences to consider what exactly the Duke wants to forget – and why. Indeed this memory work begins not only with chosen recollections but also conspicuous ellipses. Amidst the haste and clamour of the play's first scene, the Duke offers a significant, if easily overlooked, aside to his newly appointed deputy: 'Our haste from hence', he declares, 'is of so quick condition / That it prefers itself, and leaves unquestioned / Matters of needful value' (1.1.53–5). A seemingly casual digression, the comment barely registers in light of the scene's momentous actions: just prior, the Duke announced his intentions to abscond from the state and transfer full authority ('Mortality and mercy in Vienna', 1.1.44) to an untested deputy, bypassing the more experienced Escalus. Plunged into chaos, the Duke's audiences – Escalus, Angelo, readers and

playgoers alike – struggle to synthesize an abruptly disordered state of affairs, to locate a thread of stability in a world suddenly gone awry. In such a situation, 'unquestioned matters' appear trivial; as a ruler rushes away, the scene produces a powerful impetus to focus upon what remains visible, upon what materializes onstage rather than offhand occlusions. Yet the Duke's aside offers a haunting reminder that matters of 'needful value' have been pointedly omitted. Far from trivial, the comment identifies a central narrative omission. If, at first glance, the Duke appears to overlook the parameters of Angelo's commission or the 'scope' of his authority as substitute ruler, he addresses these issues moments later by ordering the deputy 'to enforce or qualify the laws / As to your soul seems good' (1.1.65–6). A troubling assertion – granting Angelo powers *carte blanche* in his absence – the claim nonetheless broadly defines the deputy's mandate. The Duke's aside thus suggests another omission, some other casualty to the imperatives of haste: amidst harried departures and substitutions, what the Duke 'leaves unquestioned' are the very grounds for his withdrawal.

The Duke addresses these motives in the play's third scene, acknowledging to Friar Thomas that he has forgotten – or failed – to enforce the 'strict statutes and most biting laws... Which for this fourteen years we have let slip' (1.3.19–21). These claims echo those of Claudio who, in the preceding scene, suffers under a 'drowsy and neglected act' and cites his persecution as an expression of 'tyranny' (1.2.151–8), thereby associating capricious enforcement with despotism. The Duke, in part, agrees: 'Sith 'twas my fault', he confesses to the Friar, ''Twould be my tyranny to strike and gall them / For what I bid them do' (1.3.35–7). The elected Angelo stands in his place. By this substitution, the Duke displaces his forgetting – and the responsibilities inherent to remembering – onto his deputy. The ruse works: the Viennese subjects never question what the Duke 'bid them do', but rather focus upon the actions of Angelo, who 'for a name' (1.2.157), they believe, resurrects the forgotten law.

Placing Angelo in his stead, the Duke elides his relations to the sexual politics of contemporary Vienna, a displacement further enacted by the play's chronology: the Duke defers explanation until meeting with the Friar (Act 1, scene 3 in modern editions), and therefore it is the citizens who first articulate the 'diseased' sexual state of Vienna (Act 1, scene 2). By the time the Duke – disguised and thus further dissociated from his official position – admits that he has 'seen corruption boil and bubble / Till it o'errun the stew' (5.1.315–16), such corruptions already have been associated with, and embodied by, his subjects. Through such deferrals, he works to forget – or, more precisely, to dissociate himself and the official narrative from – Viennese sexual 'corruption': that which 'o'errun[s]' sanctioned boundaries, desires or practices.

The Duke's denial – or elision – of his own desires mirrors these sexual politics. In conversation with Friar Thomas, the Duke notes:

> No, holy father, throw away that thought.
> Believe not that the dribbling dart of love
> Can pierce a complete bosom. Why I desire thee
> To give me secret harbor hath a purpose
> More grave and wrinkled than the aims and ends
> Of burning youth . . .   (1.3.1–6)

Actively repudiating 'love' and erotic 'desire', he instructs the Friar to 'believe not' that the Duke possesses the 'aims and ends / Of burning youth'. Yet just as Viennese sexual commerce persists beyond the frame of the play – as Leah Marcus notes, 'despite all the initial talk about the rigid enforcement of law, the Viennese statute punishing fornication with death is forgotten'[13] – the Duke's own 'desire[s]' return with force in the dénouement, when he shockingly expresses an intention to wed Isabella. The play thus associates forgetting not with oblivion but rather with persistence and the possibility of return. Indeed, just as the Duke attempts to contain the sexual and social memories of Vienna, his actions simultaneously reveal and encounter sites of (sexual) memory beyond his authoritarian grasp, including mnemonics that shift, transfer, reside elsewhere

and even – much like the Duke himself – assume a certain disguise in other names, spaces and bodies.

SEXUAL GEOGRAPHIES, URBAN PALIMPSESTS

Literary historians seeking to date and localize *Measure for Measure* often turn to the play's second scene, especially Pompey's famed reference to a state 'proclamation' that demands the razing of 'all houses in the suburbs of Vienna' (1.2.87–8). Scholars have long read this citation – in conjunction with Mistress Overdone's references to the 'war', 'sweat', 'gallows' and 'poverty' (1.2.80–2) – as an allusion to events contemporary to the play's first known performance before the court of King James I on 26 December 1604.[14] In a gloss that has become essentially *de rigueur*, J. W. Lever links Pompey's proclamation to a contemporary Stuart Royal Proclamation that calls for the 'pulling down of houses and rooms in the suburbs of London as a precaution against the spread of plague by "dissolute and idle persons"' (xxxii). I will return to such proclamations momentarily, but first propose another narrative, one that stresses less the possibilities for topical allusion than the memorial and geographic presences of prostitutions past, especially as related to the politics of erasure in Shakespeare's Vienna and Tudor London. To do so, I turn to London's famed chronicler of urban memory, John Stow.

As is well known, Stow's *Survey of London* (1598/1603) constructs an early modern city in and of memory, wherein present buildings, geographies and edifices 'stand as monumental signposts to a community, a culture, a history defined and embodied by the traces it has left behind'.[15] Yet

---

[13] Leah S. Marcus, *Puzzling Shakespeare: Local Reading and Its Discontents* (Berkeley, 1988), p. 178.

[14] See Lever, *Measure for Measure*, p. xxxii: 'Overdone's complaint links a number of factors operative in the winter of 1603–4: the continuance of the war with Spain; the plague in London; the treason trials and executions at Winchester in connection with the plots of Raleigh and others; the slackness of trade in the deserted capital.'

[15] Mullaney, *The Place of the Stage*, p. 6.

scholars have overlooked the manner in which Stow describes commercial sex both in absence and as memory – an approach invoked, in part, by a shift in verb tenses as he perambulates through the present spaces of London's sexual past.[16] Stow begins in the present, noting 'I **am** now to cross over the said river into the borough of Southwark', where 'There **be** also these five prison or gaols'. He soon declares that the 'Houses most notable **be** these', including 'The Stewes on the bank of the Thames', yet abruptly shift tenses when entering this latter geography:

Next on this bank **was sometime** the Bordello, or Stewes, a place so called of certain stew-houses privileged there, for the repair of incontinent men to the like women . . . These allowed stew-houses **had** signs on their fronts, towards the Thames, not hanged out, but painted on the walls, as a Boar's Head, the Cross Keys, the Gun, the Castle, the Crane, the Cardinal's Hat, the Bell, the Swan, &c. **I have heard** of ancient men, of good credit, report that these single women were forbidden the rites of the church so long as they continued that sinful life, and **were** excluded from Christian burial if they **were** not reconciled before their death. And therefore there **was** a plot of ground called the Single Woman's Churchyard, appointed for them far from the church . . . In the year of Christ, 1546, the 37th of Henry VIII., this row of stews in Southwark **was** put down by the king's commandment, which **was** proclaimed by sounds of trumpet, no more to be privileged, and used as a common brothel . . .

Moving to the next location, Stow returns to the present tense ('next **is** the Clink, a jail or prison for the trespassers in those parts'), but even these present constructions incorporate the traces of past prostitutions: an existing jail had served 'in old time' to house the rabble who might 'break the peace' in 'brothel-houses' and '**were** straightly imprisoned'. Moving forward, he again returns to the present tense: 'Next **is** the Bishop of Winchester's house' (374).

Within this peripatetic memory narrative, where Stow walks readers through the present spaces of London's sexual past, these brothels assume an absent materiality. Whereas other buildings are present, this section of the bankside exists as a type of cartographic lacuna, a gap filled solely with memory narratives centred upon the suppression and persistence of commercial sex in early modern London. If the material spaces of prostitution have been razed from the face of London, these buildings remain a ghostly presence – urban palimpsests occupying the gap between hospital and jail; erased but not gone in Stow's narrative, the 'Stewes on the bank of the Thames' remain present in his earlier inventory of 'Houses most notable' that '**be**' in Southwark. Whereas Steven Mullaney has argued that early modern London was haunted by the 'traces of a past whose outlines were daily growing more tenuous',[17] Stow's brothels appear as a curious exception – a durable, even interminable, urban memory.[18]

I rehearse Stow's memorial journeys less to ascribe causal links between texts and contexts than to illustrate four points: first, to note how material records participate in the reproduction and dissemination of English sexual memory;[19] second, to foreground Stow's reference to the official suppression of prostitution – previously 'privileged' and 'allowed' – under Henry VIII; third, to highlight his emphases on visibility and erasure; and fourth, to stress his configuration of prostitution as a present-absence haunting the early modern city. While I do not suggest that *Measure for Measure* – including the play's 'seedy' second scene[20] – reflects

---

16 All citations from John Stow, *A Survey of London* (1598/1603), ed. Henry Morley (Dover, 1994). My use of bold font highlights Stow's verbal shifts.

17 Mullaney, *The Place of the Stage*, p. 15.

18 See for example William Camden, *Britannia* (London, 1586), p. 322. Thomas Fuller, *Church-History of Britain* (1655), vol. 2, section V, pp. 39–41.

19 See the essays collected in David Middleton and Derek Edwards, eds., *Collective Remembering* (London, 1990), *passim*.

20 In a telling editorial move, Gary Taylor and Stanley Wells isolate Act 1 scene 2 to suggest that 'someone – perhaps Thomas Middleton, to judge by the style – seems to have supplied a new, seedy opening' to the scene (843). Such a practice replicates the very displacements enacted by the 'playwright'–Duke of Vienna, shifting responsibility for sexual content from the privileged figure of Shakespeare to an alternative writer.

such memories, it does participate in the memorial cultures of English sexual practices. It also construes sexual memory as simultaneously contested and opaque, as a persistent if evasive cultural form that continually disrupts the dominant memory narratives of state authority.

As noted, the proclamation of Act 1, scene 2 arguably invited playgoers to recall a Stuart Royal Proclamation, issued 16 September 1603, that called for the dissolution of plague-ridden buildings in the city and suburbs of London. Upon closer examination, however, the alleged reference proves a surprisingly imprecise match for the play, testifying less to prostitution than to plague, less to topicality than to persistence – an extended royal campaign, spanning the entirety of the Tudor monarchy, focused upon the unsuccessful suppression of undesirable diseases, spaces and persons: 'excessive numbers of idle, indigent, dissolute, and dangerous persons . . . in the Citie of London, and in about the Suburbes', it alleges, 'have bene one of the chiefest occasions of the great Plague and mortality'. As such, 'His Majestie . . . to avoide the continuance or renewing of such mortalitie . . . doth straightly prohibit and forbid, That no new Tenant or Inmate, or other person or persons, be admitted to inhabite or reside in any such house or place in the saide Citie, Suburbes . . . which have been so infected.' Attempting to limit the spread of 'great Plague and mortality', the proclamation adopts a diseased rhetoric similar to that of the play, yet explicitly emphasizes 'mortality' over sexual commerce; neither brothels nor sexual practices are mentioned. When this privileged document finally refers to the razing of houses, moreover, it cites this practice not as an intervention but as an extension of previous edicts: 'the said Roomes, Houses, or places as by *any Proclamation heretofore published*, are ordered or appointed to be rased or pulled down' (emphasis added). Such predecessors include not only the contemporary – Elizabeth I issued a similar edict on 22 June 1602 – but also the historical: the nearly forty Royal Proclamations attending to these and related issues published between 1487 and 1603.[21] If early modern playgoers associated Pompey's claim with the Stuart proclamation, the

reference likely stimulated memories not simply of suppression but also persistence: an authoritarian failure to extirpate that which was seen as dissolute and diseased.

Pompey's allusion likely stimulated two further memories, both of which significantly alter the play's representation of prostitution: first, the 1546 abolition of state-sanctioned prostitution by royal proclamation under Henry VIII and, second, its perceived persistence throughout the remainder of the sixteenth century. As the Stow account suggests, when writers of the period remembered the official suppression of sexual commerce, they spoke not of 1603, but of 1546. These memories allude to another proclamation – TRP 265, 'Ordering London Brothels Closed', issued 14 April 1546 – that resonates more precisely with the world of Shakespeare's Vienna, and one that also situates itself within an extended legacy of authoritarian failures to suppress the London sex trade. The document remains, to this day, an extant, material mnemonic of English sexual practice in the sixteenth century (see illustrations 16 and 17).

In 1546, the 'King's most excellent majesty, considering how by toleration of such dissolute and miserable persons . . . have been suffered to dwell beside London and elsewhere in common, open places called the stews, and there without punishment or correction exercise their abominable and detestable sin . . . thought [it] requisite utterly to extinct such abominable license'. If the playwrights, actors and playgoers of 1603–4 likely did not have direct access to this text, TRP 265 and *Measure for Measure*'s Duke nonetheless describe state prostitution in strikingly similar language. Closer akin to one another than to the favoured Stuart proclamation, the two in tandem, as well as in combination with other textual traces spanning the century, reveal an array of complex cultural, sexual and political memories swirling at the site of sexual commerce. Focused specifically on the

---

21 Paul L. Hughes and James F. Larkin, eds., *Tudor Royal Proclamations* (New Haven, 1964–9), and *Stuart Royal Proclamations, Vol. I: Royal Proclamations of King James I, 1603–1625* (Oxford, 1973). Citations from SRP 25 (1973).

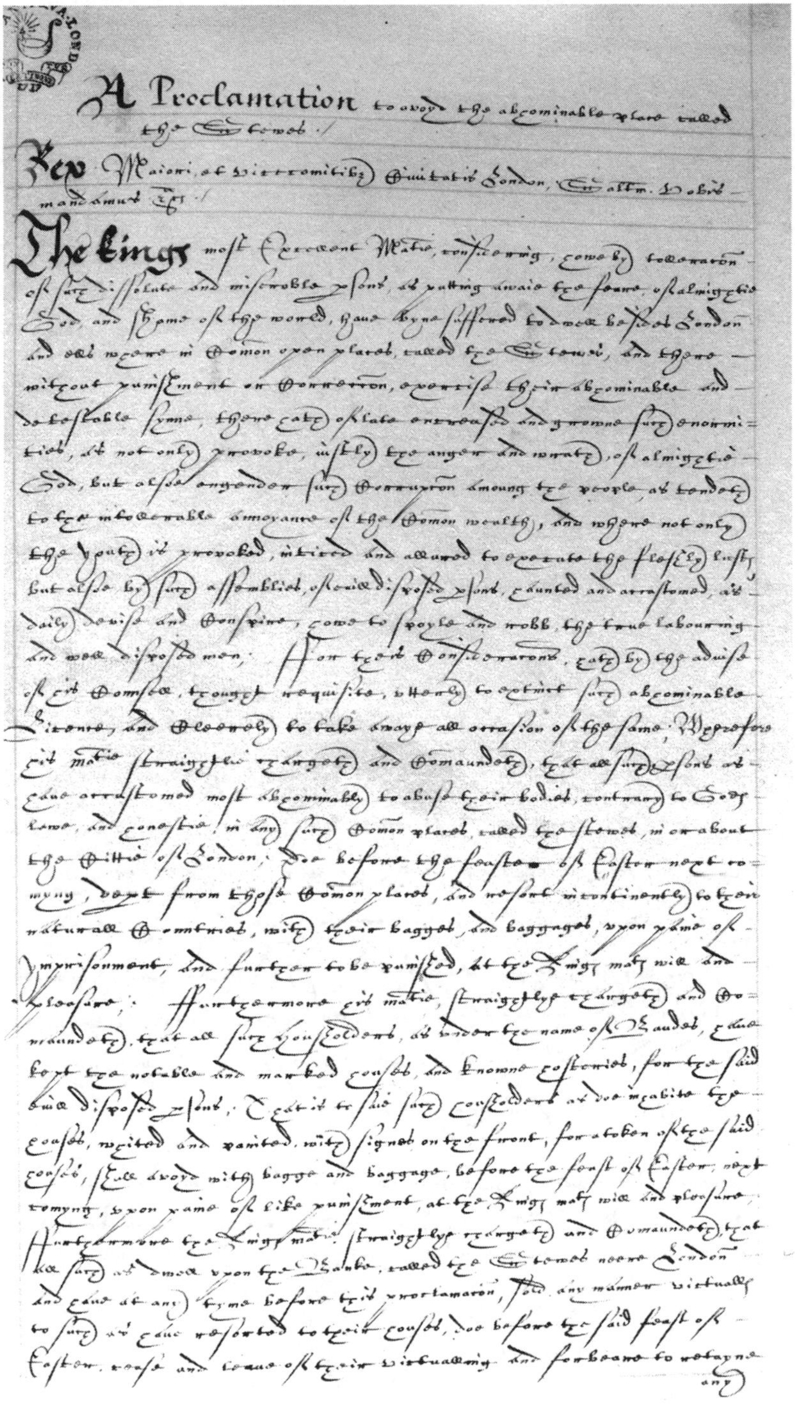
A Proclamation to avoyde the abhominable place called the Stewes./

Rex Maiori et Vicecomitibus Ciuitatis London, Salutem. Vobis mandamus &c. /

The kinges most excellent Maiestie, considering, howe by toleracion of such dissolute and miserable persons, as putting awaie the feare of almightie God, and shame of the worlde, have bene suffered to dwell beside London and els where in common open places, called the Stewes, and there without punishement or correction, exercise their abhominable and detestable synne, there hath of late encreased and growne such enormities, as not only provoke, iustly the anger and wrath, of almightie God, but also engender such corruption amonge the people, as tendeth to the intollerable annoyance of the Common wealth, and where not only the youth is provoked, intised and allured to execute the fleshly lustes, but also by such assemblies of evill disposed persons, haunted and accustomed, is daily devised and conspired, howe to spoyle and robb the true labouring and well disposed men; For these consideracions, hath by the advise of his Counsell, thought requisite, utterly to exterminate such abhominable licence, and clerely to take awaye all occasion of the same; Wherefore his maiestie straightlie chargeth and commaundeth, that all such persons as have accustomed most abhominably to abuse their bodies, contrary to Godes lawe, and honestie, in any such common places, called the stewes, in or about the Cittie of London, doe before the feaste of Easter next commyng, depart from those common places, and resort incontinently to their naturall Countries, with their bagges, and baggages, upon paine of ymprisonment, and further to be punished, at the Kinges maiesties will and pleasure; Furthermore his maiestie, straightlye chargeth and commaundeth, that all such householders, as under the name of Baudes, have kept the notable and marked houses, and knowne hostelries, for the said evill disposed persons, That is to saie such householders as doe inhabite the houses, whited and painted, with signes on the front, for a token of the said houses, shall avoyde with bagge and baggage, before the feast of Easter next comyng, upon paine of like punishment, at the Kinges maiesties will and pleasure; Furthermore the Kinges maiestie straightlye chargeth and commaundeth, that all such as dwell upon the Banke, called the Stewes neere London and have at any tyme before this proclamacion, sold any manner victualles to such as have resorted to their houses, doe before the said feast of Easter, cease and leave of their victualling and forbeare to retayne any

16. Manuscript copy of TRP 265, *c.*late sixteenth century.

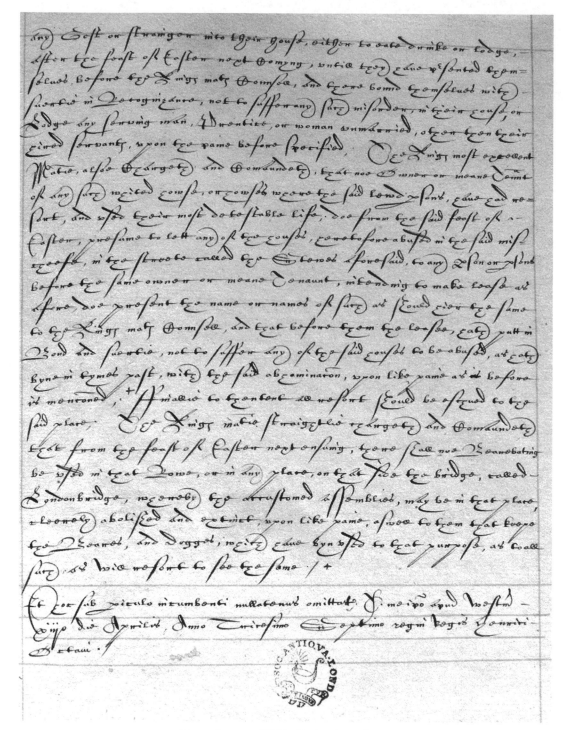

17. Manuscript copy of TRP 265, *c.*late sixteenth century.

London suburbs, the Tudor proclamation decries the 'abominable and detestable sin' of 'persons as have accustomed most abominably to abuse their bodies contrary to God's law and honesty', sentiments quite similar to those of a Duke who castigates the 'abominable and beastly touches' of those who 'believe thy living is a life, / So stinkingly depending' (3.1.292–5). The proclamation also infers the trade's 'abominable license' by state authority. This brief reference, easily overlooked amidst an invective-filled opening paragraph, could indicate a general licentiousness. Yet given the long-standing practice of officially sanctioned prostitution in medieval and early modern London, dating at least as far back as 1276,[22] the allusion possesses further resonances: as in Shakespeare's play, an official proclamation suppressing prostitution simultaneously encodes, and memorializes, state involvement ('license') in sexual commerce. Indeed, *Measure for Measure*'s proclamation itself stimulates memories of past Viennese sexual practices: 'Why', Mistress Overdone notes, 'here's a change indeed in the commonwealth!' (1.2.96–7).

The Henrician suppression appears to have succeeded, at least on one level: following the 1546 proclamation, prostitution disappears from the royal record.[23] The document thus memorializes a pivotal moment, or transition, in the histories of London prostitution: the date upon which the Tudor monarchy formally revoked its 'abominable license' of London sex work. Yet the cultural memories associated with this suppression – including those potentially stimulated and produced in and by *Measure for Measure* – offer an alternative narrative, one that posits the proclamation not as an end but a beginning, not as an erasure but as the inauguration of an official forgetting, an ongoing memory practice that actively enabled the unofficial toleration of sexual commerce. Silenced within one medium of cultural memory (Tudor records), the proclamation took on new life in other discursive fields,[24] including the London stage.

While such memories enrich *Measure for Measure*'s second scene, they also raise important conceptual and epistemological concerns. Slotted between the Duke's narrative deferral (1.1) and

the acknowledgement of his complicity (1.3), this scene provides the essential content of Viennese sexual memory, touching upon issues of fornication, prostitution, venereal disease, sexual geography, bawdy language, marriage, lechery, desire, religion and authority. Yet just as the scene progresses towards the potential fatal significance of Juliet's (absent) pregnant body, it simultaneously questions whether sexual practices signify and, if so, where and how they might be remembered.

The scene begins by exploring the materiality of memory. In a humorous if seemingly trivial exchange, Lucio opens by discussing a prospective war with Hungary, arguing that his hawkish counterparts, like 'sanctimonious' pirates who head out 'to sea with the Ten Commandments', conveniently ignore injunctions that counter their material or martial desires. In so doing, pirate and soldier alike symbolically 'raze' the letter of Divine Law, scraping undesirable prohibitions from the surface 'of the table' (1.2.7–9). The intense materiality of this image – an audacious sinner chiselling commandments from Moses's tablet – emphasizes the labour necessary to banish unwanted edicts into absentia. Adopting the languages of *ars memoria*, the exchange speaks to a central legal, ethical and memorial concern raised in several Shakespearian works: can one effectively raze or erase that which exists in memory?[25] Macbeth hopes to 'pluck' the 'rooted sorrow' from his wife's 'memory', yet can find no 'antidote' to 'raze out the written troubles' plaguing her conscience (*Macbeth*, 5.3.43–4). Upon his father's death, Prince Hal declares his intention

---

22 Ruth Mazo Karras, *Common Women: Prostitution and Sexuality in Medieval England* (New York, 1996).

23 Hughes and Larkin, *Tudor Royal Proclamations*.

24 See for example Hugh Latimer, 'The Third Sermon of M. Hugh Latimer, Preached before King Edward (1549)', in *Sermons by Hugh Latimer Sometime Bishop of Worcester* (London, 1906). John Taylor, 'A Whore', in *The Works of John Taylor, The Water-Poet, not included in the Folio Volume of 1630* (Manchester, 1870–1888).

25 Cf. Peter Stallybrass, Roger J. Chartier, Franklin Mowery and Heather Wolfe, 'Hamlet's Tables and the Technologies of Writing in Renaissance England', *Shakespeare Quarterly*, 55 (1996), 379–419.

to 'raze' the memory of his former 'vanity' in *2 Henry IV* (5.2.126–9), yet the Dauphin attests to its clear persistence in *Henry V*, noting that 'as matching to his youth and vanity, / I did present him with the Paris balls' (2.4.130–1). Gloucester, shocked to hear of the king's marriage to Margaret in *2 Henry VI*, argues that this marital alliance will blot their 'names from books of memory, / razing the characters of [their] renown', only to find himself razed from their presence (1.1.97–8). And, perhaps most famously, the speaker of Sonnet 122 ('Thy gift, thy tables, are within my brain') argues that one's internal memory far outlasts the external mnemonic.

Throughout Shakespeare's works, memories persist 'Beyond all date, even to eternity', even in the face of external forces seeking 'razed oblivion'. Only death, the sonnet speaker implies, can defeat memory: 'so long as brain and heart / Have faculty by nature to subsist ... thy record never can be missed' (Sonnet 122, lines 4–8). From such a perspective, Lucio's suggestions of erasure encode as well the possibilities – indeed likelihood – of remembrance and return: not only of Viennese sexual law, whose 'enrolled penalties' have 'like unscoured armour, hung by th' wall / So long that fourteen zodiacs have gone round' (1.2.143–4), but also, and paradoxically, the practices of prostitution that demanded such penalties in the first place. His comments, moreover, suggest that practices of forgetting themselves depend upon, and may well solidify, the very memories they seek to suppress. To forget divine law, he argues, the sinner must scrape the table itself; analogously, when Angelo attempts to erase the places and practices of prostitution from the face of the city, he recognizes their presence. Indeed, the very authority he draws upon to suppress prostitution derives from two mnemonics that testify to its presence and ensure its memorial persistence: the original edict outlawing fornication and the subsequent proclamation suppressing sexual commerce.

Focused upon official statutes, whether material or ethereal, this humorous exchange moreover highlights relations of the individual and the collective: what happens when the pirate simply ignores or reconfigures a mandate from above? Given the play's religious allusions, especially conceptions of justice rooted in the biblical phrase 'measure for measure', the Gentlemen's philosophy appears foolish. Yet the episode pointedly distinguishes between human and divine law: just as Lucio opens the scene by defending the authority of divine law, he closes it by decrying the application of a pointedly human law – absent from the Ten Commandments – that erroneously equates human 'life' with a 'game of tick-tack' (1.2.177–8). The double-entendre, one of many that saturate the particular scene, proves especially significant. In their semiotic imprecision, such metaphors posit the scene's central dramatic, political and epistemological questions: to what, exactly, does Lucio refer? How does – or does – 'tick-tack' signify sex? How might these exchanges remember and forget Viennese sexual practice? How, ultimately, does one know the sexual practices of another?

In addition to official edicts, whether divine commandment or state proclamation, this early scene also introduces an array of sexual mnemonics that enclose their own polymorphous narratives. Centred upon the conspicuous visibility of Juliet and Claudio's sexual relations – their 'most mutual entertainment / With character too gross is writ' upon her swelling womb – the scene locates the body itself as one memorial register (1.2.142–3). This exemplary case foregrounds gender as a critically operative category, yet exactly what Juliet's pregnant body signifies remains in question.[26] Indeed, where 'pregnant' in the play indicates both a parturient condition and the possession of knowledge – as noted, the Duke opens by praising Escalus's 'pregnant ... art and practice' – Juliet's mnemonic body proves both symbolically rich and polyvalent. Whereas Angelo reads it as the sign of abhorrent fornication (2.2.23), Claudio cites

---

[26] Mario DiGangi, 'Pleasure and Danger: Measuring Female Sexuality in *Measure for Measure*', *ELH* 60 (1993), 589–609.

it as a reminder of their mutual enjoyment. Speaking to Isabella, Lucio remembers Juliet's womb as the expression of natural growth and fecundity, a construction the pious Isabella immediately associates with marriage (1.4.39–48).

Acknowledging the polyvalent memorial possibilities of the parturient woman, the scene further complicates its sexual hermeneutics by considering other bodies and practices. Following their opening repartee, Lucio and the gentlemen debate just how and whether their (male) bodies bear the traces of past sexual practices – whether they 'art tainted or free' (1.2.41–2). When the first Gentleman claims he can read syphilis in Lucio's absent hair – or, more specifically, in the velvet used to cover his bald spots – his counterpart responds by detecting the signs of disease in their symptomatic absence: the Gentleman is 'sound as things that are hollow – thy bones are hollow, impiety has made a feast of thee' (1.2.53–5). This dialogue soon incorporates Mistress Overdone, whose sciatic hips the men attempt to read as indicators of venereal disease (1.2.56–7).

The scene's constant punning and double entendres foreground the play's epistemological and memorial politics. Just as the gentlemen appear to speak of and about sex, sexuality, fornication, prostitution, whoredom, syphilis, brothels and desire, these terms are conspicuously absent from their dialogue – they are, quite literally, never spoken in this exchange. Instead, sexual memories assume alternative shapes and forms, appearing opaquely in bodies, bawdy allusions, clothing, proclamations, taverns and even names themselves: Mistress Overdone bears the traces of her marital and sexual past in an infamous appellation, one further supplemented by the moniker 'Madam Mitigation' (1.2.42). Through such polymorphous traces and polyvalent mnemonics, Viennese sexual practices surface everywhere and nowhere at once. Like Lucio's Ten Commandments, the state may scrape commercial sexuality from the face of the city table, yet its practices and languages persist in this scene, as ethereal as they are material. When Pompey introduces the proclamation, he famously notes that the brothels inside the city 'shall stand for seed', but also suggests that those of the suburbs will survive by adopting new forms, names or locales: 'Come, fear you not. Good counselors lack no clients. Though you change your place, you need not change your trade' (1.2.91–100). By suppressing the visible sites and standard mnemonics of illicit sexuality, he argues, state authorities have merely catalysed the evolution and adaptation of sexual commerce in the early modern city. 'I'll be your tapster still' (1.2.100), he claims, inferring that Viennese prostitution will be re-membered – quite literally, put back together – under the guise of tavern keeping.[27]

Pompey's suggestion, neither contested nor negated by the citizens of Vienna, explicates a curious side-note in TRP 265: bawds must 'leave off their victualing and forbear to retain any guest or stranger into their house either to eat and drink or lodge'. In a pointed effort to divorce food and housing from sites of sexual commerce, the proclamation reveals an anxiety that, once the 'houses white and painted with signs on the front for a token' are removed, all houses will prove sexually suspect. From this perspective, Pompey's comments can be seen to participate in the vast conceptual distribution of urban prostitution in late Elizabethan and early Jacobean literature: even if working brothels were generally restricted to a few select areas in early modern London, often along or outside the city walls (Southwark, Aldgate, Cock Lane, Ram Alley, Smithfield, Clerkenwell, Whitefriars), they could be imagined anywhere. Thus one finds, in the literary records of the time, dozens of city spaces associated with sexual commerce, including such prominent locations as Bishopsgate, Cheapside, Fleet Street, Guildhall, Holborn, Tabard Street, Lambeth Marsh, Paris Garden, the Royal Exchange, Shoreditch, Spitalfields, St Thomas's Hospital, Westminster and

---

[27] On the association of brothels and taverns in early modern England, see especially Howard, *Theatre of a City*, and Alan Bray, *Homosexuality in Renaissance England* (New York, 1982).

even St Paul's Cathedral.[28] *Measure for Measure*'s proclamation participates in this memorial tradition: far from restricting or razing sexual spaces, the Viennese proclamation catalyses their literal and conceptual distribution throughout the city. In the attempt to elide its own explicit relations to sexual commerce, the play suggests, the state further relinquishes its capacity to identify, control and/or contain practices of illicit sexuality. Arguing that prostitution will not only persist but permeate Vienna, *Measure for Measure* encourages readers and playgoers to consider just how sex will be remembered – not only recollected, that is, but also assume new shapes and relations in the early modern city.

NOTORIOUS BODIES

Like *Pericles* and *Troilus and Cressida*, discourses of prostitution in *Measure for Measure* conspicuously associate sexual commerce with death and disease. Yet even as Lucio claims that he has 'purchased' multiple 'diseases' from Mistress Overdone (1.2.44), he and his fellow citizens do not seem particularly concerned about their physical health; it is the interventions of the state, not their own sexual practices, that threaten their well-being. The men joke about syphilis and mock one another's potential contagion, and while the play's sexual discourses are infused with a diseased rhetoric, not a single character articulates pain or suffering associated with venereal infections – even as the play explicitly recognizes that illicit sexual activities have occurred, not only between Juliet and Claudio, but Angelo and Mariana as well as Lucio and Kate Keepdown. Instead, the gravity of the play's sexual politics derives not from, in Angelo's words, a 'stained' body, but rather a condemned one (2.4.55). As Claudio is paraded through the streets, his shackled body exemplifies state intercession in the sexual practices of its citizens. Witness to such punitive and capricious sexual politics, Lucio decries authoritarian hypocrisy, as well as, in his terms, an unhealthy, puritanical approach to human sexual practices.

While Lucio playfully debates his own potentially diseased status, he also derides Angelo as a 'man whose blood is very snow-broth: one who never feels the wanton stings and motions of the sense' (1.4.56–8). Speaking to the disguised Duke later in the play, he draws on contemporary humoral discourses to construct the deputy as an unnatural, almost inhuman figure: 'they say this Angelo was not made by man and woman . . . some report a sea-maid spawned him, some that he was begot between two stockfishes. But it is certain that when he makes water his urine is congealed ice; that I know to be true. And he is a motion unregenerative; that's infallible' (3.1.368–76). It is an opinion ratified by the Duke and even, albeit implicitly, Angelo himself: 'Lord Angelo is precise', the Duke informs the Friar, he 'stands at a guard with envy, scarce confesses / That his blood flows, or that his appetite / Is more to bread than stone' (1.3.50–3). In contrast to the porous body of early medical discourses, one whose health depends upon the steady flow or movement of bodily humours, Angelo is stopped, frozen and unnatural. If coldness could, in some instances, indicate the healthy moderation of unruly desires, Angelo represents not moderation but extremism.[29] Once stirred by desires, Angelo's erotic subjectivity shifts dramatically from an almost inhuman abstemiousness ('his appetite / is more bread than stone') to an uncontrolled and rapacious gluttony: 'And now I give my sensual race the rein', he tells Isabella, 'fit thy consent to my sharp appetite' (2.4.160–1).

In this immoderate rejection of sexual desire and practice, Angelo again substitutes for the Viennese Duke: both fashion themselves as possessors of a 'complete bosom' impermeable to desire. Yet as

---

[28] In addition to studies previously cited, see Gustav Ungerer, 'Prostitution in Late Elizabethan London: The Case of Mary Newborough', *Medieval and Renaissance Drama in England*, 15 (2002), 138–223; Peter Ackroyd, *London: A Biography* (London, 2000); Wallace Shugg, 'Prostitution in Shakespeare's London', *Shakespeare Studies*, 10 (1977), 291–313.

[29] Michael C. Schoenfeldt, *Bodies and Selves in Early Modern England: Physiology and Inwardness in Spenser, Shakespeare, Herbert, and Milton* (Cambridge, 1999).

they do so, an array of Viennese subjects – Lucio, Pompey and Overdone, but also Escalus, Isabella and the Provost – openly critique such extreme views, especially from those empowered to police others; in their manifold rejoinders, these figures allege that to 'measure' the practices or desires of another, one must first remember sex, both on an individual and cultural scale. While the Duke and Angelo actively attempt to forget sex, Isabella and the Provost frame Claudio's punishment in direct relation to Viennese sexual history: 'all sects, all ages smack of this vice', the Provost decries, yet Claudio will 'die for it!' (2.2.5–6). Isabella then echoes this sentiment, imploring Angelo to remember 'who is it that hath died for this offence? / There's many that have committed it' (2.2.90–1). Such recollections foreground notions of justice and equity – as Lucio notes, 'for the rebellion of a codpiece to take away the life of a man!' (3.1.378–9) – but also of empathy: an ability to see oneself in the actions of another. Even Escalus, who invariably supports the Duke's positions and policies, encourages Angelo to remember his own temptations when judging Claudio, to envision himself in the place of the man he condemns (2.1.8–16). When Angelo disregards the entreaty, he sets the stage for his fall from grace and power.

To remember sex in *Measure for Measure* is neither to celebrate nor recuperate prostitution as a cultural institution, but rather to examine how cultures and institutions recall, identify, enable, suppress, forget and overlook sexual commerce. Moreover, to position Lucio as a figure of memory seeks not to valorize his actions, including his notorious denigration and abandonment of Kate Keepdown, but to adopt an alternative framework through which audiences might perceive the sexual politics of Shakespeare's Vienna. From such a perspective, Lucio can be seen as a libertine Antigone: a figure of counter-memory who conspicuously challenges the state's proclaimed disinterest in sexual desire and commerce, an incessant voice – 'not bid to speak' – who speaks precisely that which state authority seeks to silence and suppress. A peripatetic figure, Lucio traverses the many sexual

spaces of Vienna, interacts with characters across the social spectrum and lays claim to an alternative understanding of 'the nature of our people, / our city's institutions, and the terms / for common justice'. Arguing on behalf of sexual practice as a natural human condition, as common as 'eating and drinking' (3.1.368), he conspicuously remembers the sex that the state seeks to forget. Crossing the many sites of sexual memory, debating the sexually mnemonic body and playing with bawdily imprecise yet evocative language, he embodies desires, practices and memories that the Duke seeks to 'extirp' (3.1.367). Proclaiming that the state itself possesses desire, he links sex and state – a union later concretized in the Duke's abrupt marriage to Isabella (5.1.491). Disregarding inferences of syphilis, he challenges constructions of sex as corrupt or diseased. Hailing Mistress Overdone as Madam Mitigation, he infers that prostitution may serve a healthy body politic.[30] Surmising that the Duke himself has patronized prostitutes, he locates Viennese authority at the very centre of the city's sex trade, foreshadowing the play's final acts of bawdry.

To restore order in the play's final scene, the Duke must reveal himself: he has to return from absence to author his narrative. Threatened with torture for articulating (as the Friar) the corruptions of his state, faced with inferences of his own licentiousness, and responsible for the sexual liaison of Angelo and Mariana, he depends upon the authority of his office to enforce his memories – and, significantly, to silence Lucio. As is well known, the Duke concludes the play by ordering the monetary and marital relations of Vienna: he aligns Claudio with Juliet, Angelo with Mariana, and himself with Isabella. Yet while marriage serves as his privileged mechanism of social reconciliation, it simultaneously conjoins sexual commerce

---

[30] See also Elbow's famous malapropism construing Pompey and Froth as 'notorious benefactors' (2.1.48), a sobriquet that alludes to the long-standing construction, derived from Augustine and remembered by Thomas Aquinas, of prostitution as a necessary evil.

with state authority. Indeed, Lucio's enforced marriage to Kate Keepdown metonymically aligns such unions with the absent prostitutions of the Viennese state: the prostitute becomes the wife, the client a husband. Gesturing towards a 'palace' offstage, the Duke promises that the narrative will continue: 'we'll show / What's yet behind that's meet you all should know' (5.1.537–8). As memory work persists beyond the world of the play, playgoers are left to wonder just how the prostitutions of past and present will be remembered – and forgotten – in the future.

OTHELLO ACROSS BORDERS: ON AN INTERLOCAL AND INTERMEDIAL EXERCISE

RUI CARVALHO HOMEM

This article discusses an appropriation of Shakespeare that is defined by a sense of liminality and transit in both its semiotic status and its referential range. *Bandanna* (1999), an opera by Daron Aric Hagen with a libretto by the Irish poet Paul Muldoon, dislocates the plot of *Othello* to the fraught setting of a town on the border of the US and Mexico in the internationally momentous year of 1968. As argued below, this borderline circumstance, its territorial perplexities compounded by the plight of illegal immigration and played out against a background of international tension, enhances the tragedy's dimension of conflict. Muldoon's concise libretto is undoubtedly a much less complex dramatic construction than the Shakespearian text of which it offers a starkly abridged rewriting, but the very need for compression sets out with particular sharpness the clashes of perception and will, and the corresponding lineaments and delineations, that inform the plot of *Othello*. *Bandanna* constantly foregrounds the notion of the boundary, both at the level of representation and in its formal enactment: indeed, this article will look into the relations between this pervasive theme and the encounter of text and music in this opera, and will hence query the extent to which a nexus of conflict can pervade and disturb the collaborative rapport between Muldoon's libretto and Hagen's score.[1]

Paul Muldoon's decision to carry out a rewriting of *Othello* is hardly a surprise, since he has long been noted for a poetics of appropriation. His poetry collections are punctuated by translations, often of an iconoclastic nature – a tendency that brings them notoriously close to his sustained practice of pastiche, parody and truncated quotation.[2] A defiant but learned confrontation with the shadow of canonical predecessors has also proved persistent in his work, as in the title sequence of his collection *Madoc* (1990), a long intertextual ramble in which each short text is placed under the aegis of a major figure in western intellectual history.[3] Further, his appropriations have occasionally included drama, as with his version of Aristophanes's *The Birds* (1999), which translates this satirical comedy into the still anxious and sometimes perplexing scenarios of post-Troubles Belfast.[4]

The year in which this Aristophanic venture came out also saw the publication of *Bandanna*, Muldoon's Shakespearian version. This was his third libretto for an opera by Daron Aric Hagen, and a confirmation that the genre has provided

---

[1] William Shakespeare, *Othello*, ed. E. A. J. Honigmann, Arden Shakespeare (London, 1997); Paul Muldoon, *Bandanna: An Opera in Two Acts and a Prologue* (London, 1999); Daron Aric Hagen's *Bandanna*, Opera in Two Acts & a Prologue, Libretto by Paul Muldoon. The UNLV Opera Theatre and Wind Orchestra. 2 Discs. (Albany, NY, 2006).

[2] See Paul Muldoon's *Poems 1968–1998* (London, 2001). Useful critical studies of his work include Jefferson Holdridge, *The Poetry of Paul Muldoon* (Dublin, 2008); Elmer Kennedy-Andrews, ed., *Paul Muldoon, Poetry, Prose*; Tim Kendall and Peter McDonald, eds., *Paul Muldoon: Critical Essays* (Liverpool, 2004).

[3] Paul Muldoon, *Madoc – A Mystery* (London, 1990).

[4] *The Birds: translated from Aristophanes by Paul Muldoon with Richard Martin* (Oldcastle, Co. Meath, 1999). For a more extended discussion of these appropriations, see the chapter on Muldoon in my *Poetry and Translation in Northern Ireland: Dislocations in Contemporary Writing* (2009), pp. 147–65.

Muldoon with an apt scope for the 'American drift' of his work of the past twenty-five years. The plots of all three operas are constructed around American settings and themes, qualified or queried by the breadth of Muldoon's allusions, textual and otherwise (including the continued undertow of Irish reference in his writing). *Shining Brow* (1993) is about a decisive period in the life and work of architect Frank Lloyd Wright, construed as an emblematic but paradoxical exponent of WASP culture. *Vera of Las Vegas* (premièred in 1996, published in 2001) concerns the present-day scene, but its contemporaneity is problematized by the omnipresence of simulacra in its named setting, against which a pair of perplexed IRA terrorists are made to interact with immigration officers, secret agents and stage entertainers.[5] Finally, *Bandanna* (1999) dramatizes private conflicts in the framework of a community under duress, a 'tiny town on the border of the US and Mexico', and it does so by calquing, inflecting and streamlining *Othello* – in its plot, characterization and defining conflicts.

The broader contours of Muldoon's sharply simplified intralingual version can be glimpsed from the outset in the opera's list of *dramatis personae*, and in the libretto's opening stage directions. The border town's 'Latino chief of police' is called Morales; should one fail to note that this hints at a 'Moro' or 'Moor' (with some possible extra wordplay on *mores* and an allusion to the character's musings over morals), the appropriation becomes transparent when one reads on to find that 'Morales' white lieutenant' goes by the name of Jake (for Iago), whereas 'Morales' white wife' is Mona (for Desdemona); her 'best friend' and 'Jake's Latino fiancée' is Emily (for Emilia); and 'Morales's Irish-American captain' is called Cassidy (for Cassio).

The nature of the setting is decisive for a recognition of the conditions under which, in *Bandanna*, an early modern English play originally placed in the Mediterranean exoticism of Venice and Cyprus is dislocated to the Hispanic underbelly of late twentieth-century America, with an Irish inflection. The little border town has enough of the characteristics of an outpost to make it a 'version' of *Othello*'s Cyprus, and in this case the plot begins already there – i.e. on the Tex-Mex border. The decision not to offer a rendering of the text, characterization and plot elements found in Shakespeare's Act 1, dispensing with its miniature romantic comedy,[6] means that Muldoon's enabling source may be, besides the Jacobean play, a hallowed nineteenth-century precedent in opera: Verdi and Arrigo Boito's *Otello* (1887).[7] Indeed, whereas Rossini and Francesco Maria Berio, in their earlier opera after Shakespeare's play (*Otello*, 1816), had opted to set the whole plot in Venice, Verdi and Boito's influential appropriation strikingly favoured the spatial economy and dramatic concentration gained by opening with the sea storm and rough sea-crossing watched from Cyprus at the beginning of (Shakespeare's) Act 2, scene 1.[8] (The argument for doing so had, in fact, its own history within Shakespeare criticism, especially as a reflection of neoclassical strictures, as attested by Samuel Johnson's belief that 'had the scene opened in Cyprus . . . there had been little wanting to a drama of the most exact and scrupulous regularity'.)[9]

---

[5] Paul Muldoon, *Shining Brow* (London, 1993); Paul Muldoon, *Vera of Las Vegas* (Loughcrew, 2001).

[6] For a 'classic' diagnosis of Shakespeare's tragic plots as evolving from a comedic first stage, see Susan Snyder's *The Comic Matrix of Shakespeare's Tragedies* (Princeton, 1979).

[7] Several comments on libretti and music scores in this article refer to Libretti d'opera italiani. www.librettidopera.it/otello/otello.html and International Music Score Library Project (IMSLP), http://imslp.org/ (accessed 31 August 2012).

[8] Compared readings of these two operas punctuate Gary Schmidgall's *Shakespeare and Opera* (New York, 1990). See also Lisa Hopkins, '"What Did thy Song Bode, Lady?": *Othello* as Operatic Text', in Holger Klein and Christopher Smith, eds., *The Opera and Shakespeare*, vol. 4 of the *Shakespeare Yearbook* (Lewiston, 1994), pp. 61–70; Roberta Montemorra Marvin, 'Shakespeare and *Primo Ottocento* Italian Opera: the Case of Rossini's *Otello*', in *The Opera and Shakespeare*, pp. 71–95; Arthur Graham, *Shakespeare in Opera, Ballet, Orchestral Music, and Song: An Introduction to Music Inspired by the Bard* (Lewiston, 1997), pp. 103–65.

[9] *The Plays of William Shakespeare*, ed. Samuel Johnson (London, 1765), vol. 8, p. 473.

Bandanna also begins with a hazardous crossing, although in this case involving a land border, the desolate location for the hardships of illegal immigrants wanting to enter the US from Mexico. Their predicament and the record of lost lives on the border are poignantly and allegorically presented in the opera's prologue through the chorus of 'Illegal Immigrants', who don 'a skeleton costume and mask associated with the Day of the Dead' (the *Dia de los Muertos*). Such a circumstance provides them with a welcome disguise, but it also adds to the gloom and eeriness of the scene. 2 November 1968 is the date given for the opera's action, and the 'chorus of the Dispossessed and the Disappeared' indeed signal this topicality by chanting, 'To live is to sleep. / To die is to awaken' (1),[10] 'We know what it's like to hover / between life and death' (2). They also recite lines in Spanish that (through a proverbial-sounding phrase) trope their land crossing in watery terms, a passage that could be a distant echo of Shakespeare's 'high-wrought flood', 'the haven and the main', the 'chidden billow' in *Othello* 2.1: 'Llegaremos de solapo / entre dos aguas' (we'll arrive in stealth / between two waters, i.e. with our fate undecided) (1).

From the outset, *Bandanna* becomes a major example of Muldoon's commitment to the theme of diffuse boundaries, a confirmation of this poet's interest in equivocal arrangements of geographic and social space. This is an aspect of Muldoon's poetics in which a specific authorial inclination converges with cultural determinants – especially the fascination, so much in evidence in areas of the humanities and social sciences in recent decades, with the ambivalent and the liminal, with practices and artifacts that resist a logic of autarky or self-containment.[11] In the particular case of *Bandanna*, the border, with its difficult transits and experienced under the particular indefiniteness of the *Dia de los Muertos*, becomes an immediately evident and all-pervasive theme. The text can in fact be said to suffer from an excessive use of phrases such as 'the liminal zone', 'a liminal place', 'the thin red line', 'this no-man's land, this *zona media*'. As suggested above, this may reflect the intellectual and cultural

favour currently enjoyed by the notion, but Jake (Iago), the police lieutenant, makes it clear that the border is here a lot more than a fashionable construct:

> They say the border is a state of mind.
> I think that's a little bit ill-defined.
> It's real enough to *mis compadres*
> who hoof it over the Sierra Madre
> for days on end. That's real enough. (7)

Jake is here resorting to irony: ambivalence is a defining trait of Iago's that cannot but persist in Muldoon's version. The use of Spanish in this passage is a mark of contempt rather than sympathy, and the fact that Jake is known to the illegal immigrants by the name of 'San Joaquín' is also sardonically considered by him in a soliloquy on his 'double life' (17); indeed, Jake's alias gives additional depth to his duplicitous nature, since it is the name of a biblical figure (Mary's father) with a twin brother called Jacob (a name of which *Iago* is a version).[12] Despite the irony and contempt that mark his pronouncements on those he manipulates, Jake also denounces suffering and oppression, and he will even claim that his plot against Morales is based on the wish to make him 'remember that he, too, was dispossessed' (18).

Indeed, double-edged behaviour affects in one way or another Muldoon's full gallery of characters, a case in point being the 'labor organizer' Kane. He is a self-appointed mouthpiece for the downtrodden – a denouncer of the iniquities of 'the land of the free' who obtains the ironical epithets of 'Citizen Kane' and 'Comrade Kanovitch' respectively from Cassidy and Morales. However,

---

[10] Bracketed references following quotations from Muldoon's text indicate page numbers.

[11] The pervasiveness of such notions in the current intellectual environment would make any list of references inadequate and unconvincing; however, if one book were to be singled out for its influence in establishing the critical productiveness of notions of liminality and transit in recent years it could arguably be Homi K. Bhabha's *The Location of Culture* (London, 1994).

[12] Cf 'Saint Joachim', *Saints.SQPN.com*. http://saints.sqpn.com/saint-joachim/ – accessed 31/08/2012.

Kane is also a racketeer who profits from the illegal immigrants that he brings over the border by night and bears a grudge against the chief of police for spoiling his trade. His presence among the *dramatis personae* foregrounds one of the most striking inflections that *Bandanna* introduces, as a rewriting of *Othello*: Muldoon largely splits the character of Iago between Jake and Kane, although the latter also integrates features that arguably derive from Shakespeare's and Verdi's Roderigo and Montano. This structural decision, which curiously runs counter to the tendency for compression and plot simplification that one otherwise finds in *Bandanna* (as in other operatic appropriations), allows Muldoon to provide a double motivation for the course of action that, in Shakespeare's play, is pursued singly by the character of Iago. The compounded rationale for Jake's and Kane's musings and deeds in *Bandanna* can almost be seen as endorsing the critical view of Iago as lacking verisimilitude – or, in other terms, as offering a response to Coleridge's much-quoted diagnosis of Iago's 'motiveless malignity' as revealed in his incessant 'motive-hunting'.[13] If Muldoon's decision indeed arises from a wish to ground Iago's plotting on an easier-to-grasp representation of human motives and behaviour, then it manifests itself paradoxically in a medium – opera – which, in its commonplace description as 'larger than life', would seem to be farther than non-musical drama from expectations of a naturalistic kind.

Throughout *Bandanna*, Kane becomes a dramatic device for bringing out some of the plot's less savoury actualities. It is also primarily through Kane that the audience is made aware of both the great causes that mark the plot's historical backdrop – 'the Kennedys or Martin Luther King' (25) – and the actual or latent conflicts of the Cold War era: 'the Commie thing', Kosygin, LBJ, 'Cambodia or Nam', chairman Mao (24–6). Through Kane's political ambivalence, the tone in which such references are summoned into the text of *Bandanna* is less defined by a sense of insurmountable otherness than was the case in *Othello* with allusions to the Ottoman, the 'malignant and turbaned Turk' of the early modern geopolitical imagination. This

combines with a likewise distinct rhetoric of war: Morales and Jake (and indeed also Cassidy) are fairly uncompromising in their assumption of the battle-field logic when they reminisce about their days as soldiers 'together in Vietnam' (29); nonetheless, their remembered martial scenarios have nothing of the 'pride, pomp and circumstance of glorious war' the loss of which Othello mourns (3.3.357). Military jargon (or 'epithets of war' – *Othello* 1.1.13), when used by characters in *Bandanna*, tends rather to have the bleak, counter-rhetorical concision of acronyms that remain unglossed in the text: 'that fateful R and R' (14 – for 'rest and recreation'), 'across the DMZ' (15 – for 'demilitarized zone').

The opera's sense of the actual is thoroughly informed by a logic of conflict, both broadly political and tragically interpersonal; it concerns the general environment that provides a backdrop to the plot of *Bandanna*, but also the particularity of Muldoon's renderings of Shakespeare's various characters, as agents of a clash of wills and of a series of incompatible readings of their circumstances from which the tragic design unfolds. The potential for conflict is closely related to the complex structure of social and ethnic divides within the mostly deprived community that composes the scene of *Bandanna*, in which Latinos coexist uneasily with 'white trash' and occasional strays from other social groups. Compounded by the rough actuality of the border (as emphasized above), this dimension of conflict has a wealth of implications for the formal and thematic specificities of this Shakespearian version.

A good critical foothold for considering such implications is provided by an element of a paratextual nature, the cover chosen for *Bandanna* (in the only edition to date). It shows an *ex voto* kept at the sanctuary of San Juan de los Lagos (in Mexico), a naïf painting of a group of illegal immigrants kneeling behind a bush to hide from the border police, while, hovering in mid-air, an apparition of the

---

[13] Samuel Taylor Coleridge, 'Lectures 1808–1819: On Literature', ed. R. A. Foakes, vol. 2, in *The Collected Works of Samuel Taylor Coleridge* (Princeton, 1987), p. 315.

Virgin Mary (surrounded by angels) shares the skies with a helicopter, complete with a spotlight; in the distance, almost like a mirage, one can glimpse the skyscrapers of an American city. The scene is captioned: 'We give thanks to Our Lady of San Juan for keeping us free from the Immigration officers on our passage to Los Angeles.'[14] The picture is the expression of an act of thanks for a successful, illegal border-crossing, experienced on hands and knees, and it merges the loyalty of religious devotion with an admission of civic transgression. Its naiveté complicates perceptions of the relation between norm and deviation, as also between Catholic submissiveness before Providence and a heroic but venal forcefulness; in doing so, it alerts us to the perplexities posed by accommodating the tragic structure to the particular social and political set-up into which Muldoon brings the plot of *Othello*.

As a verbal and dramatic artifact, Muldoon's libretto is plainly much less complex than Shakespeare's *Othello*; but one of the implications of this obvious difference in scope and elaborateness is that the tragic design can become more immediately apparent.[15] This could arguably reflect the foreshortening imposed by translating (intralingually) a five-act early modern tragedy into a libretto for 'an opera in two acts & a prologue' (total duration: less than two hours) – even though the rewriting was carried out by a hailed exponent of poetic postmodernism whose work often seems to thrive on formal transgressiveness. However, some of the aspects that make the tragedy (even) more clear-cut in *Bandanna* derive from adding rather than subtracting plot features. Muldoon builds up the plausibility and the rational grounds for Jake's plotting (no 'motiveless malignity' here, to echo Coleridge again) by enhancing the element of corruption, since Jake is involved in the illegal immigration scheme and aware that Morales will sooner or later arrest him, unless he destroys him first (18, 30). Additionally, this dimension of the plot involves unqualified victims – unlike Shakespeare's Roderigo, construed as partly responsible for his own victimhood because of his folly – and this means that Jake's criminal guilt as a profiteer is a lot more evident than Iago's abuse of Roderigo's

'purse' (a plot strand that stems from the traditions of comedy[16]). Another, possibly even more telling example of Muldoon's practice in this regard is made apparent in an additional retributive feature, indeed made into the opera's iconic artifact and its title reference: the bandanna – a Tex-Mex correlative of Shakespeare's 'handkerchief', supposed proof of infidelity – becomes the weapon with which Morales strangles Mona (51). Through this particular inflection to the plot, it is as if Muldoon were maximizing the element of nemesis and design by adding a quasi-fastidious twist to Iago's suggestion, 'strangle her in her bed – even the bed she hath contaminated' (*Othello*, 4.1.204–5).

Such thicker dramatic contours might seem to lend an ironical tinge to a statement that Muldoon includes in an early stage direction, specifically bearing on stage design, but clearly informed by a broader compositional ambition: 'the essence of the design is understatement' (5). However, those elements of a sharper (also rougher) plot delineation in *Bandanna* are played out against the traits of indefiniteness derived from the pervasive theme of borderlines. These prove alternately imposing and porous, sharply drawn and under erasure: the text is insistent on notions of 'draw[ing] a line' (6), as against seeing 'the lines ... begin to blur', in particular 'the line between what's true / and false' (7). The moral definiteness of both Othello and Desdemona, the uncompromising nature of their love, the absolutes ('the cause', 5.2.1) that make Othello a would-be justified murderer and

---

[14] My version of the inscription, in Spanish: 'Damos gracias a la Virjen [sic] de San Juan por librarnos de los de la Migracion al pasar a Los Anjeles [sic]' (Muldoon, 1999, jacket cover).

[15] The sense in which I here refer to 'tragic design' is traditionally Aristotelian, i.e. involving a plot ruled by an unwavering logic of retribution (nemesis), and by a sense of 'probability and necessity' that entails the mutual necessitation of *hamartia* and *catastrophe*, of error and outcome.

[16] Or indeed one of the features of Shakespeare's plot that allowed Shaw to argue, provocatively, that 'instead of [Verdi's] *Otello* being an Italian opera written in the style of Shakespear [sic], *Othello* is a play written by Shakespear in the style of Italian opera.... [T]he plot is pure farce plot' (George Bernard Shaw, *The Great Composers: Reviews and Bombardments*, ed. Louis Crompton (Berkeley, 1978), p. 224).

Desdemona an uncomprehending victim (as made poignantly evident in 4.3) – all of these are starkly absent from the venal and all too human world of *Bandanna*. All characters are tainted, and Morales voices his consciousness of a moral (and erotic) perspective which moves from forgiving his 'little bride of the borderline' for a past 'peccadillo' to indeed desiring her all the more for that (real? supposed?) transgression: 'I love you, Mona, not despite / but because of your fouling our nest' (16). This ethical fuzziness, averse to a logic of black-and-white (or black *vs* white) is at several points directly associated with the *ethnic* element, the theme of hybridity that at all times comes to the fore with a cast of (sometimes self-dubbed) 'mestizos', '"mongrels" or "mutts"' (26).

The inter-ethnic conflict inevitably derived from rewriting *Othello* involves in the case of *Bandanna* more characters than the central pair, since Emily (Jake's fiancée) is also Hispanic, and the figure that corresponds to Cassio, *Capitan* Cassidy, is Irish-American. This makes Morales's deputy a member of a community with its own ancestral memory of oppression, and a history of social and economic peripherality in America that also involved participating in networks of ethnic bias. Cassidy's derogatory remarks on the Hispanics around him as 'greasy wetbacks', and on his own Chief as 'a greaseball himself' and a 'dago' (8), in fact casts an ethical shadow over the character that one hardly associates with his Shakespearian antecedent. Muldoon is therefore found to be aware of how slanted the discourses of prejudice can be: the oppressed in one circumstance easily turn into the oppressors and agents of iniquity elsewhere.

Cassidy thus embodies and focuses the perception that identities vary according to the relationships that characterize the spaces against which we read them. Such spaces are hardly just referential: they also pertain to the formal conditions of representation, which in the case of *Bandanna* are of an intermedial nature. A libretto is an element of a collaborative artistic venture that awaits a full dramatic and musical actualization, and this is ideally to be considered in the fullness of its semiotic range –

access to which, however, is often piecemeal and uncertain. The arguments put forward in this essay rest predominantly on a critical consideration of texts; this final stage, however, will venture a few notes on the encounter between Muldoon's verbal construct and Daron Aric Hagen's score (on the basis of the 2006 recording by the UNLV Opera Theatre and Wind Orchestra, directed by the composer).

Readers of Muldoon's libretto are bound to feel that the challenges posed by the text's relation to Hagen's score are primarily of the sort that vocal music has traditionally prompted (at least in the past four centuries, i.e. since the debates over the primacy of words or music that found a focus in Monteverdi's advocacy of what he styled the *seconda prattica*[17]). To what extent can/should the score assist the clarity of verbal enunciation? In cases when the two media prove less than mutually enhancing, at what point can the intermedial relation between words and music be said to break down (if not become outright conflict)? Opera audiences used to a long consolidated canon hardly ever face these perplexities, since they have always known the plot (if not details of the libretto) and, in any case, the language in which most of it is sung may remain utterly foreign to them. It is new repertoire that can pose the problem afresh. As regards the matter of its newness, however, an opera like *Bandanna*, as a version of one of the best-known tragedies of all times (with famous operatic versions by none other than Rossini and Verdi), can be said to hold an equivocal position. Further, the clarity with which the text relates to the music derives in this case an enhanced importance from the fact that the librettist is a prominent poet, known for his iconoclastic bent, who departs rather markedly from his Shakespearian source in ways that have to be verbally clear for the deviation to be gauged and the nature of the rewriting recognized.

At several key points in *Bandanna*, Hagen writes for the voice in terms that allow Muldoon's rhetoric, his ironies and poignancies, to be matched

---

[17] Cf Massimo Ossi, *Divining the Oracle: Monteverdi's 'Seconda Prattica'* (Chicago, 2003), pp. 27–57, 189–210.

and conveyed in some detail, as if to gratify expectations of a mutually enhancing (almost calqued) relation between the two media. This compositional practice can be found both in passages that one might dub 'lyrical' and in stretches that are arguably more 'epic'. Examples of the latter include Kane's long speech (half recitative, half aria) at the opening of 1.4, which seems to be composed so as to ensure the clarity and rhetorical clout of his politically explicit address (this passage of the libretto includes Kane's apparently impassioned complaint that 'Marx . . . is out of favour today / because of the Commie thing', 24).[18] The satirical traits of this stretch of Muldoon's text are also musically endorsed and emphasized by the inclusion of a parody of a few bars of the American national anthem. As for the 'lyrical' element, the ethical uncertainty signalled above for Morales seems adequately served by the score composed for his musings and anxieties in 1.2 (12–15)[19] and his emotional extremity at the end of Act 1, the passage in which he vows to kill Mona.[20] Further, the minimalist score of Morales's final aria (sung almost all *a cappella*) underlines his pre-suicidal serenity – which matches indeed, but with stark verbal economy, the self-representation that marks Othello's final speech.[21] Symmetrically, this aptness might equally be acknowledged with regard to the melodic line written for the emotional, though dismayed, dialogue involving Mona and Emily, followed by Mona's last soliloquy/aria, in 2.3 (corresponding to *Othello* 4.3.9–104).[22]

The passages that are bound to prove more challenging to the word-and-music rapport are those in which Hagen writes polyphonically, such as his choruses in the prologue to the opera. A case in point is provided by the first intervention of the 'chorus of the Dispossessed and the Disappeared'.[23] It provides the opera with a stentorian, indeed memorable opening, in which percussion, wind instruments and high voices seem to be stretched to the limit in terms of volume and pitch. The impact of this opening somehow matches the stormy setting of *Othello* 2.1, which indeed became Act 1, scene 1 in Verdi's *Otello*, consensually one of the most memorable inaugural scenes in the

opera repertoire. In Verdi's 1.1, a chorus of male voices (punctuated by curt solo remarks by Jago, Roderigo, Cassio and Montano) concurs with the orchestra in a crescendo that follows the trepidation of the storm and of the glimpsed sail in its midst, through terror to the exultation of Othello's safe and victorious arrival. In Hagen's score, however, the composer's formal options, and in particular the characteristics of his polyphonic writing – the way in which he composes for voices, as regards tempo, rhythm, pitch – greatly limit an audience's ability to follow the text sung by the chorus. The reason for this may be that the piece in question is a 'Prologue', which Hagen may have construed as an overture; but, if so, it is a *sung* and *acted* overture, in which the illegal immigrants arrive, describe their plight and are welcomed by Jake – and this makes it an opening segment of the plot, and indeed the functional correlative of the observed stormy crossing and eventual arrival dramatized in Shakespeare's 2.1 and Verdi's 1.1.

Hagen's writing for his opening chorus thus compromises, to some extent, the impact of Muldoon's lines, attributed as they are to a collective with such an obviously politicized designation as the 'Dispossessed'. However, the segment of the chorus that immediately follows, couched in the voices of 'Illegal Immigrants', already amounts to a compromise: it allows more easily for an identification of its referential import, and this proves crucial for the audience's perception of the dislocation on which the opera rests. The references embedded in the relevant lines include Mexican toponyms, promptly identifiable names of autochthonous historical leaders – 'Cabeza de Vaca', 'Benito Juarez', 'Santa Anna', 'Pancho Villa' – and aspects of topography that acquire an iconic value – 'mesas', 'mesillas', 'canyons and arroyos' (1–2). Nonetheless, the complexity of the choruses, quartets and duets that

---

[18] CD 1, no.10, 'Stump Aria (Kane)'.

[19] CD 1, no.5, 'Aria (Morales)'.

[20] CD 1, no.12, 'Aria (Morales)'.

[21] CD 2, no.11, 'Fracture and Epilogue (Morales)'.

[22] CD 2, no.9, 'Scene and Duet (Mona/Emily)'.

[23] CD 1, no.1, 'Chorus'.

Hagen writes for *Bandanna*, to the extent that they often involve *different* stretches of Muldoon's text being sung by distinct, juxtaposed voices, arguably validates, in this opera, the critically popular notion that the intermedial nexus is often of an agonistic nature, indeed the site of a 'struggle for dominance' in which a broadly collaborative design derives an additional, intriguing tension from the fact that it is punctuated by instances of inter-artistic 'friction'.[24] Productive semiotic conflict of this kind may in fact be read as an enhanced but also challenged instance of the fundamentally 'collaborative' nature of Shakespeare's drama, verified both under the historical conditions of its inception on the early modern stage (with its characteristically fluid rapport between text and performance, and revealing the playwright as 'himself . . . an adapter'[25]) and all through the process of ever-renewed 'imagining[s]' that it has since fostered and undergone.[26]

Addressing a Shakespearian operatic rewriting like *Bandanna* from a perspective that sees the tropes of both collaboration and conflict as productive and interchangeable, or (in plainer terms) as two sides of the critical coin, also confirms the proneness of the Shakespearian text, in its manifold afterlives, to become a privileged ground for momentous critical discussions. The discussion, in this case, ponders the alternatives posed by an agonistic rationale for tackling intermedial relations and the current 'tendency rather to deconstruct the dissimilarities of various arts and media'.[27] But further perplexities, of varying range, arise from Paul Muldoon's decision to take the basic lineaments of the plot and characterization of *Othello* – with its known political, cultural and ethnic tensions, played out against turbulent scenarios of early modern history and couched in the agonistic mould of tragedy – and translate them into a distinct medium, time and setting.

Indeed, the compounded effect of this medial and referential diversity prompts more queries than it enables answers to be offered. Such queries bear on genre, both literary and musical: does the ideological stance that *Bandanna* seems to adopt on conflicts and major movements that have marked contemporary history find a productive accommodation within the tragic design? And does the representation of conflicts lived by all too ordinary beings (rather than princely generals or daughters of Venetian *magnifici*) match the cultural and aesthetic expectations posed by opera, which has long been the object of an arch-commonplace – that it is 'larger than life'? But those queries also bear on the nature and feasibility of creative collaboration and the intermedial nexus: do the various subtleties of the (re)writer, wavering between a 'design' based on 'understatement' and the clarity of definite form, match the compositional requirements of a fellow artist (the composer) in the intrinsically collaborative medium of musical drama? Irrespective of the tentative answers they may find, the range and depth of such questions confirm the ability of the Shakespearian text, granted by the wealth of its many avatars, to be invested with the concerns and expressive needs of a variety of audience and to become that vast hoard of imaginative possibilities that we recurrently ransack so as better to read ourselves.

---

[24] Cf W. J. T. Mitchell, *Iconology: Image, Text, Ideology* (Chicago and London, 1986), p. 43 and *passim*; James Heffernan, *Museum of Words: the Poetics of Ekphrasis from Homer to Ashbery* (Chicago, 1993), p. 19 and *passim*. I am here invoking notions that have acquired critical currency in the field of word-and-image studies, but that I believe can be productively appropriated into a discussion of tensions that characterise the word-and-music nexus.

[25] *Adaptations of Shakespeare: A Critical Anthology of Plays from the Seventeenth Century to the Present*, ed. Daniel Fischlin and Mark Fortier (London, 2000), p. 1.

[26] Stephen Orgel, *Imagining Shakespeare: A History of Texts and Visions* (Houndmills, 2003), p. 1. See Douglas Lanier, *Shakespeare and Modern Popular Culture* (Oxford, 2002).

[27] Lars Elleström, ed., *Media Borders, Multimodality and Intermediality* (Houndmills, 2010), p. 11.

JOHN BERRYMAN'S EMENDATION OF *KING LEAR* 4.1.10 AND SHAKESPEARE'S SCIENTIFIC KNOWLEDGE

B. J. SOKOL

'Ghastly, / with open eyes, he attends, blind.'[1]

Nearly seventy years ago John Berryman proposed an intriguing emendation to a textually difficult line in *King Lear*. But, ever since, his proposal has been overlooked by editors. Here I will attempt to re-situate the line as it was emended by Berryman within broader contexts in *King Lear*, and also in relation to a wider cultural framework. This perspective, if accepted, will strongly corroborate Berryman's proposal.

My attention was drawn to Berryman's several emendations of *King Lear* by John Roe's recent, elegant chapter on how the American poet worked on and responded to Shakespeare's texts.[2] Moreover, the following study of Berryman's repeated efforts to emend *King Lear* 4.1.10 relies crucially on John Haffenden's annotated edition of a selection of Berryman's writings about Shakespeare, which includes letters and other unpublished items.[3] In addition, three experts respectively on Elizabethan–Jacobean drama, on Shakespeare's communicative modes and on Shakespearian textual problems, have kindly allowed me to quote from their private communications. So the following will be in a real sense a collaborative effort. That, I hope, may excuse the fact that to proceed I must also include a summary at some length of some of my own former work on details of another Shakespeare play.

I. THE CRUX

Varied readings of *King Lear* 4.1.10 (TLN 2189) appear in the Folio and in two differing press variants of the first Quarto. In the second Quarto dated 1619 and in the 1623 Folio text derived from it the line contains Edgar's puzzled observation 'But who comes heere? My Father poorely led?' But the 1608 Quarto has either 'Who's here, my father poorlie, leed', or in some copies corrected for the press (including B.L. C.34.k.18, sig. H2r) 'Who's here, my father parti,eyd,'.[4] In a 1997 article, R. J. C. Watt judged all of the Folio and Quarto variants corrupted, and moreover 'not a credible piece of human speech' (52).[5] Watt also cited a range of scholars who concur, on varied technical bases,

---

[1] John Berryman, *The Dream Songs*, introduced by W. S. Merwin (New York, 2007), p. 29.

[2] John Roe, 'John Berryman', *Great Shakespeareans*, vol. 8, ed. Peter Rawlings (London, 2011), pp. 133–80.

[3] John Haffenden, *Berryman's Shakespeare* (New York, 1999), contains only the most coherent fraction of Berryman's manuscript and other writings on Shakespeare. Some of the huge mass of less coherent materials are reported on in Theodore Leinwand, 'Berryman's Shakespeare/Shakespeare's Berryman', *Hopkins Review*, 2 (2009), 374–403.

[4] I will be using the lineation and abbreviations LRF and LRQ for the Folio and Quarto texts in Stanley Wells and Gary Taylor, eds. *William Shakespeare: The Complete Works* (Oxford, 1986); this line, Folio TLN 2189, will be referred to here as F 4.1.10. I will also cite Charlton Hinman, *The First Folio of Shakespeare* (New York, 1968) and William Shakespeare, *True Chronicle Historie . . . of King Lear*, 'Pide Bull' Quarto, British Library C.34.k.18. (London, 1608) where appropriate. On the Quarto press variants see Stanley Wells and Gary Taylor, *William Shakespeare: A Textual Companion* (Oxford, 1987), p. 519.

[5] R. J. C Watt, 'Neither Parti-Eyed nor Poorly Led: Edgar Meets the Blind Gloucester', *Review of English Studies*, 48 (1997), 51–6.

that the printing house manuscript sources of the text at that point must have been 'uncertain' (52–4). 'Uncertain' for Watt is a broad term, covering one or more forms of 'illegibility'. These, he said, 'may come from hasty writing or damage to the manuscript' or from other 'possibilities such as revision, deletion, correction, overwriting, [and] interlineation'.

Of course it is widely accepted by now that where the Quarto and Folio texts of *King Lear* diverge it is possible that *both* versions represent intentional (and possibly authorial) responses to the demands of differing times or circumstances of preparation or presentation. For instance, in a less widely discussed example of this than the matter of the French invasion, the entire scene containing a mock State Trial of the usurpers (LRQ 13) does not appear in the Folio text. In consequence there is no indication in the Folio version of the play of the 'commission' or mixed tribunal appointed in the Quarto scene by the hallucinating Lear, a tribunal that included (as was indeed the norm for English State Trials) both common law and equity judges. As Lear puts it in the Quarto: 'Thou robèd man of justice, take thy place; / And thou, his yokefellow of equity, / Bench by his side' (Q 13.32–4). The removal of this trial scene from the Folio text was almost certainly prudent; after 1606 its imagery had become too hot to handle because the formerly good relations between the common law and equity jurisdictions were fast degenerating. This was on account of an acute, and dangerous, new conflict between champions of the common law and champions of the Royal Prerogative, shadowing the interests of very different parts of society.[6]

Yet, despite a large number of such divergences, a substantial portion of *King Lear* remains nearly the same in its early texts – a point emphasised by R. A. Foakes in the Introduction to his Third Arden edition of the play.[7] The question here has to be whether there is some good reason for the lines corresponding to 4.1 to diverge in the corrected first Quarto and the Folio *Lear*. It is true that the dramatic context immediately preceding 4.1.10 does vary somewhat between the Quarto and Folio

versions. That context is the end of the blinding scene, and there the Quarto alone contains several resonant lines absent from the Folio. In those lines, two attending servants (rather than the one who had been killed by Regan when attempting to defend Gloucester) condemn his cruel blinding, and one of them says he will 'fetch some flax and whites of eggs' to dress his wounds (LRQ 14.97–105). However it is far from obvious why this kinder ending to the blinding scene, in R. J. C. Watt's words, a 'moment of pity and lowered tension' (51), would alter Edgar's remarks when he sees Gloucester.[8] Thus it would seem that any emendation of 4.1.10 should apply to both the Folio and Quarto texts.[9]

Broadly, the options for emendation of 4.1.10 separate into two categories. In one Edgar comments immediately on his father's damaged eyes, as suggested by the rather mysterious 'parti,eyd' in the corrected first Quarto text. In the other, which

---

[6] For details see B. J. Sokol and Mary Sokol, 'Shakespeare and the English Equity Jurisdiction: *The Merchant of Venice* and the Two Texts of *King Lear*', *Review of English Studies*, 50 (1999), 417–39. Indeed the mock trial scene in the *King Lear* Quarto contains Shakespeare's sole reference to 'equity' in its legal sense, and this arises where equity judges are cooperating with common law ones. Since Shakespeare or his editors cut out the reference to their good relations only after politics led to conflicts between those jurisdictions, an ideological divergence having to do with sovereign power, doubt is cast on a wide swathe of recent critical conjectures that Shakespeare was obsessed with the jurisprudential problem of 'equity versus law'.

[7] Thus in the third Arden edition of King Lear (London, 2001), Foakes argues against the 'dogmatic and purist stance, which abandons the idea of *King Lear* as a single work of which we have variant versions', and proposes instead that 'we have two versions of the same play' (118–19).

[8] Berryman suggested to W. W. Greg that '"flax and whites of eggs" applied to Gloucester's eyes might give, at first glance, precisely such an appearance [pearly]' (245–6), but Greg rejected that (247), and Berryman did not pursue the suggestion. Also, as Watt argues, 'there are strong [textual] indications that on Shakespeare's stage Gloucester's eyes were not bandaged at any point': 'Neither Parti-Eyed nor Poorly Led', p. 51.

[9] This accords with Greg's analysis, which is used as the starting point for a recent update on the status of 4.1.10 in Watt, 'Neither Parti-Eyed nor Poorly Led', p. 52.

corresponds better with the other early texts, Edgar comments on his father's scant or ragged attendance. And indeed Edgar noting his father 'poorly led' does accord with the first Quarto stage direction 'Enter Glost. led by an old man', or (to a slightly lesser degree) with the Folio stage direction 'Enter Gloucester, and an Oldman'.

There are additional attractions in the 'poorly led' reading, aside from its conservative nature, which, I confess, I found compelling prior to coming across Berryman's final, stronger, emendation. My attraction to 'poorly led' was based on the fact that if Edgar first notices only that his father is ill-attended, a very interesting dramatic pattern emerges in which he only by degrees sees Gloucester's physical wounds and realizes he has been cruelly blinded. Such a process of coming gradually to awareness follows a dynamic similar to the one seen in Spenser's *Faerie Queene* (1.7.29–32), where Prince Arthur is first described as he is seen at long range, then at medium range, and lastly in extreme close-up, and the details of his magic equipage emerge only gradually.

More familiarly to us now, the same sequencing appears in the language of cinema when a new scene is first established in outline using a long shot, is then shown in greater detail using a mid-shot, and is finally revealed in terms of its fullest emotional impact in a tight close-up. Corresponding to an 'establishing shot' or 'long shot' in *King Lear* would be Edgar first noticing only the grosser set-up, the absence of his father's accustomed retinue: 'But who comes heere? My Father poorely led?' Such a detail-obscuring long perspective, productive of fertile puzzlement, could be understood to be followed by a closer view in 4.1.19–25, where Edgar overhears talk of, and then obtains visual evidence of, his father's blinding. In such a reading, Edgar's aside in 4.1.27–8 would then correspond with a kind of extreme close-up framing his anguished face, and revealing his emotional response. That response, given in the text, is his appalled: 'O Gods, Who is't can say that I am at the worst? / I am worse then eer I was'. (It might be of interest, by the way, to compare Edgar's words here with the final chorus

in *Oedipus Rex*, following Oedipus's blinding: 'Count no mortal happy till / he has passed the final limit of his life secure from pain' (1129–30).[10])

Yet I have become persuaded that even greater artistic gains arise from Berryman's best emendation of *King Lear* 4.1.10, although in this Edgar sees immediately that his father's eyes are damaged and that precludes him from a gradual realization that Gloucester has been blinded.

2. BERRYMAN'S EMENDATIONS

In a letter to Mark Van Doren dated 22 March 1945, Berryman called the Folio version of *King Lear* 4.1.10 'the feeblest phrase in Shak, I suppose'.[11] His view here echoed that of W. W. Greg, another of Berryman's valued correspondents. The resulting riddle engaged Berryman, who evidently hoped to produce an edition of the (conflated) text of *King Lear* that would contain optimal solutions to all textual questions. Thus, in a 1944 typescript headed 'Project: An Edition of *King Lear*', Berryman wrote, 'If I have now the temerity to propose an edition of *King Lear* where so many masters have failed, it is because for the first time success is possible.'[12] And in the earliest draft of his Commentary for the proposed edition Berryman particularly noted that, 'As Greg says, one of the worst cruxes in the play' appears at 4.1.10.[13] Then, as recorded in several letters, he attempted a series of possible emendations of this line.

Thus, in March 1945 Berryman wrote excitedly to his 'much loved'[14] mentor and former teacher Mark Van Doren: 'One of the strongholds of

---

[10] Sophocles, 'Oedipus the King', *The Complete Greek Tragedies: Sophocles I*, trans. David Grene, ed. David Grene and Richmond Lattimore (Chicago, 1954), p. 76.

[11] Berryman, *Berryman's Shakespeare*, p. 226.

[12] Berryman, *Berryman's Shakespeare*, p. 175.

[13] This early version of the Commentary, written in about March 1945, is quoted in Berryman, *Berryman's Shakespeare*, 1999, p. xxix.

[14] The apt description 'much loved mentor' is used in Roe, 'John Berryman', p. 156.

corruption in *Lear* fell I think this morning', and offered up his first conjectured emendation.[15] But in a follow-up letter, sent two months later to Van Doren, Berryman confessed that his initial enthusiasm had flagged and he was no longer 'so happy about [the emendation] as on the day it occurred to me'. Yet he continued in the same letter that 'Greg is certain that F cannot be right, and I don't believe it can.'[16]

And so Berryman went on seeking a more perfect emendation of 4.1.10, and in February 1946 even wrote to W. W. Greg that 'my notes show six conjectures seriously entertained'. In that letter Berryman also admitted that his aim was to beat his editorial 'competitors'.[17]

Berryman's first attempts to emend 4.1.10 are recorded in letters that he sent to Van Doren in March 1945 and to Greg in February 1946. These emendations were, respectively, 'My father, bloody-eyed' and '[my father] emptie-ey'd'.[18] Clearly, at that stage, Berryman thought that the line shows Edgar reacting immediately upon their encounter on the heath to his realization that Gloucester has been cruelly blinded.[19]

Berryman's final proposal, made in a letter to Greg on 4 June 1946, was that 4.1.10 should be revised to 'My father pearly-ey'd'.[20] This proposal (which will be supported here) was both strange and unexpected. The image it introduces is quite eerie or uncanny.[21] And what led to it is unknown. Yet many critics have speculated about the drive behind Berryman's extended, laborious and perhaps quixotic Shakespearian quests, and in the midst of those speculations may lay a clue to his strange 'pearly-ey'd'.

In his recent chapter on Berryman and Shakespeare John Roe attributes the poet's fascination with Shakespeare to (among other things) his own Hamlet-like situation vis-à-vis his mother, father and stepfather.[22] Roe further suggests that Berryman's efforts to solve the editorial problems of *King Lear* had twin roots: '(1) the story and content [of the play] spoke to Berryman in a particular way, just as did that of *Hamlet*, (2) *Lear* exercised a particular fascination as the *cause célèbre* of the New Bibliography'.[23] Roe finds many links between

Berryman's engagement with these plays and the issues of passion, guilt, shame, horror, creativity and incomprehension treated in his own poetry. I might add that Berryman, himself a Freudian in his understanding of the unconscious process (as Roe points out),[24] may have merged the sources of his poetic myth-making and his scholarly drives in so far as the latter channelled his rivalry with father-teachers in the world of Shakespeare studies.[25]

Many others have discussed Berryman on Shakespeare, although surely the last word on that topic has not been heard. These include Theodore Leinwand, who described the passion and 'grandiosity' of Berryman's never completed ambition to be a heroic, all-conquering textual critic and editor of *King Lear*. Leinwand illustrated his points by reproducing or describing some of the multitude of obsessive notes and marginalia left by Berryman, amongst which some concerning 'sin' in *The Tempest* may bear on our present topic. Leinwand described a comment written by Berryman on the page of the Introduction to Frank Kermode's Arden edition of *The Tempest*, where Kermode asserts that 'Prospero, like Adam, fell from

---

[15] Letter to Mark Van Doren of 22 March 1945 in Berryman, *Berryman's Shakespeare*, p. 226.

[16] Berryman, *Berryman's Shakespeare*, p. 228.

[17] Letter to W. W. Greg of 16 February 1946, in Berryman, *Berryman's Shakespeare*, p. 236.

[18] Letters of 22 March 1945 and 16 February 1946 in Berryman, *Berryman's Shakespeare*, pp. 226 and 237.

[19] The same reading is said in Watt, 'Neither Parti-Eyed nor Poorly Led', p. 54, to convey the self-evident '*thought*' of the passage, although, as we shall see, alternative views are possible.

[20] Berryman, *Berryman's Shakespeare*, pp. 245–6.

[21] That the image of a gem should be aligned here with a physical loss or affliction accords with observations and analyses made by Lisa Hopkins in her 'Beautiful Scars: Jewels in English Renaissance Drama'. These conclude: 'jewels in English Renaissance drama function not only as adornment, but also as beautiful scars, marking sites of loss and lack'. I have been kindly allowed to quote this in advance of publication.

[22] Roe, 'John Berryman', pp. 143–51.

[23] Roe, 'John Berryman', p. 152.

[24] Roe, 'John Berryman', p. 146.

[25] Roe hints at this, 'John Berryman', p. 179.

his kingdom by an inordinate thirst for knowledge'. Berryman's annotation beside this reads: 'no sense of *sin* in Prosp.'[26] It is most interesting that Berryman saw Prospero not afflicted by a sense of sin, for that makes him a contrast in the play with his antagonists Alonso, Sebastian and Antonio, who are distinctly labelled 'three men of sin' (3.3.53). Yet, among those three antagonists, only one eventually comes to see himself as sinning: parallel structures of disowning or acknowledgement of sinfulness will become prominent in the following argument.

Berryman's poetry shows an intense awareness of the inner sense of having sinned. Thus in Berryman's *Dream Song* 29, quoted in the epigraph above, an alter-ego named Henry is beset by an undefined, unprovable but unshakeable sense of wrongdoing. This leaves him, appallingly, open-eyed yet blind. No doubt a conscience beset by his alcoholism, his adulteries and his undelivered literary projects (often supported by generous grants) contributed to Berryman's notorious depression, and his eventual suicide. But on another side, and importantly for present purposes, Berryman's poetry delves deeply into an anguished sense of having committed an untraceable or occluded wrong. That may have given him special insight into the plight of several sin-shaken Shakespearian characters who are, I will argue, at the same time blind and open-eyed.

In one sense all of the obsessiveness and gruelling labour that went into Berryman's attempt to edit *King Lear* came, as John Roe put it, 'to nothing in the end' (156–7), for the *Lear* edition was neither completed nor published. But Roe, as well as Leinwand and such critics as Haffenden, Hedrick, Maber and Logan, all agree that Berryman's fervent but abortive attempts to produce a critical edition of *King Lear* (as well as a literary biography of Shakespeare) had a major and positive impact on his own development as a poet.[27] My own claim is that the converse was true as well: that Berryman's poet's sensibility (perhaps similarly to Pope's[28]) led to valuable intuitions concerning both Shakespeare's language and Shakespeare's wider intentions.

Any such special editorial abilities functioned in tandem, in Berryman's case, with a particular drive to acquire and to show off his professional abilities in textual scholarship. So, as Roe put it, when Berryman proposed his final emendation of 4.1.10 to Greg, he first 'goes into impressive detail, in the course of which he tries to win his bibliographical spurs by demonstrating the different possible errors [in transmission] that might have occurred between [*King Lear*] Q and F'.[29] Such technical competence stands strangely beside a boyish-seeming earnestness and an eager hopefulness that he has cracked longstanding mysteries, also evident in Berryman's letters about his *Lear* edition.

Yet something entirely different from either his bumptious, boastful tendencies or his detailed, technical forays, indeed a whole other side of Berryman's Shakespearian endeavour, reveals itself in the letter in which Berryman replaces his earlier emendations of *Lear* 4.1.10 with the 'quite unprecedented "pearly eyed"'. For in this letter, as Roe further puts it, Berryman's 'imagination takes flight'.[30] And indeed Berryman actually identified his new proposal as 'imaginative', telling Greg that[31]

the [pearly-ey'd] reading has singular imaginative interest. It enriches the destruction of sight imagery (dart your blinding flames into her scornful eyes – the web and pin – squenes the eye – I'll pluck ye out – turn our imprest lances in our eyes – see thy cruel nails Pluck out his poor old eyes) which embodies a chief moral theme

---

[26] Leinwand, 'Berryman's Shakespeare', pp. 382–3.

[27] Donald K. Hedrick, 'Berryman Text Dreams', *New Literary History*, 12 (1981), 289–301; Peter Maber, 'John Berryman and Shakespearean Autobiography', *'After thirty Falls': New Essays on John Berryman*, ed. Philip Coleman and Philip McGowan (Amsterdam and New York, 2007), pp. 209–23; William Logan, 'Berryman at Shakespeare: Review of *Berryman's Shakespeare*', *The New Criterion* (May (1999), retrieved at www.newcriterion.com/articles.cfm/berryman-logan-2871, 11 September 2012.

[28] See Simon Jarvis, 'Alexander Pope', *Great Shakespeareans*, ed. Claude Rawson (London, 2010), vol. 1, pp. 66–114, 96–7 and *passim*, on Pope editing Shakespeare.

[29] Roe, 'John Berryman', p. 162.

[30] Roe, 'John Berryman', p. 162.

[31] Berryman, *Berryman's Shakespeare*, 246.

and supplies the context of Gloucester's actual blinding. The weeping & pearls nexus is so frequent that it may suggest Gloucester's weeping. And considering the quibble in *Two Gentlemen*, it does not need a Blunden to imagine that Shakespeare remembered in the last Act, when describing this scene, his language in it, and with a meaning of his hovering under Edgar's, wrote of 'his bleeding rings, Their precious stones new lost'.

Seemingly, Greg was intrigued by this. So, unlike Van Doren who expressed disbelief that a poet like Berryman could transform himself into a productive textual scholar,[32] Greg encouraged Berryman (but warned him about overselling his idea). Thus, a couple of weeks after he received Berryman's letter, Greg wrote briefly in reply that he found the 'pearly-ey'd' suggestion 'quite promising', and added: 'I like the way you connect it up with the imagery and the "precious stones"'. This letter ended 'Good luck!'[33]

3. JUSTIFYING BERRYMAN'S FINAL AND PREFERRED EMENDATION

His 'pearly-ey'd' emendation of 4.1.10 was the last and I think the best that Berryman offered. The reason for my preference is complexly thematic.

Berryman appreciated the theme at issue, at least in part. For he reminded Greg that in Shakespeare's time: '*Pearl* was "a thin white film or opacity growing over the eye: a kind of cataract"' (here he quoted the *OED* without attribution). Berryman then added that 'Nashe has it, and Middleton, and there is a dialectical combination "pearl-blind"'.[34] Greg, in his letter of reply, cautioned Berryman against more remote suggestions, but accepted that having pearly eyes 'might mean simply "blind"'.[35]

In the same 4 June 1946 letter in which Berryman proposed 'pearly-ey'd', he reminded Greg that Shakespeare used this eye-damaging meaning of 'pearl' when dark-complexioned Thurio in *Two Gentlemen of Verona* is reassured by Proteus in terms of an 'old saying' that '"Black men are pearls in beauteous ladies' eyes"' and Julia derides Thurio's aside with: '"Tis true, such pearls as put out ladies'

eyes' (5.2.11–14). In fact the proverb travestied here is Tilley's M79 (408), which is also echoed in *Titus Andronicus* 5.1.42.[36]

We may add to Berryman's observations that Shakespeare closely noted some of the Geneva Bible's marginalia,[37] and that the Genevan marginal comment on 'bleare eyed' at Lev. 21:20 is 'Or that hath a web, or pearle'.[38] This was despite the fact that 'pearls' in English Bible translations were always images of perfection.

The confusion in Elizabethan imagery, wherein pearls could represent either bright eyes or else dimmed and diseased eyes, resulted from the lexical doubleness wherein pearls were connected both with the eye's clear lens (*OED* II.4.a) and with the visible signs of cataracts (*OED* II.4.b). Poets or playwrights who associated pearls with defective or ugly eyes included Middleton in *Women Beware Women* (2.2.105–6), Heywood in *Loves Maistresse or The Queens Masque* (4.1.52–5), King James VI of Scotland in his poem 'The Furies' (682–4), and John Davies of Hereford in his 1609 'Picture of the Plague' which asserts that 'damn'd disguis'd, man-pleasing Sanctitie' and 'Simony' are 'Pearles that quite put out the eies / Of Piety in Christian Common-wealths'.[39]

---

32 Roe, 'John Berryman', p. 156.

33 Letter of 22 June 1946, Berryman, *Berryman's Shakespeare*, p. 247.

34 Letter of 4 June 1946, Berryman, *Berryman's Shakespeare*, p. 245.

35 Letter of 22 June 1946, Berryman, *Berryman's Shakespeare*, p. 247.

36 Morris Palmer Tilley, *A Dictionary of the Proverbs in England in the Sixteenth and Seventeenth Centuries* (Ann Arbor, 1950).

37 See B. Sokol, 'Prejudice and Law in *The Merchant of Venice*', in *Shakespeare Survey 51* (Cambridge, 1998), pp. 159–73, and Roger Stritmatter, 'By Providence Divine: Shakespeare's Awareness of Some Geneva Marginal Notes of I Samuel', *Notes and Queries*, 245 (2000), 97–100.

38 *The Bible*, known as the Geneva Bible (London, 1587).

39 Thomas Middleton, *Women Beware Women*, ed. J. R. Mulryne (Manchester, 1981), p. 52; Thomas Heywood, *Loves Mistress or The Queens Masque* (London, 1792), sig. I4v; James VI of Scotland, *Poems of James VI of Scotland*, ed. James Craigie, 2 vols. (Edinburgh, 1947–1958), 1: 150, transliterated 'The Pearl upon the eie, / That dimmes the shine, and Cataract, / That dark and cloudie bee'; John Davies of

But, in addition to paralleling other Elizabethan poets' frequent uses of negative pearl/eye imagery, there is much more to be said about Shakespeare's linking of non-functioning eyes with pearls. As I have formerly shown, in *The Tempest* Shakespeare associates pearls with destroyed vision in a very surprising way. Ariel's beautiful second song tells Prince Ferdinand that 'Those are pearles that were his eies', referring to 'your father', who is King Alonso. But, actually Alonso is alive and has not been drowned 'Full fadom five'. Yet, I have argued, the ditty of Ariel's song is also profoundly true metaphorically, because the play at large implies that Alonso has long been blinded in a peculiarly pearly way.

To understand this, it is necessary to take note of certain scientific insights newly arising in Shakespeare's time concerning the nature of pearls and the causes of pearl formation. Among other fresh and empirically based insights into biology and zoology, was a new scientific understanding arising in the late sixteenth or early seventeenth century that 'pearls were merely an oyster's way of dealing with irritants'.[40] Thus, by Shakespeare's time, a theory holding that pearl formation was simply the internal depositing by a shellfish of shell-like materials following disease or injury had displaced a long-held and fanciful, or mythic, theory of pearl formation that derived from Pliny's *Natural History*. This new theory or understanding arose independently in several places in Europe and the New World, and could have reached Shakespeare's England either through traceable published channels, or through untraceable oral ones.[41]

However it arrived, the theory seems to have impressed Shakespeare. Its essence, that gem pearls are the products of a shellfish's disease, seems to be reflected in Touchstone's 'your Pearle in your foule oyster' (*As You Like It*, 5.4.61). In *King Lear* itself the Fool asks a correlative question: 'Can'st tell how an Oyster makes his shell?' (LRQ, 5.2; LRF, 1.5.26). Just before raising that matter the Fool asserts that the purpose of the arrangement of human eyes flanking the nose is to uncover unsavoury truths: 'that what a man cannot smell out, a may spy into' (LRQ, 5.22–3; LRF, 1.5.23–4). Here a question

from natural history is concatenated with a question about moral awareness, and both have possible resonances with the powers or weaknesses of eyes. And indeed an uncomfortable moral truth is enunciated by Lear just between these two 'nonsense' comments of the Fool (on oysters making shells and on eyes detecting wrongs). For just then Lear expresses seeing that 'I did her wrong' (LRQ, 5.24; LRF, 1.5.25), no doubt thinking of Cordelia. This concatenation of an allusion to a new theory from natural history, the notion that the use of eyesight is to realize wrongs, and a sudden upsurge of remorse, encapsulates almost all I will have to say hereafter, but in so concentrated a form that unravelling it will be necessary.

The new scientific theory, that smooth pearls are deposited inside shellfish using the same materials with which they make their shells, and for the purpose of reliving pain and inflammation caused by intrusions of grit or other contamination in their sensitive flesh, has in itself no ethical content. But it can acquire the power of a moral fable if it is linked to two additional ideas: (1) that 'pearls' may signify dimmed or diseased human eyes; (2) that clear human vision may signify clear moral awareness (and diseased eyesight the opposite).

Bringing all these together, I have argued at length that Ariel's image of Alonso's eyes having

---

Hereford, *Humours Heau'n on Earth: The Picture of the Plague, according to Life, as it was Anno Domini 1603* (London, 1609), pp. 203–4.

[40] Martin Holden, *Encyclopedia of Gemstones and Minerals* (Philadelphia, 1991), p. 192.

[41] B. Sokol, 'Shakespearian Sources in "Obscure" Continental European Publications', in *Not of an Age, but for All Time: Shakespeare Across Lands and Ages*, ed. S. Coelsch-Foisner and G. E. Szőnyi (Vienna, 2004), pp. 65–75, discusses transmission through many printed texts, and also how these revelations about pearl formation were often included in accounts of New World travels. Perhaps unpublished New World travel accounts were also significant, and both Geoffrey Bullough in *Narrative and Dramatic Sources of Shakespeare*, 8 vols. (London, 1957–75) and *The Jamestown Voyages Under the First Charter 1606–1609*, ed. Philip L. Barbour, 2 vols. (Cambridge, 1969), vol. 1, p. 68, suggest that Shakespeare conducted unrecorded conversations with New World voyagers.

become pearls quite precisely represents the moral condition of the king at the play's start. Alonso has long ignored or rejected full awareness of his part in Prospero's and Miranda's unjust exile. By disowning knowledge of that, metaphorically obscuring his own vision, Alonso has made his eyes (meaning his moral sensibilities) stony, hard and opaque. Or, one might say, due to a self-protective reflex he has transformed his (morally) sensitive eyes into pearls, defending himself from the pain of a moral 'beam in the eye', or, one might say, smoothing over an intrusion of gritty truth.[42]

Indeed, well before Ariel sings his second song in *The Tempest*, Prospero has explained that, although Alonso was not himself the usurper, he did at first confederate with, and has since accepted both annual tribute and a new vassal's homage from, the usurping brother Antonio (1.2.111–16). In due course Alonso shows signs of becoming painfully and fully cognizant of this; he repents of it bitterly, and then begs and obtains forgiveness for it. So in a sense Alonso's moral eyes, although at the outset afflicted with (or become) blind, hard pearls, turn back into seeing and feeling ones. But no similar restoration of moral vision and sensibility is seen in Antonio or his henchman Sebastian, who remain smooth and smug and unremembering of their guilt.

In *King Lear* a very similar kind of disowning of sensibilities as seen in *The Tempest*, involving a morally calcifying, perhaps pain-relieving but blinding cover-up, is implied by the actions and reactions of Gloucester. But (unlike Alonso) Gloucester does not acquire moral vision and so never perceives or repents of his faults. At the play's very start, a bland encasement of any awareness of having harmed others is seen in Gloucester's boastfulness about fathering his bastard son Edmund. Thus, with obvious relish, he quips (perhaps even within Edmund's hearing): 'though this Knave came something sawcily to the world before he was sent for: yet was his Mother fayre, there was good sport at his making, and the horson must be acknowledged' (LRQ, 1.21–4, 1.1.20–3). It should be noted that the first audiences of these lines lived precisely at the historical juncture when social disapproval had greatly increased throughout Europe of the formerly widely tolerated acknowledgements, by the highborn, of having fathered illegitimate children.[43]

The tone of bland arrogance and crudity in Gloucester's remarks about impregnating Edmund's mother is of a piece with the exceptionally low perspective that misleads him into believing the false evidence of cupidity contrived by Edmund against Edgar. It is not just that Gloucester, like Lear, makes bad judgements but that at the play's outset neither of them seems to have the moral equipment for making good ones.

3. CAN WE UNDERSTAND LEAR AS SINFUL WITHOUT SINNING AGAINST LITERARY PROPRIETY?

The paralleling of Lear and Gloucester, although clearly implied by the structure of the play, may lead us into a problem of literary interpretation. Certainly Lear is at least as heedless and foolish as Gloucester is at the play's start. But more is needed to support the above argument that, like Gloucester, Lear has formerly sinned and has then arrogantly and blandly hidden this from himself with obliviousness. But there is nothing like the 'horson' speech to make it evident that Lear has formerly sinned.

Of course it could be said that these missing specifics do not matter. Certainly, Elizabethan religious outlooks found all men and women, and especially those wielding power, prone to sin. And, indeed, when raging against the hypocrisies of power and authority on the heath, Lear states specifically how sin can be hidden thanks to a hardening of the eyes: 'Get thee glasse-eyes, and like a scurvy Politian, seeme to see the things thou doest

---

[42] This is argued in detail, and the natural history background described at length in B. J. Sokol, *A Brave New World of Knowledge: Shakespeare's 'The Tempest' and Early Modern Epistemology* (London, 2003) and *Pearls, Shakespeare, and Epistemology in Harriot's Time* (Durham, 2005), pp. 30–49.

[43] B. Sokol, *Art and Illusion in The Winter's Tale* (Manchester, 1994), pp. 121–5, 225, 226, provides statistics, references and a discussion of this (as bearing on *The Winter's Tale*).

not' (4.5.166–8). Here again imagery of hardened eyes appears.

Nevertheless, all the texts of *King Lear* provide very few specifics of Lear's former misdeeds. A sole exception, often-noted, is that Lear comes to regret that 'O I have ta'en / Too little care of this' (LRQ 11.29–30; LRF 3.4.32–3), 'this' being homeless poverty. But it seems that more bad intentions than social blindness, or placing unfair demands upon and then vindictively mistreating Cordelia, are implied by Lear's confession: 'I am a man, / More sinn'd against, than sinning' (LRQ 9.60; LRF 3.2.59–60).

The sketchiness of *King Lear* concerning Lear as a sinner can be addressed in several ways. One would be to imagine or invent the details of Lear's former sins, as for instance did the poet Gordon Bottomley in his powerful 1915 verse drama 'King Lear's Wife'.[44] This portrayed (through dramatic dialogue and action, not novelistic expositions of inwardness) a headstrong and adulterous younger Lear mistreating his wife and winning the lasting hatred of Goneril. If it is thought that using the imagination in that way is impossibly naive, it might be useful to recall, as Gail Marshall and Ann Thompson do in a chapter on Mary Cowden Clarke, that despite the strictures of literary criticism 'modern actors still routinely invent "back stories" for their characters'.[45] A second approach might be to employ a more than verisimiltudinous imagination when confronting Shakespeare plays, as was suggested by David Bell, president of the British Psychoanalytic Society, when considering 'character' aspects of *Hamlet*:

to what extent we can be free to think of the *dramatis personae* [Hamlet] . . . as having an inner world, hidden motives, so that we can wonder what goes on inside such a character; whether he might, for example, reveal things to us that he does not know himself? . . . This difficulty can be avoided if we take the play itself (not the characters) as its object, viewing it rather like a dream or the movements of psychic objects in the mind . . . However, I think we can never really get away from thinking of Shakespeare's characters as people . . . They often surprise us with what they say and do, and the fact that we are surprised reveals that we have formed a sense of what

might be expected of such a character. Their speech can express an inner logic that may be unclear not only to those around them but even to themselves . . . We are familiar with the ways in which dream life, unconscious fantasy, can appear to be real, but perhaps somewhat under-emphasised is how external reality, when it gives form to that which is normally unconscious, can seem like a dream . . . Perhaps to decide whether or not to view *Hamlet* as a dreamscape, or as a world of real characters going about their lives, is somehow to miss the point, which is that the play achieves its mysterious quality and dramatic force through its capacity to maintain the tension between these different dimensions of our existence.[46]

Or, thirdly, we may adopt the position that the local logic of character or motivation in a Shakespeare play may sometimes be subordinated to a more global logic of meaning, structure and theme. In accord with either this or Dr Bell's more ramified view, the play may *need* Lear to have had some history of misdeeds which are, at its start, overlooked or buried in self-esteem, regardless of its giving no details of this.

Gloucester himself may well be, like Lear, 'More sinn'd against than sinning', but what each character does with those circumstances differs radically. Gloucester shows hardly any evidence of having seen that he has sinned, and can only 'seeme to see' both before and after being blinded. Lear's responses are very different; thus I would argue (certainly not originally) that the outwardly parallel stories of Gloucester and Lear are set up primarily to be contrasted. For, although both figures are cruelly abused by their 'bad' children and protected by 'good' ones whom they have abused, and although both are cast out to wander on the Kentish heath, Lear alone eliminates the pearls that have formed in his eyes, the hard unseeing that has protected him from intrusions of painful knowledge.

---

44 Gordon Bottomley, 'King Lear's Wife', in *Georgian Poetry 1913–1915*, ed. E[dward] M[arsh]. (London, 1915), pp. 1–47.

45 See Gail Marshall and Ann Thompson, 'Mary Cowden Clarke', *Great Shakespeareans* (London, 2011), vol. 7, pp. 58–91, 63, in a commentary on Clarke's notorious *The Girlhood of Shakespeare's Heroines* (1850–52).

46 Sent to me by email, with kind permission for use.

This contrast is a major engine of the play's meaning, but more importantly it also drives the terrific suffering Lear undergoes when he, eventually, comes to 'See better', as Kent early on demanded of him (LRQQ 1.150; 1.1.158).

So, in addition to its affinity with the play's imagery of 'precious stones' as noted by Berryman and approved by Greg, Gloucester being described as 'pearly eyed' sets him up in contrast with what Lear finally achieves. All Gloucester's losses do not disturb his purblind pearliness, and so he dies meekly. Lear – who is, more than Gloucester, dispossessed of glamour, grandeur and power – smashes up 'pomp's' encasement in self-beguilement. His suffering then is so terrific that it has startled all its witnesses, either other characters onstage, audiences or readers safe in their studies.

The big potential gain, then, in Berryman's 'pearly eyed' emendation (interpreted as it is here) lies in a symbolic underscoring of a complex theme and complex antithetical structuring.

One might ask if adopting Berryman's emendation and accepting the present reading of it would reinforce old-fashioned notions in which *King Lear* is more a dramatic poem than poetic drama. Perhaps we should leave such hoary distinctions aside – or has a recent Lucas Erne-led revolution made them up-to-date again? In any case, enhancing *King Lear* by adding poetic complexity to the pattern in which purblind Gloucester functions as a foil to King Lear 'seeing better' might even further strengthen the standing of that dual-text play as a high water mark for both poetic drama and dramatic poetry.

4. TEXTUAL APPENDIX

Direct bibliographical support for Berryman's proposed emendation would be marvellous, but I have not yet seen it, and it most likely will never appear. What I have been shown is that Berryman's 1946 proposal is still permissible in the light of subsequent knowledge of the *King Lear* texts and their transmission. That is, it is still possible to accept Berryman's claim, made to Greg, that there is 'no Elizabethan objection to it'.[47]

In the letter to Greg in which he proposed 'pearly-ey'd', Berryman also proposed that 'the compositor got the first part nearly right (allowing oo:ea), whereas the press reader messed it up (the compositor perhaps helping) but got the second part exactly right except for the hyphen, which he thought was a comma'.[48] Remarking on this in a private communication, Gabriel Egan has kindly commented:[49]

Firstly there is at least one case in Q1 where the uncorrected reading is closer to the truth than the corrected one while not being exactly right. At 11.6 Q1u has Lear refer to the 'crulentious' storm and Q1c has him call it 'tempestious', and assuming that F's reading of 'contentious' is correct it would seem that the first stab (although nonsense) shows more letters correctly read from the manuscript ("-entious") than the second stab. As Greg pointed out, we shouldn't here assume that the proof-reader did not consult the copy. He might simply have been unable to read it much better than the compositor had, and decided that they at least should set a real word.

Secondly, I think Berryman has a point in saying that the proof-reader perhaps picked up something more from the copy than the original compositor did in his alteration of 'leed' to 'eyd'. A parallel for that exists in the proofreader turning 'vntender' into 'vntented' and 'peruse' into 'pierce' (4.294–5) yet still leaving the passage incomprehensible. That is, a second stab recovered something from the copy without getting the whole passage right.

Putting those examples of the compositor's and proof-reader's behaviour together it is not unreasonable to accept Berryman's claim of a compositor getting his first setting nearly right in one word ('poorlie' for 'pearlie') and wrong in the next ('leed' for 'eyd') and then the proof-reader managing to decipher a bit more of the copy to change 'leed' to 'eyd', and then messing the reading up by rejecting 'poorlie eyd' as impossible and settling on 'parti eyd'.

So Berryman's proposal is not only still allowable but may have some limited bibliographical support.

---

[47] In a letter from Berryman to W. W. Greg of 4 June 1946, reprinted in Berryman, *Berryman's Shakespeare*, p. 246.

[48] Berryman, *Berryman's Shakespeare*, p. 246.

[49] Sent to me by email, with kind permission for use.

SPECTACLE, REPRESENTATION AND LINEAGE IN *MACBETH* 4.1

WILLIAM C. CARROLL

The first known illustration of a scene from Shakespeare's *Macbeth* is the frontispiece, engraved by Elisha Kirkall,[1] to Nicholas Rowe's edition of the play in his complete *Works* of 1709 (illustration 18).[2]

The scene depicted is not among what are now considered the most memorable or most iconic scenes in the play, such as Lady Macbeth's handwashing or sleepwalking scenes, Macbeth's first confrontation with the witches, or the banquet scene when he sees Banquo's ghost; all of these scenes were in fact described in some detail by Simon Forman in his eyewitness account of a 1611 performance.[3] Instead, Rowe's edition depicts Act 4 scene 1 but, again, it does not show any of the much-commented on prophecies emanating from the witches' cauldron – 'Beware the Thane of Fife', 'none of woman born / Shall harm Macbeth', and so on, or the visions of the '*armed head*', the '*bloody child*' and the '*child crowned*'. Rather, it represents the key moment later in the scene – the show of kings, a spectacle that has seemed more or less transparent in its meaning to most scholars. Rowe's unusual choice of illustration, I will argue, emphasizes the scene's centrality in the history of the Stuart dynasty, and provides a way of reading the scene's significance in Shakespeare's play in 1606, 1709 and beyond.

Rowe's choice of 4.1 as *the* scene to illustrate his *Macbeth* reflects in part the political and historical context of 1707–9. The Act of Union had finally been agreed to by the Scottish and English parliaments, and the two nations became one realm, a united kingdom called Great Britain,

on 1 May 1707. James I had introduced the first Act of Union in 1604, only to have the English parliament debate the measure for three years, and finally take no action at all. Thus the last Stuart monarch finally completed the first Stuart's imperial design of union. In October 1708, Queen Anne's husband, Prince George of Denmark, died. The 1701 Act of Settlement had settled the succession to the English throne on the Electress Sophia of Hanover and her Protestant heirs if there were, as the Act put it, 'default of issue of the said Princess

---

[1] See Stuart Sillars, *The Illustrated Shakespeare, 1709–1875* (Cambridge, 2008), p. 33.

[2] Although the figure of Macbeth had been depicted in Holinshed's 1577 *Chronicles*, several of the images in the Macbeth section are recycled from elsewhere in Holinshed's collection. The famous scene of the encounter with the witches is the one original image of Macbeth in Holinshed's account of his reign. Whether Rowe's illustration reflects the actual stage practice of the Davenant/Betterton production has been disputed. See Bernice W. Kliman, *Shakespeare in Performance* (Manchester, 1992), pp. 20–4, and 'The Nicholas Rowe *Macbeth* Illustration Corroborated', *Shakespeare Newsletter* 42 (1992), 23. In 'Engraving for *Macbeth* 4.1', *Shakespeare Newsletter*, 43 (1993), 3, George Walton Williams corrected Kliman's misidentification of Banquo as Hecate. John H. Astington challenged Kliman's argument in '*Macbeth* and the Rowe Illustrations', *Shakespeare Quarterly*, 49 (1998), 83–6. Kliman responded to Astington in 'Rowe 1709 *Macbeth* Illustration Again', *Shakespeare Newsletter*, 48 (1998–99), 59–60.

[3] See A. R. Braunmuller, ed., *Macbeth* (Cambridge, 1997), pp. 57–8 for the full text of Forman's account. All quotations from the play are from the Oxford *Complete Works*, 2nd edn, ed. John Jowett, William Montgomery, Gary Taylor and Stanley Wells (Oxford, 2005) and cited in the text.

18. Rowe 1709.

Anne'.[4] With Anne's husband dead and none of their thirteen children surviving beyond the year 1700, the 44-year old Queen represented, as all now recognized, the end of the Stuart line, and some of the same anxieties that had attended the beginning of the Stuart line were again in evidence.[5] Although he would become Poet Laureate in 1715, Rowe was in 1709 a devout Whig, his party loyalty being recognized in February 1709 when James Douglas, the secretary of state for Scotland, took him on as his under-secretary, and Rowe had dedicated his 1709 edition of Shakespeare to the prominent Whig politician the Duke of Somerset.[6] Rowe's choice of the show of kings, then, in part reflects the succession crises of the late Stuarts, just as the scene, in the *Macbeth* of 1606, responds in many respects to the succession crisis of the first Stuart. Indeed, 4.1 forms a key part of *Macbeth*'s interrogation of the origins of the Stuarts – represented, to Macbeth's horror, in the line of kings before him. For Rowe, by contrast, the line of kings would have represented the true succession of the Protestant Stuart line. Ultimately, the show of kings enacts a fantasy of patrilineal succession that neither the play nor the historical record sustains.

In the third edition (1714) of his Shakespeare edition, Rowe's text featured a different illustration of the same scene, this one engraved by Louis du Guernier[7] (illustration 19).

Here there are more witches (four rather than the three of 1709), a skull, crossed bones and a serpent at Macbeth's feet, all signifying mortality and evil. Macbeth's own pose is more 'dramatic', the cauldron vastly larger and the curling smoke even more powerfully ominous. And there are more kings: Banquo plus five (and just the edge of a sixth) in 1714 as against Banquo plus four in 1709. The engraver can't quite get all of Shakespeare's '*eight Kings, and Banquo last*' (Folio TLN 1604sd.) into the frame, but not for lack of trying. We do not know whether Rowe or his publisher Tonson offered any specific instructions to du Guernier,[8] but this scene, in its enhanced repetition, must have been even more compelling in 1713–14, when the third edition was being prepared, as Queen Anne's

death was imminent. The additional kings represent a now futile fantasy of the Stuart line's orderly continuation, even as it reached its extinction point. The skull at Macbeth's feet in the 1714 illustration might be that of one of his victims (though the play text mentions no skull in 4.1, much less a serpent), but proleptically it figures the end of the Stuarts.

Shakespeare had found versions of the earlier prophecies in 4.1 in Holinshed and other sources of the play, yet the show of kings is purely Shakespeare's invention, nowhere present in his sources.[9] Without question one of the play's signal moments, the show of kings provides a link to the world outside the play, to past and present, to discourses of sovereign power. The scene certainly represents Stuart royal genealogy, but its meaning, for

[4] www.legislation.gov.uk/aep/Will3/12-13/2/section/I, accessed 23 August 2012.

[5] Much had changed, of course. Howard Nenner notes that, unlike Elizabeth, Anne was not urged to name her successor (p. 256), and that from 1689 there had been a notable shift from accepting hereditary to a preference for Parliamentary authority in terms of the succession: after the Pretender announced in March 1714 that he would not renounce his Catholic faith, 'the nation did not, as some were afraid that it might, succumb misguidedly to the thrall of heredity' (*The Right To Be King* (Chapel Hill, 1995), p. 248).

[6] On Rowe's shifting political position in the 1709–14 period, see Paulina Kewes, '"The State Is out of Tune": Nicholas Rowe's "Jane Shore" and the Succession Crisis of 1713–14', *Huntington Library Quarterly*, 64:3/4 (2001), 283–308, and Brett Wilson, 'Jane Shore and the Jacobites: Nicholas Rowe, the Pretender, and The National She-Tragedy', *ELH*, 72 (2005), 823–43. Also, Arthur Sherbo, 'Rowe, Nicholas (1674–1718)', *Oxford Dictionary of National Biography, Online*, www.oxforddnb.com/view/article/24203.

[7] Sillars, *Illustrated Shakespeare*, p. 33.

[8] See Robert B. Hamm, Jr., 'Rowe's *Shakespear* (1709) and the Tonson House Style', *College Literature*, 31:3 (2004), 179–205, on the general characteristics of a Tonson publication.

[9] The first three prophecies of 4.1 are in Holinshed, Shakespeare's primary source (via Hector Boece's *Chronicles of Scotland*, translated into Scots in 1540), but George Buchanan declined to repeat them in his *Rerum Scoticarum historia* (1582, a probable source) since they are merely 'Fables, which are like *Milesian* Tales, and fitter for the Stage, than an History; and therefore I omit them' (Geoffrey Bullough, *Narrative and Dramatic Sources of Shakespeare*, 8 vols. (New York, 1957–75), vol. 7, p. 517).

U 6. p. 233

Lud. Du Guernier inv. et Sculp.

19. Rowe 1714.

Rowe as well as Shakespeare, remains far from transparent.

* * *

On 24 March 1603, after the long-anticipated death of Queen Elizabeth, Robert Cecil proclaimed that James VI, 'the K[ing] of Scots', had succeeded to the throne of England as James I. Trumpets and heralds proceeded to the various city gates to repeat the proclamation, which was heard, according to one observer, 'with grate expectacion, and silent joye'.[10] Elizabeth's approaching death had been accompanied by dire predictions of chaos and bloodshed, perhaps even civil war, for Elizabeth had failed in what many saw as the chief duty of the monarch: to produce a viable heir and continue the lineal succession of sovereign power. But James VI of Scotland, descended from the line issuing from Henry VIII's sister Margaret, Henry VII's eldest daughter, claimed the crown on the grounds of direct lineal descent.[11] Parliament quickly passed the Succession Act that, after tracing James's line on the English side, pronounced a 'most joyful and just recognition of [James's] immediate, lawful, and undoubted Succession, Descent, and Right of the Crown . . . as . . . next and sole heir of the blood royal of this realm'.[12] In addition to the blood royal, James possessed two other considerable and more practical assets: he was male, and he had two male sons – plus a spare daughter, just in case of emergency.

Recent scholarly work by Harry Berger, Jonathan Goldberg and David Norbrook,[13] among others, has drastically undermined the traditional reading of the play – the so-called King James or Authorized Version, i.e. that the play was written in early 1606 to 'flatter' or 'please' the 'recently-crowned'[14] King James, and that its setting in Scotland and its thickly embedded allusions to contemporary events cater to James's own intellectual 'interests', such as witchcraft.[15] The play, it was argued, affirms an orthodox Stuart interpretation of history, showing that royal legitimacy won in the end; the overthrow of the usurper Macbeth not only led to the rightful succession of Malcolm but more importantly, as we shall see, to the

ascendancy of the Stuarts from the descendants of Banquo – hence to the very monarch who was perhaps viewing the play with complacent satisfaction in 1606.

That normalized reading of *Macbeth* now seems impossible to sustain. The play seems less a piece of flattery to James than a synecdoche of the conflicting early modern discourses that constituted sovereignty. The gaps, fissures and contradictions within the contested political discourse of the period, particularly as they relate to James's own views, have become increasingly apparent.[16]

---

[10] *The Diary of John Manningham of the Middle Temple 1602–1603*, ed. Robert P. Sorlien (Hanover, 1976), pp. 208–9.

[11] In contrast to Queen Elizabeth herself, whose primary claim to the throne derived from her father's will; see Nenner, *The Right To Be King*, and Mortimer Levine, *Tudor Dynastic Problems 1460–1571* (London, 1973).

[12] *Statutes of the Realm*, 4.1017 (*I Jac. I, c.1*).

[13] Harry Berger, 'The Early Scenes of *Macbeth*: Preface to a New Interpretation', *ELH*, 47 (1980), 1–31; Jonathan Goldberg, 'Speculations: *Macbeth* and Source', in Jean Howard and Marion F. O'Connor, eds., *Shakespeare Reproduced: The Text in History and Ideology* (London, 1987), pp. 242–64; David Norbrook, '*Macbeth* and the Politics of Historiography', in *Politics of Discourse: The Literature and History of Seventeenth-Century England*, ed. Kevin Sharpe and Steven N. Zwicker (Berkeley, 1987).

[14] In the nearly three years that had elapsed since James's accession, however, much had happened and he had become widely unpopular to various constituencies; hence the usual qualifiers, 'recently' or 'newly' crowned, seem to beg a key question of chronology and influence.

[15] This view of the play is perhaps best represented in Henry N. Paul, *The Royal Play of 'Macbeth'* (New York, 1950). A more recent version of the argument may be found in Alvin Kernan, *Shakespeare, the King's Playwright* (New Haven, 1995). James's work on witchcraft was the *Daemonology, In Form of a Dialogue* (Edinburgh, 1597). Scholars advancing this view of the play often assume that *Macbeth* was performed (even *first* performed) at Hampton Court on 7 August 1606, near the end of the visit of James's brother-in-law, King Christian IV of Denmark; however, while this is a plausible conjecture, the existing records do not mention the titles of the three plays for which Shakespeare's company was paid. See Braunmuller, *Macbeth*, pp. 8–9.

[16] For one example, powerful arguments by James Buchanan (King James's childhood tutor in Scotland) and many Continental writers had justified tyrannicide – the idea that a monarch who had become a tyrant could lawfully be deposed – a position King James specifically attempts to

Shakespeare's play, in any event, stages the murder of not one but two kings, amply justifies tyrannicide and seems to suggest that Duncan's institution of patrilineal succession is a disaster. If this be flattery . . .

Pushing further against the normalized reading of the play, I contend here that *Macbeth* scrutinizes different, often irreconcilable conceptions of succession and, in particular, interrogates the ways in which sovereign power justified itself through genealogical narratives such as the 'show of kings'. The historical moment of the play I consider, then, is not the aftermath of the Gunpowder Plot or the context of the Union debates – though both are crucial, and both relate to my concern – but more narrowly the genealogical battlefield from the 1570s that ultimately leads to *Macbeth* 4.1 in 1606 and 1709–14.

I begin this analysis with an obvious question: Given James's substantial assets – royal blood, two sons and the alleged death-bed approval of Queen Elizabeth – the question arises in retrospect why there was ever any doubt that he would be Elizabeth's successor? James's royal succession looked, on paper, quite clear, as the genealogy drawn up by Robert Cotton, deriving James's claim through the Saxon line, was meant to show (illustration 20).

Cotton's chart is a paradigm of clarity and logic: it omits the legitimate children who did not figure in the eventual history of succession, it omits the bastard children and adulterous lovers, and it is drawn in clear, elegant lines, moving top to bottom in chronological order, suggesting to (if not persuading) the viewer the absolute clarity of descent, culminating in the assertion at the bottom: 'Robert who was King of Scots from whom the kingdom is descended to James the six the lineall heir of all the Saxon kings which race is now again in him restored to the Crown'. Cotton's chart is genealogy as teleology, the end justified by the beginning. But this type of chart also deploys genealogy as an expression of ideology. It represents politics as natural destiny, a visual incarnation of the Succession Act that had proclaimed James to be king.[17]

In the decade before Elizabeth's death, however, other observers did not find the genealogical picture to be quite so clear. For example, in his incendiary work *A Conference about the Next Succession to the Crown of England* (1595),[18] the Jesuit intellectual and polemicist Robert Parsons (using the pseudonym 'Doleman') challenged James's possible succession, arguing that as many as a dozen people had substantial claims, especially his preferred candidate, the eldest daughter to the King of Spain, the Infanta Isabel, who would, he hoped, return England to Catholic rule. But even some Protestants, such as Thomas Wilson in 1600, observed that 'there are 12 competitors that gape for the death of that good old Princess the now Queen'.[19] Here then (illustration 21) is Parsons's considerably more muddled genealogical image.

This chart is virtually a whole forest, so heavy it has to be turned on its side: the legend at the upper left claims that this is 'A Perfect and Exact Arbor and Genealogy of all the Kings, Queens, and Princes of the Blood-Royal of England'. At

refute in his own writing. And second, polemicists asserted that the kingship itself, far from being an absolute, divine right, was to some extent a constructed relationship between the people and the monarch, and that the people, as in any contractural relationship, had the right to change monarchs when they felt it necessary. James had worked hard to counter these ideas in his political writings, especially *The True Law of Free Monarchies*, but his position was losing ground historically, as his son Charles I pointedly discovered in 1649.

17 Modern genealogical charts, with their clean straight lines and sharp right angles, imply an even more 'scientific' analysis, though in fact they always have similar omissions and exclusions. See Eviatar Zerubavel, *Time Maps: Collective Memory and the Social Shape of the Past* (Chicago, 2003).

18 It was published, as the title-page claims, in 1594, but distribution was delayed until 1595 until authorities in Rome approved. See Peter Holmes, 'The Authorship and Early Reception of *A Conference About the Next Succession to the Crown of England*', *Historical Journal*, 23 (1980), 415–29; and Michael L. Carrafiello, *Robert Parsons and English Catholicism, 1580–1610* (Selinsgrove, 1998), pp. 33–55.

19 Thomas Wilson, *The State of England A.D. 1600*, ed. F. J. Fisher, Camden Miscellany, 3rd ser., lii, p. 2. Elizabeth's own godson, Sir John Harington, said in 1602 that it had been 'the policy of the state' that as a 'counterpoise to the [claim of Mary,] Queen of Scots' [James's mother] . . . some other titles should underhand[edly] be set on foot at home' (*A Tract on the Succession to the Crown (A.D. 1602)* (London, 1880), pp. 41–2).

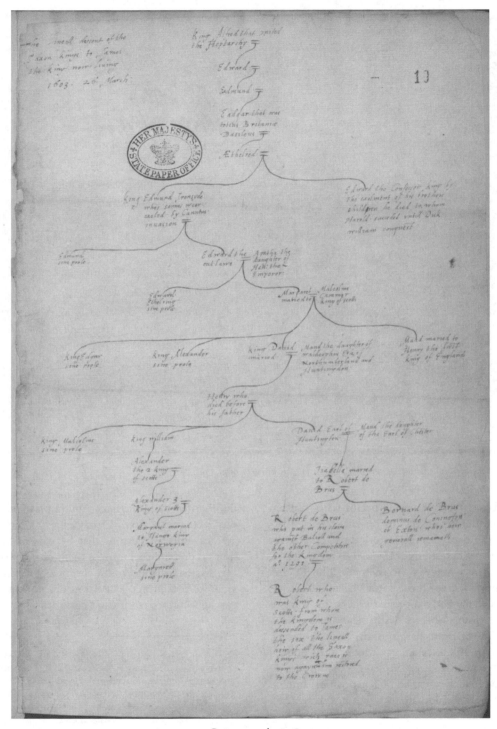

20. Cotton genealogy 1603.

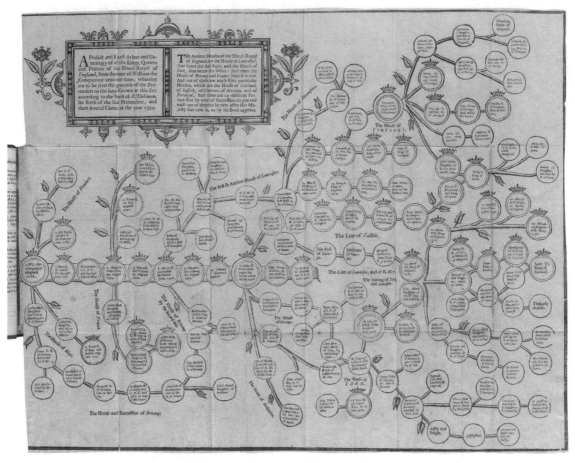

21. Parsons genealogy 1595.

the left margin, the arbour begins with William the Conqueror; but just to his left, off the margins of the page, lies the historical period actually covered in Shakespeare's *Macbeth*, in the reign of Edward the Confessor (1042–1066), 'the English king' in *Macbeth* to whose court Malcolm flees. (As with so many early modern writers, for Parsons English 'history' begins with the Norman invasion.) On the right margin of the chart, however, there is an efflorescence of chaotic, even embarrassing growth – strong saplings, noxious weeds, withered branches starved of genetic nourishment. Here too are illegitimate sons (but not daughters), disinherited sons, and pointed personal histories: '*Edw. V* put to death by his Unkle *Richard*'; 'Hoël

disinherited by his Father'. And in place of the ex post facto perspective of James's inevitability, there are '12 different Persons that by way of Succession do pretend each one of them to be next after Her Majesty that now is' – clearly a quite different view from Cotton's, as Parsons did not intend to cast light but to mystify and confuse.[20]

---

[20] The succession issues in this period have received substantial commentary: e.g. Joel Hurstfield, 'The Succession Struggle in Late Elizabethan England', in S. T. Bindoff et al., eds., *Elizabethan Government and Society: Essays Presented to Sir John Neale* (London, 1961), pp. 369–96; Marie Axton, *The Queen's Two Bodies: Drama and the Elizabethan Succession* (London, 1977); Levine, *Tudor Dynastic Problems*

James and his supporters therefore had to demolish the succession claims of several others as well as to fend off attacks on his own claims. His liabilities as lineal successor were in fact nearly as great as his assets, as Parsons and other opponents delighted in pointing out: there were nearer claimants in the House of Lancaster; he was excluded by the common law of England, which barred all foreigners born outside the realm from inheriting within the realm; James's mother, Mary Queen of Scots, had been put to death for conspiring against the life of Queen Elizabeth and, hence, by act of Parliament she and all her heirs lost all right, title, pretence or claim to the crown of England; and perhaps most importantly, Henry VIII's will, confirmed by two acts of Parliament, had established his sister Mary's line as having a prior claim to Margaret's.

Even those who supported James's claim, like the Scottish theologian John Leslie in 1584, a Catholic supporter of Mary, produced genealogical charts (illustration 22) that obfuscated James's claim as much as they supported it. Like Parsons's, Leslie's tree also begins with William the Conqueror, but his position now represents the ground, the beginning, of present history; not a branch, but the root. At the top is a similar arboreal plentitude and confusion. As similar as the Parsons and Leslie genealogies are, however, they were used – by two Catholic polemicists – to prove exactly the *opposite* points in terms of the English (via Scotland) succession: for Parsons, James should not be king; for Leslie, James (with his mother Mary first regaining the throne) should be king.[21]

To short-circuit now a long historical narrative, two things made possible James's peaceful ascent to the throne and his triumph over all the other claimants: his claim, though shaky in many ways, was nonetheless a very strong one; and he had reached a secret agreement with Elizabeth's chief minister, Robert Cecil, who stage-managed the succession for James, and then announced it to the nation.[22] The unruly genealogical arbours of Leslie, Parsons and others would eventually be pruned and thinned out by the authority of historical hindsight: genealogy would be written by the winners. The issue of succession would be transmuted through possession, and genealogies representing symmetry and harmony were produced where there really was none, as in the 1603 engraving by Renold Elstrak (illustration 23), which reverses direction from Cotton's genealogy, moving chronologically from the bottom up. This chart doesn't merely rewrite history but cleanses and purifies it as a 'seuen-fold golden chain ... in seven discents', with Mary Queen of Scots unembarrassedly linked to both her husbands (Francis II's presence seems purely for the sake of symmetry). The chart culminates with James and Anna ascendant, at the summit, alone, just below the eye of heaven, not even acknowledging the children who would succeed them.

Genealogy had indeed become a familiar practice in sixteenth-century England.[23] The very identity of the nation was based on the invented genealogy of Geoffrey of Monmouth, who claimed that Britain was founded by the imaginary Brut(e), or Brutus, great-grandson of Aeneas, twelve hundred years before the Christian era. Brut supposedly founded London as 'Troynovant' and begat a long line of kings, not ending until the death of Cadwallader. Several historians of the Tudor

---

1460–1571; Nenner, *The Right To Be King*; Jean-Christophe Mayer, ed., *The Struggle for the Succession in Late Elizabethan England* (Montpellier, 2004); and Lisa Hopkins, *Drama and the Succession to the Crown, 1561–1633* (Burlington, VT, 2011).

[21] Such division within Catholic discourse is yet another caution against totalizing historical claims.

[22] See *The secret correspondence of Sir Robert Cecil with James VI. King of Scotland. Now first published* (Edinburgh, 1766).

[23] On genealogy and heraldry in the period, see A. R. Wagner, *English Genealogy*, 2nd edn (Oxford, 1972), pp. 358–66; Michael Maclagan, 'Genealogy and Heraldry in the Sixteenth and Seventeenth Centuries', in Levi Fox, ed., *English Historical Scholarship in the Sixteenth and Seventeenth Centuries* (London, 1956), pp. 31–48; D. R. Woolf, *The Idea of History in Early Stuart England* (Toronto, 1990), pp. 73–137; Joan Evans, *A History of the Society of Antiquaries* (Oxford, 1956), pp. 1–32; and J. F. R. Day, 'Primers of Honor: Heraldry, Heraldry Books, and English Renaissance Literature', *Sixteenth Century Journal*, 21:1 (1990): 93–103. For Shakespeare's own pursuit of a coat of arms, see the account in Samuel Schoenbaum, *William Shakespeare: A Compact Documentary Life* (Oxford, 1977), pp. 228–32.

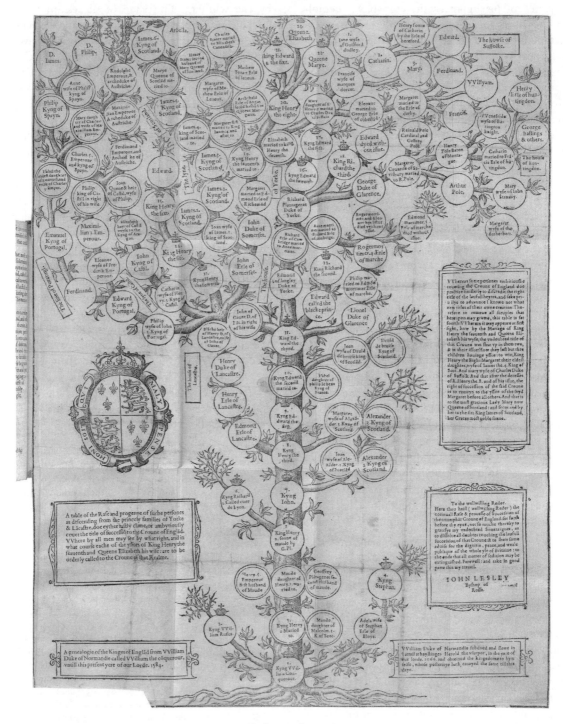

22. Leslie genealogy 1584.

23. Renold Elstrak 1603.

period, such as Polydore Vergil, disputed this claim, but it remained in literary and historical works throughout the period, and served as a powerful genealogical narrative of national identity.[24] James and his followers would repeatedly link him to the tradition of Brut, indeed as Brut's lineal successor. James's campaign, beginning in 1604, to rename England, Wales and Scotland as 'Great Britain' was much more than a simple invocation of past glories, but part of an elaborate campaign to establish the grounds on which imperial expansion (in America and Ireland particularly) could take place.[25] And the Brut tradition, above all, provided genealogical ratification of James's legitimacy.

Genealogical discourse was in general masculine discourse, written by men about male descent. Descent through the female line was not impossible, of course, but never desirable. James and his supporters argued the case for his royal blood on several fronts, above all through the English line from Margaret, but also, as seen in illustration 20, from the pre-Norman Saxon kings. James was also at pains to establish the lines of his Scottish descent – which could, it was claimed, be traced back to Noah (or at least Fergus). Thus, prior to and even after his ascent to the English throne, James's supporters began to publish ever more elaborate royal genealogies of both the English and the Scottish lines. It would not be an exaggeration to say that a campaign of lineal cleansing was undertaken. In 1604, George Owen Harry published perhaps the *ne plus ultra* of such works, entitled *The Genealogy of the High and Mighty Monarch, James*, with forty pages of genealogical narrative, in multiple columns, from Noah to James (illustrations 24a, 24b), followed by an additional twenty-four pages showing James's royal descent from French, Welsh, Saxon and Spanish lines.[26]

Panegyric welcomings of James written in the first few years of his new reign in England also presented the genealogical imperative at length, congratulating him for bringing such a pure hereditary line to the job; most also hailed him as 'the new Brut'.[27] James and his supporters thus continued to fight the genealogical battle against Parsons and others for decades after his ascent, in fact far into the next century, well after both Parsons and James were dead; Parsons was still being reprinted, attacked and defended in the years from the Exclusion Crisis to the publication of Rowe's edition of Shakespeare's plays.[28]

---

[24] See Woolf, *The Idea of History in Early Stuart England*, and Roger A. Mason, 'Scotching the Brut: Politics, History and National Myth in Sixteenth-Century Britain', in *Scotland and England, 1286–1815*, ed. Roger A. Mason (Edinburgh, 1987). For typical early modern comments on Brut, see, for example, William Camden, *Britain* (London, 1610), p. 8, where he summarizes the arguments against the Brut legend; Peter Heylyn, *Microcosmos* (Oxford, 1625), like many other writers, would cite Camden's commentary, and then dismiss or omit the legend of Brut as 'rather a fabulous report, then a well grounded historicall truth' (p. 458). On the other side of the debate, Richard Harvey published (against Buchanan's rejection of the legend) *Philadelphus, or A Defence of Brutes, and the Brutans History* (London, 1593).

[25] See, among many works on this topic, Tristan Marshall, *Theatre and Empire* (Manchester, 2000).

[26] The title, virtually an essay in itself, continues: *by the grace of God, King of great Brittayne, &c. with his lineall descent from Noah, by divers direct lynes to Brutus, first Inhabiter of this Ile of Brittayne; and from him to Cadwalader, the last King of the Brittish bloud; and from thence, sundry wayes to his Maiesty: wherein is playnly shewed his rightfull Title, by lawfull descent.* These genealogical claims would be repeated, with even less justification, at the end of the Stuart dynasty, and especially at key points of stress, such as the Exclusion Crisis.

[27] E.g. Samuel Daniel, *A Panegyrik Congratulatory delivered to the King's most excellent Majesty* (London, 1603), Thomas Dekker, *The Magnificent Entertainment* (London, 1604) and Anthony Munday, *The Triumphs of Re-United Brittania* (London, 1605).

[28] As the following titles indicate: *The Royal Apology or, An Answer to the Rebels Plea: Wherein, The Most Noted Anti-Monarchical Tenents, First, Published by Doleman the Jesuite, to promote a Bill of Exclusion against King James* etc. (London, 1684; probably written by William Assheton); Sir George Mackenzie, *Jus Regium: Or, the Just, and Solid Foundations of Monarchy. In General, and more especially of the Monarchy of Scotland: Maintain'd against Buchannan, Naphthali, Dolman, Milton, &c.* (Edinburgh, 1684) and *That the Lawful Successor Cannot be Debarr'd From Succeeding to the Crown: Maintained against Dolman, Buchannan, and others* (Edinburgh, 1684); *The Apostate Protestant: A Letter to a Friend, Occasioned By the late Reprinting of a Jesuites Book. About Succession To The Crown of England, Pretended to have been written by R. Doleman* (London, 1682; probably written by Edward Pelling). Sir Thomas Craig's *The Right of Succession to the Kingdom of England . . . Against the Sophisme of Parsons the Jesuite* – a

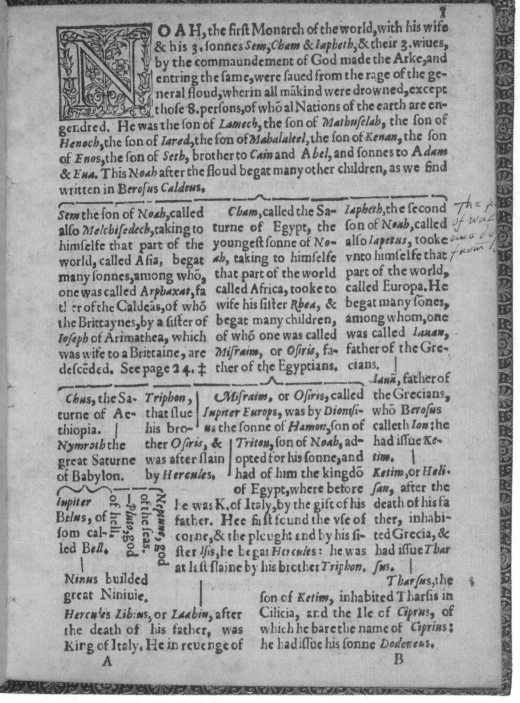

NOAH, the first Monarch of the world, with his wife & his 3. sonnes *Sem, Cham* & *Iapheth*, & their 3. wiues, by the commaundement of God made the Arke, and entring the same, were saued from the rage of the generall floud, wherin all mākind were drowned, except those 8. persons, of who al Nations of the earth are engendred. He was the son of *Lamech*, the son of *Mathuselah*, the son of *Henoch*, the son of *Iared*, the son of *Mahalaleel*, the son of *Kenan*, the son of *Enos*, the son of *Seth*, brother to *Cain* and *Abel*, and sonnes to Adam & Eua. This *Noah* after the floud begat many other children, as we find written in *Berosus Caldeus*.

Sem the son of *Noah*, called also *Melchisedech*, taking to himselfe that part of the world, called Asia, begat many sonnes, among whō, one was called *Arphaxat*, father of the Caldeas, of whō the Brittaynes, by a sister of *Ioseph* of Arimathea, which was wife to a Brittaine, are descēded. See page 24. ‡

Cham, called the Saturne of Egypt, the youngest sonne of *Noah*, taking to himselfe that part of the world called Africa, tooke to wife his sister *Rhea*, & begat many children, of whō one was called *Misraim*, or *Osiris*, father of the Egyptians.

Iapheth, the second son of *Noah*, called also *Iapetus*, tooke vnto himselfe that part of the world, called Europa. He begat many sones, among whom, one was called *Iauan*, father of the Grecians.

Chus, the Saturne of Aethiopia. | *Nymroth* the great Saturne of Babylon. |

Triphon, that slue his brother *Osiris*, & was after slain by *Hercules*.

Misraim, or *Osiris*, called *Iupiter Europs*, was by *Dionisius* the sonne of *Hamon*, son of *Triton*, son of *Noah*, adopted for his sonne, and had of him the kingdō of Egypt, where before he was K. of Italy, by the gift of his father. Hee first found the vse of corne, & the plough: and by his sister *Isis*, he begat *Hercules*: he was at last slaine by his brother *Triphon*.

Iauan, father of the Grecians, whō *Berosus* calleth *Ion*: he had issue *Ketim*. |

Ketim, or *Helisan*, after the death of his father, inhabited Grecia, & had issue *Thar sus*. |

Iupiter Belus, of whō sō cal-led Bell. |

Neptune, god of the seas. | *Pluto*, god of hell.

Ninus builded great Niniuie.

Hercules Libius, or *Laabin*, after the death of his father, was King of Italy. He in reuenge of

Tharsus, the son of *Ketim*, inhabited Tharsis in Cilicia, and the Ile of *Ciprus*, of which he bare the name of *Ciprus*: he had issue his sonne *Dodoneus*.

A

B

24a. George Owen Harry 1604.

24b. George Owen Harry 1604.

Stuart anxieties of origin, descent and legitimacy long predated James's ascent to the English crown. Peter Lake has convincingly argued that James's most foundational political text, *The True Law of Free Monarchies* (published Edinburgh, 1598), was itself written in large part as a response to Parsons's book (as well as against Buchanan), though Parsons is never mentioned.[29] James had received a copy of Parsons's work shortly after it was published and had immediately commissioned responses by loyalists to be printed by Robert Waldegrave, the king's printer.[30] *True Law*'s starting point is that of possession, articulating monarchical power and privilege rather than analysing the road to kingship via succession theory.

Among the most important claims supporting Jacobean succession in England was the descent of the house of Stuart in the aftermath of the reign of Macbeth, King of Scotland, as most famously represented by John Leslie, the Catholic supporter of Mary (illustration 25).

major early rebuttal of Parsons – was written *c.*1602–3 but only first published in London in 1703, while Sir John Hayward's rebuttal of Parsons, *An Answer to the First Part of a Certain Conference Concerning Succession* (1603), was reprinted in 1683. Parsons's *Conference* had been reprinted in 1681, and his *Jesuit's Memorial*, written in 1596, was for the first time published in 1690, with a copy presented to James II.

29 Peter Lake, 'The King (The Queen) and the Jesuit: James Stuart's 'True Law of Free Monarchies' in Context/s', *Transactions of the Royal Historical Society*, Ser. 6:14 (2004), 243–60.

30 Writing to Burghley in February 1596, John Carey reported a friend's comment that James 'keeps it [Parsons's book] so "charely" that it cannot be "wanting" from his keeper "above one night"'; Carey then offers a lengthy summary 'from one that saw the book', in which 'there is a blot in the King's title for his mother was attainted, convicted, and executed for treason against the Queen': *Calendar of Letters and Papers Relating to the Affairs of the Borders of England and Scotland*, vol. 2, pp. 102–4. George Nicolson reported that on 29 Dec. 1595 'The King has given it [Parsons's book] to Mr. John Sharpe to answer', and a few weeks later Robert Aston wrote that 'The King is highly offended at Dolman's book in so much as the ministers speaks [sic] of it

25. John Leslie 1578.

This famous image purports to represent the origin of the Stuarts. At the very top of the flourishing tree is 'Jacobus', James, and next his mother Mary Queen of Scots. We move down from James through the line of Stuart monarchs, and then through others to 'Fleanchus', or Fleance, and at the foundation, solid as a rock, is 'BANQV°H', the Banquo of Shakespeare's play. Thus this genealogical tree establishes the link from Banquo, in the reign of Macbeth, who was 85th king of Scotland, to James VI, the 108th (or 107th) king of Scotland.[31]

The link between Banquo and James, however, was not ultimately one of legitimate blood, but of merit or effort. As Holinshed told the tale, when Banquo was murdered by Macbeth's men, Fleance fled to Wales, where he impregnated the Welsh princess; the furious father 'conceived such hatefull displeasure towards Fleance, that he finallie slue him, & held his daughter in most vile estate of seruitude, for that she had consented to be on this wise defloured by a stranger'. The daughter delivered a bastard and now fatherless son, Walter. When he was a young man, Walter was taunted 'that he was a bastard, and begotten in unlawfull bed', and in anger he killed his tormentor, afterwards fled Wales for Scotland, achieved honour and reputation there, and so was made 'lord steward of Scotland', hence the family name Steward or Stuart.[32] Several generations later, one of the Stuart descendants married Marjorie Bruce, daughter of Robert Bruce and their offspring became Robert II, and the rest followed in more or less orderly fashion, one assassination or deposition following the next, leading finally to James.

One wonders why this genealogy would have been a comforting narrative of origin for James, or any of the Stuarts, as it involves illegitimacy, murder and the kind of rags-to-riches story that hardly reflects ancient nobility. But even this genealogy, the founding myth of the Stuart dynasty, was a product of the imagination, not historical fact. Banquo and Fleance were apparently invented by the early Scottish historian, Hector Boece in 1527; prior to his work, no such persons had ever appeared in chronicles, court records, or any

other document.[33] Boece's manufacturing of Banquo and Fleance solidified the line of Stuart succession and also, importantly, produced a direct derivation from the Welsh, hence English, line for the Stuarts; it also connected the Stuarts to the long Scottish line back to Noah. Within a few decades, the Banquo–Fleance myth had congealed into accepted historical fact – except for the muted voices of a few sceptical historians.[34]

Yet even after 1603, the Jacobean regime and its supporters continued to assert, reaffirm and in all ways pronounce as absolute the lineal blood legitimacy of their monarch. These anxieties of origin could not be muted, the thirst for lineal legitimacy never quite quenched, by the power of possession. In dozens of texts and genealogical charts, James's claim was propped up, and even extended so

---

in pulpit, persuading the people that that book makes the Spaniard the lawful successor of England, which may be said their intent is nothing but conquest. The ministers and the King were never so great' (*Calendar of State Papers Relating to Scotland . . . 1547–1603*, vol. 12, pp. 100, 126).

31 The usual designation was 108, as in Buchanan; however, in his *Inscriptiones historicae regum Scotorum* (Edinburgh, 1602), John Johnston placed James as number 107 by skipping over Mary, apparently judged unworthy of royal enumeration (p. *6). When John Taylor visited Holyrood Palace, Edinburgh, in 1618, he referred to the 'one hundred and seven descents' of unconquered rulers that have led to 'our peacefull king' James, quoted in P. Hume Brown, ed., *Early Travellers in Scotland* (Edinburgh, 1891), p. 111.

32 Raphael Holinshed, *The Chronicles of England, Scotland, and Ireland* (London, 1587; 6 vols., London, 1808), vol. 5, p. 272.

33 See R. J. Adam, 'The Real Macbeth: King of Scots, 1040–1054', *History Today*, 7:6 (1957), 381–7; Kenneth D. Farrow, 'The Historiographical Evolution of the Macbeth Narrative', *Scottish Literary Journal*, 21 (1994), 5–23; and Nick Aitchinson, *Macbeth: Man and Myth* (Sutton, 1999). Boece also provided, for the first time, the names and dates of the mythical first forty-five kings between Fergus I and Fergus II.

34 Such as Sir George Buc, who in 1605, in a work otherwise rhapsodic in its praises of James and his royal blood, discreetly said that this alleged descent, in which 'Fleanchus thane . . . begat unlawfully a sonne, whoe should be ancestor to all the Chiefe Stewards to his day . . . being not acknowledged by the best Scotish Historiographers, & the thing not honourable, I may well pretermit [i.e. omit] it' (*Daphnis Polystephanos. An Eclog treating of Crowns, and of Garlands* (London, 1605), A4v).

far that one sympathetic Scottish historian claimed that 'the title of *every* race which . . . has at different times ruled England is united in the person of our most gracious king'.[35] And an equally enthusiastic Scottish poet, Alexander Craig, published in 1604 a poem entitled 'Elizabeth, Late Queene of England, Her Ghost', in which the dead but surprisingly loquacious queen speaks the words that James had longed to hear but which she never in her life had actually spoken:

So now my ghost is glad, that by my care his pain,
My countries have their lawful King, the King his crowns
    again . . .
A godly David ruleth now, a Prophet and a Prince
All you my subjects dear, do homage due to him,
And that shall make my blessed ghost in boundless joys
    to swim.[36]

This *post hoc* spectral authorization of James's succession is genealogical fantasy of the highest order, apparently validating the Jacobean claim that had been contested throughout the last decades of the sixteenth century. Elizabeth's ghost, then, speaks what many readers have assumed is the meaning of the show of kings in 4.1: that James's descent legitimated his ascent to the throne.

* * *

The principle of royal succession in *Macbeth* has seemed self-evident to many readers, especially those invested in the Authorized Version: Malcolm is the rightful king, and his crowning at the end represents a restitution of the legitimate line that Macbeth has interrupted. Certainly Davenant and Stuart royalists saw the play in this light, and the structure of the play lends itself to this reading. I would argue, however, that Shakespeare mystifies the principles of succession, and therefore legitimacy, in the play, offering disparate visions of how sovereignty constitutes itself. In Holinshed, the key moment in the transformation of succession theory comes in the reign of Kenneth, when he attempts to change the ancient Scottish system of tanistry – a form of election, usually of the worthiest thane, and not necessarily (in some accounts, never) the sovereign's first-born[37] – to

one of hereditary, patrilineal succession, when he names his son (also a Malcolm) to succeed him.[38] Duncan succeeds Malcolm II, but he is not the son but a nephew. Duncan's naming of *his* son Malcolm as Prince of Cumberland is therefore the first Scottish attempt at a patrilineal succession without interruption.

Shakespeare suppresses many of the details in Holinshed's account but still places a contested view of succession at the heart of Macbeth's ambition. Malcolm, moreover, was in the chronicle sources a minor, 'not of able age' (Holinshed), 'scarce yet out of his Childhood' (Buchanan) and thus prohibited from inheriting.[39] In the public ceremony in 1.4 – 'We will establish our estate upon / Our eldest, Malcolm, whom we name hereafter / The Prince of Cumberland' (1.4.37–9) – Duncan's action both alters the ancient Scottish succession system, and at the same time seems to

---

35 Sir Thomas Craig, *A Treatise on the Union of the British Realms*, trans. C. Sanford Terry (Edinburgh, 1909), pp. 267–8 (my emphasis), translation of *De unione regnorum Britanniae tractatus* (c.1602–3).

36 Alexander Craig, *The Poeticall Essayes of Alexander Craige* (London, 1604), C4r–v.

37 See (among others) Norbrook, '*Macbeth* and the Politics of Historiography'; Nenner, *The Right To Be King*; J. H. Stevenson, 'The Law of the Throne: Tanistry and the Introduction of the Law of Primogeniture: A Note on the Succession of the Kings of Scotland from Kenneth MacAlpin to Robert Bruce', *The Scottish Historical Review*, 25:97 (1927), 1–12; and Albert Rolls, '*Macbeth* and the Uncertainties of the Succession Law', *Shakespeare Bulletin*, 52:2 (2002), 43–4, 48. According to the theory, the kingship was to alternate between parallel lines of descent, and Duncan and Macbeth were cousins.

38 The initial attempt fails, however, and the kingship reverts to the old system until later, when Kenneth's son Malcolm refused to receive the crown 'except the law established by his father Kenneth for the succession thereof were first confirmed and approved, whereupon the lords bound themselves by solemne othes to perform the same' (Holinshed 5.255).

39 James himself had been an infant when he became king. Holinshed marvelled that 'in all the kings of Scotland descended of the Stewards: that never anie one of them except the first & second king of that name was of the age of man, or of one and twentie yeeres when they put on the kinglie ornaments. A rare thing, and not unmeet to be considered of' (Holinshed 5.629–30).

observe the later normative system of primogeniture and inheritance. Shakespeare's careful phrasing of Duncan's declaration inspires some doubt, however: why must Duncan *name* his son the Prince of Cumberland, if inheritance is the ruling system? And why does Duncan employ the Lear-like language ('we shall . . . we have this hour a constant will' etc.) of 'We will establish our estate' if the recipient was clear in the eyes of the law?

Perhaps my quibbles with Duncan's language over-complicate the moment, but the analogue in Lear's attempt to determine his own succession should give us pause. Macbeth, in any event, recognizes this move for what it is, 'a step / On which I must fall down or else o'erleap, / For in my way it lies' (1.4.48–50). Beyond his violation of traditional political form, Duncan makes the very mistake that Queen Elizabeth had been so careful not to make, naming one's own successor: urged to name Mary Queen of Scots her heir presumptive, Elizabeth replied 'Think you that I could love my own winding-sheet? Princes cannot like their own children, those that should succeed unto them . . . in assuring her of the succession we might put our present state in doubt.'[40] As Elizabeth had feared and Macbeth's aside reveals, Duncan has just spoken his own death warrant.

After Duncan's murder, which Macbeth blames on Duncan's sons, Malcolm and Donalbain (who have fled), Macduff reports without comment that Macbeth 'is already named and gone to Scone / To be invested' (2.4.31–2). Macbeth thus becomes the lawful king – recognized as such by everyone in the play, even when his crimes are public, and recognized as such in every chronicle of the time. He becomes king not through inheritance but through a form of election. He too has been 'named', as Malcolm had been. The subject of this passive construction, though unstated, is no doubt the other thanes, who have apparently stripped Malcolm of his hereditary right – certainly not a possibility for those who believed in divine right. The anonymous Lord, speaking carefully with Lennox, later identifies Malcolm as 'The son of Duncan / From whom this tyrant holds the due of birth' (3.6.24–5), thus reinstating

the concept of kingship as hereditary debt, and at the same time beginning the crescendo of invocations of the ideologically charged term 'tyrant' and its variants,[41] the necessary groundwork in preparing justification for the play's murder of Macbeth not as a regicide but as a tyrannicide.

But while Macbeth has now become the lawful king, he cannot rest, for he soon recalls the witches' prophecy about Banquo:

> Then, prophet-like,
> They hailed him father to a line of kings.
> Upon my head they placed a fruitless crown,
> And put a barren sceptre in my grip,
> Thence to be wrenched with an unlineal hand,
> No son of mine succeeding. If 't be so,
> For Banquo's issue have I filed my mind;
> For them the gracious Duncan have I murdered . . .
> To make them kings, the seeds of Banquo kings.
>
> (3.1.60–71)

Ironically, Macbeth now wishes that *he* had a son who would succeed him in the kingship. The dream of patrilineal succession that might retroactively justify Macbeth's actions falters, as he realizes that 'this bank and shoal of time' is, as he feared, far from 'the be-all and the end-all' (1.7.5–6) that he had hoped. Worse, his crown will be 'wrenched' by 'an unlineal hand', an odd phrase suggesting that he had already established his own lineage; whosever 'hand' it may be, it will be without any more legitimacy than his own 'hand'. The dream of succession requires 'seeds', a son, but there is none. To enhance Macbeth's desire and anxiety, Shakespeare erased the existence of Lady Macbeth's son from her first marriage, Lulach, who is fully present in Holinshed but not in the play.[42]

---

[40] Quoted in Levine, *Tudor Dynastic Problems 1460–1571*, pp. 177–8.

[41] The words *tyranny* and *tyrant* occur 18 times in the play; 16 of those instances are from 4.3 and the fifth act following.

[42] 'Thus while Malcolm was busied in setting orders amongst his subjects, tidings came that one Lugtake [i.e. Lulach] surnamed the fool, being either the son, or (as some write) the cousin of the late mentioned Macbeth, was conveyed, with a great number of such as had taken part with the said Macbeth, unto Scone, and there by their support received the crown, as lawful inheritor thereto. To appease this business,

Here, in Macbeth's contradictory desire for his own patrilineal succession, may be the explanation for Banquo's unusual prominence in Shakespeare's play. Shakespeare's sources describe Banquo as an active co-conspirator against Duncan, not the moral figure of Shakespeare's play who experiences some temptation but, in contrast to Macbeth, would do only that which would 'still keep / My bosom franchised and allegiance clear' (2.1.26–7).[43] Shakespeare thus decontaminates the Banquo of his sources, perhaps because the chronicles pronounced him the origin of the Stuart line. Moreover, Shakespeare does not show Macbeth haunted by the ghost of Duncan – the Scottish king, father-figure and kinsman, who has been 'So clear in his great office, that his virtues / Will plead like angels, trumpet-tongued against / The deep damnation of his taking-off' (1.7.18–20). Wouldn't an audience expect to see, if not angelic trumpets, at least the ghost of the murdered *king*, as in *Hamlet*? Or as in *Julius Caesar*, the ghost of the murdered Caesar? But after Fleance's escape, Macbeth is haunted instead by that ghost of history, Banquo – especially by the manner of his appearance. According to the Folio stage direction, the ghost of Banquo enters '*and sits in Macbeths place*' (Folio TLN 1251sd.) at the banquet table; such figures, once thought dead, Macbeth says, now 'rise again / With twenty mortal murders on their crowns, / And push us from our stools' (3.4.79–81). Macbeth refers to the twenty or more mortal gashes that Banquo has in his head, but the line also suggests, by the word 'crowns', that Banquo has in effect been 'crowned' by his murder, and that he will push Macbeth from his stool or place, just as Macbeth pushed Duncan from his place.

Unnerved by the ghastly sight of Banquo's ghost, Macbeth seeks out the witches himself. The 'unknown power' that speaks the second set of prophecies tells him the future. The last prophecy – 'Macbeth shall never vanquished be until / Great Birnam Wood to high Dunsinane Hill / Shall come against him' (4.1.108–10) – accompanies the apparition of '*a child crowned, with a tree in his hand*', that 'rises like the issue of a king, / And wears upon his baby-brow the round / And top of sovereignty' (4.1.103–5). This 'tree' signifies how Malcolm's troops will become Great Birnam wood on the move, but it also suggests the genealogical tree, itself figuring the 'top of sovereignty', that defeats Macbeth's ambitions.

Finding these prophecies inadequate, Macbeth demands more: 'Yet my heart / Throbs to know one thing. Tell me, if your art / Can tell so much, shall Banquo's issue ever / Reign in this kingdom?' (4.1.116–19). At which point the witches call forth '*A shew of eight Kings, and Banquo last, with a glasse in his hand*', according to the Folio stage direction (most editors emend the stage direction so that the eighth king, not Banquo, carries the glass). As I noted earlier, the show of kings is purely Shakespeare's invention, a gesture towards Jacobean discourses of sovereign power, and an enactment of Jacobean fantasies of genealogical purity on a par with the supposed prophecy of Elizabeth's ghost. This vision of Banquo's progeny stretching 'out to th' crack of doom', with the eighth king holding a 'glass' in which 'many more' appear, some carrying 'twofold balls and treble sceptres', overcomes Macbeth.[44] Extended over five centuries, the line

---

was Macduff Earl [his new title, granted by Malcolm] of Fife sent with full commission in the king's name, who encountering with Lugtake at a village called Essen in Bogdale, slew him, and discomfited his whole power, ordering the matter with them in such wise, that afterwards there was no more trouble attempted in that behalf' (Holinshed 5.278).

43 Holinshed: 'Communicating his purposed intent with his trustie friends, amongst whome Banquho was the chiefest, upon confidence of their promised aid, he [Macbeth] slue the king at Envernes, or (as some say) at Botgosuane, in the sixt yeare of his reigne' (Holinshed 5.269); George Buchanan, *Rerum Scoticarum Historia*: '*Bancho*, who was his Companion in the Kings Parricide' (Bullough, 7.514).

44 The three sceptres reflect James's rule over Great Britain (as he now called it), France and Ireland, while the double orbs reflect the union of Scotland and England. The 'glass', as Braunmuller glosses, was not a mirror but a 'magic crystal permitting visions of the future' (4.1.110sd.1n.). But see also Iain Wright, '"Come like shadowes, so depart": The Ghostly Kings in *Macbeth*', *Shakespearean International Yearbook*, 6 (2006), 215–29; and Mitsuru Kamachi, 'Banquo's Glass: The King of Anamorphosis on the First Night of *Macbeth*', *Shakespeare Studies* (The Shakespeare Society of Japan), 38 (2000): 39–53.

would reach even to the reigning monarch, James himself.

Shakespeare's audience would surely not have been surprised to encounter this genealogical chorus-line, for the show of kings – the visual representation of royal genealogical descent – had been a recurring feature of English and European royal discourse for two centuries and more. Such kingly processions purported to show royal succession as an orderly, naturalized sequence without gaps or interlopers, draining all anxiety out of what was historically contingent. In his analysis of the legal fiction of the King's Two Bodies and the Crown that never dies, Ernst Kantorowicz connected the legal logic to the show of kings in Shakespeare's play in a passage worth quoting in full:

By maintaining the fictitious oneness of the predecessors with potential successors, all of whom were present and incorporated in the actual incumbent of the Dignity, the jurists constructed a fictitious person, a 'corporation by succession' composed of all those vested successively with that particular Dignity – a fiction which makes us think of the witches in Shakespeare's *Macbeth* (IV.i.112ff), who conjure up that uncanny ghostly procession of Macbeth's [sic] predecessor kings whose last one bears the 'glass' showing the long file of successors. By this fiction, at any rate, the plurality of persons necessary to make up a corporation was achieved.[45]

Kantorowicz's mental slip is instructive, for the show of kings does not display *Macbeth*'s but rather James's 'predecessor kings', nor do they emanate from (or to) Macbeth, but from Banquo. Kantorowicz's slip ironically reproduces Macbeth's desire to be part of a 'line' of kings himself, while inadvertently linking Macbeth, not Banquo, with James.

Still, Kantorowicz's analysis remains valid: the concept of patrilineal succession requires every point on the 'line' to be full, hence the monarchical 'show' in public pageants. Henry VI's 1432 entry into London, for example, featured, among other spectacles, two 'trees of royal lineage with children in their branches stand[ing] at conduits whose water, at the advent of the king, [was] transformed into wine, both red and white'. The paired trees of lineage, Richard Osberg has noted, with 'the king's lineage facing back in the direction from which the king has come and the Jesse Tree [showing the descent from Christ through David and Mary] facing forward towards the last pageant and St Paul's', represent the king as Messiah, 'the one [tree] establishing Christ's title to the throne of Israel, the other establishing Henry's right to the titles of England and France'.[46] Closer to home, in their royal entry into Edinburgh, on 19 May 1590, James and Anna were greeted by 'historical figures personating all the previous kings of Scotland [who] sat at the Salt Throne, "one of them lying along at their feete, as if he had been sick . . . [who] arose, and made [Queen Anna] an oration in Latine"'.[47] In London, Anthony Munday's Lord Mayor's pageant of 1605, *The Triumphs of Re-united Brittania* (which heralded James as 'our second Brute'[48]), included a show of 'seven king[s] that did in England reign', from Edward the Third through to Henry VII (though of course omitting Richard III), all previous 'Free Brethren' of the Merchant Taylors' Company that produced the show. When Charles I entered Edinburgh in 1633 he was greeted with a civic display painted by George Jamesone in which 'the Theater (a Courten drawne) manifested Mercury, with his feathered hat, and his Caduceus, with an hundred and seven Scottish Kings, which hee had

---

45 Ernst Kantorowicz, *The King's Two Bodies* (Princeton, 1957), p. 387.

46 Richard Osberg, 'The Jesse Tree in the 1432 London Entry of Henry VI: Messianic Kingship and the Rule of Justice', *Journal of Medieval and Renaissance Studies*, 16:2 (1986), pp. 214, 228–30.

47 Quoted in David Bergeron, *English Civic Pageantry 1558–1642* (Columbia, SC, 1971), p. 69.

48 As Munday wrote, James was 'truly and rightfully descended: by whose happy coming to the crown, England, Wales, and Scotland, by the first Brute severed and divided, is in our second Brute re-united and made one happy Britannia again', in *Renaissance Drama*, ed. Arthur F. Kinney (Oxford, 1999), p. 377.

brought from the Elisian fields, Fergus the first had a speech in Latine'.[49] Later in the century, Charles II in 1684 commissioned Jacob De Wet to paint the now 110 kings of Scotland to hang in Holyrood, 'all presented', as Steve Bruce and Steven Yearley note, 'in an orderly manner as if they had come to the throne by those Anglo-Norman primogeniture rules of succession so strongly, disingenuously and (in the case of the kings pre-House of Canmore) anachronistically asserted by the Scots parliament in 1681'.[50]

De Wet had not yet produced his portraits when the then Princess Anne visited Edinburgh in 1681–2, but as Queen Anne she had in 1710 – to return to our beginning – welcomed a show of actual kings to her court, the Four Indian Kings: four Iroquois chiefs on a diplomatic embassy from America.[51] It was hoped that they would assist in expelling the French from Canada – which was precisely the reason the Four Kings themselves had come to London, to seek the support of their 'GREAT QUEEN', who had unaccountably delayed in sending 'an Army to reduce Canada', as had been promised.[52]

One pamphlet published on the occasion of their visit[53] shows them, like the Magi, 'Prostrating themselves before Her Majesty' (illustration 26). In order for the Kings to be legible as royalty to the British public, the 'Dressers at the Play-house were consulted', on the Queen's orders, 'about the clothing of these Monarchs, and it was determined that part of their Dress should be a Royal Mantle'.[54] Hence they assumed theatrical garb signifying European royalty, in an irony further marked by their appearance in advertising for one of the entertainments scheduled in their honour, a puppet-show, where the exotic feathers by their ears were domesticated by their generic 'European' royal crowns and robes (illustration 27). Thus did the Four Kings themselves become an entertainment, dressed 'like other Kings of the Theatre', as John Oldmixon noted.[55]

As part of their entertainment while in London, the Four Kings were taken to a performance of – what else? – *Macbeth*, in Davenant's version, at the

[49] *The Entertainment of the High and Mighty Monarch Charles* (Edinburgh, 1633), pp. 12–13; Fergus's speech, unfortunately, is not included. See also Elizabeth McGrath, 'Local Heroes: The Scottish Humanist Parnassus for Charles I', in *England and the Continental Renaissance*, ed. Edward Chaney and Peter Mack (Woodbridge, Suffolk, 1990), pp. 257–70.

[50] Steve Bruce and Steven Yearley, 'The De Wet Portraits of the Scottish Kings', *Review of Scottish Culture*, 6 (1990), 15. Charles died before the series was completed. One hundred of the portraits are still in existence, eighty-nine of them in the Gallery (p. 18). As John Macky reported in *A Journey Through Scotland* (London, 1723), the figures stretched from 'Fergus their first King, 320 Years before the Birth of Christ, down to the Revolution' (p. 59).

[51] The four were not, strictly speaking, 'kings', as Eric Hinderaker points out in his excellent essay placing their visit in terms of the construction of a British empire: the 'impulse to project political sovereignty onto native leaders was entirely consistent . . . with the desire to extend English imperial authority in America: it posited the existence of native peoples who were capable of serving as effective allies and agents of the crown in the empire-building process' ('The "Four Indian Kings" and the Imaginative Construction of the First British Empire', *The William and Mary Quarterly*, 53:3 (1996), 488). Moreover, 'only one could be described as a sachem, and even that was stretching the truth' (p. 490). The 'essential characteristic of the four Indian kings in these contexts was that they be kings. They were treated as agents of state power and as potential allies and clients of the crown, roles Native Americans had never before been asked to play for an English audience' (p. 494).

[52] See the Four Kings' 'Speech to Her Majesty' of 20 April (London, 1710). On the politics of empire surrounding their visit, see Barbara Shapiro, *A Culture of Fact: England, 1550–1720* (Ithaca, 2000), pp. 21–34, as well as Hinderaker. The delay was perhaps the result of mourning duties following the death of Prince George in October 1708.

[53] On the Four Kings' visit, see Richmond P. Bond, *Queen Anne's American Kings* (Oxford, 1952) and John G. Garratt, *The Four Indian Kings* (Ottawa, 1985). In *Cities of the Dead: Circum-Atlantic Performance* (New York, 1996), Joseph Roach offers a provocative and illuminating account of the visit in terms of 'mutually intelligible beliefs about the afterlife' (p. 170), though that is only one strand in his rich study.

[54] John Oldmixon, *The British Empire in America* (London, 1741), p. 247. Oldmixon goes on to note that since 'The Court was then in Mourning' over the death of Prince George of Denmark, the royal consort, 'they were clothed with black Breeches, Waistcoat, Stockings, and Shoes, after the English Fashion'.

[55] John Oldmixon, *The History of England During the Reigns of King William and Mary, Queen Anne, King George I* (London, 1735), p. 452.

26. Four Indian Kings 1710.

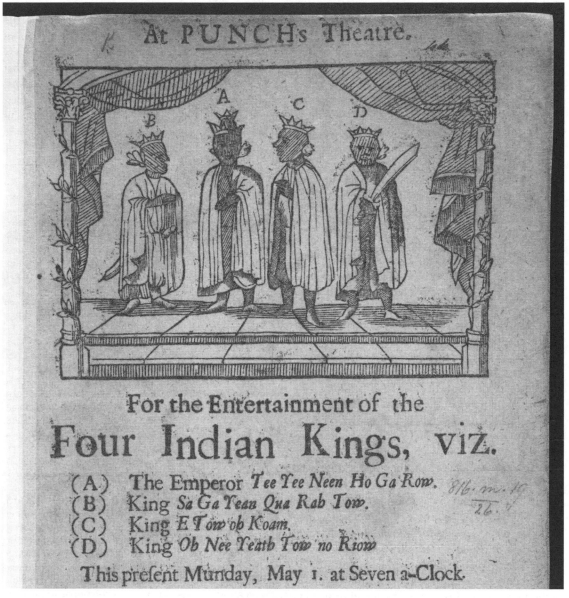

At PUNCHs Theatre.

For the Entertainment of the

Four Indian Kings, viz.

(A) The Emperor *Tee Yee Neen Ho Ga Row*.
(B) King *Sa Ga Yean Qua Rab Tow*.
(C) King *E Tow oh Koam*.
(D) King *Oh Nee Yeath Tow no Riow*

This prefent Munday, May 1. at Seven a-Clock.

27. At Punch's Theatre 1710.

Queen's Theatre in Haymarket.[56] Upset because they could not clearly see the Four Kings, who had become a sensation in London, the audience in the Queen's Theatre grew unruly and demanded satisfaction: 'the Mob', one report noted, 'declared that they came to see the Kings, "and since we have paid our money, the Kings we will have"', so

[56] Originally the Kings were to have seen Congreve's *Old Bachelor*, but Betterton was ill, so the play was changed to *Macbeth*, with Robert Wilks in the title role. See Bond, *Queen Anne's American Kings*, pp. 3–4. In the week following the *Macbeth* production, the Kings were taken to the opera *Almahide*, Otway's *Venice Preserved*, *Hamlet* (replacing, one would say thankfully, Shadwell's *Squire of Alsatia*), Mancini's

Robert Wilks (the actor playing Macbeth himself) 'got four chairs, and placed the Kings on the stage, to the no small satisfaction of the Mob'.[57] Thus the Four Kings were seated on the stage, forming a second show of kings that would have looked on, in 4.1, at Shakespeare's show of kings, making it an even dozen on the stage.[58] Both sets of kings performed in actors' clothing, and more than one line in the play ('Why do you dress me / In borrowed robes?' 1.3.106–7) must have had special resonance. The contemporary representations of the Four Kings, and their appearance literally on the stage of Davenant's production, reconfirm what we might term the theatricalization of genealogy: patrilineal succession may be something that is primarily *performed*, its impossibly seamless continuities an illusion of costume, script and staging.[59]

While the primary purpose of a state-sponsored show of kings was, as in Henry VI's entry, to represent uninterrupted lineage, divine origin and therefore legitimacy, such shows could also be less pleasing. Henry Howard, Earl of Northampton, reported the 'notable example of a Conjurer' who in about 1559 represented to Catherine de Medici 'all those personnes, as it were in a dumbe show, which should possesse the crowne in this our age, caused the king of Navarre [that is, her enemy], or rather a wicked spirite in his stedde to appeare in the fifth place, to none other ende (as I beleeve) then that she might attempt, the rydding him out of the way, by greater store of indirect devises, whom the destinies reserved to so great and honour'.[60] A letter of 1610 by Nicolas Pasquier offers the further details that the conjuror 'showed her in a room, round a circle which he had drawn, all the Kings of France who had been and would be; and they made as many turns round the circle as the number of years they had reigned or would reign'; eventually, '[Catherine] did not want to see any more'.[61]

Such genealogical lineups, presenting the unbroken line of kings from Noah to the present, had been prominently displayed throughout the Tudor period, and during James's reign, particularly in Scotland, as part of his own campaign of lineal reaffirmation. For Macbeth, however, the

show of kings is truly the 'fatal vision' (2.1.36) that shatters him; so devastating is it that, at the end of 4.1, he sweeps off to even greater acts of tyranny and savagery, beginning with the wholly unnecessary slaughter of Macduff's family, so that Macduff, too, will have no children to succeed *him*: 'give to th'edge o'th'sword / His wife, his babes, and all unfortunate souls / That trace him in his line' (4.1.167–9). Again, the 'line' is both desired

---

opera *Hydaspes*, *The Amorous Widow*, *Aurengzebe*, and, as a final treat, a new comedy, *Squire Brainless*; see Bond, p. 98n. The Four Kings were also treated to a full range of London curiosities, including (among many others) the mathematical instruments of the Astronomer Royal at Greenwich, Bedlam Hospital, the Tower, St Paul's, a fight of bears and the market at Leadenhall. Their return to their ship in Southampton included tours of Windsor and Hampton Court (Bond, pp. 3–9, 101–2n.).

57 John Genest, *Some Account of the English Stage, from the Restoration in 1660 to 1830*, 10 vols. (Bath, 1832), vol. 2, p. 451.

58 Or perhaps only eleven. While Genest, *Some Account*, vol. 2, p. 450 n. 45, refers to the 'four' chairs, Bond notes (p. 3 and 98n.) that one of the Kings fell ill on the visit, and it's possible the illness occurred before the *Macbeth* production. The epilogue to the play, however, also refers to the 'Four' who sought 'Protection on *Britannia's* Shore' (quoted in Bond, p. 4). Roach, *Cities of the Dead*, brilliantly describes one of the implications of the Four Kings' presence on the stage as 'offering to the public eye a symbolic reiteration, an intercultural doubling, of the legitimacy and the inevitability of the "empire of the world" as reflected in the cultural mirror of its allied peoples' (p. 171).

59 James I's *Basilikon Doron* (1599; republished in London 1603), in its advice to Henry, is one of the foremost statements on how kingship should be performed through gesture, speech and action. One political pamphlet, contrary to the official exaltations of the Four Kings, instead saw their visit as part of a conspiratorial plan of undermining monarchy and 'introducing a Commonwealth . . . [by] bringing over hither four unknown Persons . . . from the *West-Indies*, under notion of Kings and Emperors, exposing 'em about the Town all four in a Hackney-Coach, and lodging them I suppose four in a Bed, with no other reasonable Design but that of lessening the Honour due to the Majesty of Kings, and rendring them little and contemptible in the Eyes of the Populace; all this while forgetting the Illustrious House of *Hannover*' (*A True and Faithful Account of the Death of Tom. Whigg, Esq.* (London, 1710), pp. 32–3).

60 Quoted in Bullough, 7.520.

61 Quoted in Bullough, 7.521.

and feared. Almost always a part of a coronation progress, the show of kings in *Macbeth* represents instead Macbeth's de-coronation progress, and ostensibly leads to James's coronation.

However the show of kings was staged in Shakespeare's theatre,[62] the result is a self-consciously theatrical spectacle: the witches bid the kings 'Come like shadows, so depart' (4.1.127), and we cannot help but hear the richly suggestive connotations of 'shadows', as in *A Midsummer Night's Dream*, where the word variously means literal shadows, spirits (shades) and actors. Davenant's emendations to the Folio text further enhanced the metatheatrical and racial aspects of the scene, for his 4.1 stage direction reads '*A shaddow of eight Kings, and Banquo's Ghost after them pass by*' rather than '*shew of eight Kings*' and his Macbeth saw Banquo's smiling as seeming 'to say / That they are all Successors of his race' (cf. Folio TLN 1616–7: '*Banquo* smiles vpon me, / And points at them for his').[63] As a 'show' (or Davenant's 'shaddow'), the shadow line of kings in *Macbeth* offers an apparently reassuring genealogical orthodoxy, bringing to life and putting on the stage the royal origins of the reigning monarch. Yet the theatricalizing language surrounding the show and the fictional nature of the ancestors, not to mention that the show is produced by demonic forces, destabilizes the alleged historical truth being represented.

The phantasmal aspect of this vision of the 'line' receives further emphasis in what it fails to show. Just as all genealogies have a major omission of some kind – the inconvenient wife or the attainted cousin – so too does Shakespeare's '*shew of eight Kings*': as many readers have noted, it is missing one (in)famous monarch, James's mother, Mary Queen of Scots, who has been thoroughly erased from the line of Banquo. Mary's disappearance is certainly a part of the more general erasure and suppression of the maternal in this play, as it has been brilliantly described by such critics as Janet Adelman.[64] The 'show' in *Macbeth* offers, above all, a parthenogenetic fantasy of male reproduction without the mediation of women. Banquo's descendants are not of woman born but seem to emanate from him alone – just as in Holinshed's

report of the witch's prophecy to Banquo: 'of thee those shall be borne which shall govern the Scottish kingdome by long order of continuall descent'.[65] Male self reproduction seems the only valid form of 'continuall descent'.

The less said about Mary, of course, the better, but her highly conspicuous absence in the procession marks both her unavoidable, disturbing presence in contemporary genealogical discourse and the artificiality of the 'show'. For in the end, James owed his own kingship to his mother's deposition, and ultimately to her death, though her treason had also been one of the bars against his own succession. Yet how else could James have become king without the death or deposition of his mother? Or how could anyone? For that is the worm at the heart of succession: succession requires, indeed it is inseparable from, death. Succession marks time, and time must have a stop. The form of death is irrelevant, whether the subject be Macbeth's own father, Finel,[66] or his father-king, Duncan. Macbeth's initial confusion –

> By [F]inel's death, I know I am Thane of Glamis,
> But how of Cawdor? The Thane of Cawdor lives,
> A prosperous gentleman, and to be king
> Stands not within the prospect of belief,
> No more than to be Cawdor   (1.3.69–73)

– soon receives an uncanny clarification in the news of Cawdor's treason. The witches' prophecy to

---

[62] Rowe had placed the scene in a cave – his stage direction (in all three of his editions) for 4.1 reads 'SCENE *A dark Cave, in the middle a great Cauldron burning*', evidently following Davenant's invented, and pretty bad line, 'Let's to the Cave and our dire Charms prepare', Davenant, *Macbeth*, p. 45. For comment on various production choices for this scene, see Marvin Rosenberg, *The Masks of Macbeth* (Berkeley, 1978); Kliman, *Shakespeare in Performance*; and Iain Wright, 'Come like shadowes, so depart'.

[63] William Davenant, *Macbeth, A Tragedy* (London, 1674), pp. 48, 49.

[64] See Janet Adelman, *Suffocating Mothers: Fantasies of Maternal Origin in Shakespeare's Plays, 'Hamlet' to 'The Tempest'* (New York, 1992).

[65] Holinshed, 5.268.

[66] Macbeth's father was Finel or Findlaech; the Folio prints the recurring error (from Holinshed) 'Sinel', which misreads the F as a long S.

Banquo at first seems different, more positive – 'Thou shalt get kings, though thou be none' (1.3.65) – but Banquo's death will also be required in order for his descendants to ascend the throne. In creating this very deliberate gap in the line of succession with Mary's omission, Shakespeare was not only avoiding an unpleasant subject[67] and exorcizing maternal origin, but also revealing the constructed, performative side of patrilineal succession.

* * *

The end of the play, as many readers have noted, accompanies Malcolm's coronation with an uncanny series of repetitions. Macduff has entered 'with Macbeth's head' (5.11.19sd.), just as Macbeth had beheaded Macdonald at the beginning of the play. Malcolm has taken no part in the battle, but left it all to Macduff, just as his father Duncan relied on Macbeth. The worthiest thane, Macduff, kneels to profess his loyalty to the passive King Malcolm, just as Macbeth had done to King Duncan. Malcolm promises rewards to his followers with the same metaphor that Duncan had used in the first act: 'What's more to do / Which would be *planted* newly with the time', he promises, he 'will perform in measure, time, and place' (5.11.30–1, 39, my emphasis; cf. 1.4.28–9). And, like Duncan before him, he hands out titles to those who have slain the enemy: 'My thanes and kinsmen, / Henceforth be earls, the first that ever Scotland / In such an honour named' (5.11.28–30), though 'earl' is an English, not a Scottish, title. Worse yet, when Macduff enters with Macbeth's head, he greets Malcolm himself with *his* new title: 'Hail, King, for so thou art' (5.11.20), a form of salutation that links Malcolm with Macbeth, who was greeted by the witches in similar terms. The plot repetitions suggest that the historical cycle of violence is about to begin again – a now standard ending for most productions – and that Malcolm's lineal succession to the throne seems to have carried with it little authority.[68] Indeed, Macduff has to *name* Malcolm king – 'for so thou art' – just as his father Duncan had announced his own previous title: 'whom we name hereafter / The Prince of Cumberland'

(1.4.38–9). Malcolm, through Macduff, has committed regicide, now rhetorically dressed up as tyrannicide, with Macbeth's head now labelled by Macduff 'Th' usurper's'. Moreover, Macbeth by this point has been so thoroughly demonized that he lacks even a name – he's just 'this dead butcher' (5.11.35). In his final speech, Malcolm conspicuously does not claim the throne through inheritance; in truth, he has gained it through conquest, the play's second foreign invasion matching Norway's at the beginning. Conquest constituted one of the multiple ways in which one might succeed to the throne, as William of Normandy – just over the horizon, historically – did, along with inheritance and election. All three of these systems seem to be present in *Macbeth*, with the saintly off-stage English king, Edward the Confessor representing a magical charismatic form of legitimacy. Indeed, the only other mode of succession available to early modern England, the one that James had so resisted acknowledging – the king receiving his crown through Parliament – is the only one not present in the play.

---

[67] Though James had in 1604 apparently supported Antoine de Montchrestien, the author of a play depicting his mother's tragedy, *Escossoise, ou le Desastre Tragedie*. See John D. Staines, *The Tragic Histories of Mary, Queen of Scots, 1560–1690* (Burlington, VT, 2009), pp. 147–63; James Emerson Phillips, *Images of a Queen: Mary Stuart in Sixteenth-Century Literature* (Berkeley, 1964), pp. 219–23; and Frances A. Yates, 'Some New Light on "L'Écossaise" of Antoine de Montchrétien', *Modern Language Review*, 22.3 (1927), 285–97. The play had been performed in Paris while Queen Elizabeth was still alive, and Sir Ralph Winwood, then the English ambassador in Paris, wrote to Cecil that he had 'complained to the French chancellor about "so lewde an Indiscretion" and was promised that "this Folly should be punished, and that the like hereafter should not be committed"' (Phillips, p. 223). When Montchrestien fled to England, he revised the play and dedicated it to James, who then intervened on his behalf, according to a French Catholic newspaper of the time. No other evidence exists to support this account of James's action; see Staines, *The Tragic Histories of Mary*, for a full discussion.

[68] Jan Kott was one of the first to make this point, in his influential analysis of the 'Grand Mechanism' which is 'the image of history itself... Every successive chapter, every great Shakespearean act is merely a repetition': *Shakespeare Our Contemporary* (New York, 1964), p. 10.

Yet the circularity of plot lines at the end of *Macbeth* masks an awkward exception to the structural symmetry: where is the founder of the Stuart line at the end of the play? Fleance is gone, fled into the darkness without a word as his father Banquo is murdered. His absence is even more significant than that of Mary Queen of Scots in the show of kings, for the gap between Malcolm's coronation and the origin of the Stuart line was precisely the vacancy that royal genealogists had filled with the invented narrative of Banquo's line, but which Shakespeare leaves empty, the future uncertain. Indeed, Fleance's absence in Shakespeare's text was found to be so odd that in the very first adaptation of Shakespeare's play, Davenant's in 1664 – the performed version of the play that Rowe and his readers, and the Four Indian Kings, would have seen – both Fleance and Donalbain are brought back in the fifth act, to confront Macbeth.[69] Davenant's Fleance comes not from Wales, however, but 'from France' – never mind that, in Holinshed, he is already dead – and joins in the battle scenes and in the general 'joyful Acclamation' to Malcolm's reign.[70] In his own edition, however, Rowe kept true to Shakespeare's vision here: Fleance has vanished. Rowe featured the show of kings in his

editions of the play, but whatever his politics might have been at a given moment, they were not strong enough to join Davenant in emending the text. Shakespeare's Young Pretender simply disappears in the text of 1606, just as the Stuart line did in 1714 when the Old Pretender (another James Stuart) went into exile – in France, coincidentally. In the end, they all became ghosts of history. Like all theatrical events, the Stuart show of kings finally came to an end, the shadows finally at rest, the fantasy of the unending line of kings over.

---

[69] For an analysis of Fleance's increasingly frequent presence in contemporary films and productions, see William C. Carroll, 'Fleance/Macbeth: The Return of the Repressed', in *Shakespeare on Screen: Macbeth*, ed. Sarah Hatchuel and Nathalie Vienne-Guerrin (Rouen, 2013).

[70] Davenant, *Macbeth*, p. 66. The effect, as Simon Williams argues, is to enhance 'the illusion that social and political retribution is the sole cause of Macbeth's downfall' ('Taking Macbeth Out of Himself: Davenant, Garrick, Schiller and Verdi', in *Shakespeare Survey 57* (Cambridge, 2004), p. 57). Davenant seems to have ignored the sharp irony of bringing these two figures into the general chorus that acclaims Malcolm's crowning. On the politics of Davenant's adaptation – 'what the play does *not* justify is Divine Right' – see Lois Potter, *Secret Rites and Secret Writing* (Cambridge, 1989), pp. 202–7.

'PLEASING STRAINS': THE DRAMATURGICAL ROLE OF MUSIC IN *THE WINTER'S TALE*

SIMON SMITH

O, but they say the tongues of dying men
Enforce attention, like deep harmony.

(*Richard II*, 2.1.5–6)

These lines, spoken by the dying John of Gaunt, contain several ideas about how a listener might respond to music. Music's power to compel attention is critical to the simile, which centres on the notion that words can command similar attention when they may be the speaker's last.[1] The idea of 'deep harmony' implies a distinction between 'deep' music that can 'enforce attention' and other music that presumably cannot, whilst the use of the word 'harmony' to signify 'music' locates music's effects in a wider framework of thought about proportional relations. Ideas such as these are important to the study of early modern playhouse practice because the dramaturgical use of music in a play often reflects contemporary expectations of how playgoers will respond to this music. Early modern responses to music are often mentioned only in passing in critical writing dealing with other aspects of playhouse music, but certain recent critics have published work specifically concerned with this topic: Linda Phyllis Austern has developed a nuanced picture of responses to staged 'female' singers in the period; Bruce R. Smith has attempted to reconstruct the soundscape of early modern London in order to offer a historicized understanding of listening that is appropriate to the early modern playhouse; David Lindley's recent 'critical companion' to Shakespeare and music maintains a consistent focus on issues of experience.[2]

I have argued elsewhere that Shakespeare utilizes early modern cultural expectations of musical response in *Antony and Cleopatra* and in *Richard III*, shaping his dramaturgy through playhouse engagements with practical music.[3] This article argues that the music used in the final scene of *The Winter's Tale* likewise draws upon contemporary expectations of everyday musical response – specifically upon the widespread view that music can compel attention – with particular dramatic effects in mind. It also makes some suggestions, in light of the scene's musical dramaturgy, about the music

---

[1] For the relation of this speech to early modern understandings of last words, see Gordon McMullan, *Shakespeare and the Idea of Late Writing: Authorship in the Proximity of Death* (Cambridge, 2007), p. 216.

[2] Linda Phyllis Austern, '"Sing Againe Syren": The Female Musician and Sexual Enchantment in Elizabethan Life and Literature', *Renaissance Quarterly*, 42 (1989), 420–48; '"Alluring the Auditorie to Effeminacie": Music and the Idea of the Feminine in Early Modern England', *Music and Letters*, 74 (1993), 343–54; '"No Women are Indeed": The Boy Actor as Vocal Seductress in Late Sixteenth- and Early Seventeenth-Century English Drama', in *Embodied Voices: Representing Female Vocality in Western Culture*, ed. Leslie C. Dunn and Nancy A. Jones (Cambridge, 1994), pp. 83–102; Bruce R. Smith, *The Acoustic World of Early Modern England: Attending to the O-Factor* (Chicago and London, 1999); David Lindley, *Shakespeare and Music* (London, 2006).

[3] Simon Smith, '"I see no instruments, nor hands that play": *Antony and Cleopatra* and Visual Musical Experience', in *The Senses in Early Modern England, 1558–1660*, ed. Simon Smith, Jackie Watson and Amy Kenny (Manchester, forthcoming 2014); '"Flourish. Enter the King sicke": Exploring Kingship through Musical Spectacle in *Richard III*', in *Spectatorship at the Elizabethan Court*, Special Issue of *Zeitsprünge: Forschungen zur Frühen Neuzeit*, 17 (2013), 84–102.

that might have been used in early performances at court and in the playhouse. The surviving evidence necessitates an argument of speculation, yet the possibilities that emerge are significant for our understanding of Shakespeare as collaborator. As Tiffany Stern has recently demonstrated, the process of collaboration between playwright(s) and composer can be as suggestive about early modern drama as can the working relationships of collaborating playwrights.[4] This article offers a view of *The Winter's Tale* in which Shakespeare's play-text and a composer's music are integrated, together shaping the dramaturgy of the play's conclusion.

I begin by recovering the early modern notion of musical compulsion. Whilst any attempt to excavate responses to music must always be speculative and qualified, significant textual traces nonetheless remain of widespread early modern understandings of everyday musical response. From these, we can recover the wider cultural currency of certain prevalent ideas about musical response, including musical compulsion. These textual traces often survive in the many extant printed music books that were originally intended for amateur, domestic performance and would therefore have reached the significant number of verbally literate individuals included in what David Price has termed the 'widespread and often intensely experienced extension of musical literacy throughout the upper regions of English society' in the second half of the sixteenth century.[5] The desire to use print as a medium to broaden access to music is admirably expressed by Thomas Morley in his *Plain and Easy Introduction to Practical Music* (1597; 1608), when he explains that he has 'omitted [certain topics] as things onely seruing to content the learned, and not for the instruction of the ignorant', with the hope that 'any of but meane capacitie . . . [can] perfectly learn to sing, make discant, and set partes well and formally togither' from his book.[6] With the help of Morley's manual, many subjects might take advantage of the flourishing music printing industry in London at the turn of the seventeenth century. In so doing, they would encounter the many ideas about music that appear in the paratexts of these books, with 'text' defined here as musical notation and accompanying words, and 'paratext' as everything else printed.

The paratexts of printed music books are extremely clear about how best to describe the experience of music: the term 'delight' is used in its various forms (delight; delightful; delighting) in relation to music at least forty-five times in the paratexts of the 159 printed musical works that I have consulted, substantially more than any comparable notion. These include William Byrd's claim that '[t]he exercise of singing is delightful to Nature' (1588), referring to performer rather than to auditor, Morley's praise for 'that vertuous minde of yours [Sir Robert Cecil's], knowing the same also to be much delighted with that of Musicke' (1595), John Farmer's praise for the 'true effect [of music and number], which is to mooue delight, which delight . . . is the daughter of Harmony' (1599), and Thomas Campion's advice that the best way to appreciate his printed songs is to 'heare / How grauely with their tunes they yeeld delight' (1613).[7]

For early modern writers, the experience of music *is* delight, and the two words are paired constantly in the period, both in music book paratexts and elsewhere. This was a linguistic commonplace so familiar to early modern subjects that any reference to one of the terms must surely have evoked its connections with the other. However, simply tracing the association of delight with music tells us very little about early modern understandings of musical compulsion. Whilst the connection is amply preserved in the textual record, the

---

[4] Tiffany Stern, 'Middleton's Collaborators in Music and Song', in *The Oxford Handbook to Middleton*, ed. Gary Taylor and Trish Thomas Henley (Oxford, 2012), pp. 64–79; *Documents of Performance in Early Modern England* (Cambridge, 2009), pp. 120–73.

[5] See David C. Price, *Patrons and Musicians of the English Renaissance* (Cambridge, 1981), pp. 205–6.

[6] Thomas Morley, *A plaine and easie introduction to practicall musicke* (1597), B1v.

[7] William Byrd, *Psalmes, sonets & songs of sadnes and pietie* (1588), A1v; Thomas Morley, *The first booke of balletts* (1595), A2r; John Farmer, *The first set of English madrigals* (1599), A2v; Thomas Campion, *Tvvo bookes of ayres* (1613), A2r.

response that musical 'delight' actually describes is by no means self-evident to a modern reader, which is perhaps reflected in the lack of critical attention to this term.[8] Nonetheless, careful consideration of exactly how and when 'delight' is used in early modern writings allows us to recover what the word actually meant to early modern readers. To twenty-first-century ears, 'delight' is usually a hyperbolic descriptor of the act of giving pleasure: 'To give great pleasure or enjoyment to; to please highly'.[9] However, a clue towards its early modern sense appears in its etymology, the *Oxford English Dictionary* citing the Latin verbs 'delectare', meaning 'to *allure, attract*, delight, *charm*, or please', and 'delicere', meaning 'to *entice away* or *allure*' (my emphasis). These italicized senses are central to the way in which 'delight' was used in the early modern period; thus, an experience emerges that not only causes pleasure but is also irresistible to the delighted subject. Furthermore, the use of 'delight' in music book paratexts often emphasizes this sense of compulsion; terms such as 'enchant', 'charm' and 'captivate' are aligned with 'delight' in order to emphasize their similarity as descriptors of music's affective power. This similarity is evident in a poem dedicated to composer Thomas Greaves, '[t]he sweet resounding of whose pleasing straines, / Delightes the sences, captiuates the braines'. This praise poem, prefacing Greaves's *Songs of Sundry Kinds* (1604), claims further that his music is 'a charme against despight', suggesting similarity between delight, charm and captivation.[10]

Indeed, the general recurrence of terms such as 'enchant' and 'charm' is itself an indication of the prevalence of the notion of musical compulsion, seen in George Eastland's suggestion that John Dowland's lute will 'arise and charme the aire' (1600), and Francis Pilkington's mentions of 'enchanting melodie' and of 'the melodius charmes of Orpheus' (1605).[11] Even more forceful is the connection between delighting and ravishing, seen when Jacques Gohory pauses to 'protest vnto you that if the songes of other Musitians do delight mee, those of Orland do rauish me', in a preface translated into English in 1574.[12] 'Ravish'

is another significant term for musical compulsion, and Gohory's construction here is illuminating. In order to show how certain songs outstrip all others, he turns to the usual term for musical experience – delight – and extends it with the strongest available version of this same experience of compulsion: ravishment. By rhetorically indicating that 'to delight' is a weaker form of 'to ravish', Gohory's comparison completes the reconstruction of delight's early modern signification as a compulsive, pleasurable experience central to successful musical response.

The *concept* of musical delight was certainly familiar to both play-makers and playgoers, but could playhouse music actually compel an audience's attention? In fact, there are several reasons to believe that playgoers were indeed often 'delighted' by musical performance. Various dramatic texts show characters responding habitually with 'delight', suggesting that such compelled pleasure was an expected, everyday reaction to music.[13] Moreover, studies of sensory experience in early modern London have excavated specific and tangible features of the soundscape in and around Jacobean playhouses that were likely to have fostered a culture of listening in which

---

[8] Terms such as 'power', 'charm' and 'allure' have variously been taken up in preference. See Austern, 'Sing Againe', p. 420; Lindley, *Shakespeare and Music*, pp. 13–15, 218–19; Christopher Marsh, *Music and Society in Early Modern England* (Cambridge, 2010), pp. 32–70; Joseph M. Ortiz, *Broken Harmony: Shakespeare and the Politics of Music* (Ithaca, 2011), p. 143; Gary Tomlinson, *Music in Renaissance Magic: Toward a Historiography of Others* (Chicago, 1993), p. 172.

[9] 'Delight, *v.* 1.a', in *Oxford English Dictionary*, www.oed.com (accessed 9 November 2013).

[10] Thomas Greaves, *Songes of sundrie kindes* (1604), A2v.

[11] John Dowland, *The second booke of songs or ayres* (1600), A2v; Francis Pilkington, *First booke of songs or ayres* (1605), A2r.

[12] Adrian Le Roy, *A briefe and plaine instruction to set all musicke of eight diuers tunes in tableture for the lute* (1574), A3r.

[13] See, for instance: John Fletcher and Philip Massinger, 'The Custom of the Country', ed. Cyrus Hoy, in *The Dramatic Works in the Beaumont and Fletcher Canon*, gen. ed. Fredson Bowers, rev. edn, vol. 8 (Cambridge, 2008), 3.2.57–60; Thomas Middleton, 'A Game at Chess: A Later Form', ed. Gary Taylor, in *Thomas Middleton: The Collected Works*, gen. eds. Gary Taylor and John Lavagnino (Oxford, 2007), 5.2.30–50.

musical delighting was common. Bruce R. Smith points out that '[t]wo inventions – electricity and the internal combustion engine – make it difficult for us even to imagine what life in early modern England would have sounded like'. Arguing that 'the very loudest sounds that a sixteenth- or seventeenth-century listener might encounter... would nowadays almost rate as normal events', he suggests that the aural stimuli of the playhouse would make a far more powerful impression on an early modern auditor than their modern equivalent, even suggesting that 'applause in an enclosed auditorium', at ninety decibels, would rank amongst the loudest sounds heard at this time.[14] This may go some way towards explaining why the power to command attention is so consistently ascribed to music in the period: in a soundscape lacking the constant, high decibel background noise of a twenty-first-century city, music may well have been one of the louder and more compelling sounds to be heard. In this context an early modern listener could be far more likely to respond to music with compelled attention than may be the case when music sounds at a theatre today. Finally, it seems unlikely that commercial play-makers would have persisted quite so determinedly with attempts to compel playgoers with music throughout the Jacobean period – as indeed they did – if the desired response of delight was not being evoked with some success in the playhouse.[15]

William Prynne gives a clear account of early modern playgoers delighted by music in his *Histriomastix*: 'lewde Spectators... are oft-times ravished with these ribaldrous pleasing Ditties'. Significantly, his reference to musical ravishment, playgoers being 'transported' into an 'extasie of uncleanesse', makes very clear that playhouse music can grasp the attention of playgoers utterly. Prynne's interest is in music between a play's acts, in the form of 'amorous Pastorals, or obscene lascivious Love-songs, most melodiously cha[n]ted out upon the Stage betweene each seuerall Action'.[16] However, this article is concerned with music compelling attention *during* dramatic performance in *The Winter's Tale*. Music often appears in Jacobean commercial drama in scenes

of particular narrative importance, when attention to the events of the play is particularly desirable; musical delighting thus helps provide focus at key playhouse moments. Given the many contemporary accounts of the difficulty of captivating playgoers in both outdoor and indoor playhouses, the successful use of music to this end would have been invaluable to playwrights with access to appropriate musical resources.[17]

In *The Winter's Tale*, playgoer attention is demanded through musical delight in 5.3. Playhouse responses to the music that sounds at the reanimation of the statue after Paulina's command, 'Music; awake her; Strike!' (5.3.98), are critical to the success of this moment in performance. Indeed, this moment is so central to the overall shape of the play that the whole work's impact is to some extent defined by the level of this success. Russ McDonald has developed the notion of 'suspension' in some detail, both as a syntactical and a narratorial feature of late Shakespeare plays, such that in these texts grammatical structure is a microcosm of the overall shape of the drama. He observes, 'What distinguishes *The Winter's Tale* is that much of the poetic language is organized periodically: convoluted sentences or difficult speeches become coherent and meaningful only in their final clauses or movements', and a 'similar principle governs the arrangement of dramatic action: the shape and meaning of events become apparent only in the final moments of the tragicomedy'. Moreover, 'Shakespeare... exaggerated the grammatical means of suspension so that sentences or

---

14 Bruce R. Smith, *Acoustic World*, pp. 49–50.

15 For instance, at either end of the Jacobean period Middleton's *The Revenger's Tragedy* (KM, 1606) and *A Game at Chess* (KM, 1624) attempted to compel playgoers with music. See: 'The Revenger's Tragedy', ed. Macdonald P. Jackson, in *Middleton: Collected Works*, 5.3.41.1–III; 'A Game at Chess', 3.1.392.1; 4.3.0.1; 5.2.37–46; 5.3.162.1.

16 William Prynne, *Histrio-mastix. The players scourge, or, actors tragædie* (1633), 2L3v.

17 See Andrew Gurr, *Playgoing in Shakespeare's London* (Cambridge, 1987), pp. 205–51. Gurr collects many contemporary references to playgoing in an appendix; examples pertaining to noisy and inattentive audiences at various playhouses include extracts 10, 11, 18 and 52.

passages in these plays gain momentum and then "discharge" powerfully or unexpectedly', but this suspension and 'discharge' is also a feature of the narrative, as 'the play . . . surprises us, denying us knowledge of Hermione's survival until the very end of the work, challenging our confidence in our superior understanding and thus transforming our comprehension of the world we thought we knew'.[18]

As McDonald shows, much weight is brought to bear upon the statue and its reanimation: only in this moment do playgoers learn that Hermione lives and that the narrative can conclude with one final reconciliation. I suggest, moreover, that between the microcosm of grammatical structure and the macrocosm of the narrative, there is another system of 'suspension' and 'discharge' at work, in the stage presentation of various moments of reconciliation in the final act. This 'suspension' is enacted when the reconciliations of 5.2 (including the father-daughter meeting) are only reported verbally, allowing the fully mimetic representation of Hermione's return to have maximum impact and enact the 'discharge' of reconciliation at precisely the same point as the narratorial discharge that McDonald identifies: when the music sounds and the statue moves.

Delighting music thus sounds at a key playhouse moment in *The Winter's Tale*, occupying a 'dramatic position' at 'the climax of the play'.[19] If successful, the music '[d]elights the sences, [and] captiuates the braines' of playgoers, compelling their attention to the single most structurally important piece of dramatic representation in the play.[20] At this key moment, the suspension of knowledge of the plot is relieved by playgoers' awareness that Hermione is alive, and the suspension of reconciliation is discharged, with its merely diegetic, suppressed presentation in 5.2 replaced with a moment of mimesis. Music is used to focus playgoers' scattered attention upon this single symbolic moment of stage business, metonymically enacting the many reversals and reconciliations upon which the conclusion of the narrative depends. From here the plot moves quickly to a close, verbalizing the reconciliations that are now possible, before the drama

ends within sixty lines. Despite this quick movement, until this point playgoers are denied the knowledge that a conclusion with such a degree of reconciliation is even possible; music's power to compel is thus required here to facilitate an abrupt, even jarring, shift in dramatic direction.

What music would have been most fitting to enact this compulsion for an early audience? Whilst recovering the delighting sound of the statue scene is by no means straightforward, I hope to demonstrate that we can get far closer to the play's musical preferences than has previously been acknowledged. We lack any textual detail beyond the word 'music' when considering what Shakespeare and the King's Men's choice might have been, and there has accordingly been little scholarly attempt to recover this music.[21] But in fact, through close consideration of the contents of the scene, of the play's early stage history at court and at the Globe, and of the King's Men's repertory in the years leading up to *The Winter's Tale*'s first known performances in 1611, a hitherto unexplored musical possibility emerges.

In 5.3, music is given the apparent diegetic power to compel life into an inanimate statue. Certain features of this animation indicate that close attention to sixteenth- and seventeenth-century hermetic-alchemical thought could help elucidate this moment of stagecraft.[22] It is long

---

[18] Russ McDonald, 'Poetry and Plot in *The Winter's Tale*', *Shakespeare Quarterly*, 36 (1985), 315–29, pp. 316, 328. See, too, his *Shakespeare's Late Style* (Cambridge, 2006), particularly pp. 149–80.

[19] Catherine M. Dunn, 'The Function of Music in Shakespeare's Romances', *Shakespeare Quarterly*, 20 (1969), 391–405, p. 399.

[20] Greaves, *Songes*, A2v.

[21] Recovery of early – and later – staging, including music, has been most comprehensively attempted in Dennis Bartholomeusz, *The Winter's Tale in Performance in England and America, 1611–1976* (Cambridge, 1982). No suggestions about pre-Restoration musical choices are offered.

[22] The fields of alchemy and Hermeticism were so closely associated that from the Middle Ages, 'effectively, alchemy was the science of hermetic philosophy', and they retained their place together within the medical and scientific discourse of the sixteenth and seventeenth centuries (Margaret Healy,

established that the scene bears strong similarities to the description of animated statues found in a hermetic-alchemical text well known in Jacobean England. As Frances A. Yates argues, 'It seems obvious . . . that Shakespeare is alluding . . . to the famous god-making passage in the *Asclepius*.'[23] Named for the classical god of healing, the *Asclepius* text was attributed to 'Hermes Trismegistus', a name not dissimilar to Leontes's queen's. Yates refers to the passage describing Egyptian 'statues . . . made alive by consciousness, and . . . filled with breath. They do mighty deeds. They have knowledge of the future . . . They bring illnesses to men and cure them.' The nature of these 'terrestrial' gods 'is derived from herbs, stones and spices', and '[b]ecause of this these gods are delighted by frequent sacrifices', as well as by 'hymns, praises and sweet sounds in tune with the celestial harmony'.[24] The statue of Hermione fulfils many of the criteria for being a 'terrestrial' god; most significantly here, it comes to life in response to 'sweet sounds in tune with the celestial harmony', when Paulina calls for music.

Notably, *The Winter's Tale* is not the only Shakespearian text that alludes to Asclepian musical animation. George Wilkins and Shakespeare's *Pericles, Prince of Tyre*, a staple of the King's Men's repertory from the late 1600s, includes a similar musical resurrection that draws yet more explicitly upon hermetic-alchemical ideas. Here, it is the corpse of Thaisa, Pericles's wife, that the physician Lord Cerimon works frantically, and ultimately successfully, to revive, she having washed ashore in a coffin:

Cerimon. Well sayd, well sayd; the fire and clothes: the rough and
Wofull Musick that we haue, cause it to sound beseech you:
The Violl once more; how thou stirr'st thou blocke?
The Musicke there: I pray you giue her ayre . . .
. . . come, come; and *Escelapius* guide vs.
(*Pericles*, Q1 (1609), TLN 1288–311)

Cerimon is extremely clear that music is key to this resurrection. In *Pericles* then, as in *The Winter's Tale*, the scene combines the staging of compulsive musical resurrection with a key playhouse moment,

in which a dead central character is given new life. Cerimon's apostrophe, '*Escelapius* guide vs', is a prayer to the classical god of healing himself, but it also gestures towards the hermetic-alchemical text of musical animation that bears the god's name as its title: *Asclepius*. Cerimon's words suggest that Wilkins, Shakespeare and the King's Men were indeed familiar with the Asclepian model of musical animation before 1611. The musical 'delight' mythologized both in *Pericles* and *The Winter's Tale*, then, takes an exceptionally specific form, that of hermetic-alchemical resurrection through music.

If both *Pericles* and *The Winter's Tale* include scenes of Asclepian resurrection, extant hermetic-alchemical texts might be of help in identifying a musical form that would have been appropriate for use in early performances of *The Winter's Tale*. The reference in *Pericles* to 'rough and / Wofull Musick' is perhaps a helpful first step, but can be no more than suggestive.[25] Music from the tradition of sixteenth- and seventeenth-century hermetic-alchemical practice, however, would have been

---

'Protean Bodies: Literature, Alchemy, Science and English Revolutions', in *Renaissance Transformations: The Making of English Writing (1500–1650)*, ed. Margaret Healy and Thomas Healy (Edinburgh, 2009), pp. 161–76; p. 165). Shakespeare's scene also has obvious resonances with notions of idolatry topical in the early seventeenth century; Joseph M. Ortiz has recently and productively interrogated the music of this scene in relation to 'Pauline Iconoclasm' (*Broken Harmony*, pp. 190–8). However, as will become apparent, hermetic-alchemical thought provides a framework of particularly immediate significance for performances of the play in the early 1610s.

[23] Frances A. Yates, *Shakespeare's Last Plays: A New Approach* (London, 1975), p. 90. This view is supported in John S. Mebane, *Renaissance Magic and the Return of the Golden Age: The Occult Tradition and Marlowe, Jonson, and Shakespeare* (Lincoln, NE, 1989), p. 193; Ekbert Faas, *Tragedy and After: Euripides, Shakespeare, Goethe* (Kingston and Montreal, 1984), pp. 143–4.

[24] Hermes Trismegistus, *Asclepius: The Perfect Discourse of Hermes Trismegistus*, trans. and ed. Clement Salaman (London, 2007), pp. 78, 95. For the source texts through which this work was known in early modern England, see Frances A. Yates, *Giordano Bruno and the Hermetic Tradition* (London, 1964), p. 37.

[25] See F. Elizabeth Hart, 'Cerimon's "Rough" Music in *Pericles*, 3.2', *Shakespeare Quarterly*, 51 (2000), 313–31.

extremely fitting for use in *The Winter's Tale*, and the work of prominent hermetic-alchemical author Michael Maier includes much music that is therefore of interest. His *Atalanta Fugiens*, published in Germany in 1617 but composed over the preceding decade, includes fifty pieces of fugal music that both represent and enact alchemy. This work 'holds a special position amongst the host of alchemical treatises', due largely to 'its presentation of the alchemical process in the form of musical fugues, emblematic copper-engravings and the accompanying discourses': a study of the fugues and their structural symbolism alongside the emblems and writings allows the initiated reader to access some of the secrets of alchemy hidden within the work.[26] Maier musically represents the myth of Atalanta collecting the golden apples as she flees Hippomenes, announcing:

My Muse gives you here three-voiced fugues in order to express this race in such musical forms as are most similar to it. One voice remains simple, still and withdrawn and presents the golden apple, but the other, Atalanta, is fugitive and the third (Hippomenes) follows directly after her. Let the fugues proclaim themselves to your ears, and the emblems to your eyes, and then let your understanding test the mysteries hidden therein.[27]

As Hildemarie Streich notes, these parts 'symbolize the alchemical raw materials: Mercury, Sulphur, and Salt', relating the myth of 'Atalanta Fugiens' to alchemical practice.[28] Maier's comments on his own fugues are extremely helpful in their indication of just how much meaningful symbolic weight could be borne by musical structure and harmonic relations during the period, as indeed we see in the familiar descending 'tear' motif in Dowland's 'Lachrimae Pavan'.[29] Music sounding during the statue scene should bear some relation in its musical structure to the hermetic-alchemical reanimation that is apparently occurring, and so the symbolism of alchemical canons, such as those from *Atalanta Fugiens*, would certainly be highly appropriate for the King's Men's early performances. Maier's music has a sound distinctive amongst extant compositions of the early modern period, making the use of alchemical

fugues like his in *The Winter's Tale* an intriguing possibility.[30]

Significantly, Maier is more than just a composer of music offering convenient generic resonances with an Asclepian statue: there may in fact be some extremely close connections between his compositions and two specific early performances of *The Winter's Tale* at the court of James I, in November 1611 and in winter 1612/13. In 1979, Adam McLean identified a manuscript 'that is an elaborate greetings card addressed to King James VI and I'.[31] Along with a Rosicrucian emblem and four Latin poems, it includes a fugue with 'the [four] fugal voices being ascribed to the Archangels' and 'the cantus firmus [ascribed] to the two Shepherds' attendant upon the nativity, musically similar to the fifty canons he would publish in 1617 (illustration 28).

The 'first two images of Atalanta: The Windgod Boreas ... and the goat Amalthaea' appear both in this manuscript, and in Emblems 1 and 2 of *Atalanta Fugiens*.[32] The document was presented

---

[26] Hildemarie Streich, 'Introduction', in *Atalanta Fugiens: An Edition of the Fugues, Emblems and Epigrams*, trans. and ed. Joscelyn Godwin (Grand Rapids, 1989), p. 33. I am grateful to Margaret Healy for introducing me to Maier's music in a workshop at the University of Basel some years ago.

[27] This translation by Streich ('Introduction', p. 34). For Godwin's verse translation of the same passage, see: Godwin, ed., *Atalanta Fugiens*, p. 97.

[28] Streich, 'Introduction', p. 35.

[29] John Dowland, *Lachrimæ, or Seauen teares figured in seauen passionate pauans* (1604), B1v.

[30] Practical investigation of Maier's music has been thought-provoking. I am extremely grateful to Philip Bird for directing a performance of the statue scene with my arrangement of an *Atalanta Fugiens* canon, upon the stage at Shakespeare's Globe on 8 February 2013.

[31] 'MS. Poems and music dedicated to King James VI by Michael Maier (the German alchemist and Roiscrucian), Count Palantine and doctor of medicine and philosophy', MS GD241/212, Records of Thomson & Baxter W. S. (incorporating Campbell Lamond C. S. and Thomson Dickson & Shaw W. S.), National Archives Scotland. See Adam McLean, 'A Rosicrucian Manuscript of Michael Maier', *Hermetic Journal*, 5 (1979), 4–7; R. A. Gilbert, 'Foreword', in J. B. Craven, *Count Michael Maier: Life and Writings*, 2nd edn, rev. R. A. Gilbert (Berwick, ME, 2003), p. xviii.

[32] Godwin, ed., *Atalanta Fugiens*, p. 207.

Fuga a 5 Vocibus

Michael Maier

Gloria_____ Summa_____ DEO_____ sit

Laus immensa_____ parentis_____

Pax vigeat_____ terris_____ bona_____

Meo mortalibus_____ adsit_____ adsit_____

Cantus Firmus

Michael Maier

Gratia_____ sit Iehoua_____

28. Canon sung by the Archangels with *cantus firmus* sung by the shepherds attending the nativity, from 'Poems and music dedicated to King James VI by Michael Maier'.

by Maier to King James, 'at Christmas 1611, on behalf of Frederick, the Elector Palatine'.[33] Maier's arrival in London, fugue in hand, as ambassador for Frederick in his marriage negotiations for Princess Elizabeth was therefore contemporaneous with the first known court performance of *The Winter's Tale*

in November 1611. Maier was in the right company for his work to be known to the King's Men a year before the next known court performance,

---

[33] Gilbert, 'Foreword', p. xviii.

in the winter 1612/13 season. This following performance was part of the nuptial celebrations for Frederick and Elizabeth, whose 'brief reign . . . in the Palatinate was a Hermetic golden age, nourished on the alchemical movement led by Michael Maier'.[34] The interchangeability of much early modern stage music – indicated by the physical detachability of songs from the rest of a play-text, for instance – has been demonstrated by Tiffany Stern.[35] It must therefore remain a strong possibility that the ambassador's hermetic-alchemical music would have been considered for use on this occasion in order to emphasize the overtones of *Asclepius* in the statue scene for a guest of honour – Frederick – attuned to such resonances. Indeed, if one were to accept the case for the final scene being a later addition to the play, taking the 1612/13 performance as the occasion for revision, as W. W. Greg found more plausible than the November 1611 showing, then the hermetic-alchemical overtones of the statue's animation are extremely significant.[36] A play performed for the celebration of this couple's wedding, a match negotiated in part by Maier, would seem an ideal opportunity for adding a living statue recalling the *Asclepius* and a suitable fugue composed by Maier, such as the one he presented to King James the previous year. The significance of Maier's alchemical fugues for *The Winter's Tale* are thus threefold: as structural and stylistic examples of the kind of music that any early performance of the scene would require; as appropriate works of a composer known to be at court and closely involved with the wedding negotiations leading up to the 1612/13 performance; and finally, possibly even as part of a collaborative revision involving both Shakespeare and Maier in 1612/13, if one were to accept the various circumstantial arguments that have been made for the later addition of the statue scene.

Michael Maier's hermetic-alchemical canons take us a little closer to the possible early sound of musical delighting in *The Winter's Tale*. But what instruments might have been used for music of this nature in court and playhouse performance? Paulina calls simply for 'Music' (5.3.98), a common

play-text cue. As Thomas Middleton's *A Game at Chess* indicates, the term 'music' does not rule out song, for the 'Trinity' manuscript of this late Jacobean play cues some 'Musique' that is described in concurrent dialogue as 'Vocall Sounds' (TLN 1536–76).[37] Paulina's 'Music' could therefore be song, and indeed Maier's extant canons are all arranged for voice, with words. If Paulina requires instrumental music, however, then a consort of viols is perhaps most likely. There are several reasons for this. First, a 1595 drawing of an alchemist's laboratory includes a treble viol in its foreground, clearly associating the instrument with Hermeticism (illustration 29).[38]

Similarly, there is Cerimon's call for a viol (or perhaps a vial of medicine) to help resurrect in *Pericles*'s scene of Asclepian reanimation (3.2).[39] Finally, and more pragmatically, there is the fact that printed music books often offer music '[a]pt both for Viols and Voyces', demonstrating the

---

[34] Frances A. Yates, *The Rosicrucian Enlightenment* (London, 1972), p. xiii.

[35] Stern, *Documents of Performance*, pp. 120–73.

[36] W. W. Greg, *The Shakespeare First Folio* (Oxford, 1955), p. 417. The provenance of the text of *The Winter's Tale* is – inevitably for Shakespeare – uncertain, and critics such as Susan Snyder have argued that the single extant Folio text is a revision for courtly performance that removes mimetic representation of the father-daughter reconciliation and adds the husband-wife reconciliation of the statue scene as an entirely new conclusion. For an overview of the evidence, see *The Winter's Tale*, ed. Susan Snyder and Deborah T. Curren-Aquino (Cambridge, 2007), p. 64.

[37] Thomas Middleton, *A Game at Chess: The Trinity Manuscript*, ed. Thomas Howard-Hill, The Malone Society Reprints, 151 (Oxford, 1990).

[38] Heinrich Khunrath, *Amphitheatrum sapientiae aeternae* (Hamburg, 1595), http://specialcollections.library.wisc.edu/khunrath/index.html (accessed 12 February 2012). The other string instruments in this image are all plucked, and thus lack the sustain of voice or bowed string.

[39] 'The Violl once more' (*Pericles*, Q1 (1609), TLN 1290). There is no distinction in early modern spelling between 'viols' and 'vials'. Suzanne Gossett preferred a viol in her Arden 3 edition (London, 2004). However, the Oxford editors preferred a vial here, asking 'what is in those boxes, if not medicines'. See: Stanley Wells and Gary Taylor, with John Jowett and William Montgomery, *William Shakespeare: A Textual Companion* (Oxford, 1987), p. 574.

29. An alchemist's laboratory with treble viol in foreground, in Heinrich Khunrath,
Amphitheatrum sapientiae aeternae (Hamburg, 1595).

suitability of viols for performances of music written originally to be sung.[40] This is due at least in part to the capacity of bowed string instruments to sustain notes as a voice can, where a plucked string instrument, for instance, could not. It is the sound of an alchemical fugue performed by voices or on viols, then, that may have been used to delight early modern audiences in the final scene of *The Winter's Tale*.

---

[40] Michael East, *The third set of bookes* (1610), A1r. See, too: William Byrd, *Psalmes, songs and sonnets: some solemn, others ioyfull* (1611), A1r; Thomas Bateson, *The second set of madrigales* (1618), A1r; East, *The seventh set of bookes* (1638), A1r.

This article has considered how *The Winter's Tale* sought to evoke musical delight from playgoers, and what this delighting could have sounded like in early performances. It now explores how musical delighting contributed to the play's dramaturgy not just by directing attention towards a significant moment, but even by shaping the meaning that playgoers found in performance. This occurs, I argue, when both playgoers and stage characters are delighted by the same music at the same time; that is, when playgoers' musically compelled responses are given an amplified, mythical co-presentation in the statue's response to the same delighting music. Here, musical 'delight' as a means of directing playhouse attention meets a dramatic account of extreme compulsive music that actually gives life to Hermione's statue. This conjunction had much significance for early modern playgoers' understandings of what happens in the scene, specifically regarding the vexed question of whether or not this is really a statue. So, in light of its music, was this scene taken by early playgoers more as a convincing presentation of fantastical resurrection, or as Paulina and Hermione's elaborate deception of Leontes?

In theatre heavily reliant on audience imagination, it is often difficult to distinguish between the deception of characters onstage that must not fool playgoers, and the deceptions to which playgoers must themselves acquiesce in order to conceive a bare stage as various locations or, in this case, to accept staged actions as supernatural activity. A. D. Nuttall argued that Shakespeare utilizes this ambiguity in *King Lear*, such that playgoers could not have been quite sure that Gloucester is on level ground, that the stage is not representing a real cliff-top with a sheer drop over which he leaps (4.5.1–80).[41] The first hundred lines of the final scene in *The Winter's Tale* play with a similar ambiguity about the nature of the statue. The breathing that Leontes thinks he sees may hint that Paulina and Hermione are deceiving him, but it may equally be a joke at the expense of the actor attempting to portray a stone statue for several minutes (5.3.63–5). Tiffany Stern's vivid description of how 'the sparkling audience – and actors – will

have emerged through a delicate haze; a confusion of smoke from candles and tobacco' indicates how a lack of visual clarity could have exacerbated this ambiguity for Blackfriars playgoers, if not at the Globe.[42]

Wider conventions of playhouse music use would certainly predispose regular playgoers to accept the statue's supernatural transformation. The music that punctuates the moment at which magic or illusion takes place in *The Winter's Tale* would recall the extremely common use of music elsewhere on the early modern stage to facilitate 'authentic' supernatural activity, with plays such as *Macbeth*, *The Tempest* and John Marston's *Sophonisba* being familiar examples. The simple fact that the conjunction of music and real magic within staged worlds was a commonplace of early modern drama, something that a playgoer may have seen enacted a dozen times before, suggests that real supernatural activity would remain uppermost in playgoers' minds when music sounded, particularly when considered alongside the culturally prevalent notion of musical compulsion through 'delight' that I have traced. Music was constantly, diversely, being presented as having real power, making it unproblematic for contemporary playgoers to accept that its quickening power in this play is genuine; as David Lindley notes, 'For a Renaissance audience, much more than a modern one, these beliefs in music's powers were possible and powerful.'[43] Of course, for alchemically informed playgoers, these dramatic conventions of supernatural music would combine with the Asclepian resonances of the animation, and the hermetic-alchemical significations of the canon form (if such music was indeed used), to suggest real magic.

The statue's nature must always remain ambiguous, for this is the enigma that gives the scene

---

[41] A. D. Nuttall, *Why Does Tragedy Give Pleasure?* (Oxford, 1996), pp. 98–100.

[42] Tiffany Stern, 'Taking Part: Actors and Audience on the Stage at Blackfriars', in *Inside Shakespeare: Essays on the Blackfriars Stage*, ed. Paul Menzer (New Jersey, 2006), pp. 35–53, p. 45.

[43] Lindley, *Shakespeare and Music*, p. 138.

its vitality. Yet even whilst two interpretations remained in balance, Jacobean playgoers' responses of musical delight would foreground one reading over the other. Critically, Paulina's command encourages playgoers to relate their delighted responses to the statue's concurrent response. By instructing the music specifically to 'awake' Hermione (5.3.98), Paulina characterizes the resurrection as an extreme form of attention grasping. Playgoers are told that what the statue feels as it is brought to life is simply a stronger version of the musical compulsion they feel as they hear music and observe the statue. If playgoers perceived their own delighted response to the play's music as a microcosm of the statue's reanimation, then one conclusion must surely have seemed particularly appealing in the moment of performance: this miracle is genuine. The verbal niggles that follow the music, likening the story to 'an old tale' (5.3.118), may therefore have functioned less as sceptical asides and more as attempts to heighten early playgoers' astonishment at the genuine magic that seems to have taken place within this fantastical story. In the stagecraft of this scene, then, Shakespeare and the King's Men combined playhouse responses of delight with a stage representation of compulsive resurrection, in an attempt to direct early modern playgoers' understandings of what actually happens in a key plot event – perhaps even *the* key plot event – of *The Winter's Tale*.

This has significance both for our own reading of Shakespeare's play, and for our understanding of the dramaturgical role of delighting music in the early modern playhouse.

Shakespeare does not appear to have collaborated with any other playwright when working on *The Winter's Tale*, yet close attention to the play's use of music reminds us of the many collaborations necessary to create performative works of art such as theatre. In a seminal study of the Children of the Queen's Revels, Lucy Munro notes that '[t]o seek a single voice behind any one play – be it writer, actor or shareholder – vastly underestimates the complexity of the way in which early modern plays reached the stage'.[44] Neither should we overlook the significance of both musicians and composers in the process of dramatic production. On a more speculative basis, this article has even suggested the possibility that the final scene of *The Winter's Tale* is a collaboration between the playwright Shakespeare and a hermetic-alchemical composer, perhaps Michael Maier. Shakespeare often cues music with dramaturgically significant audience responses in mind. In the case of *The Winter's Tale*, it is just possible that he may have shaped such a cue in collaboration.

---

44 Lucy Munro, *Children of the Queen's Revels: A Jacobean Theatre Repertory* (Cambridge, 2005), p. 53.

CONFINEMENT AND FREEDOM IN *THE TEMPEST*

LESLIE THOMSON

With the last words of *The Tempest* – Prospero's 'set me free' – Shakespeare, with some irony, concludes a play deeply concerned with the power to confine and release. At every level and in ways significant and incidental, the play is overtly and expressly an exercise in control by not only the protagonist but also the playwright. The actions and language of containment and liberty function in a classical structure and occur in a plot that unfolds in an enclosed, contained location. That is, not only is the plot one in which the main character deliberately and explicitly controls the others; in various thematically and physically significant ways the play itself makes the methods of control part of the experience of those watching it. From the most basic and literal elements to the most abstract and figurative, the play is about and calls attention to the limits or restrictions – of genre, plot, structure, time, space, place – that control it.[1] Furthermore, the dominant concern with issues of freedom and confinement is expressed in staging that repeatedly illustrates them.[2] All the characters somehow face limitations on their actions, a fact to which their language and situations consistently call attention. As the character who is most powerful but also finally powerless, Prospero is at the centre of this thematic and aesthetic framework from start to finish. His control over the movements of the others is conveyed by both his commands and their obedience.[3] At the same time, images of confinement and encirclement recur in the staging and dialogue in ways that convey Prospero's power to manage the others. More broadly, in a play that is both explicitly 'artificial' and concerned with the

power of art and the artist, Shakespeare repeatedly invokes the interrelated controlling forces of Time and Fortune, emblematic concepts that permeate the tragicomic structure. *The Tempest* is also insistently teleological, a fact emphasized by language that repeatedly calls explicit attention to the control by time – structurally, thematically and metatheatrically – over a process that culminates in a literal, performed discovery that leads to a literally liberating resolution. Furthermore, by emphasizing and capitalizing on the island-stage-playhouse analogy,

---

[1] In his study of 'lexical repetition' in the play, Russ McDonald says, 'this is one of the most knowing, most self-conscious texts in the canon' (27). He observes that 'The prominence of the figure of repetition in both the verbal style and dramatic structure of *The Tempest* leads perforce to the question of its importance – what does the figure import through the text to the audience? what is its function? how does it mean?' (*Shakespeare Survey 43* (Cambridge, 1990), pp. 15–28, pp. 20, 23). My aim here is to address these questions by considering some of the play's most essential and meaningful kinds of repetition.

[2] One of the few critics to focus explicitly on the play's concern with freedom is Harry Berger, Jr. although his discussion of the significance is very different from mine ('Miraculous Harp: A Reading of Shakespeare's Tempest', *Shakespeare Studies*, 5 (1969), 253–83, p. 258). For David Lindley the play 'seems like a hall of mirrors in which reflection is added to reflection in a curiously claustrophobic dramatic world. This sense of confinement is furthered by Prospero's domination of the action' (*The Tempest*, ed. David Lindley (Cambridge, 2002), p. 3).

[3] Keith Sturgess observes that 'Only Prospero, a "god of power", can take significant action. The plot in effect is his, and the other *personae*, caught out of contingent time and confined by his experiment, can only react' (*Jacobean Private Playhouses* (London and New York, 1987), p. 75).

Shakespeare seems to have wanted to make his audience conscious of their own 'captivity'. While these might seem disparate elements, all are integral parts of one work of art that concludes with an epilogue in which Shakespeare has his protagonist acknowledge that it is time for him to give up control and request permission to depart from playgoers who, in giving it, also free themselves.

I. ENTRANCES AND EXITS

Character entrances and exits are of course fundamental to most kinds of drama; but in the plays of Shakespeare and his contemporaries these actions are both plentiful and regularly signalled by dialogue cues, which make them a very effective means of using action to reinforce meaning. Because the basic structural unit of these plays is the scene, the playwright has repeated opportunities to dramatize the control exerted by some characters over others, typically by making one or more characters manage the exits of others at the end of scenes. Similar indications of relative power can also be made evident by managing exits (or entrances) within scenes. And because early modern staging relied solely on dialogue cues to manage the characters' onstage actions, there are many occasions when the language emphasizes the power relationships. Although an entrance or exit itself takes only a few moments, the business and language of motivating and cueing an arrival or departure offer considerable opportunities for dialogue and action with thematic implications. By the time Shakespeare came to write *The Tempest* he had long since learned how the control of arrivals and departures could be used as a subtle visual and verbal means of dramatizing thematic concerns.[4] But in this play he put this basic staging element to particular and unique use by creating a protagonist who explicitly – often insistently – manages virtually every entrance and exit.

The exchanges in 1.2 between first Prospero and Ariel, then Prospero and Caliban clearly show how Shakespeare introduces and interconnects the confinement motif, the concern with time, and the protagonist's control over entrances and exits. After he has put Miranda to sleep, Prospero calls, 'Come away, servant, come! I am ready now. / Approach, my Ariel, come!' and Ariel immediately enters saying 'I come / To answer thy best pleasure' (1.2.188–9, 190–1). Prospero hears how Ariel has dealt with the victims of the shipwreck and, after asking the time, says 'The time 'twixt six and now / Must by us both be spent most preciously' (241–2). At this point, Ariel first asks for 'My liberty' and Prospero angrily responds, 'Before the time be out?' and 'Dost thou forget / From what a torment I did free thee?' (246–7, 251–2). He reminds Ariel that Sycorax 'did confine thee, / . . . / Into a cloven pine; within which rift / Imprisoned thou didst painfully remain / A dozen years' until 'It was mine art, / When I arrived and heard thee, that made gape / The pine and let thee out' (276, 279–81, 293–5). When Prospero threatens 'If thou more murmur'st, I will rend an oak, / And peg thee in his knotty entrails till / Thou has howled away twelve winters', Ariel promises to 'be correspondent to command' and Prospero responds 'Do so, and after two days / I will discharge thee' (296–9, 301–2). Ariel asks 'What shall I do?' and Prospero commands 'Go make thyself like a nymph o'th' sea' and 'Go take this shape, / And hither come in't. Go; hence with diligence!' (303–4, 306–7). As always, Ariel exits 'on cue'. This exchange articulates how Prospero's control over Ariel is a paradigm of the necessary mix of coercion and compliance that the successful exercise of power requires. Furthermore, Ariel is the first character to be promised freedom and the last to be given it. Both these elements can be related to the way in which Shakespeare works to manage playgoer response. By introducing the possibility of Ariel's freedom near the start of the play, then having Ariel refer to it repeatedly, but not fulfilling the promise until the end (and not even then, since Ariel has one more task to perform as the play ends), Shakespeare creates suspense – perhaps the most basic device of audience control.

Although the contrast between Ariel's obedience and Caliban's resistance is obvious in this

---

4 See Leslie Thomson, 'Shakespeare and the Art of Making an Exit', *University of Toronto Quarterly*, 69 (2000), 540–59.

establishing scene, the way Shakespeare uses their entrances and exits to create it repays attention. When Prospero calls Caliban and he responds from '*within*', Prospero says 'Come forth, I say! . . . / Come, thou tortoise! When?' (1.2.318–19). But instead of the reluctant Caliban, the obedient Ariel enters '*like a water-nymph*', is sent off again by Prospero and again exits on cue, after which Prospero once more calls Caliban to 'come forth!' and he finally enters (319.1, 323–3.1). The contrast continues to be developed when Sycorax's son complains to Prospero, 'here you sty me / In this hard rock' and Prospero responds that Caliban was 'Deservedly confined into this rock, / Who hast deserved more than a prison' for his attempt to 'violate' Miranda (345–6, 364–5, 350).[5] Unlike the quick, three-line group of cues that signal Ariel's departure, Prospero first commands Caliban 'Hag-seed, hence!' and threatens him with punishments, then nine lines later again says 'So, slave, hence!' before Caliban finally exits (368, 377). This sequence of contrasts is still not complete, however, because Caliban's exit is immediately followed by '*Enter Ariel [like a water-nymph] playing and singing, invisible to Ferdinand, who follows*' (377.2–3). Not only does Caliban's delayed exit here anticipate his later attempts to escape Prospero's control, but the entrance of Ariel with Ferdinand is also the first time a character arrives who is controlled by Prospero through the 'invisible' Ariel, who comes and goes on his command.

Ferdinand's description of how Ariel's music has affected him is also an implicit stage direction for how he enters: 'Thence have I followed it − / Or it hath drawn me rather' (1.2.397–8).[6] Like Miranda's earlier inability to resist sleep, Ferdinand's powerlessness over his movements here is a demonstration of Prospero's imposition of control over others through his 'art'. In the final segment of this long scene, Prospero first awakens Miranda, who immediately falls in love with Ferdinand, who instantly reciprocates. Shakespeare not only makes it clear that this is what Prospero intended − 'It goes on, I see, / As my soul prompts it' − but also that love itself is a kind of confinement − 'They are both in either's powers' (423–4, 454).

Ironically and significantly, this process of romantic entrapment is punctuated by Prospero's 'Spirit, fine spirit, I'll free thee / Within two days for this' and 'Delicate Ariel, / I'll set thee free for this' (424–5, 445–6). The scene is not finished, however, and Shakespeare next uses Ferdinand to reinforce the essential concepts and methods of the play's projects of control. As part of his testing of Ferdinand, Prospero commands 'Follow me', and 'Come! / I'll manacle thy neck and feet together', before repeating 'Follow' (463–5). When Ferdinand says he will 'resist . . . till / Mine enemy has more power', '*He draws, and is charmed from moving*' (469–70.1). Ferdinand stands thus, immobile, until Prospero breaks the spell − an early action that very effectively emblematizes his power to confine and free his captives.[7] Ferdinand's description of the experience both uses and helps to reinforce key ideas and images: 'My spirits, as in a dream, are all bound up' (490); but, he continues, being 'subdued' (493) to Prospero would matter little,

> Might I but through my prison once a day
> Behold this maid. All corners else o'th' earth
> Let liberty make use of; space enough
> Have I in such a prison. (494–7)

Shakespeare's technique of using the exits at the end of a scene to visually and orally encapsulate power relationships is evident in the final sequence

---

[5] Here and throughout this study my focus is on the internal workings of the play in the theatrical context for which it was written; I am aware of the many treatments concerned with Caliban as a victim of oppressive colonialism, but my interest in him here is as one of the figures who is held captive and released by Prospero in the action that playgoers see.

[6] In concluding his analysis of 'the power Prospero exercises through music', David Lindley comments that 'Not only are the characters on stage pushed hither and thither by Prospero's music, but it works its end upon our senses also, with an undeniable insinuation' ('Music, Masque, and Meaning in *The Tempest*', in *The Court Masque*, ed. David Lindley (Manchester, 1984), pp. 47–59, pp. 49, 58).

[7] There is no clear indication of how long this spell lasts, but the longer Ferdinand is unable to move, the stronger the visual impression and the more dramatically effective his release.

of 1.2. Prospero says to Ferdinand, 'Come on'. He then turns to praise Ariel, then back to Ferdinand with 'Follow me' (497–8). While Prospero whispers to Ariel, Miranda reassures Ferdinand. Prospero then promises Ariel freedom for doing 'All points of my command' (504). Ariel agrees, and Prospero turns again to Ferdinand – 'Come, follow' (506). Prospero's last words in the scene are to Miranda, forbidding her to 'speak for' (506) Ferdinand, which calls attention to the latter's silent and compliant exit behind Prospero – ahead of Ariel and Miranda, each of whom has a strong motive to follow them off. The image that concludes the first act thus exemplifies the different methods of control exercised by Prospero (and by Shakespeare) throughout the play.

Significantly, in Act 2 Ariel obeys Prospero's 'command', but Prospero himself never appears, suggesting that he is leaving things to Ariel at this point. In the act's first scene, when Ariel charms Alonso and his followers asleep, they drop 'as by a thunder-stroke' (2.1.209), and the consequent powerlessness of the bodies lying on the stage is emphasized not only by the plotting of Sebastian and Antonio standing above them, but also by the absence of Ariel as protector.[8] At the same time, Prospero's promise to free Ariel for his service has an ironic echo in the inducement Sebastian offers Antonio: 'Draw thy sword. One stroke / Shall free thee from the tribute which thou payest' (297–8). But it is the sleeping figures who are freed when Ariel re-enters, explaining to Gonzalo that 'My master through his art foresees the danger / That you his friend are in – and sends me forth, / For else his project dies, to keep them living' (302–4). Ariel's brief absence might be intended to suggest Prospero's temporary loss of control, or at least a threat to it; certainly there is a contrast with the next sequence, when Ariel remains on stage watching while Gonzalo awakens and then rouses the others. Thus while Alonso might seem to be in control at the end of the scene when he says 'Lead off this ground, and let's make further search / For my poor son' and 'Lead away', it is Ariel who has the final couplet: 'Prospero my lord shall know what I have done. / So, King, go safely on to seek

thy son' (328–9, 330–2) – a clear reminder of who is actually in charge.

The concern with confinement and freedom, the matter of Prospero's control, and the business of character exits are explicitly linked at the end of 2.2 – which is also the end of an act, when exits have more impact and are therefore especially useful for emphasizing key points.[9] The only suggestion of Prospero's presence in this scene is the *'noise of thunder'*[10] that prompts Caliban's description of how Prospero's 'spirits' govern his actions.[11] Indeed, 2.2 is one of only two scenes in the play (the other being 1.1) in which neither Prospero nor Ariel appears. The likelihood that this is meant to suggest the continuing tenuousness of Prospero's control is enhanced when the exits that end the act are initiated by Caliban's offer to Stephano and Trinculo: 'let me bring thee where crabs grow', 'I'll bring thee', and 'Wilt thou go with me?' followed by Stephano's 'lead the way' (166, 169, 171, 172). The drunken Caliban's joyous singing of ''Ban, 'ban, Ca-caliban / Has a new master. – Get

---

8   Although the Folio has no exit stage direction for Ariel, it does have a direction for the spirit's re-entrance, and editors since Malone have inserted the necessary exit. For whatever reason(s), Shakespeare seems to have wanted Ariel to be off-stage while Antonio tempts Sebastian to murder Alonso and the others.

9   The emphasis provided by act breaks would have been especially effective in an indoor theatre such as the Blackfriars, for which *The Tempest* might have been designed. Andrew Gurr states that this was 'the first play Shakespeare unquestionably wrote for the Blackfriars rather than the Globe'. As evidence he cites the play's use of music and the fact that it is 'the first of [Shakespeare's] plays to show unequivocal evidence that it was conceived with act breaks in mind' ('*The Tempest*'s Tempest at Blackfriars', in *Shakespeare Survey 41* (Cambridge, 1988), pp. 91–102, pp. 92, 93). See also Frank Kermode, '*The Tempest* on the Jacobean Stage', in *The Tempest*, ed. Frank Kermode, 6th edn (London, 1958), pp. 150–1.

10   In the Folio this is part of the stage direction that begins the scene; the *Oxford Shakespeare*, 2nd edn, gen. eds. Gary Taylor and Stanley Wells, moves it to 2.2.3.1.

11   Stage directions for thunder and lightning are always linked to the supernatural in plays of the period. See Leslie Thomson, 'The Meaning of *Thunder and Lightning*: Stage Directions and Audience Expectations', *Early Theatre*, 2 (1999), 11–24.

a new man! / Freedom, high-day! High-day, freedom! Freedom, high-day, freedom!' (183–6) is pointedly ironic, however, and although Stephano gives Caliban control over their exits ('Lead the way', 187), it is only because Caliban has agreed to serve him. The ironized 'freedom' demonstrated by Caliban in 1.2 in his repeated refusal to exit when Prospero first tells him to is also evident in Caliban's willing obedience to Stephano here at the end of Act 2, and both moments anticipate the threat posed by Caliban in 4.1.

The play's interest in what constitutes freedom is again apparent at the start of Act 3 when Ferdinand enters alone and of his own volition, expressing his willingness to serve Miranda. Nevertheless, as the focus switches to the lovers, Prospero also returns to the stage, but now is seen and heard only by the audience as he monitors the lovers' exchange of vows – which concludes with Ferdinand saying he will be Miranda's husband, 'with a heart as willing / As bondage e'er of freedom' (3.1.89–90). And although Ferdinand and Miranda seem to manage their own exits, when Prospero remains on stage until the end of the scene his control over their actions is emphasized visually. Also worth noting here is how he cues his own exit and subsequent actions with an acknowledgement of time's tyranny: 'I'll to my book, / For yet ere supper-time must I perform / Much business appertaining' (95–7). But whereas at the end of 2.2 Stephano, Trinculo and Caliban cued and managed their own exits, at the end of 3.2, although they sing 'Thought is free' (125), they exit very much under Ariel's control:

TRINCULO. The sound is going away. Let's follow it, and after do our work.
STEPHANO. Lead, monster; we'll follow. – I would I could see this taborer. He lays it on.
TRINCULO. Wilt come? I'll follow Stephano. *Exeunt.*
(3.2.151–5)

If, as seems likely, 'Wilt come?' is addressed to Caliban, the suggestion is that rather than responding to Stephano's invitation, he is enthralled by the music (which his failure to respond might confirm) and Trinculo must prompt him – a nice

use of exit business as a reminder of Prospero's control.

Prospero's entrance invisible to all but the audience in 3.1 begins a sequence that continues in the next scene when Ariel enters '*invisible*' (3.2.41.2), and again in the next when Prospero enters '*on the top, invisible*' (3.3.18.1–2). The use of such an overtly theatrical device three times in close succession suggests significance. In this case, these entrances further the sense of Prospero's and Ariel's control of the others while also fostering a special connection between these two figures and the audience. Certainly the spectacular events of this scene have the effect of confirming Prospero's power over the other characters. This impression is emphasized when Prospero cues his own exit before the end of the scene, confident that his power over the court group is so complete he need not wait around to manage their subsequent exits:

> My high charms work,
> And these mine enemies are all knit up
> In their distractions. They now are in my power;
> And in these fits I leave them, while I visit
> Young Ferdinand . . .   (3.3.88–92)

From the start of Act 4 to the end of the play Ariel repeatedly comes and goes at Prospero's command. The first time Prospero calls, Ariel enters immediately and is told 'Go bring the rabble, / O'er whom I give thee power, here to this place', to which Ariel responds, 'Before you can say, "Come" and "Go"' (4.1.37–8, 44). As Ariel departs, Prospero explicitly directs the timing of the spirit's return: 'Do not approach / Till thou dost hear me call' (49–50).[12] When Ferdinand asks if those in the masque are 'spirits', Prospero's answer not only includes a key image – 'Spirits, which by mine art / I have from their confines called to enact / My present fancies' (120–2) – but also suggests how sure he is of his control. This creates a certain irony when he interrupts the masque upon remembering the 'foul

---

[12] When Prospero does call – 'Now come, my Ariel! / . . . Appear, and pertly' (4.1.57–8) – it is Iris who enters, so perhaps Ariel played Iris. On the other hand, Ariel mentions having 'presented' Ceres (4.1.167).

conspiracy' (138); but his next words show that he is still in charge of the timing – 'The minute of their plot / Is almost come' – and in control of the spirits: 'Well done, avoid. No more' (141–2). Furthermore, after Prospero's 'Our revels now are ended' speech, he politely requests that Miranda and Ferdinand leave rather than issuing a command – 'If you be pleased, retire into my cell'. Thereupon the lovers exit and Prospero quickly calls, 'Come with a thought! I thank thee, Ariel. Come!' and Ariel immediately enters (148, 161). On being told by Prospero to 'go' and 'bring' the 'trumpery', the spirit exits with 'I go, I go' (186–7) and then returns almost instantly.

The end of 4.1 provides a vivid demonstration of how the business of an exit can be not only a means of getting characters off stage but also a visual encapsulation of thematic material. First there is the direction for Caliban, Stephano and Trinculo's chaotic forced departure: '*A noise of hunters heard. Enter divers spirits in shape of dogs and hounds, hunting them about, Prospero and Ariel setting them on*' (4.1.253.2–4). This is followed by Prospero's exit cue for Ariel and himself, which not only ends both scene and act but also combines language and action to emphasize the play's concern with time, constraint and freedom, and the exercise of power:

> At this hour
> Lies at my mercy all mine enemies.
> Shortly shall all my labours end, and thou
> Shalt have the air at freedom. For a little,
> Follow, and do me service.   (260–4)

These ideas are important enough for Shakespeare to have Prospero echo them at the beginning of Act 5: 'Now does my project gather to a head. / My charms crack not, my spirits obey, and time / Goes upright with his carriage' (5.1.1–3). And when Prospero asks about Alonso and his followers, Ariel reports that they are 'Confined together', 'all prisoners', and 'They cannot budge till your release' (7, 9, 11). Then after deciding that 'The rarer action is / In virtue than in vengeance', Prospero sends Ariel off: 'Go release them' (27–8, 30). Before abjuring his 'rough magic' he uses similar images of confinement and freedom to recall how

'graves at my command / Have waked their sleepers, oped, and let 'em forth / By my so potent art' (48–51). Following this, the detailed stage direction for the entrance of the court party again describes an enactment of the play's central methods and motifs:

Here enters first Ariel, invisible; then Alonso, with a frantic gesture, attended by Gonzalo; Sebastian and Antonio, in like manner, attended by Adrian and Francisco. They all enter the circle which Prospero had made, and there stand charmed; which Prospero observing, speaks . . .   (57.1–6)

The audience sees captive figures being led on in a particular order and in meaningful groupings, who then enter a circle inside which they are immobilized while for the last time the figure controlling them stands watching.

At this point Shakespeare has Prospero begin the process of release by using actions and language that both echo and contrast with what has come before. For example, after freeing the courtiers from the spell and the circle Prospero says he will 'discase' (85) – a word that does not occur elsewhere in the Shakespeare canon but is particularly appropriate in a play that includes so many other terms denoting confinement or release. Perhaps the suggestion is that Prospero has been figuratively 'encased' by his magician's robe (and responsibilities), so that returning to his duke's clothing and role is a kind of freedom from the supernatural power he has wielded. Prospero again assures Ariel 'Thou shalt ere long be free' and 'But yet thou shalt have freedom' (87, 98). But first he sends the spirit to 'find the mariners asleep / Under the hatches' and 'enforce them to this place' (100–2) – that is, release them but bring them here under control. Finally, when Prospero praises Gonzalo as one 'whose honour cannot / Be measured or confined' (123–4), a key word is used negatively to describe an important moral ideal.[13]

---

[13] My emphasis is on confinement as a demonstration of Prospero's control, but the play does not suggest that such power is any more wholly positive than is complete freedom. Prospero trusted Antonio with 'a confidence sans bound' (1.2.97), after all, and Gonzalo's idea of a 'commonwealth' without constraints is self-evidently impossible. As elsewhere

Significantly, the focus then shifts to Prospero's 'cell' (5.1.168). He tells Alonso and the others to 'look in' and that he will 'bring forth a wonder', then '*discovers Ferdinand and Miranda, playing at chess*' (169, 172, 174.1–2). I will return to this event in the next section, but here it is important to recognize that Prospero performs a physical act of release that initiates the more metaphoric releases of forgiveness to follow. The confinement and freedom motif is picked up again when Ariel returns with the Master and Boatswain, who describes how they were 'clapped under hatches', then awakened and 'straightway at liberty' (234, 238). Prospero once more promises Ariel, 'Thou shalt be free'; but first sends the spirit off again to 'Set Caliban and his companions free. / Untie the spell', at which Ariel obediently exits and soon re-enters with them (244, 255–6). These are the last character entrances in the play, but Prospero's management of exits is still very much a factor. He tells Caliban, 'Go, sirrah, to my cell. / Take with you your companions', and cues their exits with 'Go to, away!' (295–6, 301). He sends Ariel off to do one more task, 'Then to the elements / Be free, and fare thou well', before inviting (rather than commanding) the court party – 'Please you, draw near' – to join him in his 'poor cell' (321–2, 305).[14] If the Folio's '*Exeunt omnes*' (TLN 2319)[15] is accepted, Prospero goes off with the others; but it is in the metatheatrical implications of his re-entrance, epilogue (to be discussed in the final section) and final exit that the play's concern with confinement and freedom reaches its intriguing conclusion. Moreover, if Prospero's brief exit and immediate return are well managed, playgoers who think they are free to go will be surprised to find themselves still under the playwright's spell.

II. TIME, TRUTH AND FORTUNE

Typically, an audience's experience of a play is sequential: a situation is first developed, then complicated and finally resolved. This structural and temporal fact is capitalized on when a play's resolution is made possible by a fifth-act discovery of an important truth (as often happens in early modern

drama), inviting the audience to share in the satisfying enactment of the allegorical concept, *veritas filia temporis* – 'Truth is the Daughter of Time'.[16] Shakespeare uses a literal, performed revelation of a crucial truth to initiate the conclusions of a number of plays.[17] As he did with any convention, each time he used a discovery as part of a dénouement he inventively reworked the device to make the business integral to the concerns of the particular play. In *The Tempest*, the idea of *veritas filia temporis* is essential to the structure; but rather than simply allowing Time to pass until Truth is eventually revealed, Prospero explicitly recognizes the opportunity and takes charge of the temporal process that

---

in Shakespeare, when all is said and done the 'golden mean' is advanced by implication – in this case, when Prospero's control is successful and leads to repentance – but it is always tenuous and temporary.

[14] It has sometimes been suggested that Prospero's 'Please you, draw near' is addressed to the playgoers, but since he has just promised to tell Alonso and the others his story, it seems much more likely that they are the 'you' he refers to. If so, by leading them off Prospero controls everyone's exit, including his own, which heightens the irony of his subsequent request in the epilogue.

[15] Some editors follow the Folio, but others have Prospero remain on stage to speak the epilogue. Lindley makes the good point that if all the players leave the stage, the playgoers 'are likely to applaud, thus rendering Prospero's request for approval redundant' (*The Tempest*, 5.1.316 note). But if Prospero leaves with the others only to surprise the playgoers by re-entering immediately and speaking directly to them, the impact would surely keep them in the theatre and under Prospero's (and Shakespeare's) control until 'set me free'.

[16] According to Samuel Chew, 'No emblem is more familiar than that of Time leading forth his daughter from a cave or dungeon. Often Envy is raving impotently behind them, or she may be accompanied by Strife and Discord or Slander' (*The Pilgrimage of Life* (New Haven and London, 1962), p. 19). Chew provides an emblem illustration (fig. 19); for other examples see William Marshall, *Goodly Prymer in Englyshe* (London, 1535), sig. π2v; Geffrey Whitney, *A choice of emblemes, and other deuises, for the moste parte gathered out of sundrie writers, Englished and moralized* (Leiden, 1586), sig. A2v.

[17] Other fifth-act discoveries in Shakespeare include those in *Two Gentlemen* (of Julia, by herself), *Romeo* (of Juliet in the tomb, by Romeo), *Much Ado* (of Hero, by herself), *Othello* (of Desdemona on the bed, by Emilia), *Lear* Q and *Lear* F (of Edgar, by himself when he raises his helmet), *Winter's Tale* (of Hermione's 'statue', by Paulina).

leads to his discovery of a truth that he has made possible. In addition, the idea that in time truth will be revealed and justice achieved is essentially comic: out of disorder and confusion, order; out of deception and evil, good. This generic fact is signalled early and emphasized often in ways that not only help to create audience expectations of an outcome fitting tragicomic romance, but also call attention to the manipulation of events by Prospero and by Shakespeare.

Shakespeare's explicit use of the three unities works in contrasting but connected ways: on the one hand, it is a demonstration of the playwright's control over his materials; but on the other, the unities are devices that constrain or limit what a playwright can do. By using them to construct a play about the exercise of power, Shakespeare not only calls attention to himself but also mirrors the thematic concerns in such a way that playgoers are made aware of these formal devices of artistic control. Because the time during which *The Tempest* is performed is virtually the same as the time it takes for Prospero's 'project' (2.1.304, 5.1.1) to succeed, playgoers are invited to be conscious of how he controls their time too. In particular, the repeated references to the present (especially the seventy-eight uses of 'now'[18]), together with the thirty occurrences of 'the/this island' or 'the/this isle', work to create a shared time and location and an immediacy that fosters a playgoer's sense of inclusion in the larger Shakespearian project. Twelve years had to pass before circumstances were right for Prospero to begin the tightly timed process that leads to the events of the dénouement; but because Prospero knows what he wants from the start, and playgoers will have a general idea what that is, the action and dialogue can be used to focus on the carefully orchestrated process by which he achieves it. When Prospero begins to tell Miranda of their past, he says ''Tis time / I should inform thee farther' and 'The *hour's now* come. / The *very minute* bids thee ope thine ear' (1.2.23–4, 36–7; emphases added). Ariel's role as Prospero's timekeeper is one of the more telling aspects of the immortal spirit's captivity by a mortal with time-sensitive plans. The clock starts

ticking, as it were, when Prospero asks Ariel the time and the latter offers a suitably vague, 'Past the mid season', but Prospero is more specific: 'At least two glasses. The *time 'twixt six and now* / Must by us both be spent most preciously' (1.2.240–2, emphasis added). During that period Ariel is still Prospero's 'servant' (1.2.188, 4.1.34), managing the process necessary to prepare both Miranda and Ferdinand on the one hand, and especially Alonso on the other, for the final revelation. In addition, the audience is given verbal signals to chart the progress to the dénouement. When Miranda and Ferdinand immediately fall in love in 1.2, Prospero's control over the timing is emphasized: 'this swift business / I must uneasy make, lest too light winning / Make the prize light' (454–6). After Ariel frightens Alonso, Sebastian and Antonio with the disappearing banquet, Gonzalo observes: 'All three of them are desperate. Their great guilt, / Like poison given to work a great time after, / *Now* 'gins to bite the spirits' (3.3.104–6, emphasis added). As Caliban, Stephano and Trinculo run off pursued by the '*diverse Spirits*', Prospero comments '*At this hour* / Lies at my mercy all mine enemies. / *Shortly* shall all my labours end' (4.1.260–2, emphasis added). And the last act begins with a clear reminder of his schedule when Prospero says '*Now* does my project gather to a head' and Ariel tells him that it is 'On the sixth hour; *at which time*, my lord, / You said our work should cease' (5.1.1, 4–5, emphasis added).

When Prospero releases Alonso and company from his charmed circle, the resulting confrontations, confessions and reunions achieve the conditions necessary for the moment when he reveals Miranda and Ferdinand playing chess in his cell. Significantly, their location is not incidental, and has been prepared for by dialogue references and the staging since the play's second scene when Prospero refers to himself as 'master of a full poor cell' and gestures towards 'this cell' (1.2.20, 39). On the

---

[18] Although not all the uses of *now* have the same force, the frequent repetition of the word enhances the sense of immediacy. Twenty-eight uses of *now* are by Prospero, mostly in Acts 1, 4 and 5.

bare stage for which Shakespeare was writing, the cell was probably the fictional designation for the central opening in the tiring-house wall.[19] Prospero's 'this' implies that he gestures towards a particular location, identifying it as his cell, and beginning in 4.1 several references serve as reminders. As previously noted, after the masque Prospero sends Miranda and Ferdinand to 'my cell', so that later in the scene when Caliban, Stephano and Trinculo enter to murder Prospero, and Caliban brings them to 'the mouth o' the cell' (4.1.216), the lovers are momentarily in danger before the would-be murderers are distracted by the 'trumpery' hung out by Ariel. These references prepare for the moment when Prospero reveals his daughter and Alonso's son in his cell, an event that calls up an earlier, parallel occurrence in the same place. When in 1.2 Caliban complains to Prospero, 'here you sty me / In this hard rock', Prospero reminds him – and informs the audience – that he 'lodged thee / In mine own cell, till thou didst seek to violate / The honour of my child' (345–6, 348–51). The important thematic contrast between the past attempted rape we are prompted to imagine and the scene of Ferdinand and Miranda playing chess is emphasized by their teasing exchange that begins, 'Sweet lord, you play me false' (5.1.174) – and it is worth noting Ferdinand's earlier promise to Prospero that 'the murkiest den, / The most opportune place, the strong'st suggestion / Our worser genius can, shall never melt / Mine honour into lust' (4.1.25–8).

In light of the carefully contrived quality of this discovery scene, the emphasis through the play on this father's 'care' of his daughter (1.2.16), and the repeated use of staging focused on his cell, it seems likely that, as he performs this action, Prospero is to be seen as enacting a particular version of the many emblems illustrating the *veritas filia temporis* motto, in which Father Time frees his daughter, Truth, from a cave. In this instance the truth revealed is that Miranda and Ferdinand are alive, which, at the ever-present metadramatic level, opens a way out of tragedy into comedy. Moreover, for both Alonso and those with him on one side of the curtain and Ferdinand and Miranda on the other side, this is a discovery of a truth that produces important

contingent comic discoveries: father and son learn that each is alive, and language linked to revelation is used by both Sebastian – 'A most high miracle', and Miranda – 'O wonder! / How many goodly creatures are there here! / How beauteous mankind is! O brave new world . . .' (180, 184–6).[20] Significantly, this moment also signals the completion of a structural and thematic arc that begins in 1.2 when Prospero uses an image of discovery – 'The fringed curtains of thine eye advance, / And say what thou seest yon' – and Miranda upon seeing Ferdinand says 'It carries a brave form. But 'tis a spirit' and 'I might call him / A thing divine, for nothing natural / I ever saw so noble' (1.2.412–3, 415, 421–3). Furthermore, by using the *coup de théâtre* of an actual discovery scene Shakespeare ensured that any audience will share the experience of the revelation and the sense of comic release it engenders.

At the emblematic level so prevalent in this play, the achievement of this dénouement-by-discovery is controlled by Time in alliance with another powerful figure with which Shakespeare's audience would have been familiar, Lady Fortune,[21] as Prospero explains in an essential early speech establishing his dependence on forces greater than himself:

> By accident most strange, bountiful Fortune,
> Now my dear lady, hath mine enemies
> Brought to this shore; and by my prescience
> I find my zenith doth depend upon

---

19 It should be noted that there is no contemporary pictorial evidence for such an opening, but that references in the dialogue and requirements of stage directions in plays written for the public stage provide considerable support for the generally accepted belief that a central 'discovery space' did exist.

20 David Bevington notes that 'The use of the word "discovers" in what may well be an authorial stage direction . . . gives substance to the idea that Shakespeare intended the stage business of uncurtaining to coincide with the structural event of *anagnorisis*' (*Action is Eloquence* (Cambridge, MA and London, 1984), p. 117).

21 John Astington observes that '*The Tempest* is pervaded with references to the mythology and iconography of Fortune': 'Fortune, the Sea, and Shakespeare's Last Plays', in *Fortune* ('*All is but Fortune*', comp. and ed. Leslie Thomson (Washington, DC, 2000), p. 24).

A most auspicious star, whose influence
If now I court not, but omit, my fortunes
Will ever after droop.   (1.2.179–85)

And as the last act begins he returns to the connection between his supernatural assistance and time; indeed, possibly the description of Time is applicable to the appearance of Prospero himself at this moment and thus anticipates the emblematic reading of the discovery scene I have suggested:

Now does my project gather to a head.
My charms crack not, my spirits obey, and time
Goes upright with his carriage.   (5.1.1–3)

Both speeches use imagery of forward or upward motion. More particularly, Prospero's language of high ('zenith') and low ('droop') in the earlier speech calls up the well-known medieval image of Fortune turning a wheel on which there are four figures: one at the top labelled 'I reign', one falling ('I reigned'), one almost off at the bottom ('I am without reign'), and one rising ('I shall reign').[22] When he speaks these words Prospero is not falling, or at his lowest (banishment), or at his highest (dukedom), but on the way up again. As he acknowledges in the last scene, however, his reascension will be brief because constrained by death – 'my grave' (5.1.311).[23] Or, as he has put it earlier, 'our little life / Is *rounded* with a sleep' (4.1.1–57, emphasis added). The wheel of Fortune is also a wheel of Time, as it were.[24] The repeated references through the play to what time it is, when something happened or will happen, and how much time is available or lapsed function not only to chart the progress of Prospero's project but also as reminders that human mortality gives time its meaning. Time makes possible the revelation of truth but it also limits that possibility, just as the constant turning of Fortune's wheel means fleeting success in a world of time and death.

Lady Fortune is also often pictured on the sea, another way of symbolizing her constant change and instability. When Prospero refers to how his enemies have been brought to 'this shore' he reminds the audience of the tempest and sinking ship of the first scene.[25] And at the start of Act 5, Prospero says it was he who 'raised the tempest' (6) with which the play began, while in his penultimate speech he promises Alonso 'calm seas, auspicious gales' (318) for his return journey. These comments confirm what the last scene shows: that Fortune is still Prospero's Lady.[26] But the play's final reference to the sea is still to come, in the epilogue when Prospero transfers control to the audience: 'gentle breath of yours my sails / Must fill, or else my project fails' (11–12).

III. FORGIVENESS AND RELEASE

When at the start of the last act Ariel describes how the prisoners are 'confined together' and tells Prospero that 'if you now beheld them, your affections / Would become tender' (5.1.7, 18–19), Prospero's response not only prepares for the carefully staged (by Prospero and Shakespeare) process of Prospero's forgiveness and release of his prisoners, but also creates a thematic context for the epilogue:

Though with their high wrongs I am struck to th' quick,
Yet with my nobler reason 'gainst my fury
Do I take part. The rarer action is

22 See Frederick Kiefer, *Fortune and Elizabethan Tragedy* (San Marino, CA, 1983), p. 194.

23 Some emblems of Fortune show a figure being thrown from the wheel into a grave; see, *Fortune: 'All is but Fortune'*, fig. 14.

24 Among the 'glor[ies]' of Time listed by Lucrece are: 'To unmask falsehood and bring truth to light' and to 'turn the giddy round of Fortune's wheel' (*The Rape of Lucrece*, lines 939, 940, 952). Emblems of Fortune often include the figure of Time or Opportunity, an hourglass, or a clock.

25 Astington notes how 'The play begins with a stage image that to Renaissance eyes immediately would have invoked the destructive power of Fortune. The foundering or sinking ship was the victim of the goddess immemorially associated with the sea' ('Fortune, the Sea, and Shakespeare's Last Plays', p. 24).

26 As Astington observes, 'The ending of the play restores the apparently wrecked ship, and the travelers resume their journey, accompanied by some new colleagues and the promise of "calm seas, auspicious gales, / And sail so expeditious, that shall catch / Your royal fleet far off" (5.1.315–17)' ('Fortune, the Sea, and Shakespeare's Last Plays', p. 24).

In virtue than in vengeance. They being penitent,
The sole drift of my purpose doth extend
Not a frown further. Go release them, Ariel.
My charms I'll break, their senses I'll restore,
And they shall be themselves.   (5.1.25–32)

As previously noted, Ariel then brings Alonso and his company onto the stage and into the circle Prospero has drawn (which not incidentally echoes the shape of Fortune's wheel and the face of a clock), where they are held until Prospero forgives and frees them. This action of Ariel bringing characters on as captives to be released by Prospero is repeated with Caliban, Stephano and Trinculo, and the process is concluded with Prospero first sending Caliban off with 'Go, sirrah, to my cell. / Take with you your companions', then turning to Alonso: 'Sir, I invite your highness and your train / To my poor cell' (295–6, 304–5). By having both groups of characters exit through that same opening, Shakespeare uses the staging to emphasize especially that Caliban has been forgiven for his attempted violation of Miranda and, more generally, that a new society is being formed.

At this point it is important to note that the significance of who controls entrances and exits in this play actually begins in the past that is prologue, when Antonio 'open[ed] / The gates of Milan' and 'hurried thence' Prospero and Miranda – a forced exit that precipitates the forced appearance of the ship's passengers and crew on the island twelve years later and ends with the willing departure of all these characters for Naples as Prospero's 'project' concludes (1.2.129, 131). And it is useful to remember how the action of the play is charted by a sequence of analogous entrances and exits controlled by one character that dramatize analogous instances of captivity that finally end in release. Furthermore, in giving Prospero control over his and the other characters' exits and entrances through the play Shakespeare made a thematic virtue of staging necessity. This device of stage management also prepares for the intriguing shift that comes when the play seems to be over but Prospero re-enters, only to ask the audience for – at the most literal level – permission to exit. He is, as it were, confined by the playgoers;

but at the same time, his reappearance on stage restrains those playgoers from leaving. This physical circumstance of performance is thereby capitalized on by Shakespeare to explore the confinement, forgiveness, release sequence a final time, but now in a way that shifts between the fiction of the play and the reality of the audience in the theatre. Although the epilogue is sometimes seen as being outside the play proper, as Shakespeare speaking through Prospero, what the speaker actually says does not support this view.[27] Throughout the speech, the use of 'I', 'me', 'my', and 'mine' (1, 2, 4, 5, 6, 9, 12, 13, 15, 16, 20), and the references to 'Naples', 'my dukedom' and 'my sails' (5, 6, 11) reinforce the impression that it is *Prospero* speaking in a very specific context. At the same time, the request for applause calls attention to the actor playing the role, and the numerous uses of 'you' and 'your' (4, 8, 10, 11, 19, 20) repeatedly remind the audience of itself.[28] Shakespeare thus highlights the play's theatricality as he uses the conventions of an epilogue to engineer a necessary and culminating instance of the play's multi-layered concern with confinement and freedom.

By beginning the speech with 'now' and using the word twice more in it (1, 3, 13), Shakespeare continues Prospero's (and the play's) concern with time. But he also capitalizes on the fact that when a figure speaking an epilogue uses the word it also

---

[27] As Kermode has commented, the idea that the epilogue 'allegorizes Shakespeare's return to Stratford' is 'harmful in so far as it deflects attention from the structure of ideas in the play, which has to be historically ascertained; and it lacks historical warrant in itself' (*The Tempest*, Epilogue headnote). While I accept that epilogues might not always have been performed (see Tiffany Stern, *Documents of Performance in Early Modern England* (Cambridge, 2009), pp. 97–119), I nevertheless contend that this epilogue is the culminating exploration of the power-confinement-freedom nexus at the heart of the action and dialogue, and therefore of an audience's visual and aural experience of the play's meaning.

[28] Lindley observes that 'the ambiguous status of the speaker' sets this apart from other Shakespearian epilogues, and that 'at the end of this play [which] has continually teased its onstage characters with the question "What have we here?", the audience is placed in exactly the same position' (*The Tempest*, p. 80).

means 'now, at the end of the play'; that is, 'now' in the real world of the actor in the theatre – in the first and most pertinent instance, Burbage at the Blackfriars playhouse.[29] But even then, for characters, players and audience this speech comes 'three hours since' (5.1.138) the play began. The particular purpose of the resulting ambivalence (or duality) becomes evident when Prospero/Burbage says 'I must be here confined by you / Or sent to Naples' (4–5), because 'you' can refer to no one but the real-world playgoers he addresses. They are thereby explicitly given a role, which is developed in a thematically relevant way with the centrally placed request: 'Let me not'

> . . . dwell
> In this bare island by your spell;
> But *release me* from my bands
> With the help of your good hands.
>
> (5–8, emphasis added)

But of course the confining and releasing are two-sided, or reciprocal, because by releasing the speaker an audience frees itself.[30] The language both puts the playgoers into the island-world of the play and also acknowledges their power as audience. Furthermore, it is important to realize that whereas epilogues typically ask for applause, at the end of this play, in which this figure has repeatedly stage-managed his own and the other characters' exits, Shakespeare has him explicitly ask the audience for permission to depart. The speech therefore emphasizes that the speaker, as both character and player, is no longer in control, having relinquished his 'charms', 'spirits' and 'art' (1, 14). But although control is ostensibly transferred to the playgoers, in fact it remains with Shakespeare where it always was. In particular, by using the epilogue to have the protagonist ask

for freedom, Shakespeare continues to confine the playgoers until, in response to a final request, they must applaud to free themselves. And the play's concluding couplet – 'As *you* from crimes would pardoned be, / Let *your* indulgence set *me* free' (19–20, emphasis added) – makes clear the conditional relationship between the protagonist-actor's freedom and the release of the audience. Moreover, the bestowal of applause not only frees the actor to leave the stage, but in the imaginations of the playgoers it also frees Prospero to return to Naples. The actor is trapped by time, in the present; but the character is both set free and captive – eternal in art.[31]

---

[29] According to Sturgess, 'The role was almost certainly written for Burbage. In 1611 he was at the height of his powers, the greatest actor of his generation, aged 37 or 38, who had played most of Shakespeare's tragic leads' (*Jacobean Private Playhouses*, p. 75).

[30] Berger comments that 'the epilogue is not easy to make out, because so much of what has happened is packed into it . . . [I]n asking to be freed, asking for auspicious winds and pardon [Prospero] places himself in the same relation to the audience as previously Ariel, the Italians, and also Caliban, had stood to him' ('Miraculous Harp', p. 278). Lindley wonders, 'who are we being asked to free from what, and what kind of freedom is it that we bestow? Even as we confer freedom on the actor/Prospero . . . we free ourselves from our voluntary imprisonment in the theatre, and give ourselves licence to return to the workaday world' (*The Tempest*, p. 81).

[31] Lindley notes that Prospero's 'retirement to his library in Milan was an effort to find freedom from the active life of office, but it delivered him to the imprisonment of the island. There, and only there, could he release an Ariel who enabled him to put his magic arts into practice, but the desire through magic to escape from human limitation must itself in the end be disowned. *The Tempest* has, especially in recent years, been seen as a play about power. Perhaps it should rather be regarded as a play about the illusion of freedom' (*The Tempest*, p. 81).

SHAKESPEARE PERFORMANCES IN ENGLAND 2013

CAROL CHILLINGTON RUTTER

Mid January. I'm sitting on a train headed for London; opposite me, a colleague who sees almost as much Shakespeare in a year as I do. We're nattering about the 'state of the art'. He says he's fed up to the back teeth with 'event' Shakespeare. 'Event' Shakespeare? The kind of theatre he thinks we had too much of last year, productions aimed at some 'event' or other – 'Globe to Globe'; the 'World Shakespeare Festival'; both attached to the London Olympics – where the 'event' seemed to be what was driving and defining and selecting the Shakespeare on offer, rather than the creative energy and imagination of actors and directors and designers. The result for spectators was a number of productions that frequently didn't work on their own terms, productions that didn't *have* to work on their own terms, but only as bits and pieces fitting up the conceit of the big corporate project. He longs, he says wistfully, for productions that give us a whole vision of a play, the kind of Shakespeare that was standard at the RSC back in . . . (the date he offers is firmly in the last century). I say I saw a few 'whole vision' productions last year; most of them, it has to be said, independent of the frenzied corporate 'event'-making. A couple of them, it's true, had been officially 'umbrella-ed' by the sponsor but remained cockily resistant to wearing the corporate logo. Still, I take his point. We sit in silence. We gaze at each other's feet, considering the bottoms of our trousers, wondering if it's time we started wearing them rolled. Maybe we're just a couple of Prufrocks.

By the time we hit Marylebone, though, we've cheered up. We're going to the theatre, and for both of us, no matter how often we do it, nothing can take the shine off that statement: 'We're going to the theatre.' In 'post-event' Britain, we're eager to see how the personnel changes announced last year (new artistic directors at the RSC, the Royal Court, the Donmar, the Almeida) are panning out. Six months earlier, back in July, we'd first been excited by the headline in the Guardian (then deflated by the article that followed) announcing that 'Michael Boyd's last RSC season' would be a 'celebration of women in theatre', because that 'huzzah-huzzah!' moment was instantly wrecked when Boyd admitted to the arts correspondent in the interview that it was – ummm, errr – only 'by accident' that Lucy Bailey, Maria Aberg, Nancy Meckler and Lyndsey Turner would be directing at the RSC in the coming season. So this 'celebration of women': it wasn't 'a conscious piece of positive action'? (Why not do the RSC a favour and pretend it was?) Still, Boyd opined, it was 'great that we [were] doing something about it with a concentration and intensity that is new for the RSC'. You had to wonder about the elusive referent. 'It'? Positive action? Sexism in the theatre? Limited opportunities, historically, for women directing Shakespeare? Fair enough, you can put Boyd's seeming woolliness down to poor transcription of an interview. But what excuse can be made for the implications of his statement that 'doing something about it' was 'new' for the RSC? Was he ignorant of the initiatives the RSC had urged upon it back in the 1980s by the likes of Juliet Stevenson and Harriet Walter to give women greater visibility through a 'women's collective'? Boyd put me in mind of those serio-comic scene captions announcing staggering revelations in Brecht's *Galileo*: 'December 1606, Galileo abolishes heaven'. So it's official, 'July 2012, RSC boss discovers gender disparity'. Just when he's on his way out the stage door. And some thirty years after the RSC first noticed and a decade after others started seriously addressing it.

Boyd's gaffes aside, my colleague and I know, as we stride through Covent Garden on that Saturday in January, that we're headed into a year (launched today, as we arrive at the Donmar where Harriet Walter is playing Brutus and Frances Barber, Caesar) that's going to give women plenty of opportunities not just to act, direct, design and compose Shakespeare but to run theatres where Shakespeare is produced, as artistic directors and administrators. We're headed into a year in which gender will be constantly investigated, interrogated, performed and re-performed. I'll see all-women productions of *Caesar* (directed by a woman) and *Shrew* (directed by a man); also all-male productions of *Henry V*, *Shrew* and *Twelfth Night* (directed by men). I'll see gender-neutral puppets performing in *A Midsummer Night's Dream* and *Macbeth*, and a hilariously 'feminist' ending to *The Two Gentlemen of Verona* that will leave all the men standing around empty-handed and gormlessly gawping. And I'll see what I'll come to think of as a 'post-racial' *Othello*, an *Othello* that understands the profound trauma of the play to be nothing so superficial as skin colour, but rather, located in masculinity, in deep-structural homo-phobia, men hating men, and using women to kill them: a tragedy in 2013, then, constructed around not race but gender. We're headed into a year where I'll be gender blind as I'm assessing the work of directors, not least because (Michael Boyd's late learning aside) it's no longer 'news' in most quarters that powerful women are directing Shakespeare, and succeeding and failing just like the boys.

COMEDIES

You know that feeling you get, half way down the first page of a new novel when you realize you're in the safe hands of a master and you'll go wherever the writing takes you? I get it sometimes in the theatre. Case in point: Phillip Breen's *The Merry Wives of Windsor* at the RST. It was the jack'o'lantern that did it: burning in the upstairs window of the otherwise dark, timber-framed Tudor house whose façade, covered in autumn-turning Virginia creeper, stretched the width of the platform stage. The grin on the pumpkin told me this production knew where it was going: to keep an appointment at Herne's oak, via guisings and disguisings, menacing tricks and bitter treats, oofs and oafs and humiliating 'outings'; no twee, self-satisfied costume drama (Globe, 2008) or romping musical in ruffs and farthingales (RSC, 2006), but an edgy look at contemporary middle-class marriage and the (disappointed) games people play, and at the male imaginary (in self-delusional mode); making close-to-the-bone jokes about sex, money and funny foreigners; written in (mostly) prose that smuggles in so much sedition between the lines that you could take it for a late-Elizabethan *samiszdat*. Breen's production took Shakespeare's play seriously. This *Wives* was revenge comedy, his 'merry' wives placed just short of 'merry', axe-wielding Clytemnestra.

Teamed up with Breen, Max Jones set this story today, in Windsor-upon-Avon, in autumn 2012, post-Jubilee, post-Olympics, a time for reckoning costs and settling accounts, his brilliantly observed design giving us a series of locations that zoomed from close-up into long shot and back again. The Tudor house-front (home to the well-heeled, well-settled, not to say terminally domestic, Pages) flew out to reveal a long view of a rugby pitch (where we saw in the foreground Meg Page receiving a letter). When the goal posts sailed out, the kitsch interior of 'ye olde' Garter public house rolled into view. Decorating the lighting grid over the snooker table hung sets of stag's antlers, trophies of male environmental domination or ironic signifiers of man's horned destiny; on the table itself was another bloated beast, Falstaff asleep. This was replaced in turn by the clinical waiting room of Dr Caius's practice, the ultra-modern Vogue-designed glass-and-white-carpet living room of the nouveau riche (and childless) Fords, the low-lying distant vistas of foggy Frogmore, the tawdry garret flat over the bar at the Garter where Falstaff lodged (his single battered suitcase shoved under an iron bedstead whose mattress looked like it had been rescued from a dosser's life on the streets), and the final mock-gothic horror-scape of Herne's blighted oak.

The folk who inhabited these locations were recognizable County types, played just short of caricature. Page and Ford (Martin Hyder, John Ramm), near enough twins who'd prove opposite sides of the same male supremacist coin, were balding boys in short trousers, Saturday morning rugger-buggers (who needed their wives to solve the mystery of how to get the top off the beer cooler). Falstaff (Desmond Barrit) was a worn-out chancer, a geriatric city lad who appeared to have spent the last of Shallow's £1000 (borrowed in the dying moments of 2 *Henry IV*) buying up sale racks of loud tweeds (so last century!), remaindered on Savile Row, to look the part among the Shire locals. A conspicuous mistake. Parson Evans (David Charles) was a weedy, reedy-voiced Welshman in a slack cardigan who arrived for his assignation with Dr Caius wobbling into view on his bicycle, his rapier stowed the length of the cross bar, while Caius (Bart Soroczynski), physician to the toffs who held clinics in formal dress, was in the full fencing rig-out of the French Olympic team, doing one hand press-ups for warm-up. Slender (Calum Findlay) was as hapless a tangle of earnest arm-swinging idiocy as you'd meet in any Sixth Form car park, batting chat-up lines wide or into the net. Anne (Naomi Sheldon), still in school uniform, was a lass who'd slip out of her front door for a quick fag and a snog with her banned boyfriend, Fenton (Paapa Essiedu). Mrs Quickly (Anita Dobson), awed by aristos, like a pigeon pecking popcorn in Trafalgar Square bobbed and curtseyed every time she mentioned 'Sir John', and wore a smile as professionally bright as her pencil skirts were tight.

And then there were the wives – the stars of this production. Sylvestra le Touzel's Burberry-and-Barbour Meg Page was as solid and sensible, watching the rugby in green gum boots and head scarf,

as her vulgarian friend Alice (Alexandra Gilbreath) was ditzy in high-heeled Hunters. (It was typical, when they showed up for the trick-or-treating at Herne's oak, that Alice would be dressed as a cunning little vixen, Meg as Bambi's mother.) Both were 50-somethings; both, 'missing out on some things'. Le Touzel's Meg was first girlishly flattered ('What, have I scaped love-letters in the holiday time of my beauty, and am I now a subject for them?') then, her brief flirtation with 'something else' humiliated, outraged at Falstaff's billet doux. Gilbreath's constitutionally suggestive Alice might be the kind of woman men call a 'go-er', but she was nevertheless instantly steeled to 'be revenged' on 'the whale' tossed 'with so many tuns of oil in his belly, ashore at Windsor' with a plot that very nearly *did* fan the 'wicked fire' of the old lecher's lust so hot that he 'melted . . . in his own grease'. Chez Ford, with Meg poised in the wings, Alice played wiggle-bum seductress in leopard print leggings to a goggle-eyed, sweating Falstaff whom she forced to frolic (more sweat) to Marvin Gaye's 'Let's Get It On' before Meg dashed out of hiding – and took pity on the now very greasy knight by dumping him in the buck-basket.

There was never any question but that the women were in charge in Breen's Windsor and would expose the jealous husband with as much wicked glee as they'd 'out' the fantasist seducer. (This Alice would sit blandly sucking chocolates from the cheap Cadbury's selection box Falstaff had brought, eating the evidence, while her husband pawed manically through a buck-basket full of dirty knickers, searching for the lover he knew must be hiding among his wife's smalls.) But what was staggering, as both the wives and we pondered the *need* for their efforts, was that both the prospective cuckolder and the prospective cuckolded expected the *same outcome*. Both operated from the same 'knowledge': that the women would be corrupted. (And if Page didn't, it was only because he thought the hey-day in his wife's blood no longer heatable: 'my wife is not young'.) Men in this play imagine themselves the masters of language: a delicious joke, given the dubious performance of little William's Latin lesson and the amount of

30. *The Merry Wives of Windsor*, 3.3, RSC, Royal Shakespeare Theatre, directed by Phillip Breen. Sylvestra le Touzel as Mistress Page, Desmond Barrit as Falstaff, Alexandra Gilbreath as Mistress Ford.

'ranting', 'drawling', 'affecting' and 'hacking' of language that goes on as English, French and Welsh alike 'fright... English out of his wits'. Falstaff is sure he can read Meg Page like a book: that he can 'construe... her familiar style' and 'English... her rightly' to 'spy entertainment'. Ford reads out of the same misogynist textbook: 'This 'tis to be married. This 'tis to have linen and buck-baskets'; 'my wife... plots... ruminates... devises'; and what women 'think in their hearts they may effect, they will break their hearts but they will effect'.

How dreary for this 'reading' to be current in 2013. How even drearier, in 2013, to be one of these men, trapped in the residual, persistent imaginary that Breen's production showed to be still current. Two of the most woeful images produced here were first, Barrit's Falstaff, contemplative predator, cranking up the charm for one more sting, perched on the edge of his bed, holding up to his girth what he'd pulled out of his suitcase, a pair of seducer-ware boxer shorts that he clearly hadn't worn since the days when he was an 'eagle's talon in the waist', and could only see the fit of now by flashing a mirror at his groin (how macro his belly; how micro his 'yard'). And second, Ramm's Ford, who'd earlier bounced like a demented rooster around his own living room crowing 'Buck?... buck! Buck buck buck!'; later at the Garter, in a fit of insane hyperactivity, snapping a snooker cue as he ranted about linen and buck-baskets, that he clapped to his head: turning himself into a horned monster. The stag on the wall didn't bat an eye. Fortunately, this production offered the antidote to toxic male delusion: Alice's laughter (Gilbreath has one of the lewdest laughs in the business), and Meg's brains (le Touzel: what an intelligent actor!).

Jones's multiple scene changes gave us a whole social world in Breen's *Wives*. Working on the same stage at the RSC designing Lucy Bailey's *The Winter's Tale*, William Dudley produced only two locations, but these were hardly conventional re-imaginings of the play's shifts from Sicilia to Bohemia and back again.

Bailey understood Sicilia and Bohemia to exist within each other, and Dudley designed a space where this could be so, Sicilia set at the top of a damsels-in-distress-knights-in-shining-armour tower, backed by a wall of CGI projection where a fish-scale sparkling sea rolled continuously across spectators' vision, giving a vista of vertiginous height (that would later darken, roil into storm waves that would shape themselves into a monstrous tsunami 'virtual' bear that would 'virtually' devour Antigonus). This was a pre-Raphaelite world, a Burne-Jones world of lush colours, decoration and idealized conduct: a faux medieval world of chivalry and courtly love. The opening stage image showed a tangle of bodies, asleep, in velvet and gold tissue and in each other's promiscuous arms, brought suddenly awake by the noise and intrusion of a small boy, dressed as some pint-pot future Henry V or Redcrosse Knight, running rings round his nanny and dashing into the scene to leap on top of his parents – and his Dad's best friend, Polixenes.

Later, the perspective would reverse. Bohemia would be found at the base of this notional ivory tower: on the rocks, so to speak, of some north-west coastline of 1860s industrial England, the tower converted to a Heath Robinson fun-fair contraption and the locals played as clog-dancing mill workers on holiday, their recreation the deliciously vulgar antics of Donald McGill's saucy seaside postcards. Here, Perdita (a winningly fresh-faced performance from Emma Noakes) was a lass with a regional accent and decidedly regional feet, stomping out the clog dance; Autolycus (Pearce Quigley), a lank, scraggle-bearded and dour-voiced 'Rajah the Mystic Oracle' in turban and harem pants, touting for custom in a collapsible tent. Instead of a sheep-shearing, then, this production gave Wakes Week, Lancashire. And if this half of the play started, as in Sicilia, with these working folk asleep in deck chairs and on rugs (from physical exhaustion, not, as in Sicilia, ennui) the scene soon enough shifted into carnival mode, the most joyous performance of Shakespeare's Act 4 since Adrian Noble's production at the RSC in 1993.

The emotional hole in this production was Jo Stone-Fewings's Leontes. He's an actor who works from the eyes and so gives spectators fleeting moments of psychological insight, micro-gestures registering pain, contempt, weariness and so on, but not the full-body stuff that shows Leontes, body, mind and soul, mowed down by the toxic super-bug that infects his blood, nerves, heart and head. When Leontes makes the appalled discovery that 'My heart dances, but not for joy, not joy', he's admitting a condition – that dancing heart – that's not simply psychological but terribly physical. (This felt condition makes him kin to Othello and Ford in *Wives*.) To show him, early on, sucking on a hookah was a mistake that gave this Leontes an easy medical diagnosis ('bad opium trip') for his later unaccountable possession-by-jealousy.

Opposite him, Tara Fitzgerald (whose biog in the programme listed only one previous Shakespeare) was as fine a Hermione as I've ever seen. In her full-blown, big-wombed, pregnancy she sprawled languidly, unselfconsciously, post-sexually among the dozing men. At her trial, she stood stony-faced, hair shorn, in plain black – Bailey wisely not following recent production trends that have the Queen of Sicilia show up to her defence as if straight from the labour ward in a gown bloody enough to look like she's given birth in an abattoir. Bailey directed the shock of this scene to be not what it looks like but what it sounds like, the story it's telling, the devastation of intimacy that happens across the verbal exchange between husband and wife, here a one-on-one show-down that Fitzgerald made electrifying. Control, dignity, grief, rage were all present line by line in this Hermione's statement of innocence. So was emotional ruin. Fitzgerald is the only Hermione I can remember to react to Leontes's stunning news about how he'd provided for her new-born 'bastard'. Only once did she lose control, suddenly lunging forward to clutch her husband's head between her hands, straining through clenched teeth, 'My life stands in the level of your dreams.'

Her emotional other half was a volatile, powerhouse Paulina (the tiny Rakie Ayola, whose voice, like Fitzgerald's, pitched half an octave lower than you expect it, can rumble up dangerously, like a premonition of the storm that's about to strike Leontes flat). This Paulina constantly punched above her weight. She had no truck with pusillanimous men but roared her conscience-flaying accusations at Leontes. When she announced the death of the queen ('The sweet'st, the dear'st creature's dead'), she plonked herself down on some steps, suddenly weary, spread her skirts wide like a fishwife, and belly-laughed the rest of the sentence, a mock to flay the mind: 'And vengeance / Not dropped down yet'.

(I happened to catch this terrific double act a second time, played in a completely different register, when Fitzgerald and Ayola appeared in the public understudy run of the play as Mopsa and Dorcas, a pair of spitfire mill-girls on holiday, skirts hiked up, fists balled, warring over the unlikely trophy body of Nick Holder's corpulent and clodhopping Young Shepherd. What a delight!)

I give Bailey's production the top award this year for the smartest programme note. Three cheers to the unacknowledged author who wrote the plot synopsis, ending it with this brilliant non-spoiler: Perdita is 'married to Florizel, Leontes [is] reconciled to Polixenes, and a statue in commemoration of Hermione [is] unveiled.' But this production also takes my 'turkey' prize for dumb direction. (Sorry, Lucy Bailey.) Shakespeare's bear is a gift to the theatre. When the bear walks on and Antigonus looks the bear in the eye, humankind confronts its opposite in the beast – but discovers the wild animal to be 'kinder' than it. To make this a virtual, CGI encounter is to remove that moment of species recognition and to deny us one of the greatest of Shakespeare's visual jokes ('it's behind you!'), a joke that explodes horrified tension in laughter, and so turns the axis of the play. (Worse still, on the RSC's new thrust stage, it was to deny a good portion of the audience any sense of the bear at all: if you happened to be sitting towards the upstage sides of the thrust, in the stalls or the galleries, you couldn't see the CGI back projection. No sea. No tower. No vertigo. No bear.)

The *ad hominem* rage that Ayola's Paulina unleashed, Saskia Portway's Hippolyta in *A Midsummer Night's Dream* at the Bristol Old Vic sublimated – to begin with. Directed by Tom Morris in association with Handspring Puppet Company and designed by Vicki Mortimer, this *Dream* was Hippolyta's dream, but in no conventional sense. For she had been 'captured' by the mechanicals. She was, like them, an artisan (as seen in the pre-set, where the mechanicals roved the stalls, chatting up the audience and calling to each other in the galleries, then in the silent opening sequence where she appeared alone on stage). We watched her, wrapped in a carpenter's apron, armed with chisel and mallet, bashing a lump of wood, sculpting a wooden face on a workbench that was littered with woodworker's tools in a workshop cluttered with half-made pieces and abandoned projects. Behind her, a linen backcloth showed a diagram of a human body. Behind that towered what looked like the rotten hull of a capsized ship, its bare wood ribs showing.

Portway's Hippolyta, then, became the 'maker' in a *Dream* presided over not by the moon but by wood/woods, a place that carried on its surface scars of the environmental disaster Titania (Portway doubling) surveyed in a speech that was both accusing and grief-stricken. In this wood there were no trees. Just rough, human body-length planks of wood that, moved and mustered and manipulated by fairy 'operators', built barriers for lovers to push through, runways for runaways to negotiate, terrifying sudden obstructions in paths – bushes made bears. These walking planks were musical instruments. Fingers from unseen bodies drumming on them produced soundscapes by turns natural and supernatural, the sound of rain, the sound of a haunting lullaby. They metamorphosed into Theseus's hunting hounds. Turned around, they showed graffiti that spelled out an invitation to the audience to attend an interval in the foyer. They spoke a kind of 'plank language' that would have given a whole new meaning to Demetrius's, 'I am wood in these woods', if the line hadn't been cut.

This place, too, was something of a derelict builder's reclamation yard. Hippolyta's tools turned up there like residual objects refashioned by her Fairy Queen alter-ego. Puck was made of junk: his head, a blow torch, his body, an upturned basket; one leg, a hammer, the other a saw; a kind of humanoid dog stuck together by the mechanicals (doubling the fairies) who manipulated him. Like the puppets in the Russian *Dream* reviewed last year (*Shakespeare Survey 66*), this Puck could explode, fly apart, 'put a girdle round the world' from several directions simultaneously.

The conceit, suggested first by Hippolyta's work, that in this *Dream* objects would turn into humans, humans into objects, came to life in the lovers' first entrance. They arrived shadowed ('If we shadows . . .'?) with their miniature puppet doubles (suggesting perhaps their under-developed selves?). All of these puppets had the inscrutable faces of Greek masks, but they were also complicated pieces of engineering that allowed for movement of heads, shoulders, elbows, hips, knees and (gendered) torsos so that while the faces gave away nothing, the bodies were expressive. The lovers (Demetrius: Kyle Lima; Lysander: Alex Felton; Helena: Naomi Cranston; Hermia: Akiya Henry), who manipulated them, talked through their puppet alter-egos. But the puppets could also stand alone while the lovers talked face to face. Or they could be parked, made observers on the scene, as when, set aside, Demetrius's puppet watched (blandly? disapprovingly? certainly not helpfully) his other half's ding-dong with Hermia ('O, why rebuke you him that loves you so?'). When she stomped off, hugging her puppet tightly, he turned to his puppet helplessly to justify himself – *to a puppet* – whining, 'There is no following her in this fierce vein.' Shifts between men and dummies produced some revealing moments. Abandoned, Hermia was kidnapped by fairies when her puppet was snatched. Set upon, Helena nearly fell for the lads' double wooing until she realized Lysander was addressing her puppet self and simply repeating Demetrius's lines, producing an echo-chamber of empty words. She literally dragged her 'self' away (and later, sleeping, had to be prised apart from the puppet she was clutching like a teddy bear).

As if answering the smallness and blandness of the mortal word, the puppets in fairyland were supersized. Portway's Titania and David Ricardo Pearce's Oberon held massive heads of Greek statues alongside their own, ventriloquizing their masks, and Oberon was equipped with one giant prosthetic arm that allowed him to stick his fingers into everyone's pies. Or if not made bigger-than-life, the puppets in fairyland were, like Puck, repurposed: Mustardseed (manipulated by David Emmings) had been salvaged from the circus, had a clown's head; Peaseblossom (Colin Michael Carmichael) was something off a rubbish tip, a vampiric manga, ribs exposed; Cobweb (Jon Trenchard) had been re-engineered, was expressionless, femininely oriental, until the red lips suddenly snapped back in a grin to show rows of pointed metal teeth.

On the other side of metamorphosis, Bottom (Miltos Yerolemou), the human, was turned into a thing. His Ass was an outrageous mechanical monster, built on a last-century hospital gurney from repurposed human body parts posed preposterously upside down. So Bottom-as-Ass presented his near-naked bottom where his head should have been. Raised in stirrups (think: gynaecological examination) his feet were ears, while his hands made hooves that reached over the sides of the contraption and turned the flange that worked the gears that drove this bizarre buggy.

This, then, was a constantly unsettling *Dream*; a spooky *Dream* (atmospherically, not to say, gloomily, lit by Philip Gladwell); a *Dream*, at the end, that was solemnly beautiful when giant-sized full-body puppets of Titania and Oberon came alive and married the lovers; a *Dream* certainly cued by emotional identification with Shakespeare's script. But all this creativity and visual playfulness came at a cost – to the script itself. Having to crouch behind their puppets put actors in the worst possible position to speak, to inhabit Shakespeare's writing – the puppets, ironically, turning the actors into dummies. Except for Puck, whose puppeteers shared his lines and used a variety of sounds, either solo or in chorus, to make him live, parts were vocally dull, the poetry flat. Not insignificantly, the most famous speech in the play – 'The lunatic, the lover, and the poet . . . ' – was cut. Perhaps as a kindness to Shakespeare? For Ricardo Pearce's Theseus was as wooden as his wooden double.

Still, I'd rather watch a production that has too many ideas than none or the single objective, like the Michael Grandage Company's *Dream* in the West End, of bums on seats. This production marked Grandage's first Shakespeare since leaving the Donmar to go commercial (with, as the press statement had it, shows 'aimed at reaching out to a whole new generation of theatregoers', which means, if this *Dream* was anything to go by, casting TV celebrities to pull in the 'yoof'). David Walliams (of *Little Britain*) was Bottom, Sheridan Smith (*Gavin & Stacey*, *Legally Blonde*) was Hippolyta/Titania, both making these roles versions of their raunchy media 'personalities'. So Bottom's Pyramus (dying) had to smother Alex Large's Thisbe (dying) face down in his crotch while Titania had constantly to grope Bottom for his next erection. What saved this production for me was that the 'star couple' had some real actors supporting them: Richard Dempsey's spruce, spectacled, bow-tied, young-fogey auteur Quince, hugging his script, imagining its great performance, registering, silently, the tragedy of its abortion, now that Bottom had gone missing; Susannah Fielding's spitfire Hermia (a metamorphosed Exocet missile); Katherine Kingsley's man-eating Helena (who managed to de-bag Stefano Braschi's priggish Demetrius even as she ripped off her own clothes); and Sam Swainsbury's love-haunted Lysander (whose hollow eyes looked like he'd spent the last five years insomniac under Hermia's balcony and who awoke transformed by Puck's love juice into up-tripping urgent adolescent gormlessness). The design (by Christopher Oram) was handsome enough: for the court, panels of black-and-gold smoked mirror surfaces arranged in a set of receding prosceniums made frames inside frames; behind, against a blue night sky, the ruins of some ancient world, a collapsed temple, perhaps, or derelict room in a forgotten palace, the back wall caved in, the rubble making a ramp to clamber up, the hole embracing what filled it and cast the place in a cold, magic light, *a full moon*. (But doesn't the script put us in the *moonless* phase of the month? 'Four nights will quickly dream away the time; / And then the moon, like to a silver bow / New bent in heaven'. So Oram's design was spectacular, but like the central casting, just plain wrong.)

Still, even the one idea of Grandage's production put it a cut above Dominic Dromgoole's off-the-peg, faux-early modern costume drama *Dream* at the Globe where John Light's Theseus/Oberon was relentlessly flat-footed and monotone and where Pearce Quigley appeared to have exhausted all his comic resources for the season playing Autolycus in Bailey's *Winter's Tale*. Quigley's Bottom had none (bottom, that is); was all surface; with two poses: a limp leg ('I'm fey'); and an index finger poking a cheek ('I'm "special"'). So tedious! The only thing that kept me watching was Michelle Terry's Hippolyta/Titania who lit up the stage and shot fireworks into the sky. Alas, even this Fairy Queen couldn't make a silk purse out of a sow's ear of Quigley's ilk. But Dromgoole (more a theatre impresario than a theatre director) clearly knows the audience he's grooming to accept what Peter Brook long ago called the 'Deadly Theatre'. He pitches his productions to them. (To reach, I'd say, not heads and hearts but netherparts.) This was a *Dream* for Dromgoole's view of the 'groundlings'. And while it did nothing for me, they had a whale of a time.

The Globe's Jacobean-dress *Tempest*, directed by Jeremy Herrin, did have ideas, though its thoughts on Caliban I found politically problematic. Max Jones's simple and beautifully useful design had the theatre building morphing into Prospero's island. (Or perhaps I should reverse the conceit and see in this design a kind of Ovidian metamorphosis, half-enacted, where the primitive was becoming the civilized, with the polished columns of the theatre 'growing' from their stone source.) At the base of the red faux-marble pillars that hold up the Globe's 'heavens', boulders of the same-coloured stone spread forward (as though melted from their crafted shape back into original form, like wax dripped down a candle) to make a rocky promontory on a seashore. Behind, the gallery had been opened up, a platform built out from it, a kind of observation deck, with stairs onto the stage. Jones, then, left plenty of stage space for this play to bustle in – as in the opening storm sequence (its sounds made by a thundersheet) where the stage was first the ship's deck where mariners were pitched and tossed across it while, by a trick of reverse perspective, across the yard sailed, uncertainly, the same ship, in miniature replica, propelled hand-over-hand by sailors who'd be 'wrecked' with her the moment she hit the stage.

This near-empty space with different levels and outcrops offered Ariel (Colin Morgan), here half bird (in feathered tunic, high cheekbones strikingly etched, heron-like), half Indian street-acrobat (in split skirt and trousers), plenty of vantage points for perching and crouching and for spectacular aerial launches that combined virile strength and exceptional grace.

But it also troped a mournful emptiness, the desolate kingdom of Prospero's memory. Roger Allam's shambling, shabby Prospero opened up its abysmal vacancy to Miranda (Jessie Buckley) – and to us – as he recounted her past. And his. Their 'origins' were a fall story, a story of fraternal betrayal (or perhaps, of double fraternal betrayal). Telling it, Allam's Prospero got stuck on words. 'Twelve years since', 'brother', 'me': these stopped him in his narrative tracks, showed him distracted by remembering, a mind cut to the quick, momentarily unable to get the next thought out. But if Allam's Prospero was a hurt Prospero, a Prospero in whom certain lights were just beginning to dawn, he was also a *hurting* Prospero, inflicting his pain on others. He was by turns waywardly affectionate (catching his feisty daughter in an embrace that she wanted to flee), tyrannical, and downright cruel. Poor bug-eyed Ferdinand – Joshua James – terrified of the island, sword shakily drawn, his body inside his doublet and hose permanently bent into a human parenthesis, discovered that none of the 'strange noises' in the ambient air were as fearsome as Prospero's roaring. Ariel, made to dredge up what his constitutional reticence had clearly suppressed, was treated like the autistic child of a brutish schoolmaster father who *knew* the kid could remember – if he'd just *apply* himself. (It was obviously this Prospero who'd taught Caliban to talk: Caliban used the same rhetoric of mockery, interruption, contradiction, repetition on Stephano.)

The Globe stage invites extrovert performances and broad comedy, the kind of thing Allam did so brilliantly as Falstaff (*Shakespeare Survey 64*) teetering his bulk on the edge of the stage, talking to the audience and 'tempering' us 'between [his] finger and [his] thumb' to soften us up like wax. Prospero's big soliloquy ('Ye elves of hills . . . ') is of a completely different order. It's more like 'Come you spirits that tend on mortal thoughts' than 'Who calls me villain, breaks my pate across . . . ?') While Falstaff in soliloquy seems always to be pushing what's inside *out*, Prospero seems to be sucking what's outside *in*, ingesting the outside world, working it up by a kind of poetics of introversion into, finally, a god-like utterance, a *fiat*: 'I'll drown my books.' Allam's voice was wonderful. (Allam's voice is always wonderful.) But he was reciting the speech, not making it, not gathering in materials to refashion a self and a future, not conjuring thought. So where I wanted to see his metamorphosis, the magic didn't happen. Still, he was excellent as the grumpy dad, watching in (hilarious) paternal alarm his daughter spin further and further out of his reach in the circle dance that was the centre of this production's wedding masque.

In this Jacobean context, what kind of 'monster' was James Garnon's Caliban? One, it appeared, whose only 'deformity' was his skin colour. In production photographs this Caliban looks tattooed, or elaborately body-painted, like the 'Indians' in the visual records brought back from the New World (Herrin evidently setting Prospero's island in the Atlantic, not the Mediterranean). But perhaps that detailed make-up was too difficult to sustain night after night; by the time I saw the show, Garnon's near-naked 'white-boy' body was 'redded-up'. It was smeared all over the same marbled colour as the boulders on the island's notional seashore, making this Caliban elementally of the island (but making him also suggestively the material origins of the theatre). He had the rolling gait Laurence Olivier adopted, playing Othello. And the 'black' speech habits of John Kani and Winston Ntshona in *Sizwe Bansi is Dead*. So he was, for me, a disturbing racialized mash-up of borrowed markers that played on the cliché of native savagery. This Caliban eye-balled the audience, or turned on them, monkey-wise, his naked bottom, or spat on them. Was he a Caliban fighting back? Or a Caliban who'd learned Prospero's language without the benefit of any of Ariel's intermediating grace?

There's a moment at the end of *The Taming of the Shrew* that gestures towards grace. 'I wonder what it bodes', Hortensio muses of Kate's capitulation. 'Peace it bodes', Petruccio answers, 'And love and quiet life'. All that's 'sweet and happy'. This certainly looked to be the direction Joe Murphy's *Shrew* was headed, until the final five minutes when the production took a sharp swerve into bleakness.

This *Shrew* was one of the year's batch of compact, scaled-down Globe touring productions (which travel the length and breadth of Britain, and abroad, but which normally don't make it into this survey simply for lack of space). I wanted to review it because, ten years after the much-touted Phyllida Lloyd-directed *Shrew* (which featured in a Globe season billed as 'Regime Change' during which, according to the then-artistic director Mark Rylance, his policies would 'be helping to realise the enormous potential of actresses who face diminishing opportunities as their expertise and life experience grow to maturity'), the Globe was repeating the experiment. This *Shrew* was an all-female *Shrew*.

So what is released when women play all the parts? In 2003, a chance (as G. B. Shand put it) for women, under cover of Rylance's 'original practices', to put on doublet and hose and 'guy the guys', lampooning masculinity with the broadest of thigh-slapping imitations and cheapest of crude (modern) behaviours: so Janet McTeer's Petruccio could turn upstage, ostentatiously adjust his codpiece, and noisily piss against the stage pillar. In 2013, a chance to move beyond such crass role reversals; to celebrate, in a play that is about acting at every level, the actor's craft where the actors happened to be women.

This production emerged from a striped circus tent, a company of eight 'players' in versions of 1930s black dress (halters, jumpsuits, pinch-waist flared skirts, wide trousers designed by Hannah Clark). They launched skiffle-band style into a ballsy rendition of 'Jack Monroe', a ballad that, with its father-defying heroine who cross-dresses and goes to sea to get her man, announced a world of bolshie, go-getting women. These 'players', then, vanished to re-enter in roles that continuously doubled (and that produced all the music in this production). The dashing 1930s design signature was fixed by Lucentio (Becci Gemmell) and Tranio (Remy Beasley) turning up in Padua as if Brideshead freshers at Oxford, in boaters and blazers. The drunk tinker Christopher Sly (Kate Lamb) returned – a neat subverting of casting cliché – as Kate Minola. The Lord (Kathryn Hunt) in traditional hunter's pinks was later a dazed-and-bewildered Baptista then a grungy, grumbling Grumio in leather bonnet, and Joy Richardson, a spiv Gremio (all in white), then a mountainous Widow (all in black). Olivia Morgan moved from wide-eyed Bianca playing up to daddy, to gormless Biondello with electrocuted hair, transformed from half-speed half-wit to hyperactive motor-mouth describing the approaching bridegroom's horse, and Nicola Sangster, as Hortensio, in the most convincingly inhabited part in this production, produced its most enduring image. Equal parts astonishment, impotence, humiliation and sour rage, Hortensio entered as failed music master, necklaced with a lute.

Given the limitations of cast size, some stories were truncated, others unfinished. (There was no Sly at the end; and the bridal dinner was short of several men who normally fill out the audience to Kate's so-called 'capitulation' speech, which starts as instruction to the other brides but increasingly interrogates the patriarchy by ranging its idealizations across the real-life examples of actual masculinity seated at the table.) But what the casting also showed is that, whether he's played by a woman or a man, Petruccio gets most of the best lines, and if he's a gorgeous 'madcap ruffian' in full-length leather coat and knee boots, swaggeringly alluring, as Leah Whitaker was, a Petruccio that any Kate would fall for (including me), we'll fall in with the taming plot, go where the game takes us, and

sacrifice our 'sister' Kate to the fun. Here, we could do it without a guilty conscience because, as Lamb and Whitaker played 2.1, the wooing scene was, performatively, evenly matched; full of banter and play, light on its feet; without the conventional brutish turn ('Will you, nill you . . . ') that ultimately allows Petruccios physically to dominate Kates (including McTeer, who towered over tiny Kathryn Hunter).

But this delicious reciprocity made the final turn (or better said, detour) the production took to bleakness at the end unaccountable, certainly unprepared for. It was as though the director suddenly realized his *Shrew* was a comedy, and needed the show to snap out of it and behave itself as a 'problem' play. So the Kate who offered her hand beneath her husband's foot was a just-broken Kate; and the Petruccio who'd seconds before been fascinated by the feisty just-married Bianca who'd stomped out of her wedding party ('I mean to shift my bush') was a Petruccio left owning wrecked goods, a shrew he'd tamed but now was devastated to claim. Only, I didn't believe it. Lamb's Kate was always as much a jack-the-lad as Whitaker's Petruccio. Proof: she came on to launch the production's final production number swinging a saxophone.

Disconcertingly, you can flip the casting of this play and produce a not dissimilar story – at least to begin with. With its regular production team in place (director: Edward Hall; designer: Michael Pavelka; lighting: Ben Ormerod; music: the company), Propeller's all-male, twelve-man *Taming of the Shrew*, a revival from 2006, put mirror-fronted wardrobes on stage (that, opened, looked into Narnias or glimpsed activities in parallel worlds; closed, reflected the audience, made us contemplate our role on stage), and a massive chest of drawers, spilling its contents. This was a place of self regard, of doubles, of costumes and disguises; a place, in short, that would celebrate acting in sequential, cumulative and alternative performances that were presided over by a near back-wall-sized canvas showing another (narratively teasing, not least because it hung there skewed) performance, Titian's Venus attempting to seduce Adonis.

31. *The Taming of the Shrew*, 5.2, Propeller, Hampstead Theatre, directed by Edward Hall. Vince Leigh as Petruchio, Dan Wheeler as Kate.

Where the Globe's *Shrew* was set up with an up-beat ballad, Propeller's started with a much more complicated backstory that both initiated role-play and put an edge on the proceedings, reconceiving play as revenge plot. A polished Dad in morning-suit paced while tuxedoed guests milled around, a wedding about to begin. The bridal song kicked in, wrists were turned, watches checked. Dad frowned, signalled. One of the tuxedos dashed out, returned, smiled limply, shrugged. No groom. The hapless soloist started over, over-brightly. A wardrobe door crashed open. The groom, reeling ripe, stumbled in. Opposite, Dad entered with the bride, barricaded behind a veil that looked as inviting as the Berlin wall while the best man tongue-lashed the tottering groom (with lines taken from *A Shrew*), 'Heaven cease this idle humour . . . ' The groom managed an indignant, if slurred, riposte, 'Am I not Christopher Sly?' before passing out. Whereupon the bride launched her bouquet at his head like a hand grenade and stomped out, leaving Dad furious ('In my house tonight he shall not lie!'), then intrigued when one of the guests proposed a retaliatory 'bedtrick': 'Wrapped in sweet clothes . . . banquet . . . brave attendants . . . when he wakes, / Would not the beggar then forget himself?' Thus, the 'jest' was born, and the guests dived into drawers to pull out costumes to create 'dreams' that would play out, but simultaneously travesty, male fantasies, the parts Sly wished he could own. (Thus, we'd see a toreador, a gowned-up academic, a chef, bell-hop, beach-comber and, mostly sensationally, the alpha-male part of Petruchio that Sly would try on for size.) One of the tuxedoed guests was handed apparel that made him smile crookedly. He'd return as a goth-queen Kate, the kind of girl you find hanging around vandalized bus shelters, in regulation black, bovver boots, halloween eyes, scarily 'butch' bleached hair, and skirts hitched up over blood-red tights.

Up to the wedding, things fairly rollicked along, the audience laughing out loud at the male posturing that just looked very silly, not least under Bianca's (Arthur Wilson) promiscuous gaze, she as manipulative a minx as you'd ever hope to see in polka dots, running rings round the men and giving her sister two for one in one of those 'snap shots' of domesticity revealed when a wardrobe door flashed open to show them at each other's throats over Baptista's (Chris Myles) embattled head. There was full-on argy-bargy in the wooing scene – but nothing Dan Wheeler's Kate couldn't handle. And there was shock and insult when Vince Leigh's Petruchio (announced by the tour de force acting exercise of Ben Allen's Biondello, trailing what was coming) turned up to the wedding in fringed cowboy jacket and bare-assed in posing pouch – but nothing Padua couldn't handle.

After the wedding though, after the family photo, after the strutting of the beaming, new-married groom across the stage, shoving his ring into everyone's faces, things flipped. Wearing the cultural badge that gave him the power to call the shots, he did. When Kate objected to his pre-dinner exit plan, he yanked her off her feet, dragged her by her hair, bellowed his biblical claim on her to the frozen, stupefied faces of her former town as she cringed from his violence. 'Touch her who dare'. Nobody did. The audience went silent.

At home, things got even nastier: Kate entered looking like she'd lived the story Grumio (Benjamin O'Mahony) told his fellow servants. And she clearly had no change of clothes for her wrecked wedding dress but seemed to shrink inside it, cowering from the noise, the verbal abuse, the household mayhem Petruchio unleashed against his hapless servants. This was a Petruchio who was playing male supremacism for real, the violence real and the cultural legitimation unassailable: Petruchio here was no psychopath. He was a pillar of the (culturally enabled misogynist) community. When he turned his sneering onto the audience ('This is a way to tame a shrew') and challenged us to 'speak', we kept quiet. And shifted in our seats.

I had forgotten how shocking this play could be. Propeller revived the shock, made us remember (via the jest to make Sly 'forget' himself) that the gender wars are not won, that 'companionate marriage' is still a long way off for many, gave us a Shakespeare analogue, in a world that flashes images globally in seconds, to the murderous misogyny that is alive and well both home and abroad. (This was the year a medical student was dragged off a New Delhi bus and gang raped to death.) Propeller can play out brutality to such shocking extremes because they're an all-male company. They can go to the physical limit knowing that the audience is seeing Kate's (female) victimization performed but not reproduced, played on and by the male body, which is surely the stunningly radical point of Shakespeare's original concept and casting. A case in point: the tailor scene. Wheeler's Kate was grabbed, shoved, manhandled into playing substitute tailor's dummy, bundled into the dress, stripped out of it, a hat jammed onto her head, head spinning, the men working over her objectified body as if she were some kind of domestic power tool with snap-on parts. It was horrible. And achieved nothing. This Kate stood up in her sister's wedding in her ruined clothes.

The 'capitulation' speech was bleak. It ended not just with Kate, hollow-eyed, hollow-voiced, offering to put her hand beneath her husband's foot but her husband taking up the offer, smirking, arrogant, a glitteringly fierce alpha-male, stomping boot down on hand as she performed full-length prostration. On 'Kiss me Kate' he shoved a fist into her raised face for her to kiss, she crawling forward on knees like some wretched pilgrim to a shrine. But then the tables turned again. One by one, the on-lookers to this charade came silently forward, eyeballed the increasingly bewildered triumphalist, turned on heels, exited. Wheeler's Kate was the last to go – but then returned, still in the dress but voice and body now 'he' again. He raked Petruchio with a look of deadly contempt, shrinking him back into his Sly reality with the withering comment: 'It's only a play.' Exited. Leaving Sly existentially wiped off the map, and the whole project of male supremacism exposed as male fantasy and male pathology. That it was men doing the 'outing' (no woman was harmed in the making of this production) was perhaps the chief spectatorly pleasure here, muted by the sombre knowledge that still in 2013 the 'outing' needs re-performance. 'Only a play'. But it's a play we need to remind us of the cultural work that remains to be done.

Propeller double-billed its extrovert *Shrew* with another revival, of *Shrew*'s delicate, introverted (at least to begin with) twin, *Twelfth Night*. Opening this production, 'When that I was and a little tiny boy' was back-story, synopsis, and front-of-cloth curtain-raiser all in one. Sung by Liam O'Brien's dead-pan, trilby-hatted, 1930s Limerick street-busker Feste like some down-and-out Bogart carrying a tiny guitar, it introduced a moth-balled world, the furniture (*Shrew*'s repurposed chest of drawers and mirror-fronted wardrobes) under dust-sheets, the grand chandelier fallen to the floor of some forgotten salon, its wires hanging limp, the back-cloth a grey storm-scape whose gloom had washed over the interior. The place felt haunted, if not by ghosts exactly, then memories, or perhaps premonitions, embodied by a gang of weird household hangers-on: the Propeller-signature 'chorus' for this production. I'll call them 'lurkers'. Inscrutable in half-masks, they crowded into scenes, then melted away only to turn up one by one elsewhere, as though enacting an idea of suspended animation that they then subverted by morphing into a raucous saxophone-and-tympani band.

Shakespeare's scene two came first here, introducing a fresh-faced Orsino (Christopher Heyward) who would have been boyish if insomnia hadn't ploughed furrows across his forehead. His mournful thoughts on love that 'receiveth like the sea' seemed magically to call up shipwreck: a boat in a bottle 'sailed' across the scene while behind, the chandelier slowly rose, swaying like a ship's lantern, as the dustsheets went live, turning into sails flapping in a storm. Two figures – Viola (Joseph Chance), Sebastian (Dan Wheeler) – launched themselves, legs kicking, hands flailing, into arms (the linked arms across double lines of the half-masked, making a ship's deck) that first held them up (like ships' spars) then pulled them under (like devouring waves). We watched the twins drown.

This sort of image-speaking physical theatre characterized the delicacy of this production: the Captain (Benjamin O'Mahony) used an over-turned chair like a piece of driftwood for a seat;

32. *Twelfth Night*, 1.1, Propeller, Hampstead Theatre, directed by Edward Hall. Christopher Heyward as Orsino, the company as 'lurkers'.

Viola-turned-Cesario, catching her reflection in a wardrobe mirror, briefly held her hand to the surface, seeing her dead brother; Orsino, self-absorbed with weeping, head in hands, at Feste's melancholic 'cypress' song, missed the embrace that Cesario, seated next to him, almost gave, but then, hearing the end of Cesario's family history, incredulously asking, 'But died thy sister . . . ?', strode over to where his servant had separated himself and wrapped him in a bear hug; Sebastian, waking alone in a strange bed, excavated a woman's high heel from under a pillow.

But if there was delicacy here (in particular, the fascinating tiny gestures Chance's Cesario made, slight moves of hands and feet, playing into, away from, attraction that discovered 'him' lapsing into 'her' then sharply 'recovering') there was also plenty of the kind of boisterous physical comedy that Propeller is known for, hilarious sequences that

captured the mourning play – where Ben Allen's gorgeous, grief-frozen Olivia really was Patience on a monument, sorrow her personal winding sheet – for life and laughter. Death was mocked when, chez Olivia, her household furniture mimicked her mental furniture – but then the lid of a coffin-shaped table was flung open and Feste leaped out. Shipwreck was mocked when Feste, Toby Belch (Vince Leigh) and Andrew Aguecheek (John Dougall, who'd later appear for the duel scene with Cesario kitted out in boxing gloves and head protector) played 'We Three' as *Three Men in a Boat*. Most deliciously, self-importance (Orsino's self-important love, Olivia's self-important grief) was thoroughly mocked in the gulling of Chris Myles's self-important Malvolio, a steward who clearly moonlighted as the officiously petty-minded chairman of Illyria's local town council. 2.5 was a full-company pre-interval production number worthy of the wildest theatrical aspirations of the mechanicals in *A Midsummer Night's Dream*. Feste, Aguecheek and Belch played themselves hiding behind topiary that grew legs and moved (without notice, leaving those exposed behind to scramble for cover). The half-mask 'lurkers' played garden furniture, similarly mobile, doubling cawing birds and buzzing insects. Olivia appeared as a statue of herself, with a *Wizard of Oz* Scarecrow's ability to change poses, in all of those poses seductively offering between curved fingers – a letter. And Malvolio strutted to his self-absorbed doom oblivious to the circus antics gambolling just behind him.

I have only one brick-bat to throw at this production – and it's aimed at the company's marketing department. The 'reveal' of Malvolio yellowed in crossed-garters is one of the great moments in the theatre. But it's got to be a surprise! Don't wreck it by putting production shots of the scene in the programme or plastering them up as front of house publicity.

Watching Propeller, I can always see that, no matter how much elaborating of play text they're doing by inventing performance text, their invention is informative and reciprocal. It fires off Shakespeare's writing. It's always 'doing' the writing. Watching a Maria Aberg Shakespeare production (*pace* her chopped-and-changed, not to say butchered *King John* at the RSC last year, *Shakespeare Survey 66*) I get the feeling that, as far as Shakespeare's writing is concerned, she'd rather be doing anything *else*. The dozen photographs in the programme showing rehearsals of her RSC *As You Like It* are surely a giveaway: shots of boisterous 'molly dancing', of camped-up bearded men in drag, of a smooth-faced 'boyed' girl in woolly hat staring coyly straight to camera. And not a script in sight.

Here, then, Aberg worked to past form. If last year she gave us '*King John: The Office Party*', this year it was '*As You Like It: Retro Rock Festival*'. She recast six of her *John* company (including Pippa Nixon, Rosalind/Bastard and Alex Waldmann, Orlando/John). And got in award-winning 23-year-old Laura Marling to write tunes and new lyrics, either remixes or replacements of Shakespeare's. (Her pedigree is out of Mumford & Sons; her brand, so-called 'nu folk', made, writes one music journalist, 'by dewy minstrels who look like they sew quilts, carve wood, bottle fruit, tame unicorns and make gloves out of butterfly wings – and that's just the boys'; her previous history with Shakespeare, evidently nil, though an interviewer who'd followed her to Los Angeles to talk about her next album saw 'a thumbed Wordsworth Classic of *As You Like It*' among her stuff.)

Aberg's Court (designed by another *John* recidivist, Naomi Dawson; her style, kitsch 'n clutter) was Duked by a totalitarian thug (John Stahl) who roughed up his niece and whose courtiers weirdly hung around in the background like automatons, silently voguing with weird hand gestures. (Well, they had to keep occupied *somehow* during the musical interludes.) Arden was 80s-style Glastonbury, the site, a squat set in mud, littered with junk: the trashed front seat of a car, a fender, a hammock, a battered refrigerator (so the lads could lounge around, pulling rings off beer cans over duologues). The 'forest' was bare upright planks (any branches, long since stripped for firewood). There was a sound stage (drum kit, double bass, piano, guitar) that rolled on and off (impervious to mud). And a gaggle of 'Forest Lords' that kept reappearing in yet another version of fancy dress – everything from 1950s Mother Hubbards to 1980s leggings to 1880s Sioux Indian head dress. (One of the things I found so dreary about this was that I'd seen it so many times before, in numbers of Bohemias in *Winter's Tale*s.)

Everybody appeared to be playing somebody else, which would have been a nice conceit, given the artifice that's built, generically, into the heart of pastoral – except that here, I got the feeling that the imitation wasn't artful. They didn't seem to have a clue that they were doing it. Thus, Cliff Burnett's Duke Senior looked like an ageing David Bowie, but for the first half hour I mistook Burnett for Greg Hicks, since Burnett was doing a spot-on impression of Hicks playing Claudius in *Hamlet* elsewhere in the RSC's current rep. Waldmann's Orlando sounded like Jonathan

Slinger's Prince (Waldmann also playing Horatio, clearly picking up Slinger's vocal tics, most maddeningly, the inability to speak an iambic pentameter line without pause . . . pause . . .). Oliver Ryan's craze-eyed Jaques, evidently veteran of too many rock concert acid trips, was Hamlet in antic mode – cradling something that looked suspiciously like a skull. Nixon's Ganymede (in Mummerset tweeds, braces and Barbour) appeared to be a stand-in for Marlin herself. When Joanna Horton's (long-suffering) Celia (who'd arrived in Arden in designer wellies, miner's head lamp, and backpack big enough to carry not just the entire contents of her royal wardrobe but the wardrobe itself) left 4.1 to 'sleep', Rosalind/Ganymede stepped centre stage. She began crooning something along four notes (sample lyric: 'Is there anything as cruel as love / That hides itself as Cupid's dove / In court or garden / pardon me/ I'm away / I'm away') to acoustic guitar while from four corners appeared four female 'torchbearers' (including poor Celia, not granted even forty winks), flames aloft, performing what I can only describe as a high school drill-team routine, step-marching to the centre, silently circling the still-droning Ganymede, then exiting. It felt like Am Dram – and deeply embarrassing.

The shame was that so much Shakespeare that makes the meaning of this play both as text and performance was axed to make way for such drivel. There was, for instance, no 2.1 ('Which is he that killed the deer?'), which triggers the all-male horn dance that operates proleptically on the marriage-coupled dance at the end, Aberg not seeing the point of it. And there was no 'lie seven times removed'. Nicolas Tennant's white-face-red-nosed Touchstone instead was, earlier on, given a Max Miller-esque turn, baiting the audience ('Is that your wife?') with tedious fake 'improv' that thereafter, tediously, had to be apologized for. 'Much virtue in "if"' may not be the key to all understanding in this play – but it certainly fits the lock. It's just daft to cut it. Worse, Aberg's additions made this the longest, slowest, and least laughter-filled *As You Like It* of all time: running 3½ hours, with, for example, the 75 lines from 'There is a man haunts

the forest . . . ' to 'Come sister will you go' taking six minutes to play. I timed it.

Then came the final fifteen minutes of the show. Aberg staged it as a rock concert rave with the full company leaping, cavorting, line dancing, vigorously snogging and, when the heavens opened, ignoring the downpour (it wouldn't be Glastonbury without a downpour), accompanied by heavy bass, big guitars, an up-beat sing-along tune, hand-clapping to a thumping rhythm and feel good lyric ('come along and marry me / underneath the greenwood tree'). A lot of the audience walked out of the theatre on a high, humming. I walked out slumped, in Prufrock mode, wondering what was going on here. Is the RSC using Aberg the way Aberg is using Shakespeare, to do other work? Specifically, to attach to the RSC by proxy something like the kind of total immersion theatre that has been Punchdrunk's line of work since 2000? If so, performed second-hand by Aberg (and without the definitive immersiveness of total immersion theatre), the aesthetic looked superficial, empty.

Maybe the best thing to come out of Aberg's *As You* was Nancy Meckler's *All's Well That Ends Well*. Following Aberg's production into the RSC rep, Meckler's derived one considerable benefit from it – that her actors had spent a lot of time on stage together. The experience showed.

Typical of Meckler, there was for openers a long performance sequence that gave a backstory to the events. There was little to locate place or time on a stage stripped minimalistically to black floorboards and, behind, a back wall inscribed with a semi-circle, bisected top to bottom, one half grey-panelled like a stable door, the other red-bricked, a window in-set at balcony level. (As things proceeded, I'd feel I was time travelling between 1938 and 2013, the women's costumes prewar, the soldier-recruits' calisthenics, kit drills and CGI battle sequences prep for manoeuvres in Afghanistan.) Instead, the design (by Katrina Lindsay) produced space and atmosphere, the atmosphere of, say, *The Pillowman* or a Paula Rego canvas. Strobe lights picked out a lad gyrating drunkenly bare-chested on a table top to a deafening beat in some dark disco dive while his over-spangled companion pawed the scantly-clad hostesses. A girl in pink – almost a human blush – came breathlessly in, tugged at the lad, who bent, opened the note she handed him, then rushed out. He was Bertram (Alex Waldmann); she, Helena (Joanna Horton), bringing word his dad had died. In a series of quick lighting exposures that worked like flash photography, we saw a sequence of poses showing the homecoming, the scapegrace at the door, still in party clothes, his mother's household in formal mourning; the penitent son flinging himself onto his mother's lap; the girl in pink, frozen, looking on, big eyes brimming. Then a further 'shot' isolated him at the door, standing below her framed above in the window.

Thus, the terms of this *All's Well* were established. We were in some never-never time. (The Countess's only home furnishing was a faux-greenhouse exposed when Lindsay's back wall opened up to show a row of glass exhibition cases full of ageless succulents and cacti.) Bertram was a lout but penetrable by remorse. Helena was all sighs and duty, but as transparent as the girl next door, without any self-loathing at her (marital) over-reaching. Framed in window and door, they were separated, but somehow belonged with each other.

Meckler, it has to be said, pulled most of the thorns out of this spikey comedy to give us something far less anguished and humiliated than Shakespeare's original. Setting off, break-neck, to the court Bertram nevertheless paused to give Helena a fond farewell and to wrap his tie, his token, around her neck. In the knock-out wooing game of 2.3, all the spruce bachelor-wards under the king's (Greg Hicks) gaze were keen to win and showed it. (Lafeu's interventions telling a different story – 'Do all they deny her? And they were sons of mine I'd have them whipp'd' – were cut.) And Bertram, grinning loopily, gave Helena a big thumbs up between every round. Even when he'd decided to dump his new wife and flee to a lad's life at war, he answered her pained farewell, 'Strangers and foes do sunder and not kiss', not with a stony rebuff ('I pray you stay not') but a long kiss that left Helena grinning as loopily as he had earlier.

This production recuperated Bertram. We saw him handed the letter from mom telling him of Helena's death just as he was headed to 'flesh . . . his will in the spoil of her honour' in bed with Diana. Reading it, he crumpled and fled to the solace of the woman he thought was Diana almost as therapy. (This was a scene played deliciously in the dark with the lights full up, the seducer's and bedtricker's hands reaching blindly, then finding each other, Bertram collapsing into what the audience could see were Helena's arms.)

But it also recuperated Helena. Horton's Helena spoke in riddles but didn't contain any: she put her secrets in the public domain. This meant that the kinds of undisclosed anxieties that, for example, tied Harriet Walter's Helena (RSC, 1981) in knots and made Michelle Terry's (National Theatre, 2009) quirkily duplicitous, were ironed out. Horton's Helena relied on the kindness of women: Charlotte Cornwell's Countess, Karen Archer's Widow, Natalie Klamar's Diana. Through them, Meckler shaped this *All's Well* into a positively pro-feminist production. The female conspirators clasped hands, bonding in solidarity, as, baiting the trap, Diana handed over Bertram's ring to the wife who'd earn it.

That didn't mean that Helena and Bertram weren't put through the wringer. The brutal letter informing her that Bertram would 'have nothing in France' until he had 'no wife' devastated Horton's Helena. It discovered to her in a cruel flash her love-blinded presumptuousness. The idea (and surely here she's heir to another of Shakespeare's Helenas, the one who wants Demetrius to use her as his spaniel) that she might win and own the object of her servile desire was a crazy mirage. Love doesn't work like that. Her penitential pilgrimage, then, routed her through a territory where she had to find out about herself. More critically, she had, unwitting, to learn some ugly home truths about her husband, truths that would knock the 'god' of her 'idolatry' off his pedestal but, ironically, would perhaps secure their futures as mere mortals in marriage.

Waldmann's journey as Bertram took much longer. He was a slow learner. The arrogant scion

33. *All's Well That Ends Well*, 4.3, RSC, Royal Shakespeare Theatre, directed by Nancy Meckler. Samuel Taylor as Soldier, Jonathan Slinger as Parolles, Daniel Easton as Soldier.

of privilege, he was mentally a delinquent kid in a hoodie (who made you think of Prince Harry in a hotel room in Las Vegas). One stupid joke said it all. Leaving home he grabbed his suitcases, groaned, couldn't shift them; flipped his chin towards the (female) servant standing in the background who (tight-lipped) easily picked up the luggage and followed behind the hysterically giggling boy. Even when the runaway was kitted up for war (across a strobe-effect sequence played against the military's version of disco music sound-tracking combat film footage thrown up on a screen behind) that had him progressively loaded up with gear, transformed by four attendant squaddies from courtier to Action Hero, Bertram was still more boy toy than man.

It took the exposure of Parolles to Bertram to begin the exposure of Bertram to himself. Here, Meckler's production tapped into gold with David Fielder's Lafeu, a foxy old career civil servant who'd seen through the brick walls of so many callow youths' testosterone-fuelled self-delusions that Parolles's 'window of lattice' hardly needed from him a second glance; and Jonathan Slinger's Parolles, the finest rendering of this role I've ever seen. With a Salvador Dali moustache, a braggart's leer (suggesting, in a Sandhurst accent, both military and sexual conquest), and a trunk stuffed with fantastic get-ups that could have dressed him for any war from Cavaliers and Round Heads to Napoleon (but not for the present one shown on the film footage, and for no other field than the parade ground), Slinger's Parolles was first cousin to Jack Falstaff, and just as dangerous a misleader of youth. Exposed as a liar, cad, slanderer and coward, abandoned, he sat in a limp, flabby heap, like a steamed pudding deflating, hands stranded in his lap like a pair of beached flat fish; pulled off his fake tash, and for the first time spoke in his own, distinctly down-market voice: 'Simply the thing I am / Shall make me live'. How fitting, then, that Bertram's final exposure as liar, cad, slanderer and coward would be partly conducted through the witness of Parolles.

In the final scene, that Bertram's despicable ducking and diving resolved to laughter was entirely due to Klamar's delightfully ditzy Diana, stringing everyone along with riddles that made them want to string her up. That it resolved finally to wonder was due to Horton's final breath-stopping entrance and the humility of winning her husband a second time, not with a statement this time ('This is the man') but, sotto voce, a question, 'Will you be mine?'

Invited to do it all again, Meckler's bachelors leaped forward eager to embark on another round of competition wooing at the end of this *All's Well*. At the end of *The Two Gentlemen of Verona* at the Tobacco Factory (director: Andrew Hilton; designer: Harriet de Winton), the suitors watched, open-mouthed, their women stride off into the sunset *without them*.

This is a company that (in my experience) works most comfortably in Edwardian dress, and here the cravats and waistcoats (brocade for the gents, cloth for their men), the tailored women's day skirts and jackets, the straw boaters, perky tilt-top bonnets and battered bowlers gave us a distinctly marked social world. Here, bright young things lounged over demitasse coffee cups at café tables set with linen cloths. Debates about life choices – love vs. honour – in this world seemed both like witty riffs on what they'd learned in public school (probably Eton) Latin lessons and perfectly normal 'laddish' chat. Here, a leave-taking between best friends would naturally be sworn upon a ceremonial sword (whose blade, turned to a mirror, caught on its bright, deadly surface, the faces of these loving lads who'd shortly be foes). Here too a prim deb like Julia (beautifully played by Dorothea Myer-Bennett, emotionally yo-yo-ing between hauteur and weak-kneed giddiness) would have to feign insult at receiving a love letter but having ripped it to shreds, would scramble in an undignified sprawl across the floor kissing each mutilated piece as she put the paper back together. The fact that Nicky Goldie's Lucetta, a hard-boiled biddy who could definitely tell a hawk from a handsaw, caught her at it was not just comic. It discovered the kinds of hypocritical cover-ups formally structuring this male-defined culture where the honour-struck guys played fast and loose with honour,

34. *The Two Gentlemen of Verona*, 2.5, Shakespeare at the Tobacco Factory, directed by Andrew Hilton. Chris Donnelly as Launce, Lollio as Crab, Marc Geoffrey as Speed.

their cover-ups hilariously parodied when Launce (Chris Donnelly on top form and in cheese-grated socks) honourably took the rap for his delinquent dog, Crab. (Lollio was brilliant; a real Don Quixote of a labrador who could sigh even as he slid horizontal, though a less likely committer of the indiscretion Crab is accused of – cocking a leg on a farthingale – you couldn't imagine.)

Watching the Tobacco Factory audience watching early (and under-performed) Shakespeare I was thrilled to be in a theatre where people were on the edges of their seats, not knowing what was going to happen next. There were audible reactions to Proteus (Piers Wehner), flat-toned, forswearing his love to Julia, coolly persuading himself into betraying Valentine in 2.6. Hilton's direction kept him on stage sitting staring silently into space throughout 2.7 as love-sick Julia, breathless, plotted to pursue him to Milan in disguise. And there

were howls of laughter at Valentine's (Jack Bannell) dim incomprehension of Silvia's (Lisa Kay) method (another cover-up) of declaring her mind by getting clerkly him to write a love letter delivered to himself. Marc Geoffrey's Speed, Jeeves to Valentine's Wooster, paced the 'discovery' of Silvia's ruse to stretch the joke to breaking point, leaving his master bug-eyed and gaping on the punch line: 'Why muse you sir?'

Equally delightful was to listen to a play – Shakespeare's *earliest*? – that feels like a first draft for the rest of a career. We watch him writing *for actors*: the sparring matches that Hilton's company clearly relished between Valentine and Proteus, Antonio (David Plimmer) and Pantino (Thomas Frere), Julia and Lucetta, Silvia and 'Sebastian'. These debates ('Home-keeping youth have ever homely wits'; 'he cannot be a perfect man / Not being tried and tutored in the world') look like rehearsals for Olivia/Cesario, Portia/Nerissa, Juliet/Nurse, Hamlet/Horatio. We watch the young playwright writing set pieces and 'turns': Launce re-performing his family farewells with his shoes playing dad and mom; Silvia's father, the Duke (Peter Clifford), backing his daughter's would-be eloper into a corner, giving him, line by line, enough rope to hang himself (here, literally, the rope ladder Valentine intended to use to spring Silvia from her chamber winding up knotted around his neck). We hear brilliantly silly one-liners: Launce telling his master 'there is a proclamation that you are vanished', corrected by Proteus to 'banished'. We hear soliloquies that predict the soul-searching of Helena (in *Dream* and *All's Well*) or Hamlet: 'Here is her picture. Let me see . . . ' And there are places where the poetry simply lifts off into the stratosphere (while remaining grounded in the theatrical ironies of performance) as when Proteus advises the nincompoop Lord Thurio (Paul Currier: torpidly toadish) to write love lines framed 'feeling[ly]': 'For Orpheus' lute was strung with poets' sinews / Whose golden touch could soften steel and stones / Make tigers tame, and huge leviathans / Forsake unsounded deeps to dance on sands.' Not bad for a beginner.

The introduction of some new lines in the closing minutes connected back to the swordplay of the opening scene and put Proteus's life, which looked like it might be ended with a thrust from Valentine's weapon, in Silvia's forgiving hands (prompted by still-disguised Julia, Mariana-like to *Measure*'s Isabella). Further interpolations had Valentine actually *asking* Silvia's consent to marry her; and Silvia, listening to the men pass her from hand to hand, quipping, 'Whose love am I?'; 'Twice this day I have been given'; 'Thrice given! I am the gift, yet would I be the giver.' No wonder, then, that when the men finally had all the deals done, the hands clapped up in bargains, and nudged and winked at one another ('What think you of this *page* my lord?'), Silvia and the 'boy' Julia traded looks, tossed heads, linked elbows and strode off arm in arm, the compleat couple, behind them, the men, spare parts to this happy ending.

HISTORIES

For poignancy, nothing could match a single performance of *Henry V* given this year at the RSC's Swan by a company of lads from King Edward VI School (former pupil: William Shakespeare). It commemorated a production put on in the school a hundred years earlier by boys, much like themselves. They would all, over the next four years, enlist to fight in a 'Great' War, recruited when it still seemed a great adventure to follow in historic, heroic footsteps, 'to join' (as a 1912 poem by Prime Minister Herbert Asquith's son had it) 'the men of Agincourt'. Seven of the cast of 1913 would die in the trenches of Northern France, along with twenty-four more classmates.

Perry Mills directed this history as an act of remembrance, where several pasts stood side by side, put into parallel predicament, framed within the venerable conceit of the end-of-year school play. Chorus (played by KES old boy, Tim Pigott-Smith) was vintage 1920-something, a beaky schoolmaster, in wire-rims and black academic gown seated upon his magister's throne (copied from the Elizabethan original back at KES) busily marking copybooks, groaning, slashing a pen across exercises; a single look freezing into slow motion the bumptious boys in caps and blazers who dashed through his schoolroom. (When these lads returned as soldiers, they'd be armed with cricket bats.) Hearing somewhere off a boy's soprano voice opening the hymn 'Come down, O love divine', the Master's head lifted, the disembodied ethereal sound capturing him for memory. He opened a pocket-book, took out a long-creased letter, read it over, then another. No doubt it was he who'd taught the class of '13 'arma virumque cano' and 'dulce et decorum est . . . ' Behind him, stage right, their portraits, from sepia photographs, some of them in *Henry V* costume, some in uniform, were displayed on a mobile publicity hoarding, the kind you see at conferences. A second hoarding, in parallel play with the first, stood stage left. Showing lads in today's army, today's combat gear, headed for today's killing fields beneath that very slogan 'pro patria mori'.

35. *Henry V*, 3.1, Edward's Boys, Swan Theatre, directed by Perry Mills. Jeremy Franklin as Henry V, with full company.

Here, then, classroom and playing field were held in tension, ludus literarius vs. games, with both of them informing how, why, with what words in their hearts and mouths young men went, go to war, and with what expectations: 'Play up, play up . . . !' Visually, Mills kept these ideas in perspective by constantly putting past and present on stage together. Jeremy Franklin's King Harry turned up to the prelates' speech (1.2) in twenty-first century business suit but set off to the French campaign in fifteenth-century heraldic surcoat. Half his soldiers were in tabards and chain mail, the other in today's camouflage fatigues or WW2 great coats. Katharine (George Hodson) wore a period gown; Alice (Barnaby Bos) was a version of Dame Edna in twin set and handbag. The Boar's Head low-lifers were skinheads in football shirts and cheap trainers (Pistol: Jack Fenwick; Nym: Elliot Tawney) or in 1970s 'professional woman' day-wear ('Hostess' Quickly, as the programme had her: Finlay Hatch) or in down-and-out Elizabethan doublet and slack hose (Bardolph: Calum Mitchell). All of them spoke Shakespeare's demotic like today's (equally rhythmic) 'yoof' street slang.

Details of staging produced significance that was by turns hilarious and heartbreaking. Canterbury (Henry Hodson), explicating 'In terram Salicam . . .' turned to a blackboard to illustrate, where, by the time he'd finished, he'd produced a diagram that looked like a plate of spaghetti. Charlie Waters's Boy, a titch in short trousers (but for all that, more of a man than Nym or Bardolph), set to guard the baggage, sat cross-legged on the ground opposite another lad, playing a kid's game of hand slap war as, off, Agincourt was fought and, in the foreground, the defeated French plotted their treacherous revenge to kill the children.

Mills cannily released into action his best resource in this production: the youth, the energy (constantly tipping into anarchy) of his 46-strong boy company, their ability to raise a shout, or a song, or perform mayhem, or muster, facing front at the foot of the Swan stage, a foot-stomping, foot-slogging army, growing exhausted, flagging, falling. But there was quite superb discipline here, too, holding story together with excellent verse and prose speaking. At the centre was Franklin's boy-king Harry. To begin with, tossing tennis balls, he was as shiningly morning-faced as Shakespeare's satchelled-up schoolboy. By the time the 'little touch of Harry in the night' was making its rounds, the shine had darkened. He'd experienced betrayal; the adrenaline rush of storming Harfleur's breaches, then the ugly business of threatening the city into submission ('What is't to me . . . If . . . you . . . see . . . Your naked infants spitted on pikes?'); he'd known retreat, an army sickening, his back against the wall. On the eve of Agincourt, hooded, walking among his men, he'd been stung by their assessment of their suicide mission. He'd been reasonable – or maybe hair-splitting ('Every subject's duty is the king's, but every subject's soul his own'). Then, left alone, furious ('Upon the king!') and finally anguished, wrapping his black cloak around him, sobbing, collapsing across the Master's desk (Chorus/Master drawing back, disconcerted, observing) before falling to a kneeling position to invoke 'O God of battles . . .', which ended with him on his back, rocking, plea-bargaining with God, 'More will I do . . . !' The awfulness of this dark night of the young king's near-broken spirit ended when he heard as if from another world a schoolboy soprano, and lines of a future hymn, 'He who would valiant be . . . / Follow the Master', which this Henry, choking back tears, finally managed to join – 'to be a pilgrim' – before exiting to the final battle.

Ultimately, this production didn't let 'the Master' (the one in school *or* in eternity) off the hook. As Pigott-Smith's Chorus spoke Shakespeare's Epilogue, a coffin was brought on. Harry's. The 'star of England' was made the father of loss. A final hymn had all the boys, returned to 'the present', laying yellow flowers on the coffin, mimicking the ritual they go through every year in Stratford-upon-Avon, remembering, in Holy Trinity church, a poet, whose grave they lay with daffodils. The last boy of all was felt by the schoolmaster, who'd returned to his marking, as a revenant. He looked up. Saw Harry. Paused. They exchanged a long

look. Perhaps accusing. Then, as the Master wiped tears from his eyes, Harry walked into the dark. By the time the Master's glasses were back on his nose, the vision had vanished. He unscrewed his fountain pen. Picked up the next exercise book.

As the lights went down on the old man hunched over his resumed task, I've rarely heard a theatre so silent.

Starting out on this project, Perry Mills probably couldn't believe his luck when the school archivist, digging among theatre records, turned up for him the original *Henry V* score from 1913 – composed by Ralph Vaughan Williams. At the Tobacco Factory, Andrew Hilton quite possibly felt something similar about another excavation. Just weeks before his production of *Richard III* opened, DNA testing proved the identity of the skeleton that archaeologists digging under a car park in Leicester had turned up in a shallow, 500-year-old grave. Its skull had been battered with eight blows, one of them slicing bone-to-bone. Its spinal vertebrae lay in the ground in an S-curve. The man, alive, had been twisted. Here, science confirmed, was what remained of the original 'crookback' 'Dickie', Shakespeare's demon king. Hitting the headlines, the news went viral on websites. As pre-publicity for a Shakespeare opening, not even Saatchi & Saatchi could have dreamed up such a sensational campaign!

But then, if you were looking for a Richard in the theatre to put flesh on these bones, it might not have been John Mackay's. Mackay underplayed the sensational. His pinched, stretched, emaciated Richard was a maggot, not a monster: skin leper white; eyes sunken, ringed in black and hollow; head so closely shaven that it looked like a skull. He had no hump, no calipered boot: he dragged one twisted foot, broken-gaited, and held next to his ribs the hand twisted backwards on its wrist, broken-winged. He was 'othered' most significantly by his Tudor-esque suit of sober black (designer: Harriet de Winton), while everyone else went dressed flashy as peacocks, seemingly costumed out of dressing-up boxes (even Dorothea Myer-Bennett's mourning Anne who followed her father-in-law's cortège not like Edward's widow but with hair down like an early modern virgin-bride, bosom heaving over her corset).

Underplaying the body, this Richard underplayed speech. He rather wormed his way through the writing, inching his way along, every once in a while pausing, as caterpillars do, as if to lift his head and wave sensor-bristles. His opening declaration of intent gestured feebly at 'arms hung up for monuments' (practically the only decoration on de Winton's set), and the pauses between 'nimbly', 'capers' and 'lascivious' slowed the delivery to a snail's pace. There was something utterly fascinating about this drawn-out performance: the raised eyebrows on 'lover', the guillotine that came down on 'lute', the caressing, obscene fondling of 'hate'.

Equally fascinating performances supported the central part: Peter Clifford's Friar (in tabard and skull cap; face like a *memento mori*) attending King Henry's body, registering horror at Anne's blasphemous cursing; Chris Donnelly's Second Murderer not getting Richard's assassination joke, glancing anxiously sideways at his partner, forcing a terrified half-smile; Paul Currier's sleek, coy Buckingham, Richard's 'pretty' 'other self', a man so politic his eyeballs could hold their breaths and the first instantly to rise on Richard's 'follow me', glancing a look at Stanley that slid across him, frozen at the council table, like a dirty joke; Christopher Bianchi's Tyrell, his straight reportage of the princes' murders utterly chilling; James Wearmouth's boy Prince Edward, the only actor in this period production to adopt period behaviours: sitting in empty space, knowing that a camp chair would instantly be unfolded underneath him to take his weight; gesturing, his hand poised as in medieval portraiture.

And there were shocking moments that stopped the play in its tracks: as when the dead king's corpse (played by Andrew Macbean), laid out on a primitive wooden bier, little more than a barrow, was exposed, near-naked, wounds bleeding on legs and chest: horrible solemnity that was wrecked when Anne started swatting Richard with the stripped-off winding sheet. This wasn't the only miscalculation. The cartoonish, halloween feinting at the audience with Hastings' head which, set down in its burlap bag, left behind a pool of blood, was just silly. And Jane Shore appearing in an IKEA bedsheet was even sillier.

If there was practically no laughter in this production, no black comedy wittily revolving in our minds before piercing our vital organs like a stiletto under the ribs, still, Hilton's company gave us a straight run at the story. Cutting Margaret, though, Lancaster's remaindered Queen, was a mistake. Without Margaret, the deep focus of memory and prophecy, history from God's point of view, is gone, and, with history, the sense that these jigging and strutting figures are all grotesques headed for the fire in a Bosch Last Judgement.

In Bristol, in the 15-foot by 18-foot Tobacco Factory space, spectators got history in close-up; in Stratford, on the two-seasons-old RST thrust stage, in wide-angle long shot. Still, Greg Doran's period-designed *Richard II* shared something with Hilton's *Richard III*, a complete absence of clutter. Indeed, Doran (nearly) emptied the stage (making, it seems, in this, only his second production in the newly redesigned theatre, a Puck-ish point of ignoring the new stage's new-fangled high-tech gadgetry, which, like some fatal Cleopatra, had so fascinated his predecessor Artistic Director, and giving me the uncanny sense of being in a Terry Hands production). Doran cleared the space for actors (cast from the top of the Equity A-list), and let them get on with that extraordinary alchemical demonstration that happens when voice, body and actorly brain sublimate the materials of Shakespeare's writing into gold. The 'set' was virtual, made of light. A CGI projection of the epic-sized outline interior of Westminster Abbey was thrown onto the far upstage backwall. It looked almost like an architect's blueprint or, in period terms, an Inigo Jones drawing, and it was projected through what hung from the flies, hundreds of chains (the kind, I discovered later, that you have in your bathtub, humbly connecting the plug to the tap: so much for high-tech wizardry!). They diffused the light into a gun-metal grey gloom, as if the sharp outlines of arch and pillar were seen through incense haze.

36. *Richard II*, 4.1, RSC, Royal Shakespeare Theatre, directed by Gregory Doran. Nigel Lindsay as Bolingbroke,
David Tennant as Richard II.

Downstage was set a coffin, almost floating in light, to which, as a three-voiced choir (dressed like the blue-robed angels in the Wilton diptych) sang medieval 'requiem', was ushered a bent, white-haired figure in deep mourning who sat silently attending the dead, half embracing the coffin, half sprawled across it. Doran's opening scene, then, played out the 'backstory' state funeral (also a family and a cross-generational affair, the grizzled and grey vs. the spruce and brown) of Thomas Woodstock, Duke of Gloucester. The dead man's brothers and nephews assembled, lining up with prelates, courtiers, barons, hangers-on – and with the man who would be accused of his murder. 'Old John of Gaunt' addressed this line-up. Bolingbroke and

Mowbray stepped out from it to threaten each other. When it dispersed, the prostrate figure – Gloucester's widow (Jane Lapotaire) – lifted her head from the coffin to address the single mourner left behind, her action dissolving one scene into the next, into Gaunt's attempt at consolation, his resignation (futile? hopeful?) silencing her (unvoiced) 'exclaims': 'Put we our quarrel to the will of heaven / . . . God's is the quarrel'.

In production terms, Stephen Brimson Lewis's austerely elegant design, enhanced by Tim Mitchell's lighting – so reticent, so understated – played mute backdrop to the vivid characters who played across it, who stood out from it. Michael Pennington (one of his generation's finest

Hamlets; now old enough to be a kingdom's memory bank) was ferocious, a growling Gaunt, clutching at life only for breath enough warningly to 'foretell' the 'rash, fierce blaze of riot' (as he termed his nephew Richard's reign) that it 'cannot last'. His son, Henry Bolingbroke (Nigel Lindsay), wore his heavy leather surcoat as lightly as a second skin: bullet-headed, bull shouldered, built like a butcher's block. He made both accusation ('Sluiced out his innocent soul through streams of blood') and persuasion ('If that my cousin king be King of England / It must be granted I am Duke of Lancaster'; 'I come for Lancaster') as irresistible as a battering ram. Later, like some siege engine who'd done its work and been trundled into the background, he grew remote, inscrutable, taciturn. His uncle, York (Oliver Ford Davies), the serio-comic family fuss-pot and quiet lifer, was as clearly exasperated by the dangerous youth ('How long shall I be patient?'; 'Tut, tut, grace me no grace nor uncle me no uncle') as he was cautious with his impatient dying kin ('Vex not yourself . . . / For all in vain comes counsel to his ear'). But even he was stung into action from observation, carrying on where brother Gaunt left off, showing how the political analysis of this play moves in speech-making from lament (grief-struck reflection on the past) to complaint (functioning as critique), until speech defers to force, the writing on the wall: 'Set on towards London, cousin: is it so?' York's son Aumerle (smoulderingly beautiful: Oliver Rix) embodied the family loyalty crisis, needing to prove allegiance to one cousin ('We did observe . . . ') by distancing himself from another ('he had none of me'); throwing in his lot and going the distance with one who was increasingly self-defeatist ('Comfort my liege: remember who you are'); carrying his torch, post-deposition (or post-abdication) to the point of homicidal conspiracy; but – hen-pecked into it by his mother? – wanting to live when his treason was discovered. Needing to throw himself on the mercy of his other cousin, newly-kinged, he needed even more to prove new allegiance to this newly kinged-kin who looked him – his 'dangerous cousin' – straight in the eye when he dismissed him to grace ('Your mother well

hath prayed'). The new King's advice sounded like instruction: 'prove you true'. What proof? How could he prove himself? It was Aumerle (not Shakespeare's Exton), discovered when his hood was pulled back by Richard's dying hand, who fetched up at Pomfret, who put the assassin's knife into the back of the man whose lips he'd once kissed. Proof, indeed.

The sun at the centre of this erratically rotating and colliding human solar system was, of course, Richard, played by David Tennant first in gorgeous robes of brocaded blues and golds, as though he'd stepped out of an illuminated manuscript (or out of one of those pop videos where the lead singer, Jagger, say, or Bowie, is strutting, retrofashioned, in medieval 'glam'). He was fascinatingly epicoene: the jawline of a hard-man Clint Eastwood cowboy; the wavy hair down his back, as of the young Queen Elizabeth in her 1558 coronation portrait; fingernails painted gold; his sceptre lying in his arms with the languid ease of a third limb. But he was no 'girly' king. He could move from 'skipping' eye-rolling flippancy ('Why uncle, what's the matter?') to the awesome rage of an absolutist, defied. (Thus, when Gaunt rebuked him, he grabbed the dying man by the scruff of his neck and shook him like a rat: 'lunatic, lean-witted fool!'). In all the court appearances his wife (Queen Anne: Emma Hamilton) was by his side, and Bushy, Bagot and Greene (Sam Marks, Jake Mann, Marcus Griffiths) were not pretty 'play' boys but clued-up spin doctors, feeding lines into Richard's ear like the medieval equivalent of the radio earpiece. Even the kiss Richard gave Aumerle, the two of them, holed up in Flint Castle, swinging their legs over the parapet, waiting for the inevitable, the king as he spoke blowing out his cheeks in mock despair, feintingly trying his crown on his cousin's head, felt less like an 'outing' of suppressed homoeroticism than a cry for comfort, or a little whimper, from a man desolated of friendship.

Tennant got Richard's arch, self-involved and constantly stimulated (by those 'advisors') petulance. And he got Richard's self-pity: the way, returning from the Irish campaign, the posturing diva collapsed into big-eyed, frightened child, hugging his knees, lashing out ('Three Judases!') then collapsing into maudlin 'poor me'-ism: 'let us . . . tell sad stories of the death of kings'; 'you have mistook me all this while.' He even caught something of Richard's political *nous*, the way he understands the writing on the wall long before Bolingbroke does; the way he required Harry to *demonstrate* what he's not saying. So in 4.1, the deposition/abdication scene, now stripped to his soiled white smock, his hair lank, a Christ-figure among his torturers as imagined by Cranach, he was his old flippant self ordering 'Give me the crown' to hand it to Bolingbroke: 'Here cousin'. But his next word froze Bolingbroke's hand in mid air: '*seize* the crown'. And when Bolingbroke went ahead, completed the action, Richard didn't let go. The crown jerked unceremoniously between them, Bolingbroke trapped into making naked his ambition.

But there is another move Richard needs to make, and that's the one into interiority that paradoxically opens him up to exteriority, to shared humanity. This journey he conducts, alone, in prison, where he studies his condition, where he 'hammer[s] it out', where he 'sets the word against the word', to discover, finally, not just self-knowledge ('I wasted time . . .'; 'Nor I, nor any man that but man is . . .') but grace and human kind-ness: 'blessing on his heart . . . 'tis a sign of love'. If Tennant, discovered as the stage trap opened to find him filthy in a dungeon, didn't finally make this move from outside to inside, but reverted to the whining adolescent of Act 3, still, his Richard was never less than watchable.

And this production, Greg Doran's curtain raiser to the RSC's next season, the first he'll have programmed since taking over as Artist Director, boded well. As it went into the rep, Doran announced the two parts of *Henry IV* for 2014, with Antony Sher as Falstaff, and the complete works to be produced across the next six years. One thing he's going to have to address urgently, though (*pace* the bear in *The Winter's Tale* and most of what happened in Arden in *As You Like It*), is sightlines in the 'transformed' theatre. If you were sitting in the stalls for Doran's *Richard*, you only saw Richard's

head when he was in prison (and knew nothing of what he was doing wrestling with his murderers). If you were sitting under the gallery, you saw only his feet when he was above ('we are amazed') at Flint Castle. If you were sitting along the sides of the thrust, you couldn't see the back projection of Westminster Abbey at all. The problem is that the 'transformed' theatre, for all Michael Boyd's claims about a 'one-room theatre', about intimacy and spectatorly proximity to the stage, is still built around a proscenium arch. The thrust thrusts out from it, and designers are using the 'behind' space to create pictures in a depth of field which spectators are now positioned *not* to see. Doran: please do something.

This was a bumper year for the Roman plays, all four staged in productions so widely various in terms of casting, directing, design and style as to demonstrate the almost 'infinite variety' of these texts (as Enobarbus might have put it) or their 'tolerance' to performance (as John Styan has written). *Coriolanus* at the Donmar, however, opened so late in the review year that I'm having to hold it over to *Survey 68*.

For anyone (like me) who knew Julie Taymor's *Titus* (1999), Michael Fentiman's *Titus Andronicus* for the RSC in the Swan felt like an homage – or straight steal. But then, Taymor's film was a re-imagining of her own stage version (for Theatre for a New Audience, 1994) which borrowed (or lightly pilfered) from both Deborah Warner's previous Swan *Titus* (1987) and Jane Howells's filmed BBC *Titus Andronicus* (1985). Like Taymor's, this *Titus* offered period mash-up, putting spectators in the Italy of Justinian, Mussolini and Berlusconi simultaneously to show militarism, violence, savage appetites and political stupidity as nothing new; like Howells's (and Taymor's), it build extra-texual performance narratives around children; like Warner's, it imagined moments of exquisite black comedy. By the end, though, it went its own way into a place of such extravagant, sweepstake violence as to kill off even the modicum of hope that earlier productions had salvaged from the wreckage.

The opening was located in what felt like the tiled basement morgue of a 1930s *ospedale* (the eagle insignia on the wall was a fascist recycling of the Roman original) where three corpses laid out on gurneys were 'entertained' by a vintage radio weirdly broadcasting muffled speeches (intimations of electioneering or rabble rousing) over tinny music as the bodies were washed, and washed, and washed by nuns in wimples and heavy habits, one of whom sat beside them to smoke a companionable cigarette before being hustled away by the arrival of the chief mourner. Still in battered 5th century AD legionnaire's breastplate and stained with battle (or maybe what I was looking at wasn't filthy skin but, on this wiry, desiccated body, skin dried to leather), Titus (Stephen Boxer) flicked off the radio and took a weary seat among his sons while on the loggia above him, Saturninus in blackshirt (John Hopkins) and Bassianus in smoke-grey Armani (Richard Goulding) launched into their campaigning. This was the last moment of repose. From now on, everything happened pell-mell, break-neck, the designer (Colin Richmond) using the theatre's balcony, trap and proscenium screen continuously to shift the vertical axis, to sink a pit or to raise a bathtub, or, opening the 'wall', to discover behind, as with the first show of defeated Goths, a vista, that one of a full-on Roman triumph. This pace didn't let up even when Tamora (Katy Stephens) issued the challenge that should have stopped Titus in his tracks: 'Wilt thou draw near the nature of the gods? / Draw near them then in being merciful.'

The trouble was not only that drawing 'near the nature of the gods' wasn't on anybody's agenda in Fentiman's Rome but that the idea didn't even give pause to anybody's thinking (*which* gods? *which* nature?). Instead, as things proceeded, Fentiman gave us a series of grotesque, snuff-film cartoons. Tamora made compelling listening in defeat, the simple picture of a mother, war-soiled, a captive leather-harnessed protesting the sacrifice (or slaughter) of her son: 'O cruel, irreligious piety!' Transformed in Rome to Empress she looked like

some parody Goth fantasy, and acted it with hyper-melodramatic eye-rollings, leg-barings and cackles, like Cruella De Vil meeting Myra Hindley dressed by Siouxsie and the Banshees. Her sons (Chiron: Jonny Weldon; Demetrius: Perry Millward, looking, from their painfully pre-adolescent mug shots in the programme, like they'd have needed permission to be let off school to work for the RSC) were feral skin-head brats in hoodies who biked to the rape scene on BMXs, a design look that exploited current anxieties about 'yoof' in modern Britain. (This was the year a rapist, described by his victims as a twelve-year-old, terrorized a Manchester university campus.) The rape itself drew on Taymor. Lavinia (Rose Reynolds) was a girl in white whose mutilation was also humiliation, her blond hair hacked off in jagged hanks and wound around her bleeding stumps, a bizarre and violent joining of grace and horror. Later, *pace* Taymor, she'd serve, like an abattoir attendant, the throat-cutting of the rapists, strung upside down by their ankles, no longer jackals but a pair of wimpering goats who'd shortly be turned into boy pie.

Comedy here was grim. Kevin Harvey's slum-side Liverpool Aaron raised laughs taunting the white boys with their whiteness (not least when they went even whiter, seeing him stab the Nurse, then for good measure spit her up the crotch (Badria Timimi)). Dwane Walcott's Clown, blind, his face disfigured with scar tissue as though he'd had acid thrown at him, cheerfully walked straight into the execution he couldn't see coming, a lynching performed on stage. Lavinia, alone at the breakfast table with her now-bound stumps, tried to eat a boiled egg. Tamora, flanked by a table-full of fascinated guests and faced by a Titus got up in drag in starched white cap and apron like a chambermaid at the Dorchester, laughed incredulously, fork half-way to her mouth, on 'Why there they are, both baked in this pie.' She forced herself to take the next bite before spewing her guts across the linen cloth.

Titus's manic glee – ''Tis true, 'tis true, witness my knife's sharp point' – did momentarily stop his show, but only for as long as it took everyone to draw breath and weapon. What ensued was

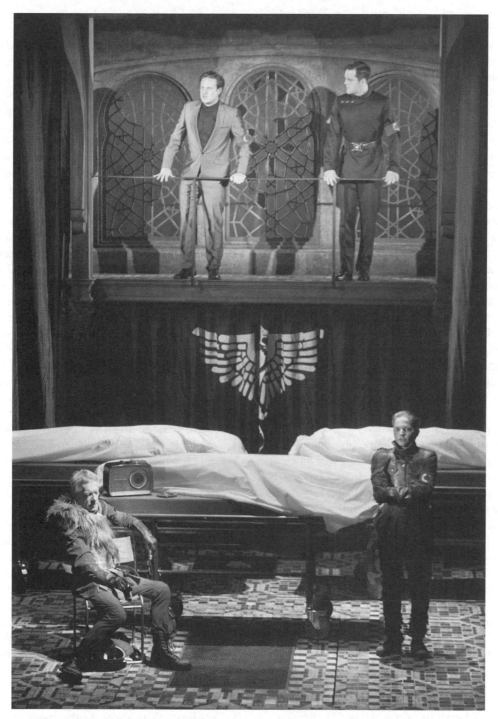

37. *Titus Andronicus*, 1.1, RSC, Royal Shakespeare Theatre, directed by Michael Fentiman. (Below) Stephen Boxer as Titus, Joe Bannister as Quintus, (above) Richard Goulding as Bassianus, John Hopkins as Saturninus.

frenzy, Roman vs. Goth, man vs. woman, ruler vs. ruled, killing (think, historically, of the scene of the Manson murders the morning after, reproduced by Polanski in his *Macbeth*) that left no one unwounded and hardly anyone alive. Lost in the mêlée was any sense of a future, any chance that the people of Rome 'By uproars severed', like 'a flight of fowl / Scattered by winds and high tempestuous gusts' or like 'scattered corn', would ever be 'knit again' into 'one mutual sheaf', their 'broken limbs again into one body'. Fentiman gave Aaron the last word – '[W]hy should wrath be mute and fury dumb?' he roared, his head revealed bizarrely sticking up out of the floor when Lucius (Matthew Needham) shoved the dinner table aside. *Pace* both Taymor and Howells, Fentiman gave little Lucius the last move. The cherubic grandson (Hal Hewetson/George David) of the dead warrior, still in school uniform, crossed the stage, carrying Aaron's baby, not dead (not, that is, executed as in Howells, by little Lucius's dad, Lucius); very much alive, as in Taymor. But not, as in Taymor, walking out of the household-slaughterhouse into a new dawn. This child Lucius paused mid-exit. He reached down among the scattered household debris. He found a piece of pointed cutlery. He raised it to the infant in his arms. Blackout.

Fentiman explored violence, institutions and play to one end; Phyllida Lloyd, to a very different end. Her all-female *Julius Caesar* at the Donmar was set in a women's prison, though it took us to the end of the play to see the twist that showed us precisely how the conceit on metatheatricality-as-therapy (or cynical institutional control) was working, which I missed, being absorbed looking elsewhere, so had to be brought up to speed on the train going home.

The cross-gender casting worked here as in a Propeller production: the women didn't impersonate men (as Propeller don't impersonate women). Lloyd's women were always women, hanging on to senses of selves by, ironically, substituting role-play for identity in a world that had stripped them of humanity *and* femininity. (And, as in Propeller, there was a particular energy released by the same-sex casting, here, a single-minded ferocity directed across the kind of mental cruelties women can excel in.)

Bunny Christie's design put actors and audience in the same space. We were visitors, they inmates in a bleak prison rec room: vomit-green walls stained with decades of cigarette smoke; plastic chairs; harsh strip lighting; stairs leading up to a metal mesh-floored gantry along the back wall; CCTV monitors showing grainy images of ghostly to-ings and fro-ings down corridors under surveillance somewhere 'off'; a sagging sofa; a hospital-style meal trolley; litter; a glass wall behind which sat the operators who pushed the levers in this institution (actually, stage management in prison uniform); beefy uniformed wardens clanking with keys, butch versions of household chatelaines.

Noises off, a flurry of movement across the monitors, a bolt shot back, a steel door slid open: a line of women, all sizes, ages, shapes, one pregnant, marched on, in singlets, tracksuits, stood to attention or slouched; waited; the door opened again; a single swaggeringly bloated 'old lag' figure appeared (long-in-the-tooth enough to be a lifer; just released from solitary?). There were roars of greeting as the door clanged shut and the muster broke up into carnival dancing paced to thumping rock music as this last 'inmate' handed out white plastic masks of herself, now recognized as prison supremo, 'Caesar' (Frances Barber). This opening captured the 'holiday humour' of Shakespeare's first scene, but replayed it with a difference that mapped Republican politics onto prison regime, suggesting (in the external narrative) totalitarianism's breathtaking efficiency while demonstrating (in the internal narrative) the corrupted system of pecking-order favours bought and sold in exchanges where the currency was the body: within seconds, everyone was dancing to Caesar's tune, morphed into mini-Caesars, faces set to Caesar's expression. Caesar signalled her 'bitch' Antony (Cush Jumbo: dangerously two-faced, and both of them beautiful) upstairs where in full view of the jeering spectators below she fondled and kissed her (Antony making 'fuck off' signs behind her back to mockers), then, silencing the music, read out over a microphone from something that looked like 'Hello!' magazine a horoscope, 'Beware the ides of March', burst into laughter, and led her 'crowd' of brown-nosers off.

Behind remained a pair of refuseniks, Brutus (Harriet Walter) and Cassius (Jenny Jules), the one white, middle-class, painfully underweight for her frame, her gaunt face permanently trapped in an anguished grimace that aged her, clearly banged up for some sort of white collar crime, the other ballsy, black, wiry, lips pulled back in the kind of grin that bares teeth, no doubt done for GBH. The tense debate that followed ('Tell me good Brutus, can you see your face?'; 'Into what dangers would you lead me, Cassius?') suggested to me that we were 'in' Shakespeare's *Caesar*, the play operating as a metaphor to explore parallel worlds of abusive power – and to offer scenarios where that power could be renegotiated. So the old lag 'Caesar' was a sadistic brute who got away with her sexual predations because, in the anti-culture of Rome-as-prison, she was the undisputed 'colossus'. An example: when she returned, interrupting Brutus and Cassius, she flourished to the crowding-in inmates a gift, a box (from beyond the prison walls) of Krispy Kreme doughnuts. Cassius sat stony. The others pounced on the goodies. Caesar eye-balled Cassius while speaking to Antony, 'Let me have men about me that are fat.' She picked up a doughnut, took a bite, then, leaning into Cassius's face, ground her lips onto Cassius's mouth before forcing the doughnut down her 'lean and hungry' throat, hissing while the other choked, 'Such men are dan-geroussssss'. In the assassination, Cassius got her own back. Caesar was forced onto a chair – her bulk telling against her – and held down by the gang who'd turned against her. Her mouth was prised open. Casca (Ishia Bennison, who'd earlier conducted conspiracy, poker faced, across a game of poker) force fed her a bottle of bleach. So: the prison 'Caesar' was dead, scores settled in poetically just, if brutal, ways.

At other times, however, I understood this performance very differently, as meta-theatre, 'play' used in this prison as *Antigone* is on John and Winston's *Island* or Marat's death is in de Sade's Charenton. In 3.3, Cinna the Poet's speech, 'I dreamt tonight . . .' suddenly broke off, interrupted by one of the Wardens entering. 'Cinna' (Carolina Valdés) was cuffed and taken away. For the first time, we spectators knew 'for real' that we were in a rehearsal, the inmates 'merely players'. With one actor down, a moment of consternation among the inmates was settled when one of them was handed a book and made to go 'on' as Second Cinna (Helen Cripps). Only, things got too 'real' when 'Tear him to pieces' launched a full-scale assault that unleashed pent-up rage that had Cinna shrieking 'fuck off you bastards!' as she fought for her life before guards descended with whistles and batons to restore order.

Only in this production's final moments did we see the final twist that located the 'meta' in respect of this theatre. Dead Caesar, post mortem, had continued to monitor the action (seated at a drum kit punching out sounds of gunshots when the trade-off executions of 4.1 – 'Prick him down' – were staged). The night before Philippi played out a bizarre fantasy sequence: Portia's ghost (Clare Dunne), round-wombed, in wedding dress, entered to Brutus who waltzed with her before finding her body-swapped, the dance cut in by Caesar's mocking ghost. Elsewhere the Soothsayer (Carrie Rock), a tiny, tubby figure, naked, wandered across the battle-field, carrying a doll like some kind of fetish, during a war staged by musicians playing rock (think: Pussy Riot) that descended into noise. Antony's and Octavius's (Clare Dunne) take-over speeches ('This was the noblest Roman of them all'; 'According to his virtue let us use him') were empty rhetoric, spin, broadcast over the CCTV and, when Casca stepped forward as if to demand 'what ceremony else?', she got a single pistol shot to the head. Spectators were still recoiling from that when the metal door opened. A warden entered. Bellowed, 'Lock-up!' (What? *Lock-up?*) The dead arose. Joined the living. Filed past the prison governor, standing in uniform at the door. *It was Caesar.* So: the penny dropped. Everything we'd seen was radically reframed, play discovered as displacement activity and perverse therapy, a regime keeping control and getting its kicks not just by permitting but playing with (and in) the playing out of inmates' fantasy, the ritual killing of hated authority.

My problem was that I didn't see the final trick of Barber-as-Caesar-turned-Governor because my eyes were riveted on Walter's Brutus. Back in the line-up, eyes facing out, her blank face registered the tragedy of this *Caesar*. The game was up. The show was over. She was back in custody. This was magnificent acting. Whether sparring with Cassius, or tying and retying the philosophical knots in her own conscience ('It must be by his death'), or drawing on red kitchen marigolds (bloody hands 'bathe[d] in Caesar's blood'), or staving off the funeral crowd that wanted to goad her ('stay here with Antony'), or struggling across the battlefield looking for a place, and the will, to fire the pistol she twice put to her temple, Walter was the actorly centre of this production, its motor and finest creation. It struck me, too, that beyond her own professional achievement, this performance gave her the opportunity personally to live up to her committed feminist politics: not just heading a company that gave women their heads but, by employing in that company actors from the women's prison theatre collective, Clean Break, giving these fellow actors dignity and a leg up into their professional futures.

In *Caesar*, in a Roman world where 'gamesome' Antony seems to have no political thoughts in his head, Brutus plots, kills and dies (as Pompey later remembers) for a deeply considered political idea: that he would 'Have one man but a man'. How satisfying to imagine Brutus getting his revenge beyond the grave on the 'play'-boy, watching Antony in the sequent history stumble unwittingly upon a political idea (of sorts) of his own worth dying for. 'Here is my space'. It is a measure of the tonal and temperamental differences between the two Roman tragedies that while we watch Brutus coming into political consciousness in a tortured, syntactically switch-tracking soliloquy ('It must be...How...And...And...But...But...So...kill him'), we hear Antony's political eye-opening told second-hand, serio-comically as erotically aroused voyeuristic barracks room gossip among NCOs: 'The barge she sat in, like a burnished throne / Burned on the water.../ Upon her landing Antony sent to her /...She replied/...Our courteous Antony, / Whom ne'er the word of "No" woman heard speak, / Being barbered ten times o'er, goes to the feast, / And for his ordinary pays his heart / For what his eyes eat only.'

It was with this memory – and this Antony told by Enobarbus – that Tarell McCraney's *Antony and Cleopatra* opened in the Swan theatre. Radically edited, even reconstructed, this version was cut for ten actors brought together in an English/American co-production involving the RSC, the Public Theatre New York and the Gable Stage, Miami. It made use of signature elements that McCraney has developed in his own playwriting, in for example, *The Brothers Size*: Yoruba iconography, African and Creole music and song, fluid physical choreography that presents bodies in space formally, even ritualistically (as during Enobarbus's opening speech, bringing Egypt alive in Rome's imagination), characters acting as Chorus, 'spoken' stage directions that serve as scene captions: 'First Scene'; 'In Rome'; 'An Interlude'.

Tom Piper's stark yet gorgeous set juxtaposed two worlds, two cultures. In the middle distance, three arches held up by bone-white romanesque columns troped the triumvirate's 'wide...ranged empire'. Seen through them, upstage and stretching across the width of the stage in front of a plain back wall that, variously lit, turned from cobalt blue to desert gold, a shallow pool gave us Cleopatra's element. Spectators first saw her (as Enobarbus narrated, 'For her own person / It beggared all description') wading across it, shaped in darkness, silhouetted naked like a hieroglyph before reclining, legs sprawled, to bathe, then to emerge like Aphrodite from the Nile. The costumes set this production in Napoleonic Haiti in the period of French colonization and black slave resistance. Samuel Collings's Octavius was a chisel-jawed Bonaparte, the width of whose magnificent epaulettes on his scarlet uniform exceeded his height. Sitting prissily ram-rod straight on a camp chair, nose in the air, hearing Antony's messenger he put me in mind of Daumier's sniffy fops.

38. *Antony and Cleopatra*, 2.5, RSC, Swan Theatre, directed by Tarell Alvin McCraney. Joaquina Kalukango as Cleopatra, Sarah Niles as Charmian, Charise Castro Smith as Iras.

Lepidus (Henry Stram) was an effete frock-coated nitwit whose periwig slid drunkenly out of kilter. Cleopatra's women (Charmian: Sarah Niles; Iras: Charise Castro Smith) wore head rags and turbans remembered from home in Nigeria and spoke, like their mistress, with slight Caribbean accents. The Soothsayer (Chivas Michael) practised voodoo. But all of this was merely gestured at, not insisted upon as some over-determining concept.

Instead, what McCraney's stripped down script gave us was a pell-mell story (in under three hours) of magnificent folly which recast political reckless-ness as personal triumph. Jonathan Cake's Antony (who towered over Octavius – Wellington, or bet-ter said, Flashman, to Napoleon) was first 'native' in Alexandria in Egyptian sarong (and literally caught with his pants down when a curtain pulled aside too soon discovered him to universal laughter step-ping out of Cleopatra's pool naked). In Rome, he was uniformed and cravatted, brass button for brass button, gold frog for gold frog Octavius's equal. But this recuperated look deceived, for in either loca-tion he wore brows permanently puckered over a laddish grin, as though utterly perplexed, 'toil'-ed by a tawny Cleopatra (the RSC's first ever black casting of Shakespeare's black queen) who filled his 'vacancy' with 'voluptuousness', and kept his 'brain' erotically over-heating, 'fuming' not with drink but with her 'salt' 'charms'. These were in the forefront of his hot thoughts even as he was making a new marriage to cold Octavia. Liter-ally distracted, he drove Collings's Caesar, a bean-counting martinet, to distraction.

But if what Antony was doing was 'ruin', it was ruin on a grand scale whose costs were more than met by the extravagant sensuous pay-out of Joaquina Kalukango's deliciously and erotically profligate Cleopatra. She was the walking embod-iment of metaphors like Rosalind's on love as bottomless as the bay of Portingale or Ulysses's on 'ticklish' reading material. This Cleopatra was cast younger than usual, a sister to Cressida, not middle-aged Beatrices or Gertrudes. She did have 'language in her eye, her cheek, her lip'; was a woman whose 'foot speaks'; whose 'wanton spir-its' did 'look out / At every joint and motive of her body' – all these in her becoming spectacu-lar recommendations of a rare gypsy queen who could turn on a sixpence ('cut my laces'; 'let it alone'). Dressed always in white, her hair a lioness's mane of plaited cornrows, Kalukango's Cleopatra moved between sluttishness ('O happy horse . . . !') and monumental dignity ('Upon your sword / Sit laurel victory'), from man-sized fury ('He is mar-ried?') to political cunning ('O') to self-ravaging grief ('Noblest of men, woot die?') and finally to apotheosis. Over one beautifully paced sequence, as Iras dressed her in her robes and attended to her 'immortal longings', Charmian upstage poured gourdful after gourdful of Nile water into a glass jar, bringing to life inside the asps that, killing Cleopa-tra, would make her immortal. Reaching into the water's depths, holding the jar against her breast like some strange pregnancy, stirring the snakes to strike her, she was not just returning to Cydnus but to her element. Dead, as Antony before her, she would rise, cross upstage to step into the pool, and wade through the water into an eternity where she met him, both turned to hieroglyphs in silhouette before the final blackout.

This Cleopatra, then, 'approve[d]' paradox, the 'common liar'. And, withall, Kalukango found the wondrous comedy of the part: she had people in the audience laughing out loud. Some of her best moments came as she sparked off Chukwudi Iwuji's bug-eyed and mercurial Enobarbus, an actor who plays the rhythms of Shakespeare's writing through his body like a dancer. This Enobarbus, who strangely died of his broken heart curled up like a child, returned post-mortem, as curtain-raiser to Cleopatra's death, now bare-torsoed in a top hat, his face made up like a skull, ribs painted on chest, Haiti's Baron Samedi, jigging broken-gaited, a carnivalized anti-masque that gave way to her magnificent triumph: 'Husband, I come.'

It struck me only later that there was no press reaction to Kalukango's casting. Back in 2000 when David Oyelowo was cast as the RSC's 'first ever black' king in *Henry VI* and in 2006 when Chuk-wudi Iwuji played Henry in the revival, there was plenty of comment. Are we in a 'post-racial' Britain? In some sense, yes (see *Othello*, later). In other senses, no. (Listen to the news from London on any day this year.) I'm rather thrilled that a black Cleopatra – a casting I've been calling for since writing about the RSC's historic whiting-out of the role in *Enter the Body: Women and Representation on Shakespeare's Stage* – today appears so obvious as to pass without notice.

In the RSC's main house, David Farr with his designer Jon Bausor pursued their fascination with cultural obsolescence and the materials of industrial dereliction (see the Shipwreck Trilogy last year and *King Lear*, *Shakespeare Survey* 66, 64) setting *Hamlet* in costumes (vaguely) of the 1970s in a gloomy down-at-heels Edwardian school gymnasium which, with a raised stage at one end, multitasked as the school theatre, and which any schools inspector would surely have condemned. Part of a wall had collapsed, the roof looked like it leaked through the plastic skylights, and the racks of fencing foils – nudge, nudge: fencing foils – that flanked the stage – nudge, nudge: we're watching a play – were unsecured.

By the interval, I'd been knocked (get it?) in the ribs so often I felt like a piece of gymnasium apparatus. A punching bag. Get it: the faded inscription over the pros arch on the school stage read 'mens sana in corpore sano'. Get it: holding their wedding reception – complete with popping confetti and champagne corks – in the gym (why? was Claudius the headmaster, Denmark a failing public school? or was this a low budget 'do' in a time of royal belt tightening?), the new-married couple welcomed faceless guests all wearing what looked suspiciously like fencing masks. (Get it?) Get it: the Ghost of old Hamlet (Greg Hicks, who doubled Claudius) came on, a faux warrior, in fencing gear and left handing his son his blood-stained face mask; Hamlet went everywhere with it thereafter, his personal memento mori, 'remember me'. Later, then, when Hamlet (Jonathan Slinger) came on mad, he was dressed like daddy (get it?), except that daddy's fencing whites were immaculate (laundry in purgatory evidently washed spotless), and Hamlet was coming apart, filthy, in mismatched slouching socks, buckles undone, straps flapping. One final 'get it': the way the boundaries between

inside/outside, known world/undiscovered country were clearly fraying. Running around the edges of the gym floor was a margin of black dirt strewn with skulls: Elsinore High built on a grave site? 'To be' literally framed by 'not to be'?

For the first ten minutes, I found this production intriguing. Into the dark gym through a pair of eerily back-lit glass-paned doors marked 'EXIT' pushed a single, balding man in an ill-fitting suit, a red carnation in his button hole, pasty-faced, a handkerchief stuffed in his mouth. He was silently sobbing; took off his thick glasses and wiped his eyes; wandered – his gait spasmodic, halting – over to the weapons rack, took down a short Greek sword, evidently wood, started flourishing it; heard a noise, barked 'Who's there?'; retreated to the foot of the thrust stage, sat, knees hunched up; wrote furiously in his pocket book, invisible for the rest of the scene as soldiers entered, raking torches across the deserted space and called 'Who's there?' Here, then, was Hamlet as myopic geek, as middle-aged Woody Allen, ideas I was interested to see panning out in Slinger's performance. Only they didn't. Because first things simply didn't connect to things later.

Thus, after his chat with dad, he'd lose the glasses, his eyesight evidently corrected. He'd lose the geekiness in his first brief encounter with Ophelia (Pippa Nixon), she in brogues and blue stockings carrying a stack of exercise books, perhaps an NQT (Newly Qualified Teacher) or geriatric head girl. Bumping into each other as they crossed paths, prince and pupil launched themselves at each other like cats on heat, Ophelia frantically unbuttoning her clothes, aiming to get down to sex on the gym floor – only to be interrupted by her brother, a dour Laertes (Luke Norris) who, in pea-jacket and university scarf, was headed off to some technical college in Paris, not the gay lights. The *coitus* here *interruptus* would be resumed later, in the nunnery scene when, not just savaging Ophelia by biffing her up and knocking her box of remembrances out of her hands, Hamlet would haul her clothes off, leave her, pathetically thin, cowering pathetically in singlet and really pathetic woolly tights, then drag her to the edge of the stage

39. *Hamlet*, 1.5, RSC, Royal Shakespeare Theatre, directed by David Farr. Jonathan Slinger as Hamlet, Greg Hicks as Ghost.

and smear her face with dirt ('I have heard of your paintings, too'), making filth her cosmetic. I can't have been the only woman in the audience wondering why Nixon's (remember those blue stockings) Ophelia kept going back for more.

There were loads of attention-seeking production ideas banging around here, but ultimately I lost patience with the adolescence ('look at me, look at me') of Farr's direction. He allowed Slinger (who never achieved more human warmth in the role than a salamander) and Hicks to act like they were in different plays (even different professions). The first over-dubbed every line with noise, moans, shrieks, strung out sound effects ('ooooooooooh'; 'yesssssssss'). The other paused pedantically between words as if he were editing the text, not speaking it and hand signalled lines like a semaphore operator ('I', 'you', 'up', 'below'; every word gestured with palm slicing air, fist to mouth, hand clutching heart, finger pointing). Farr allowed Hicks to over-indulge his habit of prissily pursing up his mouth like he was sucking sour grapes to smirk through lines like 'My offence is rank' as though smelling what's rotten in the state of Denmark – and it's the lavatory drains – while making the 'couch' of Denmark sound like X-rated furniture. He allowed Charlotte Cornwell's aimless Gertrude to wander around the stage like a stray cow in ruffled silk. He allowed – or directed – actors to make one bad acting choice after another. On 'Give me some light', Alex Waldmann's completely forgettable Horatio leaped into Claudius's face and snapped a flash polaroid. On ''tis unmanly grief', Claudius handed Hamlet a glass to drain. 'This' in 'That it should come to this' was the empty glass. Did I actually hear Nixon's Ophelia, entering, mad in a white wedding dress and veil, say 'I'm really well'? I know I saw her toss her bouquet – which Hicks (the actor), not Claudius (the character), retrieved leaving Claudius awkwardly standing there holding it. For anyone who'd slept through the 'nudge, nudge; wink, winks' of the previous two and three quarter hours, Ophelia's second mad scene would have brought them swiftly up to speed on where things were heading. Instead of distributing memory flowers, she took down

from the weapons rack a rapier, held it up (look, see: get it?), drew with it a circle in the dirt where Claudius's court were all now standing, revealed when Elsinore's floorboards were ripped up. She removed the button from the rapier's tip, sliced her hand, and 'saw' her blood 'blooming' in flowers – rue, rosemary – that she ritually smeared on the faces and foreheads of the acquiescent courtiers. Later, while his sister lay exposed in a shallow grave in the dirt margin on the forestage (the Gravedigger having unaccountably stomped off before the funeral got going, his job unfinished) Laertes would retrieve the unbated weapon Ophelia had discarded – and (get it?) a penny would drop.

I jotted in my programme during the interval, 'Question: have I come to a point in my spectatorly life where I just shut my eyes and ears and let the *Hamlet* tape play in my mind for the duration – drowning out the noise, missed beats and silly spectacle? Such a bloody great script for the nonsense boys to be getting their hands on! I could weep!' I think I got a kind of answer at the end when, on 'Why does the drum come hither?', we heard the sound of rain first beating on the roof then – oh my god! – pouring in sheets THROUGH IT. Lights exploded. Cables fizzled. There was spectacular electrical short-circuiting. Blackout.

I had it from someone in the company that Bausor explained the effect to actors as the 'Theatre weeping'. So: the theatre and I were of one mind. What a washout.

As so often recently, the tragedy I found most searchingly intelligent, substantial and memorable this year was produced at the National Theatre, not the RSC. Nicholas Hytner's modern dress *Othello* was a tragedy of big men trapped into small mindedness, crediting the incredible, and not one man's tragedy only, but another man's, and another's and another's. Brabantio (William Chubb), sitting at the far end of the board room table around which the Senate gathered listening stony-faced to the story of a wooing that had gone on under his nose *and that he'd known nothing about*, imperceptibly turned his head away and closed his eyes against the knowledge. We saw in the eyes squeezing shut a father's heart breaking. Roderigo (Tom

Robertson) hearing that Desdemona was 'directly in love' with Cassio groaned as though his chest had been carved open. The deeply painful dupability of these two dupes predicted the more than painful duping to come.

Vicki Mortimer designed for the NT's Olivier stage a highly functional space of component parts, first opening on the façade of a public house out of which tipped Iago (Rory Kinnear in civvies, clearly on R&R) and Roderigo, the two escaping from the deafening beat inside. This then gave way to the Senate interior, which trundled on inside a contained box set. Later the box would be re-dressed as the officers' headquarters on Cyprus, the squaddie's rec room, the rudimentary porch of Othello's married quarters, then the bedroom's interior. Outside the box, the camp compound suggested Basra: a concrete bunker behind high barbed-wire-topped steel-mesh fencing, under siege, expecting terrorist attack, suspicious, alert to 'intelligence' that would instruct action. This army – wearing today's British combat gear, recruited to today's military operations – was fully integrated. Not just racially. Women served here. Among them, Emilia (Lyndsey Marshal), who'd be given extra duties when the general came back on base with a wife in tow, Desdemona (Olivia Vinall), blonde, big-eyed, arriving with a Toys-R-Us pack on her back, colour coordinated to her slacks and pumps, as though headed for a gap year in the wilds of Disneyland.

We got the measure of Kinnear's pink piggy-faced Iago in the Venice scenes, watching him cadge a cigarette from Roderigo, then pocket the pack; observing his micro-gestures, tics of hand and shoulder betraying, against his inscrutable mask-like face, interior restlessness; hearing plosives come out of his mouth like grenades detonating ('put...purse') and pauses that left listeners forced to hang on his next word ('Oh sssssirrrrrr....') in a manufactured accent that sounded like jumped-up working class. In the Senate he stood by the door, flattened motionless against the wall, ludicrously out of place amongst the toffs, eyes swivelling, capturing classified information for future use. On Cyprus he was a bluff lad among lads getting his junior squaddies drunk

then adroitly pulling rank – the only one sober in what he'd turned into an ugly brawl – to advise his superior on what had transpired. *Of course* Othello would take this honest ensign, who'd so often covered his back, at his word.

Alongside Kinnear's Iago, Adrian Lester's Othello was the biggest of this production's big men (the actor himself fresh from playing Ira Aldridge playing Othello in *Red Velvet*). On leave in Venice, recalled to duty by his civic masters but required to account for his domestic business, he registered the merest flicker, something between bemusement and weariness, at racist slurs long ago consigned by all but the lunatic fringe to 'alehouse...ignorance', Brabantio's claims that a white girl loving a black man was 'Against all rules of nature'. Coming back on base, uniformed like his men who'd clearly follow him across hell and high water, only his beret and his stripes showing his superior rank, he seemed to tower over them – until shockingly reduced in their eyes when he kissed his wife. While the others shifted away embarrassed from looking, Iago gazed hungrily from under hooded eyes on the hungry kiss, confirming the 'violent commencement' he'd already diagnosed, and mentally storing up what would be 'answerable'.

In Kinnear's performance, it wasn't race hatred that made Iago destroy Othello. It was something much simpler – and more complex. He hated him as a man. And destroyed the man by making him unknow what he knew of himself as a man by unknowing what he knew of Desdemona: 'She did deceive her father, marrying you'. Was that true? Or was it (if the suggestive logic following on from it was that Desdemona-the-super-subtle-Venetian's next deception was to be her husband) 'an odious damned lie'? That line was the turning point, the point of no return.

Set in office headquarters between desks piled with reports and dispatches, the boring admin stuff of 'closet war', 3.3 was less a seduction than a briefing scene, Iago impassively feeding intelligence into a mind forced to process it. The chink and fall of sounds that brought ideas into terrible alignment unsettled Othello's attention – 'dotes',

40. *Othello*, 3.3, National Theatre, Olivier Theatre, directed by Nicholas Hytner. Rory Kinnear as Iago, Adrian Lester as Othello.

'doubts'. Left on his own, he blundered about the place, the furniture getting in his way (so he overturned it), his uniform sticking to him like the shirt of Nessus (so he twisted it like he was trying to wring water out of it), his gut suddenly rancid from the evacuation of a poisoned imagination (so he rushed to the lavvie, stuck his head down the toilet and vomited), his soldier's hands trying to figure out how to behave now that his 'occupation's gone' (his body constantly reverting to his military training, standing to attention, hands clasped behind back, his physical default position).

The man who went to kill his wife was on a military mission. His married quarters were comfortless, like a room in an undergraduate dorm or a budget motel: bed, MFI wardrobe, chair. 'It is the cause, it is the cause' was the companion to Iago's earlier briefing, this a briefing speech to his soul and whatever stars happened to be listening. (And what was astonishing about this whole sequence was Lester's Othello discovering words as they arrived on his lips.) Astonishing too: he flipped *on* the light to see what he was doing. Desdemona, who'd earlier in 4.2 gathered the evidence of her innocence in her arms by ripping the sheets off the bed, now knelt paralysed. Too late.

Still, for a professional killer, he was almost ludicrously inept. It took him three attempts: straddling her on the bed, suffocating then strangling her, then checking the pulse in the throat (his military training kicking in), then finishing the job, then (more training) covering his tracks: straightening the bed, straightening himself, remembering to turn off the light before opening the door to the squaddie who was beating on it: Emilia.

For her part, it was the body on the bed that made her finally break ranks, go AWOL on the military, opt out of the boys' war games and the need to be one of the lads to accuse her commanding officer with such vehement insubordination that

Othello, exasperated, consulted dead Desdemona with a gesture that said, 'what are we going to do with this loose cannon?' before pulling his service revolver and aiming it at Emilia's head. She just laughed. 'Do thy worst.'

Desdemona had said it earlier: 'O, these men, these *men*'. And later Emilia would finish the thought: 'As ignorant as dirt'. Too true. Here, the tragedy was not a tragedy of race but masculinity. Men, taught to trust men, to depend on men, believe men, bond with men, know their male code which defined *vir*-tue, had simultaneously to *mistrust*, suspect, anticipate betrayal, know knowledge. Men displaced betrayal onto women, but the women here were merely 'collateral damage' sustained under 'friendly fire'. 'My lord, you know I love you' was a statement whose hypocrisy was unpicked only when another statement fell into place: 'What you know you know.' Male love here was the mask hatred wore, deep, inveterate homophobia. And the pity of it? That the poisoner, poisoning, poisoned the poisoner. That the man Iago hated most of all was himself.

I end this year with two *Macbeth*s that couldn't have been further apart on the performance spectrum. Eve Best made her directing debut at the Globe with a workman-like period dress production that set things in a Scotland under siege, in a stockade of whitewashed paling, cut rough and jagged at the top, mud splattered at the bottom, running the width of the stage (designer: Mike Britton).

Some interesting choices were made by actors. Malcolm (Philip Cumbus) was a scholar, not a soldier, who constantly had his nose in a book and was staggered by his father nominating him future king. Colin Ryan, as 'cream faced loon', had a brilliant moment of strangled silence, facing Macbeth, when he could only jerk his head backward over his shoulder spasmodically in the direction of a wood he couldn't find words to say was on the move. The witches (Moyo Akandé, Cat Simmons, Jess Murphy: otherwise looking like the Sirens out of *Oh Brother, Where Art Thou?* and singing 'Kyrie Eleison' so that you had to wonder who they were

working for) at the end hauled off the boy Siward's corpse, perhaps to harvest its body parts.

Plenty of predictable or silly choices were made, too. Samantha Spiro was more of a shrew, Kate Minola on speed, than a Lady Macbeth. The witches, miming the cauldron and the apparitions, weren't expert enough in physical theatre to make the encounter with the metaphysical work. Mostly, the acting was worthy.

And then there was Joseph Millson. His Macbeth was rivetting, both speaking and playing, and more than made up for the worthiness of the rest. 'If it were done . . . ' spoken at double speed gave a mind on over-drive. 'We'll not fail' showed a listening body entranced, paralysed. Examining his bloody hands, things of terror to his sight, he stroked them as if unable to feel them, to connect them to his nervous system. Crowned king, he immediately made gestures to undo himself: wrenching off his crown ('To be thus is *nothing*!') and yanking open his ruff collar as if to give himself space to breathe. When he confessed to 'scorpions' in his mind, he was seeing seething infestation. 'I have lived long enough', flat-lined, gave emptiness. His snapped neck at the end was a relief.

Moving from the wide, outdoor Globe stage to the one-room converted Temperance Hall that's home to the Little Angel puppet theatre in Islington is to experience a Gulliver-esque reversal of perspective, from Brobdingnag to Lilliput. The Little Angel's auditorium seats 100 in pews; its stage is only 15 by 10 feet, its players two feet tall. This is the outfit that collaborated with the RSC on *Venus and Adonis* and *The Tempest*, constructing my all time favourite Caliban (*Shakespeare Survey 65*). But my heart sank when my London producer daughter informed me that what I'd be seeing at the Little Angel was '*Macbeth* with chickens'. Chickens?

It was terrifying. The warriors – Macbeth, Banquo, Macduff: all of them rod or bunraku puppets designed by master puppet maker, Lyndie Wright – had the (slightly stylized) articulated bodies of humans but the heads of cocks, their bird eyes fiercely reptilian, their combs aggressively engorged, their beaks hooked and razor

41. *Macbeth*, 1.2, Little Angel Theatre, directed by Peter Glanville. Claire Harvey, Lori Hopkins, Lowri James as Puppeteers.

sharp. When Macbeth slew the rebel Macdonald he spitted him through the eye, yanked the head off the body, and held it aloft like a trophy. When Banquo was ambushed as he climbed the steep slope to the castle gate, he was dive-bombed by a phantasmagoric bat-winged raptor bird who struck, and struck again. Wounded he slid down the incline, struggled back to his feet, only to be hit again and fall again. When the raven-like Witches ended their opening tale of Macbeth's victory, they bent like carrion crows dining on the guts of a rabbit, pulling at the white pile of wool on which they stood, the bloodied beak-fuls reading like skeins twisted by Clotho and her sister Fates.

Not everything was bleak in this Scotland. But goodness was ironized. Duncan was an over-plump white goose, his sons, a pair of fledged goslings who worked out the family pecking order (literally) in the background like a couple of stroppy kids while their father spoke, but joined him in gorgeously swooping flight to travel to Dunsinane, first circling the castle before landing in the keep. The mistress of that place wore white, but was a hen who more than pecked – she *raked* her husband's conscience with her sarcasm. She had the same snake eyes as the chicken warriors, the same single expression of blank ferocity, and her weapon of choice was her beak. Sitting at the far end of the dining table as Macbeth leaned toward her to hiss, 'We will proceed no further in this business', she suddenly yanked the tablecloth, pulling him sprawling across the surface, forcing him beak to beak to answer her challenge, 'Was the hope . . . ?'

All the deaths were horrific, none more so than the slaughter of Macduff's family, a clutch of cheeping chicks who bobbed up and down in the nest while their hen-ly mother protested cluckingly to messenger bird Ross before he flew off that her husband 'wants the natural touch'. Moments later the languidly flapping raptor bird swung into view. It descended 'in one fell swoop', ripped the head off the mother hen and carried her off in its talons after dropping a suffocating cloak over the nest. The cheeps grew fainter. The bobs faltered. The nest stilled. (I sensed everyone around me holding their breaths.) For the final show-down – 'lay on Macduff' – the puppet warriors, retreating upstage to an empty space that opened out, lost human shape, turned into veritable chickens, the battle-to-the-death staged as a cock fight, spurs viciously striking in a mêlée of flying feathers until one body fell, twitched, lay limp.

For the many children in the Little Angel's sell-out audience, this *Macbeth*, directed by long-time Artistic Director Peter Glanville in his final production for the company, offered them Shakespeare full-on if cut down, an hour of story-telling that changed none of Shakespeare's language, told in voice-over by voices that will stay with them: Nathaniel Parker was Macbeth; Helen McCrory, Lady Macbeth; Donald Sumpter, Duncan; Christopher Staines, Macduff. And they saw sights to populate nightmares: most of them played out on a table surface set downstage, but others using Peter O'Rourke's cunningly simple archi-tectural design of small-scale wooden tower, cupboard, plinth and connecting runways that could be elevated or inclined. 'She should have died hereafter' put Macbeth at the top of Dunsinane's tower. Below his feet, a wall lowered, revealing on the rake his wife's body sprawled as though she'd thrown herself off the battlements – absolutely dead. There's nothing deader than a dead puppet.

Adults might have been equally fascinated by the silent shadow-people behind the puppets, three women in black, eyes heavily kohled, hair pulled back from faces: Claire Harvey, Lori Hopkins, Lowri James. They had a trick of catching each other's eyes and giving a little nod over each yanked-off head, each dead body held upturned by its ankles going limp. They presented as the three Weird Sisters (not least because one of them at the end returned, Clotho-like, to wool picking). For any who imagines Shakespeare's Macbeth the mere puppet of some 'juggling . . . fiends', this production told that story. But of course we could see the puppet manipulation as entirely the work of human choice, human agency. This was a *Macbeth* told by women. Pondering that fact, I realize I have come full circle, to where my review year began. Which must mean that it's time to look at what's on in 2014.

PROFESSIONAL SHAKESPEARE PRODUCTIONS IN THE BRITISH ISLES JANUARY–DECEMBER 2012

JAMES SHAW

Most of the productions listed are by professional companies, but some amateur productions are included. The information is taken from *Touchstone* (www.touchstone.bham.ac.uk), a Shakespeare resource maintained by the Shakespeare Institute Library. Touchstone includes a monthly list of current and forthcoming UK Shakespeare productions from listings information. The websites provided for theatre companies were accurate at the time of going to press.

ALL'S WELL THAT ENDS WELL

Theatr Clwyd. Theatr Clwyd Cymru, Mold, 9 February–10 March and tour.
www.clwyd-theatr-cymru.co.uk
Director: Terry Hands

Arpana at the World Shakespeare Festival, Globe to Globe 2012, Shakespeare's Globe, London, 23–24 May.
www.worldshakespearefestival.org.uk
In Gujarati.

The Berkshire Shakespeare Festival. South Hill Park Arts Centre Grounds, Bracknell, 18–22 July.
www.southhillpark.org.uk

Gentleman Jack Theatre Company. Unitarian Chapel, Brunswick Square, Bristol, 27 November–8 December.
www.gentlemanjacktheatre.co.uk
Director: Philip Perry

ANTONY AND CLEOPATRA

Oyun Atölyesi (Istanbul) at the World Shakespeare Festival, Globe to Globe 2012, Shakespeare's Globe, London, 26–27 May.
www.worldshakespearefestival.org.uk
Director: Kemal Aydogan
In Turkish.

Chichester Festival Theatre Company. Chichester Festival Theatre, Chichester, 7–29 September.
www.cft.org.uk
Director: Janet Suzman
Antony: Michael Pennington
Cleopatra: Kim Cattrall
Revival of 2010 Liverpool Playhouse Production.

AS YOU LIKE IT

Clwyd Theatr Cymru. Anthony Hopkins Theatre, Mold, 9 February–10 March and Welsh tour.
www.clwyd-theatr-cymru.co.uk
Director: Terry Hands
Rosalind: Hedydd Dylan

Custom/Practice and Graffiti Productions. The Lion and Unicorn Theatre, London, 24 April–19 May.
www.giantolive.com
Director: Rae McKen
Rosalind: Rebecca Loudon

Marjanishvili State Drama Theatre (Tbilisi) at the World Shakespeare Festival, Globe to Globe

2012, Shakespeare's Globe, London,
18–19 May.
www.worldshakespearefestival.org.uk
Director: Levan Tsuladze
In Georgian.

Rain or Shine Theatre Company,
Touring 24 May–2 September.
www.rainorshine.co.uk

Lazarus Theatre Company. The Space,
Canary Wharf, 29 May–16 June.
www.lazarustheatrecompany.webs.com
Director: Gavin Harrington-Odedra

TakeOver12 Festival. Theatre Royal Studio
Theatre, York, 1–9 June.
www.yorktheatreroyal.co.uk

Iris Theatre. Garden of St Paul's Church, London,
28 June–4 August.
www.iristheatre.com
Director: Dan Winder
Promenade performance.

Bard in the Botanics, Botanic Gardens, Glasgow.
13–28 July.
http://bardinthebotanics.co.uk
Director: Gordon Barr

Shakespeare's Globe Company. Theatre
Royal, Margate, 5–7 July and tour until
September.
www.shakespearesglobe.com
Director: James Dacre

THE COMEDY OF ERRORS

National Theatre. Olivier Theatre, London,
1 November–1 April.
www.nationaltheatre.org.uk
Director: Dominic Cooke.
Antipholus of Syracuse: Lenny Henry

Rose Theatre, Bankside, 3 April–4 May.
www.rosetheatre.org.uk
Director: David Pearce

Royal Shakespeare Company. Royal
Shakespeare Theatre, Stratford-upon-Avon,

16 March–6 October; Roundhouse, London,
13 June–1 July.
www.rsc.org.uk

Roy-e-Sabs at the World Shakespeare Festival,
Globe to Globe 2012, Shakespeare's Globe,
London 30–31 May.
www.worldshakespearefestival.org.uk
Director: Amir Nizar Zuabi
In Dari Persian.

CORIOLANUS

Chiten Theatre Company (Kyoto) at the World
Shakespeare Festival, Globe to Globe 2012,
Shakespeare's Globe, London, 21–22 May.
www.worldshakespearefestival.org.uk
Director: Motoi Miura
In Japanese.

Coriolan/us
National Theatre Wales and the Royal
Shakespeare Company at the World
Shakespeare Festival, Hangar 858, Picketson,
St Athan, Vale of Glamorgan, South Wales,
9–18 August.
www.rsc.org.uk
Director: Mike Pearson and Mike Brookes
Coriolanus: Richard Lynch
Set in an aircraft hanger. Audience members
listened to the play through headphones with
the action displayed on video screens.

Adaptation
OVO. Maltings Arts Centre, St Albans,
16–31 March.
www.maltingsartstheatre.co.uk
Director: Adam Nichols
Set in modern day Italy among crowds of
football hooligans.

CYMBELINE

South Sudan Theatre Company at the World
Shakespeare Festival, Globe to Globe 2012,
Shakespeare's Globe, London, 2–3 May.
www.worldshakespearefestival.org.uk
First Shakespeare production performed in
Juba Arabic.

Ninagawa Company. Barbican Theatre, London,
    29 May–1 June and on tour.
www.worldshakespearefestival.org.uk
Director: Yukio Ninagawa
Part of the World Shakespeare Festival.

HAMLET

Young Vic Company. Young Vic Theatre,
    London, 28 October–21 January 2012.
www.youngvic.org
Director: Ian Rickson
Hamlet: Michael Sheen

The Factory. Norrington Room,
    Blackwell's Bookshop, Oxford, 5–24 March.
www.factorytheatre.co.uk
Director: Tim Carroll

Meno Fortas at the World Shakespeare Festival,
    Globe to Globe 2012, Shakespeare's Globe,
    London, 2–3 June.
www.menofortas.lt
Director: Eimuntas Nekrosius
In Lithuanian.

Shakespeare's Globe Company. Shakespeare's
    Globe, London, 11 June–1 September and tour.
www.shakespeares-globe.org
Director: Dominic Dromgoole
Hamlet: Michael Benz

Bedouin Shakespeare Company. Network
    Theatre, London, 17 December–12 January
    2013.
www.networktheatre.org
Director: Jimmy Walters

Adaptation
Kings Head Theatre Company, Islington,
    London, 17 December.
www.kingsheadtheatre.org
60-minute version for younger audiences.

Kupenga Kwa Hamlet
Two Gents Productions. The Studio, Hawth,
    14 May and tour through May.
www.twogentsproductions.com

First Quarto production set in pre-colonial
    Zimbabwe.

Hamlet: The Undiscovered Country
PBSK Partnership with Fosters Solicitors,
    30 October–3 November.
www.hostryfestival.org
Director: Stash Kirkbride
Playwright: Stash Kirkbride and Peter Beck
New play commissioned for the Hostry Festival.
    A sequel featuring the characters in purgatory.

Ophelia, Princess of Denmark
Old Joint Stock Theatre, Birmingham, 27–28 July.
www.oldjointstocktheatre.co.uk
Playwright: Frank Bramwell
Following Ophelia, Hamlet and Claudius in the
    afterlife.

The Rest Is Silence
dreamthinkspeak. Riverside Studios, 13–23 June;
    Northern State, Newcastle-upon-Tyne,
    26–30 June.
www.worldshakespearefestival.org.uk
Director: Tristan Sharps
London International Festival of Theatre (LIFT) –
    World Shakespeare Festival.

The Tiger Lillies Perform Hamlet
Republique Theatre. Queen Elizabeth Hall,
    Southbank Centre, London, 18–21 September.
Director: Martin Tulinius
Danish company incorporating puppets,
    circus skills and video projections.

HENRY IV, PART I

Compañia Nacional de Teatre at the World
    Shakespeare Festival, Globe to Globe 2012,
    Shakespeare's Globe, London, 14–15 May.
www.worldshakespearefestival.org.uk
Director: Hugo Arrevillaga
In Mexican Spanish.

Film
BBC2, broadcast 7 July 2012.
Director: Richard Eyre
Falstaff: Simon Russell Beale

Henry IV: Jeremy Irons
Prince Hal: Tom Hiddleston
Part of the *Hollow Crown* season.

HENRY IV, PART 2

Elkafka Espacio Teatral at the World Shakespeare
Festival, Globe to Globe 2012, Shakespeare's
Globe, London, 15–16 May.
www.worldshakespearefestival.org.uk
Director: Ruben Szuchmacher
In Argentinian Spanish.

Film
BBC2, broadcast 14 July 2012.
Director: Richard Eyre
Falstaff: Simon Russell Beale
Henry IV: Jeremy Irons
Prince Hal: Tom Hiddleston
Part of the *Hollow Crown* season.

HENRY V

Propeller Theatre Company. Everyman Theatre,
Cheltenham, 19–28 January and tour until
August.
www.propeller.org.uk
Director: Edward Hall

Shakespeare's Globe. Liverpool Playhouse,
Liverpool, 12–28 April and tour until August.
www.shakespeares-globe.org
Director: Dominic Dromgoole
Henry V: Jamie Parker

Theatre Delicatessen. Marylebone High Street,
London, 22 May–30 June.
www.theatredelicatessen.co.uk
Director: Roland Smith
Henry V: Philip Desmeulles

Illyria Shakespeare Company. The Gardens of
Crosby Hall, Little Crosby, 1 July and tour until
September.
www.illyria.uk.com

Old Red Lion Theatre. Old Red Lion Pub,
Islington, London, 26 July–29 September.

www.oldredliontheatre.co.uk
Director: Henry Filloux-Bennett
Henry V: Mark Field and Jack Morris
Separate actors play Henry as politician and
general.

Adaptation
Pocket Henry V
Propeller Theatre Company. ProTrinity Theatre
& Arts Centre, Tunbridge Wells, 27 September
and tour to November.
http://propeller.org.uk
Director: Edward Hall
Adaptors: Roger Warren and Edward Hall
Abbreviated version for younger audiences.

Film
BBC 2, broadcast 21 July 2012.
Director: Thea Sharrock
Henry V: Tom Hiddleston
Part of the *Hollow Crown* season.

HENRY VI, PART I

Henry VI, Part 1: The Occupation
National Theatre of Belgrade at the World
Shakespeare Festival, Globe to Globe 2012,
Shakespeare's Globe, London, 11–13 May.
www.worldshakespearefestival.org.uk
Director: Nikita Milivojevic
In Serbian.

HENRY VI, PART 2

Henry VI, Part 2: England's Fall
National Theatre of Albania at the World
Shakespeare Festival, Globe to Globe 2012,
Shakespeare's Globe, London, 12–13 May.
www.worldshakespearefestival.org.uk
Director: Adonis Filipi
In Albanian.

HENRY VI, PART 3

Henry VI, Part 3: The Chaos
National Theatre of Bitola at the World
Shakespeare Festival, Globe to Globe 2012,
Shakespeare's Globe, London, 12–13 May.

www.worldshakespearefestival.org.uk
In Macedonian.

HENRY VIII

Rakatá (Madrid) at the World Shakespeare
 Festival, Globe to Globe 2012, Shakespeare's
 Globe, London, 29–30 May.
www.worldshakespearefestival.org.uk
In Spanish.

JULIUS CAESAR

Immersion Theatre Ltd. Brockley Jack Studio
 Theatre, London, 22 February–10 March.
www.immersiontheatre.co.uk
Directors: James Tobias and Roderick Morgan

Royal Shakespeare Company. Royal Shakespeare
 Theatre, Stratford-upon-Avon, 28 May–7 July
 and tour.
www.rsc.org.uk
Director: Gregory Doran
Mark Antony: Ray Fearon
Brutus: Paterson Joseph
Caesar: Jeffery Kissoon
All black cast.

I Termini Company (Italy) at the World
 Shakespeare Festival, Globe to Globe 2012,
 Shakespeare's Globe, London, 1–2 May.
www.worldshakespearefestival.org.uk
In Italian.

Principal Theatre Company. Coram's Fields,
 London, 20 July–4 August.
Director: Paul Gladwin

Donmar Warehouse, London,
 29 November–9 February 2013.
www.donmarwarehouse.com
Director: Phyllida Lloyd
Julius Caesar: Frances Barber
Brutus: Harriet Walter

Opera
English National Opera. London Coliseum,
 West End, London, 1 October–2 November.
www.eno.org

Director: Michael Keegan-Dolan
Composer: George Handel

Adaptation
I, Cinna (The Poet)
Royal Shakespeare Company. Swan Theatre,
 13 June–6 July.
www.rsc.org.uk
Playwright and Director: Tim Crouch
One man show featuring Cinna's story.

KING JOHN

Steam Industry. Union Theatre, London,
 17 January–11 February.
www.steamindustryfreetheatre.org.uk
Director: Phil Willmott

Royal Shakespeare Company. Swan Theatre,
 Stratford-upon-Avon, 6 April–15 September.
www.rsc.org.uk
Director: Maria Aberg
King John: Alex Waldman
Philip the Bastard: Pippa Nixon
Pandulph: Paola Dionisotti

Gabriel Sundukyan National Academic Theatre
 (Armenia) the World Shakespeare Festival,
 Globe to Globe 2012, Shakespeare's Globe,
 London, 16–17 May.
www.worldshakespearefestival.org.uk
In Armenian.

KING LEAR

Shakespeare at the Tobacco Factory. The Tobacco
 Factory, Bristol, 9 February–24 March.
http://sattf.org.uk
Director: Andrew Hilton
Lear: John Shrapnel

House on the Hill Productions. Rose Theatre,
 London, 1–31 March.
www.rosetheatre.org.uk
Director: Grace Wessels

Citizens Company. Citizens Theatre, Glasgow,
 20 April–12 May.
http://citz.co.uk

Director: Dominic Hill
Lear: David Hayman

Lazarus Theatre Company. The Space,
Canary Wharf, 1 May–2 June.
www.lazarustheatrecompany.webs.com
Director: Ricky Dukes

Belarus Free Theatre at the World Shakespeare
Festival, Globe to Globe 2012, Shakespeare's
Globe, London, 17–18 May.
www.worldshakespearefestival.org.uk
In Belarusian.

Almeida Theatre Company, Almeida, London,
31 August–3 November.
www.almeida.co.uk
Director: Michael Attenborough
Lear: Jonathan Pryce

Adaptation
King Lear: Young People's Shakespeare
Royal Shakespeare Company. Nuffield Theatre,
Southampton, 12–15 September and tour until
December.
www.rsc.org.uk
Adaptor: Tim Crouch

The Madness of King Lear
CW Productions. Arts Theatre, London, 19
October–3 November.
www.artstheatrewestend.co.uk
Director: Sara Fernandez Reyes
Two-hander focusing on Lear and the Fool.

The Serpent's Tooth
Almeida Theatre, in association with Talawa
Theatre Company. Almeida Theatre,
13–17 November.
www.almeida.co.uk
Playwright: David Watson

LOVE'S LABOUR'S LOST

Northern Broadsides. New Victoria Theatre,
Newcastle-under-Lyme,
27 January–18 February and tour until May.
northern-broadsides.co.uk
Director: Barrie Rutter

Adaptation
Deafinitely Theatre at the World Shakespeare
Festival, Globe to Globe 2012, Shakespeare's
Globe, London, 22–23 May.
www.deafinitelytheatre.co.uk
Director: Paula Garfield
Performed in British Sign Language.

MACBETH

Octagon Bolton. Octagon Theatre, Bolton,
23 February–17 March.
Director: David Thacker
www.octagonbolton.co.uk
Lady Macbeth: Suzan Sylvester
Macbeth: Robert Cavanagh

Teatr im. Kochanowskiegp (Opole) at the World
Shakespeare Festival, Globe to Globe 2012,
Shakespeare's Globe, London, 8–10 May.
www.worldshakespearefestival.org.uk
In Polish.

Icarus Theatre Collective. Brewhouse Theatre
and Arts Centre, Taunton, 17 April;
Greenwich Theatre, Greenwich, 21–23 May.
www.icarustheatre.org

Lord Chamberlain's Men. Cawdor Castle,
31 May and tour to September.
www.tlcm.co.uk
Director: Andrew Normington

National Theatre of Scotland. The Tramway,
Glasgow, 14–30 June.
www.nationaltheatrescotland.com
Director: John Tiffany and Alan Goldberg
Macbeth: Alan Cumming
Virtually a one-man show.

New London Company, The Lion and Unicorn
Theatre (Giant Olive Theatre), Inner London,
19 June–7 July
www.giantolive.com

Crucible Studio Theatre, Sheffield,
5 September–6 October.
www.sheffieldtheatres.co.uk
Director: Daniel Evans

Macbeth: Geoffrey Streatfeild
Lady Macbeth: Claudie Blakeley

Lodestar Theatre Company. Royal Court,
    Liverpool, 21 September–13 October.
www.lodestartheatre.co.uk
Director: Max Rubin

Lyric Belfast. Northern Bank Stage, Belfast,
    21 October–24 November.
www.lyrictheatre.co.uk
Director: Lynne Parker

Opera
Opra Cymru. Chapter Arts Centre, Cardiff,
    13 September.
http://opracymru.org.uk
Composer: Giuseppe Verdi

Adaptation
Baz Productions. The Crypt, St Andrew's
    Church, Holborn Viaduct, London,
    18 October–5 November.
www.bazproductions.co.uk
Director: Sarah Bedi
A company of five swapping roles throughout
    the play.

Lady M: His Fiend-Like Queen
Theatre Jezebel, Tron Theatre, Glasgow,
    25–28 April.
Director and Adaptor: Mary McCluskey
60-minute version featuring only Macbeth,
    Lady Macbeth and the witches.

2008: Macbeth
TR Warszawa. Lowland Hall, Royal Highland
    Centre, Edinburgh International Festival,
    11–18 August.
Performed in Polish with English subtitles.
    Updated to a Middle East conflict.

Lady M
Het Vijfde Bedrijf – The Fifth Act, Ceca,
    Edinburgh, 1–18 August.
www.edfringe.com
Solo comic performance featuring Lady
    Macbeth's Lady-in-Waiting.

Lady MacWata
Exchange Theatre Company. The Lion and
    Unicorn Theatre, London, 8–11 February.
www.exchangetheatre.com
Playwright: Magali Muxart
Director: David Furlong
An actress turns to African witchcraft to inspire
    her performance as Lady Macbeth.

Macbeth: Leila & Ben – A Bloody History
Artistes Producteurs. Riverside Studios, London
    4–7 July; Northern Stage,
    Newcastle-upon-Tyne, 12–14 July.
Director: Lotfi Achour
Tunisian version. Part of the London
    International Festival of Theatre and the World
    Shakespeare Festival.

MEASURE FOR MEASURE

Royal Shakespeare Company. Swan Theatre,
    Stratford-upon-Avon, 17 April–15 September.
www.rsc.org.uk
Director: Roxana Silbert

Vakhtangov Theatre (Moscow) at the World
    Shakespeare Festival, Globe to Globe 2012,
    Shakespeare's Globe, London, 24–25 April.
www.worldshakespearefestival.org.uk
In Russian.

F.A.M.E (Fusion Acting & Musical Exploration).
    Bierkeller Theatre, Bristol, 29–30 July.
www.fame-totnes.co.uk
Part of the Bristol Shakespeare Festival.

Dark Corner Theatre. Cockpit Theatre,
    Gateforth Street, Marylebone, London,
    28 August–1 September.
www.thecockpit.org.uk

THE MERCHANT OF VENICE

Vox Humana Theatre Company. Rose Theatre,
    London, 1–26 February.
Director: David Weinberg

Cut to the Chase. Queen's Theatre, Hornchurch, London, 20 April–12 May.
www.queens-theatre.co.uk

Habima National Theatre (Tel Aviv) at the World Shakespeare Festival, Globe to Globe 2012, Shakespeare's Globe, London 28–29 May.
www.worldshakespearefestival.org.uk
Director: Ilan Ronen
In Hebrew.

Creation Theatre Company. The Said Rooftop Ampitheatre, Oxford, 7 July–1 September.
www.creationtheatre.co.uk
Director: Natalie Abrahami

Goodmann Productions. Studio at the Courtyard Theatre, London, 18–30 September.
www.thecourtyard.org.uk
Director: Petina Hapgood and Sharon Burrell

Adaptation
Shylock
Theatre Tours International. Theatre Royal, Margate, 27 March and tour to June.
www.theatretoursinternational.com
Director and Playwright: Gareth Armstrong

Shylock's Appeal
A. E. Harris Building, Birmingham, 13 October.
www.fred-theatre.co.uk
Playwright: John Curtis
Shylock appeals the original judgement.

THE MERRY WIVES OF WINDSOR

Royal Shakespeare Company. Royal Shakespeare Theatre, Stratford-upon-Avon, 25 October–12 January 2013.
www.rsc.org.uk
Director: Phillip Breen
Falstaff: Desmond Barrit
Mistress Quickly: Anita Dobson
Mistress Ford: Alexandra Gilbreath

Bitter Pill Productions (Kenya) at the World Shakespeare Festival, Globe to Globe 2012, Shakespeare's Globe, London, 25–26 April.

www.worldshakespearefestival.org.uk
In Swahili.

Opera
Falstaff
Royal Opera House. London, 15–30 May.
www.roh.org.uk
Director: Robert Carsen
Composer: Giuseppe Verdi

A MIDSUMMER NIGHT'S DREAM

Filter Theatre Company with The London Snorkelling Team. Lyric Hammersmith, London, 9 February–17 March; Royal Exchange, Manchester, 28 July–4 August.
www.filtertheatre.com
Director: Sean Holmes

Antic Disposition. Middle Temple Hall, London, 6–14 April.
www.anticdisposition.co.uk
Director: Ben Horslen and John Risebero.

Yohangza Theatre Company (South Korea) at the World Shakespeare Festival, Globe to Globe 2012, Shakespeare's Globe, London, 30 April–1 May.
www.worldshakespearefestival.org.uk
In Korean.

Open Air Theatre, Regent's Park, London, 2 June–5 September.
http://openairtheatre.com
Director: Matthew Dunster

Chapterhouse Theatre. St Andrews Castle, St Andrews, 7–8 June and tour September.
www.chapterhouse.org

ACS Random. Chelsea Theatre, World's End Place, King's Road, London, 12–23 June.
www.acsrandom.co.uk

The Faction Theatre Company. The Copse, Brockwell Park Open Air, London, 12 June–1 July.
www.thefaction.org.uk
Director: Mark Leipacher

Little English Theatre. The Corse Lawn, Tewkesbury, 1 July and tour to September.
www.thelittleenglishtheatre.co.uk

Oxford Shakespeare Company. Wadham College Gardens, Oxford, 3 July–26 August.
www.oxfordshakespearecompany.co.uk
Director: Gemma Fairlie

Guildford Shakespeare Company, Guildford College of Law, Guildford, 12–22 July
www.guildford-shakespeare-company.co.uk

Custom/Practice. Almeida Theatre, London, 16–21 July.
www.custompractice.co.uk
Director: Rae Mcken

The Movement. Courtyard Theatre, London, 19–30 September.
www.thecourtyard.org.uk/whatson/255/midsummer-nights-dream

Lodestar Theatre Company. Royal Court, Liverpool, 21 September–13 October.
www.lodestartheatre.co.uk

Blue Orange Theatre Company. Blue Orange Theatre, Birmingham, 27 September–6 October.
www.blueorangetheatre.co.uk
Director: Oliver Hume

Mappa Mundi & Torch Theatre. Torch Theatre, Milford Haven, 3–20 October; The Opera House, Buxton, 26–27 November.
www.mappa-mundi.org.uk
Director: Peter Doran

The Lyceum. Royal Lyceum Theatre, Edinburgh, 19 October–17 November.
www.lyceum.org.uk
Director: Matthew Lenton
Set in the middle of winter.

Lazarus Theatre Company. The Blue Elephant, London, 27 November–15 December.
http://lazarustheatrecompany.webs.com
Director: Ricky Dukes

The Lion and Unicorn Theatre. The Giant Olive Theatre, London, 11 December–5 January 2013.
http://giantolive.com

Ballet
The Royal Ballet. Royal Opera House, London, 1 February–7 March.
www.roh.org.uk
Choreography: Sir Kenneth MacMillan

Adaptation
After the Dream
Hand in Hand Theatre Productions. Tour across the Wirral, 19 June–1 July.
www.handinhandtheatreproductions.co.uk
Sequel to *A Midsummer Night's Dream*.

A Dream On A Midsummer's Night
Wee Stories. Portobello, Washhouse, London, 13 September.
Director: Iain Johnstone
An abbreviated version for teenagers, without the Mechanicals.

A Midsummer Night's Dream (As You Like It)
Chekhov International Theatre Festival / Dmitry Krymov's Laboratory / School of Dramatic Art Theatre Production. Royal Shakespeare Theatre, Stratford-upon-Avon, 10–18 August; Festival Theatre, Edinburgh, 24–26 August 2012.
www.worldshakespearefestival.org.uk
Director: Dmitry Krymov
In Russian.

MUCH ADO ABOUT NOTHING

Compagnie Hypermobile at the World Shakespeare Festival, Globe to Globe 2012, Shakespeare's Globe, London, 1–2 June.
www.worldshakespearefestival.org.uk
Director: Clement Poiree
In French.

Heartbreak Productions. Tour 5 June–2 September.

www.heartbreakproductions.co.uk
Director: Maddy Kerr

Royal Shakespeare Company. Courtyard Theatre,
    Stratford-upon-Avon. 26 July–15 September;
    Noel Coward Theatre, London,
    22 September–27 October.
www.rsc.org.uk
Director: Iqbal Khan
Benedick: Paul Battacharjee
Beatrice: Meera Syal

Folksy Theatre Company. Boiling Wells
    Amphitheatre, Bristol, 28–29 July and tour.
www.folksytheatre.co.uk

Opera
Beatrice and Benedict
Welsh National Opera. Welsh Millennium
    Centre, Cardiff, 12 and 26 February and tour
    until April.
www.wno.org.uk
Composer: Hector Berlioz
Director: Elijah Moshinsky

Adaptation
Beatrice on Fire
The Blue Elephant, London, 12–13 October.
Performer: Hattie Thomas
Comic retelling.

OTHELLO

The Questors. Questors Theatre, London,
    2–17 March.
www.questors.org.uk

White Bear Theatre, London, 24–29 April
www.whitebeartheatre.co.uk

The Faction Theatre Company. The Copse,
    Brockwell Park Open Air, London,
    15 June–1 July.
www.thefaction.org.uk
Director: Rachel Valentine Smith

York Shakespeare Project. Theatre Royal Studio,
    York, 23–27 October.
www.yorktheatreroyal.co.uk
Director: Mark France

Opera
Otello
Royal Opera House. Royal Opera House,
    London, 12–24 July.
www.roh.org.uk
Composer: Giuseppe Verdi
Director: Elijah Moshinsky

Adaptation
Q Brothers, Chicago Shakespeare Theatre at the
    World Shakespeare Festival, Globe to Globe
    2012, Shakespeare's Globe, London, 5–6 May.
www.worldshakespearefestival.org.uk
Hip hop version.

The Watermill & The Rose Theatre Kingston.
    The Watermill Theatre, Bagnor,
    5–9 November.
www.watermill.org.uk
Director: Beth Flintoff
Cast of three.

PERICLES

National Theatre of Greece at the World
    Shakespeare Festival, Globe to Globe 2012,
    Shakespeare's Globe, London, 26–27 April.
www.worldshakespearefestival.org.uk
In Greek.

Vox Humana Theatre Company. Rose Theatre,
    London, 2–28 October.
Director: David Weinberg

RICHARD II

Donmar Warehouse, London,
    1 December–4 February 2012.
www.donmarwarehouse.com
Director: Michael Grandage
Richard II: Eddie Redmayne

Ashtar (Ramallah, Palestine) at the World
    Shakespeare Festival, Globe to Globe 2012,
    Shakespeare's Globe, London, 4–5 May.
www.worldshakespearefestival.org.uk
Director: Conall Morrison
In Palestinian Arabic.

Film
BBC2, broadcast 30 June 2012.
Director: Rupert Goold
Richard II: Ben Wishaw
Bolingbroke: Rory Kinnear
Part of the *Hollow Crown* season.

RICHARD III

Guildford Shakespeare Company. Holy Trinity
    Church, Guildford, 10–25 February.
www.holytrinityguildford.org.uk

Royal Shakespeare Company. Swan Theatre,
    Stratford-upon-Avon, 22 March–15 September.
www.rsc.org.uk
Director: Roxana Silbert
Richard: Jonjo O'Neill

National Theatre of China at the World
    Shakespeare Festival, Globe to Globe 2012,
    Shakespeare's Globe, London, 28–29 April.
www.worldshakespearefestival.org.uk
Director: Wang Xiaoying
In Mandarin.

Shakespeare's Globe Company. Shakespeare's
    Globe Theatre, London, 14 July–13 October;
    Apollo Theatre, West End,
    2 November–10 February 2013.
www.shakespeares-globe.org
Director: Tim Carroll
Richard: Mark Rylance

Adaptation
The Resistible Rise of Arturo Ui
Minerva Theatre, Chichester, 29 June–28 July.
www.cft.org.uk
Playwright: Bertolt Brecht
Director: Jonathan Church
Arturo Ui: Henry Goodman

The Trial of Ubu
Hampstead Theatre. Hampstead Theatre,
    London, 18 January–18 February.
Playwright: Simon Stephens
Director: Katie Mitchell
Ubu is tried by an international tribunal.

Two Roses for Richard III
Companhia Bufomecanica. The Courtyard
    Theatre, Stratford-upon-Avon, 7–12 May;
    Roundhouse-Studio 42, The Clore West End,
    18–23 May.
Directors: Claudio Baltar and Fabio Ferreira
Inspired by Shakespeare's history plays.

ROMEO AND JULIET

Broadway Studio Theatre Production. Broadway
    Studio Theatre, London, 1–26 February.
www.broadwaytheatre.org.uk
Director: Asia Osborne

Thrice Three Muses. The Bierkeller Theatre,
    Bristol, 14–23 February.
www.bierkellertheatre.com

Headlong Theatre. Nuffield, Southampton,
    2–18 February and tour to April.
www.headlongtheatre.co.uk
Director: Robert Icke

Grupo Galpao (Brazil) at the World Shakespeare
    Festival, Globe to Globe 2012, Shakespeare's
    Globe, London, 19–20 May.
www.worldshakespearefestival.org.uk
Director: Gabriel Villela
In Brazilian Portuguese.

The Rose Theatre, Bankside, London, 5–30 June.
www.rosetheatre.org.uk

Chapterhouse. St Andrews Castle, St Andrews,
    9 June and tour to September.
www.chapterhouse.org

Bard in the Botanics. Botanic Gardens, Glasgow,
    22 June–20 July.
http://bardinthebotanics.co.uk
Director: Gordon Barr

Icarus Theatre Collective & Kings Theatre
    Southsea. Kings Theatre, Portsmouth,
    19–20 September and tour to May 2013
www.icarustheatre.org
Director: Max Lewendel

Rosemary Branch Theatre Company.
Rosemary Branch Theatre, London,
10 October–4 November.
www.rosemarybranch.co.uk
Director: Bryony J. Thompson

Ballet
The Royal Ballet. Royal Opera House, London,
10 January–3 April.
www.roh.org.uk
Composer: Sergei Prokofiev

Moscow City Ballet. Chichester Festival Theatre,
Chichester, 3–4 January and tour to March.
Composer: Sergei Prokofiev
Director: Victor Smirnov-Golovanov

Adaptation
Box Clever. The Egg, Bath, 3–8 March and
touring schools.
www.boxclevertheatre.co.uk
Director: Ria Parry
Abbreviated version for a young audience.

Facsimile Productions. Guerilla Shakespeare.
Roundhouse, London, 19 February.
www.facsimileproductions.co.uk/
guerilla-shakespeare
A 'Guerilla Shakespeare' production – performed
with no rehearsal or direction.

Romeo & Juliet in Baghdad
Baghdad Iraqi Theatre. The Swan Theatre,
Stratford-upon-Avon, 26 April–5 May;
Riverside Studios, 28–30 June.
www.worldshakespearefestival.org.uk
Directed: Monadhil Daood
Set in Iraq against Sunni and Shia tensions. Part of
the World Shakespare Festival.

Romeo and Juliet for all Time
Old Joint Stock Theatre, Birmingham, 20–21 July.
www.oldjointstocktheatre.co.uk
Playwright: Frank Bramwell

Star-Cross'd
Oldham Coliseum, Alexandra Park, Oldham,
12–22 July.

http://coliseum.org.uk
Playwright: Ian Kershaw
Director: Kevin Shaw
Outdoor promenade production, updated to
contemporary Oldham.

A Tender Thing
Swan Theatre, Stratford-upon-Avon,
27 September–20 October.
www.rsc.org.uk
Playwright: Ben Power
Director: Helena Kaut-Howson
Romeo: Richard McCabe
Juliet: Kathryn Hunter
An adaptation, first seen in 2009, depicting the
characters in old age.

THE TAMING OF THE SHREW

Royal Shakespeare Company. Royal Shakespeare
Theatre, Stratford-upon-Avon,
19 January–18 February; Theatre Royal,
Newcastle-upon-Tyne, 23 February–3 March;
Theatre Royal, Nottingham, 13–17 March;
Richmond Theatre, London, 20–24 March.
www.rsc.org.uk
Director: Lucy Bailey
Petruchio: David Caves
Katherine: Lisa Dillon

Derby Live. Derby Playhouse, 7–25 February.
www.derbylive.co.uk
Director: Peter Meakin

New Rep Theatre Company. St Leonard's
Church, Shoreditch High St, London,
10–27 May.
www.thenewrepcompany.co.uk
Director: Graham Hubbard

Theatre Walley-KASHIF (Islamabad) at the World
Shakespeare Festival, Globe to Globe 2012,
Shakespeare's Globe, London, 25–26 May.
www.worldshakespearefestival.org.uk
Director: Haissam Hussain

GB Theatre Company. Exeter Castle, Devon,
6–7 June and tour to September.

www.gbtheatrecompany.com
Director: Jenny Stephens

Shakespeare's Globe Theatre Company.
Shakespeare's Globe, London,
23 June–13 October.
www.shakespeares-globe.org
Director: Toby Frow

Adaptation
Cygnet Theatre. Sweet Grassmarket, Edinburgh,
13–24 August.
www.edfringe.com
Gender reversal production.

Kiss Me, Kate
Chichester Festival Theatre, Chichester,
18 June–1 September; Old Vic Theatre,
London, 30 November–3 March 2013.
www.cft.org.uk
Director: Trevor Nunn
Composer: Cole Porter

THE TEMPEST

Dhaka Theatre at the World Shakespeare Festival,
Globe to Globe 2012, Shakespeare's Globe,
London, 7–8 May.
www.worldshakespearefestival.org.uk
Director: Nasir Uddin Yousuff
In Bengali.

Dundee Rep Ensemble. Dundee Repertory
Theatre, 6–23 June.
www.dundeerep.co.uk
Director: Jemima Levick

MadCaps Theatre Productions. Number
8 Community Arts Centre, Pershore,
12 May and tour to July.
http://madcaptheatreproductions.co.uk

Bard in the Botanics. Botanic Gardens, Glasgow,
22 June–7 July.
http://bardinthebotanics.co.uk
Director: Jennifer Dick

The Drayton Theatre, London, 3–21 July.
www.thedraytontheatre.co.uk

GB Theatre Company. Thistle Rougemont
Hotel, Queen's Street, Exeter 9 June and tour
to September.
www.gbtheatrecompany.com
Director: Jack Shepherd

Royal Shakespeare Company. Roundhouse,
London, 9 June–5 July; Royal Shakespeare
Theatre, Stratford-upon-Avon,
13 July–7 October.
www.rsc.org.uk
Director: David Farr
Prospero: Jonathan Slinger

Theatr Genedlaethol Cymru, National Eisteddfod
Maes, Llandow, Wales, 8 August and on tour.
www.theatr.com
Director: Ellen Bowman
In Welsh.

Theatre Royal Bath. Theatre Royal, Bath,
23 August–8 September.
www.theatreroyal.org.uk
Director: Adrian Noble
Prospero: Tim Pigott-Smith

Watermill Theatre, Bangor,
27 September–3 November.
www.watermill.org.uk
Director: Paul Hart

The Lion & Unicorn Theatre. The Giant Olive
Theatre, London, 11 December–5 January
2013.
http://giantolive.com

Ballet
Ballet Cymru, Gordon Craig Theatre, Stevenage,
8 May; Northcott Theatre, Exeter, 22 June.
www.welshballet.co.uk

Adaptation
Network Theatre Company, in association with
the Royal Shakespeare Company. The
Network Theatre, London,
9 February–3 March.
www.networktheatre.org

Director and Adaptor: Bernie C. Byrnes
A jazz version, featuring musical interludes, nine
    Ariels, and female Caliban as Miranda's
    step-sister.

The Magician's Daughter
Little Angel Theatre Company in association with
    the Royal Shakespeare Company. Underbelly,
    Edinburgh, 1–27 August.
www.littleangeltheatre.com
Playwright: Michael Rosen
Puppet version. The story of Miranda's daughter.

The Nine Lessons of Caliban
Firebird Poets in collaboration with poet Claire
    Williamson. Firebird Theatre. Old Vic, Bristol,
    29 February–3 March.
www.firebird-theatre.com
An evening of poetry inspired by *The Tempest*.

Return to the Forbidden Planet
Queen's Theatre, Hornchurch,
    25 August–22 September.
www.queens-theatre.co.uk
Director and Composer: Bob Carlton

Prospero's Library
RETZ, 297 Hoxton Street, London, 14–23 June.
Directors: Felix Mortimer and Simon Ryninks.
Art installation. Part of *O Brave New World* project
    which retells *The Tempest* in monthly
    instalments in a shop in Hackney.

The Tempest – The Two Man Tempest
AJTC Theatre Company. The Riverfront,
    Newport, 15 November. Arts Centre,
    Aberystwyth, 7 December.
www.aberystwythartscentre.co.uk
Director: Geoff Bullen

TIMON OF ATHENS

National Theatre Company. Olivier Theatre,
    London, 10 July–1 November.
www.nationaltheatre.org.uk
Director: Nicholas Hytner
Timon: Simon Russell Beale
Flavia: Deborah Findlay

Bremer Shakespeare Company at the World
    Shakespeare Festival, Globe to Globe 2012,
    Shakespeare's Globe, London, 31 May–1 June.
www.worldshakespearefestival.org.uk
In German.

TITUS ANDRONICUS

Tang Shu-wing Theatre Studio (Hong Kong) at
    the World Shakespeare Festival, Globe to Globe
    2012, Shakespeare's Globe, London, 3–4 May.
www.worldshakespearefestival.org.uk
Director: Tang Shu-wing
In Cantonese.

Hiraeth Artistic Productions. Etcetera Theatre,
    London, 8–27 May.
www.hiraeth-theatre.co.uk
Director: Zoe Ford

TROILUS AND CRESSIDA

Ngakau Toa (Aukland) at the World Shakespeare
    Festival, Globe to Globe 2012, Shakespeare's
    Globe, London, 23–24 April.
www.worldshakespearefestival.org.uk
In Maori.

Royal Shakespeare Company and The Wooster
    Group. Swan Theatre, Stratford-upon-Avon,
    3–18 August; Riverside Studios, London,
    24 August–8 September.
www.rsc.org.uk
Directors: Mark Ravenhill and Elizabeth
    LeCompte
Helen/Ulysses: Scott Handy

TWELFTH NIGHT

Faction Theatre Company. New Diorama
    Theatre, London, 4 January–18 February;
    Theatre Royal, Bath, 20–21 February.
www.thefaction.org.uk
Director: Mark Leipacher

The Movement. Mumford Theatre, Cambridge,
    16 January; Norwich Playhouse, Norwich,

23–25 January; Gulbenkian Theatre,
Canterbury, 26 January.

Swivel Theatre Company. Cockpit Theatre,
London, 29 February–18 March.
www.thecockpit.org.uk

Royal Shakespeare Company. Royal Shakespeare
Theatre, Stratford-upon-Avon,
8 March–15 May; Roundhouse, London,
5 June–5 July; Royal Shakespeare Theatre,
Stratford-upon-Avon, 12 July–6 October.
www.rsc.org.uk
Director: David Farr
Viola: Emily Taaffe
Malvolio: Jonathan Slinger

The Company Theatre (Mumbai) at the World
Shakespeare Festival, Globe to Globe 2012,
Shakespeare's Globe, London, 27–28 April.
www.worldshakespearefestival.org.uk
Director: Atul Kumar
In Hindi.

Grosvenor Park Open Air Theatre. Grosvenor
Park Open Air Theatre, Chester,
6 July–18 August.
www.grosvenorparkopenairtheatre.co.uk
Director: Alex Clifton

Shakespeare's Globe Company. Apollo Theatre,
West End, London. 2 November–9 February
2013.
www.shakespeares-globe.org
Director: Tim Carroll
Olivia: Mark Rylance
Malvolio: Stephen Fry
All-male company.

Propeller. Belgrade Theatre, Coventry,
8–10 November to June 2013.
http://propeller.org.uk
Director: Edward Hall and Dugald Bruce
Lockhart
All-male company.

Bingo Dragon Theatre Company. The Dukes,
Lancaster, 12–15 December.
www.dukes-lancaster.org

Adaptation
I, Malvolio
Unicorn Theatre, London,
3 October–11 November.
Performer: Tim Crouch
Directors: Karl James and A Smith

Masters Are You Mad?
Grosvenor Park Theatre, Chester,
13 July–19 August.
www.grosvenorparkopenairtheatre.co.uk
Director: Robin Norton-Hale
A sequel, featuring Malvolio's revenge.

THE TWO GENTLEMEN
OF VERONA

Vakomana Vaviri ve Zimbabwe
Two Gents Productions at the World Shakespeare
Festival, Globe to Globe 2012, Shakespeare's
Globe, London, 9–10 May.
www.worldshakespearefestival.org.uk
In Shona.

Perfect Shadow Mingled Yarn. Jack Studio
Theatre, Brockley, London,
21 August–8 September.
www.perfectshadowmingledyarn.weebly.com
Directors: Rafaella Marcus and Matthew
Monaghan
In rep. with *The Two Noble Kinsmen*.

THE TWO NOBLE KINSMEN

Just Enough Theatre. Theatre Royal Bath and
The Space Arts Centre, London
February–March.
http://justenoughtheatre.wordpress.com
Director: John East

Perfect Shadow Mingled Yarn. Jack Studio
Theatre, Brockley, London,
21 August–8 September.
www.perfectshadowmingledyarn.weebly.com
Directors: Rafaella Marcus and Matthew
Monaghan
In rep. with *The Two Gentlemen of Verona*.

THE WINTER'S TALE

Propeller Theatre. Everyman Theatre,
Cheltenham, 19–28 January and tour until
August.
www.propeller.org.uk
Director: Edward Hall
All male company.

Renegade Theatre (Lagos) at the World
Shakespeare Festival, Globe to Globe 2012,
Shakespeare's Globe, London, 24–25 May.
www.worldshakespearefestival.org.uk
Director: Wole Oguntokun
In Yoruba.

Adaptation
A Winter's Tale
Unicorn Theatre, London,
19 September–16 November.
http://unicorntheatre.com
Adaptor: Ignace Corneilssen
Director: Purni Morell
A play-within-a-play as four actors put on *The
Winter's Tale* at the Unicorn Theatre.

POEMS

(in alphabetical order)

L.O.V.E.
Volcano Theatre. Unity Theatre, Liverpool,
5 October.
www.volcanotheatre.co.uk
Director: Nigel Charnock
Selected sonnets performed by three actors.

The Rape of Lucrece
Makin Projects Production. The Egg, Bath,
15 February; Alleyn's School Theatre, London,
27 March; Yvonne Arnaud Theatre (Mill
Studio), Surrey, 14–16 June; Rose Theatre,
Bankside, 7–12 August.
www.therapeoflucrece.co.uk
Performer: Gerard Logan

Venus and Adonis
Isango Ensemble at the World Shakespeare
Festival, Globe to Globe 2012, Shakespeare's
Globe, London, 21–22 April.

www.worldshakespearefestival.org.uk
Director: Mary Dornford-May
In various South African dialects.

Venus and Adonis
Rose Theatre. 2–25 August.
www.rosetheatre.org.uk
Director: David Pearce

MISCELLANEOUS

(in alphabetical order)

Bingo
The Young Vic, London, 16 February–31 March.
www.youngvic.org
Playwright: Edward Bond
Director: Angus Jackson
Shakespeare: Patrick Stewart
Ben Jonson: Richard McCabe
Revival of the 2010 Chichester Festival Theatre
production.

Cesario
National Theatre, London, The Shed,
22–25 August.
Director: Anthony Banks
A play about Shakespeare's children, Judith,
Hamnet and Susannah, set in 1596.

*The Complete Reworks of Shakespeare: A Live Art
William Shake-up*
Colston Hall, Bristol, 7 July.
A range of 15-minute pieces based on many of
Shakespeare's works. Part of the Bristol
Shakespeare Festival.

Dr. Dee
Coliseum, London, 25 June–7 July.
Composer: Damon Albarn
Director: Rufus Norris
Opera based on life of John Dee.

Forests
Birmingham Repertory Theatre Company and
Barcelona Internacional Teatre production in
association with the Royal Shakespeare
Company. Old Rep Theatre, Birmingham,
31 August–15 September.
www.rsc.org.uk

SHAKESPEARE PRODUCTIONS IN THE BRITISH ISLES

Director: Calixto Bieito
Collage of Shakespeare selections with the theme of forests. In Catalan and English.

The Half
Guy Masterson. Assembly George Square, Edinburgh, 1–26 August.
www.edfringe.com
Performer: Guy Masterson
Playwright: Richard Dormer
A fifty-year-old actor performs his one man *Hamlet*.

In a Pickle
Oily Cart Theatre Company and Royal Shakespeare Company. Swan Room, Stratford-upon-Avon, 23 May–17 June.
www.oilycart.org.uk
Selections for pre-school children.

Maclamear
TRB Engage, Theatre Royal (Ustinov Studio, The Egg), Bath, 15 February–4 March.
www.theatreroyal.org.uk
Playwright: Jim Graham Brown
Shakespeare as TV soap opera featuring Ken Lear as the pub landlord.

The Shakespeare Conspiracy
ACS Random. Chelsea Theatre, World's End Place, King's Road, London, 6–24 November.
www.acsrandom.co.uk
Playwright: Andrew Shepherd
Shakespeare's characters are real: Iago is trying to destroy the world and mankind's last hope is a travel agent called Martin.

Shakespeare Unbound and *The Lover, the Wife*
The London Theatre, 14–19 February.
www.thelondontheatre.co.uk
Playwright and Director: Colin David Reese
In 1623 John Heminges reminisces about his life with Shakespeare.

Shakespeare's Queens
Straylight Australia, Arts Theatre, London, 19 October–3 November.
www.artstheatrewestend.co.uk
Director: Roz Riley
Featuring Elizabeth I, Mary Queen of Scots and Shakespeare.

Silent Shakespeare
To the Moon Company. Lion and Unicorn Theatre, London, 4–8 September.
Director: Petros Michael
Selected scenes performed without words.

A Soldier in Every Son – An Aztec Trilogy
Compañía Nacional de Teatro de México and Royal Shakespeare Company Co-production. Swan Theatre, Stratford-upon-Avon, 29 June–28 July.
www.rsc.org.uk
Playwright: Luis Mario Moncada
Closely inspired by Shakespeare's plays.

What You Will
CMP Productions. Apollo Theatre, London, 18 September–8 October.
Performer: Roger Rees
Shakespeare selections and theatrical anecdotes. One-man show.

THE YEAR'S CONTRIBUTION TO
SHAKESPEARE STUDIES

1. CRITICAL STUDIES
reviewed by CHARLOTTE SCOTT

This has been a refreshingly good year for critical studies: refreshing because many of this year's
books have made me think and feel differently
about Shakespeare's work, but also, perhaps most
surprisingly, about the field of Shakespeare studies itself. While there have been a number of very
scholarly, and in some cases very brilliant, books on
the subject of melancholy, the medieval or the law,
there have also been a couple of books that have
caught me by surprise – not simply in their subject
matter but in their author's ability to write beyond
the perimeters of academic prose and into the kind
of intimate space of belief, thought and feeling
that becomes companionable. Two such books are
David Schalkwyk's *Hamlet's Dreams* and Richard
McCoy's *Faith in Shakespeare*. *Hamlet's Dreams:
The Robben Island Shakespeare* charts what becomes
a deeply personal exploration of pre- and post-
Apartheid South Africa. Beginning with a journey into Schalkwyk's childhood and his encounters
with the plays, the book goes on to examine the
circulation and role of the Alexander text in the
lives of the prisoners on Robben Island. Although
Schalkwyk is deeply and movingly invested in the
story he is also a very self-reflective critic who
wants to interrogate the validity of the often rather
sentimental and patronizing claims for the status
of *The Complete Works* in the daily consciousness of political prisoners. Revealing the ways in
which the media largely contributed to this notion
of a humanist Shakespeare, rescuing the minds of

the oppressed and speaking with solidarity to the
abused, Schalkwyk shows how certain ideals have
been created by the idea of the eloquent, suffering and educated black man: a more contemporary
version of Uncle Tom, but no less sentimentalized.
Focusing on his own often conflicted relationship
with South Africa, Schalkwyk identifies a much
less romantic encounter with the Bard than we
have been initially led to believe. Reading quotations from Matthew Hahn's interview with some of
the signatories on the Robben Island Shakespeare,
including Ahmed Kathrada, Andrew Mlengeni and
Kwede Mkalipi, can be an uncomfortable experience: 'We were ill prepared for this interview',
says Mlengeni, 'especially because I don't think
we were well informed as to what it is you people want . . . "What is the Robben Island Bible?"
What is it that people want to do?'

Are we such 'people' and what is it that we
want? Part of Schalkwyk's project is to uncover
the meaning of the signatures on this text; why
it circulated in the ways that it did and what was
the significance of those passages that were 'chosen' by prisoners. As Mlengeni's comment makes
clear, however, this is not a straightforward task –
much has been invented, extrapolated and invested
in a text that apparently humanized those who
read it as much as he who wrote it. For Schalkwyk, the presence of those signatures reshapes the
text itself, creating a palimpsest of 'personal history,
political conscience, and the peculiar hardships and

possibilities for human companionship in an extremely localized space'. Most importantly, perhaps, the book becomes about the textual, intellectual, aesthetic and ethical relationships that signatures reveal between 'I' (the writer) and 'we' (the readers) and the ways in which these dynamics mark 'Shakespeare' himself. Setting parts of the text against glimpses into the brutal and dehumanizing space of the prison, Schalkwyk interrogates the powerful, often vital, ways in which fictions, dreams and passions make space for the soul in peril; the 'I' that binds us to a version of ourselves and the 'we' that ushers us into the company of others. Taking responsibility for language, for memory (its preservation and erasure), for history and for fiction drives much of the captivating narrative of *Hamlet's Dreams*. Such a journey reveals, I think, and by his own admission, as much (and as little) about the author as about the figures who signed the Robben Island Bible: 'the wide world dreaming on things to come'.

Although very different in its objectives, Richard McCoy's *Faith in Shakespeare* shares an interest with Schalkwyk in the relationship between belief and language. Setting out to explore how the drama sustains our conviction to fictions while at the same time sharpening our awareness of illusion takes McCoy away from historicist interrogations of religious controversy and into the more existential territory of consciousness. Focusing on a range of plays, McCoy examines the most elusive and inscrutable of conditions, the 'willing suspension of disbelief'. Beginning with what constitutes 'faith'; the conditions of its arousal; the creation of 'numinous energy'; and the rapacious appetite for illusion, McCoy sets out the terms of his investigation. Like Schalkwyk's, his is a personal as well as intellectual mission: frustrated, dare I say disillusioned, by the excavations of historicism and the search for Shakespeare's denomination, McCoy finds that it is faith in drama, not God, that drives the trajectory of Shakespeare's career. But it is also about our faith, as readers and interpreters, of literature and the ways in which we commit to and invest in its commitments to illusion. Attending to some of the most explicit invocations of faith in the late plays, as well as the more diverse demands from gods, ghosts or witches, the book traces the extent to which faith manifests as distinct from religion, yet requires, demands even, the same commitment. For McCoy, poetic faith is not a happy accident of aesthetic pleasure but something that 'demands serious intellectual engagement and active goodwill'. In pursuit of the contingents of both McCoy demonstrates not only his ability to possess all the requisites of poetic faith but a deeply personal commitment to the study of literature. Isolating some key terms in his debate – play, illusion, imitation, faith, devotion, belief – McCoy focuses his argument on specific plays, including *As You Like It*, *The Comedy of Errors*, *Othello*, *The Winter's Tale* and *The Tempest*. What he produces is a series of thoughtful, engaging and beautifully written essays which tease out the complexities of what it means to believe in something, as well as to doubt it. Each chapter unpacks one of the central tensions of his thesis, which is the difference between poetic and religious faith (although many Anglicans would dispute such rigorous difference; and many poets have made a career on collapsing it). Exploring forms of mystery allows McCoy to move deftly in and out of the text: despite his overarching commitment to close textual analysis he is very aware of context and frequently situates the plays within the conditions, social, cultural and theatrical, of their performance.

Turning to the explicitly religious, however, we encounter *Shakespeare's Common Prayers: The Book of Common Prayer and the Elizabethan Age*. Here Daniel Swift negotiates 'the hidden history' of the 1549 Book of Common Prayer. The tone of the book may not be to everyone's taste – Swift's writing is often journalistic (he writes at one point of 'My Shakespeare') and he makes rather grand statements to the reader about what they should or should not care about. 'You must begin by tracing what mattered', he declares, 'not by holding onto what appears relevant now.' Having put the reader in his or her place, Swift goes on to compare the Book of Common Prayer to the Magna Carta, the United States Constitution or the Communist Manifesto as a foundational institutional document: 'It mattered more deeply than any other written text of its age precisely because it was where and how the age defined itself.' Produced under the ardent eye of Cranmer this slender volume came to establish one of the central contracts of Protestantism, namely the faithful relationship between the individual and God. Focusing in on Shakespeare, however, Swift traces a 'collision between the playwright and the prayer book in order to portray the writer at work . . . [and establish] that the Book of Common Prayer is his great forgotten source'. Although I imagine that the notion of the Book of Common Prayer as a 'forgotten source' will be irksome to those who have long acknowledged the importance of this subject, Swift's focus on the fluid relationship between drama and liturgy is refreshing if not revolutionary. Finding particular resonance in Shakespeare's dramatic interest in marriage, ceremony, rites and a 'powerful symbolic vocabulary of politics and guilt', he traces a particular narrative in Shakespeare's plays in which we observe clusters of interest in liturgy. Observing such clusters Swift chooses to focus largely on the tragedies. Most interestingly, I think, on *Macbeth*, which he describes as 'centrally formed by interaction with liturgy – by the adoption of its motifs, by the explosion of its tropes and tensions – that the play is a kind of parasite'. This is not a history of the Book of Common Prayer, but it is an often absorbing reminder of the ways in which the Book of Common Prayer, especially for the Elizabethans, promoted a language for living as well as for dying.

By contrast, in Dympna Callaghan's *Who Was William Shakespeare?* the Book of Common Prayer features only rarely, and most specifically, in relation to *The Taming of the Shrew* and *Hamlet*. But despite the inquisitive title, Callaghan is less invested in life writing than in putting the plays in the context of the social, cultural, political and religious institutions through which they emerged. Taking a wider perspective than conventional biographies, Callaghan follows the trajectory of the English Renaissance. The first half of the book focuses on certain aspects or conditions of Elizabethan culture – writing, theatre, status etc. – while the second half of the book provides more specific analyses of the plays. Even here, however, Callaghan follows a generic structure to provide a series of short essays on most of the plays. In this way the book takes on a more obviously didactic element, focusing on many of the plays and issues that support undergraduate work, particularly helpful I think in this respect is the focus on Ovid's *Metamorphoses* and the ways in which Shakespeare imports aesthetic, dramatic and intellectual transformations into his plays. This makes it a very valuable introduction to Shakespeare's plays as well as to some of the most significant ideological imperatives of his age. In search of Shakespeare, however, as her title suggests, Callaghan does not resist the biographer's temptation to make sometimes rather tendentious links between his life and art – the two daughters called Joan (one dead and the other alive) and *The Comedy of Errors*; Shakespeare's 'aged parents' and *King Lear*. They are not as heavy-handed as this may imply but I think the real quality of this book is in the lucid survey of the period.

A cheerful companion to Callaghan's search might be Laurie Maguire and Emma Smith's *30 Great Myths about Shakespeare*. Also published by Wiley Blackwell, this energetic and astutely pitched book offers prescient, humorous, concise and clever essays on conventional assumptions about Shakespeare. Many of these are not strictly 'myths' but what the collection offers is a light-hearted and erudite angle on Shakespeare's work that certainly demystifies some dearly held assumptions. Among my favourites are: 'Hamlet was named after Shakespeare's son'; 'The coarse bits are for the groundlings . . .'; 'If Shakespeare were writing now, he'd be writing for Hollywood'; and 'Shakespeare hated his wife'. As this brief list might suggest, the essays are not simply about refuting certain assumptions, but clarifying, nuancing or exploring them. On the 'myth' entitled 'Boy actors played women's roles', for example, Maguire and Smith do not contest this but explore the commonly held belief that all such boy actors had to be pre-pubescent, and the notion that Elizabethans looked 'past' their males actors to observe them as sexually neutral in the roles of women. The authors of this collection also present that rare ability of being able to cut through much of the ponderous navel-gazing that can accompany Shakespeare criticism and tell it how it is. On the subject of the Sonnets, for example, and whether they are autobiographical, Maguire and Smith simply state: 'some of them are; some of them are not; and some have the appearance (or are designed to have the appearance) of the former'. Such a straightforward approach means that these essays can move from the relatively simple to the complex, and by giving the reader a greater sense of security they are, I suspect, much more receptive to the more complex conditions of authorship, names and narrative that the chapter on the Sonnets then tells. The sanguine and intelligent responses to the 'myths' explored here diffuses much of the anxiety that surrounds the study of Shakespeare, especially for students. There is a jocular emphasis in all these essays on the value of curiosity but also on the value of acceptance, and while we may relentlessly seek to know 'that which we cannot know' there is also much we can and do know about Shakespeare which here is surprising, enlightening and immensely rewarding.

Aimed at a similar readership, and composed with equal clarity, is a new series from Arden called Language and Writing, which takes as its focus a single play. So far titles on *Macbeth* and *The Tempest* have been published, written by Emma Smith and Brinda Charry respectively, but the series promises more, including *Othello*, *Lear* and *Hamlet*. The series offers a formula which provides a very specific focus on language, and each section is broken down to provide different perspectives on or approaches to Shakespeare's semantic art. It is a series that is clearly aimed at students and attempts to provide a concise and fluent account of the play, its contexts (historical and material), sources, genre, character and language. Smith's contribution on *Macbeth* is characteristically well-pitched and clever. She is exceptionally good at writing to a wide audience and providing an erudite survey without taking refuge in complex terminology or knotted interpretations. In one section Smith

draws on an 'internet advice guide to would-be horror film screen writers', which highlights the ways in which Shakespeare's tragedy creates now familiar patterns of suspense and anxiety, attack and aftermath. The point here, as elsewhere, is not that students can only understand Shakespeare through a modern idiom (which would be patronizing indeed) but that Shakespeare's tragedy shares, develops even, a dramatic structure which would become fundamental to its translation into film. Scholars have long acknowledged this period in Shakespeare's career as working towards a certain psychological depth, which Smith exposes as fundamental to suspense fiction – gothic, crime, detective. Smith's focus on the vertiginous experience of the play's language, moving us between moments of clarity and confusion, acceptance and repulsion, is very well expressed and explained. The skill of this volume is that it opens up the interpretative spaces for students, rather than closing them down: there are no critical answers here but permission to see the multi-facetted nature of studying literature and the creative gift that is Shakespeare's drama. Charry's book on *The Tempest* follows the same general formula but is slightly more prescriptive. Her focus is on critical reception, as well as offering a more obviously pedagogic and directive approach in formulating questions for analysis, suggesting ideas and themes to think about and offering alternative approaches to the play. Charry also provides a basic but useful guide to poetic language in the form of some of the key aspects of rhetoric as well as metre and metaphor. In these ways, her edition is probably more appropriate for the transition from school to university. Both books, however, include an essay-writing section, which gives possible questions and ways of approaching or answering them. What will be a relief to many teachers of Shakespeare is that both books repeatedly emphasize the need for students to think through the connections between language and concept, methodology and interpretation.

In contrast, *Medieval Shakespeare: Pasts and Presents*, edited by Ruth Morse, Helen Cooper and Peter Holland, asks more questions than it provides in answers. Rethinking the usefulness of historical periodization, this excellent collection of essays suggests, in often divergent ways, that we rethink certain assumptions about the periodization of Shakespeare studies. As Helen Cooper's introduction argues, Shakespeare's 'whole conception of language and theatre and culture' was saturated by 'the medieval': but what we understand this to mean, however, is the subject of this volume and, as Morse points out, it is a rather roomy and almost exclusively literary term: 'There are no Middle Ages but we cannot do without them.' Rather than provide readers with an alternative model for the historical categorization of thought, this collection of essays proposes that we understand the 'Middle Ages' as a primarily literary concept defined by a particular view of the present as well as the past. The past itself comes under scrutiny as many of the contributors here (especially Morse) consider what informs, creates and defines notions of the past. Here the relationship between historiography and fiction is reconsidered through an analysis of 'Shakespeare as historian'. As Morse wittily notes, however, 'sometimes history contains too many distractions for the stage'. Alongside Shakespeare's direct engagements with history, however, the book focuses in on the semantics through which we have come to understand historical categories. Bruce Smith's essay examines the language of the 'middle', as a point in space and time, as well as the linguistic relationships between antic and antique. Teasing out the complexities of middles, Smith looks at what constitutes a medium, mode and mean. Within this matrix, he reveals the vast and often nebulous nature of the middle (including day, night, age, space, position, average, etc.). Perhaps most compellingly, Smith reveals that the middle is always the present − neither the past nor the future − it is a space of subjectivity. In Smith's readings of the phenomenal past, Hamlet becomes a refugee inhabiting the fiction of his father's past and who moves, both anticly and antiquely, between space and time. For Smith, the middle is not the median but the multiple: in other words, a position of perception which 'encouraged a reader, a watcher, a listener to keep in play multiple themes and multiple ways

of responding, all at the same time'. Smith's perspective leads us into the volume in which follows various and excellent essays: Bart van Es on *Pericles* and the seventeenth century's reconceptualization of the past, including 'a new literary category of "the medieval"'. A. E. B. Coldiron writes on the copious texture of the past, through reprinting and retaining books, and the ways in which 'medieval material came to be vividly present for Shakespeare's world'. Most interesting in this respect is her focus on the Roman plays and the ways in which print facilitated and rehabilitated the Trojan past. Jonathan Hope explores assumptions about the status of Shakespeare's language and the ways in which editorial (and critical) traditions have created a spurious idea of the modern and an ideology of standardization. Hope's essay raises significant questions for the future of the Shakespeare text and to what extent we accept the 'modern' Shakespeare when 'modernized Shakespeare is not "modern" at all'. Cooper provides a wide-ranging essay that explores, by way of personification, iconoclasm and abstraction the migration and development of abstract qualities to states of mind and physical attributes. A subtle and penetrating essay, it takes account of the psychosomatic, grammatical, textual, Christian, allegorical and mythological conditions that inform and direct the representation of both feeling and condition in art. Where the first half of the book asks us to reconsider our assumptions about the medieval past, what it means, when it was and how Shakespeare's work belongs to a culture saturated in the texts and images of the medieval, the second half focuses more specifically on particular plays, the most prominent of which is *King Lear*. Here we meet my favourite essay − although not necessarily the most perfect of the collection − which examines the dynamic between pre- and post-Christian thought in *Lear*. In this chapter Margreta de Grazia understands the tragedy as belonging, very precisely, to what she calls 'the BC/AD partition'. The importance of this double vantage point is that it allows for two potentially contradictory visions: the resurrection and the apocalypse; one vision observes the beginning, the other the end. For de Grazia:

The BC setting licenses Lear to push suffering to an extreme, to make it interminably and irreparably insufferable. The withholding of the salvation programme allows for atrocities that would in its presence have been averted or mitigated, or at least somehow rendered meaningful or redemptive.

Where the characters in the play may have no 'access to salvational history' we, the audience, do but in a move of spectacular skill we set that faith aside 'to make believe the Incarnation had never been anticipated, much less witnessed'. In a double-blow for the audience which reflects the terrifying intensity of this play, the gates are shut on the sunny side.

The last section of this collection focuses on theatre and includes essays from Peter Holland, Tom Bishop, Michael O'Connell and Janette Dillon. As such a line-up suggests, there are some terrific essays here which focus, respectively, on the visual tropes of history in performance and the ways in which we have been fed the medieval through Shakespeare; the vocabulary of 'play', rather than performance, and its moral and spiritual implications as a form of both inquiry and revelation; the influence of mystery theatre on Shakespeare's drama and the particular legacy of blood as a signifier of both brutality and innocence, often beyond the control of the characters; the discovery-space and the ways in which the uses of the stage (what Dillon terms 'a dialogue between place and scaffold') changed as well as accommodated its recent past. David Bevington concludes the volume with a focus on *Richard III* and the first tetralogy, in which he understands history as 'existential', that is, resisting the 'generic shapes of comedy and tragedy'. Inheriting an essentially medieval form of history, Shakespeare's art 'can offer audiences assurance and consolation and a hope tempered by patience and realistic expectations'.

CLOSE ENCOUNTERS

In *Shakespearean Sensations: Experiencing Literature in Early Modern England*, edited by Katherine Craik and Tanya Pollard, the contributors identify space as formative in the arousal of sensation. The volume divides its focus into three: the plays, the playhouse and the poems, in order to examine the ways in which literature affects the reader or observer. Central to this book is the claim that 'Late sixteenth- and early seventeenth-century writers not only identified emotional experience firmly within the body, but also privileged the sensations aroused by imaginative literature.' Privileging a symbiotic relationship between the body and the mind, this collection explores early modern responses to fiction, primarily construed as the dynamic between imagination and emotion. Although the contributors outline the different ways in which emotion can manifest – tears, rage, silence, creeping skin, laughter, involuntary movement etc. – the point of this book is to highlight the interconnectedness between the body and the mind and to demonstrate how drama represents and explores this. Tracing the ways in which such eruptions could be interpreted as moral signifiers, the editors identify certain anxieties about the ways in which literature could jeopardize bodily integrity. As an 'excellent stir-passion', reading was a 'potentially hazardous' experience. Drawing on a wide range of material, including humanist, Latin, medical, Platonic, humeral, anti-theatricalist and philological, the essays in this collection expose the range of human emotion that literature both elicits and represents. While the first section focuses on the plays, providing essays which explore in some detail the sensational effects of *Macbeth*, *Othello* and *Twelfth Night*, the second section on playhouses turns its attention to the audience and what they experience as witnesses, guests and participants in the performance of feeling. Most intriguing here, I think, is Matthew Steggle's analysis of early modern applause which tries to reimagine the audibility and frequency of this most sociable of bodily responses. At the centre of this essay is an analysis of the dynamic between individual reflex and group affiliation, which, as he says, is particularly fascinating in the context of early modern theatre and its alleged role in the formation of early modern subjectivity. Developing his argument through references to applause, Steggle identifies the ways in which the volubility of this action or reflex became a selling point in the reproduction of a play in print. As a sign of quality, 'applause, or its absence, at the end of the first outing of a play was economically important, a make or break moment'. To that end, Steggle argues for an understanding of applause as a form of audience participation – the moments when we raise our hands to share in the performance and recognize our own bodily eruptions as a version of the self in space. The third section, which focuses on poetry, produces some very fine essays, not least of all Michael Schoenfeldt's exploration of empathy in Shakespeare's dramas of pain. Attending to the aesthetic reproduction of suffering in *The Rape of Lucrece*, Schoenfeldt suggests that articulating suffering can produce a kind of prosthetic pain-relief. There is no value, physical or moral, in stoic silence since witnessing suffering produces the most important of human sensations – compassion. A fascinating argument in itself, Schoenfeldt's essay touches on some provocative and perhaps unresolvable issues about exposure and expression.

Broadening such an analysis of feeling through a highly intelligent and rewarding analysis is Drew Daniel's book, *The Melancholy Assemblage: Affect and Epistemology in the English Renaissance*. My favourite book of the year, *The Melancholy Assemblage* is a humorous, scholarly and immensely articulate exploration of melancholy. The book begins with an interrogation of the capacious nature of melancholy; not only the multiple ways in which it can manifest in the human subject but the various means by which we recognize the affliction: 'melancholy as a multiplicity, an expressive array of materials and postures and cases distributed across the social surround'. It is this expressive array that leads Daniel into his theories of assemblage and how early modern melancholy is less a defined set of symptoms (although instantly recognizable) and more a flow of 'on-going, fragile, and reversible correlations between bodies and languages'. Here is the crux, I think, of Daniel's thesis and what makes it so compelling, which is that, although entire and complete in themselves, it is the relational position of objects and subjects,

bodies and feelings that expose their melancholy and not the singular existence of a state of mind. It is a condition or state that is itself in search of some other form of expression or existence – Hamlet's 'seems', Jacques's variable world, Dürer's isolated figures who gaze, together, in competing directions, or Montaigne's rationalism. Moving as it does between the body and the mind, the objects and subjects of our physical realities, it also becomes, crucially, a necessary condition of 'human excellence': 'melancholy becomes the consequence of, and evidence for, commitment to a scholarly ego ideal: a sign that one was bookish, profound, withdrawn, learned, elite, aloof, and ill'. Such behaviours and symptoms, of course, persist today as marks of the academic – to be withdrawn, strange, gauche, depressed, anti-social and brilliant is a requisite of the academy. What, Daniel's book asks, makes it so? And why have we seemingly so readily accepted, recognized and assimilated the melancholy assemblage into our aesthetic and intellectual worlds? The book moves through a range of attitudes to and theories on melancholy, from the philosophical, medical, theoretical and psychoanalytical. It is by way of psychoanalysis, however, that Daniel seems to observe the most fascinating and complex affinities between the body and the mind, the subject and the object. He offers some wonderful insights on *Love's Labour's Lost* as well as *The Merchant of Venice*, where his exploration of the Antonio problem is deeply trenchant and makes sense of the character and the play in a refreshing and penetrating way. For Daniel, Antonio's opening melancholy ushers us into a corrupt and masochistic play-world where self-suffering, obedience and trauma link the protagonists on their punitive journeys through both pain and fantasy: 'what comes into view . . . is a critical sense of Antonio's melancholy and masochism as modes of subjectivity whose insistence upon participation and collaboration force into the open the disavowed conflicts at the heart of the society that surrounds him'. But it is his chapter on *Hamlet* that really stands out as Daniel takes an apparently hackneyed subject – the prince's saturnine mood – and examines precisely what the play does with a character who has 'that within which passes show'. Focusing, for example, on whether Hamlet's first line – 'a little more than kin and less than kind' – should be taken as an aside or a direct address to Claudius is symptomatic of the play's wider investment in the multiplicity of melancholy. Coming down on the side of the 'aside', Daniel asserts:

This speech is in fact an aside, in that it is a speech marked as 'private', but that it is specifically a melancholic aside, and that as such it must be necessarily public, overheard, and shareable, precisely because melancholy as such abides in an interstitial diagnostic and discursive space between the private self and the social body.

Exploring this 'discursive space', Daniel reveals how ideas of melancholy – from the manifest to the imagined – constantly mark not only our relationships to the material or physical world but also our human understanding of conditions like feeling, fulfilment, intellect, pain, mourning and justice. In these ways *The Melancholy Assemblage* brings together its own assemblage of theory and thought in often very brilliant ways. Daniel's is one of those rare voices which emerge perhaps once in a generation to change the way you think not only about Shakespeare but scholarship itself.

Continuing this year's interest in the relationships between the subjective and objective worlds is Margherita Pascucci's *Philosophical Readings of Shakespeare: 'Thou Art the Thing Itself'* and Katharine Eisaman Maus's *Being and Having in Shakespeare*. Although divergent in their methodologies, both books attend to the ways in which Shakespeare's plays can produce an ontological discourse of possession and condition. Pascucci's interest, however, is in reading Shakespeare philosophically, by which she means that we attend to the multiple ways in which the poet–playwright provokes and creates ontological debates. Pascucci's prose may not be to everyone's taste – she enjoys the flamboyant and, by her own admission, being left 'speechless' by a speech – but her commitment to Shakespeare as 'a generator of continuous new thought' can be infectious. She imagines the book as a character who 'had escaped from the

play and had brought us that atmosphere under the form of thought', which, as this quotation implies, often makes it difficult to separate out her argument from her own attachment to the subject. If you can progress, however, through the sometimes hazardous prose you discover some very insightful observations on Time, allegory and poverty. Pascucci understands her own project not as a work of literary criticism but as one of philosophy: to this end she often unhinges the plays from their context or treats them anecdotally but she does offer some decent readings of the plays, especially *Timon of Athens*. In this chapter she examines the way in which 'money is substituted for humanity' and the implications this has for essentialist readings of the play. In *Being and Having in Shakespeare*, however, Maus is much more specifically – and clearly – invested in the dramatic dynamic between subjectivity and possession. Her book, taken from the most recent Oxford Wells Shakespeare Lectures, sets out to unpack a 'poetics of property'. Neither the poetics nor the property, however, can be understood in isolation – in exclusively materialist or rhetorical terms – but only in recourse to the specific constructs of the play-worlds and the ways in which the various characters inhabit, reject, inventory or examine the properties of their dramas. To this end, it is less 'a study of things than of relationships mediated by things'. In what follows, Maus largely focuses on *Richard II*, *The Merchant of Venice* and *King Lear* (as well as a foray into the second tetralogy). In *Richard II*, she explores royal power and the play's representation of the relationship between property holding and power. Maus's take on a slightly hackneyed subject, however, is to define Richard's subjectivity through loss, rather than possession. In *Merchant* she explores forms of obligation, entitlement and obedience through the transmission of property in marriage. Here Maus identifies the ways in which the patrilineal system is affected by 'the abrupt alienation of family wealth accompanying the marriage of a daughter'. *Being and Having* follows an interpretative trajectory by way of the question of inheritance through which Maus brings a number of the plays into conversation with each other and the ways in which 'property transfers' create and direct Shakespeare's drama.

Following a similar and, to use Maus's phrase, 'unashamedly anthropocentric' perspective is *Shakespeare's Sense of Character: On the Page and from the Stage*, edited by Yu Jin Ko and Michael W. Shurgot. Picking up on the renewed interest in character-based criticism this collection brings together a range of contributors, including new and established scholars, as well as theatre practitioners. It is perhaps the latter perspective that is most refreshing about this book. An actor and director, Eunice Roberts, for example, provides an engaging glimpse into the art of playing – how to think through and beyond the perimeters of the self into something or someone else: to become a character, it seems, is to confront two conventionally opposed worlds of theory and practice. The question she frequently returns to is the extent to which actors should analyse or theorize their character and the processes by which they do it.

> Actors may not refer to liminality, but the word does point to what is happening: a journeying from one moment to the next, one character to another, a transformation, stepping over the threshold from the waiting actor, to the actor in action – applying what has been embedded on the 'slate' [sic] in rehearsal into the moment of performance.

Such a process or journey is, of course, at the centre of much of Shakespeare's most penetrating characters and Roberts explores the ways in which by divesting actors of the context of selfhood and leaving them only with the terms of response they are forced to reconsider the very processes by which they identify themselves as a particular character in a particular situation. Some of the essays here, including Roberts's, are very existential and work hard to think through the conditions of characterization. Others, including contributions by Tiffany Stern and Michael Bristol, observe the processes (material and dramaturgical) by which Shakespeare constructs the persona on- (and off-) stage. Bristol's essay confronts the scenes that Shakespeare

'didn't write': the off-stage dark rooms of the bed trick in *All's Well*, for example, and whether it is possible to perform those scenes on stage. Stern examines the actor and director's search for 'original practice' and how we might recover a sense of the early modern actor in rehearsal. Central to her essay is a re-evaluation of the role of 'spontaneity' and Stanislavski in the reimagining of a character's emotional realism. Focusing on cues she identifies how such lines or speech acts prompted as well as contained 'emotional switches'. Cary Mazer's essay, on the other hand, takes issue with many of the terms explored by Stern and suggests that in resuscitating the language of spontaneity, for example, we are 'merely substituting one historical period for another'. The structure of this collection sets up certain debates within the terms through which we approach ideas of character, how – and whether – it is possible to recreate the conditions of early modern theatre practice and to what extent this helps us understand plays and performance. *Shakespeare's Sense of Character* also reinvents the nature of our approaches to character study and the many and wonderful ways in which it feeds into and builds upon putatively competing methodologies. The editors' introduction provides a very cogent summary of the ways in which character-based criticism has fallen in and out of favour and the often unhelpful ways in which it has accompanied an intellectual divide between academic and performance-based criticism. What this collection demonstrates, however, is that the boundaries of character criticism are far wider and far more inclusive than we might have – post-Bradley – been inclined to admit.

Alongside Daniel's *Melancholy Assemblage* perhaps one of the most rewarding of this year's close encounters is a collection called *Shakespeare Up Close: Reading Early Modern Texts* (to which Daniel contributes a wonderful essay on Marlowe). Edited by Russ McDonald, Nicholas D. Nace and Travis D. Williams, this book of nearly forty short essays began in honour of Stephen Booth. Although many of the individual authors do not cite Booth's work, the kinds of approaches that characterized much of Booth's writing – perspicacity, wit, lucidity and precision – are all over this collection. Much like *Shakespeare's Sense of Character*, the editors of this book address and explore the ways in which close-reading has fallen in and out of critical favour in the last century, as well as what we mean by close textual analysis (the three words that make most undergraduates turn pale) and, perhaps most importantly, what the point of it is. Like character criticism, close analysis has taken a beating with many of the most celebrated 'new critics' and formalist critics having been assigned to the scrap heap of Shakespeare studies. What the editors point out here, however, is not only that we all do it most of the time but that learning to read, and learning to interpret, is a fundamentally rewarding part of literary studies. How we use our interpretations, of course, are idiosyncratic and defined by our methodological and ideological leanings but we must necessarily become good readers before we can become good writers. The stated aim of this collection is to redress the balance between text and context and to reinvent the pleasures of language. To that end the book includes a wide range of scholars, many of whom would not be conventionally associated with the kinds of disciplines or 'literary' values that such a collection represents. Nor is it exclusively Shakespearian – to the contrary there are some wonderful essays on Marvell, Marlowe, Milton, Fletcher, Jonson and Herbert. Neither are the essays exhaustive and minute analyses; Michael Schoenfeldt's reading of Herbert's 'Love (III)' is a brilliantly concise but more general survey of the poet's reliance on the pun that is and is not – the idea or image that we all think about but that Herbert never mentions. Looking at the organization of Herbert's poetry, its mysteries, semantics and structures, Schoenfeldt demonstrates how the 'word was made flesh, and still dwells among us, in decidedly human gestures of love and hospitality'. More conventionally technical and detailed in its approach is an explication of Sonnet 60 by Brian Gibbons: here Gibbons unpacks the syntax, metre and meta-poetics of the sonnet to then explore the wider conceptual images at work in the later, metaphysical poetry of Vaughan and Marvell. Most of these essays are masterly exercises in compression and precision but they also demonstrate the rich texture of language analysis through the identification of key skills. A. R. Braunmuller gives a mesmerizing reading of the two couplets that end Act 1 scene 5 of *The Two Noble Kinsmen*. Rather than propose any grand narrative for the interpretation of the play as a whole, Braunmuller deconstructs the apparently proverbial wisdom of the third queen. What he reveals is a remarkable demonstration of the multiple ways in which a word, or words, can perform various meanings beyond the semantic networks of the pun and into the wider, rockier terrain of association and suggestion. But where Braunmuller tenaciously hunts down the topography of the third queen's 'straying streets', McDonald attends to the pleasures of fiction in *Measure for Measure*; Paul Alpers thinks through the point of 'some similes' in Book 9 of *Paradise Lost*; and Brett Gamboa takes on the paradox in *Romeo and Juliet*. Gamboa's essay is particularly good for students, I think, in the ways that it exemplifies and demonstrates the relationship between a close-up and a wide shot. The penultimate section focuses exclusively on *Hamlet*, with contributions by Garrett Stewart, James Grantham Turner, Tiffany Stern, Coppélia Kahn and Lena Cowen Orlin. Kahn gives a beautiful reading of Claudius's speech when he attempts to pray, and Orlin focuses on the signifiers of the space in which Hamlet confronts his mother – closet or gallery. The final section is devoted to endings and exits – largely attending to *King Lear* or Prospero. There are a great many merits to this collection of essays – not only the focus, precision and detail of some of the essays but also the many various and sometimes conflicting approaches they present. Under the auspice of the close reading we encounter the text through the divergent perspectives of materialism, historicism, feminism, performance, formalism – to name but a few. And one of the great achievements here, I think, is not only the quality and range of many of the essays themselves but the renewed and vigorous claim that you can have your text and context, or cake and eat it.

THE TURN OF THE CRITIC

If there is a 'theme' this year then it is one of returning: of turning back to something that was once privileged but has since become at best unfashionable and at worst despised. While some of the books this year have turned us back to the character or the text, Michael Alexander's *Reading Shakespeare* turns us away from the stage and back to the page. Although many of this year's best essays and books work hard to demonstrate that such divisions or oppositions are critically redundant, for Alexander reading is what we largely do with Shakespeare and he is therefore at pains to keep his eye on the text as an article for interpretation: 'for reading and performing are not opposites but different parts of the same process'. Citing various performances in which text has been cut, emended or moved around, Alexander announces, 'in cases such as these, the reader of a full text has everything that Shakespeare wrote (or as close as we can get to this), not a cut-down text or one doctored for cultural reasons'. A provocative comment, and one that makes a nonsense of almost every edition of Shakespeare currently on the market – such a 'full text' is of course the holy grail of Shakespeare editorial scholarship and no mean feat! Alexander's point, however, is that the page is – ultimately – more loyal to Shakespeare than the stage. The problem with such a position is not one of aesthetics or formalism but one of critical integrity: Alexander's observation that 'someone who wants to get at what Shakespeare wrote has to read him' seems grossly at odds with much of the best work of the last ten years, which has worked hard to reposition the Shakespeare text within the theatre as well as the conditions of reading themselves. To this end, *Reading Shakespeare* provides a series of brief introductions or overviews to many of the plays – certainly the most studied plays. The book follows a chronological structure, in which Alexander observes certain clusters of interest or themes within the plays that extend beyond genre. The nature of the book means that it is necessarily general and seeks to close down certain ambiguities rather than open them up. In this way, I imagine, it will be of great service and comfort to students, as it offers clear and concise information regarding sources, context and critical approaches. Alexander is necessarily selective in what he chooses to include and to that end the book tends to reproduce conventional wisdom rather than challenge it. He writes, for example, that the 'theatre Shakespeare wrote for was bare of scenery', a widely held claim that Maguire and Smith complicate in their *30 Great Myths*; and that 'the heart of . . . [Hamlet's] mystery' is an allusion to the disembowelling of Catholic priests, something Drew Daniel might contest. Alexander's book does away with a lot of ambiguity and to that end provides a sure-footed and solid guide to Shakespeare; in the process, however, it also closes down some of the most provocative and fertile areas of discussion. Questions of gender or illusion are dispensed with: 'the audience did not suspend disbelief within a darkened theatre: it collaborated in daylit make-believe' and even on such a stage girls will be girls, even if they are played by boys. Alexander deals with controversy cursorily; from the status of the text to the question of authorship, he will not generally be drawn: 'the idea that "Shakespeare" was written by someone else is a fantasy which appeals to a taste for conspiratorial explanation – and to those who exploit that taste'. Although I agree with Alexander on this point of authorship, such a dismissal can seem irresponsible. Happily, however, it finds a much more fulsome treatment in *Shakespeare Beyond Doubt: Evidence, Argument, Controversy*, edited by Paul Edmondson and Stanley Wells. Setting out the various strands of the authorship controversy, or what the editors prefer to call 'anti-Shakespearean', the book is structured along the lines of a debate, setting out the arguments for possible contenders, the history and context of anti-Shakespeare theories, and then more generally ideas of authorship, education, bibliography and biography. Most of the scholars who have contributed to this collection are very well established Shakespearians who have made their careers on the basis of Shakespeare having written Shakespeare. Although, for example, Alan Stewart presents the case for Bacon and Charles Nicholl for Marlowe both scholars (as does Alan H. Nelson on the subject of Edward de Vere) adopt a suitably laconic tone as they unfold the multiple complexities and incredulities that support the claims of those writers on Shakespeare's work. That's not to suggest, however, that these essays are in any way mocking or derisory of the controversy that has surrounded the plays' authorship; to the contrary, the book takes the subject very seriously but what it aims to do is to unpack the often deeply bizarre assumptions that lie behind such claims (my favourites being that de Vere managed to squirrel away ten plays in a drawer before he died; and that Marlowe was not dead in Deptford but happily living on the continent, 'there to spend the next twenty years penning plays and poems under the borrowed name of a dull-witted but usefully compliant actor called William Shakespeare'). Stewart's scholarly and detailed essay points to a much more revealing phenomenon in the authorship debate, which is that there is a sporadic but nevertheless powerful collection of people who need to keep reinventing an alternative Shakespeare. Defined by all kinds of prejudice – academic, social, economic – ideas about what sort of person could have written these plays and poems are continually reinvented according to the values of any given age. When, as Stewart explores, the cipher theories that had supported Francis Bacon as a contender collapsed, 'It was time for a new William Shakespeare.' This collection of essays charts that search and what it reveals about both believers and non-believers in the hunt for an 'authentic' Shakespeare. Central to the second half of this book is an exploration of some of the ways in which questions of authorship can be determined: Macdonald P. Jackson examines the role of stylometrics and computational analysis; James Mardock and Eric Rasmussen on 'textual evidence' (here, a rather rangy term for how the practicalities of the dramaturgy are incorporated into the plays and could only be done by someone who knew about the theatre). Carol Chillington Rutter's essay identifies and examines one of the

prevailing prejudices against Shakespeare, namely his status and his schooling – how could anyone so provincial and unsophisticated write such material? As her essay makes clear, however, such an attitude tends to reveal more about the sceptic than it does about the playwright. Focusing on the requisites of grammar school education, and the provisions of the King's School, Stratford, Rutter reveals the extent to which Shakespeare would have learned the 'art', of what would become his 'nature'. Barbara Everett provides a wonderful essay on what she calls Shakespeare's 'lies', which are in fact the many and various ways in which the characters in the plays depend on fiction or fantasy. Attending to Ariel's 'song', she observes the '"lie" transforming into play and magic, and leaving behind its base in the story of the play'. Pursuing the idea of the lie in Shakespeare, she asserts: 'the Ghost of Hamlet's royal father is – like much else in the play – less of a problem than a lie; a lie meaning in this context a conventional or fictional vehicle standing in for the many things which actual human beings may experience without being able to categorize or analyse them rationally'. Such a definition of the 'lie' extends the discourse of imagination into a deeper realm which Everett traces with characteristic alacrity. Her point is that the slippage between truth and fiction invites us into the 'most sceptical and hostile elements' of the play-worlds as it also celebrates the 'abundance' of his 'creativity'. Reluctant as I am to give the film *Anonymous* any more air-time, Douglas Lanier's essay on its 'cultural politics' is very good: here he examines how the film stages its own version of authenticity and historical 'accuracy' through a long list of 'intercinematic references'. In other words, we the spectators have formulated an idea of what Shakespearian authorship might look like – gentlemanly, romantic, conflicted and biographical. To that end, Lanier suggests, the iconoclasm of *Anonymous* is pretty conventional stuff, recreating its notion of the ideal author in de Vere instead. What many of these essays reveal – in learned and sanguine ways – is that the authorship controversy is of such stuff as dreams are made on; and that those dreams reveal more about our own cultural politics than they ever do about Shakespeare's.

Moving beyond the boundaries of Everett's 'lie' into an altogether more complex 'fiction', we discover Gillian Woods's *Shakespeare's Unreformed Fictions*. Here, the unreformed refers to what we might call residual Catholicism, although, as Woods takes care to point out, such sectarian or denominational titles can be misleading. Much of the book centres on the often opaque space between pre- and post-Reformation Christianity and precisely what this might have meant for the status of long and fully assimilated traditions. For Woods, fiction takes the place of many of these traditions because it supports the continued existence of certain myths, ceremonies and beliefs whilst at the same time endorsing a politically correct distance through the recognition that no such beliefs contain a 'real presence'. Focusing on the ways in which Shakespeare's drama utilizes and exploits motifs and stories of a recent Catholic past, she identifies the multiple ways in which the 'unreformed' mobilizes meaning in the plays. Woods gives a very trenchant and thoughtful account of the variegated nature of both Christianity and sectarianism. Her articulate introduction establishes that this is not a book on the hunt for Shakespeare's personal faith, or indeed intent on revealing the plays as partisan; what she produces is a much more literary analysis which focuses on the 'imaginative function of the Catholicism in Shakespeare's drama'. The boundaries of this 'imaginative function' are very wide and the Catholic past emerges through multiple signifiers from swearing to saints; and from representations of the past to the structural expectations of genre. In a chapter on *Henry VI*, for example, Woods examines the character of Joan la Pucelle and the way in which this play rehabilitates 'the pleasures and threats of recent unorthodoxy'. In her chapter on *Love's Labour's Lost*, she traces the onomastic significance of the characters and the disjunction between character and role: 'As misnamed theatrical signs, the lords reproduce the violence their characters do to linguistic signs.' In this way, Woods argues, the play redefines 'topical names as comic characterisation'.

Arguing that drama allows for the intrusion of Catholicism into the plays, in ways that were 'prohibited in "real-life"', Woods develops her thesis through the moral and epistemological complexities of *Measure for Measure* and *All's Well That Ends Well*. But, as she reminds us, Catholics looked no different to Protestants and this lack of defining racial or sartorial distinction compounded theories of duplicity. 'Dazzling displays', she writes, 'produced moral and semantic corruption as gullible viewers were drawn to papist hypocrisy.' The second half of the book focuses on *King Lear* and *The Winter's Tale*. Here, she traces the idea and status of fiction within both plays, examining forms of possession in *Lear*, and interpretation in *The Winter's Tale*. Woods's book forms an excellent bridge between McCoy's theatrical faith and Cooper, Holland and Morse's past: collectively these books reinforce the multivalent nature of fiction, form and faith in Shakespeare's drama.

PROXIMITIES: SPACE, FAMILY AND COMPANY IN SHAKESPEARE

Perhaps a motley crew to bring together but some of this year's books tackle, in divergent ways, people, places and things in Shakespeare's drama. Two books to take on members of Shakespeare's families are Tom MacFaul's *Problem Fathers in Shakespeare and Renaissance Drama* and Jennifer Higginbotham's *The Girlhood of Shakespeare's Sisters: Gender, Transgression and Adolescence*. In *Problem Fathers*, MacFaul sets out to examine the role and representation of the father in late sixteenth- and early seventeenth-century drama. Following a trajectory that begins with Gorboduc, and ends with Massinger's Malefort, 'the worst father in all Renaissance drama', the book explores a range of brutal, emotional, punitive, tender and largely tragic paternal relationships. There is of course no father without the child, so much of MacFaul's work is invested in unpacking the dramatic tensions of those relationships, which, as he observes, are largely male (daughters are in the minority and appear largely in discussions of *Titus*, *Lear*, *The Winter's Tale* and *The*

Tempest). Although he doesn't invest in any particular theoretical model, MacFaul is clearly interested in the psychology, as well as pathology, of this relationship and his focus moves between historicized and theorized versions of the dramatic father. The range of the book is impressive since MacFaul manages to cover or at least touch on a good many plays – some of them relatively obscure – but what he builds up is an extensive portrait of the presence of the father in early modern drama. The structure of the book follows a linear narrative in which MacFaul identifies a pattern of interest in the representation of fathers on stage. Largely informed by the social and cultural structures through which the plays are produced, much of the drama discussed here seems to reflect visions and versions of early modern patriarchy: in other words, the drama tends to buy into the culture's expectations of fatherhood, rather than challenge them. Although MacFaul identifies the father as 'sacred', he also acknowledges that 'fathers are the real and original nothing':

The role of fathers in drama is rather like the role of kings in chess: they are crucial to the structure of the game, yet their scope of action is limited; much of their value comes from their vulnerability, and the necessity of either defending them (in comedy), or attacking them (in tragedy).

But as the book goes on to demonstrate, the representation and idea of the father supports – although not exclusively – a psychological and emotional development in drama that extends beyond the structural and into discourses of feeling, obligation, denial, blessing and horror. What is perhaps most revealing here is that the 'father' is not a fixed state determined by reproduction but a role in which it is notions of 'fatherhood' that confer the terms of value. With this in mind we can see the complexities of Lear or Titus or Shylock unravel, caught as these characters are in a seemingly endless struggle between revulsion and need; authority and abnegation. For MacFaul, *King Lear* brings many of the book's concerns into a single focus: '*King Lear*, like the parable, can be seen as a kind of tragicomedy – that is, the genre that

tries to resolve the tensions inherent in the age's tragedies and comedies.' The women of the book are certainly in the minority and MacFaul observes a quite specific division between the sexes, perhaps most tellingly in the observation that marriage may release daughters from their fathers but it does not release sons in the same way. More specifically focused on women, however, and gender in general, is Jennifer Higginbotham's *The Girlhood of Shakespeare's Sisters: Gender, Transgression and Adolescence*. Although both these books take one gender or the other as their focus, Higginbotham is more widely interested in the question of gender itself – biological, social, cultural or mutable. This book examines what it means to be a 'girl', and within those terms what it also means to be a woman. Higginbotham's thesis is that the terms by which the female sex is identified confer very specific (although not unchanging) values upon the female body and that by examining those terms, and those values, we discover some of the ways in which the early modern period was both defining and separating the girls from the boys. In pursuit of her argument she uncovers the often nuanced and subtle ways in which women were typified: to be called a girl, damsel, maid or wench, for example, is to be identified as belonging to a certain age, status or attitude. But, more revealingly, these terms are not fixed but are always in the process of redefinition according to who is speaking (and what they are speaking about). In this way, a 'wench' can be a term of endearment, an indictment of a woman's sexuality, a recognition of social status or youth – or indeed an insult. Similarly, the term 'girl', which is the real focus of this book, is revealed to be a multifunctional word which nevertheless goes through its most profound transition at the beginning of the seventeenth century. Unsurprisingly, Higginbotham uncovers the virulent sexism behind the organisation of such signs; she is less forthcoming, however, on the troubling ways in which women are infantilized in the male erotic imagination. To be a girl is – as this book lucidly argues – to be vulnerable in ways that support subservience but it is also to be child-like in a way that promotes rather than inhibits sexuality. Higginbotham is perhaps at her best when exploring the question of gender more generally in the period and she supports her analysis with some very insightful comments on the plays. Through an exploration of Shakespeare's representation of Joan la Pucelle in *1 Henry VI*, for example, she examines the troubling presence of the fictionalized female body: as a 'girl' Joan is figured as transgressive and threatening; she is also understood as masculine and pregnant to the extent that, for Higginbotham, 'Joan's girlishness helps to deconstruct the masculine/feminine binary in ways that render both terms virtually empty of meaning.' Perhaps most importantly in the discourses of gender that this book proposes, *The Girlhood of Shakespeare's Sisters* traces how the life cycles of the female body did not define the terms of its representation until the seventeenth century: in other words, puberty, pregnancy or the menopause were not recognized as informing the signs through which women were defined. The progress from infant to adulthood was regarded as continuous 'rather than marked by a break'; to this end words like 'girl' were largely used to locate the subject in a state of disempowerment rather than at a specific age. Taking in a wide range of texts from the sixteenth and seventeenth centuries, Higginbotham shows how 'girl' is a highly nuanced and historically complex term that not only 'enabled early modern texts to acknowledge the roles of female characters in liminal social and sexual positions' but also charted the 'general push to fashion the English language into a vernacular replacement for Latin [which] worked in concert with an interconnected shift in cultural constructions of gender'. In the course of her analysis she confronts some of the most instrumental processes by which meaning is made and the changing social vistas through which we have observed, as well as defined, the 'girl'.

Although Higginbotham focuses specifically on the term girl, rather than women or females, she shows how certain cultural constructions of gender take place both in and around the drama of this period and the ways in which the seventeenth century produces a marked shift in perceptions towards women. In *Shakespeare and Outsiders*, however,

Marianne Novy includes 'women' as a category in her exploration of 'outsider issues'. For Novy, women inhabit 'the ambiguous semi-outsider status' in Shakespeare's plays because they can move between institutional spaces of both acceptance and rejection; they can criticize conventional expectations but remain firmly embedded in them. Such a degree of fluidity and ambiguity is central to Novy's thesis, since her definition of the outsider is not someone who is always or absolutely excluded from the societies they live with but someone (and it is usually an individual, rather than a collective) who is moved in and out of positions of acceptance. Crucially, of course, such an outsider has seemingly little control over their own status, defined as they are by the social expectations of the play-worlds to which they belong. To this end, the outsiders in each play may change, moving like chess pieces from the periphery to the middle, or, less frequently, out of the game altogether. In this way the definition of an outsider is somewhat slippery so Novy organizes her book according to certain themes, genres or attitudes which allow her to locate key conflicts in Shakespeare's drama. As she points out, all of the plays are concerned in some way with the tensions produced by a conflict between the individual and the collective: much of this tension resides in the clash of competing expectations and needs, whether to reign, love, marry, succeed or destroy, and how the plays chart an individual's search for fulfilment necessarily re-evaluates certain structures of cohesion. She takes on the more obvious outsiders: 'those who are part of a resented or subordinated group' as well as those who become so emotionally powerful within the plays that they redefine the perimeters of inclusion and exclusion. It is through this perspective that the book is at its most interesting: exploring 'outsider issues' in *King Lear* and *Twelfth Night*, for example, Novy uncovers the complex and often relentless ways in which the space of the outsider is continually occupied and reoccupied by different characters. In *Lear* she notes that unlike many of Shakespeare's outsiders the greatest division occurs not between classes or ethnicities but between family members; such divisions are so profound and far-reaching that they introduce the more conventional conditions of madness, poverty or exile. Novy focuses on Shakespeare's treatment of the interrelationships between emotional, social, situational and economic forms of exclusion and the ways in which the play-world renegotiates conventional terms of sympathy. Understanding or sympathizing with the condition of the outsider is central to Novy's book and to that end she positions her readings of four plays largely within their historical context. What she reveals is that despite the apparently fixed status of the outsider – beggar, Jew, Moor, bastard, melancholic or unmarried, for example – characters may move quite easily between inclusion and exclusion and that Shakespeare's drama is perhaps most invested in exploring the extent to which we empathize with or rehabilitate the alienated figure of the outsider.

Less existential, but none the less concerned with key figures in Shakespeare's theatre, is Bart van Es's *Shakespeare in Company*. From the outset, van Es declares that this book is 'about the meeting of a classically educated poet and a company of actors. That meeting was not unusual.' Recasting Shakespeare as a 'classically educated poet', rather than an 'actor' is somewhat unusual in Shakespeare studies, even though scholars have tried assiduously to prove Shakespeare's credentials as an intellectual as well as an artist. But what van Es goes on to demonstrate, however, is that much of what we thought exceptional about Shakespeare is quite ordinary and much of what we thought ordinary is, in fact, exceptional. Following the development of the public theatre and the companies of actors who began to establish themselves there, this book repositions Shakespeare within a thriving cohort of very clever men, who, as products of their grammar school education, began to develop and explore the ever-expanding possibilities of the new public stage. In line with a number of recent books on the subject of Shakespeare's education, van Es shows that Shakespeare's interest in rhetoric, his explorations of passion and his intellectually affective landscape of history and emotion were entirely in-line with the expectations of the period. The first half of the book focuses

on the 'conventional' Shakespeare, who begins to develop his drama through what van Es calls 'normative imitation'; in other words, 'For all its brilliance, Shakespeare's writing in the first few years of the 1590s follows the compositional habits of its time.' Unexceptional Shakespeare is, for van Es, the starting point for what would become one of Shakespeare's greatest theatrical legacies – the development of a symbiotic relationship between character, actor and text. The book follows the roles of repertory companies, as well as individual actors, in shaping Shakespeare's drama. Van Es's structure is largely chronological, which allows him to discern a specific narrative not only within the creation of a thriving public theatre but also in the work of the playwright himself. To that end, van Es reveals how becoming a shareholder in the Chamberlain's Men, for example, impacted on his dramatic development of character; how a play's adaptation for certain companies could be orchestrated by someone other than its author; and how certain moments, 1594 for example, would become a watershed in Shakespeare's career. Here van Es follows the recent work of Alan Farmer, Zachary Lesser and Holger Symes and identifies that 'the events of this year . . . transformed, in an instant, his day-to-day working practice', though for van Es 1594 marks the end of Shakespeare's interest in print – rather than its beginning. *Shakespeare in Company* is at its most fascinating, however, on the actors that would come to define and shape the characterization of many of his most powerful plays. Identifying certain 'clusters of characters with their own distinctive locale and ethos' van Es observes an 'author who is himself bound up in a sustained relationship with the actors for whom he writes'. It is from this standpoint that we move from unexceptional Shakespeare to 'Shakespeare's singularity' – not only as 'sharer, performer and dramatist' but also as someone who used these positions to develop his own unique style and practice. The chapters on Burbage and Armin, particularly, provide fascinating insights into the men behind the roles and the ways in which Shakespeare developed both his comic and tragic heroes. On Armin, van Es claims, 'The Fool in *Lear* offers the most powerful and complex example of the influence that the actors had on Shakespeare': on the Children's Companies, van Es observes Shakespeare borrowing from and competing with 'the cynical and misogynistic comedies of the boys' stage'. Ending with an analysis of Shakespeare's later work, van Es argues that this phase in Shakespeare's career reveals that 'Not only did the playwright frequently collaborate with other writers, he can also be seen to imitate them much more closely than before.' Above all, however, *Shakespeare in Company* reveals that – contrary to our modern creative sensibilities – it was Shakespeare's entrepreneurialism that made him a great writer, and that his business acumen and financial success gave him the liberty and the experience to develop the plays that would come to define much of western drama.

From the people and places of Shakespeare's working life, however, we move to the 'things' that shape and direct early modern drama on stage. In *Shakespeare and the Materiality of Performance* Erika T. Lin turns her gaze towards the networks of signs and images that inform the experiences of early modern audiences. Rather than offering a homogenized view of theatre, however, where modern audiences are encouraged to identify with early modern ones, Lin establishes that our theatrical experiences are radically different and how we enter into, perceive and understand the dramatic stage has little in common with our ancestors. To that end, she aims to uncover or recover the signs, sensations, staging practices and codes that governed early modern perceptions of the public theatre. In assessing this 'theatrical language', Lin turns to the notion of materiality itself, something which she rightly points out has become a significant focus of Shakespeare studies. But for Lin, the material can be more than the object or the thing; it can be a semiotic system in which meaning becomes intelligible through the shared cultural or 'presentational process[es]' in which drama is performed. Perhaps the most significant aspects of the book are those which focus on redefining our understanding of the performance space; foremost here is her re-evaluation of Weimann's *locus* and *platea*. Contrary to Weimann's widely

adopted theories of how we can read the spaces of action on stage, Lin suggests that 'theatrical authority' derived from 'the dynamic interplay between representation and presentation'; this she explores through various 'privileged' moments or scenes. Equally important is Lin's thesis that metatheatrical allusions or commentaries within the plays are not self-referential explorations of the relationship between illusion and reality but explorations of the ways in which early modern spectators responded to their own status as audience, and the questions – moral and epistemological – that such awareness provokes. Central to Lin's book is an understanding of early modern performance as something that extends beyond the stage and into the wider fabric of entertainment – jigs, progresses, bearbaiting, execution, dismemberment or indeed anything that takes place as a communal social practice. To this end, she emphasizes the role of the theatre and 'entertainment' in the construction of early modern lives, a role – and a visual vocabulary – that we need to learn in order to fully appreciate the differences, rather than the similarities, of our play-worlds.

Keeping such differences in mind, I turn to Colin Burrow's *Shakespeare and Classical Antiquity*, which is one of the finest books to have reached my desk this year. The idea of historical and cultural difference is perhaps nowhere more sharply defined than in the study of classics. Having dropped almost entirely out of our modern curriculum even Shakespeare's 'small Latin and less Greek' would now be something to be proud of. And even more so, having read Burrow's book. In this learned, witty, engaging and eloquent contribution to the Oxford Topics Series, Burrow establishes that not only should we re-read Jonson's comment in the light of changing attitudes to the classics but that Shakespeare was writing during a period of transition in England where certain classical aesthetics, including art and architecture, had yet to become established in the public imagination. Examining which elements of classical antiquity most influenced Shakespeare's works, including their translations and adaptations, Burrow establishes the vast impact that certain classical writers had on his dramatic imagination. As each chapter focuses on a particular writer – Seneca, Virgil, Plutarch and Ovid, for example, as well as offering explorations of Cicero, Terence and Plautus – Burrow establishes that what defines Shakespeare's relationship with the classics is not so much what he knew but what he did with that knowledge. Above all, as this book beautifully demonstrates, Shakespeare, like any very brilliant writer, learned to use, abuse, imitate, mangle, forget and celebrate the stories that shaped his creativity and the medium he worked in.

AND FINALLY . . .

A brief round-up of some of this year's other highlights: John Michael Archer's *Technically Alive: Shakespeare's Sonnets* is a dense but mostly rewarding exploration of Heidegger's 'technology' within the context of the *Sonnets*. Examining various forms of technology – from the practical to the esoteric – Archer considers the terms, conditions and values of 'life' within the *Sonnets*. Two other books that are also, though perhaps more variously, concerned with 'technology' are *Making Space Public in Early Modern Europe: Performance, Geography and Privacy*, edited by Angela Vanhaelen and Joseph P. Ward, and *Shakespeare, Jonson, and the Claims of the Performative*, by James Loxley and Mark Robson. In *Making Space Public* we find a collection of essays which explore the idea of space in divergent ways: from the theoretical, practical, geographical, social and imagined these essays variously consider the instability of spaces and how we come to define as well as behave in them. Drawing on a range of early modern European texts, including Steven Mullaney on *Hamlet*, this book focuses on the volatile dynamics between the private and the public. In *Shakespeare, Jonson and the Claims of the Performative*, the contributors reassess certain theoretical claims about the performative and the conditions by which we both identify and understand its existence in and outside language. Heavily influenced by Cavell as well as De Man, Derrida and Heidegger, they offer interpretations of a range of plays by Shakespeare, including *Hamlet*, *Richard III* and *A Midsummer Night's Dream*. Lastly on my whistle-stop tour is *Shakespeare and Donne: Generic Hybrids and the Cultural Imaginary*, edited by Judith H. Anderson and Jennifer C. Vaught. A wonderful topic in itself, but the essays largely play it safe by offering a range of instances where the two writers might display an affectionate bent for the same subject. Most of the essays approach their subjects through formal, theoretical or philosophical perspectives and to that end they occasionally offer really fascinating readings of the ways in which language and theory can behave in these poems. Most compelling here is the final essay on the 'imagination', a capacious form of both thinking and being, which, as Judith H. Anderson observes, manifests in the works of these two writers quite differently as well as comparably: 'in the soliloquies, however, Shakespeare might be said to have moved onto this stage what Donne engaged in a more intimate medium, and Donne might be said to have brought speaking fictions into contemporary life.'

WORKS REVIEWED

Alexander, Michael, *Reading Shakespeare* (Basingstoke, 2013)

Anderson, Judith H. and Jennifer C. Vaught, eds., *Shakespeare and Donne: Generic Hybrids and the Cultural Imaginary* (New York, 2013)

Archer, John Michael, *Technically Alive: Shakespeare's Sonnets* (New York, 2013)

Burrow, Colin, *Shakespeare and Classical Antiquity* (Oxford, 2013)

Callaghan, Dympna, *Who Was William Shakespeare? An Introduction to his Life and Works* (Chichester, 2013)

Charry, Brinda, *The Tempest: Language and Writing* (London, 2013)

Craik, Katherine A. and Tanya Pollard, *Shakespearean Sensations: Experiencing Literature in Early Modern England* (Cambridge, 2013)

Daniel, Drew, *The Melancholy Assemblage: Affect and Epistemology in the English Renaissance* (New York, 2013)

Edmondson, Paul and Stanley Wells, eds., *Shakespeare Beyond Doubt: Evidence, Argument and Controversy* (Cambridge, 2013)

Eisaman Maus, Katharine, *Being and Having in Shakespeare* (Oxford, 2013)

Higginbotham, Jennifer, *The Girlhood of Shakespeare's Sisters: Gender, Transgression, Adolescence* (Edinburgh, 2013)

Ko, Yu Jin, and Michael W. Shurgot, eds., *Shakespeare's Sense of Character: On the Page and From the Stage* (Farnham, 2012)

Lin, Erika T., *Shakespeare and the Materiality of Performance* (Basingstoke, 2012)

Loxley, James and Mark Robson, *Shakespeare, Jonson and the Claims of the Performative* (Abingdon, 2013)

MacFaul, Tom, *Problem Fathers in Shakespeare and Renaissance Drama* (Cambridge, 2012)

Maguire, Laurie and Emma Smith, *30 Great Myths About Shakespeare* (Chichester, 2013)

McCoy, Richard C., *Faith in Shakespeare* (New York, 2013)

McDonald, Russ, Nicholas D. Nace and Travis D. Williams, eds., *Shakespeare Up Close: Reading Early Modern Texts* (London, 2012)

Morse, Ruth, Helen Cooper and Peter Holland, eds., *Medieval Shakespeare: Pasts and Presents* (Cambridge, 2013)

Novy, Marianne, *Shakespeare and Outsiders* (Oxford, 2013)

Pascucci, Margherita, *Philosophical Readings of Shakespeare: 'Thou art the thing itself'* (Basingstoke, 2013)

Schalkwyk, David, *Hamlet's Dreams: The Robben Island Shakespeare* (London, 2012)

Smith, Emma, *Macbeth: Language and Writing* (London, 2013)

Swift, Daniel, *Shakespeare's Common Prayers: The Book of Common Prayer and the Elizabethan Age* (Oxford, 2013)

Van Es, Bart, *Shakespeare in Company* (Oxford, 2013)

Vanhaelen, Angela and Joseph P. Ward, eds., *Making Space Public in Early Modern Europe: Performance, Geography and Privacy* (Abingdon, 2013)

Woods, Gillian, *Shakespeare's Unreformed Fictions* (Oxford, 2013)

2. SHAKESPEARE IN PERFORMANCE
reviewed by RUSSELL JACKSON

This year's books include some notable collections of essays on early modern theatres; expert, searching and enjoyable coverage of the Shakespearian contribution to the 'cultural Olympiad' that accompanied the athletic goings-on in and around the arenas of the capital; an important monograph reorienting approaches to journalistic reviewing; stimulating work on Shakespeare in the cinema and the (even) newer media; and the more lapidary reflections of one of the great theatre-makers of our time.

The polysemous potential of the early modern stage is a recurring theme in the essays collected in *Shakespeare's Theatres and the Effects of Performance*, edited by Farah Karim-Cooper and Tiffany Stern. At once imposing in its material presence and available for multiple and shifting identities, the very framework of the theatre was more than an empty space. Discussing the scene in which Pindarus goes up a hill to observe the battle while remaining on stage (*Julius Caesar*, 5.3) Stern suggests that the actor's ascending a ladder and then coming down as

he reports the fall of Titinius embodies the action described: 'If Pindarus approaches and then rises up a ladder while making this speech [5.3.25–30], that places his motion in opposition to Titinius', his "up" ironizing the way Titinius has been forced down; while the fact that he is on a hill that is not a hill draws attention to the way things are not as they seem' (28). Although the specific effect suggested here may be too subtle, Stern's general point holds: 'The same theatrical prop can hold two different functions: when it is part of the story, it worryingly literalizes the tale; when it is a metaphor for something else it queries the drama's reality but, by calling attention to seeming and being, can intensify the meaning of the poetic or dramatic language used around it' (28–9). Lucy Munro, examining special effects under the arresting title '"*They eat each other's arms*": Stage Blood and Body Parts', suggests convincingly that 'the force of the early modern stage's use of blood and dismembered body parts lies in its capacity for simultaneous naturalism and stylization' (77), a perception that supports a reading of such episodes as Imogen's discovery of Cloten's headless corpse as sophisticated rather than infelicitous or clumsy. In 'Within, Without, Withinwards: The Circulation of Sound in Shakespeare's Theatre' Bruce Smith develops a similarly persuasive argument for the versatility of the audience's understanding of the significance of the exchange of looks among characters as indications of inwardness, and of on- and off-stage (and extra-theatrical) sounds, as signifiers both literal (someone is knocking at the door) and metaphorical, components of the plays' poetic fabric. In the scene of Duncan's murder, the knocking at the gate, the bell and the noise made by the actor's feet on the boards of the stage accompanying Macbeth's address to the 'sure and firm-set earth' (*Macbeth*, 2.1.56) are 'sounds that exceed the meaning of the words being spoken, as sounds that fix the scene in the perceiver's ears'. Like the actor's words describing the vision of the dagger, they linger after the actor has left the stage: 'The dagger, the bell, the footsteps: it is not just words and non-verbal sounds that are fused and confused but things heard and things seen' (188). The essays in this volume are rich in such suggestions of the complex effects of material elements of the theatre and their relationship with the poetic discourse of the works performed, a stage (literally) beyond the exposition of meanings in the playhouse according to their simpler diegetic function as doors, balconies and so on. Farah Karim-Cooper's 'Touch and Taste in Shakespeare's Theatres', although persuasive in its presentation of the physical experience of playgoing, and the proposition that 'contact among the audience was a condition of performance' (235), is less convincing in demonstrating 'how tactility might affect the reception of plays'. Nevertheless, consciousness of the ways in which the audience was described – 'an aggressive crowd of people, pushing, shoving and buzzing with sounds, smells and tactile energy' – is valuable as a reminder of the nature of the 'live event' in the period. Like Holly Dugan, in her essay on the smell of the Hope Theatre, 'As dirty as Smithfield and as stinking every whit' (171), Karim-Cooper places the drama in an immediate, powerful and at times pungent context, that can only have enhanced appeals to the senses of taste, scent and touch within the diegesis.

In many respects *Shakespeare and the Making of Theatre*, edited by Stuart Hampton-Reeves and Bridget Escolme, complements *Shakespeare's Theatres and the Effects of Performance*, although its contributors range beyond the early modern theatre to take in more recent performances and other media. There is a similar attention to the multiple ways in which visual and other signs function, exemplified in Christie Carson's discussion of 'the extent to which Shakespeare's plays *play* with our vision, our expectations and our understanding of the way the theatre can make us "See better" (*King Lear*, 1.1.152) by seeing differently' (69, emphasis in the original). Again, attention is drawn to the traffic between metaphorical and literal meaning, the flexibility of the medium and the playwright's enjoyment of the opportunities it offers. In essays on exits and entrances, sound and silence (to be set alongside Bruce Smith's in the Stern and Karim-Cooper volume) and other poetic practicalities, the reader's attention is focused on the Protean potentiality of theatres of the period. Taken together, these volumes bring together some of the best scholarship and liveliest and most suggestive work being done currently on Shakespearian performance in its own time.

From one Globe to its successor: *A Year of Shakespeare: Re-living the World Shakespeare Festival*, edited by Paul Edmondson, Paul Prescott and Erin Sullivan, collects reviews by a team of contributors of the productions that constituted the combined contributions of the Royal Shakespeare Company and Shakespeare's Globe (thirty-eight productions in six weeks at the latter) and the BBC to the 2012 Cultural Olympiad. The spirit of the thirty reporters is one of generosity towards the performers and their audiences, while at the same time a keen watch is kept on the cultural and artistic faultlines revealed by many of the events.

In 'Olympic Performance in the Year of Shakespeare' Erin Sullivan draws attention to the significance, sometimes beguiling and often downright puzzling, of the opening and closing ceremonies for the Olympics and Paralympics, not least the declamation in Danny Boyle's inaugural spectacular of Caliban's 'Be not afraid. The isle is full of noises' by Kenneth Branagh disguised as Isambard Kingdom Brunel. This established Shakespeare as a presence, if not a presiding genius, though it was not clear quite why we should *not* be afraid of the spectacle of an Industrial Revolution that was destroying a folksy but at least peaceable, green and pleasant land. The Globe's contribution was one among many in this 'Year of Shakespeare', which included a 'blockbuster exhibition' at the British Museum, a season of history plays on BBC TV under the familiar title of 'The Hollow Crown', and many other performances, digital projects and exhibitions. Whatever one made of it – and there was a lot of unravelling of agendas and analysis of impact to be done – the year marked, in Sullivan's words, 'the most intensive investigation of Shakespeare's relevance to modern global culture that any of us have ever seen, the fruits of which will remain subjects of discussion, delight and debate for many years to come' (11).

The reviews in *A Year of Shakespeare*, a valuable and engaging record in themselves, can be read alongside the essays in *Shakespeare Beyond English: A Global Experiment*, edited by Susan Bennett and Christie Carson. Whereas the former are primarily reports, albeit with an appropriate evaluative content, the latter engage more fully in discussions of the political and social implications of the performances. *A Year of Shakespeare* ranges beyond Stratford and the South Bank, to take in other productions during the *annus mirabilis*, but *Shakespeare Beyond English* is Globe-centred. Many of its contributors offer little by way of description, but provide important information on the background of versions the effects of which were sometimes compromised to a degree by brief transposition to a theatre whose configuration did not always serve them well, or whose significance in their own society was appreciated fully only by spectators from their country of origin. This dimension of 'festival Shakespeare' has been the subject of lively debate for some time, and the 'afterwords' by Abigail Rokison and Bridget Escolme focus attention on the promises and frustrations of the event, not least the brevity of the visits and the fact that only Shakespeare was on view. As Escolme observes, 'The Globe to Globe Festival has provoked some questions its audiences might not otherwise have thought to ask about history and its uses' (310). In 'From Thence to England' Rokison reflects on the Globe's own *Henry V*, the opening production, and on the festival as a whole, not least because of the 'pervading sense of nationalistic fervor and its influence on the moods of audiences and reviewers' (306). Some performances at the Globe are more easily apprehended through the necessarily briefer reports in *A Year of Shakespeare*: Sarah Olive's account there (125–7) of the Vakhtangov Theatre's *Measure for Measure* gives details of the action not available in Kevin A. Quarmby's essay in *Shakespeare beyond English* (48–52); the discussion of the significance of the Maori *Troilus and Cressida* (*Shakespeare Beyond English*, 35–46) gives hardly any sense of what was seen and heard by the audience, for which one has to turn to Stephen Purcell in *A Year of Shakespeare* (210–12), where it is followed by Paul Prescott's review of the Wooster Group's deconstructive version of the same play in Stratford-upon-Avon. Peter Kirwan and Suzanne Gossett offer differing but complementary perspectives on the Habima's *Merchant of Venice* at the Globe and the demonstrations that accompanied the performance (Kirwan in *A Year of Shakespeare*, 128–32; Gossett in *Shakespeare beyond English*, 269–72). The essays in *Shakespeare Beyond English*, each given with a title appropriate to its theme, are arranged according to the six weeks of the Globe's schedule, while those in *A Year of Shakespeare* are arranged in alphabetical order of the plays. Between them, and taken together with the web-based site www.yearofshakespeare.com set up as part of the project funded jointly by the Arts and Humanities Research Council and the universities of Birmingham and Warwick, these volumes constitute a major resource for the study of the manifold ramifications of 'global Shakespeare' as it existed during the period of the Olympiad. Until the end of 2014 the web site can be accessed on line, and after that will be preserved by the Shakespeare Birthplace Trust. As Paul Edmondson concludes in the final essay in *A Year of Shakespeare*, 'Isles will always be full of noises, sweet, delightful, unhurtful, twangling, humming, dreamlike, even festive' (270). The prospect seems more inviting than the invitation to applaud the Industrial Revolution for which Caliban's speech was co-opted in Danny Boyle's Olympic ceremony.

Global – or at least, not English – Shakespeare features as one might expect in Estelle Rivier's *Shakespeare dans la maison de Molière*, a survey of productions of the plays by the Comédie-française. Although she provides an authoritative overview of the history of Shakespearian performance by the company before 1900, the emphasis is very much on the twentieth and twenty-first centuries. Shakespeare can hardly be said to have been a staple of the company's repertoire, but has been 'continually present' (36) since 1904, the date chosen by Rivier as a starting point. The presence of contemporary dramatists in its repertoire was stipulated in the Napoleonic 'Moscow decree' of 1812, in which the Emperor turned aside from the cares of campaigning to consider the cultural needs of his country. The principle of '*alternance*' makes the company's programme what is known in English as 'true repertory', with a frequent turnover of productions accumulated in the course of seasons, and it achieves the round figure of 750 performances a year across three currently available venues in Paris (30). The choice of plays across the decades since 1904 may surprise: four productions of *Hamlet*, one of *Pericles*, two of *Coriolanus* (one of them the controversial 1932–3 staging), three of *Twelfth Night*, two each of *The Taming of the Shrew*, *A Midsummer Night's Dream*, *The Merchant of Venice*, *As You Like It* and *The Winter's Tale* – but no *King Lear* or *Julius Caesar* and only one history play, *Richard III*, directed by Terry Hands in 1972 (223). Rivier identifies six stages in the company's dealings with Shakespeare: a preponderance of tragedies, often heavily 'adapted' to contemporary thinking, between the turn of the century and the Second World War; a postwar period dominated by comedies presented without significant innovation; the stir caused by a free-wheeling version of *A Midsummer Night's Dream* in the 1960s; a succession

of radical productions, often with directors from overseas, in the 1970s; and a return to the comedies after the *Hamlet* of 1994 (37).

Some of the most significant productions since the turn of the twenty-first century, though not necessarily those most successful in terms of their reception, have been those by directors from outside France, including the Romanian Andrei Serban (*The Merchant of Venice*, 2001), the German-born Pole Andrzej Seweryn (*Twelfth Night*, 2004), the Lithuanian Oskaras Korsunovas (*The Taming of the Shrew*, 2007) and the Spaniard Andres Lima (*The Merry Wives*, 2009).[1] Like the Belgian francophone director Daniel Mesguich, whose *Tempest* was seen in 1998, the visiting directors have brought radically different approaches to theatrical art as well as to the plays, so that rather than establishing some kind of parallel Shakespearian tradition, which would have complemented the already contested 'house' approach to the French classics, an 'open' and mutable Shakespeare has been offered. Rivier characterizes this as a combination of the near and the distant, adopting the binary of '*le proche et le lointain*' memorably proposed by Richard Marienstras in a study of English sixteenth- and seventeenth-century drama published in 1981.[2] Shakespeare is *closer*, because the plays have been accommodated to modern times, with new translations and mixed registers of playing; because the settings are more abstract, frequently metonymic and derived from the culture, approach and ambitions of each individual director; and because more in accord with developing methods of rehearsal and preparation. More *distant*, because the visions of the directors have conferred a diversity, figuring the Elizabethan playwright as being all the more *métamorphique* (169–70).

Rivier's detailed discussion of individual productions, grounding them in the artistic (or in-house) and social politics of their time, is especially

---

[1] A naturalized French citizen, Seweryn is a Pole born in Germany; he became the 493rd *sociétaire* of the company in 1995; in 1994 he had played the title role in *Hamlet*.

[2] *Le proche et le lointain: Sur Shakespeare, le drame élisabéthain et l'idéologie anglaise aux XVIe et XVIIe siècles* (Paris, 1981).

valuable in the earlier part of the period, notably in the case of the *Coriolanus* that occasioned rancour, rioting and governmental intervention in 1933–4: performances were banned on 9 February 1934, and the artistic director Émile Fabre was removed from his post, which was taken over by the head of the *Sûreté générale*. The installation of the chief of the state security forces was of course an absurdly blatant political move, and Fabre was subsequently reinstated, but the point had been made – Shakespeare's play, with its hero openly contemptuous of the common people, was all too easily taken as an intervention in the nation's turbid politics, a provocation to the vocal and aggressive right-wing forces marshalled against the compromises of the liberal regime. Much of this story is familiar to Anglophone readers, but one element of Rivier's account may place the production in a slightly different light: she notes that Charles Granval's production of *Hamlet* had presented a decidedly grim view of the play, in tune with the tenor of the times and reflected in the revivals in 1942 and 1945, during the 'dark years' of the Occupation (54). Overall, *Shakespeare dans la maison de Molière* provides an informed and sophisticated insight into the complexities of the playwright's reception within the theatrical culture of a country that is both near and far from Britain.

The afterlives of the plays in a theatrical culture that shared some of the assumptions of the founders of the Comédie-française figure largely in Michael Caines's *Shakespeare and the Eighteenth Century* in the 'Oxford Shakespeare Topics' series. The remit is to consider both 'what the eighteenth century did to Shakespeare – and vice-versa', a generously conceived topic that Caines tackles with wit and economy. Such texts as Cibber's *Richard III*, a version considered stageworthy well into the nineteenth century, are approached with an understanding of their significance in terms of the aesthetics and politics of the time. Attention to the influence of theatre on editorial practices is an important element in the book's success in bringing together the various events in publishing, performance and celebration that marked the century's engagement with the poet then emerging

as 'national'. David Garrick's career is identified as Janus-like, at the end of one tradition in accepting that the plays needed reworking for the stage, and the beginning of another by his innovations in acting and the restoration of some elements of the texts that had customarily been omitted: 'Forward- or backward-looking, Garrick certainly managed to make Shakespeare *his* own' (93).

Unavoidable dependence on contemporary witnesses in approaches to Garrick and his contemporaries raises more general questions about the status and nature of the evidence. In *Reviewing Shakespeare*, Paul Prescott identifies changes in the practice of newspaper criticism of Shakespearian performance from the eighteenth century to the present, showing the relationships between individual judgements and the institutions of journalism. Taking reviews of *Macbeth* as an example across successive periods, Prescott asks 'What did it mean to be a great Macbeth in the mid eighteenth century?' (33) The answer leads to conclusions about 'societal conceptions of what is acceptable or laudable in human, specifically male, behaviour'. In institutional terms, a major factor is the shift in journalism in the late nineteenth century from anonymous reviewing to 'the informal (and identified) critical voice' (175), and Prescott examines in detail the strategies by which George Bernard Shaw and Max Beerbohm established themselves as distinctive presences. Among mid-twentieth century critics, James Agate stands out as a carefully cultivated 'personality', frankly claiming descent from a line of distinguished predecessors from Hazlitt and Leigh Hunt, and intent on celebrating the pre-eminent (mainly male) actor as an index of Shakespearian interpretation. Kenneth Tynan, advertised by his employers in the 1950s as a new Shaw, began by celebrating heroic individualism in *He That Plays the King* (1953) but soon became a champion of a new, collective spirit, 'a tradition of production and reception . . . increasingly dominated by new playwrights, ensemble acting and the pre-eminence of the director' (95). But the older tradition persisted alongside the new in Tynan's writing and in his involvements with the theatre on a practical level, notably in his often fraught relationship with Olivier. The privileging of definitions of masculinity is reflected in Tynan's marginalization and habitual disparagement of Vivien Leigh in reviews of performances in which she appeared alongside Olivier, and the sexual subtext (not always very *sub*) in many of his notices takes us further into the psyche of the reviewer than that of the players. Many British newspaper readers of the 1950s and 1960s looked forward to comparing the *Observer* (Tynan) with the *Sunday Times* (Harold Hobson) as an important element of their Sunday mornings. These were star journalists, fulfilling severally and jointly what Prescott identifies as the duty 'to respond to performance immediately, to keep people talking about theatre, and to circulate pleasure' (11).

An account of this subject in some 200 pages must be selective, but returning to accounts of *Macbeth* as a touchstone affords a focus on a drama where concepts of masculinity and heroism are always in play, and which has been notorious for limiting both the male actor's opportunities to make a good end as a hero ('*Exit fighting*' – and therefore not, unless one follows Garrick's lead, achieving an onstage death) and the possibilities for a fuller exploration of the Macbeths as a tragic couple. *Reviewing Shakespeare* suggests a valuable paradigm for similar discussion of both critics and performers, and the ways in which we might scan a period's horizon of expectations. The accounts of the reviewers' culture and background are exemplary in themselves and new light is shed on the performances seen through – or refracted by – their reports.

American theatrical and cinematic treatments of Shakespeare's most popular Roman play are discussed in Maria Wyke's *Julius Caesar in the USA*, which places performances in the context of political culture and – intriguingly – the classroom teaching of Latin. For the revolutionaries, 'the Roman dictator and aspirant to kingship was displayed as an icon of what needed to be overcome in order for the new republic to emerge' (2). Wyke documents the ways in which 'Caesar's life provide[d] a whole vocabulary with which to articulate or to challenge conquest, imperialism,

usurpation, dictatorship, tyranny and assassination' (8). The ultimate irony was the declaration, in its original Latin, by Lincoln's assassin that tyrants should always be dealt with thus – '*sic semper tyrannis*'. (Along with '*e pluribus unum*' on the banknotes this must be one of the most familiar Latin tags in North America.) In the classroom Caesar's account of his Gallic wars, with its military narrative and relatively simple Latin, remained a staple until the years after the First World War, after which its currency diminished, while Shakespeare's play held its ground. Wyke traces the narrative of the Latin lessons and their textbooks alongside the production history of Shakespeare's play and the silent films that represented it or claimed to show the historical events directly. One especially interesting example of the latter, Enrico Guazzoni's film *Cajus Julius Caesar* (Italy, 1914), was issued in the USA in a version recut to follow Shakespeare more closely for Anglo-American audiences, with most of the nationalist rhetoric removed from its intertitles and Shakespearian quotations inserted in the scene of Mark Antony's funeral oration (89).

In such productions as Orson Welles and John Houseman's Mercury Theatre anti-fascist version in modern dress (New York, 1937) and Joseph L. Mankiewicz's film (MGM, 1953), the play and its subject matter retained their force and, in the case of the film, much of their ambiguity. To what extent was the film a 'Cold War' reading? Wyke concludes that the 'physical frailty of the aged leader, a nascent conspiracy against him, and his own concern at the dangerous men who surround him would have tied the Roman dictator more closely to Stalin and the present tense of 1953' than to the other European dictatorships of the 1930s (149). This is especially interesting in the light of its relationship with the 1937 production, given that John Houseman, Welles's associate in the Mercury Theatre, was its producer. Wyke's most telling point is that the film is an example of the way in which 'the Roman past has continually been represented and consumed as America's future, especially at times of political and social crisis' (131). The contradictions of the Cold War mentality are reflected in the film: 'pride in revolutionary beginnings and fear of revolutionary endings; revulsion from foreign dictators and attraction to general presidents [i.e. Eisenhower]; support of both democratic government and demagogic illegality [i.e. McCarthy]; distaste for imperialism and embrace of global dominance' (166). The CBS TV series *You Are There*, in which Walter Cronkite and other familiar television journalists presented on-the-spot coverage of historical events as breaking news, aired 'The Assassination of Julius Caesar' on 8 March 1953, with Paul Newman as Brutus. The three principal scriptwriters for the series were on the blacklist and working under pseudonyms, and *You Are There* 'cleverly camouflaged its attacks on McCarthyism with the aesthetic cover of history' (161).

Camouflaged protest on the other side of the 'Iron Curtain' figures prominently in the account given by Tiffany Ann Conroy Moore, in *Kozintsev's Shakespeare Films: Russian Political Protest in 'Hamlet' and 'King Lear'*. Unlike Jan Kott, whose work he knew and admired, Grigori Kozintsev had no room in his outlook for 'fatalism, pessimism or nihilism', but was 'a realist who honestly confronted the problems of his times, but always remained hopeful, believing in human agency and the power of artistic expression to effect positive changes in society' (14). Moore describes the relationship between the two films and the film-maker's situation before and during Stalin's rule, and during the 'thaw' under Nikita Khrushchev and its repressive aftermath after Leonid Brezhnev took over. The author draws attention to the long-standing Russian tradition of the 'holy fool' as a licensed commentator and the 'Aesopian' habit of interpretation, by which subversive stories could be identified below the surface of work that was seemingly inoffensive or even appeared to follow enthusiastically the party line of the time. Unfortunately, the study is burdened with long and somewhat repetitive introductory sections on the Russian reception since the eighteenth century of Shakespeare in general and the two tragedies in particular. All of this is assembled diligently from secondary sources in English, and no material in the original language is drawn

on. Of the book's 181 pages of text, only 23 deal directly with the *Hamlet* film, and 40 with *King Lear*. Good points are made, for example in relating the second film to Christian and 'Jewish themes' and to the production of the play by the State Jewish Theatre in the 1920s and 1930s, but pages in the account of Shostakovich's score for *King Lear* return to ground already covered in an earlier outline of his fraught relationship with Stalin, and the scandal caused by the opera *The Lady Macbeth of the Mtsensk District*.

A briefer but more incisive discussion of the director's work, equally alert to its political meanings, is Courtney Lehmann's chapter in volume XVII of the *Great Shakespeareans* series, edited by Mark Thornton Burnett. Lehmann deals deftly with the background but takes the analysis into the broader realm of cinematic genre and the international as well as Soviet context. 'Hamletism', a by-word in nineteenth-century and Soviet Russia for inertia and lack of resolve, attached undesirable associations to the play and accounted for Stalin's loathing of it: to stage and film *Hamlet* was in itself a more courageous undertaking than has generally been understood. As Lehmann points out, in the establishing sequence of the film 'Hamlet's ambivalent positioning between the relentlessly forward movement of the Western [as he and his attendants gallop across 'a desert dotted with sagebrush'] and the debilitating stasis of Olivier's "Hamletism" points to the film's own historical conditions of production, for these opposing temporalities parallel the discontinuity that resulted from the collision of Khrushchev's thaw with Stalin's freeze' (104).

Lehmann joins precise and perceptive examination of scenes and sequences to an appreciation of the complex circumstances and carefully placed ambiguities of the films. Although (unlike Moore) she does not specifically cite the 'Aesopian' mode of thought, Lehmann's analysis effectively reveals its operation, for example in the epic scale of the opening of *King Lear*, with its crowd of the distressed poor gathering in hope of a sign from the king in his formidable fortress, only to receive what is effectively an ineffective raising of his arms from the diminutive figure seen at a distance on the battlements. In *Hamlet*, the romantic Ghost, with his cloak billowing behind him, is also robotic, and as Lehmann points out, the moment when we see his eyes, shadowed as if by a mask under his helmet is followed by the sight of the ornate moulded face that forms his raised visor. Whether or not the former intentionally invokes the Lone Ranger, it is plausible to argue that Kozintsev's 'life-long fascination with Noh theatre', with which he would 'fully engage' in his *King Lear*, informs the design of the 'face' (109–10). There are a few moments of uncertainty in Lehmann's account of the Russian context: Kozintsev's recollection of 'going to school in a gymnasium' perhaps needs the use of italics to indicate that this is a high school rather than a gym (93); Stanislavksi did not create 'the school of "method acting"' (94), a later American development from his work; the 'superfluous man' of nineteenth-century literary and political discourse was not the kind of bureaucrat represented by the men around Claudius's council table (106); the eponymous hero of Ivan Goncharov's 1859 novel *Oblomov*, whose defining characteristic is an inability to get out of bed, is hardly a cog in any bureaucratic machine and does not correspond to the toadying courtiers through whom Kozintsev's Hamlet passes as he thinks his first soliloquy (107). These are minor points: in its 52 pages, this is a valuable brief study, with persuasive readings of the films supported by alertness to their intertextual dimensions and a shrewd understanding of the political engagement of this richly gifted and eloquent director.

The other essays in this volume – Mark Thornton Burnett on Kurosawa, Marguerite H. Rippy on Welles and Ramona Wray on Zeffirelli – are of a comparable quality. In each case, critical analysis of the films is supported by concise biographical and other contextual information. Burnett's analysis of Kurosawa's films combines sensitive response to cinematic strategies with persuasive argument for their wider significance, rooted in the director's experience of the world and the anxieties of his times. In *Ran*, 'actions . . . are defined through a concentration on bigger processes that dwarf articulations of human need and will', so that 'repeated cloud images, in addition to refracting *King Lear*'s realization of the "to-and-fro conflicting wind and rain" (3.1.11) as pathetic fallacy, invite contemporary readings and conjure the terrifying nuclear emblems of the cessation of World War II' (80). Rippy's readings of Welles's films locate in their biographical context the ways in which the Shakespearian adaptations 'explore issues of alienation, spiritual and moral corruption, self-creation, and tension between the individual and society' to bring out the rationale according to which the texts were cut and reshaped (16). In radio and TV performances of the title role of *King Lear* and in his unrealized plans for a film of the play, Rippy traces the director's 'interest in Lear as a representation of humanity in decline'. The perceived connection with his own situation is inescapable: 'Unjust disempowerment was a situation that Welles himself came increasingly to identify with, and even in 1946 he was starting to investigate the perspective of being an outsider in an entertainment world that had once celebrated him' (48). Welles was in many respects the ultimate insider's outsider, and his post-Hollywood career as international celebrity, *bon viveur* and artistic chancer was bodied forth in his teasing presentations of himself and his works, including the faux-documentary *F is for Fake* and the plea in his 1995 television programme *Filming 'Othello'* for our recognition of a craftiness that hides craft in the film's discontinuities and fragmentation.

Abigail Rokison's *Shakespeare for Young People: Productions, Versions and Adaptations*, offers sympathetic and discerning analyses of a number of feature films that have targeted children and teenagers, though arguably Luhrmann's *William Shakespeare's Romeo+Juliet* (1996) and Almereyda's *Hamlet* (2000) differ in the extent to which they address such an audience. Christine Edzard's *The Children's Midsummer Night's Dream* (2001), unique in being performed by as well as for children, comes closer to the kind of work represented by the theatrical adaptations and reworkings examined by Rokison. Problems may be caused for some of their target audience by the familiarity with details of the

Shakespearian texts required for a full appreciation of Sharman MacDonald's *After Juliet* (1999), Lucinda Coxon's *The Eternal Not* (2009 – an alternative view of *All's Well*) and Michael Lesslie's *Prince of Denmark* (2010), the last two designed to run alongside National Theatre productions of the Shakespearian plays. *The Eternal Not*, as sequel to its 'parent' play, may be proposed as a 'way in' but depends to a very considerable extent on knowledge of it, while there are moments in Lesslie's play that rival Stoppard's *Rosencrantz and Guildenstern Are Dead* in witty allusion. Although Rokison's emphasis is on the ways their audience is addressed in the plays, films, graphic novels, animations and other retellings she examines, her lucid, readable analyses are a contribution to the more general critical debate on adaptation. Maurizio Calbi's *Spectral Shakespeares: Media Adaptations in the Twenty-First Century* is designed for a more specialized readership, with writing underpinned but at times obscured by theoretical sophistication. It is good to have a discussion of Alexander Fodor's *Hamlet* (released on DVD in 2006), identified by its director as 'extreme', but many of those intrigued by the observation that 'redness colors and permeates everything, from the mise-en-scène to the logic of the signifier' (103) may begin to lose touch with the argument when Calbi goes on to suggest that 'One could go so far as to argue, from a Lacanian perspective, that some kind of *jouis-sense* – the enjoyment of the signifier "impregnated" with *jouissance*; the enjoyment of what is left from the signifier's ability to signify – infiltrates and undermines the circuit of communication and meaning (cf. Zizek, *Looking* 39, 129).' But readers to whom this is not helpful should stay with the author, as the chapter is an acute exposition of the paradox by which Fodor's *Hamlet* is 'simultaneously iconoclastic and reverential' (112). Under his introduction's rubric of 'Shakespeare, Spectro-Textuality, Spectro-Mediality', Calbi discusses *The King is Alive*, *Scotland PA* and the BBC 'Shakespeare Retold' *Macbeth* as well as some less widely known remediations.

'Marlowe the mirror in which Shakespeare finds himself', Derek Jarman jotted in his diary after the first screening of the completed film of *Edward II*.[3] Pascale Aebischer's *Screening Early Modern Drama: Beyond Shakespeare* includes a detailed study, supported by intensive archival research as well as sophisticated analysis of the films, that places Jarman's remarkable film of *The Tempest* in the context of the director's other work and also, as the book's title implies, the cinema versions of other plays by dramatists from the period. In the final masque of Jarman's film, which culminates its 'celebration of historical and cultural diversity', Elizabeth Welch, in a costume described by its designer Yolanda Sonnabend as 'an Inigo Jones creation filtered through the movies', makes a grand entrance to salute the lovers with a rendition of 'Stormy Weather'. It is, as Aebischer points out, the first time in Jarman's cinema when 'the early modern period fully shapes and inhabits the present, using the frame of the camera as the equivalent of Inigo Jones's proscenium arch' (16). Jarman's films might be said to be a mirror in which (relatively) big-budget Shakespeare-on-film sees itself, or rather avoids doing so. Given his distaste for the kind of 'heritage cinema' that commandeered funding he might hope to get – the cost of his eleven features taken together has been reckoned as a mere £3,270,000 – Jarman's *oeuvre* stands as a challenge to independent and dependent filmmakers alike.[4] It is appropriate that in her final section Aebischer considers the would-be rebuke to the playwright's own authority offered by Roland Emmerich's *Anonymous*, an anti-Stratfordian epic that, she suggests, 'makes it ever more unproductive to distinguish between Shakespeare and his more marginal contemporaries and to view them as opposed cultural forces' (224). 'Mainstream' and its opposition to the 'marginal' here might be extended to the film and TV (or video) versions of Shakespeare that position themselves as countercultural and resistant to the imperatives of commercial movie culture.

---

[3] Derek Jarman, *Smiling in Slow Motion*, edited by Keith Collins (London, 2000), p. 30.

[4] The figure is quoted by Rowland Wymer, *Derek Jarman* (Manchester, 2005), p. 15 n. 3.

Anonymous figures in Richard Burt and Julian Yates's *What's the Worst Thing You Can Do to Shakespeare?*, a 'project of un/reading the Bard, through reverent and irreverent discourses' (as the blurb on the back of the book describes it). The series of riffs on critical discourses around WS and all his works, on diverse mediatizations and other jerks of invention, is at times maddening, often suggestive and never dull – if only because of a novel mode of writing, in which the co-authors (beginning in their acknowledgements) manage to avoid making division between themselves: 'cowriting an essay at what may only be described as telepathic speed' in 18 months, communicating by telephone, answering machines, fax, email and – once only and that two months before submitting the manuscript – in a face-to face meeting. (xi) The title page joins/separates their names by a slash. If the re/reader is prepared to stay the course, along the way there are insights into familiar films, including Luhrmann's *William Shakespeare's Romeo+Juliet*, Greenaway's *Prospero's Books* and, yes, *Anonymous* – the last in a chapter entitled 'Anonymous/Anony/mess'. The ideal viewer of Emmerich's film 'remains, apparently, the one who sees everything but witnesses nothing. The archive remains emphatically complete but unreadable' (134). Burt has long been a tenacious seeker-out and provocative analyst of (to put it mildly) unusual Shakespeares, and his hand has clearly not lost its cunning. In this volume the combined Burt/Yates deploy(s) a formidable range of scholarship and theory, both familiar and abstruse, even if at times readers may find the hyperactive self-consciousness more wearing than enlivening.

By contrast, Peter Brook's *The Quality of Mercy: Reflections on Shakespeare* comes as a calming, undemonstrative personal account of a lifetime's engagement with an author whose plays he has never ceased to respect but not hesitated to reconstruct. When he first worked at Stratford-upon-Avon, 'the middle-class spectators were still Victorians and quite naturally viewed the plays in the way Romantic painters had shown them', but his first production, a Watteauesque *Love's Labour's Lost* (1946), 'was also influenced by the post-war

reaction against four years of drabness and austerity. We longed for elegance and charm' (29). There are reflections on the reception of his early productions by audiences who refused to accept innovation, but also on the lessons he was learning as he went along. His Stratford *Romeo and Juliet* (1947) had 'plenty of fire, colour and energy', but 'what was missing was an overall tempo, and irresistible pulse to lead from one scene to another. I had not yet learned that this was the basis of all Elizabethan theatre, and so began a long period of discovery.' The theatre, dominated by the well-made West End play, 'had long lost contact with the relentless Elizabethan rhythm' (25). Brook is passionate and incisive in his comments on the speaking of the text, and some of the information about productions may be new to most readers: the possibility, not pursued, that a film would be made of the 1955 Stratford *Titus Andronicus* is especially intriguing. The most valuable passages, though, are those in which he reflects on discoveries made in thinking through the plays, and the advice given to him when as a young man he approached the producer Alexander Korda with an idea for a film. Korda cut him off: 'Even a cook can have an idea. Come back when you have developed your "idea" enough to have a real story to offer me' (76). *The Quality of Mercy* describes some of Brook's most notable attempts to respond to this imperative and, although he subsequently paraphrases 'have a real story' as 'into a more powerful form' (83), Brook's pursuit of ideas through story-telling has remained his overall goal. *The Quality of Mercy* shares with Brook's previous publications, interviews and notes his thoughtful, candid consideration of work that in itself has been a profitably restless journey of discovery. The final chapter, which shares the book's title, has a sage-like quality in its meditation on the epilogue to *The Tempest*, and Brook is not afraid of a touch of mysticism: 'The moment that one tries to pinpoint with one's ordinary argumentative understanding, one takes a step away from the possibility of another understanding' (107). The 'epilogue' looks forward from what might seem to be simple conclusions: 'Shakespeare. Quality. Form. This is where our work begins. It can never end' (110).

WORKS REVIEWED

Aebischer, Pascale, *Screening Early Modern Drama: Beyond Shakespeare* (Cambridge, 2013)

Bennett, Susan and Christie Carson, eds., *Shakespeare Beyond English: A Global Experiment* (Cambridge, 2013)

Brook, Peter, *The Quality of Mercy: Reflections on Shakespeare* (London, 2013)

Burnett, Mark Thornton *et al.*, *Great Shakespeareans, Volume XVII. Kurosawa, Welles, Kozintsev, Zeffirelli* (London, 2013)

Burt, Richard and Julian Yates, *What's the Worst Thing You Can Do to Shakespeare?* (Houndmills and New York, 2013)

Caines, Michael, *Shakespeare and the Eighteenth Century* (Oxford, 2013)

Calbi, Maurizio, *Spectral Shakespeares: Media Adaptations in the Twenty-first Century* (New York and Houndmills, 2013)

Edmondson, Paul, Paul Prescott and Erin Sullivan, eds., *A Year of Shakespeare: Re-living the World Shakespeare Festival* (London, 2013)

Hampton-Reeves, Stuart and Bridget Escolme, eds., *Shakespeare and the Making of Theatre* (Houndmills and New York, 2013)

Karim-Cooper, Farah and Tiffany Stern, eds., *Shakespeare's Theatre and the Effects of Performance* (London, 2013)

Moore, Tiffany Ann Conroy, *Kozintsev's Shakespeare films: Russian Political Protest in 'Hamlet' and 'King Lear'* (Jefferson NC and London, 2012)

Prescott, Paul, *Reviewing Shakespeare: Journalism and Performance from the Eighteenth Century to the Present* (Cambridge, 2013)

Rivier, Estelle, *Shakespeare dans la maison de Molière* (Rennes, 2012)

Rokison, Abigail, *Shakespeare for Young People: Productions, Versions and Adaptations* (London, 2013)

Wyke, Maria, *Caesar in the USA* (Berkeley, Los Angeles and London, 2012)

3. EDITIONS AND TEXTUAL STUDIES
reviewed by SONIA MASSAI

COPERNICAN REVOLUTIONS

The last twelve months have witnessed momentous changes in the fields of Shakespeare editing and textual studies, a veritable shift in our perception of their central concerns and the conceptual categories caught in their gravitational pull. Although some of these changes became foreseeable around the time when Shakespeare textual scholars and editors were confronted by, and readjusted to, the 'materialist turn' in the mid-1980s, their impact has only recently started to manifest itself in all its magnitude. As the scholarship reviewed in this essay shows, earlier notions of the 'work' as fixed and immaterial and of 'text' and 'performance' as material manifestations of the work have given way to the opposite view that text and performance, for all their multiplicities and instabilities, are the gravitational centres that constantly reshape and redefine our understanding of what constitutes 'Shakespeare', both as an author and as a body of works. The sections into which this essay is divided explore the impact of these changes in four main areas: textual studies that focus on the transmission of Shakespeare and early modern English drama in print and manuscript; attribution studies and their impact on recent editions of the collected works; editions of individual works; and interdisciplinary studies that draw on book history and digital humanities in order to reconsider the place of Shakespeare in print and digital cultures.

TEXTUAL STUDIES

The most unapologetically field-redefining study this year is Paul Werstine's *Early Modern Playhouse Manuscripts and the Editing of Shakespeare*. In this book, Werstine urges editors of Shakespeare to approach their task *empirically* by 'meticulous comparison of the printed plays with surviving theatrical [playbooks]' (231) and to distance themselves from editorial approaches that 'depend on [Walter] Greg's understanding of "foul papers" (with its attendant idealization of authorial and some-times literary agency) and "promptbooks" (often attended by an idealization of the theatrical)' (221). Werstine has critiqued these categories before but in this book he defuses once and for all polemi-cal attacks on his work as being unduly informed by post-structuralist theory and deconstruction by using the very New Bibliographical methods devised by Greg to postulate these categories in the first place.

The first two chapters in Werstine's book are indeed 'an extended essay in New Bibliography' (1) and focus on a close study of Edward Knight's transcription of Fletcher's *Bonduca* (British Library, Add MS 36758), the very source of the phrase 'foul papers' which Greg associated with 'a copy representing the play more or less as the author intended it to stand, but not itself clear or tidy enough to serve as a promptbook' (14). Werstine faults Greg's influential definition on two counts. First, he magisterially demonstrates that adaptation by theatrical agents and scribal habits 'provid[e] a fuller and more economical description of the source of the transcript's errors', as identified by comparison with the version of the play preserved in the 1647 Beaumont and Fletcher First Folio, 'than do Greg's inferences about alternations in the "foul papers" that cannot be visualized' in any of the other extant dramatic manuscripts from the period (89). Werstine then shows that, although Greg had detected non-authorial alterations in Knight's transcription while preparing his Malone Society edition of 1951, 'he never revisited his earliest definition of "foul papers" to bring it into line with this thinking' (24). Werstine interestingly adds that Greg's definition of "foul papers" also remained inaccessible to fresh scrutiny by others because the original essay where Greg formulated it was never published (and is now deposited at the Huntington Library as MS RB112111 PF). Werstine therefore concludes that '[c]ontrary to Greg's assumption, "foul papers" need not refer exclusively to authorial drafts, whether these are messy or not; the term simply describes papers that, for whatever reason, are to be, are being, or have already been transcribed' (98). The implications of

Werstine's definition of 'foul papers' can hardly be overestimated. As he explains, 'foul papers', as a term, 'has little role to play in Shakespeare textual criticism and editing because his canonical plays descend to us only in printed form' (100). Besides, once the term 'foul papers' has stopped 'desig-nat[ing] a particular class of authorial manuscripts with identifiable features analogous to those in Knight's exemplar for his *Bonduca* transcript' (100), it can no longer be used by editors of Shakespeare to postulate the use of an authorial manuscript as printer's copy for early editions that exhibit similar features.

Werstine is just as persuasive when he turns his attention to the category of 'promptbooks', which is generally used by Shakespeare scholars to identify early playhouse manuscripts that provide a guide to, or even a record of, performance and to estab-lish theatrical provenance of the printer's copy of early editions that share some of their features. Rather than being responsible for the formulation of this category of theatrical manuscripts, Greg felt compelled, according to Werstine, to 'assim-ilate his own knowledge of early modern play-house documents to an existing Shakespeare tex-tual criticism founded on an understanding of such documents that was badly skewed by this transhis-torical conception of "promptbook"' (108). By closely analysing nineteen playhouse manuscripts and three printed quarto playbooks annotated for performance, Werstine argues in Chapter 3 that 'theatrical texts need not be [and were not] tidy' (113), because other theatrical documents, pri-marily backstage plots, cast lists and actors' parts, were used to regulate performance. In Chapter 4, Werstine then goes on to give examples of how annotations added by the bookkeeper to playhouse manuscripts, instead of resolving, in fact increased ambiguity in speech prefixes and stage directions. Although Chapter 5 shows that extant playhouse manuscripts 'can illuminate to some limited extent their function as guides to performance' (200), the presence of loose ends, false starts and ambigui-ties, once associated with authorial manuscripts, in the playhouse manuscripts discussed by Werstine makes any attempt to identify the printer's copy underlying early editions of Shakespeare as either authorial or theatrical simply wrong-headed.

What lies ahead for Shakespeare textual scholars and editors is the daunting challenge of establishing how the collapse of the Gregian distinction between 'foul papers' and 'promptbooks' affects not only their choice of what early edition of Shakespeare's works they should re-present to modern readers, but also what rationale should inform their editorial approach. Werstine proposes 'empirical editing' as an alternative to 'copy-text' editing, without providing a new, fully-fledged rationale. While Werstine's book has undoubtedly effected a Copernican revolution, by placing the indomitable complexity of early modern playhouse manuscripts (and what they cannot tell us about the authority underlying early modern printed playbooks) at the centre of our field of inquiry, it leaves the question as to what it practically means to edit *empirically* wide open.

ATTRIBUTION STUDIES AND THE SHAPE OF THE CANON

Traditionally viewed as author-centric, attribution studies in fact confront us with the instabilities of what is taken to constitute the body of works legitimately gathered under an authorizing patronymic and marker of literary value. The impact of Shakespeare attribution studies has been particularly noteworthy this year. The publication of *William Shakespeare & Others: Collaborative Plays*, edited by Jonathan Bate and Eric Rasmussen, with Jan Sewell and Will Sharpe, as a companion volume to Bate and Rasmussen's 2007 *William Shakespeare: Complete Works*, has stretched the patronym 'Shakespeare' to include plays like *Locrine* and *Thomas Lord Cromwell*, which were 'plausibly passed off as his' (10–11), but also plays like *A Yorkshire Tragedy*, whose 'raw scripts' he may have 'polished up' (11), or plays like *The London Prodigal*, which Shakespeare 'as a key member of the company . . . explicitly or implicitly signed . . . off for performance' (11), and, most controversially, plays like *The Spanish Tragedy* and *Mucedorus*, which

he may have revised for a revival by the King's Men.

Bate and Rasmussen's *William Shakespeare & Others*, as much as their 2007 edition of the *Complete Works*, provides a snapshot of 'the state of play' in the field of attribution studies, which is in constant flux, as illustrated by the principles of inclusion and exclusion underlying these two major editions. Among the most arresting decisions taken by Bate and Rasmussen, their omission of *A Lover's Complaint* from the *Complete Works* and their inclusion of the Additions to *The Spanish Tragedy* in *William Shakespeare & Others* are worth considering in light of recent and current debates in the field of attribution studies.

Bate and Rasmussen's controversial decision to omit *A Lover's Complaint* from *The Complete Works* was primarily prompted by the publication of Brian Vickers's *Shakespeare, 'A Lover's Complaint' and John Davies of Hereford* in 2007. It is interesting to note that the pendulum might now be swinging back towards the attribution of *A Lover's Complaint* to Shakespeare. Using rare-words frequency and word-pairs tests to analyse the poem in the context of a large corpus of 129 plays dated between 1580 and 1619 and 54 poems, within which likely candidates George Chapman and John Davies, as well as Shakespeare, feature more largely than any other author, Hugh Craig has established that *A Lover's Complaint* 'cannot be by Chapman or Davies, but it could be by Shakespeare' (168). Taking his cue from Marina Tarlinskaja, Craig also believes that the deeply-rooted resistance against attribution of *A Lover's Complaint* to Shakespeare, despite its inclusion in the 1609 edition of *The Sonnets*, might be due to the fact that 'the author of [this poem] was imitating Spenser' (170), an influential model for the genre of complaint poetry. What is hard to accept, according to Craig, is the realization that Shakespeare may have 'departed from his regular prosodic patterns to imitate Spenser' (170).

Similarly, Bate and Rasmussen's decision to include the text of the 1602 quarto edition of *The Spanish Tragedy*, with the Additions printed in a different font from the rest of the play, in *William Shakespeare & Others*, is supported by mounting critical opinion in favour of Shakespearian attribution. Brian Vickers is the latest scholar to have contributed to the debate about the authorship of the Additions, which he uses as a testing ground for a 'new(er)' approach, 'a "holistic" method that can respect the phenomenon of language as words that a speaker or writer has joined together in unique sequences' (24). Vickers favours this method, which originates in the fields of corpus linguistics and collocation studies (25), over the more emphatically quantitative methods used in stylometry or computational linguistics and which, according to Vickers, reach unreliable results by systematically 'separat[ing] single words...from the context of utterance in which the author placed them' (24). By applying his 'new(er)' method to a close study of the Additions to *The Spanish Tragedy*, Vickers identifies distinctively Shakespearian groupings of words, or 'N-grams', and concludes that 'the results for Shakespeare...provide overwhelming evidence for his having written these five enlarged scenes' (29).

Vickers's conclusions are indeed extremely suggestive. However, his defence of his methodology rests on a problematic assumption. As Vickers reminds us, stylometric approaches focus on grammatical or functional words, rather than lexical words, because 'they identify features of language that no one would think of manipulating, whereas...larger phrasal structures are open to appropriation, imitation and parody' (23). Possibly in order to defend his own approach from this very objection, Vickers adds a startling corollary to his conclusions, namely that 'Shakespeare could not possibly have been aware of the idiosyncratic lexicon of collocations that constituted his "phraseognomy"...[and] distinguished his language from that of his contemporaries' (32). Implicit in Vickers's corollary is the assumption that other writers could not have imitated and reproduced Shakespeare's "phraseognomy". Vickers's corollary flies in the face of a well-established understanding of early modern literary cultures as fundamentally imitative. In a feisty rebuttal of Vickers's critique of computational stylistics, John Burrows launches into a counter-attack aimed at Vickers, by arguing

that 'moments of identity', that is shared grouping of words, 'need not betoken the larger identity of shared authorship'. In fact, he goes on to explain, 'one may distinguish four kinds of resemblance between texts,...single-author and collaborative work,...imitation...[and] plagiarism' (369). Imitation, as mentioned above, seems to be crucially important in the context of early modern literary cultures. I was therefore surprised to find that Vickers dismisses it altogether when it comes to groupings of words which are so clearly distinctive and recognizable, including, just to take an example out of the verbal matches identified by Vickers, 'a thing of nothing', which the Additions share, most recognizably, with *Hamlet*.

As this year's contributions to attribution studies show, the relative viability and accuracy of the different methods used by scholars engaged in this field are still very much open to debate. I do, however, subscribe to Burrows's optimistic and conciliatory view that 'the relationship between [them]...is complementary not adversarial, mutually corroborative at most times, mutually interrogative at others' (392) and welcome Burrows's report that the methods currently used by computational stylistics scholars are reaching levels of accuracy hovering around 95 per cent (366). Progress in this field of studies can hardly be denied and the impact that attribution studies have on the editing of Shakespeare cannot be overestimated. It is therefore with these insights in mind that I return to *William Shakespeare & Others* in order to show how the benefits of reconsidering what may or may not constitute the Shakespeare canon far outweigh the inevitable to-ing and fro-ing in the attribution of target texts, such as *A Lover's Complaint* or the Additions to *The Spanish Tragedy* (or *Mucedorus*!).

Two major benefits of *William Shakespeare & Others* are eloquently highlighted in Jonathan Bate's characteristically inspired and inspiring general introduction to the volume. First, Bate argues that the broader understanding of collaboration that informs this edition allows its readers to reconsider works traditionally attributed to Shakespeare in the wider context of late Elizabethan and early

Jacobean drama more generally. Listing all the plays included in *William Shakespeare & Others*, Bate sums up this argument as follows:

> *The Spanish Tragedy*, *Arden of Faversham* and *Locrine* take us to the foundations of Elizabethan tragedy, leading us on the path towards *Hamlet*, *Othello* and *King Lear*. *Edward III* complements the English history plays. *Thomas Lord Cromwell* and *Sir Thomas More*, like Shakespeare and Fletcher's later *Henry VIII*, stand among a group of intriguing plays about Tudor politics. *The London Prodigal* in comedy and *A Yorkshire Tragedy* in darker vein are excellent examples of the work of the King's Men at the height of their fame. *Mucedorus* and *Cardenio/Double Falsehood* are intimately bound to the turn to romance in the last years of Shakespeare's career. Whether or not some or all of them were indeed part-written or 'newly set forth' or 'overseen' by Shakespeare, the reading of them cannot fail to illuminate his theatrical world.
>
> (30)

Given the compelling quality of this argument, one might wonder why other plays, like *The Merry Devil of Edmonton*, which was apparently prepared for publication but then omitted from this edition at the last minute, were not included. The mere fact that 'the evidence linking *Merry Devil* to Shakespeare's company . . . is very strong; but the evidence linking it to Shakespeare's pen is very weak' (726) has not pre-empted inclusion of plays with a similar profile, most obviously *Mucedorus*. One therefore suspects that the main reason for exclusion stems not from the play being *less* interesting as an example of the type of comedy on which Shakespeare's company built their reputation but from the fact that '[n]o real stylistic analysis on the play has been done in the last fifty years' (727). This candid statement confirms that inclusion is determined by the current state of play in attribution studies, which this edition reflects but does not aim to develop or to query.

The other major benefit rightly highlighted by Bate is that *William Shakespeare & Others* is the first edition to gather plays attributed to Shakespeare since C. F. Tucker Brooke's *The Shakespeare Apocrypha* (1908) and the very first one to offer 'a modern spelling (and thus theatrically usable), or an annotated, or a critically and theatrically introduced, edition of the so-called apocrypha' (15). The need to fill what Bate goes on to describe, possibly a little over-emphatically, as 'the single most significant lacuna in twenty-first-century Shakespearean scholarship' (15), has led to interesting editorial decisions. The texts of the plays are, for example, sparsely but helpfully glossed (and glosses are repeated – as for 'targe' in *Locrine* at 3.3.56 and 5.5.75 – rather than cross-referenced, so readers are not obliged to move backwards and forwards to find help). Only basic entry and exit directions, mostly already present in the early editions, are embedded within the main body of the dialogue, while editorial stage directions suggesting stage business, mode of delivery or blocking, the type of directions which directors and actors find notoriously intrusive, are placed in the right margin and printed in a different font. Punctuation is fairly conservatively reproduced, on the grounds that the original punctuation, though more likely to be compositorial than authorial or the product of printing-house style than theatrical practice, 'reflects the usage of the period' (29). While a mixture of rhetorical and grammatical punctuation may indeed be helpful to actors, other readers might find it a little odd, especially in the context of modernized texts where one would expect punctuation to be grammatical, and not grammatical *and* rhetorical, as in Shakespeare's time. I adjusted to it reasonably well and found it problematic only very occasionally. In *Arden of Faversham*, for example, the 1592 quarto reads:

> I cannot long be from thee gentle Ales,
> Whilest, Michel fetch our horses from the field,
> Franklin and I will down vnto the key: . . .   (A3)

The edited text preserves the punctuation, thus refraining from signalling that the second and third lines are syntactically and logically independent from the first:

> I cannot long be from thee gentle Alice,
> Whilst Michael fetch our horses from the field,
> Franklin and I will down unto the quay, . . .
>
> (1.87–9)

In this instance, the original punctuation is unlikely to be helpful either to modern actors or to the general reader, because it is neither rhetorical nor grammatical.[1]

Also original and praiseworthy is the editorial decision to interfere as little as possible with the original layout used in the original editions to signal the frequent switch between verse and prose. A conservative approach to lineation does indeed do justice to the mingling of verse and prose that was quite common in non-Shakespearian drama, and more prominently so in the work of some of his contemporaries. This enlightened policy is mostly consistently applied throughout. Only very occasionally is it overruled by the wish to rearrange the original lineation, even in passages where a peculiar pattern of verse and prose is left unaltered elsewhere. In *The London Prodigal*, for example, the layout of Flowerdale's speech at 2.104–12 is set exactly as in the 1605 quarto, where the first of the three lines are set in verse and are informed by the register of courtly love – 'Nay, if you say so, fairest of all fairs' – while the remaining lines, where Flowerdale berates his tailor and his goldsmith, are set in prose. In *Mucedorus*, Segasto's speech at 4.49–54 similarly switches between verse and prose, when, from extolling his valour and his fame 'through all the kingdom of Aragon', Segasto moves on to plotting Mucedorus's murder. This speech is rearranged as prose, presumably because it does not scan regularly. However, Segasto's next speech at 4.65–74, which does not scan regularly either, is nevertheless reproduced as verse. My preference would have been for non-intervention even in passages that are predominantly, but not entirely, set in prose. In *A Yorkshire Tragedy*, for example, a line that is tinged by a touching lyricism and is spoken by Husband in a moment of genuine lucidity and insight, 'And I am mad to think that moon was mine' (4.54–5), scans perfectly as a regular iambic pentameter and is interestingly set as a verse line, in the midst of a sea of prose, in the quarto edition of 1608. Adopting a more conventional approach to lineation, Bate and Rasmussen reset this line as prose. I must, however, stress that the editors' decision to retain the original layout as often as

they did is extremely helpful and that the layout of the dialogue in this edition does generally help readers detect changes of register, humour or tragic insight.

In short, this edition provides a wonderful resource for actors, readers and scholars alike. It is impeccably edited by Eric Rasmussen[2] and it includes features that serve different users equally well. The editorial decisions discussed above, as well as Peter Kirwan's interviews with directors who have staged these eleven plays, are bound to prompt and revive interest in them (with the exception of *Edward III* and *Cardenio/Double Falsehood*, which have received unprecedented critical and theatrical attention over the last few years, and *The Spanish Tragedy*, which is one of the best known non-Shakespearian plays from the period).

Also worth mentioning is Will Sharpe's comprehensive survey of the 'Authorship and Attribution' debates surrounding these plays, which is instead bound to appeal to students and scholars, who will find a refreshing amount of wit as well as informed critical views in its densely set pages. Representative of Sharpe's balanced reassessment of recent developments in the attribution of these eleven plays is his sense that there might very well be 'sound evidence to suggest strongly

---

[1] Re-punctuation normally clarifies. An exception occurs in *Locrine*, where the 1595 quarto reads 'Since mightie kings are subiect to mishap, / I mightie kings are subiect to mishap, / Since martiall *Locrine* is bereft of life, / Shall *Estrild* liue then after *Locrines* death?' (K2r–K2v) and the edited text emends as follows: 'Since mighty kings are subject to mishap – / Ay, mighty kings are subject to mishap – / Since martial Locrine is bereft of life. / Shall Estrild live then after Locrine's death?' (5.5.121–4).

[2] I should note that the logic informing a handful of local editorial decisions was not entirely clear to me. At 1.417 in *Arden of Faversham*, for example, 'brake' in the quarto of 1592 is modernized as 'break' in 'But did you mark me then how I break off?', where 'broke' would have seemed to be the most obvious choice of tense. In *Mucedorus*, I was not quite sure why the abbreviation 'Q' is used for the quarto text of 1598 and 'Q1' for the second quarto of 1606. Also in *Mucedorus*, I wondered whether the Prologue, which was added to the 1610 edition, should have been printed in a different typeface, like all the additional or variant passages that found their way into this edition.

Shakespeare's involvement in scene 8 [in *Arden of Faversham*]', but that we nevertheless 'do not know by whom, and under what circumstances, the rest of the play was written'. Sharpe therefore hastens to add that 'we still offer it to readers of this volume as one of the finest plays that a young Shakespeare, possibly, never wrote' (657). Only occasionally do Sharpe's perceptive observations seem a little impulsive: when writing about *Mucedorus*, for example, he wonders whether 'this shop-worn relic of a play may well have become the greatest publishing success enjoyed by an acting troupe in Renaissance England after the period's greatest writer reworked it' (716). It is worth stressing that only the stationers who published the ten early editions of this play would have benefited from its 'publishing success'; the acting company would have undoubtedly benefited from it too, but only from the publicity generated by these reprints and not from the income generated by their sale. Similarly, in the opening section of his essay on *Mucedorus* Sharpe asks, 'Could something regarding the possibility of Shakespearean involvement help account for the huge increase in the play's popularity following the appearance of this substantially revised text, on which all subsequent reprints were based, on booksellers' stalls?' (710) The answer is most certainly not, given that neither the title-page nor the paratext in the 1610 edition, or any of the subsequent reprints, attributes the additions to Shakespeare (or even to 'W. S.', as is the case with other plays included in this edition). Sharpe does add a proviso at the end of this essay that redeems the slightly tendentious quality of this opening question: 'It is curious to consider', he adds, almost as an afterthought, at the very end of this essay, that if Shakespeare did rework this play, 'his involvement would almost certainly have been as obscured to the legions of reader who bought the refurbished *Mucedorus* as it remains to us' (716).

SINGLE-TEXT EDITIONS

Peter Holland's edition of *Coriolanus* in the Arden Shakespeare (third series) represents another major,

paradigm-shifting intervention in the field. It is both a terrific contribution to the scholarship on the play and a radical challenge to the principles that currently inform the editing of Shakespeare and early modern drama more generally. Under the influence of the New Bibliography, scholarly editions of Shakespeare and early modern drama from the mid- to the late twentieth century aimed first and foremost to establish (or re-establish) the text of the play and routinely opened with lengthy overviews of the challenges associated with this task, often omitting to mention the history of the play's critical and theatrical reception altogether. Starting from the 1980s, performance history, along with an exploration of the text of a play as a script originally written to be performed, have slowly found their way into the introductions and commentaries that surround, frame and explicate the dramatic dialogue. Editors have also gradually given more prominence to the critical and theatrical reception of the play by moving their commentaries on the textual and bibliographical features of the early editions to the final sections of their introductions. However, Holland's edition of *Coriolanus* represents a much more radical, not to say genuinely revolutionary, move towards reversing the centrality of the text over performance. Holland does not simply relegate matters of purely textual and bibliographical interest to the outskirts of his edition – his 'Textual Analysis' is, for example, placed between the 'Longer Notes' and 'Appendix 1' at the back of the book, while a short 'Note on the Text' is discreetly nested in the preliminaries – nor does he merely provide a detailed account of the theatrical reception of the play. Holland instead uses a broad understanding of performance as 'the complex cultural work this play has been seen as able to perform' (8) as the main organizing principle of his editorial approach to the play. The introduction, which is framed by an opening discussion of the play's reception in the 1930s and a final section on Ralph Fiennes's film of *Coriolanus* (2011), certainly feels unmapped and refreshing. But far more crucial is Holland's use of performance as a powerful, and so far mostly overlooked, point of access into the very heart of the play, understood as a protean cultural field, constantly shifting as a result of creative, critical and theatrical responses and re-makings.

The central concerns in the play are, for example, identified not by means of a survey of the critical tradition but by paying attention to the aural dimension of the play as spoken. The section on 'Voting and Citizenship' opens with Holland's interesting and haunting suggestion that 'there is a powerful sound of sounds, a speaking of speech across the play' (77). This observation then leads him to note that 'the ritual of selection' for consulship in the play consists in the 'giving of voices' rather than votes (80), and that '[t]here is a strange passivity in the mechanization of the individual's choice in this electoral process' (95). This 'strange passivity' is perpetuated, rather than redeemed, by the creation of the tribunate, which has the very noticeable theatrical effect of 'render[ing] the people themselves voiceless' (94). Another important critical insight in Holland's introduction comes from the emphasis he places on the casting of onstage crowds by directors ranging from William Charles Macready in 1838 to Tim Supple and Robert Lepage in 1992. By turning to theatre history to gain critical insights into the play, Holland shows how some directors, unlike most critics and editors, have allowed their realization that 'plebeians' are not necessarily 'proletarians' (88) to inform their subtler interpretation of the role of citizens and citizenship in the play as a whole. Holland also points out that this reading of the mixed social make-up of the crowds in the play would have spoken more directly to the concerns of the urban middling sort for whom the play was first written and performed. Equally enlightening is Holland's acute sensitivity to the play as a series of structured sequences that produce meaning as they unfold in time. By taking his cue from Emrys Jones, he agrees that '[i]t would clarify the design if the fourth act were to begin with . . . [4.3]' (Jones, quoted in Holland, 110). He then turns to the uncertain provenance of act divisions in the text of the play as it was first printed in the First Folio as either 'Shakespeare's own failure with an unfamiliar mode of dramatic form' in what was possibly

his first Blackfriars play or the later intervention of a 'playhouse or printing-house employee' (111). Instead of lingering on this 'known unknown', Holland brilliantly demonstrates how this feature of the play is a master stroke of theatrical ingenuity:

[W]e can complain of someone else's ineptness – or indeed Shakespeare's own . . . – or we can praise him for the brilliance with which he recognized that a play of three cities, divided perhaps into two parts, shaped in five acts, was a mathematical problem incapable of comfortable solution, that two into five won't go and that the unevenness, the inexactitude, the sense of fascinatingly disrupted rhythms, is a central element in the way the play argues for the imprecision, the impossibility of Coriolanus being either a Roman or a Volscian and/or both at once . . . The problem of prefractional mathematics . . . is then exactly the point. This is the play of remainders, of what is left over when divisions are made, of the social difficulties of superfluity and inequitable division, of the class and wealth basis structured into Roman society that leaves most people as the remainder. (111)

One suspects that 'brilliance' is as much a quality of Holland's object of study as it is distinctive of his inspiring approach to the play throughout this edition.

The text of the play is flawlessly edited and generously glossed. As with Bate and Rasmussen's *William Shakespeare & Others*, I would have welcomed an even more tolerant approach to lineation as preserved in the early editions. Holland certainly makes clear his intention to keep an open mind when it comes to lineation of irregular verse lines. In his 'Textual Analysis', Holland explains his editorial strategy as follows:

Caught between the opposing dynamics of F's lineation and the relineation of subsequent editors, my policy in this edition has been to remain resolutely inconsistent, content at times to ascribe the problems to, for example, Compositor A's errors and therefore relineate, willing at other moments to leave F unaltered on the grounds that the relineated text of the editorial tradition is not entirely convincing. (449)

Very occasionally, though, Holland follows the editorial tradition, even as he notes how the irregularity of the verse may suggest a mode of delivery that relineation makes unavailable to actors. A good example occurs at 1.1.50–1, where, as Holland points out, 'the problems with lineation which occur throughout the play start' (154n). Holland here rearranges Menenius's first speech as it appears in the Folio – 'What work's my Countrimen in hand? / Where go you with Bats and Clubs? The matter / Speake I pray you' – into two hypermetrical iambic pentameters – 'What work's, my countrymen, in hand? Where go you / With bats and clubs? The matter? Speak, I pray you' (1.1.50–1). In doing so, he follows Theobald, 'though only hesitantly', as he adds, 'since the establishment of the verse rhythm takes a while to develop, perhaps as Menenius begins to gain control of the situation' (154n). It seems to me that the layout in F, where Menenius speaks three irregular verse lines, gives as good a clue about Menenius's temporary struggle to 'gain control of the situation' as does his second speech at 1.1.57–8. In this second speech, again following Theobald, Holland adjusts lineation less intrusively, by moving 'neighbours', the first word in the second line as printed in the Folio ('Why Masters, my good Friends, mine honest / Neighbours, will you vndo your selues?'), to the end of Menenius's first line ('Why, masters, my good friends, mine honest neighbours, / Will you undo yourselves?' (1.1.57–8). Menenius's first speech could similarly be more lightly relined, keeping closer to the Folio, by moving 'The matter' from the second to the third line. As a result, Menenius would have three short lines, which have a distinctive iambic beat to them, while falling short of the more conventionally full measure of the pentameters that Menenius starts to speak, consistently and regularly, as soon as he gets into his rhetorical stride in his third speech at 1.1.60–73. Following Holland's own logic and intuition, I would have thought shorter lines to be preferable to editorially reconstructed hypermetrical iambic pentameters for Menenius's first, metrically stunted, speech, made up almost entirely by questions, suggesting his temporary loss of composure at being faced by a crowd of rioting citizens. The impact of the lineation of a few lines on the overall experience of

reading Holland's and Bate and Rasmussen's editions is of course minimal and I warmly welcome these editors' willingness to refrain from rearranging verse lines into metrical forms that are more in keeping with our sense of poetic decorum but further removed from the often suggestive lineation preserved in the early editions.

Other single-text editions of Shakespeare were published earlier this year. David Bevington's *As You Like It* is the first in a new series which stems from a collaboration between the Internet Shakespeare Editions and the Broadview Editions series. Although in book form, editions in this series will use the texts, introductions and commentaries prepared by their editors for the Internet Shakespeare Editions and will be 'integrated' with the fuller resources and research materials available online. The publication of Bevington's edition is a very welcome event, which gives me the opportunity to celebrate the visionary efforts of Michael Best, coordinating and founding editor of the Internet Shakespeare Editions, a unique and pioneering resource for Shakespeare scholars and students alike, Eric Rasmussen's general editorship, yet another of Rasmussen's manifold remarkable achievements, as well as Bevington's extraordinary contributions, both as an editor and as a scholar, to the fields of Shakespeare and early modern drama. Supporting this new series by preparing its first edition to be published both in print and digitally is characteristic of Bevington's generosity as a scholar, while the lucidity of the editing and the annotation is typical of Bevington's exacting and rigorous approach to the editorial task. In book form, this edition offers a useful introduction to the main characters, to the classical and vernacular traditions that affected Shakespeare's conception of the 'green world' and to the critical and theatrical reception of the play.

One aspect of this series that may deserve further thought is how the printed and the digital versions of its editions relate to each other. Most conspicuously, Bevington's textual introduction and notes are not included in the printed version of his edition. This editorial policy, while possibly justified by the perceived needs of undergraduate students, the main target readership of this series, inevitably gives the text of the play an aura of finality and stability which is effectively dispelled by the availability of pop-up notes online. Editorial intervention is instead never signalled in the printed edition, even in exceptionally, but notoriously, difficult passages, like Silvius's speech at 5.2.84–9, which reads:

> It is to be all made of fantasy,
> All made of passion, and all made of wishes;
> All adoration, duty, and observance,
> All humbleness, all patience and impatience,
> All purity, all trial, all obedience;
> And so am I for Phoebe.

Both the digital and the printed edition emend line 88 as it appears in the Folio, 'All puritie, all triall, all obseruance' (TLN 2505), in order to avoid the repeated use of 'observance', which also features at line 86. But while readers of the printed edition are not alerted to the presence of editorial emendation in this speech, users of the digital edition can, if they decide to activate the 'Show Variants' function, detect intervention and will find a note explaining that 'F's "obseruance" looks like a compositor's erroneous repetition of the word in TLN 2503'. Users of the digital edition are also made aware of the fact that 'other emendations have been proposed, including "perseverance", "obeisance", and "endurance"'. Digital users are finally invited to refer to the 'collations' or to Richard Knowles's *Variorum* edition of the play (which will eventually become accessible to internet users, since the digitization of the *Variorum Shakespeare* is now underway) to find out who first suggested or used these emendations. I should also point out that users of the digital edition can find out, by accessing Bevington's textual introduction, that the decision to emend this line must have been far from straightforward and that neither the printed nor the digital version of this edition has ended up matching their editor's sense that, because 'there is no textual authority for "obedience", nor can one be sure which "obseruance" should be replaced ... one option (adopted by this present edition) is to print "observance" in both places and', as Bevington

crucially adds, 'note the textual problem in the commentary'.[3] This minor inconsistency between the text of the play and the textual apparatus is clearly just a local oversight, but it is worth mentioning it because it shows how deeply the lack of a textual apparatus, though available online, may affect readers of the printed version who do not consult the digital version. These readers are not only unaware of editorial intervention but also of the fact that emendation is problematic and that it seems to have been at least initially rejected. It would therefore seem to be highly desirable for future editions in this series to retain at least a minimal number of textual notes, which could be placed, helpfully and inconspicuously, among the glosses currently printed underneath the dramatic dialogue.

One other single-text edition was prepared by S. P. Cerasano for the Norton Critical Editions series. Like Bevington's *As You Like It*, Cerasano's *Julius Caesar* is bound to prove very useful to students of the play. Cerasano writes at length about the role of Rome, and of one of its most famous generals and controversial leaders, Julius Caesar, in the collective imagination of Shakespeare and his contemporaries. Cerasano also devotes a significant amount of space to the play's 'Performance History' and to 'Elements of Production', the latter being a welcome addition, particularly in light of the tendency to provide fuller accounts of the theatrical reception of Shakespeare's plays in recent editions in this series, as noted in my review essay last year. The editing of the text of the play is thorough and leaning towards non-intervention, which seems highly desirable for a play like *Julius Caesar*, which was well printed from a seemingly tidy and legible copy when it was first published in the Folio of 1623. Only very occasionally did I feel that editorial intervention could have been justified more clearly. Cerasano, for example, adds '[POPILLIUS, LIGARIUS]' to the opening stage direction in 3.1, but does not explain that these two

---

3 http://internetshakespeare.uvic.ca/Library/Texts/AYL/ intro/TextIntro/default/, accessed on 18 December 2013

characters, while missing from the original direction in the Folio, have a slightly different status, in that the former speaks but the latter is a ghost character and is therefore often not added to this direction in other editions of the play. Although the size of the textual apparatus in this series is traditionally succinct, the decision underlying the emendation of this direction, which has vexed earlier generations of editors before Cerasano, was probably worth recording.

AFTER THE REVOLUTION: FINE-TUNING NEW ORTHODOXIES

The perception that Shakespeare was already regarded as a 'literary dramatist' by those who published the first printed editions of his plays and by his first readers is probably the most significant revolution to have occurred in the fields of Shakespeare editing and textual studies since the 'materialist turn' in the mid-1980s. And the sheer fact that fewer Shakespeare scholars would now question the opening statement in Lukas Erne's new book, *Shakespeare and the Book Trade*, namely that 'Shakespeare was a man of the theatre who wrote plays for the stage, but he was also a dramatist and poet who wanted to be read' (1), is a testament to the importance and the sheer impact of Erne's work to date. *Shakespeare and the Book Trade* builds on Erne's earlier book, *Shakespeare as Literary Dramatist* (2003), by establishing the 'bibliographic presence' of Shakespeare in the London of his time (1). In other words, Erne, having made a strong argument to demonstrate Shakespeare's active interest in the fashioning of his literary persona as a print-published author in his first book, now sets out to show that Shakespeare's interest in dramatic publication would not have turned him into the most frequently printed and reprinted playwright in his own lifetime, had the book trade not taken an interest in him too. Erne's new book, much needed, thoroughly researched and beautifully argued, brilliantly demonstrates that 'Shakespeare's

early bibliographical reception ... anticipates his eighteenth-century canonization' (2) and that '[t]he view that Shakespeare was not discovered by the book trade until after his death ... is thus precisely wrong' (18).

What readers of Erne's new book might find mildly contentious is his claim that Shakespeare was uniformly popular in his own lifetime. The following is a representative statement about Shakespeare's 'bibliographic presence' in his own time: 'During the time of his active career, not only was Shakespeare the most published playwright, but his bibliographic presence compared with that of his contemporaries was massive' (42). Admittedly, Erne's book provides a much needed 'overall picture' (5) of the early fortunes of Shakespeare in print, but this 'overall picture' may need tweaking to reflect local variation in the dynamics of Shakespeare's rising popularity as a print-published author. It is, for example, open to debate whether reprints rates can be taken to represent a measure of popularity, if considered in isolation from, for example, the frequency of the publication of first editions during Shakespeare's lifetime, or the varying length of time that elapsed between first performance and first print edition. It is well known, for example, that the number of first editions of Shakespeare's plays dropped dramatically after the turn of the century, so Erne's claim, at the end of Chapter 1, that 'Shakespeare's popularity called for a steady supply of new editions' (54) up to 1660 elides the important difference between first editions and reprints, especially during Shakespeare's lifetime.

Later chapters do refine Erne's 'overall picture' of Shakespeare's print popularity in the period. Chapter 2, for example, is devoted to a close study of apocryphal plays attributed to Shakespeare prior to the publication of the First Folio. Erne is quite right to point out that no other dramatist had any playbook misattributed to him between 1595 (when *Locrine* was first published as '*newly set forth, overseen and corrected, by W. S.*') and 1622 (when the third quarto edition of *1 and 2 The Troublesome Reign of John, King of England*, attributed to 'W.Sh' in the 1611 edition, was more explicitly offered to its readers as by 'W. Shakespeare'). However, he is also fully justified in noting that Shakespeare no longer features among those playwrights who had plays misattributed to them between 1634 and 1660, thus concluding that 'the misattribution of playbooks in the 1630s and the following decades suggest that . . . Shakespeare was no longer in a class of his own' (67). He also admits, when reflecting on the lack of reprints of any of the apocrypha inside ten years, that 'Shakespearean authorship, or perceived Shakespearean authorship . . . was not enough to guarantee the success of individual playbooks' (82).

In his chapter about 'The Bibliographic and Paratextual Makeup of Shakespeare's Quarto Playbooks', Erne helpfully considers other features besides authorial attribution on title-pages and the notorious lack of authorial paratextual materials in the early editions of Shakespeare's plays in order to prove that Shakespeare's playbooks 'were endowed with literary cachet' (99). He, for example, regards continuous printing of shared verse lines, the presence of act divisions and commonplace marking in some of Shakespeare's early printed playbooks as markers of literary status. However, he does revisit the vexed issue as to why Shakespeare may have refrained from penning even a single line of paratext to furnish the printed editions of his plays. Erne rejects the view that the sheer lack of any dramatic paratext by Shakespeare is simply bizarre, because, as he rightly points out, dramatic paratext became established around the time when the number of first editions of Shakespeare's plays dropped. Erne therefore argues that we should not be surprised by the lack of dramatic paratexts in playbooks printed during the late Elizabethan period. However, it does seem worth pointing out that even the few first editions of Shakespeare's plays that reached the press during the early Jacobean period include no authorial paratext. Erne might be closer to the mark when he argues that Shakespeare, 'given his close involvement with his company, had no reason to wish his printed plays to appear in a form which would estrange them from the theatre' (123).

The last two chapters add depth and detail to the 'overall picture' put forward by the book as a whole by focusing on the stationers who invested more often and more consistently in the publication of Shakespeare's early playbooks[4] and on those collectors who must have regarded his playbooks as worth preserving. These two chapters rely more directly than the first three chapters on recent scholarship on the book trade and on reading and collecting practices in the early modern period, but they add important local insights. I welcomed, for example, Erne's re-evaluation of Thomas Pavier as a 'pioneer' (179), a view which departs quite starkly from his earlier assessment of Pavier as a rogue stationer. I would also agree with Erne that the distinction of having first collected Shakespeare's separately printed plays in a single volume should go to Frances Egerton (205) rather than Pavier, although it is probably worth bearing in mind that the former collected the plays for her personal consumption while the latter was the first stationer to envisage a collection of Shakespearian (and apocryphal) dramatic works as a potentially profitable commodity. All in all, *Shakespeare and the Book Trade* not only complements *Shakespeare as Literary Dramatist* but also provides a timely and much needed 'overall picture' of Shakespeare's 'bibliographical presence' in the late sixteenth and in the early seventeenth centuries, which will undoubtedly prompt and inform further studies in the field for years to come.

Other studies published this year have already started to revisit the question of Shakespeare's early popularity in print, which is explored so thoroughly in Erne's book. Two essays included in Andy Kesson and Emma Smith's *The Elizabethan Top Ten: Defining Print Popularity in Early Modern England* are particularly helpful. In 'Shakespeare's

---

[4] I have refrained, with regret, from reviewing a new collection of essays, *Shakespeare's Stationers: Studies in Cultural Bibliography*, edited by Marta Straznicky and published by the University of Pennsylvania Press in 2013, which also provides an overview of all stationers who contributed to the rise of Shakespeare in print, because I am one of its contributing authors.

Popularity and the Origins of the Canon', Neil Rhodes offers some interesting insights into what may have been Shakespeare's own perception of his popularity as a print-published poet and playwright, by considering print popularity as a phenomenon that, as Rhodes argues, is best measured in social and literary, as well as in economic and bibliographical, terms. According to Rhodes, 'Shakespeare's writing life is underscored by a narrative about popularity and its attendant anxieties' (120), which were sharpened by 'Shakespeare's engagement with three interrelated professional roles as actor, playwright, and poet' and by his own 'fantasies of social transformation' (117). In 'What is Print Popularity: A Map of the Elizabethan Book Trade', Alan Farmer and Zachary Lesser offer another important 'overall picture' of the popularity of different types of books in the period, against which the significance of Erne's book stands out even more clearly, and against which the popularity of any specific genre should be measured. In this essay, Farmer and Lesser show 'which books were most prevalent in the book trade as a whole' (market shares) and 'how eager were customers to buy [the different categories of books] that were for sale in bookshops' (reprint rates). Building on their earlier work, they also warn us that reprint rates were affected by what they call 'structures of popularity', with descending levels of reprints characterizing 'monopolistic' books, such as Bibles, New Testaments and law books, 'mature' genres, including 'steady sellers' such as Catechisms and cook books, 'innovative' genres, including professional plays, poetry and sermons, and 'topical' items, such as news and almanacs (40–8). Last, but not least, Farmer and Lesser explain that, while their map enables us to make comparisons and to gain a sense of the relative popularity of different types of books, it does not always offer simple answers, and they briefly revisit the vexed question as to whether sermons or professional plays were more popular and more profitable. However, they quite rightly end by stressing the fact that their methodology does provide some important, straightforward answers and, most crucially, it 'leads . . . to a host of interesting new

questions that . . . could not have [been] asked before' (54).

One other book invites its readers to reflect on the impact of early modern print cultures on the transmission of Shakespeare's works. Jeffrey Todd Knight's *Bound to Read: Compilations, Collections, and the Making of Renaissance Literature* challenges earlier assumptions about the impact of print in the production and consumption of literary artifacts as promoting the values of standardization and fixity by showing how 'unsettled conventions of book assembly' meant that 'books in early print culture were relatively open-ended and to a great extent bound (in both senses) by the desires of readers' (9). Chapter 2, which originally appeared in *Shakespeare Quarterly* in 2009, is devoted to the reception of Shakespeare and special attention is paid to *1* and *2 Henry IV* and *The Rape of Lucrece*. By regarding book assembly and book collecting as interpretative practices, Knight reconstructs historical interpretations of these works by considering how differently they must have signified as part of the multibook compilations (or *Sammelbände*) in which they were originally bound. Most refreshing is yet another re-evaluation of the Pavier Quartos, whose 'inconsistencies' are no longer regarded as symptomatic of badly concealed piracy but of 'nonteleological notions of book assembly' and which, in turn, suggest that these quartos 'might be more profitably understood and read as a consumer-driven compilation rather than a never-realized "Works"' (69). Shakespeare scholars will also find inspiring insights in the last chapter, 'The Custom-Made Corpus: English Collected Works in Print, 1532–1623', where Knight shows the influence of the 'fluid canonicity' of medieval manuscript cultures even in the most self-consciously 'modern' and 'author-centric' collections from the period, including Ben Jonson's 1616 Folio, which, by giving each play in it its own title page and imprint, preserved a 'distant semblance of detachability' (179). Shakespeare's First Folio, in this respect, did mark an important departure from customizable collections, because it prints Shakespeare's plays continuously and in such a way that makes extraction or recombination difficult, if not impossible, as shown by the fact that, as

Knight points out, three of Shakespeare's plays from the First Folio – *Othello*, *King Lear* and *Antony and Cleopatra* – are still preserved as a separate bundle at the Beinecke Library at Yale.

Re-assembly, re-presentation and re-mediation are also the central concerns explored by contributors to Brent Nelson and Melissa Terras's collection of essays about the opportunities and challenges associated with *Digitizing Medieval and Early Modern Material Culture*. The collection editors offer a salutary warning to their readers by pointing out that our unprecedented ability to digitize material artifacts, including books, should not lead us to fetishize their materiality but to study it in relation to 'the social networks that created, circulated, and received' them (4). The first chapter, co-authored by Alan Galey, Richard Cunningham, Brent Nelson, Ray Siemens and Paul Werstine, endorses this view by pointing out that the current impetus to digitize material cultures should not be understood 'in terms of new digital technologies acting upon passive written records, but as the imaginative investments of the past meeting those of the present' (22). The third chapter, 'More than Was Dreamt in Our Philosophy: Encoding *Hamlet* for the *Shakespeare Quartos Archive*', is not only the most immediately relevant to Shakespearian scholars but is also most interesting in that it matches the salutary reminders offered by the introduction and by the first chapter about the principles that should inform the digitization of early material cultures with a sense of the practical challenges faced by those who are directly involved in projects aimed at digitizing early modern artifacts. The authors of this chapter, Judith Siefring and Pip Willcox, digital editors at the Digital Library of the Bodleian Library, are just as eloquent when they explain the benefits of presenting 'as far as possible the textual and the material aspects of individual quartos' by offering users of this resource transcriptions of thirty-two, pre-1642 copies of the five editions of *Hamlet* preserved in participating institutions alongside digital images of the same editions, as they are when they discuss challenges which they had barely foreseen when they started working on this project.

Interpretation, as Siefring and Willcox admit, was one such challenge, because even when tasked with developing encoding on descriptive rather than interpretative principles, they had to make interpretative decisions every time they needed to identify different types of stage directions or to expand abbreviations, let alone the encoding of metrical forms, which they did not even attempt. All in all, I would say that the benefits of having made Shakespeare's early quartos available to the wider community of scholars and students who would not otherwise have free and easy access to the early editions far outweigh the inevitable interpretative mediation discussed by Siefring and Willcox and my hope is that the pilot project on *Hamlet* will be extended to the editions of the other plays currently available as digital images in the *Shakespeare Quartos Archive* (accessible at http://quartos.org/).

WORKS REVIEWED

Bate, Jonathan and Eric Rasmussen, with Jan Sewell and Will Sharpe, eds., *William Shakespeare & Others* (Basingstoke, 2013)

Bevington, David, ed., *As You Like It*, Broadview / Internet Shakespeare Editions (Peterborough, Ontario, 2012)

Burrows, John, 'A Second Opinion on "Shakespeare and Authorship Studies in the Twenty-First Century"', *Shakespeare Quarterly*, 63 (2012), 355–92

Cerasano, S. P., ed., *Julius Caesar*, The Norton Critical Editions series (New York and London, 2012)

Craig, Hugh, 'George Chapman, John Davies of Hereford, William Shakespeare, and *A Lover's Complaint*', *Shakespeare Quarterly*, 63 (2012), 147–74

Erne, Lukas, *Shakespeare and the Book Trade* (Cambridge, 2013)

Farmer, Alan and Zachary Lesser, 'What is Print Popularity? A Map of the Elizabethan Book Trade', in Andy Kesson and Emma Smith, eds., *The Elizabethan Top Ten: Defining Print Popularity in Early Modern England* (Farnham, 2013), pp. 19–54

Galey, Alan, Richard Cunningham, Brent Nelson, Ray Siemens and Paul Werstine, 'Beyond Remediation: The Role of Textual Studies in Implementing New Knowledge Environments', in Brent Nelson and Melissa Terras, eds., *Digitizing Medieval and Early Modern Culture* (Toronto, 2012), pp. 21–48

Holland, Peter, ed., *Coriolanus*, The Arden Shakespeare, third series (London, 2013)

Kesson, Andy and Emma Smith, *The Elizabethan Top Ten: Defining Print Popularity in Early Modern England* (Farnham, 2013)

Knight, Jeffrey Todd, *Bound to Read: Compilations, Collections, and the Making of Renaissance Literature* (Philadelphia, 2013)

Nelson, Brent and Melissa Terras, eds., *Digitizing Medieval and Early Modern Culture* (Toronto, 2012)

Rhodes, Neil, 'Shakespeare's Popularity and the Origins of the Canon', in Kesson and Smith, *Elizabethan Top Ten*, pp. 101–22

Siefring, Judith and Pip Willcox, 'More than Was Dreamt in Our Philosophy: Encoding *Hamlet* for the *Shakespeare Quartos Archive*', in Nelson and Terras, *Digitizing Medieval and Early Modern Culture*, pp. 83–112

Straznicky, Marta, ed., *Shakespeare's Stationers: Studies in Cultural Bibliography* (Philadelphia, 2013)

Vickers, Brian, 'Identifying Shakespeare's Additions to *The Spanish Tragedy* (1602): A New(er) Approach', *Shakespeare*, 8 (2012), 13–43

Werstine, Paul, *Early Modern Playhouse Manuscripts and the Editing of Shakespeare* (Cambridge, 2013)

INDEX

INDEX

INDEX

INDEX

INDEX

INDEX

INDEX

INDEX

INDEX

INDEX